AESTHETICS
A CRITICAL ANTHOLOGY

AESTHETICS
A CRITICAL ANTHOLOGY

Second Edition

George Dickie

Richard Sclafani

Ronald Roblin

EDITORS

BEDFORD / ST. MARTIN'S   *Boston* ◆ *New York*

Editor: Mark Gallaher

Project Management: Rachel Hockett, Spectrum Publisher Services, Inc.

Cover Design: John Jeheber/Jeheber & Peace, Inc.

Library of Congress Catalog Card Number: 88-60543

Manufactured in the United States of America.

4 3 2 1 0
h g f e d

For information write: Bedford/St. Martin's
75 Arlington St., Boston, MA 02116   (617-399-4000)

ISBN: 0-312-00309-9

Frontispiece: Paul Cézanne, *Mont Sainte-Victoire*, 1886–1887. The Phillips Collection, Washington, DC. Reprinted with permission.

PREFACE

When the original edition was published in 1977, *Aesthetics: A Critical Anthology* was the first text of its kind to combine historical materials, works of recent scholarship, and contemporary critical analyses in an effort to present a comprehensive account of the field of aesthetics as it is understood primarily in the Anglo-Saxon world. Beyond its uniquely broad scope, the first edition was also distinguished by several critical essays written specially for the volume and by the pairing of virtually every historical selection with a contemporary discussion of that selection.

This second edition has been prepared with the same guiding principles in mind. While preserving many of the classical writings in aesthetics—such as works by Plato, Aristotle, Hume, and Kant—the second edition includes as well a generous portion of important and influential discussions by contemporary aestheticians mainly in the "analytical tradition," more than a dozen of which have been written in the past ten years. Among the essays composed specifically for this volume are several retained from the first edition—Stanley Bates on Tolstoy, Monroe C. Beardsley on literature, Peter Kivy on the logic of taste, and Richard Schacht on Nietzsche—along with seven new contributions appearing here for the first time—Stanley Bates on Cavell's film theory, Noël Carroll on Bell, Renee Cox on musical expressionism, George Dickie's reply to Robert Stecker, Mary Mothersill on Hume, Anita Silvers on Danto, and Benjamin R. Tilghman on contemporary aesthetic theory—and several new pages by Alan Tormey on Collingwood's version of the expression theory of art.

In presenting historical materials, the second edition continues to be governed by two policies. First, philosophical works of historical interest are in no case presented in snippets; the selections are uniformly substantial. Second, the "dialectical-critical" structure of the anthology has been preserved. In some instances, the contemporary discussion offers a direct philosophical critique of the historical thesis; in others, the discussion is of a more exegetical nature. The purpose of the pairings in every case is to stimulate further thought and to reinforce the sense of ongoing debate over many of the central issues in the field.

In revising the contents for the second edition, we have taken account of continuing developments in the field of aesthetics in order to include a variety of fresh contributions. As in the case of the first edition, the book—while containing much material suitable for graduate-level study—is designed primarily for undergraduate courses; and to this end, updated translations of Plato, Kant, and Eduard Hanslick have been added. In addition, the organization has been streamlined somewhat. Five broad part divisions now focus on three central areas: traditional and contemporary theories of art, traditional and contemporary theories of the aesthetic, and theories of the individual arts. In the last of these, a new section has been added on aesthetics of dance.

The apparatus in the new edition closely follows the format of that in the first. The General Introduction and part introductions provide an overview of the issues for study and alert the reader to explicit cross-references and less obvious relationships among selections throughout the text. Photographs have been included to illustrate and complement various selections. Finally, the bibliography—the most substantial available in a collection of this kind—has been thoroughly updated to reflect new publications and important recent developments in the field.

The editors have benefited enormously from the suggestions and advice of numerous aestheticians, including Philip Alperson, Arnold Berleant, Robert Cantrick, Noël Carroll, Stanley Cavell, Ted Cohen, Renée Cox, T. J. Diffey, Jack Glickman, Garry Hagberg, Peter Kivy, Carolyn Korsmeyer, Colin Lyas, Mary Mothersill, Anita Silvers, Milton Snoeyenbos, and Francis Sparshott. Our special thanks to Geoffrey Payzant, Jenefer Robinson, and Richard Schacht, who assisted invaluably in the preparation of and editorial work for, respectively, the chapters on music, literature, and drama. The editors, of course, assume sole responsibility for the book's contents.

Finally, thanks are due to Mary F. Hewett, who assisted at every stage throughout the development of the text.

CONTENTS

General Introduction

"Aesthetics" is a term commonly used to refer to such diverse matters as theories of beauty and the elegance of a logician's axiomatic system. Philosophically, the term has a far more precise designation. Today, those philosophers called aestheticians are concerned with two general enterprises—the theory of art and the theory of the aesthetic that emerged in the eighteenth and nineteenth centuries from the theory of beauty. In this volume the division of selections into theories of art (Parts One and Two), theories of the aesthetic (Parts Three and Four), and theories of the individual arts (Part Five) is one of two large-scale organizational features. The other organizational feature of the book is the practice, when possible, of presenting a selection followed by a critique of that selection. The two central philosophical concerns—the theory of art and the theory of the aesthetic—have their origin, as does so much in philosophy, in the thought of Plato. Accordingly, the first two selections in Part One are from Plato.

The history of the theory of art can be divided into three phases of vastly different lengths of time. The first phase begins with Plato's association of the arts with imitation, in ancient Greece, and ends in the twentieth century with various formulations of the view of art as expression. (It should be noted that Plato held nothing like a modern conception of the arts, and that he identified what we call art with a form of craft.) The central feature of these theories has been an attempt to capture the *essence* of art in a definition. In one form or another, Plato's view of the arts as imitative in character remained unchallenged until the nineteenth century, when various competing theories began to be presented. They are represented in Part One of this volume by Clive Bell's theory of art as significant form and by Leo Tolstoy's and R. G. Collingwood's expressive theories of art.

The second phase in the history of art theory is really an antitheory movement. In the early 1950s a series of articles by various philosophers contended that "art" could not be defined in the manner that the earlier theorists had assumed. Morris Weitz, who denied that there are necessary and sufficient conditions for the concept of art, was one of the most influential of the antitheorists.

Maurice Mandelbaum opened the third phase of the history of art theory by arguing against Weitz and others to the effect that it may be possible to define "art" after all. Arthur Danto's "The Artworld" (Part Two) also belongs to the early stage of this third phase, as it argues that works of art exist within a complex matrix he calls "the artworld." Drawing on both Mandelbaum and Danto, George Dickie (Part Two)

1

attempts to formulate what he calls an institutional definition of art. Thus, the third phase has in common with the first the view that art can be defined, but the manner of definition is of a very different sort from traditional attempts.

Parts One through Four provide sufficient material for a course on the philosophy of art and the theory of the aesthetic.

The reader may have been surprised when at the beginning of this introduction it was asserted that the theory of the aesthetic originated in the philosophy of Plato, since the notion of the aesthetic as it is currently understood did not come into use until the nineteenth century. What was meant by that assertion was that Plato was the first to develop a theory of *beauty*, which during the eighteenth and nineteenth centuries was transformed into a theory of the aesthetic. Until the beginning of the eighteenth century, the theory of beauty along with the theory of art continued to be the twin concerns of those philosophers who today would be called aestheticians.

At that time such philosophers as Francis Hutcheson (Part Three) began developing philosophies of *taste*. The theorists of taste continued to employ the notion of beauty, but for them beauty was not an objective property of things as it was for Plato; rather it was a complicated matter involving the reaction of subjects of aesthetic perception (persons) to aesthetic phenomena. In addition, these philosophers introduced additional concepts of appreciation—the sublime, the picturesque, and others—within the theory of taste. Beauty as well as these other concepts was subjectivized, and beauty became just one among a host of other concepts. *Taste* had replaced beauty as the central organizing concept of the theory of the appreciation of art and nature. From the beginning to the end of the eighteenth century, theories of taste were offered one after another. Eventually, that manner of philosophizing ended. During the nineteenth century, theories of aesthetic attitude replaced theories of taste as the dominant method of philosophizing about the appreciation of art and nature. In this fashion the notion of the aesthetic replaced the notion of taste, which had earlier displaced the concept of beauty. It is through this complicated route that the theory of the aesthetic can be traced to the philosophy of Plato.

Theories of the aesthetic attitude continued to enjoy great popularity well into the twentieth century. During the past two decades or more, some doubts have been raised about the adequacy of aesthetic-attitude theories. Part Three of this volume deals with eighteenth-century theories of taste. Part Four deals with twentieth-century versions of the aesthetic-attitude theory, as well as with a recent attempt of a somewhat different kind to characterize the aesthetic, as in Frank Sibley's seminal article "Aesthetic Concepts." Sibley takes it for granted that we distinguish between the aesthetic and the nonaesthetic qualities of things, and he investigates the relation between these two different kinds of qualities. Whether Sibley's account of aesthetic qualities is related to, or derived from, theories of the aesthetic attitude is difficult to ascertain. Sibley holds that it would be natural enough to say that our ability to perceive aesthetic qualities, which he regards as a "characteristically human kind of awareness and activity," is notably different from "the use of the five senses" and "requires the exercise of taste, perceptivity or sensitivity, of aesthetic discrimination or appreciation." This may suggest that his account owes more to the eighteenth- than to the nineteenth-century theory of the appreciation of art and nature. Thus, the debate over the nature of the aesthetic, like that over the philosophy of art, continues.

Thus far this introduction has been concerned with art in general. Much writing about art, however, has taken the form of discussions of the particular arts. Part Five consists of essays devoted to the theories of literature, drama, the plastic arts, film, music, and dance. These essays reflect the great variety of the arts as well as significant differences among them. On some occasions, however, they reveal important insights about art in general and about specific problems relevant to aesthetics in particular: the section on literature focuses on intention and style; the chapter on drama is concerned with the nature of tragedy; the locus of the papers on painting and architecture is the question of representation in those arts; the chapter on music deals with expression; and that on dance concentrates on the problem of definition and the relationship of action theory to dance. Consequently, each of the individual arts is profiled in relation to a particular question in aesthetics, while the individuality of each art form is preserved in relation to the rest.

PART ONE

———◆◆◆◆———

Traditional Theories of Art and Contemporary Critiques of These Theories

In the General Introduction we outlined the two basic features of this book: (1) the division of our subject into theories of art and theories of the aesthetic and (2) the critical format around which our selections are structured. In Part One we begin by presenting a number of prominent traditional theories of art, each followed by a contemporary critique. The traditional theories—those of Plato, Aristotle, Leo Tolstoy, Clive Bell, and R. G. Collingwood—have been selected both for their inherent philosophical interest and for their historical value. Moreover, these traditional theories have received much attention from philosophers during the last few decades, and as we have stated, this collection aims at reflecting and crystallizing the current state of the discipline.

We ask the reader to bear in mind that several other traditional theorists who might once have been loosely called art theorists are presented, under the more philosophically precise division of this collection, as theorists of the aesthetic. The theories of Francis Hutcheson, David Hume, and Immanuel Kant are crucial to our subject, and we have included them in the collection. As we have suggested, however, they are better understood as theorists of the aesthetic, not as theorists of art.

Plato and Aristotle on the Arts

It is not an understatement to say that Plato's view of poetry and painting as imitative in nature set the stage for practically all discussions of the nature of Western art for the next two thousand years. We include here Plato's brief dialogue, *Ion*, as well as the first part of *Republic*, Book X. In the *Ion*, a characteristically Socratic dialogue, Plato deals with a number of issues critical to our understanding of art: the nature of artistic inspiration, the relationship of art to the emotions, and the question of poetry's claim to impart knowledge. In typical Socratic fashion, Plato's Socrates cross-examines Ion's claim as a rhapsodist to be the "mouthpiece" of philosophical truths as revealed in Homer. Plato concludes, ironically, that Ion is "inspired" by Homer's poetry and that he communicates his inspirations to his audience by arousing their passions in a way analogous to the attraction of iron filings to a magnet. The result of Socrates' inquiry is explicitly negative: the rhapsodist has no privileged access to any sort of philosophical truth; his "knowledge" is a sham. Implicitly the outcome of the dialogue is constructive. Plato clearly implies that knowledge is the result of rational inquiry alone and is not emotional in its content or acquisition.

The *Ion* is hardly more than an early chapter of Plato's philosophical quarrel with the poets. In the *Republic* this quarrel becomes entirely open and is couched in terms of Plato's ontology, in which poetry and painting are assigned an inferior status by comparison with the forms (the realities upon which the world of the senses is modeled) and, even further, with everyday objects and events in the sensible world. Since these objects and situations are themselves imitations of ideal forms that transcend the world we see and hear about us, poetry and painting turn out to be imitations of imitations.

We should note here that Plato held nothing like a modern understanding of the arts, which evolved after the Renaissance. Instead, he identified the "fine arts" with crafts such as furniture making or shipbuilding—a view characteristic of the ancients. His comparison of paintings, for example, to mirror images and illusions enables him to incorporate his view of them into his ontology. Thus, an aesthetic theory is often attributed to Plato that he could not in the nature of the case have expounded. It is, however, a useful starting point in the philosophy of art to understand Plato's view that poems and paintings have an inferior ontological status compared with other things in the ordinary world.

Aristotle in the *Poetics* offers a very different vision of the place of art in the world. Aristotle's chief concern is to redeem the arts, in large measure, from Plato's criticism of their value in human society. Although Aristotle's account of poetry centers upon tragedy, he attempts to dispel Plato's view of their questionable origins and effects on people as well as their inferior ontological status. Aristotle's *Poetics* is probably the most famous work in the history of art criticism. His definition of tragedy as the dramatic imitation of a serious action that brings about a catharsis of pity and fear has had a tremendous impact on literature and criticism from the Renaissance to this day. The notion of catharsis in particular has been the source of centuries-old debates among philosophers, critics, and playwrights. In the twentieth century, Bertolt Brecht went so far as to write a specifically non-Aristotelian drama.

The *Poetics* does not exhibit the tightness of structure, the rigor of argument, and the systematic exposition of typically Aristotelian works. This condition is probably due to the fact that the manuscript from which the *Poetics* was passed down to us was a series of lecture notes from which Aristotle intended to write a complete treatise. Thus, the *Poetics* contains flashes of brilliance, but at times it is repetitive and seemingly contradictory. Nevertheless, it is still the first work in the history of the subject to treat, in one form or another, virtually every problem with which the theory of art has subsequently been concerned.

Although the *Poetics* is un-Aristotelian in some ways, it is still a highly formal work in which Aristotle searches for first principles and a complete definition of his subject. In this case his subject is the art of poetry in general, and the art of tragedy in particular. For Aristotle, a complete definition of any subject proceeds according to genus and species. First, Aristotle determines to which general category, or genus, a subject belongs. He then isolates his specific subject within that genus. For Aristotle, the genus of the art of tragedy is imitation; the species of the art is dramatic imitation (as opposed to painting and sculpture, which, for example, imitate by means of color and shape). Because tragedy is a species of imitation, Aristotle finds it necessary to compare and contrast tragedy with other forms of imitation throughout his *Poetics*. This procedure provides a way of determining the general theory of art that underlies his treatment of the poetic art.

Eva Schaper contrasts Aristotle's view of poetry in the *Poetics* with Plato's views on the same themes. She finds that Aristotle did not merely modify some of the more extreme conceptions in Plato's approach, he transformed them in the light of the principles of his own philosophy. Consequently, Aristotle conceived the origin, nature, and effects of the poetic art in a way radically different from Plato. He understood the poetic-craft as a genuine kind of making, the poetic work as an organic unity, and the effects of poetry, specifically tragedy, as cathartic rather than emotionally harmful. Schaper thus envisages Aristotle as the first formalist in the history of aesthetics. His notion of organic unity in tragedy and other literary forms such as epic paved the way for future developments, which culminated in the formalism of contemporary aesthetics.

Art, Feeling, and Experience

Leo Tolstoy is justifiably famous as perhaps the greatest novelist in the history of Western literature. This is a principal reason, no doubt, why his theory of art continues to receive the attention it does, for few philosophers believe there is great philosophical merit to Tolstoy's theoretical writings on art. Tolstoy is usually considered to hold a naive and confused view of art as the communication of feeling through some sensuous medium. As Stanley Bates points out about Tolstoy's book *What Is Art?*, "It sometimes seems as though the chief function of this work for later aesthetic theory has been to provide a rich storehouse of examples of aesthetic fallacies." Nevertheless, Bates argues that Tolstoy's theory cannot be dismissed, and not simply because Tolstoy was a great novelist—he has valuable philosophical insights to offer as well. Bates gives us an illuminating exposition of Tolstoy's theory of art, distinguishing several questions Tolstoy was concerned to answer, questions many philosophers have overlooked. Bates shows us that Tolstoy's theory is more complex than philosophers have hitherto thought it to be; he shows us that certain criticisms philosophers have accepted as a conclusive refutation of Tolstoy fail to address a number of crucial considerations of Tolstoy's theory. Bates does, however, go on to state what he takes to be the "deepest failure" of Tolstoy's theory: "that he does not recognize a potential tension, or, even incompatibility, between the artist's sincerity and the infectiousness of the work of art."

Art and Significant Form

Clive Bell, a twentieth-century writer closely associated with the famous art critic Roger Fry, argued that "significant form" defines the nature of art. In so arguing, Bell stressed the importance of purely formal, i.e., nonrepresentational, elements of works of art (visual art in particular). Bell helped pave the way in the English-speaking world for the acceptance of Postimpressionist works as fully legitimate works of art.

In his discussion of Bell, Noël Carroll places Bell squarely within the tradition of aestheticism that has its origins in Hutcheson and finds its clearest expression in the sophisticated formalism of Monroe Beardsley. But Carroll does far more than "place" Bell within a certain strain in aesthetics: he engages in a detailed critique of Bell's essentialism, showing in the process how Bell's attempt to define art as significant form, and significant form in relationship to the "aesthetic emotion," leads to insuperable difficulties. Carroll's discussion thus amounts to a sustained criticism of the entire conception of aesthetics in which Bell has a prominent and influential place.

Art and Expression

R. G. Collingwood's theory of art as the expression of emotion is the most sophisticated theory of art produced in the twentieth century. Collingwood's distinction between art and craft and his critique of what he calls the "technical theory" of art have become commonplace in aesthetic thought since the publication of *The Principles of Art* in 1938. Collingwood's theory is frequently thought to be a mere reiteration of the views of Benedetto Croce, whom Collingwood acknowledged as his single most influential intellectual progenitor on aesthetic matters. However, the so-called "Croce-Collingwood" philosophy of art is a misnomer—Collingwood was influenced by a number of important philosophers, including Plato, Spinoza, Hume, Kant, and Hegel, as is evident in Part II of *The Principles of Art*.

In our lengthy selection from Collingwood, we include not merely his discussion of art and craft but also the application of this distinction to what Collingwood calls magic on the one hand, and amusement on the other. He attempts to show that magical art results from the attempt to evoke emotions that "spill over" into practical life, while amusement art maintains a "bulkhead" between the vicarious emotions aroused in the audience and the emotions of practical life. By contrast, "art proper" is the expression of emotion, which for Collingwood and many who followed him constitutes a psychological process in which dim and confused feelings become lucid and articulate through the act of expression.

Alan Tormey, in his critique of the expression theory, points to a number of critical difficulties that Collingwood and others encounter. While Tormey's essay focuses on John Dewey's view of expression, he devotes several pages, written specifically for this edition, to Collingwood's theory as well. Among his many criticisms of the theory, Tormey attacks the distinction between expressing and merely betraying emotions, which appears to be more a matter of definition than a viable philosophical distinction. Tormey's criticisms suggest that the expression theory must be defended on other than purely definitional grounds if it is to be tenable. Otherwise, there are no valid reasons for maintaining that the artist expresses his own emotions, as opposed to creating expressiveness in his work in other ways. The expression theory of art has been discredited because of the apparent discrepancy between any contingent emotions the artist might feel in the course of artistic creation and the expressive character of his or her work, including the emotions we attribute to characters in a story, etc.

Instead of construing the relation between the artist's emotions and the emotive qualities of his work *transitively*, Tormey insists that any emotions the artist may feel are irrelevant to the properties actually possessed by the work. These properties, such as sadness or joyousness, are relevant solely to the work itself and make no elliptical comments about the artist. Tormey is particularly effective in arguing this point with respect to musical compositions. He shows that despite the composer Carl Neilson's depression during a certain period of his compositional life, he was able to compose music that was often humorous and possessed characteristics diametrically opposed to those revealed by a study of biographical data. Consequently, Tormey concludes, it is necessary to view the qualities of musical works as phenomenal qualities of the works themselves rather than to project them into the mind of the composer. In this way we can speak of the expressiveness of works of art cut off from any alleged attribution of feelings to the artist which may find their way into his or her work.

Plato

POETIC INSPIRATION: THE *ION*

Socrates. Ion! Hello. Where have you come from to visit us this time? From your home in Ephesus?

Ion. No, no, Socrates. From Epidaurus, from the festival of Asklepius.

S. Don't tell me the Epidaurians hold a contest for *rhapsodes* in honor of the god?

I. They certainly do! They do it for every sort of poetry and music.

S. Really? Did you enter the contest? And how did it go for you?

I. First prize, Socrates! We carried it off.

S. That's good to hear. Well, let's see that we win the games at Athens, next.

I. We'll do it, Socrates, god willing.

S. You know, Ion, many times I've envied you rhapsodes your profession. Physically, it is always fitting for you in your profession to be dressed up to look as beautiful as you can; and at the same time it is necessary for you to be at work with poets—many fine ones, and with Homer above all, who's the best poet and the most divine—and you have to learn his thought, not just his verses! Now that is something to envy! I mean, no one would ever get to be a good rhapsode if he didn't understand what is meant by the poet. A rhapsode must come to present the poet's thought to his audience; and he can't do that beautifully unless he knows what the poet means. So this all deserves to be envied.

I. That's true, Socrates. And that's the part of my profession that took the most work. I think I speak more beautifully than anyone else about Homer; neither Metrodorus of Lampsacus nor Stesimbrotus of Thasos nor Glaucon nor anyone else past or present could offer as many beautiful thoughts about Homer as I can.

S. That's good to hear, Ion. Surely you won't begrudge me a demonstration?

I. Really, Socrates, it's worth hearing how well I've got Homer dressed up. I think I'm worthy to be crowned by the Sons of Homer with a golden crown.

S. Really, I shall make time to hear that later. Now I'd just like an answer to this: Are you so wonderfully clever about Homer alone—or also about Hesiod and Archilochus?

I. No, no. Only about Homer. That's adequate, I think.

Plato, Ion, *translated by Paul Woodruff, in* Two Comic Dialogues *(Indianapolis and Cambridge: Hackett, 1983), pp. 21–35. Reprinted by permission of Hackett Publishing Company. (Footnotes omitted.)*

S. Is there any subject on which Homer and Hesiod both say the same things?

I. Yes, I think so. A good many.

S. Then, on those subjects, would you explain Homer's verse more beautifully than Hesiod's?

I. Just the same Socrates, on those subjects, anyway, where they say the same things.

S. And how about the subjects on which they do not say the same things? Divination, for example. Homer says something about it and so does Hesiod.

I. Certainly.

S. Well. Take all the places where those two poets speak of divination, both where they agree and where they don't: who would explain those more beautifully, you, or one of the diviners if he's good?

I. One of the diviners.

S. Suppose *you* were a diviner: if you were really able to explain the places where the two poets agree, wouldn't you also know how to explain the places where they disagree?

I. That's clear.

S. Then what in the world is it that you're clever about in Homer but not in Hesiod and the other poets? Does Homer speak of any subjects that differ from those of *all* the other poets? Doesn't he mainly go through tales of war, and of how people deal with each other in society—good people and bad, ordinary folks and craftsmen? And of the gods, how *they* deal with each other and with men? And doesn't he recount what happens in heaven and in hell, and tell of the births of gods and heroes? Those are the subjects of Homer's poetry-making, aren't they?

I. That's true, Socrates.

S. And how about the other poets? Didn't they write on the same subjects?

I. Yes, but Socrates, they didn't do it the way Homer did.

S. How, then? Worse?

I. Much worse.

S. And Homer does it better?

I. *Really* better.

S. Well now, Ion, dear heart, when a number of people are discussing arithmetic, and one of them speaks best, I suppose *someone* will know how to pick out the good speaker.

I. Yes.

S. Will it be the same person who can pick out the bad speakers, or someone else?

I. The same, of course.

S. And that will be someone who has mastered arithmetic, right?

I. Yes.

S. Well. Suppose a number of people are discussing healthy nutrition, and one of them speaks best. Will one person know that the best speaker speaks best, and another that an inferior speaker speaks worse? Or will the same man know both?

I. Obviously, the same man.

S. Who is he? What do we call him?

I. A doctor.

S. So, to sum it up, this is what we're saying: when a number of people speak on the same subject, it's always the same person who will know how to pick out good speakers and bad speakers. If he doesn't know how to pick out a bad speaker, he certainly won't know a good speaker—on the same subject, anyway.

I. That's so.

S. Then it turns out that the same person is "wonderfully clever" about both speakers.

I. Yes.

S. Now *you* claim that Homer and the other poets (including Hesiod and Archilochus) speak on the same subjects, but not equally well. *He's* good, and they're inferior.

I. Yes, and it's true.

S. Now if you really do know who's speaking well, you'll know that the inferior speakers are speaking worse.

I. Apparently so.

S. You're superb! So if we say that Ion is equally clever about Homer and the other poets, we'll make no mistake. Because you agree yourself that the same person will be an adequate judge of all who speak on the same subjects, and that almost all the poets *do* treat the same subjects.

I. Then how in the world do you explain what *I* do, Socrates? When someone discusses another poet I pay no attention, and I have no power to contribute anything worthwhile: I simply doze off. But let someone mention Homer and right away I'm wide awake and I'm paying attention and I have plenty to say.

S. That's not hard to figure out, my friend. Anyone can tell that you are powerless to speak about Homer on the basis of knowledge or mastery. Because if your ability came by mastery, you would be able to speak about all the other poets as well. Look, there is an art of poetry as a whole, isn't there?

I. Yes.

S. And now take the whole of *any* other subject: won't it have the same discipline throughout? And this goes for every subject that can be mastered. Do you need me to tell you what I mean by this, Ion?

I. Lord, yes, I do, Socrates. I love to hear you wise men talk.

S. I wish that were true, Ion. But wise? Surely you are the wise men, you rhapsodes and actors, you and the poets whose work you sing. As for me, I say nothing but the truth, as you'd expect from an ordinary man. I mean, even this question I asked you—look how commonplace and ordinary a matter it is. Anybody could understand what I meant: don't you use the same discipline throughout whenever you master the whole of a subject? Take this for discussion—painting is a subject to be mastered as a whole, isn't it?

I. Yes.

S. And there are many painters, good and bad, and there have been many in the past.

I. Certainly.

S. Have you ever known anyone who is clever at showing what's well painted and what's not in the work of Polygnotus, but who's powerless to do that for other painters? Someone who dozes off when the work of other painters is displayed, and is lost, and has nothing to contribute—but when he has to give judgment on Polygnotus or any other painter (so long as it's just *one*), he's wide awake and he's paying attention and he has plenty to say—have you ever known anyone like that?

I. Good lord no, of course not!

S. Well. Take sculpture. Have you ever known anyone who is clever at explaining which statues are well made in the case of Daedalus, son of Metion, or Epeius, son of Panopeus, or Theodorus of Samos, or any other *single* sculptor, but who's lost when he's among the products of other sculptors, and he dozes off and has nothing to say?

I. Good lord no. I haven't.

S. And further, it is my opinion, you've never known anyone ever—not in flute-playing, not in cithara-playing, not in singing to the cithara, and not in rhapsodizing—you've never known a man who is clever at explaining Olympus or Thamyrus or Orpheus or Phemius, the rhapsode from Ithaca, but who has nothing to contribute about Ion, the rhapsode from Ephesus, and cannot tell when he does his work well and when he doesn't—you've never known a man like that.

I. I have nothing to say against you on that point, Socrates. But *this* I know about myself: I speak about Homer more beautifully than anybody else and I have lots to say; and everybody says I do it well. But about the other poets I do not. Now see what that means.

S. I do see, Ion, and I'm going to announce to you what I think that is. As I said earlier, that's not a subject you've mastered—speaking well about Homer; it's a divine power that moves you, as a "Magnetic" stone moves iron rings. (That's what Euripides called it; most people call it "Heracleian.") This stone not only pulls those rings, if they're iron, it also puts power *in* the rings, so that they in turn can do just what the stone does—pull other rings—so that there's sometimes a very long chain of iron pieces and rings hanging from one another. And the power in all of them depends on this stone. In the same way, the Muse makes some people inspired herself, and then through those who are inspired a chain of other enthusiasts is suspended. You know, none of the epic poets, if they're good, are masters of their subject; they are inspired, possessed, and that is how they utter all those beautiful poems. The same goes for lyric poets if they're good: just as the Corybantes are not in their right minds when they dance, lyric poets, too, are not in their right minds when they make those beautiful lyrics, but as soon as they sail into harmony and rhythm they are possessed by Bacchic frenzy. Just as Bacchus worshippers when they are possessed draw honey and milk from rivers, but not when they are in their right minds—the soul of a lyric poet does this too, as they say themselves. For of course poets tell us that they gather songs at honey-flowing springs, from glades and gardens of the Muses, and that they bear songs to us as bees carry honey, flying like bees. And what they say is true. For a poet is an airy thing, winged and holy, and he is not able to make poetry until he becomes inspired and goes out of his mind and his intellect is no longer in him. As long as a human being has his intellect in his possession he will always lack the power to make poetry or sing prophecy. Therefore because it's not by mastery that they make poems or say many lovely things about their subjects (as you do about Homer)—but because it's by a divine gift—each poet is able to compose beautifully only that for which the Muse has aroused him: one can do dithyrambs, another encomia, one can do dance songs, another, epics, and yet another, iambics; and each of them is worthless for the other types of poetry. You see, it's not mastery that enables them to speak those verses, but a divine power, since if they knew how to speak beautifully on one type of poetry by mastering the subject, they could do so for all the others also. That's why the god takes their intellect away from them when he uses them as his servants, as he does prophets and godly diviners, so that we who hear should know that *they* are not the ones who speak those verses that are of such high value, for their intellect is not in them: the god himself is the one who speaks, and he gives voice through them to us. The best evidence for this account is Tynnichus from Chalcis, who never made a poem anyone would think worth mentioning, *except* for the praise-song everyone sings, almost the most beautiful lyric-poem there is, and simply, as he says himself, "an invention of the Muses." In this more than anything, then, I think, the god is showing us, so that we should be in no doubt about it, that these beautiful poems are not human, not even *from* human beings, but are divine and from gods; that poets are nothing but representatives of the gods, possessed by whoever possesses them. To show *that*, the god deliberately sang the most beautiful lyric poem through the most worthless poet. Don't you think I'm right, Ion?

I. Lord yes, I certainly do. Somehow you touch my soul with your words, Socrates, and I do think it's by a divine gift that good poets are able to present these poems to us from the gods.

S. And you rhapsodes in turn present what the poets say.

I. That's true too.

S. So you turn out to be representatives of representatives.

I. Quite right.

S. Hold on, Ion; tell me this. Don't keep any secrets from *me*. When you recite epic poetry well and you have the most stunning effect on your spectators, either when you sing of Odysseus—how he leapt into the doorway, his identity now obvious to the suitors, and he poured out arrows at his feet—or when you sing of Achilles charging at Hector, or when you sing a pitiful episode about Andromache or Hecuba or Priam, are you at that time in your right mind, or do you get beside yourself? And doesn't your soul, in its enthusiasm, believe that it is present at the actions you describe, whether they're in Ithaca or in Troy or wherever the epic actually takes place?

I. What a vivid example you've given me, Socrates! I won't keep secrets from *you*. Listen, when *I* tell a sad story, my eyes are full of tears; and when I tell a story that's frightening or awful, my hair stands on end with fear and my heart jumps.

S. Well, Ion, should we say this man is in his right mind at times like these: when he's at festivals or celebrations, all dressed up in fancy clothes, with golden crowns, and he weeps, though he's lost none of his finery—or when he's standing among millions of friendly people and he's frightened, though no one is undressing him or doing him any harm? Is he in his right mind then?

I. Lord no, Socrates. Not at all, to tell the truth.

S. And you know that you have the same effects on most of your spectators too, don't you?

I. I know very well that we do. I look down at them every time from up on the rostrum, and they're crying and looking terrified, and as the stories are told they are filled with amazement. You see I must keep my wits and pay close attention to them: if I start them crying, *I* will laugh as I take their money, but if *they* laugh, I shall cry at having lost money.

S. And you know that this spectator is the last of the rings, don't you—the ones that I said take their power from each other by virtue of the Heracleian stone [the magnet]? The middle ring is you, the rhapsode or actor, and the first one is the poet himself. The god pulls people's souls through all these wherever he wants, looping the power down from one to another. And just as if it hung from that stone, there's an enormous chain of choral dancers and dance teachers and assistant teachers hanging off to the sides of the rings that are suspended from the Muse. One poet is attached to one Muse, another to another (we say he is "possessed," and that's near enough, for he is *held*). From these first rings, from the poets, *they* are attached in their turn and inspired, some from one poet, some from another: some from Orpheus, some from Musaeus, and many are possessed and held from Homer. You are one of *them*, Ion, and you are possessed from Homer. And when anyone sings the work of another poet, you're asleep and you're lost about what to say; but when any song of that poet is sounded, you are immediately awake, your soul is dancing, and you have plenty to say. You see it's not because you're a master of knowledge about Homer that you can say what you say, but because of a divine gift, because you are possessed. That's how it is with the Corybantes, who have sharp ears only for the specific song that belongs to whatever god possesses them; they have plenty of words and movements to go with *that* song; but they are quite lost if the music is different. That's how it is with you, Ion: when anyone mentions Homer, you have plenty to say, but if he mentions the others you are lost; and the explanation of this, for which you ask me—why it is that you have plenty to say about Homer but not about the others—is that it's not mastering the subject, but a divine gift, that makes you a wonderful singer of Homer's praises.

I. You're a good speaker, Socrates. Still, I would be amazed if you could speak well enough to convince me that I am possessed or crazed when I praise Homer. I don't believe you'd think so if you heard me speaking on Homer.

S. And I really do want to hear you, but not before you answer me this: on which of Homer's subjects do you speak well? I don't suppose you speak well on *all* of them.

I. I do, Socrates, believe me, on every single one!

S. Surely not on those subjects you happen to know nothing about, even if Homer does speak of them.

I. And these subjects Homer speaks of, but I don't know about—what are they?

S. But doesn't Homer speak about professional subjects in many places, and say a great deal? Chariot driving, for example. I'll show you, if I can remember the lines.

I. No, I'll recite them. I *do* remember.

S. Then tell me what Nestor says to his son Antilochus, when he advises him to take care at the turning post in the horse race they held for Patroclus's funeral.

I. "Lean," he says,

> Lean yourself over on the smooth-planed chariot
> Just to the left of the pair. Then the horse on the right—
> Goad him, shout him on, easing the reins with your hands.
> At the post let your horse on the left stick tight to the turn
> So you seem to come right to the edge, with the hub
> Of your welded wheel. But escape cropping the stone . . .

S. That's enough. Who would know better, Ion, whether Homer speaks correctly or not in these particular verses—a doctor or a charioteer?

I. A charioteer, of course.

S. Is that because he is a master of that profession, or for some other reason?

I. No. It's because he's a master of it.

S. Then to each profession a god has granted the ability to know a certain function. I mean, the things navigation teaches us—we won't learn them from medicine as well, will we?

I. Of course not.

S. And the things medicine teaches us we won't learn from architecture.

I. Of course not.

S. And so it is for every other profession: what we learn by mastering one profession we won't learn by mastering another, right? But first, answer me this. Do you agree that there are different professions—that one is different from another?

I. Yes.

S. And is this how you determine which ones are different? When *I* find that the knowledge [involved in one case] deals with different subjects from the knowledge [in another case], then I claim that one is a different profession from the other. Is that what you do?

I. Yes.

S. I mean if there is some knowledge of the same subjects, then why should we say there are two different professions?—Especially when each of them would allow us to know the same subjects! Take these fingers: I know there are five of them, and you know the same thing about them that I do. Now suppose I asked you whether it's the same profession—arithmetic—that teaches you and me the same things, or whether it's two different ones. Of course you'd say it's the same one.

I. Yes.

S. Then tell me now what I was going to ask you earlier. Do you think it's the same way for every profession—the same profession must teach the same subjects, and a different profession, if it *is* different, must teach not the same subjects, but different ones?

I. That's how I think it is, Socrates.

S. Then a person who has not mastered a given profession will not be able to be a good judge of the things which belong to that profession, whether they are things said or things done.

I. That's true.

S. Then who will know better whether Homer speaks beautifully or not in the lines you quoted? You, or a charioteer?

I. A charioteer.

S. That's because you're a rhapsode, of course, and not a charioteer.

I. Yes.

S. And the rhapsode's profession is different from the charioteer's.

I. Yes.

S. If it's different, then its knowledge is of different subjects also.

I. Yes.

S. Then what about the time Homer tells how Hekamede, Nestor's woman, gave barley-medicine to Machaon to drink? He says something like this—

> Over wine of Pramnos, she grated goat's milk cheese
> With a brazen grater. . . . And onion relish for the drink . . .

Is Homer right or not: would a fine diagnosis here come from a doctor's profession or a rhapsode's?

I. A doctor's.

S. And what about the time Homer says:

> Leaden she plunged to the floor of the sea like a weight
> That is fixed to a field cow's horn. Given to the hunt
> It goes among ravenous fish, carrying death.

Should we say it's for a fisherman's profession or a rhapsode's to tell whether or not he describes this beautifully?

I. That's obvious, Socrates. It's for a fisherman's.

S. All right, look. Suppose you were the one asking questions, and you asked me, "Socrates, since you're finding out which passages belong to each of the professions Homer treats—which are the passages that each profession should judge—come tell me this: which are the passages that belong to a diviner and to divination, passages he should be able to judge as to whether they're well or badly composed?" Look how easily I can give you a true answer. Often, in the *Odyssey*, he says things like what Theoklymenus says—the prophet of the sons of Melampus:

> Are you mad? What evil is this that's upon you? Night
> Has enshrouded your hands, your faces, and down to your knees.
> Wailing spreads like fire, tears wash your cheeks.
> Ghosts fill the dooryard, ghosts fill the hall, they rush
> To the black gate of hell, they drop below darkness. Sunlight
> Has died from a sky run over with evil mist.

And often in the *Iliad*, as in the battle at the wall. There he says:

> There came to them a bird as they hungered to cross over.
> An eagle, a high-flier, circled the army's left
> With a blood-red serpent carried in its talons, a monster,
> Alive, still breathing, it had not yet forgotten its warlust,
> For it struck its captor on the breast, by the neck;
> It was writhing back, but the eagle shot it groundwards
> In agony of pain, and dropped it in the midst of the throng,
> Then itself, with a scream, soared on a breath of the wind.

I shall say that these passages and those like them belong to a diviner. They are for him to examine and judge.

I. That's a true answer, Socrates.

S. Well, *your* answers are true, too, Ion. Now *you* tell me—just as I picked out for you, from the *Odyssey* and the *Iliad*, passages that belong to a diviner and ones that belong to a doctor and ones that belong to a fisherman—in the same way, Ion, since you have more experience with Homer's work than I do, you pick out for me the passages that belong to the rhapsode and to his profession, the passages a rhapsode should be able to examine and to judge better than anyone else.

I. My answer, Socrates, is "all of them."

S. That's not *your* answer, Ion. Not "all of them." Or are you really so forgetful? But no, it would not befit a *rhapsode* to be forgetful.

I. What do you think I'm forgetting?

S. Don't you remember you said that a rhapsode's profession is different from a charioteer's?

I. I remember.

S. And didn't you agree that because they are different they will know different subjects?

I. Yes.

S. So a rhapsode's profession, on *your* view, will not know everything, and neither will a rhapsode.

I. But things like that are exceptions, Socrates.

S. By "things like that" you mean that almost all the subjects of the other professions are exceptions, don't you? But then what sort of thing *will* a rhapsode know, if not everything?

I. My opinion, anyhow, is that he'll know what it's fitting for a man or a woman to say—or for a slave or a freeman, or for a follower or a leader.

S. So—what should a leader say when he's at sea and his ship is hit by a storm—do you mean a rhapsode will know better than a navigator?

I. No, no. A navigator will know *that*.

S. And when he's in charge of a sick man, what should a leader say—will a rhapsode know better than a doctor?

I. Not that, either.

S. But he *will* know what a slave should say. Is that what you mean?

I. Yes.

S. For example, what should a slave who's a cowherd say to calm down his cattle when they're going wild—will a rhapsode know what a cowherd does not?

I. Certainly not.

S. And what a woman who spins yarn should say about working with wool?

I. No.

S. And what a man should say, if he's a general, to encourage his troops?

I. Yes! That's the sort of thing a rhapsode will know.

S. What? Is a rhapsode's profession the same as a general's?

I. Well, I certainly would know what a general should say.

S. Perhaps that's because you're also a general by profession, Ion. I mean, if you were somehow both a horseman and a cithara-player at the same time, you would know good riders from bad. But suppose I asked you: "Which profession teaches you good horsemanship—the one that makes you a horseman, or the one that makes you a cithara-player?"

I. The horseman, I'd say.

S. Then if you also knew good cithara-players from bad, the profession that taught you *that* would be the one which made you a cithara-player, not the one that made you a horseman. Wouldn't you agree?

I. Yes.

S. Now, since you know the business of a general, do you know this by being a general or by being a good rhapsode?

I. I don't think there's any difference.

S. What? Are you saying there's no difference? On your view is there one profession for rhapsodes and generals, or two?

I. One, I think.

S. So anyone who is a good rhapsode turns out to be a good general too.

I. Certainly, Socrates.

S. It also follows that anyone who turns out to be a good general is a good rhapsode too.

I. No. This time I don't agree.

S. But you do agree to this: anyone who is a good rhapsode is a good general too.

I. I quite agree.

S. And aren't you the best rhapsode in Greece?

I. By far, Socrates.

S. Are you also a general, Ion? Are you the best in Greece?

I. Certainly, Socrates. That, too, I learned from Homer's poetry.

S. Then why in heaven's name, Ion, when you're both the best general *and* the best rhapsode in Greece, do you go around the country giving rhapsodies but not commanding troops? Do you think Greece really needs a rhapsode who is crowned with a golden crown? And does not need a general?

I. Socrates, *my* city is governed and commanded by you [by Athens]; we don't need a general. Besides, neither your city nor Sparta would choose me for a general. You think you're adequate for that yourselves.

S. Ion, you're superb. Don't you know Apollodorus of Cyzike?

I. What does *he* do?

S. He's a foreigner who has often been chosen by Athens to be their general. And Phanosthenes of Andros and Herakleides of Clazomenae—they're also foreigners; they've demonstrated that they are worth noticing, and Athens appoints them to be generals or other sorts of officials. And do you think that *this* city, that makes such appointments, would not select Ion of Ephesus and honor him, if they thought he was worth noticing? Why? Aren't you people from Ephesus Athenians of long standing? And isn't Ephesus a city that is second to none?

But *you*, Ion, you're doing me wrong, if what you say is true that what enables you to praise Homer is knowledge or mastery of a profession. You assured me that you knew many lovely things about Homer, you promised to give a demonstration; but you're cheating me, you're a long way from giving a demonstration. You aren't even willing to tell me what it is that you're so wonderfully clever *about*, though I've been begging you for ages. Really, you're just like Proteus, you twist up and down and take many different shapes, till finally you've escaped me altogether by turning yourself into a general, so as to avoid proving how wonderfully wise you are about Homer.

If you're really a master of your subject, and if, as I said earlier, you're cheating me of the demonstration you promised about Homer, then you're doing me wrong. But if you're not a master of your subject, if you're possessed by a divine gift from Homer, so that you make many lovely speeches about the poet without knowing anything—as *I* said about you—then you're not doing me wrong. So choose, how do you want us to think of you—as a *man* who does wrong, or as someone *divine*?

I. There's a great difference, Socrates. It's much lovelier to be thought divine.

S. Then *that* is how we think of you, Ion, the lovelier way: it's as someone divine, and not as master of a profession, that you are a singer of Homer's praises.

Plato

THE QUARREL BETWEEN PHILOSOPHY AND POETRY: FROM THE *REPUBLIC*, BOOK X

How Representation in Art Is Related to Truth

Readers who take this chapter as stating, for its own sake, an aesthetic theory of the nature of art are surprised and shocked: the point of view seems as perverse, and even stupid, as Tolstoy's in What Is Art? *The main object of attack, however, is the claim, currently made by sophists and professional reciters of the Homeric poems,[1] that Homer in particular, and in a less degree the tragedians, were masters of all technical knowledge, from wagon-building or chariot-driving to strategy, and also moral and religious guides to the conduct of life. As such, the poet becomes the rival of the philosopher as conceived by Plato, and the study of poetry an alternative to the severe intellectual training of the Academy. If wisdom is to be gained only through knowledge of the real world of Forms disclosed by Dialectic, the claim that the poet can educate mankind to virtue must be as hollow as the pretence that the artist knows all about shoemaking because he can paint a life-like picture of a shoemaker. How much knowledge of ultimate values does the poet need in order to paint in words his pictures of human life?*

The painter is taken first by way of illustration. A picture of a bed is a two-dimensional representation of the appearance of a solid object seen at a certain angle. The object itself is only a particular bed, which, as a part of the material world, is not a wholly real thing, since it comes into being and perishes and is perpetually changing; it belongs to the realm of Becoming. This actual bed, however, is nearer to reality than the picture, because it is one of many embodiments of the essential nature common to all beds. Beds can be made of wood or iron or canvas and may vary indefinitely in size,

From The Republic of Plato, *translated by Francis M. Cornford (London: Oxford University Press, 1941), pp. 321–340. Reprinted with permission of Oxford University Press. (Some footnotes omitted.) The italicized introductions to each section of the dialogue are the comments of Professor Cornford.*

[1]Such as Ion in Plato's dialogue of that name.

shape, colour, etc. But they cannot be called beds at all unless they serve the purpose of a bed, a thing designed to be slept on. This purpose, however hard to define, may be called the essence or Form of Bed, and in Plato's view it is the unique and unvarying reality which must be, however imperfectly, embodied in any bed, and is in one sense the meaning of the word "Bed." (Plato speaks here of this essential Bed as "in the nature of things," i.e., in the real world of Forms, and as made by a god, though the Forms are elsewhere described as not made by anyone, but eternal, and there is a difficulty in supposing eternal Forms of the products of human workmanship. These points, however, need not be pressed. The bed was perhaps chosen for illustrative purposes because beds are obviously made by a practical craftsman, whom Plato wishes to contrast with the fine artist, whereas the maker of natural objects, the divine Demiurge of the Timaeus, is a mythical figure who could not be introduced without a long explanation.) The upshot is that the artist's picture of a bed is at two removes from the essential Form. It is only as it were a mirror-image of a sensible thing, which itself is only one embodiment (with many accidental features) of the real Form, the object of knowledge.

Poetry is like a picture in words, a representation of life. However skillfully executed, it is no evidence that the poet really possessed the knowledge required for the right conduct of actual life. This knowledge is not to be gained by studying his portraits of heroic characters, any more than we can learn how to drive a chariot or conduct a campaign from his descriptions of a chariot-race or of the Trojan war. Socrates' examination of the poets had convinced him that they worked, not with conscious intelligence, but from inspiration, like seers and oracle-mongers who do not understand the meaning of the fine language they use.

In this chapter mimesis has a wider sense than dramatic impersonation: the nearest English word is "representation," applicable to many forms of fine art. The usual rendering "imitation" is misleading. We do not say that Garrick, still less that Shakespeare, imitated the character of Hamlet; or that Raphael imitated Julius II; or that the Passion music imitates religious emotion. In all these cases mimesis would be used. The substantive mimetes can be rendered in this context by "artist." On the other hand, mimesis does also mean "imitation," and this encourages the suggestion that tragic acting is on a level with mimicry and that fine art in general is no more than a copying of external appearances. The view that a work of art is an image or likeness (eikon) of some original, or holds a mirror up to nature, became prominent towards the end of the fifth century together with the realistic drama of Euripides and the illusionistic painting of Zeuxis. Plato's attack adopts this theory. The art which claims to be "realistic" is, in his view, as far as possible from reality.

Indeed, I continued, our commonwealth has many features which make me think it was based on very sound principles, especially our rule not on any account to admit the poetry of dramatic representation.[2] Now that we have distinguished the several parts of the soul, it seems to me clearer than ever that such poetry must be firmly excluded.

---

[2]At 398 A Plato seemed to exclude all dramatic poetry because this contains no narrative but involves the impersonation (mimesis) of all types of character, good or bad; whereas epic, for instance, can limit speeches in character to the representation of virtuous or heroic types. He will now argue that all poetry and other forms of art are essentially mimesis. The meaning of the word is obviously enlarged where he speaks just below of "representation in general."

What makes you say so?

Between ourselves—for you will not denounce me to the tragedians and the other dramatists—poetry of that sort seems to be injurious to minds which do not possess the antidote in a knowledge of its real nature.

What have you in mind?

I must speak out, in spite of a certain affection and reverence I have had from a child for Homer, who seems to have been the original master and guide of all this imposing company of tragic poets.[3] However, no man must be honoured above the truth; so, as I say, I must speak my mind.

Do, by all means.

Listen then, or rather let me ask you a question. Can you tell me what is meant by representation in general? I have no very clear notion myself.

So you expect me to have one!

Why not? It is not always the keenest eye that is the first to see something.

True; but when you are there I should not be very desirous to tell what I saw, however plainly. You must use your own eyes.

Well then, shall we proceed as usual and begin by assuming the existence of a single essential nature or Form for every set of things which we call by the same name? Do you understand?

I do.

Then let us take any set of things you choose. For instance there are any number of beds or of tables, but only two Forms, one of Bed and one of Table.

Yes.

And we are in the habit of saying that the craftsman, when he makes the beds or tables we use or whatever it may be, has before his mind the Form[4] of one or other of these pieces of furniture. The Form itself is, of course, not the work of any craftsman. How could it be?

It could not.

Now what name would you give to a craftsman who can produce all the things made by every sort of workman?

He would need to have very remarkable powers!

Wait a moment, and you will have even better reason to say so. For, besides producing any kind of artificial thing, this same craftsman can create all plants and animals, himself included, and earth and sky and gods and the heavenly bodies and all the things under the earth in Hades.

That sounds like a miraculous feat of virtuosity.

Are you incredulous? Tell me, do you think there could be no such craftsman at all, or that there might be someone who could create all these things in one sense, though not in another?[5] Do you not see that you could do it yourself, in a way?

---

[3]The plots of Greek tragedy were normally stories borrowed from epic poetry. Hence Homer was spoken of as the first tragic poet.

[4]"Form" does not mean "shape," but the essential properties which constitute what the thing, by definition, is.

[5]The divine Demiurge of the creation-myth in the *Timaeus* is pictured as fashioning the whole visible world after the likeness of the eternal Forms, which he does not create but uses as models. He is thus the maker of natural objects, corresponding to the carpenter who makes artificial objects; and both, as makers of actual things, are superior to the painter or poet, who makes all things only "in a way," by creating mere semblances like images in a mirror.

In what way, I should like to know.

There is no difficulty; in fact there are several ways in which the thing can be done quite quickly. The quickest perhaps would be to take a mirror and turn it round in all directions. In a very short time you could produce sun and stars and earth and yourself and all the other animals and plants and lifeless objects which we mentioned just now.

Yes, in appearance, but not the actual things.

Quite so; you are helping out my argument. My notion is that a painter is a craftsman of that kind. You may say that the things he produces are not real; but there is a sense in which he too does produce a bed.

Yes, the appearance of one.

And what of the carpenter? Were you not saying just now that he only makes a particular bed, not what we call the Form or essential nature of Bed?

Yes, I was.

If so, what he makes is not the reality, but only something that resembles it. It would not be right to call the work of a carpenter or of any other handicraftsman a perfectly real thing, would it?

Not in the view of people accustomed to thinking on these lines.[6]

We must not be surprised, then, if even an actual bed is a somewhat shadowy thing as compared with reality.

True.

Now shall we make use of this example to throw light on our question as to the true nature of this artist who represents things? We have here three sorts of bed: one which exists in the nature of things and which, I imagine, we could only describe as a product of divine workmanship; another made by the carpenter; and a third by the painter. So the three kinds of bed belong respectively to the domains of these three: painter, carpenter, and god.

Yes.

Now the god made only one ideal or essential Bed, whether by choice or because he was under some necessity not to make more than one; at any rate two or more were not created, nor could they possibly come into being.

Why not?

Because, if he made even so many as two, then once more a single ideal Bed would make its appearance, whose character those two would share; and that one, not the two, would be the essential Bed. Knowing this, the god, wishing to be the real maker of a real Bed, not a particular manufacturer of one particular bed, created one which is essentially unique.

So it appears.

Shall we call him, then, the author of the true nature of Bed, or something of that sort?

Certainly he deserves the name, since all his works constitute the real nature of things.

And we may call the carpenter the manufacturer of a bed?

Yes.

Can we say the same of the painter?

---

[6]Familiar with the Platonic doctrine, as opposed to current materialism, which regards the beds we sleep on as real things and the Platonic Form as a mere "abstraction" or notion existing only in our minds.

Certainly not.

Then what is he, with reference to a bed?

I think it would be fairest to describe him as the artist who represents the things which the other two make.

Very well, said I; so the work of the artist is at the third remove from the essential nature of the thing?

Exactly.

The tragic poet, too, is an artist who represents things; so this will apply to him: he and all other artists are, as it were, third in succession from the throne of truth.

Just so.

We are in agreement, then, about the artist. But now tell me about our painter: which do you think he is trying to represent—the reality that exists in the nature of things, or the products of the craftsman?

The products of the craftsman.

As they are, or as they appear? You have still to draw that distinction.[7]

How do you mean?

I mean: you may look at a bed or any other object from straight in front or slantwise or at any angle. Is there then any difference in the bed itself, or does it merely look different?

It only looks different.

Well, that is the point. Does painting aim at reproducing any actual object as it is, or the appearance of it as it looks? In other words, is it a representation of the truth or of a semblance?

Of a semblance.

The art of representation, then, is a long way from reality; and apparently the reason why there is nothing it cannot reproduce is that it grasps only a small part of any object, and that only an image. Your painter, for example, will paint us a shoemaker, a carpenter, or other workman, without understanding any one of their crafts;[8] and yet, if he were a good painter, he might deceive a child or a simple-minded person into thinking his picture was a real carpenter, if he showed it them at some distance.

No doubt.

But I think there is one view we should take in all such cases. Whenever someone announces that he has met with a person who is master of every trade and knows more about every subject than any specialist, we should reply that he is a simple fellow who has apparently fallen in with some illusionist and been tricked into thinking him omniscient, because of his own inability to discriminate between knowledge and ignorance and the representation of appearances.

Quite true.

Then it is now time to consider the tragic poets and their master, Homer, because we are sometimes told that they understand not only all technical matters but also all about human conduct, good or bad, and about religion; for, to write well, a good poet,

---

[7]The distinction is needed to exclude another possible sense of *mimesis*, the production of a complete replica.

[8]Knowledge of carpentry is the essence of the carpenter, what makes him a carpenter. The painter could not reproduce this knowledge in his picture, even if he possessed it himself. This may sound absurd as an objection to art, but Plato is thinking rather of the application to the poet, for whom it was claimed that he both possessed technical and moral knowledge and reproduced it in his work.

so they say, must know his subject; otherwise he could not write about it. We must ask whether these people have not been deluded by meeting with artists who can represent appearances, and in contemplating the poets' work have failed to see that it is at the third remove from reality, nothing more than semblances, easy to produce with no knowledge of the truth. Or is there something in what they say? Have the good poets a real mastery of the matters on which the public thinks they discourse so well?

It is a question we ought to look into.

Well then, if a man were able actually to do the things he represents as well as to produce images of them, do you believe he would seriously give himself up to making these images and take that as a completely satisfying object in life? I should imagine that, if he had a real understanding of the actions he represents, he would far sooner devote himself to performing them in fact. The memorials he would try to leave after him would be noble deeds, and he would be more eager to be the hero whose praises are sung than the poet who sings them.

Yes, I agree; he would do more good in that way and win a greater name.

Here is a question, then, that we may fairly put to Homer or to any other poet. We will leave out of account all mere matters of technical skill: we will not ask them to explain, for instance, why it is that, if they have a knowledge of medicine and not merely the art of reproducing the way physicians talk, there is no record of any poet, ancient or modern, curing patients and bequeathing his knowledge to a school of medicine, as Asclepius did. But when Homer undertakes to tell us about matters of the highest importance, such as the conduct of war, statesmanship, or education, we have a right to inquire into his competence. "Dear Homer," we shall say, "we have defined the artist as one who produces images at the third remove from reality. If your knowledge of all that concerns human excellence was really such as to raise you above him to the second rank, and you could tell what courses of conduct will make men better or worse as individuals or as citizens, can you name any country which was better governed thanks to your efforts? Many states, great and small, have owed much to a good lawgiver, such as Lycurgus at Sparta, Charondas in Italy and Sicily, and our own Solon. Can you tell us of any that acknowledges a like debt to you?"

I should say not, Glaucon replied. The most devout admirers of Homer make no such claim.

Well, do we hear of any war in Homer's day being won under his command or thanks to his advice?

No.

Or of a number of ingenious inventions and technical contrivances, which would show that he was a man of practical ability like Thales of Miletus or Anacharsis the Scythian?

Nothing of the sort.

Well, if there is no mention of public services, do we hear of Homer in his own lifetime presiding, like Pythagoras, over a band of intimate disciples who loved him for the inspiration of his society and handed down a Homeric way of life, like the way of life which the Pythagoreans called after their founder and which to this day distinguishes them from the rest of the world?

No; on the contrary, Homer's friend with the absurd name, Creophylus, would look even more absurd when considered as a product of the poet's training, if the story is true that he completely neglected Homer during his lifetime.

Yes, so they say. But what do you think, Glaucon? If Homer had really possessed the knowledge qualifying him to educate people and make them better men, instead of merely giving us a poetical representation of such matters, would he not have attracted a host of disciples to love and revere him? After all, any number of private teachers like Protagoras of Abdera and Prodicus of Ceos[9] have succeeded in convincing their contemporaries that they will never be fit to manage affairs of state or their own households unless these masters superintend their education; and for this wisdom they are so passionately admired that their pupils are all but ready to carry them about on their shoulders. Can we suppose that Homer's contemporaries, or Hesiod's, would have left them to wander about reciting their poems, if they had really been capable of helping their hearers to be better men? Surely they would sooner have parted with their money and tried to make the poets settle down at home; or failing that, they would have danced attendance on them wherever they went, until they had learnt from them all they could.

I believe you are quite right, Socrates.

We may conclude, then, that all poetry, from Homer onwards, consists in representing a semblance of its subject, whatever it may be, including any kind of human excellence, with no grasp of the reality. We were speaking just now of the painter who can produce what looks like a shoemaker to the spectator who, being as ignorant of shoemaking as he is himself, judges only by form and colour. In the same way the poet, knowing nothing more than how to represent appearances, can paint in words his picture of any craftsman so as to impress an audience which is equally ignorant and judges only by the form of expression; the inherent charm of metre, rhythm, and musical setting is enough to make them think he has discoursed admirably about generalship or shoemaking or any other technical subject. Strip what the poet has to say of its poetical colouring, and I think you must have seen what it comes to in plain prose. It is like a face which was never really handsome, when it has lost the fresh bloom of youth.

Quite so.

Here is a further point, then. The artist, we say, this maker of images, knows nothing of the reality, but only the appearance. But that is only half the story. An artist can paint a bit and bridle, while the smith and the leather-worker can make them. Does the painter understand the proper form which bit and bridle ought to have? Is it not rather true that not even the craftsmen who make them know that, but only the horseman who understands their use?

Quite true.

May we not say generally that there are three arts concerned with any object—the art of using it, the art of making it, and the art of representing it?

Yes.

And that the excellence or beauty or rightness of any implement or living creature or action has reference to the use for which it is made or designed by nature?

Yes.

It follows, then, that the user must know most about the performance of the thing he uses and must report on its good or bad points to the maker. The flute-player, for example, will tell the instrument-maker how well his flutes serve the player's purpose, and the other will submit to be instructed about how they should be made. So the man who uses any implement will speak of its merits and defects with knowledge, whereas the maker will take his word and possess no more than a correct belief, which he is obliged to obtain by listening to the man who knows.

Quite so.

But what of the artist? Has he either knowledge or correct belief? Does he know from direct experience of the subjects he portrays whether his representations are good and right or not? Has he even gained a correct belief by being obliged to listen to someone who does know and can tell him how they ought to be represented?

No, he has neither.

If the artist, then, has neither knowledge nor even a correct belief about the soundness of his work, what becomes of the poet's wisdom in respect of the subjects of his poetry?

It will not amount to much.

And yet he will go on with his work, without knowing in what way any of his representations is sound or unsound. He must, apparently, be reproducing only what pleases the taste or wins the approval of the ignorant multitude.[10]

Yes, what else can he do?

We seem, then, so far to be pretty well agreed that the artist knows nothing worth mentioning about the subjects he represents, and that art is a form of play, not to be taken seriously. This description, moreover, applies above all to tragic poetry, whether in epic or dramatic form.

Exactly.[11]

Dramatic Poetry Appeals to the Emotions, Not to the Reason

The psychological objections to poetry in this and the following chapter are based on the earlier division of the soul into three parts, and apply especially to the drama and the element of dramatic impersonation in epic poetry. The appeal of dramatic poetry is not to the reason but to a lower part, the emotions, which, like the senses, are subject to illusions. As optical and other such illusions can be corrected by the calculating and reflective part (logistikon) which ascertains the true facts by measurement, so illusory exaggerations of feeling should be corrected by reflection. But the dramatist is concerned rather to rouse sympathetic emotion than to check its excesses, and while we enter into the joys or sorrows of a hero on the stage, the reason is held in abeyance. Thus drama is as far removed as visual art from true reality and from wisdom.

But now look here, said I; the content of this poetical representation is something at the third remove from reality, is it not?

---

[10]Living in the world of appearances, the poet reproduces only "the many conventional notions of the mass of mankind about what is beautiful or honourable or just" (479 D).

[11]It should now be clear that this chapter is not concerned with aesthetic criticism, but with extravagant claims for the poets as moral teachers. It may leave the impression that Plato has been irritated by some contemporary controversy, and is overstating his case with a slightly malicious delight in paradox. . . .

Yes.

On what part of our human nature, then, does it produce its effect?

What sort of part do you mean?

Let me explain by an analogy. An object seen at a distance does not, of course, look the same size as when it is close at hand; a straight stick looks bent when part of it is under water; and the same thing appears concave or convex to an eye misled by colours. Every sort of confusion like these is to be found in our minds; and it is this weakness in our nature that is exploited, with a quite magical effect, by many tricks of illusion, like scene-painting and conjuring.

True.

But satisfactory means have been found for dispelling these illusions by measuring, counting, and weighing. We are no longer at the mercy of apparent differences of size and quantity and weight; the faculty which has done the counting and measuring or weighing takes control instead. And this can only be the work of the calculating or reasoning element in the soul.

True.

And when this faculty has done its measuring and announced that one quantity is greater than, or equal to, another, we often find that there is an appearance which contradicts it. Now, as we have said, it is impossible for the same part of the soul to hold two contradictory beliefs at the same time. Hence the part which agrees with the measurements must be a different part from the one which goes against them; and its confidence in measurement and calculation is a proof of its being the highest part; the other which contradicts it must be an inferior one.

It must.

This, then, was the conclusion I had in view when I said that paintings and works of art in general are far removed from reality, and that the element in our nature which is accessible to art and responds to its advances is equally far from wisdom. The offspring of a connexion thus formed on no true or sound basis must be as inferior as the parents. This will be true not only of visual art, but of art addressed to the ear, poetry as we call it.

Naturally.

Then, instead of trusting merely to the analogy from painting, let us directly consider that part of the mind to which the dramatic element in poetry appeals, and see how much claim it has to serious worth. We can put the question in this way. Drama, we say, represents the acts and fortunes of human beings. It is wholly concerned with what they do, voluntarily or against their will, and how they fare, with the consequences which they regard as happy or otherwise, and with their feelings of joy and sorrow in all these experiences. That is all, is it not?

Yes.

And in all these experiences has a man an undivided mind? Is there not an internal conflict which sets him at odds with himself in his conduct, much as we were saying that the conflict of visual impressions leads him to make contradictory judgements? However, I need not ask that question; for, now I come to think of it, we have already agreed that innumerable conflicts of this sort are constantly occurring in the mind. But there is a further point to be considered now. We have said that a man of high character will bear any stroke of fortune, such as the loss of a son or of anything else he holds dear, with more equanimity than most people. We may now ask: will he feel no pain, or is that impossible? Will he not rather observe due measure in his grief?

Yes, that is nearer the truth.

Now tell me: will he be more likely to struggle with his grief and resist it when he is under the eyes of his fellows or when he is alone?

He will be far more restrained in the presence of others.

Yes; when he is by himself he will not be ashamed to do and say much that he would not like anyone to see or hear.

Quite so.

What encourages him to resist his grief is the lawful authority of reason, while the impulse to give way comes from the feeling itself; and, as we said, the presence of contradictory impulses proves that two distinct elements in his nature must be involved. One of them is law-abiding, prepared to listen to the authority which declares that it is best to bear misfortune as quietly as possible without resentment, for several reasons: it is never certain that misfortune may not be a blessing; nothing is gained by chafing at it; nothing human is matter for great concern; and, finally, grief hinders us from calling in the help we most urgently need. By this I mean reflection on what has happened, letting reason decide on the best move in the game of life that the fall of the dice permits. Instead of behaving like a child who goes on shrieking after a fall and hugging the wounded part, we should accustom the mind to set itself at once to raise up the fallen and cure the hurt, banishing lamentation with a healing touch.

Certainly that is the right way to deal with misfortune.

And if, as we think, the part of us which is ready to act upon these reflections is the highest, that other part which impels us to dwell upon our sufferings and can never have enough of grieving over them is unreasonable, craven, and faint-hearted.

Yes.

Now this fretful temper gives scope for a great diversity of dramatic representation; whereas the calm and wise character in its unvarying constancy is not easy to represent, nor when represented is it readily understood, especially by a promiscuous gathering in a theatre, since it is foreign to their own habit of mind. Obviously, then, this steadfast disposition does not naturally attract the dramatic poet, and his skill is not designed to find favour with it. If he is to have a popular success, he must address himself to the fretful type with its rich variety of material for representation.

Obviously.

We have, then, a fair case against the poet and we may set him down as the counterpart of the painter, whom he resembles in two ways: his creations are poor things by the standard of truth and reality, and his appeal is not to the highest part of the soul, but to one which is equally inferior. So we shall be justified in not admitting him into a well-ordered commonwealth, because he stimulates and strengthens an element which threatens to undermine the reason. As a country may be given over into the power of its worst citizens while the better sort are ruined, so, we shall say, the dramatic poet sets up a vicious form of government in the individual soul: he gratifies that senseless part which cannot distinguish great and small, but regards the same things as now one, now the other; and he is an image-maker whose images are phantoms far removed from reality.

Quite true.

The Effect of Dramatic Poetry on Character

A further psychological objection is that dramatic poetry, tragic or comic, by encouraging the sympathetic indulgence of emotions which we are ashamed to give way to in our own lives, undermines the character. If poetry cannot be defended from this charge, it must be restricted to celebrating the praises of the gods and of good men.

But, I continued, the heaviest count in our indictment is still to come. Dramatic poetry has a most formidable power of corrupting even men of high character, with a few exceptions.

Formidable indeed, if it can do that.

Let me put the case for you to judge. When we listen to some hero in Homer or on the tragic stage moaning over his sorrows in a long tirade, or to a chorus beating their breasts as they chant a lament, you know how the best of us enjoy giving ourselves up to follow the performance with eager sympathy. The more a poet can move our feelings in this way, the better we think him. And yet when the sorrow is our own, we pride ourselves on being able to bear it quietly like a man, condemning the behaviour we admired in the theatre as womanish. Can it be right that the spectacle of a man behaving as one would scorn and blush to behave oneself should be admired and enjoyed, instead of filling us with disgust?

No, it really does not seem reasonable.

It does not, if you reflect that the poet ministers to the satisfaction of that very part of our nature whose instinctive hunger to have its fill of tears and lamentations is forcibly restrained in the case of our own misfortunes. Meanwhile the noblest part of us, insufficiently schooled by reason or habit, has relaxed its watch over these querulous feelings, with the excuse that the sufferings we are contemplating are not our own and it is no shame to us to admire and pity a man with some pretensions to a noble character, though his grief may be excessive. The enjoyment itself seems a clear gain, which we cannot bring ourselves to forfeit by disdaining the whole poem. Few, I believe, are capable of reflecting that to enter into another's feelings must have an effect on our own: the emotions of pity our sympathy has strengthened will not be easy to restrain when we are suffering ourselves.

That is very true.

Does not the same principle apply to humour as well as to pathos? You are doing the same thing if, in listening at a comic performance or in ordinary life to buffooneries which you would be ashamed to indulge in yourself, you thoroughly enjoy them instead of being disgusted with their ribaldry. There is in you an impulse to play the clown, which you have held in restraint from a reasonable fear of being set down as a buffoon; but now you have given it rein, and by encouraging its impudence at the theatre you may be unconsciously carried away into playing the comedian in your private life. Similar effects are produced by poetic representation of love and anger and all those desires and feelings of pleasure or pain which accompany our every action. It waters the growth of passions which should be allowed to wither away and sets them up in control, although the goodness and happiness of our lives depend on their being held in subjection.

I cannot but agree with you.

If so, Glaucon, when you meet with admirers of Homer who tell you that he has been the educator of Hellas and that on questions of human conduct and culture he deserves to be constantly studied as a guide by whom to regulate your whole life, it is well to give a friendly hearing to such people, as entirely well-meaning according to their lights, and you may acknowledge Homer to be the first and greatest of the tragic poets; but you must be quite sure that we can admit into our commonwealth only the poetry which celebrates the praises of the gods and of good men. If you go further and admit the honeyed muse in epic or in lyric verse, then pleasure and pain will usurp the sovereignty of law and of the principles always recognized by common consent as the best.

Quite true.

So now, since we have recurred to the subject of poetry, let this be our defence: it stands to reason that we could not but banish such an influence from our commonwealth. But, lest poetry should convict us of being harsh and unmannerly, let us tell her further that there is a long-standing quarrel between poetry and philosophy. There are countless tokens of this old antagonism, such as the lines which speak of "the cur which at his master yelps," or "one mighty in the vain talk of fools" or "the throng of all-too-sapient heads," or "subtle thinkers all in rags." None the less, be it declared that, if the dramatic poetry whose end is to give pleasure can show good reason why it should exist in a well-governed society, we for our part should welcome it back, being ourselves conscious of its charm; only it would be a sin to betray what we believe to be the truth. You too, my friend, must have felt this charm, above all when poetry speaks through Homer's lips.

I have indeed.

It is fair, then, that before returning from exile poetry should publish her defence in lyric verse or some other measure; and I suppose we should allow her champions who love poetry but are not poets to plead for her in prose, that she is no mere source of pleasure but a benefit to society and to human life. We shall listen favourably; for we shall clearly be the gainers, if that can be proved.

Undoubtedly.

But if it cannot, then we must take a lesson from the lover who renounces at any cost a passion which he finds is doing him no good. The love for poetry of this kind, bred in us by our own much admired institutions, will make us kindly disposed to believe in her genuine worth; but so long as she cannot make good her defence we shall, as we listen, rehearse to ourselves the reasons we have just given, as a counter-charm to save us from relapsing into a passion which most people have never outgrown. We shall reiterate that such poetry has no serious claim to be valued as an apprehension of truth. One who lends an ear to it should rather beware of endangering the order established in his soul, and would do well to accept the view of poetry which we have expressed.

I entirely agree.

Yes, Glaucon; for much is at stake, more than most people suppose: it is a choice between becoming a good man or a bad; and poetry, no more than wealth or power or honours, should tempt us to be careless of justice and virtue.

Your argument has convinced me, as I think it would anyone else.

Aristotle

THE NATURE OF POETIC IMITATION: FROM THE *POETICS*

1 Our subject being Poetry, I propose to speak not only of the art in general but also of its species and their respective capacities; of the structure of plot required for a good poem; of the number and nature of the constituent parts of a poem; and likewise of any other matters in the same line of inquiry. Let us follow the natural order and begin with the primary facts.

Epic poetry and Tragedy, as also Comedy, Dithyrambic poetry, and most flute-playing and lyre-playing, are all, viewed as a whole, modes of imitation. But at the same time they differ from one another in three ways, either by a difference of kind in their means, or by differences in the objects, or in the manner of their imitations. . . .

I. Just as colour and form are used as means by some, who (whether by art or constant practice) imitate and portray many things by their aid, and the voice is used by others; so also in the above-mentioned group of arts, the means with them as a whole are rhythm, language, and harmony—used, however, either singly or in certain combinations. A combination of harmony and rhythm alone is the means in flute-playing and lyre-playing, and any other arts there may be of the same description, e.g. imitative piping. Rhythm alone, without harmony, is the means in the dancer's imitations; for even he, by the rhythms of his attitudes, may represent men's characters, as well as what they do and suffer. There is further an art which imitates by language alone, without harmony, in prose or in verse, and if in verse, either in some one or in a plurality of metres. This form of imitation is to this day without a name. We have no common name for a mime of Sophron or Xenarchus and a Socratic Conversation; and we should still be without one even if the imitation in the two instances were in trimeters or elegiacs or some other kind of verse—though it is the way with people to take on "poet" to the name of a metre, and talk of elegiac-poets and epic-poets, thinking that they call them poets not by reason of the imitative nature of their work, but indiscriminately by reason of the metre they write in. Even if a theory of medicine or physical philosophy be put forth in a metrical form, it is usual to

From The Works of Aristotle, *edited by* W. D. Ross, *vol. XI.* Poetics, *translated by Ingram Bywater (London: Oxford University Press, 1966). Reprinted with permission of Oxford University Press.* (Footnotes omitted.)

describe the writer in this way; Homer and Empedocles, however, have really nothing in common apart from their metre; so that, if the one is to be called a poet, the other should be termed a physicist rather than a poet. We should be in the same position also, if the imitation in these instances were in all the metres, like the *Centaur* (a rhapsody in a medley of all metres) of Chaeremon; and Chaeremon one has to recognize as a poet. So much, then, as to these arts. There are, lastly, certain other arts, which combine all the means enumerated, rhythm, melody, and verse, e.g. Dithyrambic and Nomic poetry, Tragedy and Comedy; with this difference, however, that the three kinds of means are in some of them employed together, and in others brought in separately, one after the other. These elements of difference in the above arts I term the means of their imitation.

2 II. The objects the imitator represents are actions, with agents who are necessarily either good men or bad—the diversities of human character being nearly always derivative from this primary distinction, since the line between virtue and vice is one dividing the whole of mankind. It follows, therefore, that the agents represented must be either above our own level of goodness, or beneath it, or just such as we are; in the same way as, with the painters, the personages of Polygnotus are better than we are, those of Pauson worse, and those of Dionysius just like ourselves. It is clear that each of the above-mentioned arts will admit of these differences, and that it will become a separate art by representing objects with this point of difference. Even in dancing, flute-playing, and lyre-playing such diversities are possible; and they are also possible in the nameless art that uses language, prose or verse without harmony, as its means; Homer's personages, for instance, are better than we are; Cleophon's are on our own level; and those of Hegemon of Thasos, the first writer of parodies, and Nicochares, the author of the *Diliad*, are beneath it. The same is true of the Dithyramb and the Nome: the personages may be presented in them with the difference exemplified in the . . . of . . . and Argas, and in the Cyclopses of Timotheus and Philoxenus. This difference it is that distinguishes Tragedy and Comedy also; the one would make its personages worse, and the other better, than the men of the present day.

3 III. A third difference in these arts is in the manner in which each kind of object is represented. Given both the same means and the same kind of object for imitation, one may either (1) speak at one moment in narrative and at another in an assumed character, as Homer does; or (2) one may remain the same throughout, without any such change; or (3) the imitators may represent the whole story dramatically, as though they were actually doing the things described.

As we said at the beginning, therefore, the differences in the imitation of these arts come under three heads, their means, their objects, and their manner.

So that as an imitator Sophocles will be on one side akin to Homer, both portraying good men; and on another to Aristophanes, since both present their personages as acting and doing. This in fact, according to some, is the reason for plays being termed dramas, because in a play the personages act the story. Hence too both Tragedy and Comedy are claimed by the Dorians as their discoveries; Comedy by the Megarians— by those in Greece as having arisen when Megara became a democracy, and by the Sicilian Megarians on the ground that the poet Epicharmus was of their country, and a good deal earlier than Chionides and Magnes; even Tragedy also is claimed by certain of the Peloponnesian Dorians. In support of this claim they point to the words "comedy" and "drama." Their word for the outlying hamlets, they say, is *comae*, whereas Athenians call them *demes*—thus assuming that comedians got the name not from their *comoe* or revels, but from their strolling from hamlet to hamlet, lack of appreciation keeping them out of the city. Their word also for "to act," they say, is *dran*, whereas Athenians use *prattein*.

So much, then, as to the number and nature of the points of difference in the imitation of these arts.

4 It is clear that the general origin of poetry was due to two causes, each of them part of human nature. Imitation is natural to man from childhood, one of his advantages over the lower animals being this, that he is the most imitative creature in the world, and learns at first by imitation. And it is also natural for all to delight in works of imitation. The truth of this second point is shown by experience: though the objects themselves may be painful to see, we delight to view the most realistic representations of them in art, the forms for example of the lowest animals and of dead bodies. The explanation is to be found in a further fact: to be learning something is the greatest of pleasures not only to the philosopher but also to the rest of mankind, however small their capacity for it; the reason of the delight in seeing the picture is that one is at the same time learning—gathering the meaning of things, e.g. that the man there is so-and-so; for if one has not seen the thing before, one's pleasure will not be in the picture as an imitation of it, but will be due to the execution or colouring or some similar cause. Imitation, then, being natural to us—as also the sense of harmony and rhythm, the metres being obviously species of rhythms—it was through their original aptitude, and by a series of improvements for the most part gradual on their first efforts, that they created poetry out of their improvisations.

Poetry, however, soon broke up into two kinds according to the differences of character in the individual poets; for the graver among them would represent noble actions, and those of noble personages; and the meaner sort the actions of the ignoble. The latter class produced invectives at first, just as others did hymns and panegyrics. We know of no such poem by any of the pre-Homeric poets, though there were probably many such writers among them; instances, however, may be found from Homer downwards, e.g. his *Margites*, and the similar poems of others. In this poetry of invective its natural fitness brought an iambic metre into use; hence our present term "iambic," because it was the metre of their "iambs" or invectives against one another. The result was that the old poets became some of them writers of heroic and others of iambic verse. Homer's position, however, is peculiar: just as he was in the serious style the poet of poets, standing alone not only through the literary excellence, but also through the dramatic character of his imitations, so too he was the first to outline for us the general forms of Comedy by producing not a dramatic invective, but a dramatic picture of the Ridiculous; his *Margites* in fact stands in the same relation to our comedies as the *Iliad* and *Odyssey* to our tragedies. As soon, however, as Tragedy and Comedy appeared in the field, those naturally drawn to the one line of poetry became writers of comedies instead of iambs, and those naturally drawn to the other, writers of tragedies instead of epics, because these new modes of art were grander and of more esteem than the old.

If it be asked whether Tragedy is now all that it need be in its formative elements, to consider that, and decide it theoretically and in relation to the theatres, is a matter for another inquiry.

It certainly began in improvisations—as did also Comedy; the one originating with the authors of the Dithyramb, the other with those of the phallic songs, which still survive as institutions in many of our cities. And its advance after that was little by little, through their improving on whatever they had before them at each stage. It was in fact only after a long series of changes that the movement of Tragedy stopped on its attaining to its natural form. (1) The number of actors was first increased to two by Aeschylus, who curtailed the business of the Chorus, and made the dialogue, or spoken portion, take the leading part in the play. (2) A third actor and scenery were due to Sophocles. (3) Tragedy acquired also its magnitude. Discarding short stories and a ludicrous diction through its passing out of its satyric stage, it assumed, though only at a late point in its progress, a tone of dignity; and its metre changed then from trochaic to iambic. The reason for their original use of the trochaic tetrameter was that their poetry was satyric and more connected with dancing than it now is. As soon, however, as a spoken part came in, nature herself found the appropriate metre. The iambic, we know, is the most speakable of metres, as is shown by the fact that we very often fall into it in conversation, whereas we rarely talk hexameters, and only when we depart from the speaking tone of voice. (4) Another change was a plurality of episodes or acts. As for the remaining matters, the superadded embellishments and the account of their introduction, these must be taken as said, as it would probably be a long piece of work to go through the details.

5 As for Comedy, it is (as has been observed) an imitation of men worse than the average; worse, however, not as regards any and every sort of fault, but only as regards one particular kind, the Ridiculous, which is a species of the Ugly. The Ridiculous may be defined as a mistake or deformity not productive of pain or harm to others; the mask, for instance, that excites laughter, is something ugly and distorted without causing pain.

Though the successive changes in Tragedy and their authors are not unknown, we cannot say the same of Comedy; its early stages passed unnoticed, because it was not as yet taken up in a serious way. It was only at a late point in its progress that a chorus of comedians was officially granted by the archon; they used to be mere volunteers. It had also already certain definite forms at the time when the record of those termed comic poets begins. Who it was who supplied it with masks, or prologues, or a plurality of actors and the like, has remained unknown. The invented Fable, or Plot, however, originated in Sicily with Epicharmus and Phormis; of Athenian poets Crates was the first to drop the Comedy of invective and frame stories of a general and non-personal nature, in other words, Fables or Plots.

Epic poetry, then, has been seen to agree with Tragedy to this extent, that of being an imitation of serious subjects in a grand kind of verse. It differs from it, however, (1) in that it is in one kind of verse and in narrative form; and (2) in its length—which is due to its action having no fixed limit of time, whereas Tragedy endeavours to keep as far as possible within a single circuit of the sun, or something near that. This, I say, is another point of difference between them, though at first the practice in this respect was just the same in tragedies as in epic poems. They differ also (3) in their constituents, some being common to both and others peculiar to Tragedy—hence a judge of good and bad in Tragedy is a judge of that in epic poetry also. All the parts of an epic are included in Tragedy; but those of Tragedy are not all of them to be found in the Epic.

6 Reserving hexameter poetry and Comedy for consideration hereafter, let us proceed now to the discussion of Tragedy; before doing so, however, we must gather up the definition resulting from what has been said. A tragedy, then, is the imitation of an action that is serious and also, as having magnitude, complete in itself; in language with pleasurable accessories, each kind brought in separately in the parts of the work; in a dramatic, not in a narrative form; with incidents arousing pity and fear, wherewith to accomplish its catharsis of such emotions. Here by "language with pleasurable accessories" I mean that with rhythm and harmony or song superadded; and by "the kinds separately" I mean that some portions are worked out with verse only, and others in turn with song.

I. As they act the stories, it follows that in the first place the Spectacle (or stage-appearance of the actors) must be some part of the whole; and in the second Melody and Diction, these two being the means of their imitation. Here by "Diction" I mean merely this, the composition of the verses; and by "Melody," what is too completely understood to require explanation. But further: the subject represented also is an action; and the action involves agents, who must necessarily have their distinctive qualities both of character and thought, since it is from these that we ascribe certain qualities to their actions. There are in the natural order of things, therefore, two causes, Thought and Character, of their actions, and consequently of their success or failure in their lives. Now the action (that which was done) is represented in the play by the Fable or Plot. The Fable, in our present sense of the term, is simply this, the combination of the incidents, or things done in the story; whereas Character is what makes us ascribe certain moral qualities to the agents; and Thought is shown in all they say when proving a particular point or, it may be, enunciating a general truth. There are six parts consequently of every tragedy, as a whole (that is) of such or such quality, viz. a Fable or Plot, Characters, Diction, Thought, Spectacle, and Melody; two of them arising from the means, one from the manner, and three from the objects of the dramatic imitation; and there is nothing else besides these six. Of these, its formative elements, then, not a few of the dramatists have made due use, as every play, one may say, admits of Spectacle, Character, Fable, Diction, Melody, and Thought.

II. The most important of the six is the combination of the incidents of the story. Tragedy is essentially an imitation not of persons but of action and life, of happiness and misery. All human happiness or misery takes the form of action; the end for which we live is a certain kind of activity, not a quality. Character gives us qualities, but it is in our actions—what we do—that we are happy or the reverse. In a play accordingly they do not act in order to portray the Characters; they include the Characters for the sake of the action. So that it is the action in it, i.e. its Fable or Plot, that is the end and purpose of the tragedy; and the end is everywhere the chief thing. Besides this, a tragedy is impossible without action, but there may be one without Character. The tragedies of most of the moderns are characterless—a defect common among poets of all kinds, and with its counterpart in painting in Zeuxis as compared with Polygnotus; for whereas the latter is strong in character, the work of Zeuxis is devoid of it. And again: one may string together a series of characteristic speeches of the utmost finish as regards Diction and Thought, and yet fail to produce the true tragic effect; but one will have much better success with a tragedy which, however inferior in these respects, has a Plot, a combination of incidents, in it. And again: the most powerful elements of attraction in Tragedy, the Peripeties and Discoveries, are parts of the Plot. A further proof is in the fact that beginners succeed earlier with the Diction and Characters than with the construction of a story; and the same may be said of nearly all the early dramatists. We maintain, therefore, that the first essential, the life and soul, so to speak, of Tragedy is the Plot; and that the Characters come second—compare the parallel in painting, where the most beautiful colours laid on without order will not give one the same pleasure as a simple black-and-white sketch of a portrait. We maintain that Tragedy is primarily an imitation of action, and that it is mainly for the sake of the action that it imitates the personal agents. Third comes the element of Thought, i.e. the power of saying whatever can be said, or what is appropriate to the occasion. This is what, in the speeches in Tragedy, falls under the arts of Politics and Rhetoric; for the older poets make their personages discourse like statesmen, and the modern like rhetoricians. One must not confuse it with Character. Character in a play is that which reveals the moral purpose of the agents, i.e. the sort of thing they seek or avoid, where that is not obvious—hence there is no room for Character in a speech on a purely indifferent subject. Thought, on the other hand, is shown in all they say when proving or disproving some particular point, or enunciating some universal proposition. Fourth among the literary elements is the Diction of the personages, i.e., as before explained, the expression of their thoughts in words, which is practically the same thing with verse as with prose. As for the two remaining parts, the Melody is the greatest of the pleasurable accessories of Tragedy. The Spectacle, though an attraction, is the least artistic of all the parts, and has least to do with the art of poetry. The tragic effect is quite possible without a public performance and actors; and besides, the getting-up of the Spectacle is more a matter for the costumier than the poet.

7 Having thus distinguished the parts, let us now consider the proper construction of the Fable or Plot, as that is at once the first and the most important thing in Tragedy. We have laid it down that a tragedy is an imitation of an action that is complete in itself, as a whole of some magnitude; for a whole may be of no magnitude to speak of. Now a whole is that which has beginning, middle, and end. A beginning is that which is not itself necessarily after anything else, and which has naturally something else after it; an end is that which is naturally after something itself, either as its necessary or usual consequent, and with nothing else after it; and a middle, that which is by nature after one thing and has also another after it. A well-constructed Plot, therefore, cannot either begin or end at any point one likes; beginning and end in it must be of the forms just described. Again: to be beautiful, a living creature, and every whole made up of parts, must not only present a certain order in its arrangement of parts, but also be of a certain definite magnitude. Beauty is a matter of size and order, and therefore impossible either (1) in a very minute creature, since our perception becomes indistinct as it approaches instantaneity; or (2) in a creature of vast size—one, say, 1,000 miles long—as in that case, instead of the object being seen all at once, the unity and wholeness of it is lost to the beholder. Just in the same way, then, as a beautiful whole made up of parts, or a beautiful living creature, must be of some size, but a size to be taken in by the eye, so a story or Plot must be of some length, but of a length to be taken in by the memory. As for the limit of its length, so far as that is relative to public performances and spectators, it does not fall within the theory of poetry. If they had to perform a hundred tragedies, they would be timed by water-clocks, as they are said to have been at one period. The limit, however, set by the actual nature of the thing is this: the longer the story, consistently with its being comprehensible as a whole, the

finer it is by reason of its magnitude. As a rough general formula, "a length which allows of the hero passing by a series of probable or necessary stages from misfortune to happiness, or from happiness to misfortune," may suffice as a limit for the magnitude of the story.

8 The Unity of a Plot does not consist, as some suppose, in its having one man as its subject. An infinity of things befall that one man, some of which it is impossible to reduce to unity; and in like manner there are many actions of one man which cannot be made to form one action. One sees, therefore, the mistake of all the poets who have written a *Heracleid*, a *Theseid*, or similar poems; they suppose that, because Heracles was one man, the story also of Heracles must be one story. Homer, however, evidently understood this point quite well, whether by art or instinct, just in the same way as he excels the rest in every other respect. In writing an *Odyssey*, he did not make the poem cover all that ever befell his hero—it befell him, for instance, to get wounded on Parnassus and also to feign madness at the time of the call to arms, but the two incidents had no necessary or probable connexion with one another—instead of doing that, he took as the subject of the *Odyssey*, as also of the *Iliad*, an action with a Unity of the kind we are describing. The truth is that, just as in the other imitative arts one imitation is always of one thing, so in poetry the story, as an imitation of action, must represent one action, a complete whole, with its several incidents so closely connected that the transposal or withdrawal of any one of them will disjoin and dislocate the whole. For that which makes no perceptible difference by its presence or absence is no real part of the whole.

9 From what we have said it will be seen that the poet's function is to describe, not the thing that has happened, but a kind of thing that might happen, i.e. what is possible as being probable or necessary. The distinction between historian and poet is not in the one writing prose and the other verse—you might put the work of Herodotus into verse, and it would still be a species of history; it consists really in this, that the one describes the thing that has been, and the other a kind of thing that might be. Hence poetry is something more philosophic and of graver import than history, since its statements are of the nature rather of universals, whereas those of history are singulars. By a universal statement I mean one as to what such or such a kind of man will probably or necessarily say or do—which is the aim of poetry, though it affixes proper names to the characters; by a singular statement, one as to what, say, Alcibiades did or had done to him. In Comedy this has become clear by this time; it is only when their plot is already made up of probable incidents that they give it a basis of proper names, choosing for the purpose any names that may occur to them, instead of writing like the old iambic poets about particular persons. In Tragedy, however, they still adhere to the historic names; and for this reason: what convinces is the possible; now whereas we are not yet sure as to the possibility of that which has not happened, that which has happened is manifestly possible, else it would not have come to pass. Nevertheless even in Tragedy there are some plays with but one or two known names in them, the rest being inventions; and there are some without a single known name, e.g. Agathon's *Antheus*, in which both incidents and names are of the poet's invention; and it is no less delightful on that account. So that one must not aim at a rigid adherence to the traditional stories on which tragedies are based. It would be absurd, in fact, to do so, as

even the known stories are only known to a few, though they are a delight none the less to all.

It is evident from the above that the poet must be more the poet of his stories or Plots than of his verses, inasmuch as he is a poet by virtue of the imitative element in his work, and it is actions that he imitates. And if he should come to take a subject from actual history, he is none the less a poet for that; since some historic occurrences may very well be in the probable and possible order of things; and it is in that aspect of them that he is their poet.

Of simple Plots and actions the episodic are the worst. I call a Plot episodic when there is neither probability nor necessity in the sequence of its episodes. Actions of this sort bad poets construct through their own fault, and good ones on account of the players. His work being for public performance, a good poet often stretches out a Plot beyond its capabilities, and is thus obliged to twist the sequence of incident.

Tragedy, however, is an imitation not only of a complete action, but also of incidents arousing pity and fear. Such incidents have the very greatest effect on the mind when they occur unexpectedly and at the same time in consequence of one another; there is more of the marvellous in them then than if they happened of themselves or by mere chance. Even matters of chance seem most marvellous if there is an appearance of design as it were in them; as for instance the statue of Mitys at Argos killed the author of Mitys' death by falling down on him when a looker-on at a public spectacle; for incidents like that we think to be not without a meaning. A Plot, therefore, of this sort is necessarily finer than others.

10 Plots are either simple or complex, since the actions they represent are naturally of this twofold description. The action, proceeding in the way defined, as one continuous whole, I call simple, when the change in the hero's fortunes takes place without Peripety or Discovery; and complex, when it involves one or the other, or both. These should each of them arise out of the structure of the Plot itself, so as to be the consequence, necessary or probable, of the antecedents. There is a great difference between a thing happening *propter hoc* and *post hoc*.

11 A Peripety is the change of the kind described from one state of things within the play to its opposite, and that too in the way we are saying, in the probable or necessary sequence of events; as it is for instance in *Oedipus*: here the opposite state of things is produced by the Messenger, who, coming to gladden Oedipus and to remove his fears as to his mother, reveals the secret of his birth. And in *Lynceus*: just as he is being led off for execution, with Danaus at his side to put him to death, the incidents preceding this bring it about that he is saved and Danaus put to death. A Discovery is, as the very word implies, a change from ignorance to knowledge, and thus to either love or hate, in the personages marked for good or evil fortune. The finest form of Discovery is one attended by Peripeties, like that which goes with the Discovery in *Oedipus*. There are no doubt other forms of it; what we have said may happen in a way in reference to inanimate things, even things of a very casual kind; and it is also possible to discover whether some one has done or not done something. But the form most directly connected with the Plot and the action of the piece is the first-mentioned. This, with a Peripety, will arouse either pity or fear—actions of that nature being what Tragedy is assumed to represent; and it will also serve to bring about the happy or unhappy

ending. The Discovery, then, being of persons, it may be that of one party only to the other, the latter being already known; or both the parties may have to discover themselves. Iphigenia, for instance, was discovered to Orestes by sending the letter; and another Discovery was required to reveal him to Iphigenia.

Two parts of the Plot, then, Peripety and Discovery, are on matters of this sort. A third part is Suffering; which we may define as an action of a destructive or painful nature, such as murders on the stage, tortures, woundings, and the like. The other two have been already explained.

12 The parts of Tragedy to be treated as formative elements in the whole were mentioned in a previous Chapter. From the point of view, however, of its quantity, i.e. the separate sections into which it is divided, a tragedy has the following parts: Prologue, Episode, Exode, and a choral portion, distinguished into Parode and Stasimon; these two are common to all tragedies, whereas songs from the stage and *Commoe* are only found in some. The Prologue is all that precedes the Parode of the chorus; an Episode all that comes in between two whole choral songs; the Exode all that follows after the last choral song. In the choral portion the Parode is the whole first statement of the chorus; a Stasimon, a song of the chorus without anapaests or trochees; a *Commos*, a lamentation sung by chorus and actor in concert. The parts of Tragedy to be used as formative elements in the whole we have already mentioned; the above are its parts from the point of view of its quantity, or the separate sections into which it is divided.

13 The next points after what we have said above will be these: (1) What is the poet to aim at, and what is he to avoid, in constructing his Plots? and (2) What are the conditions on which the tragic effect depends?

We assume that, for the finest form of Tragedy, the Plot must be not simple but complex; and further, that it must imitate actions arousing fear and pity, since that is the distinctive function of this kind of imitation. It follows, therefore, that there are three forms of Plot to be avoided. (1) A good man must not be seen passing from happiness to misery, or (2) a bad man from misery to happiness. The first situation is not fear-inspiring or piteous, but simply odious to us. The second is the most untragic that can be; it has no one of the requisites of Tragedy; it does not appeal either to the human feeling in us, or to our pity, or to our fears. Nor, on the other hand, should (3) an extremely bad man be seen falling from happiness into misery. Such a story may arouse the human feeling in us, but it will not move us to either pity or fear; pity is occasioned by undeserved misfortune, and fear by that of one like ourselves; so that there will be nothing either piteous or fear-inspiring in the situation. There remains, then, the intermediate kind of personage, a man not pre-eminently virtuous and just, whose misfortune, however, is brought upon him not by vice and depravity but by some error of judgement, of the number of those in the enjoyment of great reputation and prosperity; e.g. Oedipus, Thyestes, and the men of note of similar families. The perfect Plot, accordingly, must have a single, and not (as some tell us) a double issue; the change in the hero's fortunes must be not from misery to happiness, but on the contrary from happiness to misery; and the cause of it must lie not in any depravity, but in some great error on his part; the man himself being either such as we have described, or better, not worse, than that. Fact also confirms our theory. Though the poets began by accepting any tragic story that came to hand, in these days the finest tragedies are always on the story of some few houses, on that of Alcmeon, Oedipus, Orestes, Meleager, Thyestes, Telephus, or any others that may have been involved, as either agents or sufferers, in some deed of horror. The theoretically best tragedy, then, has a Plot of this description. The critics, therefore, are wrong who blame Euripides for taking this line in his tragedies, and giving many of them an unhappy ending. It is, as we have said, the right line to take. The best proof is this: on the stage, and in the public performances, such plays, properly worked out, are seen to be the most truly tragic; and Euripides, even if his execution be faulty in every other point, is seen to be nevertheless the most tragic certainly of the dramatists. After this comes the construction of Plot which some rank first, one with a double story (like the *Odyssey*) and an opposite issue for the good and the bad personages. It is ranked as first only through the weakness of the audiences; the poets merely follow their public, writing as its wishes dictate. But the pleasure here is not that of Tragedy. It belongs rather to Comedy, where the bitterest enemies in the piece (e.g. Orestes and Aegisthus) walk off good friends at the end, with no slaying of any one by any one.

14 The tragic fear and pity may be aroused by the Spectacle; but they may also be aroused by the very structure and incidents of the play—which is the better way and shows the better poet. The Plot in fact should be so framed that, even without seeing the things take place, he who simply hears the account of them shall be filled with horror and pity at the incidents; which is just the effect that the mere recital of the story in *Oedipus* would have on one. To produce this same effect by means of the Spectacle is less artistic, and requires extraneous aid. Those, however, who make use of the Spectacle to put before us that which is merely monstrous and not productive of fear, are wholly out of touch with Tragedy; not every kind of pleasure should be required of a tragedy, but only its own proper pleasure.

The tragic pleasure is that of pity and fear, and the poet has to produce it by a work of imitation; it is clear, therefore, that the causes should be included in the incidents of his story. Let us see, then, what kinds of incident strike one as horrible, or rather as piteous. In a deed of this description the parties must necessarily be either friends, or enemies, or indifferent to one another. Now when enemy does it on enemy, there is nothing to move us to pity either in his doing or in his meditating the deed, except so far as the actual pain of the sufferer is concerned; and the same is true when the parties are indifferent to one another. Whenever the tragic deed, however, is done within the family—when murder or the like is done or mediated by brother on brother, by son on father, by mother on son, or son on mother—these are the situations the poet should seek after. The traditional stories, accordingly, must be kept as they are, e.g. the murder of Clytaemnestra by Orestes and of Eriphyle by Alcmeon. At the same time even with these there is something left to the poet himself; it is for him to devise the right way of treating them. Let us explain more clearly what we mean by "the right way." The deed of horror may be done by the doer knowingly and consciously, as in the old poets, and in Medea's murder of her children in Euripides. Or he may do it, but in ignorance of his relationship, and discover that afterwards, as does the Oedipus in Sophocles. Here the deed is outside the play; but it may be within it, like the act of the Alcmeon in Astydamas, or that of the Telegonus in *Ulysses Wounded*. A third possibility is for one meditating some deadly injury to another, in ignorance of his relationship, to make the discovery in time to draw back. These exhaust the possibilities, since the deed must necessarily be either done or not done, and either knowingly or unknowingly.

The worst situation is when the personage is with full knowledge on the point of doing the deed, and leaves it undone. It is odious and also (through the absence of suffering) untragic; hence it is that no one is made to act thus except in some few instances, e.g. Haemon and Creon in *Antigone*. Next after this comes the actual perpetration of the deed mediated. A better situation than that, however, is for the deed to be done in ignorance, and the relationship discovered afterwards, since there is nothing odious in it, and the Discovery will serve to astound us. But the best of all is the last; what we have in *Cresphontes*, for example, where Merope, on the point of slaying her son, recognizes him in time; in *Iphigenia*, where sister and brother are in a like position; and in *Helle*, where the son recognizes his mother, when on the point of giving her up to her enemy.

This will explain why our tragedies are restricted (as we said just now) to such a small number of families. It was accident rather than art that led the poets in quest of subjects to embody this kind of incident in their Plots. They are still obliged, accordingly, to have recourse to the families in which such horrors have occurred.

On the construction of the Plot, and the kind of Plot required for Tragedy, enough has now been said.

15 In the Characters there are four points to aim at. First and foremost, that they shall be good. There will be an element of character in the play, if (as has been observed) what a personage says or does reveals a certain moral purpose; and a good element of character, if the purpose so revealed is good. Such goodness is possible in every type of personage, even in a woman or a slave, though the one is perhaps an inferior, and the other a wholly worthless being. The second point is to make them appropriate. The Character before us may be, say, manly; but it is not appropriate in a female Character to be manly, or clever. The third is to make them like the reality, which is not the same as their being good and appropriate, in our sense of the term. The fourth is to make them consistent and the same throughout; even if inconsistency be part of the man before one for imitation as presenting that form of character, he should still be consistently inconsistent. We have an instance of baseness of character, not required for the story, in the Menelaus in *Orestes*; of the incongruous and unbefitting in the lamentation of Ulysses in *Scylla*, and in the (clever) speech of Melanippe; and of inconsistency in *Iphigenia at Aulis*, where Iphigenia the suppliant is utterly unlike the later Iphigenia. The right thing, however, is in the Characters just as in the incidents of the play to endeavour always after the necessary or the probable; so that whenever such-and-such a personage says or does such-and-such a thing, it shall be the necessary or probable outcome of his character; and whenever this incident follows on that, it shall be either the necessary or the probable consequence of it. From this one sees (to digress for a moment) that the Dénouement also should arise out of the plot itself, and not depend on a stage-artifice, as in *Medea*, or in the story of the (arrested) departure of the Greeks in the *Iliad*. The artifice must be reserved for matters outside the play—for past events beyond human knowledge, or events yet to come, which require to be foretold or announced; since it is the privilege of the Gods to know everything. There should be nothing improbable among the actual incidents. If it be unavoidable, however, it should be outside the tragedy, like the improbability in the *Oedipus* of Sophocles. But to return to the Characters. As Tragedy is an imitation of personages better than the ordinary man, we in our way should follow the example of good portrait-painters, who reproduce the distinctive features of a man, and at the same time, without losing the likeness, make him handsomer than he is. The poet in like manner, in portraying men quick or slow to anger, or with similar infirmities of character, must know how to represent them as such, and at the same time as good men, as Agathon and Homer have represented Achilles. . . .

23 As for the poetry which merely narrates, or imitates by means of versified language (without action), it is evident that it has several points in common with Tragedy.

I. The construction of its stories should clearly be like that in a drama; they should be based on a single action, one that is a complete whole in itself, with a beginning, middle, and end, so as to enable the work to produce its own proper pleasure with all the organic unity of a living creature. Nor should one suppose that there is anything like them in our usual histories. A history has to deal not with one action, but with one period and all that happened in that to one or more persons, however disconnected the several events may have been. Just as two events may take place at the same time, e.g. the sea-fight off Salamis and the battle with the Carthaginians in Sicily, without converging to the same end, so too of two consecutive events one may sometimes come after the other with no one end as their common issue. Nevertheless most of our epic poets, one may say, ignore the distinction.

Herein, then, to repeat what we have said before, we have a further proof of Homer's marvellous superiority to the rest. He did not attempt to deal even with the Trojan war in its entirety, though it was a whole with a definite beginning and end—through a feeling apparently that it was too long a story to be taken in in one view, or if not that, too complicated from the variety of incident in it. As it is, he has singled out one section of the whole; many of the other incidents, however, he brings in as episodes, using the Catalogue of the Ships, for instance, and other episodes to relieve the uniformity of his narrative. As for the other epic poets, they treat of one man, or one period; or else of an action which, although one, has a multiplicity of parts in it. This last is what the authors of the *Cypria* and *Little Iliad* have done. And the result is that, whereas the *Iliad* or *Odyssey* supplies materials for only one, or at most two tragedies, the *Cypria* does that for several and the *Little Iliad* for more than eight: for an *Adjudgment of Arms*, a *Philoctetes*, a *Neoptolemus*, a *Eurypylus*, a *Ulysses as Beggar*, a *Laconian Women*, a *Fall of Ilium*, and a *Departure of the Fleet*; as also a *Sinon*, and a *Women of Troy*.

24 II. Besides this, Epic poetry must divide into the same species as Tragedy; it must be either simple or complex, a story of character or one of suffering. Its parts, too, with the exception of Song and Spectacle, must be the same, as it requires Peripeties, Discoveries, and scenes of suffering just like Tragedy. Lastly, the Thought and Diction in it must be good in their way. All these elements appear in Homer first; and he has made due use of them. His two poems are each examples of construction, the *Iliad* simple and a story of suffering, the *Odyssey* complex (there is Discovery throughout it) and a story of character. And they are more than this, since in Diction and Thought too they surpass all other poems.

There is, however, a difference in the Epic as compared with Tragedy, (1) in its length, and (2) in its metre. (1) As to its length, the limit already suggested will suffice: it must be possible for the beginning and end of the work to be taken in in one view—a condition which will be fulfilled if the poem be shorter than the old epics, and about as long as the series of tragedies offered for one hearing. For the extension of its length epic poetry has a special advantage, of which it makes large use. In a play one cannot represent an action with a number of parts going on simultaneously; one is limited to the part on the stage and connected with the actors. Whereas in epic poetry the narrative form makes it possible for one to describe a number of simultaneous incidents; and these, if germane to the subject, increase the body of the poem. This then is a gain to the Epic, tending to give it grandeur, and also variety of interest and room for episodes of diverse kinds. Uniformity of incident by the satiety it soon creates is apt to ruin tragedies on the stage. (2) As for its metre, the heroic has been assigned it from experience; were any one to attempt a narrative poem in some one, or in several, of the other metres, the incongruity of the thing would be apparent. The heroic in fact is the gravest and weightiest of metres—which is what makes it more tolerant than the rest of strange words and metaphors, that also being a point in which the narrative form of poetry goes beyond all others. The iambic and trochaic, on the other hand, are metres of movement, the one representing that of life and action, the other that of the dance. Still more unnatural would it appear, if one were to write an epic in a medley of metres, as Chaeremon did. Hence it is that no one has ever written a long story in any but heroic verse; nature herself, as we have said, teaches us to select the metre appropriate to such a story.

Homer, admirable as he is in every other respect, is especially so in this, that he alone among epic poets is not unaware of the part to be played by the poet himself in the poem. The poet should say very little *in propria persona*, as he is no imitator when doing that. Whereas the other poets are perpetually coming forward in person, and say but little, and that only here and there, as imitators, Homer after a brief preface brings in forthwith a man, a woman, or some other Character—no one of them characterless, but each with distinctive characteristics.

The marvellous is certainly required in Tragedy. The Epic, however, affords more opening for the improbable, the chief factor in the marvellous, because in it the agents are not visibly before one. The scene of the pursuit of Hector would be ridiculous on the stage—the Greeks halting instead of pursuing him, and Achilles shaking his head to stop them; but in the poem the absurdity is overlooked. The marvellous, however, is a cause of pleasure, as is shown by the fact that we all tell a story with additions, in the belief that we are doing our hearers a pleasure.

Homer more than any other has taught the rest of us the art of framing lies in the right way. I mean the use of paralogism. Whenever, if A is or happens, a consequent, B, is or happens, men's notion is that, if the B is, the A also is—but that is a false conclusion. Accordingly, if A is untrue, but there is something else, B, that on the assumption of its truth follows as its consequent, the right thing then is to add on the B. Just because we know the truth of the consequent, we are in our minds led on to the erroneous inference of the truth of the antecedent. Here is an instance, from the *Bath-story* in the *Odyssey*.

A likely impossibility is always preferable to an unconvincing possibility. The story should never be made up of improbable incidents; there should be nothing of the sort in it. If, however, such incidents are unavoidable, they should be outside the piece, like the hero's ignorance in *Oedipus* of the circumstances of Laius' death; not within it, like the report of the Pythian games in *Electra*, or the man's having come to Mysia from Tegea without uttering a word on the way, in *The Mysians*. So that it is ridiculous to say that one's Plot would have been spoilt without them, since it is fundamentally wrong to make up such Plots. If the poet has taken such a Plot, however, and one sees that he might have put it in a more probable form, he is guilty of absurdity as well as a fault of art. Even in the *Odyssey* the improbabilities in the setting-ashore of Ulysses would be clearly intolerable in the hands of an inferior poet. As it is, the poet conceals them, his other excellences veiling their absurdity. Elaborate Diction, however, is required only in places where there is no action, and no Character or Thought to be revealed. Where there is Character or Thought, on the other hand, an over-ornate Diction tends to obscure them.

25 As regards Problems and their Solutions, one may see the number and nature of the assumptions on which they proceed by viewing the matter in the following way. (1) The poet being an imitator just like the painter or other maker of likenesses, he must necessarily in all instances represent things in one or other of three aspects, either as they were or are, or as they are said or thought to be or to have been, or as they ought to be. (2) All this he does in language, with an admixture, it may be, of strange words and metaphors, as also of the various modified forms of words, since the use of these is conceded in poetry. (3) It is to be remembered, too, that there is not the same kind of correctness in poetry as in politics, or indeed any other art. There is, however, within the limits of poetry itself a possibility of two kinds of error, the one directly, the other only accidentally connected with the art. If the poet meant to describe the thing correctly, and failed through lack of power of expression, his art itself is at fault. But if it was through his having meant to describe it in some incorrect way (e.g. to make the horse in movement have both right legs thrown forward) that the technical error (one in a matter of, say, medicine or some other special science), or impossibilities of whatever kind they may be, have got into his description, his error in that case is not in the essentials of the poetic art. These, therefore, must be the premisses of the Solutions in answer to criticisms involved in the Problems.

I. As to the criticisms relating to the poet's art itself. Any impossibilities there may be in his descriptions of things are faults. But from another point of view they are justifiable, if they serve the end of poetry itself—if (to assume what we have said of that end) they make the effect of either that very portion of the work or some other portion more astounding. The Pursuit of Hector is an instance in point. If, however, the poetic end might have been as well or better attained without sacrifice of technical correctness in such matters, the impossibility is not to be justified, since the description should be, if it can, entirely free from error. One may ask, too, whether the error is in a matter directly or only accidentally connected with the poetic art; since it is a lesser error in an artist not to know, for instance, that the hind has no horns, than to produce an unrecognizable picture of one.

II. If the poet's description be criticized as not true to fact, one may urge perhaps that the object ought to be as described—an answer like that of Sophocles, who said that he drew men as they ought to be, and Euripides as they were. If the description, however, be neither true nor of the thing as it ought to be, the answer must be then, that it is in accordance with opinion. The tales about Gods, for instance, may be as wrong as Xenophanes thinks, neither true nor the better thing to say; but they are certainly in accordance with opinion. Of other statements in poetry one may perhaps say, not that they are better than the truth, but that the fact was so at the time; e.g. the description of the arms: "their spears stood upright, butt-end upon the ground"; for that was the usual way of fixing them then, as it is still with the Illyrians. As for the question whether something said or done in a poem is morally right or not, in dealing with that one should consider not only the intrinsic quality of the actual word or deed, but also the person who says or does it, the person to whom he says or does it, the time, the means, and the motive of the agent—whether he does it to attain a greater good, or to avoid a greater evil. . . .

Speaking generally, one has to justify (1) the Impossible by reference to the requirements of poetry, or to the better, or to opinion. For the purposes of poetry a convincing impossibility is preferable to an unconvincing possibility; and if men such as Zeuxis depicted be impossible, the answer is that it is better they should be like that, as the artist ought to improve on his model. (2) The Improbable one has to justify either by showing it to be in accordance with opinion, or by urging that at times it is not improbable; for there is a probability of things happening also against probability. (3) The contradictions found in the poet's language one should first test as one does an opponent's confutation in a dialectical argument, so as to see whether he means the same thing, in the same relation, and in the same sense, before admitting that he has contradicted either something he has said himself or what a man of sound sense assumes as true. But there is no possible apology for improbability of Plot or depravity of character, when they are not necessary and no use is made of them, like the improbability in the appearance of Aegeus in *Medea* and the baseness of Menelaus in *Orestes*.

The objections, then, of critics start with faults of five kinds: the allegation is always that something is either (1) impossible, (2) improbable, (3) corrupting, (4) contradictory, or (5) against technical correctness. . . .

26 The question may be raised whether the epic or the tragic is the higher form of imitation. It may be argued that, if the less vulgar is the higher, and the less vulgar is always that which addresses the better public, an art addressing any and every one is of a very vulgar order. It is a belief that their public cannot see the meaning, unless they add something themselves, that causes the perpetual movements of the performers— bad flute-players, for instance, rolling about, if quoit-throwing is to be represented, and pulling at the conductor, if Scylla is the subject of the piece. Tragedy, then, is said to be an art of this order—to be in fact just what the later actors were in the eyes of their predecessors; for Mynniscus used to call Callippides "the ape," because he thought he so overacted his parts; and a similar view was taken of Pindarus also. All Tragedy, however, is said to stand to the Epic as the newer to the older school of actors. The one, accordingly, is said to address a cultivated audience, which does not need the accompaniment of gesture; the other, an uncultivated one. If, therefore, Tragedy is a vulgar art, it must clearly be lower than the Epic.

The answer to this is twofold. In the first place, one may urge (1) that the censure does not touch the art of the dramatic poet, but only that of his interpreter; for it is quite possible to overdo the gesturing even in an epic recital, as did Sosistratus, and in a singing contest, as did Mnasitheus of Opus. (2) That one should not condemn all movement, unless one means to condemn even the dance, but only that of ignoble people—which is the point of the criticism passed on Callippides and in the present day on others, that their women are not like gentlewomen. (3) That Tragedy may produce its effect even without movement or action in just the same way as Epic poetry; for from the mere reading of a play its quality may be seen. So that, if it be superior in all other respects, this element of inferiority is no necessary part of it.

In the second place, one must remember (1) that Tragedy has everything that the Epic has (even the epic metre being admissible), together with a not inconsiderable addition in the shape of the Music (a very real factor in the pleasure of the drama) and the Spectacle. (2) That its reality of presentation is felt in the play as read, as well as in the play as acted. (3) That the tragic imitation requires less space for the attainment of its end; which is a great advantage, since the more concentrated effect is more pleasurable than one with a large admixture of time to dilute it—consider the *Oedipus* of Sophocles, for instance, and the effect of expanding it into the number of lines of the *Iliad*. (4) That there is less unity in the imitation of the epic poets, as is proved by the fact that any one work of theirs supplies matter for several tragedies; the result being that, if they take what is really a single story, it seems curt when briefly told, and thin and waterish when on the scale of length usual with their verse. In saying that there is less unity in an epic, I mean an epic made up of a plurality of actions, in the same way as the *Iliad* and *Odyssey* have many such parts, each one of them in itself of some magnitude; yet the structure of the two Homeric poems is as perfect as can be, and the action in them is as nearly as possible one action. If, then, Tragedy is superior in these respects, and also, besides these, in its poetic effect (since the two forms of poetry should give us, not any or every pleasure, but the very special kind we have mentioned), it is clear that, as attaining the poetic effect better than the Epic, it will be the higher form of art.

So much for Tragedy and Epic poetry—for these two arts in general and their species; the number and nature of their constituent parts; the causes of success and failure in them; the Objections of the critics, and the Solutions in answer to them.

Eva Schaper

PLATO AND ARISTOTLE ON THE ARTS: FROM *PRELUDE TO AESTHETICS*

1. Introductory

No single work has been more influential in the development of Western thought on aesthetic and critical principles than Aristotle's *Poetics*. To add yet another chapter to the existing libraries of books, commentaries, essays, and articles can only be justified, if at all, by being severely selective. My aim will be twofold: to show how Aristotle dealt with the questions Plato had raised about art, and to discuss some contributions of the *Poetics* which are still living issues in the contemporary debate of philosophical aesthetics. This excludes at least two major approaches to the *Poetics*, both of which have been followed with great competence by distinguished scholars: to assess Aristotle's treatise in the light of and as part of classical Greek thought, and to trace its influence on later theories of literature and drama, and of tragedy in particular. Whilst some consideration of these topics will necessarily have to enter into what follows, my interest in them will be only marginal. When discussing Aristotle's transformation of the Platonic legacy, I am already restricted . . . to those issues in Plato's controversial thought about art which, I believe, still figure among the problems of contemporary aesthetics. Aristotle removed for good some of the difficulties Plato had raised; others, however, have become more deeply entrenched through Aristotle's treatment. To deal with the *Poetics* as if it were contemporary thought might appear gravely anachronistic. Yet, it is one thing to attribute to Aristotle our own problems and perplexities, and our own pre-occupation with certain sorts of question; it is quite another to select and use those arguments from Aristotle which can throw light on such problems. Only the latter is attempted here.

The emphasis will be on the *Poetics* as a treatise on the *art of* poetry, not as a treatise on poetry, or drama, or tragedy. Aristotle has as much to say on the species of this art as on its generic nature, but what he says concerns *ars poetica* and *its* species, not poems, and plays or tragedies as objects of direct literary criticism. Of course, poems and plays

Eva Schaper, Prelude to Aesthetics *(London: Unwin Hyman, 1968), pp. 57–67, 143–147. Reprinted by permission of Unwin Hyman Ltd. (Some footnotes omitted.)*

figure prominently, and their discussion is exciting for the history of criticism. To treat them here as illustrations only is not to deny the eminently practical approach of Aristotle's treatise. He considers existing works and draws conclusions about their nature. But this is no reason why we should read the *Poetics* as no more than a compendium for the fourth-century drama critic. Aristotle both derived his principles from an existing literature and applied them to it. They are principles, however, of *art* as a productive capacity which such works exemplify. The application of them as touchstones to any thought about art is as legitimate as is the testing of them against later evaluations of the contemporary dramatic and epic examples which Aristotle himself used.

2. Aristotle and Plato

Aristotle gave us the first defence of creative literature, and the first constructive account of the art of fiction. He defended poetry and the poets against the charges Plato had brought against them, and he did this by assessing the principles of the art of his day in the light of his own philosophy. Of course Aristotle is not merely engaged in a polemic against Plato. In fact, Plato's name is not even mentioned in the *Poetics*. Yet in his own way he is concerned with the central issues which were first raised by Plato: the nature of artistic creation, the structure of the work of art, and the character of the impact of and reaction to art. On all three scores Plato had not been able to assess positively what he found. The irrationality of creative enthusiasm had led him to a highly ambiguous evaluation of the artistic gift; the imitative nature of art works had provoked a complicated and eventually negative assessment of them; and the emotional effectiveness of art had provided one among many reasons for Plato's condemnation of it as morally detrimental. The *Poetics* shirks none of these issues. But Aristotle can show persuasively that the Platonic consequences need not follow, even if we accept, as Plato did, that artistic creation is not a form of cognitive understanding, that poems are mimetic, and that they have deep emotional impact. Aristotle also apparently accepted these basic distinctions and assumptions. Yet for him they carry none of the alarming suggestions already present in Plato's barest statement of them. That is because Aristotle redefined the distinction between art and knowledge, drastically re-interpreted the meaning of "mimetic," and supplied a different conceptual framework for his findings about the emotional effects of art. Thus despite a large area of apparent agreement between Plato and Aristotle,[1] Aristotle's conclusion about the status and rôle of creation, about artistic structure and about audience reaction are so unlike Plato's that they can be used polemically against the Platonic view.

---

[1]On the fundamental points of agreement between Plato and Aristotle in this respect, see Humphry House, *Aristotle's Poetics* (Rupert Hart-Davis, London, 1956). On p. 27 he lists the following:
    "(1) That poetry is an 'imitative' art.
    (2) That poetry rouses the emotions.
    (3) That poetry *gives pleasure*, both as an imitation and as rousing the emotions through imitative means.
    (4) That the rousing of the emotions by poetry has an effect upon the whole personality (of the spectator or reader) and on his emotional behaviour in real life."
House argues that Aristotle accepts these premises, but differs in the conclusions he draws from them. I would want to argue that Aristotle only apparently accepts these premises, since what he means by them is
(continued)

Aristotle like Plato thinks that there is a fundamental distinction between artistic creation and discursive reasoning. He does not doubt that theory and art are distinct, or that giving a reasoned account of something is a very different activity from making a poem or a play or singing a song. Unlike Plato, however, Aristotle does not therefore hold that the non-theoretical must belong to the irrational. Art, a form of making, together with doing belongs to the practical side of man's rational behaviour, and this must be distinguished from theoretical understanding. Both are rational, and amenable to rational investigation; both can result in knowledge, but in two different kinds of knowledge, practical and theoretical. *That* there is a sharp distinction between art and theory, Aristotle does not deny. The terms in which he draws the distinction, however, are opposed to Plato's dichotomy of reason and non-reason. Like many other works of Aristotle, the *Poetics* entails a radical criticism of Plato's split of all there is into two worlds—that of the real, to which only reason can give approximate access, and that of the not-so-real, in which we get deeper and deeper enmeshed the further we move away from the realm of pure contemplation. Against this, Aristotle does maintain a distinction of art and theory, but for him this is based on the distinction between practical and theoretical reason. The productive act of the artist is therefore naturally different from the tasks involved in theoretical understanding. Yet this does not remove the artist from the sphere of reason.

Agreement with Plato that the artist's activity is non-theoretical thus furnishes no ground for alarm about the poet's sanity or his trustworthiness, or his being a danger to the society in which he works. The artist is simply a man with a special capacity, and Aristotle does not even deny him what Plato would have called inspiration. Occasionally he speaks in a language echoing Plato's attribution of divine madness to the poet, but without any disparaging intentions. In Chapter 17, for instance, we find a passage with a very Platonic ring:

> Hence it is that poetry demands a man with a special gift for it, or else one with a touch of madness in him; the former can easily assume the required mood, and the latter may be actually beside himself with emotion.[2]

But Aristotle leaves it at that. He refuses to read the distinction between making and theory as one between irrationality and rationality. And he refuses to let the difference in origin between art works and theoretical statements determine his approach to the products of the artistic activity—art works themselves. One might assume that Aristotle realized that there was no valid line of argument leading from the recognition of either "a special gift" or "a touch of madness" to an assessment of the structure and the impact of the artistic products. This is one of the many sane insights of Aristotle by which he avoided the road Plato forced his followers to travel. When Plato insisted on irrational inspiration, he connected this with the stimulation of irrational forces in the poet's

significantly different, so that it cannot be maintained that he draws different conclusions from the same premises. Even the "fundamental agreement between Plato and Aristotle" must not be stressed too much. There certainly is some agreement, and Aristotle uses Platonic terms. On the whole, however, Aristotle's "solving" of Plato's problems usually takes the form of passing them by. He can do this by redrawing Plato's distinctions and redefining his key concepts. Thus, as Marjorie Grene puts it in a general context, "*Plato's problems are not problems for Aristotle* at all" (A *Portrait of Aristotle*, Faber, London, 1963, p. 41).

[2]Chap. 17, 1455a 33–34. Ingram Bywater's translation of the *Poetics* (edited by Hamilton Fyfe, Oxford, Clarendon Press, 1940, also edited by Richard McKeon, in *The Basic Works of Aristotle*, Random House, New York, 1941) is used in all quotations, except when otherwise stated. . . .

audiences, and poems then became mere mediating links between creation and emotional experience. Many later theories following Plato in this respect have also been in danger of losing sight of the work itself and its structure. An analysis which concentrates on origin and response tends to see the work either as a manifestation of its origin, or as an occasion for response. Aristotle proceeds on the eminently sensible assumption that whatever may be the peculiarity of the art work's origin, it is its structure and formal configuration that is available for analysis. The mystery of creation, whilst no doubt an interesting and even fascinating topic, can be left aside as largely irrelevant to the study of the created thing. The finished work is there for inspection—as the artistic process is not. And of the structural principles of works of art, Aristotle's *Poetics* provides the first theoretical discussion.

Here too, Aristotle is in apparent agreement with Plato: works of art are mimetic for both philosophers. But what this means in their respective theories is very different. For Plato the view that art works imitate the real had damaging consequences, due to his conception of reality in the Ideas or Forms. For Aristotle the implications of the mimetic assumption were entirely positive, due to *his* conception of forms in the real. Aristotle could quite readily agree with the Platonic—and generally Greek—belief that fine art is mimetic, without thereby having to agree that it is only derivatively real and not worthy of serious consideration. Of course art works are mimetic for Aristotle. There must be, he insists, a relation of relevance between art and life, or how else could anybody be interested in what art presents? Provided we do not regard all imitation as the making of useless replicas, or as mirroring what we have got already, the relation of art and life or of art and nature through imitation is as important for Aristotle as it was for Plato. But what such imitation means is understood by Aristotle in a sense which allows him to ignore most of the Platonic difficulties about *mimesis*.

Plato saw art as imitating, and gratuitously so, the products of nature and of human making which were themselves related to the reality of the ideal Forms by imitation. For Aristotle, what art imitates is nature's productive activity. Since nature in the Aristotelian scheme is a way of acting, art does not directly imitate what nature is in its products, but how nature acts. Imitation, in this usage, is not the production of a likeness, but the creation of a work of *poiesis*. The poet imitates not by reason of copying or trying to copy, but by reason of making something, of creating a new thing. This is a new sense of the concept of *mimesis*, and Aristotle restricts its application to the field of the productive arts. Whilst the difficulties of interpreting Plato's conception of artistic imitation arose from the fact that in the Platonic scheme *everything* was mimetic, in one way or another, the difficulty with Aristotle seems to be now that in his scheme *only* art is mimetic, only the arts produce works of *mimesis*. Plato could provide no differentiae of art among all the other forms of imitation, or of art works among all the other imitative things. Aristotle makes imitation *the* differentia of *ars poetica*.[3] He defines art as mimetic, and he does so by rejecting some and retaining others of the established senses of the concept of imitation. For in this new Aristotelian sense, "imitation" has not entirely lost its connection with more common usage. Though it no longer means "copy" or "likeness," it still means "representation"; not, however, in the reproductive sense, but in the sense of "presenting something as if it

---

[3]John Herman Randall, Jr, *Aristotle* (Columbia University Press, 1960) provides the most "functionalist" interpretation of Aristotle known to me. Whilst not subscribing to his view *in toto*, I find his account of artistic imitation (e.g. pp. 275, 276, 290, 291) very convincing.

were real," in other words, of presenting a semblance. This is why Aristotle can see it as *the* differentia by which we distinguish art works from other things: art works alone present to us what convinces, not through likeness to what already exists or has taken place, but because it might well be or have been. They convince by the internal coherence with which they present a fiction: they convince through what Aristotle later calls the "probability or necessity" of poetic events. They succeed when they show something as if it had taken place, as if it might be the case, as if it were real. In this sense of imitation and not in the copy sense, *mimesis* defines *poiesis*.

How the characteristics of being mimetic differentiate in detail poetic constructs from other constructed accounts of something (e.g. historical and philosophical writing) is worked out by Aristotle in his investigation of the structural requirements and formal principles of poetic works. That is the natural place for it, since it is only by considering the structure and form of works that the difference can be fully formulated. It is the work which counts, and general principles must be, as it were, read off individual structures. General principles are exemplified in successful instances.

Mimesis in the Aristotelian understanding of the word refers primarily not to an activity of imitating, but to the character of the work: *it* is mimetic, *it* represents, *it* is a semblance. In contrast to Plato's, the Aristotelian concept mainly characterizes the *work* as a product of poetic art. Plato referred the term primarily to the *genesis* and *origin* of the work in the artist's activity of copying. A mimetic work, for Plato, was a work through which the artist had copied or was trying to copy something else. In Aristotle's conception the derivation is reversed: the artist can be said to practice *mimesis*, but that simply means that what he produces are mimetic works. The Aristotelian poet is an imitator because he is a maker—whilst the Platonic poet was an imitator because he tried to copy, unsuccessfully at that, what was already there. And although Aristotle is fond of saying that "art imitates nature," this must be understood in a decidedly non-Platonic sense. Art does not imitate either Platonic forms or Platonic appearances of nature—or, in more Aristotelian terms, art does not imitate either concepts or things; it shows, however, *how* nature works, and it does this by constructing its own creations. They are "imitations" in that they are semblances, not replicas or copies; they are fictions. There are no models to be copied or to be approached by degrees of verisimilitude. What Aristotle calls the "objects" of imitation are human actions;[4] not human actions as already performed, not actions as events in history or as occurrences in nature, but actions as they are possible or as they might have been. Thus, though mimetic, though "imitating nature," the work is always a new fact, a fact of the productive imagination.

With this new slant on the conception of artistic *mimesis* Aristotle forestalls any criticism of the artist as unnecessarily duplicating what exists already. On this new view, the artist has something important to say, and his success or failure in saying it cannot be judged by comparing his products with any models he copied. The art work, mimetic as it is, makes a statement in its own right, and according to Aristotle it contributes importantly to the understanding of how we live, and of what makes living

---

[4]That human actions constitute the "objects" of imitation seems to hold for all mimetic arts, although this is discussed explicitly only in connection with dramatic art. Only in drama, of course, are human persons directly presented as acting. See also Richard McKeon, "Literary Criticism and the Concept of Imitation in Antiquity" ". . . the object of imitation, according to the statement of the *Poetics* which seems to be intended to apply to all the fine arts, is the actions of men."

actions significant. There is no need for Aristotle to defend the artist against the specific Platonic charge that his imitation is at second-hand, for what the artist imitates is not the world as we have it, but the possibilities of this world, enacted and presented in an artistic construct. Plato modelled his account of artistic imitation on the paradigm of the painter who represents what he sees. The visual orientation of both Plato's account of the arts and his condemnation of them as deceptive conditioned his view of art as preoccupied with the making of images of things and of people. Painting and sculpture for Plato were the most mimetic of the arts. When we come to Aristotle, we find a profound difference: not painting, but music figures in his scheme as the most highly mimetic art form. This brings out clearly again that by *mimesis* he did not mean reproduction, or the making of faithful copies. If music is to be counted as imitation at all, then the relation between the musical work and what it imitates can only be that of representing human feelings and their emotional form. Aristotle makes it plain that he is not thinking of music as copying auditory events or natural sounds, but as presenting musical analogues to the composition of human feelings.[5] In contrast to Plato, Aristotle assigned to painting the lowest degree of mimetic power, presumably because of its static elements which limit the representation of action and function to some extent. The entire notion of imitation is tied to action in Aristotle's scheme, and that is why drama can function as such an excellent exemplification of the principles that matter in different specifications in all the arts.

Art then is concerned with the formative principles which operate in nature and life. Art imitates them by embodying them in structures made by man. Thus the art work is first and foremost a structured thing, something deliberately made by the *techne* of the artist, and this *techne* is that of imitation. We can therefore, if we wish, speak of *mimesis* as the artist's technique of making something. On the whole, however, Aristotle in the *Poetics* prefers to discuss these matters from the other end, namely by investigating what can be found in the products of such making, in the works of poetry. But *mimesis* is a *techne*, and in other places Aristotle has stated what according to him distinguishes human making from acting or doing:[6] whilst the intransitive activity of *doing* something remains within that which it brings about, namely human action, *making* is essentially transitive, productive of artefacts which are themselves neither ingredients in human action nor parts of nature. Their perfection as artefacts lies outside the moral as well as the natural sphere. Yet to both they are importantly related: to the moral sphere by their effects and consequences (which will be discussed later): to the sphere of nature by being mimetic, that is to say, by representing how nature works, in things which are not themselves physically or biologically within nature. Making is neither of nature nor against nature: art proceeds *as* nature does, takes its clue for organized construction from nature, but produces that which is not a natural fact, produces it freely and not according to any necessity of nature. *Mimesis*, seen as a process, as the activity and *techne* of making, is therefore *imitation* of nature and of life, and its products are neither natural nor alive—the mimetic products are works of art. Among them we can make further distinctions, according to how the generally mimetic result is achieved. This brings us back to the *Poetics*.

---

[5]That music "imitates" human feeling (and not any particular auditory event) is clearly stated by Aristotle in the *Politics*, VIII, 5, 1340a.

[6]E.g. *Nicomachean Ethics*, Bk. VI, Chap 4.

There Aristotle simply tells us that the arts differ in respect of the "means," the "objects," and the "modes" of imitation. The "means" differ: colour and shape for the visual arts, sound for music, rhythm for the dance, words for literature, with sound and rhythm supplementing words in some poetic kinds. Poetic literature includes prose literature, though there is, as Aristotle points out, no common name for poetic literature as a whole.[7] "Poetry" therefore covers any mimetic product expressed in words—though not just anything expressed in words, "mimetic" being the necessary qualification—even if Aristotle often seems to use the term poetry in a popularly accepted sense which restricts it to imitation in verse. The "objects" of imitation are not existing things or persons which the arts copy, but human actions mimetically represented. In the arts which imitate the actions of men by verbal means, it is the different kinds of men imaginatively envisaged and the different kinds of incidents which differentiate, for instance, tragedy from comedy. Mainly the verbal arts are considered in respect of their "objects" in the passage under discussion, though different objects in the non-verbal arts are mentioned. The third distinction, that of "modes" of imitation, also stresses the verbal arts; narrative and dramatic presentation are specified as modal differences in works whose means of imitation are the same. But these modal differences too must be understood as having their parallels in the different tonal, pictorial, and rhythmic modalities of the other arts.

In these passages Aristotle provides a skeleton for a classification of the mimetic arts. The invitation to elaborate it has not been missed through the centuries of Aristotle interpretation. Despite its fossilization in so many theories of literary and artistic *genres*, it still is a remarkably flexible scheme for the discussion of the stratification of the arts and their sub-species and the cross-relations between them. That the scheme has proved valuable through the ages in its application to fields so much wider than those of Greek literature testifies to Aristotle's greatness, and he should not be held responsible for its abuse. The influence he has exerted on the study and criticism of literature is at least as much due to his passion for classification (to which he brought the subtlety of a mind trained in the observation of biological phenomena)[8] as it is to his proposal of a theory of the nature of literature and, by implication, of all art. It is only the latter which forms the basis for the present study, and Aristotle's important contributions to the theory of literary *genres* will not be further discussed.[9] But it is

[7]*See* Chap. 2, 1448a10: ". . . the nameless art that uses language, prose or verse without harmony, as its means." We are still without a word to distinguish a work of literature *qua* art from anything else written in words. This may be due to excessive reverence for the classificatory terms used by Aristotle. There is a pointed comment on this lack of progress since classical antiquity in Northrop Frye, *The Anatomy of Criticism* (Princeton University Press, 1957, p. 13): "We then discover that we have no word, corresponding to 'poem' in poetry or 'play' in drama, to describe a work of literary art. It is all very well for Blake to say that to generalize is to be an idiot, but when we find ourselves in the cultural situation of savages who have words for ash and willow and no word for tree, we wonder if there is not such a thing as being *too* deficient in the capacity to generalize."

[8]Marjorie Grene, *A Portrait of Aristotle* (Faber, London, 1963), is one of those who see in Aristotle's biological interest the moving force and shaping principle of his entire philosophy. I have found her formulation of this approach illuminating throughout.

[9]For a good discussion and summary of development and problems of the theory of *genres*, see René Wellek and Austin Warren, *Theory of Literature* (Harcourt, New York, 1942), chapter 17, "Literary Genres." See also Elder Olson, "An Outline of Poetic Theory" (*Critics and Criticism*, ed. R. S. Crane, pp. 546–66), who proposes a sketch for a modern theory of genres based explicitly on what he believes to be the Aristotelian method. For a contemporary example of "Aristotelian" procedure, see the polemical and highly controversial proposals towards a "science of criticism" by Northrop Frye, *Anatomy of Criticism*, a book
(continued)

worth noting that Aristotle, who has only too often been accused of rigid dogmatism in respect of definitorial and classificatory procedure, never suggests that definitions within the arts can be gained by single lines of criteria, or that we can rely on single sets of essential characteristics in establishing either the definition of an art form or that of a sub-species. The intricacies of his suggested definitions make the *Poetics* still relevant today, quite apart from the Greek context for which it was designed. Aristotle's modernity, or rather, his timelessness, finds perhaps no better exemplification than in those brief statements of the possibilities open to us to compare, to contrast, to consider apart or together—under aspects which unite or in terms which cut across established boundaries—the multifarious phenomena of the arts.[10]

It may appear that with Aristotle's redefinition of "imitation," we have lost a criterion or a whole set of criteria for critical judgement which the Platonic theory of imitation as copying provided. On the Platonic view, it is in principle possible to grade art works by the degree of likeness to their independently available originals or models. This approach is not open to an Aristotelian critic, but that does not mean that he has no criteria at all by which to distinguish good and bad in art, more from less successful works, successful that is as imitations in the new sense. It is one of Aristotle's central undertakings to show that art works *can* be assessed in actual criticism as being more or less adequate imitations, of meeting or failing to meet the standards of artistic competence, though this competence is no longer that of faithful copying. What, then, is it? Aristotle's analysis provides an answer which, in its subtlety and precision, completely by-passes the Platonic dilemma—i.e. that art is either false or irrational—without giving up some of the sounder insights from which this dilemma was supposed to follow. For Aristotle, adequacy and significance in the arts has little, if anything, to do with correspondence to pre-existing models; but it *has* to do with establishing convincing representations. To show this, it is necessary first to see how Aristotle undertakes the formal analysis of works of literature. This is Aristotle's own way of arriving at the point where questions of criteria can be asked and answered. This will bring us back to questions of the relation between art and life, in terms of the imitation of one by the other, though not of copying or reproduction.

Aristotle's *Poetics* is the first formalist critique of art. To say this is to take "form" in the widest possible sense, in the sense in which Aristotle thinks of the "form" of something as its nature, and of the specific "nature" of something as its peculiar way of acting and functioning. "Form" of something is that which makes it what it is, both in its unity and in its difference from anything else. The form of something—for Aristotle as for Plato—is that which we can know. And for Aristotle that means the form as embodied in the thing, the individual, whether this be a living thing or a man-made construct. Form is that which is intelligible, and in understanding it, we understand what it means to be that kind of thing. Understanding art therefore means understanding artistic form. Aristotle deliberately places the weight of his entire investigation on the structure of the poem, the play, the work of art, for in no other way can "formal"

---

which, setting out to discover the organizing principles and conceptual frameworks of criticism, does not hesitate to schematize, classify, and reclassify, in terms of almost all available approaches, the materials of the literary critic. Although modestly called "Four Essays," it aims at being the Prolegomena to a new Poetics.

[10]*See* for instance Chap. 3, 1448a25: "So that as an imitator Sophocles will be on one side akin to Homer, both portraying good men; and on another to Aristophanes, since both present their personages as acting and doing."

principles be shown and stated.[11] By concentrating on the structural requirements of a literary work, Aristotle was able to clarify what it meant for such a thing to be a work and not merely a counterfeit thing, a work of fiction with an organization which is open to rational investigation whilst not itself an instance of theoretical reasoning. . . .

[11]A consideration of form in the sense of artistic structure had been hinted at very tentatively by Plato in the *Ion*, when he made the rhapsode defend himself against Socrates' attack by pointing out that the artist is, after all, an expert in knowing "what is fitting and becoming," and by reminding his critic that Homer may handle the same subject-matter as other poets, but does so infinitely better. . . . The suggestion, however, that what counts in a poem may not be what it is about, but how it is constructed, was not allowed to develop. For Aristotle it becomes one of the main themes of the *Poetics*.

Leo Tolstoy

ART AS THE COMMUNICATION
OF FEELING: FROM *WHAT IS ART?*

In order correctly to define art, it is necessary, first of all, to cease to consider it as a means to pleasure and to consider it as one of the conditions of human life. Viewing it in this way we cannot fail to observe that art is one of the means of intercourse between man and man.

Every work of art causes the receiver to enter into a certain kind of relationship both with him who produced, or is producing, the art, and with all those who, simultaneously, previously, or subsequently, receive the same artistic impression.

Speech, transmitting the thoughts and experiences of men, serves as a means of union among them, and art acts in a similar manner. The peculiarity of this latter means of intercourse, distinguishing it from intercourse by means of words, consists in this, that whereas by words a man transmits his thoughts to another, by means of art he transmits his feelings.

The activity of art is based on the fact that a man, receiving through his sense of hearing or sight another man's expression of feeling, is capable of experiencing the emotion which moved the man who expressed it. To take the simplest example: one man laughs, and another who hears becomes merry; or a man weeps, and another who hears feels sorrow. A man is excited or irritated, and another man seeing him comes to a similar state of mind. By his movements or by the sounds of his voice, a man expresses courage and determination or sadness and calmness, and this state of mind passes on to others. A man suffers, expressing his sufferings by groans and spasms, and this suffering transmits itself to other people; a man expresses his feeling of admiration, devotion, fear, respect, or love to certain objects, persons, or phenomena, and others are infected by the same feelings of admiration, devotion, fear, respect, or love to the same objects, persons, and phenomena.

And it is upon this capacity of man to receive another man's expression of feeling and experience those feelings himself, that the activity of art is based.

From What is Art? *by Leo Tolstoy, translated by Aylmer Maude (Indianapolis: Hackett Publishing Company, 1960), pp. 49–52, 139–145, 159. Reprinted by permission of Macmillan Publishing Company.*

If a man infects another or others directly, immediately, by his appearance or by the sounds he gives vent to at the very time he experiences the feeling; if he causes another man to yawn when he himself cannot help yawning, or to laugh or cry when he himself is obliged to laugh or cry, or to suffer when he himself is suffering—that does not amount to art.

Art begins when one person, with the object of joining another or others to himself in one and the same feeling, expresses that feeling by certain external indications. To take the simplest example: a boy, having experienced, let us say, fear on encountering a wolf, relates that encounter; and, in order to evoke in others the feeling he has experienced, describes himself, his condition before the encounter, the surroundings, the wood, his own lightheartedness, and then the wolf's appearance, its movements, the distance between himself and the wolf, etc. All this, if only the boy, when telling the story, again experiences the feelings he had lived through and infects the hearers and compels them to feel what the narrator had experienced, is art. If even the boy had not seen a wolf but had frequently been afraid of one, and if, wishing to evoke in others the fear he had felt, he invented an encounter with a wolf and recounted it so as to make his hearers share the feelings he experienced when he feared the wolf, that also would be art. And just in the same way it is art if a man, having experienced either the fear of suffering or the attraction of enjoyment (whether in reality or in imagination), expresses these feelings on canvas or in marble so that others are infected by them. And it is also art if a man feels or imagines to himself feelings of delight, gladness, sorrow, despair, courage, or despondency and the transition from one to another of these feelings, and expresses these feelings by sounds so that the hearers are infected by them and experience them as they were experienced by the composer.

The feelings with which the artist infects others may be most various—very strong or very weak, very important or very insignificant, very bad or very good: feelings of love for one's own country, self-devotion and submission to fate or to God expressed in a drama, raptures of lovers described in a novel, feelings of voluptuousness expressed in a picture, courage expressed in a triumphal march, merriment evoked by a dance, humor evoked by a funny story, the feeling of quietness transmitted by an evening landscape or by a lullaby, or the feeling of admiration evoked by a beautiful arabesque—it is all art.

If only the spectators or auditors are infected by the feelings which the author has felt, it is art.

To evoke in oneself a feeling one has once experienced, and having evoked it in oneself, then, by means of movements, lines, colors, sounds, or forms expressed in words, so to transmit that feeling that others may experience the same feeling—this is the activity of art.

Art is a human activity consisting in this, that one man consciously, by means of certain external signs, hands on to others feelings he has lived through, and that other people are infected by these feelings and also experience them.

Art is not, as the metaphysicians say, the manifestation of some mysterious Idea of beauty or God; it is not, as the aesthetical physiologists say, a game in which man lets off his excess of stored-up energy; it is not the expression of man's emotions by external signs; it is not the production of pleasing objects; and, above all, it is not pleasure; but is a means of union among men, joining them together in the same feelings, and indispensable for the life and progress toward well-being of individuals and of humanity.

As, thanks to man's capacity to express thoughts by words, every man may know all that has been done for him in the realms of thought by all humanity before his day, and can in the present, thanks to this capacity to understand the thoughts of others, become a sharer in their activity and can himself hand on to his contemporaries and descendants the thoughts he has assimilated from others, as well as those which have arisen within himself; so, thanks to man's capacity to be infected with the feelings of others by means of art, all that is being lived through by his contemporaries is accessible to him, as well as the feelings experienced by men thousands of years ago, and he has also the possibility of transmitting his own feelings to others. . . .

Art, in our society, has been so perverted that not only has bad art come to be considered good, but even the very perception of what art really is has been lost. In order to be able to speak about the art of our society, it is, therefore, first of all necessary to distinguish art from counterfeit art.

There is one indubitable indication distinguishing real art from its counterfeit, namely, the infectiousness of art. If a man, without exercising effort and without altering his standpoint on reading, hearing, or seeing another man's work, experiences a mental condition which unites him with that man and with other people who also partake of that work of art, then the object evoking that condition is a work of art. And however poetical, realistic, effectful, or interesting a work may be, it is not a work of art if it does not evoke that feeling (quite distinct from all other feelings) of joy and of spiritual union with another (the author) and with others (those who are also infected by it).

It is true that this indication is an *internal* one, and that there are people who have forgotten what the action of real art is, who expect something else from art (in our society the great majority are in this state), and that therefore such people may mistake for this aesthetic feeling the feeling of diversion and a certain excitement which they receive from counterfeits of art. But though it is impossible to undeceive these people, just as it is impossible to convince a man suffering from "Daltonism" that green is not red, yet, for all that, this indication remains perfectly definite to those whose feeling for art is neither perverted nor atrophied, and it clearly distinguishes the feeling produced by art from all other feelings.

The chief peculiarity of this feeling is that the receiver of a true artistic impression is so united to the artist that he feels as if the work were his own and not someone else's—as if what it expresses were just what he had long been wishing to express. A real work of art destroys, in the consciousness of the receiver, the separation between himself and the artist—not that alone, but also between himself and all whose minds receive this work of art. In this freeing of our personality from its separation and isolation, in this uniting of it with others, lies the chief characteristic and the great attractive force of art.

If a man is infected by the author's condition of soul, if he feels this emotion and this union with others, then the object which has effected this is art; but if there be no such infection, if there be not this union with the author and with others who are moved by the same work—then it is not art. And not only is infection a sure sign of art, but the degree of infectiousness is also the sole measure of excellence in art.

The stronger the infection, the better is the art as art, speaking now apart from its subject matter, i.e., not considering the quality of the feelings it transmits.

And the degree of the infectiousness of art depends on three conditions:

1. On the greater or lesser individuality of the feeling transmitted;
2. On the greater or lesser clearness with which the feeling is transmitted;
3. On the sincerity of the artist, i.e., on the greater or lesser force with which the artist himself feels the emotion he transmits.

The more individual the feeling transmitted the more strongly does it act on the receiver; the more individual the state of soul into which he is transferred, the more pleasure does the receiver obtain, and therefore the more readily and strongly does he join in it.

The clearness of expression assists infection because the receiver, who mingles in consciousness with the author, is the better satisfied the more clearly the feeling is transmitted, which, as it seems to him, he has long known and felt, and for which he has only now found expression.

But most of all is the degree of infectiousness of art increased by the degree of sincerity in the artist. As soon as the spectator, hearer, or reader feels that the artist is infected by his own production, and writes, sings, or plays for himself, and not merely to act on others, this mental condition of the artist infects the receiver; and con-trariwise, as soon as the spectator, reader, or hearer feels that the author is not writing, singing, or playing for his own satisfaction—does not himself feel what he wishes to express—but is doing it for him, the receiver, a resistance immediately springs up, and the most individual and the newest feelings and the cleverest technique not only fail to produce any infection but actually repel.

I have mentioned three conditions of contagiousness in art, but they may be all summed up into one, the last, sincerity, i.e., that the artist should be impelled by an inner need to express his feeling. That condition includes the first; for if the artist is sincere he will express the feeling as he experienced it. And as each man is different from everyone else, his feeling will be individual for everyone else; and the more individual it is—the more the artist has drawn it from the depths of his nature—the more sympathetic and sincere will it be. And this same sincerity will impel the artist to find a clear expression of the feeling which he wishes to transmit.

Therefore this third condition—sincerity—is the most important of the three. It is always complied with in peasant art, and this explains why such art always acts so powerfully; but it is a condition almost entirely absent from our upper-class art, which is continually produced by artists actuated by personal aims of covetousness or vanity.

Such are the three conditions which divide art from its counterfeits, and which also decide the quality of every work of art apart from its subject matter.

The absence of any one of these conditions excludes a work from the category of art and relegates it to that of art's counterfeits. If the work does not transmit the artist's peculiarity of feeling and is therefore not individual, if it is unintelligibly expressed, or if it has not proceeded from the author's inner need for expression—it is not a work of art. If all these conditions are present, even in the smallest degree, then the work, even if a weak one, is yet a work of art.

The presence in various degrees of these three conditions—individuality, clearness, and sincerity—decides the merit of a work of art as art, apart from subject matter. All works of art take rank of merit according to the degree in which they fulfill the first, the second, and the third of these conditions. In one the individuality of the feeling transmitted may predominate; in another, clearness of expression; in a third, sincerity; while a fourth may have sincerity and individuality but be deficient in clearness; a fifth, individuality and clearness but less sincerity; and so forth, in all possible degrees and combinations.

Thus is art divided from that which is not art, and thus is the quality of art as art decided, independently of its subject matter, i.e., apart from whether the feelings it transmits are good or bad.

But how are we to define good and bad art with reference to its subject matter? . . .

Art, like speech, is a means of communication, and therefore of progress, i.e., of the movement of humanity forward toward perfection. Speech renders accessible to men of the latest generations all the knowledge discovered by the experience and reflection, both of preceding generations and of the best and foremost men of their own times; art renders accessible to men of the latest generations all the feelings experienced by their predecessors, and those also which are being felt by their best and foremost contemporaries. And as the evolution of knowledge proceeds by truer and more necessary knowledge, dislodging and replacing what is mistaken and unnecessary, so the evolution of feeling proceeds through art—feelings less kind and less needful for the well-being of mankind are replaced by others kinder and more needful for that end. That is the purpose of art. And, speaking now of its subject matter, the more art fulfills that purpose the better the art, and the less it fulfills it, the worse the art.

And the appraisement of feelings (i.e., the acknowledgment of these or those feelings as being more or less good, more or less necessary for the well-being of mankind) is made by the religious perception of the age.

In every period of history, and in every human society, there exists an understanding of the meaning of life which represents the highest level to which men of that society have attained, an understanding defining the highest good at which that society aims. And this understanding is the religious perception of the given time and society. And this religious perception is always clearly expressed by some advanced men, and more or less vividly perceived by all the members of the society. Such a religious perception and its corresponding expression exists always in every society. If it appears to us that in our society there is no religious perception, this is not because there really is none, but only because we do not want to see it. And we often wish not to see it because it exposes the fact that our life is inconsistent with that religious perception.

Religious perception in a society is like the direction of a flowing river. If the river flows at all, it must have a direction. If a society lives, there must be a religious perception indicating the direction in which, more or less consciously, all its members tend.

And so there always has been, and there is, a religious perception in every society. And it is by the standard of this religious perception that the feelings transmitted by art have always been estimated. Only on the basis of this religious perception of their age have men always chosen from the endlessly varied spheres of art that art which transmitted feelings making religious perception operative in actual life. And such art has always been highly valued and encouraged, while art transmitting feelings already outlived, flowing from the antiquated religious perceptions of a former age, has always been condemned and despised. All the rest of art, transmitting those most diverse feelings by means of which people commune together, was not condemned, and was tolerated, if only it did not transmit feelings contrary to religious perception. Thus, for instance, among the Greeks art transmitting the feeling of beauty, strength, and courage (Hesiod, Homer, Phidias) was chosen, approved, and encouraged, while art transmitting feelings of rude sensuality, despondency, and effeminacy was condemned and despised. Among the Jews, art transmitting feelings of devotion and submission to the God of the Hebrews and to His will (the epic of Genesis, the prophets, the Psalms) was chosen and encouraged, while art transmitting feelings of idolatry (the golden calf) was condemned and despised. All the rest of art—stories, songs, dances, ornamentation of houses, of utensils, and of clothes—which was not contrary to religious perception was neither distinguished nor discussed. Thus, in regard to its subject matter, has art been appraised always and everywhere, and thus it should be appraised; for this attitude toward art proceeds from the fundamental characteristics of human nature, and those characteristics do not change.

I know that according to an opinion current in our times religion is a superstition which humanity has outgrown, and that it is therefore assumed that no such thing exists as a religious perception, common to us all, by which art, in our time, can be evaluated. I know that this is the opinion current in the pseudo-cultured circles of today. People who do not acknowledge Christianity in its true meaning because it undermines all their social privileges, and who, therefore, invent all kinds of philosophic and aesthetic theories to hide from themselves the meaninglessness and wrongness of their lives, cannot think otherwise. These people intentionally, or sometimes unintentionally, confusing the conception of a religious cult with the conception of religious perception think that by denying the cult they get rid of religious perception. But even the very attacks on religion and the attempts to establish a life-conception contrary to the religious perception of our times most clearly demonstrate the existence of a religious perception condemning the lives that are not in harmony with it.

If humanity progresses, i.e., moves forward, there must inevitably be a guide to the direction of that movement. And religions have always furnished that guide. All history shows that the progress of humanity is accomplished not otherwise than under the guidance of religion. But if the race cannot progress without the guidance of religion—and progress is always going on, and consequently also in our own times— then there must be a religion of our times. So that, whether it pleases or displeases the so-called cultured people of today, they must admit the existence of religion—not of a religious cult, Catholic, Protestant, or another, but of religious perception—which, even in our times, is the guide always present where there is any progress. And if a religious perception exists among us, then our art should be appraised on the basis of that religious perception; and, as has always and everywhere been the case, art transmitting feelings flowing from the religious perception of our time should be chosen from all the indifferent art, should be acknowledged, highly esteemed, and encouraged, while art running counter to that perception should be condemned and despised, and all the remaining indifferent art should neither be distinguished nor encouraged. . . .

Whatever the work may be and however it may have been extolled, we have first to ask whether this work is one of real art or a counterfeit. Having acknowledged, on the basis of the indication of its infectiousness even to a small class of people, that a certain production belongs to the realm of art, it is necessary, on the basis of the indication of its accessibility, to decide the next question, Does this work belong to the category of bad, exclusive art, opposed to religious perception, or to Christian art uniting people? And having acknowledged an article to belong to real Christian art, we must then, according to whether it transmits the feelings flowing from love to God and man, or merely the simple feelings uniting all men, assign it a place in the ranks of religious art or in those of universal art.

Only on the basis of such verification shall we find it possible to select from the whole mass of what in our society claims to be art those works which form real, important, necessary spiritual food, and to separate them from all the harmful and useless art and from the counterfeits of art which surround us. Only on the basis of such verification shall we be able to rid ourselves of the pernicious results of harmful art and to avail ourselves of that beneficent action which is the purpose of true and good art and which is indispensable for the spiritual life of man and of humanity.

Stanley Bates

TOLSTOY EVALUATED:
TOLSTOY'S THEORY OF ART

Tolstoy's *What Is Art?* has provoked controversy from the time of its original publication. It is a work which cannot be ignored because of the gigantic stature of its author. Even those who would dismiss it as the product of the troubled religious conscience of its author's old age must recognize that Tolstoy was rational when he wrote it, and that he regarded it as his definitive statement on aesthetics. Any work on aesthetics written by a man generally regarded as one of world literature's supreme artists has a *prima facie* claim to our attention. (Ironically, such aesthetic canonization is one of Tolstoy's targets of attack in the book.) And yet—it is rare for a reader of this work not to feel outraged by its theory, and dumbfounded by its critical judgments. Indeed, it sometimes seems as though the chief function of this work for later aesthetic theory has been to provide a rich storehouse of examples of aesthetic fallacies. (Mill's *Utilitarianism*, for a very long time, played a similar role for ethical theorists.) In this essay, I would like to separate out a number of different aspects of Tolstoy's thoughts on art in order to be able to say clearly why I think that *What Is Art?* is still a work worth encountering.

Tolstoy published *What Is Art?* at a critical point in the history of art. (Incidentally, I shall use "art" here to cover all of the fine arts as Tolstoy does. He draws his examples chiefly from literature, drama, opera, painting, and concert and chamber music. This may unjustly presuppose a unity in the different arts which they do not, in fact, possess. However, the presupposition is Tolstoy's, and it is not only his. Anyone who supposes that there is some single answer to Tolstoy's title question seems to share this presupposition.) The various movements in the arts that are subsumed under the rubric of modernism were either gathering force or well on their way to establishing a position which would dominate subsequent critical discussion, and dominate the practice of subsequent "advanced" artists. Tolstoy was uniformly hostile to the "advanced" art of his day in *What Is Art?* as we shall see. He did not base his hostility, however, on the fact that this art deviated from the standards of "high" art as laid down over the previous centuries. This kind of reaction, of course, did occur during this period; it finds its most characteristic expression in the hostility of official art schools to

This essay was written for the first edition of this collection.

the new art, and in the outrage of some audiences when exposed to new music. Tolstoy rather was moved from his rejection of much of the art of his own time, to deal with a problem which Stanley Cavell calls, " 'the threat of fraudulence,' something I take to be endemic to modern art."[1] There was a great deal of what purported to be art, that Tolstoy wanted to reject as art at all.

> Both Tolstoy's *What is Art?* and Nietzsche's *Birth of Tragedy* begin from an experience of the fraudulence of the art of their time. However obscure Nietzsche's invocation of Apollo and Dionysus and however simplistic Tolstoy's appeal to the artist's sincerity and the audience's "infection" their use of these concepts is to specify the genuine in art in opposition to specific modes of fraudulence and their meaning is a function of that opposition.[2]

Tolstoy finds that he cannot deal with the art of his time without at the same time raising the same questions about the traditions of high art and the works canonized as masterpieces within those traditions.

Let me now turn to an account of Tolstoy's theory of art. It would be useful to begin by separating a number of different questions to which he addresses himself in *What Is Art?* Having done this we can then consider Tolstoy's answers to these questions and try to say what issues these answers raise for us.

1. What is art as opposed to non-art? What is the criterion for something's being a work of art? Tolstoy claims that previous theories in the history of aesthetics have been hopelessly confused in their answers to this question.
2. What is good art as opposed to bad art? He makes an effort (not always successful) to keep this question separate from the question above.
3. What are the highest feelings of humanity? Tolstoy is led to this question by (2) above. It is here that he introduces his own religious views.
4. Which works are examples of good art, bad art, and non-art? It is here that Tolstoy makes his critical judgment on works of art or pseudo-works of art.

These seem to be the crucial questions dealt with in the book, though, of course, Tolstoy touches on many other topics.

The answer to the first question is somewhat complicated. Tolstoy begins by rejecting all accounts which try somehow to base the criterion for a work of art on the concept of beauty. Though beauty may be important in our judgment of works of art, it cannot by itself, according to Tolstoy, provide the defining characteristic of art. A reason why this must be so can be seen immediately if we simply recall to ourselves that other things than works of art (for example, natural phenomena: sunsets, animals, human beings, mountains) can be beautiful. It might be possible to define beauty by, in some way, relating it to human pleasure, but this will fail to distinguish art from non-art. Tolstoy says, "The inaccuracy of all these definitions arises from the fact that in them all . . . the object considered is the pleasure art may give, and not the purpose it may serve in the life of man and humanity . . . [Art is] one of the conditions of human life. Viewing it in this way we cannot fail to observe that art is one of the means of intercourse between man and man."[3] This is, of course, not yet a definition, but it does begin to point to that of which a definition of art must take account.

[1]Stanley Cavell, *Must We Mean What We Say?* (New York: Charles Scribner's Sons, 1969), p. 176.
[2]Ibid., p. 189.
[3]Leo Tolstoy, *What Is Art? and Essays on Art*, translated by Aylmer Maude (London: Oxford University Press, 1930), p. 120.

What specifically is the purpose which art serves? What kind of intercourse is it? Tolstoy here introduces, and depends on, a distinction between thoughts and feelings. Speech is the medium of the communication of thoughts; art is the means of communicating feelings. However, and this must be emphasized very strongly for Tolstoy has been misunderstood on this point, not all communication of feeling is art. Art is based on the human capacity to share the feelings of a fellow human being. (This is the capacity called sympathy by David Hume.) However, this capacity extends far beyond artistic activity. The critical paragraphs in Tolstoy's exposition, which he italicized himself and which constitutes his definition of art are:

> To evoke in oneself a feeling one has once experienced and having evoked it in oneself then by means of movements, lines, colours, sounds, or forms expressed in words, so to transmit that feeling that others experience the same feeling—this is the activity of art.
>
> Art is a human activity consisting in this, that one man consciously by means of certain external signs, hands on to others feelings he has lived through, and that others are infected by these feelings and also experience them.[4]

I have a number of observations to make on this definition. First, it requires the audience to receive the *same* feeling that the artist has felt. Here is the point at which the human capacity to receive the feelings of others is brought into play. Also it leads immediately to the conclusion that all genuine art requires *sincerity* on the part of the artist—a conclusion which Tolstoy shortly makes explicit. Second, a part of Tolstoy's definition which has been less often noted is that he includes a reference to the media of the various arts ("movements, line, colors, sounds, or forms expressed in words"). Tolstoy is often criticized for neglecting certain formal aspects of art, but he does include this reference in his basic definition. Third, Tolstoy requires a *conscious* manipulation of the medium by the artist. These second and third features of Tolstoy's definition are the specific features of art which enable Tolstoy to distinguish it from the human communication of feeling in general. Of course, this conscious manipulation of the medium does not need to include the intention to create a work of art; it only needs to include the conscious aim to communicate to another the feeling which the artist has had. Hence, in addition to feeling or emotion we require something like the Wordsworthian addition "recollected in tranquility." I say "something like" because Tolstoy may not require tranquility, but he does require more than the natural overt, expression of emotion, which some critics charge he makes equivalent to artistic activity.

It should also be noted, though, that this definition does cover more activity than is traditionally considered a part of the "fine arts." Tolstoy's own example of artistic activity is of a boy recounting his encounter with a wolf and trying to evoke in his audience the feelings that he experienced. This feature of his theory does not trouble the author, who decries the assumption that only the fine arts are art, and who denounces the claim that artistic activity is the exclusive province of the professional artist.

Finally, I shall simply point to the fact that Tolstoy relies on a largely uncriticized conception of feeling, and a distinction between feeling and thought, which would require very careful investigation before we could be in a position to judge his

---

[4]Ibid., p. 123.

definition. Tolstoy does not have a philosophical account of feeling to offer, but in order to respond critically to his definition we would need such an account.

The second question I isolated above was: What is good art as opposed to bad art? Here we bring to bear standards of value on the products of artistic activity which have been identified in terms of his criterion of art. The activity of art involves the "infection" of an audience with a feeling experienced by the artist and re-presented by him or her. It would be very natural to suppose that the value of such a re-presentation would be determined by the value of the feeling or feelings which are communicated by it. Such, indeed, is the position which Tolstoy adopts. Hence, we move immediately to a broader conception of value than "aesthetic" value—and it is in terms of this broader conception that aesthetic value is to be determined. This seems to imply a complete subjection of art to nonartistic evaluation, and this seeming implication is, of course, what many of Tolstoy's critics find most objectionable about his entire theory of art as we shall see below. What does Tolstoy propose as the standard? "In every age and in every human society there exists a religious sense of what is good and what is bad common to that whole society, and it is this religious conception that decides the value of the feelings transmitted by art."[5] Here we seem not only to have a subjection of art to morality, but also a subjection of morality to religion. I have used the word "seems" here because I believe Tolstoy's position is somewhat more complex than it first appears, though these "seeming" characterizations have a great deal of truth in them. One indication that Tolstoy does not have a simple equation of artistically good to morally good is given when he writes, "If a work is a good work of art, then the feeling expressed by the artist—be it moral or immoral—transmits itself to other people."[6] This suggests that it is possible for there to be an immoral, good work of art and that this possibility would have been foreclosed by the equation. If we look more closely at Tolstoy's statement that it is "this religious conception that decides the value of the feelings transmitted by art," we shall see that it is the "feelings transmitted" rather than the work of art whose evaluation is being discussed. Tolstoy himself separates two aspects of evaluation in a later part of *What Is Art?* He writes of (1) the quality of art (which depends on its form) considered apart from its subject matter[7] and (2) the quality of the feelings which form the subject matter of these works.[8] It is the latter which is determined, according to him, by the religious conception; the former depends upon how well a particular work of art fulfills what has been determined by Tolstoy to be the necessary function of all works of art, that is, the infection of an audience with the author's "condition of soul" or feeling. "And not only is infection a sure sign of art, but the degree of infectiousness is also the sole measure of excellence in art."[9] He goes on to add, *The stronger the infection the better is the art,* as art, speaking of it now apart from its subject-matter—that is, not considering the value of the feelings it transmits." It may seem strange to us to see this being advanced as Tolstoy's candidate for what is being judged when we talk about the *form* of a work of art. Many might consider this to be totally irrelevant to the consideration of the work of art "in itself." I would suggest that this indicates that we shall need to undertake an

[5]Ibid., pp. 128ff.
[6]Ibid., p. 194.
[7]Ibid., p. 227.
[8]Ibid., p. 231.
[9]Ibid., p. 228.

investigation of such a phrase as "the work of art in itself." Certainly Tolstoy's conception of it is broad enough to embrace those aspects which he includes under the concept of infection. Tolstoy goes further and gives three conditions which, he says, determine the degree of infectiousness. They are (1) the individuality of the feeling transmitted, (2) the clarity with which the feeling is transmitted, and (3) the sincerity of the artist. We are probably accustomed to thinking in such a way that only the second of these conditions seems relevant to the formal properties of the work of art. Part of the investigation into the concept of "the work of art in itself" would involve showing why we have become thus accustomed. For Tolstoy, the most important of these conditions is the sincerity of the artist, and he even claims that it—sincerity—includes the first two, for if the artist is sincere, he will express his own feeling in all its individuality, and he will be impelled to clarity in expressing his feelings.

I would argue that the two aspects of evaluation which Tolstoy separates are, ultimately, inextricably connected for him. (Again, this should not surprise us since most of us now probably assume that a form/subject-matter distinction is ultimately artificial.) We can see why this is so by turning to what he has to say about the religious conception in terms of which we are to evaluate the feelings communicated. At this point, we are led to Tolstoy's answer to the third of the questions I distinguished: What are the highest feelings of humanity? One of the briefest statements of his answer to this question is the following:

> The religious perception of our time in its widest and most practical application is the consciousness that our well-being, both material and spiritual, individual and collective, temporal and eternal, lies in the growth of brotherhood among men—in their loving harmony with one another . . . And it is on the basis of this perception that we should appraise all the phenomena of our life and among the rest our art also . . .[10]

Now, I shall not undertake a critical examination of Tolstoy's religious belief here. What is crucial for us is to realize that he does have a definite view of what the religious truth is and that this is what allows him to evaluate human feelings. The standard is not a relativistic one, nor is it set by any standardized body of opinion. Those feelings which are valuable because they contribute to the growth of the brotherhood among men are the ones which are good. So far it seems as though we have two separate standards which may not be in agreement. One standard evaluates how infectious a work of art is; the other evaluates what is communicated by the work of art. However, I believe that these two standards must, in a certain way, come together. This is because Tolstoy has a normative view of sincerity. By this I mean that Tolstoy holds that his religious perception is based on the way the world is—that all men *are* brothers (and, presumably, that all men and women *are* brothers and sisters). Hence, someone whose feelings are not in accordance with this perception is wrong—Tolstoy's word is "perverted." Now it is clear that ultimately the "sincere" expression of "perverted" feelings cannot be rated as highly as the sincere expression of correct feelings. Hence, though there is a limited sense in which you can have an immoral, good work of art, in a broader sense this is not possible. Tolstoy is inclined to call the moral, good work of art "true" art or real art. Hence, ultimately the two different standards of evaluation come together through the concept of sincerity and the religious perception of life.

[10]Ibid., pp. 234ff.

Now we come to Tolstoy's judgments of particular works of art. Tolstoy complained at the beginning of *What Is Art?* about the procedure of aesthetic theorists who assumed that they had a canon of works of art (or, of great art) and then tailored their theories to fit this canon. Since he refuses to do this it should not surprise or shock us that his judgments about the value of particular works of art are radically at variance with the usual judgments about our high culture. As I said at the beginning, this is probably the aspect of *What Is Art?* that produces the strongest immediate resistance on the part of the reader. Surely no theory which culminates in the outrageous claims that Tolstoy makes can be, in any way, acceptable. Let me give a list of some of the artists whose work Tolstoy condemns as pseudo-art or bad art: Aeschylus, Sophocles, Euripides, Aristophanes, Dante, Tasso, Shakespeare, Milton, Goethe, Baudelaire, Mallarmé, Maeterlinck, Ibsen, Hauptmann, Michelangelo, Raphael, Manet, Monet, Renoir, Pissarro, Sisley, most of Bach, late Beethoven, Liszt, Berlioz, Wagner, Brahms, Zola, Kipling, and almost all of the literary works of Leo Tolstoy (including *Anna Karenina* and *War and Peace*.) Though there have been and continue to be critical disputes over the relative merits of particular works of these artists, or over their claims to be considered as great artists, I can think of no one else beside Tolstoy who would reject so much of what has been thought to be the great art of the past. What this amounts to, as Tolstoy realizes, is a wholesale repudiation of the tradition of high art. Indeed, it is a rejection of most of Western and Russian cultural history for centuries and centuries. I am not going to defend these judgments of Tolstoy's. I only want to make two points about them.

First, although Tolstoy does indulge in this mass condemnation, he also gives examples of works of art that satisfy his criteria of arthood and value. These include primarily folk art and religious literature of great antiquity (e.g., Genesis, the *Iliad*, some vedic hymns) as well as such works as *Les Misérables*, a number of works by Dickens, the works of Dostoyevsky, George Eliot's *Adam Bede*, *Don Quixote*, Molière's comedies, and stories by Pushkin, Gogol, and Maupassant. Tolstoy used the "religious perception of our time" to judge these works and finds them good. Hence, his rejection of "high" art is not complete.

My second point is of more theoretical importance. If we resist Tolstoy's judgment, then we should be prepared to say why we value those works which he rejects. Most of us, most of the time, may be willing to accept the canonization of these masterpieces just *because* they play no important role in our lives. The only response in defense of these works, from us, that Tolstoy will accept, is one which links our experience of the work of these artists to our fundamental ethical, social, and religious concerns as human beings. Even if we reject his theory, we need our *own* experiences of art as data and some account of them in order to have responded to Tolstoy's challenge. Stanley Cavell writes:

> The list of figures whose art Tolstoy dismisses as fraudulent or irrelevant or bad, is, of course, unacceptably crazy . . . But the sanity of his procedure is this: it confronts the fact that we often do not find, and have never found, works we would include in a canon of works of art to be of importance or relevance to us. And the implication is that apart from this, we cannot know that they are art, or what makes them art.[11]

---

[11]Cavell, *Must We Mean What We Say?* p. 193.

This seems to me Tolstoy's deepest relevance for us in thinking about art.

There are many questions that can be raised, and criticisms that can be made, of Tolstoy's theorizing. Indeed, we may feel as Turgenev did when he wrote, "It is a great misfortune when a self-educated man of Tolstoy's type sets out to philosophize. He invariably climbs onto any old broomstick [and] invents some universal system that seems to provide a solution to every problem in three easy steps. . . ."[12] Many would object to the Platonizing assumption of the question, "What is art?" Tolstoy's account of history is impressionistic. His statement of his own religious views is as dogmatic as any made by a member of the churches which he attacks. He relies, as I have said earlier, at the critical point of his theory on a conception of feeling which needs considerable elucidation. However, I would like to concentrate on what seems to me to be the two most commonly made complaints about Tolstoy's theory, which are connected to each other.

First, it seems that, by invoking such concepts as "sincerity" and "infection" as both defining and evaluative standards of art, we deflect our attention from "the work of art itself" to its aesthetically irrelevant accompaniments. Various forms that this objection to Tolstoy might take would include charging him with committing some among the various aesthetic "fallacies" which critics and philosophers have attacked—for example, the "intentional fallacy," the "affective fallacy," the "pathetic fallacy."

The second commonly encountered charge against Tolstoy is that he introduces a moral criterion into the evaluation of art. There is, of course, a long tradition in philosophy extending from Plato through Rousseau to Sartre which does exactly this, but many people think that an important modern discovery is of the autonomy of art, and that moral criticism of art deflects us from the "work of art itself" as art. This second criticism, thus stated, can be seen as a special case of the first. The concept of the "work of art itself" is employed in each of these charges to help establish what is relevant and what is irrelevant for aesthetic judgment.

Obviously, I cannot even attempt to settle any of these issues here, but I do believe it is worth attempting to understand why someone could think that "sincerity," "infection," and moral criticism are irrelevant to aesthetics.

Suppose that we think of the relationship of the artist/work of art/audience as correctly modeled on the relationship of craftsman (say, shoemaker)/product (say, shoes)/customer (shoe buyer and user). The artist makes something; the "something" is more or less like a physical object (a painting, a statue, a poem, a symphony); the something is then encountered by someone who apprehends it through his senses. (The last clause doesn't seem, even initially, to work very well for literary works of art, but we shall ignore that for the moment.) The relationship of the maker to the made, in this schematized account, is that of cause to effect. The relationship of the thing made to the person who encounters it is that of causing some effect in the spectator. If we add to this account a Humian assumption about the nature of the causality— namely, that all cause/effect relationships are contingent and that it must be possible to identify (and, perhaps, to understand) each of the elements in these relationships independently of the other in order to assure this contingency—then we can better understand how one might come to think that the relationship of the artist to what he or she produces and the relationship of the work of art to its audience are irrelevant.

---

[12]Quoted in Henri Troyat, *Tolstoy* (Garden City: Doubleday, 1967), p. 300.

Let me give one example of this sort of criticism of Tolstoy. Monroe Beardsley remarks, "Tolstoy's criteria of genuineness fail for well-known reasons—most decisively because the sincerity of the artist is seldom verifiable."[13] Cavell suggests that the "well-known" reason Beardsley has in mind are those advanced by him and W. K. Wimsatt in their celebrated article, "The Intentional Fallacy," wherein they claim to establish the irrelevance of an artist's intentions for understanding or evaluating a work of art. Cavell's response is, "It is still worth saying about such remarks that they appeal to a concept of intention as relevant to art which does not exist elsewhere. . . ."[14] This, I believe, is correct. Certainly, Tolstoy, in his account of art as a means of human intercourse and a condition of human life, rejects the schematized account I gave above.

I do not insist that simply because someone held something like the schematized account he would then be led to reject Tolstoy's theory because it commits the "intentional fallacy," and that those who do make this objection to Tolstoy do hold the schematized account. *That* would be to commit a real fallacy, the fallacy of affirming the consequent. However, I must say that this is the only plausible reason that presents itself to me, to account for a remark like Beardsley's.

If we wish to reject Tolstoy's theory of art, we should look closely and see the point at which we wish to demur. Perhaps, we would wish to say against him that *King Lear* or Beethoven's Ninth Symphony is a supreme work of art. But, if we feel that it is a supreme work of art precisely because it does convey to us the artist's own feeling of unity with all of humanity, then we are rejecting a particular judgment of Tolstoy's and not his theory. Perhaps we wish to disagree with him about what the religious perception of our time is—perhaps, we may even think our time has no religious perception and this is what makes it unique. But, if we think that *this* condition of our time (i.e., that it has no religious perception) is crucially relevant to its supreme works of art, we may still be accepting a considerable part of Tolstoy's theory. Only now, in order to argue with him, we shall have to articulate our own vision of history, society, and religion.

My own judgment of the deepest failure of Tolstoy's account is that he does not recognize a potential tension, or even incompatibility, between the artist's sincerity and the infectiousness of the work of art. Tolstoy's theory rests on the assumption that the real artist could never find himself in a position in which it is really true that the times are out of joint and that the audience for genuine art may be missing. This, I suppose, is a function of his religious views. It relates to the relative neglect of formal considerations in his aesthetic theory.

Theorists like Tolstoy may show us why an "art for art's sake" theory is ultimately untenable. However, his explanations of the untenability of such a view tend to make it incomprehensible as to how this kind of "aestheticism" could have ever arisen. (It is important to remember that this claim about the autonomy of art and of the work of art is not just a view of philosophers and critics but that it has characteristically been a view of modernist artists.) Surely, the historical attraction of aestheticism requires explanation. John Dewey, for example, does attempt such an explanation by reference to such phenomena of modern times as nationalism, imperialism, capitalism, and the use of

---

[13]Quoted in Cavell, *Must We Mean What We Say?* p. 226.
[14]Ibid., p. 226.

the museum system. Certainly, these phenomena have a role in our ultimate understanding of the history of the arts and of aesthetic theory. However, they belong to what I should call the external history of the arts.

To draw a very crude distinction, all of the arts have both an external and an internal history. (The ultimate point of drawing the distinction is to show how intimately these two histories may be related to each other.) The external history includes such factors as the system of patronage, the political restrictions placed on the arts, the movement of ideas in other areas, the historical position of the artist. The internal history of the art includes the evolution of the solutions to problems of form which are presented by artists in succeeding generations as they attempt to continue to write, to paint, to compose. One of the characteristic features of modernism in all of the arts is not just the coming to self-consciousness of the formal problems of the particular art but the acknowledgment of that self-consciousness in the work of art. Moreover, the formal problems are often no longer particular problems to be solved within the limits of acknowledged conventions, but fundamental problems about the possibility of any conventions at all through which serious conviction can be conveyed. Thus, it seems that an artist might be forced to choose between sincerity in how he can continue to write, to paint, to compose (what forms he can believe are available to him in those arts) and infecting an audience. (The dilemma is falsely posed because even in the sincere expression the concept of communicating to an audience is needed. But the artist may realize that the audience is not there, but has to be created—perhaps, in part, by his art.)

This is what Stanley Cavell is writing of when he says:

> Tolstoy called for sincerity from the artist and infection from his audience; he despised taste just because it revealed, and concealed, the loss of our *appetite* for life and consequently for art that matters. But he would not face the possible cost of the artist's radical, unconventionalized sincerity—that his work may become uninfectious and even (and even deliberately) unappetizing, forced to defeat the commonality which was to be art's high function, in order to remain art at all (art in exactly the sense Tolstoy meant, directed from and to genuine need).[15]

Cavell's own writing is the best on the philosophy of art that I know which deals with just this situation of the artist.

[15]Cavell, *Must We Mean What We Say?* p. 206.

Clive Bell

ART AS SIGNIFICANT FORM:
FROM ART

It is improbable that more nonsense has been written about aesthetics than about anything else: the literature of the subject is not large enough for that. It is certain, however, that about no subject with which I am acquainted has so little been said that is at all to the purpose. The explanation is discoverable. He who would elaborate a plausible theory of aesthetics must possess two qualities—artistic sensibility and a turn for clear thinking. Without sensibility a man can have no aesthetic experience, and, obviously, theories not based on broad and deep aesthetic experience are worthless. Only those for whom art is a constant source of passionate emotion can possess the data from which profitable theories may be deduced; but to deduce profitable theories even from accurate data involves a certain amount of brain-work, and, unfortunately, robust intellects and delicate sensibilities are not inseparable. As often as not, the hardest thinkers have had no aesthetic experience whatever. I have a friend blessed with an intellect as keen as a drill, who, though he takes an interest in aesthetics, has never during a life of almost forty years been guilty of an aesthetic emotion. So, having no faculty for distinguishing a work of art from a handsaw, he is apt to rear up a pyramid of irrefragable argument on the hypothesis that a handsaw is a work of art. This defect robs his perspicuous and subtle reasoning of much of its value; for it has ever been a maxim that faultless logic can win but little credit for conclusions that are based on premises notoriously false. Every cloud, however, has its silver lining, and this insensibility, though unlucky in that it makes my friend incapable of choosing a sound basis for his argument, mercifully blinds him to the absurdity of his conclusions while leaving him in full enjoyment of his masterly dialectic. People who set out from the hypothesis that Sir Edwin Landseer was the finest painter that ever lived will feel no uneasiness about an aesthetic which proves that Giotto was the worst. So, my friend, when he arrives very logically at the conclusion that a work of art should be small or round or smooth, or that to appreciate fully a picture you should pace smartly before it

From Art (London: Chatto and Windus, 1914), pp. 13–37. Reprinted with permission of Chatto and Windus and the estate of Clive Bell.

73

or set it spinning like a top, cannot guess why I ask him whether he has lately been to Cambridge, a place he sometimes visits.

On the other hand, people who respond immediately and surely to works of art, though, in my judgment, more enviable than men of massive intellect but slight sensibility, are often quite as incapable of talking sense about aesthetics. Their heads are not always very clear. They possess the data on which any system must be based; but, generally, they want the power that draws correct inferences from true data. Having received aesthetic emotions from works of art, they are in a position to seek out the quality common to all that have moved them, but, in fact, they do nothing of the sort. I do not blame them. Why should they bother to examine their feelings when for them to feel is enough? Why should they stop to think when they are not very good at thinking? Why should they hunt for a common quality in all objects that move them in a particular way when they can linger over the many delicious and peculiar charms of each as it comes? So, if they write criticism and call it aesthetics, if they imagine that they are talking about Art when they are talking about particular works of art or even about the technique of painting, if, loving particular works they find tedious the consideration of art in general, perhaps they have chosen the better part. If they are not curious about the nature of their emotion, nor about the quality common to all objects that provoke it, they have my sympathy, and, as what they say is often charming and suggestive, my admiration too. Only let no one suppose that what they write and talk is aesthetics; it is criticism, or just "shop."

The starting-point for all systems of aesthetics must be the personal experience of a peculiar emotion. The objects that provoke this emotion we call works of art. All sensitive people agree that there is a peculiar emotion provoked by works of art. I do not mean, of course, that all works provoke the same emotion. On the contrary, every work produces a different emotion. But all these emotions are recognisably the same in kind; so far, at any rate, the best opinion is on my side. That there is a particular kind of emotion provoked by works of visual art, and that this emotion is provoked by every kind of visual art, by pictures, sculptures, buildings, pots, carvings, textiles, &c., &c., is not disputed, I think, by anyone capable of feeling it. This emotion is called the aesthetic emotion; and if we can discover some quality common and peculiar to all the objects that provoke it, we shall have solved what I take to be the central problem of aesthetics. We shall have discovered the essential quality in a work of art, the quality that distinguishes works of art from all other classes of objects.

For either all works of visual art have some common quality, or when we speak of "works of art" we gibber. Everyone speaks of "art," making a mental classification by which he distinguishes the class "works of art" from all other classes. What is the justification of this classification? What is the quality common and peculiar to all members of this class? Whatever it be, no doubt it is often found in company with other qualities; but they are adventitious—it is essential. There must be some one quality without which a work of art cannot exist; possessing which, in the least degree, no work is altogether worthless. What is this quality? What quality is shared by all objects that provoke our aesthetic emotions? What quality is common to Sta. Sophia and the windows at Chartres, Mexican sculpture, a Persian bowl, Chinese carpets, Giotto's frescoes at Padua, and the masterpieces of Poussin, Piero della Francesca, and Cézanne? Only one answer seems possible—significant form. In each, lines and colours combined in a particular way, certain forms and relations of forms, stir our aesthetic emotions. These relations and combinations of lines and colours, these aesthetically moving forms, I call "Significant Form"; and "Significant Form" is the one quality common to all works of visual art.

At this point it may be objected that I am making aesthetics a purely subjective business, since my only data are personal experiences of a particular emotion. It will be said that the objects that provoke this emotion vary with each individual, and that therefore a system of aesthetics can have no objective validity. It must be replied that any system of aesthetics which pretends to be based on some objective truth is so palpably ridiculous as not to be worth discussing. We have no other means of recognising a work of art than our feeling for it. The objects that provoke aesthetic emotion vary with each individual. Aesthetic judgments are, as the saying goes, matters of taste; and about tastes, as everyone is proud to admit, there is no disputing. A good critic may be able to make me see in a picture that had left me cold things that I had overlooked, till at last, receiving the aesthetic emotion, I recognise it as a work of art. To be continually pointing out those parts, the sum, or rather the combination, of which unite to produce significant form, is the function of criticism. But it is useless for a critic to tell me that something is a work of art; he must make me feel it for myself. This he can do only by making me see; he must get at my emotions through my eyes. Unless he can make me see something that moves me, he cannot force my emotions. I have no right to consider anything a work of art to which I cannot react emotionally; and I have no right to look for the essential quality in anything that I have not *felt* to be a work of art. The critic can affect my aesthetic theories only by affecting my aesthetic experience. All systems of aesthetics must be based on personal experience—that is to say, they must be subjective.

Yet, though all aesthetic theories must be based on aesthetic judgments, and ultimately all aesthetic judgments must be matters of personal taste, it would be rash to assert that no theory of aesthetics can have general validity. For, though A, B, C, D are the works that move me, and A, D, E, F the works that move you, it may well be that x is the only quality believed by either of us to be common to all the works in his list. We may all agree about aesthetics, and yet differ about particular works of art. We may differ as to the presence or absence of the quality x. My immediate object will be to show that significant form is the only quality common and peculiar to all the works of visual art that move me; and I will ask those whose aesthetic experience does not tally with mine to see whether this quality is not also, in their judgment, common to all works that move them, and whether they can discover any other quality of which the same can be said.

Also at this point a query arises, irrelevant indeed, but hardly to be suppressed: "Why are we so profoundly moved by forms related in a particular way?" The question is extremely interesting, but irrelevant to aesthetics. In pure aesthetics we have only to consider our emotion and its object: for the purposes of aesthetics we have no right, neither is there any necessity, to pry behind the object into the state of mind of him who made it. Later, I shall attempt to answer the question; for by so doing I may be able to develop my theory of the relation of art to life. I shall not, however, be under the delusion that I am rounding off my theory of aesthetics. For a discussion of aesthetics, it need be agreed only that forms arranged and combined according to certain unknown and mysterious laws do move us in a particular way, and that it is the business of an artist so to combine and arrange them that they shall move us. These moving combinations and arrangements I have called, for the sake of convenience and for a reason that will appear later, "Significant Form."

A third interruption has to be met.

"Are you forgetting about colour?" someone inquires. Certainly not; my term "significant form" included combinations of lines and of colours. The distinction between form and colour is an unreal one; you cannot conceive a colourless line or a colourless space; neither can you conceive a formless relation of colours. In a black and white drawing the spaces are all white and all are bounded by black lines; in most oil paintings the spaces are multi-coloured and so are the boundaries; you cannot imagine a boundary line without any content, or a content without a boundary line. Therefore, when I speak of significant form, I mean a combination of lines and colours (counting white and black as colours) that moves me aesthetically.

Some people may be surprised at my not having called this "beauty." Of course, to those who define beauty as "combinations of lines and colours that provoke aesthetic emotion," I willingly concede the right of substituting their word for mine. But most of us, however strict we may be, are apt to apply the epithet "beautiful" to objects that do not provoke that peculiar emotion produced by works of art. Everyone, I suspect, has called a butterfly or a flower beautiful. Does anyone feel the same kind of emotion for a butterfly or a flower that he feels for a cathedral or a picture? Surely, it is not what I call an aesthetic emotion that most of us feel, generally, for natural beauty. I shall suggest, later, that some people may, occasionally, see in nature what we see in art, and feel for her an aesthetic emotion; but I am satisfied that, as a rule, most people feel a very different kind of emotion for birds and flowers and the wings of butterflies from that which they feel for pictures, pots, temples and statues. Why these beautiful things do not move us as works of art move us is another, and not an aesthetic, question. For our immediate purpose we have to discover only what quality is common to objects that do move us as works of art. In the last part of this chapter, when I try to answer the question—"Why are we so profoundly moved by some combinations of lines and colours?" I shall hope to offer an acceptable explanation of why we are less profoundly moved by others.

Since we call a quality that does not raise the characteristic aesthetic emotion "Beauty," it would be misleading to call by the same name the quality that does. To make "beauty" the object of the aesthetic emotion, we must give to the word an over-strict and unfamiliar definition. Everyone sometimes uses "beauty" in an un-aesthetic sense; most people habitually do so. To everyone, except perhaps here and there an occasional aesthete, the commonest sense of the word is unaesthetic. Of its grosser abuse, patent in our chatter about "beautiful huntin'" and "beautiful shootin'," I need not take account; it would be open to the precious to reply that they never do so abuse it. Besides, here there is no danger of confusion between the aesthetic and the non-aesthetic use; but when we speak of a beautiful woman there is. When an ordinary man speaks of a beautiful woman he certainly does not mean only that she moves him aesthetically; but when an artist calls a withered old hag beautiful he may sometimes mean what he means when he calls a battered torso beautiful. The ordinary man, if he be also a man of taste, will call the battered torso beautiful, but he will not call a withered hag beautiful because, in the matter of women, it is not to the aesthetic quality that the hag may possess, but to some other quality that he assigns the epithet. Indeed, most of us never dream of going for aesthetic emotions to human beings, from whom we ask something very different. This "something," when we find it in a young woman, we are apt to call "beauty." We live in a nice age. With the man-in-the-street "beautiful" is more often than not synonymous with "desirable"; the word does not necessarily connote any aesthetic reaction whatever, and I am tempted to believe that in the minds of many the sexual flavour of the word is stronger than the aesthetic. I have noticed a consistency in those to whom the most beautiful thing in the world is a beautiful woman, and the next most beautiful thing a picture of one. The confusion between aesthetic and sensual beauty is not in their case so great as might be supposed. Perhaps there is none; for perhaps they have never had an aesthetic emotion to confuse with their other emotions. The art that they call "beautiful" is generally closely related to the women. A beautiful picture is a photograph of a pretty girl; beautiful music, the music that provokes emotions similar to those provoked by young ladies in musical farces; and beautiful poetry, the poetry that recalls the same emotions felt, twenty years earlier, for the rector's daughter. Clearly the word "beauty" is used to connote the objects of quite distinguishable emotions, and that is a reason for not employing a term which would land me inevitably in confusions and misunderstandings with my readers.

On the other hand, with those who judge it more exact to call these combinations and arrangements of form that provoke our aesthetic emotions, not "significant form," but "significant relations of form," and then try to make the best of two worlds, the aesthetic and the metaphysical, by calling these relations "rhythm," I have no quarrel whatever. Having made it clear that by "significant form" I mean arrangements and combinations that move us in a particular way, I willingly join hands with those who prefer to give a different name to the same thing.

The hypothesis that significant form is the essential quality in a work of art has at least one merit denied to many more famous and more striking—it does help to explain things. We are all familiar with pictures that interest us and excite our admiration, but do not move us as works of art. To this class belongs what I call "Descriptive Painting"—that is, painting in which forms are used not as objects of emotion, but as means of suggesting emotion or conveying information. Portraits of psychological and historical value, topographical works, pictures that tell stories and suggest situations, illustrations of all sorts, belong to this class. That we all recognise the distinction is clear, for who has not said that such and such a drawing was excellent as illustration, but as a work of art worthless? Of course many descriptive pictures possess, amongst other qualities, formal significance, and are therefore works of art: but many more do not. They interest us; they may move us too in a hundred different ways, but they do not move us aesthetically. According to my hypothesis they are not works of art. They leave untouched our aesthetic emotions because it is not their forms but the ideas or information suggested or conveyed by their forms that affect us.

Few pictures are better known or liked than Frith's "Paddington Station"; certainly I should be the last to grudge it its popularity. Many a weary forty minutes have I whiled away disentangling its fascinating incidents and forging for each an imaginary past and an improbable future. But certain though it is that Frith's masterpiece, or engravings of it, have provided thousands with half-hours of curious and fanciful pleasure, it is not less certain that no one has experienced before it one half-second of aesthetic rapture— and this although the picture contains several pretty passages of colour, and is by no means badly painted. "Paddington Station" is not a work of art; it is an interesting and amusing document. In it line and colour are used to recount anecdotes, suggest ideas, and indicate the manners and customs of an age: they are not used to provoke aesthetic emotion. Forms and the relations of forms were for Frith not objects of emotion, but means of suggesting emotion and conveying ideas.

The ideas and information conveyed by "Paddington Station" are so amusing and so well presented that the picture has considerable value and is well worth preserving. But, with the perfection of photographic processes and of the cinematograph, pictures of this sort are becoming otiose. Who doubts that one of those *Daily Mirror* photographers in collaboration with a *Daily Mail* reporter can tell us far more about "London day by day" than any Royal Academician? For an account of manners and fashions we shall go, in future, to photographs, supported by a little bright journalism, rather than to descriptive painting. Had the imperial academicians of Nero, instead of manufacturing incredibly loathsome imitations of the antique, recorded in fresco and mosaic the manners and fashions of their day, their stuff, though artistic rubbish, would now be an historical gold-mine. If only they had been Friths instead of being Alma Tademas! But photography has made impossible any such transmutation of modern rubbish. Therefore it must be confessed that pictures in the Frith tradition are grown superfluous; they merely waste the hours of able men who might be more profitably employed in works of a wider beneficence. Still, they are not unpleasant, which is more than can be said for that kind of descriptive painting of which "The Doctor" is the most flagrant example. Of course "The Doctor" is not a work of art. In it form is not used as an object of emotion, but as a means of suggesting emotions. This alone suffices to make it nugatory; it is worse than nugatory because the emotion it suggests is false. What it suggests is not pity and admiration but a sense of complacency in our own pitifulness and generosity. It is sentimental. Art is above morals, or, rather, all art is moral because, as I hope to show presently, works of art are immediate means to good. Once we have judged a thing a work of art, we have judged it ethically of the first importance and put it beyond the reach of the moralist. But descriptive pictures which are not works of art, and, therefore, are not necessarily means to good states of mind, are proper objects of the ethical philosopher's attention. Not being a work of art, "The Doctor" has none of the immense ethical value possessed by all objects that provoke aesthetic ecstasy; and the state of mind to which it is a means, as illustration, appears to me undesirable.

The works of those enterprising young men, the Italian Futurists, are notable examples of descriptive painting. Like the Royal Academicians, they use form, not to provoke aesthetic emotions, but to convey information and ideas. Indeed, the published theories of the Futurists prove that their pictures ought to have nothing whatever to do with art. Their social and political theories are respectable, but I would suggest to young Italian painters that it is possible to become a Futurist in thought and action and yet remain an artist, if one has the luck to be born one. To associate art with politics is always a mistake. Futurist pictures are descriptive because they aim at presenting in line and colour the chaos of the mind at a particular moment; their forms are not intended to promote aesthetic emotion but to convey information. These forms, by the way, whatever may be the nature of the ideas they suggest, are themselves anything but revolutionary. In such Futurist pictures as I have seen—perhaps I should except some by Severini—the drawing, whenever it becomes representative as it frequently does, is found to be in that soft and common convention brought into fashion by Besnard some thirty years ago, and much affected by Beaux-Art students ever since. As works of art, the Futurist pictures are negligible; but they are not to be judged as works of art. A good Futurist picture would succeed as a good piece of psychology succeeds; it would reveal, through line and colour, the complexities of an interesting state of mind. If Futurist pictures seem to fail, we must seek an explanation, not in a lack of artistic qualities that they never were intended to possess, but rather in the minds the states of which they are intended to reveal.

Most people who care much about art find that of the work that moves them most the greater part is what scholars call "Primitive." Of course there are bad primitives. For instance, I remember going, full of enthusiasm, to see one of the earliest Romanesque churches in Poitiers (Notre-Dame-la-Grande), and finding it as ill-proportioned, over-decorated, coarse, fat and heavy as any better class building by one of those highly civilised architects who flourished a thousand years earlier or eight hundred later. But such exceptions are rare. As a rule primitive art is good—and here again my hypothesis is helpful—for, as a rule, it is also free from descriptive qualities. In primitive art you will find no accurate representation; you will find only significant form. Yet no other art moves us so profoundly. Whether we consider Sumerian sculpture or pre-dynastic Egyptian art, or archaic Greek, or the Wei and T'ang masterpieces, or those early Japanese works of which I had the luck to see a few superb examples (especially two wooden Bodhisattvas) at the Shepherd's Bush Exhibition in 1910, or whether, coming nearer home, we consider the primitive Byzantine art of the sixth century and its primitive developments amongst the Western barbarians, or, turning far afield, we consider that mysterious and majestic art that flourished in Central and South America before the coming of the white men, in every case we observe three common characteristics—absence of representation, absence of technical swagger, sublimely impressive form. Nor is it hard to discover the connection between these three. Formal significance loses itself in preoccupation with exact representation and ostentatious cunning.

Naturally, it is said that if there is little representation and less saltimbancery in primitive art, that is because the primitives were unable to catch a likeness or cut intellectual capers. The contention is beside the point. There is truth in it, no doubt, though, were I a critic whose reputation depended on a power of impressing the public with a semblance of knowledge, I should be more cautious about urging it than such people generally are. For to suppose that the Byzantine masters wanted skill, or could not have created an illusion had they wished to do so, seems to imply ignorance of the amazingly dexterous realism of the notoriously bad works of that age. Very often, I fear, the misrepresentation of the primitives must be attributed to what the critics call, "wilful distortion." Be that as it may, the point is that, either from want of skill or want of will, primitives neither create illusions, nor make display of extravagant accomplishment, but concentrate their energies on the one thing needful—the creation of form. Thus have they created the finest works of art that we possess.

Let no one imagine that representation is bad in itself; a realistic form may be as significant, in its place as part of the design, as an abstract. But if a representative form has value, it is as form, not as representation. The representative element in a work of art may or may not be harmful; always it is irrelevant. For, to appreciate a work of art we need bring with us nothing from life, no knowledge of its ideas and affairs, no familiarity with its emotions. Art transports us from the world of man's activity to a world of aesthetic exaltation. For a moment we are shut off from human interests; our anticipations and memories are arrested; we are lifted above the stream of life. The pure mathematician rapt in his studies knows a state of mind which I take to be similar, if not identical. He feels an emotion for his speculations which arises from no perceived relation between them and the lives of men, but springs, inhuman or super-human, from the heart of an abstract science. I wonder, sometimes, whether the appreciators of art and of mathematical solutions are not even more closely allied. Before we feel an aesthetic emotion for a combination of forms, do we not perceive intellectually the rightness and necessity of the combination? If we do, it would explain the fact that passing rapidly through a room we recognise a picture to be good, although we cannot say that it has provoked much emotion. We seem to have recognised intellectually the rightness of its forms without staying to fix our attention, and collect, as it were, their emotional significance. If this were so, it would be permissible to inquire whether it was the forms themselves or our perception of their rightness and necessity that caused aesthetic emotion. But I do not think I need linger to discuss the matter here. I have been inquiring why certain combinations of forms move us; I should not have travelled by other roads had I enquired, instead, why certain combinations are perceived to be right and necessary, and why our perception of their rightness and necessity is moving. What I have to say is this: the rapt philosopher, and he who contemplates a work of art, inhabit a world with an intense and peculiar significance of its own; that significance is unrelated to the significance of life. In this world the emotions of life find no place. It is a world with emotions of its own.

To appreciate a work of art we need bring with us nothing but a sense of form and colour and a knowledge of three-dimensional space. That bit of knowledge, I admit, is essential to the appreciation of many great works, since many of the most moving forms ever created are in three dimensions. To see a cube or a rhomboid as a flat pattern is to lower its significance, and a sense of three-dimensional space is essential to the full appreciation of most architectural forms. Pictures which would be insignificant if we saw them as flat patterns are profoundly moving because, in fact, we see them as related planes. If the representation of three-dimensional space is to be called "repre-sentation," then I agree that there is one kind of representation which is not irrelevant. Also, I agree that along with our feeling for line and colour we must bring with us our knowledge of space if we are to make the most of every kind of form. Nevertheless, there are magnificent designs to an appreciation of which this knowledge is not necessary: so, though it is not irrelevant to the appreciation of some works of art it is not essential to the appreciation of all. What we must say is that the representation of three-dimensional space is neither irrelevant nor essential to all art, and that every other sort of representation is irrelevant.

That there is an irrelevant representative or descriptive element in many great works of art is not in the least surprising. Why it is not surprising I shall try to show elsewhere. Representation is not of necessity baneful, and highly realistic forms may be extremely significant. Very often, however, representation is a sign of weakness in an artist. A painter too feeble to create forms that provoke more than a little aesthetic emotion will try to eke that little out by suggesting the emotions of life. To evoke the emotions of life he must use representation. Thus a man will paint an execution, and, fearing to miss with his first barrel of significant form, will try to hit with his second by raising an emotion of fear or pity. But if in the artist an inclination to play upon the emotions of life is often the sign of a flickering inspiration, in the spectator a tendency to seek, behind form, the emotions of life is a sign of defective sensibility always. It means that his aesthetic emotions are weak or, at any rate, imperfect. Before a work of art people who feel little or no emotion for pure form find themselves at a loss. They are deaf men at a concert. They know that they are in the presence of something great, but they lack the power of apprehending it. They know that they ought to feel for it a tremendous emotion, but it happens that the particular kind of emotion it can raise is one that they can feel hardly or not at all. And so they read into the forms of the work those facts and ideas for which they are capable of feeling emotion, and feel for them the emotions that they can feel—the ordinary emotions of life. When confronted by a picture, instinctively they refer back its forms to the world from which they came. They treat created form as though it were imitated form, a picture as though it were a photograph. Instead of going out on the stream of art into a new world of aesthetic experience, they turn a sharp corner and come straight home to the world of human interests. For them the significance of a work of art depends on what they bring to it; no new thing is added to their lives, only the old material is stirred. A good work of visual art carries a person who is capable of appreciating it out of life into ecstasy: to use art as a means to the emotions of life is to use a telescope for reading the news. You will notice that people who cannot feel pure aesthetic emotions remember pictures by their subjects; whereas people who can, as often as not, have no idea what the subject of a picture is. They have never noticed the representative element, and so when they discuss pictures they talk about the shapes of forms and the relations and quantities of colours. Often they can tell by the quality of a single line whether or not a man is a good artist. They are concerned only with lines and colours, their relations and quantities and qualities; but from these they win an emotion more profound and far more sublime than any that can be given by the description of facts and ideas.

This last sentence has a very confident ring—over-confident, some may think. Perhaps I shall be able to justify it, and make my meaning clearer too, if I give an account of my own feelings about music. I am not really musical. I do not understand music well. I find musical form exceedingly difficult to apprehend, and I am sure that the profounder subtleties of harmony and rhythm more often than not escape me. The form of a musical composition must be simple indeed if I am to grasp it honestly. My opinion about music is not worth having. Yet, sometimes, at a concert, though my appreciation of the music is limited and humble, it is pure. Sometimes, though I have poor understanding, I have a clean palate. Consequently, when I am feeling bright and clear and intent, at the beginning of a concert for instance, when something that I can grasp is being played, I get from music that pure aesthetic emotion that I get from visual art. It is less intense, and the rapture is evanescent; I understand music too ill for music to transport me far into the world of pure aesthetic ecstasy. But at moments I do appreciate music as pure musical form, as sounds combined according to the laws of a mysterious necessity, as pure art with a tremendous significance of its own and no relation whatever to the significance of life; and in those moments I lose myself in that infinitely sublime state of mind to which pure visual form transports me. How inferior is my normal state of mind at a concert. Tired or perplexed, I let slip my sense of form, my aesthetic emotion collapses, and I begin weaving into the harmonies, that I cannot grasp, the ideas of life. Incapable of feeling the austere emotions of art, I begin to read into the musical forms human emotions of terror and mystery, love and hate, and spend the minutes, pleasantly enough, in a world of turbid and inferior feeling. At such times, were the grossest pieces of onomatopoeic representation—the song of a bird, the galloping of horses, the cries of children, or the laughing of demons—to be introduced into the symphony, I should not be offended. Very likely I should be pleased; they would afford new points of departure for new trains of romantic feeling or heroic thought. I know very well what has happened. I have been using art as a means to the emotions of life and reading into it the ideas of life. I have been cutting blocks with a razor. I have tumbled from the superb peaks of aesthetic exaltation to the snug foothills of warm humanity. It is a jolly country. No one need be ashamed of enjoying himself there. Only no one who has ever been on the heights can help feeling a little crestfallen in the cosy valleys. And let no one imagine, because he has made merry in the warm tilth and quaint nooks of romance, that he can even guess at the austere and thrilling raptures of those who have climbed the cold, white peaks of art.

About music most people are as willing to be humble as I am. If they cannot grasp musical form and win from it a pure aesthetic emotion, they confess that they understand music imperfectly or not at all. They recognise quite clearly that there is a difference between the feeling of the musician for pure music and that of the cheerful concert-goer for what music suggests. The latter enjoys his own emotions, as he has every right to do, and recognises their inferiority. Unfortunately, people are apt to be less modest about their powers of appreciating visual art. Everyone is inclined to believe that out of pictures, at any rate, he can get all that there is to be got; everyone is ready to cry "humbug" and "impostor" at those who say that more can be had. The good faith of people who feel pure aesthetic emotions is called in question by those who have never felt anything of the sort. It is the prevalence of the representative element, I suppose, that makes the man in the street so sure that he knows a good picture when he sees one. For I have noticed that in matters of architecture, pottery, textiles, &c., ignorance and ineptitude are more willing to defer to the opinions of those who have been blest with peculiar sensibility. It is a pity that cultivated and intelligent men and women cannot be induced to believe that a great gift of aesthetic appreciation is at least as rare in visual as in musical art. A comparison of my own experience in both has enabled me to discriminate very clearly between pure and impure appreciation. Is it too much to ask that others should be as honest about their feelings for pictures as I have been about mine for music? For I am certain that most of those who visit galleries do feel very much what I feel at concerts. They have their moments of pure ecstasy; but the moments are short and unsure. Soon they fall back into the world of human interests and feel emotions, good no doubt, but inferior. I do not dream of saying that what they get from art is bad or nugatory; I say that they do not get the best that art can give. I do not say that they cannot understand art; rather I say that they cannot understand the state of mind of those who understand it best. I do not say that art means nothing or little to them; I say they miss its full significance. I do not suggest for one moment that their appreciation of art is a thing to be ashamed of; the majority of the charming and intelligent people with whom I am acquainted appreciate visual art impurely; and, by the way, the appreciation of almost all great writers has been impure. But provided that there be some fraction of pure aesthetic emotion, even a mixed and minor appreciation of art is, I am sure, one of the most valuable things in the world—so valuable, indeed, that in my giddier moments I have been tempted to believe that art might prove the world's salvation.

Yet, though the echoes and shadows of art enrich the life of the plains, her spirit dwells on the mountains. To him who woos, but woos impurely, she returns enriched what is brought. Like the sun, she warms the good seed in good soil and causes it to bring forth good fruit. But only to the perfect lover does she give a new strange gift—a gift beyond all price. Imperfect lovers bring to art and take away the ideas and emotions of their own age and civilisation. In twelfth-century Europe a man might have been greatly moved by a Romanesque church and found nothing in a T'ang picture. To a man of a later age, Greek sculpture meant much and Mexican nothing, for only to the former could he bring a crowd of associated ideas to be the objects of familiar emotions. But the perfect lover, he who can feel the profound significance of form, is raised above the accidents of time and place. To him the problems of archaeology, history, and hagiography are impertinent. If the forms of a work are significant its provenance is irrelevant. Before the grandeur of those Sumerian figures in the Louvre he is carried on the same flood of emotion to the same aesthetic ecstasy as, more than four thousand years ago, the Chaldean lover was carried. It is the mark of great art that its appeal is universal and eternal. Significant form stands charged with the power to provoke aesthetic emotion in anyone capable of feeling it. The ideas of men go buzz and die like gnats; men change their institutions and their customs as they change their coats; the intellectual triumphs of one age are the follies of another; only great art remains stable and unobscure. Great art remains stable and unobscure because the feelings that it awakens are independent of time and place, because its kingdom is not of this world. To those who have and hold a sense of the significance of form what does it matter whether the forms that move them were created in Paris the day before yesterday or in Babylon fifty centuries ago? The forms of art are inexhaustible; but all lead by the same road of aesthetic emotion to the same world of aesthetic ecstasy.

Noël Carroll

CLIVE BELL'S AESTHETIC HYPOTHESIS

Clive Bell's *Art*—from which "The Aesthetic Hypothesis" is excerpted—is a book that helped to change the taste of the English-speaking world with respect to fine art; effectively, it was a powerful and popular brief in behalf of what we now call Modern Art. Bell's *Art* is, on one level, a polemic in favor of what Roger Fry, Bell's mentor in the Bloomsbury brand of art criticism, dubbed Postimpressionism: a style of painting pioneered especially by Cézanne that stresses the form or architectonic of the picture plane over and above representational accuracy. This emphasis on form and the correlative demotion of verisimilitude, of course, advances one of the key operating premises of Modern Art—i.e., the abstract (rather than representational) art of figures ranging from Mondrian to Pollock and Stella. For, in situating the value of art in formal invention—and, correspondingly, in denying aesthetic worth to pictorial representation—Bell implicitly encourages the artist to explore pictorial design and dynamics with utter indifference to mimetic content.

One way in which to locate Bell's book historically is to recall that he is writing, so to speak, in the shadow of photography. As his asides about photography indicate, Bell thinks that the popularity of this relatively recent medium shows, once and for all, that one view of art—that art should hold a mirror up to nature—is at least obsolete. Photography renders painting, conceived of in terms of imitation theories of art, superfluous. If the appearance of the world can be captured automatically, why labor over canvases? Modern Art should find some other arena of value to explore, one that preferably does not traffic in the sort of descriptive enterprises photography achieves mechanically. And, of course, Modern Art did just that—evolving projects as varied as expressionism, cubism, and minimalism in the pursuit of other than merely representational value.

However, though one may reinterpret Bell as a sign of his times, in his own view, his position is not a recommendation about the direction that art should take now that photography is on the scene. That is, he is not simply saying that *henceforth* art should be devoted to formal invention. Rather, he wants to claim that genuine art throughout history, despite spurious beliefs about the centrality of representation, has always been concerned exclusively with formal values. His claim is philosophical rather than

This essay was written for the second edition of this collection and is being published for the first time.

strategical; his aesthetic hypothesis is meant to apply universally to all art of all ages. The advent of photography, in his view, is not the pretext for a new kind of art; rather, at best, it affords us the opportunity to see that which art, all along, has been about. Art, in his estimation, does not change; it remains eternally concerned with form.

If Bell's book holds a central place in the history of taste in the twentieth century, it has an equally important place in the history of philosophical aesthetics. There are a number of reasons for this. First, much modern philosophy of art, especially as that is practiced in the Anglo-American tradition, presumes that a major question for the field is "What is Art?" and that the answer to this question will take the form of an essential definition. Some theorists argue that there can be no such definition; but even in making their point they agree that the debate about the nature of art is to be staged over the issue of an essential definition. Whether all the discussants in the history of art theory—including Plato and Tolstoy—were in fact concerned to isolate the essential definition of art may be open to dispute. However, it is clear that Clive Bell was explicitly committed to this sort of essentialism in the formulation of his aesthetic hypothesis, and it may well be that subsequent theorists were tempted to construe the bulk of the history of art theory in terms of Bell's essentialist construction of the problem.

Bell also occupies a special position in the history of empiricist aesthetics as that trajectory reaches from Francis Hutcheson[1] to Monroe Beardsley.[2] Like them—and this is the root of his empiricism—Bell is concerned to build his theory on the basis of a distinct feeling or experience, which he calls the aesthetic emotion. This response is to be distinguished from a cognitive response. Moreover, Bell thinks of this aesthetic emotion as a subjective state that is brought about causally by something in the structure of the artwork. That is, Bell's theory is functionalist as well as empiricist; the aesthetic emotion is a function of the structure of the artwork (a function of significant form for Bell in a manner analogous to Hutcheson's belief that taste is triggered by unity and diversity).

Of course, Bell's theory differs from Hutcheson's in a number of respects. Hutcheson talks of beauty, while Bell prefers to speak of aesthetic emotions, and where Hutcheson's theory applies to our response to nature as well as art, Bell restricts his purview to artworks. Hutcheson analyzes the sense of beauty in terms of disinterested pleasure, whereas Bell dispenses with the element of pleasure in his account of the aesthetic emotion; but Bell, nevertheless, retains the notion of a divorce from practicality, undoubtedly owing to the influence of Kant.

Bell is an interesting way station between Hutcheson and Beardsley. Thinkers like Hutcheson and Kant were concerned with what we might characterize as the aesthetic response to art and nature. But with Bell two crucial moves are made: the analysis of something like taste is tied to artworks, and, even more important, the provocation of that emotion becomes the mark by which art is identified. Bell, in other words, introduces what has come to be called an aesthetic theory of art of the sort later developed with great sophistication by Beardsley. And, like Beardsley and the tradition of New Criticism of which Beardsley was the major theorist, Bell excludes questions of the artist's intention as well as other questions concerning the genesis of the artwork,

---

[1]See Francis Hutcheson's "An Initial Theory of Taste" in this volume.
[2]See Monroe Beardsley's "The Philosophy of Literature" in this volume. Unlike Bell, Beardsley thinks aesthetic value is instrumental, not intrinsic.

and also questions of the intellectual and/or sociopolitical significance of the artwork, as proper objects of aesthetic appreciation. Bell, in short, like Beardsley, is a formalist. Thus, in Bell we find the rudiments of a very powerful theory of art, one that has its origin in the empiricist concern to distinguish aesthetic taste from other mental capacities or states and that, in turn, transforms that Enlightenment attempt to differentiate the aesthetic into a means to differentiate art objects from all other objects. That is, Bell, operating within the empiricist tradition, develops a theory of art that is both functionalist and formalist in ways that anticipate the spirit, though not the details, of the very challenging contemporary theory of art that was defended by Monroe Beardsley.

So far we have discussed the historical importance of Bell's theory, but the theory itself remains to be explicated. For the purpose of this article, attention will concern primarily Bell's aesthetic hypothesis, leaving aside, for the most part, discussion of his metaphysical hypothesis except where allusion to it is necessary to illuminate certain obscurities in what Bell says about the aesthetic hypothesis.

As has already been mentioned, Bell's theory of art is developed to account for visual art, though he says things about music, dance, and the verbal art in literature that suggest that the theory might be extrapolated to cover other art forms. The central question that the aesthetic hypothesis is intended to answer is: What makes a picture, a sculpture, or an architectural design a member of the class of artworks? In Bell's opinion, if aestheticians cannot answer this question, they gibber. Moreover, Bell thinks that the answer to the question involves finding a property common to all the visual objects we are willing to include in the class of artworks—a property without which an object cannot be a work of art. In other words, Bell is after the essential identifying feature of visual artworks.

You might think that if Bell wants a definition of visual art, he should say that a work of visual art is any picture, sculpture, or architectural ensemble. But this will not do. For there are many pictures (e.g., Garbage Pail Kid trading cards), sculptures (lawn reindeer at Yuletide), and architectural structures (Wendy's hamburger shops) that are not art. So what leads us to classify a Poussin painting as art while denying that status to the cartoon series *Zippy*, and, furthermore, what property does the Poussin painting share with Romanesque cathedrals that allows works of such different art forms to nevertheless be counted as artworks?

Bell believes that we have only one clue to go by here. Our experience. He asserts it as given that when sensitive people confront artworks, they undergo a peculiar emotion. Bell, of course, is not alone in this supposition; many of us have at least been tempted to believe that there is a special kind of experience to be had from art that is categorically unlike other types of experience. Bell assumes that his readers will have had this experience—that they will, on the basis of their own case, recognize what he is talking about. This emotion may be hard to pinpoint in language (in the French tradition of aesthetics, it would be identified as a certain *I know not what*). But it is a feeling with which art goers are putatively familiar and that can be called the aesthetic emotion. Moreover, Bell hypothesizes, this emotion correlates with encounters with all and only artworks.

Bell would not want to deny that each artwork has, in a manner of speaking, its own particular emotional flavor. But these emotions, he thinks—presumably on phenomenological grounds—all belong to the same recognizable kind. Furthermore, if all artworks cause this kind of aesthetic emotion, they must have some common property that brings about or provokes the uniform effect of aesthetic emotion. The solution to the problem of aesthetics, then, becomes the identification of this common property.

As is well known, Bell's candidate here is what he calls *significant form*. It is the essential differentiating feature of the artwork, by hypothesis, because it is the causal trigger that gives rise to the unique experience—the having of aesthetic emotions—that invariably accompanies encounters with artworks. Bell portrays his method as a species of induction. Objects that bring about the same effect must have something in common that accounts for that recurring effect. The aesthetic hypothesis *conjectures*, in terms of a generalization, that the common cause must be significant form. It is the essential feature of artworks because it is the agency that brings about the essential experience that distinguishes art from everything else.

In order to get a handle on this hypothesis, as well as the reasons for believing it, we need some inkling of what Bell means by significant form. *Significant form* pertains to the combination of lines, colors, shapes, and spaces; characteristic achievements with respect to securing significant form would include balancing harmonies, reconciling dissonances, and discovering rhythms. In all probability, Bell, like Kant,[3] believes that one cannot supply rules for what forms will count as significant; rather, the ultimate test of whether something is an instance of significant form depends upon whether it provokes an aesthetic emotion: a sense of ecstasy divorced from practical concerns and interests, a sense of being lifted out of the stream of life, and a feeling of the rightness of the formal design before you. Moreover, this experience is not a function of an attitude that we bring to artworks, but rather is the effect that artworks, by virtue of significant form, have on us.

Though significant form sounds like what many philosophers would prefer to call a relation, Bell speaks of it as a quality of the artwork. It is a formal property. It applies to the design of the work. Here, the design or form of the artwork is supposed to be contrasted to the content of the work, where "content" is to be narrowly construed in terms of the reference of the representation and/or the ideas presented by the work. Furthermore, this crude (many would argue insupportable) distinction between the content of the artwork and its design can perhaps give us some insight into why Bell opts for significant form as the best solution to the problem of aesthetics.

Given the distinction between form and content, Bell has at least two sorts of reasons to believe that his aesthetic hypothesis is stronger than competing hypotheses. Here it pays to remember that the major rival hypothesis to Bell's own is the view that the essential feature of visual art is representation—that visual art is dedicated to referring to the world by way of verisimilitude. However, on the one hand, not all representations, as noted above, are art. So the representation hypothesis is too broad in some cases. On the other hand, in further cases it is not broad enough—there are types of primitive art that do not strive after verisimilitude. So representation—which Bell associates with content—cannot be the essential feature of art. By elimination, form is. Moreover, this hypothesis can be fleshed out by concrete acts of criticism that reveal, time and again, that it is the form of the work of art that engages our attention.

As well, Bell seems to believe that content—projected by means of representation—is apt to engage our practical emotions or our powers of cognition. But these, Bell

[3]See Immanuel Kant's "A Theory of Aesthetic Judgment" in this volume.

believes, perhaps by definition, are contrary to aesthetic feelings. So, presumably, representational content is an unlikely source of aesthetic emotions, whereas the formal properties of an object do not evince this liability. And this lends further conviction to the conjecture that it is the design elements, the significant form of the artifact, that qualify it as a work of art.

Undoubtedly the most remembered portions of *Art* are Bell's vituperations against representation. Representation is for photographers; it is apt to engage human interest rather than aesthetic emotions. Sixth-century Byzantine art, which on Bell's account employed distortion for the sake of form, excels, whereas Frith's *Paddington Station* could be outclassed by a photojournalist. But Bell is not an iconoclast; he is not opposed to representation (though he is suspicious of it). Great paintings may be representational. However, the representation in such paintings is no part of their greatness; it is their design that deserves commendation. Representation is irrelevant when it comes to artistic merit. Significant form is the only genuine locus of value in visual art. Moreover, since significant form is the essential identifying feature of any work of visual art, every work of visual art, by definition, has some good in it.

Bell's case for the irrelevance of representation is supported by a distinction that he makes between artworks that are the objects of an emotion and artworks that suggest emotions. Any emotion, including the aesthetic emotion, has an object toward which it is directed. Moreover, the kind of object an emotion takes is, in part, constitutive of the emotion itself; that is, we individuate emotions, in part, in terms of their objects. If I am overjoyed at the fecundity of spring, the fecundity of spring is the object of my joy, and, as well, I identify my feelings as those of joy, in part, because the fecundity of spring is the sort of thing toward which feelings of joy are appropriate.

When we are moved by a painting, our emotion has an object. The object may be the painting itself; we may be moved by the rightness of the combination of lines and colors. In this case, significant form is the object of our aesthetic emotion. However, with representational paintings we may take as the object of our emotion the referent of the representation. For example, we may be saddened by the slaughter of Marat. But here our emotion is not an aesthetic emotion; it is the emotion of sadness. This is an emotion that has been *suggested* by the incident in the painting. It does not have the painting as its object, but rather the assassination of Marat. In general, the emotions that attach to the representational elements of the painting will be ordinary human emotions just because what representations often represent are human incidents that call for everyday emotions. But the emotion that is central to art is the aesthetic emotion, which is divorced from everyday emotions. Thus, representation will be irrelevant to aesthetic appreciation because it provokes emotions that are not germane to the aesthetic experience. Indeed, representations may even distract one from experiencing aesthetic emotions by portraying incidents that suggest overwhelming but everyday human emotions.

That is, artworks prompt emotions, and emotions have objects. The objects of the emotions with respect to an artwork can be the artwork itself or the events, persons, places, and so on that are portrayed in an artwork. The aesthetic emotion takes the artwork (i.e., its significant form) as its object. Suggested emotion takes portrayed events as its object. Only aesthetic emotion is genuinely directed at the painting; suggested emotion is concerned not with the painting but with that to which the painting refers. Suggested emotion is never directed at the painting as such. The representation in artworks traffics solely in suggested emotions. The representation in artworks does not engage the aesthetic emotion. The representation in artworks is irrelevant to aesthetic emotion. And, of course, the aesthetic emotion is the only emotion relevant to the artwork as such, because it is the only emotion that takes the artwork itself as its object.

The aesthetic emotion is not identified with a feeling of pleasure. Nor, even though it sounds like what a Kantian might wish to call a subjective feeling of beauty, does Bell want to describe it in terms of beauty. For Bell worries that "Beauty" has the connotation in common language of desirability. Rather, for Bell, the aesthetic is a *good* state of mind that, following G. E. Moore, Bell contends we all recognize to be intrinsically good. That is why Bell thinks that appreciating art is an ethical act in and of itself; experiencing aesthetic emotion gives us access to the intrinsically good.

One may wonder what the role of the critic can be in this context, if appreciation is really a matter of having aesthetic emotions. Bell makes a very ingenious suggestion here, one that will be developed later with influential consequences by Arnold Isenberg. The critic, according to Bell, proceeds by effectively inducing aesthetic emotions in her audience. She does this by pointing to the picture—by literally showing the relation of this line to that line—in such a way that her auditor comes to have an aesthetic emotion. If you and I disagree that a given painting is a work of art, then it is up to me to point out the significant form in the painting to you in such a way that an aesthetic emotion is prompted in you. Moreover, Bell defends the general claims of the aesthetic hypothesis by conjecturing that even if there is some residual disagreement among us about which objects are artworks, he predicts that all the claimants will be said, by their defenders, to have significant form, despite the fact that it may be the case that not everyone is sensitive to the significant form in every artwork so defended. That is, it will in fact turn out that there will be agreement that significant form is the distinguishing mark of art, even if there is some remaining dispute over certain candidates.

Perhaps the most popular objection to Bell's aesthetic hypothesis is to point out that, though it appears to be a straightforward causal generalization, it does not meet the criteria many would demand of such a hypothesis. In order to test whether or not one set of phenomena is the cause of another set of phenomena, we expect to be able to identify the cause and effect independently of each other. For example, if we wish to ascertain whether amphetamine stimulates the central nervous system, we will want a way in which to identify the substance amphetamine apart from its putative capacity to stimulate the central nervous system. For if we do not have such a means of in- dependent identification, we will worry that the term "amphetamine" just means "whatever stimulates the central nervous system." And this, of course, will make it impossible to falsify the claim that it stimulates the central nervous system. But causal generalizations have to be falsifiable if they are to be informative.

A famous satiric example of the problem here is Molière's "Soporific drugs cause sleep." On the face of it, this seems to be a causal generalization. But upon scrutiny, it is really a definition. For "soporific" means "causes sleep" and vice versa. Thus, if you find a drug that does not cause sleep, you have not challenged the supposed generaliza- tion because it is not, by definition, soporific. Because the assertion is really a definition, there is no way to falsify it, but also no way to verify it. It is a definition masquerading as a causal generalization.

Now the relevance of this to Bell's aesthetic hypothesis is that significant form behaves rather like "soporific" in the preceding example. Bell says precious little by way of independently identifying it. Significant form is said to be the cause of aesthetic emotion. But how do you know that you've found an instance of significant form unless there is a corresponding aesthetic emotion? It would appear that there is no way to do this. If two qualified parties disagree about whether an object has significant form, and one claims to have experienced the aesthetic emotion, there is no independent characterization of significant form to which either party can advert in order to undermine the claims of the other party.

We are told that significant form pertains to the combination of lines, and to the combination of colors and spaces where these are design elements. But this is of no help. For every work of visual artifice will involve a combination of design elements, yet surely not every one of these displays significant form. Or to put the matter alternatively, every visual artifice will have form, in the sense of an external configuration, but not every form is significant form. What defines the difference between mere form and significant form? Bell never says. Roger Fry, at one point, says that our interest in El Greco is purely psychological. But what if I say my interest is in El Greco's twisted linear forms, which I claim are significant? How will we settle our dispute? Bell may say it all depends on whether those twisted linear forms elicit aesthetic emotion. But then again it seems that significant form cannot be identified independently of aesthetic emotion (and vice versa), and that the putative causal correspondence between significant form and aesthetic emotion is definitional and not empirical.

Here one might think there is a way out of this problem. We might say that, though Bell's way of speaking makes it sound as though he is propounding a causal generalization, he is really doing something else, namely, attempting to offer a conceptual analysis of what it is to have an aesthetic emotion. This interpretation of Bell might be supported by recalling his discussion of objects of emotion. Bell maintained that the aesthetic emotion takes the artwork itself—specifically its significant form—as its object. We also noted that the object of an emotion is what, in part, individuates a given emotion. Thus, the relation of the object of an emotion to the emotion as a whole is not contingent in the way that the relation of a cause to an effect is thought to be. The object of the emotion is, in part, constitutive of the emotion at hand. Thus, if we take Bell to be offering an analysis of the aesthetic emotion by elucidating the object of that emotion—for him, significant form—then it may be unproblematic that the relation between the aesthetic emotion and significant form is not independent.

However, it is not clear that this maneuver is open to Bell. For though it is true that the object of an emotion gives the emotion its identity, the object has to be appropriate to the emotion under consideration. A tank hurtling at me with guns blazing is an appropriate object of fear; a wet noodle is not. If someone is said to be frightened by a wet noodle, that can only be due to some very deviant beliefs he has about wet noodles. But they are not completely deviant; they are such that if they were true, we would all be frightened of wet noodles. Perhaps he believes that wet noodles are radioactive. That is, fear would be appropriate to wet noodles, if his beliefs about wet noodles were true. In other words, the objects of an emotion that individuate the emotion are ruled by criteria of appropriateness. If the emotion is fear, the object must be of a sort that is potentially harmful, or, at least, the emoter must believe that the object meets those criteria.

But with respect to Bell, this sends us back to the problem that we have no idea of the criteria an object must meet in order to be an instance of significant form. Bell thinks that our experiences of significant form constitute a recognizable category of experience; but without characterizing the criteria that the objects of this experience must meet in order for us to be legitimately responding to significant form, or, at least, for us to think that we are responding to significant form, Bell leaves us in the lurch about what constitutes the aesthetic emotion. That is, if the concept of significant form is not ruled by specifying criteria, then the notion of an aesthetic emotion that takes significant form as its appropriate object is empty. The problem here is not that significant form and the aesthetic emotion are conceptually bound; the problem is that if significant form is supposed to define the aesthetic emotion and significant form is not specified, then the aesthetic emotion is conceptually without substance.

Bell offers us little guidance about the nature of the aesthetic emotion. His statements about its divorce from practical affairs and interests make it sound rather like the sensation of beauty in the works of preceding aestheticians, though Bell is averse to beauty talk because he fears it is misleading. However, it is difficult to have confidence that a notion that is so vaguely defined can, in turn, be useful in tracking something as elusive as significant form.

Furthermore, even the few hints that Bell does provide concerning the aesthetic emotion are troublesome. Bell speaks as though this state is marked by some special aura of disinterest. But many philosophers, perhaps most notably George Dickie, have argued that no sense whatever can be made of the notion of disinterested psychological states—whether they be attitudes, perceptions, modes of attention, or emotion. For example, is there any coherent and principled way in which to separate our interest in having aesthetic emotions from other interests, such as practical interests? Bell speaks as though through having aesthetic emotions we are afforded a way in which to escape the pressures of everyday human affairs. But that sounds very practical, in at least one very respectable sense of the term; certainly when we schedule vacations into our activities, that is part of evolving a practical—advisable and sensible—life plan. (Indeed, Bell himself speaks of art as a means of securing the good, and one would suppose that contact with the good, if there is such a thing, would also be part of a practical life plan.)

However, even if these problems with the concepts of disinterest and practicality could be worked out, and we could come to some homey consensus about what is disinterested and divorced from practical concern, *and* if we could agree that these concepts can actually be applied to human life, further problems will still arise. For in all probability, if there is any workable distinction in this area, it is likely to apply not only to aesthetic responses to artworks but to the responses of *pure* mathematicians to their theorems and systems in unapplied (nonpractical) fields of research, such as the foundations of arithmetic or symbolic logic.[4] Bell more or less admits this in his analogies between the aesthete and the mathematician. But he fails to realize the

---

[4]This is a standard objection to aesthetic theories of art. By analogizing the artist and the mathematician, Bell is leading with his jaw.

damning consequences these remarks have for his project. For if the disinterested response is supposed to pick out all and only artworks, it will not work in the way that Bell predicts. For if it picks out anything, it will pick out artworks *and* research in the more theoretical and nonapplied branches of mathematics. Nor should we regard Bell's analogies between mathematicians and aesthetes as dispensable extravagances. For Bell is logically compelled to make them, given his use of notions like the divorce from practicality in his characterization of the aesthetic emotion. In short, in his own terms, Bell gibbers.

Bell's reliance on notions like disinterest, of course, is connected to his extreme formalism. Visual artworks like paintings are to be evaluated exclusively in virtue of their design elements. Good paintings are good because they have significant form. And significant form is good because it produces good states of mind, namely aesthetic emotions. This, of course, at best tells us why significant form is good, but not why it is the only good-making feature with respect to things like paintings. After all, some paintings may promote moral or intellectual insight; but a formalist such as Bell does not regard these as merits that count in the paintings' favor—indeed, he seems to worry that they may be pernicious distractions.

Bell's reasons for regarding significant form as the only locus of value in fine art stem from two sources: his concept of aesthetic emotion and the essentialist bent in answering the question "What is art?" Formalism follows from his notion of the aesthetic emotion, since, by definition (or what there is of it), said emotion is divorced from practical life; that is, from morality and inquiry into the working of things. Also, aesthetic emotions are distinct from everyday emotions of the sort that might be churned up by political or otherwise humanly concerned paintings. Moreover, formalism is not only implied by Bell's view of aesthetic emotion; it follows from his desire to identify an essential feature of art that differentiates it from other forms of activity. And, of course, moral and intellectual insight, along with political viewpoints, can be found outside the domain of art.

Clearly, if the concept of aesthetic emotion, characterized in terms of notions like disinterest, cannot be sustained, then Bell's formalism cannot get support from it. This is not to deny that we may appreciate art because of its design properties and call it good in virtue of its form. Rather, it is to deny that formal appreciation precludes the fact that particular artworks might have other value resources, such as providing moral and intellectual insight. That is, we can admit that form is a good-making feature in art without maintaining that it is the only good-making feature, if we challenge the position that formal appreciation mandates indifference to the moral and intellectual values that may be connected to specific works of art.

Bell's formalism is also motivated by his essentialism. He believes that in order for discourse about art to be intelligible, we need a characterization of it that distinguishes art from everything else. Moreover, he connects the distinguishing mark of art, significant form, with the basis of value in art. In this way, the goodness of a work of art is unique to art—i.e., the good of a painting is the good of a painting *qua* painting; the good of a painting is not of a sort that could also be the good of something else (in the way that moral or intellectual merit could be good-making features of a philosophical essay).

That the distinguishing mark of a painting, however, is also a good-making feature puts Bell's theory in the unenviable position of being forced to admit that there is no bad art. For, by definition, to be a work of art is already to have significant form, which is something that calls for commendation. As soon as Bell identifies a painting as a work of art, he is compelled to say it is good. But this surely rubs our intuitions that there can be bad works of art the wrong way.

Perhaps an even deeper question about Bell's essentialism, however, concerns his motive for adopting this approach to begin with. That is, why does Bell believe that he can draw a sharp boundary between all other human practices and art, or even fine art? Art quite clearly has played and continues to play an integral role in diverse social practices such as religion, morality, and politics. It is not, on the face of things, a totally autonomous practice. And, as a result, one would not expect its concerns, communicative processes, and sources of value to be utterly discrete from those of other cultural practices. Bell is undoubtedly possessed by an Enlightenment pre-occupation with differentiating things—art from other objects, and aesthetic emotions (or taste) from other mental states (such as cognitive states). But it appears likely that this is just a prejudice about how things should go and not a reflection of the way that either the world or the artworld really is. The expectation that these neat distinctions can be drawn may encourage a prejudice in the theorist that is ultimately distorting. That is, rather than providing a framework that illuminates the variety of the functions and of the subtending values evident in art as we know it, the theorist will be tempted to offer a reductive account. Such an account says what art is and why art is valuable in terms of what differentiates it from other things, thereby excluding many of its characteristic features (e.g., representation) and their subtending values as almost vestigial curiosities.

From what might be thought of as an external viewpoint, Bell's essentialism leads him to attempt to answer the question "What is art?" in terms of what differentiates fine art from other things, such as mere pictures. This leads to some radically counterintuitive results concerning representation as well as the moral and intellectual values of at least some art. From an internal viewpoint, Bell's essentialism commits him to discovering a common feature among all works of art, which feature he identifies as significant form, the possession of which he regards as the sole grounds for positive critical evaluation.

Here it is important to note that this aspect of Bell's approach to theory leads him to search for the least common denominator among all the objects he regards to be art. Since he counts nonmimetic primitive artifacts and Postimpressionist painting as art, fidelity in representation cannot be the identifying feature of art. Significant form is. Moreover, this essentialism with respect to the ontological question of identifying artworks is paralleled by a species of formalism with respect to the question of evaluating art. Namely, it seems that it is being presupposed that anything that is to be accepted as an evaluative criterion for artworks must be applicable to all works of art, or, in Bell's case, to all works of fine art.

The search for a least common denominator in regard to evaluation leads quickly to formalism. For if there are some works of art to which standards of moral and intellectual knowledge do not apply, then these criteria do not meet the expectation of being common denominators of value. They are not viable criteria for artistic evalua-tion. That is, if a candidate for an evaluative criterion of artistic value does not apply uniformly to all art, then it is not an artistic standard. Since not all art aspires to moral or intellectual value, these criteria are not acceptable. On the other hand, since all art does evince some formal aspiration, form meets the requirement of being relevant to the evaluation of all art.

However, the presupposition that the only legitimate criteria for evaluating art must meet the test of being a least common denominator seems suspect. The principle is unargued for, and it appears false. We would not embrace it in evaluative contexts outside the artworld. At a sporting event, the high jump does not demand endurance. But does this entail that endurance is never a pertinent criterion of evaluation when assessing other sports? If a basketball player lacked endurance, wouldn't this be a relevant consideration in evaluating her performance? Similarly, some genres of fine art may, as a consequence of the class of art to which they belong, imply evaluative standards that would be inappropriate for other genres. Minimal art may have to meet certain intellectual standards of self-consciousness that would be outlandish to apply to primitive art, while political art may be evaluated morally in a way that will make no sense when it comes to minimal art or primitive art. Moreover, it may be the case that we find examples of political art or minimal art that do, in fact, score well on these standards just because they are intellectually or morally valuable.

Formalism tells us to ignore these values. But if these recommendations are based on the principle that any value criterion must meet the test of the least common denominator, the argument seems unpersuasive. It says we should ignore the moral value of painting x because paintings a, b, and c lack moral value. But this makes as much sense as saying that we should not appreciate the high-speed maneuvering capabilities of a Porsche because this evaluative criterion is irrelevant when it comes to tractors! In short, insofar as Bell's formalism is based on the expectation of finding a uniformly applicable evaluative standard, it is misguided, because the least common denominator approach is flawed (even if it had been the case that some sense could be made of aesthetic emotion as a source of value).

We began this essay by emphasizing the historical importance of Clive Bell's *Art*. And in the course of our discussion, we have unearthed a series of problems with its general approach. Thus, since the book holds a central position in the evolution of modern aesthetic theory, the question arises as to whether or not the problems of Bell's approach infect subsequent theorizing. My own sense is that they do have such effects, especially in terms of what are called aesthetic theories of art.

As has already been mentioned, Bell's notion of the aesthetic emotion strongly reminds one of earlier attempts to analyze beauty, even though Bell eschews beauty talk. Invocation of the divorce from practicality is especially relevant here. One way of diagnosing the genealogy of Bell's position is to say that he redeploys certain elements of the analysis of beauty, as found in figures like Hutcheson and Kant, as the basis for his concept of the aesthetic emotion; and he then goes on to take the provocation of the aesthetic emotion as the quiddity of art.

If this interpretation of Bell is correct, then his theory of art, in one sense, is essentially a beauty theory (though that term is shunned). That beauty might be a function solely of form, of course, is not outlandish (though it may be false). What becomes problematic is to take the response to beauty as the model for every type of genuine response one might make to an artwork and to take the capacity to provoke a sense of beauty as the defining feature of every artwork. This is likely to get you formalism, but it is not helpful for deriving a general theory of art. In Bell, I would argue that what has happened is that, albeit inadvertently, the entire theory of art and of our response to artworks has been reduced to a theory of beauty, reconstrued as aesthetic emotion. This camouflaged survival of beauty theory, I submit, continues in contemporary ventures in the aesthetic theory of art. These, in effect, attempt to provide a unified theory of art on the basis of a conception of the aesthetic response that is rooted in earlier theorizing, which sought to analyze the concept of beauty and which explicitly did not intend the analysis of beauty to be an account either of art or of the range of our responses to artworks. In narrowing art theory to what is essentially beauty theory, Bell impoverished the field in a way that made formalism almost inevitable. Bell's *Art* represents a historic turn in art theory, but I think it is a wrong turn—wrong, in part, because Bell misunderstood previous aesthetic research that was devoted to the analysis of beauty as a general attempt to analyze the entire compass of our response to art. And, though this problem may not be as initially obvious in contemporary versions of aesthetic theories of art, it continues to be built in to them in a way that makes one sort of formalism a perennial temptation.

R. G. Collingwood

ART AS THE EXPRESSION OF EMOTION: FROM *THE PRINCIPLES OF ART*

Introduction

1. THE TWO CONDITIONS OF AN AESTHETIC THEORY

The business of this book is to answer the question: What is art?

A question of this kind has to be answered in two stages. First, we must make sure that the key word (in this case "art") is a word which we know how to apply where it ought to be applied and refuse where it ought to be refused. It would not be much use beginning to argue about the correct definition of a general term whose instances we could not recognize when we saw them. Our first business, then, is to bring ourselves into a position in which we can say with confidence "this and this and this are art; that and that and that are not art."

This would be hardly worth insisting upon, but for two facts: that the word "art" is a word in common use, and that it is used equivocally. If it had not been a word in common use, we could have decided for ourselves when to apply it and when to refuse it. But the problem we are concerned with is not one that can be approached in that way. It is one of those problems where what we want to do is to clarify and systematize ideas we already possess; consequently there is no point in using words according to a private rule of our own, we must use them in a way which fits on to common usage. This again would have been easy, but for the fact that common usage is ambiguous. The word "art" means several different things; and we have to decide which of these usages is the one that interests us. Moreover, the other usages must not be simply jettisoned as irrelevant. They are very important for our inquiry; partly because false theories are generated by failure to distinguish them, so that in expounding one usage we must give a certain attention to others; partly because confusion between the

From The Principles of Art *(Oxford: Clarendon Press, 1938), Book I. Reprinted with permission of Oxford University Press. (Some footnotes omitted.)*

various senses of the word may produce bad practice as well as bad theory. We must therefore review the improper senses of the word "art" in a careful and systematic way; so that at the end of it we can say not only "that and that and that are not art," but "that is not art because it is pseudo-art of kind A; that, because it is pseudo-art of kind B; and that, because it is pseudo-art of kind C."

Secondly, we must proceed to a definition of the term "art." This comes second, and not first, because no one can even try to define a term until he has settled in his own mind a definite usage of it: no one can define a term in common use until he has satisfied himself that his personal usage of it harmonizes with the common usage. Definition necessarily means defining one thing in terms of something else; therefore, in order to define any given thing, one must have in one's head not only a clear idea of the thing to be defined, but an equally clear idea of all the other things by reference to which one defines it. People often go wrong over this. They think that in order to construct a definition or (what is the same thing) a "theory" of something, it is enough to have a clear idea of that one thing. That is absurd. Having a clear idea of the thing enables them to recognize it when they see it, just as having a clear idea of a certain house enables them to recognize it when they are there; but defining the thing is like explaining where the house is or pointing out its position on the map; you must know its relations to other things as well, and if your ideas of these other things are vague, your definition will be worthless.

2. ARTIST-AESTHETICIANS AND PHILOSOPHER-AESTHETICIANS

Since any answer to the question "What is art?" must divide itself into two stages, there are two ways in which it is liable to go wrong. It may settle the problem of usage satisfactorily but break down over the problem of definition; or it may deal competently with the problem of definition but fail over the problem of usage. These two kinds of failure may be described respectively as knowing what you are talking about, but talking nonsense; and talking sense but not knowing what you are talking about. The first kind gives us a treatment which is well informed and to the point, but messy and confused; the second, one which is neat and tidy, but irrelevant.

People who interest themselves in the philosophy of art fall roughly into two classes: artists with a leaning towards philosophy and philosophers with a taste for art. The artist-aesthetician knows what he is talking about. He can discriminate things that are art from things that are pseudo-art, and can say what these other things are: what it is that prevents them from being art, and what it is that deceives people into thinking that they are art. This is art-criticism, which is not identical with the philosophy of art, but only with the first of the two stages that go to make it up. It is a perfectly valid and valuable activity in itself; but the people who are good at it are not by any means necessarily able to achieve the second stage and offer a definition of art. All they can do is to recognize it. This is because they are content with too vague an idea of the relations in which art stands to things that are not art: I do not mean the various kinds of pseudo-art, but things like science, philosophy, and so forth. They are content to think of these relations as mere differences. To frame a definition of art, it is necessary to think wherein precisely these differences consist.

Philosopher-aestheticians are trained to do well just the thing that artist-aestheticians do badly. They are admirably protected against talking nonsense: but there is no security that they will know what they are talking about. Hence their theorizing, however competent in itself, is apt to be vitiated by weakness in its foundation of fact. They are tempted to evade this difficulty by saying: "I do not profess to be a critic; I am not equal to adjudging the merits of Mr. Joyce, Mr. Eliot, Miss Sitwell, or Miss Stein; so I will stick to Shakespeare and Michelangelo and Beethoven. There is plenty to say about art if one bases it only on the acknowledged classics." This would be all right for a critic; but for a philosopher it will not do. Usage is particular, but theory is universal, and the truth at which it aims is *index sui et falsi*. The aesthetician who claims to know what it is that makes Shakespeare a poet is tacitly claiming to know whether Miss Stein is a poet, and if not, why not. The philosopher-aesthetician who sticks to classical artists is pretty sure to locate the essence of art not in what makes them artists but in what makes them classical, that is, acceptable to the academic mind.

Philosophers' aesthetic, not having a material criterion for the truth of theories in their relation to the facts, can only apply a formal criterion. It can detect logical flaws in a theory and therefore dismiss it as false; but it can never acclaim or propound any theory as true. It is wholly unconstructive; *tamquam virgo Deo consecrata, nihil parit.* Yet the fugitive and cloistered virtue of academic aesthetic is not without its uses, negative though they are. Its dialectic is a school in which the artist-aesthetician or critic can learn the lessons that will show him how to advance from art-criticism to aesthetic theory.

3. THE PRESENT SITUATION

The division between artist-aestheticians and philosopher-aestheticians corresponds fairly well with the facts as they stood half a century ago, but not with the facts of to-day. In the last generation, and increasingly in the last twenty years, the gulf between these two classes has been bridged by the appearance of a third class of aesthetic theorists: poets and painters and sculptors who have taken the trouble to train themselves in philosophy or psychology or both, and write not with the airs and graces of an essayist or the condescension of a hierophant, but with the modesty and seriousness of a man contributing to a discussion in which others beside himself are speaking, and out of which he hopes that truths not yet known even to himself will emerge.

This is one aspect of a profound change in the way in which artists think of themselves and their relation to other people. In the later nineteenth century the artist walked among us as a superior being, marked off even by his dress from common mortals; too high and ethereal to be questioned by others, too sure of his superiority to question himself, and resenting the suggestion that the mysteries of his craft should be analysed and theorized about by philosophers and other profane persons. To-day, instead of forming a mutual admiration society whose serene climate was broken from time to time by unedifying storms of jealousy, and whose aloofness from worldly concerns was marred now and then by scandalous contact with the law, artists go about like other men, pursuing a business in which they take no more than a decent pride, and criticizing each other publicly as to their ways of doing it. In this new soil a new growth of aesthetic theory has sprung up; rich in quantity and on the whole high in quality. It is too soon to write the history of this movement, but not too late to contribute to it; and it is only because such a movement is going on that a book like this can be published with some hope of its being read in the spirit in which it is written.

4. HISTORY OF THE WORD "ART"

In order to clear up the ambiguities attaching to the word "art," we must look to its history. The aesthetic sense of the word, the sense which here concerns us, is very recent in origin. Ars in ancient Latin, like τέχνη in Greek, means something quite different. It means a craft or specialized form of skill, like carpentry or smithying or surgery. The Greeks and Romans had no conception of what we call art as something different from craft; what we call art they regarded merely as a group of crafts, such as the craft of poetry (ποιητική τέχνη, ars poetica), which they conceived, sometimes no doubt with misgivings, as in principle just like carpentry and the rest, and differing from any one of these only in the sort of way in which any one of them differs from any other.

It is difficult for us to realize this fact, and still more so to realize its implications. If people have no word for a certain kind of thing, it is because they are not aware of it as a distinct kind. Admiring as we do the art of the ancient Greeks, we naturally suppose that they admired it in the same kind of spirit as ourselves. But we admire it as a kind of art, where the word "art" carries with it all the subtle and elaborate implications of the modern European aesthetic consciousness. We can be perfectly certain that the Greeks did not admire it in any such way. They approached it from a different point of view. What this was, we can perhaps discover by reading what people like Plato wrote about it; but not without great pains, because the first thing every modern reader does, when he reads what Plato has to say about poetry, is to assume that Plato is describing an aesthetic experience similar to our own. The second thing he does is to lose his temper because Plato describes it so badly. With most readers there is no third stage.

Ars in medieval Latin, like "art" in the early modern English which borrowed both word and sense, meant any special form of book-learning, such as grammar or logic, magic or astrology. That is still its meaning in the time of Shakespeare: "lie there, my art," says Prospero, putting off his magic gown. But the Renaissance, first in Italy and then elsewhere, reestablished the old meaning; and the Renaissance artists, like those of the ancient world, did actually think of themselves as craftsmen. It was not until the seventeenth century that the problems and conceptions of aesthetic began to be disentangled from those of technic or the philosophy of craft. In the late eighteenth century the disentanglement had gone so far as to establish a distinction between the fine arts and the useful arts; where "fine" arts meant, not delicate or highly skilled arts, but "beautiful" arts (les beaux arts, le belle arti, die schöne Kunst). In the nineteenth century this phrase, abbreviated by leaving out the epithet and generalized by substituting the singular for the distributive plural, became "art."

At this point the disentanglement of art from craft is theoretically complete. But only theoretically. The new use of the word "art" is a flag placed on a hill-top by the first assailants; it does not prove that the hill-top is effectively occupied.

5. SYSTEMATIC AMBIGUITY

To make the occupation effective, the ambiguities attaching to the word must be cleared away and its proper meaning brought to light. The proper meaning of a word (I speak not of technical terms, which kindly god-parents furnish soon after birth with neat and tidy definitions, but of words in a living language) is never something upon which the word sits perched like a gull on a stone; it is something over which the word hovers like a gull over a ship's stern. Trying to fix the proper meaning in our minds is like coaxing the gull to settle in the rigging, with the rule that the gull must be alive when it settles: one must not shoot it and tie it there. The way to discover the proper meaning is to ask not, "What do we mean?" but, "What are we trying to mean?" And this involves the question "What is preventing us from meaning what we are trying to mean?"

These impediments, the improper meanings which distract our minds from the proper one, are of three kinds. I shall call them obsolete meanings, analogical meanings, and courtesy meanings.

The obsolete meanings which every word with a history is bound to possess are the meanings it once had, and retains by force of habit. They form a trail behind the word like that of a shooting star, and divide themselves according to their distance from it into more and less obsolete. The very obsolete are not a danger to the present use of the word; they are dead and buried, and only the antiquary wishes to disinter them. But the less obsolete are a very grave danger. They cling to our minds like drowning men, and so jostle the present meaning that we can only distinguish it from them by the most careful analysis.

The analogical meanings arise from the fact that when we want to discuss the experience of other people we can only do so in our own language. Our own language has been invented for the purpose of expressing our own experience. When we use it for discussing other people's we assimilate their experience to our own. We cannot talk in English about the way in which a negro tribe thinks and feels without making them appear to think and feel like Englishmen; we cannot explain to our negro friends in their own language how Englishmen think and feel without making it appear to them that we think and feel like themselves.[1] Or rather, the assimilation of one kind of experience to another goes smoothly for a time, but sooner or later a break comes, as when we try to represent one kind of curve by means of another. When that happens, the person whose language is being used thinks that the other has gone more or less mad. Thus in studying ancient history we use the word "state" without scruple as a translation of πόλις. But the word "state," which comes to us from the Italian Renaissance, was invented to express the new secularized political consciousness of the modern world. The Greeks had no such experience; their political consciousness was religious and political in one; so that what they meant by πόλις was something which looks to us like a confusion of Church and State. We have no words for such a thing, because we do not possess the thing. When we use for it words like "state," "political," and so forth, we are using them not in their proper sense, but in an analogical sense.

Courtesy meanings arise from the fact that the things we give names to are the things we regard as important. Whatever may be true of scientific technicalities, words in a living language are never used without some practical and emotional colouring, which sometimes takes precedence of its descriptive function. People claim or disclaim such titles as gentleman, or Christian, or communist, either descriptively, because they

---

[1]"Let the reader consider any argument that would utterly demolish all Zande claims for the power of the oracle. If it were translated into Zande modes of thought [which is the same thing as saying, if it were translated into the Zande language] it would serve to support their entire structure of belief." Evans-Pritchard, *Witchcraft, Oracles and Magic among the Azande* (1937), pp. 319–20.

think they have or have not the qualities these titles connote; or emotionally, because they wish to possess or not to possess these qualities, and that irrespectively of whether they know what they are. The two alternatives are very far from being mutually exclusive. But when the descriptive motive is overshadowed by the emotional one, the word becomes a courtesy title or discourtesy title as the case may be.

Applying this to the word "art," we find its proper meaning hedged about with well-established obsolete, analogical, and courtesy meanings. The only obsolete meaning of any importance is that which identifies art with craft. When this meaning gets tangled up with the proper one, the result is that special error which I call the technical theory of art; the theory that art is some kind of craft. The question then, of course, arises: What kind of craft is it? and here is vast scope for controversy between rival views as to its differentia. To that controversy this book will contribute nothing. The question is not whether art is this or that kind of craft, but whether it is any kind at all. And I do not propose even to refute the theory that it is some kind of craft. It is not a matter that stands in need of demonstration. We all know perfectly well that art is not craft; and all I wish to do is to remind the reader of the familiar differences which separate the two things.

Analogically, we use the word "art" of many things which in certain ways (important ways, no doubt) resemble what we call art in our own modern European world, but in other ways are unlike it. The example which I shall consider is magical art. I will pause to explain what this means.

When the naturalistic animal-paintings and sculptures of the upper palaeolithic age were discovered in the last century, they were hailed as representing a newly found school of art. Before long, it was realized that this description implied a certain misunderstanding. To call them art implied the assumption that they were designed and executed with the same purpose as the modern works from which the name was extended to them; and it was found that this assumption was false. When Mr. John Skeaping, whose manner is obviously indebted to these palaeolithic predecessors, makes one of his beautiful animal-drawings, he frames it under glass, exhibits it in a place of public resort, expects people to go and look at it, and hopes that somebody will buy it, take it home, and hang it up to be contemplated and enjoyed by himself and his friends. All modern theories of art insist that what a work of art is for is to be thus contemplated. But when an Aurignacian or Magdalenian painter made such a drawing he put it where nobody lived, and often where people could never get near it at all without great trouble, and on some special occasion; and it appears that what he expected them to do was to stab it with spears or shoot arrows at it, after which, when it was defaced, he was ready to paint another on the top of it.

If Mr. Skeaping hid his drawings in a coal-cellar and expected anybody who found them to shoot them full of bullet-holes, aesthetic theorists would say that he was no artist, because he intended his drawings for consumption, as targets, and not for contemplation, as works of art. By the same argument, the palaeolithic paintings are not works of art, however much they may resemble them: the resemblance is super-ficial; what matters is the purpose, and the purpose is different. I need not here go into the reasons which have led archaeologists to decide that the purpose was magical, and that these paintings were accessories in some kind of ritual whereby hunters prefigured and so ensured the death or capture of the animals depicted.

A similar magical or religious function is recognizable elsewhere. The portraits of ancient Egyptian sculpture were not designed for exhibition and contemplation; they were hidden away in the darkness of the tomb, unvisited, where no spectator could see them, but where they could do their magical work, whatever precisely that was, uninterrupted. Roman portraiture was derived from the images of ancestors which, keeping watch over the domestic life of their posterity, had a magical or religious purpose to which their artistic qualities were subservient. Greek drama and Greek sculpture began as accessories of religious cult. And the entire body of medieval Christian art shows the same purpose.

The terms "art," "artist," "artistic," and so forth are much used as courtesy titles. When we consider in bulk the things which claim them, but, on the whole, claim them without real justification, it becomes apparent that the thing which most constantly demands and receives the courtesy title of art is the thing whose real name is amusement or entertainment. The vast majority of our literature in prose and verse, our painting and drawing and sculpture, our music, our dancing and acting, and so forth, is quite plainly and often quite explicitly designed to amuse, but is called art. Yet we know that there is a distinction. The gramophone trade, a recent one which has the outspokenness of an *enfant terrible*, actually states the distinction, or tries to, in its catalogues. Nearly all its records are issued frankly as amusement music; the small remainder is marked off as "connoisseur's records" or the like. Painters and novelists make the same distinction, but not so publicly.

This is a fact of great interest for the aesthetic theorist, because, unless he grasps it, it may debauch his conception of art itself by causing him to identify art proper with amusement; and of equal interest to the historian of art, or rather of civilization as a whole, because it concerns him to understand the place which amusement occupies in relation to art and to civilization in general.

Our first business, then, is to investigate these three kinds of art falsely so called. When that has been done, we must see what there is left to be said about art proper.

Art and Craft

1. THE MEANING OF CRAFT

The first sense of the word "art" to be distinguished from art proper is the obsolete sense in which it means what in this book I shall call craft. This is what *ars* means in ancient Latin, and what τεχνη means in Greek: the power to produce a preconceived result by means of consciously controlled and directed action. In order to take the first step towards a sound aesthetic, it is necessary to disentangle the notion of craft from that of art proper. In order to do this, again, we must first enumerate the chief characteristics of craft.

(1) Craft always involves a distinction between means and end, each clearly conceived as something distinct from the other but related to it. The term "means" is loosely applied to things that are used in order to reach the end, such as tools, machines, or fuel. Strictly, it applies not to the things but to the actions concerned

with them: manipulating the tools, tending the machines, or burning the fuel. These actions (as implied by the literal sense of the word means) are passed through or traversed in order to reach the end, and are left behind when the end is reached. This may serve to distinguish the idea of means from two other ideas with which it is sometimes confused: that of part, and that of material. The relation of part to whole is like that of means to end, in that the part is indispensable to the whole, is what it is because of its relation to the whole, and may exist by itself before the whole comes into existence; but when the whole exists the part exists too, whereas, when the end exists, the means have ceased to exist. As for the idea of material, we shall return to that in (4) below.

(2) It involves a distinction between planning and execution. The result to be obtained is preconceived or thought out before being arrived at. The craftsman knows what he wants to make before he makes it. This foreknowledge is absolutely indispensable to craft: if something, for example stainless steel, is made without such foreknowledge, the making of it is not a case of craft but an accident. Moreover, this foreknowledge is not vague but precise. If a person sets out to make a table, but conceives the table only vaguely, as somewhere between two by four feet and three by six, and between two and three feet high, and so forth, he is no craftsman.

(3) Means and end are related in one way in the process of planning; in the opposite way in the process of execution. In planning the end is prior to the means. The end is thought out first, and afterwards the means are thought out. In execution the means come first, and the end is reached through them.

(4) There is a distinction between raw material and finished product or artifact. A craft is always exercised upon something, and aims at the transformation of this into something different. That upon which it works begins as raw material and ends as finished product. The raw material is found ready made before the special work of the craft begins.

(5) There is a distinction between form and matter. The matter is what is identical in the raw material and the finished product; the form is what is different, what the exercise of the craft changes. To describe the raw material as raw is not to imply that it is formless, but only that it has not yet the form which it is to acquire through "transformation" into finished product.

(6) There is a hierarchical relation between various crafts, one supplying what another needs, one using what another provides. There are three kinds of hierarchy: of materials, of means, and of parts. (*a*) The raw material of one craft is the finished product of another. Thus the silviculturist propagates trees and looks after them as they grow, in order to provide raw material for the felling-men who transform them into logs; these are raw material for the saw-mill which transforms them into planks; and these, after a further process of selection and seasoning, become raw material for a joiner. (*b*) In the hierarchy of means, one craft supplies another with tools. Thus the timber-merchant supplies pit-props to the miner; the miner supplies coal to the blacksmith; the blacksmith supplies horseshoes to the farmer; and so on. (*c*) In the hierarchy of parts, a complex operation like the manufacture of a motor-car is parcelled out among a number of trades: one firm makes the engine, another the gears, another the chassis, another the tyres, another the electrical equipment, and so on; the

final assembling is not strictly the manufacture of the car but only the bringing together of these parts. In one or more of these ways every craft has a hierarchical character; either as hierarchically related to other crafts, or as itself consisting of various heterogeneous operations hierarchically related among themselves.

Without claiming that these features together exhaust the notion of craft, or that each of them separately is peculiar to it, we may claim with tolerable confidence that where most of them are absent from a certain activity that activity is not a craft, and, if it is called by that name, is so called either by mistake or in a vague and inaccurate way.

2. THE TECHNICAL THEORY OF ART

It was the Greek philosophers who worked out the idea of craft, and it is in their writings that the above distinctions have been expounded once for all. The philosophy of craft, in fact, was one of the greatest and most solid achievements of the Greek mind, or at any rate of that school, from Socrates to Aristotle, whose work happens to have been most completely preserved.

Great discoveries seem to their makers even greater than they are. A person who has solved one problem is inevitably led to apply that solution to others. Once the Socratic school had laid down the main lines of a theory of craft, they were bound to look for instances of craft in all sorts of likely and unlikely places. To show how they met this temptation, here yielding to it and there resisting it, or first yielding to it and then laboriously correcting their error, would need a long essay. Two brilliant cases of successful resistance may, however, be mentioned: Plato's demonstration (*Republic*, 330 D–336 A) that justice is not a craft, with the pendant (336 E–354 A) that injustice is not one either; and Aristotle's rejection (*Metaphysics*, Λ) of the view stated in Plato's *Timaeus*, that the relation between God and the world is a case of the relations between craftsman and artifact.

When they came to deal with aesthetic problems, however, both Plato and Aristotle yielded to the temptation. They took it for granted that poetry, the only art which they discussed in detail, was a kind of craft, and spoke of this craft as ποιητικὴ τέχνη, poet-craft. What kind of craft was this?

There are some crafts, like cobbling, carpentering, or weaving, whose end is to produce a certain type of artifact; others, like agriculture or stock-breeding or horse-breaking, whose end is to produce or improve certain non-human types of organism; others again, like medicine or education or warfare, whose end is to bring certain human beings into certain states of body or mind. But we need not ask which of these is the genus of which poet-craft is a species, because they are not mutually exclusive. The cobbler or carpenter or weaver is not simply trying to produce shoes or carts or cloth. He produces these because there is a demand for them; that is, they are not ends to him, but means to the end of satisfying a specific demand. What he is really aiming at is the production of a certain state of mind in his customers, the state of having these demands satisfied. The same analysis applies to the second group. Thus in the end these three kinds of craft reduce to one. They are all ways of bringing human beings into certain desired conditions.

The same description is true of poet-craft. The poet is a kind of skilled producer; he produces for consumers; and the effect of his skill is to bring about in them certain states of mind, which are conceived in advance as desirable states. The poet, like any other kind of craftsman, must know what effect he is aiming at, and must learn by experience and precept, which is only the imparted experience of others, how to produce it. This is poet-craft, as conceived by Plato and Aristotle and, following them, such writers as Horace in his *Ars Poetica*. There will be analogous crafts of painting, sculpture, and so forth; music, at least for Plato, is not a separate art but is a constituent part of poetry.

I have gone back to the ancients, because their thought, in this matter as in so many others, has left permanent traces on our own, both for good and for ill. There are suggestions in some of them, especially in Plato, of a quite different view; but this is the one which they have made familiar, and upon which both the theory and the practice of the arts has for the most part rested down to the present time. Present-day fashions of thought have in some ways even tended to reinforce it. We are apt nowadays to think about most problems, including those of art, in terms either of economics or of psychology; and both ways of thinking tend to subsume the philosophy of art under the philosophy of craft. To the economist, art presents the appearance of a specialized group of industries; the artist is a producer, his audience consumers who pay him for benefits ultimately definable in terms of the states of mind which his productivity enables them to enjoy. To the psychologist, the audience consists of persons reacting in certain ways to stimuli provided by the artist; and the artist's business is to know what reactions are desired or desirable, and to provide the stimuli which will elicit them.

The technical theory of art is thus by no means a matter of merely antiquarian interest. It is actually the way in which most people nowadays think of art; and especially economists and psychologists, the people to whom we look (sometimes in vain) for special guidance in the problems of modern life.

But this theory is simply a vulgar error, as anybody can see who looks at it with a critical eye. It does not matter what kind of craft in particular is identified with art. It does not matter what the benefits are which the artist is regarded as conferring on his audience, or what the reactions are which he is supposed to elicit. Irrespectively of such details, our question is whether art is any kind of craft at all. It is easily answered by keeping in mind the half-dozen characteristics of craft enumerated in the preceding section, and asking whether they fit the case of art. And there must be no chopping of toes or squeezing of heels; the fit must be immediate and convincing. It is better to have no theory of art at all, than to have one which irks us from the first.

3. BREAK-DOWN OF THE THEORY

(1) The first characteristic of craft is the distinction between means and end. Is this present in works of art? According to the technical theory, yes. A poem is means to the production of a certain state of mind in the audience, as a horseshoe is means to the production of a certain state of mind in the man whose horse is shod. And the poem in its turn will be an end to which other things are means. In the case of the horseshoe, this stage of the analysis is easy: we can enumerate lighting the forge, cutting a piece of iron off a bar, heating it, and so on. What is there analogous to these processes in the case of a poem? The poet may get paper and pen, fill the pen, sit down and square his

elbows; but these actions are preparatory not to composition (which may go on in the poet's head) but to writing. Suppose the poem is a short one and composed without the use of any writing materials; what are the means by which the poet composes it? I can think of no answer, unless comic answers are wanted, such as "using a rhyming dictionary," "pounding his foot on the floor or wagging his head or hand to mark the metre," or "getting drunk." If one looks at the matter seriously, one sees that the only factors in the situation are the poet, the poetic labour of his mind, and the poem. And if any supporter of the technical theory says "Right: then the poetic labour is the means, the poem the end," we shall ask him to find a blacksmith who can make a horseshoe by sheer labour, without forge, anvil, hammer, or tongs. It is because nothing corresponding to these exists in the case of the poem that the poem is not an end to which there are means.

Conversely, is a poem means to the production of a certain state of mind in an audience? Suppose a poet had read his verses to an audience, hoping that they would produce a certain result; and suppose the result were different; would that in itself prove the poem a bad one? It is a difficult question; some would say yes, others no. But if poetry were obviously a craft, the answer would be a prompt and unhesitating yes. The advocate of the technical theory must do a good deal of toe-chopping before he can get his facts to fit his theory at this point.

So far, the prospects of the technical theory are not too bright. Let us proceed.

(2) The distinction between planning and executing certainly exists in some works of art, namely those which are also works of craft or artifacts; for there is, of course, an overlap between these two things, as may be seen by the example of a building or a jar, which is made to order for the satisfaction of a specific demand, to serve a useful purpose, but may none the less be a work of art. But suppose a poet were making up verses as he walked; suddenly finding a line in his head, and then another, and then dissatisfied with them and altering them until he had got them to his liking: what is the plan which he is executing? He may have had a vague idea that if he went for a walk he would be able to compose poetry; but what were, so to speak, the mea-surements and specifications of the poem he planned to compose? He may, no doubt, have been hoping to compose a sonnet on a particular subject specified by the editor of a review; but the point is that he may not, and that he is none the less a poet for composing without having any definite plan in his head. Or suppose a sculptor were not making a Madonna and child, three feet high, in Hoptonwood stone, guaranteed to placate the chancellor of the diocese and obtain a faculty for placing it in the vacant niche over a certain church door; but were simply play-ing about with clay, and found the clay under his fingers turning into a little danc-ing man: is this not a work of art because it was done without being planned in advance?

All this is very familiar. There would be no need to insist upon it, but that the technical theory of art relies on our forgetting it. While we are thinking of it, let us note the importance of not over-emphasizing it. Art as such does not imply the distinction between planning and execution. But (*a*) this is a merely negative characteristic, not a positive one. We must not erect the absence of plan into a positive force and call it inspiration, or the unconscious, or the like. (*b*) It is a permissible characteristic of art, not a compulsory one. If unplanned works of art are possible, it does not follow that no planned work is a work of art. That is the logical fallacy that underlies one, or some, of the various things called romanticism. It may very well be true that the only works of art which can be made altogether without a plan are trifling ones, and that the greatest and most serious ones always contain an element of planning and therefore an element of craft. But that would not justify the technical theory of art.

✻ ✻ ✻

Art as Magic

1. WHAT MAGIC IS NOT: (I) PSEUDO-SCIENCE

Representation, we have seen, is always means to an end. The end is the re-evocation of certain emotions. According as these are evoked for their practical value or for their own sake, it is called magic or amusement.

My use of the term "magic" in this connexion is certain to cause difficulty; but I cannot avoid it, for reasons which I hope will become clear. I must therefore see to it that the difficulty does not amount to misunderstanding, at any rate in the case of readers who wish to understand.

The word "magic" as a rule carries no definite significance at all. It is used to denote certain practices current in "savage" societies, and recognizable here and there in the less "civilized" and less "educated" strata of our own society, but it is used without any definite conception of what it connotes; and therefore, if some one asserts that, for example, the ceremonies of our own church are magical, neither he nor any one else can say what the assertion means, except that it is evidently intended to be abusive; it cannot be described as true or false. What I am here trying to do is to rescue the word "magic" from this condition in which it is a meaningless term of abuse, and use it as a term with a definite meaning.

Its degradation into a term of abuse was the work of a school of anthropologists whose prestige has been deservedly great. Two generations ago, anthropologists set themselves the task of scientifically studying the civilizations different from our own which had been lumped together under the unintelligently depreciatory (or, at times, unintelligently laudatory) name of savage. Prominent among the customs of these civilizations they found practices of the kind which by common consent were called magical. As scientific students, it was their business to discover the motive of these practices. What, they asked themselves, is magic for?

The direction in which they looked for an answer to this question was determined by the prevailing influence of a positivistic philosophy which ignored man's emotional nature and reduced everything in human experience to terms of intellect, and further ignored every kind of intellectual activity except those which, according to the same philosophy, went to the making of natural science. This prejudice led them to compare the magical practices of the "savage" (civilized men, they rashly assumed, had none, except for certain anomalous things which these anthropologists called survivals) with the practices of civilized man when he uses his scientific knowledge in order to control nature. The magician and the scientist, they concluded, belong to the same genus. Each is a person who attempts to control nature by the practical application of scientific knowledge. The difference is that the scientist actually possesses scientific knowledge, and consequently his attempts to control nature are successful: the magician possesses none, and therefore his attempts fail. For example, irrigating crops really makes them grow; but the savage, not knowing this, dances at them in the false belief that his example will encourage in the crops a spirit of emulation, and induce them to grow as high as he jumps. Thus, they concluded, magic is at bottom simply a special kind of error: it is erroneous natural science.

* * *

3. WHAT MAGIC IS

The only profitable way of theorizing about magic is to approach it from the side of art. The similarities between magic and applied science, on which the Tylor-Frazer theory rests, are very slight, and the dissimilarities are great. The magician as such is not a scientist; and if we admit this, and call him a bad scientist, we are merely finding a term of abuse for the characteristics that differentiate him from a scientist, without troubling to analyse those characteristics. The similarities between magic and neurosis, on which the Freudian theory rests, are just as strong or as weak as one pleases; for neurosis is a negative term, covering many different kinds of departure from our rough-and-ready standard of mental health; and there is no reason why one item in the list of qualifications demanded by a standard of mental health should not be a disbelief in magic. But the similarities between magic and art are both strong and intimate. Magical practices invariably contain, not as peripheral elements but as central elements, artistic activities like dances, songs, drawing, or modelling. Moreover, these elements have a function which in two ways resembles the function of amusement. (i) They are means to a preconceived end, and are therefore not art proper but craft. (ii) This end is the arousing of emotion.

* * *

4. MAGICAL ART

A magical art is an art which is representative and therefore evocative of emotion, and evokes of set purpose some emotions rather than others in order to discharge them into the affairs of practical life. Such an art may be good or bad when judged by aesthetic standards, but that kind of goodness or badness has little, if any, connexion with its efficacy in its own proper work. The brilliant naturalism of the admittedly magical palaeolithic animal paintings cannot be explained by their magical function. Any kind of scrawl or smudge would have served the purpose, if the neophyte on approaching it had been solemnly told that it "was" a bison. When magical art reaches a high aesthetic level, this is because the society to which it belongs (not the artists alone, but artists and audience alike) demands of it an aesthetic excellence quite other than the very modest degree of competence which would enable it to fulfill its magical function. Such an art has a double motive. It remains at a high level only so long as the two motives are felt as absolutely coincident. As soon as a sculptor thinks to himself "surely it is a waste of labour to finish this portrait with such care, when it is going to be shut up in a tomb as soon as it leaves my hand," the two motives have come apart in his mind. He has conceived the idea that something short of his best work, in the aesthetic sense of that phrase, would satisfy the needs of magic; and decadence at once begins. Indeed, it has begun already; for ideas of that kind only come up into consciousness long after they have begun to influence conduct.

Art as Amusement

1. AMUSEMENT ART

If an artifact is designed to stimulate a certain emotion, and if this emotion is intended not for discharge into the occupations of ordinary life, but for enjoyment as something of value in itself, the function of the artifact is to amuse or entertain. Magic is useful, in the sense that the emotions it excites have a practical function in the affairs of every day; amusement is not useful but only enjoyable, because there is a watertight bulkhead between its world and the world of common affairs. The emotions generated by amusement run their course within this watertight compartment.

Every emotion, dynamically considered, has two phases in its existence: charge or excitation, and discharge. The discharge of an emotion is some act done at the prompting of that emotion, by doing which we work the emotion off and relieve ourselves of the tension which, until thus discharged, it imposes upon us. The emotions generated by an amusement must be discharged, like any others; but they are discharged within the amusement itself. This is in fact the peculiarity of amusement. An amusement is a device for the discharge of emotions in such a way that they shall not interfere with the concerns of practical life. But since practical life is only definable as that part of life which is not amusement, this statement, if meant for a definition, would be circular. We must therefore say: to establish a distinction between amusement and practical life[2] is to divide experience into two parts, so related that the emotions generated in the one are not allowed to discharge themselves in the other. In the one, emotions are treated as ends in themselves; in the other, as forces whose operation achieves certain ends beyond them. The first part is now called amusement, the second part practical life.

✳ ✳ ✳

4. REPRESENTATION AND THE CRITIC

The question may here be raised, how the practice of art-criticism is affected by identifying art with representation in either of its two forms. The critic's business, as we have already seen, is to establish a consistent usage of terms: to settle the nomenclature of the various things which come before him competing for a given name, saying, "this is art, that is not art," and, being an expert in this business, performing it with

---

[2] Aestheticians who discuss the relation between two mutually exclusive things called "Art" and "Life" are really discussing this distinction.

authority. A person qualified so to perform it is called a judge; and judgement means verdict, the authoritative announcement that, for example, a man is innocent or guilty. Now, the business of art-criticism has been going on ever since at least the seventeenth century; but it has always been beset with difficulties. The critic knows, and always has known, that in theory he is concerned with something objective. In principle, the question whether this piece of verse is a poem or a sham poem is a question of fact, on which every one who is properly qualified to judge ought to agree. But what he finds, and always has found, is that in the first place the critics as a rule do not agree; in the second place, their verdict is as a rule reversed by posterity; and in the third place it is hardly ever welcomed and accepted as useful either by the artists or by the general public.

When the disagreements of critics are closely studied, it becomes evident that there is much more behind them than mere human liability to form different opinions about the same thing. The verdict of a jury in court, as judges are never tired of telling them, is a matter of opinion; and hence they sometimes disagree. But if they disagreed in the kind of way in which art-critics disagree, trial by jury would have been experimented with only once, if that, before being abolished for ever. The two kinds of disagreement differ in that the juror, if the case is being handled by a competent judge, has only one point at which he can go wrong. He has to give a verdict, and the judge tells him what the principles are upon which he must give it. The art-critic also has to give a verdict; but there is no agreement between him and his colleagues as to the principles on which it must be given.

*　*　*

Art Proper: (1) as Expression

1. THE NEW PROBLEM

We have finished at last with the technical theory of art, and with the various kinds of art falsely so called to which it correctly applies. We shall return to it in the future only so far as it forces itself upon our notice and threatens to impede the development of our subject.

That subject is art proper. It is true that we have already been much concerned with this; but only in a negative way. We have been looking at it so far as was necessary in order to exclude from it the various things which falsely claimed inclusion in it. We must now turn to the positive side of this same business, and ask what kinds of things they are to which the name rightly belongs.

In doing this we are still dealing with what are called questions of fact, or what in the first chapter were called questions of usage, not with questions of theory. We shall not be trying to build up an argument which the reader is asked to examine and criticize, and accept if he finds no fatal flaw in it. We shall not be offering him information which he is asked to accept on the authority of witnesses. We shall be trying as best we can to remind ourselves of facts well known to us all: such facts as this, that on occasions of a certain kind we actually do use the word art or some kindred word to designate certain kinds of things, and in the sense which we have now isolated as the proper sense of the word. Our business is to concentrate our attention on these usages until we can see them as consistent and systematic. This will be our work throughout this chapter and the next. The task of defining the usages thus systematized, and so constructing a theory of art proper, will come later.

* * *

This method will now be applied to the technical theory of art. The formula for the distortion is known from our analysis of the notion of craft . . . Because the inventors of the theory were prejudiced in favour of that notion, they forced their own ideas about art into conformity with it. The central and primary characteristic of craft is the distinction it involves between means and end. If art is to be conceived as craft, it must likewise be divisible into means and end. We have seen that actually it is not so divisible; but we have now to ask why anybody ever thought it was. What is there in the case of art which these people misunderstood by assimilating it to the well-known distinction of means and end? If there is nothing, the technical theory of art was a gratuitous and baseless invention; those who have stated and accepted it have been and are nothing but a pack of fools; and we have been wasting our time thinking about it. These are hypotheses I do not propose to adopt.

(1) This, then, is the first point we have learnt from our criticism: that there is in art proper a distinction resembling that between means and end, but not identical with it.

(2) The element which the technical theory calls the end is defined by it as the arousing of emotion. The idea of arousing (i.e. of bringing into existence, by determinate means, something whose existence is conceived in advance as possible and desirable) belongs to the philosophy of craft, and is obviously borrowed thence. But the same is not true of emotion. This, then, is our second point. Art has something to do with emotion; what it does with it has a certain resemblance to arousing it, but is not arousing it.

(3) What the technical theory calls the means is defined by it as the making of an artifact called a work of art. The making of this artifact is described according to the terms of the philosophy of craft: i.e. as the transformation of a given raw material by imposing on it a form preconceived as a plan in the maker's mind. To get the distortion out of this we must remove all these characteristics of craft, and thus we reach the third point. Art has something to do with making things, but these things are not material things, made by imposing form on matter, and they are not made by skill. They are things of some other kind, and made in some other way.

We now have three riddles to answer. For the present, no attempt will be made to answer the first: we shall treat it merely as a hint that the second and third should be treated separately. In this chapter, accordingly, we shall inquire into the relation between art and emotion; in the next, the relation between art and making.

2. EXPRESSING EMOTION AND AROUSING EMOTION

Our first question is this. Since the artist proper has something to do with emotion, and what he does with it is not to arouse it, what is it that he does? It will be remembered that the kind of answer we expect to this question is an answer derived from what we all know and all habitually say; nothing original or recondite, but something entirely commonplace.

Nothing could be more entirely commonplace than to say he expresses them. The idea is familiar to every artist, and to every one else who has any acquaintance with the arts. To state it is not to state a philosophical theory or definition of art; it is to state a fact or supposed fact about which, when we have sufficiently identified it, we shall have later to theorize philosophically. For the present it does not matter whether the fact that is alleged, when it is said that the artist expresses emotion, is really a fact or only supposed to be one. Whichever it is, we have to identify it, that is, to decide what it is that people are saying when they use the phrase. Later on, we shall have to see whether it will fit into a coherent theory.

They are referring to a situation, real or supposed, of a definite kind. When a man is said to express emotion, what is being said about him comes to this. At first, he is conscious of having an emotion, but not conscious of what this emotion is. All he is conscious of is a perturbation or excitement, which he feels going on within him, but of whose nature he is ignorant. While in this state, all he can say about his emotion is: "I feel . . . I don't know what I feel." From this helpless and oppressed condition he extricates himself by doing something which we call expressing himself. This is an activity which has something to do with the thing we call language: he expresses himself by speaking. It has also something to do with consciousness: the emotion expressed is an emotion of whose nature the person who feels it is no longer unconscious. It has also something to do with the way in which he feels the emotion. As unexpressed, he feels it in what we have called a helpless and oppressed way; as expressed, he feels it in a way from which this sense of oppression has vanished. His mind is somehow lightened and eased.

This lightening of emotions which is somehow connected with the expression of them has a certain resemblance to the "catharsis" by which emotions are earthed through being discharged into a make-believe situation; but the two things are not the same. Suppose the emotion is one of anger. If it is effectively earthed, for example by fancying oneself kicking some one down stairs, it is thereafter no longer present in the mind as anger at all: we have worked it off and are rid of it. If it is expressed, for example by putting it into the hot and bitter words, it does not disappear from the mind; we remain angry; but instead of the sense of oppression which accompanies an emotion of anger not yet recognized as such, we have that sense of alleviation which comes when we are conscious of our own emotion as anger, instead of being conscious of it only as an unidentified perturbation. This is what we refer to when we say that it "does us good" to express our emotions.

The expression of an emotion by speech may be addressed to some one; but if so it is not done with the intention of arousing a like emotion in him. If there is any effect which we wish to produce in the hearer, it is only the effect which we call making him understand how we feel. But, as we have already seen, this is just the effect which expressing our emotions has on ourselves. It makes us, as well as the people to whom we talk, understand how we feel. A person arousing emotion sets out to affect his audience in a way in which he himself is not necessarily affected. He and his audience stand in quite different relations to the act, very much as physician and patient stand in quite different relations towards a drug administered by the one and taken by the other. A person expressing emotion, on the contrary, is treating himself and his audience in the same kind of way; he is making his emotions clear to his audience, and that is what he is doing to himself.

It follows from this that the expression of emotion, simply as expression, is not addressed to any particular audience. It is addressed primarily to the speaker himself, and secondarily to any one who can understand. Here again, the speaker's attitude towards his audience is quite unlike that of a person desiring to arouse in his audience a certain emotion. If that is what he wishes to do, he must know the audience he is addressing. He must know what type of stimulus will produce the desired kind of reaction in people of that particular sort; and he must adapt his language to his audience in the sense of making sure that it contains stimuli appropriate to their peculiarities. If what he wishes to do is to express his emotions intelligibly, he has to express them in such a way as to be intelligible to himself; his audience is then in the position of persons who overhear[3] him doing this. Thus the stimulus-and-reaction terminology has no applicability to the situation.

The means-and-end, or technique, terminology too is inapplicable. Until a man has expressed his emotion, he does not yet know what emotion it is. The act of expressing it is therefore an exploration of his own emotions. He is trying to find out what these emotions are. There is certainly here a directed process: an effort, that is, directed upon a certain end; but the end is not something foreseen and preconceived, to which appropriate means can be thought out in the light of our knowledge of its special character. Expression is an activity of which there can be no technique.

3. EXPRESSION AND INDIVIDUALIZATION

Expressing an emotion is not the same thing as describing it. To say "I am angry" is to describe one's emotion, not to express it. The words in which it is expressed need not contain any reference to anger as such at all. Indeed, so far as they simply and solely express it, they cannot contain any such reference. The curse of Ernulphus, as invoked by Dr. Slop on the unknown person who tied certain knots, is a classical and supreme expression of anger; but it does not contain a single word descriptive of the emotion it expresses.

This is why, as literary critics well know, the use of epithets in poetry, or even in prose where expressiveness is aimed at, is a danger. If you want to express the terror which something causes, you must not give it an epithet like "dreadful." For that describes the emotion instead of expressing it, and your language becomes frigid, that is inexpressive, at once. A genuine poet, in his moments of genuine poetry, never mentions by name the emotions he is expressing.

Some people have thought that a poet who wishes to express a great variety of subtly differentiated emotions might be hampered by the lack of a vocabulary rich in words referring to the distinctions between them; and that psychology, by working out such a vocabulary, might render a valuable service to poetry. This is the opposite of the truth. The poet needs no such words at all; the existence or non-existence of a scientific terminology describing the emotions he wishes to express is to him a matter of perfect

---

[3]Further development of the ideas expressed here will make it necessary to qualify this word and assert a much more intimate relation between artist and audience.

indifference. If such a terminology, where it exists, is allowed to affect his own use of language, it affects it for the worse.

The reason why description, so far from helping expression, actually damages it, is that description generalizes. To describe a thing is to call it a thing of such and such a kind: to bring it under a conception, to classify it. Expression, on the contrary, individualizes. The anger which I feel here and now, with a certain person, for a certain cause, is no doubt an instance of anger, and in describing it as anger one is telling truth about it; but it is much more than mere anger: it is a peculiar anger, not quite like any anger that I ever felt before, and probably not quite like any anger I shall ever feel again. To become fully conscious of it means becoming conscious of it not merely as an instance of anger, but as this quite peculiar anger. Expressing it, we saw, has something to do with becoming conscious of it; therefore, if being fully conscious of it means being conscious of all its peculiarities, fully expressing it means expressing all its peculiarities. The poet, therefore, in proportion as he understands his business, gets as far away as possible from merely labelling his emotions as instances of this or that general kind, and takes enormous pains to individualize them by expressing them in terms which reveal their difference from any other emotion of the same sort.

This is a point in which art proper, as the expression of emotion, differs sharply and obviously from any craft whose aim it is to arouse emotion. The end which a craft sets out to realize is always conceived in general terms, never individualized. However accurately defined it may be, it is always defined as the production of a thing having characteristics that could be shared by other things. A joiner, making a table out of these pieces of wood and no others, makes it to measurements and specifications which, even if actually shared by no other table, might in principle be shared by other tables. A physician treating a patient for a certain complaint is trying to produce in him a condition which might be, and probably has been, often produced in others, namely, the condition of recovering from the complaint. So an "artist" setting out to produce a certain emotion in his audience is setting out to produce not an individual emotion, but an emotion of a certain kind. It follows that the means appropriate to its production will be not individual means but means of a certain kind: that is to say, means which are always in principle replaceable by other similar means. As every good craftsman insists, there is always a "right way" of performing any operation. A "way" of acting is a general pattern to which various individual actions may conform. In order that the "work of art" should produce its intended psychological effect, therefore, whether this effect be magical or merely amusing, what is necessary is that it should satisfy certain conditions, possess certain characteristics: in other words be, not this work and no other, but a work of this kind and of no other.

This explains the meaning of the generalization which Aristotle and others have ascribed to art. We have already seen that Aristotle's *Poetics* is concerned not with art proper but with representative art, and representative art of one definite kind. He is not analysing the religious drama of a hundred years before, he is analysing the amusement literature of the fourth century, and giving rules for its composition. The end being not individual but general (the production of an emotion of a certain kind) the means too are general (the portrayal, not of this individual act, but of an act of this sort; not, as he himself puts it, what Alcibiades did, but what anybody of a certain kind would do). Sir Joshua Reynolds's idea of generalization is in principle the same; he expounds it in connexion with what he calls "the grand style," which means a style intended to produce emotions of a certain type. He is quite right; if you want to produce a typical case of a certain emotion, the way to do it is to put before your audience a representation of the typical features belonging to the kind of thing that produces it: make your kings very royal, your soldiers very soldierly, your women very feminine, your cottages very cottagesque, your oak-trees very oakish, and so on.

Art proper, as expression of emotion, has nothing to do with all this. The artist proper is a person who, grappling with the problem of expressing a certain emotion, says, "I want to get this clear." It is no use to him to get something else clear, however like it this other thing may be. Nothing will serve as a substitute. He does not want a thing of a certain kind, he wants a certain thing. This is why the kind of person who takes his literature as psychology, saying "How admirably this writer depicts the feelings of women, or busdrivers, or homosexuals . . .," necessarily misunderstands every real work of art with which he comes into contact, and takes for good art, with infallible precision, what is not art at all.

4. SELECTION AND AESTHETIC EMOTION

It has sometimes been asked whether emotions can be divided into those suitable for expression by artists and those unsuitable. If by art one means art proper, and identifies this with expression, the only possible answer is that there can be no such distinction. Whatever is expressible is expressible. There may be ulterior motives in special cases which make it desirable to express some emotions and not others; but only if by "express" one means express publicly, that is, allow people to overhear one expressing oneself. This is because one cannot possibly decide that a certain emotion is one which for some reason it would be undesirable to express thus publicly, unless one first becomes conscious of it; and doing this, as we saw, is somehow bound up with expressing it. If art means the expression of emotion, the artist as such must be absolutely candid; his speech must be absolutely free. This is not a precept, it is a statement. It does not mean that the artist ought to be candid, it means that he is an artist only in so far as he is candid. Any kind of selection, any decision to express this emotion and not that, is inartistic not in the sense that it damages the perfect sincerity which distinguishes good art from bad, but in the sense that it represents a further process of a non-artistic kind, carried out when the work of expression proper is already complete. For until that work is complete one does not know what emotions one feels; and is therefore not in a position to pick and choose, and give one of them preferential treatment.

From these considerations a certain corollary follows about the division of art into distinct arts. Two such divisions are current: one according to the medium in which the artist works, into painting, poetry, music, and the like; the other according to the kind of emotion he expresses, into tragic, comic, and so forth. We are concerned with the second. If the difference between tragedy and comedy is a difference between the emotions they express, it is not a difference that can be present to the artist's mind when he is beginning his work; if it were, he would know what emotion he was going to express before he had expressed it. No artist, therefore, so far as he is an artist proper, can set out to write a comedy, a tragedy, an elegy, or the like. So far as he is an artist proper, he is just as likely to write any one of these as any other; which is the truth that Socrates was heard expounding towards the dawn, among the sleeping figures in

Agathon's dining-room.[4] These distinctions, therefore, have only a very limited value. They can be properly used in two ways. (1) When a work of art is complete, it can be labelled *ex post facto* as tragic, comic, or the like, according to the character of the emotions chiefly expressed in it. But understood in that sense the distinction is of no real importance. (2) If we are talking about representational art, the case is very different. Here the so-called artist knows in advance what kind of emotion he wishes to excite, and will construct works of different kinds according to the different kinds of effect they are to produce. In the case of representational art, therefore, distinctions of this kind are not only admissible as an *ex post facto* classification of things to which in their origin it is alien; they are present from the beginning as a determining factor in the so-called artist's plan of work.

The same considerations provide an answer to the question whether there is such a thing as a specific "aesthetic emotion." If it is said that there is such an emotion independently of its expression in art, and that the business of artists is to express it, we must answer that such a view is nonsense. It implies, first, that artists have emotions of various kinds, among which is this peculiar aesthetic emotion; secondly, that they select this aesthetic emotion for expression. If the first proposition were true, the second would have to be false. If artists only find out what their emotions are in the course of finding out how to express them, they cannot begin the work of expression by deciding what emotion to express.

In a different sense, however, it is true that there is a specific aesthetic emotion. As we have seen, an unexpressed emotion is accompanied by a feeling of oppression; when it is expressed and thus comes into consciousness the same emotion is accompanied by a new feeling of alleviation or easement, the sense that this oppression is removed. It resembles the feeling of relief that comes when a burdensome intellectual or moral problem has been solved. We may call it, if we like, the specific feeling of having successfully expressed ourselves; and there is no reason why it should not be called a specific aesthetic emotion. But it is not a specific kind of emotion pre-existing to the expression of it, and having the peculiarity that when it comes to be expressed it is expressed artistically. It is an emotional colouring which attends the expression of any emotion whatever.

*   *   *

7. EXPRESSING EMOTION AND BETRAYING EMOTION

Finally, the expressing of emotion must not be confused with what may be called the betraying of it, that is, exhibiting symptoms of it. When it is said that the artist in the proper sense of that word is a person who expresses his emotions, this does not mean that if he is afraid he turns pale and stammers; if he is angry he turns red and bellows;

---

[4]Plato, *Symposium*, 223 D. But if Aristodemus heard him correctly, Socrates was saying the right thing for the wrong reason. He is reported as arguing, not that a tragic writer as such is also a comic one, but that ὁ τέχνῃ τραγῳΔοποιός is also a comic writer. Emphasis on the word τέχνῃ is obviously implied; and this, with a reference to the doctrine (*Republic*, 333 ᴇ–334 ᴀ) that craft is what Aristotle was to call a potentiality of opposites, i.e. enables its possessor to do not one kind of thing only, but that kind and the opposite kind too, shows that what Socrates was doing was to assume the technical theory of art and draw from it the above conclusion.

and so forth. These things are no doubt called expressions; but just as we distinguish proper and improper senses of the word "art," so we must distinguish proper and improper senses of the word "expression," and in the context of a discussion about art this sense of expression is an improper sense. The characteristic mark of expression proper is lucidity or intelligibility; a person who expresses something thereby becomes conscious of what it is that he is expressing, and enables others to become conscious of it in himself and in them. Turning pale and stammering is a natural accompaniment of fear, but a person who in addition to being afraid also turns pale and stammers does not thereby become conscious of the precise quality of his emotion. About that he is as much in the dark as he would be if (were that possible) he could feel fear without also exhibiting these symptoms of it.

Confusion between these two senses of the word "expression" may easily lead to false critical estimates, and so to false aesthetic theory. It is sometimes thought a merit in an actress that when she is acting a pathetic scene she can work herself up to such an extent as to weep real tears. There may be some ground for that opinion if acting is not an art but a craft, and if the actress's object in that scene is to produce grief in her audience; and even then the conclusion would follow only if it were true that grief cannot be produced in the audience unless symptoms of grief are exhibited by the performer. And no doubt this is how most people think of the actor's work. But if his business is not amusement but art, the object at which he is aiming is not to produce a preconceived emotional effect on his audience but by means of a system of expressions, or language, composed partly of speech and partly of gesture, to explore his own emotions: to discover emotions in himself of which he was unaware, and, by permitting the audience to witness the discovery, enable them to make a similar discovery about themselves. In that case it is not her ability to weep real tears that would mark out a good actress; it is her ability to make it clear to herself and her audience what the tears are about.

This applies to every kind of art. The artist never rants. A person who writes or paints or the like in order to blow off steam, using the traditional materials of art as means for exhibiting the symptoms of emotion, may deserve praise as an exhibitionist, but loses for the moment all claim to the title of artist. Exhibitionists have their uses; they may serve as an amusement, or they may be doing magic. The second category will contain, for example, those young men who, learning in the torment of their own bodies and minds what war is like, have stammered their indignation in verses, and published them in the hope of infecting others and causing them to abolish it. But these verses have nothing to do with poetry.

Thomas Hardy, at the end of a fine and tragic novel in which he has magnificently expressed his sorrow and indignation for the suffering inflicted by callous sentimentalism on trusting innocence, spoils everything by a last paragraph fastening his accusation upon "the president of the immortals." The note rings false, not because it is blasphemous (it offends no piety worthy of the name), but because it is rant. The case against God, so far as it exists, is complete already. The concluding paragraph adds nothing to it. All it does is to spoil the effect of the indictment by betraying a symptom of the emotion which the whole book has already expressed; as if a prosecuting counsel, at the end of his speech, spat in the prisoner's face.

The same fault is especially common in Beethoven. He was confirmed in it, no doubt, by his deafness; but the cause of it was not his deafness but a temperamental inclination to rant. It shows itself in the way his music screams and mutters instead of speaking, as in the soprano part of the Mass in D, or the layout of the opening page in the *Hammerklavier* Sonata. He must have known his failing and tried to overcome it, or he would never have spent so many of his ripest years among string quartets, where screaming and muttering are almost, one might say, physically impossible. Yet even there, the old Adam struts out in certain passages of the *Grosse Fuge*.

It does not, of course, follow that a dramatic writer may not rant in character. The tremendous rant at the end of *The Ascent of F6*, like the Shakespearian[5] ranting on which it is modelled, is done with tongue in cheek. It is not the author who is ranting, but the unbalanced character he depicts; the emotion the author is expressing is the emotion with which he contemplates that character; or rather, the emotion he has towards that secret and disowned part of himself for which the character stands.

[5]Shakespeare's characters rant (1) when they are characters in which he takes no interest at all, but which he uses simply as pegs on which to hang what the public wants, like Henry V; (2) when they are meant to be despicable, like Pistol; or (3) when they have lost their heads, like Hamlet in the graveyard.

Alan Tormey

ART AND EXPRESSION: A CRITIQUE: FROM *THE CONCEPT OF EXPRESSION*

1   If the analysis developed [earlier] is correct in its general outlines, it should be possible to derive from it a number of implications bearing on the adequacy of attempts to understand art as a form of expression.

The history of the philosophy of art could, without excessive distortion, be written as a study of the significance of a handful of concepts. The successive displacement of "imitation" by "representation," and of "representation" by "expression," for example, marks one of the more revealing developments in the literature of aesthetics; and it would be only a slight exaggeration to claim that from the close of the eighteenth century to the present "expression" and its cognates have dominated both aesthetic theorizing and the critical appraisal of the arts. One purpose of this chapter will be to explore the claim that works of art or the activities of the artist can best be understood as a form of expression.

2   Let us first consider some of the contentions of philosophers who have advanced expression theories of art. It has generally been recognized that some distinction must be made at the outset between the process and the product of art: we must distinguish between the artist's activity in constructing a work of art and the outcome of that activity, the work itself. It matters, that is, whether "expression" is predicated of the process, the product, or both. Many, including Dewey, Reid, Ducasse, Santayana, and Collingwood, have been explicit about this distinction, and have advocated predicating "expression" of both process and product. These writers are committed to maintaining that there is a noncontingent and specifiable relation between the artist's activity and the work of art. More precisely, they are committed to the position that the artist, in creating the work, is expressing something,[1] which is then to be found "embodied," "infused," or "objectified" in the work itself. For such theorists, the

From "Art and Expression: A Critique," in *Alan Tormey*, The Concept of Expression: A Study in Philosophical Psychology and Aesthetics *(Princeton: Princeton University Press, 1971). Reprinted with permission of Princeton University Press. (Some footnotes omitted.)*

[1]There is a range of values for the variable here; "feeling," "attitude," "idea," "mood," and "outlook" have all been suggested at some time, but "feeling" is the favored substitution.

"central problem of the aesthetic attitude" is "how a feeling can be got into an object"[2] or, alternately, how the artist in expressing his feelings embodies them in the art work.

Common to all theories of this type are two assumptions: (1) that an artist, in creating a work of art, is invariably engaged in expressing something; and (2) that the expressive qualities of the art work are the direct consequence of this act of expression. I shall argue that there is no reason to accept these assumptions; but first we must consider a logically prior contention which is almost universally accepted by Expression theorists. This contention is that aesthetic, or artistic expression is something quite different from the symptomatic behavioral display of inner states. Vincent Tomas summarizes this view in these words:

> . . . behavior which is merely symptomatic of a feeling, such as blushing when one is embarrassed or swearing when one is angry, is not artistic expression of feeling. Collingwood says it is just a "betrayal" of feeling. Dewey says it is "just a boiling over" of a feeling, and Ducasse says it is "a merely impulsive blowing off of emotional steam." As Hospers says, "A person may give vent to grief without expressing grief." Unlike merely giving vent to or betraying a feeling, artistic expression consists in the deliberate creation of something which "embodies" or "objectifies" the feeling.[3]

The corollary is that "embodying" or "objectifying" a feeling is equivalent to (artistically) expressing it. It is important to notice that these distinctions have been made in the interest of sustaining some favored version of the Expression theory; and since the appropriation of "expression" for this purpose involves a significant departure from ordinary usage, we may reasonably demand some justification for this procedure.

On this point Dewey and Collingwood are the most thorough and articulate, and I shall confine my criticism to their versions of the argument. Dewey writes that:

> Not all outgoing activity is of the nature of expression. At one extreme, there are storms of passion that break through barriers and that sweep away whatever intervenes between a person and something he would destroy. There is activity, but not, from the standpoint of the one acting, expression. An onlooker may say "What a magnificent expression of rage!" But the enraged being is only raging, quite a different matter from *expressing* rage. Or, again, some spectator may say "How that man is expressing his own dominant character in what he is doing or saying." But the last thing the man in question is thinking of is to express his character; he is only giving way to a fit of passion.[4]

Dewey is concerned to protect us from the "error" which has invaded aesthetic theory ". . . that the mere giving way to an impulsion, native or habitual, constitutes expression."[5] He adds that "emotional discharge is a necessary but not a sufficient condition of expression" on the grounds that: "While there is no expression, unless there is urge from within outwards, the welling up must be clarified and ordered by

---

[2]Bernard Bosanquet, *Three Lectures on Aesthetic* (London: Macmillan, 1915), p. 74.

[3]"The Concept of Expression in Art," *Philosophy Looks at the Arts*, ed. Joseph Margolis (New York: Scribner's, 1962), p. 31. The quotations are taken from Collingwood, *The Principles of Art*; Dewey, *Art as Experience*; Ducasse, *Art, the Critics, and You*; and Hospers, *Meaning and Truth in the Arts*.

[4]*Art as Experience*, p. 61.

[5]*Loc. cit.*

taking into itself the values of prior experiences before it can be an act of expression."[6] There can be no expression without inner agitation then, but the mere discharging of inner impulsions is insufficient to constitute an expression. ". . . to express is to stay by, to carry forward in development, to work out to completion";[7] and, "Where there is . . . no shaping of materials in the interest of embodying excitement, there is no expression."[8]

Dewey offers these remarks as *evidence* for the adequacy of the Expression theory, whereas they follow in fact only if one has already assumed its truth. They are thinly disguised stipulations and not, as Dewey would have it, independently discoverable truths *about* expression. The circularity of this procedure can best be seen in his refusal to admit anything as an expression which does not result in the production of an object or state of affairs that embodies some aesthetically valuable quality.[9] But there are more serious objections. Dewey clearly wants to confine "expression" to activities which are intentionally or voluntarily undertaken. (It must be an expression "from the standpoint of the one acting"; the involuntary venting of rage is ruled out with the comment that "the last thing the man in question is thinking of is to express his character; he is only giving way to a fit of passion.") But there is an existing distinction, and one which we would normally employ here, between voluntary and involuntary expression. Dewey offers us no reason for abandoning this in favor of his stipulative restriction, other than an implicit appeal to the very theory which requires the sacrifice, and we are entitled to a more compelling argument before adopting this way of speaking.[10]

One reason for Dewey's insistence on this restriction is obvious. Many activities and behavioral patterns that are called "expressions" are irrelevant to the production of aesthetically interesting objects. Most Expression theorists agree that the artist is engaged in doing something quite different from the man who merely vents his rage or airs his opinions—that he is doing something which bears little resemblance to commonly recognized varieties of expressive behavior. But the fact that the artist *is* doing something so apparently different ought to suggest not that he alone is expressing while others are not, but that the aesthetically relevant activity of the artist may not be an expression at all. Rather than being shown in creative activity the real meaning of "expression," we are offered a stipulation which would undermine most of the paradigmatic examples of expressive behavior in the interests of promoting a debatable theory.

Collingwood echoes Dewey's insistence that expressing an emotion must not be confused with betraying it, by which he means merely exhibiting symptoms of the emotion. So, presumably, the artist "proper" cannot express his feelings in the same way that the devotee of a fanatical religion might express his anger or disgust by smashing the sacred icons of a rival religion. Collingwood argues that ". . . just as we distinguish proper and improper senses of the word 'art,' so we must distinguish proper

---

[6]*Loc. cit.*
[7]*Ibid.*, p. 62.
[8]*Loc. cit.*
[9]Chs. IV and V of *Art as Experience*.
[10]Dewey makes more of this than most Expression theorists, but even those, like Ducasse, who admit the use of "expression" to describe involuntary revelations of inner states have argued that *aesthetic* expression is something quite distinct, and not to be confused with the former.

and improper senses of the word 'expression.'" This is reminiscent of Dewey but goes boldly beyond the views of that cautious pragmatist. It is also a curious maneuver on Collingwood's part, and amounts to what philosophers have long recognized as "persuasive definition," the attempt to promote an argument by insisting that the real or proper meaning of a term is just the one that conveniently suits the theoretical presuppositions of the author. There is, of course, nothing inherently wrong with the tactic of stipulation in philosophical discourse, but persuasive definitions are normally secreted, as they are here, behind the facade of an objective search for semantic validity.

Collingwood's strategy is particularly surprising since it appears to be in conflict with his insistence elsewhere that in attempting to reach an adequate understanding of "art" or "expression" we are dealing with questions of fact—facts that are well known to us and that are evidenced by the manner in which we commonly speak about art. Questions of fact, for Collingwood, are questions of usage and not questions of theory. What he appears to have overlooked is that usage is theoretically independent of philosophical theory, and that the appeal to "what everyone knows" is both provincial and potentially fatal to a theory confronted with the inevitable drift of linguistic usage. Serious theories of art, of course, come and go. Those that pretend to permanence must face the dilemma of being rooted in a timeless, unshakable frame of Platonic essences inhospitable to innovation, or being uprooted by the unpredictable flux of art and the attendant mutations of the talk of critics and connoisseurs.

Another problematic aspect of Collingwood's theory is his claim that ". . . a person who expresses something thereby becomes conscious of what it is that he is expressing," a view that we might usefully characterize as "No expression *proper* without clarification of emotion." In addition to its artificial formulation in defiance of common usage, this also threatens the exclusion of many acknowledged works from the catalog of "art proper." (One need think only of the notable frescoes of Mantegna in Mantova for which the artist was paid by the square meter and for his compliance with his patron's prescriptions about matters of both form and content. Or, to take more recent examples, we might seriously wonder about the plausibility of construing Cristo's *Running Fence* or John Cage's 4' 33" as products of the artists' attempts to clarify their emotions.)

Paradoxically, on Collingwood's theory, an artist "proper" should be someone who is *not* emotionally engaged with his work, or at least someone whose emotions are appropriately aesthetic and restrained from spilling over into the passions of real life. Artists, he insists, never rant. They are neither exhibitionists nor propagandists. He refers, I assume, to such renowned First World War poets as Rupert Brooke, as ". . . those young men who, learning in the torment of their own bodies and minds what war is like, having stammered their indignation in verses, [have] published them in the hope of infecting others and causing them to abolish it. But these verses have nothing to do with poetry." Is poetry then to be restricted to apolitical themes, to love lyrics, pastoral fantasies, and confessional couplets? More generally, is "art proper" to have no palpable political, religious, or moral content? Collingwood does not tell us explicitly, but it is clear that on his view any work that prominently exhibits these qualities is immediately under suspicion of being merely an instance of the craft of magic or amusement.

Finally, Collingwood's myopic insistence that all "art proper" must be the (successful) product of an effort at personal expression runs headlong into history. It fails to account for the vast number of accepted art works that were created on commission, under duress, or for nonaesthetic reasons. Witness Mozart's flute quartets, written to make money for an instrument he disliked and for a patron he distrusted. And it fails to account for the numerous works that must be credited not to an individual genius working out his personal feelings, but to an assemblage of artists, as in the Renaissance *botteghe*, or workshops, in one of which Leonardo da Vinci was apprenticed for years to his maestro Verrocchio. All this, and much more, we must assume was for Collingwood simply not art, or, to beg the question in a now transparent way, not art "proper." But, as I have argued earlier, there is art without expression just as there is expression without art.

The upshot of this is that, if "aesthetic expression" as a process is not to be understood in relation to pre-analytic notions of expressive behavior, then it must be understood in relation to something else—the something else here being the aesthetic qualities of the created product, the work of art.

In turning to the expressive qualities of the object we are not leaving behind the act of expression, for even if we center attention on the properties of the work itself ("the object that is expressive, that says something to us"[11]) Dewey reminds us that "isolation of the act of expressing from the expressiveness possessed by the object leads to the notion that expression is merely a process of discharging personal emotion"[12]; and that, "Expression as personal act and as objective result are *organically connected* with each other [italics added]."[13] But it is just here that Expression theories fail to convince, for the nature of this supposed connection is far from obvious, and no adequate analysis has yet been offered by anyone committed to this view. The argument for such a connection is usually established somewhat in the following way: aesthetic objects, including works of art, are said to possess certain perceptible physiognomic or "expressive" qualities such as "sadness," "gaiety," "longing"; and where these are qualities of intentionally structured objects it is reasonable to assume that their presence is the intended consequence of the productive activity of the artist. But the Expression theorist is not content with this; he will go on to assert that, since the aesthetically relevant qualities of the object are *expressive* qualities, the productive activity must have been an act of expression and, moreover, an act of expressing just those feeling states whose analogues are predicated of the object. The situation can be represented more schematically in the following way:

(E-T) If art object O has expressive quality Q, then there was a prior activity C of the artist A such that in doing C, A expressed his F for X by imparting Q to O (where F is a feeling state and Q is the qualitative analogue of F).

The *E-T* represents a core-theory which I believe to be shared e.g. by Dewey, Ducasse, Collingwood, Carritt, Gotshalk, Santayana, Tolstoy, and Véron, whatever their further differences might be.[14] I shall argue that the *E-T* contains an error traceable to the tendency to treat all of the cognate forms of "expression" as terms whose logical behavior is similar. The particular mistake here arises from assuming that the existence of *expressive qualities* in a work of art implies a prior act of *expression*.

[11]Dewey, *Art as Experience*, p. 82.
[12]*Loc. cit.*
[13]*Loc. cit.*
[14]Harold Osborne has summarized the Expression theory in a somewhat different manner: "The underlying theory is, in its baldest form, that the artist lives through a certain experience; he then makes an

(continued)

Now, to say that an object has a particular expressive quality is to say something, first of all, about the object. (Even those who argue that "the music is sad" can be translated as "the music makes me feel sad" or ". . . has a disposition to make me, or others, feel sad" will agree that their accounts are only plausible on the assumption that the object has *some* properties which are at least causally relevant to the induced feeling.) But the Expression theorist is committed to the further assumption of a *necessary* link between the qualities of the art work and certain states of the artist. Critics of this theory have been quick to observe that this would commit us to treating all art works as auto-biographical revelations. Moreover, it would entail that descriptions of the expressive qualities of an art work were falsifiable in a peculiar way. If it turned out that Mahler had experienced *no* state of mind remotely resembling despair or resignation during the period of the composition of *Das Lied von der Erde*, the Expression theorist would be obliged to conclude that we were mistaken in saying that the final movement (*Der Abschied*) of that work was expressive of despair or resignation; and this seems hardly plausible, since it implies that statements ostensibly about the music itself are in fact statements about the composer.[15] If works of art *were* expressions, in the way that behavior and language are expressions of states of a person, that is precisely what we would say. Normal imputations of expression *are* falsifiable, and the assertion that a person's behavior constitutes an expression of something is defeated when it can be shown that the imputed inference is unwarranted. But statements about the expressive qualities of an art work remain, irresolutely, statements *about* the work, and any revision or rejection of such statements can be supported only by referring to the work itself. "That's a sad piece of music" is countered not by objections such as, "No, he wasn't" or "He was just pretending" (referring to the composer), but by remarking "You haven't listened carefully" or "You must listen again; there are almost no minor progressions and the tempo is *allegro moderato.*"

Descriptions attributing expressive qualities to works of art then are not subject to falsification through the discovery of any truths about the inner life of the artist. An Expression theorist could of course grasp the other horn, arguing that the presence of quality Q in O is *sufficient* evidence of the occurrence of state S in A, such that A felt F for X. But in ruling out the possibility of independent and conflicting evidence of the artist's feeling states, the Expression theorist secures his position by the simple expedient of making it analytically true; and no one, to my knowledge, has wished to claim that the E-T is an empty, though indisputable truth.

That a theory of art-as-expression which entails these difficulties should have been embraced so widely is due in part to a misunderstanding of the logic of "expression" and "expressive." I would argue that statements attributing expressive (or physiognomic) properties to works of art should be construed as statements about the works

artifact which in some way embodies that experience; and through appreciative contemplation of this artifact other men are able to duplicate in their own minds the experience of the artist. What is conveyed to them is . . . an experience of their own as similar as possible to the artist's experience in all its aspects . . ." (*Aesthetics and Criticism* [London: Routledge and Kegan Paul, 1955], p. 143). My formulation is constructed to call attention to the Expression theorist's view of the relation between the activity of the artist and the expressive qualities of the work.

[15]If it is objected that the composer is expressing some *remembered* or unconscious feelings of this sort, we can strengthen the example by supposing it to be false that the composer had ever experienced, consciously or otherwise, the feeling corresponding to the feeling-quality attributed to the music. The logical point remains untouched in any case.

themselves; and that the presence of expressive properties does not entail the occurrence of a prior *act* of expression. Misunderstanding of this latter point has contributed greatly to the uncritical acceptance of the E-T.

3 "Expressive," despite its grammatical relation to "expression," does not always play the logical role that one might expect. There are occasions on which the substitution of one term for the other is semantically harmless. "His gesture was an expression of impatience" may in some contexts be replaced without noticeable alteration in meaning by "His gesture was expressive of impatience." But there are other contexts in which "expression" and "expressive" are significantly disparate. The remark that "Livia has a very expressive face" does not entail that Livia is especially adept at expressing her inner states, nor does it entail that she is blessed with an unusually large repertoire of moods and feelings which she displays in a continuous kaleidoscope of facial configurations.

To make this clear I shall need to appeal to another distinction . . . between the two syntactic forms, "ϕ expression" *(A)* and "expression of ϕ" *(B)*. That distinction was intended to establish that instances of *B* are inference-warranting while instances of *A* are descriptive, and that *A* and *B* are logically independent in the sense that no statement containing an instance of *A* (or *B*) entails another statement containing an instance of *B* (or *A*). (A cruel expression in a human face does not automatically entitle us to infer that cruelty is being expressed.)

Now, the assertion that a person has an expressive face is not equivalent to the assertion that he is expressing, or is disposed to express, his inner states through a set of facial configurations; or rather the equivalence is not guaranteed. The difficulty is that "expressive" is systematically ambiguous. It *may* be an alternate reading of "is an expression of . . ." or it may be understood as a one-place predicate with no inferential overtones. Which of these meanings it has in a particular instance will depend upon what substitutions we are willing to make and what further questions we are prepared to admit. If, for example, the question "expressive of what?" is blocked, we can conclude that "expressive" is not functioning here in a variant of syntactic form *B*. "X is expressive" does not *entail* that there is an inner state *S* such that *S* is being expressed, any more than the appearance of a cruel expression in a face entails that cruelty is being expressed.

The statement that "X is express*ive*" then may be logically complete, and to say of a person's gesture or face that it is *expressive* is not invariably to legitimize the question "expressive of what?" In such cases we may say that "expressive" is used intransitively. Still, we would not call a face (intransitively) expressive unless it displayed considerable mobility. A face that perpetually wore the *same* expression would not be expressive, and appreciation of this point should contribute to an understanding of the intransitive *(I)* sense of "expressive." A face is expressive *(I)* when it displays a wide range of expressions *(A)*. Thus the successive appearance of sad, peevish, sneering, and puzzled expressions on the face of a child may lead us to say that he has an expressive face without committing us to a set of implications about the inner state of the child.

The meaning of "expressive" *(I)* is not exhausted, however, through correlation with indefinitely extended sets of expressions *(A)*. A face may be expressive merely in virtue of its mobility or its range of perceptible configurations, even though it presents no recognizable expressions *(A)* for which there are established names. To this extent, "expressive" *(I)* is dispositional. It refers to the disposition of a face (or a body) to assume a variety of plastic configurations regardless of whether any momentary aspect of the face is describable as an expression *(A)* or not; and since it is clear that we have neither names nor definite descriptions for many of the geometrical patterns the human face and body can assume, the domain of "expressive" *(I)* is both wider and less precise than "expression" *(A)*. It may refer at times simply to the capacity or disposition of a person to move or use his body in varied and perceptually interesting ways.[16] But whatever the correct analysis of "expressive" *(I)*, the fact remains that its use imposes no inferential commitments, and we may use it, just as we use "expression" *(A)* to refer to certain qualities of persons and objects without implying the existence of some correlated *act* of expression. . . .

4   It may be objected that all this, at best, discloses some interesting features of the use of "expression" and "expressive" in ordinary language which, from the standpoint of the Expression theorist, are entirely irrelevant. On the contrary, I believe these distinctions are crucial for an understanding of the very art form to which Expression theorists have made most frequent appeal. The point I want to develop here is that the language used by composers and performers of music is at variance with the conception of musical activity derivable from the *E-T*. This is not merely an instance of the naïveté of artists in contrast with the ability of philosophers to provide reflective analyses of a complex enterprise. It is rather that "expressive" has a particular and quasi-technical meaning *within* the language used by musicians—a meaning which is logically similar to the intransitive sense of "expressive," which is clearly distinguishable from "expression" *(B)*, and whose use does not therefore commit us to any version of the *E-T*.

There are numerous passages in the music of the Romantic period (and later) which are marked *espressivo* ("expressively" or "with expression"). Now this is a particular instruction for the performance of the indicated passage or phrase, and as such it can be compared with the instructions *agitato, grazioso, dolce, leggiero, secco, stürmisch, schwer,* and *pesante.* All of these are indications to the performer that the passage is to be played in a certain manner, and to play *espressivo* is merely to play in one manner rather than another. It is not to play well rather than badly, or to play with, rather than without some particular feeling, nor is it to succeed rather than fail to communicate the composer's intentions, feelings, or ideas. All of these misconceptions are the result of a category mistake. One does not play *agitato* or *pesante and espressivo*; the choice must come from among alternatives all of which are logically similar members of a single category.[17] Moreover, to play *espressivo* is not to be engaged in expressing anything, any more than to play *leggiero* is to express lightness. (Nor, similarly does the composition of an expressive work entail that the *composer* be expressing anything.) Failure to realize this has led some adherents of the Expression theory into associating an expressive musical performance with some presumed *act* of expression on the part

---

[16]Notice e.g. that we can refer to the movements of a Thai dancer performing a *Lakon* as expressive even though we may have no idea what the movements "mean" and no precise language in which to describe them.

[17]Many of the commonly encountered instructions for performance are incompatible, though of course this is not true of all. *Leggiero* and *animoso* are clearly compatible, and the opening bars of Debussy's *Prélude à L'Après-Midi d'un Faune* are marked *doux et expressif*; but the indication '*ecco, espressivo*' would be contradictory, and contradictory in the same way that incompatible imperatives are contradictory—the performer could not simultaneously carry out both instructions.

of the performer, the composer, or both, and thence with some particular feeling state which is attributable to them.[18]

It would follow from the E-T that we might always be mistaken in thinking that a performer had played a phrase expressively, since the correctness of this belief would depend on the truth of some psychological statement about the performer's inner states. But *espressivo* (expressively) is an adverbial characterization of a *manner* of performance, and the suggestion that follows from the E-T, that an expressive performance *must* be linked noncontingently to some particular inner state of the performer, is untenable.

It might be objected at this point that both the Expression theorist and I have misconceived the role of "expressive," for in critical usage "expressive" may characterize entire performances or personal styles of performance (one might argue that Oistrakh's performance of the Sibelius *Violin Concerto* was more expressive than Heifetz's, or that generally, A's playing was more expressive than B's). "Expressive" is still intransitive in this role, but it resists reduction to specific occurrences of passages played *espressivo*.[19] And it is this usage which may lead to the suggestion that "expressive" has a primarily *evaluative* function in critical discourse. "Expressive" does not, on this view, license inferences nor label particular or even general features of the object to be assessed, rather it does the assessing. Thus, calling a performance expressive would be to approve, applaud, or commend, not to detect, notice, or describe.

But there are two related and, I think, decisive objections to this suggestion. For even where "expressive" is used to characterize a style or an entire performance and cannot be explicated by reference to particular occurrences of *espressivo* passages, the possibility remains that the expressiveness may be misplaced. There are omnipresent opportunities for misplaced expressiveness in musical performances, and we should find something peculiarly offensive in an expressive performance of Stravinsky's *L'Histoire du Soldat* or Bartok's *Allegro Barbaro*. Appropriate and effective performances of such works require the absence, or perhaps even the deliberate suppression of expressiveness. Similarly, austere performances of austere works are not *bad* performances; and to call performances of such works expressive may well be to condemn them. If "expressive" were primarily an evaluative device, the notion of misplaced expressiveness would be self-contradictory, or at best paradoxical. Similar remarks apply to works as well as performances, and describing a particular work as nonexpressive is not equivalent to condemning it, nor is it prima facie evidence of its lack of artistic worth.

The second error results from failure to notice the first. Whether "expressive" may be correctly *used* to praise a performance is a function of whether an expressive performance is appropriate to the work being performed. Where it *is* appropriate, and the performance commensurately expressive, *calling* it so may also serve to commend it. But this does no more to show that "expressive" is an essentially evaluative predicate of our critical language than commending figs for their sweetness shows that "sweet" is

---

[18]When the difficulty of naming particular feeling states becomes apparent, the Expression theorist may resort to the sui generis category of "aesthetic emotions."

[19]There is a strong analogy between the intransitively expressive performance and the intransitively expressive face.

an essentially evaluative predicate of our culinary language. That we prefer expressive to nonexpressive performances of Rachmaninoff and Chopin implies that we regard expressiveness as required for an appropriate reading of the Romantic architecture of their works; it does not imply that "expressive" is an aesthetic variant of "good."

We shall gain a better view of the issue, I think, if we consider how we might teach someone to play expressively or, conversely, how we might teach someone to recognize an expressive performance. If a student asks: "What must I do to play this passage expressively?" we cannot give him a rule to follow such as: "You must always play such passages in *this* way . . ." Of course we can give him a rule of sorts—"To play expressively you must vary the dynamics of the phrase; you must stress some notes more than others, and you must not play with rhythmic rigidity"—but we cannot give him a precise rule specifying *which* notes to stress or where and how to vary the dynamics. There are no paradigmatic examples of expressive playing from which a universal rule could be extracted and applied to other phrases. No phrase can be played expressively without *some* deviation from literal note values, without *some* modulations in the dynamic level, but the choice of where and how is not rule-governed.[20] The student who merely follows our second-order rule and plays the passage with rhythmic freedom and some dynamic modulation may produce a grotesquely unmusical and inexpressive result.

The problem is analogous to teaching someone to recognize an expressively played passage. There are no rules that will help here either. (If someone had no idea what to listen for, we might say: "It happens when the pianist closes his eyes" or "Watch for him to sway from the waist" and so on.) It may be thought that the difficulty here is much the same as that of showing the face in the cloud to someone whose aspect-blindness allows him to perceive only the cloud. There is an analogous kind of expression-deafness, but the analogy is only partial, and it is apt to mislead. Expression-deafness is closer to aspect-blindness than to color-blindness. There is no way to *teach* a color-blind person to see the normal range of colors, but we may succeed in getting someone to see the face in the cloud or the "aspects" of the duck-rabbit figure; and we may succeed, analogously, in teaching someone to recognize an expressive performance. But the analogy cannot be stretched to a perfect fit. Recognition of the expressiveness in Grumiaux's performance of the Debussy *Sonata for Violin and Piano* presupposes that we are able to discriminate among a number of qualities that are predicable of musical performances. To hear a performance as expressive is also to hear that it is *not* dry, strained, heavy, agitated, or hollow. The identification presupposes, in other words, that we are conversant with a highly complex set of predicates and with their logical relations to one another. Recognition of the duck in the duck-rabbit figure, on the other hand, seems not to presuppose any comparably complex discriminatory abilities. Ducks and duck-like shapes may be recognizable even to those whose acquaintance with the zoological world is limited to ducks. But talk of expressive performances or works can occur meaningfully only within a developed language of musical criticism, and it implies an ability to discriminate and select from among a number of logically similar predicates.

There is no possibility that someone should learn to use "expressive" correctly and yet be unable correctly to apply any other aesthetic predicate, as one might learn to use

[20]See Frank Sibley, "Aesthetic Concepts," *Philosophical Review*, LXVIII (1959), 421–50, for a cogent discussion of the general question of rule-governed and sufficient conditions in aesthetic discourse.

"duck" correctly without at the same time being able to correctly apply other zoological predicates. (Seeing the figure as a duck is more closely analogous to hearing the sounds as music than to hearing the music as expressive.)

Aesthetic predicates are not learned independently of one another in some discursive or ostensive fashion. They acquire significance for us only in relation to one another as we become reflective and articulate participants in the art world.[21]

Despite the popularity of aspect and "seeing-as" models in recent discussions of aesthetic perception, considerations such as this seriously impair the attempt to explain our perception of aesthetic qualities by analogy with the perception of aspects, or as instances of "seeing-as."[22] Aspect perception has been a useful model in freeing us from the temptation to think of aesthetic objects as ontologically peculiar and distinct from, say, the material objects we hang on our walls; but it is misleading when it suggests that seeing, or hearing, an art work as *expressive* (or garish, or sentimental) is no different from spotting the face in the cloud or the duck in the figure.

5   The Expression theorist of course may object that he is not concerned so much with the language of musicians or critics as with the possibility of giving a theoretical description of the art which would enable us to grasp certain aesthetically relevant features of the processes of creating, performing, and attending to musical compositions. We must, I think, admit that there is a sense in which it would be correct to say that a piece of music may be an expression (B); the account I have given in the preceding chapters leaves open this possibility. But this admission concedes nothing to the E-T, for the only sense in which "expression" (B) is admissible here is inconsistent with the E-T.

The admission amounts to this: Aside from certain occurrences of nonverbal behavior and linguistic utterances there is a class of things we may call indirect or secondary expressions. The manner of a woman's dress, the way she wears her hair, or the arrangement of her room may "express" some aspect of her character. My handwriting, my preferences in literature, my style at poker, and my choice of friends may likewise reveal something of my inner states and dispositions. It is legitimate to speak of these as expressions (B) where they satisfy the conditions of being evidential or inference-warranting, and lead, correctly, to the attribution of an intentional state. It is clear that this is often the case, that we do make such inferences, and that the conditions for expression are satisfied here as well as in cases of direct or primary expression in language and behavior.

And if my style of playing poker expresses my temerity or my avarice, why should not my style of painting landscapes express something of me as well? Or my style of playing the flute? The conditions of a warranted inference to an intentional state may be as well met by art as by action; and there are impressive examples in the literature of psychoanalysis of the use of art works to unlock the psychic labyrinths of the artist.[23] It

---

[21]See also Arthur C. Danto, "The Artworld," *Journal of Philosophy*, LXI (1964), 571–84.

[22]See e.g. B. R. Tilghman, "Aesthetic Perception and the Problem of the 'Aesthetic Object,' " *Mind*, LXXV (1966), 351–68; and Virgil C. Aldrich, *Philosophy of Art* (Englewood Cliffs: Prentice-Hall, 1963). An illustration of some of the limitations of aspect-perception models in aesthetics may be found in Peter Kivy, "Aesthetic Aspects and Aesthetic Qualities," *Journal of Philosophy*, LXV (1968), 85–93. The *locus classicus* for discussions of the problem is Wittgenstein, *Philosophical Investigations*, Part II.

[23]Freud's study of Leonardo is perhaps the best known of such attempts; but Jung has made more consistent use of art works in his routine analytic practice. Cf. particularly *Symbols of Transformation*, tr. R. F. C. Hull, Bollingen Series XX:5 (New York: Pantheon, 1956).

is this sense in which I concede that an art work may be an expression of something: it may contribute material leading to a correct inference to an intentional state of the artist. But I contend that this does nothing to support the E-T, and further, that it does nothing to distinguish art from any other product of human activity.

We should recall that the E-T entails that the (successful) artist, by his creative activity, imparts a quality to the work which is *descriptively analogous* to the feeling state expressed by him (sadness-"sadness") and ought therefore to be recognizable as the embodiment of his feeling without assistance from extra-perceptual sources of knowledge. But, far from being clear that this is always the case with successful works of art, it would seem in some instances to be impossible. It will be best to illustrate this point with an example. Carl Nielsen completed his Sixth Symphony during the years 1924–25, and it was during this period of the composer's life that "he was harassed by ill health and depression, puzzled by the notoriety enjoyed by what seemed to him to be musical nihilism, and upset over the seeming failure of his own work to take hold beyond the borders of his native land. . . . It is not unreasonable to suppose that this is the source of some of the exasperation that manifests itself particularly in the second and final movements of the Sixth Symphony."[24] (The second movement is referred to later as ". . . a bitter commentary on the musical modernism of the 1920's.")

Now the second movement of the Nielsen symphony is marked *Humoresque*, and the prevailing impression left by the music itself is that of lighthearted buffoonery. It may not be unreasonable as the program notes suggest, to conclude that Nielsen was venting exasperation, bitterness, or disappointment here, but it is difficult to see how such an inference could have been suggested by attending to the qualities of the music alone. The music does not *sound* exasperated or disappointed, nor can I see how any piece of music *could* have these as perceptible qualities. The movement sounds humorous, and there is an obvious reference to Prokofiev's *Peter and the Wolf*; but the suggestion that Nielsen was manifesting exasperation or commenting bitterly on musical modernism in this piece can have arisen only with the acquisition of some extra-musical information about the composer's life. If the critic *now* wants to maintain that the Sixth Symphony is an expression of Nielsen's bitterness and disappointment, we may agree that this is at least a plausible inference given the truth of the biographical data. But we must also point out that this has little to do with the aesthetically relevant expressive qualities of the music itself. This is something of a paradox for the E-T. In order for the Nielsen symphony to be an expression of the composer's bitterness and disappointment (i.e., to be a secondary expression) it must have certain perceptible qualities which, together with the biographical data, will yield an inference. But the qualities of the music here are not, and *cannot* be analogues of the intentional state of the composer. The music is humorous, the composer is disappointed. And he cannot inject his bitterness and disappointment into the music in the way that is required by the E-T. There is no sense in which the *music* is disappointed. Even if we suppose it to be true that Nielsen was disappointed, exasperated, or bitter, and that the critic's inferences are correct, there is nothing in this to establish the presence of a noncontingent relation between the perceptible qualities of the music and any particular state of mind of the composer. Such linkages are contingent, and dependent in every case on the possession of some extra-musical

[24]Quoted from the notes to *Music of the North*, Vol. VIII: Carl Nielsen, Symphony No. 6, "Sinfonia Semplice," Mercury Classics Recording, MG 10137.

knowledge of the composer's life. In itself, humor in a piece of music no more guarantees the presence of bitterness than it invariably betrays a carefree state of mind. Paralleling the distinction between syntactic forms A and B, the expressive qualities of a work of art are logically independent of the psychological states of the artist, and humor (or sadness) in a madrigal is neither necessary nor sufficient for amusement (or despair) in a Monteverdi.

Thus, even where we speak of a piece of music as an expression *(B)* of some state of mind, this use fails to meet the requirements of the *E-T*. There is no direct, noncontingent relation between qualities of the work and states of the artist as the *E-T* supposes (*F* and *Q* are not related in the required way). The relation is contingent and mediated by extra-musical considerations, including in some instances appeal to psychological theories. Secondly, it is often *impossible* to impart a feeling quality to a work which will perceptually reflect the artist's feeling state (e.g. disappointment). And, finally, the presence of an expressive quality in a work of art is never sufficient to guarantee the presence of an analogous feeling state in the artist. What the music "expresses" is logically independent of what, if anything, the composer expresses.[25]

It follows from this that statements of the form, "The music expresses ϕ," or "The music is expressive of ϕ" must, if we are to understand them as making relevant remarks about the music and not as making elliptical remarks about the composer, be interpreted as intentionally equivalent to syntactic form A; that is, they are to be understood as propositions containing "expression" or "expressive" as syntactic parts of a one-place predicate denoting some perceptible quality, aspect, or *gestalt* of the work itself. Moreover, "The *music* expresses ϕ" cannot be interpreted as an instance of the use of "expression" *(B)* since it would make no sense to ask for the *intentional object* of the music. The sadness of the music is not sadness *over* or *about* anything.[26] I am not claiming that everyone who uses these constructions does in fact understand them to have this meaning, but I am contending that this is the only interpretation which is both coherent and which preserves the aesthetic relevance of such assertions.

6   To recapitulate, neither playing expressively nor composing "expressive" music entails that one *be* expressing anything.[27] They require only that the product of the relevant activity have certain phenomenal properties that can be characterized as noninferentially expressive. And once we have shed the tendency to look behind the expressive qualities in an art object for some correlated act of expression we shall be closer to a correct understanding of the relation of the artist to his work; or rather, we shall be relieved at least of a persistent misunderstanding of that relation. Musicians, and artists generally, do not "express" themselves in their work in any sense that is

---

[25]Many of these points may be extended beyond music, though I am not concerned to argue here for the applicability of all of these remarks to the other arts. Freud's analysis of Leonardo, for example, makes use of certain features of the paintings (the similarity of facial expression in the *Gioconda* and the *Madonna and Child with St. Anne*; the incompleteness of many of the canvases, etc.); yet none of Freud's analytic inferences are based on qualities of the paintings alone. They are rooted in his interpretation of the available biographical material. I would suggest, though I cannot pursue it here, that inferences from works of *art alone*—whether from music, fiction, or architecture—to the character of the artist are generally suspect.

[26]Much has been made of the difference between "real" feelings and "aesthetic" feelings; between, for instance, life-sadness and music-sadness; and I would suggest that at least the promise of an explanation lies in the fact that intentional objects are present in the former and absent from the latter.

[27]There is a trivial sense in which these activities may always be an expression of something—an expression of the desire to get the phrase right, for instance—but such expressions are irrelevant to the *E-T* for reasons given above.

intelligible, consistent, and aesthetically relevant. This is not to say that there is no relation between the artist's activity and the resultant expressive qualities of the work, but rather to argue that it must be something other than that envisaged by the E-T. It would be less misleading, if a little archaic, to say simply that the relation is one of making or creating. The artist is not expressing something which is then infused into the work by alchemical transformation; he is making an expressive object. What he does to accomplish this remains, of course, as complex and mystifying as before, and I have nothing to add to the numerous attempts to explain the "creative process" except to argue that, whatever it may be, it is not identical with some act or process of expression.

One aspiration of aesthetics has always been to demonstrate that the creation of art works is a unique and exalted form of human activity. Even those like Dewey who have been determined to narrow the gap between art and ordinary experience reflect the urge to find something extraordinary in art. To conclude that the traditional concept of art-as-expression fails to realize this aim is not to abandon the conviction that there is something singular in the creative process; it is only to abandon a theory which fails to do justice to that conviction, and to reveal the need to give it more trenchant and persuasive formulation.

The theory that art is an or *the* expression of the human spirit is either trivial or false; for the sense in which art is an expression of a state of mind or character of the artist does not establish a relevant distinction between art and any other form of human activity, and the attempt to utilize the concept of expression to distinguish artistic or creative activity from more mundane affairs leads only to incoherence and absurdity. If there is a residue of truth in the E-T, it is that works of art often have expressive qualities. But so do natural objects, and there is nothing in this to compel us to the conclusion entailed by the E-T. The only way that we can interpret the notion of art-as-expression which is both coherent and aesthetically relevant is to construe statements referring to works of art and containing some cognate form of "expression" as references to certain properties of the works themselves; and it is to a consideration of this class of properties that we shall turn [later].

PART TWO

———◆—◦•◦—◆———

Contemporary Theories of Art and Contemporary Critiques of These Theories

As most of the traditional theories of art presented here demonstrate, it is generally assumed that the art theorist should provide a definition that enables us to distinguish art from nonart. Historically, such definitions have been "essentialist," that is, they presuppose that there is a complete set of necessary and sufficient conditions for something to be a work of art. A necessary condition is simply a condition that *must* be met if an object is to qualify as a work of art. A sufficient condition is a condition that, if met, *guarantees* that the object is a work of art. It is clear, however, that traditional theories of art differ radically on just what the necessary and sufficient conditions of art may be. As we shall see, this is evident, for example, in the opposition between formalist and expressive theories of art. Given these radical disagreements, perhaps we should cease asking, "What is the true definition of the nature of art?" and ask instead, "Does it even *make sense* to seek a true definition of art's nature?" For a quarter of a century after World War II, aestheticians in the English-speaking world concentrated on this latter question. In effect, aesthetic theory became the starting point for the question "Is it possible, or for that matter desirable, to seek a definition of art or the concept of art?" These two questions as we shall see are distinguishable.

In the period 1945–1960 a score of important essays appeared challenging the assumption of traditional art theory that a true definition of art could be formulated. Among the most important of these essays are "The Function of Philosophical Aesthetics" and "Art as an Essentially Contested Concept" by W. B. Gallie; "The Task of Defining a Work of Art" by Paul Ziff; "The Role of Theory in Aesthetics" by Morris Weitz. We have not reprinted these essays in this collection for three reasons. (1) They are widely anthologized, and thus easily obtainable elsewhere. (2) Maurice Mandelbaum's essay in this part ("Family Resemblances and Generalization Concerning the Arts") discusses several of these essays in detail, concentrating on those by Ziff and Weitz in particular. And (3) these essays have been superseded by the two selections we have chosen, Weitz's reformulation of his earlier views and his response to Mandelbaum in his book *The Opening Mind,* and Benjamin R. Tilghman's "Reflections on Aesthetic Theory."

Some explanation of the background of Weitz's antitheoretical stance may be helpful here. Weitz was deeply influenced by the philosophy of Ludwig Wittgenstein, as is clear in his influential "The Role of Theory in Aesthetics." Using as a model Wittgenstein's analysis of the concept of a game in the *Philosophical Investigations,* and borrowing the expression "open-textured concept" from another Wittgensteinian, Friedrich Waismann, Weitz argued that the concept of art cannot be defined because it is an open-textured concept. Such a concept, as Weitz understood it, has no necessary and sufficient conditions for its application; it is a concept whose conditions of application are perennially changeable. Because the concept of art in general and subconcepts such as novel, tragedy, and so on could be shown to be open-textured, Weitz maintained that none of them could be defined in the traditional manner. Thus in one fell swoop Weitz argued to put an end to the traditional search for true definitions of art and its subconcepts. Although Weitz's view was deeply influential for an extended period, he and other aestheticians came to see that the antidefinitionalist position was not immune to criticism. Nonetheless, in the Anglo-American philosophical world, Weitz's work, along with others, convinced many that an essentialist approach in the traditional sense was untenable.

Maurice Mandelbaum, in the essay reprinted here, refutes the de-definitionalist positions held by Weitz and W. E. Kennick, arguing that they are inconclusive, although in different ways. Kennick, Mandelbaum maintains, actually sets forth the underpinnings of an aesthetic theory while simultaneously denying that such a theory is possible. On the other hand, Mandelbaum argues that Weitz's attempt to show that there are no necessary and sufficient criteria for art is inconclusive. (Here Mandelbaum does not distinguish, as does Weitz, the attempt to define art in an essentialist fashion from the denial that the *concept* of art has necessary and sufficient criteria.)

Mandelbaum holds that Kennick, Weitz, and other "de-definitionalists" do not prove their cases. In fact, Mandelbaum argues against Wittgenstein himself, claiming that Wittgenstein failed to recognize important differences among different kinds of features that games, art, and other things possess. When these distinctions are taken into account, Mandelbaum sees no reason why the possibility of defining art cannot be realized. The thrust of Mandelbaum's argument is to show that one cannot prove in advance that no definition of art could be correct, as Weitz tried to do. From the fact that no satisfactory definition of art has yet been found, it does not follow that it is logically impossible to find one. Mandelbaum's essay thus served to revive interest in the problem of defining art and introduced a new chapter in the critical discussion of this problem.

Weitz's discussion in *The Opening Mind* of the conceptual problems involved in defining art is included here for three reasons. First, Weitz recapitulates his earlier theory; second, he updates his earlier views, indicating in what respects they were defective; and third, he astutely responds to Mandelbaum's criticisms of his views on aesthetic theory.

Benjamin R. Tilghman, a contemporary aesthetician, adopts a similar Wittgensteinian position in his essay "Reflections on Aesthetic Theory." Tilghman argues that traditional aesthetic theories have not merely failed to produce an accurate statement of the necessary and sufficient criteria for the concept of art, but they have in addition failed to have a significant bearing on the practice of the arts themselves. In his discussion Tilghman singles out John Dewey's aesthetics as a case in point. Dewey proposed his theory of art on the assumption that it would have an important bearing on the everyday practice of the arts, but Tilghman shows that such theories as Dewey's have had little impact on the work of artists themselves and have contributed in no fruitful way to the development of the arts in contemporary society.

In "The Artworld" Arthur Danto initiates a further stage in the movement away from antidefinitionalism. Danto's very provocative work is a contemporary classic that served to stimulate a fresh approach to art theory via the conception of an "artworld" that provides an atmosphere for the artistic enterprise. Danto introduced this novel idea in order to embrace an informal group of institutions that he maintains are responsible for the fact that certain artifacts in our society may be identified as artworks. The artworld includes not merely artists, critics, curators, and audiences, but orchestras, theaters, museums, dance companies, etc. It is the artworld that enables artworks to enjoy a specific kind of existence. Thus, an ordinary blue tie purchased in a department store is no work of art; but if Picasso paints a tie blue and exhibits it in a gallery, however indistinguishable it may be from an ordinary necktie, Picasso's work becomes art.

How can this be? According to Danto, the possession of a theory of art is required in order to explain this paradoxical situation. The cave painters of Lascaux, because they (presumably) lacked a theory of art, failed to create art! However, we who are denizens of the artworld have incorporated their "paintings" into our institution of art. In this way Danto requires that we examine the history of art theory in order to understand and explain how the kind of reality that artworks possess depends upon social institutions.

In "Once Upon a Time in the Artworld," Anita Silvers critically discusses Danto's views of art history, the tasks of the art historian and the role which artistic theories play in this situation. Silvers interprets Danto's influential statement, "To see something as art requires something the eye cannot decry—an atmosphere of artistic theory, a knowledge of the history of art: an artworld," to imply that "while artistic theory implies an atmosphere, art history is afforded the status of knowledge." As a result, art history, according to Danto, functions in the artworld as a neutral frame or ground, stable in an age of artistic revolutions. Danto therefore allows for the possibility of changes in aesthetic style which correspond to the transitoriness in the history of art itself.

In order to clarify this view, Danto examines the way in which art historical knowledge functions. Danto writes: ". . . I shall think of interpretations as functions which transform material objects into works of art. . . . Only in relation to an interpretation is a material object an artwork. . . ." Therefore, there are no pure aesthetic responses to art—to eliminate interpretation is to blind ourselves. But how are we to distinguish between plausible and implausible interpretations? Danto's answer, according to Silvers, is that "art historical references fulfill this role." It is history itself which imposes knowledge to guide and limit the interpretation of artworks. As a result, Danto appeals to historical explanation as informing interpretation and appreciation, thereby providing a stable ground for truth claims. Art historical explanation is developmental: "It must show how and why successor styles grow out of their predecessors."

Much of the remainder of Silvers' discussion centers on showing that it is impossible to remove the evaluative aspect from judgments of art works. She turns to a number of telling historical examples to show that different periods of art history judged works according to their own distinctive evaluative standards. In this way, she counters Danto's claim that it is possible to demarcate the descriptive and evaluative components in the interpretation of art works. Silvers shows that the "disparity in the importance attributed to certain works . . . reveals how infused with evaluation are historical renderings of art's past." The evolutionary model of art history espoused by Danto is thus criticized by Silvers on the grounds that different eras infuse works of art with their own distinctive evaluations and that no linear model of art history is available.

The most widely debated institutional theory of art is George Dickie's. Over the past generation Dickie has developed a clearly stated definition of art that has attracted widespread attention and criticism. Dickie's account is restricted to the "classificatory" as opposed to the "evaluative" sense, and embraces the latter. The term "work of art" is used by Dickie to describe how something becomes a member of the class of artworks rather than to explain what makes it good or bad. Thus works of art in the classificatory sense embrace good as well as bad and indifferent art; the traditional conception of what makes something a good work of art are its "good-making" characteristics, such as significant form, is on this view mistaken.

The first requirement that anything must meet to be a work of art is *artifactuality*. In his earlier writings Dickie allowed that the property of artifactuality could simply be conferred on an object, but this view left open the possibility that virtually anyone could create art, even without a minimum of skill or craftsmanship; however, in *The Art Circle* (1984) Dickie tightens his notion of artifactuality so as to exclude many contemporary works, including "conceptual art," "found art," and other work that involves no craftsmanship on the part of the "artist." More important, Dickie revises his initial definition of a work of art in *Art and the Aesthetic* (1974), in which he conceived of the second requirement for something's being a work of art as the conferring of the status of "candidate for appreciation" upon certain aspects of a work. This conferring, however, necessarily takes place against the background of the artworld, which is an informal social practice or institution.

In *The Art Circle* Dickie further modifies his theory; he abandons the notion of conferring the status of candidacy for appreciation and instead offers a series of definitions that bend in on each other in a circular fashion. His new definition of a work of art encompasses the numerous agents and agencies of the artworld (including artists, an art public or audience, critics, curators, etc.), pointing up the interrelationships among these agents in the artworld and clearly exhibiting their respective functions. Thus the circularity created by Dickie's new institutional theory of art attempts to capture the "Byzantine complexity" of the artworld in all its richness and variety.

Dickie's version of the institutional theory has given rise to much criticism and controversy over the past decade. In "The End of an Institutional Theory of Art" Robert Stecker argues against Dickie along three major lines. First, he contends that Dickie's reformulated version of the theory fails to distinguish works of art from many other artifacts. Second, Stecker maintains that Dickie's new account turns out to be closer to the views of the antidefinitionalists than to Dickie's own earlier approach.

Third, according to Stecker, Dickie "fails to show that existing in an institutional framework is a necessary condition for being art." Stecker's paper is valuable in several ways: it calls attention to the question of how it is possible to distinguish between those artifacts that are and those that are not works of art; it relates Dickie's work to that of the antitheorists and points up the similarities and differences between them; it raises questions about what works, particularly those of contemporary art, can be included in the corpus of artworks; and finally, Stecker at least suggests some important questions about the relationship between the classificatory and evaluative senses of art.

In his response to Stecker, Dickie attempts to answer a number of the more serious criticisms posed by Stecker. The reader will find Dickie's discussion provocative and informative. Thus, the controversy over the institutional theory of art continues in contemporary aesthetics.

Maurice Mandelbaum

FAMILY RESEMBLANCES AND GENERALIZATION CONCERNING THE ARTS

In 1954 William Elton collected and published a group of essays under the title *Aesthetics and Language*. As his introduction made clear, a common feature of these essays was the application to aesthetic problems of some of the doctrines characteristic of recent British linguistic philosophy.[1] While this mode of philosophizing has not had as pervasive an influence on aesthetics as it has had on most other branches of philosophy,[2] there have been a number of important articles which, in addition to those contained in the Elton volume, suggest the direction in which this influence runs. Among these articles one might mention "The Task of Defining a Work of Art" by Paul Ziff,[3] "The Role of Theory in Aesthetics" by Morris Weitz,[4] Charles L. Stevenson's "On 'What Is a Poem' "[5] and W. E. Kennick's "Does Traditional Aesthetics Rest on a Mistake?"[6] In each of them one finds a conviction which was also present in most of the essays in the Elton volume: that it is a mistake to offer generalizations concerning the arts, or, to put the matter in a more provocative manner, that it is a mistake to attempt to discuss what art, or beauty, or the aesthetic, or a poem, *essentially* is. In partial support of this contention, some writers have made explicit use of Wittgenstein's doctrine of *family resemblances*; Morris Weitz, for example, has placed it in the forefront of his discussion. However, in that influential

Maurice Mandelbaum, "Family Resemblances and Generalization Concerning the Arts." Reprinted from The American Philosophical Quarterly, *vol. 2, no. 3 (1965), by permission of* The American Philosophical Quarterly.

[1] See William Elton (ed.), *Aesthetics and Language* (Oxford, Basil Blackwell, 1954), p. 1, n. 1 and 2.

[2] A discussion of this fact is to be found in Jerome Stolnitz, "Notes on Analytic Philosophy and Aesthetics," *British Journal of Aesthetics*, vol. 3 (1961), pp. 210–222.

[3] *Philosophical Review*, vol. 62 (1953), pp. 58–78.

[4] *Journal of Aesthetics and Art Criticism*, vol. 15 (1956), pp. 27–35.

[5] *Philosophical Review*, vol. 66 (1957), pp. 329–362.

[6] *Mind*, vol. 67 (1958), pp. 317–334. In addition to the articles already referred to, I might mention "The Uses of Works of Art" by Teddy Brunius in *Journal of Aesthetics and Art Criticism*, vol. 22 (1963), pp. 123–133, which refers to both Weitz and Kennick, but raises other questions with which I am not here concerned.

and frequently anthologized article, Professor Weitz made no attempt to analyze, clarify, or defend the doctrine itself. Since its use with respect to aesthetics has provided the means by which others have sought to escape the need of generalizing concerning the arts, I shall begin my discussion with a consideration of it.

I

The *locus classicus* for Wittgenstein's doctrine of family resemblances is in Part I of *Philosophical Investigations*, sections 65–77.[7] In discussing what he refers to as language-games, Wittgenstein says:

> Instead of producing something common to all that we call language, I am saying that these phenomena have no one thing in common which makes us use the same word for all—but they are *related* to one another in many different ways. And it is because of this relationship, or these relationships, that we call them all "language." (§65)

He then illustrates his contention by citing a variety of *games*, such as board games, card games, ball games, etc., and concludes:

> We see a complicated network of similarities overlapping and criss-crossing: sometimes overall similarities of detail. (§66)
> I can think of no better expression to characterize these similarities than "family resemblances": for the various resemblances between members of a family: build, features, colour of eyes, gait, temperament, etc., etc. overlap and criss-cross in the same way.—And I shall say: "games" form a family. (§67)

In short, what Wittgenstein aims to establish is that one need not suppose that all instances of these entities to which we apply a common name do in fact possess any one feature in common. Instead, the use of a common name is grounded in the criss-crossing and overlapping of resembling features among otherwise heterogeneous objects and activities.

Wittgenstein's concrete illustrations of the diversity among various types of games may at first make his doctrine of family resemblances extremely plausible. For example, we do not hesitate to characterize tennis, chess, bridge, and solitaire as games, even though a comparison of them fails to reveal any specific feature which is the same in each of them. Nonetheless, I do not believe that his doctrine of family resemblances, as it stands, provides an adequate analysis of why a common name, such as "a game," is in all cases applied or withheld.

Consider first the following case. Let us assume that you know how to play that form of solitaire called "Canfield"; suppose also that you are acquainted with a number of other varieties of solitaire (Wittgenstein uses "patience," i.e., "solitaire," as one instance of a form of game). Were you to see me shuffling a pack of cards, arranging the cards in piles, some face up and some face down, turning cards over one-by-one,

---

[7]Ludwig Wittgenstein, *Philosophical Investigations*, translated by G. E. M. Anscombe (New York, Macmillan, 1973), pp. 31–36. A parallel passage is to be found in "The Blue Book": see *Preliminary Studies for the "Philosophical Investigations," Generally Known as The Blue and Brown Books* (Oxford, Basil Blackwell, 1958), pp. 17–18.

sometimes placing them in one pile, then another, shifting piles, etc., you might say: "I see you are playing cards. What game are you playing?" However, to this I might answer: "I am not playing a game; I am telling (or reading) fortunes." Will the resemblances between what you have seen me doing and the characteristics of card games with which you are familiar permit you to contradict me and say that I am indeed playing some sort of game? Ordinary usage would not, I believe, sanction our describing fortune-telling as an example of playing a game, no matter how striking may be the resemblances between the ways in which cards are handled in playing solitaire and in telling fortunes. Or, to choose another example, we may say that while certain forms of wrestling contests are sometimes characterized as games (Wittgenstein mentions "*Kampfspiele*")[8] an angry struggle between two boys, each trying to make the other give in, is not to be characterized as a game. Yet one can find a great many resembling features between such a struggle and a wrestling match in a gymnasium. What would seem to be crucial in our designation of an activity as a game is, therefore, not merely a matter of noting a number of specific resemblances between it and other activities which we denote as games, but involves something further.

To suggest what sort of characteristic this "something further" might possibly be, it will be helpful to pay closer attention to the notion of what constitutes a family resemblance. Suppose that you are shown ten or a dozen photographs and you are then asked to decide which among them exhibit strong resemblances.[9] You might have no difficulty in selecting, say, three of the photographs in which the subjects were markedly round-headed, had a strongly prognathous profile, rather deep-set eyes, and dark curly hair.[10] In some extended, metaphorical sense you might say that the similarities in their features constituted a family resemblance among them. The sense, however, would be metaphorical, since in the absence of a biological kinship of a certain degree of proximity we would be inclined to speak only of resemblances, and not of a *family* resemblance. What marks the difference between a literal and a metaphorical sense of the notion of "family resemblances" is, therefore, the existence

---

[8]Ludwig Wittgenstein, *Philosophical Investigations*, ∫66, p. 31. For reasons which are obscure, Miss Anscombe translates "*Kampfspiele*" as "Olympic games."

[9]In an article which is closely related to my discussion, but which uses different arguments to support a similar point, Haig Khatchadourian has shown that Wittgenstein is less explicit than he should have been with respect to the levels of determinateness at which these resemblances are significant for our use of common names. See "Common Names and 'Family Resemblances,'" *Philosophy and Phenomenological Research*, vol. 18 (1957–58), pp. 341–358. (For a related, but less closely relevant article by Professor Khatchadourian see "Art-Names and Aesthetic Judgments," *Philosophy*, vol. 36 [1961], pp. 30–48.)

[10]It is to be noted that this constitutes a closer resemblance than that involved in what Wittgenstein calls "family resemblances," since in my illustration the specific similarities all pertain to a single set of features, with respect to each one of which all three of the subjects directly resemble one another. In Wittgenstein's use of the notion of family resemblances there is, however, no one set of resembling features common to each member of the "family"; there is merely a criss-crossing and overlapping among the elements which constitute the resemblances among the various persons. Thus, in order to conform to his usage, my illustration would have to be made more complicated, and the degree of resemblance would become more attenuated. For example, we would have to introduce the photographs of other subjects in which, for example, recessive chins would supplant prognathous profiles among those who shared the other characteristics; some would have blond instead of dark hair, and protuberant instead of deep-set eyes, but would in each case resemble the others in other respects, etc. However, if what I say concerning family resemblances holds of the stronger similarities present in my illustration, it should hold *a fortiori* of the weaker form of family resemblances to which Wittgenstein draws our attention.

of a genetic connection in the former case and not in the latter. Wittgenstein, however, failed to make explicit the fact that the literal, root notion of a family resemblance includes this genetic connection no less than it includes the existence of noticeable physiognomic resemblances.[11] Had the existence of such a *twofold* criterion been made explicit by him, he would have noted that there is in fact an attribute common to all who bear a family resemblance to each other: they are related through a common ancestry. Such a relationship is not, of course, one among the specific features of those who share a family resemblance; it nonetheless differentiates them from those who are not to be regarded as members of a single family.[12] If, then, it is possible that the analogy of family resemblances could tell us something about how games may be related to one another, one should explore the possibility that, in spite of their great dissimilarities, games may possess a common attribute which, like biological connection, is not itself one among their directly exhibited characteristics. Unfortunately, such a possibility was not explored by Wittgenstein.

To be sure, Wittgenstein does not explicitly state that the resemblances which are correlated with our use of common names must be of a sort that are directly exhibited. Nonetheless, all of his illustrations in the relevant passages involve aspects of games which would be included in a description of how a particular game is to be played; that is, when he commands us to "look and see" whether there is anything common to all games,[13] the "anything" is taken to represent precisely the sort of manifest feature that

---

[11]Although Wittgenstein failed to make explicit the fact that a genetic connection was involved in his notion of "family resemblances," I think that he did in fact presuppose such a connection. If I am not mistaken, the original German makes this clearer than does the Anscombe translation. The German text reads:

> Ich kann diese Ähnlichkeiten nicht besser charakterisieren, als durch das Wort "Familienähnlichkeiten"; denn so übergreifen und kreuzen sich die verschiedenen Ähnlichkeiten, die zwischen den Gliedern einer Familie bestehen: Wuchs, Gesichtzüge, Augenfarbe, Gang, Temperament, etc., etc. (§67).

Modifying Miss Anscombe's translation in as few respects as possible, I suggest that a translation of this passage might read:

> I can think of no better expression to characterize these similarities than "family resemblances," since various similarities which obtain among the members of a family—their build, features, color of eyes, gait, temperament, etc., etc.—overlap and criss-cross in the same way.

This translation differs from Miss Anscombe's (which has been quoted above) in that it makes more explicit the fact that the similarities are similarities among the members of a single family, and are not themselves definitive of what constitutes a *family* resemblance.

[12]Were this aspect of the twofold criterion to be abandoned, and were our use of common names to be solely determined by the existence of overlapping and criss-crossing relations, it is difficult to see how a halt would ever be called to the spread of such names. Robert J. Richman has called attention to the same problem in " 'Something Common,' " *Journal of Philosophy*, vol. 59 (1962), pp. 821–830. He speaks of what he calls "the Problem of Wide-Open Texture," and says: "the notion of family resemblances may account for our extending the application of a given general term, but it does not seem to place any limit on this process" (p. 829).

In an article entitled "The Problem of the Model-Language Game in Wittgenstein's Later Philosophy," *Philosophy*, vol. 36 (1961), pp. 333–351, Helen Hervey also calls attention to the fact that "a family is so-called by virtue of its common ancestry" (p. 334). She also mentions (p. 335) what Richman referred to as the problem of "the wide-open texture."

[13]Ludwig Wittgenstein, *Philosophical Investigations*, §66, p. 31.

is described in rule-books, such as Hoyle. However, as we have seen in the case of family resemblances, what constitutes a *family* is not defined in terms of the manifest features of a random group of people; we must first characterize the *family* relationship in terms of genetic ties, and then observe to what extent those who are connected in this way *resemble* one another.[14] In the case of games, the analogue to genetic ties might be the purpose for the sake of which various games were formulated by those who invented or modified them, e.g., the potentiality of a game to be of absorbing non-practical interest to either participants or spectators. If there were any such common feature one would not expect it to be defined in a rule book, such as Hoyle, since rule books only attempt to tell us how to play a particular game: our interest in playing a game, and our understanding of what constitutes a game, is already pre-supposed by the authors of such books.

It is not my present concern to characterize any feature common to most or all of those activities which we call games, nor would I wish to argue on the analogy of family resemblances that there *must be* any such feature. If the question is to be decided, it must be decided by an attempt to "look and see." However, it is important that we look in the right place and in the right ways if we are looking for a common feature; we should not assume that any feature common to all games must be some manifest characteristic, such as whether they are to be played with a ball or with cards, or how many players there must be in order for the game to be played. If we were to rely exclusively on such features we should, as I have suggested, be apt to link solitaire with fortune-telling, and wrestling matches with fights, rather than (say) linking solitaire with cribbage and wrestling matches with weight-lifting. It is, then, my contention that Wittgenstein's emphasis on directly exhibited resemblances, and his failure to consider other possible similarities, led to a failure on his part to provide an adequate clue as to what—in some cases at least—governs our use of common names.[15]

If the foregoing remarks are correct, we are now in a position to see that the radical denigration of generalization concerning the arts, which has come to be almost a hallmark of the writings of those most influenced by recent British philosophy, may involve serious errors, and may not constitute a notable advance.

II

In turning from Wittgenstein's statements concerning family resemblances to the use to which his doctrine has been put by writers on aesthetics, we must first note what these writers are *not* attempting to do. In the first place, they are not seeking to clarify

---

[14]Although I have only mentioned the existence of genetic connections among members of a family, I should of course not wish to exclude the effects of habitual association in giving rise to some of the resemblances which Wittgenstein mentions. I have stressed genetic connection only because it is the simplest and most obvious illustration of the point I have wished to make.

[15]I do not deny that directly exhibited resemblances often play a part in our use of common names: this is a fact explicitly noted at least as long ago as by Locke. However, similarities in origin, similarities in use, and similarities in intention may also play significant roles. It is such factors that Wittgenstein overlooks in his specific discussions of family resemblances and of games.

the relationships which exist among the many different senses in which the word "art" is used. Any dictionary offers a variety of such senses (e.g., the art of navigation, art as guile, art as the craft of the artist, etc.), and it is not difficult to find a pattern of family resemblances existing among many of them. However, an analysis of such resemblances, and of their differences, has not, as a matter of fact, been of interest to the writers of the articles with which we are here concerned. In the second place, these writers have not been primarily interested in analyzing how words such as "work of art" or "artist" or "art" are ordinarily used by those who are neither aestheticians nor art critics; their concern has been with the writing which makes up the tradition of "aesthetic theory." In the third place, we must note that the concern of these writers has not been to show that family resemblances do in fact exist among the various arts, or among various works of art; on the contrary, they have used the doctrine of family resemblances in a *negative* fashion. In this, they have of course followed Wittgenstein's own example. The position which they have sought to establish is that traditional aesthetic theory has been mistaken in assuming that there is any essential property or defining characteristic of works of art (or any set of such properties or characteristics); as a consequence, they have contended that most of the questions which have been asked by those engaged in writing on aesthetics are mistaken sorts of questions.

However, as the preceding discussion of Wittgenstein should have served to make clear, one cannot assume that if there is any one characteristic common to all works of art it must consist in some specific, directly exhibited feature. Like the biological connections among those who are connected by family resemblances, or like the intentions on the basis of which we distinguish between fortune-telling and card games, such a characteristic might be a relational attribute, rather than some characteristic at which one could directly point and say: "It is this particular feature of the object which leads me to designate it as a work of art." A relational attribute of the required sort might, for example, only be apprehended if one were to consider specific art objects as having been created by someone for some actual or possible audience.

The suggestion that the essential nature of art is to be found in such a relational attribute is surely not implausible when one recalls some of the many traditional theories of art. For example, art has sometimes been characterized as being one special form of communication or of expression, or as being a special form of wish-fulfillment, or as being a presentation of truth in sensuous form. Such theories do not assume that in each poem, painting, play, and sonata there is a specific ingredient which identifies it as a work of art; rather, that which is held to be common to these otherwise diverse objects is a relationship which is assumed to have existed, or is known to have existed, between certain of their characteristics and the activities and the intentions of those who made them.[16]

[16]I know of no passage in which Wittgenstein takes such a possibility into account. In fact, if the passage from "The Blue Book" to which I have already alluded may be regarded as representative, we may say that Wittgenstein's view of traditional aesthetic theories was quite without foundation. In that passage he said:

> The idea of a general concept being a common property of its particular instances connects up with other primitive, too simple, ideas of the structure of language. It is comparable to the idea that *properties* are *ingredients* of the things which have the properties, e.g., that beauty is an ingredient of all beautiful things as alcohol is of beer and wine, and that we therefore could have pure beauty, unadulterated by anything that is beautiful (p. 17).

(continued)

While we may acknowledge that it is difficult to find any set of attributes—whether relational or not—which can serve to characterize the nature of a work of art (and which will not be as vulnerable to criticism as many other such characterizations have been),[17] it is important to note that the difficulties inherent in this task are not really avoided by those who appeal to the notion of family resemblances. As soon as one attempts to elucidate how the term "art" is in fact used in the context of art criticism, most of the same problems which have arisen in the history of aesthetic theory will again make their appearance. In other words, linguistic analysis does not provide a means of escape from the issues which have been of major concern in traditional aesthetics. This fact may be illustrated through examining a portion of one of the articles to which I have already alluded, Paul Ziff's article entitled "The Task of Defining a Work of Art."

To explain how the term "a work of art" is used, and to show the difficulties one encounters if one seeks to generalize concerning the arts, Professor Ziff chooses as his starting point one clear-cut example of a work of art and sets out to describe it. The work he chooses is a painting by Poussin, and his description runs as follows:

> Suppose we point to Poussin's "The Rape of the Sabine Women" as our clearest available case of a work of art. We could describe it by saying, first, that it is a painting. Secondly, it was made, and what is more, made deliberately and self-consciously with obvious skill and care, by Nicolas Poussin. Thirdly, the painter intended it to be displayed in a place where it could be looked at and appreciated, where it could be contemplated and admired. . . . Fourthly, the painting is or was exhibited in a museum gallery where people do contemplate, study, observe, admire, criticize, and discuss it. What I wish to refer to here by speaking of contemplating, studying, and observing a painting, is simply what we may do when we are concerned with a painting like this. For example, when we look at this painting by Poussin, we may attend to its sensuous features, to its "look and feel." Thus we attend to the play of light and color, to dissonances, contrasts, and harmonies of hues, values, and intensities. We notice patterns and pigmentation, textures, decorations, and embellishments. We may also attend to the structure, design, composition, and organization of the work. Thus we look for unity, and we also look for variety, for balance and movement. We attend to the formal interrelations and cross connexions in the work, to its underlying structure. . . . Fifthly, this work is a representational painting with a definite subject matter; it depicts a certain mytholog-

I fail to be able to identify any aesthetic theory of which such a statement would be true. It would not, for example, be true of Clive Bell's doctrine of "significant form," nor would it presumably be true of G. E. Moore's view of beauty, since both Bell and Moore hold that beauty depends upon the specific nature of the other qualities which characterize that which is beautiful.

However, it may be objected that when I suggest that what is common to works of art involves reference to "intentions," I overlook "the intentional fallacy" (see W. K. Wimsatt, Jr., and Monroe C. Beardsley, "The Intentional Fallacy," *Sewanee Review*, vol. 54 [1946], pp. 468–488). This is not the case. The phrase "the intentional fallacy" originally referred to a particular method of criticism, that is, to a method of interpreting and evaluating given works of art; it was not the aim of Wimsatt and Beardsley to distinguish between art and non-art. These two problems are, I believe, fundamentally different in character. However, I do not feel sure that Professor Beardsley has noted this fact, for in a recent article in which he set out to criticize those who have been influenced by the doctrine of family resemblances he apparently felt himself obliged to define art *solely* in terms of some characteristic in the object itself (see "The Definition of the Arts," *Journal of Aesthetics and Art Criticism*, vol. 20 [1961], pp. 175–187). Had he been willing to relate this characteristic to the activity and intention of those who make objects having such a characteristic, his discussion would not, I believe, have been susceptible to many of the criticisms leveled against it by Professor Douglas Morgan and Mary Mothersill (*ibid.*, pp. 187–198).

[17]I do not say "*all*" such definitions, for I think that one can find a number of convergent definitions of art, each of which has considerable merit, though each may differ slightly from the others in its emphasis.

Nicolas Poussin, Rape of the Sabine Women. *The Metropolitan Museum of Art, Harris Brisbane Dick Fund, 1946. All rights reserved, The Metropolitan Museum of Art.*

ical scene. Sixthly, the painting is an elaborate and certainly complex formal structure. Finally, the painting is a good painting. And this is to say simply that the Poussin painting is worth contemplating, studying, and observing in the way I have ever so roughly described.[18]

With reference to this description we must first note that it is clearly not meant to be anything like a complete description of the Poussin painting; it is at most a description of those aspects of that painting which are relevant to its being called a work of art. For example, neither the weight of the painting nor its insurable value is mentioned. Thus, whether because of his own preconceptions, or because of our ordinary assumptions concerning how the term "work of art" is to be used, Professor Ziff focuses more attention on some aspects of the Poussin painting than upon others. In doing so, he is making an implicit appeal to what is at least a minimal aesthetic theory, that is, he is supposing that neither weight nor insurable value need be mentioned when we list the characteristics which lead us to say of a particular piece of painted canvas that it is a work of art. In the second place, we must note that of the seven characteristics which he mentions, not all are treated by Professor Ziff as being independent of one another; nor are all related to one another in identical ways. It will be instructive to note some of

[18]*Op. cit.*, pp. 60–61. It is an interesting problem, but not germane to our present concerns, to consider whether Poussin's painting should be classified as a "mythological" painting, as Professor Ziff describes it, or whether it should be regarded as an historical painting.

the differences among their relationships, since it is precisely here that many of the traditional problems of aesthetic theory once again take their rise.

For example, we are bound to note that Professor Ziff related the seventh characteristic of the Poussin painting to its fourth characteristic: the fact that it is a good painting is, he holds, related to the characteristics which we find that it possesses when we contemplate, observe, and study it. Its goodness, however, is not claimed to be related to its first, third, or fifth characteristics: in other words, Professor Ziff is apparently not claiming that the goodness of this particular work of art depends upon its being a painting rather than being some other sort of work of art which is capable of being contemplated, studied, etc.; nor is he claiming that its goodness is dependent upon the fact that it was intended to be hung in a place where it can be observed and studied; nor upon the fact that it is a representational painting which depicts a mythological scene. If we next turn to the question of how the goodness of this painting is related to the fact that it was "made deliberately and self-consciously, with obvious skill and care by Nicolas Poussin," Professor Ziff's position is somewhat less explicit, but what he would say is probably quite clear. Suppose that the phrase "obvious skill" were deleted from the description of this characteristic: would the fact that this painting had been deliberately and self-consciously made, and had been made with care (but perhaps not with skill), provide a sufficient basis for predicating goodness of it? I should doubt that Professor Ziff would hold that it would, since many bad paintings may be supposed to have been made deliberately, self-consciously, and with care. Yet, if this is so, how is the maker's skill related to the object's goodness? Perhaps the fact that "obvious skill" is attributed to Poussin is meant to suggest that Poussin intended that "The Rape of the Sabine Women" should possess those qualities which Professor Ziff notes that we find in it when we contemplate, study, and observe it in the way in which he suggests that it should be contemplated. If this is what is suggested by attributing skill to the artist, it is surely clear that Professor Ziff has without argument built an aesthetic theory into his description of the Poussin painting. That theory is implicit both in the characteristics which he chooses as being aesthetically relevant, and in the relations which he holds as obtaining among these characteristics.

If it be doubted that Professor Ziff's description contains at least an implicit aesthetic theory, consider the fact that in one of the passages in which he describes the Poussin painting (but which I did not include in my foreshortened quotation from that description), he speaks of the fact that in contemplating, studying, and observing this painting "we are concerned with both two-dimensional and three-dimensional movements, the balance and opposition, thrust and recoil, of spaces and volumes." Since the goodness of a painting has been said by him to depend upon the qualities which we find in it when we contemplate, study, and observe it, it follows that these features of the Poussin painting contribute to its goodness. And I should suppose that they are also included in what Professor Ziff calls the sixth characteristic of the Poussin painting, namely its "complex formal structure." Thus, presumably, the goodness of a painting does depend, in part at least, upon its formal structure. On the other hand, Professor Ziff never suggests that the goodness of the Poussin painting depends upon the fact that it is a representational painting, and that it has a mythological (or historical) subject matter, rather than some other sort of subject matter. In fact, when he discusses critics such as Kenyon Cox and Royal Cortissoz, Professor Ziff would apparently—and quite properly—wish to separate himself from them, rejecting the view that what makes a painting a good painting has any necessary relation to the fact that it is or is not a representational painting of a certain sort. Thus, Professor Ziff's account of the aesthetically relevant features of the Poussin painting, and his statements concerning the interrelationships among the various features of that painting, define a particular aesthetic position.

The position which I have been attributing to him is one with which I happen to agree. However, that fact is not of any importance in the present discussion. What is important to note is that Professor Ziff's characterization of the Poussin painting contains an implicit theory of the nature of a work of art. According to that theory, the goodness of a painting depends upon its possession of certain objective qualities, that these qualities are (in part at least) elements in its formal structure, and that the artist intended that we should perceive these qualities in contemplating and studying the painting. (Had he not had this intention, would we be able to say that he had made the object self-consciously, deliberately, *and* with skill?) Further, this implicit theory must be assumed to be a theory which is general in import, and not confined to how we should look at this one painting only. Were this not so, the sort of description of the Poussin painting which was given by Professor Ziff would not have helped to establish a clear-cut case of what is to be designated as a work of art. For example, were someone to describe the same painting in terms of its size, weight, and insurable value (as might be done were it to be moved from museum to museum), we would not thereby learn how the term "work of art" is to be used. In failing to note that his description of the Poussin painting actually did involve a theory of the nature of art, Professor Ziff proceeded to treat that description as if he had done nothing more than bring forward a list of seven independent characteristics of the painting he was examining. In so doing, he turned the question of whether there are any features common to all works of art into a question of whether one or more of these seven specific indices could be found in all objects to which the term "work of art" is applied. Inevitably, his conclusion was negative, and he therefore held that "no one of the characteristics listed is necessarily a characteristic of a work of art."[19]

However, as we have seen, Professor Ziff's description of the Poussin painting was not actually confined to noting the specific qualities which were characteristic of the pictorial surface of that painting; it included references to the relations between these qualities and the aim of Poussin, and references to the ways in which a painting having such qualities is to be contemplated by others. Had he turned his attention to examining these relationships between object, artist, and contemplator, it would assuredly have been more difficult for him to assert that "neither a poem, nor a novel, nor a musical composition can be said to be a work of art in the same sense of the phrase in which a painting or a statue or a vase can be said to be a work of art."[20] In fact, had he carefully traced the relationships which he assumed to exist among some of the characteristics of the Poussin painting, he might have found that, contrary to his

[19]*Ibid.*, p. 64.
[20]*Ibid.*, p. 66. For example, Ziff denies that a poem can be said to be "exhibited or displayed." Yet it is surely the case that in printing a poem or in presenting a reading of a poem, the relation between the work and its audience, and the relation between artist, work, and audience, is not wholly dissimilar to that which obtains when an artist exhibits a painting. If this be doubted, consider whether there is not a closer affinity between these two cases than there is between a painter *exhibiting* a painting and a manufacturer *exhibiting* a new line of fountain pens.

inclinations, he was well advanced toward putting forward explicit generalizations concerning the arts.

III

While Professor Ziff's argument against generalization depends upon the fact that the various artistic media are significantly different from one another, the possibility of generalizing concerning the arts has also been challenged on historical grounds. It is to Morris Weitz's use of the latter argument that I shall now turn.

In "The Role of Theory in Aesthetics" Professor Weitz places his primary emphasis on the fact that art forms are not static. From this fact he argues that it is futile to attempt to state the conditions which are necessary and sufficient for an object to be a work of art. What he claims is that the concept "art" must be treated as an open concept, since new art forms have developed in the past, and since any art form (such as the novel) may undergo radical transformations from generation to generation. One brief statement from Professor Weitz's article can serve to summarize this view:

> What I am arguing, then, is that the very expansive, adventurous character of art, its ever-present changes and novel creations, makes it logically impossible to ensure any set of defining properties. We can, of course, choose to close the concept. But to do this with "art" or "tragedy" or portraiture, etc. is ludicrous since it forecloses the very conditions of creativity in the arts.[21]

Unfortunately, Professor Weitz fails to offer any cogent argument in substantiation of this claim. The lacuna in his discussion is to be found in the fact that the question of whether a particular concept is open or closed (i.e., whether a set of necessary and sufficient conditions can be offered for its use) is not identical with the question of whether future instances to which the very same concept is applied may or may not possess genuinely novel properties. In other words, Professor Weitz has not shown that every novelty in the instances to which we apply a term involves a stretching of the term's connotation.

By way of illustration, consider the classificatory label "representational painting." One can assuredly define this particular form of art without defining it in such a way that it will include only those paintings which depict either a mythological event or a religious scene. Historical paintings, interiors, fête-champêtres, and still life can all count as "representational" according to any adequate definition of this mode of painting, and there is no reason why such a definition could not have been formulated prior to the emergence of any of these novel species of the representational mode. Thus, to define a particular form of art—and to define it truly and accurately—is not necessarily to set one's self in opposition to whatever new creations may arise within that particular form.[22] Consequently, it would be mistaken to suppose that all attempts

---

[21]*Op. cit.*, p. 32.

[22]To be sure, if no continuing characteristic is to be found, the fact of change will demand that the concept be treated as having been an open one. This was precisely the position taken by Max Black in a discussion of the concept "science." (See "The Definition of Scientific Method," in *Science and Civilization*, edited by Robert C. Stauffer [Madison, Wisconsin, 1949].) Paul Ziff refers to the influence of Professor Black's discussion upon his own views, and the views of Morris Weitz are assuredly similar. However, even if Professor Black's view of the changes in the concept "science" is a correct one (as I should be prepared to think that it may be), it does not follow that the same argument applies in the case of art. Nor does the fact that the meaning of "science" has undergone profound changes in the past imply that further analogous changes will occur in the future.

to state the defining properties of various art forms are prescriptive in character and authoritarian in their effect.

This conclusion is not confined to cases in which an established form of art, such as representational painting, undergoes changes; it can also be shown to be compatible with the fact that radically new art forms arise. For example, if the concept "a work of art" had been carefully defined prior to the invention of cameras, is there any reason to suppose that such a definition would have proved an obstacle to viewing photography or the movies as constituting new art forms? To be sure, one can imagine definitions which might have done so. However, it was not Professor Weitz's aim to show that one or another definition of art had been a poor definition; he wished to establish the general thesis that there was a necessary incompatability, which he denoted as a logical impossibility, between allowing for novelty and creativity in the arts and stating the defining properties of a work of art. He failed to establish this thesis since he offered no arguments to prove that new sorts of instantiation of a previously defined concept will necessarily involve us in changing the definition of that concept.

To be sure, if neither photography nor the movies had developed along lines which satisfied the same sorts of interest that the other arts satisfied, and if the kinds of standards which were applied in the other arts were not seen to be relevant when applied to photography and to the movies, then the antecedently formulated definition of art would have functioned as a closed concept, and it would have been used to exclude all photographers and all motion-picture makers from the class of those who were to be termed "artists." However, what would the defender of the openness of concepts hold that one should have done under these circumstances? Suppose, for example, that all photographers had in fact been the equivalent of passport photographers, and that they have been motivated by no other interests and controlled by no other standards than those which govern the making of photographs for passports and licenses: would the defender of open concepts be likely to have expanded the concept of what is to count as an art in order to have included photography? The present inclusion of photography among the arts is justified, I should hold, precisely because photography arises out of the same sorts of interest, and can satisfy the same sorts of interest, and our criticism of it employs the same sorts of standards, as is the case with respect to the other arts.

Bearing this in mind, we are in a position to see that still another article which has sometimes been cited by those who argue for the openness of the concept "a work of art" does not justify the conclusions which have been drawn from it. That article is Paul Oskar Kristeller's learned and informative study entitled "The Modern System of the Arts."[23] The way in which Professor Kristeller states the aim of his article suggests that he too would deny that traditional aesthetic theory is capable of formulating adequate generalizations concerning the arts. He states his aim in saying:

> The basic notion that the five "major arts" constitute an area all by themselves, clearly separated by common characteristics from the crafts, the sciences and other human activities has been taken for granted by most writers on aesthetics from Kant to the present day. . . .
> It is my purpose to show that this system of the five major arts, which underlies all modern aesthetics and is so familiar to us all, is of comparatively recent origin and did not assume

[23]*Journal of the History of Ideas*, vol. 12 (1951), pp. 496–527, and vol. 13 (1952), pp. 17–46. This study has been cited by both Elton (*op. cit.*, p. 2) and Kennick (*op. cit.*, p. 320) in substantiation of their views.

definite shape before the eighteenth century, although it had many ingredients which go back to classical, mediaeval, and Renaissance thought.[24]

However, the fact that *the classification of the arts* has undoubtedly changed during the history of Western thought, does not of itself suggest that *aesthetic theory* must undergo comparable changes. Should this be doubted, one may note that Professor Kristeller's article does not show in what specific ways attempts to classify or systematize the arts are integral to, or are presupposed by, or are consequences of, the formulation of an aesthetic theory. This is no minor cavil, for if one examines the writers on aesthetics who are currently attacked for their attempts to generalize concerning the nature of art, one finds that they are not (by and large) writers whose discussions are closely allied to the discussions of those with whom Kristeller's article was primarily concerned. Furthermore, it is to be noted that Kristeller did not carry his discussion beyond Kant. This terminal point was justified by him on the ground that the system of the arts has not substantially changed since Kant's time.[25] However, when one recalls that Kant's work is generally regarded as standing near the beginning of modern aesthetic theory— and surely not near its end—one has reason to suspect that questions concerning "the system of the arts" and questions concerning aesthetic theory constitute distinct, and probably separate sets of questions. A survey of recent aesthetic theory bears this out. Since the time of Hegel and of Schopenhauer there have been comparatively few influential aesthetic theories which have made the problem of the diversity of art forms, and the classification of these forms, central to their consideration of the nature of art.[26] For example, the aesthetic theories of Santayana, Croce, Alexander, Dewey, Prall, or Collingwood cannot be said to have been dependent upon any particular systematic classification of the arts. In so far as these theories may be taken as representative of attempts to generalize concerning the arts, it is strange that current attacks on traditional aesthetics should have supposed that any special measure of support was to be derived from Kristeller's article.

Should one wish to understand why current discussions have overlooked the gap between an article such as Kristeller's and the lessons ostensibly derived from it, an explanation might be found in the lack of concern evinced by contemporary analytic philosophers for the traditional problems of aesthetic theory. For example, one looks in vain in the Elton volume for a careful appraisal of the relations between aesthetic theory and art criticism, and how the functions of each might differ from the functions of the other. A striking example of the failure to consider this sort of problem is also to be found in John Wisdom's often cited dicta concerning "the dullness" of aesthetic theory.[27] In examining his views one finds that the books on art which Wisdom finds *not* to be dull are books such as Edmund Wilson's *Axel's Castle*, in which a critic "brings out features of the art he writes about, or better, brings home the character of

[24]*Op. cit.*, vol. 12, p. 497.
[25]*Op. cit.*, vol. 13, p. 43; also, pp. 4 ff.
[26]One exception is to be found in T. M. Greene: *The Arts and the Art of Criticism* (Princeton, 1940). This work is cited by Kristeller, and is one of the only two which he cites in support of the view that the system of the arts has not changed since Kant's day (*op. cit.*, vol. 12, p. 497, n. 4). The other work cited by him is Paul Franke's *System der Kunstwissenschaft* (Brünn/Leipzig, 1938), which also offers a classification of the arts, but only within a framework of aesthetic theory which could easily embrace whatever historical changes the arts undergo.
[27]See "Things and Persons," *Proceedings of the Aristotelian Society, Supplementary Volume XXII* (1948), pp. 207–210.

what he writes about."[28] In short, it is not theory—it is not aesthetic theory at all—that Wisdom is seeking: he happens to be interested in criticism.

I do not wish to be taken as denying the importance of criticism, nor as belittling the contribution which a thorough acquaintance with the practice of criticism in all of the arts may make to general aesthetic theory. However, it is important to note that the work of any critic presupposes at least an implicit aesthetic theory, which—as critic—it is not his aim to establish or, in general, to defend. This fact can only be overlooked by those who confine themselves to a narrow range of criticism: for example, to the criticism appearing in our own time in those journals which are read by those with whom we have intellectual, political, and social affinities. When we do not so confine ourselves, we rapidly discover that there is, and has been, an enormous variety in criticism, and that this variety represents (in part at least) the effect of differing aesthetic preconceptions. To evaluate criticism itself we must, then, sometimes undertake to evaluate these preconceptions. In short, we must do aesthetics ourselves.

However, for many of the critics of traditional aesthetics this is an option which does not appeal. If I am not mistaken, it is not difficult to see why this should have come to be so. In the first place, it has come to be one of the marks of contemporary analytic philosophy to hold that philosophic problems are problems which cannot be solved by appeals to matters of fact. Thus, to choose but a single instance, questions of the relations between aesthetic perception and other instances of perceiving—for example, questions concerning psychical distance, or empathic perception, or the role of form in aesthetic perception—are not considered to be questions with which a philosopher ought to try to deal. In the second place, the task of the philosopher has come to be seen as consisting largely of the unsnarling of tangles into which others have gotten themselves. As a consequence, the attempt to find a synoptic interpretation of some broad range of facts—an attempt which has in the past been regarded as one of the major tasks of a philosopher—has either been denigrated or totally overlooked.[29] Therefore, problems such as the claims of the arts to render a true account of human character and destiny, or questions concerning the relations between aesthetic goodness and standards of greatness in art, or an estimate of the significance of variability in aesthetic judgments, are not presently fashionable. And it must be admitted that if philosophers wish not to have to face either factual problems or synoptic tasks, these are indeed questions which are more comfortably avoided than pursued.

[28]*Ibid.*, p. 209.

[29]For example, W. B. Gallie's "The Function of Philosophical Aesthetics," in the Elton volume, argues for "a journeyman's aesthetics," which will take up individual problems, one by one, these problems being of the sort which arise when a critic or poet gets into a muddle about terms such as "abstraction" or "imagination." For this purpose the tools of the philosopher are taken to be the tools of logical analysis (*op. cit.*, p. 35); a concern with the history of the arts, with psychology, or a direct and wide-ranging experience of the arts seems not to be presupposed.

A second example of the limitations imposed upon aesthetics by contemporary linguistic analysis is to be found in Professor Weitz's article. He states that "the root problem of philosophy itself is to explain the relation between the employment of certain kinds of concepts and the conditions under which they can be correctly applied" (*op. cit.*, p. 30).

Morris Weitz

ART AS AN OPEN CONCEPT:
FROM *THE OPENING MIND*

Aesthetics and logic have not been friends. Instead, their relation historically has been one of indifference, mutual suspicion or contempt, and at times even open warfare. Such hostility is a pity, since logic has as much to learn from aesthetics as aesthetics has from logic. Many, perhaps the most fundamental, problems of aesthetics are conceptual, not empirical; and some of the concepts of aesthetics are especially relevant to logic in its indigenous quest for the limits and scope of valid argument. Thus, if logic requires of aesthetics, as it does of all forms of discourse, adherence to rigorous standards of acceptable inference, aesthetics at least invites logic to consider, if not ultimately to accommodate, certain irreducibly open concepts that do not simply dissolve into the traditional notions of ambiguity and vagueness.

That logic and aesthetics do have much to say to each other I shall illustrate by turning once again to the concept of art. Because I have already argued for the conceptual rather than factual character of the central question of traditional aesthetics, What is art? and for the openness of that concept in "The Role of Theory in Aesthetics" (1956)—an essay that is easily accessible—I shall not reproduce the argument here. Rather, I shall summarize it and shall then state and examine certain major objections to it, including my own. My aim, however, is to strengthen, not repudiate, the open character of the concept of art. The fundamental thesis of that essay remains intact: that all theories of art—past, present, and future—fail and are doomed to fail in their putative real definitions of art because they misconceive the concept of art.

The search for a theory of art, I claimed, has been and remains the preoccupation of aesthetics or the philosophy of the arts. Theory has been variously construed in the history of aesthetics as real definition of the nature of art or as a statement about the essence, necessary and sufficient properties, or common denominator of art. Every theory of art or of a particular art, such as poetry or tragedy, from Plato and Aristotle to modern aesthetic theories of the fine arts, either states or converges on a statement of

Reprinted from The Opening Mind *by Morris Weitz (Chicago: University of Chicago Press, 1977), by permission of the University of Chicago Press and the estate of the author. Copyright © 1977 by the University of Chicago Press.*

the nature of art: what it is and how it differs from what is not art. Without a theory, intelligible talk and thought about art are impossible; thus, a theory of art is a necessary condition for the cogency of criticism and appreciation of the arts. If we generalize to all of the arts Clive Bell's remark about visual art, we have a succinct summative statement of the overriding importance of a theory of art: "For either all works of visual art have some common quality, or when we speak of 'works of art' we gibber" (*Art*, p. 7).

Is there a true theory of art? Can there be such a theory? Need there be such a theory in order to render talk and thought about the arts intelligible? The history of aesthetics or, since this history is recent, the history of philosophy of the arts is in large part a history of successive competing affirmative answers to these three questions. And it was the main burden of my essay to reject these answers, not by offering different affirmative ones, but by giving negative replies to these three questions.

That there is no extant true theory of art is supported by the disagreements among the theories themselves. Each theory purports to enumerate the defining properties of art and to succeed in this endeavor as its competing theories do not. Yet we are as far from unanimity on a true theory as ever we have been. More important, though, is the range and assortment of deficiencies regarding the defining terms which are expressed in the disagreements, for there is not in the entire history of aesthetics a putatively true statement about the nature of art that has not been castigated by its opponents as incomplete, too inclusive, circular, founded on dubious features or principles, vague, or untestable.

These objections to traditional theories, each made by one theorist or another in his efforts to secure a new true theory of art, though they cast serious doubt on an affirmative answer to the question, Is there a true theory of art? do not, so I argued, go far enough, since they allow that further research and probing into the complexities of art can remedy the flaws of extant theories. For them, the difficulties remain factual.

The problem, however, is not factual. It is conceptual. There is no true theory of art, not because no one has yet produced it, but because such a theory forecloses on the concept of art. A theory of art—a true statement of its necessary and sufficient properties, its essence, its nature, its common denominator—is not simply difficult to formulate; it is logically impossible because it states the definitive criteria of a concept whose very use depends upon there being no such set. There is no true theory of art, then, because there cannot be one. The concept of art, as its use reveals, is open; a theory of art presupposes or entails the false claim that the concept of art is closed, governed by necessary and sufficient criteria, corresponding to the definitive properties of art, which criteria can be formulated into a definition of "art" that can then legislate correct talk about art. That the concept of art is open, that it functions under less than definitive conditions, and, consequently, that art can no more be defined in terms of a set of definitive properties than "art" can be defined in terms of a set of definitive criteria: this was the central thesis of my essay.

What is art? entails What is the concept of art? which in turn yields What is the role of "art" in discourse about the arts? Traditional aesthetic theory, I said, gave the wrong answer to What does "art" do? and What are the conditions under which it does it? What, then, did I offer as the right answer? That "art" and its subconcepts, such as "novel," "drama," "music," "tragedy," "painting," and so forth, are employed either to describe or to evaluate certain objects and that, though this description or evaluation is dependent on certain criteria, these criteria are neither necessary nor sufficient. All, therefore, are open in the sense that they perform their descriptive and appraisive jobs on the overall condition that new cases with their new properties can be accommodated by the addition of new criteria for these terms. The history of the arts is in part the history of the creation of new objects with their new properties. The history of the concept of art reflects this origination of the new, which, until it occurs, is unpredictable and unforeseeable, yet must be accommodated by the concept of art. In effect, then, I identified the openness of the concept of art with its open texture, as indeed I assimilated all the subconcepts of art, such as tragedy, to Waismann's notion of open texture. Neither "art" nor any of its subterms, "tragedy," "drama," "music," "painting," etc., could be defined, since their criteria had to allow for the possibility of new ones that render definitive sets of them violations of the concepts they convey.

This wholesale reading of open concepts in aesthetics as open-texture concepts was a mistake. Not that it is a mistake that there are open concepts in aesthetics; the mistake was rather in conflating the open with the open-texture concepts. Some aesthetic concepts are open in the sense that they must allow for the unforeseeably new. But some are also and more radically open in the sense that they must allow for the possibility of the rejection of any of the prevailing criteria as well. Thus, "tragedy," for example, differs from "drama" and even "art" in that it has no unchallengeable criterion; whereas the other two, though also without necessary or sufficient criteria, have some unrejectable criteria, such as "has a plot" or "is made by human skill."

My blunder in not distinguishing in this early essay between the perennially flexible and the perennially debatable—indeed, in assuming that they entail each other—led to another bad mistake, this time about certain concepts that I said were closed, among them "ancient Greek tragedy." This concept is closed, I argued, because the prefix sets boundaries to the concept of tragedy; and within the boundaries and with all the cases in, we could state the necessary and sufficient properties of all the extant ancient Greek tragedies. Having identified open with open texture, "ancient Greek tragedy" (equated with its extant examples) could hardly be perennially flexible; so I concluded that it is closed. The mistake was in not realizing that "ancient Greek tragedy," though closed in its cases, each of which is indisputable as a Greek tragedy, is nevertheless as open as "tragedy" because each of the reasons given for any of its indisputable examples' being tragic is challengeable and rejectable. That "ancient Greek tragedy" is open in the sense of perennially debatable, as open as "tragedy," can be seen when we shift from the question, absurd as it is, Is *Oedipus Rex* tragic? to the question, intelligible and as alive as it was to Aristotle, Why is *Oedipus Rex* tragic? Even a cursory survey of the reasons that have been given and of the range of disagreement over these reasons points to nothing short of the perennial debatability of the concept of tragedy.

I was wrong about "tragedy" as only a perennially flexible concept. It is that; but it is also a perennially debatable one. But I still think that the concept of art is open in Waismann's sense of open texture: perennially flexible. In my essay, in characterizing the logic of the sets of conditions under which "art" is employed to describe or to evaluate, I said that there are these conditions—which I referred to as "criteria of recognition" and "criteria of evaluation"—but that they do not add up to a definitive set: there are no necessary or sufficient conditions or criteria for the correct use of "art" to describe or to evaluate works of art. "This is a work of art" can be joined with "and it was made by no one," "and it is not an artifact," "and it was created by accident," or with a denial of any statement about a putatively necessary property of a work of art, without misuse of the concept of art, and occasionally to make a true statement about art.

Do we need a theory of art? If there cannot be such a theory and there is not such a theory—whether we deduce the latter from the former or generalize it from the failures of past theories to formulate true definitions of art—then we have no definitive properties to fall back on as we buttress our talk about art. If we require a theory of art to talk about art and there is no such theory, then we cannot talk about art. But we do talk about art. We describe objects as works of art, and we praise certain features of works of art. We also interpret and explain works of art. Is it a necessary condition of our doing these things that we possess a true theory or that we must assume that such a theory is forthcoming? Here—this time with the help of Wittgenstein's talk about games—I argued that we do not need a theory, nor do we have to assume that there is such a theory, in order to talk and argue intelligently about art. My negative answer to this third question of traditional aesthetics—Do we need a theory of art?—was not, however, a negative answer to the ontological question Does art have an essence? Rather, it was a negative answer to the conceptual question Must we assume that art has an essence in order to be able to talk about it? Consequently, to substitute family resemblances for essences or, in the case of art, indisputable examples of works of art and their strands of nonnecessary, nonsufficient properties for sets of definitive properties was to substitute one overall condition of intelligible discourse for another; it was not to supplant one ontological view by an anti-ontological one. Thus, a negative answer to Do we need a theory of art in order to talk cogently about art? is absolutely independent of a negative (or, for that matter, an affirmative) answer to the question, Is there a true theory of art? Even if, then, there were a true theory of art or there could be one, it would still not follow that it was required—that this theory is a necessary condition—for being able to say all that we want to say or that needs saying about the arts.

Not all of my observations on classical theories of art were negative. Despite their logically vain attempts to define the indefinable, to state the necessary and sufficient properties of art and, by implication, the definitive criteria of "art," or to construe the openness of the concept of art as closed, I suggested at the end of my essay that each of these classical theories and of those to come could be read as a series of invaluable pedagogic directions for attending to art. I did not intend my suggestion to be a correct reading of classical misreadings of the concept of art; it was instead a recommendation to salvage the illuminating criteria proffered by the theories by converting them from necessary and sufficient into honorific criteria for a stipulated or legislated use of "art."

As everyone knows, it is notoriously difficult and treacherous for an author to expound his early work. I hope my summary of "The Role of Theory in Aesthetics" belies this observation. I think my central thesis was that art is an open concept: that it performs its main jobs of describing and evaluating certain objects under conditions less than definitive and, in particular, under sets of conditions, none of which is necessary or sufficient, but some of which are not rejectable, and others of which must accommodate the unforeseeably new works that are demanded by the development of art. The concept of art and some of its subconcepts, like the novel and drama, music and painting, sculpture and architecture, are open in the precise sense of "perennially flexible." This thesis, especially if it is divorced from the wholly incorrect thesis that perennial flexibility entails perennial debatability, which I built into my essay, remains firm and, if true as well, a contribution to the elucidation of the concept of art and, through that concept, to the elucidation of the major issues of aesthetics.

But is it true that the concept of art is open? The confidence I retain in my affirmative answer is clearly not shared by all. Indeed, if one can judge from the vehemence of the objections that have appeared since the publication of that essay (and expansions of it in *Hamlet and the Philosophy of Literary Criticism*), the openness of the concept of art and of its subconcepts, along with the consequent denial of the possibility of a theory of art or of some of its subconcepts, has been accepted by very few! Perhaps the authors of these objections are right. At any rate, the issues they raise are eminently worth examining, since they embrace the overriding theme of the nature and role of concepts in aesthetics and related humanistic disciplines.

I begin with Maurice Mandelbaum's criticism of my thesis of the openness of the concept of art in his important paper "Family Resemblances and Generalization Concerning the Arts" (1965). Mandelbaum does not affirm a theory of art. Instead he argues against certain contemporary rejections, including mine, of the possibility of a theory of art.

Is it a mistake to offer generalizations concerning the arts? Mandelbaum identifies this question with the entirely different question, Is it a mistake to discuss what art essentially is?—which he regards as only "a more provocative" form of the first question. But surely these questions are different, as their answers show. How, for example, could anyone challenge the making of some generalizations about the arts? There must be literally thousands of these, such as "The arts are enjoyable" or "The arts are more accessible today than they were a hundred years ago." Some of these generalizations are more interesting than others, some are more true than false, some less trivial than others.

So it is not generalizations about the arts that are suspect but only certain kinds of generalizations—those about the essence of art: what all works of art share, by virtue of which they are works of art and without which they would not be works of art. And the mistake that Mandelbaum says opponents of essentialistic generalizations attribute to such generalizations cannot be simply in the "attempt to discuss what art . . . *essentially* is"; it must be in statements about the essence of art, in formulations of the necessary and sufficient properties of art. But why are these statements a mistake? Not because art has no such definitive sets of properties, but because the statements that it does entail that the concept of art and the word "art" in any language are governed by definitive criteria that correspond to the definitive properties where the concept and its conveying words are not so governed. The mistake, when it is a mistake, committed by essentialistic generalizations about the arts, is the mistake of implying that there are definitive criteria for a concept when there are no such criteria. It is therefore a mistake about the concept, not the nature, of art.

I emphasize this distinction between ontological and conceptual affirmation and its truth or falsity (mistake) because it is precisely this distinction that Mandelbaum, I think, conflates in arguing that no one has yet showed that it is a mistake to generalize about the arts. In effect, he construes essentialistic generalization as ontological (which it is) and the contemporary attack on it as anti-ontological (which it is not). For him, the opponent of essentialistic generalization argues as follows: Art has no essence, only family resemblances; so it is a mistake to say it has an essence when it does not. It is because he interprets the issue as ontological rather than conceptual that he quite rightly claims that the contemporary attack rests on the truth of the doctrine of family resemblances.

Mandelbaum's next step is not to refute this doctrine but to tighten it up so that it becomes a version of essentialism. He says that family resemblances are manifest similarities that embody unexhibited genetic connections. Wittgenstein's strands of similarities cannot, without the genetic ties, explain what he claimed they explained, that is, why we apply or withhold, in all cases, certain common names, such as "game."

What is Wittgenstein's doctrine of family resemblances? It is a doctrine about the criteria of certain terms, names, or concepts. He holds that these criteria comprise a family, not an essence; or, to express it nonmetaphorically, that many terms, words, or concepts are employed correctly to name certain members of certain classes under disjunctive sets of nonnecessary, nonsufficient conditions rather than under sets of necessary and sufficient conditions. The doctrine, then, is one about the logical grammar of certain words or concepts, not about the less-than-essential ontology of things. It is Wittgenstein's answer to Do we need a theory—a true statement about essences—in order to be able to talk about, name, refer to, certain things, such as games? It is not an answer to Is there such a theory? And his answer is that, if we look and see instead of impose an overall necessary condition for the intelligibility of discourse, we do find, at least in many cases, that many terms are employed correctly without sets of definitive criteria that can be formulated into essentialistic definitions.

Now, according to Mandelbaum, Wittgenstein's doctrine of family resemblances is inadequate. He offers the example of a man who looks as if he were playing solitaire but who, when asked what he is doing, replies that he is reading his fortune. If we go by ostensible resemblances alone, we cannot, Mandelbaum claims, explain why we withhold "game" and apply "fortune-telling." In order to decide whether this case is a case of one rather than the other, we need to know the man's intention; and the man's intention is a nonmanifest feature of the situation that serves as the decisive criterion in our use of "fortune-telling" rather than "game." Likewise, in all games, all activities, a necessary criterion for correct characterization of them is that of intention or purpose, which is not a criterion of a manifest resemblance. It is rather a criterion of a hidden genetic tie that makes the resemblances a family. Indeed, the tie—in this case, a common ancestry—is what makes the resemblances a family in its literal, not metaphorical, sense.

It is not clear whether Mandelbaum is claiming that there are family resemblances, in his sense of genetic connections among manifest similarities, and that this relationship is what Wittgenstein left out of his account, thereby rendering it inadequate, or whether he is contending instead that it is a necessary condition for the cogent use of certain common names that the criteria for this use must include the necessary criterion of a genetic tie or relationship among the disjunctive sets of nonnecessary, nonsufficient criteria. In any case, it seems to me, the first objection is irrelevant, since Wittgenstein neither affirmed nor denied, or needed to affirm or deny, that there are strands of similarities among members of certain classes but no hidden ties or essences. And the second contention is false: it is not a necessary condition for our correct, intelligible, and cogent employment of common names, such as "game," that all the criteria for this employment—for example, "skill," "amusement," "competition," etc.—be linked together by a necessary criterion of some sort of tie or connection among the criteria. What Mandelbaum must demonstrate but does not and, I believe, cannot is that Wittgenstein's doctrine of family resemblances is incoherent without an overall necessary condition that ties together the disjunctive conditions.

That it is not incoherent can be seen even from Mandelbaum's example of the fortune-teller. For in that example it is not the man's hidden intention that decides whether "solitaire" or "fortune-telling" applies to what he is doing; it is what he says when asked or provoked by another's utterance. And what he says is decisive only if we believe him or have no reason not to. What he says—"I'm telling my fortune"—is one (and here the most crucial) among manifest criteria, none necessary, none sufficient, for applying, withholding, or retracting a common name. Moreover, if he won't tell us what he is doing, we may not be able to decide what the correct term to apply is. Or, suppose he does tell us he is telling his fortune: how does he, or do we, decide to apply or to reject "You have been playing solitaire all this time and didn't even know it"?

Contemporary repudiations of traditional aesthetic theory, Mandelbaum contends, rest on Wittgenstein's doctrine of family resemblances. This doctrine, as Wittgenstein formulated it, is inadequate; so the arguments based on it are also inadequate. Art may yet have an essence; art may yet have manifest strands of similarity united by un-exhibited relations that embody its essence while at the same time providing the concept of art and the word "art"—like the concept of game and the word "game"—with a set of necessary and sufficient criteria for their correct use. At any rate, no one has yet showed that such a theory is a mistake or that, in particular, it involves a confusion between essence and strands of similarity.

Is Mandelbaum correct in attributing to contemporary attacks on aesthetic theory the wholesale acceptance of Wittgenstein's doctrine of family resemblances as basic? I cannot speak for the other opponents of aesthetic theory, but I can say that he is not at all accurate in his interpretation of my essay, which he singles out as an argument against aesthetic theory that is rooted in Wittgenstein's inadequate conception of family resemblances. For my argument against theories of art was (and is) that they attempt to state definitive criteria for a concept whose use has depended on and continues to depend, not on its having such a set, but rather on its being able, for its correct use, to accommodate new criteria that are derived, or derivable, from new art forms whose features demand emendation, rejection, or expansion of extant criteria. However, it is not the history and the future of art but what that history and the unforeseeable possibilities of the future reveal about the functioning or role of the concept of art that are fundamental to my thesis that the concept of art is not amenable to definitive criteria and, therefore, that definitions or theories of art are conceptually, not empirically, impossible.

Mandelbaum is thus in error, at least in my opinion, in thinking that my argument against traditional aesthetic theory rests on Wittgenstein's doctrine of family resem-blances or even, as he shifts in his analysis of my essay, on the history and continuing development of art. I hope it is now clear that it rests on neither, but only on what it can be based on: the use and conditions of use of the concept of art. Indeed, Wittgenstein's doctrine of family resemblances is wholly irrelevant to two of the questions I asked: Is there a theory of art? and Can there be such a theory? (I am not even sure that Wittgenstein would have tolerated my negative answers to these two questions.) It is relevant only to the question: Do we need a theory of art? My answer, borrowed from Wittgenstein, was (and is): No; we can get along quite nicely in talking about art—in asking and answering What is art?, Is this a work of art?, and Why is this a work of art?—with reasons that relate to disjunctive sets of nonnecessary, nonsufficient criteria and to their corresponding properties in the works of art that have them.

That there is not and cannot be a true theory of art is not a mistake. It is nothing short of a valid inference from the true description of the logical grammar of "art." The mistake consists in confusing this conceptual truth about "art" with a factual claim about art.

Benjamin R. Tilghman

REFLECTIONS ON AESTHETIC THEORY

Questions about the nature of theories in aesthetics and the philosophy of art and skeptical doubts about whether such theories are even possible did not become serious issues until Wittgenstein's *Philosophical Investigations* began to be influential in that area of philosophy in the 1950s.[1] Wittgenstein's work suggested to a number of philosophers of art that the kinds of theories aestheticians have so often sought are either not possible or, more cautiously, of little help. Despite the considerable measure of debate, those who are skeptical about the role of theories in aesthetics have clearly been in the minority in the last thirty-five years or so. The prevailing opinion seems to be that theories are not only possible, but are essential to the philosophical enterprise of thinking about art and aesthetics. There are, nevertheless, questions about theories that still need to be raised, and I intend to raise some of them here.

What is an aesthetic theory, and what do we want of one? A good place to begin is with a distinction made by the historian of recent American art, Stewart Buettner. Buettner distinguishes between two kinds of theory; on the one hand there is what he calls *aesthetics*, and on the other, *art theory:*

> As opposed to aesthetics, which is the philosophic inquiry into art and beauty, art theory investigates the ideas of artists in an effort to explain a variety of phenomena in both an artist's life and work that may help to further the appreciation of an artist or a group of artists. The difference, then, between aesthetics and art theory rests almost exclusively upon the profession of the individuals concerned.[2]

It is important to make some kind of distinction along these lines between philosophical theories and those that are intended to help us understand and appreciate individual works of art, the *oeuvre* of an artist, or an artistic period or movement. Buettner, I would suggest, has mistaken the principle of the distinction, for it has nothing to do with anyone's profession. The distinction is, rather, in the broadest sense, a logical one.

This essay was written for the second edition of this collection and is being published for the first time.

[1]See, for example, Morris Weitz, "The Role of Theory in Aesthetics," *Journal of Aesthetics and Art Criticism* (1956), and William Kennick, "Does Traditional Aesthetics Rest on a Mistake?," *Mind* (1958).

[2]Stewart Buettner, *American Art Theory* (Ann Arbor: University of Michigan Research Press, 1981), pp. ix–x.

If this point about Buettner's distinction is to have any interest for us, it has to amount to more than the recognition of the obvious fact that one person can wear two hats, that a professional philosopher, for example, can write for the philosophical journals on Monday, Wednesday, and Friday, and then write criticism for the art and literary magazines the rest of the week. What has to be shown is that the kind of procedure that is characteristic of the critical, the appreciative, and the art-historical discussion of particular artists and works, styles, and the like is sometimes an integral part of the philosophical investigation of the arts, and, conversely, that philosophical issues and contentions often enter into the discussion of artists, critics, and historians, even if the philosophical character of those issues and contentions is frequently not recognized. Granted that this kind of distinction is important, it remains to show why it is important and also how it resolves itself into additional distinctions of a complexity not made out by Buettner.

Before we can say much about theories in the arts, we have to say something about just what it is we are willing to call a theory. One paradigm of what a theory is or ought to be is frequently taken from the physical sciences, where we think of the theory of mechanics, atomic theory, quantum theory, and so on. Aesthetic theories are only too obviously different from these; such models do not even represent all the different varieties of scientific theories, biological theories, and theories in the social sciences, for example. The examples of the paradigmatic theories of physics will, nevertheless, allow us to make three important points about theories.

In the first place, these theories aim at a high level of generality; they seek to tell us something about the nature and behavior of *all* things of a certain sort; e.g., Newtonian mechanics defines and relates the notions of velocity, acceleration, mass, and force for *all* bodies whatsoever. This is not to say, of course, that such laws and theories are generalizations arrived at inductively. In the second place, a theory involves several concepts or notions that are represented as logically interrelated. Mechanics, to use the Newtonian example once again, can be formulated with the concepts of space, time, and mass as its primitive concepts, and the ideas of velocity, acceleration, and force can then be introduced in terms of them; the familiar laws of motion then state the relations between all those concepts.

Finally, no theory is self-explanatory or carries the conditions of its application within itself. These theories exist within a context of scientific tradition and practice that determines how the theory is to be used. To make anything of classical mechanics, one must know how velocities and masses are to be measured, how the appropriate mathematics is to be applied and results calculated; and one must also be aware of the limitations on the theory's application and how it does not work for velocities approaching the speed of light, for certain subatomic phenomena, and so on. One does not learn physics merely by learning the statement of its theories, for one must in addition learn something of the problems the theory was designed to solve, how the theory works to describe and explain particular phenomena, how experiments are set up in the laboratory, and, in short, how one becomes a participant in that human activity we call physical science.

Despite the great differences between physical theory and aesthetic theory, there is something to be learned about the latter from what we have just said about generality, logical structure, and practice in the former. To understand an aesthetic theory, we must know something about the human practice in which it is embedded. This remark is no more than a reminder of what we have learned from Wittgenstein, that an expression can have a sense only in the context of an activity, that is, a language game or even a form of life, if you will. This point needs repeating only because it is so often overlooked by philosophers and aestheticians who go on as if their theories and comments can be understood in isolation from any context in which they might have a role to play.

Both Buettner's art theories and aesthetic theories are frequently encapsulated in the formula "Art is . . .," where the ellipsis is satisfied by the meat of the theory, "imitation," "expression," "significant form," or whatever it happens to be. Sometimes the theory may instead be a theory of some subclass of art, and then we find corresponding formulas such as "Poetry is the expression of the imagination," and "Sculpture is the abstract reconstruction of the planes and volumes that determine form." We should be struck by the fact that these theories all have the same grammatical form in that they all take the form of generalizations about either the whole of art or one of the arts. But if we must understand an expression—or an entire theory—in terms of the role it plays in the context of a practice, then the fact that these theoretical expressions share a common surface grammar is not necessarily a clue to how they are actually used and hence how they must actually be understood.

How are they to be understood? Or, better, how can they be understood? Consider the contention that sculpture is the abstract reconstruction of the planes and volumes that determine form. Here we can think of several situations in which this remark could be made. Imagine this being said by a teacher to a student in the studio as a way of encouraging the student to sculpt in a certain way—perhaps the teacher is trying to wean the student away from the classicism of Canova or the beaux arts tradition of Harriet Hosmer to something more characteristically twentieth century. Now imagine the remark being made by a lecturer explaining twentieth-century developments to a popular audience where the intention is not to influence anyone's sculptural practice, but is instead to point out to the audience the significant differences between, say, Canova and Henry Moore. As a matter of fact, the statement was made by Umberto Boccioni as part of his Futurist Manifesto.[3]

We have now indicated three distinct situations or contexts that determine three distinct uses of the common formula "Sculpture is . . ." In one case it is an instruction for using hammer and chisel to achieve certain results and is roughly equivalent to "Try to get it to come out this way rather than that." In the second case it comes to the advice "If you wish to understand and appreciate some of the more influential trends in twentieth-century sculpture, look for and concentrate on these features." In the third situation Boccioni in his manifesto is expressing a decision or an intention to sculpt in a certain fashion.

In none of these contexts does the formula carry with it any high level of generality. If the instructor finds that the students have little feel for modern abstract values, students may be encouraged in other directions or advised to seek another studio more congenial to their talents and inclinations. Art historians lecturing to their audience need not, and probably would not, commit themselves to the claim that theirs is the

---

[3]The complete statement is "The aim of sculpture is the abstract reconstruction of the planes and volumes which determine form, not their figurative value": Umberto Boccioni, "Technical Manifesto of Futurist Sculpture," in *Modern Artists on Art*, ed. Robert L. Herbert (Englewood Cliffs, N.J.: Prentice-Hall, 1964), p. 55.

only thing going on in recent sculpture. Nor can we understand Boccioni to be making a truth claim about all sculptural art; his words, after all, are a *manifesto*. He may even be charitable enough to say, although disapprovingly, that others are quite free to go their own way.

It is only by sorting out the various roles that such expressions play and by getting some sense of the various contexts that determine their roles that we can begin to assess and evaluate them; needless to say, it is the context of their use that determines what is relevant to that assessment. Is the instructor giving the student good advice, and is this the most effective way to get the student to do what is wanted? This is a different question from the one we ask of the lecturer when we want to know whether he or she has focused on those features of recent sculpture that will in fact put it all in the best perspective for us and thereby help us to a better understanding of the art of this century. Our concern with the manifesto is again of a different kind: has Boccioni committed himself to a worthwhile project, and will we as artists want to follow him in that direction?

At this point in the discussion it may be tempting to suppose that what is wanted to answer these questions is some higher-level theory of aesthetic value in general, a theory about what determines significance and what is artistically worthwhile. It can thus be made to appear that an art theory presupposes a philosophical aesthetic theory. I shall return to a discussion of this point.

Boccioni's formula about sculpture is certainly one that Buettner would comprehend under the heading of art theory, for all of the uses that we have imagined for it do aim at calling our attention to particular examples of art, to particular movements within art, or the work of particular artists for the advancement of appreciation and, I would add, the practice of the art itself.

There may, however, be something a bit out of order, if not pretentious, in calling such a statement a theory; for one thing, we have seen that we can understand the formula only in particular contexts, and in them we find none of the generality that characterizes other theories. Nor in Boccioni do we find his "definition" of sculpture linked to other notions so as to form a systematic network of ideas to help us in understanding his program. What we do find is a species of argument for his position that consists in pejorative descriptions of traditional sculpture that amount to the contention that the work of the past that Boccioni sees as based on the Greeks and Michelangelo has lost its vitality and that something new is needed. But this kind of reason-giving does not show the kind of logical linking of ideas characteristic of so much scientific theory.

It is certainly not the sort of thing that we find, for example, in Aristotle's *Poetics*. Aristotle maps for us a system of relationships between the plot structure of tragedy, the kinds of incidents that produce the tragic emotions of pity and fear, and the kinds of characters that can play appropriate roles in these incidents. This systematic mapping of dramatic relationships allows Aristotle to explain how a tragedy works and why some plays are better than others. Whether it is an adequate representation and explanation of what we know of Greek drama is not to the point; there is still every reason to describe it as a theory.

Should we describe the *Poetics*, in Buettner's terms, as aesthetic theory or as art theory? Aristotle, to be sure, was a professional philosopher, but the *Poetics* does not offer a general theory of art nor even a general theory of poetry; in the form that we have, it addresses only tragedy (although a lost second book may have been about comedy). There is reason to suppose that it was designed to further the appreciation of drama, at least of tragedy, and may even have been intended as a guide for authors. This is additional reinforcement of my contention that while Buettner's distinction between types of theory points to something important, the profession of the theorist is quite irrelevant to it.

Let us turn now to aesthetic theory, those philosophical theories of art and beauty. It is by no means clear just exactly what a philosophical theory of art is. One way to construe such a theory is to take it as a definition. The formula common to so many theories, "Art is . . .," is thus often understood to be a statement of the properties that all works of art and only works of art have in common by virtue of which they are works of art, or to put it in the formal mode, a statement of the necessary and sufficient conditions for the application of the word "art." Conceived of as definitions, philosophical theories of art and aesthetics have frequently been supposed to allow us to distinguish art from what is not art. If we do not have a definition of art, it has been claimed, we will be unable to delimit a subject matter for art history, art criticism, and so on.[4] Theories are also required, it has been thought, to provide standards of aesthetic and artistic value and to provide philosophical justification for value judgments. It has been said in addition that theories are needed to determine what is and what is not relevant to the understanding, interpretation, and appreciation of works of art.

The standard objections to this kind of theory as definition have too often been ill-conceived. It won't do to claim that such a definition is fated to be either too wide or too narrow, admitting things as art that are not or eliminating things that clearly are art, before we have a pretty good idea of what can qualify as a viable candidate for a defining characteristic. Such a characteristic certainly cannot be anything such as rhyme scheme, space composition, or harmonic intervals. Note that it is false to say that this painting has such and such a rhyme scheme, and consequently, the denial that at this level all works of art have something in common is simply unintelligible.

To forestall a possible objection, it should be pointed out that not infrequently works of art of one form are described in the vocabulary appropriate to another form. Thus we sometimes speak of the *rhythm* of the fenestration of an architectural facade or of the poet's use of *chiaroscuro* in the "painting" of his subject. I would suggest, however, that these appropriations or borrowings of words that have their home base somewhere else are properly understood as metaphorical, or better, as secondary uses of those bits of language, and one cannot make theory out of that.

Nor do we fare any better if we give up the search for common defining properties among such "directly exhibited" features of works of art as rhyme scheme in favor of seeking them in the background of artists' intentions.[5] The only way to understand and identify an intention is in terms of what it is an intention to do. The intention of the

---

[4]This claim has been made, for example, by Lewis K. Zerby, "A Reconsideration of the Role of Theory in Aesthetics—a Reply to Morris Weitz," *Journal of Aesthetics and Art Criticism* (1957).

[5]Maurice Mandelbaum ("Family Resemblances and Generalization Concerning the Arts," *American Philosophical Quarterly*, vol. 2, no. 3 [1965]) argued that Wittgenstein's notion of family resemblance could not be used as an objection to the search for definition in the arts on the grounds (1) that the only properties between which Wittgenstein sees a family resemblance are "directly exhibited" ones, (2) that sharing "directly exhibited" properties is not sufficient to justify calling different things by the same name, and (3) that we may need to seek the defining properties of art in the nonexhibited intentions and purposes of artists.

(continued)

poet, then, is to write a poem with such and such a rhyme scheme, the intention of the painter is to paint a canvas with this kind of space composition, and so on. What we find, consequently, is that the very same diversity and logical disparity among the characteristics of works of art is duplicated at the level of intentions.

As a matter of fact, theories and definitions of art have never been formulated in terms of the particulars of the various arts such as rhyme scheme, space composition, and the like. Instead we are more likely to find much broader notions such as imitation, expression, significant form, and their ilk, which are intended to have application across the full range of the arts.

Again the question is not the one of mistakenly trying to specify necessary and sufficient conditions for what is really a family resemblance concept. The theory that art is imitation is not the false generalization that all art is representational, nor is the theory that art is expression the commonplace that artists frequently are inspired by their emotional responses to situations they have lived through. The former is embedded in a whole metaphysics of reality (e.g., Plato), and the latter presupposes an entire philosophical psychology and philosophy of language and communication (e.g., Croce and Collingwood).

It is in theories such as these that we find the generality and web of logical relations typical of our paradigmatic theories. One aim of these theories is to relate art to other aspects of the world and human life and to explain the nature of artistic and aesthetic value. There nevertheless remain questions about how we are to understand and apply these theories. If we are to pursue the analogy with physical theories, then we should expect, indeed demand, that these theories have a use and an application. We should expect them to help us to understand the phenomena of art. We must remember that those phenomena are simply the entirety of the human practices in which art is embedded, that is, practices of painting, writing, composition, commissioning, criticizing, appreciating, writing art history, and so on.

It seems to me that there are at least two major difficulties with these philosophical theories of art and aesthetics. The phenomena of art are diverse and, indeed, logically diverse; that is, the characteristics of painting cannot intelligibly be ascribed to poetry in a way that could serve theory, and so on. We would thus expect the terms of the theory to be just as diverse as the phenomena it is supposed to explain. But any general theory seeks to unify a range of phenomena; it seeks the unity in variety, the common form behind an apparently disparate variety of phenomena. This is certainly true of much scientific theory. Newton was not content merely to describe and catalogue the various kinds of motion, e.g., that stones fall straight down, projectiles trace parabolas, planets move in ellipses, etc., but was able to show that these are all special cases of a more fundamental set of basic laws. Newton's scientific achievement was in part the result of the introduction of a new set of concepts for dealing with motion. And we must remind ourselves that a new set of concepts must bring with it a new practice; the new way of thinking about motion must bring with it new ways of measuring, predicting, conducting experiments, and so on.

Mandelbaum, however, has seriously misunderstood Wittgenstein. Wittgenstein does not restrict family resemblances to "directly exhibited" properties—the concept of number is a family resemblance concept—and he never attempts to use it as a justification for calling different things by the same name, but only as a description of how it often is with our language. I have discussed Mandelbaum's paper as well as other problems of definition in more detail in *But Is It Art?* (Oxford: Basil Blackwell, 1984), especially chapter 2.

When we try to apply this conception of theory to the explanation of human practices, whether artistic or otherwise, certain special problems arise. What a theory would be called upon to explain is not simply some different set of *phenomena*, but human *practices*, that is, what we do. We must remind ourselves that works of art are not just there in the world, like the planets and their motions, waiting to be investigated, but are instead the intentional products of artists and are inseparably connected with the reactions of audiences; they are part and parcel of a web of human practices. The kind of theory I have been talking about will have to understand the diversity of actual practices as surface appearance hiding some underlying unity that it is the task of the theory to reveal. In other words, it will be committed to showing that what we are doing is not what we thought we were doing, that our practices were not what we took them to be. (I thought I was just being nice to the chap, but it seems I was really manifesting latent sexual desire, or seeking ego satisfaction, or the like.)

The basic notions of Newtonian mechanics, mass, velocity, etc., are new, technical terms introduced into the language together with their criteria of application as part of the theory. Sexual desire and self-interest are notions that already have a place in our language and represent only two of many possible motives with which we are familiar and between which we can discriminate. The contention that my "just being nice" is really a case of ego satisfaction can be saved from obvious falsehood only by stretching the notion of self-interest completely out of shape and draining it of all content. We have to reject the assumption that behind our practices there is a latent essence that will make everything clear once it is brought to light. With respect to human beings and human practices, we can say that nothing is hidden,[6] at least not in any philosophically significant way.

The concepts that make up the stuff of so many philosophical theories of art and aesthetics (e.g., imitation/representation, expression of emotion, form) are notions that already have a place in the language, and we should be able to distinguish between an artist expressing his feelings in his work and one who is concerned, say, only with problems of formal design. The expression theory saves itself from empirical disconfirmation not by making the notion of expression vacuous, but by making expression into a technical notion by embedding it in a more general philosophical theory. The problem with this latter move is that the philosophical theory of art and aesthetics is precisely that, a *philosophical* theory grounded in metaphysics, epistemology, and all the rest of what we think of as the core of the philosophical tradition. As part of a general philosophical theory, the aesthetic theory shares in all the conceptual confusion that is the trademark of that kind of thinking. A theory that results from conceptual confusion can have no use or application, no role to play in the stream of life; it is language gone on holiday, it is like an idling wheel that does not work, to parade all the familiar conceits.[7]

Nor can aesthetic theories do for us what has been wanted of them. No theory can help us pick out works of art from things that are not art. The uses of the word "art" are more subtle and complex than most theorists have intimated and are inextricably

---

[6]This expression is an invitation to refer to Norman Malcolm's recent book *Nothing Is Hidden* (Oxford: Basil Blackwell, 1986) for an extended examination of this idea in the work of Wittgenstein.

[7]It should be obvious that the view of philosophy, of its problems, methods, and theories, expressed in this paper follow that of Wittgenstein in the *Philosophical Investigations*.

tied to practices of evaluation and appreciation.[8] Evaluation and appreciation depend upon our reactions to works of art, and our reactions are not determined by any theory. Neither can a philosophical theory justify our value judgments—theory can't show that our ways of dealing with art and reacting to it are the correct ones.

It has to remain a curious fact, then, that philosophical theories of art and aesthetics have sometimes apparently played a role in the practical affairs of art. Clive Bell's theory of art as significant form is a case in point. It is generally recognized that Bell was influenced by G. E. Moore, and, following Moore, the term "significant form" is doubtless intended to denote a simple, unanalyzable, and hence indefinable quality that not all of us are capable of apprehending. The philosophical hopelessness of all that needs no additional comment. But "significant form" nevertheless did play a role in practical criticism; Bell did put it to use in explaining and defending Postimpressionist painting. How are we to account for this?

I suggest that it can be accounted for very simply. When Bell got around to applying his theory, that is, to practical criticism, all the philosophical baggage of the theory was simply set aside, and the notion of "form" was cashed in terms of relations of line, mass, shape, and color, and the design and composition that can be constructed out of them, notions that were already perfectly familiar to artists even if their audience had never paid much attention to them. Thus Bell could come to grips with the particulars of paint and canvas when he talked about how Cézanne painted mountains, how his forms are like Giotto's, and how both painters differ from Raphael. The modifier "significant" merely trades upon our nontheoretical sense of the difference between good, bad, and better. To describe a painting as having significant form, then, is to say that it makes good use of the formal elements of painting by contrast with one that, let us say, tries to get by solely on its historical, literary, or sentimental connotations.

Another interesting example of a philosophical theory that has had a considerable practical impact is John Dewey's theory of art as experience. Dewey's book *Art as Experience* was published in 1934 and was read and discussed by a number of American artists during the thirties and forties. The reception of the book and its subsequent influence has been traced in some detail by Stewart Buettner.[9] Even if the theory had no *direct* influence on the practice of American artists, it served to bring into focus many ideas that were already in the air and to articulate thoughts that artists were already thinking. Thomas Hart Benton, for one, was both thoroughly familiar with Dewey and sympathetic to his ideas, and it was thus easy enough to read *Art as Experience* as providing a justification for American Regionalism. Buettner also suggests that *Art as Experience* is consistent with Action Painting, and may have had some indirect influence on that movement. It is known, in addition, that the book did have an influence on some of the administrators of the Federal Art Project and encouraged them in their support of American artists during the Depression.

Dewey's book, like the rest of his thought, is philosophically exasperating. It is never clear how we are supposed to understand his use of the word "experience" or even whether he has provided a use for it. The word "experience" comes into our language

[8]See *But Is It Art?*, chapter 3.
[9]Stewart Buettner, "John Dewey and the Visual Arts in America," *Journal of Aesthetics and Art Criticism* (Summer 1975).

in many different ways. I may relate the intriguing experience I had the other day ("When on my way to the university, this stunning blonde in the open touring car pulled up and said . . ."), or we read the notice that says, "Dishwasher wanted, no experience necessary." "Experience" by and large does duty for things that have happened to us, events we have lived through, skills we have acquired, and the like, but Dewey's notion of experience as an entity with an ontological status all its own is a mare's nest and, I suspect, is at least partially planted in the tradition of Cartesianism that he wanted to abjure.

An ontology and metaphysics of experience fares no better than Bell's appeal to unanalyzable qualities, but it was evidently not the metaphysics of *Art as Experience* that affected American artists. Dewey's book is full of remarks to the effect that art belongs in the mainstream of life and not just museums, those "beauty parlors of civilization," and that artists should engage themselves in the fullness of life at all its levels. A remark such as "But one of the functions of art is precisely to sap the moralistic timidity that causes the mind to shy away from some materials and refuse to admit them into the clear and purifying light of perceptual consciousness" was welcomed as a justification of the artistic subjects dear to the Regionalists and to the muckraking and reforming tendencies of Depression era artists out to exalt the working classes and to portray the seamier underside of American life.

The remark just cited is a useful one for emphasizing the point that our understanding of an expression must be a function of the context of its use. We understand Dewey's statement in that we know how to use it, that is, we can describe situations in which it would have a use, but we do not understand what anyone means by it in abstraction from all specified contexts. The concerns of American artists in the 1930s provided one such context in which the statement could function as a defense of their themes and as an encouragement to go on with their artistic program. We can also easily imagine others. Such a statement—its anachronistic tone aside—could just as well have served as a defense of the introduction of Christian themes into the art of a late antiquity still dominated by paganism. Or it could have played a role in the debate about the increasing tendency to treat religious themes naturalistically in the fifteenth century by contrast to the otherworldly styles of the preceding periods. And doubtless other examples will not be wanting. Without some context that determines a use, Dewey's statement is quite empty and devoid of content.

If I am right that it was these various reflections and admonitions rather than the philosophical theory itself that made the impact on the American art scene, then it becomes clear that all those remarks are logically quite independent of any assumptions about the ontology of experience. That an artist should undertake to work in the way that he does or to concern himself with this or that subject matter neither follows from the contention that experience arises from tensions between a living organism and its environment nor presupposes it as a condition of intelligibility. Dewey's comments about the proper place and role of artists and art in society could be understood and advocated by anyone innocent of philosophical theory in general and his version of pragmatism in particular.

I have suggested that what Buettner calls art theories need have little about them that is theoretical in any interesting sense, and I have also suggested that philosophical theories of aesthetics are conceptual confusions and that when we try to untangle and apply them, they tend to turn into particular remarks and comments for particular occasions, This does not entail that there is no place for serious thinking, for rational reflection, even for philosophy, about matters of art and aesthetics; but it does mean that the kind of thinking and the kind of philosophy required must not take the form they have taken in so much of the aesthetic theory we are familiar with. What is wanted instead is, first, a closer look at the problems that a theory was generated to solve. Are these problems themselves perhaps the result of conceptual confusion, of a failure to understand something about the workings of our language? Are the problems really the kind that a theory can solve? (Do we really need a *theory* to tell us when something is a work of art or when one work is better than another?)

Along with raising questions such as these goes the need for conceptual clarification. There is, for example, a belief widely shared among philosophers that all human action and everything that is a product of intentional action requires *interpretation* if it is to be intelligible. But interpreting is something we have to do when we fail to understand what someone means or what he is up to when he speaks or acts. Interpretation has to stand in contrast to the immediate understanding, seeing, hearing, etc., of what is going on. Interpretation makes no sense unless there is a bedrock of more fundamental reaction (seeing, reading, hearing, understanding, etc.). If everything has to be interpreted, then we could never find our feet with our own cultural practices.

Examples of the importance of conceptual clarification in the philosophy of art and aesthetics can be multiplied many times over, but one of its most useful applications is in the sorting out of the different kinds of expressions found in theorizing and the different uses to which they can be put. We must be prepared to distinguish the conclusion of an argument from a grammatical remark, a conceptual issue from an empirical generalization, and expressions of advice, evaluation, intention, and so on from all the others. I have tried to do a certain amount of this in this paper, in order to repeat a suggestion made earlier that only when such logical sorting out is done can we assess the merits of whatever is being said.

There is yet another project that may fall under the heading of philosophy, and that is taking a careful look at the place of art and its importance in our lives. What roles have the arts played in life in the past, and what roles do they play now? What do we want from the arts, and what are their possibilities for entering into our lives in significant ways? These are questions that recent theory, especially analytical philosophy of art, has tended to ignore. These questions lead us into a kind of cultural criticism that is of the greatest importance, but one that must be carried out in the language that belongs to our ordinary life and functions in our day-to-day human relationships rather than in the jargon borrowed from some philosophical system that has no role in the very circumstances it is supposed to illuminate.

When we do aesthetics and the philosophy of art in the ways I have just been describing, the inquiry has to begin with and eventually return to our actual commerce with art—and that includes the practices of artists and critics and all the rest of us who have any concern for that aspect of our lives. It follows from this that the philosopher doing aesthetic theory is also going to have to do a certain amount of Buettner's art theory; he is going to have to consider art in the ways that artists and critics and appreciators do.

When we look at this the other way round, we often find art theorists involved in what are really philosophical questions. Unfortunately it generally proves to be the kind of philosophy that springs from conceptual confusion rather than the kind that seeks to identify and diagnose confusion. An example of this is the critic Clement Greenberg's contention that "it seems to be a law of modernism . . . that the conventions not essential to the viability of a medium be discarded as soon as they are recognized."[10] This looks suspiciously like the philosophical thesis that the various art forms have an essence, and the philosophical problems in that kind of view are well known. There is nothing to indicate that Greenberg was aware of his transition from explaining certain developments in the abstract painting of this century, i.e., art theory, to the move into philosophy, i.e., aesthetic theory.

I will end this paper with two pleas. The first is that discussions of art (or art theory, in Buettner's parlance) be disentangled from philosophical theory and that all who undertake to think seriously about art—artist, critic, historian, and philosopher—learn to recognize when they are taking that step into philosophy and conceptual confusion so that they can back out of it before they become trapped in whatever fly bottle they were headed into. The second plea is that all who undertake to think seriously about art be absolutely clear about what they are doing and prepare themselves to articulate it clearly, whether it be making empirical generalizations about history or styles, doing conceptual analysis, giving advice to artists or their public, or committing themselves to an artistic course of action.

Both of these recommendations chart a difficult course and call for resolve, for, as Wittgenstein pointed out, philosophy is a constant battle against the bewitchment of our intelligence by language.

---

[10]Clement Greenberg, " 'American-Type' Painting," in *Art and Culture: Critical Essays* (Boston: Beacon Press, 1961), p. 208.

Arthur Danto

THE ARTISTIC ENFRANCHISEMENT OF
REAL OBJECTS: THE ARTWORLD

> *Hamlet:*
>   Do you see nothing there?
> *The Queen:*
>   Nothing at all; yet all that is I see.
>
> Shakespeare: Hamlet, Act III, Scene IV

Hamlet and Socrates, though in praise and deprecation respectively, spoke of art as a mirror held up to nature. As with many disagreements in attitude, this one has a factual basis. Socrates saw mirrors as but reflecting what we can already see; so art, insofar as mirrorlike, yields idle accurate duplications of the appearances of things, and is of no cognitive benefit whatever. Hamlet, more acutely, recognized a remarkable feature of reflecting surfaces, namely that they show us what we could not otherwise perceive—our own face and form—and so art, insofar as it is mirrorlike, reveals us to ourselves, and is, even by socratic criteria, of some cognitive utility after all. As a philosopher, however, I find Socrates' discussion defective on other, perhaps less profound grounds than these. If a mirror image of *o* is indeed an imitation of *o*, then, if art is imitation, mirror images are art. But in fact mirroring objects no more is art than returning weapons to a madman is justice; and reference to mirrorings would be just the sly sort of counterinstance we would expect Socrates to bring forward in rebuttal of the theory he instead uses them to illustrate. If that theory requires us to class *these* as art, it thereby shows its inadequacy: "is an imitation" will not do as a sufficient condition for "is art." Yet, perhaps because artists *were* engaged in imitation, in Socrates' time and after, the insufficiency of the theory was not noticed until the invention of photography. Once rejected as a sufficient condition, mimesis was quickly discarded as even a necessary one; and since the achievement of Kandinsky, mimetic features have been relegated to the periphery of critical concern, so much so that some

Arthur Danto, "The Artworld," from The Journal of Philosophy 61, no. 19 (1964): 571–584. *Reprinted by permission of* The Journal of Philosophy *and the author.*

works survive in spite of possessing those virtues, excellence in which was once celebrated as the essence of art, narrowly escaping demotion to mere illustrations.

It is, of course, indispensable in socratic discussion that all participants be masters of the concept up for analysis, since the aim is to match a real defining expression to a term in active use, and the test for adequacy presumably consists in showing that the former analyzes and applies to all and only those things of which the latter is true. The popular disclaimer notwithstanding, then, Socrates' auditors purportedly knew what art was as well as what they liked; and a theory of art, regarded here as a real definition of "Art," is accordingly not to be of great use in helping men to recognize instances of its application. Their antecedent ability to do this is precisely what the adequacy of the theory is to be tested against, the problem being only to make explicit what they already know. It is *our* use of the term that the theory allegedly means to capture, but we are supposed able, in the words of a recent writer, "to separate those objects which are works of art from those which are not, because . . . we know how correctly to use the word 'art' and to apply the phrase 'work of art.' " Theories, on this account, are somewhat like mirror images on Socrates' account, showing forth what we already know, wordy reflections of the actual linguistic practice we are masters in.

But telling artworks from other things is not so simple a matter, even for native speakers, and these days one might not be aware he was on artistic terrain without an artistic theory to tell him so. And part of the reason for this lies in the fact that terrain is constituted artistic in virtue of artistic theories, so that one use of theories, in addition to helping us discriminate art from the rest, consists in making art possible. Glaucon and the others could hardly have known what was art and what not: otherwise they would never have been taken in by mirror images.

I. Suppose one thinks of the discovery of a whole new class of artworks as something analogous to the discovery of a whole new class of facts anywhere, viz., as something for theoreticians to explain. In science, as elsewhere, we often accommodate new facts to old theories via auxiliary hypotheses, a pardonable enough conservatism when the theory in question is deemed too valuable to be jettisoned all at once. Now the Imitation Theory of Art (IT) is, if one but thinks it through, an exceedingly powerful theory, explaining a great many phenomena connected with the causation and evaluation of artworks, bringing a surprising unity into a complex domain. Moreover, it is a simple matter to shore it up against many purported counterinstances by such auxiliary hypotheses as that the artist who deviates from mimeticity is perverse, inept, or mad. Ineptitude, chicanery, or folly are, in fact, testable predications. Suppose, then, tests reveal that these hypotheses fail to hold, that the theory, now beyond repair, must be replaced. And a new theory is worked out, capturing what it can of the old theory's competence, together with the heretofore recalcitrant facts. One might, thinking along these lines, represent certain episodes in the history of art as not dissimilar to certain episodes in the history of science, where a conceptual revolution is being effected and where refusal to countenance certain facts, while in part due to prejudice, inertia, and self-interest, is due also to the fact that a well-established, or at least widely credited theory is being threatened in such a way that all coherence goes.

Some such episode transpired with the advent of post-impressionist paintings. In terms of the prevailing artistic theory (IT), it was impossible to accept these as art unless inept art: otherwise they could be discounted as hoaxes, self-advertisements, or the visual counterparts of madmen's ravings. So to get them accepted *as* art, on a footing with the *Transfiguration* (not to speak of a Landseer stag), required not so much a revolution in taste as a theoretical revision of rather considerable proportions, involving not only the artistic enfranchisement of these objects, but an emphasis upon newly significant features of accepted artworks, so that quite different accounts of their status as artworks would now have to be given. As a result of the new theory's acceptance, not only were post-impressionist paintings taken up as art, but numbers of objects (masks, weapons, etc.) were transferred from anthropological museums (and heterogeneous other places) to *musées des beaux arts*, though, as we would expect from the fact that a criterion for the acceptance of a new theory is that it account for whatever the older one did, nothing had to be transferred out of the *musée des beaux arts*—even if there were internal rearrangements as between storage rooms and exhibition space. Countless native speakers hung upon suburban mantelpieces innumerable replicas of paradigm cases for teaching the expression "work of art" that would have sent their Edwardian forebears into linguistic apoplexy.

To be sure, I distort by speaking of a theory: historically, there were several, all, interestingly enough, more or less defined in terms of the IT. Art-historical complexities must yield before the exigencies of logical exposition, and I shall speak as though there were one replacing theory, partially compensating for historical falsity by choosing one which was actually enunciated. According to it, the artists in question were to be understood not as unsuccessfully imitating real forms but as successfully creating new ones, quite as real as the forms which the older art had been thought, in its best examples, to be creditably imitating. Art, after all, had long since been thought of as creative (Vasari says that God was the first artist), and the post-impressionists were to be explained as genuinely creative, aiming, in Roger Fry's words, "not at illusion but reality." This theory (RT) furnished a whole new mode of looking at painting, old and new. Indeed, one might almost interpret the crude drawing in Van Gogh and Cézanne, the dislocation of form from contour in Rouault and Dufy, the arbitrary use of color planes in Gauguin and the Fauves, as so many ways of drawing attention to the fact that these were *non-imitations*, specifically intended not to deceive. Logically, this would be roughly like printing "Not Legal Tender" across a brilliantly counterfeited dollar bill, the resulting object (counterfeit *cum* inscription) rendered incapable of deceiving anyone. It is not an illusory dollar bill, but then, just because it is non-illusory it does not automatically become a real dollar bill either. It rather occupies a freshly opened area between real objects and real facsimiles of real objects: it is non-facsimile, if one requires a word, and a new contribution to the world. Thus, Van Gogh's *Potato Eaters*, as a consequence of certain unmistakable distortions, turns out to be a non-facsimile of real life potato eaters; and inasmuch as these are not facsimiles of potato eaters Van Gogh's picture, as a non-imitation, had as much right to be called a real object as did its putative subjects. By means of this theory (RT), artworks re-entered the thick of things from which socratic theory (IT) had sought to evict them: if no *more* real than what carpenters wrought, they were at least no *less* real. The Post-Impressionist won a victory in ontology.

It is in terms of RT that we must understand the artworks around us today. Thus Roy Lichtenstein paints comic-strip panels, though ten or twelve feet high. These are reasonably faithful projections onto a gigantesque scale of the homely frames from the daily tabloid, but it is precisely the scale that counts. A skilled engraver might incise *The Virgin and the Chancellor Rollin* on a pinhead, and it would be recognizable as such to the keen of sight, but an engraving of a Barnett Newman on a similar scale would be a blob, disappearing in the reduction. A *photograph* of a Lichtenstein is indiscernible from a photograph of a counterpart panel from *Steve Canyon*; but the photograph fails to capture the scale, and hence is as inaccurate a reproduction as a black-and-white engraving of Botticelli, scale being essential here as color there. Lichtensteins, then, are not imitations but *new entities*, as giant whelks would be. Jasper Johns, by contrast, paints objects with respect to which questions of scale are irrelevant. Yet his objects cannot be imitations, for they have the remarkable property that any intended copy of a member of this class of objects is automatically a member of the class itself, so that these objects are logically inimitable. Thus, a copy of a numeral just *is* that numeral: a painting of 3 is a 3 made of paint. Johns, in addition, paints targets, flags, and maps. Finally, in what I hope are not unwitting footnotes to Plato, two of our pioneers—Robert Rauschenberg and Claes Oldenburg—have made genuine beds.

Rauschenberg's bed hangs on a wall, and is streaked with some desultory house-paint. Oldenburg's bed is a rhomboid, narrower at one end than the other, with what one might speak of as a built-in perspective: ideal for small bedrooms. As beds, these sell at singularly inflated prices, but one *could* sleep in either of them: Rauschenberg has expressed the fear that someone might just climb into his bed and fall asleep. Imagine, now, a certain Testadura—a plain speaker and noted philistine—who is not aware that these are art, and who takes them to be reality simple and pure. He attributes the paintstreaks on Rauschenberg's bed to the slovenliness of the owner, and the bias in the Oldenburg bed to the ineptitude of the builder or the whimsy, perhaps, of whoever had it "custom-made." These would be mistakes, but mistakes of rather an odd kind, and not terribly different from that made by the stunned birds who pecked the sham grapes of Zeuxis. They mistook art for reality, and so has Testadura. But it was meant to *be* reality, according to RT. Can one have mistaken reality for reality? How shall we describe Testadura's error? What, after all, prevents Oldenburg's creation from being a misshapen bed? This is equivalent to asking what makes it art, and with this query we enter a domain of conceptual inquiry where native speakers are poor guides: *they* are lost themselves.

II. To mistake an artwork for a real object is no great feat when an artwork is the real object one mistakes it for. The problem is how to avoid such errors, or to remove them once they are made. The artwork is a bed, and not a bed-illusion; so there is nothing like the traumatic encounter against a flat surface that brought it home to the birds of Zeuxis that they had been duped. Except for the guard cautioning Testadura not to sleep on the artworks, he might never have discovered that this was an artwork and not a bed; and since, after all, one cannot discover that a bed is not a bed, how is Testadura to realize that he has made an error? A certain sort of explanation is required, for the error here is a curiously philosophical one, rather like, if we may assume as correct some well-known views of P. F. Strawson, mistaking a person for a material body when the truth is that a person *is* a material body in the sense that a whole class of predicates, sensibly applicable to material bodies, are sensibly, and by appeal to no different criteria, applicable to persons. So you cannot *discover* that a person is not a material body.

We begin by explaining, perhaps, that the paintstreaks are not to be explained away, that they are *part* of the object, so the object is not a mere bed with—as it happens—streaks of paint spilled over it, but a complex object fabricated out of a bed and some paintstreaks: a paint-bed. Similarly, a person is not a material body with—as it happens—some thoughts superadded, but is a complex entity made up of a body and some conscious states: a conscious-body. Persons, like artworks, must then be taken as irreducible to *parts* of themselves, and are in that sense primitive. Or, more accurately, the paintstreaks are not part of the real object—the bed—which happens to be part of the artwork, but are *like* the bed, part of the artwork as such. And this might be generalized into a rough characterization of artworks that happen to contain real objects as parts of themselves: not every part of an artwork A is part of a real object R when R is part of A and can, moreover, be detached from A and seen *merely* as R. The mistake thus far will have been to mistake A for *part* of itself, namely R, even though it would not be incorrect to say that A is R, that the artwork is a bed. It is the "is" which requires clarification here.

There is an *is* that figures prominently in statements concerning artworks which is not the *is* of either identity or predication; nor is it the *is* of existence, of identification, or some special *is* made up to serve a philosophic end. Nevertheless, it is in common usage, and is readily mastered by children. It is the sense of *is* in accordance with which a child, shown a circle and a triangle and asked which is him and which his sister, will point to the triangle saying "That is me"; or, in response to my question, the person next to me points to the man in purple and says "That one is Lear"; or in the gallery I point, for my companion's benefit, to a spot in the painting before us and say "That white dab is Icarus." We do not mean, in these instances, that whatever is pointed to stands for, or represents, what it is said to be, for the *word* "Icarus" stands for or represents Icarus: yet I would not in the same sense of *is* point to the word and say "That is Icarus." The sentence "That *a* is *b*" is perfectly compatible with "That *a* is not *b*" when the first employs this sense of *is* and the second employs some other, though *a* and *b* are used nonambiguously throughout. Often, indeed, the truth of the first *requires* the truth of the second. The first, in fact, is incompatible with "That *a* is not *b*" only when the *is* is used nonambiguously throughout. For want of a word I shall designate this the *is of artistic identification*; in each case in which it is used, the *a* stands for some specific physical property of, or physical part of, an object; and, finally, it is a necessary condition for something to be an artwork that some part or property of it be designable by the subject of a sentence that employs this special *is*. It is an *is*, incidentally, which has near-relatives in marginal and mythical pronouncements. (Thus, one *is* Quetzalcoatl; those *are* the Pillars of Hercules.)

Let me illustrate. Two painters are asked to decorate the east and west walls of a science library with frescoes to be respectively called *Newton's First Law* and *Newton's Third Law*. These paintings, when finally unveiled, look, scale apart, as follows:

As objects I shall suppose the works to be indiscernible: a black horizontal line on a white ground, equally large in each dimension and element. *B* explains his work as follows: a mass, pressing downward, is met by a mass pressing upward: the lower mass reacts equally and oppositely to the upper one. *A* explains his work as follows: the line through the space is the path of an isolated particle. The path goes from edge to edge, to give the sense of its *going beyond*. If it ended or began within the space, the line would be curved: and it is parallel to the top and bottom edges, for if it were closer to one than to another, there would have to be a force accounting for it, and this is inconsistent with its being the path of an *isolated* particle.

Much follows from these artistic identifications. To regard the middle line as an edge (mass meeting mass) imposes the need to identify the top and bottom half of the picture as rectangles, and as two distinct parts (not necessarily as two masses, for the line could be the edge of *one* mass jutting up—or down—into empty space). If it is an edge, we cannot thus take the entire area of the painting as a single space: it is rather composed of two forms, or one form and a non-form. We could take the entire area as a single space only by taking the middle horizontal as a *line* which is not an edge. But this almost requires a three-dimensional identification of the whole picture: the area can be a flat surface which the line is *above (Jet-flight)*, or *below (Submarine-path)*, or *on (Line)*, or *in (Fissure)*, or *through (Newton's First Law)*—though in this last case the area is not a flat surface but a transparent cross section of absolute space. We could make all these prepositional qualifications clear by imagining perpendicular cross sections to the picture plane. Then, depending upon the applicable prepositional clause, the area is (artistically) interrupted or not by the horizontal element. If we take the line as *through* space, the edges of the picture are not really the edges of the space: the space goes beyond the picture if the line itself does; and we are in the same space as the line is. As *B*, the edges of the picture can be *part* of the picture in case the masses go right to the edges, so that the edges of the picture are *their* edges. In that case, the vertices of the picture would be the vertices of the masses, except that the masses have four vertices more than the picture itself does: here four vertices would be part of the artwork which were not part of the real object. Again, the faces of the masses could be the face of the picture, and in looking at the picture, we are looking at these faces: but *space* has no face, and on the reading of *A* the work has to be read as faceless, and the face of the physical object would not be part of the artwork. Notice here how one artistic identification engenders another artistic identification and how, consistently with a given identification, we are *required* to give others and *precluded* from still others: indeed, a given identification determines how many elements the work is to contain. These different identifications are incompatible with one another, or generally so, and each might be said to make a different artwork, even though each artwork contains the identical real object as part of itself—or at least parts of the identical real object as parts of itself. There are, of course, senseless identifications: no one could, I think, sensibly read the middle horizontal as *Love's Labour's Lost* or *The Ascendency of St. Erasmus*. Finally, notice how acceptance of one identification rather than another is in effect to exchange one *world* for another. We could, indeed, enter a quiet poetic world by identifying the upper area with a clear and cloudless sky, reflected in the still surface of the water below, whiteness kept from whiteness only by the unreal boundary of the horizon.

And now Testadura, having hovered in the wings throughout this discussion, protests that *all he sees is paint*: a white painted oblong with a black line painted across it. And how right he really is: that is all he sees or that anybody can, we aesthetes included. So, if he asks us to show him what there is further to see, to demonstrate through pointing that this is an artwork *(Sea and Sky)*, we cannot comply, for he has overlooked nothing (and it would be absurd to suppose he had, that there was something tiny we could point to and he, peering closely, say "So it is! A work of art after all!"). We cannot help him until he has mastered the *is of artistic identification* and so *constitutes* it a work of art. If he cannot achieve this, he will never look upon artworks: he will be like a child who sees sticks as sticks.

But what about pure abstractions, say something that looks just like A but is entitled No. 7? The 10th Street abstractionist blankly insists that there is nothing here but white paint and black, and none of our literary identifications need apply. What then distinguishes him from Testadura, whose philistine utterances are indiscernible from his? And how can it be an artwork for him and not for Testadura, when they agree that there is nothing that does not meet the eye? The answer, unpopular as it is likely to be to purists of every variety, lies in the fact that this artist has returned to the physicality of paint through an atmosphere compounded of artistic theories and the history of recent and remote painting, elements of which he is trying to refine out of his own work; and as a consequence of this his work belongs in this atmosphere and is part of this history. He has achieved abstraction through rejection of artistic identifications, returning to the real world from which such identifications remove us (he thinks), somewhat in the mode of Ch'ing Yuan, who wrote:

> Before I had studied Zen for thirty years, I saw mountains as mountains and waters as waters. When I arrived at a more intimate knowledge, I came to the point where I saw that mountains are not mountains, and waters are not waters. But now that I have got the very substance I am at rest. For it is just that I see mountains once again as mountains, and waters once again as waters.

His identification of what he has made is logically dependent upon the theories and history he rejects. The difference between his utterance and Testadura's "This is black paint and white paint and nothing more" lies in the fact that he is still using the *is* of artistic identification, so that his use of "That black paint is black paint" is not a tautology. Testadura is not at that stage. To see something as art requires something the eye cannot descry—an atmosphere of artistic theory, a knowledge of the history of art: an artworld.

III. Mr. Andy Warhol, the Pop artist, displays facsimiles of Brillo cartons, piled high, in neat stacks, as in the stockroom of the supermarket. They happen to be of wood, painted to look like cardboard, and why not? To paraphrase the critic of the *Times*, if one may make the facsimile of a human being out of bronze, why not the facsimile of a Brillo carton out of plywood? The cost of these boxes happens to be 2×10^3 that of their homely counterparts in real life—a differential hardly ascribable to their advantage in durability. In fact the Brillo people might, at some slight increase in cost, make their boxes out of plywood without these becoming artworks, and Warhol might make *his* out of cardboard without their ceasing to be art. So we may forget questions of intrinsic value, and ask why the Brillo people cannot manufacture art and why Warhol cannot *but* make artworks. Well, his are made by hand, to be sure. Which is like an insane reversal of Picasso's strategy in pasting the label from a bottle of

Andy Warhol, Campbell Soup Can—Tomato (green and purple version), *1965. Private Collection, USA. The Menil Foundation, Houston.*

Suze onto a drawing, saying as it were that the academic artist, concerned with exact imitation, must always fall short of the real thing: so why not just *use* the real thing? The Pop artist laboriously reproduces machine-made objects by hand, e.g., painting the labels on coffee cans (one can hear the familiar commendation "Entirely made by

Claes Oldenburg, Two Cheeseburgers, with Everything (Dual Hamburgers), 1962. *Burlap soaked in plaster, painted with enamel, 7 × 14 3/4 × 8 5/8". Collection, The Museum of Modern Art, New York. Philip Johnson Fund.*

hand" falling painfully out of the guide's vocabulary when confronted by these objects). But the difference cannot consist in craft: a man who carved pebbles out of stones and carefully constructed a work called *Gravel Pile* might invoke the labor theory of value to account for the price he demands; but the question is, What makes it art? And why need Warhol *make* these things anyway? Why not just scrawl his signature across one? Or crush one up and display it as *Crushed Brillo Box* ("A protest against mechanization . . .") or simply display a Brillo carton as *Uncrushed Brillo Box* ("A bold affirmation of the plastic authenticity of industrial . . .")? Is this man a kind of Midas, turning whatever he touches into the gold of pure art? And the whole world consisting of latent artworks waiting, like the bread and wine of reality, to be trans-figured, through some dark mystery, into the indiscernible flesh and blood of the sacrament? Never mind that the Brillo box may not be good, much less great art. The impressive thing is that it is art at all. But if it is, why are not the indiscernible Brillo boxes that are in the stockroom? Or *has* the whole distinction between art and reality broken down?

Suppose a man collects objects (ready-mades), including a Brillo carton; we praise the exhibit for variety, ingenuity, what you will. Next he exhibits nothing but Brillo cartons, and we criticize it as dull, repetitive, self-plagiarizing—or (more profoundly) claim that he is obsessed by regularity and repetition, as in *Marienbad*. Or he piles them high, leaving a narrow path; we tread our way through the smooth opaque stacks and find it an unsettling experience, and write it up as the closing in of consumer products, confining us as prisoners: or we say he is a modern pyramid builder. True, we don't say these things about the stockboy. But then a stockroom is not an art gallery, and we cannot readily separate the Brillo cartons from the gallery they are in, any more than we can separate the Rauschenberg bed from the paint upon it. Outside the gallery, they are pasteboard cartons. But then, scoured clean of paint, Rauschenberg's bed is a bed, just what it was before it was transformed into art. But then if we think this matter through, we discover that the artist has failed, really and of necessity, to produce a mere real object. He has produced an artwork, his use of real Brillo cartons being but an expansion of the resources available to artists, a contribution to *artists' materials*, as oil paint was, or *tuche*.

What in the end makes the difference between a Brillo box and a work of art consisting of a Brillo Box is a certain theory of art. It is the theory that takes it up into the world of art, and keeps it from collapsing into the real object which it is (in a sense of *is* other than that of artistic identification). Of course, without the theory, one is unlikely to see it as art, and in order to see it as part of the artworld, one must have mastered a good deal of artistic theory as well as a considerable amount of the history of recent New York painting. It could not have been art fifty years ago. But then there could not have been, everything being equal, flight insurance in the Middle Ages, or Etruscan typewriter erasers. The world has to be ready for certain things, the artworld no less than the real one. It is the role of artistic theories, these days as always, to make the artworld, and art, possible. It would, I should think, never have occurred to the painters of Lascaux that they were producing *art* on those walls. Not unless there were neolithic aestheticians.

IV. The artworld stands to the real world in something like the relationship in which the City of God stands to the Earthly City. Certain objects, like certain individuals, enjoy a double citizenship, but there remains, the RT notwithstanding, a fundamental contrast between artworks and real objects. Perhaps this was already dimly sensed by the early framers of the IT who, inchoately realizing the nonreality of art, were perhaps limited only in supposing that the sole way objects had of being other than real is to be sham, so that artworks necessarily had to be imitations of real objects. This was too narrow. So Yeats saw in writing "Once out of nature I shall never take / My bodily form from any natural thing." It is but a matter of choice: and the Brillo box of the artworld may be just the Brillo box of the real one, separated and united by the *is* of artistic identification. But I should like to say some final words about the theories that make artworks possible, and their relationship to one another. In so doing, I shall beg some of the hardest philosophical questions I know.

I shall now think of pairs of predicates related to each other as "opposites," conceding straight off the vagueness of this *demodé* term. Contradictory predicates are not opposites, since one of each of them must apply to every object in the universe, and neither of a pair of opposites need apply to some objects in the universe. An object must first be of a certain kind before either of a pair of opposites applies to it, and then at most and at least one of the opposites must apply to it. So opposites are not contraries, for contraries may both be false of some objects in the universe, but opposites cannot both be false; for of some objects, neither of a pair of opposites *sensibly* applies, unless the object is of the right sort. Then, if the object is of the required kind, the opposites behave as contradictories. If F and non-F are opposites, an object o must be of a certain kind K before either of these sensibly applies; but if o is a member of K, then o either is F or non-F to the exclusion of the other. The class of pairs of opposites that sensibly apply to the ($ô$) Ko I shall designate as the class of *K-relevant predicates*. And a necessary condition for an object to be of a kind K is that at least one pair of K-relevant opposites be sensibly applicable to it. But, in fact, if an object is of kind K, at least and at most one of each K-relevant pair of opposites applies to it.

I am now interested in the K-relevant predicates for the class K of artworks. And let F and non-F be an opposite pair of such predicates. Now it might happen that, throughout an entire period of time, every artwork is non-F. But since nothing thus far is both an artwork and F, it might never occur to anyone that non-F is an artistically relevant predicate. The non-F-ness of artworks goes unmarked. By contrast, all works up to a given time might be G, it never occurring to anyone until that time that something might both be an artwork and non-G; indeed, it might have been thought that G was a *defining trait* of artworks when in fact something might first have to be an artwork before G is sensibly predicable of it—in which case non-G might also be predicable of artworks, and G itself then could not have been a defining trait of this class.

Let G be "is representational" and let F be "is expressionist." At a given time, these and their opposites are perhaps the only artrelevant predicates in critical use. Now letting "+" stand for a given predicate P and "−" for its opposite non-P, we may construct a style matrix more or less as follows:

F	G
+	+
+	−
−	+
−	−

The rows determine available styles, given the active critical vocabulary: representational expressionistic (e.g., Fauvism); representational nonexpressionistic (Ingres); nonrepresentational expressionistic (Abstract Expressionism); nonrepresentational nonexpressionist (hard-edge abstraction). Plainly, as we add artrelevant predicates, we increase the number of available styles at the rate of 2^n. It is, of course, not easy to see in advance which predicates are going to be added or replaced by their opposites, but suppose an artist determines that H shall henceforth be artistically relevant for his paintings. Then, in fact, both H and non-H become artistically relevant for *all* painting, and if his is the first and only painting that is H, every other painting in existence becomes non-H, and the entire community of paintings is enriched, together with a doubling of the available style opportunities. It is this retroactive enrichment of the entities in the artworld that makes it possible to discuss Raphael and De Kooning together, or Lichtenstein and Michelangelo. The greater the variety of artistically relevant predicates, the more complex the individual members of the artworld become; and the more one knows of the entire population of the artworld, the richer one's experience with any of its members.

In this regard, notice that, if there are m artistically relevant predicates, there is always a bottom row with m minuses. This row is apt to be occupied by purists. Having scoured their canvasses clear of what they regard as inessential, they credit themselves with having distilled out the essence of art. But this is just their fallacy: exactly as many artistically relevant predicates stand true of their square monochromes as stand true of any member of the Artworld, and they can *exist* as artworks only insofar as "impure" paintings exist. Strictly speaking, a black square by Reinhardt is artistically as rich as Titian's *Sacred and Profane Love*. This explains how less is more.

Fashion, as it happens, favors certain rows of the style matrix: museums, connoisseurs, and others are makeweights in the Artworld. To insist, or seek to, that all artists become representational, perhaps to gain entry into a specially prestigious exhibition, cuts the available style matrix in half: there are then $2^n/2$ ways of satisfying the requirement, and museums then can exhibit all these "approaches" to the topic they have set. But this is a matter of almost purely sociological interest: one row in the matrix is as legitimate as another. An artistic breakthrough consists, I suppose, in adding the possibility of a column to the matrix. Artists then, with greater or less alacrity, occupy the positions thus opened up: this is a remarkable feature of contemporary art, and for those unfamiliar with the matrix, it is hard, and perhaps impossible, to recognize certain positions as occupied by artworks. Nor would these things be artworks without the theories and the histories of the Artworld.

Brillo boxes enter the artworld with that same tonic incongruity the *commedia dell'arte* characters bring into *Ariadne auf Naxos*. Whatever is the artistically relevant predicate in virtue of which they gain their entry, the rest of the Artworld becomes that much the richer in having the opposite predicate available and applicable to its members. And, to return to the views of Hamlet with which we began this discussion, Brillo boxes may reveal us to ourselves as well as anything might: as a mirror held up to nature, they might serve to catch the conscience of our kings.

Anita Silvers

ONCE UPON A TIME IN THE ARTWORLD

Esthetics is for the artists like ornithology is for the birds.
A saying attributed to the twentieth-century painter Barnett Newman

Soon after World War II, Anglo-American aestheticians considered the history of their field. They gave it a dismal review and an even more dismal prognosis: aesthetic theorizing was dismissed as logically incapable of playing the roles in which it traditionally had been cast. A very influential and typical expression of this conclusion was offered by Morris Weitz in "The Role of Theory in Aesthetics":

> Is aesthetic theory, in the sense of a true definition or set of necessary and sufficient properties of art, possible? If nothing else does, the history of aesthetics itself should give one enormous pause here. For, in spite of the many theories, we seem no nearer our goal today than we were in Plato's time. Each age, each art-movement, each philosophy of art, tries over and over again to establish the stated ideal only to be succeeded by a new or revised theory, rooted, at least in part, in the repudiation of preceding ones.[1]

Overall, the arguments raised against aesthetic theory did not vary very much from Weitz's. If traditional essentialist[2] definitions suffer from an Achilles' heel, it is that the future of art appears always to be nipping away at them. The conviction that the anti-essentialist analytic aestheticians[3] of the postwar period inspired undoubtedly drew strength from the force their thesis brought to bear in explaining a phenomenon that had been familiar throughout the history of art but that seemed to have intensified during the previous century of art history. In essay after essay Weitz and other postwar analytic aestheticians cited this phenomenon: the repetitious overthrow of one aesthet-

---

This essay was written for the second edition of this collection and is being published for the first time. An earlier version was presented at the October 1985 annual meeting of the American Society for Aesthetics.
[1]*The Journal of Aesthetics and Art Criticism* 15 (1956): 27–35.

[2]An essentialist definition is one that purports to define necessary and sufficient conditions for the thing defined. This set of conditions is said to be essential to the thing (or type of thing) defined. Weitz and other analytic aestheticians believed that traditional evaluative aesthetic theories were disguised proposals of essentialist definitions of art.

[3]Analytic aestheticians characteristically employed the philosophical technique of analyzing ordinary language and then accepting or rejecting philosophical theory on the basis of its accuracy in reflecting language use.

ic theory by another, which they took as a history of failure and thus as evidence of why traditional aesthetic theorizing was doomed to fail. They insisted that no essentialist definition could account for this history in which the expression of art theories seemed itself to stimulate artistic progress, but in which progress occurs at the cost of provoking the creation of counterexamples to the theories themselves.

The analytic aestheticians neglected explaining why, during the preceding thousands of years since the Greek philosophers began theorizing about art, the futility of the enterprise was not widely remarked and accepted. Possibly, recent developments in the history of art induced Weitz and his postwar contemporaries to think they viewed the history of aesthetics in a new light. It is fair to say that the century prior to their arrival on the scene seethed with aesthetic revolution. But, arguably, events like the victory of perspectival painting, which marked the Italian Renaissance, had been, relative to their time, equally revolutionary. Yet, far from having little effect, theoretical studies, some by artists of such stature as Leonardo, played a central role in the development of Italian Renaissance art.

Moreover, the aesthetic revolutions of the late nineteenth and early twentieth centuries occurred not in aesthetic theory but in art itself. Although designed to promote the ways in which innovative artists like Cézanne, James Joyce, or John Cage departed abruptly from tradition, the aesthetic theories that served this purpose did not themselves diverge radically from the aesthetic concepts of the eighteenth or earlier centuries. So the succession of aesthetic theories to which Weitz refers is not itself revolutionary; rather, it appears caused by the need to revise theory in order to reflect revolutions in art.

As it happens, the very same art-historical record that seems to render each prevailing aesthetic theory as eventually subject to the creation or discovery of counterexamples also offers counterexamples to the "anything goes" theory on which no distinction can be drawn between art and non-art. There is no difficulty in providing sufficient context and history to be persuasive in claiming that some objects simply could not be viewed as art. For example, it is perfectly plausible to propose that a shovel purchased at the neighborhood ironmonger's in England in 1860 could not, in 1860, have been art, even though an indiscernible shovel purchased by the artist Marcel Duchamp in the twentieth century is art. (Called *In Advance of the Broken Arm*, this latter shovel now is owned by the Yale University Art Gallery.) And if there is a case for believing that a shovel looking just like *In Advance of the Broken Arm* could not have been art in Victorian England, one needs to explain what differentiates the twentieth-century object from the nineteenth-century one. In his 1964 essay "The Artworld," Arthur Danto turned the tide for aesthetic theory by arguing that a decisive factor in determining whether any object counts as art is whether the history of the artworld has rendered the art public ready to accept the object as art.

To see something as art requires something the eye cannot decry—an atmosphere of artistic theory, a knowledge of the history of art: an artworld.[4]

---

[4]"The Artworld" first appeared in *The Journal of Philosophy*, vol. 61 (1964), and is reprinted in this volume. The quotation can also be found on p. 135 of Danto's *The Transfiguration of the Commonplace* (Cambridge: Harvard University Press, 1981).

Marcel Duchamp, In Advance of the Broken Arm. *Yale University Art Gallery, Collection Société Anonyme.*

It is important to notice the distinction Danto introduces in this very influential statement. While artistic theory supplies an atmosphere, art history is afforded the status of knowledge. Consequently, through reference both to theoretical trends and to particular events or facts, art-historical study should be able to function in artworld contexts as a neutral frame or ground, free from the vagaries of artistic revolution, stable rather than transitory. After all, regardless of whether one style of art replaces another, and of whether an aesthetic theory that admits the value of a recent, innovative art style subsequently replaces an aesthetic theory that does not, the fact of the earlier art style's existence cannot itself be eliminated or replaced. Nor, one expects, can the contributions of predecessor to successor, any more than a child's genetic inheritance from its parents is eliminated or replaced just because the child succeeds the parent in certain social roles.

In a later work, *The Transfiguration of the Commonplace*, Danto expands on the function of art-historical explanation:

> It is not . . . simply that he happens to be an artist that Picasso's necktie, but not that of the child, is a work of art, for the thing has to stand in the right relationship to the person who causes it to come into existence, even if he or she happens to be an artist. There was a certain sense of unfairness felt at the time when Warhol piled the Stable Gallery full of his Brillo boxes; for the commonplace Brillo container was actually *designed* by an artist, an Abstract Expressionist driven by need into commercial art; and the question was why Warhol's boxes should have been worth $200 when that man's products were not worth a dime.
>
> In part, the answer to this question has to be historical. Not everything is possible at every time, as Heinrich Wölfflin has written, meaning that certain artworks simply could not be inserted as artworks into certain periods of art history, though it is possible that objects identical to artworks could have been made at that period. A sculptor who produced an archaic torso of Apollo in the period of Praxiteles would have gone hungry, since the artworld by then had evolved so as to exclude this as a possible artwork unless it had been made when appropriate, and lingered on as an antique . . . these examples involve going against the direction of evolution. . . . I am more struck by the reverse direction, in which we are to imagine an object from a much later art-historical stage having emerged at an earlier one. . . . it is not difficult to conceive of objects which, though they would not have been works of art at the time they were made, can have in a later period objects precisely like them which are works of art.[5]

But to what logical role in the formulation and justification of aesthetic judgments does Danto assign art-historical references? He does not seem to offer a thoroughly explicit account. Taken by itself, his caution in not stating exactly how art-historical claims function is not a flaw. For it is preferable to acknowledge the influence of art history on art appreciation, and so reflect what seems to be a fact of most art-critical thinking, even if one is not prepared to delineate precisely the logical standing of beliefs about art history. There are, nevertheless, places where Danto expands and explicates his views, and it is useful to examine these, even if they are less than explicit about how art-historical knowledge functions. One such place is an article published in 1983, "The Appreciation and Interpretation of Works of Art," in which Danto supposes art history to ground interpretation and, by doing so, ground art itself:

> I shall think of interpretations as functions which transform material objects into works of art.

---

[5]Arthur Danto, *The Transfiguration of the Commonplace*, pp. 44–45.

Interpretation is, in effect, the lever with which an object is lifted out of the real world and into the artworld. . . . Only in relation to an interpretation is a material object an artwork, which of course does not entail that what is an artwork is relative in any further interesting way. The artwork a thing becomes may, in fact, have a remarkable stability.[6]

To understand the import of this view, one must comprehend that, in Danto's opinion, there should be no pure aesthetic responses to art. To eliminate interpretation is to blind ourselves, he suggests:

Suppose it is established by psychologists and anthropologists . . . that there is a universal spontaneous aesthetic preference for just the object Duchamp happens to have chosen for *Fountain*, invariably as to questions of meaning and background metaphysics. . . . All this is meant to get us as close as possible to an aesthetic tabula rasa, and my only purpose is to show that nothing remotely like this is available for *Fountain* itself, regardless of whatever delight the object it is materially related to may bring to the uncontaminated seventh sense of newborn babies and bushmen. . . . There is something to which the neonate is blind that the critic of *Blind Man* could see. . . . It is at this, rather than at what we can nakedly aestheticize, that we must look to see what an artwork is. And it will call for a very different sort of aesthetic from what pure aesthetic responses exemplify.[7]

What do interpretations do?

Interpretations pivot on artistic identifications, and these in turn determine which parts and properties of the object in question belong to the work of art into which the interpretation transfigures it. We could as easily characterize interpretations as functions which impose artworks onto material objects, in the sense of determining which properties and parts of the latter are to be taken as part of the work and as significant within the work in a way they characteristically are not outside the work.[8]

But if interpretation is transfigurative in the sense that it transforms objects into works of art,[9] then interpretation itself cannot be grounded in its objects. Given Danto's insistence on the power of interpretation to transform the commonplace into art, what kinds of considerations constrain interpretation and permit us to distinguish between plausible and implausible interpretive accounts? Danto's answer seems to be that art-historical references fulfill this role. Before we explore his proposal more thoroughly, it is useful to illustrate it with at least one case in which historical knowledge appears to function as he suggests.

One interesting case that illustrates the impact of art-historical knowledge on both interpretation and appreciation involves the recent discovery that the American composer Charles Ives tampered with his autograph scores, adding notes and dates in the margins in order to make it seem as if their composition predated the premiere of Stravinsky's *Sacré du Printemps* and consequently anticipated, rather than followed, the polytonal clashes prominent in Stravinsky's work. Historical research recently has revealed that these marginal notations are in Ives' later handwriting and, in some cases, have been inscribed over another date. In reporting this research, the *New York Times* music critic Donal Henahan comments:

---

[6]Danto, "The Appreciation and Interpretation of Works of Art," in *Relativism in the Arts*, ed. Betty Jean Craige (Athens: University of Georgia Press, 1983), p. 37.
[7]Ibid., pp. 36–37.
[8]Ibid., p. 40.
[9]Ibid., p. 43.

In the pantheon of American heroes there is no more appealing figure than Charles Ives, the iconoclastic Yankee insurance man and spare-time composer who, though supposedly unaware of avant-garde developments in European music, anticipated many innovations credited to Debussy, Mahler, Scriabin, Stravinsky, Schoenberg and Hindemith. Indeed, scholarly detective work . . . has verified what music historians long suspected: that Ives worked assiduously and deviously, if often rather clumsily, to create his own legend, predating and secretly "modernizing" many of his scores by adding dissonances, polyrhythms and polytonal passages. . . . it is going to be impossible for many of us ever again to hear an Ives piece in quite the same way as before.[10]

This case suggests that history restrains theory by imposing knowledge to guide and limit interpretation. Consistent with the phenomena manifested by the Ives case, Danto says:

> The interpretation is not something outside the work: work and interpretation arise together in aesthetic consciousness. As interpretation is inseparable from work, it is inseparable from the artist if it is the artist's work.
>   The possible interpretations are constrained by the artist's location in the world, by when and where he lived, by what experiences he could have had.[11]

The Ives case, and others like it (for instance, the failed attempt by the Russian painters Larinov and Goncharova to supersede Picasso and Braque as cubist innovators by changing the dates on their 1912–13 paintings to 1909–10), indicate the dangers of emphasizing the artist's own interpretation, as well as the virtues of focusing on the artist's location in the historical world. The artist's interpretation may be as untruthful as any other. But the historical time of the work's creation seems to provide a point of certain reference. Danto acknowledges this point as follows:

> The work itself could not have come about in many ways at many times and be the work it is. There is a truth to interpretation and a stability to works of art which are not relative at all.[12]

Note that Danto unequivocally takes historical explanation as informing interpretation and appreciation in a way that is prophylactic against relativism. But how is it that art-historical explanation functions to provide a stable ground for truthful claims? In this regard, we should notice Danto's assumption that the history of art manifests an evolutionary pattern. To provide the proper framework, he assumes, art-historical explanation must be developmental: it must show how and why successor styles grow out of their predecessors. Within such a framework, successor artworks are linked to their predecessors by a theory on which the successors are as they are by virtue of their following their predecessors. Thus, although the history of art may appear startlingly revolutionary, as innovations appear again and again to replace art that once upon a time counted but no longer counts as innovative, art-historical theory can make out such change to be intelligible and even systematic. A quotation from Danto's 1973 article "The Last Work of Art: Artworks and Real Things" illustrates this point:

> But Picasso's artworld was ready to receive, at Picasso's hand, a necktie: for he had made a chimpanzee out of a toy, a bull out of a bicycle seat, a goat out of a basket, a venus out of a gasjet: so why not a *tie out of a tie?* It had room not only in the artworld, but in the corpus of the artist, in a way in which the identical object, from the hands of Cézanne, would have had

[10]*New York Times*, February 21, 1988, section 2, p. 1.
[11]Danto, "The Appreciation and Interpretation of Works of Art," p. 44.
[12]Ibid.

room for neither. Cézanne could only have made a mountain out of paint, in the received and traditional manner of such transformations. He did not have the option even of making paint out of paint, in the later manner of the Abstract Expressionists.

Part at least of what Picasso's statement is about is art, and art had not developed appropriately by the time of Cézanne for such a statement to have been intelligible. . . . Picasso's work stands at just the right remove from reality for it to *be* a statement, indeed a statement in part about reality and art sufficiently penetrating to enable its own enfranchisement into the world of art. It enters at a phase of art-history when the consciousness of the difference between reality and art is part of what makes the difference between art and reality.[13]

Danto assumes art evolves, a thought not unique to him. Indeed, developmental models similar to that Danto adopts have been accepted at least since Aristotle and have persisted, have even flourished, to explain the artistic events of the modern and postmodern periods. In the fourth century B.C. Aristotle framed his *Poetics* by offering an account of the historical development of tragedy and by supposing that the development of tragedy finally had attained its natural form in his day.[14] Within this framework he identified the distinctive features of tragic drama by explaining how its archaic forms related to its classical ones and why the innovation through which one form replaced another occurred.

With remarkable similarity, in 1962 the art critic Clement Greenberg explained the development of abstract expressionism as the only way New York painters of the 1940s and 1950s could find "to say something personal, therefore new, therefore worth saying," in order to transcend not only whatever representationalism survived in the cubists but also cubism's "cleanly marked contours, closed and more or less regular shapes, and flat colour."[15] Greenberg offered an explanatory framework according to which "more and more of the conventions of the art of painting have shown themselves to be dispensable," so that "by now it has been established . . . that the irreducible essence of pictorial art consists in but two constitutive conventions or norms: flatness and the delimitation of flatness."[16]

Both Aristotle and Greenberg assume their explanations derive from empirical generalizations, not from evaluative aesthetic theories. Greenberg makes this point explicitly, and Artistotle's approach to understanding tragedy employs some of the investigative strategies he applies to biological entities. It is just this point, that developmental or evolutionary explanation appears always to function descriptively, that promises to permit Danto's artworld theory to escape the shortcomings of essentialism. While an *evaluative* theory on which Warhol's Brillo cartons are more worthy than those designed by the nameless abstract expressionist seems inconsistent, an *explanatory* theory that makes us understand why Warhol's, but not the other artist's, Brillo boxes excite appreciation has no such logical problems. The difference here is that any evaluative theory is hard put to defend inconsistency in the valuation of indiscernibles. However, all an explanatory theory need do is illuminate why people happen to make inconsistent judgments. The explanation may, but need not, show

---

[13]Danto, "The Last Work of Art: Artworks and Real Things," *Theoria* 39 (1973), 10–12.
[14]See the Bywater translation of Aristotle's *Poetics*, reprinted in this volume.
[15]From "After Abstract Expressionism," originally published in *Art International*, vol. 6, no. 8 (1962). Reprinted in the first edition of this work, p. 424.
[16]Ibid., p. 435.

that apparently inconsistent valuations actually are compatible because historical differences render the seemingly identical objects different from one another. Thus, developmental theories can actually feed on revolution rather than be fed upon by it, for such theories display their worth by accounting for innovative change.

Moreover, while facts can contribute to any theory's being displaced by a successor, there is a sense in which facts also insulate descriptive, but not evaluative, theorizing from total revolution. Although one explanatory theory may be replaced by a better confirmed or more illuminating one, the entities to whose behavior both predecessor and successor theories are supposed to apply remain constant. Improvements in observation or refinements in theory itself may revise the way these entities are described. Nevertheless, when we say that one explanatory theory replaces another because it offers a preferable (on some ground or other) explanation (as the Copernican theory replaced the Ptolemaic one, and Einstein's physics succeeded Newton's), we can do so only within a historical framework given stability by the persistence of the objects or events to be explained.

So, although art-historical study itself has evolved from Burckhardt's mid-nineteenth-century political and cultural approach through Berenson's scientific connoisseurship and Wölfflin's formalism at the turn of the century, and Panofsky's iconography[17] in the next generation, to the socioeconomic revisionism of T. J. Clark today, these explanatory methodologies all seem to enjoy a counterrevolutionary stability because they all are supposed to explain the same phenomena, events, or things. While the set of objects whose occurrence must be explained constantly expands, this no more destabilizes the artworld than the constant occurrence of new viruses destabilizes the biological domain. Whereas the counterexemplary force of innovative art can overthrow prevailing evaluative theory, creating the sense that such theorizing is futile as long as art has a future, the worst that innovation can do to historical explanation is really a blessing in disguise, for only if art has a future will it also have a constantly enlarging past, a growing history always in need of further study.

Presumably, an unaccountable aesthetic innovation might force a revolution in prevailing art-historical explanation, but the presumed virtue of its doing so is that, in discovering a hypothesis to explain the innovation along with preceding artworld events, art historians are able to view their field as making progress. So the same phenomena that herald the futility of evaluative aesthetic theories promote the promise of explanatory theories. Thus, the art-historical knowledge that Danto proclaims to be essential to art apparently takes the form of developmental art-historical explanation,[18] which escapes the analytic aestheticians' criticisms because it is descriptive and empirical, merely reporting what has occurred, not attempting, and consequently not failing, to constrain the future of art.

So Danto proposes to return aesthetic theory to center stage by distinguishing between artistic theory, which is atmospheric, and art history, which is a source of knowledge.

---

[17]In "Art, Evolution, and History," Danto observes first that Panofsky holds a "deeply discontinuous theory" of art history, but then goes on to say that Panofsky actually had little to say about the level to which deep interpretation takes us and at which causality takes place. This essay is found in *The Philosophical Disenfranchisement of Art* (New York: Columbia University Press, 1986), pp. 201–203.

[18]"The Artworld," *The Transfiguration of the Commonplace*, and *The Philosophical Disenfranchisement of Art*, passim.

The former pervades the contexts in which aesthetic appreciation occurs so that good and bad aesthetic experiences can be differentiated. The latter grounds the former, introducing intelligibility by offering reasons for changes in valuation or taste. In the selection of such reasons, art-historical studies must contain formulations of historical generalizations and so must include theoretical knowledge as part of their contribution. But to be informative enough to succeed in this role, art-historical theory has to satisfy the following condition: the selection of objects for historical study must be independent of any evaluative aesthetic criteria whose plausibility is, in turn, supported by art-historical examples. To violate this condition is to embed evaluative aesthetic theory in art-historical studies, so that describing the past is the outcome of evaluating it.

As it happens, however, art-historical studies themselves reveal great numbers of cases in which this condition is violated. The British philosopher Roger Scruton insists in "Art History and Aesthetic Judgment" that aesthetic evaluation is indispensable to the practices of art history.

> A more complex case: it used to be thought that Constable's finished paintings constitute his principle *ouevre*; looking at these we might consider Constable to be at the end of a tradition, with a pastoral and at the same time social flavour which sets him in relation to his eighteenth century English forebears. His sketches, by contrast, used to be seen as *incomplete*: as gestures toward the finished product. As a result of a revolution in taste, such sketches as the "Seascape Study with Rain Clouds" (Royal Academy, London) or the landscape sketches in the Victoria and Albert Museum, London, have come to be seen, not as incompleted gestures toward some other thing, but as works of art complete in themselves. Hence Constable is perceived as the great originator of nineteenth-century landscape painting, and as the true forerunner of impressionism.[19]

Scruton observes:

> The aesthetic perception changes the whole history of the subject. This is because the historical order perceived in painting is an aesthetic order, and the creation of a discipline of taste.[20]

Undoubtedly, much art study resembles Scruton's example. Typically, such studies focus either on objects already accepted as canonical, or else on objects that will be revealed in the course of the study as worthy of canonization. Objects of meager value usually are deemed unworthy of study. Often, interest in studying an object waxes and wanes over the centuries as evaluative criteria change, or the lessons drawn from the object shift so dramatically to reflect changes in taste that one wonders whether it can really be the same object that has been studied from century to century.

For instance, the roller coaster reputation of the early Florentine painter Giotto (1266/67–1337) determines whether his work is recommended for study. In 1558 the Renaissance art critic Giorgio Vasari began his "Life of Giotto" by saying:

> In my opinion painters owe to Giotto, the Florentine painter, exactly the same debt they owe to nature, which constantly serves them as a model and whose first and most beautiful objects they are always striving to imitate and reproduce.[21]

[19]This essay appears in Roger Scruton, *The Aesthetic Understanding* (London: Methuen, 1983). The quotation is from p. 177.
[20]Ibid.
[21]Giorgio Vasari, *The Lives of the Artists*, tr. George Bull (Harmondsworth: Penguin, 1965), p. 57.

Vasari goes on to cite Giotto's contribution to the developmental history of art:

> Giotto not only captured his master's style but also began to draw so ably from life that he made a decisive break from the crude traditional Byzantine style and brought to life the great art of painting as we know it today, introducing the technique of drawing accurately from life, which had been neglected for more than two hundred years.[22]

From a perspective of 250 years Giotto appears progressive to Vasari, but with the passage of another 300 years, we find the influential Victorian *Art-Journal* dismissing Giotto:

> The present generation are looking forward—not backward. The only advantage our painters will gain from studying the various works of Giotto is to learn what to avoid, and this, to one class will be something, *if they learn it*.[23]

And also in the nineteenth century Sir Charles Eastlake, president of the Royal Academy and director of the National Gallery, who considered early Florentine pictures to be "full of affectation and grimace," remarked, on the occasion of his acquiring one such painting for the National Gallery:

> I take occasion here to remark that while it is desirable that a museum of pictures should in its completeness contain examples of every school and period, it by no means follows that all such examples are fit objects of study for young artists.[24]

Why, then, did Sir Charles bother to preserve archaic art such as Giotto's? One familiar nineteenth-century argument went like this: Raphael was a great painter, but artists after him were bad. This was taken to indicate the presence of something wonderfully instructive in the work of Raphael's predecessors.[25] But instruction was not necessarily to be gained through emulating earlier work; rather, some artists affected art history by revealing artistic problems that they bequeathed to their successors to solve. Indeed, Danto's own view of how art evolves progressively is not too far removed from this Victorian account. Nevertheless, the typical history of Italian painting written during the Victorian era differs noticeably from our contemporary accounts of the history of Italian painting. It is the divergence of Victorian taste from our own that causes us to remark on this difference, and it is the disparity in the importance attributed to certain works that reveals how infused with valuation are historical renderings of art's past.

One fact that should worry proponents of the evolutionary model of art history accounts is that change in artistic reputation is not uni-directional. Reputations do not necessarily decay progressively. To illustrate this point, we can compare how Giotto was viewed by the most distinguished of Victorian genre painters, the creator of *Paddington Station*, William Frith, and the most respected of Edwardian art theorists, Clive Bell, of the Bloomsbury circle. In 1875 Frith confessed that he was sick of Giotto, whose pictures "are curiosities, and not works of art in the true sense of the

[22]Ibid., p. 58.
[23]My source for this quotation and other information about the Victorian artworld is Francis Haskell, *Rediscoveries in Art* (Ithaca: Cornell University Press, 1976). This quotation appears on p. 100.
[24]Ibid., pp. 101, 103.
[25]Ibid., p. 103.

term."[26] But in his influential 1914 book *Art*, Clive Bell praises Giotto's frescoes for possessing the quality essential to art,[27] saying:

> Go to Santa Croce or the Arena Chapel and admit that if the greatest name in European painting is not Cézanne it is Giotto.[28]

At the same time, Bell contends that

> "Paddington Station" is not a work of art. . . . with the perfection of photographic processes and of the cinematograph, pictures of this sort are becoming otiose.[29]

Is there any methodology for art-historical study that can free it from changes of taste such as those illustrated by the rise and fall and rise of Giotto's reputation? Is any art-historical study scientific? The art historian Mark Roskill believes

> art history is a science, with definite principles and techniques . . . though the artist is long since dead, like the corpse in a mystery.[30]

Roskill says art historians solve puzzles such as

> problems of attribution, "reassembly" of an artist's work leading to the discovery of a virtually unknown genius, the reconstruction of complex works to arrive at an understanding of how they originally looked and were taken in by the viewer, the detection of forgery.[31]

For Roskill, the method of Bernard Berenson exemplifies scientific art history. But there are many instances where Berenson unabashedly relies on his taste as when, after proving that a triptych of Christ, St. Peter, and St. James dates from the last quarter of the thirteenth century, he makes an attribution to Cimabue solely on the ground of Cimabue's being the only painter at that date with enough genius to paint such a masterpiece.[32] Even more revealing of the evaluation infusing his study is his complaint that the work of the Sienese painters of the trecento is difficult to attribute because the quality of these painters' work is so uneven.[33] These examples suggest that even scientific art history does not display sufficient independence from evaluation.

One final example deserves attention. It might be thought that at least the detection of copies and forgeries is scientific. After all, doesn't the discovery that a work with the identifying marks of one artist actually was made by someone else suffice to result in the knowledge that the object is a forgery or at least a copy, not an original work of art? Apparently not. As early as the 1960s Elaine Sturtevant, a founder of the "image appropriation" movement, began making virtually identical copies of works of Duchamp, Warhol, Stella, Lichtenstein, and Oldenburg, and signing them herself. These still are shown and sold as original art. In 1987 Sherrie Levine showed a series entitled "Untitled (After Alexander Rodchenko)," which consisted of photographs of Rodchenko's photographs. What distinguishes the objects made by Sturtevant and Levine from copies or forgeries? That these are deemed art worthy of study results from

[26]Ibid., p. 106.
[27]Clive Bell, *Art* (New York: Capricorn Books, 1958), pp. 17–18.
[28]Ibid., p. 104.
[29]Ibid., p. 23.
[30]Mark Roskill, *What Is Art History?* (New York: Harper and Row, 1976), p. 9.
[31]Ibid., p. 9.
[32]Bernard Berenson, *Studies in Medieval Painting* (New York: Da Capo Press, 1975), p. 25.
[33]Ibid., p. 89.

the application of evaluative criteria derived from the aesthetic of image appropriation.[34]

On the view that has dominated aesthetics since World War II, art history provides knowledge only if evaluative judgment does not defeat the possibility of knowledge. Need we examine every art-historical study to discover whether all are as pervaded by an atmosphere of artistic theory as those we have just reviewed? Even if all existing art-historical methodologies were represented by these cases, it could always be contended that it will be possible in future to formulate a value-free methodology. Fortunately, we can avoid having to deal with speculation by recognizing why art-historical study cannot avoid evaluation.

What if the very purpose art-historical study is purported to serve renders it incapable of extrication from evaluation? From Aristotle through the analytic aestheticians to Danto, from Vasari through Eastlake to Bell, the history of art is seen as a history of revolutionary change, with new types of objects replacing old in a systematic, or at least in a constant, way. Because art-historical accounts characteristically are designed to explain what "is" in terms of what "was," and because in art what "is" often is so innovative that it introduces values foreign to what "was," the past can be relevantly explanatory only if ordered by reference to the values of the future. So art historians seem required to revise history in light of changed valuation as the future of art unfolds. If this is the case, any contribution attributed to art-historical knowledge is undermined by the very weakness in theory the analytic aestheticians decried: the failure of aesthetic theory to constrain the future of art.

And so aesthetic theory once more seems doomed, unless one notices that its failure, in the terms accepted by postwar aestheticians, is by no means a universal fact. Whereas contemporary aestheticians in the Western tradition try to disassociate evaluation from theory in the belief that their field thus will gain stability by this means, style in Chinese art remained stable for nearly two thousand years because of, rather than despite, an unabashedly evaluative aesthetics that succeeded in constraining art.

> The early stage of landscape painting dates back to the Southern and Northern dynasties period (c. 5th–6th cent.). Tsung Ping and Wang Wei were among the early art critics and were especially important for their studies on perspective as well as space-consciousness in Chinese art. Moreover, their discoveries and discussions greatly influenced the future development of Chinese art, and formed decisive guidelines for the artists who followed.
>
> One thousand years earlier than in the West, Tsung Ping had already discovered the realistic approach of including perspective in painting. He used a piece of silk through which he looked out to a distant mountain and then painted the scenery on the silk as it loomed before his eyes. In his treatise on the theory of painting, he notes: "The farther an object recedes, the smaller it appears to your eyes." He goes on to suggest that the painter "detail the near, and suggest the distant."
>
> His contemporary, Wang Wei, on the other hand, was strongly opposed to the idea of emphasizing perspective in painting. Wang thought that if one paints from a fixed spot and paints the immediate scene before him, he can only see the mountain before him, not the many, many mountains beyond his panorama. To him, painting was meant to convey the poetic quality of a scene. Above all, the spiritual quality seen by the mind's eye and the space

---

[34]From an article by Lawrence Weschler entitled "Value: A Fool's Questions," *The New Yorker*, January 18, 1988.

filled by the eternal Ch'i, or Tao, should likewise be rendered and to depict these realities should be the goal which all artists should pursue. Therefore, he advocated that a "bird's eye" view should be adopted in order to liberate the artist from the bondage of perspective view which is too limited in scope. This was an advanced and intellectual point of view. Chinese artists have followed his counsel ever since.[35]

Much about this example, and about the history of Chinese art, needs to be better understood. One important question is why evaluative aesthetic theory prevailed in China but not in the West. But a second important question is whether evaluative theory actually failed in the West. For the crucial difference between the histories of Chinese and Western art may lie in the fact that the fundamental aesthetic theory dominating Western art itself incorporates a criterion valuing change above stability. In this light, aesthetic theorizing can be seen to have prevailed as decisively in the West as in the East, although a crucial difference between the theories has led to different historical results.

In addition, the line of thought initiated by this comparison mitigates the disturbing prognosis offered by Danto in "The Last Work of Art: Artworks and Real Things"[36] and in "The End of Art."[37] For let us suppose that somehow, as Danto predicts, Western art theory bankrupts itself by dissolving the difference between reality and art, or by reaching a point where innovation or progress becomes impossible. Should such an art-historical moment threaten to occur, at least Western art has available the adoption of a conservative aesthetic theory like the Chinese, which in context might appear less revolutionary than some other events in Western art history have seemed. And, at worst, should the world of Western art actually self-destruct, there remain many other traditions for immigrants from our artworld to explore. At any rate, the comparison should remind us that, in drawing philosophical lessons from art's past, we must not overlook how diverse are the stories that legitimately begin "Once upon a time in the artworld."

[35]Da-wei Kwo, *Chinese Brushwork: Its History, Aesthetics, and Techniques* (Montclair, N.J.: Allanheld and Schram, 1981), pp. 66–67.

[36]Danto, op cit., pp. 16–17.

[37]Danto, "The End of Art," in *The Philosophical Disenfranchisement of Art* (New York: Columbia University Press), 1986, pp. 70–81, passim.

George Dickie

THE NEW INSTITUTIONAL THEORY OF ART

The version of the institutional theory that I worked out in 1974 in *Art and the Aesthetic*[1] was defective in several respects, but the institutional approach is, I think, still viable. By an institutional approach I mean the idea that works of art are art as the result of the position they occupy within an institutional framework or context. I have tried in a forthcoming book, *The Art Circle*, to work out a revised version of the theory. In this paper, I shall attempt to give a summary account of the new version of the institutional theory of art.

It should be made clear here at the beginning that the theory of art I am trying to work out is a classificatory one. Some theories of art have assumed that a work of art is necessarily a good thing, but this assumption would leave unaccounted for all the mediocre, bad, and worthless art. It is the wider class of objects which contain the worthless, the indifferent, the mediocre, the good, and the masterpieces about which I am concerned to theorize.

Traditional theories of art place works of art within simple and narrowly-focused networks of relations. The imitation theory, for example, suspends the work of art in a three-place network between artist and subject matter, and the expression theory places the work of art in a two-place network of artist and work. The institutional theory attempts to place the work of art within a multi-placed network of greater complexity than anything envisaged by the various traditional theories. The networks or contexts of the traditional theories are too "thin" to be sufficient. The institutional theory attempts to provide a context which is "thick" enough to do the job. The network of relations or context within which a theory places works of art I shall call "the framework" of that theory.

Despite my reservations about the traditional theories of art, they were, I believe, on the right track about the group of objects they focus on. All of the traditional theories assume that works of art are artifacts, although they differ about the nature of the artifacts. There is, then, a sense in which the institutional approach is a return to the

From Aesthetics, *Proceedings of the Eighth International Wittgenstein Symposium, Part I, edited by Rudolf Haller (Vienna: Holder-Pichler-Temsky, 1984), pp. 57–64. Reprinted with permission of Holder-Pichler-Temsky and the author.*
[1]Dickie, G., *Art and the Aesthetic* (Ithaca and London, 1974).

traditional way of theorizing about art for it too maintains that works of art are artifacts. By the way, what is meant by "artifact" here is the ordinary dictionary definition: "an object made by man, especially with a view to subsequent use." Furthermore, although many are, an artifact need not be a physical object: for example a poem is not a physical object, but it is, nevertheless, an artifact. Still further, things such as performances, for example, improvised dances, are also "made by man" and are, therefore, artifacts.

In the 1950s, first Paul Ziff and then Morris Weitz challenged the assumption of artifactuality, claiming that being an artifact is not a necessary condition of art. Although Ziff's and Weitz's views differ somewhat, they have in common the claim that there is no necessary condition for something's being art, not even artifactuality. Their common view can be called "the new conception of art." This new view conceives of the members of the class of works of art as having no common feature of any theoretical significance. The members of the class are related only by means of similarities: work of art A resembles work of art B and work of art B resembles work of art C, but A does not have to resemble C. According to the new view, an object becomes a work of art by sufficiently resembling a prior-established work of art.

The new conception speaks of sufficient resemblance as the only way that a work of art can come into being. An examination of the new view reveals, however, that it entails that there must be another way than sufficient resemblance to a prior-established work of art for a work of art to come into being. That two ways of becoming art are required by the new conception of art can be shown in the following way. Suppose that work of art A had become art by sufficiently resembling prior-established work of art B. Work of art B would have had to become art by sufficiently resembling an earlier prior-established work of art, call it C. If resemblance to a prior-established work of art is the only way of becoming art, then the way back in time from work of art A to work of art B to work of art C generates an infinite regress of works of art receding into the past. If resemblance to a prior-established work of art were the only way of becoming art, there could be no first work of art and, consequently, there could not be any art at all. Some way of becoming art other than resemblance to a prior-established work is required for resemblance to a prior-established work to function as a way of becoming art. Works of art which become art by sufficiently resembling prior-established works may be called "similarity art." In order for there to be similarity art there must be at least one work of art which did not become art in virtue of its similarity to a prior-established work of art. Consequently, the new conception of art really requires two ways of becoming art: the similarity way and some nonsimilarity way. The new conception is an unacknowledged "double" theory of art.

What is the nature of the nonsimilarity art required by the new conception? Since neither Ziff nor Weitz was aware that their view requires nonsimilarity art, it is not surprising that they said nothing about it. The nature of nonsimilarity art will have to be inferred from the stated theory. First, nonsimilarity art is primary within the theory—there could not be similarity art unless there is first nonsimilarity art. Second, the class of works of art, according to the new conception, consists of two distinct subsets of which one (nonsimilarity art) is more basic than the other (similarity art). Finally, there is nothing in the new conception of art or outside of it which requires nonsimilarity art to be a one-time sort of thing the only function of which is to block the regress and get the art process going. Although nothing in the new conception entails that it is, the only plausible account of the nature of nonsimilarity art that I can think of is that it is art which is art as the result of someone's creating an artifact. This, of course, does not prove that nonsimilarity art is to be identified with what may be called "artifactual art," but artifactual art seems to be the only real contender. The new conception of art involves two distinct kinds of art—artifactual art and similarity art—with the former being primary. Artifactual art is clearly not confined to the beginning of the art process, because such art is being created at the present and has been created throughout the history of art.

Ziff and Weitz demand that if one is to theorize about art, one must produce a theory which encompasses all members of the class of works of art. And according to their view, the members of the class have no common feature or features. Consequently, they claim that one cannot theorize about art in the traditional manner of discovering necessary and sufficient features. The closest they can come to theorizing about art is to say that there is a class of objects to which the terms "art" and "work of art" meaningfully apply and that this class cannot be theoretically characterized further.

The earlier examination of the new conception of art has shown that the class of objects to which the terms "art" and "work of art" meaningfully apply divides into two distinct subclasses of art. This division shows that the class can be theoretically characterized further. The first thing to be noted about the subclasses is that the two activities which generate the two subclasses are very different. Artifactual art is generated by the human activity of making. Similarity art is generated by the human activity of noticing similarities. The strikingly different activities which generate the two subclasses suggest that the two classes are not literally subclasses of a single class. The two classes seem more like a class picked out by the literal uses of a term and a derivative class picked out by the metaphorical uses of the same term. I will not, however, pursue this point here.

Even if one were to agree with Ziff and Weitz that artifactual art and similarity art are both literally art, why should this persuade philosophers to abandon their traditional concern with theorizing about what is in effect artifactual art? From Plato's time forward, philosophers of art have been concerned to theorize about the class of objects which is generated by a particular kind of human making. Philosophers have been interested in these objects precisely because they are human artifacts. The fact that there is another class of objects which is in some way derivative by means of similarities from the class of objects they have traditionally been interested in is not surprising and is no reason to divert philosophers of art from their traditional activity. That traditional activity is the attempt to describe correctly the nature of the making of artifactual art and, consequently, the nature of the objects made. Artifactuality is, in effect, a "built-in" characteristic of the interest of philosophers in works of art.

On the surface anyway, there is no mystery about the making of the great bulk of works of artifactual art; they are crafted in various traditional ways—painted, sculpted, and the like. (Later, I will attempt to go below the surface a bit.) There is, however, a puzzle about the artifactuality of some relatively recent works of art: Duchamp's readymades, found art, and the like. Some deny that such things are art because, they claim, they are not artifacts made by artists. It can, I think, be shown that they are the artifacts of artists. (In *Art and the Aesthetic* I claimed, I now think, mistakenly, that artifactuality is *conferred* on things such as Duchamp's *Fountain* and found art, but I will not discuss this here.)

Typically an artifact is produced by altering some preexisting material: by joining two pieces of material, by cutting some material, by sharpening some material, and so on. This is typically done so that the altered material can be used to do something. When materials are so altered, one has clear cases which neatly fit the dictionary definition of "artifact"—"An object made by man, especially with a view to subsequent use." There are other cases which are less clear-cut. Suppose one picks up a piece of driftwood and without altering it in any way digs a hole or brandishes it at a threatening dog. The unaltered driftwood has been *made* into a digging tool or a weapon by the use to which it is put. These two cases do not conform to the nonnecessary clause of the definition "especially with a view to subsequent use" because they are pressed into service on the spot. There does seem to be a sense in which something is made in these cases, but what is it that has been made if the driftwood is unaltered? In the clear cases in which material is altered, a complex object is produced: the original material is for present purposes a simple object and its being altered produces the complex object— altered material. In the two less clear-cut cases, complex objects have also been made—the wood used as a digging tool and the wood used as a weapon. In neither of the two less clear-cut cases is the driftwood alone the artifact; the artifact in both cases is the driftwood manipulated and used in a certain way. The two cases in question are exactly like the sort of thing that anthropologists have in mind when they speak of unaltered stones found in conjunction with human or human-like fossils as artifacts. The anthropologists assume that the stones were used in some way. The anthropologists have in mind the same notion of a complex object made by the use of a simple (i.e., unaltered) object.

A piece of driftwood may be used in a similar way within the context of the artworld, i.e., picked up and displayed in the way that a painting or a sculpture is displayed. Such a piece of driftwood would be being used as an artistic medium and thereby would become part of the more complex object—the-driftwood-used-as-an-artistic-medium. This complex object would be an artifact of an artworld system. Duchamp's *Fountain* can be understood along the same lines. The urinal (the simple object) is being used as an artistic medium to make *Fountain* (the complex object) which is an artifact within the artworld—Duchamp's artifact. The driftwood would be being used and the urinal was used as artistic media in the way that pigments, marble, and the like are used to make more conventional works of art.

Thus far, I have talked of artifactuality as a necessary condition of art, but this discussion does not distinguish the institutional theory from the traditional theories, as the latter have assumed or implied that being an artifact is a necessary condition of art. In the last paragraph, however, I introduced without explanation the notion of the *artworld*, and it is now time to turn to a discussion of the artworld, for it is this notion which lies at the heart of the institutional theory.

Perhaps the best way to begin a discussion of the artworld is to quote the now-abandoned definition of "work of art" from the earlier version of the institutional theory. "A work of art in the classificatory sense is (1) an artifact (2) a set of the aspects of which has had conferred upon it the status of a candidate for appreciation by some

person or persons acting on behalf of a certain social institution (the artworld)."[2]
Monroe Beardsley has observed that in the discussion which surrounds the definition
in the earlier version of the theory I characterized the artworld as an "established
practice" which is to say, an informal kind of activity. He then goes on to point out that
the quoted definition makes use of such phrases as "conferred status" and "acting on
behalf of." Such phrases typically have application within formal institutions such as
states, corporations, universities, and the like. Beardsley correctly notes that it is a
mistake to use the language of formal institutions to try to describe an informal
institution as I conceive the artworld to be. Beardsley queries, ". . . does it make sense
to speak of acting on behalf of a practice? Status-awarding authority can center in [a
formal institution], but practices, as such, seem to lack the requisite source of
authority."[3]

Accepting Beardsley's criticism, I have abandoned as too formal the notions of *status
conferral* and *acting on behalf of* as well as those aspects of the earlier version which
connect up with these notions. Being a work of art is a status all right, that is, it is the
occupying of a position within the human activity of the artworld. Being a work of art is
not, however, a status which is conferred but is rather a status which is achieved as the
result of creating an artifact within or against the background of the artworld.

The claim is then that works of art are art as the result of the position or place they
occupy within an established practice, namely, the artworld. There are two crucial
questions about the claim. (1) Is the claim true and (2) if the claim is true, how is the
artworld to be described?

The claim is a claim about the existence of a human institution, and the test of its
truth is the same as for any other claim about human organization—the test of
observation. "Seeing" the artworld and the works of art embedded in its structures,
however, is not as easy as "seeing" some of the other human institutions which we are
more accustomed to thinking about.

Arthur Danto has invented an argument which helps somewhat in "seeing" the
structure in which works of art are embedded. (I must note, however, that what Danto
himself "sees" with the use of his argument is quite different from what I "see," but I
will not here attempt to rebut Danto's theory.) My version of Danto's argument runs as
follows. Consider a painting and another object which looks exactly like it but which
was produced accidentally and is, therefore, not a work of art. Or consider *Fountain*
and a urinal which is its twin but is not a work of art. Here are two pairs of objects with
visually indistinguishable elements, but the first element in each pair is a work of art
and the second element is not. The fact that the first element of each pair is a work of
art and the second element is not although the elements of each pair are visually
indistinguishable shows that the first object in each pair must be enmeshed in some
sort of framework or network of relations in which the second element is not. It is the
first element's being enmeshed in the framework which accounts for its being a work of
art, and it is the second element's not being enmeshed in the framework which
accounts for its not being a work of art. The framework in question is not, of course,
visible to the eye in the way that the colors of the two objects are.

[2]Ibid., p. 34.
[3]"Is Art Essentially Institutional?," in *Culture and Art*, Lars Aagaard-Mogensen (ed.) (Atlantic Highlands, N.J. 1976), p. 202.

Some will argue that the *Fountain*/urinal pair does not show anything because *Fountain* is not a work of art. Fortunately, the other hypothetical pair is sufficient to get the argument off the ground. The *Fountain*/urinal pair, however, can also be shown to suffice even if *Fountain* is not a work of art. *Fountain* does not actually have to be a work of art to show the necessity of a context or framework. It is sufficient for the argument that at some time some person mistakenly thought *Fountain* to be a work of art. The framework within which *Fountain* apparently had a place would in this case explain the mistake. And, some persons have thought *Fountain* to be a work of art.

Danto's argument shows that works of art exist within a context or framework, but it does not reveal the nature of the elements which make up the framework. Moreover, many different frameworks are possible. Each of the traditional theories of art, for example, implies its own particular framework. For one example, Susanne Langer's view that "Art is the creation of forms symbolic of human feeling" implies a framework of artist (one who creates) and a specific kind of subject matter (human feeling). And as I noted at the beginning of the paper, the imitation theory and the expression theory each implies a particular framework. Langer's theory and the other traditional theories, however, fall easy prey to counterexamples, and, consequently, none of the frameworks they imply can be the right one. The reason that the traditional theories are easy prey for counterexamples is that the frameworks implied by the theories are too narrowly focused on the artist and various differences of the more obvious characteristics which works of art may have rather than on *all* the framework elements which surround works of art. The result is that it is all too easy to find works of art which lack the properties seized upon by a particular traditional theory as universal and defining.

The frameworks of the traditional theories do lead in the right direction in one respect. Each of the traditional theories conceives of the making of art as a human practice, as an established way of behaving. The framework of each of these theories is conceived of, then, as a cultural phenomenon which persists through time and is repeatable. The persistence of a framework as a cultural practice is enough, I think, to make the traditional theories themselves quasi-institutional. That is to say, each of the traditional theories purports to describe an established cultural practice. In every one of the traditional theories, however, there is only one established role envisioned and that is the role of the artist or the maker of artifacts. And in every case, the artist is seen as the creator of an artifact with a property such as being representative, being symbolic, or being an expression. For the traditional theories the artist role is envisaged as simply that of producing representations, producing symbolic forms, producing expressions, or some such thing. It is this narrow conception of the artist role which is responsible for the ease with which counterexamples can be produced. Since the traditional theories are inadequate, there must be more to the artist role than the producing of any, or even all, of these kinds of things which the traditional theories envisage. What an artist understands and does when he creates a work of art far exceeds the simple understanding and doing entailed by the traditional theories.

Whenever art is created there is, then, an artist who creates it, but an artist always creates for a *public* of some sort. Consequently, the framework must include a role for a *public* to whom art is presented. Of course, for a variety of reasons many works of art are never in fact presented to any public. Some works just never reach their public although their makers intended for them to do so. Some works are withheld from their publics by their creators because they judge them to be in some way inferior and unworthy of presentation. The fact that artists withhold some of their works because they judge them unworthy of presentation shows that the works are things of a *kind* to be presented, otherwise, it would be pointless to judge them unworthy of presentation. Thus, even art not intended for public presentation presupposes a public, for not only is it possible to present it to a public (as sometimes happens), it is a thing of a type which has as a goal presentation to a public. The notion of a public hovers always in the background, even when a given artist refuses to present his work. In those cases in which works of art are withheld from a public, there is what might be called a "double intention"—there is an intention to create a thing of a kind which is presented, but there is also an intention not to actually present it.

But what is an artworld public? Such a public is not just a collection of people. The members of an artworld public are such because they know how to fulfill a role which requires knowledge and understanding similar in many respects to that required of an artist. There are as many different publics as there are different arts, and the knowledge required for one public is different from that required by another public. An example of one bit of knowledge required of the public of stage plays is the understanding of what it is for someone to act a part. Any given member of a public would have a great many such bits of information.

The artist and public roles are the minimum framework for the creation of art, and the two roles in relation may be called "the presentation group." The role of artist has two central aspects: first, a general aspect characteristic of all artists, namely, the awareness that what is created for presentation is art, and, second, the ability to use one or more of a wide variety of art techniques which enable one to create art of a particular kind. Likewise, the role of a public has two central aspects: first, a general aspect characteristic of all publics, namely, the awareness that what is presented to it is art and, second, the abilities and sensitivities which enable one to perceive and understand the particular kind of art with which one is presented.

In almost every actual society which has an institution of art-making, in addition to the roles of artist and public, there will be a number of supplementary artworld roles such as those of critic, art teacher, director, curator, conductor, and many more. The presentation group, i.e., the roles of artist and public in relation, however, constitutes the essential framework for art-making.

Among the more frequent criticisms of *Art and the Aesthetic* was that it failed to show that art-making is institutional because it failed to show that art-making is rule-governed. The underlying assumption of the criticism is that it is rule-governedness which distinguishes institutional practices such as, say, promising from noninstitutional ones such as, say, dog-walking. And it is true that *Art and the Aesthetic* did not bring out the rule-governedness of art-making and this requires correcting. There are rules implicit in the theory developed in the earlier book, but unfortunately I failed to make them explicit. There is no point in discussing the rules governing art-making implicit in the earlier theory, but those of the present revised theory can be stated. Earlier in this paper I argued that artifactuality is a necessary condition for being a work of art. This claim of necessity implies one rule of art-making: if one wishes to make a work of art, one must do so by creating an artifact. Also earlier in this paper I claimed that being a thing of a kind which is presented to an artworld public is a necessary condition for being a work of art. This claim of necessity implies another rule of art-making: if one wishes to create a work of art, one must do so by creating a thing of a kind which is presented to an artworld public. These two rules are jointly sufficient for making works of art.

The question naturally arises as to why the framework described as the institutional one is the correct essential framework rather than some other framework. The framework of the traditional theories is clearly inadequate, but its inadequacy does not prove the correctness of the framework of the present version of the institutional theory. Proving that a theory is true is notoriously difficult to do, although proving that a theory is false is sometimes easy to do. It can be said of the present version of the institutional theory that it is a conception of a framework in which works of art are clearly embedded and that no other plausible framework is in the offing. For lack of a more conclusive argument that the institutional theory's framework is the right one, I shall have to rely on the description of it I have given to function as an argument as to its rightness. If the description is correct, or approximately so, then it should evoke a "that's right" experience in the listener. In the remainder of the paper I shall, in effect, continue my description of the essential framework for the creation of art.

In *Art and the Aesthetic* I talked a great deal about conventions and how they are involved in the institution of art. In that book, I tried to distinguish between what I called "the primary convention" and other "secondary conventions" which are involved in the creation and presentation of art. One example of the so-called secondary conventions discussed there is the Western theatrical convention of concealing stagehands behind the scenery. This Western convention was there contrasted with that of classical Chinese theater in which the stagehand (called the property man) appears on stage during the action of the play and rearranges props and scenery. These two different theatrical solutions for the same task, namely, the employment of stagehands, brings out an essential feature of conventions. Any conventional way of doing something could have been done in a different way.

The failure to realize that things of the kind just discussed are conventions can result in confused theory. For example, it is another convention of Western theater that spectators do not participate in the action of a play. Certain aesthetic-attitude theorists failed to realize that this particular convention is a convention and concluded that the nonparticipation of spectators is a rule derived from aesthetic consciousness and that the rule must not be violated. Such theorists are horrified by Peter Pan's request for the members of the audience to applaud to save Tinkerbell's life. The request, however, merely amounts to the introduction of a new convention which small children, but not some aestheticians, catch on to right away.

There are innumerable conventions involved in the creation and presentation of art, but there is not, as I claimed in my earlier book, a *primary* convention to which all the other conventions are secondary. In effect, in *Art and the Aesthetic* I claimed that not only are there many conventions involved in the creation and presentation of art, but that at bottom the whole activity is completely conventional. But theater, painting, sculpting, and the like, are not ways of doing something which could be done in another way, and, therefore, they are not conventional. If, however, there is no *primary* convention, there is a primary *something* within which the innumerable conventions that there are have a place. What is primary is the understanding shared by all involved that they are engaged in an established activity or practice within which there is a variety of roles: artist roles, public roles, critic roles, director roles, curator roles, and so on. Our artworld consists of the totality of such roles with the roles of artist and public at its core. Described in a somewhat more structured way, the artworld consists of a set of individual artworld systems, each of which contains its own specific artist and public roles plus other roles. For example, painting is one artworld system, theater is another, and so on.

The institution of art, then, involves rules of very different kinds. There are conventional rules which derive from the various conventions employed in presenting and creating art. These rules are subject to change. There are more basic rules which govern the engaging in an activity, and these rules are not conventional. The artifact rule—if one wishes to make a work of art, one must do so by creating an artifact—is not a conventional rule, it states a condition for engaging in a certain kind of practice.

As I remarked earlier, the artifact rule and the other nonconventional rule are sufficient for the creating of art. And, as each rule is necessary, they can be used to formulate a definition of "work of art."

A work of art is an artifact of a kind created to be presented to an artworld public.

This definition explicitly contains the terms "artworld" and "public," both of which have been discussed but not defined in this paper. The definition also involves the notions of *artist* and *artworld system*, both of which have been discussed but not definitionally characterized in this paper. I shall not attempt to define either "artist," "public," "artworld," or "artworld system" here, as I do in my book manuscript, but the definition of "work of art" given here and the definitions of these other four central terms provide the leanest possible description of the institutional theory of art.

To forestall an objection to the definition, let me acknowledge that there are artifacts which are created for presentation to the artworld publics which are not works of art: for example, playbills. Such things are, however, parasitic or secondary to works of art. Works of art are artifacts of a primary kind in this domain, and playbills and the like which are dependent on works of art are artifacts of a secondary kind within this domain. The word "artifact" in the definition should be understood to be referring to artifacts of a primary kind.

The definition of "work of art" given in *Art and the Aesthetic* was, as I affirmed there, circular, although not viciously so. The definition of "work of art" just given is also circular, although again not viciously so. In fact, the definitions of the five central terms constitute a logically circular set of terms.

There is an ideal of noncircular definition which assumes that the meaning of terms used in a definition ought not to lead back to the term originally defined, but rather ought to be or lead to terms which are more basic. The ideal of noncircular definition also assumes that we ought to be able to arrive at terms which are primitive in the sense that they can be known in some nondefinitional way, say, by direct sensory experience or by rational intuition. There may be some sets of definitions which satisfy this ideal, but the definitions of the five central terms of the institutional theory do not. Does this mean that the institutional theory involves a vicious circularity? The circularity of the definitions shows the interdependency of the central notions. These central notions are *inflected*, that is, that they bend in on, presuppose, and support one another. What the definitions reveal is that art-making involves an intricate, correlative structure which cannot be described in the straightforward, linear way envisaged by the ideal of noncircular definition. The inflected nature of art is reflected in the way we learn about art. This learning is sometimes approached through being taught how to be an artist—learning how to draw pictures which can be displayed, for example. This learning is sometimes approached through being taught how to be a member of an artworld public—learning how to look at pictures which are presented as the intentional products of artists. Both approaches teach us about artists, works, and publics all at the same time, for these notions are not independent of one another. I suspect that many areas within the cultural domain also have the same kind of inflected nature that the institution of art has. For example, the area which involves the notions of *law, legislative, executive,* and *judiciary.*

The ideal of noncircular definition holds also that sets of circular definitions cannot be informative. This may be true of some sets of definitions, but it is not, I think, true of the definitions of the institutional theory. For these definitions just mirror the mutually dependent items which constitute the art enterprise, and, thereby, informs us of its inflected nature.

Robert Stecker

THE END OF AN INSTITUTIONAL
DEFINITION OF ART

When George Dickie originally proposed an institutional definition of art, he was offering an alternative to two other views about the definition of art. He opposed traditional definitions which look for defining properties of art in one or more perceptible features shared in common by works of art. He also opposed views like those of Morris Weitz who denied that there are necessary and sufficient conditions for being a work of art.

Dickie has now written a new book[1] which purports to pursue the same goals with an institutional "account" revised in the light of criticism of his earlier definition.

I will argue for three claims: first, if we consider the letter of Dickie's new account, it fails to distinguish works of art from many other artefacts. Second, if we consider its spirit, the new account turns out to be closer to the approach of those who claim that art cannot be defined than to Dickie's own earlier approach. Third, Dickie fails to show that existing in an institutional framework is a necessary condition for being art.

I

Dickie's old project centred on giving a definition of "work of art."[2] While this new account contains something resembling a definition of "work of art," Dickie no longer claims that the main point of his present project is to formulate and defend such a definition. Rather, the main point now is to give "the leanest possible description" of "the essential framework of art" (82) and to argue that works of art can only exist within this framework. The description is summed up in a set of five definitions:

Robert Stecker, "The End of an Institutional Definition of Art," from British Journal of Aesthetics 26, *no. 2 (Spring 1986): 124–132. Reprinted by permission of Oxford University Press.*

[1]George Dickie, *The Art Circle* (New York, 1984). Parenthetical page references are to this work.
[2]See George Dickie, *Art and the Aesthetic* (Ithaca, 1974), pp. 19–52 for the most authoritative statement of the project.

1. An artist is a person who participates with understanding in the making of a work of art (80). 2. A work of art is an artefact of a kind created to be presented to an artworld public (80). 3. A public is a set of persons members of which are prepared in some degree to understand an object which is presented to them (81). 4. The artworld is the totality of artworld systems (81). 5. An artworld system is a framework of the presentation of a work of art by an artist to an artworld public (82).

The most glaring feature of this set of definitions is the circularity of the set. *Artist* is defined in terms of *work of art* and that in turn is defined in terms of *artworld public*. To find out what an artworld public is we look to the definitions of *public* and *the artworld*. *The artworld* is defined in terms of *artworld systems*, and it, in turn, is defined in terms of *artist*, *work of art* and, once again, *artworld public*.

Dickie readily acknowledges the circularity of the set of definitions but denies that this poses a problem. I will return to this issue later in the section. There is a preliminary problem that should be dealt with first.

Dickie is not altogether clear about what his definitions are definitions of. When he introduces his definitions, he usually suggests they are definitions of words or expressions, e.g., "I shall begin with the definition of the term 'artist' " (80). Also, in his discussion of circularity, Dickie speaks exclusively of the definition of words. However, the definitions themselves never mention words. Taken literally, they appear to be attempts to tell us what an artist is, what a work of art is, etc. The definitions themselves suggest that Dickie is more concerned with the nature of art rather than the meaning of certain expressions. Dickie does sometimes describe what he is doing in these terms. He tells us he is trying "to describe the conditions necessary for a particular activity or practice . . . the enterprise of art" (111).

Dickie may think that the nature of art is revealed in the meaning of certain words. However, he does not argue that this is so, and it does not seem obvious that it is. I believe Dickie is mainly concerned with the nature of art. In any case, that is my concern, and so the question I want to answer is: how well do Dickie's definitions of what an artist is, what a work of art is, etc. reveal the nature of art?

We may now return to the circularity of the set of definitions 1–5. Dickie points out that the main reason that this circularity may seem to be a problem is that it renders the set of definitions uninformative. Dickie appears to be in two minds about this problem. On the one hand he says that an informative definition is not needed. (I will be concerned with this claim in section II.) On the other hand, he says, "there is a sense in which the definitions are informative; if they accurately reflect the nature of art and the relations which hold among the various elements of the artworld. . . ."(82).

The set of definitions do give us information. It tells us that works of art are artefacts, are typically made for some public, and so the "enterprise of art" has a role for makers of certain artefacts, for a public they are made for, and for middlemen who facilitate the presentation of the artefacts to the public. The only important notion found in Dickie's definitions that I may seem to have left out is that of artworld system. But in fact that notion has already been captured by pointing out that, given that works of art are typically made for a public, art production creates roles not only for producers but also for consumers and middlemen.

Certainly, these are facts about art as we know it, but does reporting these tell us anything about the nature of art? Granting that works of art are necessarily artefacts, it remains true that many other artefacts exist within systems in which producers' products are presented to consumers via middlemen. Unless artworld systems can be distinguished from non-art artefact presentation systems, the framework Dickie gives us tells us no more than that art resembles many other kinds of artefacts. It is true that Dickie tells us in the discussion a little about some artworld systems that everyone recognizes as such (or at least as arts or art forms), e.g., painting, the theatre. But what Dickie claims cannot be done is to give a principled way of distinguishing artworld systems from systems that exist to present artefacts that are not art to a public. "What has to be accepted is the 'arbitrariness' of being an artworld system" (77). This seems to me to be an admission that there simply is no such thing as the nature of art—at least nothing that is sufficient for being art. So the set of definitions do not reflect a nature.

Against this, it may be said that Dickie gives us a definition of art much like his old definition even though the new one is part of a specification of a broader framework. The new definition also states two conditions: (a) being an artefact; (b) being something of a kind created to be presented to an artworld public. Dickie claims these two conditions are sufficient for defining art.

I have been arguing, however, that these conditions are at best unilluminating. If the distinction between artworld systems and non-artworld systems for presenting artefacts is arbitrary, then the expression "artworld public" in condition (b) is no more informative than "public." It can be added that Dickie's definition of public is so vague that it is not clear who would be excluded from the artworld public. Dickie's discussion of the public sometimes suggests that a public for a particular artworld system possesses a good deal of specialized knowledge of the system, but in other places he emphasizes that even very small children have a basic understanding of the institution of art which may suffice to satisfy the definition of the public.

There are also problems with the expression "kind created to be presented." Is there really such a kind? Dickie tells us what he does not mean by the expression. It does not mean that every instance of the kind is presented or is even intended for presentation. It does not refer to sub-categories of art like that of novel or sculpture. I am inclined to think it does not mean that instances of the kind are typically presented because whether that is so for works of art is an empirical question about how many make it to a public. From Dickie's discussion I suspect he means a kind whose instances are typically, though not invariably, made with the intention that they be presented. This appears factually true of works of art. However, if the intention is sometimes absent, it is not clear why we cannot imagine it often or even typically absent, although the artworld would then be radically different. An alternative conception of the kind would be one whose instances have the potential to exist in the sort of framework Dickie describes. On this conception, however, it may be that all artefacts are of this kind. No doubt, not every artefact, or even every kind of artefact, is made to be presented to a public. But artefacts are usually made for some purpose which is not wholly idiosyncratic so that there will be a potential public for them and so a potential for an institution with makers, consumers and middlemen to arise.

If being a kind that is created to be presented is a consequence of being an artefact and if there is no non-arbitrary distinction between artworld systems and non-artworld systems, Dickie's definition of work of art tells us only that such works are artefacts. Even if the definition tells us a bit more than this, the fact that Dickie's gives no way of distinguishing between artworld and non-artworld systems guarantees that the definition fails to distinguish art from many other artefacts.

Even if we waive doubts about the significance of the expressions "artworld public," "kind created to be presented," it should be noted that Dickie gives no argument for the claim that 2. gives sufficient conditions for being a work of art. Dickie himself, in passing, gives us grounds for doubting that it does.

Duchamp's *Fountain* is one of the inspirations for the institutional theory of art. In passing Dickie acknowledges that some have doubts whether it is a work of art (63). Dickie now appears not to insist it is a work of art; he recognizes that it may not be.

However, if 2. gives us sufficient conditions for being a work of art there could be no doubt that *Fountain* is a work of art. It is an artefact. It was exhibited by Duchamp, an artist, at a famous art exhibition at Duchamp's insistence. So there is no doubt that it was intended to be presented to an artworld public and succeeded in being presented. I assume that makes *Fountain* an artefact of a kind created to be presented to an artworld public.

We cannot doubt that *Fountain* satisfies 2. We can doubt it is a work of art. I draw two conclusions.

These facts about *Fountain* show beyond doubt that 2. does not give the meaning of the *expression* "work of art."

They do not *prove* that 2. does not provide sufficient conditions for being art, but they place it in serious doubt. It seems possible to imagine many artefacts made by artists to be presented to a public interested in and knowledgeable about art that are not works of art. Such artefacts may question, criticize, attack a conception of art without being art. Alternatively, they may be intended as art but simply fail as works of art. (I say more about this in section IV.)

Dickie has not provided an illuminating sufficient condition for being art. It is doubtful that he has provided a sufficient condition of any sort.

II

Dickie claims that institutional facts about art reveal a sufficient condition for being art while at the same time insisting that the institution cannot be distinguished from other systems in an informative, non-circular, non-arbitrary way. I have argued that if the second claim is true the first should be recognized as unilluminating. If that is so, the question arises whether there is a more attractive way of viewing Dickie's present account of art. I will argue in this section that, although Dickie does not acknowledge it, he is best construed as holding a position similar to one that he once opposed, viz., that the project of defining art is misconceived.

The starting point is Dickie's *response* to his claim that the distinction between artworld systems and non-artworld systems is arbitrary. He responds to this claim by asking whether it renders his account circular, admitting that it does but claiming that this is not a defect. Circularity undermines the informativeness of the account, but, "virtually everyone can recognize some things as works of art, know how some works of art are made, and the like. Thus no one needs a definition of 'works of art' which would inform them which things are works of art" (79). The inference from the fact that we all recognize *some* things as works of art to the conclusion we do not need an informative definition strikes me as shaky. Aren't there *other* things about which we are uncertain whether or not they are works of art, e.g., avant-garde experiments, exquisite pieces of furniture? Might one not look to a definition to resolve the uncertainty? More important than this is understanding the way Dickie is relying on the common ability to recognize art. Since nothing that can be spelled out in a definition distinguishes in an informative way art from non-art, it appears to be our recognitional ability itself that maintains the distinction, the brute fact that we do classify in a certain way. In particular, whatever practice deems an artworld system is an artworld system (apparently) at least within the constraint that the objects presented in the system are artefacts. Theory can only reflect this practice.[3] Since the practice is not based on crucial similarities that distinguish artworld systems from non-artworld systems, theory cannot do this by stating a principle of classification. Nor can theory reflect practice by stating a definitive list of artworld systems since practice is constantly evolving new systems. All theory can do is reflect what Dickie calls the "inflected nature of art," i.e., resign itself to giving an uninformative circular definition.

Except for calling the end product of theory a definition, the views just expressed strikingly resemble the views of the "anti-definitionists." For example, Dickie's reason why *no informative definition* is necessary strikingly resembles some anti-definitionist arguments why *no definition* is necessary, e.g., Kennick's warehouse argument.[4] Kennick claimed that, if placed in a warehouse full of objects, we would all be able to distinguish the art works from the non-art works. So we do not need a definition that tells us how to do this. Though Dickie would claim that we need more background knowledge than would be provided by the warehouse, his point is essentially similar to Kennick's. Both agree that an (informative) definition is not needed because we already know how to classify and that if one were needed it would not be forthcoming. (Kennick thinks this is directly true of art while for Dickie, we might say, it is indirectly true of art because it is directly true of artworld systems.) The concept of art that emerges from Dickie's account resembles Weitz's open concept. Which things turn out to be art is a function of practice, not a function of statable conditions for arthood.

It does have to be admitted that the concept of art on Dickie's view is not as *wide* open as it is on Weitz's. There are two necessary conditions for being art on Dickie's view, even if it has been placed in doubt that they are jointly sufficient. One condition is artefactuality. The other is being made within an institutional framework. I now want to consider whether this second condition is necessary for being art.

III

Dickie gives two arguments for the view that art can only exist within an institutional framework. One argument tries to refute the possibility of a "romantic" artist—one

---

[3]Dickie tells us that philosophical definitions are attempts to make explicit "what we already in some sense know" (79). However, in one passage he seems to deny that this amounts to saying that theory follows practice: ". . . a philosopher . . . should look to the actual practices of artists, the sayings of critics, and so on. It does not follow, however, that a philosopher must take seriously *everything* that the denizens of the artworld do . . . just because something is treated as a thing of a certain type (art) by someone (art critics) does not necessarily mean that something is a thing of that kind" (60). The remark is made in the context of a dispute with T. Binkley over the artefactuality condition. When that condition is not violated, I can think of no instance where Dickie would not defer to the practice of artists and critics.

[4]W. E. Kennick, "Does Traditional Aesthetics Rest on a Mistake?" reprinted in *Collected Papers on Aesthetics*, C. Barrett (ed.) (New York, 1966), pp. 6–7.

who works completely outside the framework. The other is based on the possibility of visually indistinguishable objects only one of which is a work of art.

To prove the impossibility of a romantic artist, Dickie asks us to imagine a primitive society in which no framework such as Dickie has described exists. Suppose an individual in that society creates a representation (of an animal, say, carved out of wood). Here is why, according to Dickie, the object is not a work of art:

> While the creator of the representation would certainly recognize the object as a representation, he would not have any cognitive structure into which to fit it so as to understand it as art. Someone might make the mistake of identifying art with representation . . . Once this temptation is put aside, we can see that the creator of the representation cannot recognize his creation as art and that, therefore, it cannot be art. (55)

I agree with Dickie that the individual would have no concept of art. I would have thought, however, that it is the inference from this fact to the conclusion that the carving is not a work of art that Dickie would take pains to defend. Instead, he simply makes the inference. But why must someone who makes art be able to understand it as art? If Dickie's institutional account is true, we would have a reason, but the point of argument is to show the account true, not to presuppose it. Dickie does not give us any other reason to accept the inference.

Suppose the carving is of a leopard and the carver succeeds not just in producing a representation that is recognizable as a big cat (if not a leopard) but puts into it something of his own attitude towards leopards: someone looking at the carving can feel something of the fearsomeness of a leopard. I agree with Dickie that being a representation is neither necessary nor sufficient for being art, but being a representation like this is a much better reason for calling something art. (This is not, however, to *identify* art with expressive representation or with anything else.) That the carving has such expressive power is a much better reason for exhibiting it in an art museum than is knowledge that it was created in a certain institutional framework. So I am inclined to reject Dickie's inference.

Is it possible for an inhabitant of modern society to create art outside an artworld framework? Because of the vagueness of the notion of artworld framework, it is much harder to answer this question. However, examples may be found in some unusual works in what are typically non-art media such as fashion or furniture. (Dickie seems to approve of Walton's exclusion of the fashion world from the artworld (75) and I assume that furniture would go the same way.) Occasionally such people may produce objects in these media which transcend the uses to which the media are usually put. The objects possess a value typical of values we seek in works of art, e.g., they have great aesthetic interest or they seem to embody or express a whole way of life.[5] Though the works possess these values and perhaps were intended to, it does not follow that their makers intended them to be works of art. Perhaps their makers are capable of thinking of them as art but that surely is not sufficient for being in an artworld framework. They were not made for an artworld public (in so far as we can make sense of that notion). By hypothesis, they were not produced within an artworld system. But it does not seem completely far fetched to claim that they are works of art.

---

[5]A discussion of what it is for an artefact to embody a way of life is found in Roger Scruton, *The Aesthetics of Architecture* (London, 1979), pp. 237–56.

Dickie's other argument for the necessity of an artworld framework is based on the existence of visually indistinguishable pairs, only one of which is a work of art. Examples of such pairs are Warhol's *Brillo Box* and an ordinary Brillo box, the painting *Polish Rider* and an accidentally produced object that looks just like it, Duchamp's *Fountain* and a similar urinal produced by the same manufacturer. What these pairs show, according to Dickie, is that: 1. "it is not the visible characteristics of an object alone which make it a work of art" and 2. "a work of art must be enmeshed in some sort of framework . . . which is responsible for its being a work of art" (62). Since I am ready to admit that artefactuality is a necessary condition for being art, I would grant 1. Does the existence of such pairs show 2.? I don't think so. First, it is not obvious that all the pairs are to be treated in the same way. The Polish Rider pair is the easiest to handle. Since the look alike is accidentally produced, it is not an artefact. Nothing more is needed to explain why it is not art. With *Fountain*, I would be inclined to say that if it is art, it is because Duchamp was able to use his particular urinal to give immediacy and force to certain questions about art. The other urinal does nothing like this. With *Brillo Box*, since I have never found it in any way valuable, I cannot say it is a work of art though I do not deny that it is.

Now I would admit that Duchamp would not have used his urinal to raise questions about art if he was not working within (or manipulating) a framework such as Dickie describes. If *Brillo Box* is a work of art, this is in part due to its existing in such a framework. However, it is hard to see that a conclusion about the necessity of such a framework for all art follows. All that follows is that certain things would not be works of art if they had not come into existence inside this framework.

IV

Dickie might object to the entire preceding section on the ground that I have confused the classificatory sense of "art" with an evaluative sense of "art" (although he is now no longer sure it is correct to speak of different *senses* of "art" [37]). It is true that I claimed that various things are art because they possessed certain valuable characteristics: expressive power in the case of the primitive carving, aesthetic interest and expression in a fashion design or a piece of furniture, immediacy and force in *Fountain*. Also, I was unable to affirm *Brillo Box* is art because I could find nothing valuable about it. Nevertheless, I would claim that I am still working with the classificatory sense of "art."

The evaluative sense of "art," as it is described by aestheticians such as Weitz and Dickie, simply uses the word "art" to praise an object. I am not using "art" in this way. I am just as concerned with classification as Dickie.

It seems to me that it is part of our common understanding of art that works of art are objects of value. Thus if an artefact is a representation with great expressive power, it is art whether or not it arose within an artworld framework. This understanding of art is reflected in the way some critics seem to think of the phenomena of the avant-garde. They seem to think of it as a series of experiments that keep raising the question: is this (still) art? Though the question is clearly raised by artists producing artefacts for an artworld public, for the question to be meaningful, the possibility must exist that the answer is: no. The way the question is answered by some critics is by looking for certain valuable qualities in the works.[6]

An objection to this way of thinking about art is that it eliminates the distinctions between art and good art and between non-art and bad art. The distinction need not be eliminated on this approach. Good art possesses a high degree of value. Bad works (as Beardsley has suggested) fall below "some rough level of . . . value expected" by critics.[7]

Another objection is that no one has ever succeeded in defining art in terms of valuable qualities it has. I believe this is true and am not hopeful that a definition will be forthcoming. However, it now appears that the institutional approach is no better off.

If my brief suggestions (no more is possible in this paper) about how we classify objects as art are correct, we have a positive reason for denying that works of art can only exist in an institutional framework. However, even if I am completely wrong, the argument of section III still shows that Dickie has not given us a positive reason for affirming that works of art can only so exist.

---

[6]Such a view is clearly suggested by Clement Greenberg in "Modernist Painting" where he defines modernism as a kind of self-criticism which is interpreted in turn as a search for the definition of an art medium. On this view a failed modernist experiment with paint is a non-painting, not a bad painting. Failure for Greenberg is clearly a question of not realizing certain formal and expressive values. I am not sure whether this view is also held by Leo Steinberg. Some remarks in "Contemporary Art and the Plight of the Public" suggest an even more radical view, viz., that Steinberg would not consider an object even a *candidate* for arthood unless he could first find value in it. Both articles are found in *The New Art*, Gregory Battcock (ed.) (New York, 1973).

[7]Monroe Beardsley, *Aesthetics* (Indianapolis, 1981), p. 501.

George Dickie

REPLY TO STECKER

Robert Stecker offers three broad areas of criticism of the institutional theory of art as I set it forth in *The Art Circle*. Each of the three areas contains subcriticisms.

The first criticism is that the theory "fails to distinguish works of art from many other artifacts." In response to a criticism Kendall Walton directed against an earlier account in *Art and the Aesthetic*, I said that there is an arbitrariness about what is or is not an artworld system. Stecker takes my remark to be "an admission that there simply is no such thing as the nature of art." Well, yes and no. Art does not have a nature in the way some have thought that natural kinds such as lions and tigers have natures, and the reason is that art is not a natural kind. Art is a cultural kind, and that is the central message of *The Art Circle*. It is often a feature of our cultural phenomena, which are our collective inventions, that they exhibit arbitrariness. This arbitrariness is sometimes subject to criticism, as, for example, when our moral institutions treat men and women differently for no good reason. Perhaps the artworld is subject to criticism for treating painting and furniture differently, but I will forgo a discussion of this issue. Stecker concludes that because of the arbitrariness involved in distinguishing artworld systems, the institutional definition of "work of art" "fails to distinguish art from many other artifacts." Well, yes, it fails to make the distinction for persons who are ignorant of the artworld culture.

Stecker is puzzled by what I said about artworld publics. He writes, "Dickie's discussion of the public sometimes suggests that a public for a particular artworld system possesses a good deal of specialized knowledge of the system, but in other places he emphasizes that even very small children have a basic understanding of the institution of art which may suffice to satisfy the definition of the public." One can be puzzled by what I said about artworld publics only if one underrates the cognitive capacities of small children. Although there is much in the content of sophisticated art that small children cannot comprehend, they have no difficulty understanding the general idea of art and enjoying works with content that interests them. Artworld publics, as is no doubt true of other kinds of publics, include a wide range of competencies.

Stecker is also puzzled by the expression "kind to be presented" in my definition of

This essay was written for the second edition of this collection and is being published for the first time.

"work of art." He concludes, "From Dickie's discussion I suspect he means a kind whose instances are typically, though not invariably, made with the intention that they be presented." This is not what I intended. What I intended is the following. Works of art are a kind of thing created for presentation. In some cases they are actually presented, and in some cases they are not. There are several possibilities in the second kind of cases. Someone might create a work of art intending to present it but be prevented from doing so. In this case there are two intentions—an intention to create a kind of thing to be presented and an intention to present it. Someone might create a work of art intending not to present it. In this case there are also two intentions—an intention to create a kind of thing to be presented and an intention not to present it.

In the first section of his paper Stecker also writes, "Dickie acknowledges that some have doubts whether it [*Fountain*] is a work of art. Dickie now appears not to insist it is

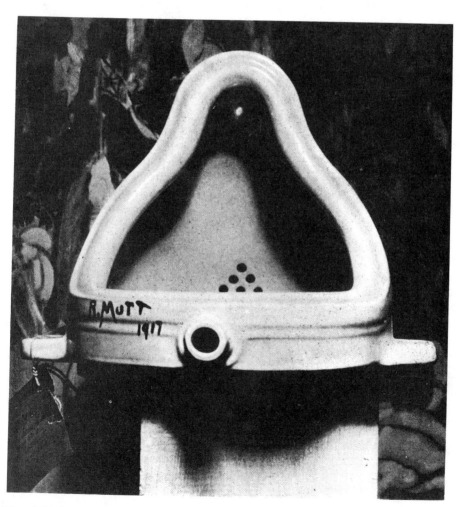

Marcel Duchamp, Fountain, 1917, *no longer extant. Photograph by Alfred Stieglitz, courtesy, The Museum of Modern Art, New York.*

a work of art; he recognizes that it may not be." Stecker has misunderstood the passage he refers to. In this passage I said that some people claim that either *Fountain* is not a work of art or it is unclear whether it is a work of art. I then said that *Fountain* did not have to be a work of art in order for *a particular argument to work*. In this passage I made no claim about whether *Fountain* is or is not a work of art. I do think *Fountain* is a work of art.

The main point of the second section of Stecker's paper is that my view resembles those of Kennick and Weitz, both of whom reject the idea of definition. I do reject the kind of definitions that Kennick and Weitz reject, and in saying that a definition is possible I move on to a different kind of definition, one that focuses on the cultural matrix in which works of art are embedded. I am trying to do something different from what both the traditional theorists and Kennick and Weitz are trying to do.

The criticism in the third section revolves around Stecker's query "Why must someone who makes art be able to understand it as art?" Analogously, one might ask, "Why must someone who makes a promise be able to understand it as a promise?" The answer in this case is that one cannot make a promise unless one understands that one is doing so. A parrot that utters the sentence "I promise to meet you at three o'clock" is not making a promise. Of course, one does not have to be saying to oneself at the time of making the promise, "I am making a promise," in order to understand that one is making a promise. Similarly, at the time of making a work of art, one does not have to be saying to oneself, "I am making art," in order to understand that one is making art. Surely in making a work of art, a person must be able to understand in a broad sense what he is doing.

In trying to refute my contention about understanding, Stecker quotes part of the passage from *The Art Circle* in which I envisage a person in a society without art who fashions a representation of something. (He does not note that in my imagined case the society without art had not previously had any representations either.) I then wrote, "We can see that the creator of the representation cannot recognize his creation as art and that, therefore, it cannot be art." I realize now, as I realized then, that my remarks are not a proof, but it seems to me that such a representation is not art. There is, of course, a "chicken and egg" problem here, and I went on to remark that the creation of such a representation might well be an initiating event in a process that ultimately would lead to the establishment of the institution of art in a society. Stecker writes, "Suppose the carving is of a leopard and the carver succeeds not just in producing a representation that is recognizable as a big cat (if not a leopard) but puts into it something of his own attitude towards leopards. . . . being a representation like this is a much better reason for calling something art." I agree that it is reasonable to judge that a representation of the kind Stecker envisages is a work of art, but this is not the kind of case I envisaged. I find it hard to imagine that the representation Stecker envisages could occur as the *first* representation made in a society. Such a representation would have to come at a much later point in a society's history than the kind of representation I was imagining. If Stecker wishes to refute my view by commenting on my imagined example, he must use my example.

Stecker remarks that "it does not seem completely far fetched to claim" that furniture with values typical of those works of art have are works of art. I agree; it is not farfetched to claim this. It is also not farfetched to claim that such furniture is not art. I do not think that we have a settled view about such items as we do about paintings.

Stecker also takes exception to my indistinguishable-pairs argument. He writes, "It is hard to see that a conclusion about the necessity of such a framework for all art follows. All that follows is that certain things [*Fountain*, for example] would not be works of art if they had not come into existence inside this framework." Perhaps it does not follow from this argument that all art requires a framework. I do think, however, that in showing that *Fountain* has an essential framework, the argument shows that it is reasonable to think that all art does. The argument is supposed to enable us to "see" the framework that all artworks are embedded in by focusing on odd ones such as *Fountain*. It would be odd, I think, if there were an essential framework for *Fountain* and its likes and that the more ordinary works of art have nothing to do with the framework. Why would an essential framework have been created only for *Fountain* and its ilk? The framework was in place long before artists began making weird works; it was what enabled them to do dada.

PART THREE

———◆◆◆◆———

Traditional Theories of the Aesthetic and Contemporary Discussions of These Theories

Part Three is concerned entirely with eighteenth-century theories of taste and aesthetic perception, which essentially give an account of what is involved in the experience and appreciation of beauty in art and nature. By contrast with the earlier Platonic conception of beauty as an objective property of things, both of these theories focus on the subject experiencing beauty. Thus, with the development of these theories, the faculties (taste) and experiences (sense perceptions) of persons became the prime subject matter of aesthetics.

The theory of taste begins, at least in Great Britain, as pointed out by Peter Kivy, with the publication in 1712 of Joseph Addison's sketchy remarks on the subject. The two most important systematic developments in this area of thought were generated by Francis Hutcheson and David Hume. The general philosophical tradition within which their theories of taste developed was the empiricism of John Locke. The other important influence on these theorists was the notion of disinterestedness introduced into the theory of the appreciation of beauty by the third Earl of Shaftesbury. Shaftesbury's view is also sometimes considered a theory of taste, but if it is so called it should be noted that it differs strikingly from those of other British thinkers who developed theories of taste. Whereas the others—Addison, Hutcheson, Hume, Edmund Burke, Alexander Gerard, and Archibald Alison—worked within the empiricist tradition of Locke, Shaftesbury was an anti-empiricist who wrote of the appreciation of beauty in Platonic or Neoplatonic terms.

The theory of taste that developed from Addison in 1712 to Alison in 1790 exhibits a constant five-part structure, although the various thinkers filled in particular parts of the structure in different ways. The first structural part is *perception*, which for all the British theorists was simply the mode whereby one knows the objects in the world and their characteristics. The second structural part is the *faculty of taste*. The theorists differ as to the nature of this faculty. Addison rather vaguely spoke of the imagination. Hutcheson wrote in considerable detail of the faculty of taste as an internal sense of beauty. An internal sense contrasts with the external senses, such as vision and hearing, which cognize the world; an internal sense reacts to what the external senses apprehend. An internal sense resembles an external sense in that the former works automatically and cannot be influenced by interest. Burke rejected the notion of the faculty of taste as a special sense and spoke simply in terms of the propensity to experience pleasure and pain. Hume did not have much to say about the nature of the faculty of taste but concentrated on other aspects of the theory. The third structural part of the theory of taste is the *mental product*, which exists when the faculty of taste reacts. The theorists generally understood this product to be pleasure. The fourth structural part is the *kind of object* in the perceived world to which the faculty of taste reacts. It is here that the theorists differ most. Hutcheson said it is based on the perception of *uniformity in variety*. Burke, rather than specifying a formula, gave a list of properties: smoothness, smallness, and the like. Hume spoke vaguely of "certain qualities in objects." Alison wrote of the perception of something that is a sign of, or is expressive of, a quality of mind (nobility, for example). The fifth and final structural part is *judgments of taste*; for example, a judgment such as "This painting is beautiful." Such a judgment means that a perceived object (the painting) in virtue of some characteristic (say, uniformity in variety) causes the faculty of taste to react and produce pleasure.

All theorists of taste make use of the notion of disinterestedness. For Hutcheson, the alleged fact that the faculty of taste was a *sense* insured disinterestedness because this meant that the faculty reacted automatically and was indifferent to interest. Hutcheson was aware, of course, that the faculty can be influenced by custom, training, and even the accidental association of ideas. By contrast with Hutcheson, Alison, at the end of the eighteenth century, rejected the notion of a special sense as the faculty of taste and instead developed an elaborate account of what goes on in the mind of a person who experiences beauty. Alison included disinterestedness in his approach by claiming that any practical interests held by a person may interfere with, and be destructive of, the experience of beauty. For Hutcheson, disinterestedness was insured by the nature of the faculty of taste; for Alison disinterestedness was something to be achieved by freeing oneself from practical interests that distract from the experience of beauty.

Mary Mothersill's "Hume and the Paradox of Taste" is a critical study of the difficulties Hume attempted to resolve in the concept of taste. In his essay "Of the Standard of Taste," Hume observes that although common sense agrees with the "skeptical philosophy" in holding it fruitless to dispute about matters of taste, common sense also dismisses certain critical judgments as not merely false but absurd and ridiculous. Hence there is an opposition that Hume sets out to resolve. This is the paradox of taste. (Immanuel Kant, who confronted the same issue, refers to it as an "antinomy.") Hume, working within a neoclassical framework, tries to show that although the judgment of taste "O is beautiful" depends not on reason but on "sentiment" (in particular, felt pleasure), nonetheless, some critics have better judgment than others. There are certain qualities that are discovered to be universally pleasing. Hence, there are laws of taste. The good critics are the ones who can detect such qualities in works of art even when present only in a small degree. The joint verdict of such critics provides us with a standard of taste.

Hume's solution, according to Mothersill, is spectacularly unsuccessful, but for that very reason is useful in making evident that no variant of his argument, nothing that depends on the notion of laws of taste, can hope to succeed. Furthermore, in the course of the discussion Hume suggests indirectly or by implication a very different line of inquiry, one that, were it developed, would avoid the paradox and provide the basis for a plausible account of critical reasoning.

We have presented a sketch of the philosophical background and structure of the theories of taste and perception offered by the philosophers of the British Enlightenment. These theories contrast markedly with the aesthetic-attitude theories of certain nineteenth-century thinkers, such as Arthur Schopenhauer, and twentieth-century theorists, such as Jerome Stolnitz and Eliseo Vivas. The structure of the aesthetic-attitude theorists is simpler than the structure of theories of taste. In attitude theories the faculty of perception assumes a more critical role. For the aesthetic-attitude theories there are two kinds of perception: ordinary and aesthetic. While ordinary perception is concerned with the practical dimension of everyday life, aesthetic perception is said to be special and distinctive insofar as its "object" is aesthetic in nature.

The theories of taste, especially when viewed in contrast with Platonic conceptions of beauty, were themselves steps in the direction of subjectivity because they centered theoretical considerations on the perceptions and reactions of subjects. The notion of disinterestedness is retained in aesthetic-attitude theories, but it is aesthetic perception that is supposed to be disinterested and, thereby, capable of determining its object as aesthetic in character or of making aesthetic qualities available to the perceiver. In this theoretical stance, judgments of taste have been replaced by aesthetic judgments, which refer to the objects of aesthetic perception.

The theory of taste of the German philosopher Immanuel Kant, published in 1790, falls both temporally and theoretically between the theories of the British philosophers of taste and the later aesthetic-attitude theorists (see Part Four). Kant's theory clearly retains the five-part structure of the earlier theories of taste. For Kant, the *faculty of taste* is the set of ordinary cognitive faculties (the understanding and the imagination) functioning in an unusual way. For him, the mental consequence of the faculty of taste's reaction is *pleasure*. Kant offers an account of judgments of taste similar to those of the earlier theorists, except that for reasons inherent in his theory he maintains that such judgments are always singular (about an individual object) and never universal (about a whole set of objects).

The kind of perceived object that, according to Kant, triggers the faculty of taste is one that exhibits the *form of purpose*. Not just any form, according to Kant, will trigger the faculty of taste, but only one that has the form of purpose. In this way Kant introduces teleology into his conception of works of fine art, as a work of art is viewed in much the same way as a living organism, although the functions of living organisms have no obvious analogy in works of "fine art." Finally, according to Kant, because judgments of taste are subjective or relative to the individual person, they nonetheless make a claim to universal assent. This contention remains a standing problem in Kant's aesthetics: how is it possible for aesthetic judgments, whether of natural phenomena or of works of art, to be "individual" and hence subjective while at the same time laying claim to universality?

Kant's conception of *perception* clearly sets him apart from the British theorists of taste and makes possible the development of the later aesthetic-attitude theories. The British theorists, working in the tradition of Locke, assumed perception to be a *passive* function of the mind that simply reveals to us the nature of the perceived world. Before he began work on the theory of taste, Kant had developed a theory of the mind according to which mind is an active force that to a large extent forms and constitutes the objects we perceive. Kant's theory of taste was then worked out within this more general philosophical framework. One of the prime functions of the mind, according to Kant, is to give to experience the spatial and temporal *form* that it has. Thus, when Kant maintained that an object's *form* of purpose triggers the faculty of taste, he was saying that the faculty of taste is triggered by an object—having such aspect (its form) as a result of the activity of a subject's mind. Thus, Kant made the aspect of the perceived world that triggers the faculty of taste to a degree subjective, that is, dependent upon the activity of a subject's mind. It was this development in Kant's general philosophy and in his theory of taste that made possible the development of the even more subjective aesthetic-attitude theories of the nineteenth and twentieth centuries.

In their introduction to *Essays in Kant's Aesthetics*, Ted Cohen and Paul Guyer present a condensed exposition of the background and themes of Kant's aesthetic theory. The problematics of the *Critique of Judgment* are dealt with in terms of a number of recurring motifs, including disinterestedness, purposiveness, and the central question of the objectivity of aesthetic judgments. Kant's view results in the dilemma that, on the one hand, aesthetic judgments are subjective and, on the other, that they command universal assent, thereby laying claim to a kind of objectivity. Cohen and Guyer explore the implications of this dilemma, and attempt to show how Kant's efforts to resolve the problem lead to a number of difficulties, which he tries to answer by incorporating the notions of teleological judgments in his analysis of the concept of taste. The authors elucidate the central concepts of Kant's aesthetics in the light of the paradox of taste and illustrate it in their discussion of Kant's psychology of the faculties, specifically his reference to the "free play" or "harmony" between imagination and understanding that is at the basis of our enjoyment of the formal qualities of both natural and artistic objects.

Cohen and Guyer are particularly astute in their analysis of the ways in which Kant prefigures contemporary aesthetics and the manner in which he formulates this problem and attempts to resolve it in various ways. Their conclusion is that Kant's resolution of the problem consists in "regarding all subjective differences between [the judge] and others as irrelevant, and the import of his judgment is the incumbency upon all others to have his feeling for [the object in question]. The basis for one's judgment is one's own personal feeling, but this feeling is, so to speak, impersonally personal." Thus, the judge is a true representative of people in general, and that judgment thereby becomes interpersonal in nature.

Francis Hutcheson

AN INITIAL THEORY OF TASTE: FROM AN INQUIRY INTO THE ORIGINAL OF OUR IDEAS OF BEAUTY AND VIRTUE

The Preface

There is no part of Philosophy of more importance, than a just Knowledge of Human Nature, and its various Powers and Dispositions. Our late Inquirys have been very much employ'd about our Understanding, and the several Methods of obtaining Truth. We generally acknowledge, that the Importance of any Truth is nothing else than its Moment, or Efficacy to make Men happy, or to give them the greatest and most lasting Pleasure; and Wisdom denotes only a Capacity of pursuing this End by the best Means. It must surely then be of the greatest importance, to have distinct Conceptions of this End it self, as well as of the Means, necessary to obtain it; that we may find out which are the greatest and most lasting Pleasures, and not employ our Reason, after all our laborious Improvements of it, in trifling Pursuits. It is to be fear'd indeed, that most of our Studys, without this Inquiry, will be of very little use to us; for they seem to have scarce any other tendency than to lead us into speculative Knowledge it self. Nor are we distinctly told how it is that Knowledge, or Truth, is pleasant to us.

This Consideration put the Author of the following Papers upon inquiring into the various Pleasures which Human Nature is capable of receiving. We shall generally find in our modern philosophick Writings, nothing farther on this Head, than some bare Division of them into Sensible, and Rational, and some trite Common-place Arguments to prove the latter more valuable than the former. Our sensible Pleasures are slightly passed over, and explain'd only by some Instances in Tastes, Smells, Sounds, or such like, which Men of any tolerable Reflection generally look upon as very trifling Satisfactions. Our rational Pleasures have had much the same kind of treatment. We are seldom taught any other Notion of rational Pleasure than that which we have upon reflecting on our Possession, or Claim to those Objects, which may be Occasions of Pleasure. Such Objects we call advantageous; but Advantage, or

From the third edition of An Inquiry into the Original of Our Ideas of Beauty and Virtue *(London: 1729)*.

Interest, cannot be distinctly conceiv'd, till we know what those Pleasures are which advantageous Objects are apt to excite; and what Senses or Powers of Perception we have with respect to such Objects. We may perhaps find such an Inquiry of more importance in Morals, to prove what we call the Reality of Virtue, or that it is the surest Happiness of the Agent, than one would at first imagine.

In reflecting upon our external Senses, we plainly see, that our Perceptions of Pleasure, or Pain, do not depend directly on our Will. Objects do not please us, according as we incline they should. The presence of some Objects necessarily pleases us, and the presence of others as necessarily displeases us. Nor can we by our Will, any otherwise procure Pleasure, or avoid Pain, than by procuring the former kind of Objects, and avoiding the latter. By the very Frame of our Nature the one is made the occasion of Delight, and the other of Dissatisfaction.

The same Observation will hold in all many other sorts of Objects, which please, our other Pleasures and Pains. For there are many other sorts of Objects which please, or displease us as necessarily, as material Objects do when they operate upon our Organs of Sense. There is scarcely any Object which our Minds are employ'd about, which is not thus constituted the necessary occasion of some Pleasure or Pain. Thus we find our selves pleas'd with a regular Form, a piece of Architecture or Painting, a Composition of Notes, a Theorem, an Action, an Affection, a Character. And we are conscious that this Pleasure necessarily arises from the Contemplation of the Idea, which is then present to our Minds, with all its Circumstances, altho some of these Ideas have nothing of what we commonly call sensible Perception in them; and in those which have, the Pleasure arises from some Uniformity, Order, Arrangement, Imitation; and not from the simple Ideas of Colour, or Sound, or mode of Extension separately consider'd.

These Determinations to be pleas'd with any Forms, or Ideas which occur to our Observation, the Author chooses to call SENSES; distinguishing them from the Powers which commonly go by that Name, by calling our Power of perceiving the Beauty of Regularity, Order, Harmony, an INTERNAL SENSE; and that Determination to approve Affections, Actions, or Characters of rational Agents, which we call virtuous, he marks by the name of a MORAL SENSE.

His principal Design is to shew, "That Human Nature was not left quite indifferent in the affair of Virtue, to form to it self Observations concerning the Advantage, or Disadvantage of Actions, and accordingly to regulate its Conduct." The weakness of our Reason, and the avocations arising from the Infirmities and Necessities of our Nature, are so great, that very few Men could ever have form'd those long Deductions of Reason, which shew some Actions to be in the whole advantageous to the Agent, and their Contrarys pernicious. The AUTHOR of Nature has much better furnish'd us for a virtuous Conduct, than our Moralists seem to imagine, by almost as quick and powerful Instructions, as we have for the preservation of our Bodys. He has given us strong Affections to be the Springs of each virtuous Action; and made Virtue a lovely form, that we might easily distinguish it from its contrary, and be made happy by the pursuit of it.

This moral Sense of Beauty in Actions and Affections, may appear strange at first View. Some of our Moralists themselves are offended at it in my LORD SHAFTESBURY; so much are they accustom'd to deduce every Approbation, or Aversion, from rational Views of Interest, (except it be merely in the Simple-Ideas of the external Senses) and have such a Horror at innate Ideas, which they imagine this borders upon. But this moral Sense has no relation to innate Ideas, as will appear in the second Treatise. Our Gentlemen of good Taste can tell us of a great many Senses, Tastes, and Relishes for Beauty, Harmony, Imitation in Painting and Poetry; and may not we find too in Mankind a Relish for a Beauty in Characters, in Manners? I doubt we have made Philosophy, as well as Religion, by our foolish management of it, so austere and ungainly a Form, that a Gentleman cannot easily bring himself to like it; and those who are strangers to it, can scarcely bear to hear our Description of it. So much it is changed from what was once the delight of the finest Gentlemen among the Antients, and their Recreation after the Hurry of publick Affairs!

In the first Treatise, the Author perhaps in some Instances has gone too far, in supposing a greater Agreement of Mankind in their Sense of Beauty, than Experience will confirm; but all he is sollicitous about is to shew "That there is some Sense of Beauty natural to Men; that we find as great an Agreement of Men in their Relishes of Forms, as in their external Senses, which all agree to be natural; and that Pleasure or Pain, Delight or Aversion, are naturally join'd to their Perceptions." If the Reader be convinc'd of such Determination of the Mind to be pleas'd with Forms, Proportions, Resemblances, Theorems; it will be no difficult matter to apprehend another superior Sense, natural also to Men, determining them to be pleas'd with Actions, Characters, Affections. This is the moral Sense, which makes the Subject of the second Treatise.

The proper Occasions of Perception by the external Senses, occur to us as soon as we come into the World; whence perhaps we easily look upon these Senses to be natural; but the Objects of the superior Senses of Beauty and Virtue generally do not. It is probably some little time before Children reflect, or at least let us know that they reflect upon Proportion and Similitude; upon Affections, Characters, Tempers; or come to know the external Actions which are Evidences of them. Hence we imagine that their Sense of Beauty, and their moral Sentiments of Actions, must be entirely owing to Instruction, and Education; whereas it is as easy to conceive, how a Character, a Temper, as soon as they are observ'd, may be constituted by NATURE the necessary occasion of Pleasure, or an Object of Approbation, as a Taste or a Sound; tho these Objects present themselves to our Observation sooner than the other.

Sect. I

Concerning some Powers of Perception, distinct from what is generally understood by Sensation

To make the following Observations understood, it may be necessary to premise some Definitions, and Observations, either universally acknowledg'd, or sufficiently prov'd by many Writers both antient and modern, concerning our Perceptions called Sensations, and the Actions of the Mind consequent upon them.

Art. I. Those Ideas which are rais'd in the Mind upon the presence of external Objects, and their acting upon our Bodys, are call'd Sensations. We find that the Mind in such Cases is passive, and has not Power directly to prevent the Perception or Idea, or to vary it at its Reception, as long as we continue our Bodys in a state fit to be acted upon by the external Object.

II. When two Perceptions are intirely different from each other, or agree in nothing but the general Idea of Sensation, we call the Powers of receiving those different Perceptions, different Senses. Thus Seeing and Hearing denote the different Powers of receiving the Ideas of Colours and Sounds. And altho Colours have great Differences among themselves, as also have Sounds, yet there is a greater Agreement among the most opposite Colours, than between any Colour and a Sound: Hence we call all Colours Perceptions of the same Sense. All the several Senses seem to have their distinct Organs, except Feeling, which is in some degree diffus'd over the whole Body.

III. The Mind has a Power of compounding Ideas, which were receiv'd separately; of comparing Objects by means of the Ideas, and of observing their Relations and Proportions; of enlarging and diminishing its Ideas at pleasure, or in any certain Ratio, or Degree; and of considering separately each of the simple Ideas, which might perhaps have been impress'd jointly in the Sensation. This last Operation we commonly call Abstraction.

IV. The Ideas of Substances are compounded of the various simple Ideas jointly impress'd, when they presented themselves to our Senses. We define Substances only by enumerating these sensible Ideas: And such Definitions may raise an Idea clear enough of the Substance in the Mind of one who never immediately perceiv'd the Substance; provided he has separately receiv'd by his Senses all the simple Ideas which are in the Composition of the complex one of the Substance defin'd: But if there be any simple Ideas which he has not receiv'd, or if he wants any of the Senses necessary for the Perception of them, no Definition can raise any simple Idea which has not been before perceived by the Senses.

V. Hence it follows, "That when Instruction, Education, or Prejudice of any kind, raise any Desire or Aversion toward an Object, this Desire or Aversion must be founded upon an Opinion of some Perfection, or of some Deficiency in those Qualitys, for Perception of which we have the proper Senses." Thus if Beauty be desir'd by one who has not the Sense of Sight, the Desire must be rais'd by some apprehended Regularity of Figure, Sweetness of Voice, Smoothness, or Softness, or some other Quality perceivable by the other Senses without relation to the Ideas of Colour.

VI. Many of our sensitive Perceptions are pleasant, and many painful, immediately, and that without any knowledge of the Cause of this Pleasure or Pain, or how the Objects excite it, or are the Occasions of it; or without seeing to what farther Advantage or Detriment the Use of such Objects might tend: Nor would the most accurate Knowledge of these things vary either the Pleasure or Pain of the Perception, however it might give a rational Pleasure distinct from the sensible; or might raise a distinct Joy, from a prospect of farther Advantage in the Object, or Aversion, from an apprehension of Evil.

VII. The simple Ideas rais'd in different Persons by the same Object, are probably some way different, when they disagree in their Approbation or Dislike; and in the same Person, when his Fancy at one time differs from what it was at another. This will appear from reflecting on those Objects, to which we have now an Aversion tho they were formerly agreeable: And we shall generally find that there is some accidental Conjunction of a disagreeable Idea, which always recurs with the Object. . . .

VIII. The only Pleasure of Sense, which many Philosophers seem to consider, is that which accompanys the simple Ideas of Sensation: But there are far greater Pleasures in those complex Ideas of Objects, which obtain the Names of Beautiful, Regular, Harmonious. Thus every one acknowledges he is more delighted with a fine Face, a just Picture, than with the View of any one Colour, were it as strong and lively as possible; and more pleas'd with a Prospect of the Sun arising among fettled Clouds, and colouring their Edges with a starry Hemisphere, a fine Landskip, a regular Building, than with a clear blue Sky, a smooth Sea, or a large open Plain, not diversify'd by Woods, Hills, Waters, Buildings: And yet even these latter Appearances are not quite simple. So in Musick, the Pleasure of fine Composition is incomparably greater than that of any one Note, how sweet, full, or swelling soever.

IX. Let it be observ'd, that in the following Papers, the Word Beauty is taken for the Idea rais'd in us, and a Sense of Beauty for our Power of receiving this Idea. Harmony also denotes our pleasant Ideas arising from Composition of Sounds, and a good Ear (as it is generally taken) a Power of perceiving this Pleasure. In the following Section, an Attempt is made to discover "what is the immediate Occasion of these pleasant Ideas, or what real Quality in the Objects ordinarily excites them."

X. It is of no consequence whether we call these Ideas of Beauty and Harmony, Perceptions of the External Senses of Seeing and Hearing, or not. I should rather choose to call our Power of perceiving these Ideas, an INTERNAL SENSE, were it only for the Convenience of distinguishing them from other Sensations of Seeing and Hearing, which Men may have without Perception of Beauty and Harmony. It is plain from Experience, that many Men have in the common meaning, the Senses of Seeing and Hearing perfect enough; they perceive all the simple Ideas separately, and have their Pleasures; they distinguish them from each other, such as one Colour from another, either quite different, or the stronger or fainter of the same Colour, when they are plac'd beside each other, altho they may often confound their Names when they occur a-part from each other; as some do the Names of Green and Blue: they can tell in separate Notes, the higher, lower, sharper or flatter, when separately sounded; in Figures they discern the Length, Breadth, Wideness of each Line, Surface, Angle; and may be as capable of hearing and seeing at great distances as any Men whatsoever: And yet perhaps they shall find no Pleasure in Musical Compositions, in Painting, Architecture, natural Landskip; or but a very weak one in comparison of what others enjoy from the same Objects. This greater Capacity of receiving such pleasant Ideas we commonly call a fine Genius or Taste: in Musick we seem universally to acknowledge something like a distinct Sense from the External one of Hearing, and call it a good Ear; and the like distinction we should probably acknowledge in other Objects, had we also got distinct Names to denote these Powers of Perception by.

XI. There will appear another Reason perhaps hereafter, for calling this Power of perceiving the Ideas of Beauty, an Internal Sense, from this, that in some other Affairs, where our External Senses are not much concern'd, we discern a sort of Beauty, very like, in many respects, to that observ'd in sensible Objects, and accompany'd with like Pleasure: Such is that Beauty perceiv'd in Theorems, or universal Truths, in general Causes, and in some extensive Principles of Action.

XII. Let every one here consider, how different we must suppose the Perception to be, with which a Poet is transported upon the Prospect of any of those Objects of natural Beauty, which ravish us even in his Description; from that cold lifeless

Conception which we imagine in a dull Critick, or one of the Virtuosi, without what we call a fine Taste. This latter Class of Men may have greater Perfection in that Knowledge which is deriv'd from external Sensation; they can tell all the specifick Differences of Trees, Herbs, Minerals, Metals; they know the Form of every Leaf, Stalk, Root, Flower, and Seed of all the Species, about which the Poet is often very ignorant: And yet the Poet shall have a much more delightful Perception of the Whole; and not only the Poet but any Man of a fine Taste. Our External Senses may by measuring teach us all the Proportions of Architecture to the Tenth of an Inch, and the Situation of every Muscle in the human Body; and a good Memory may retain these: and yet there is still something farther necessary, not only to make a Man a compleat Master in Architecture, Painting or Statuary, but even a tolerable Judge in these Works; or capable of receiving the highest Pleasure in contemplating them. Since then there are such different Powers of Perception, where what are commonly called the External Senses are the same; since the most accurate Knowledge of what the External Senses discover often does not give the Pleasure of Beauty or Harmony, which yet one of a good Taste will enjoy at once without much Knowledge; we may justly use another Name for these higher, and more delightful Perceptions of Beauty and Harmony, and call the Power of receiving such Impressions, an Internal Sense. The Difference of the Perceptions seems sufficient to vindicate the Use of a different Name, especially when we are told in what meaning the Word is applied.

XIII. This superior Power of Perception is justly called a Sense, because of its Affinity to the other Senses in this, that the Pleasure does not arise from any Knowledge of Principles, Proportions, Causes, or of the Usefulness of the Object; but strikes us at first with the Idea of Beauty: nor does the most accurate Knowledge increase this Pleasure of Beauty, however it may superadd a distinct rational Pleasure from prospects of Advantage, or from the Increase of Knowledge.

XIV. And farther, the Ideas of Beauty and Harmony, like other sensible Ideas, are necessarily pleasant to us, as well as immediately so; neither can any Resolution of our own, nor any Prospect of Advantage or Disadvantage, vary the Beauty or Deformity of an Object: For as in the external Sensations, no View of Interest will make an Object grateful, nor View of Detriment, distinct from immediate Pain in the Perception, make it disagreeable to the Sense; so propose the whole World as a Reward, or threaten the greatest Evil, to make us approve a deform'd Object, or disapprove a beautiful one; Dissimulation may be procur'd by Rewards or Threatenings, or we may in external Conduct abstain from any pursuit of the Beautiful, and pursue the Deform'd; but our Sentiments of the Former and our Perceptions, would continue invariably the same.

XV. Hence it plainly appears, "that some Objects are immediately the Occasions of this Pleasure of Beauty, and that we have Senses fitted for perceiving it; and that it is distinct from that Joy which arises upon prospect of Advantage." Nay, do not we often see Convenience and Use neglected to obtain Beauty, without any other prospect of Advantage in the Beautiful Form, than the suggesting the pleasant Ideas of Beauty? Now this shews us, that however we may pursue beautiful Objects from Self-love, with a view to obtain the Pleasures of Beauty, as in Architecture, Gardening, and many other Affairs; yet there must be a Sense of Beauty, antecedent to Prospects even of this Advantage, without which Sense, these Objects would not be thus Advantageous, nor excite in us this Pleasure which constitutes them advantageous. Our Sense of Beauty from Objects, by which they are constituted good to us, is very distinct from our Desire of them when they are thus constituted: Our Desire of Beauty may be counter-balanc'd by Rewards or Threatnings, but never our Sense of it; even as Fear of Death may make us desire a bitter Potion, or neglect those Meats which the Sense of Taste would recommend as pleasant; and yet no prospect of Advantage, or Fear of Evil, can make that Potion agreeable to the Sense, or Meat disagreeable to it, which was not so antecedently to this Prospect. The same holds true of the Sense of Beauty and Harmony; that the Pursuit of such Objects if frequently neglected, from prospects of Advantage, Aversion to Labour, or any other Motive or Interest, does not prove that we have no Sense of Beauty, but only that our Desire of it may be counter-balanc'd by a stronger Desire. . . .

XVII. Beauty is either Original or Comparative; or, if any like the Terms better, Absolute, or Relative: Only let it be observ'd, that by Absolute or Original Beauty, is not understood any Quality suppos'd to be in the Object, which should itself be beautiful, without relation to any Mind which perceives it: For Beauty, like other Names of sensible Ideas, properly denotes the Perception of some Mind; so Cold, Hot, Sweet, Bitter, denote the Sensations in our Minds, to which perhaps there is no resemblance in the Objects, which excite these Ideas in us, however we generally imagine otherwise. The Ideas of Beauty and Harmony being excited upon our Perception of some primary Quality, and having relation to Figure and Time, may indeed have a nearer resemblance to Objects, than these Sensations, which seem not so much any Pictures of Objects, as Modifications of the perceiving Mind; and yet were there no Mind with a Sense of Beauty to contemplate Objects, I see not how they could be call'd beautiful. We therefore by Absolute Beauty understand only that Beauty, which we perceive in Objects without comparison to any thing external, of which the Object is suppos'd an Imitation, or Picture; such as that Beauty perceiv'd from the Works of Nature, artificial Forms, Figures, Theorems. Comparative or Relative Beauty is that which we perceive in Objects, commonly considered as Imitations or Resemblances of something else. These two Kinds of Beauty employ the three following Sections.

Sect. II

Of Original or Absolute Beauty

I. Since it is certain that we have Ideas of Beauty and Harmony, let us examine what Quality in Objects excites these Ideas, or is the occasion of them. And let it be here observ'd, that our Inquiry is only about the Qualitys which are beautiful to Men; or about the Foundation of their Sense of Beauty: for, as was above hinted, Beauty has always relation to the Sense of some Mind; and when we afterwards shew how generally the Objects which occur to us, are beautiful, we mean that such Objects are agreeable to the Sense of Men: for there are many Objects which seem no way beautiful to Men, and yet other Animals seem delighted with them; they may have Senses otherwise constituted than those of Men, and may have the Ideas of Beauty excited by Objects of a quite different Form. We see Animals fitted for every Place; and what to Men appears rude and shapeless, or loathsom, may be to them a Paradise.

II. That we may more distinctly discover the general Foundation or Occasion of the Ideas of Beauty among Men, it will be necessary to consider it first in its simpler Kinds, such as occurs to us, in regular Figures; and we may perhaps find that the same Foundation extends to all the more complex Species of it.

III. The Figures which excite in us the Ideas of Beauty, seem to be those in which there is Uniformity amidst Variety. There are many Conceptions of Objects which are agreeable upon other accounts, such as Grandeur, Novelty, Sanctity, and some others, which shall be mention'd hereafter. But what we call Beautiful in objects, to speak in the Mathematical Style, seems to be in a compound Ratio of Uniformity and Variety: so that where the Uniformity of Bodys is equal, the Beauty is as the Variety; and where the Variety is equal, the Beauty is as the Uniformity. . . .

V. The same Foundation we have for our Sense of Beauty in the Works of NATURE. In every Part of the World which we call Beautiful, there is a surprizing Uniformity amidst an almost infinite Variety. Many Parts of the Universe seem not at all design'd for the use of Man; nay, it is but a very small Spot with which we have any acquaintance. The Figures and Motions of the great Bodys are not obvious to our Senses, but found out by Reasoning and Reflection, upon many long Observations: and yet as far as we can by Sense discover or by Reasoning enlarge our Knowledge, and extend our Imagination, we generally find their Structure, Order, and Motion, agreeable to our Sense of Beauty. Every particular Object in Nature does not indeed appear beautiful to us; but there is a great Profusion of Beauty over most of the Objects which occur either to our Senses, or Reasonings upon Observation: For not to mention the apparent Situation of the heavenly Bodys in the Circumference of a great Sphere, which is wholly occasion'd by the Imperfection of our Sight in discerning Distances; the Forms of all the great Bodys in the Universe are nearly Spherical; the Orbits of their Revolutions generally Elliptick, and without great Eccentricity, in those which continually occur to our Observation: now these are Figures of great Uniformity, and therefore pleasing to us. . . .

XIV. But in all these Instances of Beauty let it be observ'd, That the Pleasure is communicated to those who never reflected on this general Foundation; and that all here alleg'd is this, "That the pleasant Sensation arises only from Objects, in which there is Uniformity amidst Variety": We may have the Sensation without knowing what is the Occasion of it; as a Man's Taste may suggest Ideas of Sweets, Acids, Bitters, tho he be ignorant of the Forms of the small Bodys, or their Motions, which excite these Perceptions in him.

Sect. III

Of the Beauty of Theorems

I. The Beauty of Theorems, or universal Truths demonstrated, deserves a distinct Consideration, being of a Nature pretty different from the former kinds of Beauty; and yet there is none in which we shall see such an amazing Variety with Uniformity: and hence arises a very great Pleasure distinct from Prospects of any farther Advantage.

II. For in one Theorem we may find included, with the most exact Agreement, an infinite Multitude of particular Truths; nay, often an Infinity of Infinites: so that altho the Necessity of forming abstract Ideas and universal Theorems, arises perhaps from the Limitation of our Minds, which cannot admit an infinite Multitude of singular

Ideas or Judgments at once, yet this Power gives us an Evidence of the Largeness of the human Capacity above our Imagination. Thus for instance, the 47th Proposition of the first Book of EUCLID's *Elements* contains an infinite Multitude of Truths, concerning the infinite possible Sizes of right-angled Triangles, as you make the Area greater or less; and in each of these Sizes you may find an infinite Multitude of dissimilar Triangles, as you vary the Proportion of the Base to the Perpendicular; all which Infinitys of Infinites agree in the general Theorem. In Algebraick, and the Fluxional Calculations, we shall still find a greater Variety of particular Truths included in general Theorems; not only in general Equations applicable to all Kinds of Quantity, but in more particular Investigations of Areas and Tangents: In which one Manner of Operation shall discover Theorems applicable to infinite Orders or Species of Curves, to the infinite Sizes of each Species, and to the infinite Points of the infinite Individuals of each Size.

III. That we may the better discern this Agreement, or Unity of an Infinity of Objects, in the general Theorem, to be the Foundation of the Beauty or Pleasure attending their Discovery, let us compare our Satisfaction in such Discoverys, with the uneasy state of Mind in which we are, when we can only measure Lines, or Surfaces, by a Scale, or are making Experiments which we can reduce to no general Canon, but only heaping up a Multitude of particular incoherent Observations. Now each of these Trials discovers a new Truth, but with no Pleasure or Beauty, notwithstanding the Variety, till we can discover some sort of Unity, or reduce them to some general Canon.

IV. Again, let us take a Metaphysical Axiom, such as this, Every Whole is greater than its Part; and we shall find no Beauty in the Contemplation. For tho this Proposition contains many Infinitys of particular Truths; yet the Unity is inconsiderable, since they all agree only in a vague, undetermin'd Conception of Whole and Part, and in an indefinite Excess of the former above the latter, which is sometimes great and sometimes small. So, should we hear that the Cylinder is greater than the inscrib'd Sphere, and this again greater than the Cone of the same Altitude and Diameter of the Base, we shall find no pleasure in this Knowledge of a general Relation of greater and less, without any precise Difference or Proportion. But when we see the universal exact Agreement of all possible Sizes of such Systems of Solids, that they preserve to each other the constant Ration of 3,2,1; how beautiful is the Theorem, and how we are ravish'd with its first Discovery.

We may likewise observe, that easy or obvious Propositions, even where the Unity is sufficiently distinct, and determinate, do not please us so much as those, which being less obvious, give us some Surprize in the Discovery: Thus we find little Pleasure in discovering that a Line bisecting the vertical Angle of an Isosceles Triangle, bisects the Base, or the Reverse; or, that Equilateral Triangles are Equiangular. These Truths we almost know Intuitively, without Demonstration: They are like common Goods, or those which Men have long possessed, which do not give such sensible Joys as much smaller new Additions may give us. But let none hence imagine, that the sole Pleasure of Theorems is from Surprize; for the same Novelty of a single Experiment does not please us much: nor ought we to conclude from the greater Pleasure accompanying a new, or unexpected Advantage, that Surprize, or Novelty is the only Pleasure of Life, or the only ground of Delight in Truth. . . .

It is easy to see how Men are charm'd with the Beauty of such Knowledge, besides its

Usefulness; and how this sets them upon deducing the Propertys of each Figure from one Genesis, and demonstrating the mechanick Forces from one Theorem of the Composition of Motion; even after they have sufficient Knowledge and Certainty in all these Truths from distinct independent Demonstrations. And this Pleasure we enjoy even when we have no Prospect of obtaining any other Advantage from such Manner of Deduction, than the immediate Pleasure of contemplating the Beauty: nor could Love of Fame excite us to such regular Methods of Deduction, were we not conscious that Mankind are pleas'd with them immediately, by this internal Sense of their Beauty.

It is no less easy to see into what absurd Attempts Men have been led by this Sense of Beauty, and an Affection of obtaining it in the other Sciences as well as the Mathematicks. 'Twas this probably which set DESCARTES on that hopeful Project of deducing all human Knowledge from one Proposition, *viz. Cogito, ergo sum;* while others with as little Sense contended, that *Impossibile est idem simul esse and non esse,* had much fairer Pretensions to the Style and Title of *Principium humanae Cognitionis absolute primum.* Mr. LEIBNITZ had an equal Affection for his favourite Principle of a sufficient Reason for every thing in Nature, and brags to Dr. CLARKE of the Wonders he had wrought in the intellectual World by its Assistance; but his learned Antagonist seems to think he had not sufficient Reason for his Boasting. If we look into particular Sciences, we may see in the Systems learned Men have given us of them, the Inconveniences of this Love of Uniformity. . . .

Sect. IV

Of Relative or Comparative Beauty

I. If the preceding Thoughts concerning the Foundation of absolute Beauty be just, we may easily understand wherein relative Beauty consists. All Beauty is relative to the Sense of some Mind perceiving it; but what we call relative is that which is apprehended in any Object, commonly consider'd as an Imitation of some Original: And this Beauty is founded on a Conformity, or a kind of Unity between the Original and the Copy. The Original may be either some Object in Nature, or some establish'd Idea; for if there be any known Idea as a Standard, and Rules to fix this Image or Idea by, we may make a beautiful Imitation. Thus a Statuary, Painter, or Poet, may please us with an HERCULES, if his Piece retains that Grandeur, and those marks of Strength, and Courage, which we imagine in that Hero.

And farther, to obtain comparative Beauty alone, it is not necessary that there be any Beauty in the Original; the Imitation of absolute Beauty may indeed in the whole make a more lovely Piece, and yet an exact Imitation shall still be beautiful, tho the Original were intirely void of it: Thus the Deformitys of old Age in a Picture, the rudest Rocks or Mountains in a Landskip, if well represented, shall have abundant Beauty, tho perhaps not so great as if the Original were absolutely beautiful, and as well represented: Nay, perhaps the Novelty may make us prefer the representation of Irregularity.

II. The same Observation holds true in the Descriptions of the Poets either of natural Objects or Persons; and this relative Beauty is what they should principally endeavour to obtain, as the peculiar Beauty of their Works. By the *Moratoe Fabulae,* we are not to understand virtuous Manners in a moral Sense, but a just Representation of Manners or Characters as they are in Nature; and that the Actions and Sentiments be suited to the Characters of the Persons to whom they are ascrib'd in Epick and Dramatick Poetry. Perhaps very good Reasons may be suggested from the Nature of our Passions, to prove that a Poet should not draw his Characters perfectly Virtuous; these Characters indeed abstractly consider'd might give more Pleasure, and have more Beauty than the imperfect ones which occur in Life with a mixture of Good and Evil: But it may suffice at present to suggest against this Choice, that we have more lively Ideas of imperfect Men with all their Passions, than of morally perfect Heroes, such as really never occur to our Observation; and of which consequently we cannot judge exactly as to their Agreement with the Copy. And farther, thro' Consciousness of our own State, we are more nearly touch'd and affected by the imperfect Characters; since in them we see represented, in the Persons of others, the Contrasts of Inclinations, and the Struggles between the Passions of Self-Love and those of Honour and Virtue, which we often feel in our own Breasts. This is the Perfection of Beauty for which HOMER is justly admir'd, as well as for the Variety of his Characters.

III. Many other Beautys of Poetry may be reduc'd under this Class of relative Beauty: The Probability is absolutely necessary to make us imagine Resemblance; it is by Resemblance that the Similitudes, Metaphors and Allegorys are made either the Subject or the Thing compar'd to it have Beauty or not; the Beauty indeed is greater, when both have some original Beauty or Dignity as well as Resemblance: and this is the foundation of the Rule of studying Decency in Metaphors and Similys as well as Likeness. The Measures and Cadence are instances of Harmony, and come under the head of absolute Beauty.

IV. We may here observe a strange Proneness in our Minds to make perpetual Comparisons of all things which occur to our Observation, even of those which are very different from each other. There are certain Resemblances in the Motions of all Animals upon like Passions, which easily found a Comparison; but this does not serve to entertain our Fancy: Inanimate Objects have often such Positions as resemble those of the human Body in various Circumstances; these Airs or Gestures of the Body are Indications of certain Dispositions in the Mind, so that our very Passions and Affections as well as other Circumstances obtain a Resemblance to natural inanimate Objects. Thus a Tempest at Sea is often an Emblem of Wrath; a Plant or Tree drooping under the Rain, of a Person in Sorrow; a Poppy bending its Stalk, or a Flower withering when cut by the Plow, resembles the Death of a blooming Hero; an aged Oak in the Mountains shall represent an old Empire, a Flame seizing a Wood shall represent other things, even the most remote, especially the Passions and Circumstances of human Nature in which we are more nearly concern'd; and to confirm this and furnish Instances of it, one need only look into HOMER or VIRGIL. A fruitful Fancy would find in a Grove, or a Wood, an Emblem for every Character in a Commonwealth, and every turn of Temper, or Station in Life.

V. Concerning that kind of comparative Beauty which has a necessary relation to some establish'd Idea, we may observe, that some Works of Art acquire a distinct Beauty by their Correspondence to some universally suppos'd Intention in the Artificers, or the Persons who employ'd him: And to obtain this Beauty, sometimes they do not form their Works so as to attain the highest Perfection of original Beauty separately consider'd; because a Composition of this relative Beauty, along with some degree of the original Kind, may give more Pleasure, than a more perfect original Beauty separately. Thus we see, that strict Regularity in laying out of Gardens in Parterres, Vistas, parallel Walks, is often neglected, to obtain an Imitation of Nature even in some of its Wildnesses. And we are more pleas'd with this Imitation, especially when the Scene is large and spacious, than with the more confin'd Exactness of regular Works. So likewise in the Monuments erected in honour of deceased Heroes, altho a Cylinder, or Prism, or regular Solid, may have more original Beauty than a very acute Pyramid or Obelisk, yet the latter pleases more, by answering better the suppos'd Intentions of Stability, and being conspicuous. For the same reason Cubes, or square Prisms, are generally chosen for the Pedestals of Statues, and not any of the more beautiful Solids, which do not seem so secure from rolling. This may be the reason too, why Columns or Pillars look best when made a little taper from the middle, or a third from the bottom, that they may not seem top-heavy and in danger of falling.

VI. The like reason may influence Artists, in many other Instances, to depart from the Rules of original Beauty, as above laid down. And yet this is no Argument against our Sense of Beauty being founded, as was above explain'd, on Uniformity amidst Variety, but only an Evidence that our Sense of Beauty of the Original Kind may be vary'd and overbalanc'd by another kind of Beauty.

Sect. VI

Of the Universality of the Sense of Beauty among Men

I. We before insinuated, "That all Beauty has a relation to some perceiving Power"; and consequently since we know not how great a Variety of Senses there may be among Animals, there is no Form in Nature concerning which we can pronounce, "That it has no Beauty"; for it may still please some perceiving Power. But our Inquiry is confin'd to Men; and before we examine the Universality of this Sense of Beauty, or their agreement in approving Uniformity, it may be proper to consider, "whether, as the other Senses which give us Pleasure do also give us Pain, so this Sense of Beauty does make some Objects disagreeable to us, and the occasion of Pain."

That many Objects give no pleasure to our Sense is obvious; many are certainly void of Beauty: But then there is no Form which seems necessarily disagreeable of itself, when we dread no other Evil from it, and compare it with nothing better of the Kind. Many Objects are naturally displeasing, and distasteful to our external Senses, as well as others pleasing and agreeable; as Smells, Tastes, and some separate Sounds: but as to our Sense of Beauty, no Composition of Objects which give not unpleasant simple Ideas, seems positively unpleasant or painful of itself, had we never observ'd any thing better of the kind. Deformity is only the absence of Beauty, or deficiency in the Beauty expected in any Species: Thus bad Musick pleases Rusticks who never heard any better, and the finest Ear is not offended with tuning of Instruments if it be not too tedious, where no Harmony is expected; and yet much small Dissonancy shall offend amidst the Performance, where Harmony is expected. A rude Heap of Stones is no way offensive to one who shall be displeas'd with Irregularity in Architecture, where

Beauty was expected. And had there been a Species of that Form which we now call ugly or deform'd, and had we never seen or expected greater Beauty, we should have receiv'd no disgust from it, altho the Pleasure would not have been so great in this Form as in those we now admire. Our Sense of Beauty seems design'd to give us positive Pleasure, but not positive Pain or Disgust, any farther than what arises from disappointment.

II. There are indeed many Faces which at first View are apt to raise Dislike; but this is generally not from any Deformity which of it self is positively displeasing, but either from want of expected Beauty, or much more from their carrying some natural indications of morally bad Dispositions, which we all acquire a Faculty of discerning in Countenances, Airs, and Gestures. That this is not occasion'd by any Form positively disgusting, will appear from this, That if upon long acquaintance we are sure of finding sweetness of Temper, Humanity and Cheerfulness, altho the bodily Form continues, it shall give us no Disgust or Displeasure; whereas if any thing were naturally disagreeable, or the occasion of Pain, or positive Distaste, it would always continue so, even altho the Aversion we might have toward it were counterbalanc'd by other Considerations. There are Horrors rais'd by some Objects, which are only the Effect of Fear for our selves, or Compassion towards others, when either Reason, or some foolish Association of Ideas, makes us apprehend Danger, and not the Effect of any thing in the Form it self: for we find that most of those Objects which excite Horror at first, when Experience or Reason has remov'd the Fear, may become the occasions of Pleasure; as ravenous Beasts, a tempestuous Sea, a craggy Precipice, a dark shady Valley.

III. We shall see hereafter, "That Associations of Ideas make Objects pleasant, and delightful, which are not naturally apt to give any such Pleasures; and the same way, the casual Conjunctions of Ideas may give a Disgust, where there is nothing disagreeable in the Form it self." And this is the occasion of many fantastick Aversions to Figures of some Animals, and to some other Forms: Thus Swine, Serpents of all Kinds, and some Insects really beautiful enough, are beheld with Aversion by many People, who have got some accidental Ideas associated to them. And for Distastes of this Kind, no other Account can be given.

IV. But as the universal Agreement of Mankind in their Sense of Beauty from Uniformity amidst Variety, we must consult Experience: and as we allow all Men Reason, since all Men are capable of understanding simple Arguments, tho few are capable of complex Demonstrations; so in this Case it must be sufficient to prove this sense of Beauty universal, "if all Men are better pleas'd with Uniformity in the simpler Instances than the contrary, even when there is no Advantage observ'd attending it; and likewise if all Men, according as their Capacity enlarges, so as to receive and compare more complex Ideas, have a greater Delight in Uniformity, and are pleas'd with its more complex Kinds, both Original and Relative."

Now let us consider if ever any Person was void of this Sense in the simpler Instances. Few Trials have been made in the simplest Instances of Harmony, because as soon as we find an Ear incapable of relishing complex Compositions, such as our Tunes are, no farther Pains are employ'd about such. But in Figures, did ever any Man make choice of a Trapezium, or any irregular Curve, for the Ichnography or Plan of his House, without Necessity, or some great Motive of Convenience? or to make the opposite Walls not parallel, or unequal in Height? Were ever Trapeziums, irregular Polygons or Curves chosen for the Forms of Doors or Windows, though these Figures might have answer'd the Uses as well, and would have often sav'd a great part of the Time, Labour and Expence to Workmen, which is now employ'd in suiting the Stones and Timber to the regular Forms? Among all the fantastick Modes of Dress, none was ever quite void of Uniformity, if it were only in the resemblance of the two Sides of the same Robe, and in some general Aptitude to the human Form. The Pictish Painting had always relative Beauty, by resemblance to other Objects, and often those Objects were originally beautiful. . . . But never were any so extravagant as to affect such Figures as are made by the casual spilling of liquid Colours. Who was ever pleas'd with an inequality of Heights in Windows of the same Range, or dissimilar Shapes of them? with unequal Legs or Arms, Eyes or Cheeks in a Mistress? It must however be acknowledg'd, "That Interest may often counter-balance our Sense of Beauty, in this Affair as well as in others, and superior good qualitys may make us overlook such Imperfections."

V. Nay farther, it may perhaps appear, "That Regularity and Uniformity are so copiously diffus'd thro' the Universe, and we are so readily determin'd to pursue this as the Foundation of Beauty in Works of Art, that there is scarcely any thing ever fancy'd as Beautiful, where there is not really something of this Uniformity and Regularity." We are indeed often mistaken in imagining that there is the greatest possible Beauty, where it is but very imperfect; but still it is some degree of Beauty, which pleases, altho there may be higher Degrees which we do not observe; and our Sense acts with full Regularity when we are pleas'd, altho we are kept by a false Prejudice from pursuing Objects which would please us more.

A goth, for instance, is mistaken, when from Education he imagines the Architecture of his Country to be the most perfect: and a Conjunction of some hostile Ideas, may make him have an Aversion to Roman Buildings, and study to demolish them, as some of our Reformers did the Popish Buildings, not being able to separate the Ideas of the superstitious Worship from the Forms of the Buildings where it was practised: and yet it is still real Beauty which pleases the GOTH, founded upon Uniformity amidst Variety. For the Gothick Pillars are uniform to each other, not only in their Sections, which are Lozengeform'd; but also in their Heights and Ornaments: Their Arches are not one uniform Curve, but yet they are Segments of similar Curves, and generally equal in the same Ranges. The very Indian Buildings have some kind of Uniformity, and many of the EASTERN NATIONS, tho they differ much from us, yet have great Regularity in their Manner, as well as the ROMANS in theirs. Our Indian Screens, which wonderfully supply our Imaginations with Ideas of Deformity, in which Nature is very churlish and sparing, do want indeed all the Beauty arising from Proportion of Parts, and Conformity to Nature; and yet they cannot disvest themselves of all Beauty and Uniformity in the separate Parts: And this diversifying the human Body into various Contortions, may give some wild Pleasure from Variety, since some Uniformity to the human Shape is still retain'd.

VI. There is one sort of Beauty which might perhaps have been better mention'd before, but will not be impertinent here, because the Taste or Relish of it is universal in all Nations, and with the Young as well as the Old, and that is the Beauty of History. Every one knows how dull a Study is to read over a Collection of Gazettes, which shall perhaps relate all the same Events with the Historian: The superior Pleasure then of History must arise, like that of Poetry, from the Manners; when we see a Character well drawn, wherein we find the secret Causes of a great Diversity of seemingly inconsistent Actions; or an Interest of State laid open, or an artful View nicely unfolded, the Execution of which influences very different and opposite Actions as the Circumstances may alter. Now this reduces the whole to an Unity of Design at least: And this may be observ'd in the very Fables which entertain Children, otherwise we cannot make them relish them.

VII. What has been said will probably be assented to, if we always remember in our Inquirys into the Universality of the Sense of Beauty, That there may be real Beauty, "where there is not the greatest; and that there are an Infinity of different Forms which may all have some Unity, and yet differ from each other." So that Men may have different Fancys of Beauty, and yet Uniformity be the universal Foundation of our Approbation of any Form whatsoever as Beautiful. And we shall find that it is so in the Architecture, Gardening, Dress, Equipage, and Furniture of Houses, even among the most uncultivated Nations; where Uniformity still pleases, without any other Advantage than the Pleasure of the Contemplation of it.

VIII. It will deserve our Consideration on this Subject, how, in like Cases, we form very different Judgments concerning the internal and external Senses. Nothing is more ordinary among those, who after Mr. LOCKE have rejected innate Ideas, than to alledge, "That all our Relish for Beauty, and Order, is either from prospect of Advantage, Custom, or Education," for no other Reason but the Variety of Fancys in the World: and from this they conclude, "That our Fancys do not arise from any natural Power of Perception, or Sense." And yet all allow our external Senses to be Natural, and that the Pleasures or Pains of their Sensations, however they may be increas'd, or diminish'd, by Custom, or Education, and counterbalanc'd by Interest, yet are really antecedent to Custom, Habit, Education, or Prospect of Interest. Now it is certain, "That there is at least as great a variety of Fancys about their Objects, as the Objects of Beauty": Nay it is much more difficult, and perhaps impossible, to bring the Fancys or Relishes of the external Senses to any general Foundation at all, or to find any Rule for the agreeable or disagreeable: and yet we all allow "that these are natural Powers of Perception."

IX. The Reason of this different Judgment can be no other than this, That we have got distinct Names for the external Senses, and none, or very few, for the Internal; and by this are led, as in many other Cases, to look upon the former as some way more fix'd and real and natural, than the latter. The Sense of Harmony has got its Name, viz. a good Ear; and we are generally brought to acknowledge this a natural Power of Perception, or a Sense some way distinct from Hearing: now it is certain, "That there is as necessary a Perception of Beauty upon the presence of regular Objects, as of Harmony upon hearing certain Sounds."

X. But let it be observ'd here once for all, "That an internal Sense no more presupposes an innate Idea, or principle of Knowledge, than the external." Both are natural Powers of Perception, or Determinations of the Mind to receive necessarily certain Ideas from the presence of Objects. The internal Sense is, a passive Power of receiving Ideas of Beauty from all Objects in which there is Uniformity amidst Variety. Nor does there seem any thing more difficult in this matter, than that the Mind should always be determin'd to receive the Idea of Sweet, when Particles of such a Form enter the Pores of the Tongue; or to have as little Connection with its Idea, as the other: And the same Power could with equal ease constitute the former the occasion of Ideas as the latter.

XI. The Association of Ideas above hinted at, is one great Cause of the apparent Diversity of Fancys in the Sense of Beauty, as well as in the external Senses; and often makes Men have an aversion to Objects of Beauty, and a liking to others void of it, but under different Conceptions than those of Beauty or Deformity. And here it may not be improper to give some Instances of some of these Associations. The Beauty of Trees, their cool Shades, and their Aptness to conceal from Observation, have made Groves and Woods, the usual Retreat to those who love Solitude, especially to the Religious, the Pensive, the Melancholy, and the Amorous. And do not we find that we have so join'd the Ideas of these Dispositions of Mind with those external Objects, that they always recur to us along with them? The Cunning of the Heathen Priests might make such obscure Places the Scene of the fictitious Appearances of their Deitys; and hence we join Ideas of something Divine to them. We know the like Effect in the Ideas of our Churches, from the perpetual use of them only in religious Exercises. The faint Light in Gothick Buildings has had the same Association of a very foreign Idea, which our Poet shews in his Epithet, A Dim religious Light.

In like manner it is known, That often all the Circumstances of Actions, or Places, or Dresses of Persons, or Voice, or Song, which have occur'd at any time together, when we were strongly affected by any Passion, will be so connected that any one of these will make all the rest recur. And this is often the occasion both of great Pleasure and Pain, Delight and Aversion to many Objects, which of themselves might have been perfectly indifferent to us: but these Approbations, or Distastes, are remote from the Ideas of Beauty, being plainly different Ideas.

XII. There is also another Charm in Musick to various Persons, which is distinct from the Harmony, and is occasion'd by its raising agreeable Passions. The human Voice is obviously vary'd by all the stronger Passions; now when our Ear discerns any resemblance between the Air of a Tune, whether sung or play'd upon an Instrument, either in its Time, or Modulation, or any other Circumstance, to the sound of the human Voice in any Passion, we shall be touch'd by it in a very sensible manner, and have Melancholy, Joy, Gravity, Thoughtfulness, excited in us by a sort of Sympathy or Contagion. The same Connexion is observable between the very Air of a Tune, and the Words expressing any Passion which we have heard it fitted to, so that they shall both recur to us together, tho but one of them affects our Senses.

Now in such a diversity of pleasing or displeasing Ideas which may be join'd with Forms of Bodys, or Tunes, when Men are of such different Dispositions, and prone to such a variety of Passions, it is no wonder "that they should often disagree in their Fancys of Objects, even altho their Sense of Beauty and Harmony were perfectly uniform"; because many other Ideas may either please or displease, according to Persons' Tempers, and past Circumstances. We know how agreeable a very wild Country may be to any Person who has spent the chearful Days of his Youth in it, and how disagreeable very beautiful places may be, if they were the Scenes of his Misery. And this may help us in many Cases to account for the Diversitys of Fancy, without denying the Uniformity of our internal Sense of Beauty.

XIII. Grandeur and Novelty are two Ideas different from Beauty, which often recommend Objects to us. . . .

Sect. VII

Of the Power of Custom, Education, and Example, as to our Internal Senses

I. Custom, Education, and Example are so often alledg'd in this Affair, as the occasion of our Relish for beautiful Objects, and for our Approbation of, or Delight in a certain Conduct in Life in a moral Species, that it is necessary to examine these three particularly, to make it appear "that there is a natural Power of Perception, or Sense of Beauty in Objects, antecedent to all Custom, Education, or Example."

II. Custom, as distinct from the other two, operates in this manner. As to Actions, it only gives a disposition to the Mind or Body more easily to perform those Actions which have been frequently repeated, but never leads us to apprehend them under any other View than what we were capable of apprehending them under at first; nor gives us any new Power of Perception about them. We are naturally capable of Sentiments of Fear, and Dread of any powerful Presence; and so Custom may connect the Ideas of religious Horror to certain Buildings: but Custom could never have made a Being naturally incapable of Fear, receive such Ideas. So had we no other Power of perceiving, or forming Ideas of Actions, but as they were advantageous or dis-advantageous, Custom could only have made us more ready at perceiving the Advan-tage or Disadvantage of Actions. But this is not to our present purpose.

As to our Approbation of, or Delight in external Objects. When the Blood or Spirits, of which Anatomists talk, are rous'd, quicken'd, or fermented as they call it, in any agreeable manner by Medicine or Nutriment; or any Glands frequently stimulated to Secretion; it is certain that to preserve the Body easy, we shall delight in Objects of Taste which of themselves are not immediately pleasant to it, if they promote that agreeable State which the Body had been accustom'd to. Farther, Custom will so alter the State of the Body, that what at first rais'd uneasy Sensations will cease to do so, or perhaps raise another agreeable Idea of the same Sense; but Custom can never give us any Idea of a Sense different from those we had antecedent to it: It will never make the Blind approve Objects as coloured, or those who have no Taste approve Meats as delicious, however they might approve them as Strengthening or Exhilarating. Were our Glands and the Parts about them void of Feeling, did we perceive no Pleasure from certain brisker Motions in the Blood, Custom could never make stimulating or intoxicating Fluids or Medicines agreeable, when they were not so to the Taste: So by like Reasoning, had we no natural Sense of Beauty from Uniformity, Custom could never have made us imagine any Beauty in Objects; if we had had no Ear, Custom could never have given us the Pleasures of Harmony. When we have these natural Senses antecedently, Custom may make us capable of extending our Views farther, and of receiving more complex Ideas of Beauty in Bodys, or Harmony in Sounds, by increasing our Attention and quickness of Perception. But however Custom may increase our Power of receiving or comparing complex Ideas, yet it seems rather to weaken than strengthen the Ideas of Beauty, or the Impressions of Pleasure from regular Objects; else how is it possible that any Person could go into the open Air on a sunny Day, or clear Evening, without the most extravagant Raptures, such as MILTON represents our ancestor upon his first Creation? For such any Person would certainly fall into, upon the first Representation of such a Scene.

Custom in like manner may make it easier for any Person to discern the Use of a complex Machine, and approve it as advantageous; but he would never have imagin'd it Beautiful, had he no natural Sense of Beauty. Custom may make us quicker in apprehending the Truth of complex Theorems, but we all find the Pleasure or Beauty of Theorems as strong at first as ever. Custom makes us more capable of retaining and comparing complex Ideas, so as to discern more complicated Uniformity, which escapes the Observation of Novices in any Art; but all this presupposes a natural Sense of Beauty in Uniformity: for had there been nothing in Forms, which was constituted the necessary occasion of Pleasure to our Senses, no Repetition of indifferent Ideas as to Pleasure or Pain, Beauty or Deformity, could ever have made them grow pleasing or displeasing.

III. The Effect of Education is this, that thereby we receive many speculative Opinions, which are sometimes true and sometimes false; and are often led to believe that Objects may be naturally apt to give Pleasure or Pain to our external Senses, which in reality have no such Qualitys. And farther, by Education there are some strong Associations of Ideas without any Reason, by mere Accident sometimes, as well as by Design, which it is very hard for us ever after to break asunder. Thus Aversions are rais'd to Darkness, and to many kinds of Meat, and to certain innocent Actions: Approbations without Ground are aris'd in like manner. But in all these Instances, Education never makes us apprehend any Qualitys in Objects, which we have not naturally Senses capable of perceiving. We know what Sickness of the Stomach is, and may without Ground believe that very healthful Meats will raise this; we by our Sight and Smell receive disagreeable Ideas of the Food of Swine, and their Styes, and perhaps cannot prevent the recurring of these Ideas at Table: but never were Men naturally Blind prejudic'd against Objects as of a disagreeable Colour, or in favour of others as of a beautiful Colour; they perhaps hear Men dispraise one Colour, and may imagine this Colour to be some quite different sensible Quality of the other Senses, but that is all. And the same way, a Man naturally void of Taste could by no Education receive the Ideas of Taste, or be prejudic'd in favour of Meats as delicious: So, had we no natural Sense of Beauty and Harmony, we could never be prejudic'd in favour of Objects or Sounds as Beautiful or Harmonious. Education may make an unattentive GOTH imagine that his Countrymen have attain'd the Perfection of Architecture; and an Aversion of their Enemys the ROMANS, may have join'd some disagreeable Ideas to their very Buildings, and excited them to their Demolition; but he had never form'd these Prejudices, had he been void of a Sense of Beauty. Did ever blind Men debate whether Purple or Scarlet were the finer Colour? or could any Education prejudice them in favour of either as Colours?

Thus Education and Custom may influence our internal Senses, where they are antecedently, by enlarging the Capacity of our Minds to retain and compare the Parts of complex Compositions: And then if the finest Objects are presented to us, we grow conscious of a Pleasure far superior to what common Performances excite. But all this presupposes our Sense of Beauty to be natural. Instruction in Anatomy, Observation of Nature, and of those Airs of the Countenance and Attitudes of Body, which accompany any Sentiment, Action, or Passion, may enable us to know where there is a just Imitation: but why should an exact Imitation please upon Observation, if we had not naturally a Sense of Beauty in it, more than the observing the Situation of fifty or a hundred Pebbles thrown at random? and should we observe them ever so often, we should never dream of their growing Beautiful.

David Hume

OF THE STANDARD OF TASTE:
FROM *FOUR DISSERTATIONS*

The great variety of Taste, as well as of opinion, which prevails in the world, is too obvious not to have fallen under every one's observation. Men of the most confined knowledge are able to remark a difference of taste in the narrow circle of their acquaintance, even where the persons have been educated under the same government, and have early imbibed the same prejudices. But those, who can enlarge their view to contemplate distant nations and remote ages, are still more surprized at the great inconsistence and contrariety. We are apt to call *barbarous* whatever departs widely from our own taste and apprehension: But soon find the epithet of reproach retorted on us. And the highest arrogance and self-conceit is at last startled, on observing an equal assurance on all sides, and scruples, amidst such a contest of sentiment, to pronounce positively in its own favour.

As this variety of taste is obvious to the most careless enquirer; so will it be found, on examination, to be still greater in reality than in appearance. The sentiments of men often differ with regard to beauty and deformity of all kinds, even while their general discourse is the same. There are certain terms in every language, which import blame, and others praise; and all men, who use the same tongue, must agree in their application of them. Every voice is united in applauding elegance, propriety, simplicity, spirit in writing; and in blaming fustian, affectation, coldness, and a false brilliancy: But when critics come to particulars, this seeming unanimity vanishes; and it is found, that they had affixed a very different meaning to their expressions. In all matters of opinion and science, the case is opposite: The difference among men is there oftener found to lie in generals than in particulars; and to be less in reality than in appearance. An explanation of the terms commonly ends the controversy; and the disputants are surprized to find, that they had been quarrelling, while at bottom they agreed in their judgment.

Those who found morality on sentiment, more than on reason, are inclined to comprehend ethics under the former observation, and to maintain, that, in all questions, which regard conduct and manners, the difference among men is really

Hume's essay is reprinted here in its entirety. This essay first appeared in 1757 in Hume's Four Dissertations. *It was later included in his* Essays and Treatises on Several Subjects.

greater than at first sight it appears. It is indeed obvious, that writers of all nations and all ages concur in applauding justice, humanity, magnanimity, prudence, veracity; and in blaming the opposite qualities. Even poets and other authors, whose compositions are chiefly calculated to please the imagination, are yet found, from Homer down to Fenelon, to inculcate the same moral precepts, and to bestow their applause and blame on the same virtues and vices. This great unanimity is usually ascribed to the influence of plain reason; which, in all these cases, maintains similar sentiments in all men, and prevents those controversies, to which the abstract sciences are so much exposed. So far as the unanimity is real, this account may be admitted as satisfactory: But we must also allow that some part of the seeming harmony in morals may be accounted for from the very nature of language. The word *virtue*, with its equivalent in every tongue, implies praise; as that of *vice* does blame: And no one, without the most obvious and grossest impropriety, could affix reproach to a term, which in general acceptation is understood in a good sense; or bestow applause, where the idiom requires disapprobation. Homer's general precepts, where he delivers any such, will never be controverted; but it is obvious, that, when he draws particular pictures of manners, and represents heroism in Achilles and prudence in Ulysses, he intermixes a much greater degree of ferocity in the former, and of cunning and fraud in the latter, than Fenelon would admit of. The sage Ulysses in the Greek poet seems to delight in lies and fictions, and often employs them without any necessity or even advantage: But his more scrupulous son, in the French epic writer, exposes himself to the most imminent perils, rather than depart from the most exact line of truth and veracity.

The admirers and followers of the Alcoran insist on the excellent moral precepts interspersed throughout that wild and absurd performance. But it is to be supposed, that the Arabic words, which correspond to the English, equity, justice, temperance, meekness, charity, were such as, from the constant use of that tongue, must always be taken in a good sense; and it would have argued the greatest ignorance, not of morals, but of language, to have mentioned them with any epithets, besides those of applause and approbation. But would we know, whether the pretended prophet had really attained a just sentiment of morals? Let us attend to his narration; and we shall soon find, that he bestows praise on such instances of treachery, inhumanity, cruelty, revenge, bigotry, as are utterly incompatible with civilized society. No steady rule of right seems there to be attended to; and every action is blamed or praised, so far only as it is beneficial or hurtful to the true believers.

The merit of delivering true general precepts in ethics is indeed very small. Whoever recommends any moral virtues, really does no more than is implied in the terms themselves. That people, who invented the word *charity*, and used it in a good sense, inculcated more clearly and much more efficaciously, the precept, *be charitable*, than any pretended legislator or prophet, who should insert such a *maxim* in his writings. Of all expressions, those, which, together with their other meaning, imply a degree either of blame or approbation, are the least liable to be perverted or mistaken.

It is natural for us to seek a *Standard of Taste*; a rule, by which the various sentiments of men may be reconciled; at least, a decision, afforded, confirming one sentiment, and condemning another.

There is a species of philosophy, which cuts off all hopes of success in such an attempt, and represents the impossibility of ever attaining any standard of taste. The difference, it is said, is very wide between judgment and sentiment. All sentiment is right; because sentiment has a reference to nothing beyond itself, and is always real, wherever a man is conscious of it. But all determinations of the understanding are not right; because they have a reference to something beyond themselves, to wit, real matter of fact; and are not always conformable to that standard. Among a thousand different opinions which different men may entertain of the same subject, there is one, and but one, that is just and true; and the only difficulty is to fix and ascertain it. On the contrary, a thousand different sentiments, excited by the same object, are all right: Because no sentiment represents what is really in the object. It only marks a certain conformity or relation between the object and the organs or faculties of the mind; and if that conformity did not really exist, the sentiment could never possibly have being. Beauty is no quality in things themselves: It exists merely in the mind which contemplates them; and each mind perceives a different beauty. One person may even perceive deformity, where another is sensible of beauty; and every individual ought to acquiesce in his own sentiment, without pretending to regulate those of others. To seek the real beauty, or real deformity, is as fruitless an enquiry, as to pretend to ascertain the real sweet or real bitter. According to the disposition of the organs, the same object may be both sweet and bitter; and the proverb has justly determined it to be fruitless to dispute concerning tastes. It is very natural, and even quite necessary, to extend this axiom to mental, as well as bodily taste; and thus common sense, which is so often at variance with philosophy, especially with the sceptical kind, is found, in one instance at least, to agree in pronouncing the same decision.

But though this axiom, by passing into a proverb, seems to have attained the sanction of common sense; there is certainly a species of common sense which opposes it, at least serves to modify and restrain it. Whoever would assert an equality of genius and elegance between Ogilby and Milton, or Bunyan and Addison, would be thought to defend no less an extravagance, than if he had maintained a mole-hill to be as high as Teneriffe, or a pond as extensive as the ocean. Though there may be found persons, who give the preference to the former authors; no one pays attention to such a taste; and we pronounce without scruple the sentiment of these pretended critics to be absurd and ridiculous. The principle of the natural equality of tastes is then totally forgot, and while we admit it on some occasions, where the objects seem near an equality, it appears an extravagant paradox, or rather a palpable absurdity, where objects so disproportioned are compared together.

It is evident that none of the rules of composition are fixed by reasonings *a priori*, or can be esteemed abstract conclusions of the understanding, from comparing those habitudes and relations of ideas, which are eternal and immutable. Their foundation is the same with that of all the practical sciences, experience; nor are they any thing but general observations, concerning what has been universally found to please in all countries and in all ages. Many of the beauties of poetry and even of eloquence are founded on falsehood and fiction, on hyperboles, metaphors, and an abuse or perversion of terms from their natural meaning. To check the sallies of the imagination, and to reduce every expression to geometrical truth and exactness, would be the most contrary to the laws of criticism; because it would produce a work, which, by universal experience, has been found the most insipid and disagreeable. But though poetry can never submit to exact truth, it must be confined by rules of art, discovered to the author either by genius or observation. If some negligent or irregular writers have pleased, they have not pleased by their transgressions of rule or order, but in spite of these transgressions: They have possessed other beauties, which were conformable to just criticism; and the force of these beauties has been able to overpower censure, and give the mind a satisfaction superior to the disgust arising from the blemishes. Ariosto pleases; but not by his monstrous and improbable fictions, by his bizarre mixture of the serious and comic styles, by the want of coherence in his stories, or by the continual interruptions of his narration. He charms by the force and clearness of his expression, by the readiness and variety of his inventions, and by his natural pictures of the passions, especially those of the gay and amorous kind: And however his faults may diminish our satisfaction, they are not able entirely to destroy it. Did our pleasure really arise from those parts of his poem, which we denominate faults, this would be no objection to criticism in general: It would only be an objection to those particular rules of criticism, which would establish such circumstances to be faults, and would represent them as universally blameable. If they are found to please, they cannot be faults; let the pleasure, which they produce, be ever so unexpected and unaccountable.

But though all the general rules of art are founded only on experience and on the observation of the common sentiments of human nature, we must not imagine, that, on every occasion, the feelings of men will be conformable to these rules. Those finer emotions of the mind are of a very tender and delicate nature, and require the concurrence of many favourable circumstances to make them play with facility and exactness, according to their general and established principles. The least exterior hindrance to such small springs, or the least internal disorder, disturbs their motion, and confounds the operation of the whole machine. When we would make an experiment of this nature, and would try the force of any beauty or deformity, we must choose with care a proper time and place, and bring the fancy to a suitable situation and disposition. A perfect serenity of mind, a recollection of thought, a due attention to the object; if any of these circumstances be wanting, our experiment will be fallacious, and we shall be unable to judge of the catholic and universal beauty. The relation, which nature has placed between the form and the sentiment, will at least be more obscure; and it will require greater accuracy to trace and discern it. We shall be able to ascertain its influence not so much from the operation of each particular beauty, as from the durable admiration, which attends those works, that have survived all the caprices of mode and fashion, all the mistakes of ignorance and envy.

The same Homer, who pleased at Athens and Rome two thousand years ago, is still admired at Paris and at London. All the changes of climate, government, religion, and language, have not been able to obscure his glory. Authority or prejudice may give a temporary vogue to a bad poet or orator; but his reputation will never be durable or general. When his compositions are examined by posterity or by foreigners, the enchantment is dissipated, and his faults appear in their true colours. On the contrary, a real genius, the longer his works endure, and the more wide they are spread, the more sincere is the admiration which he meets with. Envy and jealousy have too much place in a narrow circle; and even familiar acquaintance with his person may diminish the applause due to his performances: But when these obstructions are removed, the beauties, which are naturally fitted to excite agreeable sentiments, immediately display their energy; and while the world endures, they maintain their authority over the minds of men.

It appears then, that, amidst all the variety and caprice of taste, there are certain general principles of approbation or blame, whose influence a careful eye may trace in all operations of the mind. Some particular forms or qualities, from the original structure of the internal fabric, are calculated to please, and others to displease; and if they fail of their effect in any particular instance, it is from some apparent defect or imperfection in the organ. A man in a fever would not insist on his palate as able to decide concerning flavours; nor would one, affected with the jaundice, pretend to give a verdict with regard to colours. In each creature, there is a sound and a defective state; and the former alone can be supposed to afford us a true standard of taste and sentiment. If, in the sound state of the organ, there be an entire or a considerable uniformity of sentiment among men, we may thence derive an idea of the perfect beauty; in like manner as the appearance of objects in day-light, to the eye of a man in health, is denominated their true and real colour, even while colour is allowed to be merely a phantasm of the senses.

Many and frequent are the defects in the internal organs, which prevent or weaken the influence of those general principles, on which depends our sentiment of beauty or deformity. Though some objects, by the structure of the mind, be naturally calculated to give pleasure, it is not to be expected, that in every individual the pleasure will be equally felt. Particular incidents and situations occur, which either throw a false light on the objects, or hinder the true from conveying to the imagination the proper sentiment and perception.

One obvious cause, why many feel not the proper sentiment of beauty, is the want of that *delicacy* of imagination, which is requisite to convey a sensibility of those finer emotions. This delicacy every one pretends to: Every one talks of it; and would reduce every kind of taste or sentiment to its standard. But as our intention in this essay is to mingle some light of the understanding with the feelings of sentiment, it will be proper to give a more accurate definition of delicacy, than has hitherto been attempted. And not to draw our philosophy from too profound a source, we shall have recourse to a noted story in Don Quixote.

It is with good reason, says Sancho to the squire with the great nose, that I pretend to have a judgment in wine: This is a quality hereditary in our family. Two of my kinsmen were once called to give their opinion of a hogshead, which was supposed to be excellent, being old and of a good vintage. One of them tastes it, considers it; and after mature reflection pronounces the wine to be good, were it not for a small taste of leather, which he perceived in it. The other, after using the same precautions, gives also his verdict in favour of the wine; but with the reserve of a taste of iron, which he could easily distinguish. You cannot imagine how much they were both ridiculed for their judgment. But who laughed in the end? On emptying the hogshead, there was found at the bottom, an old key with a leathern thong tied to it.

The great resemblance between mental and bodily taste will easily teach us to apply this story. Though it be certain, that beauty and deformity, more than sweet and bitter, are not qualities in objects, but belong entirely to the sentiment, internal or external; it must be allowed, that there are certain qualities in objects, which are fitted by nature to produce those particular feelings. Now as these qualities may be found in a small degree, or may be mixed and confounded with each other, it often happens, that the taste is not affected with such minute qualities, or is not able to distinguish all the particular flavours, amidst the disorder, in which they are presented. Where the organs are so fine, as to allow nothing to escape them; and at the same time so exact as to perceive every ingredient in the composition: This we call delicacy of taste, whether we employ these terms in the literal or metaphorical sense. Here then the general rules of beauty are of use; being drawn from established models, and from the observation of what pleases or displeases, when presented singly and in a high degree: And if the same qualities, in a continued composition and in a smaller degree, affect not the organs with a sensible delight or uneasiness, we exclude the person from all pretensions to this delicacy. To produce these general rules or avowed patterns of composition is like finding the key with the leathern thong; which justified the verdict of Sancho's kinsmen, and confounded those pretended judges who had condemned them. Though the hogshead had never been emptied, the taste of the one was still equally delicate, and that of the other equally dull and languid: But it would have been more difficult to have proved the superiority of the former, to the conviction of every by-stander. In like manner, though the beauties of writing had never been methodized, or reduced to general principles; though no excellent models had ever been acknowledged; the different degrees of taste would still have subsisted, and the judgment of one man been preferable to that of another; but it would not have been so easy to silence the bad critic, who might always insist upon his particular sentiment, and refuse to submit to his antagonist. But when we show him an avowed principle of art; when we illustrate this principle by examples, whose operation, from his own particular taste, he ac-knowledges to be conformable to the principle; when we prove, that the same principle may be applied to the present case, where he did not perceive or feel its influence: He must conclude, upon the whole, that the fault lies in himself, and that he wants the delicacy, which is requisite to make him sensible of every beauty and every blemish, in any composition or discourse.

It is acknowledged to be the perfection of every sense or faculty, to perceive with exactness its most minute objects, and allow nothing to escape its notice and observa-tion. The smaller the objects are, which become sensible to the eye, the finer is that organ, and the more elaborate its make and composition. A good palate is not tried by strong flavours; but by a mixture of small ingredients, where we are still sensible of each part, notwithstanding its minuteness and its confusion with the rest. In like manner, a quick and acute perception of beauty and deformity must be the perfection of our mental taste; nor can a man be satisfied with himself while he suspects, that any excellence or blemish in a discourse has passed him unobserved. In this case, the perfection of the man, and the perfection of the sense or feeling, are found to be united. A very delicate palate, on many occasions, may be a great inconvenience both to a man himself and to his friends: But a delicate taste of wit or beauty must always be a desirable quality; because it is the source of all the finest and most innocent enjoyments, of which human nature is susceptible. In this decision the sentiments of all mankind are agreed. Wherever you can ascertain a delicacy of taste, it is sure to meet with approbation; and the best way of ascertaining it is to appeal to those models and principles, which have been established by the uniform consent and experience of nations and ages.

But though there be naturally a wide difference in point of delicacy between one person and another, nothing tends further to encrease and improve this talent, than *practice* in a particular art, and the frequent survey or contemplation of a particular species of beauty. When objects of any kind are first presented to the eye or imagina-tion, the sentiment, which attends them, is obscure and confused; and the mind is, in a great measure, incapable of pronouncing concerning their merits or defects. The taste cannot perceive the several excellences of the performance; much less distinguish the particular character of each excellency, and ascertain its quality and degree. If it pronounce the whole in general to be beautiful or deformed, it is the utmost that can be expected; and even this judgment, a person, so unpractised, will be apt to deliver with great hesitation and reserve. But allow him to acquire experience in those objects, his feeling becomes more exact and nice: He not only perceives the beauties and defects of each part, but marks the distinguishing species of each quality, and assigns it suitable praise or blame. A clear and distinct sentiment attends him through the whole survey of the objects; and he discerns that very degree and kind of approbation or displeasure, which each part is naturally fitted to produce. The mist dissipates, which seemed formerly to hang over the object: The organ acquires greater perfection in its operations; and can pronounce, without danger of mistake, concerning the merits of every performance. In a word, the same address and dexterity, which practice gives to the execution of any work, is also acquired by the same means, in the judging of it.

So advantageous is practice to the discernment of beauty, that, before we can give judgment on any work of importance, it will even be requisite, that that very individual performance be more than once perused by us, and be surveyed in different lights with attention and deliberation. There is a flutter or hurry of thought which attends the first perusal of any piece, and which confounds the genuine sentiment of beauty. The relation of the parts is not discerned: The true characters of style are little distinguished: The several perfections and defects seem wrapped up in a species of confusion, and present themselves indistinctly to the imagination. Not to mention, that there is a species of beauty, which, as it is florid and superficial, pleases at first; but being found incompatible with a just expression either of reason or passion, soon palls upon the taste, and is then rejected with disdain, at least rated at a much lower value.

It is impossible to continue in the practice of contemplating any order of beauty, without being frequently obliged to form *comparisons* between the several species and degrees of excellence, and estimating their proportion to each other. A man, who has had no opportunity of comparing the different kinds of beauty, is indeed totally unqualified to pronounce an opinion with regard to any object presented to him. By comparison alone we fix the epithets of praise or blame, and learn how to assign the due degree of each. The coarsest daubing contains a certain lustre of colours and exactness of imitation, which are so far beauties, and would affect the mind of a peasant or Indian with the highest admiration. The most vulgar ballads are not entirely destitute of harmony or nature; and none but a person, familiarized to superior beauties, would pronounce their numbers harsh, or narration uninteresting. A great inferiority of beauty gives pain to a person conversant in the highest excellence of the kind, and is for that reason pronounced a deformity: As the most finished object, with which we are acquainted, is naturally supposed to have reached the pinnacle of perfection, and to be entitled to the highest applause. One accustomed to see, and examine, and weigh the several performances, admired in different ages and nations, can only rate the merits of a work exhibited to his view, and assign its proper rank among the productions of genius.

But to enable a critic the more fully to execute this undertaking, he must preserve his mind free from all *prejudice*, and allow nothing to enter into his consideration, but the very object which is submitted to his examination. We may observe, that every work of art, in order to produce its due effect on the mind, must be surveyed in a certain point of view, and cannot be fully relished by persons, whose situation, real or imaginary, is not conformable to that which is required by the performance. An orator addresses himself to a particular audience, and must have a regard to their particular genius, interests, opinions, passions, and prejudices; otherwise he hopes in vain to govern their resolutions, and inflame their affections. Should they even have entertained some prepossessions against him, however unreasonable, he must not overlook this disadvantage; but, before he enters upon the subject, must endeavour to conciliate their affection, and acquire their good graces. A critic of a different age or nation, who should peruse this discourse, must have all these circumstances in his eye, and must place himself in the same situation as the audience, in order to form a true judgment of the oration. In like manner, when any work is addressed to the public, though I should have a friendship or enmity with the author, I must depart from this situation; and considering myself as a man in general, forget, if possible, my individual being and my peculiar circumstances. A person influenced by prejudice, complies not with this condition; but obstinately maintains his natural position, without placing himself in that point of view, which the performance supposes. If the work be addressed to persons of a different age or nation, he makes no allowance for their peculiar views and prejudices; but, full of the manners of his own age and country, rashly condemns what seemed admirable in the eyes of those for whom alone the discourse was calculated. If the work be executed for the public, he never sufficiently enlarges his comprehension, or forgets his interest as a friend or enemy, as a rival or commentator. By this means, his sentiments are perverted; nor have the same beauties and blemishes the same influence upon him, as if he had imposed a proper violence on his imagination, and had forgotten himself for a moment. So far his taste evidently departs from the true standard; and of consequence loses all credit and authority.

It is well known, that in all questions, submitted to the understanding, prejudice is destructive of sound judgment, and perverts all operations of the intellectual faculties: It is no less contrary to good taste; nor has it less influence to corrupt our sentiment of beauty. It belongs to *good sense* to check its influence in both cases; and in this respect, as well as in many others, reason, if not an essential part of taste, is at least requisite to the operations of this latter faculty. In all the nobler productions of genius, there is a mutual relation and correspondence of parts; nor can either the beauties or blemishes be perceived by him, whose thought is not capacious enough to comprehend all those parts, and compare them with each other, in order to perceive the consistence and uniformity of the whole. Every work of art has also a certain end or purpose, for which it is calculated; and is to be deemed more or less perfect, as it is more or less fitted to attain this end. The object of eloquence is to persuade, of history to instruct, of poetry to please by means of the passions and the imagination. These ends we must carry constantly in our view, when we peruse any performance; and we must be able to judge how far the means employed are adapted to their respective purposes. Besides, every kind of composition, even the most poetical, is nothing but a chain of propositions and reasonings; not always, indeed, the justest and most exact, but still plausible and specious, however disguised by the colouring of the imagination. The persons introduced in tragedy and epic poetry, must be represented as reasoning, and thinking, and concluding, and acting, suitably to their character and circumstances; and without judgment, as well as taste and invention, a poet can never hope to succeed in so delicate an undertaking. Not to mention, that the same excellence of faculties which contributes to the improvement of reason, the same clearness of conception, the same exactness of distinction, the same vivacity of apprehension, are essential to the operations of true taste, and are its infallible concomitants. It seldom, or never happens, that a man of sense, who has experience in any art, cannot judge of its beauty; and it is no less rare to meet with a man who has a just taste without a sound understanding.

Thus, though the principles of taste be universal, and, nearly, if not entirely the same in all men; yet few are qualified to give judgment on any work of art, or establish their own sentiment as the standard of beauty. The organs of internal sensation are seldom so perfect as to allow the general principles their full play, and produce a feeling correspondent to those principles. They either labour under some defect, or are vitiated by some disorder; and by that means, excite a sentiment, which may be pronounced erroneous. When the critic has no delicacy, he judges without any distinction, and is only affected by the grosser and more palpable qualities of the object: The finer touches pass unnoticed and disregarded. Where he is not aided by practice, his verdict is attended with confusion and hesitation. Where no comparison has been employed, the most frivolous beauties, such as rather merit the name of defects, are the object of his admiration. Where he lies under the influence of prejudice, all his natural sentiments are perverted. Where good sense is wanting, he is not qualified to discern the beauties of design and reasoning, which are the highest and most excellent. Under some or other of these imperfections, the generality of men labour; and hence a true judge in the finer arts is observed, even during the most polished ages, to be so rare a character: Strong sense, united to delicate sentiment, improved by practice, perfected by comparison, and cleared of all prejudice, can alone entitle critics to this valuable character; and the joint verdict of such, wherever they are to be found, is the true standard of taste and beauty.

But where are such critics to be found? By what marks are they to be known? How distinguish them from pretenders? These questions are embarrassing; and seem to throw us back into the same uncertainty, from which, during the course of this essay, we have endeavoured to extricate ourselves.

But if we consider the matter aright, these are questions of fact, not of sentiment. Whether any particular person be endowed with good sense and a delicate imagination, free from prejudice, may often be the subject of dispute, and be liable to great discussion and enquiry: But that such a character is valuable and estimable will be agreed in by all mankind. Where these doubts occur, men can do no more than in other disputable questions, which are submitted to the understanding: They must produce the best arguments, that their invention suggests to them; they must acknowledge a true and decisive standard to exist somewhere, to wit, real existence and matter of fact; and they must have indulgence to such as differ from them in their appeals to this standard. It is sufficient for our present purpose, if we have proved, that the taste of all individuals is not upon an equal footing, and that some men in general, however difficult to be particularly pitched upon, will be acknowledged by universal sentiment to have a preference above others.

But in reality the difficulty of finding, even in particulars, the standard of taste, is not so great as it is represented. Though in speculation, we may readily avow a certain criterion in science and deny it in sentiment, the matter is found in practice to be much more hard to ascertain in the former case than in the latter. Theories of abstract philosophy, systems of profound theology, have prevailed during one age: In a successive period, these have been universally exploded: Their absurdity has been detected: Other theories and systems have supplied their place, which again gave place to their successors: And nothing has been experienced more liable to the revolutions of chance and fashion than these pretended decisions of science. The case is not the same with the beauties of eloquence and poetry. Just expressions of passion and nature are sure, after a little time, to gain public applause, which they maintain for ever. Aristotle, and Plato, and Epicurus, and Descartes, may successively yield to each other: But Terence and Virgil maintain an universal, undisputed empire over the minds of men. The abstract philosophy of Cicero has lost its credit: The vehemence of his oratory is still the object of our admiration.

Though men of delicate taste be rare, they are easily to be distinguished in society, by the soundness of their understanding and the superiority of their faculties above the rest of mankind. The ascendant, which they acquire, gives a prevalence to that lively approbation, with which they receive any productions of genius, and renders it generally predominant. Many men, when left to themselves, have but a faint and dubious perception of beauty, who yet are capable of relishing any fine stroke, which is pointed out to them. Every convert to the admiration of the real poet or orator is the cause of some new conversion. And though prejudices may prevail for a time, they never unite in celebrating any rival to the true genius, but yield at last to the force of nature and just sentiment. Thus, though a civilized nation may easily be mistaken in the choice of their admired philosopher, they never have been found long to err, in their affection for a favorite epic or tragic author.

But notwithstanding all our endeavours to fix a standard of taste, and reconcile the discordant apprehensions of men, there still remain two sources of variation, which are not sufficient indeed to confound all the boundaries of beauty and deformity, but will often serve to produce a difference in the degrees of our approbation or blame. The one is the different humours of particular men; the other, the particular manners and opinions of our age and country. The general principles of taste are uniform in human nature: Where men vary in their judgments, some defect or perversion in the faculties may commonly be remarked; proceeding either from prejudice, from want of practice, or want of delicacy; and there is just reason for approving one taste, and condemning another. But where there is such a diversity in the internal frame or external situation as is entirely blameless on both sides, and leaves no room to give one the preference above the other; in that case a certain degree of diversity in judgment is unavoidable, and we seek in vain for a standard, by which we can reconcile the contrary sentiments.

A young man, whose passions are warm, will be more sensibly touched with amorous and tender images, than a man more advanced in years, who takes pleasure in wise, philosophical reflections concerning the conduct of life and moderation of the passions. At twenty, Ovid may be the favourite author; Horace at forty; and perhaps Tacitus at fifty. Vainly would we, in such cases, endeavour to enter into the sentiments of others, and divest ourselves of those propensities, which are natural to us. We choose our favourite author as we do our friend, from a conformity of humour and disposition. Mirth or passion, sentiment or reflection; whichever of these most predominates in our temper, it gives us a peculiar sympathy with the writer who resembles us.

One person is more pleased with the sublime; another with the tender; a third with raillery. One has a strong sensibility to blemishes, and is extremely studious of correctness: Another has a more lively feeling of beauties, and pardons twenty absurdities and defects for one elevated or pathetic stroke. The ear of this man is entirely turned towards conciseness and energy; that man is delighted with a copious, rich, and harmonious expression. Simplicity is affected by one; ornament by another. Comedy, tragedy, satire, odes, have each its partizans, who prefer that particular species of writing to all others. It is plainly an error in a critic, to confine his approbation to one species or style of writing, and condemn all the rest. But it is almost impossible not to feel a predilection for that which suits our particular turn and disposition. Such preferences are innocent and unavoidable, and can never reasonably be the object of dispute, because there is no standard, by which they can be decided.

For a like reason, we are more pleased, in the course of our reading, with pictures and characters, that resemble objects which are found in our own age or country, than with those which describe a different set of customs. It is not without some effort, that we reconcile ourselves to the simplicity of ancient manners, and behold princesses carrying water from the spring, and kings and heroes dressing their own victuals. We may allow in general, that the representation of such manners is no fault in the author, nor deformity in the piece; but we are not so sensibly touched with them. For this reason, comedy is not easily transferred from one age or nation to another. A Frenchman or Englishman is not pleased with the Andria of Terence, or Clitia of Machiavel; where the fine lady, upon whom all the play turns, never once appears to the spectators, but is always kept behind the scenes, suitably to the reserved humour of the ancient Greeks and modern Italians. A man of learning and reflection can make allowance for these peculiarities of manners; but a common audience can never divest themselves so far of their usual ideas and sentiments, as to relish pictures which in no wise resemble them.

But here there occurs a reflection, which may, perhaps, be useful in examining the celebrated controversy concerning ancient and modern learning; where we often find the one side excusing any seeming absurdity in the ancients from the manners of the age, and the other refusing to admit this excuse, or at least, admitting it only as an apology for the author, not for the performance. In my opinion, the proper boundaries in this subject have seldom been fixed between the contending parties. Where any innocent peculiarities of manners are represented, such as those above mentioned, they ought certainly to be admitted; and a man, who is shocked with them, gives an evident proof of false delicacy and refinement. The poet's *monument more durable than brass*, must fall to the ground like common brick or clay, were men to make no allowance for the continual revolutions of manners and customs, and would admit of nothing but what was suitable to the prevailing fashion. Must we throw aside the pictures of our ancestors, because of their ruffs and fardingales? But where the ideas of morality and decency alter from one age to another, and where vicious manners are described, without being marked with the proper characters of blame and disapprobation; this must be allowed to disfigure the poem, and to be a real deformity. I cannot, nor is it proper I should, enter into such sentiments; and however I may excuse the poet, on account of the manners of his age, I never can relish the composition. The want of humanity and of decency, so conspicuous in the characters drawn by several of the ancient poets, even sometimes by Homer and the Greek tragedians, diminishes considerably the merit of their noble performances, and gives modern authors an advantage over them. We are not interested in the fortunes and sentiments of such rough heroes: We are displeased to find the limits of vice and virtue so much confounded: And whatever indulgence we may give to the writer on account of his prejudices, we cannot prevail on ourselves to enter into his sentiments, or bear an affection to characters, which we plainly discover to be blameable.

The case is not the same with moral principles, as with speculative opinions of any kind. These are in continual flux and revolution. The son embraces a different system from the father. Nay, there scarcely is any man, who can boast of great constancy and uniformity in this particular. Whatever speculative errors may be found in the polite writings of any age or country, they detract but little from the value of those compositions. There needs but a certain turn of thought or imagination to make us enter into all the opinions, which then prevailed, and relish the sentiments or conclusions derived from them. But a very violent effort is requisite to change our judgment of manners, and excite sentiments of approbation or blame, love or hatred, different from those to which the mind from long custom has been familiarized. And where a man is confident of the rectitude of that moral standard, by which he judges, he is justly jealous of it, and will not pervert the sentiments of his heart for a moment, in complaisance to any writer whatsoever.

Of all speculative errors, those, which regard religion, are the most excusable in compositions of genius; nor is it ever permitted to judge of the civility or wisdom of any people, or even of single persons, by the grossness or refinement of their theological principles. The same good sense, that directs men in the ordinary occurrences of life, is not hearkened to in religious matters, which are supposed to be placed altogether above the cognizance of human reason. On this account, all the absurdities of the pagan system of theology must be overlooked by every critic, who would pretend to form a just notion of ancient poetry; and our posterity, in their turn, must have the same indulgence to their forefathers. No religious principles can ever by imputed as a fault to any poet, while they remain merely principles, and take not such strong possession of his heart, as to lay him under the imputation of *bigotry* or *superstition*. Where that happens, they confound the sentiments of morality, and alter the natural boundaries of vice and virtue. They are therefore eternal blemishes, according to the principle above mentioned; nor are the prejudices and false opinions of the age sufficient to justify them. . . .

Religious principles are also a blemish in any polite composition, when they rise up to superstition, and intrude themselves into every sentiment, however remote from any connection with religion. It is no excuse for the poet, that the customs of his country had burthened life with so many religious ceremonies and observances, that no part of it was exempt from that yoke. It must for ever be ridiculous in Petrarch to compare his mistress Laura, to Jesus Christ. Nor is it less ridiculous in that agreeable libertine, Boccace, very seriously to give thanks to God Almighty and the ladies, for their assistance in defending him against his enemies.

Peter Kivy

RECENT SCHOLARSHIP AND THE
BRITISH TRADITION:
A LOGIC OF TASTE
—THE FIRST FIFTY YEARS

". . . the logic of Taste, if I may be allowed the expression . . ."
Edmund Burke

(1) A Logic of Taste?

In an obviously uncomplimentary characterization* of what he described a few years back as "the present trend" in philosophy of science, Paul K. Feyerabend wrote, "Take a subject that is full of unsatisfactory features, where pseudo explanations abound and non sequiturs are the rule, and many philosophers will point out that the subject is not so bad after all, that it possesses a 'logic of its own' and must be judged by the standards of this logic."[1] Shorn of its exaggeration and innuendo, this is a fairly accurate reflection not only of recent trends in philosophy of science but in other branches of philosophy as well, for titles which begin "The Logic of . . ." are as common these days in philosophical journals and publishers' lists as fleas on a dog.

It is of course clear that Professor Feyerabend's rather overdrawn caricature does contain a warning that must be heeded. To defend astrology or entrail reading on the grounds that each has a "logic of its own" and therefore should not be judged harshly because it violates our standards of good inductive inference is, doubtless, carrying the "Logic of . . ." movement to its logically absurd conclusion. But, whether we are

---

*This essay was written for the first edition of this collection.
   [1] Paul K. Feyerabend, "Comments on Baker's 'The Role of Simplicity in Explanation,' " *Current Issues in the Philosophy of Science: Proceedings of Section L of the American Association for the Advancement of Science, 1959*, Herbert Feigl and Grover Maxwell, eds. (New York: Holt, Rinehart and Winston, 1961), p. 279.

commiting this kind of logical howler when, for instance, we insist that there is a "logic of moral discourse" or that explanations in physics and psychology may be, in some deep sense, different in kind, is not all that obvious.

So it seems to me that the discovery of what might be called a "logic of aesthetic discourse"—in other words, a "logic of taste"—is not, at least on first reflection, a foredoomed and misguided endeavor. But my subject here is not what I have discovered the logic of taste to be; rather, it is some of the kinds of things it was thought to be during a crucial period in the history of modern aesthetic theory: from the publication of Joseph Addison's paper on taste and those *On the Pleasures of the Imagination*, in 1712, to Alexander Gerard's dissertation "Of the Standard of Taste," added to the third edition of his *Essay on Taste*, in 1780. I shall not, however, be a neutral observer of these proceedings, for, if I am not entirely clear about what the logic of taste is, I have a pretty good idea of some of the things it is not. And my examination of this seminal period in the history of aesthetics is motivated not merely by historical curiosity (which is a worthwhile enough motive) but by a desire to know the answer to the question that some of the most talented men of the British Enlightenment failed to answer. How they failed is as important to me as what they said in failing.

But why begin with Addison, and why in Britain?

Most philosophers who worry about such things seem to agree that the discipline of aesthetics, as practiced by professional philosophers today, came into being in Britain early in the eighteenth century and that Addison's *Spectator* papers *On the Pleasures of the Imagination* is the inaugural work, if any single work is.[2] So part of the answer to our question is: begin with Addison because he is the beginning of the discipline to which this study is intended to contribute.

But there is more to be said than that, and it involves asking ourselves why such a contemporary-sounding phrase as "the logic of taste" should ever have been coined in the eighteenth century at all. The answer, I would suggest, is that philosophers start trying to demonstrate the logic of this or that in response to philosophical skepticism. And it is only in the presence of aesthetic skepticism that the quest for an aesthetic logic will arise as such. At other times it is simply taken for granted. It was the climate of aesthetic skepticism at the beginning of the eighteenth century which gave rise to Burke's phrase and the philosophical inquiry which it (somewhat belatedly) baptized.

I think we can, now, frame a more satisfactory justification for beginning a study of the logic of aesthetic discourse with Addison. Part of the justification is, indeed, that Addison marks the beginning of modern aesthetics, if anyone does. But we can add that necessary for a philosophically interesting theory of the logic of taste is a climate of philosophical skepticism which casts serious doubt on its possibility. Such a climate existed in the early years of the eighteenth century as never before, except perhaps in the *Ion* and the skeptical Socrates. But Plato is a plausible starting place for *anything* in philosophy. And the reasons for not *always* starting with Plato are obvious enough to permit me to pass them over in silence.

---

[2]Jerome Stolnitz, for example, calls Addison's *On the Pleasures of the Imagination* "the starting point of modern aesthetics," in "On the Origins of 'Aesthetic Disinterestedness,' " *Journal of Aesthetics and Art Criticism*, XX (1961), 143.

(2) Addison: Materials for a Theory

What, then, is Addison's account of taste? And can it really be thought of as (in Burke's phrase) a "logic" of the thing?

In his paper on taste, Addison begins by defining taste as "that faculty of the soul, which discerns the beauties of an author with pleasure, and the imperfections with dislike."[3] Hutcheson and his followers would have read "sense" for "faculty" here. But there is no evidence that Addison meant anything more by "faculty" than "ability,"[4] or, rather, a combination of an ability and a propensity, for, while we *discern* beauty with our taste, and we *discern* imperfection with it, we also enjoy the former when we discern it, and dislike the latter. And, although it seems all right to call discernment an ability, it hardly seems appropriate to talk about an ability to like or dislike or enjoy. So we may conclude that for Addison, "taste" for the beautiful is an ability to discern and a propensity for enjoying it, and, conversely, an ability to discern its absence and a propensity for disliking this lack.

So much, then, for what taste is. How do I know if I possess it? Addison offers us three tests, but I shall pass over the third as it is not, I think, of any particular interest.[5] The first is the familiar "test of time":

> If a man would know whether he is possessed of this faculty, I would have him read over the celebrated works of antiquity, which have stood the test of so many different ages and countries, or those works among the moderns which have the sanction of the politer part of our contemporaries. If, upon perusal of such writings, he does not find himself delighted in an extraordinary manner, or if, upon reading the admired passages in such authors, he finds a coldness and indifference in his thoughts, he ought to conclude, not (as is too usual among tasteless readers) that the author wants those perfections which have been admired in him, but that he himself wants the faculty of discovering them.[6]

One test, then, for the presence of taste is to see if you are delighted by those works whose excellence is generally agreed upon. It is, on first reflection, an egregious example of either the *vox populi* argument (if you emphasize the reference to "so many different ages and countries") or the argument from authority (if you fix your eye on "the politer part of our contemporaries"). But more of that in a moment.

The second taste test, a refinement, really, of the first, is to determine if you are pleased with the *proper* qualities of what you are perceiving. It is no good just to be pleased, say, by Bach; you must be pleased by what he is universally admired for. Thus, the taste tester must, Addison writes, "in the second place, be very careful to observe, whether he tastes the distinguishing perfections, or, if I may be allowed to call them so, the specific qualities of the author whom he peruses; whether he is particularly pleased with Livy for his manner of telling a story, with Sallust for his entering into

---

[3]*The Spectator*, Alexander Chalmers, ed. (New York: D. Appleton, 1879), vol. V, p. 20 (Paper No. 409).

[4]Stolnitz ("On the Origins of 'Aesthetic Disinterestedness,'" pp. 139–140), quite rightly, I think, argues that for Addison "taste" and "imagination" are names for the same faculty; and thus the pleasure of taste for the beautiful in Paper 409 is one of the pleasures of the imagination which give Papers 411–422 their name.

[5]The third test presupposes that a thought expressed by a great writer will have a different effect on the reader than the same thought expressed by "a person of ordinary genius" (Addison, *On the Pleasures of the Imagination*, p. 21); hence, if the thoughts of great writers have the appropriate effect on me, then I know that I have taste. But what the specific nature of this effect is Addison does not make clear.

[6]Addison, *On the Pleasures of the Imagination*, pp. 20–21.

those internal principles of action which arise from characters and manners of the persons he describes, or with Tacitus for his displaying those outward motives of safety and interest, which give birth to the whole series of transactions which he relates."[7] In other words, we are to render unto Caesar that which is Caesar's and unto Livy that which is Livy's.

Three questions may now occur to the thoughtful reader of Addison's essay on taste. First, How do I know when I am experiencing the pleasure of taste in the beautiful? I can, after all, be reading a beautiful book, be experiencing pleasure in the reading, and yet my pleasure may be sexual pleasure, because the book is sexually arousing, or ego satisfaction, if it is a book I have written, or any number of other things. Is there any particular "feel" that pleasure in the beautiful has, that other pleasures do not? Does it have some special *quale?*

Second, What is the "excellence" in books, and other beautiful objects, that occasions the pleasure? Addison promises at the close of the paper on taste to answer this question in the succeeding papers *On the Pleasures of the Imagination.*

Third, Is there any special state of mind which renders us particularly receptive to the beautiful? For, clearly, there are states of mind that would be completely inimical either to its perception or to its enjoyment. A cutpurse, about to be drawn and quartered, is not likely to perceive or enjoy the beauty of the Twenty-third Psalm, no matter how eloquently it is rendered by the *clergyman* in attendance.

To all of these questions we can detect at least the trace of an answer in *On the Pleasures of the Imagination.* And when, with the help of a little hindsight, we combine these with what we already have in the paper on taste, the bare bones of a "logic of taste" will begin to emerge.

First, then, What is the "phenomenology" of the feeling of beauty? It is, Addison says, "an inward joy, . . . a cheerfulness and delight. . . ."[8] Not much of a description, you will say, but I am not really concerned here with its adequacy—merely that a description is attempted at all, for it is the logical structure of Addison's theory that concerns me, not the details of its working out.

Second, What is it in objects that causes us to feel this "inward joy," this peculiar "cheerfulness and delight"? Here we must recognize a division of beauties into three kinds: (1) The beauty that creatures perceive in members of their own species, which is caused, Addison tells us, by "several modifications of matter which the mind, without any previous consideration, pronounces at first sight beautiful or deformed."[9] (2) The "beauty that we find in the several productions of art and nature," which "consists either in the gaiety or variety of colours, in the symmetry and proportion of parts, in the arrangement and disposition of bodies, or in a just mixture and concurrence of all together."[10] (3) The beauty of resemblance, which may be the result of a work of nature resembling a work of art, or a work of art resembling a work of nature, for "the productions of nature rise in value according as they more or less resemble those of art . . . ," and "artificial works receive a greater advantage from their resemblance of such as are natural. . . ."[11]

[7]Ibid., p. 21.
[8]Ibid., p. 36 (Paper No. 412).
[9]Ibid.
[10]Ibid., pp. 37–38.
[11]Ibid., p. 47 (Paper No. 414).

Third, What is the optimal state of the perceivers of beauty? What renders them most receptive? We enter dangerous territory here. But it is territory that has been explored carefully before, and I am not so much interested in a detailed map as merely the general lie of the land. Briefly, then, there is a doctrine, familiar to philosophers of art, called the doctrine of "aesthetic disinterestedness." It has existed in various forms, it is still alive (but not so well as it used to be), and it holds that there is a special attitude of disengagement from practical concerns, which has as its ultimate result the perception of aesthetic "qualities."[12]

There are at least two forms that the doctrine might take as regards what happens when we assume the aesthetic attitude of disinterestedness. It might be that in taking the attitude we make ourselves receptive to aesthetic qualities, or that in taking the attitude we (one way or another) "transform" the ordinary qualities of the world into aesthetic ones. I take it that Addison, and the others with whom we will be concerned here, held the former version of the doctrine, namely, that there is an attitude which renders us receptive to the perception of aesthetic qualities. In Addison's case it is an attitude in which the demands of the understanding are put aside so that the pleasures of taste, which are pleasures of perception, may be experienced unimpeded.[13] By such means "A man of polite imagination is let into a great many pleasures that the vulgar are not capable of receiving."[14] The pleasure of beauty is one of this number.

To put these pieces together into a "logic of taste" was not in Addison's nature to do, and to seek it in the *Spectator* would be like looking for a metaphysical treatise in "Talk of the Town."[15] But two thinkers more systematic than Addison, Francis Hutcheson and David Hume, did fashion a "logic" of aesthetic discourse, the materials of which, I would argue, were waiting to be synthesized in Addison's papers. We have these materials before us. Let us see how they can be manipulated.

Addison begins, as we have seen, with the "test of time": if we are pleased with what has pleased our ancestors, then our taste is sound. It is an obvious appeal to authority, for, clearly, when Addison talks about what has continued to please since antiquity, he is talking about what has pleased the people worth pleasing. And it takes no Doctor of Subtleties to see that such an argument is not going to satisfy the aesthetic skeptic. If you tell him that he proves his taste by comparing it with someone else's, he will surely want to know how *that* person's taste is to be proved, and we will clearly be in danger of either begging the question or being drawn into an infinite regress.

But with a little jostling, the appeal to authority can become something much more philosophically respectable: the appeal to some kind of ideal observer or normal perceiver. When the oculist tests your eyes, after all, he is proving them against what others have perceived in the past. But it is not an argument from authority: he is not committing an elementary logical fallacy.

---

[12]If Professor Stolnitz is right, the doctrine originates in Shaftesbury. See his "On the Significance of Lord Shaftesbury in Modern Aesthetic Theory," *Philosophical Quarterly*, XI (1961). If George Dickie is right, the British version of the doctrine in the eighteenth century was more markedly different from the modern version than Professor Stolnitz makes out. See Professor Dickie's "Taste and Attitude: The Origin of the Aesthetic," *Theoria*, XXXIX (1973). I have purposely kept my statement of the doctrine as vague as intelligibility permits in order to avoid a philosophical detour so extensive that we will never get back to the subject at hand.

[13]Following Stolnitz, "On the Origins of 'Aesthetic Disinterestedness,' " pp. 139–143.

[14]Addison, *On the Pleasures of the Imagination*, p. 31 (Paper No. 411).

[15]I am speaking of it as in the days of Ross. Today, likely as not, you *would* find one.

Suppose, then, that there are seeds of an appeal to the normal or ideal aesthetic perceiver in Addison. What more is needed for us to have a reasonably complete perceptual model of aesthetic value judgment? And do we find it in Addison?

Well, besides our oculist having the notion of a normal or ideal perceiver, he has, of course, a rather sophisticated theory of what happens when, for example, his subject sees (or fails to see) the color red. Part of that theory is a specification of those properties that cause his subject to perceive colors. And Addison has, as we have seen, a theory about what causes us to feel the pleasure of beauty. Our oculist must also assume that his subject knows the sensation of redness when he has it, and Addison provides us with a description that enables us to identify the pleasure of beauty. (Of course the sensation of redness, unlike the feeling of beauty in Addison's papers, is simple, and hence no description of it is possible.) But even if there is a red object before my eyes, and I am a normal or ideal perceiver, I may still fail to see the red; sufficient conditions for the perception of color must prevail. And here too we can find an analogue in Addison, in the notion of the aesthetic attitude. It can be seen as the condition under which the normal aesthetic perceiver will experience the pleasure of beauty when the proper object is being attended to.

So we have, in Addison's *On the Pleasures of the Imagination*, the building blocks for a logic of taste, using, as its model, the logic of perceptual judgments such as "X is red." What is required is the philosophical mortar to assemble them into a viable structure. That mortar was supplied by Hutcheson and Hume who, each in his own way, constructed a perceptual "logic of taste."

(3) Hutcheson and Hume: Taste as Perception

If Addison's *On the Pleasures of the Imagination* marks the beginning of modern aesthetic theory, Francis Hutcheson's *Inquiry Concerning Beauty, Order, Harmony, Design* is the first milestone—the first systematic philosophical treatise.[16] That Hutcheson's logic of taste embodies a perceptual model hardly requires stating, for, although he did not coin the phrase "sense of beauty," and he was not the first to make philosophical use of it, he made it so much his own that his age and his century thought of him as the founder of the tradition which it named. But, whereas Hutcheson had the logic of sense perception in mind when he explicated the logic of taste, he by no means thought that "X is beautiful" could be analyzed point for point as (for example) "X is red" could.

To take the most obvious (but by no means trivial) difference, the oculist can examine my organs of sight for physical defects, but the critic cannot examine my sense of beauty in any closely analogous way. So to say that Hutcheson utilized a perceptual model for his analysis of aesthetic value judgments is to say that he thought of them as crucially similar to perceptual judgments, not that he was foolish enough to think them identical. Our task, then, is to extract Hutcheson's analysis of "X is beautiful," keeping in mind the rough outline of the perceptual model which we

---

[16]This is the first of two treatises (the second being *An Inquiry Concerning Moral Good and Evil*) which Hutcheson published together under the title *Inquiry into the Original of our Ideas of Beauty and Virtue*. It went through four editions during his lifetime, all under his supervision: 1725, 1726, 1729, 1738.

distilled from Addison, the main characteristics being (1) an identifiable sensation of the beautiful, (2) an identifiable cause of the sensation, (3) an ideal or normal perceiver of the sensation, and (4) the conditions under which the cause of the sensation produces it in the ideal or normal perceiver.

The crucial passage for any analysis of Hutcheson on aesthetic discourse begins, "the word *beauty* is taken for *the idea raised in us.* . . ."[17] We can immediately conclude from this statement that when I assert that something is beautiful, I am, to begin with, either *describing* or *expressing* a feeling or idea of beauty. This part of the meaning of "X is beautiful" I call the "feeling moment," and it is this I first want to isolate.

The content of the feeling moment of "X is beautiful" may have reference either to the speaker's feeling or to the feeling of some other individual (the ideal observer) or group of individuals (the majority of normal observers). If it is the first, we would be giving a first person interpretation of the feeling moment; if the second, a third person interpretation. The first person interpretation can be understood in either a cognitive or a noncognitive way. In the cognitive interpretation, "X is beautiful" is thought to describe the state of mind of the speaker and, hence, is true or false, depending upon the accuracy or inaccuracy of the description. In the noncognitivist interpretation, however, "X is beautiful" is thought to express or evince and not describe the state of mind of the speaker and, hence, cannot be true or false.

Suppose now, for the sake of argument, that we opt for a first person interpretation. Are we to choose the cognitive or the noncognitive variety? I shall argue here for a cognitive analysis on the grounds that it is the only one Hutcheson's underlying commitments would allow. And, although this is not the place to raise the question, I think that similar considerations rule out recent attempts to prove that Hutcheson was an ethical noncognitivist.[18]

In a passage which closely parallels Locke's account of language in Book III of the *Essay Concerning Human Understanding*, Hutcheson pretty much closes the door on any noncognitive linguistic expressions. He writes:

> we know that by custom words or sounds are made signs of ideas and combinations of words signs of judgments. We know that men generally by words express their sentiments and profess to speak, as far as they know, according to what is matter of fact, so that their profession is to speak the truth.[19]

Bearing in mind that in this context to "express" one's "sentiments" means to express one's opinions, we can summarize Hutcheson's account of language as follows: (1) Words signify ideas. (2) Sentences (i.e., "combinations of words") signify judgments. (3) Judgments are made by men to convey matters of fact and, hence, are either true or false. There is, then, no room in Hutcheson's account of language for expressions of a

---

[17]Francis Hutcheson, *Inquiry Concerning Beauty, Order, Harmony, Design*, Peter Kivy, ed. (The Hague: Martinus Nijhoff, 1973), p. 34. The text quoted in the present paper is always that of the first edition (1725). For a more detailed and comprehensive account of Hutcheson's views, along similar lines, see my *The Seventh Sense: A Study of Francis Hutcheson's Aesthetics, and Its Influence in Eighteenth-Century Britain* (New York: Lenox Hill, 1976), Chapters II–IV.

[18]William Frankena, "Hutcheson's Moral Sense Theory," *Journal of the History of Ideas*, XVI (1955); William T. Blackstone, *Francis Hutcheson and Contemporary Ethical Theory* (Athens, Ga.: Univ. of Georgia Press, 1965); Bernard Peach, ed., *Francis Hutcheson: Illustrations on the Moral Sense* (Cambridge, Mass.: Harvard Univ. Press, 1971).

[19]*Letters Between the Late Mr. Gilbert Burnet and Mr. Hutcheson Concerning the True Foundation of Virtue or Moral Goodness* (1735), reprinted in Peach, ibid., p. 212.

noncognitive kind. All linguistic utterances are utterances either of truth or falsity. And what *we* would construe as linguistic expressions of emotion could only be construed by Hutcheson as statements about emotions, true or false as the case might be. If this is a correct characterization of Hutcheson's linguistic views, a noncognitive interpretation of his aesthetics is simply out of the question.

If we opt for a first person analysis, then, we are committed to a cognitive analysis of the feeling moment of "X is beautiful," and the next order of business is to decide between a first person and a third person analysis. This decision is complicated additionally by a further distinction that we must make between the idea of beauty as "occurrent" or as "dispositional,"[20] for, when we ascribe the idea of beauty to ourselves or others in the statement "X is beautiful," we may mean that the idea is presently being experienced by ourselves or others, or that we or others have a disposition to experience it under appropriate conditions. I would interpret Hutcheson as giving a first person analysis since, unlike Hume, he does not suggest that beauty be defined in terms of a consensus of feelings. And I would further suggest that it is a dispositional account, thus allowing for the instances in which Hutcheson is clearly talking about objects being beautiful although unperceived.

The feeling moment of "X is beautiful" can be interpreted, then, as "I have the feeling of beauty whenever contemplating X." But now two further questions press themselves upon us: As in the case of Addison, we will want to know what it is that distinguishes the feeling of beauty from the other pleasurable feelings we might experience in the perception of X. And we will want to know, as well, what else there is to the assertion "X is beautiful" besides the feeling moment.

In answer to the first question, two responses seem plausible on first reflection: that the idea of beauty is identified by its cause, or by its peculiar subjective "feel."

Hutcheson, as is well known, believed that the idea of beauty is raised by a complex quality which he called *uniformity amidst variety*. Thus the possibility immediately suggests itself that I recognize the idea of beauty by identifying it as a pleasurable feeling caused by uniformity amidst variety. This does not, however, seem to be the answer Hutcheson intends, for we can know that X is beautiful, in Hutcheson's view, without first knowing that the cause of the feeling of beauty is uniformity amidst variety: "We may have the sensation without knowing what is the occasion of it," Hutcheson writes, "as a man's taste may suggest ideas of sweets, acids, bitters, though he be ignorant of the forms of the small bodies, or their motions, which excite these perceptions in him,"[21] the implication being here, clearly, that we can identify the sensation of beauty without knowing that uniformity amidst variety is its cause.

What Hutcheson seems to be maintaining, rather, is that the sensation of beauty is identified by some felt quality of the sensation itself. Thus he writes on one occasion that "this pleasure of beauty . . . is distinct from that *joy* which arises upon prospect of advantage."[22] I would suggest the passage be understood in this way. The pleasure of beauty has a distinctly different feel—a different "taste," if you will—from another pleasure, "joy," which is experienced in perceiving objects from the practical point of

---

[20]See C. D. Broad, "Some Reflections on Moral-Sense Theories in Ethics," *Proceedings of the Aristotelian Society*, XLV (1944–45).

[21]Hutcheson, *Inquiry Concerning Beauty*, p. 47.

[22]Ibid., p. 37.

view, rather than simply for their own sake. This attitude, which is, of course, Hutcheson's version of the attitude of "aesthetic disinterestedness," renders us susceptible of receiving a particular kind of pleasure, namely, the pleasure of beauty, upon perceiving objects with uniformity amidst variety—the latter being construed as the cause of the former.

Let us return now to the analysis of "X is beautiful," and to the problem of determining what further content besides the feeling moment it reveals. I do not believe it reveals anything further. It is Hutcheson's view that those objects giving rise to the idea of beauty are by and large those in which there is *uniformity amidst variety*, a conclusion, I presume, reached by inductive inference and stated as a causal law. However, this does not imply that when we assert that "X is beautiful," we are asserting anything about uniformity amidst variety. The connection between the idea of beauty and uniformity amidst variety is a contingent one. Just as I can know that fire engines are red without having a theory of perception, so too I can know that something is beautiful without knowing that the idea of beauty is caused by uniformity amidst variety. And the fact that I assert "X is beautiful" when X lacks uniformity amidst variety does not mean that I have made a mistake—only that I differ from the normal. There is, to be sure, an elaborate explanation, on Hutcheson's view, as to *why* such deviations occur, relying heavily on the principle of the association of ideas. But the details of this explanation cast no further light on Hutcheson's logic of taste.

The time perhaps is late for a refutation of Hutcheson's aesthetic sense doctrine, for, although individual insights of value may remain, no one, I expect, will be tempted to adopt Hutcheson's system as a plausible account of an aesthetic experience. Thus, extended criticism is scarcely needed here. But just as certain of Hutcheson's isolated remarks point in promising directions, so certain of his mistakes prove instructive; both serve as a warning to contemporary workers in the field, and in helping us understand the advance made by Hume in dealing with the problem of taste. Let me briefly touch on two such mistakes before leaving Hutcheson for his more illustrious contemporary. The two mistakes, as we shall see, are closely related.

Hutcheson's logic of taste, I have argued, is derived from a perceptual model. His emphasis lies heavily on the property which causes us to have the sensation of beauty. And one element of the model, although available to Hutcheson in Addison's seminal reflections, is completely lacking, namely, the notion of an ideal or normal aesthetic perceiver.

The property itself, *uniformity amidst variety*, strikes us, on first reflection, as an entirely relevant one. But the way Hutcheson deals with it seems perverse. For we do not imagine ourselves, I would think, adducing the presence of *uniformity amidst variety* as part of a *causal explanation* of our aesthetic feelings. Rather, its presence is adduced as a *reason* for making a particular aesthetic judgment. When I say "It is beautiful because it has *uniformity amidst variety*," the "because" is not a causal one (as in "He died because his kidneys failed") but rather a justifactory one (as in "It is right because it will benefit mankind"). It is not a causal theory that is wanted here. And although Hutcheson has certainly provided us with *one* of the criteria for aesthetic merit, he has presented it in the completely unacceptable role of a causal property with which we (often unknowingly) interact, rather than an aesthetic feature which we perceive and adduce in defending our aesthetic judgments.

This leads us directly to the second of Hutcheson's mistakes, namely, the lack of a qualified aesthetic observer, for it is this concept that would, in the perceptual model, bear the weight of the standard of correctness and incorrectness that Hutcheson's theory essentially ignores. A causal theory such as Hutcheson is giving can provide criteria of taste only if there is some ideal or normal perceiver to serve as the standard against which our success or failure to causally interact with objects of aesthetic perception can be measured and evaluated. I do not think such a theory will work for aesthetics, even if this missing link is put in, but without it the theory is doomed from the start. In the absence of such a standard, our successes and failures can deviate from the normal but not from the correct.[23] It is this issue that Hume saw far more clearly than did Hutcheson, as is evidenced by the fact that his emphasis was in just the opposite direction: on the qualified observer and away from the possible cause of the sensation of beauty.

Hume, who, by his own admission, found close affinities with Hutcheson, produced in his essay "Of the Standard of Taste" the most mature aesthetic document to come out of the British Enlightenment, and one of the few real masterpieces of which the philosophy of art can boast. Beneath its mask of easy-going literary charm lies a solid philosophical core that can sustain close and critical scrutiny. The task Hume set himself was to steer a safe course between an out-and-out aesthetic relativism and a rigid aesthetic rationalism, neither of which he thought tenable. The problem is still with us, and Hume's answer still worth the trouble of considering.

It is clear from the way Hume introduces the problem of taste that he cannot accept a straightforward first person analysis of "X is beautiful." Although he recognizes its prima facie plausibility, as expressed in the old adage that there is no disputing about tastes, he recognizes too that there is a counterintuition which balks at the idea of indifference in the choice between pushpin and poetry or *King Lear* and breaking crockery. Thus, although it might seem on first reflection that "the proverb has justly determined it to be fruitless to dispute concerning tastes . . . ," Hume insists nevertheless that "there is a species of common sense, which opposes it, at least serves to modify and restrain it."[24] Hume was already committed in the *Treatise of Human Nature* to the view that matters of taste are determined by feelings of pleasure or, to use the more generic term, "sentiment." The problem he faced in the essay on taste was how to escape what appeared to be the inevitable but unpalatable conclusion of this view: *de gustibus non est disputandum.*

A classic interpretation of Hume's ethics infers that Hume is maintaining that there would be general agreement in matters of morals *if* there were agreement in the relevant matters of fact which attend moral decision making and that, since all matters of fact are, at least in principle, susceptible of a rational determination, all moral disagreements are also, in principle, resolvable by rational means. I believe that Hume is maintaining something like this with regard to aesthetic disputes. In questions

[23]See Carolyn Wilker Korsmeyer, "Relativism and Hutcheson's Aesthetic Theory," *Journal of the History of Ideas*, XXXVI (1975). Ms. Korsmeyer's conclusions are marred, it seems to me, by the failure to distinguish, in her discussion of the standard of taste, between the "normal" and the "correct."

[24]David Hume, "Of the Standard of Taste," *Essays, Moral, Political and Literary* (Oxford Univ. Press, 1963), p. 235.

concerning beauty and deformity, Hume is arguing, we can "translate" (so to speak) matters of sentiment into matters of fact.[25]

Now the difference between a judgment of sentiment and a "scientific" or "factual" judgment is, as Hume puts it, that in the latter "the mind does nothing but run over its objects, as they are supposed to stand in reality, without adding any thing to them, or diminishing any thing from them," whereas "In the former case, the mind is not content with merely surveying its objects, as they stand in themselves: it also feels a sentiment of delight or uneasiness, approbation or blame, consequent to that survey; and this sentiment determines it to affix the epithet *beautiful or deformed, desirable or odious*."[26] But although a feeling of delight or uneasiness may of course arise in anyone, and perhaps license anyone, on this basis, to affirm that something *appears* to them beautiful (or deformed), it does not license them to affirm that it *is* so. For the standard of taste, according to which the reality is known from the appearance, is not established simply by anyone's feeling: as Hume remarks, "few are qualified to give judgment on any work of art, or establish their own sentiment as the standard of beauty."[27]

We may, then, analyze "X seems beautiful" in a straightforward subjectivist way as something like "I experience delight in contemplating X." But when it comes to the assertion "X is beautiful," it is not my approval, or yours, but the qualified observer's that decides the case. The correct analysis of "X is beautiful" seems to be something along the lines of "X would give pleasure to the majority of qualified observers." And the question immediately arises as to how we are to determine who the qualified observers are. But as difficult as this question may be, it is, Hume claims, a more tractable one because it is a question "of fact, not sentiment." "It is sufficient for our present purpose," Hume argues, "if we have proved, that the taste of all individuals is not upon equal footing, and that some men in general, however difficult to be particularly pitched upon, will be acknowledged by universal sentiment [opinion] to have a preference above others."[28]

Whether the features that make a qualified aesthetic observer are as universally acknowledged and above controversy as Hume suggests is questionable. In any event, Hume isolates five such features as definitive of the guardians of taste: "*strong sense*, united to *delicate sentiment*, improved by *practice*, perfected by *comparison* [of one art work with another], and *cleared of all prejudice*, can alone entitle critics to this character; and the joint verdict of such, wherever they are to be found, is the true standard of taste and beauty."[29]

At this point in Hume's argument, the objection has frequently been made in the past that a vicious circle is being drawn whereby beauty is analyzed in terms of the qualified observer and the qualified observer in terms of the ability to recognize beauty. I shall not rehash this objection here[30] but, rather, press Hume on another point,

---

[25]I have presented a similar interpretation of Hume in a somewhat different way in "Hume's Standard of Taste: Breaking the Circle," *British Journal of Aesthetics*, VII (1967).

[26]Hume, "The Sceptic," *Essays*, pp. 166–167.

[27]Hume, "Of the Standard of Taste," *Essays*, pp. 246–247.

[28]Ibid., p. 248.

[29]Ibid., p. 247; italics mine.

[30]For a discussion of this objection, and a possible answer to it, see "Hume's Standard of Taste: Breaking the Circle," pp. 60–63.

namely, whether or not an attempt to establish a qualified observer is a plausible strategic move in the game Hume is playing.

If we recall once more the materials which Addison provided for a perceptual logic of taste—a means for identifying the sensation of beauty, a theory of what it is that causes the sensation, an account of what conditions are most favorable to the arousal of the sensation, and, finally, appeal to the normal or ideal perceiver—we are, I think, impressed not by how *many* of them Hume took up but, rather, how *few*. Of a "phenomenology" of the sentiment of beauty, there is not a trace, as far as I can make out, in Hume's writings. And although there are some half-hearted attempts, here and there, at isolating the quality (or qualities) in objects that give rise to the sentiment,[31] there is no real systematic effort, suggesting, I would think, Hume's low opinion of the problem's importance. The notion of "optimal conditions" does indeed play a part, but it has been conflated with the notion of the ideal or normal observer. So what becomes apparent is that Hume has put all of his aesthetic eggs in one basket: the major operator, indeed almost the *only* operator, in Hume's philosophy of taste is the ideal aesthetic observer. The rest, he seems to be implying, does not belong in philosophy at all, and the details of its working out are irrelevant to the logical problem of the beautiful.

I think that Hume's instincts here are correct, for, as I argued previously, it is the ideal or normal observer that, in the perceptual model, transforms a causal theory of what properties generate what sensations into a *standard* which tells us what responses are correct and what ones mistaken. Having chosen the perceptual model in aesthetics, and realizing that the problem of taste was a problem of *justification*, not *explanation*, Hume had no other choice than to direct his full attention to the ideal or optimal aesthetic observer. And, if we can show that the notion of an ideal or normal aesthetic observer will not wash, we will, at a single stroke, have also shown that the logic of taste cannot be accommodated by a perceptual model.

Now I believe that there are many indications that the ideal or normal aesthetic observer cannot do for the judgment "X is beautiful" what its nonaesthetic prototype can do for "X is red." I shall confine myself here to one of these.

In a recent and influential paper called (appropriately enough) "The Logic of Aesthetic Concepts," Isabel C. Hungerland writes of the notion of the normal aesthetic observer,

> But a rebel from within, or a Philistine from without, may dispute my standards of [aesthetic] "normality." Time and again the rebel or the Philistine has partly or wholly prevailed. . . . In the end, Sensibility does not function like Sense![32]

What Mrs. Hungerland is driving at here, I think, is that there is, in aesthetic contexts, a kind of basic vulnerability about the (so-called) "normal" or "ideal" perceiver which his counterpart, say, in color perception does not have. We can reasonably dispute about whether an object is red, but not about whether a certain kind of perceiver should or should not count as normal. That is why appealing to the normal perceiv-

---

[31]For a recent account of Hume's efforts in this direction, see William H. Halberstadt, "A Problem in Hume's Aesthetics," *Journal of Aesthetics and Art Criticism*, XXX (1971).

[32]Isabel C. Hungerland, "The Logic of Aesthetic Concepts," *Proceedings and Addresses of the American Philosophical Association*, XXXVI (1962–63), p. 58.

er settles the question. But in the aesthetic case we are just as likely to be arguing about what kind of perceiver should be recommended or admired as what kind of object.

Should the ideal aesthetic observer be passionate or cold-blooded, emotional, or cerebral? Poet or peasant, of the elite or the masses? In the ivory tower, or in the ash can? Political or apolitical, moral or immoral? Sensitive to craftsmanship or aesthetic surface, technique or impression? Quick to judge or slow in judgment? All these are questions that have been part and parcel of the evolution of artistic and aesthetic movements and schools, just as much as have questions about the recommended aesthetic properties of works of art. We need not—and should not—conclude from this that there is no reason giving in criticism, but what we must conclude is that the reason giving cannot consist in an appeal to a normal or ideal aesthetic perceiver. Hume was certainly right on the mark in seeing the question of taste as a question of reason giving. Where he erred was in his choice of a reason giving model. In this Mrs. Hungerland is correct. Sensibility does not function like "Sense."

(4) Kames and Gerard: Taste as Science

In 1759, Alexander Gerard published one of the more important and interesting aesthetic treatises of the British Enlightenment, *An Essay on Taste*. The third edition of the work (1780) contained an extended disquisition called, not very surprisingly, "Of the Standard of Taste."[33] As we have seen, Hutcheson and Hume, each in his own way, represents a development of the perceptual model of taste adumbrated by Addison. Gerard introduces a new model: the inductive one. But its seeds are already present in Addison, in his empirical predispositions; in Hutcheson and Hume, it exists as an implied part of the perceptual logic.

The pleasures of taste, according to Gerard, cannot be distinguished from one another subjectively; that is, we cannot tell simply by the felt quality of the pleasure whether it is, say, the pleasure of beauty or the pleasure of grandeur or whatever. "The gratifications of taste agree in this, that they are all pleasant; they are likewise analogous in other respects." But there are, he maintains, certain groups of qualities that produce pleasure, and an object, depending upon which group it might contain, is called "beautiful," or "grand," and so on.

> If the object which pleases us, possess uniformity, variety, and proportion, we are sure that it is beautiful. If it possess amplitude along with simplicity, we know that it is grand.[34]

---

[33] As the title of this paper indicates, I have wished to confine myself to the fifty-year period beginning in 1712 with Addison's *On the Pleasures of the Imagination*, which would put the 1780 edition of Gerard's work well out of range. But W. J. Hipple, who has a knack for knowing this kind of thing, assures us that the argument, and perhaps even the text itself of this edition to the original *Essay*, "had been worked out years before, at the time of discussions in the Aberdeen Philosophical Society." This could place Gerard's "Of the Standard of Taste" as early as 1758–1759, well within my purview. See Hipple's introduction to Alexander Gerard, *An Essay on Taste* (Gainsville, Fla.: Scholars' Facsimiles and Reprints, 1963), p. xxii.

[34] Gerard, *An Essay on Taste*, p. 255. The pagination of the edition cited corresponds to that of the third edition (1780).

Now we discover which groups of qualities please by induction: from our own experience and "from the general experience of mankind. . . ."[35] Thus,

> All objects which produce the same species of pleasure however different in other respects, have some qualities in common. It is by means of these qualities, that they produce this pleasure. It belongs to criticism to investigate and ascertain these qualities.[36]

And it is the discovery of these qualities that provides us with a standard of taste: "principles for deciding between discordant appreciations."

We can imagine the inductive process going something like this. Objects A, B, C, and D all cause Mr. Smith, Mr. Jones, Ms. Doe, and Ms. Roe to be pleased and to pronounce the objects beautiful. Objects E, F, G, and H all cause Mr. Smith, Mr. Jones, Ms. Doe, and Ms. Roe to be pleased and to pronounce the objects grand. We discover, on closer scrutiny, that objects A, B, C, and D have in common uniformity, variety, and proportion, and only those, and we find that objects E, F, G, and H have in common amplitude and simplicity, and only those. We conclude by the method of sameness that the conjunction of uniformity, variety, and proportion causes the pleasure of beauty and that the conjunction of amplitude and simplicity causes the pleasure of grandeur.[37]

It is possible at this point to enunciate two principles of taste in the form of hypothetical imperatives: (1) To cause the pleasure of beauty, make an object with uniformity, variety, and proportion. (2) To cause the pleasure of grandeur, make an object with amplitude and simplicity.

There are, to be sure, very obvious difficulties with these two induction-based imperatives. It is certain that they are not valid, and it is doubtful that any valid ones very much like them could ever be established. But let us put these scruples aside, accept the imperatives with all their crimes broad blown, and see what logical model they yield for judgments of taste.

Clearly, these practical imperatives are directed to the makers of art, not to the perceivers. And *if* such imperatives were possible, they would indeed provide a standard of "correct" and "incorrect" judgment for *them*. If, for example, the physician accepts the "end" of the hypothetical imperative, "To calm a hysteric, administer a tranquilizer," and adopts as his means the administering of caffeine, he has made a mistake. Likewise, given the validity of the practical imperative "To raise the pleasure of beauty, make objects with uniformity, variety, and proportion," I would be making a mistake if I accepted the end and adopted as my means the fashioning of objects with amplitude and simplicity, but without uniformity, variety, and proportion.

But we are equally, if not *more* interested in the other party to taste: the perceiver of the object. And here our troubles really start. Suppose the physician administers Valium to the hysteric, and he fails to respond. Would we say that the hysteric has "made a mistake" by ignoring the valid practical imperative? No more, then, would we say that the Philistine has "made a mistake" by not responding with the pleasure of beauty when he is confronted with uniformity, variety, and proportion. If our induc-

[35]Ibid., p. 261.
[36]Ibid., p. 253.
[37]There is no reason why we cannot, in Gerard's view, use more complex inductive procedures. I choose the method of sameness, in its most primitive form, for simplicity of exposition only.

tion is a good one, and the imperative valid, he has reacted *abnormally*—but not *incorrectly*. We believe, to be sure, that aesthetic reactions are more in our power to change than our reactions to drugs. And so we might say to the Philistine, "If you want to be *normal*, take steps to react the way we do to 'beautiful' objects." But the Philistine may not accept the end of normality as a particularly desirable one, and there our argument with him terminates. Normality, after all, is not, like health and happiness, an end we have a right to expect all of us share.

Lord Kames must have been well aware of this problem when he posed to himself the question, "doth it not seem whimsical, and perhaps absurd, to assert, that a man *ought not* be pleased when he is, or that he *ought* to be pleased when he is not?"[38] And as Lord Kames, by Gerard's own admission,[39] was espousing a view very similar to his own with regard to the logic of taste, it is not inappropriate to conclude these remarks on Gerard with Kames's strikingly Humean answer to his own question. (I say strikingly Humean because it is reminiscent of Hume's "retreat to psychology," best exemplified by the celebrated treatment of causality.)

Kames essentially admits that there is no rational justification for calling deviations from the normal aesthetic response "incorrect." It is indeed "whimsical" and "absurd" to do so. But we have a psychological compulsion to do so, nevertheless, just as, according to Hume, we have a psychological compulsion to expect events in the future to follow those they have followed in the past, even though there is no "rational" justification for it. So, says Kames, "my disgust is raised . . . by differing from what I judge to be the common standard [the normal]";[40] that is, I am psychologically repelled by the abnormal, in myself as well as in anyone else: "Every remarkable deviation from the standard [the normal] is disagreeable, and raises in us a painful emotion: monstrous births, exciting the curiosity of a philosopher, fail not at the same time to excite a sort of horror."[41] And we are left, then, with a psychological explanation for why we condemn aberrant tastes as mistaken: it is to rid ourselves of a psychological irritant by negative reinforcement. But we remain without the sought-after rational justification for doing so. The inductive model, like the perceptual one, fails to reveal a proper "logic of taste" but leads, rather, to a Humean skepticism.

Where, then, do we go from here? We can, of course, accept the skeptical conclusion and give up the quest. Or we can, in the face of Feyerabend's warning, widen our notion of rationality to encompass other "logical" models. The latter alternative is today being vigorously exploited. Whether or not success lies in that direction is yet to be determined.[42]

[38]Henry Home, Lord Kames, *Elements of Criticism*, 6th ed. (Edinburgh, 1785), vol. II, p. 488. The first edition of Kames's influential book appeared in 1762.

[39]Gerard, *An Essay on Taste*, p. 247n.

[40]Kames (Home), *Elements of Criticism*, vol. II, p. 494.

[41]Ibid., vol. II, p. 492.

[42]An earlier version of the present paper was presented to the Columbia University Seminar on Eighteenth Century European Culture, 20 March, 1975. I am extremely grateful to all those in attendance, for a valuable and stimulating discussion, and, especially, to Professor John H. Middendorf for his encouragement. I also want to express my thanks to Professor Jack Glickman for reading and commenting on another early version of this paper.

Mary Mothersill

HUME AND THE PARADOX OF TASTE

1

"Of the Standard of Taste" was one of a set of essays published under the title *Four Dissertations* in 1757. Hume had achieved that "literary fame" to which he aspired and was beginning for the first time in his life to be free of financial worries. The essays—roughly forty in number, which he had written on political, literary, moral, and philosophical topics in the aftermath of the *Treatise of Human Nature*—were from the beginning a popular success and went through many editions. The *History of England*, though controversial, was widely read and discussed; the final two volumes were to appear in 1762. Although the *Treatise*, his great philosophical work, was still neglected, Hume had established an international reputation as a scholar and man of letters. He remained, it is true, a target for the bigots, those zealous men of God who had twice blocked his appointment to a professorial post, and this has a bearing on the "Taste" essay. The original title had been *Five Dissertations*, but Hume was persuaded to withdraw "Of Suicide" and "Of the Immortality of the Soul." Hume explains in a letter: "I wrote a new Essay on the Standard of Taste to supply their place."[1] The essay was written in the summer of 1756 and appeared together with the three remaining essays, "Natural History of Religion," "Of Tragedy," and "Of the Passions." Nineteen years later in the memoir written just before his death, Hume remarks, "In this interval, I published . . . my Natural History of Religion, along with some other small pieces."[2] The "Natural History" was in the forefront for the "bigots" as well as for Hume, and while that was attacked in print with, as Hume puts it, "illiberal petulance, arrogance and scurrility,"[3] the other three essays went largely unnoticed. Subsequent editions, although closely supervised by Hume, contain no variant readings or revisions of the "Taste" essay, nor did he, as far as I know, ever return to the issues discussed there. But his interest in these issues was lifelong: in the *Treatise* he discusses

---

This essay was written for the second edition of this collection and is published here for the first time.
[1]Ernest Campbell Mossner, *The Life of David Hume* (Austin: University of Texas Press, 1954), p. 325.
[2]David Hume, "My Own Life" (1776), reprinted in Hume, *An Inquiry Concerning Human Understanding,* ed. Charles W. Hendel (New York: Liberal Arts Press, 1957).
[3]Ibid.

the relation of taste to sentiment, and "beauty and deformity" play a substantial role in his account of the passions. A fair number of the essays deal with literary topics, and Hume frequently puts forward his own forceful opinions of particular authors or passages. Nonetheless, "Of the Standard of Taste" is his final and indeed his only attempt to deal with questions in critical theory, and I think we may take it as definitive of Hume's position. What is difficult is to make out what that position is.

One can see in a general way what creates a problem for Hume. (For one thing, it remains a problem for many philosophers and students of the arts.) The question is this: given that aesthetic preference depends on feeling, as distinct from factual evidence or observation, and given that individuals differ conspicuously with respect to what they like or dislike in the way of poetry or the other arts, how does it happen that there are some opinions—not many, perhaps, but some—that are instantly dismissed as false (or agreed to as true) by anyone who has a right to be listened to at all? It is clear enough that this is a problem for Hume, but it is difficult to understand why he thinks "Taste" offers a solution, since on the most natural interpretation, it obviously does not. Can Hume have failed to notice this? It seems implausible, and yet he does not concede failure or even any doubts.

"Of the Standard of Taste" is a curious production: its mannered Addisonian style and air of putting everything in its place, far from concealing, brings to attention a series of bad arguments, non sequiturs, and inconsistencies, including an apparent reversal halfway through the essay of his initial position. The mistakes are *so* gross as to make it possible to entertain the thought that Hume's "solution" is intended as a sort of parody on the model of Cleanthes' spirited defense of the argument from design in the *Dialogues Concerning Natural Religion* (a work Hume arranged to have published posthumously together with the essays withdrawn from *Four Dissertations*). And yet that interpretation cannot be right: Hume is not, as in the case of religion, challenging accepted pieties; it is true that the neoclassical doctrine that emerges from his account as a ramshackle ad hoc theory was the establishment view, but then Hume was and felt honored to be a *member* of the establishment. Nothing in his writings suggests anything but respect for the opinions of Dryden, Pope, Fontenelle, Samuel Johnson, Joshua Reynolds. I think what happened is that Hume—who all his life was preoccupied by what he saw as a conflict between serious philosophy, which is "accurate," "abstruse," and often "unintelligible" to the educated layman, and philosophy that treats its "subject in an easy and obvious manner"—had never really considered the official neoclassical doctrine. When he did, he discovered—could not have *failed* to discover—that it was embarrassingly incoherent. But to get to the heart of the problem would have meant going back to the kind of detailed analysis practiced in the *Treatise*, and he was unwilling to do that. Kant recognized as Hume did not (or did not quite) that beauty is a good that is distinct from moral good, and when faced with Hume's problem (which he presents as "The Antinomy of Taste"),[4] Kant saw that any plausible solution would have to be pretty complicated and so devoted the first part of *The Critique of Judgment* to a new "transcendental deduction."

 Whatever his reasons for keeping it short and informal, Hume's essay has more

---

[4]Immanuel Kant, *The Critique of Judgment* (1790), tr. James C. Meredith (Oxford: Clarendon Press, 1964), p. 205.

substance than first appears; it is not a superficial work. In trying to figure out the obliquities of the argument, one discovers a systematic ambiguity that provides the ground for a subtext—or at least for an interpretation—that differs radically from what appears at first reading. Hume, for example, equivocates on at least two crucial terms: "standard of taste" hovers between "rule" and "paradigm"; "particular forms or qualities" can be construed as "specifiable properties" or as "the properties of a particular individual." There is also an unresolved question about what the "standard" is to be used for. Is it to help us assess the beauty of works that we encounter, or is it to enable us to decide whose critical judgments are authoritative? Other questions remain open because they are rooted in unresolved issues in Hume's basic theory. How, for example, are we to relate information about what people actually like with our conception of what is worthy of being liked? Why should what motivates an utterance be thought to impose limits on its claims to have a truth value?

The paradox of taste is generated for Hume by conjoining his general theory with his own critical convictions. The conjunction does yield a contradiction, although Hume does not acknowledge that it does. Something has to give: either the theory must be modified or Hume's convictions have to be reclassified as affective states neither true nor false, justified nor unjustified. Hume does neither; he tries to smooth things over by bringing what I have called the "official doctrine" into play. The outcome can be summarized as follows: there are certain properties—truth to nature in painting, verisimilitude in poetry, unity of action in drama—that are universally pleasing. You find out what these properties are by studying classical models and then generalizing your results. For poets these yield "rules of composition" that guide their creative efforts; from the same source critics derive "principles of taste" that determine the merits of particular poems. The essential properties are, however, very difficult to discern, and it requires native ability and exhaustive training and practice to be able to recognize them. Hence, qualified critics (Hume's phrase is "true judges") are rare. Where disputes about taste arise, it is the joint verdict of the true judges that settles the matter: that verdict is the "standard of taste."

The alternative reading, the subtext retrievable from the equivocations mentioned above, is, in outline, as follows. There are particular works that have stood the test of time because they are truly beautiful. What make them beautiful are the properties they have, but such properties must be picked out by indexical predicates. No two great works of art have any properties that are both shared and contribute to the beauty of each individual work. Hence, there are nontrivial "rules of composition" and no nontrivial "principles of taste." True judges are indeed rare, and their verdicts provide no criterion for beauty but at most serve to recommend the work judged to our attention. The judgment of taste is confirmed or disconfirmed only through the experience of subjects, taken one by one, who are acquainted with the works in question. Standards of taste are set by particular works of great and lasting beauty. Every epic poem stands, for example, in the shadow of the *Iliad*.

If the subtext can be derived from "Taste" and compared with the official doctrine with which it is obviously at odds, then Hume entertained, at least in outline, a view that is much closer to Kant than has been supposed. I will argue, moreover, that the subtext, suitably amplified, provides the clue to a solution of the paradox that is both simpler and more intuitive than anything to be gleaned from the third *Critique*.

2

"Of the Standard of Taste" opens with some general observations. Even in the most narrow circles, Hume says, there is a great variety of taste, and when we contemplate "distant ages and remote nations," we are surprised by "the great inconsistence and contrariety of taste." We begin by thinking that what differs from our own taste is "barbarous," but when we find that aliens think *we* are barbarous and that there is an "equal assurance on all sides," we become less arrogant in our pronouncements.

We are less impressed than we ought to be by the extent to which tastes vary because "there are certain terms in every language which import blame and others praise":

> Every voice is united in applauding elegance, propriety, simplicity, spirit in writing and in blaming fustian, affectation, coldness, and a false brilliancy. But when the critics come to particulars, this seeming unanimity vanishes and it is found that they have affixed a very different meaning to their expressions.[5]

The reverse is said to hold "in matters of opinion and science" where differences are "less in reality than in appearance." In morals as in taste, the appearance of harmony is deceptive and is explained by "the very nature of language." "Virtue" implies praise in every language, and "vice" blame, but we find great differences in criteria for application. (Hume is right about the critical vocabulary: two poems admired for their elegance may be very, very different. As for moral questions, he may be right about virtue and vice, but the specific virtues—he mentions "justice, humanity, magnanimity, prudence, veracity"—are not free-floating: they are vague to be sure, but a chronic liar cannot be admired for his veracity, nor a torturer for being humane.)

Next Hume announces his main theme:

> It is natural for us to seek a *Standard of Taste*, a rule by which the various sentiments of men may be reconciled, at least a decision afforded confirming one sentiment and condemning another.

It seems an odd statement: the only rule required to *reconcile* "various sentiments" is that we should agree to differ, which is what Hume suggested in the opening paragraph. But to look for a rule that will authorize us to "confirm" one sentiment and "condemn" another looks like a *retreat* from tolerance—as if we were out to *prove* that alien tastes really are "barbarous." Of course, what is "natural" may be unwarranted—like thinking one has good reasons for expecting the future to resemble the past. Is that what Hume means? Consider the immediate sequel in which the paradox of taste emerges:

> There is a species of philosophy which cuts off all hopes of success in such an attempt and represents the impossibility of ever attaining any standard of taste. The difference, it is said, is very wide between judgment and sentiment. All sentiment is right; because sentiment has a reference to nothing beyond itself and is always real wherever a man is conscious of it. But all determinations of the understanding are not right because they have a reference to something beyond themselves, to wit, real matter of fact; and are not always conformable to that standard. Among a thousand different opinions which different men may entertain of the

---

[5]David Hume, "Of the Standard of Taste" (1757), reprinted in *Of the Standard of Taste and Other Essays*, ed. John W. Lenz (New York: Bobbs-Merrill, Library of Liberal Arts, 1965). (Since the essay is not very long and repays close study, I have not footnoted quotations from the text.)

same subject, there is one and but one that is just and true; and the only difficulty is to fix and ascertain it. On the contrary, a thousand different sentiments, excited by the same object, are all right because no sentiment represents what is really in the object. It only marks a certain conformity or relation between the objects and organs or faculties of the mind; and if that conformity did not really exist, the sentiment could never possibly have being. Beauty is no quality of things themselves; it exists merely in the mind which contemplates them; and each mind perceives a different beauty. One person may even perceive deformity where another is sensible of beauty; and every individual ought to acquiesce in his own sentiment without pretending to regulate those of others. To seek the real beauty or real deformity is as fruitless an inquiry as to pretend to ascertain the real sweet or real bitter. According to the disposition of the organs, the same object may be both sweet and bitter; and the proverb has justly determined it to be fruitless to dispute concerning tastes. It is very natural and even quite necessary to extend this axiom to mental as well as bodily taste; and thus common sense, which is so often at variance with philosophy, especially of the skeptical kind, is found in one instance at least, to agree in pronouncing the same decision.

But though this axiom, by passing into a proverb, seems to have attained the sanction of common sense, there is certainly a species of common sense, which opposes it, at least serves to modify and restrain it. Whoever would assert an equality of genius between Ogilby and Milton, or Bunyan and Addison, would be thought to defend no less an extravagance than if he had maintained a mole-hill to be as high as Teneriffe or a pond as extensive as the ocean. Though there may be found persons who give the preference to the former authors, no one pays attention to such a taste and we pronounce without scruple, the sentiment of these pretended critics to be absurd and ridiculous. The principles of the natural equality of tastes is then totally forgot, and while we admit it on some occasions, where the objects seem near an equality, it appears an extravagant paradox, or rather a palpable absurdity, where objects so disproportioned are compared together.

We have then two "species of common sense"; the first finds support in philosophy of the "skeptical kind," while the second lacks a philosophical sponsor. Although Hume does not endorse the skeptical philosophy here, it is the position that is defended at length in all his earlier writings beginning with the *Treatise*.[6] The account in "Taste" follows almost word for word what he wrote in "The Skeptic" (1742) and reaffirmed in *An Inquiry Concerning the Principles of Morals* (1751). Hume's overall theory is too complicated to be easily summarized, but what pertains to "Taste" is roughly as follows: Hume's project in the *Treatise* was to derive entirely from "experience and observation" a "science of man," which would be the basis for "a complete system of the sciences."[7] In the less ambitious program announced in the *Inquiry Concerning Human Understanding* (1748), he speaks of "mental geography or a delineation of the distinct parts and powers of the mind."[8] The main boundary line divides reason from the passions (or sentiments). Reason distinguishes truth from falsehood under two categories: (1) "relations of ideas" such as "that three times five equals one half of thirty" and (2) "matters of fact" such as "that the sun will rise tomorrow."[9]

Since Hume was not interested in theory of meaning or logic, he concentrates on (2) and in particular on the analysis of causal relations. On the other side of the dividing line are the passions and sentiments, what we would call affects. The passions are what

[6]*Hume's Treatise of Human Nature*, ed. L. A. Selby-Bigge (Oxford: Clarendon Press, 1941).
[7]*Treatise*, Preface, p. xx.
[8]*Human Understanding*, p. 22.
[9]Ibid., p. 40.

move us to action; reason itself is motivationally inert. The two basic passions are pain and pleasure, the two primitive motives. Complex passions such as pride, humility, love, hatred, pity, and so forth are analyzable in terms of beliefs related directly or indirectly through the "association of ideas" to pleasure and pain.

Once the relation of a particular passion to pleasure and pain has been established, there is nothing more to explain. Thus, for example, to be proud of my beautiful house is to be pleased with myself because the house that is *mine* is beautiful, i.e., a cause of pleasure.[10]

Moral good and evil, virtue and vice, beauty and deformity, are all to be explained on the model of the passions. Often the relevant passions are "calm," not "violent," and so may be mistaken for reason, a confusion to be avoided:

> Reason is the discovery of truth or falsehood. Truth or falsehood consists in an agreement or disagreement either to the real relations of ideas or to real existence and matter of fact. Whatever therefore, is not susceptible of this agreement or disagreement is incapable of being true or false and can never be an object of our reason. Now 'tis evident our passions, volitions, and actions are not susceptible of any such agreement or disagreement; being original facts and realities complete in themselves, and implying no reference to other passions, volitions, or actions. 'Tis impossible, therefore, they can be pronounced either true or false and be either contrary to or conformable to reason.[11]

Thus, *a fortiori*, the judgment of taste lacks a truth value. It manifests itself in a sentiment and "contains not any representative quality."[12] I will argue later that one of the two elements of Hume's theory that give rise to the paradox of taste is his notion of what is "representative," a confused notion based on a metaphor that distinguishes qualities "in" the object from those "in" the subject. Had he been willing to switch to the mode in which predicates are said to be true of an object (or of a subject), he could have avoided many problems without giving up the important distinction between reason and the passions. But although his practice, as we shall see, belies his principle, Hume was wedded to the "inside-outside" distinction. Hume gives an example that he must have liked, since he repeats it:

> A man may know all the circles and ellipses of the Copernican system and all the irregular spirals of the Ptolemaic, without perceiving that the former is more beautiful than the latter. Euclid has fully explained every quality of the circle but has not in any proposition, said a word of its beauty. The reason is evident. Beauty is not a quality of the circle. It lies not in any part of the line whose parts are all equally distant from a common centre. It is only the effect which that figure produces upon a mind whose particular fabric or structure renders it susceptible of such sentiments.[13]

In fact, this is not such a good example for Hume: the qualities of the circle explained by Euclid are not parts of any line, are not *visual* properties. Why should there be a distinction between them and the (nonvisual) dispositional property of appearing beautiful, i.e., being a cause of pleasure to the observer?

What "cuts off all hope of success" (to return to "Taste") and "represents the impossibility of ever attaining any Standard of Taste" is the skeptical philosophy, i.e., Hume's own theory. Common sense (first species) comes in, not as endorsing the

[10]*Treatise*, pp. 275ff.
[11]*Treatise*, p. 458.
[12]*Treatise*, p. 415.
[13]"The Skeptic" (1742), reprinted in *Taste*, p. 125.

whole analysis of reason and sentiment but only as agreeing that it is "fruitless to dispute concerning tastes." Notice that one might well hold to the proverb and yet think, contrary to Hume's theory, that judgments of taste are either true or false. You claim to have seen Mother Teresa riding a bicycle in Central Park; you also claim to have failed an exam not because you did not study but because Thursday is an inauspicious day for Scorpios. Both claims are either true or false, as I see them, respectively unlikely and absurd, and yet I might well think it silly to *argue* with you. Prejudice, misperception, and fanciful, ungrounded beliefs are common as grass. If we undertook to unmask every falsehood, there would be time for very little else. Aesthetic preferences, whatever one may think of their truth claims, are difficult to explain. As Hume says, good critics are rare, and it takes time and concentration to get to be one. In many cases—here again moral and aesthetic interests differ—it does not matter. If you admire what I take to be junk, we can still (up to a point) be friends. What "the proverb has justly determined" has less to do with epistemology than with tolerance reinforced by indolence. I assume that Hume is right about Ogilby and Milton (all that I have been able to discover about Ogilby is that he translated Homer). I think Hume is wrong about Bunyan and Addison. Perhaps I could have persuaded him that "elegance" is not everything and not what Bunyan is about, or that Addison, though good in his way, lacks depth—but I might very well fail.

The second species of common sense, the one that takes certain judgments to be false, Hume describes as one that "opposes" the first species "or at least serves to modify and restrain it." That is an understatement: it cannot be both that "a thousand sentiments excited by the same object, are all right" and that to compare Ogilby with Milton is a "palpable absurdity." The conjunction entails a contradiction. Hence, the paradox of taste. I suggested earlier that it is Hume's theory—in particular, his assumption that utterances that manifest sentiments cannot, for that reason, be truth-valued—that gives rise to the paradox. But it would be a mistake to think that the problem is factitious—one of those rootless wonders that can impress only those who are in the grip of some theory. I believe that common sense really *is* divided, although of course the issue is not very sharp, along the lines laid down by Hume. Without any well-defined commitments, we do tend to be relativists "in principle" and absolutists when it comes to opinions of particular works or authors that we know and love (or hate). That is what makes the paradox worth unscrambling.

Everything that Hume had written before 1757 would lead one to think that he would simply discount the second species of common sense as human (therefore natural) error. The only fact of the matter is that while most people find Milton better than Ogilby, some find Ogilby the equal of Milton. What follows? On Hume's account, nothing: nobody is in error because nothing is "represented," and, following the celebrated passage in the *Treatise*,[14] what *is* the case grounds no inferences about what *ought* to be the case. With respect to the findings of the second species of common sense, Hume could have used the steamroller tactics that he used in analogous situations in ethics. In the *Treatise* he says that the common sense notion that some actions are more in accord with reason than others is just a plain *mistake*:

'Tis not contrary to reason to prefer the destruction of the whole world to the scratching of my finger. 'Tis not contrary to reason for me to choose my total ruin to prevent the least

---

[14]*Treatise*, p. 469.

uneasiness of an Indian or a person totally unknown to me. 'Tis as little contrary to reason to prefer even my own acknowledged lesser good to my greater, and have a more ardent affection for the former than the latter.[15]

Why does he not dispose of the Ogilby-Milton question in the same way? Perhaps the fact that his examples are comparative rather than categorical judgments is relevant: "*Paradise Lost* is beautiful" is easier to assimilate than "Ogilby is the equal of Milton." Beauty, however analyzed, is a matter of degree, and the two authors are simply, in Hume's word, "disproportioned." It is like saying that "a mole-hill is as high as Teneriffe or a pond as extensive as the ocean." Although it does not follow from "*x* is more beautiful than *y*" that *x* is beautiful, still it would need an argument to show that while the comparative judgment is truth-valued, the categorical is not.

3

The two species of common sense and the problem created by their "opposition" are never mentioned again in "Taste," but the only way to understand the argument that ensues is to suppose that Hume, in the face of his own theory, is bent on discovering the standard of taste. In the immediate sequel to the passage quoted above, he writes:

> It is evident that none of the rules of composition are fixed by reasoning *a priori* or can be esteemed abstract conclusions of the understanding. . . . Their foundation is the same with that of all the practical sciences, experience; nor are they any thing but general observations concerning what has been universally found to please in all countries and in all ages.

Here Hume turns to the official doctrine of neoclassicism. To make out his case, he needs some distinctions that he does not draw but perhaps would not object to. First there is what we may call a "law of taste" to the effect that any work characterized by property *F* will please universally. The law can be pressed into service both by the poet who wants to please and by the critic who wants to settle disputed questions. In the hands of the poet the law becomes a "rule of composition"; for the critic it becomes a "principle of taste," i.e., a candidate major premise for an argument that has a judgment of taste for its conclusion. Of course if the rules of composition are to be effective and the principles of taste valid, then there must *be* laws of taste, i.e., law-like generalizations that are *true*. As noted in the summary offered above, there were several familiar candidate laws, and since Hume himself, later in "Taste" and elsewhere, approves "exactness of imitation," "consistence and uniformity," and "unity of action," one would expect him to offer some examples here. Instead, he continues:

> Many of the beauties of poetry and even of eloquence are founded on falsehood and fiction, on hyperboles, metaphors and an abuse or perversion of language. . . . But though poetry can never submit to exact truth, it must be confined by rules of art discovered to the author either by genius or by observation."

The disjunction is significant: in neoclassical jargon, "genius" is the term reserved for "irregular" authors like Shakespeare who mix up genres, fail to preserve the unities, and yet produce great works. But it is not open to Hume to speak of laws of taste

[15]*Treatise*, p. 416.

discovered "by genius" as distinct from "observation." That would be as if to say that Adam on first acquaintance with water could discover by genius that if he fell in he would drown.

Hume tries to save his position by suggesting that while breaking a rule is always bad, there are many rules, and a work may succeed overall despite blemishes. If some negligent or irregular writers have pleased, they have not pleased by their transgressions of rules or order, but in spite of these transgressions.

> Ariosto pleases; but not by his monstrous and improbable fictions, by his bizarre mixture of the serious and comic styles, by the want of coherence in his stories, or by the continual interruption of his narration. He charms by the force and clearness of his expression, by the readiness and variety of his inventions, and by his natural picture of the passions . . . and however his faults may diminish our satisfaction, they are not able entirely to destroy it.

But what if the very things that we like in Ariosto are his "faults"?

> Did our pleasure really arise from those parts of his poem which we denominate faults, this would be no objection to criticism in general; it would only be an objection to those particular rules of criticism, which would establish such circumstances to be faults and represent them as universally blamable. If they are found to please, they cannot be faults, let the pleasure they produce be ever so unexpected and unaccountable.

In other words: you have a principle of taste to the effect that monstrous and improbable fictions are faults; the principle derives from a law that such fictions displease "in all countries and in all ages." Then you find that in Ariosto's case, his monstrous and improbable fictions give pleasure. The law is disconfirmed and you have an "objection" to the particular "rule of criticism" (principle of taste). Suppose you find some further counterexamples: *Gulliver's Travels, Alice in Wonderland*, perhaps. Now you have evidence that supports a new law and new principles to the effect that monstrous and improbable fictions are good-making characteristics, not blemishes but beauties. But it will not take long to find a counterexample to the new law either.

Hume seems to be on the verge of recognizing an important truth, namely that there are no laws of taste on which to ground rules of composition and principles of taste. All the time-honored candidate laws are, if testable, plainly false, and if not testable then uninformative. There are indefinitely many true descriptions of any poem or other work of art. None give me reason to think that what satisfies the description will please me or anyone else. Being true to nature, instantiating the "golden section," manifesting unity in variety, are qualities randomly distributed over good works and bad. If this is true, why is its truth not obvious? The explanation is as follows: the test of whether a poem pleases you requires that you read the poem (listen to the music, look at the painting, etc.). The hypothesis, based on a putative law of taste, is that it pleases you in virtue of property F. F is either a property discoverable only by reading, e.g. (Hume's example), elegance, propriety, simplicity, and spirit, or it is not, e.g., being in iambic pentameter, having been written by a Soviet dissident, etc. Laws of the second type are not very plausible since they are so easily disconfirmed. Laws of the first type do not allow the antecedent of the conditional to be confirmed without at the same time confirming (or disconfirming) the consequent.

It is not that I check the poem out first to see whether it has elegance, propriety, simplicity, and so forth, and read it a second time to see whether it pleases me. I read the poem; if it pleases me, I try to identify the features that account for my pleasure by mentioning elegance, propriety, simplicity, etc. As Hume points out at the beginning of "Taste," these terms import praise; we are dealing with "relations of ideas." We agree in advance that what is elegant is beautiful, but, as Hume points out, when it comes to particulars our agreement may vanish. Of course it is true that some beautiful things are elegant and that their elegance contributes to their beauty. Any plausible account of critical reasoning—i.e., of claims put forward in support of a judgment of taste— will have to explain how this squares with the fact that every elegant thing is, so to speak, elegant in its own way, that two elegant things may have no other interesting properties in common.

Hume moves smoothly on to another troublesome topic. The question (which he does not raise but tries to answer) is this: suppose that there *are* laws of taste based on observation about what has been found "to please universally." Why do we need critics? Why indeed do we need a "standard"? Works that have the pleasing properties will be liked by everyone; works that have some but lack others will have a mixed reaction. What is there to decide?

Hume writes:

> But though all the general rules of art are founded only on experience and on the observation of the common sentiments of human nature, we must not imagine that on every occasion, the feelings of men will be conformable to those rules. Those finer emotions of the mind are of a very tender and delicate nature and require the concurrence of many favorable circumstances to make them play with facility and exactness according to their general and established principles. Many and frequent are the defects in the internal organs which prevent or weaken the influence of those general principles on which depends our sentiment of beauty or deformity.

In other words, the laws of taste tell us not what qualities *do* please universally but what *would* please universally if everyone could discern them, but the vast majority are unable to discern them. In a way, Hume's intuitions are sound: popularity does not establish worth. On the other hand, it is hard to see how the new subjunctive conditional laws are going to be established by observation. Hume goes on to list five conditions that must be satisfied by the qualified critic, what he calls "the true judge." They are "delicacy of taste," "perfect serenity of mind," "practice," "comparison," "freedom from prejudice," and "good sense." (Hume's explanation of each of these is excellent and deserves careful study.) People who do not meet the conditions are "defective"; a man in a fever is not a good judge of flavor, nor one who has jaundice a good judge of color. But for the analogy to hold, we have to suppose that *most* of us are chronically feverish and jaundiced—which raises questions about what is "normal."

Hume summarizes his discussion and offers an answer to the main question:

> Thus, though the principles of taste be universal and nearly if not entirely the same in all men, yet few are qualified to give judgment on any work of art or establish their sentiment as the standard of beauty.

(He then reviews the criteria for being a true judge and shows for each what failure or "imperfection" amounts to.)

> Under some or other of these imperfections the generality of men labor; and hence a true judge in the finer arts is observed, even during the most polished ages, to be so rare a

character: strong sense, united to delicate sentiment, improved by practice, perfected by comparison and cleared of all prejudice, can alone entitle critics to this valuable character; and the joint verdict of such, wherever they are to be found, is the true standard of taste and beauty.

Hume then admits (for the first time in the essay) that there are difficulties:

> But where are such critics to be found? By what marks are they to be known? How distinguish them from the pretenders? These questions are embarrassing; and seem to throw us back into the same uncertainty which, during the course of this *Essay*, we have endeavored to extricate ourselves.

It is strange that Hume does not give examples: there were Dryden and Pope and Dennis and Addison, to mention only those who were famous. Instead, he says that, after all, the question whether someone meets the qualifications is a "question of fact, not of sentiment." This is true of *some* of the requirements. Whether a critic has practiced assiduously or has worked on comparisons or is free from prejudice may be questions of fact; not so for "delicacy of taste," which is the crucial qualification. Delicacy of taste, on Hume's account, involves the capacity to respond to beauties that are nonobvious, unfamiliar, or subtle and the further capacity to pick out the particular features of a work that explain its overall beauty. (Imagine getting an audience deafened, as might be, by Beethoven, to see that there is something to Monteverdi and then going on to show exactly what that something is.) Delicacy of taste is displayed only in critical performance and in the light of a particular work. It is only to the extent that through your help I come to appreciate Monteverdi that I am warranted in crediting you with delicacy of taste. Thus, there is no way to distinguish the "true judges" from the "pretenders" that does not depend on a judgment of taste—hence, of sentiment—as a touchstone.

Hume concludes:

> Whether any particular person be endowed with good sense and a delicate imagination, free from prejudice, may often be the subject of dispute, and be liable to great discussion and inquiry; but that such a character is valuable and estimable will be agreed in by all mankind.

But that was not the issue. Besides, given that most of us are dull normals and lack these virtues, why should we agree that such a character is "valuable and estimable"?

The joint verdict of the "true judges" is not a matter of indifference. If it confirms my findings, I will feel more confident; if it clashes, I will wonder whether I have made a mistake. Hearing of their verdict and not knowing the work may make me eager to *get* to know it. But it cannot, as Hume claims, be the standard of taste. If it were, then without having ever read or appreciated any poetry at all, I could claim to know which poems are beautiful and which not, and that is absurd.

4

Hume's solution fails; his theory cannot be brought into line with the official neoclassical doctrine, and the latter, although it embodies some insights, is a logical mess. I want now to sketch a strategy that Hume might have adopted that does solve the paradox and to show, by reference to what I called the "subtext" of the essay, that Hume had a conception, albeit inchoate, of what the strategy is.

The basic idea is that for each of the two opposed positions, you keep something and jettison something. That beauty depends on sentiment, in particular on pleasure, is the element of Hume's theory to be retained. That the judgment of taste is either true or false, either defensible or indefensible, is the element of the official doctrine that should be retained. That means that Hume has to give up the notion that a judgment based on sentiment has no truth value. What has to be deleted from the official doctrine is the assumption that there are any nontrivial laws or principles of taste. My strategy is not purely ad hoc: the elements to be deleted have very feeble claims to truth. What emerges from the process is the conjunction, "Judgments of taste are either true or false and there are no principles of taste." As those familiar with these troubled issues will notice, this conjunction is one short step away from Kant's "Antinomy of Taste," and a solution that consists of replacing a paradox with an antinomy does not look like a step forward. On the other hand, Kant's antinomy is factitious and, I think, easily disposed of.

Here is his formulation:

> *Thesis.* The judgment of taste is not based upon concepts; for if it were, it would be open to dispute (decision by means of proofs).
> *Antithesis.* The judgment of taste is based on concepts; for otherwise, despite diversity of judgment, there could be no room even for contention in the matter (a claim to the necessary agreement of others with this judgment).[16]

The thesis is unexceptionable, provided one accepts Kant's claim that the judgment of taste is not derivable by inference, a claim that by this time—the antinomy comes close to the end of the First Part of the *Critique*—he has repeated, by a rough count, forty-seven times. But what is one to make of the *Antithesis?* The idea is that without *some* sort of concept, it would not make sense to defend a particular judgment, and it does make sense. Kant speaks of judgments not as "true" but as "valid," but his phrase "claim to the necessary agreement of others" would seem as appropriate to truth as to validity. There are passages where Kant suggests that the demands we make on the agreement of others with respect to the judgment of taste are parallel to those involved in ordinary empirical judgments. Thus he writes:

> A singular empirical judgment, as, e.g. the judgment of one who perceives a movable drop of water in a rock-crystal, rightly looks to everyone finding the fact as stated, since the judgment has been formed according to the universal conditions of the determinant judgment under the laws of a possible experience generally. In the same way, one who feels pleasure in simple reflection on the form of an object, without having any concept in mind, rightly lays claim to the agreement of everyone, although this judgment is empirical and a singular judgment.[17]

But Kant's proposed solution to the antinomy moves in a different direction. It is extremely brief: "concept," he says, means different things in the *Thesis* and the *Antithesis*. In the *Thesis* it is just what is picked out by an ordinary predicate that can function in a law-like generalization. It is a "determinable" concept. But "concept" in the *Antithesis* is something else: it is "indeterminable," which is to say that it is "the transcendental rational concept of the supersensible which lies at the basis of sensible

---

[16]Kant, *Critique*, p. 206.
[17]Ibid., p. 32.

intuition and is, therefore, incapable of being further determined theoretically." So the antinomy just needs to be rephrased.

> The *Thesis* should read: The judgment of taste is not based on *determinate* concepts; and the *Antithesis* should read: The judgment of taste does rest upon a concept, although an *indeterminate* one (that namely of the supersensible substrate of phenomena). Thus, there would be no conflict between them.[18]

Kant repeats the point: ordinary concepts would provide "objective principles of taste" and these are impossible, but the subjective principle—that is to say, the indeterminate idea of the supersensible within us—"can only be indicated as the unique key to the riddle of this faculty, itself concealed from us in its sources; and there is no means of making it any more intelligible."[19]

Well, of course, if you toss "the unique key" into the noumenal world, you *guarantee* that "there is no means of making it more intelligible." The "supersensible substrate" is a refuge for ignorance if there ever was one, and while intelligent philosophers may differ about the value of this conception for epistemology and ethics, its introduction into the third *Critique* strikes one as mechanical and rather high-handed. It is as though Kant thought that for the sake of symmetry the third *Critique* needed to have a concluding "Dialectic" in which the noumenal world figured prominently and then devised a way to make it relevant to his discussion of aesthetic judgment. However that may be, there is a way—Hume points the way—to a solution that is less burdensome and more intuitive. Keep the *Thesis*, drop the *Antithesis*, and recognize that a judgment of taste may be truth-valued without being provable, i.e., without "resting upon concepts" in the *Thesis* sense of "concept." Kant does not recognize beauty as a concept because he thinks that if it were, then it would have to have criteria for application that could serve as major premises for a syllogism. (See his statement of the *Thesis*.) He also thought that the sole alternative was a conception of beauty that reduces it to "the merely agreeable" and assimilates the judgment of taste to a confession of "private feeling."[20] But these alternatives are not exhaustive: except in logic and the formal sciences, very few singular judgments are derivable by deduction from principles. On this point, Frege is a better guide than Kant: if we think of a concept as "a function whose value is always a truth-value,"[21] then we can accommodate such concepts as generosity, intelligence, unhappiness, and so on. Beauty will certainly qualify. What is the test for whether some expression qualifies as a Fregean concept? We have only to consider whether we allow the appropriate judgment, in this case the judgment of taste, to play a role in ordinary deductive inference and in practical reasoning. Are we prepared to sanction an inference from "The *Iliad* is beautiful" to "At least one poem written in Greek is beautiful" or to "And so our students ought to read it"? If the answer is yes, then beauty is a concept. Hume, in every informal context, treats it as one. In the *Treatise*, for example, he entertains the

---

[18]Ibid., p. 208.
[19]Ibid.
[20]Ibid., p. 51.
[21]Gottlob Frege, "Function and Concept" (1891), reprinted in *Philosophical Writings of Gottlob Frege*, ed. P. T. Geach and Max Black (Oxford: Basil Blackwell, 1960), p. 30. (I am indebted to Sue Larson for drawing my attention to the bearing of Frege's conception on problems related to the judgment of taste and on philosophical aesthetics in general.)

thought that we find something (his example is a house) beautiful when we perceive it as beneficial, well suited to its purpose, a house that would be nice to live in. He then notices that we attach the term to houses that belong to strangers and cites this fact as evidence of the operation of "a delicate sympathy." What if there is no one to sympathize with?

> 'Tis sufficient if everything be complete in the object itself. A house that is contrived with great judgment for all the commodities of life, pleases us upon that account; though perhaps we are sensible that no one will ever dwell in it. A fertile soil, and a happy climate delight us by a reflection on the happiness which they would afford the inhabitants, though at present the country be desert and uninhabited.[22]

Hume's analysis is open to question. Kant, for one, makes a point of denying that the beautiful serves some determinate purpose. But how could one take *sides* on the issue, argue for or against a proposed analysis, without taking beauty to be eligible for analysis, i.e., without taking beauty to be a concept?

Hume, as we have seen, keeps saying that there are laws and principles of taste but does not mention any, and his discussion serves chiefly to show how ill-considered and confused the whole notion is. In "The Skeptic" Hume had written:

> There is something approaching to principles in mental taste; and critics can reason and dispute more plausibly than cooks or perfumers.[23]

But being a principle is not a matter of *degree:* only what fits the prescribed logical form will qualify. Kant's great contribution was to be absolutely clearheaded and explicit with respect to the pretensions of the official doctrine. He cites the passage quoted above and remarks that while Hume may be right in thinking that critics reason more plausibly than cooks, "they must still share the same fate":

> For the determining ground of their judgment they are not able to look to the force of demonstration, but only to the reflection of the subject upon his own state (of pleasure or displeasure), to the exclusion of precepts and rules.[24]

And from the same section:

> A principle of taste would mean a fundamental premiss under the condition of which one might subsume the concept of an object, and then, by syllogism, draw the inference that it is beautiful. That, however, is absolutely impossible.

One can hardly blame Hume for not having anticipated Kant, and Kant, after all, was the first person ever to demonstrate without hedging that the conception of principles is empty. There is less excuse for the generations of post-Kantian philosophers who *still* do not get the point. (When people say that there are no principles of taste, they mean that art is a free-for-all, anything goes—which is to say that there are no *standards*, a very different claim and one that is false.) Even serious philosophers are misled: C. I. Lewis, otherwise very perceptive about problems of aesthetics,

---

[22]*Treatise*, p. 584.
[23]"The Skeptic," *Taste*, p. 122.
[24]Kant, *Critique*, p. 141.

believed that there were laws of taste (hence principles) but that they have yet to be discovered.[25] More modish aestheticians reject the *term* "principles of taste" as antiquarian but suppose that there are "criterial features" or "good-making characteristics" that, when relativized to particular art forms, genres, and subgenres, and hedged by *ceteris paribus* clauses, provide for exactly the kind of deductive support for the judgment of taste that Kant recognized to be impossible.

Hume is saddled with the notion of principles and laws of taste with their attendant embarrassments only because of his commitment to the official doctrine. His own theory not only does not require that there be principles, but rather, as we have seen, precludes them. What about laws of taste, those inductive generalizations on which principles are supposed to be grounded? Here Hume's theory is interestingly ambiguous. In characterizing the skeptical position, he writes:

> No sentiment represents what is really in the object. It only marks a certain conformity or relation between the object and the organs and faculties of the mind and if that conformity did not really exist, the sentiment could never possibly have being.

What is this "conformity or relation"? It is cause and effect: my reading of a poem gives me pleasure and that it should do so is a necessary condition for my judging it beautiful. (I have been assuming that Hume, along with Kant, Plato, Aristotle, Aquinas, and almost everybody else, is right in taking the beautiful, whatever else it may be, to be a cause of pleasure.) The passage quoted has many parallels in Hume, and all of them are warped in a funny way. To put it in current jargon, Hume is so preoccupied by the thought that response is conditioned by "the organs and faculties of the mind," which vary from person to person, that he forgets that it is also conditioned by the character of the stimulus. It is as if to the question "Why does this poem please me?" there was only one answer and that tautological, namely, "Because it conforms to the organs and faculties of the mind." But that is unrealistic: very often I can say what it is about a poem (a person, a landscape) that pleases me (or displeases me). Such informal amplifications are the nucleus of criticism. Suppose you love *Die Walküre* and I hate it. Here are two facts but facts that quite naturally give rise to questions. No doubt there are psychological differences between us, but what does that explain? What I am curious about is not the state of your organs and faculties: what I want to know is what you find in *Die Walküre* (perhaps it is something I missed) that makes you love it. Hume could take account of this without giving up anything in his theory (except the mistakes). Taste depends not on reason but on sentiment; I call something beautiful only if it pleases me. Does it follow that nothing further can be said? Of course not. I can, for example, wonder whether Ariosto pleases *despite* his monstrous and improbable fictions or *because* of his monstrous and improbable fictions.

When Hume embraces the official doctrine, he has to change his tack and commend attention to "what has been universally found to please in all countries and in all ages." What he has in mind are properties common to great works of art, and when he cannot come up with any, he is driven to a fallback position, namely, there are some such properties but they are very hard to discern, which is why we need critics. But the "what" in "what pleases universally" is ambiguous, and Hume suddenly has a cheering thought:

---

[25]Clarence Irving Lewis, *An Analysis of Knowledge and Valuation* (La Salle: Open Court, 1946), p. 109.

The same Homer who pleased at Athens and Rome two thousand years ago, is still admired at Paris and London. All the changes of climate, government, religion and language have not been able to obscure his glory. Authority or prejudice may give a temporary vogue to a bad poet or orator; but his reputation will never be durable or general. . . .

A real genius may suffer from the results of envy and jealousy, but when these obstructions are removed, the beauties, which are naturally fitted to excite agreeable sentiments, immediately display their energy; and while the world endures, they maintain their authority over the minds of men.

Here Hume, it seems to me, is on the right track: the qualities found to please universally are, for example, the qualities peculiar to the *Iliad*. It is true that they are not discernible to every single human being. (For one thing, one has to know Greek.) On the other hand, there is nothing arcane about them; they are there for anyone who takes the trouble to find them. That "delicacy of taste" that we hope for in a critic is directed not at finding the secret ingredient common to Homer and Milton but rather at identifying and describing in perspicuous language the qualities that make the *Iliad* beautiful.

Hume's insight enables him to sketch a conception of the standard of taste that is quite different from that allegedly provided by the joint verdict of the critics. On this new conception, the standard of taste for each of the arts is set by the works that are acknowledged masterpieces, as the *Iliad* for epic poetry. This view I believe to be correct. T. S. Eliot remarked that in the history of poetry, the advent of a major artist, a Milton or a Wordsworth, alters our perspective on the past and leads to a review of our rankings. Try to imagine eighteenth-century opera without Mozart, Elizabethan drama without Shakespeare, American popular music without Irving Berlin: for me this leads to feelings of disorientation. What would things be like? Would minor figures suddenly become major figures? The thought is slightly eerie: nothing has changed but everything would look or sound different. Loss of standards breeds confusion and anxiety.

But if a standard is a paradigm, a shining example, could one not derive from it a principle? Yes, but the principle will not be adjudicative. If the *Iliad* is beautiful, then whatever is indistinguishable from the *Iliad* is beautiful. Here we have a principle but not a principle of taste (or perhaps the only legitimate principle of taste). The error of the official neoclassical doctrine is to suppose that since Milton is better than Ogilby, there must be something that Milton has *more of* than Ogilby. This error has proved hard to eradicate.

Hume's insight leads him to a dramatic, though unacknowledged, reversal of his position with respect to the contrast between "opinion and science" and sentiment:

In reality, the difficulty of finding, even in particulars, the standard of taste is not so great as it is represented. Though in speculation we may readily avow a certain criterion in science and deny it in sentiment, the matter is found in practice to be much more hard to ascertain in the former case than in the latter. Theories of abstract philosophy, systems of profound theology, have prevailed during one age: in a successive period these have been universally exploded. . . .

The case is not the same with the beauties of eloquence and poetry. Just expressions of passion and nature are sure, after a little time, to gain public applause which they maintain forever. Aristotle and Plato, and Epicurus and Descartes, may successively yield to each other: but Terence and Virgil maintain a universal, undisputed empire over the minds of men. The abstract philosophy of Cicero has lost its credit: the vehemence of his oratory is still the object of our admiration.

In summary, the nominal argument of "Taste" is as follows: the judgment of taste manifests a sentiment and is neither true nor false. There are laws of taste based on observation that specify properties common to works that please. The laws provide a foundation for rules of composition and principles of taste. The properties in question are difficult to discern: only the qualified critic recognizes them, and hence he is the only one competent to apply the principles. The joint verdict of qualified critics is authoritative in deciding disputes and constitutes the standard of taste.

The argument of the subtext is as follows: there are no laws of taste, hence no principles or rules of composition. There are particular works, such as the *Iliad*, which please universally "in all countries and in all ages." "The *Iliad* is beautiful" is not merely true; it is an eternal truth. A critic who failed to recognize this would be a "pretender" and not a "true judge." The critic with "delicacy of taste" is known by his ability to identify the particular features of, say, the *Iliad* that contribute to its beauty. The standard of taste is set for each of the arts by the works that are acknowledged masterpieces, as is the *Iliad* for epic poetry. The subtext is in part explicit (e.g., the bits about Homer) and in part derived by implication (e.g., the vacuity of principles as it emerges from the discussion of Ariosto).

To what extent was Hume aware of the subtext of "Taste"? There is no way of knowing. Since the subtext is flatly inconsistent with the nominal text, either Hume did not notice that he was subverting *en passant* the position he had set out to defend, or having noticed it, he did not care. As noted at the outset, the essay was written under pressure to fill a gap, and perhaps this explains its want of coherence.

Hume was preoccupied all his life with the tension between the demands of serious philosophy and the need for easy communication between philosophers and cultivated amateurs:

> The elegant part of mankind who are not immersed in mere animal life, but employ themselves in the operations of the mind may be divided into the *learned* and the *conversable*. The learned are such as have chosen for their portion the higher and more difficult operations of the mind, which require leisure and solitude and cannot be brought to perfection without long preparation and severe labor. The conversable world join to a social disposition and a taste for pleasure, an inclination for the easier and more gentle exercises of the understanding, for obvious reflections on human affairs and the duties of common life, and for observation of the blemishes and perfections of the particular objects that surround them.[26]

Hume worked hard at developing a style that would please the "conversable" audience, and his efforts were successful. Of course, he also chose for his essays topics that were nontechnical and suited to a fairly casual treatment. Philosophy brought to the coffee houses is bound, one might say, to be damaged in transit, but in a way Hume is right—it does not matter. There is little point in a comparative evaluation of the essays and the *Treatise*; they belong to different genres. But there is a related and less innocent distinction that Hume describes at the beginning of *An Inquiry Concerning Human Understanding*: the opposition between philosophy that is "accurate" and "abstruse" and philosophy that is "easy and obvious" is tied into a division of *subject-*

---

[26]"Of Essay Writing" (1742), *Taste*, p. 38.

matters.[27] When considering man as a "reasonable rather than active being," then rigor is called for and the criterion is "the approbation of the learned." But if one's concern is man as active, as "influenced by taste and sentiment," then the aim will be to treat the subject in the way "best fitted to please the imagination and engage the affections." Epistemology and metaphysics, in other words, are difficult and demanding and for the select few; ethics and aesthetics are comparatively easy and tractable in a manner that will make them appealing to the general educated public. This, I think, is a serious mistake. The problems connected with sentiment and the judgment of taste are not less complicated or deserving than those connected with the operations of reason. This is something Hume recognized in the *Treatise:* there is no change of key or lowering of standards when he moves from his discussion of the understanding to his analysis of the passions and of morals. The trouble with the "easy and obvious philosophy" is that it is inattentive to questions of evidence and to questions of consistency. It is no doubt silly to speculate, but one cannot help wondering what the outcome would have been had Hume been willing to apply to the problem of taste the philosophy that is "accurate" and "abstruse."

What is fascinating about "Of the Standard of Taste" as it stands is the unresolved (perhaps unrecognized) dissonance between philosophical insight and bad theory. Hume's great genius is occluded but never eclipsed, and the essay offers us, or so I have argued, almost all that is required for a solution to one of the central problems of philosophical aesthetics.

[27]*Human Understanding*, pp. 15ff.

Immanuel Kant

A THEORY OF AESTHETIC JUDGMENT: FROM THE *CRITIQUE OF JUDGMENT*

1

A Judgment of Taste Is Aesthetic

If we wish to decide whether something is beautiful or not, we do not use understanding to refer the presentation to the object so as to give rise to cognition; rather, we use imagination (perhaps in connection with understanding) to refer the presentation to the subject and his feeling of pleasure or displeasure. Hence a judgment of taste is not a cognitive judgment and so is not a logical judgment but an aesthetic one, by which we mean a judgment whose determining basis *cannot be other* than *subjective*. But any reference of presentations, even of sensations, can be objective (in which case it signifies what is real [rather than formal] in an empirical presentation); excepted is a reference to the feeling of pleasure and displeasure—this reference designates nothing whatsoever in the object, but here the subject feels himself, [namely] how he is affected by the presentation.

To apprehend a regular, purposive building with one's cognitive power (whether the presentation is distinct or confused) is very different from being conscious of this presentation with a sensation of liking. Here the presentation is referred only to the subject, namely to his feeling of life, under the name feeling of pleasure or displeasure, and this forms the basis of a very special power of discriminating and judging. This power does not contribute anything to cognition, but merely compares the given presentation in the subject with the entire presentational power, of which the mind becomes conscious when it feels its own state. The presentations given in a judgment may be empirical (and hence aesthetic), but if we refer them to the object, the judgment we make by means of them is logical. On the other hand, even if the given presentations were rational, they would still be aesthetic if, and to the extent that, the subject referred them, in his judgment, solely to himself (to his feeling).

From Critique of Judgment, *translated by Werner S. Pluhar (Indianapolis: Hackett, 1987), selections from* Book I. *Reprinted with permission of Hackett Publishing Company. (Footnotes omitted.)*

2

The Liking That Determines a Judgment of Taste Is Devoid of All Interest

Interest is what we call the liking we connect with the presentation of an object's existence. Hence such a liking always refers at once to our power of desire, either as the basis that determines it, or at any rate as necessarily connected with that determining basis. But if the question is whether something is beautiful, what we want to know is not whether we or anyone cares, or so much as might care, in any way, about the thing's existence, but rather how we judge it in our mere contemplation of it (intuition or reflection). Suppose someone asks me whether I consider the palace I see before me beautiful. I might reply that I am not fond of things of that sort, made merely to be gaped at. Or I might reply like that Iroquois *sachem* who said that he liked nothing better in Paris than the eating-houses. I might even go on, as *Rousseau* would, to rebuke the vanity of the great who spend the people's sweat on such superfluous things. I might, finally, quite easily convince myself that, if I were on some uninhabited island with no hope of ever again coming among people, and could conjure up such a splendid edifice by a mere wish, I would not even take that much trouble for it if I already had a sufficiently comfortable hut. The questioner may grant all this and approve of it; but it is not to the point. All he wants to know is whether my mere presentation of the object is accompanied by a liking, no matter how indifferent I may be about the existence of the object of this presentation. We can easily see that, in order for me to say that an object is *beautiful,* and to prove that I have taste, what matters is what I do with this presentation within myself, and not the [respect] in which I depend on the object's existence. Everyone has to admit that if a judgment about beauty is mingled with the least interest then it is very partial and not a pure judgment of taste. In order to play the judge in matters of taste, we must not be in the least biased in favor of the thing's existence but must be wholly indifferent about it.

There is no better way to elucidate this proposition, which is of prime importance, than by contrasting the pure disinterested liking that occurs in a judgment of taste with a liking connected with interest, especially if we can also be certain that the kinds of interest I am about to mention are the only ones there are.

3

A *Liking* for the Agreeable *Is Connected with Interest*

Agreeable is what the senses like in sensation. Here the opportunity arises at once to censure and call attention to a quite common confusion of the two meanings that the word sensation can have. All liking (so it is said or thought) is itself sensation (of a pleasure). Hence whatever is liked, precisely inasmuch as it is liked, is agreeable (and, depending on the varying degrees or on the relation to other agreeable sensations, it is *graceful, lovely, delightful, gladdening, etc.*). But if we concede this, then sense impressions that determine inclination, or principles of reason that determine the will, or mere forms of intuition that we reflect on [and] that determine the power of judgment, will all be one and the same insofar as their effect on the feeling of pleasure is concerned, since pleasure would be the agreeableness [found] in the sensation of one's state. And since, after all, everything we do with our powers must in the end aim at the practical and unite in it as its goal, we could not require them to estimate things and their value in any other way than by the gratification they promise; how they provided it would not matter at all in the end. And since all that could make a difference in that promised gratification would be what means we select, people could no longer blame one another for baseness and malice, but only for foolishness and ignorance, since all of them, each according to his own way of viewing things, would be pursuing one and the same goal: gratification.

When [something determines the feeling of pleasure or displeasure and this] determination of that feeling is called sensation, this term means something quite different from what it means when I apply it to the presentation of a thing (through the senses, a receptivity that belongs to the cognitive power). For in the second case the presentation is referred to the object, but in the first it is referred solely to the subject and is not used for cognition at all, not even for that by which the subject *cognizes* himself.

As I have just explicated it [i.e., for the second case], the word sensation means an objective presentation of sense; and, to avoid constantly running the risk of being misinterpreted, let us call what must always remain merely subjective, and cannot possibly be the presentation of an object, by its other customary name: feeling. The green color of meadows belongs to *objective* sensation, i.e., to the perception of an object of sense; but the color's agreeableness belongs to *subjective* sensation, to feeling, through which no object is presented, but through which the object is regarded as an object of our liking (which is not a cognition of it).

Now, that a judgment by which I declare an object to be agreeable expresses an interest in that object is already obvious from the fact that, by means of sensation, the judgment arouses a desire for objects of that kind, so that the liking presupposes something other than my mere judgment about the object: it presupposes that I have referred the existence of the object to my state insofar as that state is affected by such an object. This is why we say of the agreeable not merely that we *like* it but that it *gratifies* us. When I speak of the agreeable, I am not granting mere approval: the agreeable produces an inclination. Indeed, what is agreeable in the liveliest way requires no judgment at all about the character of the object, as we can see in people who aim at nothing but enjoyment (this is the word we use to mark the intensity of the gratification): they like to dispense with all judging.

4

A Liking for the Good Is Connected with Interest

Good is what, by means of reason, we like through its mere concept. We call something (viz., if it is something useful) *good for* [this or that] if we like it only as a means. But we call something *intrinsically good* if we like it for its own sake. In both senses of the term, the good always contains the concept of a purpose, consequently a relation of reason to a volition (that is at least possible), and hence a liking for the existence of an object or action. In other words, it contains some interest or other.

In order to consider something good, I must always know what sort of thing the object is [meant] to be, i.e., I must have a [determinate] concept of it. But I do not need this in order to find beauty in something. Flowers, free designs, lines aimlessly intertwined and called foliage: these have no significance, depend on no determinate concept, and yet we like them. A liking for the beautiful must depend on the reflection, regarding an object, that leads to some concept or other (but it is indeterminate which concept this is). This dependence on reflection also distinguishes the liking for the beautiful from [that for] the agreeable, which rests entirely on sensation.

It is true that in many cases it seems as if the agreeable and the good are one and the same. Thus people commonly say that all gratification (especially if it lasts) is intrinsically good, which means roughly the same as to be (lastingly) agreeable and to be good are one and the same. Yet it is easy to see that in talking this way they are merely substituting one word for another by mistake, since the concepts that belong to these terms are in no way interchangeable. Insofar as we present an object as agreeable, we present it solely in relation to sense; but if we are to call the object good [as well], and hence an object of the will, we must first bring it under principles of reason, using the concept of a purpose. [So] if something that gratifies us is also *good*, it has a very different relation to our liking. This is [also] evident from the fact that in the case of the good there is always the question whether it is good merely indirectly or good directly (i.e., useful, or intrinsically good), whereas in the case of the agreeable this question cannot even arise, since this word always signifies something that we like directly. (What we call beautiful is also liked directly.)

5

Comparison of the Three Sorts of Liking, Which Differ in Kind

Both the agreeable and the good refer to our power of desire and hence carry a liking with them, the agreeable a liking that is conditioned pathologically by stimuli *(stimuli)*, the good a pure practical liking that is determined not just by the presentation of the object but also by the presentation of the subject's connection with the existence of the object; i.e., what we like is not just the object but its existence as well. A judgment of taste, on the other hand, is merely *contemplative*, i.e., it is a judgment that is indifferent to the existence of the object: it [considers] the character of the object only by holding it up to our feeling of pleasure and displeasure. Nor is this contemplation, as such, directed to concepts, for a judgment of taste is not a cognitive judgment (whether theoretical or practical) and hence is neither *based* on concepts, nor directed to them as *purposes*.

Hence the agreeable, the beautiful, and the good designate three different relations that presentations have to the feeling of pleasure and displeasure, the feeling by reference to which we distinguish between objects or between ways of presenting them. The terms of approbation which are appropriate to each of these three are also different. We call *agreeable* what GRATIFIES us, *beautiful* what we just LIKE, *good* what we ESTEEM, or *endorse* [*billigen*], i.e., that to which we attribute [*setzen*] an objective value. Agreeableness holds for nonrational animals too; beauty only for human beings, i.e., beings who are animal and yet rational, though it is not enough that they be rational (e.g., spirits) but they must be animal as well; the good, however, holds for every rational being as such, though I cannot fully justify and explain this proposition until later. We may say that, of all these three kinds of liking, only the liking involved in taste for the beautiful is disinterested and *free*, since we are not compelled to give our approval by any interest, whether of sense or of reason. So we might say that [the term] liking, in the three cases mentioned, refers to *inclination*, or to *favor*, or to *respect*. For FAVOR is the only free liking. Neither an object of inclination, nor one that a law of reason enjoins on us as an object of desire, leaves us the freedom to make an object of pleasure for ourselves out of something or other. All interest either presupposes a need or gives rise to one; and, because interest is the basis that determines approval, it makes the judgment about the object unfree.

EXPLICATION OF THE BEAUTIFUL INFERRED FROM THE FIRST MOMENT

Taste is the ability to judge an object, or a way of presenting it, by means of a liking or disliking *devoid of all interest*. The object of such a liking is called *beautiful*.

6

The Beautiful Is What Is Presented Without Concepts as the Object of a Universal *Liking*

This explication of the beautiful can be inferred from the preceding explication of it as object of a liking devoid of all interest. For if someone likes something and is conscious that he himself does so without any interest, then he cannot help judging that it must contain a basis for being liked [that holds] for everyone. He must believe that he is justified in requiring a similar liking from everyone because he cannot discover, underlying this liking, any private conditions, on which only he might be dependent, so that he must regard it as based on what he can presuppose in everyone else as well. He cannot discover such private conditions because his liking is not based on any inclination he has (nor on any other considered interest whatever): rather, the judging person feels completely *free* as regards the liking he accords the object. Hence he will talk about the beautiful as if beauty were a characteristic of the object and the judgment were logical (namely, a cognition of the object through concepts of it), even though in fact the judgment is only aesthetic and refers the object's presentation merely to the subject. He will talk in this way because the judgment does resemble a logical judgment inasmuch as we may presuppose it to be valid for everyone. On the other hand, this universality cannot arise from concepts. For from concepts there is no transition to the feeling of pleasure or displeasure (except in pure practical laws; but these carry an interest with them, while none is connected with pure judgments of taste). It follows that, since a judgment of taste involves the consciousness that all interest is kept out of it, it must also involve a claim to being valid for everyone, but without having a universality based on concepts. In other words, a judgment of taste must involve a claim to subjective universality.

7

Comparison of the Beautiful with the Agreeable and the Good
in Terms of the Above Characteristic

As regards the *agreeable* everyone acknowledges that his judgment, which he bases on a private feeling and by which he says that he likes some object, is by the same token confined to his own person. Hence, if he says that canary wine is agreeable he is quite content if someone else corrects his terms and reminds him to say instead: It is agreeable to *me*. This holds moreover not only for the taste of the tongue, palate, and throat, but also for what may be agreeable to any one's eyes and ears. To one person the color violet is gentle and lovely, to another lifeless and faded. One person loves the sound of wind instruments, another that of string instruments. It would be foolish if we disputed about such differences with the intention of censuring another's judgment as incorrect if it differs from ours, as if the two were opposed logically. Hence about the agreeable the following principle holds: *Everyone has his own taste* (of sense).

It is quite different (exactly the other way round) with the beautiful. It would be ridiculous if someone who prided himself on his taste tried to justify [it] by saying: This object (the building we are looking at, the garment that man is wearing, the concert we are listening to, the poem put up to be judged) is beautiful *for me*. For he must not call it *beautiful* if [he means] only [that] *he* likes it. Many things may be charming and agreeable to him; no one cares about that. But if he proclaims something to be beautiful, then he requires the same liking from others; he then judges not just for himself but for everyone, and speaks of beauty as if it were a property of things. That is why he says: The *thing* is beautiful, and does not count on other people to agree with his judgment of liking on the ground that he has repeatedly found them agreeing with him; rather, he *demands* that they agree. He reproaches them if they judge differently, and denies that they have taste, which he nevertheless demands of them, as something they ought to have. In view of this, we cannot say that everyone has his own particular taste. That would amount to saying that there is no such thing as taste at all, no aesthetic judgment that could rightfully lay claim to everyone's assent.

And yet, even about the agreeable we can find people standing in agreement, and because of this we do, after all, deny that some people have taste while granting it to others; in speaking of taste here we do not mean the sense of taste, which involves an organ, but an ability to judge the agreeable in general. Thus we will say that someone has taste if he knows how to entertain his guests [at a party] with agreeable things (that they can enjoy by all the senses) in such a way that everyone likes [the party]. But here it is understood that the universality is only comparative, so that the rules are only *general* (as all empirical rules are), not *universal*, as are the rules that a judgment about the beautiful presupposes or lays claim to. Such a judgment of taste about the agreeable refers to sociability as far as that rests on empirical rules. It is true that judgments about the good also rightfully claim to be valid for everyone, but in presenting the good as the object of a universal liking we do so *by means of a concept*, whereas this is the case neither with the beautiful nor with the agreeable.

8

In a Judgment of Taste the Universality of the Liking Is Presented Only as Subjective

This special characteristic of an aesthetic judgment [of reflection], the universality to be found in judgments of taste, is a remarkable feature, not indeed for the logician but certainly for the transcendental philosopher. This universality requires a major effort on his part if he is to discover its origin, but it compensates him for this by revealing to him a property of our cognitive power which without this analysis would have remained unknown.

We must begin by fully convincing ourselves that in making a judgment of taste (about the beautiful) we require *everyone* to like the object, yet without this liking's being based on a concept (since then it would be the good), and that this claim to universal validity belongs so essentially to a judgment by which we declare something to be *beautiful* that it would not occur to anyone to use this term without thinking of universal validity; instead, everything we like without a concept would then be included with the agreeable. For as to the agreeable we allow everyone to be of a mind of his own, no one requiring others to agree with his judgment of taste. But in a judgment of taste about beauty we always require others to agree. Insofar as judgments about the agreeable are merely private, whereas judgments about the beautiful are put forward as having general validity (as being public), taste regarding the agreeable can be called taste of sense, and taste regarding the beautiful can be called taste of reflection, though the judgments of both are aesthetic (rather than practical) judgments about an object, [i.e.,] judgments merely about the relation that the presentation of the object has to the feeling of pleasure and displeasure. But surely there is something strange here. In the case of the taste of sense, not only does experience show that its judgment (of a pleasure or displeasure we take in something or other) does not hold universally, but people, of their own accord, are modest enough not even to require others to agree (even though there actually is, at times, very widespread agreement in these judgments too). Now, experience teaches us that the taste of reflection, with its claim that its judgment (about the beautiful) is universally valid for everyone, is also rejected often enough. What is strange is that the taste of reflection should nonetheless find itself able (as it actually does) to conceive of judgments that can demand such agreement, and that it does in fact require this agreement from everyone for each of its judgments. What the people who make these judgments dispute about is not whether such a claim is possible; they are merely unable to agree, in particular cases, on the correct way to apply this ability.

Here we must note, first of all, that a universality that does not rest on concepts of the object (not even on empirical ones) is not a logical universality at all, but an aesthetic one; i.e., the [universal] quantity of the judgment is not objective but only subjective. For this quantity I use the expression *general validity*, by which I mean the validity that a presentation's reference to the feeling of pleasure and displeasure [may] have for every subject, rather than the validity of a presentation's reference to the cognitive power. (We may, alternatively, use just one expression, universal validity, for both the aesthetic and the logical quantity of a judgment, provided we add *objective* for the logical universal validity, to distinguish it from the merely subjective one, which is always aesthetic.)

Now a judgment that is *universally valid objectively* is always subjectively so too, i.e., if the judgment is valid for everything contained under a given concept, then it is also valid for everyone who presents an object by means of this concept. But if a judgment has *subjective*—i.e., aesthetic—*universal validity*, which does not rest on a concept, we cannot infer that it also has logical universal validity, because such judgments do not deal with the object [itself] at all. That is precisely why the aesthetic universality we attribute to a judgment must be of a special kind; for although it does not connect the predicate of beauty with the concept of the *object*, considered in its entire logical sphere, yet it extends that predicate over the entire sphere *of judging persons.*

In their logical quantity all judgments of taste are *singular* judgments. For since I must hold the object directly up to my feeling of pleasure and displeasure, but without using concepts, these judgments cannot have the quantity that judgments with objective general validity have. On the other hand, once we have made a judgment of taste about an object, under the conditions characteristic for such judgments, we may then convert the singular presentation of the object into a concept by comparing it [with other presentations] and so arrive at a logically universal judgment. For example, I may look at a rose and make a judgment of taste declaring it to be beautiful. But if I compare many singular roses and so arrive at the judgment, Roses in general are beautiful, then my judgment is no longer merely aesthetic, but is a logical judgment based on an aesthetic one. Now the judgment, The rose is agreeable (in its smell), is also aesthetic and singular, but it is a judgment of sense, not of taste. For a judgment of taste carries with it an *aesthetic quantity* of universality, i.e., of validity for everyone, which a judgment about the agreeable does not have. Only judgments about the good, though they too determine our liking for an object, have logical rather than merely aesthetic universality; for they hold for the object, as cognitions of it, and hence for everyone.

If we judge objects merely in terms of concepts, then we lose all presentation of beauty. This is why there can be no rule by which someone could be compelled to acknowledge that something is beautiful. No one can use reasons or principles to talk us into a judgment on whether some garment, house, or flower is beautiful. We want to submit the object to our own eyes, just as if our liking of it depended on that sensation. And yet, if we then call the object beautiful, we believe we have a universal voice, and lay claim to the agreement of everyone, whereas any private sensation would decide solely for the observer himself and his liking.

We can see, at this point, that nothing is postulated in a judgment of taste except such a *universal voice* about a liking unmediated by concepts. Hence all that is postulated is the *possibility* of a judgment that is aesthetic and yet can be considered valid for everyone. The judgment of taste itself does not *postulate* everyone's agreement (since only a logically universal judgment can do that, because it can adduce reasons); it merely *requires* this agreement from everyone, as an instance of the rule, an instance regarding which it expects confirmation not from concepts but from the agreement of others. Hence the universal voice is only an idea. (At this point we are not yet inquiring on what this idea rests.) Whether someone who believes he is making a judgment of taste is in fact judging in conformity with that idea may be uncertain; but by using the term beauty he indicates that he is at least referring his judging to that idea, and hence that he intends it to be a judgment of taste. For himself, however, he can attain certainty on this point, by merely being conscious that he is separating whatever belongs to the agreeable and the good from the liking that remains to him after that. It is only for this that he counts on everyone's assent, and he would under these conditions [always] be justified in this claim, if only he did not on occasion fail to observe these conditions and so make an erroneous judgment of taste.

9

Investigation of the Question Whether in a Judgment of Taste the Feeling of Pleasure Precedes the Judging of the Object or the Judging Precedes the Pleasure

The solution of this problem is the key to the critique of taste and hence deserves full attention.

If the pleasure in the given object came first, and our judgment of taste were to attribute only the pleasure's universal communicability to the presentation of the object, then this procedure would be self-contradictory. For that kind of pleasure would be none other than mere agreeableness in the sensation, so that by its very nature it could have only private validity, because it would depend directly on the presentation by which the object *is given*.

Hence it must be the universal communicability of the mental state, in the given presentation, which underlies the judgment of taste as its subjective condition, and the pleasure in the object must be its consequence. Nothing, however, can be communicated universally except cognition, as well as presentation insofar as it pertains to cognition; for presentation is objective only insofar as it pertains to cognition, and only through this does it have a universal reference point with which everyone's presentational power is compelled to harmonize. If, then, we are to think that the judgment about this universal communicability of the presentation has a merely subjective determining basis, i.e., one that does not involve a concept of the object, then this basis can be nothing other than the mental state that we find in the relation between the presentational powers [imagination and understanding] insofar as they refer a given presentation to *cognition in general*.

When this happens, the cognitive powers brought into play by this presentation are in free play, because no determinate concept restricts them to a particular rule of cognition. Hence the mental state in this presentation must be a feeling, accompanying the given presentation, of a free play of the presentational powers directed to cognition in general. Now if a presentation by which an object is given is, in general, to become cognition, we need *imagination* to combine the manifold of intuition, and *understanding* to provide the unity of the concept uniting the [component] presentations. This state of *free play* of the cognitive powers, accompanying a presentation by which an object is given, must be universally communicable; for cognition, the determination of the object with which given presentations are to harmonize (in any subject whatever) is the only way of presenting that holds for everyone.

But the way of presenting [which occurs] in a judgment of taste is to have subjective universal communicability without presupposing a determinate concept; hence this subjective universal communicability can be nothing but [that of] the mental state in which we are when imagination and understanding are in free play (insofar as they harmonize with each other as required for *cognition in general*). For we are conscious that this subjective relation suitable for cognition in general must hold just as much for everyone, and hence be just as universally communicable, as any determinate cognition, since cognition always rests on that relation as its subjective condition.

Now this merely subjective (aesthetic) judging of the object, or of the presentation by which it is given, precedes the pleasure in the object and is the basis of this pleasure, [a pleasure] in the harmony of the cognitive powers. But the universal subjective validity of this liking, the liking we connect with the presentation of the object we call beautiful, is based solely on the mentioned universality of the subjective conditions for judging objects.

That the ability to communicate one's mental state, even if this is only the state of one's cognitive powers, carries a pleasure with it, could easily be established (empirically and psychologically) from man's natural propensity to sociability. But that would not suffice for our aim here. When we make a judgment of taste, the pleasure we feel is something we require from everyone else as necessary, just as if, when we call something beautiful, we had to regard beauty as a characteristic of the object, determined in it according to concepts, even though in fact, apart from a reference to the subject's feeling, beauty is nothing by itself. We must, however, postpone discussion of this question until we have answered another one, namely, whether and how aesthetic judgments are possible a priori.

At present we still have to deal with a lesser question, namely, how we become conscious, in a judgment of taste, of a reciprocal subjective harmony between the cognitive powers: is it aesthetically, through mere inner sense and sensation? or is it intellectually, through consciousness of the intentional activity by which we bring these powers into play?

If the given presentation that prompts the judgment of taste were a concept which, in our judgment of the object, united understanding and imagination so as to give rise to cognition of the object, then the consciousness of this relation would be intellectual (as it is in the objective schematism of judgment, with which the *Critique* [*of Pure Reason*] deals). But in that case the judgment would not have been made in reference to pleasure and displeasure and hence would not be a judgment of taste. But in fact a judgment of taste determines the object, independently of concepts, with regard to liking and the predicate of beauty. Hence that unity in the relation [between the cognitive powers] in the subject can reveal itself only through sensation. This sensation, whose universal communicability a judgment of taste postulates, is the quickening of the two powers (imagination and understanding) to an activity that is indeterminate but, as a result of the prompting of the given presentation, nonetheless accordant: the activity required for cognition in general. An objective relation can only be thought. Still, insofar as it has subjective conditions, it can nevertheless be sensed in the effect it has on the mind; and if the relation is not based on a concept (e.g., the relation that the presentational powers must have in order to give rise to a power of cognition in general), then the only way we can become conscious of it is through a sensation of this relation's effect: the facilitated play of the two mental powers (imagination and understanding) quickened by their reciprocal harmony. A presentation that, though singular and not compared with others, yet harmonizes with the conditions of the universality that is the business of the understanding in general, brings the cognitive powers into that proportioned attunement which we require for all cognition and which, therefore, we also consider valid for everyone who is so constituted as to judge by means of understanding and the senses in combination (in other words, for all human beings).

EXPLICATION OF THE BEAUTIFUL INFERRED FROM THE SECOND MOMENT

Beautiful is what, without a concept, is liked universally.

10

On Purposiveness in General

What is a purpose? If we try to explicate it in terms of its transcendental attributes (without presupposing anything empirical, such as the feeling of pleasure), then a purpose is the object of a concept insofar as we regard this concept as the object's cause (the real basis of its possibility); and the causality that a *concept* has with regard to its *object* is purposiveness *(forma finalis)*. Hence we think of a purpose if we think not merely, say, of our cognition of the object, but instead of the object itself (its form, or its existence), as an effect that is possible only through a concept of that effect. In that case the presentation of the effect is the basis that determines the effect's cause and precedes it. Consciousness of a presentation's causality directed at the subject's state so as to *keep* him in that state, may here designate generally what we call pleasure; whereas displeasure is that presentation which contains the basis that determines [the subject to change] the state [consisting] of [certain] presentations into their own opposite (i.e., to keep them away or remove them).

The power of desire, insofar as it can be determined to act only by concepts, i.e., in conformity with the presentation of a purpose, would be the will. On the other hand, we do call objects, states of mind, or acts purposive even if their possibility does not necessarily presuppose the presentation of a purpose; we do this merely because we can explain and grasp them only if we assume that they are based on a causality [that operates] according to purposes, i.e., on a will that would have so arranged them in accordance with the presentation of a certain rule. Hence there can be purposiveness without a purpose, insofar as we do not posit the causes of this form in a will, and yet can grasp the explanation of its possibility only by deriving it from a will. Now what we observe we do not always need to have insight into by reason (as to how it is possible). Hence we can at least observe a purposiveness as to form and take note of it in objects—even if only by reflection—without basing it on a purpose (as the matter of the *nexus finalis*).

11

A Judgment of Taste Is Based on Nothing but the Form of Purposiveness *of an Object (or of the* Way of Presenting It)

Whenever a purpose is regarded as the basis of a liking, it always carries with it an interest, as the basis that determines the judgment about the object of the pleasure.

Hence a judgment of taste cannot be based on a subjective purpose. But a judgment of taste also cannot be determined by a presentation of an objective purpose, i.e., a presentation of the object itself as possible according to principles of connection in terms of purposes, and hence it cannot be determined by a concept of the good. For it is an aesthetic and not a cognitive judgment, and hence does not involve a *concept* of the character and internal or external possibility of the object through this or that cause; rather, it involves merely the relation of the presentational powers to each other, so far as they are determined by a presentation.

Now this relation, [present] when [judgment] determines an object as beautiful, is connected with the feeling of a pleasure, a pleasure that the judgment of taste at the same time declares to be valid for everyone. Hence neither an agreeableness accompanying the presentation, nor a presentation of the object's perfection and the concept of the good, can contain the basis that determines [such a judgment]. Therefore the liking that, without a concept, we judge to be universally communicable and hence to be the basis that determines a judgment of taste, can be nothing but the subjective purposiveness in the presentation of an object, without any purpose (whether objective or subjective), and hence the mere form of purposiveness, insofar as we are conscious of it, in the presentation by which an object is *given* us.

* * *

13

A Pure Judgment of Taste Is Independent of Charm and Emotion

All interest ruins a judgment of taste and deprives it of its impartiality, especially if, instead of making the purposiveness precede the feeling of pleasure as the interest of reason does, that interest bases the purposiveness on the feeling of pleasure; but this is what always happens in an aesthetic judgment that we make about something insofar as it gratifies or pains us. Hence judgments affected in this way can make either no claim at all to a universally valid liking, or a claim that is diminished to the extent that sensations of that kind are included among the bases determining the taste. Any taste remains barbaric if its liking requires that *charms* and *emotions* be mingled in, let alone if it makes these the standard of its approval.

And yet, (though beauty should actually concern only form), charms are frequently not only included with beauty, as a contribution toward a universal aesthetic liking, but are even themselves passed off as beauties, so that the matter of the liking is passed off as the form. This is a misunderstanding that, like many others having yet some basis in truth, can be eliminated by carefully defining these concepts.

A *pure judgment of taste* is one that is not influenced by charm or emotion (though these may be connected with a liking for the beautiful), and whose determining basis is therefore merely the purposiveness of the form.

14

Elucidation by Examples

Aesthetic judgments, just like theoretical (i.e., logical) ones, can be divided into empirical and pure. Aesthetic judgments are empirical if they assert that an object or a way of presenting it is agreeable or disagreeable; they are pure if they assert that it is beautiful. Empirical aesthetic judgments are judgments of sense (material aesthetic judgments); only pure aesthetic judgments (since they are formal) are properly judgments of taste.

Hence a judgment of taste is pure only insofar as no merely empirical liking is mingled in with the basis that determines it. But this is just what happens whenever charm or emotion have a share in a judgment by which something is to be declared beautiful.

Here again some will raise objections, trying to make out, not merely that charm is a necessary ingredient in beauty, but indeed that it is sufficient all by itself to [deserve] being called beautiful. Most people will declare a mere color, such as the green color of a lawn, or a mere tone (as distinct from sound and noise), as for example that of a violin, to be beautiful in themselves, even though both seem to be based merely on the matter of presentations, i.e., solely on sensation, and hence only deserve to be called agreeable. And yet it will surely be noticed at the same time that sensations of color as well as of tone claim to deserve being considered beautiful only insofar as they are *pure*. And that is an attribute that already concerns form, and it is moreover all that can be universally communicated with certainty about these presentations; for we cannot assume that in all subjects the sensations themselves agree in quality, let alone that everyone will judge one color more agreeable than another, or judge the tone of one musical instrument more agreeable than that of another.

But what we call pure in a simple kind of sensation is its uniformity, undisturbed and uninterrupted by any alien sensation. It pertains only to form, because there we can abstract from the quality of the kind of sensation in question (as to which color or tone, if any, is presented). That is why all simple colors, insofar as they are pure, are considered beautiful; mixed colors do not enjoy this privilege, precisely because, since they are not simple, we lack a standard for judging whether we should call them pure or impure.

But the view that the beauty we attribute to an object on account of its form is actually capable of being heightened by charm is a vulgar error that is very prejudicial to genuine, uncorrupted, solid taste. It is true that charms may be added to beauty as a supplement: they may offer the mind more than that dry liking, by also making the presentation of the object interesting to it, and hence they may commend to us taste and its cultivation, above all if our taste is still crude and unpracticed. But charms do actually impair the judgment of taste if they draw attention to themselves as [if they were] bases for judging beauty. For the view that they contribute to beauty is so far off the mark that it is in fact only as aliens that they must, indulgently, be granted admittance when taste is still weak and unpracticed, and only insofar as they do not interfere with the beautiful form.

In painting, in sculpture, indeed in all the visual arts, including architecture and horticulture insofar as they are fine arts, *design* is what is essential; in design the basis for any involvement of taste is not what gratifies us in sensation, but merely what we like because of its form. The colors that illuminate the outline belong to charm. Though they can indeed make the object itself vivid to sense, they cannot make it beautiful and worthy of being beheld. Rather, usually the requirement of beautiful form severely restricts [what] colors [may be used], and even where the charm [of colors] is admitted it is still only the form that refines the colors.

All form of objects of the senses (the outer senses or, indirectly, the inner sense as well) is either *shape* or *play;* if the latter, it is either play of shapes (in space, namely, mimetic art and dance), or mere play of sensations (in time). The *charm* of colors or of the agreeable tone of an instrument may be added, but it is the *design* in the first case and the *composition* in the second that constitute the proper object of a pure judgment of taste; that the purity of the colors and of the tones, or for that matter their variety and contrast, seem to contribute to the beauty, does not mean that, because they themselves are agreeable, they furnish us, as it were, with a supplement to, and one of the same kind as, our liking for the form. For all they do is to make the form intuitable more precisely, determinately, and completely, while they also enliven the presentation by means of their charm, by arousing and sustaining the attention we direct toward the object itself.

* * *

16

A Judgment of Taste by Which We Declare an Object Beautiful under the Condition of a Determinate Concept Is Not Pure

There are two kinds of beauty, free beauty *(pulchritudo vaga)* and merely accessory beauty *(pulchritudo adhaerens).* Free beauty does not presuppose a concept of what the object is [meant] to be. Accessory beauty does presuppose such a concept, as well as the object's perfection in terms of that concept. The free kinds of beauty are called (self-subsistent) beauties of this or that thing. The other kind of beauty is accessory to a concept (i.e., it is conditioned beauty) and as such is attributed to objects that fall under the concept of a particular purpose.

Flowers are free natural beauties. Hardly anyone apart from the botanist knows what sort of thing a flower is [meant] to be; and even he, while recognizing it as the reproductive organ of a plant, pays no attention to this natural purpose when he judges the flower by taste. Hence the judgment is based on no perfection of any kind, no intrinsic purposiveness to which the combination of the manifold might refer. Many birds (the parrot, the humming-bird, the bird of paradise) and a lot of crustaceans in the sea are [free] beauties themselves [and] belong to no object determined by concepts as to its purpose, but we like them freely and on their own account. Thus designs *à la grecque*, the foliage on borders or on wallpaper, etc., mean nothing on their own: they represent [*vorstellen*] nothing, no object under a determinate concept, and are free beauties. What we call fantasias in music (namely, music without a topic [*Thema*]), indeed all music not set to words, may also be included in the same class.

When we judge free beauty (according to mere form) then our judgment of taste is pure. Here we presuppose no concept of any purpose for which the manifold is to serve the given object, and hence no concept [as to] what the object is [meant] to represent; our imagination is playing, as it were, while it contemplates the shape, and such a concept would only restrict its freedom.

But the beauty of a human being (and, as kinds subordinate to a human being, the beauty of a man or woman or child), or the beauty of a horse or of a building (such as a church, palace, armory, or summer-house) does presuppose the concept of the purpose that determines what the thing is [meant] to be, and hence a concept of its perfection, and so it is merely adherent beauty. Now just as a connection of beauty, which properly concerns only form, with the agreeable (the sensation) prevented the judgment of taste from being pure, so does a connection of beauty with the good (i.e., as to how, in terms of the thing's purpose, the manifold is good for the thing itself) impair the purity of a judgment of taste.

It is true that taste gains by such a connection of aesthetic with intellectual liking, for it becomes fixed and, though it is not universal, rules can be prescribed for it with regard to certain objects that are purposively determined. By the same token, however, these rules will not be rules of taste but will merely be rules for uniting taste with reason, i.e., the beautiful with the good, a union that enables us to use the beautiful as an instrument for our aim regarding the good, so that the mental attunement that sustains itself and has subjective universal validity may serve as a basis for that other way of thinking that can be sustained only by laborious resolve but that is universally valid objectively. Actually, however, neither does perfection gain by beauty, nor beauty by perfection. Rather, because in using a concept in order to compare the presentation by which an object is given us with that object itself (with regard to what it is [meant] to be), we inevitably hold the presentation up to the sensation in the subject, it is the *complete power* of presentation that gains when the two states of mind harmonize.

* * *

17

On the Ideal of Beauty

There can be no objective rule of taste, no rule of taste that determines by concepts what is beautiful. For any judgment from this source [i.e., taste] is aesthetic, i.e., the basis determining it is the subject's feeling and not the concept of an object. If we search for a principle of taste that states the universal criterion of the beautiful by means of determinate concepts, then we engage in a fruitless endeavor, because we search for something that is impossible and intrinsically contradictory. The universal communicability of the sensation (of liking or disliking)—a universal communicability that is indeed not based on a concept—[I say that] the broadest possible agreement among all ages and peoples regarding this feeling that accompanies the presentation of certain objects is the empirical criterion [for what is beautiful]. This criterion, although weak and barely sufficient for a conjecture, [does suggest] that a taste so much confirmed by examples stems from [a] deeply hidden basis, common to all human beings, underlying their agreement in judging the forms under which objects are given them.

That is why we regard some products of taste as *exemplary*. This does not mean that taste can be acquired by imitating someone else's. For taste must be an ability one has oneself; and although someone who imitates a model may manifest skill insofar as he succeeds in this, he manifests taste only insofar as he can judge that model himself. From this, however, it follows that the highest model, the archetype of taste, is a mere idea, an idea which everyone must generate within himself and by which he must judge any object of taste, any example of someone's judging by taste, and even the taste of everyone [else]. *Idea* properly means a rational concept, and *ideal* the presentation of an individual being as adequate to an idea. Hence that archetype of taste, which does indeed rest on reason's indeterminate idea of a maximum, but which still can be presented not through concepts but only in an individual exhibition, may more appropriately be called the ideal of the beautiful. Though we do not have such an ideal in our possession, we do strive to produce it within us. But it will be merely an ideal of the imagination, precisely because it does not rest on concepts but rests on an exhibition, and the power of exhibition is the imagination. How, then, do we arrive at such an ideal of beauty? Do we do so a priori or empirically? Also, which type of the beautiful admits of an ideal?

We must be careful to note, first of all, that if we are to seek an ideal of beauty then the beauty must be *fixed* rather than *vague*, fixed by a concept of objective purposiveness. Hence this beauty must belong not to the object of an entirely pure judgment of taste, but to the object of a partly intellectual one. In other words, if an ideal is to be located in any kind of bases for judging, then there must be some underlying idea of reason, governed by determinate concepts, that determines a priori the purpose on which the object's inner possibility rests. An ideal of beautiful flowers, of beautiful furnishings, or of a beautiful view is unthinkable. But an ideal of a beauty that is accessory to determinate purposes is also inconceivable, e.g., an ideal of a beautiful mansion, a beautiful tree, a beautiful garden, etc., presumably because the purposes are not sufficiently determined and fixed by their concept, so that the purposiveness is nearly as free as in the case of *vague* beauty. [This leaves] only that which has the purpose of its existence within itself—*man*. Man can himself determine his purposes by reason; or, where he has to take them from outer perception, he can still compare them with essential and universal purposes and then judge the former purposes' harmony with the latter ones aesthetically as well. It is *man*, alone among all objects in the world, who admits of an ideal of *beauty*, just as the humanity in his person, [i.e., in man considered] as an intelligence, is the only [thing] in the world that admits of the ideal of *perfection*.

But we must still distinguish the *ideal* of the beautiful, which for reasons already stated must be expected solely in the *human figure*. Now the ideal in this figure consists in the expression of the *moral*; apart from the moral the object would not be liked universally and moreover positively (rather than merely negatively, when it is exhibited in a way that is [merely] academically correct). Now it is true that this visible expression of moral ideas that govern man inwardly can be taken only from experience. Yet these moral ideas must be connected, in the idea of the highest purposiveness, with everything that our reason links with the morally good: goodness of soul, or purity, or fortitude, or serenity, etc.; and in order for this connection to be made visible, as it were, in bodily expression (as an effect of what is inward), pure ideas of reason must be united with a very strong imagination in someone who seeks so much as to judge, let alone exhibit, it. The correctness of such an ideal of beauty is proved by its not permitting any charm of sense to be mingled with the liking for its object, while yet making us take a great interest in it. This in turn proves that a judging by such a standard can never be purely aesthetic, and that a judging by an ideal of beauty is not a mere judgment of taste.

EXPLICATION OF THE BEAUTIFUL INFERRED FROM THE THIRD MOMENT

Beauty is an object's form of *purposiveness* insofar as it is perceived in the object *without the presentation of a purpose.*

18

What the Modality of a Judgment of Taste Is

About any presentation I can say at least that there is a *possibility* for it (as a cognition) to be connected with a pleasure. About that which I call *agreeable* I say that it *actually* gives rise to pleasure in me. But we think of the *beautiful* as having a *necessary* reference to liking. This necessity is of a special kind. It is not a theoretical objective necessity, allowing us to cognize a priori that everyone *will feel* this liking for the object I call beautiful. Nor is it a practical objective necessity, where, through concepts of a pure rational will that serves freely acting beings as a rule, this liking is the necessary consequence of an objective law and means nothing other than that one absolutely (without any further intention) ought to act in a certain way. Rather, as a necessity that is thought in an aesthetic judgment, it can only be called *exemplary*, i.e., a necessity of the assent of *everyone* to a judgment that is regarded as an example of a universal rule that we are unable to state. Since an aesthetic judgment is not an objective and cognitive one, this necessity cannot be derived from determinate concepts and hence is not apodeictic. Still less can it be inferred from the universality of experience (from a thorough agreement among judgments about the beauty of a certain object). For not only would experience hardly furnish a sufficient amount of evidence for this, but a concept of the necessity of these judgments cannot be based on empirical judgments.

19

The Subjective Necessity That We Attribute to a Judgment of Taste Is Conditioned

A judgment of taste requires everyone to assent; and whoever declares something to be beautiful holds that everyone *ought* to give his approval to the object at hand and that he too should declare it beautiful. Hence the *ought* in an aesthetic judgment, even once we have all the data needed for judging, is still uttered only conditionally. We solicit everyone else's assent because we have a basis for it that is common to all. Indeed, we could count on that assent, if only we could always be sure that the instance had been subsumed correctly under that basis, which is the rule for the approval.

20

The Condition for the Necessity Alleged by a Judgment of Taste Is the Idea of a Common Sense

If judgments of taste had (as cognitive judgments do) a determinate objective principle, then anyone making them in accordance with that principle would claim that his judgment is unconditionally necessary. If they had no principle at all, like judgments of the mere taste of sense, then the thought that they have a necessity would not occur to us at all. So they must have a subjective principle, which determines only by feeling rather than by concepts, though nonetheless with universal validity, what is liked or disliked. Such a principle, however, could only be regarded as a *common sense*. This common sense is essentially distinct from the common understanding that is sometimes also called common sense *(sensus communis)*; for the latter judges not by feeling but always by concepts, even though these concepts are usually only principles conceived obscurely.

Only under the presupposition, therefore, that there is a common sense (by which, however, we [also] do not mean an outer sense, but mean the effect arising from the free play of our cognitive powers)—only under the presupposition of such a common sense, I maintain, can judgments of taste be made.

* * *

22

The Necessity of the Universal Assent That We Think in a Judgment of Taste Is a Subjective Necessity That We Present as Objective by Presupposing a Common Sense

Whenever we make a judgment declaring something to be beautiful, we permit no one to hold a different opinion, even though we base our judgment only on our feeling rather than on concepts; hence we regard this underlying feeling as a common rather than as a private feeling. But if we are to use this common sense in such a way, we cannot base it on experience; for it seeks to justify us in making judgments that contain an ought: it does not say that everyone *will* agree with my judgment, but that he *ought* to. Hence the common sense, of whose judgment I am at that point offering my judgment of taste as an example, attributing to it *exemplary* validity on that account, is a mere ideal standard. With this standard presupposed, we could rightly turn a judgment that agreed with it, as well as the liking that is expressed in it for some object, into a rule for everyone. For although the principle is only subjective, it would still be assumed as subjectively universal (an idea necessary for everyone); and so it could, like an objective principle, demand universal assent insofar as agreement among different judging persons is concerned, provided only we were certain that we had subsumed under it correctly.

That we do actually presuppose this indeterminate standard of a common sense is proved by the fact that we presume to make judgments of taste. But is there in fact such a common sense, as a constitutive principle of the possibility of experience, or is there a still higher principle of reason that makes it only a regulative principle for us, [in order] to bring forth in us, for higher purposes, a common sense in the first place? In other words, is taste an original and natural ability, or is taste only the idea of an ability yet to be acquired and [therefore] artificial, so that a judgment of taste with its requirement for universal assent is in fact only a demand of reason to produce such agreement in the way we sense? In the latter case the *ought*, i.e., the objective necessity that everyone's feeling flow along with the particular feeling of each person, would signify only that there is a possibility of reaching such agreement; and the judgment of taste would only offer an example of the application of this principle. These questions we neither wish to nor can investigate at this point. For the present our task is only to analyze the power of taste into its elements, and to unite these ultimately in the idea of a common sense.

EXPLICATION OF THE BEAUTIFUL INFERRED FROM THE FOURTH MOMENT

Beautiful is what without a concept is cognized as the object of a *necessary* liking.

GENERAL COMMENT ON THE FIRST DIVISION OF THE ANALYTIC

If we take stock of the above analyses, we find that everything comes down to the concept of taste, namely, that taste is an ability to judge an object in reference to the *free lawfulness* of the imagination. Therefore, in a judgment of taste the imagination must be considered in its freedom. This implies, first of all, that this power is here not taken as reproductive, where it is subject to the laws of association, but as productive and spontaneous (as the originator of chosen forms of possible intuitions). Moreover, [second,] although in apprehending a given object of sense the imagination is tied to a determinate form of this object and to that extent does not have free play (as it does [e.g.,] in poetry), it is still conceivable that the object may offer it just the sort of form in the combination of its manifold as the imagination, if it were left to itself [and] free, would design in harmony with the *understanding's lawfulness* in general. And yet, to say that the *imagination* is *free* and yet *lawful of itself*, i.e., that it carries autonomy with it, is a contradiction. The understanding alone gives the law. But when the imagination is compelled to proceed according to a determinate law, then its product is determined by concepts (as far as its form is concerned); but in that case the liking, as was shown above, is a liking not for the beautiful but for the good (of perfection, at any rate, formal perfection), and the judgment is not a judgment made by taste. It seems, therefore, that only a lawfulness without a law, and a subjective harmony of the imagination with the understanding without an objective harmony—where the presentation is referred to a determinate concept of an object—is compatible with the free lawfulness of the understanding (which has also been called purposiveness without a purpose) and with the peculiarity of a judgment of taste.

* * *

Ted Cohen and Paul Guyer

INTRODUCTION TO KANT'S AESTHETICS: FROM *ESSAYS IN KANT'S AESTHETICS*

In 1735 Alexander Gottlieb Baumgarten's dissertation, *Philosophical Reflections on some matters pertaining to Poetry*, first used the name for the modern discipline of aesthetics.[1] But the first work that gives a sense of the actual content and shape of modern aesthetics is Immanuel Kant's *Critique of Judgment of 1790,* or, more specifically, its first half, the *Critique of Aesthetic Judgment.*[2] Though published only four decades after Baumgarten began publishing his mature statement of his own views in the *Aesthetica* of 1750–58, Kant's book is separated by far more than a single intellectual generation from its predecessor: for Baumgarten's work, though many interesting ideas still lay buried beneath its baroque surface, is a late product of a rationalist model of mind that is essentially alien to anything we now entertain; but Kant's work, though its language and its arguments often reflect its times, delineates conceptions of mind and art, of aesthetic response and aesthetic judgment, with which we are still at home and with which we can still do much useful work. Kant's thinking was directed to problems of aesthetics by the writings of Baumgarten and his German-

From Ted Cohen and Paul Guyer, Essays in Kant's Aesthetics (Chicago: University of Chicago Press, 1982), pp. 1–12. Reprinted by permission of the University of Chicago Press and the authors. Copyright © 1982 by the University of Chicago Press. Some footnotes omitted.

[1]Baumgarten first mentions the name "aesthetics" in his *Meditationes philosophicae de nonnullis ad poema pertinentibus* of 1735 . . . where §116 defines "aesthetic" as the science of perception in general, and §117 defines "general poetics," also called "philosophical poetics" in §9, as that branch of aesthetics dealing with "perfected presentation of sensate [or sensitive] representations," i.e., the works of art which correspond to the ultimate objects of discussion in our modern discipline (if discipline it is) of aesthetics, The *Aesthetica* of 1750–58 retains the definition of aesthetics as the general science of perception or knowledge through the senses (§1), but also implies that this "science" is coextensive with what was formerly classified only as a part of it, namely "poetics," by defining the "perfection of sensitive cognition" and then even beauty *(pulcritudo)* as the proper object *(finis)* of the science of aesthetics itself (§14). This corresponds more closely to the use of the term "aesthetics" that was firmly entrenched, if not by the time of Kant himself, then certainly by the time of Hegel.

[2]The *Critique of Judgment* consists of two parts, a *Critique of Aesthetic Judgment and a Critique of Teleological Judgment,* which are preceded by a general Preface and Introduction—the latter of which itself exists in two versions, that originally published with the work and Kant's first draft of the Introduction, which was published in its entirety only in this century and which is generally known as the *First Introduction to the Critique of Judgment.* The essays in this collection are primarily concerned with the views expressed by Kant and the topics addressed by him in the *Critique of Aesthetic Judgment,* although of course some of the papers draw on material included in the *Critique of Teleological Judgment* as well as in other Kantian texts.

writing collaborator and sometime translator Georg Friedrich Meier,[3] and many of Kant's early reflections[4] on these problems reflect the now lost intellectual world of these thinkers. And the final form which Kant's exposition of his thoughts on aesthetic judgment and its objects took is also strange for us, for the whole of the *Critique of Judgment* embeds its first part's discussion of aesthetic issues in a larger theory of the teleological judgment of nature which is even more alien to us than is the eighteenth century philosophy of mind. But in its actual content Kant's critical theory of aesthetic judgment substantially departed from its early roots in rationalism, and it was not irremediably distorted by Kant's late decision to connect it with his attempt to solve outstanding problems in his theory of natural science by a halfhearted resurrection of teleological reasoning.[5] Although the *Critique of Judgment* must naturally be read against the background of Kant's other major works, it does stand on its own in the sense of circumscribing a set of intellectual challenges which must be faced by anyone who thinks about certain regions of our feelings, thought, discourse, and action, and it does propose answers to these challenges which can be evaluated, if not always interpreted, independently of our attitudes to many other aspects of Kant's philosophy. Thus the *Critique of Aesthetic Judgment* is a fundamental text for our ongoing occupation with aesthetics, although some considerable interpretation is required to render it accessible for contemporary use.

What are the issues on which the *Critique of Judgment* is focused and which remain fundamental even to our contemporary concerns in aesthetics? Modern aesthetics is constituted by a nest of problems and approaches, and this image is applicable to Kant's foundational work. As in all of his major writings Kant expounds his views and arguments in an apparently highly structured manner, dividing up his text in a way which conveys the impression that a very tightly defined problem is being solved in a number of specifically differentiated steps. The problem which plays this central role in the *Critique of Aesthetic Judgment* is the problem of taste. How can we issue judgments which speak with a "universal voice" (*CJ*, §8, 216) or which claim "general" or "universal validity" (*CJ*, §7, 214–15), but are grounded on what is apparently the most subjective of all our responses to objects, namely, pleasure? How can we rationally make judgments "whose determining ground *cannot be other than sub-jective*" (*CJ*, §1, 203)? Or, to put the problem in Kant's official language of the synthetic *a priori*, the issue on which all appears to be focused is this:

> How is a judgment possible which, going merely upon the individual's *own* feeling of pleasure in an object independent of the concept of it, estimates this as a pleasure attached to the representation of the same object in *every other individual*, and does so *a priori*, i.e., without being allowed to wait and see if other people will be of the same mind? (*CJ*, §36, 288).

[3]G. F. Meier, a student of Baumgarten's though only four years his junior, translated Baumgarten's *Metaphysica* into German (in 1767), and also presented his three volume work on the *Foundations of All Beautiful Arts and Sciences* (*Anfangsgründe aller schönen Künste und Wissenschaften*) as if it were little more than a German version of the lectures his mentor had been giving, even though he began publishing this work in 1748, two years before Baumgarten published the first of the two volumes of his own never-completed *Aesthetica*. In fact, there are interesting differences between the views expressed by the two authors, although of course the framework of their thought is essentially the same.

[4]This material consists of notes written by Kant in the late 1760s and early 1770s, preserved and edited by Erich Adickes in volumes 15 and 16 of the *Akademie* edition of Kant's works, and of materials in Kant's lectures on logic, recorded in various surviving student notebooks and now published in volume 24 of the *Akademie* edition. . . .

[5]For further discussion, see Guyer, *Kant and the Claims of Taste*, chapter 2.

In outward form, the whole text of the *Critique of Aesthetic Judgment* is organized as if it were the exposition of, and then answer to, this question. Kant's text opens with an "Analytic of the Beautiful" (*CJ*, §§1–22) which first analyzes our judgments about the beauty of various objects as claiming universal intersubjective validity for the pleasure that those objects occasion, in spite of the apparent ontological subjectivity or innerness of feelings of pleasure and their epistemological freedom from any conceptual rules which could govern their occurrence, and which then sketches out certain indeterminate criteria—disinterestedness and finality of form—meant to insure intersubjective validity for responses of pleasure. Kant then proceeds, in his "Analytic of the Sublime" (*CJ*, §§23–29), to explain why certain other subjective responses to objects, namely, feelings of sublimity, though they had been linked to feelings of beauty in the philosophical tradition,[6] and are indeed similar to them in certain salient ways, do not in fact present the problem of taste in the same pressing form as judgments of beauty. That issue out of the way, but with the heading of "Analytic of the Sublime" confusingly retained, Kant proceeds to the "Deduction of Pure Aesthetic Judgments" (*CJ*, §§30–40), in which the assumption of intersubjective validity for pure judgments of taste and the procedures suggested for attaining such agreement in the case of particular judgments are to be defended by an examination of the epistemological structure of the frame of mind which underlies aesthetic response. Then, after what are apparently some mere digressions on some specific issues raised by judgments about works of art rather than about natural beauty (*CJ*, §§41–54), Kant turns from the "Deduction" of pure aesthetic judgments to their "Dialectic" (*CJ*, §§55–59), in which the argument is made that the solution to the same problem of taste which has been the focus of attention all along—here cast in the form of an antinomy arising from the tension between taste's claim to the "necessary agreement of others" with its exclusion of "decision by means of proofs" (*CJ*, §56, 338)—cannot be completed until the epistemological deduction of taste is supplemented by an interpretation of its metaphysical significance and its symbolic connection with morality.

But this appearance of a single-minded development of such a narrowly defined issue is misleading. The underlying issue in the problem of taste, namely, the reconciliation of the apparent conflict between the demands of the subjective or private in our responses to objects and of the objective or public in our discourse about both objects and ourselves, is indeed never far from Kant's mind. What he actually presents, however, is not a continuous pursuit of this issue but rather a more loosely constructed nest of ideas which has its core in the exposition and solution of the problem of taste, but which then wraps around this core a further skein of thoughts focusing on the complex relations between feeling and reason that manifest themselves in the creation and appreciation of the arts and in the interconnections of the arts with other areas of human concern. Throughout his work, Kant is concerned to show how the phenomena of taste and art can be incorporated into a general model of rationality and publicity without a loss of that delicate balance between the spontaneity of feeling and the order of rules—or, as he sometimes puts it in his language of mental faculties, between the faculty of feeling on the one hand and the faculties of understanding and

---

[6]The most important representative of this tradition for Kant was Edmund Burke, whose *Philosophical Enquiry into the Origin of Our Ideas of the Sublime and the Beautiful* was first published in 1757 and translated into German in 1773.

reason on the other—which is actually responsible for our pleasure in and fascination with the aesthetic. Thus, the problem of justifying judgments of taste is not so much the sole question to which Kant singlemindedly subordinates his discussion as it is the paradigmatic question of his aesthetics, on which each of the other issues he discusses has some bearing but which also provides a model for the solution of independent questions about these other matters.

If we conceive of the *Critique of Aesthetic Judgment* as a broader exploration of the relations between pleasure and objectivity than its official dedication to the single issue of the justification of judgments of taste would suggest, the progress of the whole work takes on a form somewhat different from that just sketched out. In those sections of its introductions[7] devoted to aesthetic rather than teleological judgment and in the "Analytic of the Beautiful," the discussion is indeed focused almost exclusively on the issue of the form and basis of the judgment of taste. In these parts of the work Kant is first concerned to advance his analysis of such a judgment as a judgment made on the basis of the pleasure felt in the experience of a particular object which then rationally imputes that pleasure to all members of the potential audience for the object. He then directs his efforts to justifying such a form of judgment by showing how, in spite of the apparent subjectivity of pleasures in general, feelings of pleasure connected to the particular and peculiarly nonconceptual disposition of our capacities for knowledge which Kant calls the "harmony" or "free play" of imagination and understanding can reasonably be expected to occur in anyone who approaches the object disinterestedly and yet properly attentive to its form. It is important to note, however, that the requirements which Kant actually takes to *define* aesthetic judgment are that it be grounded in and concerned with a feeling of pleasure while claiming the universal validity of that very feeling; that the ground of a particular pleasure lie in the harmony of the faculties, however, is necessary to justify a claim to universal validity but is not in itself sufficient to make its expression a pure judgment of taste. This has the consequence that, in Kant's initial consideration of the matter, judgments about works of art are not even candidates for the status of pure judgments of taste, for our pleasures in art, though actually produced by a harmony of the faculties, are to some degree at least constrained by the concepts we must apply to works of art in order to recognize them as such and to properly describe them (this is the lesson of Kant's discussion of "dependent beauty" in §16) and may thus vary in different persons depending on the concepts with which they approach these works. Initially, then, aesthetic judgments on Kant's conception, in radical contrast to what had been assumed by most writers since classical times, are more properly applied to objects of nature than to works of art.

This acute separation of art from nature has become a staple of aesthetics. An ironic twist, however, has blocked Kant's text from its proper audience in the twentieth century. In our time aesthetics has been concerned principally—if not exclusively—with art, and the beauty of nature has been a secondary, derivative concern. (In fact, most major contemporary aestheticians have taken no interest at all in natural beauty.) But the most compelling parts of Kant's analysis are directed at objects of nature, and this has made it singularly difficult for contemporary theorists to assimilate Kant's work, for they have read these passages as if Kant were talking about art. Only very recently has the philosophy of art begun to be able to integrate Kant's actual insights

---

[7]In the published Introduction, section VII; in the First Introduction, sections VII and VIII.

about art rather than simply contend with his claims for the superiority of natural beauty.

In the later parts of his text, however, Kant himself loosens the connection between the aesthetic and that which can be guaranteed to be universally valid because of its minimal conceptual content. That is, in spite of his initial emphasis on natural beauty, Kant himself comes to recognize that the underlying grounds of pleasure in works of art are fundamentally similar to those at the basis of our aesthetic response to nature, and he devotes more attention to the delicate balance between feeling and the conceptual order of understanding and reason in the case of art. But before he does this, Kant first reveals the full breadth of his real concern by digressing on our experience of the sublime. If Kant's sole concern were the possibility—or rationality—of a judgment which predicates universal validity of our response to a given object without actually predicating any determinate property of that object, then, on Kant's own account, he would not have to discuss the case of the sublime at all, for his view is that in expressing feelings of sublimity we do not say anything at all about the objects which occasion— and in this case *merely* occasion—those feelings. But it is clear that the phenomenon introduced in the "Analytic of the Beautiful" apparently just to justify claims to the intersubjective validity of certain pleasures produced by objects, namely, the delicate balance between the spontaneity of feeling and the demand for conceptualizability imposed by our cognitive faculties, is becoming a sign of the aesthetic itself, and an independent topic for investigation in the "Analytic of the Sublime." Here, however, Kant's chief concern is not that balance as it exists in the relation between imagination and what we might call the discriminating or particularizing interests of the un- derstanding, but instead the balance that may be achieved between the sensory aspects of the imagination and the universalizing or infinitizing interests of the faculty of reason and its pure ideas, and the subsequent impact of this relation on our capacity to take pleasure in our own cognitive abilities. Just as in the case of his discussion of beauty, however, Kant's concern is to show how there is a special source of feeling in the free interaction between the sensory basis of our imagination and our other cognitive faculties, and then to make the revolutionary suggestion that a full un- derstanding of the rational development of human capacities requires not the sub- ordination of all feeling to understanding—or the reverse—but interaction between these capacities. In this way, Kant's explanation of the phenomena underlying the recognition and enjoyment of both beauty and sublimity implies a rejection of the Platonic conception of the desirable subordination of feeling to reason as well as of the Humean conception of the necessary submission of reason to passion.

After returning to the specific issue of intersubjectivity for the ten sections (*CJ*, §§30–40) that properly constitute his "Deduction of Pure Aesthetic Judgments," Kant resumes the expansion of his discussion into new aspects of the relations between feeling and rules, widening his initially restrictive conception of the aesthetic until it takes in a range of issues underlying much of modern aesthetics. He begins by considering the nature of an "intellectual" interest in the beautiful, or the way in which the aesthetic employment of the imagination can interact with moral as well as with purely theoretical considerations. At this stage Kant still persists in his apparent denigration of merely human art, for he suggests that an interest in the arts is typically self-serving, while only an interest in natural beauty has any moral significance (*CJ*, §§41–42). Immediately after this discussion, however, Kant begins to give serious consideration to the actual nature of both the response to art and its creation; and the remainder of the book is largely informed by the tacit assumption that, although there is one fundamental difference between the judgment and creation of works of art on the one hand, and the evaluation and origination of natural beauty on the other— namely, that concepts have some irreducible role in the former although they are totally absent from the latter—there are also profound similarities between the forms which human rationality takes in these two domains and their significance for the whole of our thought and action.

The focus of Kant's discussion of art is the idea of genius, an idea generated by a simple, powerful argument. Kant's presentation of the argument is invalid, but with the necessary premises articulated the argument runs like this: the assessment of beauty cannot be made according to a rule (a concept). If it is assumed that some beautiful objects are made, and that at least some of these objects are made by people acting purposively to make such objects, then a special explanation is needed of the creation of beauty. Ordinarily in purposive making an agent brings into existence an object matching an antecedent concept—but what concept could be used to make a beautiful object? None, it would seem, for if there were any concept of beauty available for this making, it could also be used in judging objects, and Kant has already argued that there can be no rule-made assessments of beauty. How, then, can anyone even in principle consciously make a beautiful thing? Only, says Kant, if there is a special capacity for this, different from the ordinary capacity to make things: a capacity to make in accordance with something like a concept but not a concept. Kant calls such a capacity or talent genius.

Kant's explicit concern here, in line with his programmatic emphasis on the judgment of taste, seems to be to show how the delicate constraint of taste on human thought and emotion is not only compatible with the free processes of artistic production but is exactly what separates genuine artistic work from the false originality of what we would now call expressionism or romanticism on the one hand, and the orderly and even mechanical processes of scientific discovery on the other (CJ, §47).[8] In actual content, however, Kant's discussion of art goes well beyond what is required to demonstrate merely that even artistic success requires a consideration of intersubjective validity. Although Kant never quite admits it, the real purpose of the larger discussion appears to be to show that even though both the judgment and creation of a work of art require that someone have a concept of what such an object should be and mean, such a concept is not in itself a sufficient condition for either appreciation or creation. Instead, both evaluation and artistic production depend upon our striking a balance between the requirements of form and content imposed by the media and intentions of art, on the one hand, and the freedom of the imagination, on the other. It is this balance which is Kant's real concern in his initial exploration of the precise role of concepts of purpose and perfection in the judgment of art, and then in his further exploration not only of the creation of art by genius but also of the proper classification and capacities of the various forms which fine art can take. There is a difference between the entirely free character of our aesthetic response to nature and the more constrained exercise of the imagination which underlies either the creation or evalua-

---

[8]A post-Kuhnian conception of the nature of scientific discovery would remove much of the sting from Kant's contrast between scientific and artistic imagination, but not at the expense of his account of the latter. . . .

tion of any particular work of art, for the former depends upon a free harmony between the effect of an object on the imagination and some very general condition of or on conceptualizability, while the latter requires a harmony between the imaginative presentation of an object and some rather more specific concept or idea. But their similarity is greater than their difference, for what is crucial in both cases is that while a balance must be struck between the imagination's demand for freedom from constraint, and rationality's demand for rule-governed order, in neither case is there any rule for striking this balance.

After his lengthy and perhaps a bit unwilling restoration of art to the sphere of the genuinely aesthetic, Kant concludes his discussion with a brief return to the question of intersubjective validity. Or at least that is the presumptive purpose of the "Dialectic of Aesthetic Judgment," which is explicitly intended to resolve the antinomy which is generated by assuming that aesthetic judgments cannot be grounded in determinate concepts of objects and yet claim universal validity in a manner ordinarily permissible only for judgments which are so grounded (*CJ*, §56). Kant's solution to this problem is to suggest that aesthetic judgment may be grounded in a concept, but an indeterminate one. The presence of a concept makes this truly a judgment and grounds the claim to universality; but the indeterminate character of the concept eliminates the possibility of proof and preserves the "aesthetic" character of the judgment. At this point, however, Kant does not reintroduce the indeterminate concept of the non-rule-governed but intersubjectively valid harmony of the imagination and the higher faculties of cognition which he has already made central to his theory, but instead introduces an indeterminate metaphysical concept—that is, a concept without specific sensible criteria for its application—of the "supersensible" ground or substratum of all phenomenal reality. And this suggests that his purpose in this concluding part of the work is not so much to complete his epistemological defense of aesthetic judgments, which is in fact already complete, as it is to read deeper significance into the delicate balance between feeling and reason, perhaps to suggest that it ultimately gives us a way of feeling at ease with, or at home in, the world, which we do not quite enjoy on his model of the theoretical intelligence as a dominant but somewhat alien ruler imposing an order of its own on the mere appearance of objects. And this reach for deeper significance is then extended when Kant concludes the book with his discussion of beauty as the symbol of the morally good, for the underlying idea here seems to be precisely that the imagination in its aesthetic employment, with that characteristic balance between feeling and rule, gives us a way of actually feeling the impact of moral ideas which otherwise might remain pure postulates of practical reason.

* * *

It is in his analysis of the judgment of taste that Kant most acutely prefigures contemporary aesthetics, and we may attempt to extract a sketch of this analysis from the text we have just outlined. Kant begins with the observation that the grammar, or logical form, of a judgment of taste does not reveal but rather masks the epistemology of the judgment. The judgment seems to have the genesis and import of any judgment in which an apprehended object is brought under some concept, and it has this look because the statement "*x* is beautiful" has the superficial form "*x* is *F*."[9] This look is partly an illusion, and partly not. The illusion concerns the act of judgment which underlies the statement "*x* is beautiful."[10] It seems characteristic of statements with the form "*x* is *F*" that behind each lies an act of judgment in which the object *x* is subsumed under the concept *F*, that is, an act of apprehension in which, by means of a rule, *x* is conceptualized as an *F*. A judgment of taste is expressed in such a statement, but the statement is based on no such subsumption. Thus a judgment of taste is not "logical" in Kant's sense but "aesthetical." One's apprehension of *x* as beautiful is not the detection of some property in *x* by means of a procedure for recognition. It is, rather, the awareness that *x* prompts some feeling in oneself. The word "beautiful" in a judgment of taste, therefore, is not the term for a proper predicate concept. It looks as if it is, but this is illusory. In classifying the judgment of taste as "aesthetical" Kant is emphasizing that it is a judgment whose "determining ground *cannot be other than subjective*" (*CJ*, §1,203). In saying this Kant is accepting the leading claim of earlier British theory of taste (a theory most elegantly expounded by Hume but better known to Kant from the works of Francis Hutcheson, Edmund Burke, and Hume's cousin Henry Home, Lord Kames), and he is entrenching the assumption of the subjective character of aesthetic judgment so strongly that by our own time it has become virtually an (unargued) commonplace.

Having consigned the judgment of taste to subjectivity, and thereby, on his terms, debarred it from even a pretension to knowledge, Kant has set himself the problem of retrieving its respectability or legitimacy. This, too, has been part of the legacy with which modern aesthetics must contend. Except for the extreme verificationist willing to settle for saying that all judgments of beauty are inherently untenable, any aesthetician must explain how one can sensibly *assert* something which is yet merely subjective. Kant's own answer has not been as widely accepted as his formulation of the question, but this answer has only recently begun to receive the kind of analysis which can allow a proper assessment of its merits.

The statement "*x* is beautiful" is deceptive, then, insofar as it may seem to signal an underlying logical (objective) judgment, but Kant's deep and radical idea is that there is no deception whatever in *using* the statement, for using it is the only way to say what one wants to say about *x*. This form of words may seem to be appropriate only if one purports to say something "objectively" true about *x*, something which has a genuine

[9]It is an arguable point of interpretation whether the judgment is accurately schematized as "*x* is *F*." Kant's examples, typically, are not "This is beautiful" but are like "This rose is beautiful," and this suggests not "*x* is *F*" but "*x*-which-is-*G* is *F*." This could accord with Kant's insistence elsewhere that the judgment is not "This is heavy" but "This body is heavy"; and it leaves those who would reconstruct Kant's theory freer to introduce concepts into the judgment by bringing them in at the subject position, as long as it is conceded that the identifying concept *G* never provides a reason for the predicate *F* ("beautiful").

[10]A double difficulty in translation and interpretation has vexed readers of Kant. First is the relation of statements to judgments. Readers of the *Critique of Pure Reason* as well as readers of the *Critique of Judgment* have often supposed that they could read "judgment" as "statement" or "proposition." This is especially tempting in the third *Critique* because it is natural to think of a judgment as a statement in which something is appraised. But a judgment, for Kant, is an act, an act of the mind, and the related statement is only a graphic record. The second difficulty is with "judgment" itself, for this English word translates both "*Urteil*" and "*Urteilskraft*" (roughly, an act of judging and the capacity to perform such acts), and then retains the ambiguity (as in "His judgment was poor"). This ambiguity is resolved in context throughout the essays in this book, but it is left to the reader to remember that "judgments" are not always or ever just statements.

contradictory, but it is in fact justified whenever one refuses the disagreement of others who judge about x, or, to put it a bit more deeply, whenever one understands a lack of similarity of feeling to be a *disagreement*. Kant is the first to formulate the point precisely, in this way: one says "x is beautiful" instead of "x pleases me" or "I like x" just when one wants to make a judgment with more than personal import. This intersubjective significance rests upon one's awareness that one's pleasure in x is constituted by the unique relation one has to x. It is a uniquely uncluttered relation, devoid of every possible condition which would necessarily distinguish the judge from other people. Because of this the judge may regard all subjective differences between himself and others as irrelevant, and the import of his judgment is the incumbency upon all others to have his feeling for x. The basis for one's judgment is one's own personal feeling, but this feeling is, so to speak, impersonally personal. Thus the judge is a true representative of people in general, and it is therefore correct of him to offer the judgment in a form which indicates a public referent, for only such a form can indicate the interpersonal bearing of his judgment.

PART FOUR

---◆◆◆---

Contemporary Theories of the Aesthetic and Contemporary Critiques of These Theories

By the time the aesthetic-attitude theories presented in this part were being written, *beauty* had ceased to be the central concept of concern. The eighteenth-century theorists of taste had distinguished new categories, such as the sublime and the picturesque, and had given them separate treatments. Because of these innovations, and for other reasons as well, theories of taste had introduced a complexity into the theory of the appreciation of art and nature that by the end of the eighteenth century must have seemed chaotic to many theorists. As a result, eighteenth-century theories of taste were replaced by nineteenth-century theories of aesthetic attitude such as Schopenhauer's. The concept of the aesthetic functioned to restore a theoretical unity that was lost in the dismantling of theories of taste. The aesthetic attitude has its proper object—the locus of aesthetic value. The approach was simple and straightforward again, or at least it seemed to be.

At this point, the distinction between strong and weak versions of aesthetic-attitude theory can be introduced. A strong version maintains that whatever is viewed with aesthetic perception is thereby made beautiful or given other aesthetic properties; a weak version maintains that viewing with aesthetic perception is a necessary condition for experiencing the aesthetic properties of things—attributes that they have independently of aesthetic perception. Many of the recent aesthetic-attitude theories are weak versions of the theory; that is, they are theories that purport to describe an attitude enabling one to become aware of, and then appreciate, the aesthetic features of things. (In George Dickie's "The Myth of the Aesthetic Attitude" both stronger and weaker varieties of aesthetic-attitude theory are discussed, but the reader is warned that what is meant there by "stronger" and "weaker" is something different from what is meant by the "strong" and "weak" versions discussed above.)

Edward Bullough's article, which presents the aesthetic attitude in terms of *psychical distance*, was published in 1912. It has been reprinted in numerous anthologies and has exerted an enormous influence on aesthetic theory. Bullough begins by asserting that psychical distance "has a *negative*, inhibitory aspect . . . and a positive side." He discusses, however, only the inhibitory aspect, and consequently "psychical distance" has come to be taken to refer to a psychological inhibitory force that, when it occurs, blocks out impulses to action and "practical" thoughts. Once this blocking has occurred, a person is in the aesthetic attitude and can focus on and appreciate the aesthetic features of things. Bullough's now-famous example of the concept of psychical distance is a performance of *Othello* attended on the one hand by a jealous husband and on the other by a lighting technician. The jealous husband, unable to detach himself from his real-life situation, "underdistances" himself, i.e., he identifies himself with the character of Othello and consequently disregards the features of the play he would normally attend to aesthetically. The lighting technician, by contrast, pays attention to a single quality, with the result that he "overdistances" himself. According to Bullough, the happy mean to be pursued is just the right or appropriate distance, which is a state in which we detach ourselves from practical concerns and attend to as many relevant aesthetic properties as possible.

In "The Myth of the Aesthetic Attitude" Dickie argues that no such psychological blocking force is at work in the appreciation of the aesthetic features of art and nature and that Bullough has mistaken certain conventions we observe in our interaction with art for a psychological force blocking thought or action. For example, theatergoers remain in their seats conventionally and do not try to interact with the actors. Bullough misinterprets our observation of this convention and maintains that we are in the grip of a psychological force that prevents us, say, from mounting the stage on certain occasions to aid a player.

Another influential variety of the weak version of aesthetic-attitude theory was developed by Jerome Stolnitz, among the most influential of the aesthetic-attitude theorists. In his book *Aesthetics and Philosophy of Art Criticism* he maintains that different attitudes determine the way in which we perceive the world. Since perception is determined by purposes, our attention is always selective. We never perceive everything in our immediate environment that is there to be sensed; rather we attend to objects and phenomena relative to whether our attitude is practical or aesthetic. When our attitude is practical, we view objects as means to further ends; when it is aesthetic, our attention becomes "disinterested and sympathetic," and we take an interest in the object "for its own sake." The role of perception is therefore crucially different in the two cases. Practical perception is always directed toward a goal beyond our immediate transaction with the objects about us; it is oriented toward some future goal. Aesthetic perception, by contrast, is its own justification.

The criterion of perceiving for its own sake leads Stolnitz to a characterization of the aesthetic attitude as "disinterested" (detached from ulterior interests and motives) and "sympathetic" (dwelling on the object's "whole nature and character"). Such active attentiveness to the object serves to insulate us from economic worries or moral concerns and brings us into an immediate relationship with the objects of our perception and imagination.

Dickie's "Myth of the Aesthetic Attitude" contains an extensive discussion and criticism of the theories of Stolnitz and his contemporary Eliseo Vivas. This school of thought has as its central conception the notion of *disinterested attention*. Unlike Bullough, whose theory maintains that there is a *special* psychological force that blocks impulses to action and practical thoughts, Stolnitz and Vivas maintain that attention may be either interested or disinterested. When it is disinterested, attention defines the aesthetic attitude.

The weak versions of the aesthetic-attitude theory discussed here purport to describe a person's state of mind, which enables that person to be aware of the aesthetic features of art and nature. Frank Sibley, in his celebrated "Aesthetic Concepts" and several follow-up essays, attempts a similar feat but does so by trying to make use of the concept of *taste* rather than the notion of aesthetic attitude. In employing the word "taste," Sibley may seem to echo the writers of the eighteenth century. But as Ted Cohen notes at the end of his critical essay on Sibley, Sibley's notion of taste is far more restricted than those of the eighteenth-century philosophers. For the eighteenth-century philosophers of taste, taste was conceived to be (1) an ability to notice, (2) a capacity to enjoy (or be pained), and (3) a faculty that is the basis for evaluations. These philosophers were, however, almost entirely concerned with the last two aspects of taste. For Sibley taste is simply an *ability* that enables one to notice or discriminate features that a person who lacks taste cannot notice.

In "Aesthetic Concepts" Sibley claims that we make a distinction between aesthetic and nonaesthetic features of art (and non-art) and that our ability to do so might be called "taste." He also tries to establish that aesthetic features of objects depend on nonaesthetic features but asserts that this relationship is not a condition-governed one. With regard to the first point, Sibley maintains, for example, that a thing may possess the aesthetic quality of delicacy, which a person with normal eyes, ears, and intelligence—but lacking taste—will be unable to notice. A person who possesses taste will be able to notice the delicate quality of the object. With regard to the second point, the aesthetic feature of the delicacy of an object depends on its nonaesthetic features—say, its thinness and slight curvature; but thinness and slight curvature are not generally sufficient conditions for producing delicacy. Consequently, no matter how full a description one might have of the nonaesthetic features of an object, one could not infer that it has some particular aesthetic feature. Only sensing or perceiving and exercising taste will reveal whether the aesthetic feature exists.

In correspondence with one of the editors, Sibley clarifies his position as follows.

> I had no intention of using some eighteenth century notion of a "faculty of taste" to make, or "derive," the initial (aesthetic-nonaesthetic) distinction. That we all make some such broad distinction (and have to, if we're to have a subject matter for aesthetics) I take as my datum. "Taste" (and a variety of other locutions I offered . . . as alternatives) serves no more than a label for a complex of widely shared human perceptual-cum-imaginative abilities and propensities (the variety of which I tried to indicate in Section 2 of the paper [between 365 and 374]. What is more, I tried to stress that these abilities are "normal" enough, widely shared and exercised; but they are different from the merely normal use of eyesight, hearing, etc. and not merely a matter of intelligence. People have constantly supposed me to be referring to something "special" or "non-normal"; but I said quite carefully and deliberately at the outset [356] that nonaesthetic (etc.) were available, *not* to "normal *abilities*," (which *would* imply taste or aesthetic perceptivity to be non-normal), but to "normal *eyes, ears,* and *intelligence.*"[1]

Ted Cohen, in his critique of Sibley's account of the aesthetic/nonaesthetic distinction, is almost solely concerned with denying the legitimacy of the distinction. Cohen

---

[1]Letter to Ronald Roblin dated April 8, 1988. See also Sibley's comments on Cohen's critique below.

maintains that Sibley's distinction between aesthetic and nonaesthetic features derives from the exercise of taste, and he contends that Sibley presents no argument for the existence of taste as an ability we may have over and above normal abilities that perceive the features of the world. Cohen's criticism thus raises important questions concerning both the interpretation of Sibley's work as well as the relationship between taste and the aesthetic features of objects. Cohen contends that the so-called aesthetic features can be discerned by normal abilities, and that Sibley's distinction, therefore, "comes to nothing." Cohen concludes his essay by maintaining that the aesthetic/nonaesthetic distinction "has been shown to be not merely a superfluity, but an impediment."

Cohen's critique is commonly viewed as the standard refutation of the view held in "Aesthetic Concepts." For this reason, we include further comments by Sibley on Cohen's critique.

> . . . his critique entirely misinterprets my paper in a cart-before-the-horse manner. That is: (1) my distinction between aesthetic and nonaesthetic does not *derive* from the exercise of taste; I take it as a given obvious starting point and I label the ability we have to discern aesthetic qualities "taste"; hence (2) I don't need to present any argument "for the existence of taste"; and (3) I don't regard it as "an ability . . . over and above *normal* abilities"; indeed I labour to argue that it is itself a very normal and widely possessed human ability. I do, however, regard it as different from (= over and above ??) the abilities merely to exercise "normal eyes, ears, and intelligence"; but this is *not* to deny that "so-called aesthetic features can be discerned by normal abilities." Taste or aesthetic sensibility, in varying degrees, *is*, like intelligence, also in varying degrees, a normal human ability or propensity.

These quotations are included in order to strike a balance between Cohen's vigorous critique of Sibley's work and the latter's equally energetic response to them. The reader will wish to consider carefully both Cohen's criticisms and Sibley's response to them.

In "Categories of Art" Kendall Walton defends a contextualist approach to the understanding of works of art. Walton distinguishes between *intrinsic* properties, such as a work's formal values, and *extrinsic* properties, which cannot be discovered by direct perception of the works themselves. According to formalists, it is only the intrinsic properties of a work that count aesthetically. By contrast, Walton maintains that art history affects our understanding and appreciation of art and that critical questions about works of art cannot be separated from their histories. While attention to the intrinsic features of objects is crucial, not all of these features are relevant for aesthetic appreciation; determining which ones count requires extrinsic information excluded by the formalist.

On Walton's view, the perception of aesthetic features depends upon which nonaesthetic features are "standard," which "variable," and which "contra-standard." Standard features, such as flatness in painting, determine which category a work belongs to. Variable features have no bearing on a work's belonging in a certain category, such as subject matter in the plastic arts. The presence of contra-standard features, however, disqualifies a work's membership in a certain category, such as three-dimensionality in painting. Walton argues, accordingly, that the aesthetic properties a work seems to have and the effect the work has upon us depend, in part, on which of its features are standard, which variable, and which contra-standard for us. Thus, we must know which features are which before we can appreciate a work aesthetically, and this cannot be discovered by viewing it in isolation from its history or cultural context. It is the history of art that determines which features are standard, variable, and contra-standard, and the external information obtained from history and social practice is therefore relevant to our understanding and experience of art.

Walton's work has often been interpreted in opposition to Sibley's. However, in many respects, "Categories of Art" can be understood as a further development and amplification of much of Sibley's work, although there is not complete agreement between the two. The reader is asked not to take the customary view of "Sibley vs. Walton" but instead to examine and assess the points of agreement and difference between the two authors.

Edward Bullough

"PSYCHICAL DISTANCE" AS A FACTOR IN ART AND AS AN AESTHETIC PRINCIPLE

I

1. The conception of 'Distance' suggests, in connexion with Art, certain trains of thought by no means devoid of interest or of speculative importance. Perhaps the most obvious suggestion is that of *actual spatial* distance, i.e. the distance of a work of Art from the spectator, or that of *represented spatial* distance, i.e. the distance represented within the work. Less obvious, more metaphorical, is the meaning of *temporal* distance. The first was noticed already by Aristotle in his *Poetics*; the second has played a great part in the history of painting in the form of perspective; the distinction between these two kinds of distance assumes special importance theoretically in the differentiation between sculpture in the round, and relief-sculpture. Temporal distance, remoteness from us in point of time, though often a cause of misconceptions, has been declared to be a factor of considerable weight in our appreciation.

It is not, however, in any of these meanings that 'Distance' is put forward here, though it will be clear in the course of this essay that the above mentioned kinds of distance are rather special forms of the conception of Distance as advocated here, and derive whatever *aesthetic* qualities they may possess from Distance in its *general* connotation. This general connotation is 'Psychical Distance.'

A short illustration will explain what is meant by 'Psychical Distance.' Imagine a fog at sea: for most people it is an experience of acute unpleasantness. Apart from the physical annoyance and remoter forms of discomfort such as delays, it is apt to produce feelings of peculiar anxiety, fears of invisible dangers, strains of watching and listening for distant and unlocalised signals. The listless movements of the ship and her warning calls soon tell upon the nerves of the passengers; and that special, expectant, tacit anxiety and nervousness, always associated with this experience, make a fog the dreaded terror of the sea (all the more terrifying because of its very silence and gentleness) for the expert seafarer no less than for the ignorant landsman.

From the British Journal of Psychology 5 *(1912), pp. 87–98, 108–117. Reprinted by permission of the British Psychological Society. Footnotes omitted.*

Nevertheless, a fog at sea can be a source of intense relish and enjoyment. Abstract from the experience of the sea fog, for the moment, its danger and practical unpleasantness, just as every one in the enjoyment of a mountain-climb disregards its physical labour and its danger (though, it is not denied, that these may incidentally enter into the enjoyment and enhance it); direct the attention to the features 'objectively' constituting the phenomenon—the veil surrounding you with an opaqueness as of transparent milk, blurring the outline of things and distorting their shapes into weird grotesqueness; observe the carrying-power of the air, producing the impression as if you could touch some far-off siren by merely putting out your hand and letting it lose itself behind that white wall; note the curious creamy smoothness of the water, hypocritically denying as it were any suggestion of danger; and, above all, the strange solitude and remoteness from the world, as it can be found only on the highest mountain tops: and the experience may acquire, in its uncanny mingling of repose and terror, a flavour of such concentrated poignancy and delight as to contrast sharply with the blind and distempered anxiety of its other aspects. This contrast, often emerging with startling suddenness, is like a momentary switching on of some new current, or the passing ray of a brighter light, illuminating the outlook upon perhaps the most ordinary and familiar objects—an impression which we experience sometimes in instants of direst extremity, when our practical interest snaps like a wire from sheer over-tension, and we watch the consummation of some impending catastrophe with the marvelling unconcern of a mere spectator.

It is a difference of outlook, due—if such a metaphor is permissible—to the insertion of Distance. This Distance appears to lie between our own self and its affections, using the latter term in its broadest sense as anything which affects our being, bodily or spiritually, e.g. as sensation, perception, emotional state or idea. Usually, though not always, it amounts to the same thing to say that the Distance lies between our own self and such objects as are the sources or vehicles of such affections.

Thus, in the fog, the transformation by Distance is produced in the first instance by putting the phenomenon, so to speak, out of gear with our practical, actual self; by allowing it to stand outside the context of our personal needs and ends—in short, by looking at it 'objectively,' as it has often been called, by permitting only such reactions on our part as emphasise the 'objective' features of the experience, and by interpreting even our 'subjective' affections not as modes of *our* being but rather as characteristics of the phenomenon.

The working of Distance is, accordingly, not simple, but highly complex. It has a *negative*, inhibitory aspect—the cutting-out of the practical sides of things and of our practical attitude to them—and a *positive* side—the elaboration of the experience on the new basis created by the inhibitory action of Distance.

2. Consequently, this distanced view of things is not, and cannot be, our normal outlook. As a rule, experiences constantly turn the same side towards us, namely, that which has the strongest practical force of appeal. We are not ordinarily aware of those aspects of things which do not touch us immediately and practically, nor are we generally conscious of impressions apart from our own self which is impressed. The sudden view of things from their reverse, usually unnoticed, side, comes upon us as a revelation, and such revelations are precisely those of Art. In this most general sense, Distance is a factor in all Art.

3. It is, for this very reason, also an aesthetic principle. The aesthetic contemplation

and the aesthetic outlook have often been described as 'objective.' We speak of 'objective' artists as Shakespeare or Velasquez, of 'objective' works or art forms as Homer's *Iliad* or the drama. It is a term constantly occurring in discussions and criticisms, though its sense, if pressed at all, becomes very questionable. For certain forms of Art, such as lyrical poetry, are said to be 'subjective'; Shelley, for example, would usually be considered a 'subjective' writer. On the other hand, no work of Art can be genuinely 'objective' in the sense in which this term might be applied to a work on history or to a scientific treatise; nor can it be 'subjective' in the ordinary acceptance of that term, as a personal feeling, a direct statement of a wish or belief, or a cry of passion is subjective. 'Objectivity' and 'subjectivity' are a pair of opposites which in their mutual exclusiveness when applied to Art soon lead to confusion.

Nor are they the only pair of opposites. Art has with equal vigour been declared alternately 'idealistic' and 'realistic,' 'sensual' and 'spiritual,' 'individualistic' and 'typical.' Between the defence of either terms of such antitheses most aesthetic theories have vacillated. It is one of the contentions of this essay that such opposites find their synthesis in the more fundamental conception of Distance.

Distance further provides the much needed criterion of the beautiful as distinct from the merely agreeable.

Again, it marks one of the most important steps in the process of artistic creation and serves as a distinguishing feature of what is commonly so loosely described as the 'artistic temperament.'

Finally, it may claim to be considered as one of the essential characteristics of the 'aesthetic consciousness,'—if I may describe by this term that special mental attitude towards, and outlook upon, experience, which finds its most pregnant expression in the various forms of Art.

II

Distance, as I said before, is obtained by separating the object and its appeal from one's own self, by putting it out of gear with practical needs and ends. Thereby the 'contemplation' of the object becomes alone possible. But it does not mean that the relation between the self and the object is broken to the extent of becoming 'impersonal.' Of the alternatives 'personal' and 'impersonal' the latter surely comes nearer to the truth; but here, as elsewhere, we meet the difficulty of having to express certain facts in terms coined for entirely different uses. To do so usually results in paradoxes, which are nowhere more inevitable than in discussions upon Art. 'Personal' and 'impersonal,' 'subjective' and 'objective' are such terms, devised for purposes other than aesthetic speculation, and becoming loose and ambiguous as soon as applied outside the sphere of their special meanings. In giving preference therefore to the term 'impersonal' to describe the relation between the spectator and a work of Art, it is to be noticed that it is not impersonal in the sense in which we speak of the 'impersonal' character of Science, for instance. In order to obtain 'objectively valid' results, the scientist excludes the 'personal factor,' i.e. his personal wishes as to the validity of his results, his predilection for any particular system to be proved or disproved by his research. It goes without saying that all experiments and investigations are undertaken out of a personal interest in the science, for the ultimate support of a definite assumption, and involve personal hopes of success; but this does not affect the 'dispassionate' attitude of the investigator, under pain of being accused of 'manufacturing his evidence.'

1. Distance does not imply an impersonal, purely intellectually interested relation of such a kind. On the contrary, it describes a *personal* relation, often highly emotionally coloured, but *of a peculiar character*. Its peculiarity lies in that the personal character of the relation has been, so to speak, filtered. It has been cleared of the practical, concrete nature of its appeal, without, however, thereby losing its original constitution. One of the best known examples is to be found in our attitude towards the events and characters of the drama: they appeal to us like persons and incidents of normal experience, except that that side of their appeal, which would usually affect us in a directly personal manner, is held in abeyance. This difference, so well known as to be almost trivial, is generally explained by reference to the knowledge that the characters and situations are 'unreal,' imaginary. In this sense Witasek, operating with Meinong's theory of *Annahmen*, has described the emotions involved in witnessing a drama as *Scheingefühle*, a term which has so frequently been misunderstood in discussions of his theories. But, as a matter of fact, the 'assumption' upon which the imaginative emotional reaction is based is not necessarily the condition, but often the consequence, of Distance; that is to say, the converse of the reason usually stated would then be true: viz. that Distance, by changing our relation to the characters, renders them seemingly fictitious, not that the fictitiousness of the characters alters our feelings toward them. It is, of course, to be granted that the actual and admitted unreality of the dramatic action reinforces the effect of Distance. But surely the proverbial unsophisticated yokel whose chivalrous interference in the play on behalf of the hapless heroine can only be prevented by impressing upon him that 'they are only pretending,' is not the ideal type of theatrical audience. The proof of the seeming paradox that it is Distance which primarily gives to dramatic action the appearance of unreality and not *vice versâ*, is the observation that the same filtration of our sentiments and the same seeming 'unreality' of *actual* men and things occur, when at times, by a sudden change of inward perspective, we are overcome by the feeling that "all the world's a stage."

2. This personal, but 'distanced' relation (as I will venture to call this nameless character of our view) directs attention to a strange fact which appears to be one of the fundamental paradoxes of Art: it is what I propose to call 'the antinomy of Distance.'

It will be readily admitted that a work of Art has the more chance of appealing to us the better it finds us prepared for its particular kind of appeal. Indeed, without some degree of predisposition on our part, it must necessarily remain incomprehensible, and to that extent unappreciated. The success and intensity of its appeal would seem, therefore, to stand in direct proportion to the completeness with which it corresponds with our intellectual and emotional peculiarities and the idiosyncracies of our experience. The absence of such a concordance between the characters of a work and of the spectator is, of course, the most general explanation for differences of 'tastes.'

At the same time, such a principle of concordance requires a qualification, which leads at once to the antinomy of Distance.

Suppose a man, who believes that he has cause to be jealous about his wife, witnesses a performance of 'Othello.' He will the more perfectly appreciate the situation, conduct and character of Othello, the more exactly the feelings and experiences of Othello coincide with his own—at least he *ought* to on the above principle of concordance. In point of fact, he will probably do anything but appreciate the play. In reality, the concordance will merely render him acutely conscious of his own jealousy; by a sudden reversal of perspective he will no longer see Othello apparently betrayed by Desdemona, but himself in an analogous situation with his own wife. The reversal of perspective is the consequence of the loss of Distance.

If this be taken as a typical case, it follows that the qualification required is that the coincidence should be as complete as is compatible with maintaining Distance. The jealous spectator of 'Othello' will indeed appreciate and enter into the play the more keenly, the greater the resemblance with his own experience—*provided* that he succeeds in keeping the Distance between the action of the play and his personal feelings: a very difficult performance in the circumstances. It is on account of the same difficulty that the expert and the professional critic make a bad audience, since their expertness and critical professionalism are *practical* activities, involving their concrete personality and constantly endangering their Distance. [It is, by the way, one of the reasons why Criticism is an art, for it requires the constant interchange from the practical to the distanced attitude and *vice versâ*, which is characteristic of artists.]

The same qualification applies to the artist. He will prove artistically most effective in the formulation of an intensely *personal* experience, but he can formulate it artistically only on condition of a detachment from the experience *quâ personal*. Hence the statement of so many artists that artistic formulation was to them a kind of catharsis, a means of ridding themselves of feelings and ideas the acuteness of which they felt almost as a kind of obsession. Hence, on the other hand, the failure of the average man to convey to others at all adequately the impression of an overwhelming joy or sorrow. His personal implication in the event renders it impossible for him to formulate and present it in such a way as to make others, like himself, feel all the meaning and fulness which it possesses for him.

What is therefore, both in appreciation and production, most desirable is the *utmost decrease of Distance without its disappearance.*

3. Closely related, in fact a presupposition to the 'antimony,' is the *variability of Distance.* Herein especially lies the advantage of Distance compared with such terms as 'objectivity' and 'detachment.' Neither of them implies a *personal* relation—indeed both actually preclude it; and the mere inflexibility and exclusiveness of their opposites render their application generally meaningless.

Distance, on the contrary, admits naturally of degrees, and differs not only according to the nature of the *object*, which may impose a greater or smaller degree of Distance, but varies also according to the *individual's capacity* for maintaining a greater or lesser degree. And here one may remark that not only do *persons differ from each other* in their habitual measure of Distance, but that the *same individual differs* in his ability to maintain it in the face of different objects and of different arts.

There exist, therefore, two different sets of conditions affecting the degree of Distance in any given case: those offered by the object and those realised by the subject. In their interplay they afford one of the most extensive explanations for varieties of aesthetic experience, since loss of Distance, whether due to the one or the other, means loss of aesthetic appreciation.

In short, Distance may be said to *be variable both according to the distancing-power of the individual, and according to the character of the object.*

There are two ways of losing Distance: either to 'under-distance' or to 'over-distance.' 'Under-distancing' is the commonest failing of the *subject*, an excess of Distance is a frequent failing of *Art*, especially in the past. Historically it looks almost as if Art had attempted to meet the deficiency of Distance on the part of the subject and had overshot the mark in this endeavour. It will be seen later that this is actually true, for it appears that over-distanced Art is specially designed for a class of appreciation which has difficulty to rise spontaneously to any degree of Distance. The consequence of a loss of Distance through one or other cause is familiar: the verdict in the case of under-distancing is that the work is 'crudely naturalistic,' 'harrowing,' 'repulsive in its realism.' An excess of Distance produces the impression of improbability, artificiality, emptiness or absurdity.

The individual tends, as I just stated, to under-distance rather than to lose Distance by over-distancing. *Theoretically* there is no limit to the decrease of Distance. In theory, therefore, not only the usual subjects of Art, but even the most personal affections, whether ideas, percepts or emotions, can be sufficiently distanced to be aesthetically appreciable. Especially artists are gifted in this direction to a remarkable extent. The average individual, on the contrary, very rapidly reaches his limit of decreasing Distance, his 'Distance-limit,' i.e. that point at which Distance is lost and appreciation either disappears or changes its character.

In the *practice*, therefore, of the average person, a limit does exist which marks the minimum at which his appreciation can maintain itself in the aesthetic field, and this average minimum lies considerably higher than the Distance-limit of the artist. It is practically impossible to fix this average limit, in the absence of data, and on account of the wide fluctuations from person to person to which this limit is subject. But it is safe to infer that, in art practice, explicit references to organic affections, to the material existence of the body, especially to sexual matters, lie normally below the Distance-limit, and can be touched upon by Art only with special precautions. Allusions to social institutions of any degree of personal importance—in particular, allusions implying any doubt as to their validity—the questioning of some generally recognised ethical sanctions, references to topical subjects occupying public attention at the moment, and such like, are all dangerously near the average limit and may at any time fall below it, arousing, instead of aesthetic appreciation, concrete hostility or mere amusement.

This difference in the Distance-limit between artists and the public has been the source of much misunderstanding and injustice. Many an artist has seen his work condemned, and himself ostracized for the sake of so-called 'immoralities' which to him were *bonâ fide* aesthetic objects. His power of distancing, nay, the necessity of distancing feelings, sensations, situations which for the average person are too intimately bound up with his concrete existence to be regarded in that light, have often quite unjustly earned for him accusations of cynicism, sensualism, morbidness or frivolity. The same misconception has arisen over many 'problem plays' and 'problem novels' in which the public have persisted in seeing nothing but a supposed 'problem' of the moment, whereas the author may have been—and often has demonstrably been—able to distance the subject-matter sufficiently to rise above its practical problematic import and to regard it simply as a dramatically and humanly interesting situation.

The variability of Distance in respect to Art, disregarding for the moment the subjective complication, appears both as a general feature in Art, and in the differences between the special arts.

It has been an old problem why the 'arts of the eye and of the ear' should have reached the practically exclusive predominance over arts of other senses. Attempts to raise 'culinary art' to the level of a Fine Art have failed in spite of all propaganda, as completely as the creation of scent or liqueur 'symphonies.' There is little doubt that, apart from other excellent reasons of a partly psycho-physical, partly technical nature, the actual, *spatial distance* separating objects of sight and hearing from the subject has contributed strongly to the development of this monopoly. In a similar manner *temporal remoteness* produces Distance, and objects removed from us in point of time are *ipso facto* distanced to an extent which was impossible for their contemporaries. Many pictures, plays and poems had, as a matter of fact, rather an expository or illustrating significance—as for instance much ecclesiastical Art—or the force of a direct practical appeal—as the invectives of many satires or comedies—which seem to us nowadays irreconcilable with their aesthetic claims. Such works have consequently profited greatly by lapse of time and have reached the level of Art only with the help of temporal distance, while others, on the contrary, often for the same reason have suffered a loss of Distance, through *over*-distancing.

Special mention must be made of a group of artistic conceptions which present excessive Distance in their form of appeal rather than in their actual presentation—a point illustrating the necessity of distinguishing between distancing an object and distancing the appeal of which it is the source. I mean here what is often rather loosely termed 'idealistic Art,' that is, Art springing from abstract conceptions, expressing allegorical meanings, or illustrating general truths. Generalisations and abstractions suffer under this disadvantage that they have too much general applicability to invite a personal interest in them, and too little individual concreteness to prevent them applying to us in all their force. They appeal to everybody and therefore to none. An axiom of Euclid belongs to nobody, just because it compels everyone's assent; general conceptions like Patriotism, Friendship, Love, Hope, Life, Death, concern as much Dick, Tom and Harry as myself, and I therefore either feel unable to get into any kind of personal relation to them or, if I do so, they become at once, emphatically or concretely, *my* Patriotism, *my* Friendship, *my* Love, *my* Hope, *my* Life and Death. By mere force of generalisation, a general truth or a universal ideal is so far distanced from myself that I fail to realise it concretely at all, or, when I do so, I can realise it only as part of my *practical actual being*, i.e. it falls below the Distance-limit altogether. 'Idealistic Art' suffers consequently under the peculiar difficulty that its excess of Distance turns generally into an *under*-distanced appeal—all the more easily, as it is the usual failing of the subject to *under*- rather than to *over*-distance. . . .

III

It remains to indicate the value of Distance as *an aesthetic principle*: as criterion in some of the standing problems of Aesthetics; as representing a phase of artistic creation; and as a characteristic feature of the 'aesthetic consciousness.'

1. The axiom of 'hedonistic Aesthetics' is that beauty is pleasure. Unfortunately for hedonism the formula is not reversible: not all pleasure is beauty. Hence the necessity

of some limiting criterion to separate the beautiful within the 'pleasure-field' from the merely agreeable. This relation of the beautiful to the agreeable is the ever recurring crux of all hedonistic Aesthetics, as the problem of this relation becomes inevitable when once the hedonistic basis is granted. It has provoked a number of widely different solutions, some manifestly wrong, and all as little satisfactory as the whole hedonistic groundwork upon which they rest: the shareableness of beauty as opposed to the 'monopoly' of the agreeable (Bain), the passivity of beauty-pleasure (Grant Allen), or most recently, the 'relative permanence of beauty-pleasure in revival' (H. R. Marshall).

Distance offers a distinction which is as simple in its operation as it is fundamental in its importance: *the agreeable is a non-distanced pleasure.* Beauty in the widest sense of aesthetic value is impossible without the insertion of Distance. The agreeable stands in precisely the same relation to the beautiful (in its narrower sense) as the sad stands to the tragic, as indicated earlier. Translating the above formula, one may say, that the agreeable is felt as an affection of our concrete, practical self; the centre of gravity of an agreeable experience lies in the self which experiences the agreeable. The aesthetic experience, on the contrary, has its centre of gravity in itself or in the object mediating it, not in the self which has been distanced out of the field of the inner vision of the experiencer: "not the fruit of experience, but experience itself, is the end." It is for this reason that to be asked in the midst of an intense aesthetic impression "whether one likes it," is like a somnambulist being called by name: it is a recall to one's concrete self, an awakening of practical consciousness which throws the whole aesthetic mechanism out of gear. One might almost venture upon the paradox that the more intense the aesthetic absorption, the less one 'likes," consciously, the experience. The failure to realise this fact, so fully borne out by all genuine artistic experience, is the fundamental error of hedonistic Aesthetics.

The problem of the relation of the beautiful and the agreeable has taken more definite shape in the question of the aesthetic value of the so-called 'lower senses' (comprising sensations of taste and temperature, muscular and tactile, and organic sensations). Sight and hearing have always been the 'aesthetic senses *par excellence.* Scent has been admitted to the status of an aesthetic sense by some, excluded by others. The ground for the rejection of the lower senses has always been that they mediate only agreeable sensations, but are incapable of conveying aesthetic experiences. Though true normally, this rigid distinction is theoretically unfair to the senses, and in practice often false. It is undoubtedly very difficult to reach an aesthetic appreciation through the lower senses, because the materialness of their action, their proximity and bodily connexion are great obstacles to their distancing. The aroma of coffee may be a kind of foretaste, taste etherialised, but still a taste. The sweetness of scent of a rose is usually felt more as a bodily caress than as an aesthetic experience. Yet poets have not hesitated to call the scents of flowers their "souls." Shelly has transformed the scent to an imperceptible sound. We call such conceptions 'poetical': they mark the transition from the merely agreeable to the beautiful by means of Distance.

M. Guyau has described the same transformation of a taste. Even muscular sensations may present aesthetic possibilities, in the free exercise of bodily movement, the swing of a runner, in the ease and certainty of the trained gymnast; nay, such diffuse organic sensations as the buoyancy of well-being, and the elasticity of bodily energy, can, in privileged moments, be aesthetically enjoyed. That they admit of no material fixation, such as objects of sight and hearing do, and for that reason form no part of Art in the narrower sense; that they exist as aesthetic objects only for the moment and for the single being that enjoys them, is no argument against their aesthetic character. Mere material existence and permanence is no aesthetic criterion.

This is all the more true, as even among the experience of lasting things, such as are generally accounted to yield aesthetic impressions, the merely agreeable occurs as frequently as the beautiful.

To begin with the relatively simple case of colour-appreciation. Most people imagine that because they are not colour-blind, physically or spiritually, and prefer to live in a coloured world rather than in an engraving, they possess an aesthetic appreciation of colour as such. This is the sort of fallacy which hedonistic art-theories produce, and the lack of an exchange of views on the subject only fosters. Everybody believes that he enjoys colour—and for that matter other things—just like anyone else. Yet rather the contrary is the case. By far the greater number, when asked why they like a colour, will answer, that they like it, because it strikes them as warm or cold, stimulating or soothing, heavy or light. They constitute a definite type of colour-appreciation and form about sixty per cent of all persons. The remainder assumes, for the greater part, a different attitude. Colours do not appeal to them as effects (largely organic) upon themselves. Their appreciation attributes to colours a kind of personality: colours are energetic, lively, serious, pensive, melancholic, affectionate, subtle, reserved, stealthy, treacherous, brutal, etc. These characters are not mere imaginings, left to the whim of the individual, romancing whatever he pleases into the colours, nor are they the work simply of accidental associations. They follow, on the contrary, definite rules in their applications; they are, in fact, the same organic effects as those of the former type, but transformed into, or interpreted as, attributes of the colour, instead of as affections of one's own self. In short, they are the result of the distancing of the organic effects: they form an aesthetic appreciation of colour, instead of a merely agreeable experience like those of the former kind.

A similar parallelism of the agreeable and the beautiful (in the widest sense of aesthetic value) occurs also within the sphere of recognised art-forms. I select for special notice *comedy* and *melodrama* (though the same observation can be made in painting, architecture and notably in music), firstly as counterparts to tragedy, secondly, because both represent admitted art-forms, in spite of their at least partially, inadequate claims to the distinction, and lastly because all these types, tragedy, comedy and melodrama, are usually grouped together as 'arts of the theatre' no less than as forms of 'literature.'

From the point of view of the present discussion, the case of *comedy* is particularly involved. What we mean by comedy as a class of theatrical entertainment covers several different kinds, which actually merge into each other and present historically a continuity which allows of no sharp lines of demarcation (a difficulty, by the way, which besets all distinctions of literary or artistic *species*, as opposed to artistic *genera*). The second difficulty is that the 'laughable' includes much more than the comic of comedy. It may enter, in all its varieties of the ridiculous, silly, naïve, brilliant, especially as the humorous, into comedy as ingredients, but the comic is not coextensive with the laughable as a whole.

The fact to be noted here is, that the different types of comedy, as well as the different kinds of the laughable, presuppose different degrees of Distance. Their tendency is to have none at all. Both to laugh and to weep are direct expressions of a thoroughly practical nature, indicating almost always a concrete personal affection. Indeed, given suitable circumstances and adequate distancing-power, both can be distanced, but only with great difficulty; nor is it possible to decide which of the two offers the greater difficulty. The balance seems almost to incline in favour of tears as the easier of the two, and this would accord with the acknowledged difficulty of producing a really good comedy, or of maintaining a consistent aesthetic attitude in face of a comic situation. Certainly the tendency to *under*distance is more felt in comedy even than in tragedy; most types of the former presenting a *non-distanced*, practical and personal appeal, which precisely implies that their enjoyment is generally hedonic, not aesthetic. In its lower forms comedy consequently is a mere amusement and falls as little under the heading of Art as pamphleteering would be considered as *belles-lettres*, or a burglary as a dramatic performance. It may be spiritualised, polished and refined to the sharpness of a dagger-point or the subtlety of foil-play, but there still clings to it an atmosphere of amusement pure and simple, sometimes of a rude, often of a cruel kind. This, together with the admitted preference of comedy for generalised types rather than for individualised figures, suggests the conclusion that its point of view is the survival of an attitude which the higher forms of Art have outgrown. It is noteworthy that this tendency decreases with every step towards high comedy, charac- ter-comedy and drama, with the growing spiritualisation of the comic elements and the first appearance of Distance. Historically the development has been slow and halting. There is no doubt that the 17th century considered the *Misanthrope* as amusing. We are nowadays less harsh and less socially intolerant and *Alceste* appears to us no longer as frankly ridiculous. The supreme achievement of comedy is unquestionably that 'distanced ridicule' which we call *humour*. The self-contradiction of smiling at what we love, displays, in the light vein, that same perfect and subtle balance of the 'antinomy of Distance' which the truly tragic shows in the serious mood. The tragic and the humorous are the genuine aesthetic opposites; the tragic and the comic are contradictory in the matter of Distance, as aesthetic and hedonic objects respectively.

A similar hedonic opposition in the other direction is to be found between tragedy and *melodrama*. Whereas comedy tends to *under*distance, melodrama suffers from *over*distancing. For a cultivated audience its overcharged idealism, the crude opposi- tion of vice and virtue, the exaggeration of its underlined moral, its innocence of *nuance*, and its sentimentality with violin-accompaniment are sufficient cause to stamp it as inferior Art. But perhaps its excessive distance is the least Distance obtainable by the public for which it is designed, and may be a great help to an unsophisticated audience in distancing the characters and events. For it is more than probable that we make a mistake in assuming an analogy between a cultivated audience at a serious drama, and a melodramatic audience. It is very likely that the lover of melodrama does not present that subtle balance of mind towards a play, implied in the 'antinomy of Distance.' His attitude is rather either that of a matter-of- fact adult or of a child: i.e. he is either in a frankly personal relation to the events of the play and would like to cudgel the villain who illtreats the innocent heroine, and rejoices loudly in his final defeat—just as he would in real life—or, he is completely lost in the excessive distance imposed by the work and watches naïvely the wonders he sees, as a child listens enchantedly to a fairy-tale. In neither case is his attitude aesthetic; in the one the object is *under*-, in the other *over*distanced; in the former he confuses it with the reality he *knows* (or thinks he knows) to exist, in the other with a reality whose existence he does *not know, but accepts*. Neither bears the twofold character of the aesthetic state in which *we know* a thing *not* to exist, but *accept its existence*. From the point of view of moral advantage—in the absence of any aesthetic advantage—the former attitude might seem preferable. But even this may be doubted; for if he believes what he sees in a great spectacular melodrama, every marble-lined hall of the most ordinary London hotel that he passes after the play must appear to him as a veritable Hell, and every man or woman in evening-dress as the devil incarnate. On either supposition, the moral effect must be deplorable in the extreme, and the melodrama is generally a much more fitting object of the censor's attention than any usually censored play. For in the one case the brutalising effect of the obtrusively visible wickedness cannot possibly be outweighed by any retaliatory poetic justice, which must seem to him singularly lacking in real life; in the other, the effect is purely negative and narcotic; in both his perspective of real life is hopelessly outfocussed and distorted.

2. The importance of Distance in artistic creation has already been briefly alluded to in connexion with the 'antinomy of Distance.'

Distancing might, indeed, well be considered as the especial and primary function of what is called the 'creative act' in artistic production: distancing is the *formal* aspect of creation in Art. The view that the artist 'copies nature' has already been dismissed. Since the 'imitation-of-nature' theory was officially discarded at the beginning of the 19th century, its place in popular fancy has been taken by the conception of the 'self-expression of the artist,' supported by the whole force of the Romantic Movement in Europe. Though true as a crude statement of the subjective origin of an artistic conception, though in many ways preferable to its predecessor and valuable as a corollary of such theories as that of the 'organic growth' of a work of Art, it is apt to lead to confusions and to one-sided inferences, to be found even in such deliberate and expert accounts of artistic production as that of Benedetto Croce. For, to start with, the 'self-expression' of an artist is not such as the 'self-expression' of a letter-writer or a public speaker: it is not the *direct* expression of the concrete personality of the artist; it is not even an *indirect* expression of his concrete personality, in the sense in which, for instance, Hamlet's 'self-expression' might be supposed to be the indirect reflexion of Shakespeare's ideas. Such a denial, it might be argued, runs counter to the observation that in the works of a literary artist, for example, are to be found echoes and mirrorings of his times and of his personal experiences and convictions. But it is to be noted that to find these *is* in fact impossible, unless you previously know what reflexions to look for. Even in the relatively most direct transference from personal experience to their expression, viz. in lyrical poetry, such a connexion cannot be established backwards, though it is easy enough to prove it forwards: i.e. given the knowledge of the experiences, there is no difficulty in tracing their echoes, but it is impossible to infer biographical data of any detail or concrete value from an author's works alone. Otherwise Shakespeare's *Sonnets* would not have proved as refractory to biographical research as they have done, and endless blunders in literary history would never have been committed. What proves so impossible in literature, which after all offers an exceptionally adequate medium to 'self-expression,' is *a fortiori* out of question in other arts, in which there is not even an equivalence between the personal experiences and the material in which they are supposed to be formulated. The fundamental two-fold error of the 'self-expression' theory is to speak of 'expression' in the sense of 'intentional communication,' and to identify straightway the artist and the man. An intentional communication is as far almost from the mind of the true artist as it would be from that of the ordinary respectable citizen to walk about naked in the streets, and the idea has repeatedly been indignantly repudiated by artists. The second confusion is as misleading in its theoretical consequences, as it is mischievous and often exceedingly painful to the 'man' as well as to the 'artist.' The numberless instances in history of the astonishing difference, often the marked contrast between the *man* and his *work* is one of the most disconcerting riddles of Art, and should serve as a manifest warning against the popular illusion of finding the 'artist's mind' in his productions.

Apart from the complication of technical necessities, of conventional art-forms, of the requirements of unification and composition, all impeding the direct transference of an actual mental content into its artistic formulation, there is the interpolation of Distance which stands between the artist's conception and the man's. For the 'artist' himself is already distanced from the concrete, historical personality, who ate and drank and slept and did the ordinary business of life. No doubt here also are *degrees* of Distance, and the 'antinomy' applies to this case too. Some figures in literature and other arts are unquestionably self-portraits; but even self-portraits are not, and cannot be, the direct and faithful cast taken from the living soul. In short, so far from being 'self-expression,' *artistic production is the indirect formulation of a distanced mental content.*

I give a short illustration of this fact. A well-known dramatist described to me the process of production as taking place in his case in some such way as follows:

The starting-point of his production is what he described as an 'emotional idea,' i.e. some more or less general conception carrying with it a strong emotional tone. This idea may be suggested by an actual experience; anyhow the idea itself *is* an actual experience, i.e. it occurs within the range of his normal, practical being. Gradually it condenses itself into a situation made up of the interplay of certain characters, which may be of partly objective, partly imaginative descent. Then ensues what he described as a "life and death struggle" between the idea and the characters for existence: if the idea gains the upper hand, the conception of the whole is doomed. In the successful issue, on the contrary, the idea is, to use his phrase, "sucked up" by the characters as a sponge sucks up water, until no trace of the idea is left outside the characters. It is a process, which, he assured me, he is quite powerless to direct or even to influence. It is further of interest to notice that during this period the idea undergoes sometimes profound, often wholesale changes. Once the stage of complete fusion of the idea with the characters is reached, the conscious elaboration of the play can proceed. What follows after this, is of no further interest in this connexion.

This account tallies closely with the procedure which numerous dramatists are known to have followed. It forms a definite type. There are other types, equally well supported by evidence, which proceed along much less definite lines of a semi-logical development, but rather show sudden flash-like illuminations and much more subconscious growth.

The point to notice is the "life and death struggle" between the idea and the characters. As I first remarked, the idea is the 'man's,' it is the reflexion of the dramatist's concrete and practical self. Yet this is precisely the part which must "die." The paradox of just the germpart of the whole being doomed, particularly impressed my informant as a kind of life-tragedy. The 'characters' on the other hand belong to the imaginary world, to the 'artist's.' Though they may be partially suggested by actuality, their full-grown development is divorced from it. This process of the 'idea' being "sucked up" by the characters and being destroyed by it, is a phase of artistic production technically known as the 'objectivation' of the conception. In it the 'man' dies and the 'artist' comes to life, and with him the work of Art. It is a change of death and birth in which there is no overlapping of the lives of parent and child. The result is the distanced finished production. As elsewhere, the distancing means the separation of personal affections, whether idea or complex experience, from the concrete personality of the experiencer, its filtering by the extrusion of its personal aspects, the throwing out of gear of its personal potency and significance.

The same transformation through distance is to be noticed in *acting*. Here, even more than in the other arts, a lingering bias in favour of the 'imitation of nature' theory has stood in the way of a correct interpretation of the facts. Yet acting supplies in this and other respects exceptionally valuable information, owing to its medium of expression and the overlapping—at least in part—of the process of producing with the finished production, which elsewhere are separated in point of time. It illustrates, as no other art can, the cleavage between the concrete, normal person and the distanced personality. [The acting here referred to is, of course, not that style which consists in 'walking on.' What is meant here is 'creative' acting, which in its turn must be distinguished from 'reproductive' acting—two different types traceable through the greater part of theatrical history, which in their highest development are often outwardly indistinguishable, but nevertheless retain traces of differences, characteristic of their procedures and psychical mechanism.] This cleavage between the two streams or layers of consciousness is so obvious that it has led to increasing speculation from the time when acting first attracted intelligent interest, since the middle of the 18th century. From the time of Diderot's *Paradoxe sur le Comédien* (itself only the last of a series of French studies) down to Mr. William Archer's *Masks or Faces* (1888) and the controversey between Coquelin and Salvini (in the nineties), theory has been at pains to grapple with this phenomenon. Explanations have differed widely, going from the one extreme of an identification of the acting and the normal personality to the other of a separation so wide as to be theoretically inconceivable and contradicted by experience. It is necessary to offer some conception which will account for the differences as well as for the indirect connexion between the two forms of being, and which is applicable not merely to acting, but to other kinds of art as well. Distance, it is here contended, meets the requirement even in its subtlest shades. To show this in detail lies outside the scope of this essay, and forms rather the task of a special treatment of the psychology of acting. . . .

4. In this way Distance represents in aesthetic appreciation as well as in artistic production a quality inherent in the impersonal, yet *so* intensely personal, relation which the human being entertains with Art, either as mere beholder or as producing artist.

It is Distance which makes the aesthetic object 'an end in itself.' It is that which raises Art beyond the narrow sphere of individual interest and imparts to it that 'postulating' character which the idealistic philosophy of the 19th century regarded as a metaphysical necessity. It renders questions of origin, of influences, or of purposes almost as meaningless as those of marketable value, of pleasure, even of moral importance, since it lifts the work of Art out of the realm of practical systems and ends.

In particular, it is Distance, which supplies one of the special criteria of aesthetic values as distinct from practical (utilitarian), scientific, or social (ethical) values. All these are concrete values, either *directly* personal as utilitarian, or *indirectly* remotely personal, as moral values. To speak, therefore, of the 'pleasure value' of Art, and to introduce hedonism into aesthetic speculation, is even more irrelevant than to speak of moral hedonism in Ethics. Aesthetic hedonism is a compromise. It is the attempt to reconcile for public use utilitarian ends with aesthetic values. Hedonism, as a practical, personal appeal has no place in the distanced appeal of Art. Moral hedonism is even more to the point than aesthetic hedonism, since ethical values, *quâ* social values, lie on the line of prolongation of utilitarian ends, sublimating indeed the *directly* personal object into the realm of socially or universally valuable ends, often demanding the sacrifice of individual happiness, but losing neither its *practical* nor even its *remotely personal* character.

In so far, Distance becomes one of the distinguishing features of the 'aesthetic consciousness,' of that special mentality or outlook upon experience and life, which, as I said at the outset, leads in its most pregnant and most fully developed form, both appreciatively and productively, to Art.

Jerome Stolnitz

THE AESTHETIC ATTITUDE: FROM
AESTHETICS AND PHILOSOPHY OF ART CRITICISM

How We Perceive the World

Aesthetic perception will be explained in terms of the aesthetic *attitude*.

It is the attitude we take which determines how we perceive the world. An attitude is a way of directing and controlling our perception. We never see or hear everything in our environment indiscriminately. Rather, we "pay attention" to some things, whereas we apprehend others only dimly or hardly at all. Thus attention is *selective*—it concentrates on some features of our surroundings and ignores others. Once we recognize this, we realize the inadequacy of the old notion that human beings are simply passive receptors for any and all external stimuli. Furthermore, what we single out for attention is dictated by the purposes we have at the time. Our actions are generally pointed toward some goal. In order to achieve its goal, the organism watches keenly to learn what in the environment will help and what will be detrimental. Obviously, when individuals have different purposes, they will perceive the world differently, one emphasizing certain things which another will ignore. The Indian scout gives close attention to markings and clues which the person who is simply strolling through the woods will pass over.

Thus an attitude or, as it is sometimes called, a "set" guides our attention in those directions relevant to our purposes. It gives direction to our behavior in still another way. It prepares us to *respond* to what we perceive, to act in a way we think will be most effective for achieving our goals. By the same token, we suppress or inhibit those responses which get in the way of our efforts. A man intent on winning a chess game readies himself to answer his opponent's moves and thinks ahead how best to do this. He also keeps his attention from being diverted by distractions.

Finally, to have an attitude is to be favorably or unfavorably oriented. One can welcome and rejoice in what he sees, or he can be hostile and cold toward it. The

From Aesthetics and Philosophy of Art Criticism *(New York: Houghton Mifflin, 1960), pp. 32–42. Reprinted with permission of Houghton Mifflin Company. (Some footnotes omitted.)*

Anglophobe is a person whose attitude toward all things British is negative, so that when he meets someone with a British accent or hears "Rule Brittania," we expect him to say something disparaging or cynical. When one's attitude toward a thing is positive, he will try to sustain the object's existence and continue to perceive it; when negative, he will try to destroy it or avert his attention from it.

To sum up, an attitude organizes and directs our awareness of the world. Now the aesthetic attitude is not the attitude which people usually adopt. The attitude which we customarily take can be called the attitude of "practical" perception.

We usually see the things in our world in terms of their usefulness for promoting or hindering our purposes. If ever we put into words our ordinary attitude toward an object, it would take the form of the question, "What can I do with it, and what can it do to me?" I see the pen as something I can write with, I see the oncoming automobile as something to avoid; I do not concentrate my attention upon the object itself. Rather, it is of concern to me only so far as it can help me to achieve some future goal. Indeed, from the standpoint of fulfilling one's purposes, it would be stupid and wasteful to become absorbed in the object itself. The workman who never gets beyond looking at his tools, never gets his job done. Similarly, objects which function as "signs," such as the dinner bell or traffic light, are significant only as guides to future behavior. Thus, when our attitude is "practical," we perceive things only as means to some goal which lies beyond the experience of perceiving them.

Therefore our perception of a thing is usually limited and fragmentary. We see only those of its features which are relevant to our purposes, and as long as it is useful we pay little attention to it. Usually perception is merely a rapid and momentary identification of the kind of thing it is and its uses. Whereas the child has to learn laboriously what things are, what they are called, and what they can be used for, the adult does not. His perception has become economized by habit, so that he can recognize the thing and its usefulness almost at once. If I intend to write, I do not hesitate about picking up the pen rather than a paper clip or the cigarette lighter. It is only the pen's usefulness-for-writing-with, not its distinctive color or shape, that I care about. Is this not true of most of our perception of the "furniture of earth?" In actual life the normal person really only reads the labels as it were on the objects around him and troubles no further."[1]

If we stop to think about it, it is astonishing how little of the world we really *see*. We "read the labels" on things to know how to act with regard to them, but we hardly see the things themselves. As I have said, it is indispensable to getting on with the "work of the world" that we should do this. However, we should not assume that perception is always habitually "practical," as it probably is in our culture. Other societies differ from our own, in this respect.[2]

But nowhere is perception exclusively "practical." On occasion we pay attention to a thing simply for the sake of enjoying the way it looks or sounds or feels. This is the "aesthetic" attitude of perception. It is found wherever people become interested in a play or a novel or listen closely to a piece of music. It occurs even in the midst of "practical" perception, in "casual truant glances at our surroundings, when the press-

---

[1]Roger Fry, *Vision and Design* (New York: Brentano's, n.d.), p. 25.
[2]Lester D. Longman, "The Concept of Psychical Distance," *Journal of Aesthetics and Art Criticism*, VI (1947), 32.

ing occupations of practical effort either tire us or leave us for a moment to our own devices, as when in the absorbing business of driving at forty or fifty miles an hour along a highway to get to a destination, the tourist on his holiday glances at the trees or the hills or the ocean."[3]

The Aesthetic Attitude

It will forward our discussion of the aesthetic attitude to have a definition of it. But you should remember that a definition, here or in any other study, is only a point of departure for further inquiry. Only the unwary or intellectually lazy student will rest content with the words of the definition alone, without seeing how it helps us to understand our experience and how it can be employed to carry on the study of aesthetics. With this word of caution, I will define "the aesthetic attitude" as "disinterested and sympathetic attention to and contemplation of any object of awareness whatever, for its own sake alone." Let us now take up in turn each of the ideas in this definition and see what they mean precisely. Since this will be a piecemeal analysis, the truth of the account must be found in the total analysis and not in any single part of it.

The first word, "disinterested," is a crucially important one. It means that we do not look at the object out of concern for any ulterior purpose which it may serve. We are not trying to use or manipulate the object. There is no purpose governing the experience other than the purpose of just *having* the experience. Our interest comes to rest upon the object alone, so that it is not taken as a sign of some future event, like the dinner bell, or as a cue to future activity, like the traffic light.

Many sorts of "interest" are excluded from the aesthetic. One of them is the interest in owning a work of art for the sake of pride or prestige. A book collector, upon seeing an old manuscript, is often interested only in its rarity or its purchase price, not its value as a work of literature. (There are some book collectors who have never *read* the books that they own!) Another nonaesthetic interest is the "cognitive," i.e., the interest in gaining knowledge about an object. A meteorologist is concerned, not with the visual appearance of a striking cloud formation, but with the causes which led to it. Similarly, the interest which the sociologist or historian takes in a work of art . . . is cognitive. Further, where the person who perceives the object, the "percipient,"[4] has the purpose of passing judgment upon it, his attitude is not aesthetic. This should be kept in mind, for, as we shall see later, the attitude of the art critic is significantly different from the aesthetic attitude.

We may say of all these nonaesthetic interests, and of "practical" perception generally, that the object is apprehended with an eye to its origins and consequences, its interrelations with other things. By contrast, the aesthetic attitude "isolates" the object and focuses upon it—the "look" of the rocks, the sound of the ocean, the colors in the painting. Hence the object is not seen in a fragmentary or passing manner, as it is in "practical" perception, e.g., in using a pen for writing. Its whole nature and

---

[3]D. W. Prall, *Aesthetic Judgment* (New York: Crowell, 1929), p. 31.

[4]This is a clumsy and largely outmoded word, but it is more convenient for our purposes than words of more limited meaning such as "spectator," "observer," "listener," and is accordingly used here and elsewhere.

character are dwelt upon. One who buys a painting merely to cover a stain on the wall paper does not see the painting as a delightful pattern of colors and forms.

For the aesthetic attitude, things are not to be classified or studied or judged. They are in themselves pleasant or exciting to look at. It should, then, be clear that being "disinterested" is very far from being "*un*-interested." Rather, as all of us know, we can become intensely absorbed in a book or a moving picture, so that we become much more "interested" than we usually are in the course of our "practical" activity.

The word "sympathetic" in the definition of "aesthetic attitude" refers to the way in which we prepare ourselves to respond to the object. When we apprehend an object aesthetically, we do so in order to relish its individual quality, whether the object be charming, stirring, vivid, or all of these. If we are to appreciate it, we must accept the object "on its own terms." We must make ourselves receptive to the object and "set" ourselves to accept whatever it may offer to perception. We must therefore inhibit any responses which are "unsympathetic" to the object, which alienate us from it or are hostile to it. A devout Mohammedan may not be able to bring himself to look for very long at a painting of the Holy Family, because of his animus against the Christian religion. Closer to home, any of us might reject a novel because it seems to conflict with our moral beliefs or our "way of thinking." When we do so, we should be clear as to what we are doing. We have *not* read the book aesthetically, for we have interposed moral or other responses of our own which are alien to it. This disrupts the aesthetic attitude. We cannot then say that the novel is *aesthetically* bad, for we have not permitted ourselves to consider it aesthetically. To maintain the aesthetic attitude, we must follow the lead of the object and respond in concert with it.

This is not always easy, for all of us have deep-seated values as well as prejudices. They may be ethical or religious, or they may involve some bias against the artist or even against his native country. (During the First World War, many American symphony orchestras refused to play the works of German composers.) The problem is especially acute in the case of contemporary works of art, which may treat of disputes and loyalties in which we are deeply engaged. When they do so, we might remind ourselves that works of art often lose their topical significance with the passing of time and then come to be esteemed as great works of art by later generations. Milton's sonnet "On the Late Massacre in Piedmont" is a ringing protest called forth by an event which occurred shortly before the writing of the poem. But the heated questions of religion and politics which enter into it seem very remote to us now. People sometimes remonstrate with a friend who seems to reject offhand works of art of which they are fond, "You don't even give it a chance." To be "sympathetic" in aesthetic experience means to give the object the "chance" to show how it can be interesting to perception.

We come now to the word "attention" in our definition of "aesthetic attitude." As has been pointed out, any attitude whatever directs attention to certain features of the world. But the element of attention must be especially underscored in speaking of aesthetic perception. For, as a former teacher of mine used to say, aesthetic perception is frequently thought to be a "blank, cow-like stare." It is easy to fall into this mistake when we find aesthetic perception described as "just looking," without any activity or practical interest. From this it is inferred that we simply expose ourselves to the work of art and permit it to inundate us in waves of sound or color.

But this is surely a distortion of the facts of experience. When we listen to a rhythmically exciting piece of music which absorbs us with its energy and movement, or when we read a novel which creates great suspense, we give our earnest attention to it to the exclusion of almost everything else in our surroundings. To be "sitting on the edge of the chair" is anything but passive. In taking the aesthetic attitude, we want to make the value of the object come fully alive in our experience. Therefore we focus our attention upon the object and "key up" our capacities of imagination and emotion to respond to it. As a psychologist says of the aesthetic experience, "Appreciation . . . is awareness, alertness, animation."[5] Attention is always a matter of *degree*, and in different instances of aesthetic perception, attention is more or less intense. A color, briefly seen, or a little melody, may be apprehended on the "fringe" of consciousness, whereas a drama will absorb us wholly. But to whatever extent it does so, experience is aesthetic only when an object "holds" our attention.

Furthermore, aesthetic attention is accompanied by activity. This is not the activity of practical experience, which seeks an ulterior goal. Rather it is activity which is either evoked by disinterested perception of the object, or else is required for it. The former includes all muscular, nervous, and "motor" responses such as feelings of tension or rhythmic movement. Contrary to what some snobs would have us believe, there is nothing inherently unaesthetic about tapping one's foot in time to the music. The theory of *empathy* points out that we "feel into" the object our muscular and bodily adjustments. We brace ourselves and our muscles become taut in the face of a sculptured figure which is tall, vigorous, and upright.[6] This does not occur in aesthetic experience alone, and it does not occur in all aesthetic experience, but when it does, it exemplifies the kind of activity which may be aroused in aesthetic perception. The direction of attention itself may not improperly be called "activity." But even overt bodily movement and effort may be required for aesthetic perception. We usually have to walk round all sides of a sculpture, or through a cathedral, before we can appreciate it. We would often reach out and touch sculptured figures if only museum guards would permit us to do so.

But focusing upon the object and "acting" in regard to it, is not all that is meant by aesthetic "attention." To savor fully the distinctive value of the object, we must be attentive to its frequently complex and subtle details. Acute awareness of these details is *discrimination*. People often miss a good deal in the experience of art, not only because their attention lapses, but because they fail to "see" all that is of significance in the work. Indeed, their attention frequently lapses for just this reason. They miss the individuality of the work, so that one symphony sounds like any other piece of "long-hair" music, and one lyric poem is indistinguishable from another, and all are equally boring. If you have had the good fortune to study literature with an able teacher, you know how a play or novel can become vital and engaging when you learn to look for details to which you were previously insensitive. But awareness of this kind is not always easily come by. It often requires knowledge about allusions or symbols which occur in the work, repeated experience of the work, and even, sometimes, technical training in the art-form.

As we develop discriminating attention, the work comes alive to us. If we can keep

---

[5]Kate Hevner, "The Aesthetic Experience: A Psychological Description," *Psychological Review*, 44 (1937), 249.

[6]Cf. Herbert S. Langfield, *The Aesthetic Attitude* (New York: Harcourt, Brace, 1920), chaps. V–VI; Vernon Lee, "Empathy," in Melvin Rader, ed., *A Modern Book of Esthetics*, rev. ed. (New York: Holt, 1952), pp. 460–65.

in mind the chief themes in the movement of a symphony, see how they are developed and altered in the course of the movement, and appreciate how they are played off against each other, then there is a great gain in our experience. The experience has greater richness and unity. Without such discrimination it is thin, for the listener responds only to scattered passages or to a patch of striking orchestral color. And it is disorganized, for he is not aware of the structure which binds the work together. His experience may be said to be intermittently and to a limited degree aesthetic, but it is not nearly as rewarding as it might be. Everybody knows how easy it is to start thinking of other things while the music is playing, so that we are really aware of it only now and again. All the more reason, then, why we should develop the capacities for appreciating its richness and profundity. Only so can we keep our experience from becoming, in Santayana's famous phrase "a drowsy revery relieved by nervous thrills."[7]

If you now understand how aesthetic attention is alert and vigorous, then it is safe to use a word which has often been applied to aesthetic experience—"contemplation." Otherwise, there is the great danger that this word will suggest an aloof, unexcited gaze which, we have seen, is untrue to the facts of aesthetic experience. Actually, "contemplation" does not so much add something new to our definition as it sums up ideas which we have already discussed. It means that perception is directed to the object in its own right and that the spectator is not concerned to analyze it or to ask questions about it. Also, the word connotes thoroughgoing absorption and interest, as when we speak of being "lost in contemplation." Most things are hardly noticed by us, whereas the object of aesthetic perception stands out from its environment and rivets our interest.

The aesthetic attitude can be adopted toward "any object of awareness whatever." This phrase need not, strictly speaking, be included in our definition. We could understand the aesthetic attitude as the kind of perceptual attention we have been talking about, without adding that "any object whatever" may be its object. But definitions are flexible to an extent. We can choose to include in them even what is not strictly necessary to identify the term being defined. The great and even limitless scope of aesthetic experience is one of the most interesting and important things about it.

The definition permits us to say that any object at all can be apprehended aesthetically, i.e., no object is inherently unaesthetic. But it might be thought odd, or even downright wrong, to say this. There are some objects which are conspicuously attractive, so that they "catch our eye" and draw attention to themselves—a bed of bright and many-colored flowers or a marching song, massive cloud formations, or a noble and stately cathedral. Certainly the same is not true of many, indeed most, other things in the world. Are we to say that a dirty, run-down slum section is to be called "aesthetic"? What about dull, unexciting things like supplies stacked row upon row in a warehouse or, if you please, the telephone directory? Indeed, the word "aesthetic" is often used in everyday speech to distinguish these objects which are delightful to look upon or listen to, from those which are not. As was pointed out [earlier], this is also the view of a good deal of traditional aesthetic theory.

This argument—that some objects do not qualify as "aesthetic"—certainly sounds

[7]George Santayana, *Reason in Art* (New York: Scribner's, 1946), p. 51.

plausible and convincing. I think that the best way to argue against it is to present evidence that human beings have contemplated disinterestedly objects which are enormously diverse. Among such objects are some which we might consider wholly uninviting. As was mentioned earlier, men have found perceptual enjoyment in things which people of earlier times or other cultures judged to be unaesthetic. The whole "history of taste" shows how the boundaries of aesthetic experience have been pushed back and have come to include a tremendous variety of things.

The best evidence of this broadening of vision is to be found in the arts. For here we have permanent records of the objects which have aroused aesthetic interest. It can also be found, however, in the appreciation of nature. The subjects chosen from nature for treatment by artists show the expansion of perceptual interest. "Social historians" can often trace changes in the appreciation of nature in other ways, e.g., memoirs and diaries, sites chosen for resort places, and so on. But let us for the moment speak solely of art. If we confine ourselves to the art of the last 150 years, we find an enormous amount of art devoted to the two sorts of objects which "common sense" considers intrinsically unaesthetic, viz., dull, commonplace objects and ugly or grotesque things and events. The poet Wordsworth, at the beginning of the nineteenth century, devoted much of his poetry to "humble and rustic life." One of van Gogh's paintings is of a perfectly prosaic yellow chair . . . , another is of the rude furniture in his bedroom. In our own day, the painter Ben Shahn has chosen as the subject of one of his works city boys playing handball . . . Instances of the depiction of ugly and macabre themes in recent art are even more obvious. The student may be able to think of some himself. I will cite Géricault's "The Raft of the *Medusa*" . . . , the harrowing treatment of a tortured and pathetic figure in Berg's opera *Wozzeck*, and such "realistic" literature as Gorki's *Lower Depths* and Farrell's *Studs Lonigan*.

To be sure, the artist apprehends such subjects with imagination and feeling. And when they emerge in the work of art, he has invested them with vividness and excitement. However, the very fact that his attention has been directed to these subjects shows how far-ranging aesthetic interest can be. Further, his use of them alters and expands the taste of the nonartist. The ordinary man now becomes newly sensitive to the perceptual interest of many different objects and events. Thus appreciation of the grandeur of mountain ranges, which is a relatively recent chapter in the history of taste, was stimulated by such works of art as Haller's poem *Die Alpen*. Less lofty objects and even scenes which are ugly become the objects of aesthetic attention. Here is the testimony of one who is not an artist:

> [The] ugliest thing in nature that I can think of at the moment is a certain street of shabby houses where a street-market is held. If one passes through it, as I sometimes do, early on a Sunday morning, one finds it littered with straw, dirty paper and the other refuse of a market. My normal attitude is one of aversion. I wish to hold myself away from the scene. . . . But I sometimes find that . . . the scene suddenly gets jerked away from *me* and on to the aesthetic plane, so that I can survey it quite impersonally. When this happens, it does seem to me that what I am apprehending looks different; it has a form and coherence which it lacked before, and details are more clearly seen. But . . . it does not seem to me to have ceased to be ugly and to have become beautiful. I can see the ugly aesthetically, but I cannot see it as beautiful.[8]

---

[8]E. M. Bartlett, *Types of Aesthetic Judgment* (London: George Allen & Unwin, 1937), pp. 211–12. Italics in original.

The student can probably think of things in his own experience—a face, a building, a landscape—which, though not conventionally "pretty" or "attractive," arouse aesthetic interest. Evidence of this kind cannot establish that *all* objects can be aesthetic objects. When such evidence is multiplied, however, it makes this assumption a reasonable one at the outset of aesthetic inquiry.

In keeping with this assumption, the word "awareness" is used in our definition of "aesthetic attitude." I have been using the word "perception" to describe aesthetic apprehension, but its meaning is too narrow. It refers to apprehension of sense-data, e.g., colors or sounds, which are interpreted or "judged" to be of a certain kind. Perception differs from sensation as the experience of an adult differs from that of the newborn infant, for whom the world is a succession of mysterious and unrelated sensory "explosions." In adult experience, we rarely apprehend sense-data without knowing something about them and interrelating them, so that they become meaning-ful. We see more than a color patch; we see a flag or a warning signal. Perception is the most usual sort of "awareness." But if sensation occurs, it too can be aesthetic.

There is another kind of "awareness" that occurs, though relatively infrequently, in adult experience. This is "intellectual," nonsensuous knowledge of "concepts" and "meanings" and their interrelations: such knowing takes place in abstract thinking, such as logic and mathematics. Even if images or "pictures" accompany such thinking, they are only secondary. When the mathematician thinks of the properties of triangles, his thought is not restricted to any particular triangle he may "see in his head" or draw on paper. A man who develops a system of mathematical logic is occupied with logical relationships which are neither sensed nor perceived. Now this kind of apprehension can also be aesthetic. If one's purpose is not, for the moment, problem solving, if he pauses to contemplate disinterestedly the logical structure before him, then his experi-ence is aesthetic. Such experience has been attested to by many mathematicians, and it is evidenced by the use of such words as "elegance" and "grace," borrowed from the realm of the aesthetic, to describe a conceptual system. The poetess Edna St. Vincent Millay says, in a line that has become famous, "Euclid alone has looked on Beauty bare." The great Greek geometrician discerned mathematical properties and relations which had no sensuous "dress" of sound or color.

To take account of such experience as well as sensation, I have used the broad term "awareness" rather than "perception." Anything at all, whether sensed or perceived, whether it is the product of imagination or conceptual thought, can become the object of aesthetic attention.

This completes the analysis of the meaning of "aesthetic attitude," the central concept in our study. "Aesthetic," understood to mean "disinterested and sympathetic attention," marks out the field of our further investigation. All the concepts to be discussed later are defined by reference to this: "aesthetic experience" is the total experience had while this attitude is being taken; "aesthetic object" is the object toward which this attitude is adopted; "aesthetic value" is the value of this experience or of its object. It is therefore imperative that the student understand and think about the meaning of "aesthetic," before going on to further discussions.

George Dickie

ALL AESTHETIC ATTITUDE THEORIES FAIL: THE MYTH OF THE AESTHETIC ATTITUDE

Some recent articles[1] have suggested the unsatisfactoriness of the notion of the aesthetic attitude and it is now time for a fresh look at that encrusted article of faith. This conception has been valuable to aesthetics and criticism in helping wean them from a sole concern with beauty and related notions.[2] However, I shall argue that the aesthetic attitude is a myth and while, as G. Ryle has said, "Myths often do a lot of theoretical good while they are still new,"[3] this particular one is no longer useful and in fact misleads aesthetic theory.

There is a range of theories which differ according to how strongly the aesthetic attitude is characterized. This variation is reflected in the language the theories employ. The strongest variety is Edward Bullough's theory of psychical distance, recently defended by Sheila Dawson.[4] The central technical term of this theory is "distance" used as a verb to denote an action which either constitutes or is necessary for the aesthetic attitude. These theorists use such sentences as "He distanced (or failed to distance) the play." The second variety is widely held but has been defended most vigorously in recent years by Jerome Stolnitz and Eliseo Vivas. The *central* technical term of this variety is "disinterested"[5] used either as an adverb or as an adjective. This weaker theory speaks not of a special kind of action (distancing) but of an ordinary kind of action (attending) done in a certain way (disinterestedly). These first two versions are perhaps not as different as my classification suggests. However, the language of the two is different enough to justify separate discussions. My discussion of this second variety

George Dickie, "The Myth of the Aesthetic Attitude," from American Philosophical Quarterly 1, no. 1 *(1964):56–66. Reprinted by permission of* American Philosophical Quarterly.

[1]See Marshall Cohen, "Appearance and the Aesthetic Attitude," *Journal of Philosophy*, vol. 56 (1959), p. 926; and Joseph Margolis, "Aesthetic Perception," *Journal of Aesthetics and Art Criticism*, vol. 19 (1960), p. 211. Margolis gives an argument, but it is so compact as to be at best only suggestive.

[2]Jerome Stolnitz, "Some Questions Concerning Aesthetic Perception," *Philosophy and Phenomenological Research*, vol. 22 (1961), p. 69.

[3]*The Concept of Mind* (London, 1949), p. 23.

[4]" 'Distancing' as an Aesthetic Principle," *Australasian Journal of Philosophy*, vol. 39 (1961), pp. 155–174.

[5]"Disinterested" is Stolnitz' term. Vivas uses "intransitive."

will for the most part make use of Jerome Stolnitz' book[6] which is a thorough, consistent, and large-scale version of the attitude theory. The weakest version of the attitude theory can be found in Vincent Tomas' statement "If looking at a picture and attending closely to how it looks is not really to be in the aesthetic attitude, then what on earth is?"[7] In the following I shall be concerned with the notion of *aesthetic* attitude and this notion may have little or no connection with the ordinary notion of an *attitude*.

I

Psychical distance, according to Bullough, is a psychological process by virtue of which a person *puts* some object (be it a painting, a play, or a dangerous fog at sea) "out of gear" with the practical interests of the self. Miss Dawson maintains that it is "the beauty of the phenomenon, which captures our attention, puts us out of gear with practical life, and forces us, if we are receptive, to view it on the level of aesthetic consciousness."[8]

Later she maintains that some persons (critics, actors, members of an orchestra, and the like) "distance deliberately."[9] Miss Dawson, following Bullough, discusses cases in which people are unable to bring off an act of distancing or are incapable of being induced into a state of being distanced. She uses Bullough's example of the jealous ("under-distanced") husband at a performance of *Othello* who is able to keep his attention on the play because he keeps thinking of his own wife's suspicious behavior. On the other hand, if "we are mainly concerned with the technical details of its [the play's] presentation, then we are said to be over-distanced."[10] There is, then, a species of action—distancing—which may be deliberately done and which initiates a state of consciousness—being distanced.

The question is: Are there actions denoted by "to distance" or states of consciousness denoted by "being distanced"? When the curtain goes up, when we walk up to a painting, or when we look at a sunset are we ever induced into a state of being distanced either by being struck by the beauty of the object or by pulling off an act of distancing? I do not recall committing any such special actions or of being induced into any special state, and I have no reason to suspect that I am atypical in this respect. The distance-theorist may perhaps ask, "But are you not usually oblivious to noises and sights other than those of the play or to the marks on the wall around the painting?" The answer is of course—"Yes." But if "to distance" and "being distanced" simply mean that one's attention is focused, what is the point of introducing new technical terms and speaking as if these terms refer to special kinds of acts and states of consciousness? The distance-theorist might argue further, "But surely you put the play

[6]*Aesthetics and Philosophy of Art Criticism* (Boston, 1960), p. 510.

[7]"Aesthetic Vision," *The Philosophical Review*, vol. 68 (1959), p. 63. I shall ignore Tomas' attempt to distinguish between appearance and reality since it seems to confuse rather than clarify aesthetic theory. See F. Sibley, "Aesthetics and the Looks of Things," *Journal of Philosophy*, vol. 56 (1959), pp. 905–915; M. Cohen, op. cit., pp. 915–926; and J. Stolnitz, "Some Questions Concerning Aesthetic Perception," op. cit., pp. 69–87. Tomas discusses only visual art and the aesthetic attitude, but his remarks could be generalized into a comprehensive theory.

[8]Dawson, op. cit., p. 158.

[9]Ibid., pp. 159–160.

[10]Ibid., p. 159.

(painting, sunset) 'out of gear' with your practical interests?" This question seems to me to be a very odd way of asking (by employing the technical metaphor "out of gear") if I attended to the play rather than thought about my wife or wondered how they managed to move the scenery about. Why not ask me straight out if I paid attention? Thus, when Miss Dawson says that the jealous husband under-distanced *Othello* and that the person with a consuming interest in techniques of stagecraft over-distanced the play, these are just technical and misleading ways of describing two different cases of inattention. In both cases something is being attended to, but in neither case is it the action of the play. To introduce the technical terms "distance," "under-distance," and "over-distance" does nothing but send us chasing after phantom acts and states of consciousness.

Miss Dawson's commitment to the theory of distance (as a kind of mental insulation material necessary for a work of art if it is to be enjoyed aesthetically) leads her to draw a conclusion so curious as to throw suspicion on the theory.

> One remembers the horrible loss of distance in *Peter Pan*—the moment when Peter says "Do you believe in fairies? . . . If you believe, clap your hands!" the moment when most children would like to slink out of the theatre and not a few cry—not because Tinkerbell may die, but because the magic is gone. What, after all, should we feel like if Lear were to leave Cordelia, come to the front of the stage and say, "All the grown-ups who think that she loves me, shout 'Yes.' "[11]

It is hard to believe that the responses of any children could be as theory-bound as those Miss Dawson describes. In fact, Peter Pan's request for applause is a dramatic high point to which children respond enthusiastically. The playwright gives the children a momentary chance to become actors in the play. The children do not at that moment lose or snap out of a state of being distanced because they never had or were in any such thing to begin with. The comparison of Peter Pan's appeal to the hypothetical one by Lear is pointless. *Peter Pan* is a magical play in which almost anything can happen, but *King Lear* is a play of a different kind. There are, by the way, many plays in which an actor directly addresses the audience (*Our Town*, *The Marriage Broker*, *A Taste of Honey*, for example) without causing the play to be less valuable. Such plays are unusual, but what is unusual is not necessarily bad; there is no point in trying to lay down rules to which every play must conform independently of the kind of play it is.

It is perhaps worth noting that Susanne Langer reports the reaction she had as a child to this scene in *Peter Pan*.[12] As she remembers it, Peter Pan's appeal shattered the illusion and caused her acute misery. However, she reports that all the other children clapped and laughed and enjoyed themselves.

II

The second way of conceiving of the aesthetic attitude—as the ordinary action of attending done in a certain way (disinterestedly)—is illustrated by the work of Jerome Stolnitz and Eliseo Vivas. Stolnitz defines "aesthetic attitude" as "disinterested and

[11]Ibid., p. 168.
[12]*Feeling and Form* (New York, 1953), p. 318.

sympathetic attention to and contemplation of any object of awareness whatever, for its own sake alone."[13] Stolnitz defines the main terms of his definition: "disinterested" means "no concern for any ulterior purpose";[14] "sympathetic" means "accept the object on its own terms to appreciate it";[15] and "contemplation" means "perception directed toward the object in its own right and the spectator is not concerned to analyze it or ask questions about it."[16]

The notion of disinterestedness, which Stolnitz has elsewhere shown[17] to be seminal for modern aesthetic theory, is the key term here. Thus, it is necessary to be clear about the nature of disinterested attention to the various arts. It can make sense to speak, for example, of listening disinterestedly to music only if it makes sense to speak of listening interestedly to music. It would make no sense to speak of walking *fast* unless walking could be done *slowly*. Using Stolnitz' definition of "disinterestedness," the two situations would have to be described as "listening with no ulterior purpose" (disinterestedly) and "listening with an ulterior purpose" (interestedly). Note that what initially appears to be a perceptual distinction—listening in a certain way (interestedly or disinterestedly)—turns out to be a motivational or an intentional distinction—listening for or with a certain purpose. Suppose Jones listens to a piece of music for the purpose of being able to analyze and describe it on an examination the next day and Smith listens to the same music with no such ulterior purpose. There is certainly a difference between the motives and intentions of the two men: Jones has an ulterior purpose and Smith does not, but this does not mean Jones's *listening* differs from Smith's. It is possible that both men enjoy the music or that both are bored. The attention of either or both may flag and so on. It is important to note that a person's motive or intention is different from his action (Jones's listening to the music, for example). There is only one way to *listen* to (to attend to) music, although the listening may be more or less attentive and there may be a variety of motives, intentions, and reasons for doing so and a variety of ways of being distracted from the music.

In order to avoid a common mistake of aestheticians—drawing a conclusion about one kind of art and assuming it holds for all the arts—the question of disinterested attention must be considered for arts other than music. How would one look at a painting disinterestedly or interestedly? An example of alleged interested viewing might be the case in which a painting reminds Jones of his grandfather and Jones proceeds to muse about or to regale a companion with tales of his grandfather's pioneer exploits. Such incidents would be characterized by attitude-theorists as examples of using a work of art as a vehicle for associations and so on, i.e., cases of interested attention. But Jones is not looking at (attending to) the painting at all, although he may be facing it with his eyes open. Jones is now musing or attending to the story he is telling, although he had to look at the painting at first to notice that it resembled his grandfather. Jones is not now looking at the painting interestedly, since he is not now looking at (attending to) the painting. Jones's thinking or telling a story about his grandfather is no more a part of the painting than his speculating about the artist's intentions is and, hence, his

[13]*Aesthetics and Philosophy of Art Criticism*, pp. 34–35.
[14]Ibid., p. 35.
[15]Ibid., p. 36.
[16]Ibid., p. 38.
[17]"On the Origins of 'Aesthetic Disinterestedness,' " *The Journal of Aesthetics and Art Criticism*, vol. 20 (1961), pp. 131–143.

musing, telling, speculating, and so on cannot properly be described as attending to the painting interestedly. What attitude-aestheticians are calling attention to is the occurrence of irrelevant associations which distract the viewer from the painting or whatever. But distraction is not a special kind of attention, it is a kind of inattention.

Consider now disinterestedness and plays. I shall make use of some interesting examples offered by J. O. Urmson,[18] but I am not claiming that Urmson is an attitude-theorist. Urmson never speaks in his article of aesthetic attitude but rather of aesthetic satisfaction. In addition to aesthetic satisfaction, Urmson mentions economic, moral, personal, and intellectual satisfactions. I think the attitude-theorist would consider these last four kinds of satisfaction as "ulterior purposes" and, hence, cases of interested attention. Urmson considers the case of a man in the audience of a play who is delighted.[19] It is discovered that his delight is *solely* the result of the fact that there is a full house—the man is the impresario of the production. Urmson is right in calling *this* impresario's satisfaction economic rather than aesthetic, although there is a certain oddness about the example as it finds the impresario sitting *in the audience*. However, my concern is not with Urmson's examples as such but with the attitude theory. This impresario is certainly an interested party in the fullest sense of the word, but is his behavior an instance of interested attention as distinct from the supposed disinterested attention of the average citizen who sits beside him? In the situation as described by Urmson it would not make any sense to say that the impresario is attending to the play at all, since his *sole* concern at the moment is the till. If he can be said to be attending to anything (rather than just thinking about it) it is the size of the house. I do not mean to suggest that an impresario could not attend to his play if he found himself taking up a seat in a full house; I am challenging the sense of disinterested attention. As an example of personal satisfaction Urmson mentions the spectator whose daughter is in the play. Intellectual satisfaction involves the solution of technical problems of plays and moral satisfaction the consideration of the effects of the play on the viewer's conduct. All three of these candidates which the attitude-theorist would propose as cases of interested attention turn out to be just different ways of being distracted from the play and, hence, not cases of interested attention to the play. Of course, there is no reason to think that in any of these cases the distraction or inattention must be total, although it could be. In fact, such inattentions often occur but are so fleeting that nothing of the play, music, or whatever is missed or lost.

The example of a playwright watching a rehearsal or an out-of-town performance with a view to rewriting the script has been suggested to me as a case in which a spectator is certainly attending to the play (unlike our impresario) and attending in an interested manner. This case is unlike those just discussed but is similar to the earlier case of Jones (not Smith) listening to a particular piece of music. Our playwright—like Jones, who was to be examined on the music—has ulterior motives. Furthermore, the playwright, unlike an ordinary spectator, can change the script after the performance or during a rehearsal. But how is our playwright's *attention* (as distinguished from his motives and intentions) different from that of an ordinary viewer? The playwright might enjoy or be bored by the performance as any spectator might be. The

---

[18]"What Makes a Situation Aesthetic?" in *Philosophy Looks at the Arts*, Joseph Margolis (ed.) (New York, 1962), pp. 13–26. Reprinted from *Proceedings of the Aristotelian Society, Supplementary Volume* 31 (1957), pp. 75–92.

[19]Ibid, p. 15.

playwright's attention might even flag. In short, the kinds of things which may happen to the playwright's attention are no different from those that may happen to an ordinary spectator, although the two may have quite different motives and intentions.

For the discussion of disinterested-interested reading of literature it is appropriate to turn to the arguments of Eliseo Vivas whose work is largely concerned with literature. Vivas remarks that "By approaching a poem in a nonaesthetic mode it may function as history, as social criticism, as diagnostic evidence of the author's neuroses, and in an indefinite number of other ways."[20] Vivas further notes that according to Plato "the Greeks used Homer as an authority on war and almost anything under the sun," and that a certain poem "can be read as erotic poetry or as an account of a mystical experience."[21] The difference between reading a poem *as* history or whatever (reading it nonaesthetically) and reading it aesthetically depends on how *we* approach or read it. A poem "does not come self-labelled,"[22] but presumably is a poem only when it is read in a certain way—when it is an object of aesthetic experience. For Vivas, being an aesthetic object means being the object of the aesthetic attitude. He defines the aesthetic experience as "an experience of rapt attention which involves the intransitive apprehension of an object's immanent meanings and values in their full presentational immediacy."[23] Vivas maintains that his definition "helps me understand better what I can and what I cannot do when I read *The Brothers* [*Karamazov*]" and his definition "forces us to acknowledge that *The Brothers Karamazov* can hardly be read as art. . . ."[24] This acknowledgment means that we probably cannot intransitively apprehend *The Brothers* because of its size and complexity.

"Intransitive" is the key term here and Vivas' meaning must be made clear. A number of passages reveal his meaning but perhaps the following is the best. "Having once seen a hockey game in slow motion, I am prepared to testify that it was an object of pure intransitive experience [attention]—for I was not *interested* in which team won the game and no external factors mingled with my interest in the beautiful rhythmic flow of the slow-moving men."[25] It appears that Vivas' "intransitive attention" has the same meaning as Stolnitz' "disinterested attention," namely, "attending with no ulterior purpose."[26] Thus, the question to ask is "How does one attend to (read) a poem or any literary work transitively?" One can certainly attend to (read) a poem for a variety of different purposes and because of a variety of different reasons, but can one attend to a poem transitively? I do not think so, but let us consider the examples Vivas offers. He mentions "a type of reader" who uses a poem or parts of a poem as a spring-board for "loose, uncontrolled, relaxed day-dreaming, wool-gathering rambles, free from the contextual control" of the poem.[27] But surely it would be wrong to say such musing is a

---

[20]"Contextualism Reconsidered," *The Journal of Aesthetics and Art Criticism*, vol. 18 (1959), pp. 224–225.

[21]Ibid., p. 225.

[22]Loc. cit.

[23]Ibid., p. 227.

[24]Ibid., p. 237.

[25]Ibid., p. 228. (Italics mine.)

[26]Vivas' remark about the improbability of being able to read *The Brothers Karamazov* as art suggests that "intransitive attention" may sometimes mean for him "that which can be attended to at one time" or "that which can be held before the mind at one time." However, this second possible meaning is not one which is relevant here.

[27]Vivas, op. cit., p. 231.

case of transitively attending to a poem, since it is clearly a case of not attending to a poem. Another supposed way of attending to a poem transitively is by approaching it "as diagnostic evidence of the author's neuroses." Vivas is right if he means that there is no critical point in doing this since it does not throw light on the poem. But this is a case of *using* information gleamed from a poem to make inferences about its author rather than attending to a poem. If anything can be said to be attended to here it is the author's neuroses (at least they are being thought about). This kind of case is perhaps best thought of as a rather special way of getting distracted from a poem. Of course, such "biographical" distractions might be insignificant and momentary enough so as scarcely to distract attention from the poem (a flash of insight or understanding about the poet). On the other hand, such distractions may turn into dissertations and whole careers. Such an interest may lead a reader to concentrate his attention (when he does read a poem) on certain "informational" aspects of a poem and to ignore the remaining aspects. As deplorable as such a sustained practice may be, it is at best a case of attending to certain features of a poem and ignoring others.

Another way that poetry may allegedly be read transitively is by reading it as history. This case is different from the two preceding ones since poetry often *contains* history (makes historical statements or at least references) but does not (usually) contain statements about the author's neuroses and so on nor does it contain statements about what a reader's free associations are about (otherwise we would not call them *"free associations"*). Reading a poem as history suggests that we are attending to (thinking about) historical events by way of attending to a poem—the poem is a time-telescope. Consider the following two sets of lines:

> In fourteen hundred and ninety-two
>   Columbus sailed the ocean blue.
> Or like stout Cortez when with eagle eyes
>   He star'd at the Pacific—and all his men
> Look'd at each other with a wild surmise—
>   Silent, upon a peak in Darien.

Someone might read both of these raptly and not know that they make historical references (inaccurately in one case)—might this be a case of intransitive attention? How would the above reading differ—so far as attention is concerned—from the case of a reader who recognized the historical content of the poetic lines? The two readings do not differ as far as attention is concerned. History is a part of these sets of poetic lines and the two readings differ in that the first fails to take account of an aspect of the poetic lines (its historical content) and the second does not fail to do so. Perhaps by "reading as history" Vivas means "reading *simply* as history." But even this meaning does not mark out a special kind of attention but rather means that only a single aspect of a poem is being noticed and that its rhyme, meter, and so on are ignored. Reading a poem as social criticism can be analyzed in a fashion similar to reading as history. Some poems simply are or contain social criticism, and a complete reading must not fail to notice this fact.

The above cases of alleged interested attending can be sorted out in the following way. Jones listening to the music and our playwright watching the rehearsal are both attending with ulterior motives to a work of art, but there is no reason to suppose that the attention of either is different in kind from that of an ordinary spectator. The reader who reads a poem as history is simply attending to an aspect of a poem. On the other hand, the remaining cases—Jones beside the painting telling of his grandfather, the gloating impresario, daydreaming while "reading" a poem, and so on—are simply cases of not attending to the work of art.

In general, I conclude that "disinterestedness" or "intransitiveness" cannot properly be used to refer to a special kind of attention. "Disinterestedness" is a term which is used to make clear that an action has certain kinds of motives. Hence, we speak of disinterested findings (of boards of inquiry), disinterested verdicts (of judges and juries), and so on. Attending to an object, of course, has its motives but the attending itself is not interested or disinterested according to whether its motives are of the kind which motivate interested or disinterested action (as findings and verdicts might), although the attending may be more or less close.

I have argued that the second way of conceiving the aesthetic attitude is also a myth, or at least that its main content—disinterested attention—is; but I must now try to establish that the view misleads aesthetic theory. I shall argue that the attitude-theorist is incorrect about (1) the way in which he wishes to set the limits of aesthetic relevance; (2) the relation of the critic to a work of art; and (3) the relation of morality to aesthetic value.

Since I shall make use of the treatment of aesthetic relevance in Jerome Stolnitz' book, let me make clear that I am not necessarily denying the relevance of the specific items he cites but disagreeing with his criterion of relevance. His criterion of relevance is derived from his definition of "aesthetic attitude" and is set forth at the very beginning of his book. This procedure leads Monroe Beardsley in his review of the book to remark that Stolnitz' discussion is premature.[28] Beardsley suggests "that relevance cannot be satisfactorily discussed until after a careful treatment of the several arts, their dimensions and capacities."[29]

First, what is meant by "aesthetic relevance"? Stolnitz defines the problem by asking the question: "Is it ever 'relevant' to the aesthetic experience to have thoughts or images or bits of knowledge which are not present within the object itself?"[30] Stolnitz begins by summarizing Bullough's experiment and discussion of single colors and associations.[31] Some associations absorb the spectator's attention and distract him from the color and some associations "fuse" with the color. Associations of the latter kind are aesthetic and the former are not. Stolnitz draws the following conclusion about associations:

> If the aesthetic experience is as we have described it, then whether an association is aesthetic depends on whether it is compatible with the attitude of "disinterested attention." If the association re-enforces the focusing of attention upon the object, by "fusing" with the object and thereby giving it added "life and significance," it is genuinely aesthetic. If, however, it arrogates attention to itself and away from the object, it undermines the aesthetic attitude.[32]

It is not clear how something could *fuse* with a single color, but "fusion" is one of those words in aesthetics which is rarely defined. Stolnitz then makes use of a more fruitful

---

[28]*The Journal of Philosophy*, vol. 57 (1960), p. 624.
[29]Loc. cit.
[30]Op. cit., p. 53.
[31]Ibid., p. 54.
[32]Ibid., pp. 54–55.

example, one from I.A. Richards' *Practical Criticism*.[33] He cites the responses of
students to the poem which begins:

> Between the erect and solemn trees
> I will go down upon my knees;
> I shall not find this day
> So meet a place to pray.

The image of a rugby forward running arose in the mind of one student-reader on
reading the third verse of this poem. A cathedral was suggested to a second reader of the
poem. The cathedral image "is congruous with both the verbal meaning of the poem
and the emotions and mood which it expresses. It does not divert attention away from
the poem."[34] The rugby image is presumably incongruous and diverts attention from
the poem.

It is a confusion to take compatibility with disinterested attention as a criterion of
relevance. If, as I have tried to show, *disinterested attention* is a confused notion, then
it will not do as a satisfactory criterion. Also, when Stolnitz comes to show why the
cathedral image is, and the rugby image is not relevant, the criterion he actually uses is
congruousness with the meaning of the poem, which is quite independent of the notion
of disinterestedness. The problem is perhaps best described as the problem of relevance
to a poem, or more generally, to a work of art, rather than aesthetic relevance.

A second way in which the attitude theory misleads aesthetics is its contention that a
critic's relationship to a work of art is different in kind from the relationship of other
persons to the work. H. S. Langfeld in an early statement of this view wrote that we
may "slip from the attitude of aesthetic enjoyment to the attitude of the critic." He
characterizes the critical attitude as "intellectually occupied in coldly estimating . . .
merits" and the aesthetic attitude as responding "emotionally to" a work of art.[35] At the
beginning of his book in the discussion of the aesthetic attitude, Stolnitz declares that if
a percipient of a work of art "has the purpose of passing judgment upon it, his attitude
is not aesthetic."[36] He develops this line at a later stage of his book, arguing that
appreciation (perceiving with the aesthetic attitude) and criticism (seeking for reasons
to support an evaluation of a work) are (1) distinct and (2) "psychologically opposed to
each other."[37] The critical attitude is questioning, analytical, probing for strengths and
weakness, and so on. The aesthetic attitude is just the opposite: "It commits our
allegiance to the object freely and unquestioningly"; "the spectator 'surrenders' himself
to the work of art."[38] "Just because the two attitudes are inimical, whenever criticism
obtrudes, it reduces aesthetic interest."[39] Stolnitz does not, of course, argue that
criticism is unimportant for appreciation. He maintains criticism plays an important
and necessary role in preparing a person to appreciate the nuances, detail, form, and so
on of works of art. We are quite right, he says, thus to read and listen perceptively and
acutely, but he questions, "Does this mean that we must analyze, measure in terms of

---

[33]Ibid., pp. 55–56.
[34]Ibid., p. 56.
[35]*The Aesthetic Attitude* (New York, 1920), p. 79.
[36]Op. cit., p. 35.
[37]Ibid., p. 377.
[38]Ibid., pp. 377–378.
[39]Ibid., p. 379.

value-criteria, etc., *during* the supposedly aesthetic experience?"[40] His answer is "No" and he maintains that criticism must occur "*prior* to the aesthetic encounter,"[41] or it will interfere with appreciation.

How does Stolnitz know that criticism will always interfere with appreciation? His conclusion sounds like one based upon the observations of actual cases, but I do not think it is. I believe it is a logical consequence of his definition of aesthetic attitude in terms of disinterested attention (no ulterior purpose). According to his view, to appreciate an object aesthetically one has to perceive it with no ulterior purpose. But the critic has an ulterior purpose—to analyze and evaluate the object he perceives—hence, in so far as a person functions as a critic he cannot function as an appreciator. But here, as previously, Stolnitz confuses a perceptual distinction with a motivational one. If it were possible to *attend* disinterestedly or interestedly, then perhaps the critic (as percipient) would differ from other percipients. But if my earlier argument about attending is correct, the critic differs from other percipients only in his motives and intentions and not in the way in which he attends to a work of art.

Of course, it might just be a fact that the search for reasons is incompatible with the appreciation of art, but I do not think it is. Several years ago I participated in a series of panel discussions of films. During the showing of each film we were to discuss, I had to take note of various aspects of the film (actor's performance, dramatic development, organization of the screen-plane and screen-space at given moments, and so on) in order later to discuss the films. I believe that this practice not only helped educate me to appreciate subsequent films but that it enhanced the appreciation of the films I was analyzing. I noticed and was able to appreciate things about the films I was watching which ordinarily out of laziness I would not have noticed. I see no reason why the same should not be the case with the professional critic or any critical percipient. If many professional critics seem to appreciate so few works, it is not because they are critics, but perhaps because the percentage of good works of art is fairly small and they suffer from a kind of combat fatigue.

I am unable to see any significant difference between "perceptively and acutely" attending to a work of art (which Stolnitz holds enhances appreciation) and searching for reasons, so far as the experience of a work of art is concerned. If I attend perceptively and acutely, I will have certain standards and/or paradigms in mind (not necessarily consciously) and will be keenly aware of the elements and relations in the work and will evaluate them to some degree. Stolnitz writes as if criticism takes place and then is over and done with, but the search for and finding of reasons (noticing this fits in with that, and so on) is continuous in practiced appreciators. A practiced viewer does not even have to be looking for a reason, he may just notice a line or an area in a painting, for example, and the line or area becomes a reason why he thinks the painting better or worse. A person may be a critic (not necessarily a good one) without meaning to be or without even realizing it.

There is one final line worth pursuing. Stolnitz' remarks suggest that one reason he thinks criticism and appreciation incompatible is that they compete with one another for time (this would be especially bad in the cases of performed works). But seeking and finding reasons (criticism) does not compete for time with appreciation. First, to seek

[40]Ibid., p. 380.
[41]Loc. cit.

for a reason means to be ready and able to notice something and to be thus ready and able as one attends does not compete for time with the attending. In fact, I should suppose that seeking for reasons would tend to focus attention more securely on the work of art. Second, finding a reason is an achievement, like winning a race. (It takes time to run a race but not to win it.) Consider the finding of the following reasons. How much time does it take to "see" that a note is off key (or on key)? How long does it take to notice that an actor mispronounces a word (or does it right)? How much time does it take to realize that a character's action does not fit his already established personality? (One is struck by it.) How long does it take to apprehend that a happy ending is out of place? It does not take time to find any of these reasons or reasons in general. Finding a reason is like coming to understand—it is done in a flash. I do not mean to suggest that one cannot be mistaken in finding a reason. What may appear to be a fault or a merit (a found reason) in the middle of a performance (or during one look at a painting and so forth) may turn out to be just the opposite when seen from the perspective of the whole performance (or other looks at the painting).

A third way in which the attitude theory misleads aesthetic theory is its contention that aesthetic value is always independent of morality. This view is perhaps not peculiar to the attitude theory, but it is a logical consequence of the attitude approach. Two quotations from attitude-theorists will establish the drift of their view of morality and aesthetic value.

> We are either concerned with the beauty of the object or with some other value of the same. Just as soon, for example, as ethical considerations occur to our mind, our attitude shifts.[42]

> Any of us might reject a novel because it seems to conflict with our moral beliefs . . . When we do so . . . We have *not* read the book aesthetically, for we have interposed moral . . . responses of our own which are alien to it. This disrupts the aesthetic attitude. We cannot then say that the novel is *aesthetically* bad, for we have not permitted ourselves to consider it aesthetically. To maintain the aesthetic attitude, we must follow the lead of the object and respond in concert with it.[43]

This conception of the aesthetic attitude functions to hold the moral aspects and the *aesthetic* aspects of the work of art firmly apart. Presumably, although it is difficult to see one's way clearly here, the moral aspects of a work of art cannot be an object of aesthetic attention because aesthetic attention is by definition disinterested and the moral aspects are somehow practical (interested). I suspect that there are a number of confusions involved in the assumption of the incompatibility of aesthetic attention and the moral aspects of art, but I shall not attempt to make these clear, since the root of the assumption—disinterested attention—is a confused notion. Some way other than in terms of the aesthetic attitude, then, is needed to discuss the relation of morality and aesthetic value.

David Pole in a recent article[44] has argued that the moral vision which a work of art may embody is *aesthetically* significant. It should perhaps be remarked at this point that not all works of art embody a moral vision and perhaps some kinds of art (music, for example) cannot embody a moral vision, but certainly some novels, some poems,

---

[42]H. S. Langfeld, op. cit., p. 73.
[43]J. Stolnitz, *Aesthetics and the Philosophy of Art Criticism*, p. 36.
[44]"Morality and the Assessment of Literature," *Philosophy*, vol. 37 (1962), pp. 193–207.

and some films and plays do. I assume it is unnecessary to show how novels and so on have this moral aspect. Pole notes the curious fact that while so many critics approach works of art in "overtly moralistic terms," it is a "philosophical commonplace . . . that the ethical and the aesthetic modes . . . form different categories";[45] I suspect that many philosophers would simply say that these critics are confused about their roles. But Pole assumes that philosophical theory "should take notice of practice"[46] and surely he is right. In agreeing with Pole's assumption I should like to reserve the right to argue in specific cases that a critic may be misguided. This right is especially necessary in a field such as aesthetics because the language and practice of critics is so often burdened with ancient theory. Perhaps *all* moralistic criticism is wrong but philosophers should not rule it out of order at the very beginning by use of a definition.

Pole thinks that the moral vision presented by a particular work of art will be either true or false (perhaps a mixture of true and false might occur). If a work has a false moral vision, then something "is lacking within the work itself. But to say that is to say that the [work] is internally incoherent; some particular aspect must jar with what—on the strength of the rest—we claim a right to demand. And here the moral fault that we have found will count as an aesthetic fault too."[47] Pole is trying to show that the assessment of the moral vision of a work of art is just a special case of coherence or incoherence, and since everyone would agree that coherence is an aesthetic category, the assessment of the moral vision is an aesthetic assessment.

I think Pole's conclusion is correct but take exception to some of his arguments. First, I am uncertain whether it is proper to speak of a moral vision being true or false, and would want to make a more modest claim—that a moral vision can be judged to be acceptable or unacceptable. (I am not claiming Pole is wrong and my claim is not inconsistent with his.) Second, I do not see that a false (or unacceptable) moral vision makes a work incoherent. I should suppose that to say a work is coherent or incoherent is to speak about how its parts fit together and this involves no reference to something outside the work as the work's truth or falsity does.

In any event, it seems to me that a faulty moral vision can be shown to be an aesthetic fault independently of Pole's consideration of truth and coherence. As Pole's argument implies, a work's moral vision is a *part* of the work. Thus, any statement—descriptive or evaluative—about the work's moral vision is a statement about the *work*; and any statement about a *work* is a critical statement and, hence, fails within the aesthetic domain. To judge a moral vision to be morally unacceptable is to judge it defective and this amounts to saying that the work of art has a defective part. (Of course, a judgment of the acceptability of a moral vision may be wrong, as a judgment of an action sometimes is, but this fallibility does not make any difference.) Thus, a work's moral vision may be an aesthetic merit or defect just as a work's degree of unity is a merit or defect. But what justifies saying that a moral vision is a part of a work of art? Perhaps "part" is not quite the right word but it serves to make the point clear enough. A novel's moral vision is an essential part of the novel and if it were removed (I am not sure how such surgery could be carried out) the novel would be greatly changed. Anyway, a novel's moral vision is not like its covers or binding. However,

---

[45]Ibid., p. 193.
[46]Loc. cit.
[47]Ibid., p. 206.

someone might still argue that even though a work's moral vision is defective and the moral vision is part of the work, that this defect is not an *aesthetic* defect. How is "aesthetic" being used here? It is being used to segregate certain aspects or parts of works of art such as formal and stylistic aspects from such aspects as a work's moral vision. But it seems to me that the separation is only nominal. "Aesthetic" has been selected as a name for a certain sub-set of characteristics of works of art. I certainly cannot object to such a stipulation, since an underlying aim of this essay is to suggest the vacuousness of the term "aesthetic." My concern at this point is simply to insist that a work's moral vision is a part of the work and that, therefore, a critic can legitimately describe and evaluate it. I would *call* any defect or merit which a critic can legitimately point out an aesthetic defect or merit, but what we call it does not matter.

It would, of course, be a mistake to judge a work solely on the basis of its moral vision (it is only one part). The fact that some critics have judged works of art in this way is perhaps as much responsible as the theory of aesthetic attitude for the attempts to separate morality from the aesthetic. In fact, such criticism is no doubt at least partly responsible for the rise of the notion of the aesthetic attitude.

If the foregoing arguments are correct, the second way of conceiving the aesthetic attitude misleads aesthetic theory in at least three ways.

III

In answer to a hypothetical question about what is seen in viewing a portrait with the aesthetic attitude, Tomas in part responds "If looking at a picture and attending closely to how it looks is not really to be in the aesthetic attitude, then what on earth is?"[48] I shall take this sentence as formulating the weakest version of the aesthetic attitude. (I am ignoring Tomas' distinction between appearance and reality. See footnote 7. My remarks, thus, are not a critique of Tomas' argument; I am simply using one of his sentences.) First, this sentence speaks only of "looking at a picture," but "listening to a piece of music," "watching and listening to a play," and so on could be added easily enough. After thus expanding the sentence, it can be contracted into the general form: "Being in the aesthetic attitude is attending closely to a work of art (or a natural object)."

But the aesthetic attitude ("the hallmark of modern aesthetics") in this formulation is a great letdown—it no longer seems to say anything significant. Nevertheless, this does seem to be all that is left after the aesthetic attitude has been purged of *distancing* and *disinterestedness*. The only thing which prevents the aesthetic attitude from collapsing into simple attention is the qualification *closely*. One may, I suppose, attend to a work of art more or less closely, but this fact does not seem to signify anything very important. When "being in the aesthetic attitude" is equated with "attending (closely)," the equation neither involves any mythical element nor could it possibly mislead aesthetic theory. But if the definition has no vices, it seems to have no virtues either. When the aesthetic attitude finally turns out to be simply attending (closely), the final version should perhaps not be called "the weakest" but rather "the vacuous version" of the aesthetic attitude.

---

[48]Thomas, op. cit., p. 63.

Stolnitz is no doubt historically correct that the notion of the aesthetic attitude has played an important role in the freeing of aesthetic theory from an overweening concern with beauty. It is easy to see how the slogan, "Anything can become an object of the aesthetic attitude," could help accomplish this liberation. It is worth noting, however, that the same goal could have been (and perhaps to some extent was) realized by simply noting that works of art are often ugly or contain ugliness, or have features which are difficult to include within beauty. No doubt, in more recent times people have been encouraged *to take an aesthetic attitude toward a painting* as a way of lowering their prejudices, say, against abstract and non-objective art. So if the notion of aesthetic attitude has turned out to have no theoretical value for aesthetics, it has had practical value for the appreciation of art in a way similar to that of Clive Bell's suspect notion of significant form.

Frank N. Sibley

AESTHETIC CONCEPTS

The remarks we make about works of art are of many kinds. In this paper I wish to distinguish between two broad groups. We say that a novel has a great number of characters and deals with life in a manufacturing town; that a painting uses pale colours, predominantly blues and greens, and has kneeling figures in the foreground; that the theme in a fugue is inverted at such a point and that there is a stetto at the close; that the action of a play takes place in the span of one day and that there is a reconciliation scene in the fifth act. Such remarks may be made by, and such features pointed out to, anyone with normal eyes, ears, and intelligence. On the other hand, we also say that a poem is tightly-knit or deeply moving; that a picture lacks balance, or has a certain serenity and repose, or that the grouping of the figures sets up an exciting tension; that the characters in a novel never really come to life, or that a certain episode strikes a false note. It would be natural enough to say that the making of judgments such as these requires the exercise of taste, perceptiveness, or sensitivity, of aesthetic discrimination or appreciation; one would not say this of my first group. Accordingly, when a word of expression is such that taste or perceptiveness is required in order to apply it, I shall call it an *aesthetic* term or expression, and I shall, correspondingly, speak of *aesthetic* concepts or *taste* concepts.[1]

Aesthetic terms span a great range of types and could be grouped into various kinds and sub-species. But it is not my present purpose to attempt any such grouping; I am interested in what they all have in common. Their almost endless variety is adequately displayed in the following list: *unified, balanced, integrated, lifeless, serene, sombre, dynamic, powerful, vivid, delicate, moving, trite, sentimental, tragic.* The list of course is not limited to adjectives; expressions in artistic contexts like "telling contrast," "sets up a tension," "conveys a sense of," or "holds it together" are equally good

From The Philosophical Review, 67 (1959): 421–450. *Reprinted with permission of* The Philosophical Review *and the author.*

[1] I shall speak loosely of an "aesthetic term," even when, because the word sometimes has other uses, it would be more correct to speak of its *use* as an aesthetic term. I shall also speak of "non-aesthetic" words, concepts, features, and so on. None of the terms other writers use, "natural," "observable," "perceptual," "physical," "objective" (qualities), "neutral," "descriptive" (language), when they approach the distinction I am making, is really apt for my purpose.

illustrations. It includes terms used by both layman and critic alike, as well as some which are mainly the property of professional critics and specialists.

I have gone for my examples of aesthetic expressions in the first place to critical and evaluative discourse about works of art because it is there particularly that they abound. But now I wish to widen the topic; we employ terms the use of which requires an exercise of taste not only when discussing the arts but quite liberally throughout discourse in everyday life. The examples given above are expressions which, appearing in critical contexts, most usually, if not invariably, have an aesthetic use; outside critical discourse the majority of them more frequently have some other use unconnected with taste. But many expressions do double duty even in everyday discourse, sometimes being used as aesthetic expressions and sometimes not. Other words again, whether in artistic or daily discourse, function only or predominantly as aesthetic terms; of this kind are *graceful, delicate, dainty, handsome, comely, elegant, garish*. Finally, to make the contrast with all the preceding examples, there are many words which are seldom used as aesthetic terms at all: *red, noisy, brackish, clammy, square, docile, curved, evanescent, intelligent, faithful, derelict, tardy, freakish*.

Clearly, when we employ words as aesthetic terms we are often making and using metaphors, pressing into service words which do not primarily function in this manner. Certainly also, many words *have come* to be aesthetic terms by some kind of metaphorical transference. This is so with those like "dynamic," "melancholy," "balanced," "tightly-knit" which, except in artistic and critical writings, are not normally aesthetic terms. But the aesthetic vocabulary must not be thought wholly metaphorical. Many words, including the most common (*lovely, pretty, beautiful, dainty, graceful, elegant*), are certainly not being used metaphorically when employed as aesthetic terms, the very good reason being that this is their primary or only use, some of them having no current non-aesthetic uses. And though expressions like "dynamic," "balanced," and so forth *have come* by a metaphorical shift to be aesthetic terms, their employment in criticism can scarcely be said to be more than quasi-metaphorical. Having entered the language of art description and criticism as metaphors they are now standard vocabulary in that language.[2]

The expressions I am calling aesthetic terms form no small segment of our discourse. Often, it is true, people with normal intelligence and good eyesight and hearing lack, at least in some measure, the sensitivity required to apply them; a man need not be stupid or have poor eyesight to fail to see that something is graceful. Thus taste or sensitivity is somewhat more rare than certain other human capacities; people who exhibit a sensitivity both wide-ranging and refined are a minority. It is over the application of aesthetic terms too that, notoriously, disputes and differences sometimes go helplessly unsettled. But almost everybody is able to exercise taste to some degree and in some matters. It is surprising therefore that aesthetic terms have been so largely neglected. They have received glancing treatment in the course of other aesthetic discussions; but as a broad category they have not received the direct attention they merit.

The foregoing has marked out the area I wish to discuss. One warning should

---

[2]A contrast will reinforce this. If a critic were to describe a passage of music as chattering, carbonated, or gritty, a painter's colouring as vitreous, farinaceous, or effervescent, or a writer's style as glutinous, or abrasive, he *would* be using live metaphors rather than drawing on the more normal language of criticism. Words like "athletic," "vertiginous," "silken" may fall somewhere between.

perhaps be given. When I speak of taste in this paper, I shall not be dealing with questions which centre upon expressions like "a matter of taste" (meaning, roughly, a matter of personal preference or liking). It is with an ability to *notice* or *see* or *tell* that things have certain qualities that I am concerned.

I

In order to support our application of an aesthetic term, we often refer to features the mention of which involves other aesthetic terms: "it has an extraordinary vitality because of its free and vigorous style of drawing," "graceful in the smooth flow of its lines," "dainty because of the delicacy and harmony of its colouring." It is as normal to do this as it is to justify one mental epithet by other epithets of the same general type, *intelligent* by *ingenious, inventive, acute,* and so on. But often when we apply aesthetic terms, we explain why by referring to features which do *not* depend for their recognition upon an exercise of taste: "delicate because of its pastel shades and curving lines," or "it lacks balance because one group of figures is so far off to the left and is so brightly illuminated." When no explanation of this latter kind is offered, it is legitimate to ask or search for one. Finding a satisfactory answer is sometimes difficult, but one cannot ordinarily reject the question. When we cannot ourselves quite say what non-aesthetic features make something delicate or unbalanced or moving, the good critic often puts his finger on something which strikes us as the right explanation. In short, aesthetic terms always ultimately apply because of, and aesthetic qualities always ultimately depend upon, the presence of features which, like curving or angular lines, colour contrasts, placing of masses, or speed of movement, are visible, audible, or otherwise discernible without any exercise of taste or sensibility. Whatever kind of dependence this is, and there are various relationships between aesthetic qualities and non-aesthetic features, what I want to make clear in this paper is that there are no non-aesthetic features which serve in *any* circumstances as logically *sufficient conditions* for applying aesthetic terms. Aesthetic concepts are not in *this* respect condition-governed at all.

There is little temptation to suppose that aesthetic terms resemble words which, like "square," are applied in accordance with a set of necessary and sufficient conditions. For whereas each square is square in virtue of the *same* set of conditions, four equal sides and four right angles, aesthetic terms apply to widely varied objects; one thing is graceful because of these features, another because of those, and so on. Recently, philosophers have broken the spell of the strict necessary-and-sufficient model by showing that many everyday concepts are not of that type, but are governed only in a much looser way by conditions. However, since these newer models provide satisfactory accounts of many concepts, it might plausibly be thought that aesthetic concepts are of some such kind and that they similarly are governed in some looser way by conditions. I want to argue that aesthetic concepts differ radically from any of these other concepts.

Amongst these concepts to which attention has recently been paid are those for which no *necessary-and-sufficient* conditions can be provided, but for which there are a number of relevant features, A, B, C, D, E, such that the presence of some groups or combinations of these features is *sufficient* for the application of the concept. The list of relevant features may be an open one; that is, given A, B, C, D, E, we may not wish to close off the possible relevance of other unlisted features beyond E. Examples of such concepts might be "dilatory," "discourteous," "possessive," "capricious," "prosperous," "intelligent." . . . If we begin a list of features relevant to "intelligent" with, for example, ability to grasp and follow various kinds of instructions, ability to master facts and marshall evidence, ability to solve mathematical or chess problems, we might go on adding to this list almost indefinitely.

However, with concepts of this sort, although decisions may have to be made and judgment exercised, it is always possible to extract and state, from cases which have *already* clearly been decided, the sets of features or conditions which were regarded as sufficient in those cases. These relevant features which I am calling conditions are, it should be noted, features which, though not sufficient *alone* and needing to be combined with other similar features, nevertheless carry some weight and count only in one direction. Being a good chess player can count only *towards* and not *against* intelligence. Whereas mention of it may enter sensibly along with other remarks in expressions like "I say he is intelligent because . . ." or "the reason I call him intelligent is that . . . ," it cannot be used to complete such negative expressions as "I say he is *un*intelligent because. . . ." But what I want particularly to emphasize about features which function as conditions for a term is that *some* group or set of them is sufficient fully to ensure or warrant the application of that term. An individual characterized by some of these features may not yet qualify to be called lazy or intelligent, and so on, beyond all question, but all that is needed is to add some further (indefinite) number of such characterizations and a point is reached where we have enough. There are individuals possessing a number of such features of whom one cannot deny, cannot but admit, that they are intelligent. We have left necessary-and-sufficient conditions behind, but we are still in the realm of sufficient conditions.

But aesthetic concepts are not condition-governed even in this way. There are no sufficient conditions, no non-aesthetic features such that the presence of some set or number of them will beyond question logically justify or warrant the application of an aesthetic term. It is impossible . . . to make any statements corresponding to those we make for condition-governed words. We are able to say "If it is true he can do this, and that, and the other, then one just cannot deny that he is intelligent," or "if he does A, B, and C, I don't see how it can be denied that he is lazy," but we cannot make *any* general statement of the form "If the vase is pale pink, somewhat curving, lightly mottled, and so forth, it will be delicate, cannot but be delicate." Nor again can one say *any* such thing here as "Being tall and thin is not enough *alone* to ensure that a vase is delicate, but if it is, for example, slightly curving and pale coloured (and so forth) as well, it cannot be denied that it is." Things may be described to us in non-aesthetic terms as fully as we please but we are not thereby put in the position of having to admit (or being unable to deny) that they are delicate or graceful or garish or exquisitely balanced.[3]

[3] In a paper reprinted in *Aesthetics and Language*, ed. by W. Elton (Oxford, 1954), pp. 131–46, Arnold Isenberg discusses certain problems about aesthetic concepts and qualities. Like others who approach these problems, he does not isolate them, as I do, from questions about verdicts on the *merits* of works of art, or from questions about *likings* and *preferences*. He says something parallel to my remarks above: "There is not in all the world's criticism a single purely descriptive statement concerning which one is prepared to say beforehand, 'if it is true, I shall *like* that work so much the better' " (p. 139, my italics). I should think *this* is highly questionable.

No doubt there are some respects in which aesthetic terms *are* governed by conditions or rules. For instance, it may be impossible that a thing should be garish if all its colours are pale pastels, or flamboyant if all its lines are straight. There may be, that is, descriptions using only non-aesthetic terms which are incompatible with descriptions employing certain aesthetic terms. If I am told that a painting in the next room consists solely of one or two bars of very pale blue and very pale grey set at right angles on a pale fawn ground, I can be sure that it cannot be fiery or garish or gaudy or flamboyant. A description of this sort may make certain aesthetic terms *in*applicable or *in*appropriate; and if from this description I inferred that the picture was, or even might be, fiery or gaudy or flamboyant, this might be taken as showing a failure to understand these words. I do not wish to deny therefore that taste concepts may be governed *negatively* by conditions.[4] What I am emphasizing is that they quite lack governing conditions of a sort many other concepts possess. Though on *seeing* the picture we might say, and rightly, that it is delicate or serene or restful or sickly or insipid, no *description* in non-aesthetic terms permits us to claim that these or any other aesthetic terms must undeniably apply to it.

I have said that if an object is characterized *solely* by certain sorts of features this may count decisively against the possibility of applying to it certain aesthetic terms. But of course the presence of *some* such features need not count decisively; other features may be enough to outweigh those which, on their own, would render the aesthetic term inapplicable. A painting might be garish even though much of its colour is pale. These facts call attention to a further feature of taste concepts. One *can* find general features or descriptions which in some sense count in one direction only, only *for* or only *against* the application of certain aesthetic terms. Angularity, fatness, brightness, or intensity of colour are typically *not* associated with delicacy or grace. Slimness, lightness, gentle curves, lack of intensity of colour are associated with delicacy, but not with flamboyance, majesty, grandeur, splendour or garishness. This is shown by the naturalness of saying, for example, that someone is graceful *because* she's so light, but in *spite of* being quite angular or heavily built; and by the corresponding oddity of saying that something is graceful *because* it is so heavy or angular, or delicate *because* of its bright and intense colouring. This may therefore sound quite similar to what I have said already about conditions in discussing terms like "intelligent." There are nevertheless significant differences. Although there is this sense in which slimness, lightness, lack of intensity of colour, and so on, count only towards, not against, delicacy, these features, I shall say, at best count only *typically* or *characteristically* towards delicacy. They do not count towards in the same sense as condition-features count towards laziness or intelligence; that is, no group of them is ever logically sufficient.

One way of reinforcing this is to notice how features which are characteristically associated with one aesthetic term may also be similarly associated with other, rather different aesthetics terms. "Graceful" and "delicate" may be on the one hand sharply contrasted with terms like "violent," "grand," "fiery," "garish," or "massive" which have characteristic non-aesthetic features, quite unlike those for "delicate" and "graceful."

---

[4]Isenberg (op. cit., p. 132) makes a somewhat similar but mistaken point: "If we had been told that the colours of a certain painting are garish, it would be *astonishing* to find that they are *all* very pale and unsaturated" (my italics). But if we say "all" rather than "predominantly," then "astonishing" is the wrong word. The word that goes with "all" is "impossible"; "astonishing" might go with "predominantly."

But on the other hand they may also be contrasted with aesthetic terms which stand much closer to them, like "flaccid," "weakly," "washed out," "lanky," "anaemic," "wan," "insipid"; and the features characteristic of *these* qualities, pale colour, slimness, lightness, lack of angularity and contrast, are virtually identical with the range for "delicate" and "graceful." Similarly many features typically associated with "joyous," "fiery," "robust," or "dynamic" are identical with those associated with "garish," "strident," "turbulent," "gaudy," or "chaotic." Thus an object described very fully, but exclusively in terms of qualities characteristic of delicacy, may turn out on inspection to be not delicate at all, but anaemic or insipid. The failures of novices and the artistically inept prove that quite close similarity in line, colour, or technique gives no assurance of gracefulness or delicacy. A failure and a success in the manner of Degas may be generally more alike, so far as their non-aesthetic features go, than either is like a successful Fragonard. But I need not go even this far to make my main point. A painting which has only the kind of features one would associate with vigour and energy but which even so fails to be vigorous and energetic *need* not be instead, say, strident or chaotic. It may fail to have any particular character whatever. It may employ bright colours and the like without being particularly lively and vigorous at all; but one may feel unable to describe it as chaotic or strident or garish either. It is, rather, simply lacking in character (though of course this too is an aesthetic judgment; taste is exercised also in seeing that the painting has no character).

There are of course many features which do not in these ways characteristically count for (or against) particular aesthetic qualities. One poem has strength and power because of the regularity of its metre and rhyme; another is monotonous and lacks drive and strength because of its regular metre and rhyme. We do not feel the need to switch from "because of" to "in spite of." However, I have concentrated upon features characteristically associated with aesthetic qualities because, if one could maintain that taste concepts are in any way governed by sufficient conditions, these would seem to be the most promising candidates for governing conditions. But to say that features are associated only *characteristically* with an aesthetic term *is* to say that they can never amount to sufficient conditions; no description however full, even in terms characteristic of gracefulness, puts it beyond question that something is graceful in the way a description may put it beyond question that someone is lazy or intelligent.

It is important to observe, however, that I am not merely claiming that no sufficient conditions can be stated for taste concepts. For if this were all, they might not be after all really different from one kind of concept recently discussed. They could be accommodated perhaps with those concepts which Professor H. L. A. Hart has called "defeasible"; it is a characteristic of defeasible concepts that we cannot state sufficient conditions for them because, for any sets we offer, there is always an (open) list of defeating conditions any of which might rule out the application of the concept. The most we can say schematically for a defeasible concept is that, for example, A, B, and C together are sufficient for the concept to apply *unless* some feature is present which overrides or voids them. But, I want to emphasize, the very fact that we *can* say this sort of thing shows that we are still to the extent in the realm of conditions.[5] The features governing defeasible concepts can ordinarily count only one way, *either* for *or* against.

---

[5] H. L. A. Hart, "The Ascription of Responsibility and Rights in *Logic and Language*," First Series, ed. by A. G. N. Flew (Oxford, 1951). Hart indeed speaks of "conditions" throughout, see p. 148.

To take Hart's example, "offer" and "acceptance" can count only towards the existence of a valid contract, and fraudulent misrepresentation, duress, and lunacy only against. And even with defeasible concepts, if we are told that there are *no* voiding features present, we can know that some set of conditions or features, A, B, C, . . ., is enough to ensure, for example, that there is a contract. The very notion of a defeasible concept seems to require that some group of features *would* be sufficient *in certain circumstances*, i.e. in the absence of voiding features. In a certain way, defeasible concepts lack sufficient conditions then, but they are still, in the sense described, condition-governed. My claim about taste concepts is stronger; that they are not, except negatively, governed by conditions at all. We could not conclude even in certain circumstances, e.g. if we were told of the absence of all "voiding" or uncharacteristic features (no angularities and the like), that an object *must* certainly be graceful, however fully it was described to us as possessing features characteristic of gracefulness.

My arguments and illustrations so far have been rather simply schematic. Many concepts, including most of the examples I have used . . . are much more thoroughly open and complex than my illustrations suggest. Not only may there be an open list of relevant conditions; it may be impossible to give precise rules telling how many features from the list are needed for a sufficient set or in which combinations; impossible similarly to give precise rules covering the extent or degree to which such features need to be present in those combinations. Indeed, we may have to abandon as futile any attempt to describe or formulate anything like a complete set of precise conditions or rules, and content ourselves with giving only a very general account of the concept, making reference to samples or cases or precedents. We cannot employ these concepts *simply* by being equipped with lists of conditions, readily applicable procedures or sets of rules, however complex. For to exhibit a mastery of one of those concepts we must be able to apply the word correctly to new individual cases, at least to central ones; and each new case may be a uniquely different object, just as each intelligent child or student may differ from others in relevant features and exhibit a unique combination of kinds and degrees of achievement and ability. In dealing with these new cases mechanical rules and procedures would be useless; we have to exercise our judgment, guided by a complex set of examples and precedents. Here then there is a marked *superficial* similarity to aesthetic concepts. For in using aesthetic terms too we learn from samples and examples, not rules, and we have to apply them, likewise, without guidance by rules or readily applicable procedures, to new and unique instances. Neither kind of concept admits of a simply "mechanical" employment.

But this is *only* a superficial similarity. It is at least noteworthy that in applying words like "lazy" or "intelligent" to new and unique instances we say that we are required to exercise *judgment*; it would be indeed odd to say that we are exercising *taste*. In exercising judgment we are called upon to examine the pros and cons, and to decide whether a quite new feature is to be counted as weighing on one side or on the other. But this goes to show that, though we may learn from and rely upon samples and precedents rather than a set of stated conditions, we are not out of the realm of general conditions and guiding principles. These precedents necessarily embody, and are used by us to illustrate, a complex web of governing and relevant conditions which it is impossible to formulate completely. To profit by precedents we have to understand them; and we must argue consistently from case to case. This is the very function of precedents. Thus it is possible, even with these very loosely condition-governed concepts, to take clear or paradigm cases of X and to say "this is X because . . .," and follow it up with an account of features which logically clinch the matter.

Nothing like this is possible with aesthetic terms. Examples undoubtedly play a crucial role in giving us a grasp of these concepts; but we do not and cannot derive from these examples conditions and principles, however complex, which will enable us, if we are consistent, to apply the terms even to some new cases. When, with a clear case of something which is in fact graceful or balanced but which I have not seen, someone tells me what features make it so, it is always possible for me to wonder whether, in spite of these features, it really is graceful or balanced.

My point may be reinforced thus. A man who failed to realize the nature of aesthetic concepts, or who, knowing he lacked sensitivity in aesthetic matters, did not want to reveal this lack might by assiduous application and shrewd observation provide himself with some rules and generalizations; and by inductive procedures and intelligent guessing, he might frequently say the right things. But he could have no great confidence or certainty; a slight change in an object might at any time unpredictably ruin his calculations, and he might as easily have been wrong as right. No matter how careful he has been about working out a set of consistent principles and conditions, he is only in a position to think that the object is very possibly delicate. With concepts like *lazy, intelligent,* or *contract,* someone who intelligently formulated rules that led him aright appreciably often *would* thereby show the beginning of a grasp of those concepts; but the person we are considering is not even beginning to show an awareness of what delicacy is. Though he sometimes says the right thing, he has not seen, but guessed, that the object is delicate. However intelligent he might be, we could easily tell him wrongly that something was delicate and "explain" why without his being able to detect the deception. (I am ignoring complications now about negative conditions.) But if we did the same with, say, "intelligent" he could at least often uncover some incompatibility which would need explaining. In a world of beings like himself he would have no use for concepts like delicacy. As it is, these concepts would play a quite different role in his life. He would for himself, have no more reason to choose tasteful objects, pictures, and so on, than a deaf man would to avoid noisy places. He could not be praised for exercising taste; at best his ingenuity and intelligence might come in for mention. In "appraising" pictures, statuettes, poems, he would be doing something quite different from what other people do when they exercise taste.

At this point I want to notice in passing that there are times when it may look as if an aesthetic word could be applied according to a rule. These cases vary in type; I shall mention only one. One might say, in using "delicate" of glassware perhaps, that the thinner the glass, other things being equal, the more delicate it is. Similarly, with fabrics, furniture, and so on, there are perhaps times when the thinner or more smoothly finished or more highly polished something is, the more certainly some aesthetic term or other applies. On such occasions someone might formulate a rule and follow it in applying the word to a given range of articles. Now it may be that sometimes when this is so, the word being used is not really an aesthetic term at all; "delicate" applied to glass in this way may at times really mean no more than "thin" or "fragile." But this is certainly not always the case; people often *are* exercising taste even when they say that glass is very delicate because it is so thin, and know that it would be less so if thicker and more so if thinner. These instances where there appear to be rules are peripheral cases of the use of aesthetic terms. If someone did merely follow a rule we should not say he was exercising taste, and we should hesitate to admit that he had any real notion of delicacy until he satisfied us that he could discern it in other instances where no rule was available. In any event, these occasions when aesthetic words can be applied by rule are exceptional not central or typical, and there is still no reason to think we are dealing with a logical entailment.[6]

It must not be thought that the impossibility of stating any conditions (other than negative) for the application of aesthetic terms results from an accidental poverty or lack of precision in language, or that it is simply a question of extreme complexity. It is true that words like "pink," "bluish," "curving," "mottled" do not permit of anything like a specific naming of each and every varied shade, curve, mottling, and blending. But if we were to give special names much more liberally than either we or even the specialists do (and no doubt there are limits beyond which we could not go), or even if, instead of names, we were to use vast numbers of specimens and samples of particular shades, shapes, mottlings, lines, and configurations, it would still be impossible, and for the same reasons, to supply any conditions.

We do indeed, in talking about a work of art, concern ourselves with its individual and specific features. We say that it is delicate not simply because it is in pale colours but because of *those* pale colours, that it is graceful not because its outline curves slightly but because of *that* particular curve. We use expressions like "because of *its* pale colouring," "because of *the* flecks of bright blue," "because of *the* way the lines converge" where it is clear we are referring not to the presence of general features but to very specific and particular ones. But it is obvious that even with the help of precise names, or even samples and illustrations, of particular shades of colour, contours and lines, any attempt ɯ state conditions would be futile. After all, the very same feature, say a colour or shape or line of a particular sort, which helps make one work may quite spoil another. "It would be quite delicate if it were not for that pale colour there" may be said about the very colour which is singled out in another picture as being largely responsible for its delicate quality. No doubt one way of putting this is to say that the features which make something delicate or graceful, and so on, are combined in a peculiar and unique way; that the aesthetic quality depends upon exactly this individual or unique combination of just these specific colours and shapes so that even a slight change might make all the difference. Nothing is to be achieved by trying to single out or separate features and generalizing about them.

[6]I cannot in the compass of this paper discuss the other types of apparent exceptions to my thesis. Cases where a man *lacking* in sensitivity might learn and follow a rule, as above, ought to be distinguished from cases where someone who *possesses* sensitivity might know, from a non-aesthetic description, that an aesthetic term applies. I have stated my thesis as though this latter kind of case never occurs because I have had my eye on the logical features of *typical* aesthetic judgments and have preferred to over- rather than understate my view. But with certain aesthetic terms, especially negative ones, there may perhaps be some rare genuine exceptions when a description enables us to visualize very fully, and when what is described belongs to certain restricted classes of things, say human faces or animal forms. Perhaps a description like "One eye red and rheumy, the other missing, a wart-covered nose, a twisted mouth, a greenish pallor" may justify in a strong sense ("must be," "cannot but be") the judgments "ugly" or "hideous." If so, such cases are marginal, form a very small minority, and are uncharacteristic or atypical of aesthetic judgments in general. Usually, when, on hearing a description, we say "it *must* be very beautiful (graceful, or the like)," we mean no more than "it surely must be, it's only remotely possible that it isn't." Different again are situations, and these are very numerous, where we can move quite simply from "bright colours" to "gay," or from "reds and yellows" to "warm," but where we are as yet only on the borderline of anything that could be called an expression of taste or aesthetic sensibility. I have stressed the importance of this transitional and border area between non-aesthetic and obviously aesthetic judgments below.

I have now argued that in certain ways aesthetic concepts are not and cannot be condition- or rule-governed.[7] Not to be so governed is one of their essential characteristics. In arguing this I first claimed in a general way that no non-aesthetic features are possible candidates for conditions, and then considered more particularly both the "characteristic" *general* features associated with aesthetic terms and the individual or *specific* features found in particular objects. I have not attempted to examine what relationship these specific features of a work do bear to its aesthetic qualities. An examination of the locutions we use when we refer to them in the course of explaining or supporting our application of an aesthetic term reinforces with linguistic evidence the fact that we are certainly not offering them as explanatory or justifying *conditions*. When we are asked why we say a certain person is lazy or intelligent or courageous, we are being asked in virtue of what we *call* him this; we reply with "because of the way he regularly leaves his work unfinished," or "because of the ease with which he handles such and such problems," and so on. But when we are asked to say why, in our opinion, a picture lacks balance or is sombre in tone, or why a poem is moving or tightly organized, we are doing a different kind of thing. We may use similar locutions: "his verse has strength and variety *because of the way* he handles the metre and employs the caesura," or "it is nobly austere *because* of the lack of detail and the restricted palette." But we can also express what we want to by using quite other expressions: "it is the handling of metre and caesura which is *responsible for* its strength and variety," "its nobly austere quality is *due to* the lack of detail and the use of a restricted palette," "its lack of balance *results from* the highlighting of the figures on the left," "those minor chords *make it* extremely moving," "those converging lines *give it* an extraordinary unity." These are locutions we cannot switch to with "lazy" or "intelligent"; to say what *makes* him lazy, is *responsible* for his laziness, what it is *due to*, is to broach another question entirely.

One after another, in recent discussions, writers have insisted that aesthetic judgments are not "mechanical": "Critics do not formulate general standards and apply these mechanically to all, or to classes of, works of art." "Technical points can be settled rapidly, by the application of rules," but aesthetic questions "cannot be settled by any mechanical method." Instead, these writers on aesthetics have emphasized that there is no "substitute for individual judgment" with its "spontaneity and speculation" and that "The final standard . . . [is] the judgment of personal taste."[8] What is surprising is that, though such things have been repeated again and again, no one seems to have said what is meant by "taste" or by the word "mechanical." There are many judgments besides those requiring taste which demand "spontaneity" and "individual judgment" and are not "mechanical." Without a detailed comparison we cannot see in what particular way *aesthetic* judgments are not "mechanical," or how

[7]Helen Knight says (Elton, op. cit., p. 152) that "piquant" (one of my "aesthetic" terms) "depends on" various features (a *retroussé* nose, a pointed chin, and the like), and that these features are *criteria* for it; this second claim is what I am denying. She also maintains that "good," when applied to works of art, depends on *criteria* like balance, solidity, depth, profundity (my aesthetic terms again; I should place piquancy in this list). I would deny this too, though I regard it as a different question and do not consider it in this paper. The two questions need separating: the relation of nonaesthetic features (*retroussé*, pointed) to aesthetic qualities, and the relation of aesthetic qualities to "aesthetically good" (verdicts). Most writings which touch on the nature of aesthetic concepts have this other (verdict) question mainly in mind. Mrs. Knight blurs this difference when she says, for example, " 'piquant' is the same kind of word as 'good.' "

[8]See articles by Margaret Macdonald and J. A. Passmore in Elton, op. cit., pp. 118, 41, 40, 119.

they differ from those other judgments, nor can we begin to specify what taste is. This I have attempted. It is a characteristic and essential feature of judgments which employ an aesthetic term that they cannot be made by appealing, in the sense explained, to non-aesthetic conditions.[9] This, I believe is a logical feature of aesthetic or taste judgments in general though I have argued it here only as regards the more restricted range of judgments which employ aesthetic terms. It is part of what "taste" means.

II

A great deal of work remains to be done on aesthetic concepts. In the remainder of this paper I shall offer further suggestions which may help towards an understanding of them.

The realization that aesthetic concepts are governed only negatively by conditions is likely to give rise to puzzlement over how we manage to apply the words in our aesthetic vocabulary. If we are not following rules and there are no conditions to appeal to, how are we to know when they are applicable? One very natural way to counter this question is to point out that some other sorts of concepts also are not condition-governed. We do not apply simple colour words by following rules or in accordance with principles. We see that the book is red by looking, just as we tell that the tea is sweet by tasting it. So too, it might be said, we just see (or fail to see) that things are delicate, balanced, and the like. This kind of comparison between the exercise of taste and the use of the five senses is indeed familiar; our use of the word "taste" itself shows that the comparison is age-old and very natural. Yet whatever the similarities, there are great dissimilarities too. A careful comparison cannot be attempted here though it would be valuable; but certain differences stand out, and writers who have emphasized that aesthetic judgments are not "mechanical" have sometimes dwelt on and been puzzled by them.

In the first place, while our ability to discern aesthetic features is dependent upon our possession of good eyesight, hearing, and so on, people normally endowed with senses and understanding may nevertheless fail to discern them. "Those who listen to a concert, walk round a gallery, read a poem may have roughly similar sense perceptions, but some get a great deal more than others," Miss Macdonald says; but she adds that she is "puzzled by this feature 'in the object' which can be seen only by a specially qualified observer" and asks, "What is this 'something more'?"[10]

It is this difference between aesthetic and perceptual qualities which in part leads to the view that "works of art are esoteric objects . . . not simple objects of sense perception."[11] But there is no good reason for calling an object esoteric simply because we discern aesthetic qualities in it. The *objects* to which we apply aesthetic words are of the most diverse kinds and by no means esoteric: people and buildings, flowers and

---

[9]As I indicated, . . . above. I have dealt only with the relation of *non-aesthetic* to aesthetic features. Perhaps a description in *aesthetic* terms may occasionally suffice for applying another aesthetic term. Johnson's Dictionary gives "handsome" as "beautiful with dignity"; Shorter O.E.D. gives "pretty" as "beautiful in a slight, dainty, or diminutive way."

[10]Macdonald in Elton, op. cit., pp. 114, 119. See also pp. 120, 122.

[11]Macdonald, ibid., pp. 114, 120–3. She speaks of non-aesthetic properties here as "physical" or "observable" qualities, and distinguishes between "physical objects" and "work of art."

gardens, vases and furniture, as well as poems and music. Nor does there seem any good reason for calling the *qualities* themselves esoteric. It is true that someone with perfect eyes or ears might miss them, but we do after all say we *observe* or *notice* them ("Did you notice how very grateful she was?," "Did you observe the exquisite balance in all his pictures?"). In fact, they are very familiar indeed. We learn while quite young to use many aesthetic words, though they are, as one might expect from their dependence upon our ability to see, hear, distinguish colours, and the like, not the earliest words we learn: and our mastery and sophistication in using them develop along with the rest of our vocabulary. They are not rarities; some ranges of them are in regular use in everyday discourse.

The second notable difference between the exercise of taste and the use of the five senses lies in the way we support those judgments in which aesthetics concepts are employed. Although we use these concepts without rules or conditions, we do defend or support our judgments, and convince others of their rightness, by talking; "disputation about art is not futile," as Miss Macdonald says, for critics do "attempt a certain kind of explanation of works of art with the object of establishing correct judgments."[12] Thus even though this disputation does not consist in "deductive or inductive inference" or "reasoning," its occurrence is enough to show how very different these judgments are from those of a simple perceptual sort.

Now the critic's talk, it is clear, frequently consists in mentioning or pointing out the features, including easily discernible non-aesthetic ones, upon which the aesthetic qualities depend. But the puzzling question remains how, by mentioning these features, the critic is thereby justifying or supporting his judgments. To this question a number of recent writers have given an answer. Stuart Hampshire, for example, says that "One engages in aesthetic discussion for the sake of what one might see on the way . . . if one has been brought to see what there is to be seen in the object, the purpose of discussion is achieved. . . . The point is to bring people to see these features."[13] The critic's talk, that is, often serves to support his judgments in a special way; it helps us to *see* what he has seen, namely, the aesthetic qualities of the object. But even when it is agreed that this is one of the main things that critics do, puzzlement tends to break out again over *how* they do it. How is it that by talking about features of the work (largely non-aesthetic ones) we can manage to bring others to see what they had not seen? "What sort of endowment is this which *talking* can modify? . . . Discussion does not improve eyesight and hearing" (my italics).[14]

Yet of course we do succeed in applying aesthetic terms, and we frequently do succeed by talking (and pointing and gesturing in certain ways) in bringing others to see what we see. One begins to suspect that puzzlement over how we can possibly do this, and puzzlement over the "esoteric" character of aesthetic qualities too, arises from bearing in mind inappropriate philosophical models. When someone is unable to see that the book on the table is brown, we cannot get him to see that it is by talking; consequently it seems puzzling that we might get someone to see that the vase is

---

[12]Ibid., pp. 115–16: cf. also John Holloway, *Proceedings of the Aristotelian Society*, Supplementary Vol. xxiii (1949), pp. 175–6.

[13]Stuart Hampshire in Elton, op. cit., p. 165. Cf. also remarks in Elton by Isenberg (pp. 142, 145), Passmore (p. 38), in *Philosophy and Psycho-analysis* by John Wisdom (Oxford, 1953), pp. 223–4, and in Holloway, op. cit., p. 175.

[14]Macdonald, op. cit., pp. 119–20.

graceful by talking. If we are to dispel this puzzlement and recognize aesthetic concepts and qualities for what they are, we must abandon unsuitable models and investigate how we actually employ these concepts. With so much interest in and agreement about *what* the critic does, one might expect descriptions of *how* he does it to have been given. But little has been said about this, and what has been said is unsatisfactory.

Miss Macdonald,[15] for example, subscribes to this view of the critic's task as presenting "what is not obvious to casual or uninstructed inspection," and she does ask the question "What sort of considerations are involved, *and how*, to justify a critical verdict?" (my italics). But she does not in fact go on to answer it. She addresses herself instead to the different, though related, question of the interpretation of art works. In complex works different critics claim, often justifiably, to discern different features; hence Miss Macdonald suggests that in critical discourse the critic is bringing us to see what he sees by offering new interpretations. But if the question is "what [the critic] does and how he does it," he cannot be represented either wholly or even mainly as providing new interpretations. His task quite as often is simply to help us appreciate qualities which other critics have regularly found in the works he discusses. To put the stress upon *new* interpretations is to leave untouched the question how, by talking, he can help us to see *either* the newly appreciated aesthetic qualities *or* the old. In any case, besides complex poems or plays which may bear many interpretations, there are also relatively simple ones. There are also vases, buildings, and furniture, not to mention faces, sunsets, and scenery, about which no questions of "interpretation" arise but about which we talk in similar ways and make similar judgments. So the "puzzling" questions remain: how do we support these judgments and how do we bring others to see what we see?

Hampshire,[16] who likewise believes that the critic brings us "to see what there is to be seen in the object," does give some account of how the critic does this. "The greatest service of the critic" is to point out, isolate, and place in a frame of attention the "particular features of the particular object which *make* it ugly or beautiful"; for it is "difficult to see and hear all that there is to see and hear," and simply a prejudice to suppose that while "things really do have colours and shapes . . . there do not exist literally and objectively, concordances of colours and perceived rhythms and balances of shapes." However, these "extraordinary qualities" which the critic "may have seen (in the wider sense of 'see')" are "qualities which are of no direct practical interest." Consequently, to bring us to see them the critic employs "an unnatural use of words in description"; "the common vocabulary, being created for practical purposes, obstructs any disinterested perception of things"; and so these qualities "are normally described metaphorically by some transference of terms from the common vocabulary."

Much of what Hampshire says is right. But there is also something quite wrong in the view that the "common" vocabulary "obstructs" our aesthetic purposes, that it is "unnatural" to take it over and use it metaphorically, and that the critic "is under the necessity of building . . . a vocabulary *in opposition to the main tendency of his language*" (my italics). First, while we do often coin new metaphors in order to

---

[15]Ibid., see pp. 127, 122, 125, 115. Other writers also place the stress on interpretation, cf. Holloway, op. cit., p. 173 ff.
[16]Op. cit., pp. 165–8.

describe aesthetic qualities, we are by no means always under the necessity of wresting the "common vocabulary" from its "natural" uses to serve our purposes. There does exist, as I observed earlier, a large and accepted vocabulary of aesthetic terms some of which, whatever their metaphorical origins, are now not metaphors at all, others of which are at most quasi-metaphorical. Second, this view that our use of metaphor and quasi-metaphor for aesthetic purposes is unnatural or a makeshift into which we are forced by a language designed for other purposes misrepresents fundamentally the character of aesthetic qualities and aesthetic language. There is nothing unnatural about using words like "forceful," "dynamic," or "tightly-knit" in criticism; they do their work perfectly and are exactly the words needed for the purposes they serve. We do not want or need to replace them by words which lack the metaphorical element. In using them to describe works of art, the very point is that we are noticing aesthetic qualities related to their literal or common meanings. If we possessed a quite different word from "dynamic," one we could use to point out an aesthetic quality unrelated to the common meaning of "dynamic," it could not be used to describe that quality which "dynamic" does serve to point out. Hampshire pictures "a colony of aesthetes, disengaged from practical needs and manipulations" and says that "descriptions of aesthetic qualities, which for us are metaphorical, might seem to them to have an altogether literal and familiar sense"; they might use "a more directly descriptive vocabulary." But if they had a new and "directly descriptive" vocabulary lacking the links with non-aesthetic properties and interests which our vocabulary possesses, they would have to remain silent about many of the aesthetic qualities we can describe; further, if they were more completely "disengaged from practical needs" and other non-aesthetic awareness and interests, they would perforce be blind to many aesthetic qualities we can appreciate. The links between aesthetic qualities and non-aesthetic ones are both obvious and vital. Aesthetic concepts, all of them, carry with them attachments and in one way or another are tethered to or parasitic upon non-aesthetic features. The fact that many aesthetic terms are metaphorical or quasi-metaphorical in no way means that common language is an ill-adapted tool with which we have to struggle. When someone writes as Hampshire does, one suspects again that critical language is being judged against other models. To use language which is frequently metaphorical might be strange for some *other* purpose or from the standpoint of doing something else, but for the purpose and from the standpoint of making aesthetic observations it is not. To say it is an unnatural use of language for doing *this* is to imply there is or could be for this purpose some other and "natural" use. But these *are* natural ways of talking about aesthetic matters.

To help understand what the critic does, then, how he supports his judgments and gets his audience to see what he sees, I shall attempt a brief description of the methods we use as critics.[17]

(1) We may simply mention or point out non-aesthetic features: "Notice these flecks of colour, that dark mass there, those lines." By merely drawing attention to those easily discernible features which make the painting luminous or warm or dynamic, we often succeed in bringing someone to see these aesthetic qualities. We get him to see B by mentioning something different, A. Sometimes in doing this we are drawing

---

[17]Holloway, op. cit., pp. 173–4, lists some of these very briefly.

attention to features which may have gone unnoticed by an untrained or insufficiently attentive eye or ear: "Just listen for the repeated figure in the left hand," "Did you notice the figure of Icarus in the Breughel? It is very small." Sometimes they are features which have been seen or heard but of which the significance or purpose has been missed in any of a variety of ways: "Notice how much darker he has made the central figure, how much brighter these colours are than the adjacent ones," "Of course, you've observed the ploughman in the foreground; but had you considered how he, like everyone else in the picture, is going about his business without noticing the fall of Icarus?" In mentioning features which may be discerned by anyone with normal eyes, ears, and intelligence, we are singling out what may serve as a kind of key to grasping or seeing something else (and the key may not be the same for each person).

(2) On the other hand we often simply mention the very qualities we want people to see. We point to a painting and say, "Notice how nervous and delicate the drawing is," or "See what energy and vitality it has." The use of the aesthetic term itself may do the trick; we say what the quality or character is, and people who had not seen it before see it.

(3) Most often, there is a linking of remarks about aesthetic and non-aesthetic features: "Have you noticed this line and that, and the points of bright colour here and there . . . don't they give it vitality, energy?"

(4) We do, in addition, often make extensive and helpful use of similes and genuine metaphors: "It's as if there are small points of light burning," "as though he had thrown on the paint violently and in anger," "the light shimmers, the lines dance, everything is air, lightness and gaiety," "his canvasses are fires, they crackle, burn, and blaze, even at their most subdued always restlessly flickering, but often bursting into flame, great pyrotechnic displays," and so on.

(5) We make use of contrasts, comparisons, and reminiscences: "Suppose he had made that a lighter yellow, moved it to the right, how flat it would have been," "Don't you think it has something of the quality of a Rembrandt?," "Hasn't it the same serenity, peace, and quality of light of those summer evenings in Norfolk?" We use what keys we have to the known sensitivity, susceptibilities, and experience of our audience.

Critics and commentators may range, in their methods, from one extreme to the other, from painstaking concentration on points of detail, line and colour, vowels and rhymes, to more or less flowery and luxuriant metaphor. Even the enthusiastic biographical sketch decorated with suitable epithet and metaphor may serve. What is best depends on both the audience and the work under discussion. But this would not be a complete sketch unless certain other notes were added.

(6) Repetition and reiteration often play an important role. When we are in front of a canvas we may come back time and again to the same points, drawing attention to the same lines and shapes, repeating the same words, "swirling," "balance," "luminosity," or the same similes and metaphors, as if time and familiarity, looking harder, listening more carefully, paying closer attention may help. So again with variation; it often helps to talk round what we have said, to build up, supplement with more talk *of the same kind*. When someone misses the swirling quality, when one epithet or one metaphor does not work, we throw in related ones; we speak of its wild movement, how it twists

and turns, writhes and whirls, as though, failing to score a direct hit, we may succeed with a barrage of near-synonyms.

(7) Finally, besides our verbal performances, the rest of our behaviour is important. We accompany our talk with appropriate tones of voice, expression, nods, looks, and gesture. A critic may sometimes do more with a sweep of the arm than by talking. An appropriate gesture may make us see the violence in a painting or the character of a melodic line.

These ways of acting and talking are not significantly different whether we are dealing with a particular work, paragraph, or line, or speaking of an artist's work as a whole, or even drawing attention to a sunset or scenery. But even with the speaker doing all this, we may fail to see what he sees. There may be a point, though there need be no limit except that imposed by time and patience, at which he gives up and sets us (or himself) down as lacking in some way, defective in sensitivity. He may tell us to look or read again, or to read or look at other things and then come back again to this; he may suspect there are experiences in life we have missed. But these are the things he does. This is what succeeds if anything does; indeed it is all that can be done.

But realizing clearly that, whether we are dealing with art or scenery or people or natural objects, this is how we operate with aesthetic concepts, we may recognize this sphere of human activity for what it is. We operate with different kinds of concepts in different ways. If we want someone to agree that a colour is red we may take it into a good light and ask him to look; if it is viridian we may fetch a colour chart and make him compare; if we want him to agree that a figure is fourteen-sided we get him to count; and to bring him to agree that something is dilapidated or that someone is lazy we may do other things, citing features and reasoning and arguing about them. These are the methods appropriate to these various concepts. But the ways we get someone to see aesthetic qualities are different; they are of the kind I have described. With each kind of concept we can describe what we do and how we do it. But the methods suited to these other concepts will not do for aesthetic ones, or vice versa. We cannot prove by argument or by assembling a sufficiency of conditions that something is graceful; but this is no more puzzling than our inability to prove, by using the methods, metaphors, and gestures of the art critic, that it will be mate in ten moves. The questions raised admit of no answer beyond the sort of description I have given. To go on to ask, with puzzlement, how it is that *when* we do these things people come to see, is like asking how is it that, when we take the book into a good light, our companion agrees with us that it is red. There is no place for this kind of question or puzzlement. Aesthetic concepts are as natural, as little esoteric, as any others. It is against the background of different and philosophically more familiar models that they seem puzzling.

I have described how people justify aesthetic judgments and bring others to see aesthetic qualities in things. I shall end by showing that the methods I have outlined are the ones natural for and characteristic of taste concepts from the start. When someone tries to make me see that a painting is delicate or balanced, I have some understanding of these terms already and know in a sense what I am looking for. But if there is puzzlement over how, by talking, he can bring me to see these qualities in this picture, there should be equal puzzlement over how I learned to use aesthetic terms and discern aesthetic qualities in the first place. We may ask, therefore, how we learn to do these things; and this is to inquire (1) what natural potentialities and tendencies people have and (2) how we develop and take advantage of these capacities in training and teaching. Now for the second of these there is no doubt that our ability to notice and respond to aesthetic qualities is cultivated and developed by our contacts with parents and teachers from quite an early age. What is interesting for my present purpose is that, while we are being taught in the presence of examples what grace, delicacy and so on are, the methods used, the language and behaviour, are of a piece with those of the critic as I have already described them.

To pursue these two questions, consider first those words like "dynamic," "melancholy," "balanced," "taut," or "gay" the aesthetic use of which is quasi-metaphorical. It has already been emphasized that we could not use them thus without some experience of situations where they are used literally. The present inquiry is how we shift from literal to aesthetic uses of them. For this it is required that there be certain abilities and tendencies to link experiences, to regard certain things as similar, and to see, explore, and be interested in these similarities. It is a feature of human intelligence and sensitivity that we do spontaneously do these things and that the tendency can be encouraged and developed. It is no more baffling that we should employ aesthetic terms of this sort than that we should make metaphors at all. Easy and smooth transitions by which we shift to the use of these aesthetic terms are not hard to find. We suggest to children that simple pieces of music are hurrying or running or skipping or dawdling, from there we move to lively, gay, jolly, happy, smiling, or sad, and, as their experiences and vocabulary broaden, to solemn, dynamic, or melancholy. But the child also discovers for himself many of these parallels and takes interest or delight in them. He is likely on his own to skip, march, clap, or laugh with the music, and without this natural tendency our training would get nowhere. In so far, however, as we do take advantage of this tendency and help him by training, *we do just what the critic does*. We may merely need to persuade the child to pay attention, to look or listen; or we may simply *call* the music jolly. But we are also likely to use, as the critic does, reiteration, synonyms, parallels, contrasts, similes, metaphors, gestures, and other expressive behavior.

Of course the recognition of similarities and simple metaphorical extensions are not the only transitions to the aesthetic use of language. Others are made in different ways; for instance, by the kind of peripheral cases I mentioned earlier. When our admiration is for something as simple as the thinness of a glass or the smoothness of a fabric, it is not difficult to call attention to such things, evoke a similar delight, and introduce suitable aesthetic terms. These transitions are only the beginnings; it may often be questionable whether a term is yet being used aesthetically or not. Many of the terms I have mentioned may be used in ways which are not straightforwardly literal but of which we should hesitate to say that they demanded much yet by way of aesthetic sensitivity. We speak of warm and cool colours, and we may say of a brightly coloured picture that at least it is gay and lively. When we have brought someone to make this sort of metaphorical extension of terms, he has made one of the transitional steps from which he may move on to uses which more obviously deserve to be called aesthetic and demand a more obviously aesthetic appreciation. When I said at the outset that aesthetic sensitivity was rarer than some other natural endowments, I was not denying that it varies in degree from the rudimentary to the refined. Most people learn easily to make the kinds of remarks I am now considering. But when someone can call bright canvasses gay and lively without being able to spot the one which is really vibrant, or can recognize the obvious outward vigor and energy of a student composition played *con fuoco* while failing to see that it lacks inner fire and drive, we do not regard his aesthetic sensitivity in these areas as particularly developed. However, once these transitions from common to aesthetic uses are begun in the more obvious cases, the domain of aesthetic concepts may broaden out, and they become more subtle and even partly autonomous. The initial steps, however varied the metaphorical shifts and however varied the experiences upon which they are parasitic, are natural and easy.

Much the same is true when we turn to those words which have no standard non-aesthetic use, "lovely," "pretty," "dainty," "graceful," "elegant." We cannot say that these are learned by a metaphorical shift. But they still are linked to non-aesthetic features in many ways and the learning of them also is made possible by certain kinds of natural response, reaction, and ability. We learn them not so much by noticing similarities, but by our attention being caught and focused in other ways. Certain phenomena which are outstanding or remarkable or unusual catch the eye or ear, seize our attention and interest, and move us to surprise, admiration, delight, fear, or distaste. Children begin by reacting in these ways to spectacular sunsets, woods in autumn, roses, dandelions, and other striking and colourful objects, and it is in these circumstances that we find ourselves introducing general aesthetic words to them, like "lovely," "pretty," and "ugly." It is not an accident that the first lessons in aesthetic appreciation consist in drawing the child's attention to roses rather than to grass; nor is it surprising that we remark to him on the autumn colour rather than on the subdued tints of winter. We all of us, not only children, pay aesthetic attention more readily to such outstanding and easily noticeable things. We notice with pleasure early spring grass or the first snow, hills of notably marked and varied contours, scenery flecked with a great variety of colour or dappled variously with sun and shadow. We are struck and impressed by great size or mass, as with mountains or cathedrals. We are similarly responsive to unusual precision or minuteness or remarkable feats of skill, as with complex and elaborate filigree, or intricate wood carving and fan-vaulting. It is at these times, taking advantage of these natural interests and admirations, that we first teach the simpler aesthetic words. People of moderate aesthetic sensitivity and sophistication continue to exhibit aesthetic interest mainly on such occasions and to use only the more general words ("pretty," "lovely," and the like). But these situations may serve as a beginning from which we extend our aesthetic interests to wider and less obvious fields, mastering as we go the more subtle and specific vocabulary of taste. The principles do not change; the basis for learning more specific terms like "graceful," "delicate," and "elegant" is also our interest in and admiration for various non-aesthetic natural properties ("She seems to move *effortlessly*, as if floating," "So very *thin* and *fragile*, as if a breeze might destroy it," "So *small* and yet so *intricate*," "So *economical* and perfectly *adapted*").[18] And even with these aesthetic terms which are not metaphorical

[18]It is worth noticing that most of the words which in current usage are primarily or exclusively aesthetic terms had earlier non-aesthetic uses and gained their present use by some kind of metaphorical shift. Without reposing too great weight on these etymological facts, it can be seen that their history reflects connections with the responses, interests, and natural features I have mentioned as underlying the learning and use of aesthetic terms. These transitions suggest both the dependence of aesthetic upon other interests, and what some of these interests are. Connected with liking, delight, affection, regard, estimation, or choice—*beautiful, graceful, delicate, lovely, exquisite, elegant, dainty*; with fear or repulsion—*ugly*; with what notably catches the eye or attention—*garish, splendid, gaudy*; with what attracts by notable rarity, precision, skill, ingenuity, elaboration—*dainty, nice, pretty, exquisite*; with adaptation to function, suitability to ease of handling—*handsome*.

themselves ("graceful," "delicate," "elegant"), we rely in the same way upon the critic's methods, including comparison, illustration, and metaphor, to teach or make clear what they mean.

I have wished to emphasize in the latter part of this paper the natural basis of responses of various kinds without which aesthetic terms could not be learned. I have also outlined what some of the features are to which we naturally respond: similarities of various sorts, notable colours, shapes, scents, size, intricacy, and much else besides. Even the non-metaphorical aesthetic terms have significant links with all kinds of natural features by which our interest, wonder, admiration, delight, or distaste is aroused. But in particular I have wanted to urge that it should not strike us as puzzling that the critic supports his judgment and brings us to see aesthetic qualities by pointing out key features and talking about them in the way he does. It is by the very same methods that people helped us develop our aesthetic sense and master its vocabulary from the beginning. If we responded to those methods then, it is not surprising that we respond to the critic's discourse now. It would be surprising if, by using this language and behavior, people could *not* sometimes bring us to see the aesthetic qualities of things; for this would prove us lacking in one characteristically human kind of awareness and activity.

Ted Cohen

A CRITIQUE OF SIBLEY'S POSITION: AESTHETICS/NON-AESTHETICS AND THE CONCEPT OF TASTE

Outline of Sibley's Theory[1]

Abstracting and condensing, to isolate the themes I will be examining, I take Sibley to be making three moves (though, as shall be seen, Sibley does not think of the first as a *move*): (1) invoking an aesthetic/non-aesthetic distinction, (2) asking whether the items thus distinguished are related in certain specific ways, (3) answering that they are not so related. In more detail—(1) The distinction works on many levels, applying at least to qualities, descriptions, judgments, terms, and concepts. Which level Sibley takes as basic or independent is unclear, in spite of the ostensible concern with concepts. (The paper is called "Aesthetic Concepts.") The most natural account I can give of the distinction, consistent with Sibley's intentions but coherent, is this.

An aesthetic quality (or feature) is one which is noted in an aesthetic judgment (or description or remark). An aesthetic judgment is a judgment in which an aesthetic concept is used. An aesthetic concept is a concept whose related term—the term used when one applies the concept—is an aesthetic term. An aesthetic term is one whose use (perhaps correct use) requires the possession of taste. Taste is perceptiveness, sensitivity, aesthetic discrimination, aesthetic appreciation. Sibley says that it is "an ability to *notice* or *see* or *tell* that things have certain qualities" (AC, p. 65). Finally, a quality, judgment, concept, or term is non-aesthetic if and only if it is not an aesthetic one.

That Sibley intends something like this quasi-formal apparatus is clear from the opening passages of "Aesthetic Concepts."

Ted Cohen, "Aesthetics/Non-Aesthetics and the Concept of Taste," from Theoria 39 *(1973):113–152. Reprinted by permission of* Theoria: A Swedish Journal of Philosophy. *This article has been abridged extensively by the author for the second edition of this volume.*

[1]As presented in "Aesthetic Concepts," *Philosophical Review*, Vol. 68, No. 4 (October, 1959); "Aesthetic Concepts: A Rejoinder," ibid., Vol. 72, No. 1 (January, 1963); "Aesthetic and Nonaesthetic," ibid., Vol. 74, No. 2 (April, 1965). Hereafter, to facilitate brief references in the body of the text, these will be referred to by "AC," "ACR," and "AN," respectively.

Shortly after its initial appearance AC was reprinted with the author's "extensive minor revisions" in *Philosophy Looks at the Arts*, edited by Joseph Margolis (New York: Scribner's, 1962). References to AC will cite pages in the Margolis volume, references to ACR and AN will be to the *Philosophical Review*.

The remarks we make about works of art are of many kinds. . . . We say that a novel has a
great number of characters and deals with life in a manufacturing town; that a painting uses
pale colors, predominantly blues and greens, and has kneeling figures in the foreground; that
the theme in a fugue is inverted at such a point and that there is a stretto at the close; that the
action of a play takes place in the span of one day and that there is a reconciliation scene in the
fifth act. Such remarks may be made by, and such features pointed out to, anyone with
normal eyes, ears, and intelligence. On the other hand, we also say that a poem is tightly-knit
or deeply moving; that a picture lacks balance, or has a certain serenity and repose, or that the
grouping of the figures sets up an exciting tension; that the characters in a novel never really
come to life, or that a certain episode strikes a false note. It would be natural enough to say
that the making of such judgments as these requires the exercise of taste, perceptiveness, or
sensitivity, of aesthetic discrimination or appreciation; one would not say this of my first
group. Accordingly, when a word or expression is such that taste or perceptiveness is required
in order to apply it, I shall call it an *aesthetic* term or expression, and I shall, correspondingly,
speak of *aesthetic* concepts or *taste* concepts. (AC, pp. 63–64)

Still, my technical-looking rectified version of Sibley's aesthetic/non-aesthetic distinction requires considerable justification, for there is no way to take it straightforwardly
from his text. Most controversial points are non-exegetical, I think, since around them
turn various possible defences of Sibley against my criticisms. So, I shall not deal with
them until they arise in the course of the argument. There are, however, two points to
be mentioned immediately.

(i) The quotation seems to show clearly that the fundamental distinction is between
concepts, or at least that concepts are as basic as terms for Sibley, while in my version
concepts are ultimately supplanted by terms. I reserve discussion of this until later,
when I hope to show that it is a critical matter. Here I simply point out that Sibley is
unclear about the relation of terms to concepts as well as about what either a term or a
concept is. In a later paper, Sibley alludes to the passages from which the above
quotation came, saying, "the distinction I set out to make in the introductory section
was between *terms* or *expressions* of two kinds" (ACR, p. 80).

(ii) Whatever the relation of terms to concepts, it seems a mistake to say for Sibley
that every aesthetic judgment contains an aesthetic term—as I do. In ACR, which is
addressed to H. R. G. Schwyzer,[2] Sibley complains of just this misinterpretation.

Nothing I said, that is, implied the doctrine Schwyzer attributes to me, that "an aesthetic
remark always involves the use of an aesthetic term." Indeed, not only did I suppose it obvious
that, as he says, "the class of remarks *the making of which* requires perceptiveness is different
from, indeed far larger than, the class of remarks that contain *words and expressions whose
application* requires perceptiveness"; I said so myself at the end of Part I where I pointed out
that I had not been discussing "aesthetic or taste judgments in general" but only "the more
restricted range of judgments which employ aesthetic terms." (ACR, p. 40)

In the context of this essay my recasting of the distinction is immune to this complaint.
It is with regard only to aesthetic judgments which do contain aesthetic terms that
Sibley takes a stand, and it is only as such that I will claim that his argument is
defective. However, more generally, Sibley and Schwyzer seem to me much too quick
to recognize aesthetic judgments which contain no aesthetic terms. They have in mind
remarks like "how very gradually the stem curves" and "it is a big picture." It is simple

[2]H. R. G. Schwyzer, "Sibley's 'Aesthetic Concepts,' " *Philosophical Review*, Vol. 72, No. 1 (January,
1963).

to imagine circumstances in which sensitivity and pedagogical insight are behind these remarks, and yet none of the constituent words seem to require for their successful use what Sibley calls taste. But this is not so clear. I shall be arguing that Sibley has no convincing reason for refusing to call these words aesthetic terms. Until that argument appears, perhaps this will suffice to preserve my rendering of Sibley's distinction; although Sibley (and Schwyzer) seem to use "term" as roughly interchangeable with "word" (or "words"), I am using it in the sense of "open sentence."[3] Thus in any remark of the form "x is F," "is F" is a *term*. This being so, it seems clear that a remark is aesthetic only if its term is aesthetic. When this construction becomes contentious I will return to it. So long as attention is confined to those judgments which, according to Sibley, are aesthetic *and* contain aesthetic terms, his terms and my terms (roughly) coincide.

(2) About aesthetic terms Sibley says "I am interested in what they all have in common" (AC, p. 64).

(3) Eleven pages later he announces that he has found it: "I have now argued that in certain ways aesthetic concepts are not and cannot be condition- or rule-governed" (AC, p. 75). (This means that the applicability of an aesthetic concept cannot be inferred, in any of a variety of standard ways, from the applicability of any number of non-aesthetic concepts.)

It should be clear that Sibley's work fits the conception and appproach sketched earlier. In his view aesthetic judgments do have truth-values. They are in the ordinary sense, descriptions; their characteristic terms—aesthetic terms—apply to certain properties—aesthetic properties. Since the presence of a particular aesthetic property is never guaranteed by the presence of any given non-aesthetic properties, it follows that neither the applicability of an aesthetic term nor the truth of an aesthetic judgment (which on my view of "term" comes to the same thing) can be inferred from the applicability of non-aesthetic terms. Only taste will suffice in making aesthetic judgments.

Seen in terms of the sketch Sibley looks like an intuitionist or non-naturalist, if one imports the all too handy categories of meta-meta-ethics, as has been noted by various readers.[4] However his characterization of aesthetic judgments and, correlatively, his conception of "taste" make Sibley's view untypical. He treats aesthetic judgments explicitly without regard to their connection with value or praise. He says,

> About a third and much-discussed class of judgments, however, I have nothing to say in this paper. These are the purely evaluative judgments: whether things are aesthetically good or bad, excellent or mediocre, superior to others or inferior, and so on. Such judgments I shall call *verdicts*. Nor shall I raise any other questions about evaluation: about how verdicts are made or supported, or whether the judgments I am dealing with carry evaluative implications. (AN, p. 136)

Then this is not so much like ethical intuitionists' discussions of "good" and "right," nor is it obviously commensurate with Hume's naturalistic account of beauty so that it

---

[3]For an account of this use see Willard Van Orman Quine, *Methods of Logic* (New York: Holt, Rinehart and Winston, 1950—revised edition, 1956), sections 12 and 17, especially pp. 64 and 89 ff.

[4]For instance, R. David Broiles in "Frank Sibley's 'Aesthetic Concepts,'" *Journal of Aesthetics and Art Criticism*, Vol. 23, No. 2 (Winter, 1964), and Peter Kivy in "Aesthetic Aspects and Aesthetic Qualities," *Journal of Philosophy*, Vol. 65, No. 4 (February 22, 1968).

might be taken as a straightforward alternative. I will return to this at the end of the essay.

Criticism of Sibley's Argument

Sibley's conclusion is that there are and can be no necessary, sufficient or defeasible non-aesthetic conditions for the use of an aesthetic term. He offers a number of observations in support of this, but until just before the conclusion is announced he presents no *argument*. In fact he says, "My arguments and illustrations so far have been rather simply schematic" (AC, p. 71). And so they have, in general coming to statements like these—

> There is little temptation to suppose that aesthetic terms resemble words which, like "square," are applied in accordance with a set of necessary and sufficient conditions. For whereas each square is square in virtue of the *same* set of conditions, four equal sides and four right angles, aesthetic terms apply to widely varied objects; one thing is graceful because of these features, another because of those, and so on almost endlessly. (AC, p. 66)

> There are no sufficient conditions, no non-aesthetic features such that the presence of some set of numbers of them will beyond question logically justify or warrant the application of an aesthetic term. It is impossible (barring certain limited exceptions, . . .) to make any statements corresponding to those we can make for condition-governed words. We are able to say "If it is true he can do this, and that, and the other, then one just cannot deny that he is intelligent," or "if he does A, B, and C, I don't see how it can be denied that he is lazy," but we cannot make *any* general statement of the form "If the vase is pale pink, somewhat curving, lightly mottled, and so forth, it will be delicate, cannot but be delicate." (AC, pp. 67–68)

> Although there is this sense in which slimness, lightness, lack of intensity of color, and so on, count only towards, not against, delicacy, these features, I shall say, at best count only *typically* or *characteristically* towards delicacy; they do not count towards in the same sense as condition-features count toward laziness or intelligence; that is, no group of them is even logically sufficient. (AC, p. 69)

> The very notion of a defeasible concept seems to require that some group of features *would* be sufficient *in certain circumstances*, that is, in the absence of overriding or voiding features. In a certain way defeasible concepts lack sufficient conditions then, but they are still, in the sense described, condition-governed. My claim about taste concepts is stronger; that they are not, except negatively, governed by conditions at all. We could not conclude even in certain circumstances, e.g., if we were told of the absence of all "voiding" or uncharacteristic features (no angularities and the like), that an object *must* certainly be graceful, no matter how fully it was described to us as possessing features characteristic of gracefulness. (AC, p. 71)

The obvious way to quarrel with these remarks is to produce a counter-example. I have none. Indeed I do not say that they are wrong (though I expect to show that they are vacuous). I note only that they are, as Sibley says, simply schematic, and pass on to what seems to me Sibley's only real argument. Perhaps Sibley does not regard this as an argument at all; he calls it a reinforcement of his argument. However, I believe it schematizes all the argument Sibley has, and it will do to show that there is no arguing, only a kind of running in place.

The point I have argued may be reinforced in the following way. A man who failed to realize the nature of aesthetic concepts, or someone who, knowing he lacked sensitivity in aesthetic matters, did not want to reveal this lack might by assiduous application and shrewd observation provide himself with some rules and generalizations; and by inductive procedures and intelligent guessing, he might frequently say the right things. But he could have no great confidence or certainty; a slight change in an object might at any time unpredictably ruin his calculations, and he might as easily have been wrong as right. No matter how careful he has been about working out a set of consistent principles and conditions, he is only in a position to think that the object is very possibly delicate. . . . Though he sometimes says the right thing, he has not seen, but guessed, that the object is delicate. (AC, pp. 72–73)

Again, I do not say that Sibley is wrong, but that he has said nothing (new). To show this concisely it will help to use some symbols.

Let "E" be an aesthetic term naming the aesthetic quality E-ness.

Let "N_1," "N_2," . . . , and "N_n" be non-aesthetic terms naming the non-aesthetic qualities N_1-ness, N_2-ness, . . . , and N_n-ness.

There are four distinct relations to consider.

(1) "E" means (or means the same as) "N_1 and N_2 and . . . and N_n."

(2) The meaning of "E" is carried in (or is contained in) the meaning of "N_1 and N_2 and . . . and N_n."

I do not claim to have an account of "meaning," "containment of meaning," etc., nor that there is an account. It will be clear that this is not an important matter.

(3) $(x) (Ex \equiv. N_1 \& N_2 \& \ldots \& N_n)$. (Things are E if and only if they are N_1 and N_2 and . . . N_n.)

(4) $(x) (N_1 \& N_2 \& \ldots \& N_n \supset E)$. (Anything which is $N_1 \& N_2 \& \ldots \& N_n$ is also E.)

With this in hand, let us argue.

Since taste is required to detect E-ness but not to detect any of N_1-ness, . . . , N_n-ness—(for that is exactly the difference between aesthetic and non-aesthetic terms)—it follows immediately that,

From the fact that someone can apply all of "N_1," . . . , "N_n" we cannot infer that he can detect E-ness.

That seems to be Sibley's point. But he must intend more, because it remains possible that,

From the fact that "N_1," . . . , "N_n" apply we can infer that "E" applies.

Why? Because it may happen that E-ness always accompanies the joint presence of N_1-ness and . . . and N_n-ness. That is, it may be that (4) or even (3) is true and is known to be true. It is senseless to suppose that (1) or (2) be true but not be known to be true, and perhaps both (1) and (2) must be false, as Sibley would have it. But the truth of (4), or even of (3), requires the truth of neither (1) or (2). Then Sibley's argument is inadequate.

The point is simple, but perhaps too simple to be appreciated easily, for it is startling to find it undercutting Sibley's argument. An illustration of the point in a parallel example is helpful.

Suppose that all cylindrical objects are red, that Smith knows this, and that Smith is blind. Now Smith can tell that something is red even though Smith can't detect redness and even though "red" and "cylindrical" are unconnected in meaning. Sibley's position is that of citing the existence of Smith as a proof, or a reinforcement of a proof, that not all cylinders are red. That is, Smith "has not seen" that the object is red. But what point could this reinforce?—beyond the claim that Smith is blind?[5]

One might feel like saying that after all Smith only guesses or predicts that a given cylinder is red because in fact it might not be red. Then suppose that cylinders have to be red, that it is a law of nature that cylinders are red. This puts it in order, I suppose, to aver that if such were the case, "cylindrical" and "red" might not be altogether unconnected in meaning. No matter: the point remains that the existence, or imaginability, of a blind man is not—as things stand—proof that some cylinders are not red.

Another possible rejoinder is that Smith can't fit the description, can't tell that something is red, because being blind Smith can't know the meaning of "red." Whether or not there is any reason to believe that "acquaintance" with something is a necessary condition of knowing the meaning of a term which applies to that thing, the point can be made irrelevant. Amend the example so that Smith occasionally has seen, and seen red things, but in this case doesn't see that the object is red. (This could be because Smith has only recently gone blind, or perhaps he is not blind but the object is poorly lit or too far away.) Then why deny that Smith can tell that "red" applies though he does not detect (see) any redness?

Sibley can be rescued—and I should like him to be rescued—in this way. Let "apply E" and "detect E-ness" be interchangeable. This will make it true that,

> From the fact that "N_1," . . . , "N_n" apply, it does not follow that "E" applies.

This is Sibley's conclusion: "E" is not condition-governed. But the maneuver which gets there, construing being able to apply "E" as being able to detect E-ness, is of no help to Sibley, for it leaves us with this:

> To apply an aesthetic term is to detect an aesthetic quality; it takes taste to do this.
>   To apply a non-aesthetic term does not require taste, only normality (whether or not one must detect N_1-ness in order to apply "N_1").

Now we can say that being able to apply non-aesthetic terms never guarantees that one can apply aesthetic terms; but we can say this because—and only because,

> From the fact that one is normal it does not follow that one has taste.

Or, to be more exact,

> From the fact that one is exercising one's normal capacities it does not follow that one is exercising taste.

This is an unhappy but telling form for Sibley's conclusion, for it is nothing but the aesthetic/non-aesthetic distinction itself. If there were no difference between exercising one's taste and exercising one's (merely) normal capacities, there would have been no difference between aesthetic and non-aesthetic terms.

This argument against Sibley is oblique and it may be misleading. I must not be taken to be advancing "naturalism" as against Sibley's "intuitionism." I have not shown

---

[5]This parallel illustration is hard to keep a grip on. Perhaps it is of help to have the analogy laid out. Being blind: Being without taste; "Red": An aesthetic term; "Cylindrical": A non-aesthetic term.

that Sibley is wrong in denying that aesthetic judgments can be inferred from non-aesthetic ones, if this would be to show that they can be inferred. One may conceive all these petrified views—naturalism, property-intuitionism, rule-intuitionism, etc.—as answers to one question: How, if at all, are aesthetic and non-aesthetic judgments, concepts, or terms related to one another? What I wish to do, if not to bury this question, is at least to divest it of its innocence. To this end I have now made clear that whatever Sibley has *shown* was shown in the drawing of the aesthetic/non-aesthetic distinction and only reflected in the putative argument following the appearance of the distinction.

Criticism of Sibley's Distinction

To rehearse: Suppose in discussing a painting someone refers to one of its lines, saying "That line is curved," and later adds "That line is graceful." The latter is an aesthetic judgment, the former is not. Why? Because only the latter (or its making) is the application of an aesthetic concept, the use of an aesthetic term. How does one tell? By noting that "graceful" is an aesthetic term while "curved" is not. Which is to say that taste is required to apply "graceful" but no more than normal eyes and intelligence is required to apply "curved."

That is the aesthetic/non-aesthetic distinction at work, identifying judgments like "That is graceful" and thereby sorting out what Sibley calls the "subject matter" of aesthetics (AN, p. 135). It is not itself part of aesthetics, on Sibley's view; rather, drawing it is a precondition of beginning aesthetics. If the preceding section of this essay succeeded, then what Sibley does after invoking the distinction is ignorable: the distinction itself is all the philosophy Sibley has and it is the ultimate cause of whatever uneasiness one feels with Sibley's position. How does one "attack" this distinction (or any other)? Only, I think, by showing that it does nothing—in particular, that it does not do what is demanded of it in its context.

One thing the distinction should do (according to my rectified version of it) is to identify a given judgment as aesthetic or non-aesthetic by discerning the presence or absence of aesthetic terms. I think the distinction fails to do this, or even to begin to do this, for there seems to me no sensible and important way of dividing terms according to whether taste or only normality is needed to apply them. (One may think that "sense" and "importance" are not definite enough notions to underwrite a critique. I had thought of supplanting them with the technical notion of an effective procedure, and then criticizing Sibley for supplying nothing remotely like even a quasi-mechanical routine. But this would be a mistake. Sibley is altogether unspecific about the nature of the distinction and its application. My leaving the terms of appraisal vague seems fairer and more generous to Sibley, and it allows me to encompass some efforts to rescue the distinction. And finally, it is the burden of this essay to persuade you that Sibley's distinction has become far too prominent and that its sense (and sensibility have been too readily acknowledged.)

With regard to the application of the distinction Sibley acknowledges "the expected debatable, ambiguous, or borderline cases" (AN, p. 135). But I cannot see that he has any clearcut cases. Take "graceful," to start, which is one of the words which, according to Sibley, "whether in artistic or daily discourse, function only or predominantly as aesthetic terms" (AC, p. 64). Suppose I show this figure and ask which is the graceful line, or whether any is a graceful line. No doubt you have taste, but do you need it? Virtual insensitivity will do, I think, to manage "(c) is the graceful one" or "(c) is graceful" or "(c) is more graceful than (a) or (b)."

(a)   (b)   (c)

If you are unsatisfied with my figure you must make your own. Keep in mind that the aim is not to make (c) better than the others, nor is it to make (c) more likeable. Good and bad, and likes and dislikes have nothing to do with the conception of taste as used in drawing the distinction. Taste is more than normal ability to notice or detect things. Taste is required to notice gracefulness (and so to use the aesthetic term "graceful"). I ask you to produce an example in which "(c) is graceful" is accessible upon a merely normal view. This may seem to beg the question against Sibley but I think it does not. It is to take the question seriously, disingenuously, pre-theoretically: is it always the case with "graceful" that taste is needed to apply it? I say no.

Sibley would say, perhaps, that in such an example "(c) is graceful" is not an aesthetic judgment. Then what about "graceful"? There are answers at Sibley's disposal. One, which seems to me painfully clumsy, is that "graceful" is a term associated with (at least) two concepts, the aesthetic concept *graceful*$_a$ and the non-aesthetic concept *graceful*$_n$. Sibley says that, given the definition of "aesthetic term" he "shall, correspondingly, speak of *aesthetic* concepts" (AC, p. 64). About the correspondence between terms and concepts Sibley says nothing; perhaps he would say that "graceful" can correspond to either of (at least) two concepts. Then he could hold that "(c) is graceful" is a non-aesthetic judgment with "graceful" a non-aesthetic term being used to apply the non-aesthetic concept *graceful*$_n$.

To this one may object that it renders the distinction inoperative. It is no longer possible to identify aesthetic judgments by noting the presence of aesthetic terms, for there is no way of noting aesthetic terms by inspection. I prefer to object that no legitimate reason has been given for claiming that "graceful" has two concepts or senses. What motivation is there for multiplying the sense of "graceful" beyond a desire to preserve the aesthetic/non-aesthetic distinction? I am not raising those involuted questions about meaning which require technical accounts of polysemy backed by a "theory of meaning." What is wanted (and, I think, is lacking) is an informal rationale for identifying extra concepts for "graceful." What *reason* is there for distinguishing *graceful*$_a$ and *graceful*$_n$? They are distinguished so far, in this hypothetical response on Sibley's behalf, by the fact that only one of them requires taste for its application. Is that sufficient? Shall we say that whenever an otherwise ordinary term is used in a context in which more than normal competence is needed to handle the term, the term has changed its meaning or been affixed to a different concept? Although I think the general answer to this question is clear, it is a vexed question even when taken informally. Since it will recur in this essay, it may be helpful to take time now to consider a battery of illustrations.

First, consider some terms which can be managed readily on the strength of normal intelligence, eyes, etc., but whose use on occasion signals more than mere normality. (I shall be claiming that this description fits virtually all of Sibley's aesthetic terms.)

The terms applying to a variety of racial, geographical, and sexual groups of people are common, and are learned and used by everyone. Some observers, however, are much more accurate than others at recognizing members of these groups. They can tell on sight, by attending to people's size, shape, posture, gestures, gait, etc., Jews, Northern Europeans, homosexuals, New Yorkers, etc. Phonetic descriptions are a special case. Some professional linguists and many amateurs with good ears can identify East Texans, Canadians, native Bavarians, etc., by hearing them speak English.

Another auditory case is pitch, in music. Regardless of what minimal ability one supposes could be cultivated in any normal person, beyond that there are differences in abilities to "hear" absolute and relative pitch, to identify pitches in chord constructions, etc.

Handwriting identification is, visually, a partial analogue. A handwriting expert can identify signatures and match writing samples with far more facility than those with no more than normal intelligence and eyes.

It is helpful to consider some terms all of whose uses are relatively esoteric. Some examples are medical terms applied to patients after examination, i.e. the names of diseases, syndromes, "conditions," etc. A few doctors, the best internists, are much better than their colleagues at detecting, say, diabetes, and hypoglycemia. From external examinations they obtain results nearly as accurate as those obtained by lesser diagnosticians aided by laboratory analysis.

The fact that these examples may involve terms which apply to properties which are not purely perceptual is irrelevant. Sibley's examples of aesthetic terms include ones which refer to qualities not literally seen or heard (e.g., "tightly-knit," said of a poem; "has characters who never really come to life," said of a novel). (A relevant passage from Sibley is quoted above, p. 376.)

Also irrelevant, but probably harder to ignore, is the fact that the examples involve terms which, allegedly unlike "graceful," seem clearly to be condition-governed. But being unconditioned is not what makes "graceful" an aesthetic term. Sibley first sorts out aesthetic terms and then argues that these terms are unconditioned. We have seen that the argument goes nowhere beyond the distinction, and we are now back at the beginning, looking into Sibley's way of sorting out aesthetic terms. Taking Sibley literally, "graceful" is an aesthetic term—whether or not it is condition-governed— because taste is needed to apply it. In response to the suggested counter-example ("(c) is graceful") one might look for two concepts to go with "graceful." The budget of cases just gone through is meant to illustrate an implausibility in that response.

The cases mainly concern terms—"Jew," "East Texan," "G-sharp," "written by Lincoln"—whose use frequently requires no special capacity, but whose use in the examples is effected by means of special capacities and talents (something beyond mere normality). The (rhetorical) question is, shall we say that in these examples the terms are being used to apply different concepts?

It may be suggested that the fact that these terms have conditions, perhaps even necessary and sufficient ones, renders the examples defective. The argument would be that each of the terms does have two senses, the proof being that in their ordinary use one applies them with reference to their defining conditions, while this does not happen when they are used by a specialist in difficult cases. This suggestion is mistaken, but it has an interesting twist.

The mistake is, simply, to conflate unreasonably the meaning of a term and the way in which—in some actual case—someone decides whether to apply it. "Square" does not change its meaning when I apply it to a figure without measuring the sides. Surely the brilliant diagnostician and the routine laboratory worker are not using "diabetes" to apply different concepts. Knowing the meaning of a term is not a guarantee of being able to decide whether it correctly applies nor is inability to tell whether a term applies a proof of ignorance of the term's meaning.

However, if the suggestion were acceptable it would have an unwanted effect on Sibley's argument. All aesthetic terms, including "graceful," are non-condition-governed, Sibley argues. Then if alteration in the conditions governing application of a term—in general, or in particular cases—were the sign of a multiplicity of concepts associated with the term, this would be of no help in urging that "graceful" is associated with more than one concept.

I conclude that Sibley has no reason to discount "(c) is graceful" (as a counter-example to "graceful's" being an aesthetic term) by claiming that it is the application of $graceful_n$, for I see no reason to suppose that there is a $graceful_n$ (or a $graceful_a$).

A simpler, more direct response, in Sibley's interest, is that "graceful" is indeed an aesthetic term but that aesthetic terms can appear in non-aesthetic judgments, as, for example, "graceful" appears in "(c) is graceful."

This response obviously ruins the program for identifying aesthetic and non-aesthetic judgments by the presence or absence of aesthetic terms. That is a minor objection. The decisive objection is not that the distinction ceases to function, but that it functions inconsistently. Sibley says that both judgments and terms are to be defined as aesthetic by means of the "Is-taste-required?" test. Since a non-aesthetic judgment can be made without exercising taste, but an aesthetic term cannot be applied without exercising taste, it follows that if "graceful" is an aesthetic term then making the judgment that (c) is graceful both does and does not require taste.

No doubt Sibley would deal with "(c) is graceful" in neither of the ways just discussed, but it is hard to see what response, right or wrong, he would find congenial. His most relevant remark occurs in a footnote. He says,

> I shall speak loosely of an "aesthetic term," even when, because the word sometimes has other uses, it would be more correct to speak of its *use* as an aesthetic term. (AC, p. 64, n. 1)

This suggests that there are times when one might speak of an aesthetic term and not be speaking loosely. This would occur, presumably, when one were speaking of a term whose use invariably requires taste. I doubt that there are any such terms, whatever taste is; and I am fairly certain that there are no such terms when the notion of taste is the one Sibley uses.

Two aspects of the notion of taste are expressly removed from consideration by Sibley (though he does not deny that they would come up in a more complete analysis of taste). The first is taste as it has to do with likes and dislikes, the second is taste as it has to do with good and bad.[6] Taste, as that which is exercised in the use of an aesthetic term, is "an ability to *notice* or *see* or *tell* that things have certain qualities" (AC, p. 65). Whether this constricts or distorts the notion of taste, and how that affects one's notion of the relative complexity of the apprehension of art works, is an implicit theme throughout his essay, and it will become explicit shortly. Here I want only to get clear about what one of Sibley's aesthetic terms would be like if there were one. If there are any, they are terms whose (successful) application invariably requires an "ability to notice" which is something more than the abilities that go with normal intelligence and sense organs. I said that I think there are no such terms. My reason is simply that I seem to be able to find, for any given term (or at least any of the terms Sibley considers), an application of it which could be managed by any normal man. I doubt that this reason will convince you straightway (though I have no idea what other reason could be given). You have to think it over until you agree that something like what I did with "graceful"—or what you did to satisfy yourself about "graceful"—can be done with any term. But what Sibley means by "taste" must be kept in mind or it may not be clear when a "non-aesthetic" use has been found. I believe Sibley himself may have overlooked this.

Sibley says that "lovely," "pretty," "beautiful," "dainty," "graceful," and "elegant" "are certainly not being used metaphorically when employed as aesthetic terms, the very good reason being that this is their primary or only use, some of them having no current non-aesthetic use" (AC, p. 65). That is, at least some of these terms are— *strictly speaking*—aesthetic terms.

We have dealt with "graceful." The others seem no more difficult. Can't you imagine situations in which it would be natural, easy, and obvious to say—"It's a lovely day today"; "This glove is too big; you have a rather dainty hand"; "He's an elegant old gentleman"; "The sun has finally broken through and now the sky is pretty"; "I couldn't see the vessels clearly on the last one, but this earthworm is a beautiful specimen."

Do you insist that taste is required to make these judgments? (In fact, do you feel like calling them aesthetic judgments at all?) Why? Remember that whether the speaker is expressing personal satisfaction or gratification and whether he is evaluating or ranking things are irrelevant. Perhaps in the situation you imagine the speaker of "It's a lovely day" is clearly happy about it and in addition is lauding the climate and ranking this day above others. Those features of the utterance seem to me the only ones which make it even faintly plausible to call it an aesthetic judgment. But those features are irrelevant (as is the fact—if you think it is one—that "lovely" is not condition-governed, that the speaker couldn't *prove* that the day is lovely). From none of these features does it follow that what Sibley calls an aesthetic judgment has been made. The only question is whether *taste* has been exercised, and it needn't have been if normal intelligence and senses are enough. I don't see why they should not be enough.

What difference does this make in the intelligibility of the aesthetic/non-aesthetic distinction? This: if no term invariably requires taste for its application, then what,

---

[6]"When I speak of taste in this paper, I shall not be dealing with questions which center upon expressions like 'a matter of taste' (meaning, roughly, a matter of personal preference or liking)" (AC, p. 65). For his extrusion of questions of evaluation, see his remark quoted above.

after all, is an *aesthetic* term? Is it a term which usually requires taste for its application? Then what of Sibley's formula for speaking correctly (not loosely) of such a term? We are, he says, to speak of a term's *use* as an aesthetic term. That, now, will be to speak of a term's being used as a term which is usually used as an aesthetic term. A minor objection to this version of the distinction is, again, that it will not support the program for identifying aesthetic judgments by picking out aesthetic terms. The major objection this time is not that the distinction functions inconsistently, but that it functions not at all: it will pick out nothing as an aesthetic term.

Before giving up on Sibley's version of the aesthetic/non-aesthetic distinction we must consider two final, meager, efforts to rescue it.

In the footnote quoted from above, Sibley says something which suggests that, speaking more correctly, the aesthetic/non-aesthetic distinction is to be made out with regard, not to terms, but to the "uses" of terms (AC, p. 64, n. 1; quoted above, p. 376). Could we say that on certain occasions the use of (some) terms manifests an exercise of taste, and thereby effect a distinction between aesthetic and non-aesthetic uses? Perhaps—though to what point I don't know, but in any case this subverts Sibley's program. All the talk of terms, judgments, descriptions, remarks, and concepts becomes idle at best. There are no terms which are always used in that way, and, I think, there are none that are never used in that way. Part of the spirit of Schwyzer's objection is right, after all (though he has left himself open to Sibley's rebuttal). He says,

> Sibley's preoccupation with words (both aesthetic and non-aesthetic) and their uses, and the features to which they allegedly "apply," has led him to lose sight of the nature of actual critical utterances.[7]

If we turn from terms to terms-as-they-are-used-in-specific-circumstances, or some such, then can we identify a class of performances, actual utterances, which are exhibitions of taste? If so, then it will be not that "graceful" is an aesthetic term, but that the use of "graceful" upon some occasion is an aesthetic use. There will also be non-aesthetic uses. There is no reason to call these *other* uses in any but a numerical sense. Still, is there now a serviceable aesthetic/non-aesthetic distinction? It will not serve Sibley's purposes, for he wants to isolate and then discuss more abstract things than particular actual uses of terms. And indeed it is only about terms considered generally that his question about conditions is sensible. We can ask, Why does Churchill call Mussolini a utensil? but we can't ask, What are the necessary and sufficient conditions for applying "utensil" to Mussolini as opposed to applying "utensil" in general?

Schwyzer's criticism fails to get deep enough, I think, because in spite of his aversion to classifying words, he is willing to classify, and to accept Sibley's formula for going about it. He agrees, that is, that

> the distinction between aesthetic and non-aesthetic discourse is clearly to be located in the area of what we can and cannot say given normal eyesight, normal hearing, normal intelligence . . .[8]

---

[7]Schwyzer, op. cit., p. 75.
[8]Ibid., p. 75.

Classifying discourse is as problematic as classifying terms. In either case the conception of taste does the work. Whatever defects have been uncovered in Sibley's distinction, it will be good to take up this conception in examining one last possible defense of the distinction.

The "(c) is graceful" judgment and all the others might be met head on: one might insist that "graceful" and the others are aesthetic terms as defined by Sibley, that these judgments are aesthetic judgments and that they can be made by any normal speaker because any normal speaker will have taste enough to do so. Sibley does say that "almost everybody is able to exercise taste to some degree and in some matters" (AC, p. 65).

This reply fails, I think, because it places on Sibley's conception of taste more weight than it can bear. A distinction is now forced between being a merely normal man and exercising one's merely normal capacities. The fact that the most pedestrian observer can manage "(c) is graceful" shows nothing; the question remains, does he in judging that (c) is graceful make use of more than "normal eyes and intelligence"? I do not know what to make of this question. I am prepared to claim (or to repeat) that Sibley has given no reason to suppose that an extra perceptivity is required—or used—in making the judgment. Why suppose that?

Again I point out that the presence or absence of conditions governing this, or any, use of "graceful" is irrelevant. It is especially likely that one will begin to think of the possibility of stating conditions when the issue concerns the relative ease with which terms can be mastered. That is, it is tempting to suppose that some terms are learned and used readily because there are clear (perhaps necessary and sufficient) conditions to be learned; and conversely, that when conditions can be given, the terms are readily mastered. This is probably, in general, an error. Sibley says, "We do not apply simple color words by following rules or in accordance with principles" (AC, p. 77). Surely he is right. Even if such words do have necessary and sufficient conditions, this is not what accounts for the ease with which they are mastered. On the other hand, various esoteric terms like "primitive recursive function," "quadrature of a parabola," and "abelian group" obviously do have necessary and sufficient conditions, having been introduced in terms of such conditions, and yet their fully competent use exceeds the competence of many people. A bothersome point here is that examples of mathematical terms are examples of terms whose necessary and sufficient conditions are themselves stated in mathematical terms, so that inability to master, say, "primitive recursive function" is likely to be accompanied by an inability to master "value of a function," etc.; while the conditions ostensibly sought for aesthetic terms are non-aesthetic conditions. This point must simply be ignored, for it is the intelligibility of the aesthetic/non-aesthetic distinction itself which is at issue; and I mean only to remind you of the irrelevance of the question of conditions (of any kind) in appraising that distinction. The distinction must be sensible antecedently. If the question of conditions is to be part of the initial characterization of aesthetic terms, then, as has been seen in the preceding section, the subsequent argument is aimless. But still, the distinction remains unclear. We shall now need a way of picking aesthetic terms out of the class of non-condition-governed terms, and this will lead us back to taste. Aesthetic terms will be those unconditioned terms whose use requires taste.

And so, what about taste? How are we to decide whether some judgment requires only normal eyes, ears, etc., or more, when any normal observer can make the judgment? I sympathize with anyone trying to give a convincing answer. It would be understandable if Sibley were to fall back on our sense that there is a difference, whether or not we can mark it. However, I do not share this sense, and I have little sympathy for anyone trying to construct a "theory" atop the distinction if it's drawn in this way.

On the strength of this and the preceding section, I conclude (1) that his aesthetic/non-aesthetic distinction is the soul of Sibley's view, and (2) that that distinction comes to nothing. If this conclusion seems hasty, perhaps the next section will help, where the question of what to require of a "distinction" is met more directly.

Discussion of the Distinction in General

Before attempting some cautious generalizations about the aesthetic/non-aesthetic distinction I would like to fend off a misunderstanding to which my view seems susceptible. I do not claim (nor do I think) that the word "aesthetic" is meaningless or ambiguous or vague. I am not asking to extrude the word from ordinary talk, or even from philosophical talk. Here are some sample remarks which, whether or not they are true, are understandable; and I have no reason or wish to ask that they not be made. (i) "Some proofs, though not defective on strictly formal grounds, are objectionable on aesthetic grounds: they are inelegant." (ii) "One must resist treating the Mass as an occasion for an aesthetic experience, for this will likely preclude a religious response." (iii) "In the first part of *Either/Or* Kierkegaard is exhibiting what it is to be a man for whom all the world's objects—including people—are aesthetic objects." (iv) "Our traditional way of approaching paintings is exactly what comes between us and much of contemporary art. This, now classical, aestheticizing compromises one's response, and destroys one's chances with a work which will submit to nothing but a perfectly human approach."

These remarks are intelligible; one can understand them, argue over them, etc.; and it isn't clear how some of them could be supplanted by substitutes devoid of "aesthetic." What follows from that? Nothing much, I think, and certainly not that people who say such things are committed to anything like the existence of a definition of "aesthetic" which would underwrite an aesthetic/non-aesthetic distinction. (An irony: if there were such things as Sibley's aesthetic terms, "aesthetic" might well be one.)

Then what of the distinction? I am not *against* it as, so to speak, a matter of principle, because I cannot see what point—or sense—there could be in saying I reject it (or I accept it)—period. There is a time to say something, and that is when the distinction is being used and it matters how far we are willing to be led. I have shown that when Sibley uses the distinction we have gone the whole route if we fail to balk at the outset. This is not because of some simple blunder of Sibley's. If he has begged an important question, it is not the ostensible question, Is the applicability of non-aesthetic terms ever sufficient to justify applying an aesthetic term?—though that question was dealt with in the asking. What has been begged is the question of raising that question, and that involves a complex of questions about what the world is like, what art is like, and what it's like to come to terms with either. It is not Sibley's conclusion but his approach which is deep, and this is especially dangerous because that approach not only looks innocuous but is explictly presented by Sibley as pre-philosophical trivia. Thus he seems to me disingenuous when he says,

> I make this broad distinction by means of *examples* of judgments, qualities, and expressions. There is, it seems to me, no need to defend the distinction. . . . Those who in their theoretical moments deny any such distinction usually show in their practice that they can make it quite adequately. (AN, p. 135)

This will not do, for these are theoretical moments. Summing up the first section of "Aesthetic Concepts," Sibley says,

> Without a detailed comparison we cannot see in what particular way *aesthetic* judgments are not "mechanical," or how they differ from those other judgments, nor can we begin to specify what taste is. This I have attempted. It is a characteristic and essential feature of judgments which employ an aesthetic term that they cannot be made by appealing, in the sense explained, to non-aesthetic conditions. This, I believe, is a logical feature of aesthetic or taste judgments in general, though I have argued it here only as regards the more restricted range of judgments which employ aesthetic terms. It is part of what "taste" means. (AC, p. 76)

These seem to be theoretical remarks concerning the nature of "aesthetic language," and I have been trying to show that the arguments supporting these remarks require that the underlying aesthetic/non-aesthetic distinction be at least relatively un-problematic. Even granting that one makes, or can make, the distinction in practice— which I do not grant—Sibley's claim that no further defense is needed warrants the (irresistible) reply, That may be well and good in practice but it seems not to work in theory. Before looking at distinctions, theoretical ones and also those obviously exemplified in one's practice, I want to try to take seriously Sibley's claim about one's practice. What does this mean, that one shows in one's practice that one can make the aesthetic/non-aesthetic distinction? That one uses "aesthetic" is not enough, nor would it help if one also used "non-aesthetic" (which no one does).

What Sibley means, I think, is that most people (or perhaps most people who have much taste) could, upon being given a series of terms, descriptions, or judgments, sort them into two groups, the aesthetic ones and the non-aesthetic ones, and that with some exceptions the groupings would be the same. Is this so? We can imagine two ways of getting started.

(1) The person is given two sheets of paper, both blank except for *aesthetic* and *non-aesthetic* written in as headings. We give him instructions: "You are to enter on the first list any term whose use requires taste. Taste is an ability to. . . . All other terms go on the second list."

I cannot accept this procedure, obviously, for I have been arguing for several pages that the given instructions are not going to produce the desired results, if indeed they produce anything at all. Perhaps it is better, and clearer, here, to object to the procedure on the grounds that the assumption that it might be implemented begs the question—regardless of what results would ensue. I say that I cannot get a grip on the notion that some terms require taste and others do not. That means that I cannot receive and use the given instructions. If this brings us to a point at which it is simply Sibley's sense that the instructions are clear and usable against my inability to find this sense, then we are at an impasse. After sketching a second way of getting started, I will try to swing the issue my way by imagining more concretely the use of the distinction in practice.

There is a feeling that the first way of getting started somehow takes too much for granted, because instead of straightforwardly resting the burden of this distinction on common practice it first indoctrinates that practice with the distinction itself. This feeling might be relieved by imagining a procedure reminiscent of one suggested by Katz in his effort to reconstitute the analytic/synthetic distinction.[9]

(2) The person is given two sheets of paper, headed *aesthetic* and *non-aesthetic*, each containing the first few entries in a list. Each begins with the terms that Sibley has already sorted for us. Under *aesthetic* are "lovely," "pretty," "beautiful," "dainty," etc.; under *non-aesthetic* are "red," "noisy," "brackish," etc.[10] We give the person instructions: "Go on making these two lists." We might add that what we mean is that he is to continue the lists in conformity with the rule obviously employed, or exhibited, in their beginnings.

What will happen? I submit that the subject will have no idea how to proceed. What if "noisy" were not on either initial list and when he came to "noisy" he happened to think not of pneumatic drills but of a section of some Mahler symphony? Or what if he came to "flat" and thought of a Mondrian?[11]

Perhaps you feel like saying: why not stop this pussyfooting, this pseudo-philosophical by-play, with the distinction without examples or examples without the distinction; Sibley is not doing technical philosophy of language, he is presenting a simple, obvious fact in the informal tone appropriate to such a right-minded announcement. This is not a novel objection. In coming to my view of the distinction (that there is none worth drawing), I have often felt that I was being perverse, raising niggling points of unimportant detail. But no longer. I can find no other way to show that there is no sensible and important way of dividing terms in line with Sibley's aesthetic/non-aesthetic distinction. Sibley says,

> Once examples have been given to illustrate it [the distinction], I believe almost anyone could continue to place further examples—barring of course the expected debatable, ambiguous, or borderline cases—in one category or the other. (AN, p. 135)

Let us try, try it with ourselves. We combine ways (1) and (2): we tell ourselves what Sibley says taste is, we illustrate for ourselves the necessity, or lack of it, of using taste with reference to any of Sibley's examples we find convincing, and then we try to go on. Try going on with these terms.

---

[9]See Jerrold J. Katz, "Some Remarks on Quine on Analyticity," *The Journal of Philosophy*, vol. 64 (1967), pp. 36–52.

[10]See AC, pp. 64–65 for Sibley's examples.

[11]Paul Ziff has intriguing remarks on the significance of flatness in Mondrian in his "Reasons in Art Criticism," first published in *Philosophy and Education*, edited by Israel Scheffler (Boston: Allyn and Bacon, Inc., 1958), and reprinted in Ziff's self-anthology *Philosophic Turnings* (Ithaca: Cornell University Press, 1966).

allegorical
baroque
by Beethoven
  (in the style of
  Beethoven)
Christian
classical
climactic
colorful
daring
derivative
didactic
dissonant
funny
geometrical
Gothic
  (Île-de-France
  Gothic
ideological
impressionist
  (impressionistic)

introspective
Kafkaesque
linear
lyrical
mechanical
metaphysical
modernist
moralistic
murky
muted
nationalistic
obscene
painterly
philosophical
poetic
pompous
popular
powerful
pretentious
realist
  (realistic)

religious
restful
rhythmic
riddle canon
Romanesque
romantic
sad
sentimental
serious
sincere
soothing
suggestive
surrealist
  (surrealistic)
suspenseful
symbolist
  (symbolistic,
  symbolical)
youthful

These terms were collected, not at random, but not with malice or contrivance either. They are terms used in talking about art works (and other things). How do you class them—aesthetic or non-aesthetic? It is important to imagine as fully as possible contexts for their use. (In cases where a term is accompanied by related terms in parentheses, try imagining cases where all the terms will do, and then where one will do but not the other.) An inexperienced listener mismanages "by Beethoven," withholding it from Beethoven's *First Symphony* and applying "by Haydn" instead. Is that a failure of taste? The fact that "by Beethoven" does not apply to a "property-of-the-work," if that fact can be made out, is irrelevant, I think. The issue concerns only the correct use of terms. We can avoid the problem by looking at "in the style of Beethoven." Not everything by Beethoven is Beethovian, nor is everything in the style of Beethoven by Beethoven. What is required to apply "in the style of Beethoven" to various works of Liszt and Brahms? Obviously some training or informed experience is needed. But what is that: the development of taste or the directed training of one's normal faculties? What kind of question is this? I want to say not that it is a hard question, but that it is a phony. To suppose that it must "in principle" have an answer is to ask to be smitten with a theory.

There is little point in my going on about these terms. At best I can help in imagining cases in which the aesthetic/non-aesthetic distinction becomes tortured. ("Stevens is metaphysical" seems harder than "Donne is metaphysical" which is harder than "Donne is Metaphysical." Is this a diminution in a term's "taste component"?) So I assert, but can only nudge you to accept, that we do not show in our practice that we make or can make Sibley's distinction.

Let us forget Sibley for a while and try to work on the aesthetic/non-aesthetic distinction in general. As the mention of Katz foreshadowed, we are led inevitably to consider the aesthetic/non-aesthetic distinction with reference to the most celebrated debate over a distinction in recent times—namely, Quine vs. nearly everyone on the analytic/synthetic distinction. [12] Since 1951, when "Two Dogmas of Empiricism" first appeared, the debate itself has become nearly an autonomous topic within professional philosophy, with a variety of writers entering on both sides, and, characteristically, a certain inner group specializing in reporting what the debate is really about, what Quine was really up to, etc. I hope to avoid entangling the aesthetic/non-aesthetic distinction and my qualms about it in this debate. It would be good, though, to "locate" the aesthetic/non-aesthetic distinction relative to the analytic/synthetic distinction, and it will be helpful to be able to refer to one aspect of Quine's attack.

Among putatively exhaustive distinctions there are two relatively clear classes. There are purely technical distinctions, like the distinction between finite and infinite sets, Descartes' distinction between clear and unclear perceptions, and the distinction within numbers between the rational and the irrational ones. On the other hand there are, so to speak, ordinary distinctions, distinctions one ordinarily makes using the ordinary terms of ordinary language in ordinary ways. (It may well be that there is no ordinary distinction which is, or which purports to be, exhaustive. But for these purposes I think we can let that pass.) Examples are blue eyes/eyes which aren't blue, people/other things, Jews (or Mormons or Catholics)/Gentiles.

Whatever else Quine has done, and whatever else his work implies, he has undermined the acceptability of the analytic/synthetic distinction *as a technical distinction*. In the texts of classical Vienna positivism, and especially in the works of Carnap, the distinction appears as a technical distinction. By that I mean that the distinction is conceived as being elaborated for the first time: it is formulated precisely—with no looseness or gaps to be filled in by a rough understanding of the distinction's import, and it gains no credibility from its application to or its use in, common practice (nor does it lose credibility by failing to be related to common practice). Against this kind of distinction Quine can make at least two points. (1) The distinction is not sufficiently precise in the manner required by the very theory in which it occurs. The distinction is supported by no effective procedure for sorting statements into the analytic ones and the synthetic ones. (2) The enterprise the distinction is meant to serve, something like the "logical analysis of the language of science," can be carried on without the distinction.

Neither of these points can be urged against the aesthetic/non-aesthetic distinction directly, for the distinction is not clearly a technical one. But what kind of distinction is it? It seems to be something of an intermediate case, not technical but not altogether

---

[12]The most discussed statement of Quine's position has been his "Two Dogmas of Empiricism" *Philosophical Review*, Vol. 60, No. 1 (January, 1951). This essay appears in several anthologies, including *Analyticity*, edited by James F. Harris, Jr. and Richard H. Severens (Chicago: Quadrangle Books, 1970), and *Necessary Truth*, edited by L. W. Sumner and John Woods (New York: Random House, 1969). These two books also contain extensive bibliographies. In appreciating Quine's position as an attack on what I call a "technical distinction" it is helpful to re-read "Two Dogmas of Empiricism" in the light of his "Truth by Convention," in Otis H. Lee (ed.), *Philosophical Essays for A. N. Whitehead* (New York: Longmans, Green and Co., 1936), and "Carnap and Logical Truth" (*Synthese*, Vol. 12, No. 4, December, 1960—but see Quine's first footnote for an account of the publishing history of this essay).

ordinary. "Aesthetic" certainly has common uses (though "non-aesthetic" has none); some illustrations were set out earlier (p. 388). Unlike "analytic," "aesthetic" has a non-theoretical use which seems related to the use it is given in theories like Sibley's. And besides this respect in which the aesthetic/non-aesthetic distinction might be said to be common, according to Sibley "aesthetic" can be used to mark a distinction made in common practice (though I have argued against this). That is, it is easy (though I think it is mistaken) to believe that the aesthetic/non-aesthetic distinction is both embedded in and applies to ordinary language. Whether or not the analytic/synthetic distinction can be applied to ordinary language, it is not embedded there. One might say that it does not live there, that whatever life it has must come from the theory which incorporates and animates it. If the distinction is not rendered unproblematic in the theory, then its claim to our attention—in fact its existence—falls away. This point (point (1) above) can be made about the aesthetic/non-aesthetic distinction, but without the same consequence.

Neither Sibley's theory nor any other theory in recent philosophy of art comes equipped with explicit semantic and syntactic requirements, a theory of meaning, etc., as did positivism—requirements that Quine then imposed on the theory itself with a devastating effect. Still, there is a theory within which, after the distinction is drawn, Sibley argues that aesthetic terms have a logical independence, that they can be learned and used in certain ways, and so on. Within the theory the distinction functions as a technical distinction, and whatever one wishes to require of such a distinction, surely it must meet at least the minimal methodological requirement that it not beg questions the theory is supposed to answer. I claim to have shown that it does not meet this requirement. But this does not wipe out the sense of "aesthetic." "Aesthetic" remains there in my language whatever any philosopher may do to mutilate its sense, and whatever I may do playing reformer. The strongest point to be made is that the argumentative use of the aesthetic/non-aesthetic distinction as a part of, or a prelude to, a "theory" cannot be justified solely on the grounds that "aesthetic" is a certified non-theoretical term. . . .

Then what of the distinction? I do not know whether it *can* be rehabilitated, but perhaps the second point made against the analytic/synthetic distinction can be made against the aesthetic/non-aesthetic distinction. I have elsewhere tried to talk about art and our apprehension of art without reliance on any substantive notion of "aesthetic" terms or concepts, and so have others. To the extent that we have succeeded, the aesthetic/non-aesthetic distinction has been shown to be not merely a superfluity, but an impediment.

Kendall L. Walton

CATEGORIES OF ART

I. Introduction

> False judgments enter art history if we judge from the impression which
> pictures of different epochs, placed side by side, make on us. . . . They
> speak a different language.[1]

Paintings and sculptures are to be looked at; sonatas and songs are to be heard. What is
important about such works of art is what can be seen or heard in them.[2] This apparent
truism has inspired attempts by aesthetic theorists to purge from criticism of works of
art supposedly extraneous excursions into matters not available to inspection of the
works, and to focus attention narrowly on the works themselves. Circumstances
connected with a work's origin, in particular, are frequently held to have no essential
bearing on an assessment of its aesthetic nature. Thus critics are advised to ignore how
and when a work was created, the artist's intentions in creating it, his philosophical
views, psychological state, personal life, the artistic traditions and intellectual atmosphere of his society, and so forth. Once produced, it is argued, a work must stand or
fall on its own; it must be judged for what it is, regardless of how it came to be as it is.

Arguments for this position need not involve the claim that how and in what
circumstances a work comes about is not of "aesthetic" interest or importance. One
might consider an artist's action of producing a work to be aesthetically interesting, an
"aesthetic object" in its own right, while vehemently denying its relevance to an
aesthetic investigation of the work. Robert Rauschenberg once carefully obliterated a
drawing by de Kooning, titled the bare canvas *Erased de Kooning Drawing*, framed it,
and exhibited it.[3] His doing this might be taken as symbolic or expressive (of an attitude

From The Philosophical Review 79 (1970):334–367. *Reprinted with permission of* The Philosophical Review
and the author.

[1] Heinrich Wölfflin, *Principles of Art History*, trans. by M. D. Hottinger (7th ed.; New York, 1929), p.
228.

[2] "[W]e should all agree, I think, . . . that any quality that cannot even in principle be heard in it [a
musical composition] does not belong to it as music." Monroe Beardsley, *Aesthetics: Problems in the
Philosophy of Criticism* (New York, 1958), pp. 31–32.

[3] Cf. Calvin Tompkins, *The Bride and the Bachelors* (New York, 1965), pp. 210–211.

toward art, or toward life in general, or whatever) in an "aesthetically" significant manner, and yet thought to have no bearing whatever on the aesthetic nature of the finished product. The issue I am here concerned with is how far critical questions about works of art can be *separated* from questions about their histories.[4]

One who wants to make a sharp separation may regard the basic facts of art along the following lines. Works of art are simply objects with various properties, of which we are primarily interested in perceptual ones—visual properties of paintings, audible properties of music, and so forth.[5] A work's perceptual properties include "aesthetic" as well as "non-aesthetic" ones—the sense of mystery and tension of a painting as well as its dark coloring and diagonal composition; the energy, exuberance, and coherence of a sonata, as well as its meters, rhythms, pitches, timbres; the balance and serenity of a Gothic cathedral as well as its dimensions, lines, and symmetries.[6] Aesthetic properties are features or characteristics of works of art just as much as nonaesthetic ones are.[7] They are *in* the works, to be seen, heard, or otherwise perceived there. Seeing a painting's sense of mystery or hearing a sonata's coherence might require looking or listening longer or harder than does perceiving colors and shapes, rhythms and pitches; it may even require special training or a special kind of sensitivity. But these qualities must be discoverable simply by examining the works themselves if they are discoverable at all. It is never even partly *in virtue of* the circumstances of a work's origin that it has a sense of mystery or is coherent or serene. Such circumstances sometimes provide hints concerning what to look for in a work, what we might reasonably expect to find by examining it. But these hints are always theoretically dispensable; a work's aesthetic properties must "in principle" be ascertainable without their help. Surely (it seems) a Rembrandt portrait does not have (or lack) a sense of mystery in virtue of the fact that Rembrandt intended it to have (or to lack) that quality, any more than a contractor's intention to make a roof leakproof makes it so; nor is the portrait mysterious in virtue of any other facts about what Rembrandt thought or how he went about painting the portrait or what his society happened to be like. Such circumstances are important to the result only in so far as they had an effect on the pattern of paint splotches that became attached to the canvas, and the canvas can be examined without in any way considering how the splotches got there. It would not matter in the least to the aesthetic properties of the portrait if the paint had been applied to the canvas not by Rembrandt at all, but by a chimpanzee or a cyclone in a paint shop.

The view sketched above can easily seem very persuasive. But the tendency of critics to discuss the histories of works of art in the course of justifying aesthetic judgments

[4]Monroe Beardsley argues for a relatively strict separation (*op. cit.*, pp. 17–34). Some of the strongest recent attempts to enforce this separation are to be found in discussions of the so-called "intentional fallacy," beginning with William Wimsatt and Beardsley, "The Intentional Fallacy," *Sewanee Review*, LIV (1946), which has been widely cited and reprinted. Despite the name of the "fallacy" these discussions are not limited to consideration of the relevance of artists' *intentions*.

[5]The aesthetic properties of works of literature are not happily called "perceptual." For reasons connected with this it is sometimes awkward to treat literature together with the visual arts and music. (The notion of perceiving a work in a category, to be introduced shortly, is not straightforwardly applicable to literary works.) Hence in this paper I will concentrate on visual and musical works, though I believe that the central points I make concerning them hold, with suitable modifications, for novels, plays, and poems as well.

[6]Frank Sibley distinguishes between "aesthetic" and "nonaesthetic" terms and concepts in "Aesthetic Concepts," *Philosophical Review*, LXVIII (1959).

[7]Cf. Paul Ziff, "Art and the 'Object of Art,'" in Ziff, *Philosophic Turnings* (Ithaca, N.Y., 1966), pp. 12–16 (originally published in *Mind*, N.S. LX [1951]).

about them has been remarkably persistent. This is partly because hints derived from facts about a work's history, however dispensable they may be "in principle," are often crucially important in practice. (One might not think to listen for a recurring series of intervals in a piece of music, until he learns that the composer meant the work to be structured around it.) No doubt it is partly due also to genuine confusions on the part of critics. But I will argue that certain facts about the origins of works of art have an *essential* role in criticism, that aesthetic judgments rest on them in an absolutely fundamental way. For this reason, and for another as well, the view that works of art should be judged simply by what can be perceived in them is seriously misleading. Nevertheless there is something right in the idea that what matters aesthetically about a painting or a sonata is just how it looks or sounds.

II. *Standard, Variable, and Contra-Standard Properties*

I will continue to call tension, mystery, energy, coherence, balance, serenity, sentimentality, pallidness, disunity, grotesqueness, and so forth, as well as colors and shapes, pitches and timbres *properties* of works of art, though "property" is to be construed broadly enough not to beg any important questions. I will also, following Sibley, call properties of the former sort "aesthetic" properties, but purely for reasons of convenience I will include in this category "representational" and "resemblance" properties, which Sibley excludes—for example, the property of representing Napoleon, that of depicting an old man stooping over a fire, that of resembling, or merely suggesting, a human face, claws (the petals of van Gogh's sunflowers), or (in music) footsteps or conversation. It is not essential for my purposes to delimit with any exactness the class of aesthetic properties (if indeed any such delimitation is possible), for I am more interested in discussing particular examples of such properties than in making generalizations about the class as a whole. It will be obvious, however, that what I say about the examples I deal with is also applicable to a great many other properties we would want to call aesthetic.

Sibley points out that a work's aesthetic properties depend on its nonaesthetic properties; the former are "emergent" or "*Gestalt*" properties based on the latter.[8] I take this to be true of all the examples of aesthetic properties we will be dealing with, including representational and resemblance ones. It is because of the configuration of colors and shapes on a painting, perhaps in particular its dark colors and diagonal composition, that it has a sense of mystery and tension, if it does. The colors and shapes of a portrait are responsible for its resembling an old man and its depicting an old man. The coherence or unity of a piece of music (for example, Beethoven's *Fifth Symphony*) may be largely due to the frequent recurrence of a rhythmic motive, and the regular meter of a song plus the absence of harmonic modulation and of large intervals in the voice part may make it serene or peaceful.

Moreover, a work *seems* or *appears* to us to have certain aesthetic properties because we observe in it, or it appears to us to have, certain nonaesthetic features (though it may not be necessary to notice consciously all the relevant nonaesthetic features). A

[8]"Aesthetic and Nonaesthetic," *Philosophical Review*, LXXII (1965).

painting depicting an old man may not look like an old man to someone who is color-blind, or when it is seen from an extreme angle or in bad lighting conditions which distort or obscure its colors or shapes. Beethoven's *Fifth Symphony* performed in such a sloppy manner that many occurrences of the four-note rhythmic motive do not sound similar may seem incoherent or disunified.

I will argue, however, that a work's aesthetic properties depend not only on its nonaesthetic ones, but also on which of its nonaesthetic properties are "standard," which "variable," and which "contra-standard," in senses to be explained. I will approach this thesis by way of the psychological point that what aesthetic properties a work seems to us to have depends not only on what nonaesthetic features we perceive in it, but also on which of them are standard, which variable, and which contra-standard *for us* (in a sense also to be explained).

It is necessary to introduce first a distinction between standard, variable, and contra-standard properties relative to perceptually distinguishable categories of works of art. A category is perceptually distinguishable if membership in it is determined solely by features of works that can be perceived in them when they are experienced in the normal manner. The categories of painting, cubist painting, Gothic architecture, classical sonatas, painting in the style of Cézanne, music in the style of late Beethoven, and most other media, genre, styles, and forms can be construed as perceptually distinguishable. If we do construe them this way, we must, for example, regard whether a piece of music was written in the eighteenth century as irrelevant to whether it belongs to the category of classical sonatas, and we must take whether or not a work was produced by Cézanne or Beethoven to have nothing essential to do with whether or not it is in the style of Cézanne or late Beethoven. The category of etchings as normally understood is not perceptually distinguishable in the requisite sense, for to be an etching is, I take it, to have been produced in a particular manner. But the category of *apparent* etchings, works which *look* like etchings from the quality of their lines, whether or not they are etchings, is perceptually distinguishable.[9]

A feature of a work of art is *standard* with respect to a (perceptually distinguishable) category just in case it is among those in virtue of which works in that category belong to that category—that is, just in case the absence of that feature would disqualify, or tend to disqualify, a work from that category. A feature is *variable* with respect to a category just in case it has nothing to do with works belonging to that category; the possession or lack of the feature is irrelevant to whether a work qualifies for the category. Finally, a *contra-standard* feature with respect to a category is the absence of a standard feature with respect to that category—that is, a feature whose presence tends to *disqualify* works as members of the category. Needless to say, it will not be clear in *all* cases whether a feature of a work is standard, variable, or contra-standard relative to a given category, since the criteria for classifying works of art are far from precise. But clear examples are abundant. The flatness of a painting and the motionlessness of its markings are standard, and its particular shapes and colors are variable, relative to the category of painting. A protruding three-dimensional object or an electrically driven twitching of the canvas would be contra-standard relative to this category. The straight

---

[9]A category will not count as perceptually distinguishable in my sense if in order to determine perceptually whether something belongs to it, it is necessary (in some or all cases) to determine, on the basis of nonperceptual considerations, which categories it is correctly perceived in. (See Section IV below.) This prevents the category of serene things, for example, from being perceptually distinguishable.

lines in stick-figure drawings and squarish shapes in cubist paintings are standard with respect to those categories respectively, though they are variable with respect to the categories of drawing and painting. The exposition-development-recapitulation form of a classical sonata is standard, and its thematic material is variable, relative to the category of sonatas.

In order to explain what I mean by features being standard, variable, or contra-standard *for a person on a particular occasion*, I must introduce the notion of perceiving a work in, or as belonging to, a certain (perceptually distinguishable) category. To perceive a work in a certain category is to perceive the *"Gestalt"* of that category in the work. This needs some explanation. People familiar with Brahmsian music (music in the style of Brahms—notably, works of Johannes Brahms) or impressionist paintings can frequently recognize members of these categories by recognizing the Brahmsian or impressionist *Gestalt* qualities. Such recognition is dependent on perception of particular features that are standard relative to these categories, but it is not a matter of *inferring* from the presence of such features that a work is Brahmsian or impressionist. One may not notice many of the relevant features, and he may be very vague about which ones are relevant. If I recognize a work as Brahmsian by first noting its lush textures, its basically traditional harmonic and formal structure, its superimposition and alternation of duple and triple meters, and so forth, and recalling that these characteristics are typical of Brahmsian works, I have not recognized it by hearing the Brahmsian *Gestalt*. To do that is simply to recognize it by its Brahmsian *sound*, without necessarily paying attention to the features ("cues") responsible for it. Similarly, recognizing an impressionist painting by its impressionist *Gestalt* is recognizing the impressionist *look* about it, which we are familiar with from other impressionist paintings; not applying a rule we have learned for recognizing it from its features.

To *perceive* a *Gestalt* quality in a work—that is, to perceive it in a certain category— is not, or not merely, to *recognize* that *Gestalt* quality. Recognition is a momentary occurrence, whereas perceiving a quality is a continuous state which may last for a short or long time. (For the same reason, seeing the ambiguous duck-rabbit figure as a duck is not, or not merely, recognizing a property of it.) We perceive the Brahmsian or impressionist *Gestalt* in a work when, and as long as, it *sounds* Brahmsian or *looks* impressionist to us. This involves perceiving (not necessarily being aware of) features standard relative to that category. But it is not *just* this, nor this plus the intellectual realization that these features make the work Brahmsian, or impressionist. These features are perceived combined into a single *Gestalt* quality.

We can of course perceive a work in several or many different categories at once. A Brahms sonata might be heard simultaneously as a piece of music, a sonata, a romantic work, and a Brahmsian work. Some pairs of categories, however, seem to be such that one cannot perceive a work as belonging to both at once, much as one cannot see the duck-rabbit both as a duck and as a rabbit simultaneously. One cannot see a photographic image simultaneously as a still photograph and as (part of) a film, nor can one see something both in the category of paintings and at the same time in the category (to be explained shortly) of *guernicas*.

It will be useful to point out some of the *causes* of our perceiving works in certain categories. (*a*) In which categories we perceive a work depends in part, of course, on what other works we are familiar with. The more works of a certain sort we have experienced, the more likely it is that we will perceive a particular work in that

category. (b) What we have heard critics and others say about works we have experienced, how they have categorized them, and what resemblances they have pointed
out to us is also important. If no one has ever explained to me what is distinctive about
Schubert's style (as opposed to the styles of, say, Schumann, Mendelssohn, Beethoven, Brahms, Hugo Wolf), or even pointed out that there is such a distinctive style, I
may never have learned to hear the Schubertian *Gestalt* quality, even if I have heard
many of Schubert's works, and so I may not hear his works as Schubertian. (c) How we
are introduced to the particular work in question may be involved. If a Cézanne
painting is exhibited in a collection of French Impressionist works, or if before seeing it
we are told that it is French Impressionist, we are more likely to see it as French
Impressionist than we would be if it is exhibited in a random collection and we are not
told anything about it beforehand.

I will say that a feature of a work is standard for a particular person on a particular
occasion when, and only when, it is standard relative to some category in which he
perceives it, and is not contra-standard relative to any category in which he perceives it.
A feature is variable for a person just when it is variable relative to *all* of the categories
in which he perceives it. And a feature is contra-standard for a person just when it is
contra-standard relative to *any* of the categories in which he perceives it.[10]

III. A Point about Perception

I turn now to my psychological thesis that what aesthetic properties a work seems to
have, what aesthetic effect it has on us, how it strikes us aesthetically often depends (in
part) on which of its features are standard, which variable, and which contra-standard
for us. I offer a series of examples in support of this thesis.

(a) Representational and resemblance properties provide perhaps the most obvious
illustration of this thesis. Many works of art look like or resemble other objects—
people, buildings, mountains, bowls of fruit, and so forth. Rembrandt's *Titus Reading*
looks like a boy, and in particular like Rembrandt's son; Picasso's *Les Demoiselles
d'Avignon* looks like five women, four standing and one sitting (though not *especially*
like any particular women). A portrait may even be said to be a *perfect* likeness of the
sitter, or to capture his image *exactly*.

An important consideration in determining whether a work *depicts* or *represents* a
particular object, or an object of a certain sort (for example, Rembrandt's son, or
simply *a* boy), in the sense of being a picture, sculpture, or whatever of it[11] is whether
the work resembles that object, or objects of that kind. A significant degree of

[10]I am ignoring some considerations that might be important at a later stage of investigation. In
particular, I think it would be important at some point to distinguish between different *degrees* or *levels* of
standardness, variableness, and contra-standardness for a person; to speak, e.g., of features being *more* or *less*
standard for him. At least two distinct sorts of grounds for such differences of degree should be recognized.
(a) Distinctions between perceiving a work in a certain category to a greater and lesser extent should be
allowed for, with corresponding differences of degree in the standardness for the perceiver of properties
relative to that category. (b) A feature which is standard relative to more, and/or more specific, categories in
which a person perceives the work should thereby count as more standard for him. Thus, if we see something
as a painting and also as a French Impressionist painting, features standard relative to both categories are
more standard for us than features standard relative only to the latter.

[11]This excludes, e.g., the sense of "represent" in which a picture might represent justice or courage, and
probably other senses as well.

resemblance is, I suggest, a necessary condition in most contexts for such representation or depiction,[12] though the resemblance need not be obvious at first glance. If we
are unable to see a similarity between a painting purportedly of a woman and women, I
think we would have to suppose either that there is such a similarity which we have not
yet discovered (as one might fail to see a face in a maze of lines), or that it simply is not
a picture of a woman. Resemblance is of course not a *sufficient* condition for
representation, since a portrait (containing only one figure) might resemble both the
sitter and his twin brother equally but is not a portrait of both of them. (The title might
determine which of them it depicts.)[13]

It takes only a touch of perversity, however, to find much of our talk about
resemblances between works of art and other things preposterous. Paintings and people
are *very* different sorts of things. Paintings are pieces of canvas supporting splotches of
paint, while people are live, three-dimensional, flesh-and-blood animals. Moreover,
except rarely and under special conditions of observation paintings and people *look*
very different. Paintings look like pieces of canvas (or anyway flat surfaces) covered with
paint and people look like flesh-and-blood animals. There is practically no danger of
confusing them. How, then, can anyone seriously hold that a portrait resembles the
sitter to any significant extent, let alone that it is a perfect likeness of him? Yet it
remains true that many paintings strike us as resembling people, sometimes very much
or even exactly—despite the fact that they look so very different!

To resolve this paradox we must recognize that the resemblances we perceive
between, for example, portraits and people, those that are relevant in determining what
works of art depict or represent, are resemblances of a somewhat special sort, tied up
with the categories in which we perceive such works. The properties of a work which
are standard for us are ordinarily irrelevant to what we take it to look like or resemble in
the relevant sense, and hence to what we take it to depict or represent. The properties
of a portrait which make it *so* different from, so easily distinguishable from, a
person—such as its flatness and its *painted* look—are standard for us. Hence these
properties just do not count with regard to what (or whom) it looks like. It is only the
properties which are variable for us, the colors and shapes on the work's surface, that
make it look to us like what it does. And these are the ones which are relevant in
determining what (if anything) the work represents.[14]

Other examples will reinforce this point. A marble bust of a Roman emperor seems
to us to resemble a man with, say, an aquiline nose, a wrinkled brow, and an
expression of grim determination, and we take it to represent a man with, or as having,

---

[12]This does not hold for the special case of photography. A photograph is a photograph of a woman no
matter what it looks like, I take it, if a woman was in front of the lens when it was produced.

[13]Nelson Goodman denies that resemblance is necessary for representation—and obviously not merely
because of isolated or marginal examples of nonresembling representations (p. 5). I cannot treat his
arguments here, but rather than reject *en masse* the common-sense beliefs that pictures do resemble
significantly what they depict and that they depict what they do partly because of such resemblances, if
Goodman advocates rejecting them, I prefer to recognize a sense of "resemblance" in which these beliefs are
true. My disagreement with him is perhaps less sharp than it appears since, as will be evident, I am quite
willing to grant that the relevant resemblances are "conventional." Cf. Goodman, *Languages of Art*
(Indianapolis, 1968), p. 39, n. 31.

[14]The connection between features variable for us and what the work looks like is by no means a
straightforward or simple one, however. It may involve "rules" which are more or less "conventional" (e.g.,
the "laws" of perspective). Cf. E. H. Gombrich, *Art and Illusion* (New York, 1960) and Nelson Goodman,
op cit.

those characteristics. But why don't we say that it resembles and represents a per-petually motionless man, of uniform (marble) color, who is severed at the chest? It is similar to such a man, it seems, and much more so than to a normally colored, mobile, and whole man. But we are not struck by the former similarity when we see the bust, obvious though it is on reflection. The bust's uniform color, motionlessness, and abrupt ending at the chest are standard properties relative to the category of busts, and since we see it as a bust they are standard for us. Similarly, black-and-white drawings do not look to us like colorless scenes and we do not take them to depict things as being colorless, nor do we regard stick-figure drawings as resembling and depicting only very thin people. A cubist work might look like a person with a cubical head to someone not familiar with the cubist style. But the standardness of such cubical shapes for people who see it as a cubist work prevents them from making that comparison.

The shapes of a painting or a still photograph of a high jumper in action are motionless, but these pictures do not look to us like a high jumper frozen in midair. Indeed, depending on features of the pictures which are variable for us (the exact positions of the figures, swirling brush strokes in the painting, slight blurrings of the photographic image) the athlete may seem in a frenzy of activity; the pictures may convey a vivid sense of movement. But if static images exactly like those of the two pictures occur in a motion picture, and we see it as a motion picture, they probably would strike us as resembling a static athlete. This is because the immobility of the images is standard relative to the category of still pictures and variable relative to that of motion pictures. (Since we are so familiar with still pictures it might be difficult to see the static images as motion pictures for very long, rather than as [filmed] still pictures. But we could not help seeing them that way if we had no acquaintance at all with the medium of still pictures.) My point here is brought out by the tremendous aesthetic difference we are likely to experience between a film of a dancer moving *very* slowly and a still picture of him, even if "objectively" the two images are very nearly identical. We might well find the former studied, calm, deliberate, laborious, and the latter dynamic, energetic, flowing, or frenzied.

In general, then, what we regard a work as resembling, and as representing, depends on the properties of the work which are variable, and not on those which are standard for us.[15] The latter properties serve to determine what *kind* of a representation the work is, rather than what it represents or resembles. We take them for granted, as it were, in representations of that kind. This principle helps to explain also how clouds can look like elephants, how diatonic orchestral music can suggest a conversation or a person crying or laughing, and how a twelve-year-old boy can look like his middle-aged father.

We can now see how a portrait can be an *exact* likeness of the sitter, despite the huge differences between the two. The differences, in so far as they involve properties standard for us, simply do not count against likeness, and hence not against exact likeness. Similarly, a boy not only can resemble his father but can be his "spitting image," despite the boy's relative youthfulness. It is clear that the notions of resem-

---

[15]There is at least one group of exceptions to this. Obviously features of a work which are standard for us because they are standard relative to some *representational* category which we see it in—e.g., the category of nudes, still lifes, or landscapes—do help determine what the work looks like to us and what we take it to depict.

blance and exact resemblance that we are concerned with are not even cousins of the notion of perceptual indistinguishability.

(*b*) The importance of the distinction between standard and variable properties is by no means limited to cases involving representation or resemblance. Imagine a society which does not have an established medium of painting, but does produce a kind of work of art called *guernicas*. Guernicas are like versions of Picasso's *Guernica* done in various bas-relief dimensions. All of them are surfaces with the colors and shapes of Picasso's *Guernica*, but the surfaces are molded to protrude from the wall like relief maps of different kinds of terrain. Some guernicas have rolling surfaces, others are sharp and jagged, still others contain several relatively flat planes at various angles to each other, and so forth. If members of this society should come across Picasso's *Guernica*, they would count it as a guernica—a perfectly flat one—rather than as a painting. Its flatness is variable, and the figures on its surface are standard relative to the category of guernicas. Thus the flatness, which is standard for us, would be variable for members of the other society, and the figures on the surface, which are variable for us, would be standard for them. This would make for a profound difference between our aesthetic reaction to *Guernica* and theirs. It seems violent, dynamic, vital, disturbing to us. But I imagine it would strike them as cold, stark, lifeless, or serene and restful, or perhaps bland, dull, boring—but in any case *not* violent, dynamic, and vital. We do not pay attention to or take note of *Guernica's* flatness; this is a feature we take for granted in paintings. But for the other society this is *Guernica's* most striking and noteworthy characteristic—what is *expressive* about it. Conversely, *Guernica's* color patches, which we find noteworthy and expressive, are insignificant to them.

It is important to notice that this difference in aesthetic response is not due *solely* to the fact that we are much more familiar with flat works of art than they are, and they are more familiar with *Guernica's* colors and shapes. Someone equally familiar with paintings and guernicas might, I think, see Picasso's *Guernica* as a painting on some occasions, and as a guernica on others. On the former occasions it will probably look dynamic, violent, and so forth to him, and on the latter cold, serene, bland, or lifeless. Whether he sees the work in a museum of paintings or a museum of guernicas, or whether he has been told that it is a painting or a guernica, may influence how he sees it. But I think he might be able to shift at will from one way of seeing it to the other, somewhat as one shifts between seeing the duck-rabbit as a duck and seeing it as a rabbit.

This example and the previous ones might give the impression that in general only features of a work that are variable for us are aesthetically important—that these are the expressive, aesthetically active properties, as far as we are concerned, whereas features standard for us are aesthetically inert. But this notion is quite mistaken, as the following examples will demonstrate. Properties standard for us are not aesthetically lifeless, though the life that they have, the aesthetic effect they have on us, is typically very different from what it would be if they were variable for us.

(*c*) Because of the very fact that features standard for us do not seem striking or noteworthy, that they are somehow expected or taken for granted, they can contribute to a work a sense of order, inevitability, stability, correctness. This is perhaps most notably true of large-scale structural properties in the time arts. The exposition-development-recapitulation form (including the typical key and thematic relationships) of the first movements of classical sonatas, symphonies, and string quartets is standard with respect to the category of works in sonata-allegro form, and standard for listeners, including most of us, who hear them as belonging to that category. So proceeding along the lines of sonata-allegro form seems *right* to us; to our ears that is how sonatas are *supposed* to behave. We feel that we know where we are and where we are going throughout the work—more so, I suggest, than we would if we were not familiar with sonata-allegro form, if following the strictures of that form were variable rather than standard for us.[16] Properties standard for us do not always have this sort of unifying effect, however. The fact that a piano sonata contains only piano sounds, or uses the Western system of harmony throughout, does not make it seem unified to us. The reason, I think, is that these properties are *too* standard for us in a sense that needs explicating (cf. note 10). Nevertheless, sonata form is unifying partly because it is standard rather than variable for us.

(*d*) That a work (or part of it) has a certain determinate characteristic (of size, for example, or speed, or length, or volume) is often variable relative to a particular category, when it is nevertheless standard for that category that the variable characteristic falls within a certain range. In such cases the aesthetic effect of the determinate variable property may be colored by the standard limits of the range. Hence these limits function as an aesthetic catalyst, even if not as an active ingredient.

Piano music is frequently marked *sostenuto, cantabile, legato,* or *lyrical.* But how can the pianist possibly carry out such instructions? Piano tones diminish in volume drastically immediately after the key is struck, becoming inaudible relatively promptly, and there is no way the player can prevent this. If a singer or violinist should produce sounds even approaching a piano's in suddenness of demise, they would be nerve-wrackingly sharp and percussive—anything but *cantabile* or lyrical! Yet piano music *can* be *cantabile, legato,* or lyrical nevertheless; sometimes it is extraordinarily so (for example, a good performance of the *Adagio Cantabile* movement of Beethoven's *Pathétique* sonata). What makes this possible is the very fact that the drastic diminution of piano tones cannot be prevented, and hence never is. It is a standard feature for piano music. A pianist can, however, by a variety of devices, control a tone's rate of diminution and length within the limits dictated by the nature of the instrument.[17] Piano tones may thus be *more or less* sustained within these limits, and *how* sustained they are, how quickly or slowly they diminish and how long they last, within the range of possibilities, is variable for piano music. A piano passage that sounds lyrical or *cantabile* to us is one in which the individual tones are *relatively* sustained, given the capabilities of the instrument. Such a passage sounds lyrical only because piano music is limited as it is, and we hear it as piano music; that is, the limitations are standard properties for us. The character of the passage is determined not merely by the

---

[16]The presence of clichés in a work sometimes allows it to contain drastically disorderly elements without becoming chaotic or incoherent. Cf. Anton Ehrenzweig, *The Hidden Order of Art* (London, 1967), pp. 114–116.

[17]The timing of the release of the key affects the tone's length. Use of the sustaining pedal can lessen slightly a tone's diminuendo by reinforcing its overtones with sympathetic vibrations from other strings. The rate of diminuendo is affected somewhat more drastically by the force with which the key is struck. The more forcefully it is struck the greater is the tone's relative diminuendo. (Obviously the rate of diminuendo cannot be controlled in this way independently of the tone's initial volume.) The successive tones of a melody can be made to overlap so that each tone's sharp attack is partially obscured by the lingering end of the preceding tone. A melodic tone may also be reinforced after it begins by sympathetic vibrations from harmonically related accompanying figures, contributed by the composer.

"absolute" nature of the sounds, but by that in relation to the standard property of what piano tones can be like.[18]

This principle helps to explain the lack of energy and brilliance that we sometimes find even in very fast passages of electronic music. The energy and brilliance of a fast violin or piano passage derives not merely from the absolute speed of the music (together with accents, rhythmic characteristics, and so forth), but from the fact that it is fast *for that particular medium.* In electronic music different pitches can succeed one another at any frequency up to and including that at which they are no longer separately distinguishable. Because of this it is difficult to make electronic music *sound* fast (energetic, violent). For when we have heard enough electronic music to be aware of the possibilities we do not feel that the speed of a passage approaches a limit, no matter how fast it is.[19]

There are also visual correlates of these musical examples. A small elephant, one which is smaller than most elephants with which we are familiar, might impress us as charming, cute, delicate, or puny. This is not simply because of its (absolute) size, but because it is small *for an elephant.* To people who are familiar not with our elephants but with a race of mini-elephants, the same animal may look massive, strong, dominant, threatening, lumbering, if it is large for a mini-elephant. The size of elephants is variable relative to the class of elephants, but it varies only within a certain (not precisely specifiable) range. It is a standard property of elephants that they do fall within this range. How an elephant's size affects us aesthetically depends, since we see it as an elephant, on whether it falls in the upper, middle, or lower part of the range.

(e) Properties standard for a certain category which do not derive from physical limitations of the medium can be regarded as results of more or less conventional "rules" for producing works in the given category (for example, the "rules" of sixteenth-century counterpoint, or those for twelve-tone music). These rules may combine to create a dilemma for the artist which, if he is talented, he may resolve ingeniously and gracefully. The result may be a work with an aesthetic character very different from what it would have had if it had not been for those rules. Suppose that the first movement of a sonata in G major modulates to C-sharp major by the end of the development section. A rule of sonata form decrees that it must return to G for the recapitulation. But the keys of G and C-sharp are as unrelated as any two keys can be; it is difficult to modulate smoothly and quickly from one to the other. Suppose also that while the sonata is in C-sharp there are signs that, given other rules of sonata form, indicate that the recapitulation is imminent (motivic hints of the return, an emotional climax, a cadenza). Listeners who hear it as a work in sonata form are likely to have a distinct feeling of unease, tension, uncertainty, as the time for the recapitulation approaches. If the composer with a stroke of ingenuity accomplishes the necessary modulation quickly, efficiently, and naturally, this will give them a feeling of relief—one might say of deliverance. The movement to C-sharp, which may have seemed

---

[18]"[T]he musical media we know thus far derive their whole character and their usefulness as musical media precisely from their limitations." Roger Sessions, "Problems and Issues Facing the Composer Today," in Paul Henry Lang, *Problems of Modern Music* (New York, 1960), p. 31.

[19]One way to make electronic music sound fast would be to make it sound like some traditional instrument, thereby trading on the limitations of that instrument.

alien and brashly adventurous at the time will have proven to be quite appropriate, and the entire sequence will in retrospect have a sense of correctness and perfection about it. Our impression of it is likely, I think, to be very much like our impression of a "beautiful" or "elegant" proof in mathematics. (Indeed the composer's task in this example is not unlike that of producing such a proof.)

But suppose that the rule for sonatas were that the recapitulation must be *either* in the original key *or* in the key one half-step below it. Thus in the example above the recapitulation could have been in F-sharp major rather than G major. This possibility removes the sense of tension from the occurrence of C-sharp major in the development section, for a modulation from C-sharp to F-sharp is as easy as any modulation is (since C-sharp is the dominant of F-sharp). Of course, there would also be no special *release* of tension when the modulation to G is effected, there being no tension to be released. In fact, that modulation probably would be rather surprising, since the permissible modulation to F-sharp would be much more natural.

Thus the effect that the sonata has on us depends on which of its properties are dictated by "rules," which ones are standard relative to the category of sonatas and hence standard for us.

(*f*) I turn now to features which are contra-standard for us—ones which have a tendency to disqualify a work from a category in which we nevertheless perceive it. We are likely to find such features shocking, or disconcerting, or startling, or upsetting, just because they are contra-standard for us. Their presence may be so obtrusive that they obscure the work's variable properties. Three-dimensional objects protruding from a canvas and movement in a sculpture are contra-standard relative to the categories of painting and (traditional) sculpture respectively. These features are contra-standard for us, and probably shocking, if despite them we perceive the works possessing them in the mentioned categories. The monochromatic paintings of Yves Klein are disturbing to us (at least at first) for this reason: we see them as paintings, though they contain the feature contra-standard for paintings of being one solid color.[20] Notice that we find other similarly monochromatic surfaces—walls of living rooms, for example—not in the least disturbing, and indeed quite unnoteworthy.

If we are exposed frequently to works containing a certain kind of feature which is contra-standard for us, we ordinarily adjust our categories to accommodate it, making it contra-standard for us no longer. The first painting with a three-dimensional object glued to it was no doubt shocking. But now that the technique has become commonplace we are not shocked. This is because we no longer see these works as *paintings*, but rather as members of either (*a*) a new category—*collages*—in which case the offending feature has become standard rather than contra-standard for us, or (*b*) an expanded category which includes paintings both with and without attached objects, in which case that feature is variable for us.

But it is not just the rarity, unusualness, or unexpectedness of a feature that makes it shocking. If a work differs *too* significantly from the norms of a certain category we do not perceive it in that category and hence the difference is not contra-standard for us, even if we have not previously experienced works differing from that category in that

---

[20]This example was suggested by Göran Hermerén.

way. A sculpture which is constantly and vigorously in motion would be so obviously and radically different from traditional sculptures that we probably would not perceive it as one even if it is the first moving sculpture we have come across. We would either perceive it as a *kinetic* sculpture, or simply remain confused. In contrast, a sculpted bust which is traditional in every respect except that one ear twitches slightly every thirty seconds would be perceived as an ordinary sculpture. So the twitiching ear would be contra-standard for us, and it would be considerably more unsettling than the much greater movement of the other kinetic sculpture. Similarly, a very small colored area of an otherwise entirely black-and-white drawing would be very disconcerting. But if enough additional color is added to it we will see it as a colored rather than a black-and-white drawing, and the shock will vanish.

This point helps to explain a difference between the harmonic aberrations of Wagner's *Tristan and Isolde* and those of Debussy's *Pelléas et Mélisande* and Schoenberg's *Pierrot Lunaire* as well as Schoenberg's later twelve-tone works. The latter are not merely *more* aberrant, *less* tonal, than *Tristan*. They differ from traditional tonal music in such respects and to such an extent that they are not heard as tonal at all. *Tristan*, however, retains enough of the apparatus of tonality, despite its deviations, to be heard as a tonal work. For this reason its lesser deviations are often the more shocking.[21] *Tristan* plays on harmonic traditions by selectively following and flaunting them, while *Pierrot Lunaire* and the others simply ignore them.

Shock then arises from features that are not just rare or unique, but ones that are contra-standard relative to categories in which objects possessing them are perceived. But it must be emphasized that to be contra-standard relative to a certain category is not merely to be rare or unique *among things of that category*. The melodic line of Schubert's song "*Im Walde*" is probably unique; it probably does not occur in any other songs, or other works of any sort. But it is not contra-standard relative to the category of songs, because it does not tend to disqualify the work from that category. Nor is it contra-standard relative to any other category to which we hear the work as belonging. And clearly we do not find this melodic line at all upsetting. What is important is not the rarity of a feature, but its connection with the classification of the work. Features contra-standard for us are perceived as misfits in a category which the work strikes us as belonging to, as doing *violence* to such a category. Being rare in a category is not the same thing as being a misfit in it.

It should be clear from the above examples that how a work affects us aesthetically— what aesthetic properties it seems to us to have and what ones we are inclined to attribute to it—depends in a variety of important ways on which of its features are standard, which variable, and which contra-standard for us. Moreover, this is obviously not an isolated or exceptional phenomenon, but a pervasive characteristic of aesthetic perception. I should emphasize that my purpose has not been to establish general principles about how each of the three sorts of properties affects us. How any particular feature affects us depends also on many variables I have not discussed. The important point is that in many cases whether a feature is standard, variable, or contra-standard for us has a great deal to do with what effect it has on us. We must now begin to assess the theoretical consequences of this.

[21]Cf. William W. Austin, *Music in the 20th Century* (New York, 1966), pp. 205–206; and Eric Salzman, *Twentieth-Century Music: An Introduction* (Englewood Cliffs, N.J., 1967), pp. 5, 8, 19.

IV. Truth and Falsity

The fact that what aesthetic properties a thing seems to have may depend on what categories it is perceived in raises a question about how to determine what aesthetic properties it really does have. If *Guernica* appears dynamic when seen as a painting, and not dynamic when seen as a guernica, is it dynamic or not? Can one way of seeing it be ruled correct, and the other incorrect? One way of approaching this problem is to deny that the apparently conflicting aesthetic judgments of people who perceive a work in different categories actually do conflict.[22]

Judgments that works of art have certain aesthetic properties, it might be suggested, implicitly involve reference to some particular set of categories. Thus our claim that *Guernica* is dynamic really amounts to the claim that it is dynamic *as a painting*, or for people who see it as a painting. The judgment that it is not dynamic made by people who see it as a guernica amounts simply to the judgment that it is not dynamic *as a guernica*. Interpreted in these ways, the two judgments are of course quite compatible. Terms like "large" and "small" provide a convenient model for this interpretation. An elephant might be both small as an elephant and large as a mini-elephant, and hence it might be called truly either "large" or "small," depending on which category is implicitly referred to.

I think that aesthetic judgments are in *some* contexts amenable to such category-relative interpretations, especially aesthetic judgments about natural objects (clouds, mountains, sunsets) rather than works of art. (It will be evident that the alternative account suggested below is not readily applicable to most judgments about natural objects.) But most of our aesthetic judgments can be forced into this mold only at the cost of distorting them beyond recognition.

My main objection is that category-relative interpretations do not allow aesthetic judgments to be mistaken often enough. It would certainly be natural to consider a person who calls *Guernica* stark, cold, or dull, because he sees it as a guernica, to be *mistaken;* he misunderstands the work because he is looking at it in the wrong way. Similarly, one who asserts that a good performance of the *Adagio Cantabile* of Beethoven's *Pathétique* is percussive, or that a Roman bust looks like a unicolored, immobile man severed at the chest and depicts one as such, is simply wrong, even if his judgment is a result of his perceiving the work in different categories from those in which we perceive it. Moreover, we do not accord a status any more privileged to our own aesthetic judgments. We are likely to regard cubist paintings, or Japanese *gagaku* music, as formless, incoherent, or disturbing on our first contact with these forms largely because, I suggest, we would not be perceiving the works as cubist paintings, or as *gagaku* music. But after becoming familiar with these kinds of art we would probably *retract* our previous judgments, admit that they were mistaken. It would be quite inappropriate to protest that what we meant previously was merely that the works were formless or disturbing for the categories in which we then perceived them, while admitting that they are not for the categories of cubist paintings, or *gagaku* music. The conflict between apparently incompatible aesthetic judgments made while perceiving a

---

[22]I am ruling out the view that the notions of truth and falsity are not applicable to aesthetic judgments, on the ground that it would force us to reject so much of our normal discourse and common-sense intuitions about art that theoretical aesthetics, conceived as attempting to understand the institution of art, would hardly have left a recognizable subject matter to investigate. (Cf. the quotation from Wölfflin, above.)

work in different categories does not simply evaporate when the difference of categories is pointed out, as does the conflict between the claims that an animal is large and that it is small, when it is made clear that the person making the first claim regarded it as a mini-elephant and the one making the second regarded it as an elephant. The latter judgments do not (necessarily) reflect a real disagreement about the size of the animal, but the former do reflect a real disagreement about the aesthetic nature of the work.

Thus it seems that, at least in some cases, it is *correct* to perceive a work in certain categories, and *incorrect* to perceive it in certain others; that is, our judgments of it when we perceive it in the former are likely to be true, and those we make when perceiving it in the latter false. This provides us with absolute senses of "standard," "variable," and "contra-standard": features of a work are standard, variable, or contra-standard absolutely just in case they are standard, variable, or contra-standard (respectively) for people who perceive the work correctly. (Thus an absolutely standard feature is standard relative to some category in which the work is correctly perceived and contra-standard relative to none, an absolutely variable feature is variable relative to all such categories, and an absolutely contra-standard feature is contra-standard relative to at least one such category.)

How is it to be determined in which categories a work is correctly perceived? There is certainly no very precise or well-defined procedure to be followed. Different criteria are emphasized by different people and in different situations. But there are several fairly definite considerations which typically figure in critical discussions and which fit our intuitions reasonably well. I suggest that the following circumstances count toward its being correct to perceive a work, W, in a given category, C:

(*i*) The presence in W of a relatively large number of features standard with respect to C. The correct way of perceiving a work is likely to be that in which it has a minimum of contra-standard features for us. I take the relevance of this consideration to be obvious. It cannot be correct to perceive Rembrandt's *Titus Reading* as a kinetic sculpture, if this is possible, just because that work has too few of the features which make kinetic sculptures kinetic sculptures. But of course this does not get us very far. *Guernica*, for example, qualifies equally well on this count for being perceived as a painting and as a guernica.

(*ii*) The fact that W is better, or more interesting or pleasing aesthetically, or more worth experiencing, when perceived in C than it is when perceived in alternative ways. The correct way of perceiving a work is likely to be the way in which it comes off best.

(*iii*) The fact that the artist who produced W intended or expected it to be perceived in C, or thought of it as a C.

(*iv*) The fact that C is well established in and recognized by the society in which W was produced. A category is well established in and recognized by a society if the members of the society are familiar with works in that category, consider a work's membership in it a fact worth mentioning, exhibit works of that category together, and so forth—that is, roughly if that category figures importantly in their way of classifying works of art. The categories of impressionist painting and Brahmsian music are well established and recognized in our society; those of guernicas, paintings with diagonal composition containing green crosses, and pieces of music containing between four and eight F-sharps and at least seventeen quarter notes every eight bars are not. The categories in which a work is correctly perceived, according to this condition, are generally the ones in which the artist's contemporaries did perceive or would have perceived it.

In certain cases I think the mechanical process by which a work was produced, or (for example, in architecture) the nonperceptible physical characteristics or internal structure of a work, is relevant. A work is probably correctly perceived as an apparent etching rather than, say, an apparent woodcut or line drawing, if it was produced by the etching process. The strengths of materials in a building or the presence of steel girders inside wooden or plaster columns counts (not necessarily conclusively) toward the correctness of perceiving it in the category of buildings with visual characteristics typical of buildings constructed in that manner. I will not discuss these considerations further here.

What can be said in support of the relevance of conditions (ii), (iii), and (iv)? In the examples mentioned above, the categories in which we consider a work correctly perceived probably meet all of these conditions. I would suppose that *Guernica* is better seen as a painting than it would be seen as a guernica (though this would be hard to prove). In any case, Picasso certainly intended it to be seen as a painting rather than a guernica, and the category of paintings is well established in his (that is, our) society, whereas that of guernicas is not. But this of course does not show that (ii), (iii), and (iv) *each* is relevant. It tends to indicate only that one or other of them, or some combination, is relevant.

The difficulty of assessing each of the three conditions individually is complicated by the fact that by and large they can be expected to coincide, to yield identical conclusions. Since an artist usually intends his works for his contemporaries he is likely to intend them to be perceived in categories established in and recognized by his society. Moreover, it is reasonable to expect works to come off better when perceived in the intended categories than when perceived in others. An artist tries to produce works which are well worth experiencing when perceived in the intended way and, unless we have reason to think he is totally incompetent, there is some presumption that he succeeded at least to some extent. But it is more or less a matter of chance whether the work comes off well when perceived in some unintended way. The convergence of the three conditions, however, at the same time diminishes the *practical* importance of justifying them individually, since in most cases we can decide how to judge particular works of art without doing so. But the theoretical question remains.

I will begin with (ii). If we are faced with a choice between two ways of perceiving a work, and the work is very much better perceived in one way than it is perceived in the other, I think that, at least in the absence of contrary considerations, we would be strongly inclined to settle on the former way of perceiving it as the *correct* way. The process of trying to determine what is in a work consists partly in casting around among otherwise plausible ways of perceiving it for one in which the work is good. We feel we are coming to a correct understanding of a work when we begin to like or enjoy it; we are finding what is really there when it seems worth experiencing.

But if (ii) is relevant, it is quite clearly not the *only* relevant consideration. Take any work of art we can agree is of fourth- or fifth- or tenth-rate quality. It is very possible that if this work were perceived in some far-fetched set of categories that someone might dream up, it would appear to be first-rate, a masterpiece. Finding such *ad hoc* categories obviously would require talent and ingenuity on the order of that necessary to produce a masterpiece in the first place. But we can sketch how one might begin searching for them. (*a*) If the mediocre work suffers from some disturbingly prominent feature that distracts from whatever merits the work has, this feature might be toned down by choosing categories with respect to which it is standard, rather than variable or contra-standard. When the work is perceived in the new way the offending feature may be no more distracting than the flatness of a painting is to us. (*b*) If the work suffers from an overabundance of clichés it might be livened up by choosing categories with respect to which the clichés are variable or contra-standard rather than standard. (*c*) If it needs ingenuity we might devise a set of rules in terms of which the work finds itself in a dilemma from which it ingeniously escapes, and we might build these rules into a set of categories. Surely, however, if there are categories waiting to be discovered which would transform a mediocre work into a masterpiece, it does not follow that the work really is a hitherto unrecognized masterpiece. The fact that when perceived in such categories it would appear exciting, ingenious, and so forth, rather than grating, cliché-ridden, pedestrian, does not make it so. It *cannot* be correct, I suggest, to perceive a work in categories which are totally foreign to the artist and his society, even if it comes across as a masterpiece in them.[23]

This brings us to the historical conditions (*iii*) and (*iv*). I see no way of avoiding the conclusion that one or the other of them at least is relevant in determining in what categories a work is correctly perceived. I consider both relevant, but I will not argue here for the independent relevance of (*iv*). (*iii*) merits special attention in light of the prevalence of disputes about the importance of artists' intentions. To test the relevance of (*iii*) we must consider a case in which (*iii*) and (*iv*) diverge. One such instance occurred during the early days of the twelve-tone movement in music. Schoenberg no doubt intended even his earliest twelve-tone works to be heard as such. But this category was certainly not then well established or recognized in his society: virtually none of his contemporaries (except close associates such as Berg and Webern), even musically sophisticated ones, would have (or could have) heard these works in that category. But it seems to me that even the very first twelve-tone compositions are correctly heard as such, that the judgments one who hears them otherwise would make of them (for example, that they are chaotic, formless) are mistaken. I think this would be so even if Schoenberg had been working entirely alone, if *none* of his contemporaries had any inkling of the twelve-tone system. No doubt the first twelve-tone compositions are much better when heard in the category of twelve-tone works than when they are heard in any other way people might be likely to hear them. But as we have seen this cannot *by itself* account for the correctness of hearing them in the former way. The only other feature of the situation which could be relevant, so far as I can see, is Schoenberg's intention.

The above example is unusual in that Schoenberg was extraordinarily self-conscious about what he was doing, having explicitly formulated rules—that is, specified standard properties—for twelve-tone composition. Artists are not often so self-conscious, even when producing revolutionary works of art. Their intentions as to which categories their works are to be perceived in are not nearly as clear as Schoenberg's were, and

---

[23]To say that it is incorrect (in my sense) to perceive a work in certain categories is not necessarily to claim that one *ought not* to perceive it that way. I heartily recommend perceiving mediocre works in categories that make perceiving them worthwhile whenever possible. The point is that one is not likely to *judge* the work correctly when he perceives it incorrectly.

often they change their minds during the process of creation. In such cases (as well as ones in which the artists' intentions are unknown) the question of what categories a work is correctly perceived in is left by default to condition (*iv*), together with (*i*) and (*ii*). But it seems to me that in almost all cases at least one of the historical conditions, (*iii*) and (*iv*), is of crucial importance.

My account of the rules governing decisions about what categories works are correctly perceived in leaves a lot undone. There are bound to be a large number of undecidable cases on my criteria. Artists' intentions are frequently unclear, variable, or undiscoverable. Many works belong to categories which are borderline cases of being well established in the artists' societies (perhaps, for example, the categories of rococo music—for instance, C.P.E. Bach—of music in the style of early Mozart, and of very thin metal sculpted figures of the kind that Giacometti made). Many works fall between well-established categories (for example, between impressionist and cubist paintings), possessing *some* of the standard features relative to each, and so neither clearly qualify nor clearly fail to qualify on the basis of condition (*i*) to be perceived in either. There is, in addition, the question of what relative weights to accord the various conditions when they conflict.

It would be a mistake, however, to try to tighten up much further the rules for deciding how works are correctly perceived. To do so would be simply to legislate gratuitously, since the intuitions and precedents we have to go on are highly variable and often confused. But it is important to notice just where these intuitions and precedents are inconclusive, for doing so will expose the sources of many critical disputes. One such dispute might well arise concerning Giacometti's thin metal sculptures. To a critic who sees them simply as sculptures, or sculptures of people, they look frail, emaciated, wispy, or wiry. But that is not how they would strike a critic who sees them in the category of thin metal sculptures of that sort (just as stick figures do not strike us as wispy or emaciated). He would be impressed not by the thinness of the sculptures, but by the expressive nature of the positions of their limbs, and so forth, so he would no doubt attribute very different aesthetic properties to them. Which of the two ways of seeing these works is correct is, I suspect, undecidable. It is not clear whether enough such works have been made and have been regarded sufficiently often as constituting a category for that category to be deemed well established in Giacometti's society. And I doubt whether any of the other conditions settle the issue conclusively. So perhaps the dispute between the two critics is essentially unresolvable. The most that we can do is to point out just what sort of a difference of perception underlies the dispute, and why it is unresolvable.

The occurrence of impasses like this is by no means something to be regretted. Works may be fascinating precisely because of shifts between equally permissible ways of perceiving them. And the enormous richness of some works is due in part to the variety of permissible, and worthwhile, ways of perceiving them. But it should be emphasized that even when my criteria do not clearly specify a *single* set of categories in which a work is correctly perceived, there are bound to be possible ways of perceiving it (which we may or may not have thought of) that they definitely rule out.

The question posed at the outset of this section was how to determine what aesthetic properties a work has, given that which ones it seems to have depends on what categories it is perceived in, on which of its properties are standard, which variable, and which contra-standard for us. I have sketched in rough outline rules for deciding in what categories a work is *correctly* perceived (and hence which of its features are absolutely standard, variable, and contra-standard). The aesthetic properties it actually possesses are those that are to be found in it when it is perceived correctly.[24]

V. Conclusion

I return now to the issues raised in Section I. (I will adopt for the remainder of this paper the simplifying assumption that there is only one correct way of perceiving any work. Nothing important depends on this.) If a work's aesthetic properties are those that are to be found in it when it is perceived correctly, and the correct way to perceive it is determined partly by historical facts about the artist's intention and/or his society, no examination of the work itself, however thorough, will by itself reveal those properties.[25] If we are confronted by a work about whose origins we know absolutely nothing (for example, one lifted from the dust at an as yet unexcavated archaeological site on Mars), we would simply not be in a position to judge it aesthetically. We could not possibly tell by staring at it, no matter how intently and intelligently, whether it is coherent, or serene, or dynamic, for by staring we cannot tell whether it is to be seen as a sculpture, a guernica, or some other exotic or mundane kind of work of art. (We could attribute aesthetic properties to it in the way we do to natural objects, which of course does not involve consideration of historical facts about artists or their societies. [Cf. section IV.] But to do this would not be to treat the object as a *work* of art.)

It should be emphasized that the relevant historical facts are not merely useful aids to aesthetic judgment; they do not simply provide hints concerning what might be found in the work. Rather they help to *determine* what aesthetic properties a work has; they, together with the work's nonaesthetic features, *make* it coherent, serene, or whatever. If the origin of a work which is coherent and serene had been different in crucial respects, the work would not have had these qualities; we would not merely have lacked a means for *discovering* them. And of two works which differ *only* in respect of their origins—ones which are perceptually indistinguishable—one might be coherent or serene, and the other not. Thus, since artists' intentions are among the relevant historical considerations, the "intentional fallacy" is not a fallacy at all. I have of course made no claims about the relevance of artists' intentions as to the aesthetic properties that their works should have. I am willing to agree that whether an artist intended his work to be coherent or serene has nothing essential to do with whether it is coherent or serene. But this must not be allowed to seduce us into thinking that *no* intentions are relevant.

---

[24]This is a considerable oversimplification. If there are two equally correct ways of perceiving a work, and it appears to have a certain aesthetic property perceived in one but not the other of them, does it actually possess this property or not? There is no easy general answer. Probably in some such cases the question is undecidable. But I think we would sometimes be willing to say that a work is, e.g., touching or serene if it seems so when perceived in one acceptable way (or, more hesitantly, that there is "something very touching, or serene, about it"), while allowing that it does not seem touching, or serene, when perceived in another way which we do not want to rule incorrect. In some cases works have aesthetic properties (e.g., intriguing, subtle, alive, interesting, deep) which are not apparent on perceiving it in any *single* acceptable way, but which depend on the multiplicity of acceptable ways of perceiving it and relations between them. None of these complications relieves the critic of the responsibility for determining in what way or ways it is correct to perceive a work.

[25]But this, plus a general knowledge of what sorts of works were produced when and by whom, might.

Aesthetic properties, then, are not to be found in works themselves in the straightforward way that colors and shapes or pitches and rhythms are. But I do not mean to deny that we perceive aesthetic properties in works of art. I *see* the serenity of a painting and *hear* the coherence of a sonata, despite the fact that the presence of these qualities in the works depends partly on circumstances of their origin which I cannot (now) perceive. Jones's marital status is part of what makes him a bachelor, if he is one, and we cannot tell his marital status just by looking at him, though we can thus ascertain his sex. Hence, I suppose, his bachelorhood is not a property we can be said to perceive in him. But the aesthetic properties of a work do not depend on historical facts about it in anything like the way Jones's bachelorhood depends on his marital status. The point is not that the historical facts function as *grounds* in any ordinary sense for aesthetic judgments. By themselves they do not, in general, count either for or against the presence of any particular aesthetic property. And they are not part of a larger body of information (also including data about the work derived from an examination of it) from which conclusions about the works' aesthetic properties are to be deduced or inferred. We must learn to *perceive* the work in the correct categories, as determined in part by the historical facts, and judge it by what we then perceive in it. The historical facts help to determine whether a painting is coherent or serene *only* (as far as my arguments go) by affecting what way of perceiving the painting must reveal these qualities if they are truly attributable to the work.

We must not, however, expect to judge a work simply by setting ourselves to perceive it correctly, once it is determined what the correct way of perceiving it is. For one cannot, in general, perceive a work in a given set of categories simply by setting himself to do it. I could not possibly, merely by an act of will, see *Guernica* as a guernica rather than as a painting, nor could I hear a succession of street sounds in any arbitrary category one might dream up, even if the category has been explained to me in detail. Indeed, I cannot even imagine except in a rather vague way what it would be like, for example, to see *Guernica* as a guernica. One cannot merely decide to respond appropriately to a work—to be shocked or unnerved or surprised by its (absolutely) contra-standard features, to find its standard features familiar or mundane, and to react to its variable features in other ways—once one knows the correct categories. Perceiving a work in a certain category or set of categories is a skill that must be acquired by training, and exposure to a great many other works of the category or categories in question is ordinarily, I believe, an essential part of this training. (But an effort of will may facilitate the training, and once the skill is acquired one may be able to decide at will whether or not to perceive it in that or those categories.) This has important consequences concerning how best to approach works of art of kinds that are new to us—contemporary works in new idioms, works from foreign cultures, or newly resurrected works from the ancient past. It is no use just immersing ourselves in a particular work, even with the knowledge of what categories it is correctly perceived in, for that alone will not enable us to perceive it in those categories. We must become familiar with a considerable variety of works of similar sorts.

When dealing with works of more familiar kinds it is not generally necessary to undertake deliberately the task of training ourselves to perceive them in the correct categories (except perhaps when those categories include relatively subtle ones). But this is, I think, only because we have been trained unwittingly. Even the ability to see paintings as paintings had to be acquired, it seems to me, by repeated exposure to a great many paintings. The critic must thus go beyond the work before him in order to judge it aesthetically, not only to discover what the correct categories are, but also to be able to perceive it in them. The latter does not require consideration of historical facts, or consideration of facts at all, but it requires directing one's attention nonetheless to things other than the work in question.

Probably no one would deny that *some* sort of perceptual training is necessary, in many if not all instances, for apprehending a work's serenity or coherence, or other aesthetic properties. And of course it is not only *aesthetic* properties whose apprehension by the senses requires training. But the kind of training required in the aesthetic cases (and perhaps some others as well) has not been properly appreciated. In order to learn how to recognize gulls of various kinds, or the sex of chicks, or a certain person's handwriting, one must have gulls of those kinds, or chicks of the two sexes, or examples of that person's handwriting pointed out to him, practice recognizing them himself, and be corrected when he makes mistakes. But the training important for discovering the serenity or coherence of a work of art that I have been discussing is not of this sort. Acquiring the ability to perceive a serene or coherent work in the correct categories is not a matter of having had serene or coherent things pointed out to one, or having practiced recognizing them. What is important is not (or not merely) experience with other serene and coherent things, but experience with other things of the appropriate categories.

Much of the argument in this paper has been directed against the seemingly common-sense notion that aesthetic judgments about works of art are to be based solely on what can be perceived in them, how they look or sound. That notion is seriously misleading, I claim, on two different counts. I do not deny that paintings and sonatas are to be judged solely by what can be seen or heard in them—when they are perceived correctly. But examining a work with the senses can by itself reveal neither how it is correct to perceive it, nor how to perceive it that way.

PART FIVE

——————◆•••◆——————

Theories of the Individual Arts

Parts One through Four deal with the theory of art and the aesthetic. Although various theorists in these sections emphasize different arts in their discussions (for example, Bell emphasizes painting, Tolstoy literature, Danto the plastic arts), the primary aim of these theories is to provide a general analysis of art and the aesthetic, setting aside whatever differences there may be among the various arts and our aesthetic perceptions. This is not to suggest that these theorists are insensitive to important differences among the literary arts, the plastic arts, the performing arts, and those arts that seem to cut across categories (film, for example). It is only to say that their main concern is to distinguish between art and non-art, the aesthetic and the nonaesthetic, and not what sets one art apart from another.

Clearly, there are enormous differences among the arts. The most casual observer could hardly fail to note that what makes literature literature differs vastly from what makes painting painting. In fact, several of the writers in this section take pains to distinguish one art form from another, such as painting from sculpture. In this part we present a variety of discussions of the different arts. It would be impossible to survey all of the arts, and we have consequently chosen to concentrate on five areas with which aestheticians have been traditionally concerned (literature, drama, painting, architecture, and music) and two areas of special importance to contemporary aesthetics (film and dance). These selections attempt to represent the diverse ways in which theorizing about the various arts has occurred. To facilitate the study of these multiple selections, we provide a brief introduction for each section of this part. Moreover, we attempt to retain the "dialectical-critical" format of the earlier chapters as far as possible. Thus, Wollheim's essay on Gombrich and the critical discussion by Carroll and Banes of Beardsley move in this direction. As in previous chapters, some of the discussion is expository and interpretative in nature, while most is more openly critical.

It is possible to read these chapters with an eye to a specific philosophical problem or problems upon which each focuses. Thus, the theory of literature consists of a number of papers whose main theme is intention and style in the literary work; the chapter on drama deals with Nietzsche and the nature of tragedy. Similarly for the other chapters: the aesthetics of painting and of architecture contain selections on the nature of representation in those arts; film theory centers on ontology and the interrelationships of film to the other arts; the chapter on musical aesthetics is directly concerned with the question of expressiveness in music; and the chapter on dance deals largely with the problem of defining this art. As a result, the chapters may be used as much to illuminate a specific problem in the philosophy of art as to teach the theory of that art itself.

THE THEORY OF LITERATURE:
INTENTION AND STYLE IN THE LITERARY WORK

This section begins with Monroe Beardsley's "The Philosophy of Literature," a piece that attempts to survey a range of problems in the theory of literature but that centers on the question "What is a literary text?" Beardsley begins his essay by raising the question "What is required for anything to be the subject matter of philosophical inquiry?" He rejects the claim that the subject of a philosophical inquiry must be governed by specific rules or principles and allows that it is sufficient for it to be an *activity* informed by rational objectives. Literature, he maintains, is such an activity because authoring (composing a literary work) and "literating" (reading or following a literary work), whether fictional or nonfictional, are governed by certain rational conditions that distinguish them from other forms of writing. Beardsley proceeds to define "literary work" in two stages by distinguishing between two subclasses of literary text—the first fictional and the second real. While the former class of texts is not intended to affect actual human behavior, the latter class contains an *artistic intention*. (Beardsley's use of the artist's intentions in this context is used to distinguish between art and non-art, while his discussion in "The Intentional Fallacy" uses the concept of intention as a method of criticism and analysis.)

Ultimately, Beardsley's problem consists in clarifying the meaning of the term "artistic intention." He does so by appealing to an "aesthetic interest" as a means of distinguishing between literary and nonliterary writing. Beardsley restricts literary works to those in which a "substantial role" in their creation is played by the artistic intention to make the work capable of satisfying an aesthetic interest. This point of view is characteristic of Beardsley's formalistic approach to the arts, in which he views the formal qualities possessed by artworks as instruments for the satisfaction of purely aesthetic interests such as wit, humor, tragic power, dramatic intensity, etc. This formalistic account Beardsley contrasts with "cognitivism," which maintains that the central concern of literature is the acquisition of knowledge, such as the understanding of human behavior.

"The Philosophy of Literature" is closely related to the Wimsatt and Beardsley essay "The Intentional Fallacy," in which the authors defend a form of aestheticism with respect to the literary work. In effect, the authors treat literary works as monads; they reject all attempts to interpret and/or evaluate poems, fictions, etc., in terms of subjective or biographical considerations. Broadly, this is meant to include not merely an author's conscious plans for his or her work, but any psychological treatment that takes us beyond the confines of the work itself. Thus, expressive qualities of the work are not to be understood as direct expressions of the writer's state of mind, but simply as properties of the work itself—as if it were a physical object. As a result, "The Intentional Fallacy" amounts to a classical statement of an anti-intentionalist position on the arts, and one that has given rise to such important questions as "How do an artist's intentions figure in our interpretation/assessment of works of art?"; "Is there a viable distinction between 'internal' and 'external' evidence in the interpretation of literature?"; "Is there really a *fallacy* in appealing to talk about the creative and expressive activities of the artist?"

Colin Lyas' "Personal Qualities and the Intentional Fallacy" deals with the ongoing controversy over the relevance of references to the intentions of artists. Lyas distinguishes various forms of the more limited claim that references to intentions are critically irrelevant from the general thesis that no reference of any sort to artists can be relevant to the evaluation of works of art. He challenges this latter thesis and argues, by reference to what he calls "personal qualities," that a *prima facie* case exists for saying that references to the fact that a work is perceptive, or glib, or pretentious, or mawkish, etc., are references to the minds of artists as they display themselves in their works.

Lyas then raises the question of why Beardsley and Wimsatt might have wished to eliminate references to artists. One answer is that they are committed to an absolute distinction between references to artists and references to works of art; this is further related to an implicit acceptance in their work of a Cartesian dualism between the mental/private and the physical/public. Such an absolute distinction between artist and work entails that for any assertion made by a would-be critic, one must be able to answer the question "Is that assertion about the artist or is it about the work?" Lyas' discussion of personal qualities argues persuasively that this question does not always admit of a clear answer. That being so, the distinction between talking about artists and talking about works is undermined, and with it is also undermined the further claim by Beardsley and Wimsatt that any talk about artists is irrelevant and fallaciously distracts attention from what they tendentiously call the work itself. For Lyas, *the work itself* can contain and display to us the mind of its artist. Any full account of what is in the work will, therefore, have to refer to that mind.

In "Style and Personality in the Literary Work" Jenefer Robinson defends the idea that the style of an individual author is an expression of qualities of mind, attitudes, interests, and personality traits in that author or "implied" author. Style in general is described as a way of *doing things*, and literary style in particular as a way of doing certain *literary* things, such as describing characters and social setting, commenting on events, and presenting various points of view. People's qualities of mind are typically expressed in what they do. Similarly, a writer's way of doing things is expressive of personality traits and qualities of mind that may be the author's or may belong to the persona the author assumes in writing (the "implied" author).

It could be argued that it is the verbal and expressive characteristics of a literary work ("Latinate," "euphonious," "dramatic," "heroic") that are its stylistic qualities and that these need not be qualities of the implied author's mind or personality. The response to this objection is that these qualities are *not* always stylistic, and that when they are, it is only because they contribute to the expression of qualities of mind, etc., in the implied author. For example, "Latinate" is a style quality only if it contributes to the expression of an abstract imagination (say) in the implied author.

The theory, according to Robinson, has a number of explanatory advantages. It explains why a correct description of a writer's style mentions some of its verbal characteristics and not others, and why the same verbal characteristic may have stylistic significance in one work and no stylistic significance or a different significance in another work. It explains unity in individual style (as the expression of a unified personality). It shows why subject matter as well as "form" can have stylistic significance, and it explains the difference between style and "signature." Finally, it enables us to distinguish clearly between a writer's *individual* style and *general* style categories such as "Elizabethan pastoral."

Monroe C. Beardsley

THE PHILOSOPHY OF LITERATURE

We might be amused at a brash barroom philosopher who announced that he could philosophize about anything—and we might even start trying to think of examples that would puncture the boast. On second thought, though, why not? Sermons in stones, they say—and, according to Walt Whitman, "a mouse is miracle enough to stagger sextillions of infidels." Perhaps a sufficiently deep or determined thinker could manage to extract some philosophical juice from even the humblest object or event. Still, on third thought—if we get that far—we had better pause to consider what actually is being claimed. What is philosophizing? The relevance of this question is pointed up by a conversation David Hume once had.

> "I am surprised, Mr. Hume," said Thomas White, a decent rich merchant of London, "that a man of your good sense should think of being a philosopher. Why, I now took it into my head to be a philosopher for some time, but tired of it most confoundedly, and very soon gave it up."
>
> "Pray, sir," said Mr. Hume, "in what branch of philosophy did you employ your researches? What books did you read?"
>
> "Books?" said Mr. White; "nay, sir, I read no books, but I used to sit you whole forenoons a-yawning and poking the fire."[1]

Before we could say with assurance whether there could be a philosophy of ———, we would want to know what a "philosophy of" something is to consist in, and what sort of word may legitimately replace that blank.

In seeking to understand what kind of inquiry philosophy of literature is, or ought to be, I know no better guide than a recent book on the philosophy of education by James McClellan—even if we can't follow his trail exactly. What properly fits into the blank in "philosophy of ———" is always (according to McClellan) the name of a practice, which is a form of activity defined by a system of rules or canons governing the actions of those engaged in the practice. The philosophy of a practice has as its purpose "to discover the distinctive form which human reason assumes in that practice."[2] In its

This essay was written for the first edition of this collection and is being reprinted here in an abridged form.
[1] From Ernest Campbell Mossner, *The Forgotten Hume* (New York: Columbia Univ. Press, 1943), p. xii.
[2] James E. McClellan, *The Philosophy of Education*, Foundations of Philosophy Series (Englewood Cliffs, N.J.: Prentice-Hall, 1976), p. 2.

"revelatory" aspect, this inquiry aims to make explicit "some general features(s) of human reason as exemplified in the practice."

> It doesn't require philosophy to point out that each of us can follow a story, a proof, and a lawyer's advice. We are engaged in philosophy of history, mathematics, and law from their revelatory aspects when we (try to) uncover the presupposed canons of reason which make "following" in each case a rational activity.

In its "critical" aspect, the philosophy of a practice examines those canons against "the most general principles of rationality we can discern"—those of logic and ethics.

When we try to fit the philosophy of literature into this pattern, some genuine difficulties arise at once; and the two most fundamental ones deserve some preliminary discussion. They center on the concepts of *practice* and *reason*.

I

A practice is an activity governed by a system of rules: "in those terms," McClellan remarks,

> law is clearly a practice, so are engineering, medicine, mathematics. . . . Neither art nor the criticism of art is clearly a practice. . . . Love is unequivocally *not* a practice, though it is often perverted into a facsimile of one or more practices.[3]

Literature can certainly be thought of as an activity. It probably comes more naturally to most of us to think of literature as a collection of objects, of books and magazines and so on stacked in libraries or homes—though if pressed we would also be willing to add stories told in various cultures but not written down or printed and tape-recordings of old radio shows never yet transcribed. All these are literary *products*, and they enter into processes of production and consumption. So—staying with our own culture for the most part—we have two basic literary activities: that of composing a literary work deliberately and that of reading it understandingly. Around these, of course, cluster other familiar activities that may justify our calling literature a social institution: those of publishers, printers, librarians, book sellers, book collectors, book reviewers, and such. But authoring (i.e., composing a literary work) and literating (i.e., reading a literary work) are central, and reciprocal.

In literature we find, apparently, a distinguishable form of activity, but is it a practice? For our present purposes we need not develop the lurking complexities of this question, but some of them may be noted for future reflection. Consider authoring, the making of literary works. It is an activity that certainly includes rule following (at least in the usual case): rules of English grammar, for example, and sometimes more contingent ones (if the short story is for a particular magazine, it may not be over 6,000 words long).

It was once thought by respected literary critics that every literary work must belong to a certain fixed type, or genre, and must follow the rules of that genre (as that a satire is to be in heroic couplets); but hardly anyone would agree with such a view now. The rules of grammar, though they impose restrictions on most authors, don't really define

---

[3]Ibid., pp. 1–2.

the activity of authoring, since, just because a paragraph is grammatical, it doesn't follow that it is a literary work. Textbooks that purport to teach people how to write fiction or poetry do often contain a lot of general advice, like "Make your characters three dimensional" or "Avoid metaphors that are clichés ('the moon looked down')." But these are not the kinds of rules that define a practice; they are (supposed to be) aids in *improving* practice. Note how in any game there are rules that define or constitute the game—rules you have to follow in order to play the game at all—and practical "rules of thumb" that experienced players bear in mind in order to play the game *well*.

So perhaps we can't really call authoring a practice. What about literating? Again, you can't read a novel in English without knowing the rules of English syntax and the semantical rules governing the words. But these rules apply to *all* reading; they are not distinctive of literating (a word I made up for this occasion). Of course, again, there are various principles, of varying degrees of usefulness, which it might in general be well to follow if we wish to read literature with the greatest possible understanding and enjoyment. But these don't make literating a practice. It has been suggested that our encounters with literary works have some features of a game; for example, in detective stories, both sides must play fair in that the author is bound by the rule that all essential clues are to be provided for the reader and the reader is bound by the rule that he is not to look at the last chapter until he gets to it. No doubt the detective story genre has a touch of game-like quality (though whether or not it is literature might be debated).

On a more sophisticated level, a view has developed (out of the contemporary movement known as "structuralism") that the literator follows certain broad "codes" or "conventions" in interpreting a literary work—and even that there is a sort of implicit "narrative contract" between author and literator, licensing certain expectations from the latter.[4] These ideas are important; I shall return to them later. If they should become confirmed, they would go far toward demonstrating that authoring-literating is a (dual) practice. In the meantime, however, we may be content to soften McClellan's requirement that the only thing we can have a philosophy of is a practice. Let us say that any distinctive form of activity (A) can be the occasion of a philosophy of A.

But this decision now raises questions about the other part of McClellan's formula: that to philosophize about A is to study "human reason as exemplified in" A. It is easy to see human reason as exemplified in a system of rules—partly because we may think (what may not be true) that the rules were deliberately devised, and that therefore there must be some reason for having them, and partly because we know (a little about) how to argue for and against rules—whether there should, or should not, for example, be a rule that all controversial articles in the high school newspaper are to be approved by the principal before publication.

Now it may be quite true that, in general, practices will provide more to philosophize about than other activities, just because they are constituted by rules. Still, an activity—if it has a distinctive form and is widely carried on—may be more or less reasonable too. It may involve, and on analysis exhibit, distinctive modes of thinking (as legal reasoning differs from that typical of experimental psychology). It may have its own special purposes and be more or less rationally ordered for the

---

[4]For an excellent discussion, see Jonathan Culler, *Structuralist Poetics: Structuralism, Linguistics, and the Study of Literature* (Ithaca, N.Y.: Cornell University Press, 1975), chapters 6–9.

successful fulfillment of those purposes. It may presuppose the truth of important general assumptions about human nature, or knowledge, or reality; and these would be subject to philosophical scrutiny.

Still, some uneasiness may linger. What, you may wonder, does reason have to do with literature at all? Why should we expect there to be any "distinctive form that reason assumes" in authoring and literating? Recall, for example, McClellan's reference to following a story—after which it turned out that he was thinking of historical narrative, which, naturally, we can philosophize about because history purports to be a branch of human knowledge obtained by characteristic methods and tested against recognized canons of historical inquiry. But when we read *Pinocchio* or *The Forsyte Saga* we are following a story too; only here the story is about events that never happened to people who never were. We have fiction. No question, it seems, of claims to knowledge about the real world, methods of investigation, or standards of truth or probability. So where does reason come into the picture, to give the would-be philosopher something to get hold of?

We must look more closely to see it—but looking closely is, after all, no novelty to the philosopher. First, in fiction writing (including tale telling) we have a very widespread form of activity, which suggests that it is not without a point. Reason appears in the tendency of this activity (if we discover that it *has* a tendency) to satisfy rather basic and pervasive human needs or to afford significant satisfactions. Second, if stories may be told well or poorly, and differences in quality can be discerned, then reason appears in whatever skills and aptitudes are required (a) to tell stories well rather than poorly and (b) to judge correctly that a particular telling is good or poor. Third, if understanding a story, in the fullest degree, is something that one person may be better at than another person, then reason appears in learning and teaching how to follow stories most understandingly.

In short, experience suggests (1) that it is possible for a justification, or adequate reason, to be given for engaging in such an activity as authoring-literating, (2) that it is possible for reasons to be given for telling a story in one way rather than another, or for telling one story rather than another, and (3) that it is possible for reasons to be given for understanding a literary work in one way rather than in another. How much of a philosophy of literature it is possible to have—how extensive, how systematic, how significant it can be—depends on the extent to which these possibilities turn out, on investigation, to be actualities.

To touch on just one of the questions I have raised, if *The Forsyte Saga* is superior as a literary work to *Pinocchio* (not better to read to children, but just better literature), then there must be some reason *why* it is better; something about it must make it better, or explain why it is better. One of the special forms reason assumes in literating (and indirectly in authoring, since the writer, as he writes, must constantly criticize his own work) is that of making reasonable judgments about the comparative literary value of novels, short stories, poems, and the like. I don't mean to imply that the literator must always be a kind of critic, only that it is natural for his interest in literature to generate questions about comparative literary value. Such questions call for reasoned answers. The sort of reasoning typically involved has its distinctive form—it is not like the reasoning in law or in experimental psychology. Thus it presents an opportunity for—it invites—philosophical reflection.

II

To fill out the foregoing rather abstract account of the philosophy of literature, we must look at some of the central and basic problems that this branch of philosophy encounters and aims to solve. Let us begin with authoring.

"Authoring" has been defined here; but the illumination provided by any definition depends on the terms it uses, and in the present case the key term is "literary work." One of the earliest questions to arise in the philosophy of literature is bound to be, What is a literary work? Until we can answer this question, we do not fully understand what authoring is.

Someone sits down, pen, pencil, or typewriter in hand (or you can supply a tape-recorder if you prefer), and writes

  a shopping list
  a note to be left on the refrigerator door for Johnny
  a letter to Senator S about taxes
  a children's story about a pair of mischievous twin wombats
  a report on some laboratory experiments designed to develop featherless chickens

There is a handy term for what is produced in all these cases: "text." Now a text is not the same thing as the particular physical object which is an instance of it. When you write down a shopping list, you are making marks on paper; the marked paper is a new object in the world. If your list is different from any previous one, you have also produced a new text. If you copy someone else's shopping list, you have produced a new instance of the same text. All copies of *The Three Musketeers* (at least, those with no really puzzling typographical errors) are examples of the same text, though there are thousands of copies. So it is useful to have two terms: "text-token" for the particular volume you presented to your nephew, "text-type" for the sequence of words common to all volumes containing *The Three Musketeers*. When I write "text" I always mean "text-type."

By the definition I have proposed, writing a shopping list is not authoring, since a shopping list is not a literary work. Or could it be? (Of course it could be a *part* of a literary work—of a short story about a compulsive shopper or of a poem about the materialistic values of contemporary America.) Here's the problem: How are we to distinguish the literary texts from all the rest?

There are various ways of trying to make such a distinction: (1) We might look for objective features of the texts themselves that are present in literary texts but not in others. For example, we might note that some texts are in meter and also rhyme (they are verse), and we might propose that any such text is a literary text. This would not cover all literary texts, but it would be a start—if we really think it reasonable to classify, say, "Thirty days hath September" as a literary work. (2) We might look for defining features in the process of creation itself, in the writer's intention. (3) We might look for distinctive effects of the text on people who read it. (4) We might look for some other more complicated relationship between the text and certain social institutions (e.g., literature is what has been given that name by reputable critics). Or (5) We might try some combination of these.

I want to give some sense of the potential complications of this apparently simple question, "What is a literary text?" even though we won't be able to pursue them very far here. Probably the most useful thing to do is to propose an answer and discuss some of its strengths and weaknesses briefly, then leave it to you to consider other strengths and (especially) weaknesses that I have overlooked. If you end up by rejecting my answer, you will at least be in a better position to suggest your own alternative.

My proposal is to approach the task of carving out the class of literary texts in two stages. Stage 1 makes use of the concept of *fictional text*—and right away another important problem in the philosophy of literature turns up. For there are a number of subtleties in this concept, which only careful analysis can cope with. The main distinction is apparent enough. The shopping list you might find crumpled on the floor near the supermarket check-out counter is a *real* text: In composing it, someone was actually recording a resolution to buy those items and, presumably, carried it out. The shopping list you might find in a short story about a compulsive shopper was never actually drawn up or used by any real person (since the character in the story doesn't exist): It is a make-believe shopping list. Again: Let's say the letter to the Senator alluded to above begins with these words:

> Dear Senator S:
> I think it is a crying shame that the legislature is once again considering the imposition of a state income tax on us hardworking citizens who are already groaning under the burden of countless oppressive taxes. . . .

You don't have to read more than a line or two to see that here someone really is complaining about the situation. Suppose the story about the mischievous twin wombats begins:

> Willie and Wanda, the wombat twins, rubbed their eyes as they awoke one spring and dashed out of their homey cave with cries of joy. . . .

You don't have to read more than a line or two to see that no one is really claiming that such a thing ever happened—in no way could this be taken for biography, zoology, or mammalian ethnology.

A real text, then, is (roughly) one used to perform an action involving an attempt to communicate, in a broad sense: it is used to deplore, to describe, to plead, to threaten, to express affection, or whatever. A fictional text is one that has the general form of a communication, but in fact is not one: no such action is being performed. It is a kind of play-acting on paper. This definition is highly simplified, but it will have to serve for the present.[5] My proposal as stage 1, then, is that all fictional texts are literary works. They are not all *good* or *great* literary works—you see that children's stories, nursery rhymes, pornographic novels, and Polish jokes are swept into my broad category. But it is a significant category, since the distinction between fictional and nonfictional texts cuts rather deep across the entire range of texts and since the appropriate response to a fictional text obviously differs so greatly from that to a nonfictional text. There are complexities here, which we must not deny, even if we set them aside. For example, a short story about a rape is fictional, a newspaper account is nonfictional; yet you might

---

[5]For further discussion, see "The Concept of Literature," in Frank Brady, John Palmer, and Martin Price, eds., *Literary Theory and Structure* (New Haven, Conn.: Yale Univ. Press, 1973) and references given there.

well have some of the same emotions in reading them. Still, in important respects your reactions must differ: for example, the actual rape may move you to write a letter to the newspaper blaming the police for inadequate patrolling, but you can't blame the police for fictional rapes.

Ordinarily, normally, the texts we encounter and expect to encounter are (in the sense used above) real. The fictional twist is special and more sophisticated. Thus for a text to be fictional, it is not enough for the *author* to know it is not real or for him not to care whether it is or not; he must signal to the reader, or potential reader, that his text is not real. A simple and common way of doing this is to attach a label: "A Novel," "A Romance," "A Fantasy," whatever. Then the librarians know which shelf to place the text-tokens on, and the reader is in no danger of mistaking fiction for fact.

But one of the ways of expanding the boundaries of literature, and one of the great opportunities for literary invention, especially in our time, is the possibility of making the text itself declare its fictionality. The wombat story is an obvious case of this: we doubt that wombats can utter "cries of joy," and this anthropomorphizing of the creatures is a cue to fictionality. More subtle devices are needed in highly realistic novels, which carefully build up an imaginary world that could easily be a real one. In an interesting and perceptive essay, Philip Stevick has discussed an apparent tendency in some contemporary fictionalists to reject the idea of building an imaginary world, and to attain a special tone of mocking, a kind of put-on.[6] He quotes from Woody Allen's account of Lord Sandwich's efforts to invent the sandwich:

> 1745: After four years of frenzied labor, he is convinced he is on the threshold of success. He exhibits before his peers two slices of turkey with a slice of bread in the middle. His work is rejected by all but David Hume, who senses the imminence of something great and encourages him. Heartened by the philosopher's friendship, he returns to work with renewed vigor.[7]

How do we know that this is, as we say, "meant to be funny"—or, more precisely, that it is humorous fiction rather than a wildly misinformed attempt at culinary history? It is, of course, no part of our present task to answer such questions—they are for the critic and literary theorist. What is to be noted here, however, is that the very status of a text as a literary work, in virtue of its fictionality, may depend on the author's ability to plant the proper cues, which can be correctly read by the literator in order to recognize the text as fictional and, thus, as literature. Here is one place where reason assumes a characteristic form in authoring, for the construction of systems of signs, and the invention and establishment of new signs, are rational activities, and traffic with signs of fictional status are inherently involved in the activity of authoring.

It must be acknowledged that the nature of fictionality, and of the innumerable conventions involved in assigning fictional status, is still far from fully understood. This is one of the items of unfinished business in the philosophy of literature. It is obvious that the absurdity (but by what standards?) of supposing that a great philosopher like David Hume, amiable though he was, would be impressed by such paltry fruit of "four years of frenzied labor" serves as a signal that the ostensible speaker in this passage does not literally believe what he is saying. But can we generalize from this? Are there underlying principles? How, for example, do we know when a text is ironic?[8]

[6]See "Lies, Fictions, and Mock-Facts," *The Western Humanities Review*, 30 (1976), 1–12.
[7]*Getting Even* (New York: Warner Paperback Library, 1972), p. 34.
[8]For an interesting recent discussion of the problem of signaling and recognizing irony, see Göran Hermerén, "Intention and Interpretation in Literary Criticism," *New Literary History*, 7 (1975–76), 71–74.

(The difficulty and subtlety of the task I have described has just been pointed up for me by a packet of mustard received—along with an imitation of the celebrated Earl's invention—on an airplane trip. It is inscribed:

MADE WITH WHITE WINE. Grey Poupon. Daring French mustard pioneer. Lived in 1777. Added white wine to mustard, creating smooth aristocratic taste. A truly great man who lent his name to a truly great mustard. Grey Poupon.

How many cues help us to take this passage straight—on the assumption that it was *not* written by Woody Allen?)

But of course the making and planting of fictional cues is by no means the only point at which we can discern reason in authoring. It is by thinking, often hard and complicated thinking, that the author shapes his plot, regulates the rhythmic variations in pace as he tells his story, selects from among the thoughts that come to him those words and actions that will most sharply reveal key traits of his characters, and, sometimes, provides us with profound visions of human life and of the universe that we are left to reflect upon. I do not mean to suggest that the process of writing a novel or a poem is purely a matter of cold calculation or of puzzle-solving; no more—and indeed much less—than most human activities is it free of sudden inspirations, feelings, and emotion of all sorts. But whatever else it also is, authoring is a mode of thinking. And wherever thinking appears, we may, as philosophers, ask how well it is done—as judged against the basic canons of logical reasoning.

III

My proposal was to define "literary work" in two stages, by marking out the two subclasses of literary texts. One subclass consists of all fictional texts: in them, however serious may be their ultimate import, we find a peculiar play with language, an imaginative invention, that justifies our considering them as works of literary art. The other subclass consists, to put it very concisely at first, of those texts in which we can discern an *artistic intention*.

What makes a text real, in the sense here assigned to this term, is that it does in fact enter into a process of linguistic interaction connected, at least indirectly, with other actual or potential behavior. Pope's *Essay on Man* expounds a philosophy and argues for it. Winston Churchill's famous radio speech after the retreat from Dunkirk summoned the people of Great Britain to rise above their crushing defeat and stand firm against Hitlerism. John Lothrop Motley's *Rise of the Dutch Republic* describes, explains, and interprets numerous historical events in the long struggle of the Low Countries to free themselves from Spain. But these are more than real texts: Pope's poem has a great deal of cleverness and wit, sharpened by the heroic couplets; Churchill's speech has powerful language and rises to a magnificent climax; Motley shapes his story artfully and exhibits a strong feeling of moral indignation through his supple and eloquent style. It is such features that (by stage 2) enable us to classify these works as literature. Even the report on a laboratory experiment designed to produce featherless chickens might conceivably rise to literature in a similar way—though the odds are against it.

The immediate problem, of course, is to clarify the key term I have introduced:

"artistic intention." The problem is, indeed, so large that we cannot hope to resolve it here, but we can get some sense of its dimensions and ramifications. To begin with, we may try expanding our stage 2 proposal in somewhat different terms:

> X is a literary work if a substantial role in X's creation was played by the intention to make it capable of satisfying an aesthetic interest.

So—you may say—we understand that an artistic intention is an intention to satisfy an aesthetic interest, but that only pushes the problem back one step: What is an aesthetic interest?

Before returning to this question, we should note some other problematic features of this proposal. First, can we tolerate the rather vague term "substantial role"? I suspect that we must. On the one hand, we wouldn't want to count the shopping list or refrigerator note to Johnny as literary texts, I should think: they are about as purely utilitarian as anything can be. On the other hand, we must make room within the class of literary texts for Pope, Churchill, and Motley, who clearly made a conscious effort to produce something more than plain philosophy, oration, and history. But it is a matter of degree how much concern the writer has with these aesthetic aspects of his work, and so the line between literary real texts and nonliterary real texts is bound to be fuzzy. Still, as long as there are many clear-cut examples on both sides, the distinction is useful: the fuzziness merely reminds us to avoid future arguments about the admittedly borderline cases (for example, some essays by Freud or some letters of William James).

Second, you may question the introduction of intention in this context: does this not risk running afoul of the so-called "intentional fallacy"? I think not. I agree fully with what is said by Maurice Mandelbaum in a fine essay that is in fact highly relevant to the problems we are now considering.

> The phrase "the intentional fallacy" originally referred to a particular method of criticism, that is, to a method of interpreting and evaluating given works of art; it was not the aim of Wimsatt and Beardsley to distinguish between art and nonart. These two problems are, I believe, fundamentally different in character. However, I do not feel sure that Professor Beardsley has noted this fact. . . .[9]

The fact is duly noted. In distinguishing between art and nonart in the particular case of literature (that is, between literary works of art and other texts), we have to appeal at some point to an artistic intention.

There are problems, however, about our knowledge of this intention. In some few cases we may have external evidence that the historian wished his narrative to have dramatic form, as well as faithfulness to fact, and may have wished his style to be not only accurate but subtle and expressive. Even if he failed to fulfill these intentions, we may charitably classify his work as literature, while rating it rather low. Mostly, of course, we discern the artistic intention in the work itself. The narrative is in fact dramatically shaped, the characters are three-dimensional and live, the style carries heavy overtones, now ironic, now compassionate, now angry, now judicious. Such works, one may say, proclaim that they are literature by being quite good literature. Since it is highly probable that the writer knew what he had done and wanted it that

---

[9]"Family Resemblances and Generalization Concerning the Arts," *American Philosophical Quarterly*, 2 (1965), 5n.

way, we can legitimately infer the intention from the deed. In cases like this, it may seem that we can for all practical purposes dispense with the appeal to intention; yet I think the literary merits betoken literary status only via the inference to artistic intention. And this is shown by the fact that some texts with (perhaps modest) literary merits are still never thought of as literature, because the intention is so concentrated on biology, social psychology, astronomy, or political propaganda.

Third, then, we return to the concept of producing a text capable of satisfying an aesthetic interest. And the effort to clarify this concept plunges us at once into one of the deepest and most controversial problems in the philosophy of literature. Consider fictional texts for the moment; they toil not, neither do they spin. They don't help us buy groceries, fight wars, stop littering the streets, learn the ways of God to man, or understand the rise of the Dutch Republic. Yet if the activity of producing them is rationally justifiable, it must have some point. A person can cut words out of the newspaper, toss them in a hat, draw them out at random, and paste them up. And there is no law against his claiming to have produced a poem. But this claim is purely verbal, and wholly empty, unless he has a concept of what a literary work is and of what value a literary work may have. His activity is simply pointless. But we do not believe it was pointless of Jane Austen to write *Persuasion* or of Keats to write his "Ode on a Grecian Urn."

Since fictional texts are good for nothing in the usual ways of being good, they must be good for something else: for satisfying an aesthetic interest. If we can come to understand what this means, we can also understand how real texts sometimes rise to literature in that they offer (or at least purport to offer) a similar satisfaction, over and above their usefulness in the context of human life.

One way to start an inquiry into the nature of aesthetic interests (or interest, if there is only one) would be to look for some very plain, simple, and uncontroversial examples. Thus consider someone who likes (or buys, or keeps, or looks at) a vase because of its delicate colors and graceful shape: no one (I suppose) will be unwilling to call his interest in the vase aesthetic. And if he is interested in the shape of a novel's plot—in the neat way the complications are developed and worked out to a dramatic climax, with a final tying up of all the threads (as in *Tom Jones*)—that interest, too, is evidently aesthetic. This is fairly easy to agree on, and we may even risk the generalization that any interest in form or quality for its own sake is an aesthetic interest. (But that begins to raise problems.) Now suppose he is interested in the philosophy of a literary work—say, Tolstoy's philosophy of history, in *War and Peace*. Then we may want to suggest a distinction: if what interests him is the truth of that philosophy or its logical consistency or its historical antecedents and influence, then his interest in the novel is not aesthetic; but if what interests him is the character of that philosophy (its bold sweep, say) or its organic relationship to the structure and recurrent themes of the novel, then his interest *is* aesthetic—indeed, it is an interest in form and quality.

How far this suggestion can be carried is a matter of some importance, ultimately, in the philosophy of literature; it is also highly debatable. Not that we must insist on a sharp line between aesthetic and other interests, of course; vagueness may be inescapable and acceptable here, too. But it seems that some line must be drawn if we are to find a point in authoring, whether of fictional texts or of nonfictional texts that aspire to literary status.

The line of thought just sketched (all too thinly) moves toward what some would call a "formalist" conception of aesthetic interest, and it has long been recognized that, of all the arts, literature is least likely, on the face of it, to take kindly to such a treatment. It may well seem to you—as you think of other features of other literary works to test the proposed analysis—that formalism is bound to leave out too much. What! Are aesthetic interests limited to form and quality alone? Even granted that this includes a lot of things—wit, humor, tragic power, dramatic intensity, style, and more—it may not include everything that you would want to say we can take an aesthetic interest in.

Therefore it may be well, in lieu of a thorough discussion of this most basic problem, to set forth (though with equal sketchiness) an alternative kind of view. Let's call it "cognitivism," since its central emphasis is on knowledge. What we ask from literature, on this theory, and what we get a good deal of from the best literature, is knowledge—more particularly, understanding of human beings, ourselves and others. The point of authoring (and of literature) is ultimately to promote this human understanding. How does this point differ from that of psychology and social science? Only in that literary works constitute a fundamentally different kind of symbol system from the texts of psychology, sociology, anthropology, and the like.

There are various ways of trying to make this distinction, and all of them have difficulties that have not yet been cleared up (more unfinished business for the philosophy of literature). For example, we might argue that psychology (taking that as a paradigm science of human behavior and human action) has its characteristic methods, involving induction, generalization, classification, and so on. But in literature persons and events and situations are given a symbolic form that enables us to obtain insights into new possibilities of human character and human life, personal and social. Stated so baldly, such a view may strike you as more problematical than plausible, and it may not even be very intelligible. My purpose is merely to point out that here is a possible way of answering our pending question: it is to say (roughly) that to take an aesthetic interest in literature is to take an interest in the understanding of human nature and the human condition that it provides, *not* in the form of general statements, but in the form of the symbolic meaning of characters and events. If it should turn out that the point of authoring is to cater to aesthetic interests, so conceived, then, very clearly indeed, we could discern in authoring a special form of reason, which it would be the task of philosophy to articulate, to explain, and to assess. . . .

William K. Wimsatt, Jr. and Monroe C. Beardsley

THE INTENTIONAL FALLACY

"He owns with toil he wrote the following scenes;
But, if they're naught, ne'er spare him for his pains:
Damn him the more; have no commiseration
For dullness on mature deliberation."

William Congreve
Prologue to *The Way of the World*

I

The claim of the author's "intention" upon the critic's judgment has been challenged in a number of recent discussions, notably in the debate entitled *The Personal Heresy*, between Professors Lewis and Tillyard. But it seems doubtful if this claim and most of its romantic corollaries are as yet subject to any widespread questioning. The present writers, in a short article entitled "Intention" for a *Dictionary*[1] of literary criticism, raised the issue but were unable to pursue its implications at any length. We argued that the design or intention of the author is neither available nor desirable as a standard for judging the success of a work of literary art, and it seems to us that this is a principle which goes deep into some differences in the history of critical attitudes. It is a principle which accepted or rejected points to the polar opposites of classical "imitation" and romantic expression. It entails many specific truths about inspiration, authenticity, biography, literary history and scholarship, and about some trends of contemporary poetry, especially its allusiveness. There is hardly a problem of literary criticism in which the critic's approach will not be qualified by his view of "intention."

[1]*Dictionary of World Literature*, Joseph T. Shipley, ed. (New York: 1942), 326–29.

"Intention," as we shall use the term, corresponds to *what he intended* in a formula which more or less explicitly has had wide acceptance. "In order to judge the poet's performance, we must know *what he intended*." Intention is design or plan in the author's mind. Intention has obvious affinities for the author's attitude toward his work, the way he felt, what made him write.

We begin our discussion with a series of propositions summarized and abstracted to a degree where they seem to us axiomatic.

1. A poem does not come into existence by accident. The words of a poem, as Professor Stoll has remarked, come out of a head, not out of a hat. Yet to insist on the designing intellect as a *cause* of a poem is not to grant the design or intention as a *standard* by which the critic is to judge the worth of the poet's performance.

2. One must ask how a critic expects to get an answer to the question about intention. How is he to find out what the poet tried to do? If the poet succeeded in doing it, then the poem itself shows what he was trying to do. And if the poet did not succeed, then the poem is not adequate evidence, and the critic must go outside the poem—for evidence of an intention that did not become effective in the poem. "Only one *caveat* must be borne in mind," says an eminent intentionalist[2] in a moment when his theory repudiates itself; "the poet's aim must be judged at the moment of the creative act, that is to say, by the art of the poem itself."

3. Judging a poem is like judging a pudding or a machine. One demands that it work. It is only because an artifact works that we infer the intention of an artificer. "A poem should not mean but be." A poem can *be* only through its *meaning*—since its medium is words—yet it *is*, simply *is*, in the sense that we have no excuse for inquiring what part is intended or meant. Poetry is a feat of style by which a complex of meaning is handled all at once. Poetry succeeds because all or most of what is said or implied is relevant; what is irrelevant has been excluded, like lumps from pudding and "bugs" from machinery. In this respect poetry differs from practical messages, which are successful if and only if we correctly infer the intention. They are more abstract than poetry.

4. The meaning of a poem may certainly be a personal one, in the sense that a poem expresses a personality or state of soul rather than a physical object like an apple. But even a short lyric poem is dramatic, the response of a speaker (no matter how abstractly conceived) to a situation (no matter how universalized). We ought to impute the thoughts and attitudes of the poem immediately to the dramatic *speaker*, and if to the author at all, only by an act of biographical inference.

5. There is a sense in which an author, by revision, may better achieve his original intention. But it is a very abstract sense. He intended to write a better work, or a better work of a certain kind, and now has done it. But it follows that his former concrete intention was not his intention. "He's the man we were in search of, that's true," says Hardy's rustic constable, "and yet he's not the man we were in search of. For the man we were in search of was not the man we wanted."

"Is not a critic," asks Professor Stoll, "a judge, who does not explore his own consciousness, but determines the author's meaning or intention, as if the poem were a will, a contract, or the constitution? The poem is not the critic's own." He has accurately diagnosed two forms of irresponsibility, one of which he prefers. Our view is yet different. The poem is not the critic's own and not the author's (it is detached from the author at birth and goes about the world beyond his power to intend about it or control it). The poem belongs to the public. It is embodied in language, the peculiar

[2]J. E. Spingarn, "The New Criticism," in *Criticism in America* (New York, 1924), 24–25.

possession of the public, and it is about the human being, an object of public knowledge. What is said about the poem is subject to the same scrutiny as any statement in linguistics or in the general science of psychology.

A critic of our *Dictionary* article, Ananda K. Coomaraswamy, has argued[3] that there are two kinds of inquiry about a work of art: (1) whether the artist achieved his intentions; (2) whether the work of art "ought ever to have been undertaken at all" and so "whether it is worth preserving." Number (2), Coomaraswamy maintains, is not "criticism of any work of art *qua* work of art," but is rather moral criticism; number (1) is artistic criticism. But we maintain that (2) need not be moral criticism: that there is another way of deciding whether works of art are worth preserving and whether, in a sense, they "ought" to have been undertaken, and this is the way of objective criticism of works of art as such, the way which enables us to distinguish between a skillful murder and a skillful poem. A skillful murder is an example which Coomaraswamy uses, and in his system the difference between the murder and the poem is simply a "moral" one, not an "artistic" one, since each if carried out according to plan is "artistically" successful. We maintain that (2) is an inquiry of more worth than (1), and since (2) and not (1) is capable of distinguishing poetry from murder, the name "artistic criticism" is properly given to (2).

II

It is not so much a historical statement as a definition to say that the intentional fallacy is a romantic one. When a rhetorician of the first century A.D. writes: "Sublimity is the echo of a great soul," or when he tells us that "Homer enters into the sublime actions of his heroes" and "shares the full inspiration of the combat," we shall not be surprised to find this rhetorician considered as a distant harbinger of romanticism and greeted in the warmest terms of Saintsbury. One may wish to argue whether Longinus should be called romantic, but there can hardly be a doubt that in one important way he is.

Goethe's three questions for "constructive criticism" are "What did the author set out to do? Was his plan reasonable and sensible, and how far did he succeed in carrying it out?" If one leaves out the middle question, one has in effect the system of Croce—the culmination and crowning philosophic expression of romanticism. The beautiful is the successful intuition-expression, and the ugly is the unsuccessful; the intuition or private part of art is *the* aesthetic fact, and the medium or public part is not the subject of aesthetic at all.

> The Madonna of Cimabue is still in the Church of Santa Maria Novella; but does she speak to the visitor of to-day as to the Florentines of the thirteenth century?
> *Historical interpretation* labors . . . to reintegrate in us the psychological conditions which have changed in the course of history. It . . . enables us to see a work of art (a physical object) as its *author saw* it in the moment of production.[4]

---

[3]Ananda K. Coomaraswamy, "Intention," in *American Bookman*, I (1944), 41–48.

[4]It is true that Croce himself in his *Ariosto, Shakespeare and Corneille* (London, 1920), Chap. VII, "The Practical Personality and the Poetical Personality," and in his *Defence of Poetry* (Oxford, 1934), 24, and elsewhere, early and late, has delivered telling attacks on emotive geneticism, but the main drive of the *Aesthetic* is surely toward a kind of cognitive intentionalism.

The first italics are Croce's, the second ours. The upshot of Croce's system is an ambiguous emphasis on history. With such passages as a point of departure a critic may write a nice analysis of the meaning or "spirit" of a play by Shakespeare or Corneille—a process that involves close historical study but remains aesthetic criticism—or he may, with equal plausibility, produce an essay in sociology, biography, or other kinds of non-aesthetic history.

III

> I went to the poets; tragic, dithyrambic, and all sorts. . . . I took them some of the most elaborate passages in their own writings, and asked what was the meaning of them. . . . Will you believe me? . . . there is hardly a person present who would not have talked better about their poetry than they did themselves. Then I knew that not by wisdom do poets write poetry, but by a sort of genius and inspiration.

That reiterated mistrust of the poets which we hear from Socrates may have been part of a rigorously ascetic view in which we hardly wish to participate, yet Plato's Socrates saw a truth about the poetic mind which the world no longer commonly sees—so much criticism, and that the most inspirational and most affectionately remembered, has proceeded from the poets themselves.

Certainly the poets have had something to say that the critic and professor could not say; their message has been more exciting: that poetry should come as naturally as leaves to a tree, that poetry is the lava of the imagination, or that it is emotion recollected in tranquillity. But it is necessary that we realize the character and authority of such testimony. There is only a fine shade of difference between such expressions and a kind of earnest advice that authors often give. Thus Edward Young, Carlyle, Walter Pater:

> I know two golden rules from *ethics*, which are no less golden in *Composition*, than in life. 1. *Know thyself*; 2dly, *Reverence thyself*.

> This is the grand secret for finding readers and retaining them: let him who would move and convince others, be first moved and convinced himself. Horace's rule, *Si vis me flere*, is applicable in a wider sense than the literal one. To every poet, to every writer, we might say: Be true, if you would be believed.

> Truth! there can be no merit, no craft at all, without that. And further, all beauty is in the long run only *fineness* of truth, or what we call expression, the finer accommodation of speech to that vision within.

And Housman's little handbook to the poetic mind yields this illustration:

> Having drunk a pint of beer at luncheon—beer is a sedative to the brain, and my afternoons are the least intellectual portion of my life—I would go out for a walk of two or three hours. As I went along, thinking of nothing in particular, only looking at things around me and following the progress of the seasons, there would flow into my mind, with sudden and unaccountable emotion, sometimes a line or two of verse, sometimes a whole stanza at once.

This is the logical terminus of the series already quoted. Here is a confession of how poems were written which would do as a definition of poetry just as well as "emotion recollected in tranquillity"—and which the young poet might equally well take to heart as a practical rule. Drink a pint of beer, relax, go walking, think on nothing in particular, look at things, surrender yourself to yourself, search for the truth in your own soul, listen to the sound of your own inside voice, discover and express the *vraie vérité*.

It is probably true that all this is excellent advice for poets. The young imagination fired by Wordsworth and Carlyle is probably closer to the verge of producing a poem than the mind of the student who has been sobered by Aristotle or Richards. The art of inspiring poets, or at least of inciting something like poetry in young persons, has probably gone further in our day than ever before. Books of creative writing such as those issued from the Lincoln School are interesting evidence of what a child can do.[5] All this, however, would appear to belong to an art separate from criticism—to a psychological discipline, a system of self-development, a yoga, which the young poet perhaps does well to notice, but which is something different from the public art of evaluating poems.

Coleridge and Arnold were better critics than most poets have been, and if the critical tendency dried up the poetry in Arnold and perhaps in Coleridge, it is not inconsistent with our argument, which is that judgment of poems is different from the art of producing them. Coleridge has given us the classic "anodyne" story, and tells what he can about the genesis of a poem which he calls a "psychological curiosity," but his definitions of poetry and of the poetic quality "imagination" are to be found elsewhere and in quite other terms.

It would be convenient if the passwords of the intentional school, "sincerity," "fidelity," "spontaneity," "authenticity," "genuineness," "originality," could be equated with terms such as "integrity," "relevance," "unity," "function," "maturity," "subtlety," "adequacy," and other more precise terms of evaluation—in short, if "expression" always meant aesthetic achievement. But this is not so.

"Aesthetic" art, says Professor Curt Ducasse, an ingenious theorist of expression, is the conscious objectification of feelings, in which an intrinsic part is the critical moment. The artist corrects the objectification when it is not adequate. But this may mean that the earlier attempt was not successful in objectifying the self, or "it may also mean that it was a successful objectification of a self which, when it confronted us clearly, we disowned and repudiated in favor of another."[6] What is the standard by which we disown or accept the self? Professor Ducasse does not say. Whatever it may be, however, this standard is an element in the definition of art which will not reduce to terms of objectification. The evaluation of the work of art remains public; the work is measured against something outside the author.

[5]See Hughes Mearns, *Creative Youth* (Garden City, 1925), esp. 10, 27–29. The technique of inspiring poems has apparently been outdone more recently by the study of inspiration in successful poets and other artists. See, for instance, Rosamond E. M. Harding, *An Anatomy of Inspiration* (Cambridge, 1940); Julius Portnoy, *A Psychology of Art Creation* (Philadelphia, 1942); Rudolf Arnheim and others, *Poets at Work* (New York, 1947); Phyllis Bartlett, *Poems in Process* (New York, 1951); Brewster Ghiselin (ed.), *The Creative Process: A Symposium* (Berkeley and Los Angeles, 1952).

[6]Curt Ducasse, *The Philosophy of Art* (New York, 1929), 116.

IV

There is criticism of poetry and there is author psychology, which when applied to the present or future takes the form of inspirational promotion; but author psychology can be historical too, and then we have literary biography, a legitimate and attractive study in itself, one approach, as Professor Tillyard would argue, to personality, the poem being only a parallel approach. Certainly it need not be with a derogatory purpose that one points out personal studies, as distinct from poetic studies, in the realm of literary scholarship. Yet there is danger of confusing personal and poetic studies; and there is the fault of writing the personal as if it were poetic.

There is a difference between internal and external evidence for the meaning of a poem. And the paradox is only verbal and superficial that what is (1) internal is also public: it is discovered through the semantics and syntax of a poem, through our habitual knowledge of the language, through grammars, dictionaries, and all the literature which is the source of dictionaries, in general through all that makes a language and culture; while what is (2) external is private or idiosyncratic; not a part of the work as a linguistic fact: it consists of revelations (in journals, for example, or letters or reported conversations) about how or why the poet wrote the poem—to what lady, while sitting on what lawn, or at the death of what friend or brother. There is (3) an intermediate kind of evidence about the character of the author or about private or semiprivate meanings attached to words or topics by the author or by a coterie of which he is a member. The meaning of words is the history of words, and the biography of an author, his use of a word, and the associations which the word had for *him*, are part of the word's history and meaning.[7] But the three types of evidence, especially (2) and (3), shade into one another so subtly that it is not always easy to draw a line between examples, and hence arises the difficulty for criticism. The use of biographical evidence need not involve intentionalism, because while it may be evidence of what the author intended, it may also be evidence of the meaning of his words and the dramatic character of his utterance. On the other hand, it may not be all this. And a critic who is concerned with evidence of type (1) and moderately with that of type (3) will in the long run produce a different sort of comment from that of the critic who is concerned with (2) and with (3) where it shades into (2).

The whole glittering parade of Professor Lowes's *Road to Xanadu*, for instance, runs along the border between types (2) and (3) or boldly traverses the romantic region of (2). " 'Kubla Khan,' " says Professor Lowes, "is the fabric of a vision, but every image that rose up in its weaving had passed that way before. And it would seem that there is nothing haphazard or fortuitous in their return." This is not quite clear—not even when Professor Lowes explains that there were clusters of associations, like hooked atoms, which were drawn into complex relation with other clusters in the deep well of Coleridge's memory, and which then coalesced and issued forth as poems. If there was nothing "haphazard or fortuitous" in the way the images returned to the surface, that may mean (1) that Coleridge could not produce what he did not have, that he was limited in his creation by what he had read or otherwise experienced, or (2) that having received certain clusters of associations, he was bound to return them in just the way

---

[7]And the history of words *after* a poem is written may contribute meanings which if relevant to the original pattern should not be ruled out by a scruple about intention.

he did, and that the value of the poem may be described in terms of the experiences on which he had to draw. The latter pair of propositions (a sort of Hartleyan associationism which Coleridge himself repudiated in the *Biographia*) may not be assented to. There were certainly other combinations, other poems, worse or better, that might have been written by men who had read Bartram and Purchas and Bruce and Milton. And this will be true no matter how many times we are able to add to the brilliant complex of Coleridge's reading. In certain flourishes (such as the sentence we have quoted) and in chapter headings like "The Shaping Spirit," "The Magical Synthesis," "Imagination Creatrix," it may be that Professor Lowes pretends to say more about the actual poems than he does. There is a certain deceptive variation in these fancy chapter titles; one expects to pass on to a new stage in the argument, and one finds—more and more sources, more and more about "the streamy nature of association."[8]

"Wohin der Weg?" quotes Professor Lowes for the motto of his book. "Kein Weg! Ins Unbetretene." Precisely because the way is *unbetreten*, we should say, it leads away from the poem. Bartram's *Travels* contains a good deal of the history of certain words and of certain romantic Floridian conceptions that appear in "Kubla Khan." And a great deal of that history has passed and was then passing into the very stuff of our language. Perhaps a person who has read Bartram appreciates the poem more than one who has not. Or, by looking up the vocabulary of "Kubla Khan" in the *Oxford English Dictionary*, or by reading some of the other books there quoted, a person may know the poem better. But it would seem to pertain little to the poem to know that *Coleridge* had read Bartram. There is a gross body of life, of sensory and mental experience, which lies behind and in some sense causes every poem, but can never be and need not be known in the verbal and hence intellectual composition which is the poem. For all the objects of our manifold experience, for every unity, there is an action of the mind which cuts off roots, melts away context—or indeed we should never have objects or ideas or anything to talk about.

It is probable that there is nothing in Professor Lowes' vast book which could detract from anyone's appreciation of either *The Ancient Mariner* or "Kubla Khan." We next present a case where preoccupation with evidence of type (3) has gone so far as to distort a critic's view of a poem (yet a case not so obvious as those that abound in our critical journals).

In a well-known poem by John Donne appears this quatrain:

> Moving of th'earth brings harmes and feares,
>   Men reckon what it did and meant,
> But trepidation of the spheares,
>   Though greater farre, is innocent.

A recent critic in an elaborate treatment of Donne's learning has written of this quatrain as follows:

> He touches the emotional pulse of the situation by a skillful allusion to the new and the old astronomy. . . . Of the new astronomy, the "moving of the earth" is the most radical principle; of the old, the "trepidation of the spheares" is the motion of the greatest complexity. . . . The poet must exhort his love to quietness and calm upon his departure; and for this purpose the

[8]Chaps. VIII, "The Pattern," and XVI, "The Known and Familiar Landscape," will be found of most help to the student of the poem.

figure based upon the latter motion (trepidation), long absorbed into the traditional astronomy, fittingly suggests the tension of the moment without arousing the "harmes and feares"
implicit in the figure of the moving earth.[9]

The argument is plausible and rests on a well substantiated thesis that Donne was
deeply interested in the new astronomy and its repercussions in the theological realm.
In various works Donne shows his familiarity with Kepler's *De Stella Nova*, with
Galileo's *Siderius Nuncius*, with William Gilbert's *De Magnete*, and with Clavius's
commentary on the *De Sphaera* of Sacrobosco. He refers to the new science in his
Sermon at Paul's Cross and in a letter to Sir Henry Goodyer. In *The First Anniversary*
he says the "new philosophy calls all in doubt." In the *Elegy* on *Prince Henry* he says
that the "least moving of the center" makes "the world to shake."

It is difficult to answer an argument like this, and impossible to answer it with
evidence of like nature. There is no reason why Donne might not have written a stanza
in which the two kinds of celestial motion stood for two sorts of emotion at parting.
And if we become full of astronomical ideas and see Donne only against the background of the new science, we may believe that he did. But the text itself remains to be
dealt with, the analyzable vehicle of a complicated metaphor. And one may observe:
(1) that the movement of the earth according to the Copernican theory is a celestial
motion, smooth and regular, and while it might cause religious or philosophic fears, it
could not be associated with the crudity and earthiness of the kind of commotion
which the speaker in the poem wishes to discourage; (2) that there is another moving of
the earth, an earthquake, which has just these qualities and is to be associated with the
tear-floods and sigh-tempests of the second stanza of the poem; (3) that "trepidation" is
an appropriate opposite of earthquake, because each is a shaking or vibratory motion;
and "trepidation of the spheares" is "greater farre" than an earthquake, but not much
greater (if two such motions can be compared as to greatness) than the annual motion
of the earth; (4) that reckoning what it "did and meant" shows that the event has passed,
like an earthquake, not like the incessant celestial movement of the earth. Perhaps a
knowledge of Donne's interest in the new science may add another shade of meaning,
an overtone to the stanza in question, though to say even this runs against the words.
To make the geocentric and heliocentric antithesis the core of the metaphor is to
disregard the English language, to prefer private evidence to public, external to
internal.

V

If the distinction between kinds of evidence has implications for the historical critic, it
has them no less for the contemporary poet and his critic. Or, since every rule for a
poet is but another side of a judgment by a critic, and since the past is the realm of the
scholar and critic, and the future and present that of the poet and the critical leaders of
taste, we may say that the problems arising in literary scholarship from the intentional
fallacy are matched by others which arise in the world of progressive experiment.

The question of "allusiveness," for example, as acutely posed by the poetry of Eliot,
is certainly one where a false judgment is likely to involve the intentional fallacy. The

[9]Charles M. Coffin, *John Donne and the New Philosophy* (New York, 1927), 97–98.

frequency and depth of literary allusion in the poetry of Eliot and others has driven so many in pursuit of full meanings to the *Golden Bough* and the Elizabethan drama that it has become a kind of commonplace to suppose that we do not know what a poet means unless we have traced him in his reading—a supposition redolent with intentional implications. The stand taken by F. O. Matthiessen is a sound one and partially forestalls the difficulty.

> If one reads these lines with an attentive ear and is sensitive to their sudden shifts in movement, the contrast between the actual Thames and the idealized vision of it during an age before it flowed through a megalopolis is sharply conveyed by that movement itself, whether or not one recognizes the refrain to be from Spenser.

Eliot's allusions work when we know them—and to a great extent when we do not know them, through their suggestive power.

But sometimes we find allusions supported by notes, and it is a nice question whether the notes function more as guides to send us where we may be educated, or more as indications in themselves about the character of the allusions. "Nearly everything of importance . . . that is apposite to an appreciation of 'The Waste Land,' " writes Matthiessen of Miss Weston's book, "has been incorporated into the structure of the poem itself, or into Eliot's Notes." And with such an admission it may begin to appear that it would not much matter if Eliot invented his sources (as Sir Walter Scott invented chapter epigraphs from "old plays" and "anonymous" authors, or as Coleridge wrote marginal glosses for *The Ancient Mariner*). Allusions to Dante, Webster, Marvell, or Baudelaire doubtless gain something because these writers existed, but it is doubtful whether the same can be said for an allusion to an obscure Elizabethan:

> The sound of horns and motors, which shall bring Sweeney to Mrs. Porter in the spring.

"Cf. Day, *Parliament of Bees*": says Eliot,

> When of a sudden, listening, you shall hear,
> A noise of horns and hunting, which shall bring
> Actaeon to Diana in the spring,
> Where all shall see her naked skin.

The irony is completed by the quotation itself; had Eliot, as is quite conceivable, composed these lines to furnish his own background, there would be no loss of validity. The conviction may grow as one reads Eliot's next note: "I do not know the origin of the ballad from which these lines are taken: it was reported to me from Sydney, Australia." The important word in this note—on Mrs. Porter and her daughter who washed their feet in soda water—is "ballad." And if one should feel from the lines themselves their "ballad" quality, there would be little need for the note. Ultimately, the inquiry must focus on the integrity of such notes as parts of the poem, for where they constitute special information about the meaning of phrases in the poem, they ought to be subject to the same scrutiny as any of the other words in which it is written. Matthiessen believes the notes were the price Eliot "had to pay in order to avoid what he would have considered muffling the energy of his poem by extended connecting links in the text itself." But it may be questioned whether the notes and the need for them are not equally muffling. F. W. Bateson has plausibly argued that Tennyson's

"The Sailor Boy" would be better if half the stanzas were omitted, and the best versions of ballads like "Sir Patrick Spens" owe their power to the very audacity with which the minstrel has taken for granted the story upon which he comments. What then if a poet finds he cannot take so much for granted in a more recondite context and rather than write informatively, supplies notes? It can be said in favor of this plan that at least the notes do not pretend to be dramatic, as they would if written in verse. On the other hand, the notes may look like unassimilated material lying loose beside the poem, necessary for the meaning of the verbal symbol, but not integrated, so that the symbol stands incomplete.

We mean to suggest by the above analysis that whereas notes tend to seem to justify themselves as external indexes to the author's *intention*, yet they ought to be judged like any other parts of a composition (verbal arrangement special to a particular context), and when so judged their reality as parts of the poem, or their imaginative integration with the rest of the poem, may come into question. Matthiessen, for instance, sees that Eliot's titles for poems and his epigraphs are informative apparatus, like the notes. But while he is worried by some of the notes and thinks that Eliot "appears to be mocking himself for writing the note at the same time that he wants to convey something by it," Matthiessen believes that the "device" of epigraphs "is not at all open to the objection of not being sufficiently structural." "The *intention*," he says, "is to enable the poet to secure a condensed expression in the poem itself." "In each case the epigraph *is designed* to form an integral part of the effect of the poem." And Eliot himself, in his notes, has justified his poetic practice in terms of intention.

> The Hanged Man, a member of the traditional pack, fits my purpose in two ways: because he is associated in my mind with the Hanged God of Frazer, and because I associate him with the hooded figure in the passage of the disciples to Emmaus in Part V. . . . The man with Three Staves (an authentic member of the Tarot pack) I associate, quite arbitrarily, with the Fisher King himself.

And perhaps he is to be taken more seriously here, when off guard in a note, than when in his Norton Lectures he comments on the difficulty of saying what a poem means and adds playfully that he thinks of prefixing to a second edition of *Ash Wednesday* some lines from *Don Juan*:

> I don't pretend that I quite understand
> My own meaning when I would be *very* fine;
> But the fact is that I have nothing planned
> Unless it were to be a moment merry.

If Eliot and other contemporary poets have any characteristic fault, it may be in *planning* too much.

Allusiveness in poetry is one of several critical issues by which we have illustrated the more abstract issue of intentionalism, but it may be for today the most important illustration. As a poetic practice allusiveness would appear to be in some recent poems an extreme corollary of the romantic intentionalist assumption, and as a critical issue it challenges and brings to light in a special way the basic premise of intentionalism. The following instance from the poetry of Eliot may serve to epitomize the practical implications of what we have been saying. In Eliot's "Love Song of J. Alfred Prufrock," toward the end, occurs the line: "I have heard the mermaids singing, each to each," and this bears a certain resemblance to a line in a Song by John Donne, "Teach me to heare Mermaides singing," so that for the reader acquainted to a certain degree with Donne's poetry, the critical question arises: Is Eliot's line an allusion to Donne's? Is Prufrock thinking about Donne? Is Eliot thinking about Donne? We suggest that there are two radically different ways of looking for an answer to this question. There is (1) the way of poetic analysis and exegesis, which inquires whether it makes any sense if Eliot-Prufrock *is* thinking about Donne. In an earlier part of the poem, when Prufrock asks, "Would it have been worth while, . . . To have squeezed the universe into a ball," his words take half their sadness and irony from certain energetic and passionate lines of Marvell's "To His Coy Mistress." But the exegetical inquirer may wonder whether mermaids considered as "strange sights" (to hear them is in Donne's poem analogous to getting with child a mandrake root) have much to do with Prufrock's mermaids, which seem to be symbols of romance and dynamism, and which incidentally have literary authentication, if they need it, in a line of a sonnet by Gérard de Nerval. This method of inquiry may lead to the conclusion that the given resemblance between Eliot and Donne is without significance and is better not thought of, or the method may have the disadvantage of providing no certain conclusion. Nevertheless, we submit that this is the true and objective way of criticism, as contrasted to what the very uncertainty of exegesis might tempt a second kind of critic to undertake: (2) the way of biographical or genetic inquiry, in which, taking advantage of the fact that Eliot is still alive, and in the spirit of a man who would settle a bet, the critic writes to Eliot and asks him what he meant, or if he had Donne in mind. We shall not here weigh the probabilities—whether Eliot would answer that he meant nothing at all, had nothing at all in mind—a sufficiently good answer to such a question—or in an unguarded moment might furnish a clear and, within its limit, irrefutable answer. Our point is that such an answer to such an inquiry would have nothing to do with the poem "Prufrock"; it would not be a critical inquiry. Critical inquiries, unlike bets, are not settled in this way. Critical inquiries are not settled by consulting the oracle.

Colin Lyas

PERSONAL QUALITIES AND THE
INTENTIONAL FALLACY

In their article "The Intentional Fallacy,"[1] Beardsley and Wimsatt raised problems about the legitimacy of certain critical practices. These problems, raised again in later writings[2] and intensively discussed in recent years, remain unsettled and this lecture is intended to throw light upon them.

1. I shall have more to say shortly by way of clarification of the theses I wish to discuss. Before that I want to mention a couple of distinctions that may need to be made in discussing the legitimacy of reference to artists and their intentions.

First, we may need to distinguish what is called "the personal heresy" from what is called "the intentional fallacy." Thus, in "The Intentional Fallacy" (p. 3) there is clearly an attack on the relevance of critical references to the author's *intentions*. "The design or intention of the author," we read, "is neither available nor desirable as a standard for judging the success of a literary work of art." To make reference to such intentions is to commit the intentional fallacy. Combined with this, however, is an attack on *any* reference to the author. "There is a danger," they write (p. 10), "of confusing personal and poetic studies."[3] To refer to the author in the course of criticism is to commit the personal heresy. We are never told, though, just what the relation is between the intentional fallacy and the personal heresy and it is not clear that both are supported by the same sort of arguments. I will discuss later some of the connections between the personal heresy and the intentional fallacy.

Secondly, in "The Intentional Fallacy" at least,[4] Beardsley and Wimsatt did not

From Royal Institute of Philosophy Lectures (London: Macmillan London, 1971–72), 6:196–219. *Reprinted with permission of Macmillan London and the author.*

[1]Reprinted in W. K. Wimsatt, *The Verbal Icon* (New York: Noonday, 1966). Page references are to that volume.

[2]Notably in M. C. Beardsley, *Aesthetics* (New York: Harcourt Brace and World, 1959) chs. i and x; W. K. Wimsatt, "Genesis: A Fallacy Revisited" in Demetz and others (eds.), *The Disciplines of Criticism* (New Haven: Yale University Press, 1968); and M. C. Beardsley, *The Possibility of Criticism* (Detroit: Wayne, 1971).

[3]Quite what is being distinguished here is not clear. I shall show however that no radical separation of personal and poetic studies can be maintained.

[4]But see Wimsatt's later article in Demetz, p. 222.

distinguish clearly between an attack on those references to intentions and personality made in the course of *evaluating* works and an attack on such references made when *interpreting* works. At the beginning of the article their claim is that intentions are irrelevant as a standard for *judging the success* of a work. As the article proceeds, however, emphasis is switched to the irrelevance of references to intention when various problems of *interpretation* are at issue.

Many of those who have attacked Beardsley and Wimsatt's views have done so on the ground that knowledge of intention and other biographical material *is* relevant to this or that problem of interpretation. In so far as interpretation is a preparation for evaluation this is to suggest that such knowledge may be a prerequisite for, and hence, indirectly at least, relevant to evaluation. There is however far less discussion of the more direct ways in which knowledge of artists and their intentions may be relevant to evaluation. What I wish later to show is not that evaluation may presuppose and so *indirectly* require knowledge of intention and other facts about artists, but that some critical evaluations are directly personalistic and as such require a certain sort of knowledge of intention.

2. As a preamble now to a further clarification of the anti-personalistic and anti-intentionalistic theses that might be proposed, I shall state a number of points about intentions. I have no time to argue these points although they can be, and have been, argued at length.

First, intentions should not be thought of as private mental events totally detached from verbal and other behavior. They are, rather, connected with such behavior and can be known only because they are so connected.

Secondly we need sometimes to distinguish between what a person explicitly tells us about his intentions prior to, during or after his actions, and what we know from his other words and deeds about his intentions. These other words and deeds can cast doubt on, and even falsify, a person's explicit claims about his intentions. Moreover if no such explicit claims are made or are available, it is through these other words and deeds that our knowledge of intention must and does come.

Thirdly we must distinguish between an intention in the sense of a plan or design formed *prior* to an action and an action done *intentionally*. Not every action done intentionally is done with prior intent. A complication here is that Austin and others have claimed that we do not anyway call an action "intentional" unless there is something "special" about it.[5] I shall, however, allow myself the use of 'intentional' to describe any action we can attribute to a person as his responsibility, as within his control or, more widely, as something *he* did. And then not every intentional action need be done with forethought, prior intent or design.

In the light of these remarks some anti-intentionalist theses may be distinguished. Since I am interested in problems about evaluation, I shall concentrate on versions of these theses that relate to critical evaluations.

First it might be argued that in critical evaluations no attention need be paid to what artists *say* about their intentions before, during or after the completion of their works. Since their claims that they intended to put certain merits in their works will always have to be checked against what they have done, i.e., the work itself, one can always

[5]For more on the debate over this matter see the papers collected in my *Philosophy and Linguistics* (London: Macmillan, 1971).

start there and dispense with quite separate enquiries into the artist's statements of intention.[6]

This first thesis rules out only the need for knowledge of and reference to *statements* of prior intention. It does not establish the dispensability of knowledge of prior intentions where this knowledge is gained in ways other than by study of *explicit* statements of intention. A second, stronger, thesis might therefore be offered. According to this thesis, knowledge of intentions had by the artist prior to producing the work, however this knowledge is obtained, is unnecessary in criticism. At best such knowledge can suggest to us things we should look for in the work. Again, however, since these things will eventually have to be found in the work itself, one can always start there. Moreover, mere successful completion of these prior intentions could never constitute the standard by which the merit of the work is determined. For the work to be meritorious the intentions would have to have been worth having, and this is to say that there must be independent standards in terms of which the intentions, and anything produced by their successful completion, can be judged.

This second, stronger, thesis would, if true, show only the dispensability of knowledge of and reference to *prior* intentions. It does not, as such, rule out reference to our knowledge of the fact that the work and some of its effects are *intentional*. For, as we have seen, this knowledge may not involve reference to prior intentions at all. Hence a third thesis might be added, namely that critical evaluations presuppose no knowledge that a work or its effects are intentional (in the wide sense of "intentional" adopted above).

To assert the strongest form of anti-intentionalism would be to assert all the theses I have mentioned. This would constitute a total elimination of reference to intention from critical talk about art and would have an interesting consequence. For since the only differences I can see between a work of art and a natural object stem from the fact that intentional human activity is involved in the making of art, so to deny the relevance of *any* knowledge of intention would be to deny the relevance of knowledge that one is dealing with *art*. If a knowledge of intention is totally dispensable in criticism then, from the point of view of evaluation, works of art are on the same footing as natural objects.[7]

In order to maintain that knowledge of intention has some relevance it is not, of course, necessary to claim that all the theses so far mentioned are false. For my part I think that the first two theses mentioned *do* have some plausibility but that the third is false. Since, as I shall show, it *is* false, no comprehensive anti-intentionalist position can be argued.

Beardsley and Wimsatt certainly subscribe to the first two theses, i.e. they certainly wish to attack references to prior intention and references to statements of prior intention. The third thesis is never *explicitly* advocated in their writings and this means that contrary to popular impression they have never argued (and possibly have never wished to argue) a comprehensive anti-intentionalist position. To show this may be to go some way to make their views more palatable to some of their critics.

---

[6]Which is not to say that in *practice* (as opposed to in *principle*) we need dispense with such references. See Wimsatt in Demetz, op. cit., p. 211 § 4 *(b)*.

[7]See §§ 5 and 10 below.

3. So far I have discussed only anti-intentionalist positions. I turn now to anti-personalist theses. I shall consider two of these. First there is the strong line that *all* references to the artist (including references to his intentions) are eliminable from critical evaluations. This thesis, approached by Beardsley and Wimsatt in their distinction between personal and poetic studies, turns the intentional fallacy into a sub-species of the personal heresy.

Secondly there is a weaker claim. It may be allowed that certain references to artists (particularly if made *in* talking of their works) are relevant. At the same time other sorts of references to artists may be excluded. Two cases may be mentioned here. First, it might be said that knowledge of the artist gained independently of a study of the work is not required for knowledge of the work itself. At best it can suggest things to look for in the work. Since this will then involve a confirming scrutiny of the work itself one could, in principle, have made do with this scrutiny alone. The move from knowledge of the artist to statements about his work (where the two are separable) is, strictly speaking, unnecessary. Secondly, knowledge of the artist gained by inference *away* from the work is irrelevant to criticism, although not perhaps to biographical interests. For the critic to move from talking of the work to talking of the artist (where these two things are separable) is for him to move from the proper object of critical study, the work itself, to a study of something else, the work's creator. In general, therefore, *where knowledge of artists and knowledge of works can be distinguished* it is unnecessary for critics to possess the former (even by inference from the latter).

In what follows I shall suggest why a strong, total anti-personalism is false and I shall say what I think is right about a weaker anti-personalism, i.e., an anti-personalism that, without eliminating all references to artists from criticism, nonetheless eliminates certain moves from work to artist and from artist to work.

4. We have therefore some possible theses. How are they to be tested? Here I begin with a general remark about the dispute over the relevance of critical references to artists and their intentions. Those who deny the relevance of such references have claimed that the outcome of the dispute has important implications for critical *practice*. Thus Beardsley and Wimsatt write ("The Intentional Fallacy," p. 3):

> There is hardly a problem of literary criticism in which the critic's approach will not be qualified by his view of intention.

For all that such claims have been made it is critical *theorists*, people arguing about criticism, who have generated the heat in this debate. Those who *practice* criticism have not suspended nor appreciably altered their activities whilst awaiting the outcome of the debate. This suggests that there is, prior to critical theory, a well-founded activity of commenting on works of art in various ways and for various purposes, that the various purposes of the various comments are well recognised and that those who engage in this activity are in principle capable of realising when various sorts of comments are clear and relevant, or obscure and irrelevant.

This in turn suggests a way of assessing critical theories of the type we are examining. Presumably since those who advocate such theories are claiming that certain sorts of references to artists and their intentions frustrate the aims of criticism, we have to ask what in fact these aims are and whether they are frustrated by the sorts of references that are under attack. We decide what these aims in fact are by reference to that well established form of activity I have mentioned, an activity that exists prior to theories about it and which, as I have said, continues uninterrupted even while theoretical debates about it continue. Reference to this activity dictates the shape of my inquiry. Before beginning it, however, I would remark that when one does look at critical practice, one is struck by the ubiquity of references to artists. Critic after critic refers to what this or that *artist* did and to what *his* work was like. Hence presumably the puzzlement felt by those who believe rightly or wrongly that Beardsley and Wimsatt wished to censure such remarks. For if such comments *do* frustrate the aim of criticism, how strange that so many critics should make them and make them so often. I shall make more comments later on the reasons for this puzzlement.

5. In line with a determination to let critical practice govern my inquiries, I begin with a reminder of the enormous vocabulary of terms and phrases by which critics attribute merits and demerits of various sorts to works of various sorts. (They do not, as is sometimes supposed, confine themselves to the terms "good" and "beautiful".) Once certain classifications of this vocabulary are observed we can begin to clarify questions about the role of references in criticism to artists and their intentions.

The task of classification may begin with what I hope is the uncontentious observation that many of the qualities for which we value works of art are also qualities for which we value natural objects, scenes and events. One group of qualities is the following:

> elegance, charm, balance, unity, proportion, grace, richness of colour, sweetness of sound, daintiness.

It is not unnatural to call these *aesthetic* qualities since they are paradigms of the sort of qualities upon which an aesthetic interest centres. Since these *are* qualities of works of art it might be thought that the value features of works of art are the same as value features of natural objects with the difference, insignificant from an evaluative point of view, that in the case of art these features characterise deliberately produced objects. If this were so, then since we clearly need no knowledge of artists and their intentions in order to attribute aesthetic qualities to natural objects, there will be a temptation[8] to suppose that such knowledge is unnecessary when aesthetic qualities are attributed to works of art.

Even if such knowledge *were* unnecessary for the attribution of aesthetic qualities to works of art this would not establish that in general knowledge of artists and their intentions is eliminable from criticism. For there may be other sorts of qualities critics attribute to works of art which *do* presuppose knowledge of and reference to artists and their intentions. I believe in fact that if we are to explain the value and importance of *art* to us we must suppose it to have values additional to any of the aesthetic values that works of art share with natural objects. Critics too have spoken thus. For example, Leavis writes:

> When we examine the formal perfection of *Emma* we find that it can be appreciated only in terms of the moral preoccupations that characterise the novelist's peculiar view of life. Those

---

[8]Although possibly a mistaken one. See on this K. Walton, "Categories of Art," *Philosophical Review,* 1971.

who suppose it to be an aesthetic matter, a beauty of composition, can give no adequate reason for the view that *Emma* is a great novel.[9]

Whether these additional values, special to art, involve knowledge of artists and their intentions is a matter that will increasingly concern us.

6. I offer now a list of merit and demerit qualities of works of art, qualities special to them as man-made things. We may, first, praise a work of art by using some of the following of it:

> responsible, mature, intelligent, sensitive, perceptive, discriminating, witty, poised, precise, self-aware, ironic, controlled, courageous.

Demerit terms include the following:

> simple-minded, shallow, diffuse, vulgar, immature, self-indulgent, uncomprehending, heavy-handed, gauche, glib, smug.

These terms characterise works of art but not natural objects. I call them *personal qualities* and I want to argue that the presence of these qualities in a work reflects the personality of an artist. Hence, if they are relevant things for critics to mention in talking of works, they become critical remarks about the work's creator.

Clearly the personal quality terms I have introduced need more treatment than I can give them here. Thus, for example, distinctions need to be made within the class of personal qualities. Again we may need to ask how we distinguish works of art which display such qualities from other things that display them, for example things like sermons, political speeches and clinical diagnoses. Here I freely admit that possession of such qualities alone may not be sufficient to make something art, but that these are qualities for which art is praised cannot I think be denied.

A cursory examination of critical writings, particularly on the literary arts, reveals the profusion of attributions of personal qualities to works of art. If anyone now says that although these *are* qualities to be found in works and *are* qualities of the work's producer, none the less it is no part of the *critic's* task to refer to them, then this seems to me merely to be stipulating a definition of "critic." I have no idea what argument one could then give to show that reference to personal qualities *is* relevant to the determination of the work's artistic merit. At best one can only draw attention to the fact that critics *do* think the citation of personal qualities is relevant and do often cite them with no widespread feeling of irrelevance. Any philosophy of art must do justice to this fact.

Two remarks by Beardsley and Wimsatt are relevant here. First, in "The Intentional Fallacy" (p. 5) they write:

> The meaning of the poem may certainly be a personal one in the sense that a poem expresses a personality or state of soul. . . . Even a short lyric poem is dramatic, the response of a speaker to a situation.[10]

In so far as the object of critical study is a response of a speaker, so it is relevant to apply personal quality terms to it. For terms like "glib," "smug" or "perceptive," for example, just are terms we have for characterising human responses.

---

[9]F. R. Leavis, *The Great Tradition* (Harmondsworth: Penguin, 1962) p. 17.
[10]The question "Response to what?" raises, of course, profound issues in the philosophy of art.

Secondly, granted that personal quality terms do apply to a speaker-response articulated in and by the work, it is tempting to fall back on the claim that no assumption need be made that the speaker-responder in the work is the creator of the work. Beardsley and Wimsatt certainly did try this. They wrote as follows in "The Intentional Fallacy":

> We ought to impute the thoughts and attitudes of the poem immediately to the dramatic speaker and if to the author at all only by an act of biographical inference. (p. 5)

The difficulty here is, as I have argued elsewhere,[11] that for certain personal quality attributions to the work itself no suitable "speaker" other than the author presents himself as the bearer of the personal qualities of the work. It is worth noting here that in his later work Wimsatt writes as follows (Demetz, p. 221):

> What we meant . . . (in "The Intentional Fallacy") . . . and what in effect I think we managed to say, was that the closest one could ever get to the artist's intending or meaning mind outside his work would still be short of his *effective* intention or *operative* mind as it appears in the work itself and can be read from the work.[12]

It does then look as if Wimsatt at least does wish to allow that the predication of personal qualities to the response-in-the-work *is* critically relevant and that no harm follows from attributing these qualities to the artist as he shows himself in the work.

Once it is admitted that personal qualities are qualities properly predicated of works by critics then certain anti-personalistic and anti-intentionalistic theses become less plausible. First in order to be able to attribute personal qualities to a thing at all one needs to know that that thing was produced by intentional human activity, rather than by natural causes. Any thesis advocating the total dispensability of knowledge of intention will then collapse.

Secondly, books *qua* ink marks on paper, paintings *qua* oil-based pigment on canvas, to take but two examples, cannot themselves be perceptive, intelligent and so on. These are *human* qualities. It is not unnatural therefore to believe that the referent of these personal quality attributions is the creator as he shows himself in his work. If this is so then to attribute personal qualities to a work in the course of critical evaluation *is* to refer to its artist and any strong anti-personalist thesis collapses. Moreover we have now found a way in which critical evaluations are directly personalistic. The only way to subvert these conclusions would be to show either that attributions of personal qualities are critically irrelevant or to show that the speaker-in-the-work should not be identified with the author. I have seen neither of these demonstrated and so far as the second alternative goes, Wimsatt at least seems unwilling to adopt it.

For the remainder of this paper I shall assume that to attribute personal qualities to a work is to speak of its artist.[13] What I want now to do is see what does and does not follow from this assumption and I shall examine this matter by examining two responses that those of an anti-personalist and anti-intentionalist persuasion might

---

[11]"Aesthetic and Personal Qualities," PAS 1971–2.

[12]This is surely not what was, even in effect, said in the earlier paper, or less controversy would have been provoked by it. Note too that Beardsley still seems to maintain that speaker-in-the-work and the author should be kept distinct. See *The Possibility of Criticism*, p. 59.

[13]I have *argued* this in the paper referred to above.

make *if* it were established that to make personal quality attributions to the work is to talk of the artist.

7. The first thing an anti-personalist might do, granted that personal quality attributions *are* made to the response articulated by the artist in the work, is modify his position. He might claim that although it is legitimate in criticism to make some references to the artist, *via* the qualities he displays in his work, a wide range of other possible references to him are critically irrelevant. In particular, reference to biographical detail discovered by independent historical research, and reference to the author by inference away from the work, are out of order for critics (although not perhaps for historical scholars).

There is something right about this. Historico-literary scholarship is often confused with, or substituted for, the task of critical judgment. Moreover historical inquiries into biography typically *follow* the completion of the critic's evaluative task. We do not e.g. research into Wordsworth's life in order to find out that his poetry was great but because we already know it is.

Although all this is doubtless true two further points need to be made. First, if I am right, then personal quality attributions characterise the *artist's* response as articulated in the work. It just is a fact about responses however that they may be more fully appreciated as the circumstances of the response are better understood. For this reason we may need extensive literary scholarship in order to reconstruct the social, intellectual and other climate within which the response occurred. Moreover in some cases our appreciation of a response is heightened if we know the circumstances in which it occurred and among these circumstances may be numbered the personal situation of the artist at the time of his writing. To claim this however is not to license the hoarding up of every literary nugget that can be mined by historical biographical inquiry. Rather it is to allow that the kind of biographical knowledge that throws light on the response articulated in the work, and that can be *connected* with the work, is relevant knowledge.

The second point I would make is that in opposing the excesses of irrelevant biographism the anti-personalist is objecting to nothing that many notable personalists have not also objected to. Take for example these comments made by E. M. W. Tillyard in the course of his debate with C. S. Lewis:

> Mr Lewis implies that "personal" as a critical term includes every accident, however trivial, connected with the author. . . . But I should guess that not a few supporters of the "personal heresy" would simply ignore such trivialities in their conception of personality. They would attach them to the sphere of literary gossip, not that of criticism.[14]

And (p. 34):

> When . . . (Mr Lewis) . . . imagines Keats reading about senators in a little brown book in a room smelling of boiled beef, he attaches these supposed facts to Keats' normal personality. I . . . call them . . . irrelevant to his normal personality. In other words by "personality" I do not mean practical or everyday personality. I mean rather some mental pattern that makes Keats Keats and not Mr Smith or Mr Jones.

[14]C. S. Lewis and E. M. W. Tillyard, *The Personal Heresy* (Oxford: Oxford paperbacks, 1965) p. 33.

What however is this mental pattern that interests the personalistic critic? Writing of Herrick (p. 47), Tillyard says

> It is not by any laborious process of induction after we have read the poem that we apprehend the qualities of unaffected sensuality, keen observation, sophistication and sense of decorum. We apprehend them from the rhythm, the vocabulary, the word arrangement, the pattern of the poem, in fact from the poem's most intimate poetical features.[15]

What Tillyard here calls the "mental pattern" is clearly related to particular instantiations of what I have called personal qualities. Although these are qualities of the artist we do not need to discover them by independent historical research, nor do we need to discover them by elaborate inferences away from the work. Hence we can attribute them when, as with Shakespeare, we know very little of the artist's life, or when, as with the ballads, we may know nothing of that life at all.

8. There is a second response that might be made to a demonstration that personal quality attributions are made to the artist's response-in-the-work. Here, although the correctness of some form of personalism may be admitted, it might then be claimed that this entails nothing about the correctness of intentionalism. Personalism and intentionalism, it may be said, are unrelated. Hence the correctness of personalism licenses no reference to the artist's intention.

In order to examine this response we need to look at the relationship between the intentional fallacy and the personal heresy. To begin with, personalism and intentionalism are independent to this extent. When we call a person's responses, say, perceptive or self-indulgent, we often need make no assumption that he had a *prior* intention to exhibit these qualities. To this extent a personalist could go along with those who argue that a knowledge of prior intentions is unnecessary when the work itself is to be studied. It also follows of course that the advice to ignore the prior intention and study "the work itself" does not rule out personalism. For the qualities found in the work itself may be personal qualities that the artist has, without prior intention, displayed there.

Although the truth of a thesis about the correctness of personalism is independent of the truth of a thesis about the relevance of knowledge of the *prior* intentions of the artist, it does not follow that personalism and other forms of intentionalism are similarly separable. Thus it seems obvious to me that we would not call an artist's productions "mature," "sensitive," "perceptive," "glib," etc., unless they were done intentionally in the wide sense of "intentional" I have adopted, that is, unless they were *his* responsibility, in *his* control and attributable *to him*. This being so, application of a wide range of personal terms to a work and many of its effects presupposes that the work and some of its effects are intentional productions.

Does anything that Beardsley and Wimsatt say have any bearing on *this* form of intentionalism? I think not. For they explicitly concern themselves only with questions about the necessity of knowledge of and reference to *prior* intentions and *statements about* prior intentions. Sometimes they argue that these statements are unhelpfully precise. This may well be so. A statement of intention before the composition of something like *War and Peace* might be a pretty vague thing. Sometimes it is argued

---

[15]It will be clear how closely this is related to the "operationalism" allowed by Wimsatt in a passage quoted above, this in spite of the fact that Tillyard appears to be under attack on p. 10 of "The Intentional Fallacy."

that knowledge of prior intentions is unavailable to the student of the work itself and is to be had only by leaving the work and conducting some separate inquiry. I doubt that this is so even for knowledge of prior intentions. These, as I said earlier, can be known from behavior and the work itself is often a substantial and revealing piece of behavior.[16] However even if prior intentions could not be known from the work, it does not follow that knowledge that the work and some of its effects are intentional, knowledge needed for the critically relevant attribution of personal qualities to the work, cannot be had from the work itself. Intention can be revealed in the work equally as well as in any other piece of human behavior.

The form of intentionalism that I am advocating survives Beardsley's "conclusive" argument against the appeal to intention. He writes (*Aesthetics*, p. 458):

> We can seldom know the intention with sufficient exactness independently of the work itself, to compare the work with it and measure its success and failure. Even where we can do so the resulting judgment is not a judgment of the work but only of the worker.

This makes it clear that Beardsley and Wimsatt are opposed to an appeal to intention that takes us away from the work or which makes mere successful fulfilment of intention the standard of success in art. The personalism and the related intentionalism that I have in mind is not of this sort. First, this personalism does not require *any* knowledge independent of the work itself. Rather the intentional effects to which the personal qualities are attributed are found in the work itself. Secondly, I do not want to say that mere successful fulfilment of prior intention is the standard of success in art, nor do I want to give the artist a privileged voice in the assessment of his work. Rather I want to claim that certain human merits are merits of the art that humans produce. To attribute these merits to a work is to suppose that the work and at least some of its effects are intentional. However, whether these intentionally produced works and effects have merits worthy of praise in personalistic terms is not a matter on which the artist has a privileged voice, no more than I have a privileged voice as to whether this "intentional" lecture is self-indulgent, precious, glib, pretentious or a host of other things.

9. I have argued so far that some forms of personalism and intentionalism have not been shown to be improper in criticism. I want now to conclude with some reflections on why Beardsley and Wimsatt may have arrived at their separation, however unclear, of personal and poetic studies and with some suggestions as to why their writings have proved, for many, so disturbing. First then, some reasons why personal and poetic studies were separated.

The first consideration applies particularly to Beardsley. There is, in his writing on art, a strong tendency to stress the aesthetic. Thus very early in his *Aesthetics* he identifies the work of art with what he calls "the aesthetic object." He writes (p. 17):

> Statements like "the play is tragic" seem to be about something . . .; let us call that something an "aesthetic object."

The danger in identifying works of art and aesthetic objects is one of thinking that the aesthetic qualities of art are the only important ones and of concentrating on these to the exclusion of other non-aesthetic qualities of art.

---

[16]See Wimsatt in Demetz, p. 210, and John Kemp, "The Work of Art and the Artist's Intentions," *British Journal of Aesthetics* (1964).

These aesthetic qualities are, as I have said, qualities that both works of art and natural objects may display. This being so, once they are made central there will be a temptation to concentrate on what works of art and natural objects have in common, indeed to put works of art and natural objects on the same footing for the purposes of evaluation. We can find some evidence of this way of thinking in Beardsley's *Aesthetics*. He writes (p. 17):

Aesthetic objects are perceptual objects, but so too are other things, e.g. cows, weeds.

Once this stage is reached it becomes tempting to believe that since in perceiving value qualities in natural objects no knowledge of or reference to a creator is needed, so in attributing these features to works of art no such knowledge or reference is needed. Further, claims about the illegitimacy of references from knowledge of the qualities of the work to statements about the qualities of art are more plausible when *aesthetic* qualities are used as examples.[17] Inferences from the elegance of Pope's writing to the elegance of Pope *are* of dubious critical relevance.

I suggest therefore that one reason why Beardsley at least was led to separate talk about artists and talk about works was that he concentrated on the *aesthetic* qualities of works. For these qualities such separation has some plausibility. Since however these qualities are only a sub-set of the qualities of art no general separation of artist and work can be argued from them. Indeed, such a separation becomes far less plausible when the personal qualities of works are singled out for study.[18]

The second reason Beardsley and Wimsatt may have been led to separate personal and poetic studies was, I think, because of a *dualistic* view of the relation between mental and non-mental phenomena. The author's personality, and in particular his intentions,[19] are "private"[20] events lying "behind"[21] the public entity, the work, so that "inferences"[22] or probabilistic inductions about the artist's mind are the best that the work would "indirectly"[23] allow. On the one hand there is the public object, the work, on the other the "private" mind of the artist.[24] Once given this inclination to dualism it follows that the critic who must concentrate on what is public, the work itself, must ignore the private mind of the artist.

It is obvious that all the recent discussions in philosophy of the privacy of experience are relevant here. Although it would take me beyond the scope of this paper to

---

[17]As a case in point here, note the terms used as examples in the argument on p. 20 of Beardsley's *Aesthetics*.

[18]Beardsley says very little about what I have called "personal qualities." Where he does touch on them the discussion is not happy, as in the following example: "Many of the regional qualities we find in art are most aptly, but of course metaphorically, named by qualities taken over from the moral aspects of human nature: they are "disciplined," "decisive," "decorous," "calm," "controlled," "sound," "strong," "bold," "healthy," to cite only positive terms. But an analogy is not a causal connection. To prove that decorous music makes us behave decorously, it is not enough to point out the similarity between the music and the hoped for behaviour." (*Aesthetics*, pp. 565–6.)

[19] "The artist's intention is a series of psychological states or events in his mind" (*Aesthetics*, p. 17). See, though, Wimsatt in Demetz, p. 220.

[20]Wimsatt in Demetz, p. 194.

[21]Ibid.

[22]"The Intentional Fallacy," p. 5.

[23]*Aesthetics*, p. 20.

[24]Note here the whole of Wimsatt's first section in Demetz, pp. 193–7.

demonstrate the matter it seems to me that at this point the philosophy of art and the philosophy of mind come together. In particular the claim some have argued, that persons are seen *in* their behavior (rather than inferred from it), is highly germane to our present inquiries. For if it is possible to replace a dualism of persons and behavior with the monism of "persons behaving," it may be possible to replace the dualism of artist and work by a monism of an artist showing himself in the response articulated by the work. If this is so, then *in* talking of the work itself we may well be talking of the artist. The separation of artist and work upon which the separation of personal and poetic studies depends may turn out to be untenable. If so, anti-personalist theses will have to be modified so as to rule out only those references to the author that are not related to a study of the work itself.

10. Why, finally, did the Beardsley-Wimsatt approach seem so disturbing? I think it was assumed that they wished totally to separate the work from the response of some actual person, so that *all* references to persons and their intentions were to be eliminated in some large scale dehumanisation of art.

I am not sure that Beardsley and Wimsatt ever intended this.[25] The temptation to believe that they did may have many sources. I mention three. First, there is Beardsley's concentration on features that works and natural objects share. This might well lead people to assume a belief on Beardsley's part that the artist is as irrelevant to the assessment of his work as he would be to the assessment of a natural object. Secondly, we have Beardsley and Wimsatt's apparently total distinction between personal and poetic studies. Thirdly, those who wished to defend intentionalism never gave a clear enough catalogue of the various possible theses about the relevance or irrelevance of appeals to intention. In consequence many seem not to have realised that Beardsley and Wimsatt argued only a relatively narrow thesis about the irrelevance of reference to prior intentions or statements of intention. They have never argued the dispensability of knowledge of other sorts of intention where this knowledge is gained from the work itself.[26]

Why however, even granted an assumption that Beardsley and Wimsatt *did* wish to argue the total eliminability of references to artists, would this seem so disturbing? One reason I think is that the belief that some works are, in part at least, important as documents of actual human responses, is deeply embedded in the concept of art as we have it. This belief is reflected in the ubiquity of references by critics to artists, that I have referred to above. To assert, as Beardsley and Wimsatt certainly did originally, that the response articulated in the work need not be thought of as some actual person's response but might be treated as the response of a dramatic speaker, a quasi-fictional *persona* detected in the work, was, for many, to urge the elimination of a centrally important feature of art.

It is perhaps relevant here to note the beginning of a possible divergence between Beardsley and Wimsatt on this matter. Wimsatt, as we have seen, does not appear to object to critical references to the mental quality shown by the artist in the work. Beardsley, on the other hand, is still exploring ways in which a wedge can be driven between the artist and the dramatic-responder-in-the-work. In his latest work he writes

---

[25]"A poem does not come into existence by accident. The words of a poem . . . come out of a head, not out of a hat." "The Intentional Fallacy," p. 4.

[26]Nor do they say much that is positive about such knowledge. See, e.g., Wimsatt in Demetz, p. 210.

The writing of a poem is, as such . . . the creation of a fictional character performing a fictional illocutionary act. (*The Possibility of Criticism*, p. 59.)

Given that there is a divergence here I am inclined to say that, without recanting his attack on irrelevant and unnecessary references to artists and their intentions, Wimsatt has come closest to recognising what an interest in art (an interest that becomes most articulate in criticism) *actually* involves. For he seems to recognise that an interest in the value of some art may be in part an interest in the response articulated by an artist *in* his work. As such he may have done more justice to "the form of life" of criticism as we have it.

Jenefer M. Robinson

STYLE AND PERSONALITY IN
THE LITERARY WORK

Introduction

In this paper I want to describe and defend a certain conception of literary style. If we look at literary style in the way I shall suggest, it will explain many of the problems that surround this elusive concept such as why something can be an element of style in the work of one author and not in another, what the difference is between individual style and general style, and how style differs from "signature." The ordinary conception of style is that it consists of nothing but a set of verbal elements such as a certain kind of vocabulary, imagery, sentence structure and so on. On my conception, however, a literary style is rather a way of *doing* certain things, such as describing characters, commenting on the action and manipulating the plot. I shall claim that an author's way of doing these things is an expression of her personality, or, more accurately, of the personality she seems to have. The verbal elements of style gain their stylistic significance by contributing to the expression of this personality, and they cannot be identified as *stylistic* elements independently of the personality they help to express.

Many theorists and critics have written as if style were an expression of personality. A good recent example is an essay on the first paragraph of Henry James' novel *The Ambassadors*, in which the writer, Ian Watt, claims that

> the most obvious and demonstrable features of James' prose style, its vocabulary and syntax, are direct reflections of his attitude to life and his conception of the novel . . .[1]

Watt lists some of the most notable elements in James' style: the preference for "non-transitive" verbs, the widespread use of abstract nouns, the prevalence of the word "that," the presence of "elegant variation" in the way in which something is referred to, and the predominance of negatives and near-negatives. Then Watt pro-

Jenefer M. Robinson, "*Style and Personality in the Literary Work,*" from The Philosophical Review 94, no. 2 (April 1985):227–247. Reprinted by permission of The Philosophical Review *and the author.*
[1]Ian Watt, "The first paragraph of *The Ambassadors*: an explication," reprinted in *Henry James,* ed. Tony Tanner (London: Macmillan, 1968), p. 301.

ceeds to show how these stylistic elements are expressive of James' *interest* in the abstract, his *preoccupation* with what is going on in the consciousness of his characters and his *attitude* of humorous compassion for them.

This essay is an attempt to explain and justify the assumption of Watt and others like him that style is essentially an expression of qualities of mind, attitudes, interests and personality traits which appear to be the author's own. My thesis is a thesis about what Richard Wollheim calls "individual style" and not about the style of periods or of groups of writers within a period.[2] I do not want to suggest that the unity of period or group styles, such as the Augustan style, can be explained in terms of the "personality" of a group or period. One other point should be mentioned. I believe that my remarks apply equally well to the non-literary arts, but for reasons of space I shall not attempt to justify this claim here.

I

Style as the Expression of Personality

In this first section I shall argue that style is essentially a way of doing something and that it is expressive of personality. Further, I shall suggest that what count as the verbal elements of style are precisely those elements which contribute to the expression of personality.

Intuitively, my style of dress, work, speech, decision-making and so on is the mode or manner or way in which I dress, work, speak and make decisions. In short it is the way I *do* these things. In ordinary contexts, then, a style is always a way of *doing* something. No less intuitively, my style of dressing, working, speaking and making decisions is typically an *expression* of (some features of) my personality, character, mind or sensibility. Thus my vulgar way of dressing is likely to be an expression of my vulgar sensibility, my witty, intellectual way of speaking an expression of my witty, intellectual mind, and my uncompromisingly courageous way of making decisions an expression of my uncompromisingly courageous character.

In saying that a person's way of doing things is an *expression* of that person's traits of mind, character or personality, I am saying (1) that the person's way of doing things exhibits or manifests these traits, and (2) that it is these traits which cause the person to do things in the way she does. Thus these traits leave a matching imprint or trace upon the actions which express them. If my timid way of behaving at parties is an expression of my timid character, then (1) my behavior exhibits or manifests timidity—I behave in a manifestly timid fashion, blushing, refusing to talk to strangers, hiding in the washrooms, etc.—and (2) my timid behavior is caused by my timid character, i.e., it is not due to the fact that (say) I am pretending to be timid, imitating a timid person or acting the part of a timid person in a play, nor is it the result of secret arrogance and contempt for parties. In general, if a person's actions are an expression of her personality, then those actions have the character that they have—compassionate,

---

[2]See Richard Wollheim, "Pictorial Style: Two Views," in *The Concept of Style*, ed. Berel Lang (Philadelphia: University of Pennsylvania Press, 1979), pp. 129–145. My chief debt in this paper is to Wollheim, whose remark that style has "psychological reality" provided its initial stimulus.

timid, courageous or whatever—in virtue of the fact that they are caused by the corresponding trait of mind or character in that person, compassion, timidity or courage. In expression, as the word itself suggests, an "inner" state is expressed or forced out into "outer" behavior. An "inner" quality of mind, character or personality causes the "outer" behavior to be the way it is, and also leaves its "trace" upon that behavior. A timid or compassionate character leaves a "trace" of timidity or compassion upon the actions which express it.[3]

Just as a person's style of dressing, working and speaking is the mode or manner or way in which she dresses, works and speaks, so an author's style of description, character delineation and treatment of a theme is the mode or manner or way in which she describes things, delineates character and treats her theme. In other words, it is her way of *doing* certain things, such as describing or characterizing a setting, delineating character, treating or presenting a theme, and commenting on the action. Moreover, the writer's way of describing, delineating, commenting and so on is typically an *expression* of (some features of) her personality, character, mind or sensibility. Thus James' humorous yet compassionate way of describing Strether's bewilderment expresses the writer's own humorous yet compassionate attitude. Jane Austen's ironic way of describing social pretension expresses her ironic attitude to social pretension.

Now, a style is not simply a way of doing something. We do not say that a person has a *style* of doing so-and-so unless that person does so-and-so in a relatively consistent fashion. Thus we say I have a vulgar and flamboyant *style* of dressing only if I consistently dress in a vulgar and flamboyant way. It may be, of course, that my way of dressing differs considerably from one day to the next: yesterday I wore a purple silk pyjama suit, today I am wearing a frilly scarlet mini-dress and tomorrow it will be leather dungarees and a transparent blouse. Despite these differences, however, we still say that I have a consistent way of dressing, because all my outfits are consistently vulgar and flamboyant. Moreover, my style of dressing is expressive of a particular feature of my personality, namely vulgarity and flamboyance. In an exactly similar way, we say that Jane Austen has a *style* of describing social pretension, because she consistently describes social pretension in an *ironic* way and the way she describes social pretension is expressive of a particular feature of her outlook, namely her irony.

So far I have talked only about a person's style of doing a particular thing, such as dressing. By contrast, when we say that a person has "a style," we normally mean that he or she has the same style of doing a number of different things. Thus when we accuse John of having a vulgar and flamboyant style, we may be referring to the vulgar and flamboyant way in which John not only dresses but also talks and entertains his dinner guests. Again, in characterizing Mary's style as generous, open, casual and easy-going, we may mean that Mary is generous, open, casual and easy-going in almost everything that she does. In this case Mary's style is expressive not of a single trait but of a number of traits which together "sum up" Mary's personality.

In just the same way, a person's literary style is their style of performing a wide range of (literary) activities. Thus, clearly, Jane Austen's style is not simply her style of doing any one thing, such as describing social pretension, but rather her style of doing a

---

[3]See especially Richard Wollheim, "Expression," in Royal Institute of Philosophy Lectures, Vol. I, 1966–67, *The Human Agent* (New York: St. Martin's Press, 1968), and *Art and Its Objects* (2nd edition; Cambridge: Cambridge University Press, 1980), sections 15–19. See also Guy Sircello, *Mind and Art* (Princeton: Princeton University Press, 1972).

number of things, such as *describing*, *portraying* and *treating* her characters, theme and social setting, *commenting* on the action, *presenting* various points of view, and so on. In short, to borrow a concept from Guy Sircello, it is the way in which she performs the various "artistic acts"[4] which constitute the writing of a literary work. Now, a style of doing a wide range of things is just like a style of doing a particular thing in that it consistently expresses certain features of the mind, personality, etc., of the agent. We say that Mary has "a style" in virtue of the consistently generous, open, casual and easy-going way in which she does a number of different things. Similarly, a writer has a literary style in virtue of the fact that her style of performing a wide variety of artistic acts expresses the same qualities of (her) mind and temperament. For example, James' style of *treating* Strether, of *portraying* the difference between what Strether thinks of Waymarsh and what he thinks he thinks, of *emphasizing* the abstract and the timeless, of *commenting* on Strether's bewilderment and so on together constitute what we call "James' style." And this style owes its coherence to the fact that all these artistic acts express the same set of attitudes, interests and qualities of mind.

Of course, not every artistic act of a writer in a particular work expresses exactly the same qualities of mind, character or personality. In *Emma*, for example, Jane Austen portrays Mrs. Elton in a quite different way from Jane Fairfax. This is because Jane Austen's attitude to Mrs. Elton is quite different from her attitude to Jane Fairfax. In the one portrayal she expresses (among other things) her love of the ridiculous, and in the other she expresses (among other things) her compassion for suffering sensibility. But Jane Austen's way of portraying Mrs. Elton and her way of portraying Jane Fairfax, as well as her way of portraying the other characters in the novel, her way of describing their personal relationships, her way of developing the plot, and all the other innumerable artistic acts which go into writing the novel *Emma* together add up to the style in which *Emma* is written, a style which expresses all those attitudes that together form the personality of the author of *Emma*.

If a writer has an individual style, then the way she writes has a certain consistency: the same traits of mind, character and personality are expressed throughout her work. Now, at a particular point in a novel, the writer may seem to express anxiety about, anger at or contempt towards a particular character, event or idea, although the writer does not seem to be a chronically anxious, angry or contemptuous sort of person. However, such "occasional" properties should not be thought of as properties of style. Only those properties which are "standing" or long-term properties can be considered stylistic. Thus stylistic qualities are likely to be qualities of mind, moral qualities and deep-seated character traits, rather than mood or emotional qualities such as "angry," "joyful" and "afraid." In the same way, we do not treat every angry, joyful or fearful action performed in real life as an expression of basic character or personality; it is only when someone consistently acts in a choleric or a cheerful way, that we infer to her essentially choleric or cheerful nature.

I have argued that a literary style is a way of performing "artistic acts," describing a setting, portraying character, manipulating plot and so on, and it is the writer's way of performing these acts which is expressive of all those standing traits, attitudes, qualities of mind and so on that together form her personality. What, then, is the relation

---

[4]Guy Sircello, *Mind and Art* (Princeton: Princeton University Press, 1972), Chapter 1. I am not sure whether Sircello would approve of the use to which I put the concept of artistic acts.

between the performance of these acts and what have traditionally been thought of as the verbal elements of style, such as a certain vocabulary, imagery and sentence structure? When a writer describes a setting and portrays character, she uses words, and the kind of word she uses, the sort of sentence structure she forms and so on together constitute the elements of verbal style. If a writer manipulates his theme from the point of view of one whose main interest is in thought and the development of consciousness (James) or if she portrays her characters with a judicious mixture of irony and compassion (Austen), then he or she does so by using language in certain ways.

Obviously the presence of certain verbal elements does not *entail* that a particular personality is being expressed.[5] If, however (on a reasonable interpretation), those verbal elements are being used by a writer to perform artistic acts in a particular way, then we can infer from the way the acts are performed to characteristics of the writer's mind, character and personality. For example, Henry James uses negatives, abstract nouns, etc., in order to describe Strether's state of consciousness, to comment on Strether's bewilderment and to characterize Strether's attitude to Waymarsh, and he thereby expresses qualities of his own mind and personality.

Moreover, negatives, abstract nouns, non-transitive verbs, elegant variation and so on are verbal elements which at first sight seem to have nothing in common. What links them all together, however, as elements of "James' style" is their use in the artistic acts James performs: they are all elements of his style because they all contribute to the expression of his personality and attitudes. For example, using these particular verbal elements, James thereby describes Strether's state of consciousness in a particular judicious, abstractive, expository way and thereby expresses his own "subjective and abstractive tendency,"[6] his interest in the relations between minds (Strether's, the narrator's, the reader's), his moral sensitivity and his cool and judicious intellect.

II

The Personality of the Implied Author

So far in this essay I have written as if the personality expressed by the style of a work were that of the writer herself. I have suggested that we infer from the way in which the writer performs the artistic acts in a work to the presence of personality traits and so on *in the writer* which cause her to perform those acts in the way that she does. But this is an oversimplification. What is more typically expressed by the style of a work is not the personality of the actual author, but of what, following Wayne Booth, we might call the "implied author,"[7] that is, the author as she seems to be from the evidence of the

---

[5]See Frank Sibley, "Aesthetic Concepts," in *Philosophy Looks at the Arts*, ed. Joseph Margolis (New York: Scribner, 1962), and a large subsequent literature [including this volume].

[6]Watt, "The first paragraph of *The Ambassadors*," p. 291.

[7]Wayne Booth, *The Rhetoric of Fiction* (Chicago: University of Chicago Press, 1961), especially pp. 70–77. Kendall Walton has developed the related, but more general notion of an "apparent artist" in his paper "Points of View in Narrative and Depictive Representation," *Nôus* 10 (1976), pp. 49–61, and elsewhere. Walton's own theory of style, in which the idea of the "apparent artist" plays an important role, is to be found in "Style and the Products and Processes of Art," in *The Concept of Style*, ed. Berel Lang (Philadelphia: University of Pennsylvania Press, 1979).

work. Thus however querulous and intolerant the actual Tolstoy may have been in real life, the implied author of *Anna Karenina* is full of compassionate understanding.

Because the way in which people act typically expresses features of their minds, attitudes and personalities, we are justified in making inferences from the way in which people perform actions to the presence in them of certain character or personality traits. If we see Mary constantly acting in a generous and compassionate way, then, barring any evidence to the contrary, it is reasonable to infer that Mary has a generous and compassionate nature which is responsible for her generous and compassionate actions.[8] The situation is more complicated, however, when we are considering acts performed by an author in the composition of a literary work. Although it may sometimes be legitimate to infer from the way these acts are performed to personality traits in the actual author, it is normally the case that the personality expressed by the style of a literary work is not that of the actual author but that of the implied author.

This might sound as if the author were trying to mislead us. After all if in real life it turns out that Mary's generous and compassionate actions are entirely due to her desire to impress John, then we might well accuse her of deceiving us—or at least John—about her true nature. She seems to be a generous and compassionate person but in fact is not. However, the situation is significantly different in the literary case. It is, after all, a commonplace convention of fiction-writing that the author more or less consciously "puts on" or "adopts" a persona to tell "her" story, but normally at any rate the author is not thereby trying to deceive us into believing that this assumed persona or personality is her own.[9] When we make inferences from the way the artistic acts in a work are performed to the personality of this implied author, the "person" who seems to be performing these acts, we are aware that the personality which leaves its "trace" on the way those acts are performed is a personality created and adopted by the author and which may be different from that of the author herself.[10] Thus, as Booth points out, even the implied author of *Emma* does not have all her qualities in common with the real Jane Austen. Both are wise, witty, unsentimental and so

---

[8]What "having a compassionate nature" means is a large question: presumably at the least it involves having certain beliefs and desires and being prone to certain kinds of behavior. For a discussion of compassion, see Lawrence Blum, "Compassion," in *Explaining Emotions*, ed. Amelie Rorty (Berkeley: University of California Press, 1980).

[9]It is not appropriate for me to argue here for any general thesis about the correct way to interpret literary texts, but it is interesting to notice that my view that style is the expression of personality fits very nicely with a plausible theory of critical interpretation recently defended by Alexander Nehamas ("The Postulated Author: Critical Monism as a Regulative Ideal," *Critical Inquiry* 8 (Autumn, 1981), pp. 133–149. In his words,

> To interpret a text is to consider it as its author's production. Literary texts are produced by agents and must be understood as such. . . . And since texts are products of expressive actions, understanding them is inseparably tied to understanding their agents.

Here Nehamas uses the word "author" to mean "implied author." His claim is that a text must be read as an expression of the attitudes and so on of the implied author. Of course it could turn out that Nehamas is wrong and the correct way to read literary texts is as the expression of attitudes in the actual author. My thesis can accommodate either view.

[10]Compare the way in which actors "adopt" the personality which they express.

on, but the implied author of *Emma* has a moral perfection beyond the scope of the real Jane Austen.[11]

Some literary works deliberately exploit a number of different styles. A good example is James Joyce's *Ulysses*. In this case the style of at least some of the different episodes of the book should be identified with the style not of the implied author "James Joyce" but of the narrator of that episode. The personality expressed by the style of the Cyclops episode, for example, is not the personality which the author seems to have; the coarse and unpleasant personality expressed belongs only to the nameless narrator of the episode. Notice, however, that this kind of case is parasitic upon the normal case: it is because a style is normally an expression of the personality of the writer that we infer from the style of the Cyclops episode to the presence of a coarse and unpleasant person writing or narrating it.[12]

Does it make sense to talk about "the style" of *Ulysses?* In a way it does not, because *Ulysses* contains so many different styles (some of which are not even "individual" styles).[13] Nevertheless, we can identify an implied author of *Ulysses* and detect the way in which he appears to *manipulate* the narrative point of view, *treat* the *Ulysses* theme, *characterize* Molly Bloom, etc. The way these artistic acts are performed is part of *the style of Ulysses*. For example, the presence of many different narrators with different styles is itself a feature of *Joyce's* style and it is expressive of certain traits that Joyce seems to have, such as a boisterous creativity, a delight in the expressive capacities of language and an interest in the way reality can be viewed and reported from so many different points of view.[14]

One of the ways in which we identify "Joyce's style" is by looking at Joyce's oeuvre as a whole. Thus we may be inclined to see the style of the early Stephen episodes in *Ulysses* (as opposed to, say, the Cyclops episode) as in "Joyce's style" partly because they are in somewhat the same style as other works by Joyce, notably A *Portrait of the Artist*. The style of an oeuvre, just like the style of an individual work, is an expression of the personality of the implied author of that oeuvre. Just as we sometimes find a variety of styles in a single work (like *Ulysses*), so it is possible to find in a single oeuvre a variety of styles corresponding to radically different implied authors. But in the normal case the implied author of different works in a single oeuvre is recognizably the "same person." Of course no two works do or even can express exactly the same personality, but there will normally be striking similarities. Typically, the personality expressed by an author's style matures over time. Thus the implied author of Jane Austen's books becomes less acerbic in her wit, more compassionate and tender;[15] the implied author of Henry James' works becomes ever more complex, subtle and abstract in his thinking and moralizing. A style grows and matures with the personality it expresses.

[11]See Booth, *The Rhetoric of Fiction*, p. 265.

[12]Compare *Tristram Shandy* which is written in Tristram's (the narrator's) style. The implied author seems to have a personality much like that of Tristram, but he is distinct from Tristram and appears from time to time to correct Tristram's opinions in helpful footnotes.

[13]See, for example, *The Oxen of the Sun* episode.

[14]Notice that plays can have individual style despite the fact that they contain many different "voices."

[15]However, the implied author of the late fragment *The Watsons* may seem less mature than the implied author of *Persuasion*.

III

An Objection Considered

My thesis has been that the defining feature of a literary work which has an individual style is that the work is an expression of the personality of the implied author,[16] and that what links the diverse verbal elements of style together into a coherent whole is that they all contribute to the expression of this particular personality. One objection to this thesis is that there are many qualities of a work which *prima facie* are qualities of its style but which do not seem to express any qualities of mind or personality in the implied author. In particular, there are formal qualities (euphonious, Latinate, colloquial, ornate) and expressive qualities (dramatic, heroic, violent) which may be attributed to the style of a work but which are not (or need not be) qualities of the implied author's mind or personality.

In this section of the paper I shall argue that such formal and expressive qualities are not always qualities of the individual style of a work, and that when they are it is only because they contribute to the expression of qualities of mind, personality, etc. in the implied author. Among works which possess striking formal or expressive qualities (euphony, violence, etc.), I distinguish three sorts of case: (1) works which have such properties but lack style altogether, (2) works which have such properties and also belong to a general style category but which lack individual style, and (3) works which have such properties and which also possess individual style.

(1) Intuitively, there could be a piece of characterless prose which nevertheless happens to be *euphonious*, i.e., the words it contains make a pleasing musical sound. Imagine, for example, an incompetent Freshman English paper in which the ideas are unclearly expressed, the sentence structure confused and the choice of words unimaginative. No one reading the paper would attribute to it an individual style. Yet, quite by chance, the ill-chosen words are euphonious: l's, m's and n's predominate, there are only a few plosives or fricatives, and the vowel sounds fit together in a melodious way. To say that this work is in a "euphonious style," however, is at best misleading, since intuitively it is not in a style at all. The possession of just one striking formal quality, such as euphony, is not normally sufficient to endow a work with style. Indeed even a string of nonsense syllables may be euphonious, although presumably they cannot be in a style. Hence euphony does not always contribute to individual style, just because it may be a quality of a work that lacks style altogether. On my view, of course, a euphonious work that lacks individual style is a euphonious work which fails to express any individual personality in the implied author.

(2) A more interesting situation arises when a work is in a "euphonious style" in the sense that it belongs to what Wollheim calls a "general" style category, although it does not possess *individual* style. General style categories, such as period or school styles, group together writers, painters or other artists who seem to the critic and historian to have important characteristics in common, for example, the Elizabethan pastoral lyric

---

[16]From now on I shall write as if the personality expressed by the style of a work were that of the implied author, because typically this is the case. However the implied author may sometimes have all his or her properties in common with the actual author. Moreover, as I have already noticed, in some cases the personality expressed is that of the narrator.

style or the style of the school of Donne (the Metaphysical style). To belong to a general category of literary style often involves obeying certain conventions and using certain techniques. Thus the style of Elizabethan pastoral love lyrics demands a certain stylized way of referring to the lover and the beloved, of describing their surroundings and so on. The imagery and the poetic forms employed all fall within a fairly narrow and predictable range. More importantly for my present argument, membership in a particular general style category often requires a work to have certain formal and expressive qualities. Thus the style of an Elizabethan pastoral love lyric is supposed to be charming and euphonious, the Metaphysical style colloquial and dramatic, and the Miltonic epic style (i.e., the style of works which imitate *Paradise Lost*) Latinate and heroic.

Now, intuitively, there is a distinction between merely belonging to a general style category and having a formed individual style. For example, although a poem must be (somewhat) colloquial and (somewhat) dramatic in order to count as a Metaphysical poem at all, it does not follow that every minor lyric by Carew or Suckling has an individual style. Indeed we may often be hard-pressed to distinguish between the lesser works of Carew and Suckling, just because they do lack "individuality." Similarly, many of the poems in the collection *England's Helicon* obey all the requirements of the Elizabethan pastoral lyric style and yet remain "characterless." They are charming and euphonious but they have an anonymous air about them: they do not seem to have been written by anyone in particular. In short, a work which belongs to a general style category may have certain striking formal or expressive qualities even though it lacks individual style. An Elizabethan love lyric may be euphonious, a Metaphysical poem dramatic, a Miltonic epic Latinate without necessarily being in an individual style.

One of the merits of my theory of style is that it allows us to define and explain this intuitive distinction between individual and general style. On my view, the crucial difference is that whereas having an individual style necessarily involves the expression of personality in the implied author, belonging to a general style category has no such implications. Elsewhere[17] I have argued for this position in much greater detail than is either possible or appropriate here. If I am right, however, it follows that there can be works belonging to a general style category which possess the formal and expressive qualities characteristic of that style but which do not express any individual personality in the implied author. Hence these formal and expressive qualities, although qualities of general style, do not contribute to any individual style in the work just because they do not contribute to the expression of an individual personality in the implied author of the work.

(3) Finally, formal and expressive qualities such as "Latinate," "euphonious" and "dramatic" may be qualities that are present in works of individual style and which do contribute to the expression of personality in those works. It does not follow, however, that the implied author is a Latinate, euphonious or dramatic sort of fellow. These

---

[17]"General and Individual Style in Literature," *The Journal of Aesthetics and Art Criticism*, 43 (1984). I argue there that if a work belongs to a general style category, such as a school or period style, then it obeys certain rules and observes certain conventions, some of which undoubtedly foster certain kinds of formal and expressive properties. However, it is possible to write works which belong to a general style category and succeed to some extent in achieving the formal and expressive goals of that category without thereby expressing an individual personality in the implied author.

qualities in themselves do not express any particular trait in the implied author. Rather they can help to express many diverse traits, depending upon the artistic acts to which they contribute. In a similar way, Henry James' fondness for negatives does not in itself express any feature of "his" personality; it is the way the negatives are used in the performance of artistic acts, such as describing Strether's state of mind, which gives this feature of James' work its stylistic significance.

The quality of euphony, for example, may indeed contribute to individual style, but it does so by contributing to the expression of individual personality in a work. Consequently the contribution it makes is very different in different works. Both Swinburne's "Garden of Proserpine" and large passages of Milton's "Paradise Lost" can be described as euphonious, but the personalities expressed in the individual style of these two works are very different. In the Swinburne poem the gentle, musical sounds help to express the implied author's sense of world-weariness, melancholy and resignation,[18] whereas the famous Miltonic melody generally serves to help express the implied author's sense of the dignity and grandeur of his theme. To say that both works are in a "euphonious style" means simply that euphony is a formal quality of both works, which in both cases contributes to individual style. The way it contributes, however, is quite different in the two cases. Similarly it could be argued that both Jane Austen and Donne have *dramatic* styles, but clearly the dramatic qualities in each help to express quite different personalities and hence contribute quite differently to the styles of each.[19]

In summary then, the formal and expressive qualities I have been discussing are not always qualities of the individual style of a work: they may be present in works lacking any style at all or in works which belong to a general style category but do not have individual style. Moreover, even when such qualities contribute to the individual style of a work, they do so in very different ways. The "same" quality in two different works may contribute to the expression of quite different traits of mind and personality in the implied authors of those works.

There are two interesting corollaries of my discussion. First, it would seem to follow that no verbal element or formal or expressive quality in a work is always and inevitably an element or quality of individual style. Even such qualities as "euphonious" and "Latinate" do not contribute to individual style wherever they appear, and even when they do contribute to individual style, they do so in virtue of how they are used in the artistic acts in the work. Secondly, it would also seem to follow that *any* verbal element or formal or expressive quality in a work *can* be an element or quality of individual style, provided it contributes in the appropriate way to the expression of personality in the implied author.

[18]There go the loves that wither,
     The old loves with wearier wings;
   And all dead years draw thither,
     And all disastrous things; . . .

[19]Sometimes a writer performs the artistic act of "expressing" some quality in the external world, as when she, for example, "expresses" the violence of a battle or the fragility of an elf. Again, however, it is not the violence or fragility themselves which contribute to style, but the way in which violence or fragility is "expressed" (in this sense) by the writer. Thus one woman may "express" the violence of a battle with gusto, thereby expressing "her" enjoyment of fast-moving action and enthusiasm for heroic exploits, whereas another may "express" the violence with cool detachment, thereby expressing "her" ironic awareness of human folly. For further discussion of this issue, see Guy Sircello, *Mind and Art*, Chapter 4, and my "Expressing the Way the World Is," *Journal of Aesthetic Education* 13 (1979), pp. 29–44.

In short, if my thesis is correct, then there is no "taxonomy" or checklist of style elements, that is, elements which contribute to individual style wherever they appear.[20] Euphony, Latinate diction and the presence of many negatives are elements of individual style only if they are used in such a way as to contribute to the expression of traits of mind and personality in the implied author.

We cannot, therefore, identify the elements of individual style merely as the most striking or salient features of a work. On the one hand there are striking features which do not invariably contribute to individual style. I have argued that euphony, for example, may be a striking feature of works which lack individual style. Again, it would be a striking feature of a work if all the proper names in it began with the letter "X," yet intuitively this would not be a feature of its *style* (although it could be if, for example, it were used to express the implied author's sense of fun).

On the other hand, moreover, there are many elements which are not particularly salient but which contribute to individual style. Thus a certain writer who has a formed individual style may have a preference for the indefinite article over the definite which contributes in a small way to the expression of her generalizing imagination and tendency to abstraction. Again, any careful, sensitive reader of *The Ambassadors* can tell that James tends to "interpolate" elements in his sentences, but we may not notice that the interpolations typically occur between verb or adjective and complement, or between auxiliary and main verb, and that they cluster towards the center of a sentence.[21] Yet it is non-salient elements such as these which contribute significantly to James' style, because they all help to express "James' " characteristic attitudes, interests and qualities of mind and personality.

IV

Some Problems Resolved

I have argued that if a literary work has an individual style, the artistic acts in the work are performed in such a way as to express qualities of mind, attitudes, personality traits, etc., which make up the individual personality of the implied author of the work. The verbal elements of (individual) style are those elements which contribute to the expression of this personality. There is no "checklist" of elements or qualities which inherently or intrinsically contribute to individual style, no matter where they appear.

So far I have merely tried to make my thesis seem reasonable and to forestall some possible objections to it. In this final section I should like to make some more positive remarks in its favor. The best reason for accepting my theory is that it answers an array of difficult questions surrounding the concept of style.

(1) First, my theory explains why a correct description of a writer's style mentions some of its verbal characteristics but not others. On my view, what count as the

---

[20]cf. Richard Wollheim, "Pictorial Style: Two Views." It is possible that there are taxonomies for *general* style categories, unlike individual style.

[21]See Seymour Chatman, *The Later Style of Henry James* (Oxford: Blackwell 1972), pp. 126–127. Chatman's book contains many more examples of non-salient (as well as salient) verbal features that are important to James' style. In his comparison between a successful parody of James' style (by Max Beerbohm) and a rather unsuccessful one (by W. H. D. Rouse), Chatman shows how Beerbohm incorporates into his parody many features of James' style which were obviously not salient to Rouse.

elements of a style are precisely those verbal elements which contribute to the expression of the implied author's personality. In Henry James, for example, the relevant verbal elements include the recurrent use of non-transitive verbs, abstract nouns, negatives and the word "that." These all help to contribute to the expression of "James' " personality. But we could, no doubt, if we searched for them, discover many recurrent elements in James' work which are not stylistically significant. Thus perhaps it would turn out that James had a penchant for nouns beginning with the letter "f" or that his sentences invariably had an even number of words in them. A description of James' style would not mention these elements, however, precisely because they do not contribute to the expression of the personality of the implied author. In short, many quite diverse and seemingly unrelated verbal elements belong to the same style in virtue of the fact that they all contribute to the expression of the same personality. It is only if the frequent use of nouns beginning with the letter "f" can be shown to contribute to this personality that this particular verbal characteristic would be an element of style.

(2) For similar reasons, my theory explains why it is that the same verbal element may have stylistic significance in one work or author and no stylistic significance, or a different significance, in another work or author. For the same stylistic element may play no expressive role in the one case and an important role in the other. Alternatively, it may simply play different expressive roles in the two cases. Suppose, for example, that two writers tend to use the indefinite article rather than the definite. In one writer, who has a formed individual style, this may contribute to the expression of her generalizing imagination and tendency to abstraction. In the other writer, it may be an accident and it may have no expressive effect in the work, or perhaps it indicates a lack of strength and precision in the style. In the first writer we have located the presence of a stylistic element; in the second writer the same element has no stylistic significance or a different one. If we were to view a person's style as consisting of a set of elements which we can check off on a checklist, then it would make no sense to say that a particular element is sometimes stylistic and sometimes not. But if we view style as a function of the literary personality expressed by a work in the way I have suggested, then the problem dissolves.

(3) It is commonly believed that if a writer or a work has an individual style, this implies that the various stylistic elements have a certain unity. Yet there are no intrinsic connections among the features of James' style, for example: why should negatives, abstract nouns and "elegant variation" go together to form a unified style? My theory explains in a clear way what stylistic unity amounts to: a style has a unity because it is the expression of the personality of the implied author. Just as we see the way a person performs the various actions of daily life as expressive of different facets of her personality, so we see the way in which a writer seems to perform the various artistic acts in a literary work as expressive of different facets of "her" personality. The many disparate elements of verbal style fit together only because they are being used to express the "same" personality: the writer uses the elements of verbal style to describe her characters, treat her theme, etc., thereby seeming to reveal a set of personality traits, qualities of mind, attitudes and so forth which "makes sense" out of (unifies) this multitude of artistic acts.

The question arises as to whether this set of "standing" traits forms a coherent personality. The concept of a "unified" or coherent personality is admittedly somewhat vague, since the most disparate and apparently inconsistent psychological traits seem capable of coexisting in normal, rational people.[22] All I need to insist on, however, is that if a work has an individual style then the different traits expressed by the various artistic acts in the work (portraying Jane Fairfax, characterizing Emma's treatment of her father, etc.) coexist in a way which is consistent with our knowledge of persons and human nature. Moreover, the same traits must be consistently expressed throughout a work. Thus the implied author of *Le Rouge et le Noir* both admires and despises the aristocratic world to which Julien Sorel aspires, but because he does so consistently and because the conflict in his attitudes is one which we recognize as possible in a basically rational person, his admiration and scorn are both part of the personality expressed by the style of the work.[23] If however, a work expresses no individual personality at all or if the personality expressed is a confusion of different traits which do not fit together in an intelligible way, then it follows from my thesis that the work in question lacks individual style.[24]

(4) It used to be a commonplace of literary theory that the subject-matter of a text is *what* the writer writes about, whereas the style is *how* she writes about it. This distinction has recently been questioned by several writers, including Nelson Goodman who argues that

> some differences in style consist entirely of differences in what is said. Suppose one historian writes in terms of military conflicts, another in terms of social changes; or suppose one biographer stresses public careers, another personalities.[25]

The theory of style which I have outlined in this essay accounts for the intuition that sometimes features of subject-matter may be stylistic features and explains which features of subject-matter will count as stylistic and why. Briefly, a feature of subject-matter is of stylistic relevance just in case it is expressive of the implied author's personality. Thus it is reasonable to construe the subject-matter of *The Ambassadors* as the development of Strether's consciousness. In this case the choice of subject-matter is clearly of stylistic relevance. Again the differences in the histories and biographies envisioned by Goodman are clearly differences in the personalities of the implied authors of these works.

(5) My theory also has a satisfying explanation for the difference between what Goodman calls "style" and "signature." A "signature" is anything which identifies a work as being by a particular author, school, or whatever, such as an actual signature. A "signature," however, may have no stylistic significance. Goodman says:

> Although a style is metaphorically a signature, a literal signature is no feature of style.[26]

It is true that a style, like a "signature," may *identify* a work or an author, but the way it performs the identification is quite different. A "signature" may have nothing to do

---

[22]See the work on emotions by Amelie Rorty, "Explaining Emotions," and Patricia Greenspan, "A Case of Mixed Feelings: Ambivalence and the Logic of Emotion," both in Rorty, ed., *Explaining Emotions*.

[23]Lee Brown brought this example to my attention.

[24]If for example, *for no apparent reason*, an author describes a certain character with unqualified approval in chapters 1, 3 and 5 and with a certain kind of qualified disapproval in chapters 2, 4 and 6, then it might be that the implied author is schizophrenic or, more likely, simply a confused creation.

[25]Nelson Goodman, "The Status of Style," *Critical Inquiry* 1 (1975), p. 801. Goodman's explanation for this fact is different from mine, however.

[26]Goodman, "The Status of Style," p. 807.

with the qualities of the implied author expressed by a work. Perhaps it is an actual signature or perhaps some other convention is used: a writer might be uniquely identifiable by the particular Latin tag which appears at the head of all her books, regardless of their subject-matter or style (if any). A style, on the other hand, identifies a work or an author because it is an expression of a set of attitudes, qualities of mind, character traits and so on which are unique to the implied author of that work or oeuvre.

(6) Finally, as I have already remarked, one of the virtues of my theory is that it allows me to clarify the distinction between general and individual style.[27] If a work belongs to a general style category, then, although it may have formal and expressive qualities that are distinctive of that style, it may nevertheless remain "characterless": no personality "informs" the work. Alternatively, there may be personality traits expressed but they do not seem to belong to any particular individual. The work has an "anonymous" air about it, because the artistic acts are performed in a way which is common to a large number of different writers.[28] By contrast, as I have argued throughout this paper, the defining quality of an individual style is that it expresses a coherent set of attitudes, qualities of mind and so on which seem to belong to the individual writer of the work: a work which has an individual style expresses the personality of the implied author of that work.[29]

[27]See also my "General and Individual Style in Literature."

[28]There are some general style categories such as the heroic epic, in which individual style is rarely found and might even be deemed inappropriate. The Homeric epics, however, do seem to contain passages that have individual style. It is interesting to note that the argument over the authorship of the *Iliad* is partly an argument about style and personality in the work. Those parts of the *Iliad* which have individual style provide a strong argument for scholars who wish to argue that there was one central author of the *Iliad* (call him "Homer") even though parts of it had been handed down by an oral tradition. By contrast, scholars who argue that there were a number of bards who contributed importantly to the creation of the *Iliad* point to the fact that there is no individual style to the *Iliad* as a whole. Interestingly, both sets of experts seem implicitly to grant the connection between individual style and an individual personality which is expressed in the style. For an introduction to the problem of multiple authorship in the *Iliad*, see E. R. Dodds, "Homer," in *The Language and Background of Homer*, ed. G. S. Kirk (Cambridge: Cambridge University Press, 1964), pp. 1–21.

[29]Many people have helped to improve this paper. I am particularly indebted to Lee Brown, Ann Clark, John Martin, Francis Sparshott, Kendall Walton, Richard Wollheim and the editors and referees of *The Philosophical Review*. I am also grateful to Berel Lang whose NEH Seminar on the Concept of Style aroused my interest in this topic.

THE THEORY OF DRAMA:
NIETZSCHE AND TRAGEDY

Nietzsche's *The Birth of Tragedy* is a passionate work wherein he sought to reach to the very depths of artistic creativity, revealing simultaneously the terrible absurdity of existence and the power that art has in transfiguring this terror. The Apollinian and the Dionysian, the dream state and the state of intoxication, intellectual vision and orgiastic ecstasy—all of these Nietzschean notions are by now commonplace in our thinking about art and the nature of tragedy. Nietzsche thus reveals the complex interrelationships between art and reality, and he does this through the concepts of overcoming and transfiguration: "Art is not merely the imitation of the reality of nature but rather a metaphysical supplement of the reality of nature. The tragic myth . . . participates freely in this metaphysical intention of art to transfigure." In tragedy, at least Attic tragedy, the Dionysian and Apollinian impulses are combined into a unique synthesis. Each of these impulses results from the force of nature and gives rise on the one hand to the "beautiful illusions" of the Apollinian dreamworld and on the other hand to the ecstatic impulse of the Dionysian.

The Birth of Tragedy is a work of Nietzsche's youth. Later in his life he refined and corrected various ideas presented there in light of subsequent developments in his philosophical career. We here add a very brief portion of Nietzsche's "Attempt at a Self-Criticism" to supplement his ideas in *The Birth of Tragedy* and to present a sample of his later work. The interested reader should consult *The Will to Power* for Nietzsche's later views on artistic creativity.

Richard Schacht's essay on *The Birth of Tragedy* illuminates these philosophical themes in Nietzsche's work. Schacht maintains that the question of the relationship between art and life guided Nietzsche's thought on art from his earliest writings. The problem Nietzsche inherited from Schopenhauer was how, given the terror and meaninglessness of existence, art could function as a means of redemption by which it could be put in the service of life. Not merely that, but Nietzsche sought to overcome the horror of existence by identifying human life with artistic creativity. This is clear in his ideas of *overcoming* and *transfiguration*, which Schacht views as the central ideas of his theory of art. Each of these impulses involves a creative transformation of everyday existence, which means that life is essentially artistic and that art is an expression of the fundamental nature of life.

In the case of Apollinian art, which Nietzsche links with the plastic arts, the creation of a "beautiful illusion" associated with *dreaming* is identified with the creative imagining that is a kind of waking dream. According to Schacht, the forms are not viewed as representations or imitations of reality in the fashion of Schopenhauer, but instead depart radically from the "real world" of ordinary experience. They are "placed alongside it for its overcoming."

According to Nietzsche, "Apollo is the transfiguring genius of the *principium individuationis* [principle of individuation] through which alone the redemption and illusion is truly to be obtained." By contrast, Dionysian art gives expression to the will in its omnipotence, breaking the spell of individuation and opening the way to "the innermost heart of things." However, neither the idealized images of Apollinian art nor the orgiastic revelry associated with Dionysus attempts to faithfully represent or express anything at all. Nor can either artistic impulse be rigidly tied to the conventional division of art forms—the plastic arts being considered Apollinian and the Dionysian arts musical. Each type of art transfigures a different vision of the world so that Nietzsche can speak of "two worlds of art differing in their intrinsic essence." Each art is thus a symbolic expression that is to be confused neither with conceptualization nor with representation. It is only through the creation of such symbolic forms that a nondestructive identification of art with the world is possible.

In Schacht's words, "In these arts, the world's nature is expressed in a form that attracts rather than repels us—a symbolic form, the attractiveness of which is bound up with the transfiguration involved in this symbolization." Moreover, *The Birth of Tragedy* for Nietzsche involved not merely the appearance of a qualitatively new art form, but also a further qualitative transformation of human life. In this way, Nietzsche prefigures his later writings in which he anticipates a new kind of human being, one that unites the Apollinian and Dionysian impulses discussed in *The Birth of Tragedy*.

Friedrich Nietzsche

APOLLINIAN AND DIONYSIAN ART:
FROM *THE BIRTH OF TRAGEDY*

We shall have gained much for the science of aesthetics, once we perceive not merely by logical inference, but with the immediate certainty of vision, that the continuous development of art is bound up with the *Apollinian* and *Dionysian* duality—just as procreation depends on the duality of the sexes, involving perpetual strife with only periodically intervening reconciliations. The terms Dionysian and Apollinian we borrow from the Greeks, who disclose to the discerning mind the profound mysteries of their view of art, not, to be sure, in concepts, but in the intensely clear figures of their gods. Through Apollo and Dionysus, the two art deities of the Greeks, we come to recognize that in the Greek world there existed a tremendous opposition, in origin and aims, between the Apollinian art of sculpture, and the nonimagistic, Dionysian art of music. These two different tendencies run parallel to each other, for the most part openly at variance; and they continually incite each other to new and more powerful births, which perpetuate an antagonism, only superficially reconciled by the common term "art"; till eventually, by a metaphysical miracle of the Hellenic "will," they appear coupled with each other, and through this coupling ultimately generate an equally Dionysian and Apollinian form of art—Attic tragedy.

In order to grasp these two tendencies, let us first conceive of them as the separate art worlds of *dreams and intoxication*. These physiological phenomena present a contrast analogous to that existing between the Apollinian and the Dionysian. . . .

The beautiful illusion[1] of the dream worlds, in the creation of which every man is truly an artist, is the prerequisite of all plastic art, and, as we shall see, of an important part of poetry also. In our dreams we delight in the immediate understanding of figures; all forms speak to us; there is nothing unimportant or superfluous. But even when this dream reality is most intense, we still have, glimmering through it, the sensation that it is *mere appearance*: at least this is my experience, and for its frequency—indeed, normality—I could adduce many proofs, including the saying of the poets.

From The Birth of Tragedy *and the* Case of Wagner *by Friedrich Nietzsche, translation and commentary by Walter Kaufmann. Copyright © 1967 by Random House Inc. Reprinted by permission of Random House Inc. (Some footnotes omitted.)*

[1]*Schein* has been rendered in these pages sometimes as "illusion" and sometimes as "mere appearance."

Philosophical men even have a presentiment that the reality in which we live and have our being is also mere appearance, and that another, quite different reality lies beneath it. Schopenhauer actually indicates as the criterion of philosophical ability the occasional ability to view men and things as mere phantoms or dream images. Thus the aesthetically sensitive man stands in the same relation to the reality of dreams as the philosopher does to the reality of existence; he is a close and willing observer, for these images afford him an interpretation of life, and by reflecting on these processes he trains himself for life.

It is not only the agreeable and friendly images that he experiences as something universally intelligible: the serious, the troubled, the sad, the gloomy, the sudden restraints, the tricks of accident, anxious expectations, in short, the whole divine comedy of life, including the inferno, also pass before him, not like mere shadows on a wall—for he lives and suffers with these scenes—and yet not without that fleeting sensation of illusion. And perhaps many will, like myself, recall how amid the dangers and terrors of dreams they have occasionally said to themselves in self-encouragement, and not without success: "It is a dream! I will dream on!" I have likewise heard of people who were able to continue one and the same dream for three and even more successive nights—facts which indicate clearly how our innermost being, our common ground, experiences dreams with profound delight and a joyous necessity.

This joyous necessity of the dream experience has been embodied by the Greeks in their Apollo: Apollo, the god of all plastic energies, is at the same time the soothsaying god. He, who (as the etymology of the name indicates) is the "shining one,"[2] the deity of light, is also ruler over the beautiful illusion of the inner world of fantasy. The higher truth, the perfection of these states in contrast to the incompletely intelligible everyday world, this deep consciousness of nature, healing and helping in sleep and dreams, is at the same time the symbolical analogue of the soothsaying faculty and of the arts generally, which make life possible and worth living. But we must also include in our image of Apollo that delicate boundary which the dream image must not overstep lest it have a pathological effect (in which case mere appearance would deceive us as if it were crude reality). We must keep in mind that measured restraint, that freedom from the wilder emotions, that calm of the sculptor god. His eye must be "sunlike," as befits his origin; even when it is angry and distempered it is still hallowed by beautiful illusion. And so, in one sense, we might apply to Apollo the words of Schopenhauer when he speaks of the man wrapped in the veil of *māyā* (*Welt als Wille und Vorstellung*, I, p. 416): "Just as in a stormy sea that, unbounded in all directions, raises and drops mountainous waves, howling, a sailor sits in a boat and trusts in his frail bark: so in the midst of a world of torments the individual human being sits quietly, supported by and trusting in the *principium individuationis*."[3] In fact, we might say of Apollo that in him the unshaken faith in this *principium* and the calm repose of the man wrapped up in it receive their most sublime expression; and we might call Apollo himself the glorious divine image of the *principium individuationis*, through whose gestures and eyes all the joy and wisdom of "illusion," together with its beauty, speak to us.

---

[2] *Der "Scheinende."* The German words for illusion and appearance are *Schein* and *Erscheinung*.
[3] Principle of individuation.

In the same work Schopenhauer has depicted for us the tremendous *terror* which seizes man when he is suddenly dumfounded by the cognitive form of phenomena because the principle of sufficient reason, in some one of its manifestations, seems to suffer an exception. If we add to this terror the blissful ecstasy that wells from the innermost depths of man, indeed of nature, at this collapse of the *principium individuationis*, we steal a glimpse into the nature of the *Dionysian*, which is brought home to us most intimately by the analogy of intoxication.

Either under the influence of the narcotic draught, of which the songs of all primitive men and peoples speak, or with the potent coming of spring that penetrates all nature with joy, these Dionysian emotions awake, and as they grow in intensity everything subjective vanishes into complete self-forgetfulness. In the German Middle Ages, too, singing and dancing crowds, ever increasing in number, whirled themselves from place to place under this same Dionysian impulse. In these dancers of St. John and St. Vitus, we rediscover the Bacchic choruses of the Greeks, with their prehistory in Asia Minor, as far back as Babylon and the orgiastic Sacaea.[4] There are some who, from obtuseness or lack of experience, turn away from such phenomena as from "folk-diseases," with contempt or pity born of the consciousness of their own "healthy-mindedness." But of course such poor wretches have no idea how corpselike and ghostly their so-called "healthy-mindedness" looks when the glowing life of the Dionysian revelers roars past them.

Under the charm of the Dionysian not only is the union between man and man reaffirmed, but nature which has become alienated, hostile, or subjugated, celebrates once more her reconciliation with her lost son, man. Freely, earth proffers her gifts, and peacefully the beasts of prey of the rocks and desert approach. The chariot of Dionysus is covered with flowers and garlands; panthers and tigers walk under its yoke. Transform Beethoven's "Hymn to Joy" into a painting; let your imagination conceive the multitudes bowing to the dust, awestruck—then you will approach the Dionysian. Now the slave is a free man; now all the rigid, hostile barriers that necessity, caprice, or "impudent convention" have fixed between man and man are broken. Now, with the gospel of universal harmony, each one feels himself not only united, reconciled, and fused with his neighbor, but as one with him, as if the veil of *māyā* had been torn aside and were now merely fluttering in tatters before the mysterious primordial unity.

In song and in dance man expresses himself as a member of a higher community; he has forgotten how to walk and speak and is on the way toward flying into the air, dancing. His very gestures express enchantment. Just as the animals now talk, and the earth yields milk and honey, supernatural sounds emanate from him, too: he feels himself a god, he himself now walks about enchanted, in ecstasy, like the gods he saw walking in his dreams. He is no longer an artist, he has become a work of art: in these paroxysms of intoxication the artistic power of all nature reveals itself to the highest gratification of the primordial unity. The noblest clay, the most costly marble, man, is here kneaded and cut, and to the sound of the chisel strokes of the Dionysian world-artist rings out the cry of the Eleusinian mysteries: "Do you prostrate yourselves, millions? Do you sense your Maker, world?"

---

[4]A Babylonian festival that lasted five days and was marked by general license. During this time slaves are said to have ruled their masters, and a criminal was given all royal rights before he was put to death at the end of the festival. For references, see, e.g., *The Oxford Classical Dictionary*.

Thus far we have considered the Apollinian and its opposite, the Dionysian, as artistic energies which burst forth from nature herself, *without the mediation of the human artist*—energies in which nature's art impulses are satisfied in the most immediate and direct way—first in the image world of dreams, whose completeness is not dependent upon the intellectual attitude or the artistic culture of any single being; and then as intoxicated reality, which likewise does not heed the single unit, but even seeks to destroy the individual and redeem him by a mystic feeling of oneness. With reference to these immediate art-states of nature, every artist is an "imitator," that is to say, either an Apollinian artist in dreams, or a Dionysian artist in ecstasies, or finally—as for example in Greek tragedy—at once artist in both dreams and ecstasies; so we may perhaps picture him sinking down in his Dionysian intoxication and mystical self-abnegation, alone and apart from the singing revelers, and we may imagine how, through Apollinian dream-inspiration, his own state, i.e., his oneness with the inmost ground of the world, is revealed to him in a *symbolical dream image*.

So much for these general premises and contrasts. Let us now approach the *Greeks* in order to learn how highly these *art impulses of nature* were developed in them. Thus we shall be in a position to understand and appreciate more deeply that relation of the Greek artist to his archetypes which is, according to the Aristotelian expression, "the imitation of nature." In spite of all the dream literature and the numerous dream anecdotes of the Greeks, we can speak of their *dreams* only conjecturally, though with reasonable assurance. If we consider the incredibly precise and unerring plastic power of their eyes, together with their vivid, frank delight in colors, we can hardly refrain from assuming even for their dreams (to the shame of all those born later) a certain logic of line and contour, colors and groups, a certain pictorial sequence reminding us of their finest bas-reliefs whose perfection would certainly justify us, if a comparison were possible, in designating the dreaming Greeks as Homers and Homer as a dreaming Greek—in a deeper sense than that in which modern man, speaking of his dreams, ventures to compare himself with Shakespeare.

On the other hand, we need not conjecture regarding the immense gap which separates the *Dionysian Greek* from the Dionysian barbarian. From all quarters of the ancient world—to say nothing here of the modern—from Rome to Babylon, we can point to the existence of Dionysian festivals, types which bear, at best, the same relation to the Greek festivals which the bearded satyr, who borrowed his name and attributes from the goat, bears to Dionysus himself. In nearly every case these festivals centered in extravagant sexual licentiousness, whose waves overwhelmed all family life and its venerable traditions; the most savage natural instincts were unleashed, including even that horrible mixture of sensuality and cruelty which has always seemed to me to be the real "witches' brew." For some time, however, the Greeks were apparently perfectly insulated and guarded against the feverish excitements of these festivals, though knowledge of them must have come to Greece on all the routes of land and sea; for the figure of Apollo, rising full of pride, held out the Gorgon's head to this grotesquely uncouth Dionysian power—and really could not have countered any more dangerous force. It is in Doric art that this majestically rejecting attitude of Apollo is immortalized.

The opposition between Apollo and Dionysus became more hazardous and even impossible, when similar impulses finally burst forth from the deepest roots of the Hellenic nature and made a path for themselves: the Delphic god, by a seasonably effected reconciliation, now contented himself with taking the destructive weapons from the hands of his powerful antagonist. This reconciliation is the most important moment in the history of the Greek cult: wherever we turn we note the revolutions resulting from this event. The two antagonists were reconciled; the boundary lines to be observed henceforth by each were sharply defined, and there was to be a periodical exchange of gifts of esteem. At bottom, however, the chasm was not bridged over. But if we observe how, under the pressure of this treaty of peace, the Dionysian power revealed itself, we shall now recognize in the Dionysian orgies of the Greeks, as compared with the Babylonian Sacaea with their reversion of man to the tiger and the ape; the significance of festivals of world redemption and days of transfiguration. It is with them that nature for the first time attains her artistic jubilee; it is with them that the destruction of the *principium individuationis* for the first time becomes an artistic phenomenon.

The horrible "witches' brew" of sensuality and cruelty becomes ineffective; only the curious blending and duality in the emotions of the Dionysian revelers remind us—as medicines remind us of deadly poisons—of the phenomenon that pain begets joy, that ecstasy may wring sounds of agony from us. At the very climax of joy there sounds a cry of horror or a yearning lamentation for an irretrievable loss. In these Greek festivals, nature seems to reveal a sentimental trait; it is as if she were heaving a sigh at her dismemberment into individuals. The song and pantomime of such dually-minded revelers was something new and unheard-of in the Homeric-Greek world; and the Dionysian *music* in particular excited awe and terror. If music, as it would seem, had been known previously as an Apollinian art, it was so, strictly speaking, only as the wave beat of rhythm, whose formative power was developed for the representation of Apollinian states. The music of Apollo was Doric architectonics in tones, but in tones that were merely suggestive, such as those of the cithara. The very element which forms the essence of Dionysian music (and hence of music in general) is carefully excluded as un-Apollinian—namely, the emotional power of the tone, the uniform flow of the melody, and the utterly incomparable world of harmony. In the Dionysian dithyramb man is incited to the greatest exaltation of all his symbolic faculties; something never before experienced struggles for utterance—the annihilation of the veil of *māyā*, oneness as the soul of the race and of nature itself. The essence of nature is now to be expressed symbolically; we need a new world of symbols; and the entire symbolism of the body is called into play, not the mere symbolism of the lips, face, and speech but the whole pantomime of dancing, forcing every member into rhythmic movement. Then the other symbolic powers suddenly press forward, particularly those of music, in rhythmics, dynamics, and harmony. To grasp this collective release of all the symbolic powers, man must have already attained that height of self-abnegation which seeks to express itself symbolically through all these powers—and so the dithyrambic votary of Dionysus is understood only by his peers. With what astonishment must the Apollinian Greek have beheld him! With an astonishment that was all the greater the more it was mingled with the shuddering suspicion that all this was actually not so very alien to him after all, in fact, that it was only his Apollinian consciousness which, like a veil, hid this Dionysian world from his vision.

To understand this, it becomes necessary to level the artistic structure of the *Apollinian culture,* as it were, stone by stone, till the foundations on which it rests become visible. First of all we see the glorious *Olympian* figures of the gods, standing on the gables of this structure. Their deeds, pictured in brilliant reliefs, adorn its friezes. We must not be misled by the fact that Apollo stands side by side with the others as an individual deity, without any claim to priority of rank. For the same impulse that embodied itself in Apollo gave birth to this entire Olympian world, and in this sense Apollo is its father. What terrific need was it that could produce such an illustrious company of Olympian beings?

Whoever approaches these Olympians with another religion in his heart, searching among them for moral elevation, even for sanctity, for disincarnate spirituality, for charity and benevolence, will soon be forced to turn his back on them, discouraged and disappointed. For there is nothing here that suggests asceticism, spirituality, or duty. We hear nothing but the accents of an exuberant, triumphant life in which all things, whether good or evil, are deified. And so the spectator may stand quite bewildered before this fantastic excess of life, asking himself by virtue of what magic potion these high-spirited men could have found life so enjoyable that, wherever they turned, their eyes beheld the smile of Helen, the ideal picture of their own existence, "floating in sweet sensuality." But to this spectator, who has already turned his back, we must say: "Do not go away, but stay and hear what Greek folk wisdom has to say of this very life, which with such inexplicable gaiety unfolds itself before your eyes.

"There is an ancient story that King Midas hunted in the forest a long time for the wise Silenus, the companion of Dionysus, without capturing him. When Silenus at last fell into his hands, the king asked what was the best and most desirable of all things for man. Fixed and immovable, the demigod said not a word, till at last, urged by the king, he gave a shrill laugh and broke out into these words: 'Oh, wretched ephemeral race, children of chance and misery, why do you compel me to tell you what it would be most expedient for you not to hear? What is best of all is utterly beyond your reach: not to be born, not to *be*, to be *nothing*. But the second best for you is—to die soon.' "

How is the world of the Olympian gods related to this folk wisdom? Even as the rapturous vision of the tortured martyr to his suffering.

Now it is as if the Olympian magic mountain had opened before us and revealed its roots to us. The Greek knew and felt the terror and horror of existence. That he might endure this terror at all, he had to interpose between himself and life the radiant dream-birth of the Olympians. That overwhelming dismay in the face of the titanic powers of nature, the Moira enthroned inexorably over all knowledge, the vulture of the great lover of mankind, Prometheus, the terrible fate of the wise Oedipus, the family curse of the Atridae which drove Orestes to matricide: in short, that entire philosophy of the sylvan god, with its mythical exemplars, which caused the downfall of the melancholy Etruscans—all this was again and again overcome by the Greeks with the aid of the Olympian *middle world* of art; or at any rate it was veiled and withdrawn from sight. It was in order to be able to live that the Greeks had to create these gods from a most profound need. Perhaps we may picture the process to ourselves somewhat as follows: out of the original Titanic divine order of terror, the Olympian divine order of joy gradually evolved through the Apollinian impulse toward beauty, just as roses burst from thorny bushes. How else could this people, so sensitive, so vehement in its desires, so singularly capable of *suffering*, have endured existence, if it had not been revealed to them in their gods, surrounded with a higher glory?

The same impulse which calls art into being, as the complement and consummation of existence, seducing one to a continuation of life, was also the cause of the
Olympian world which the Hellenic "will" made use of as a transfiguring mirror. Thus
do the gods justify the life of man: they themselves live it—the only satisfactory
theodicy! Existence under the bright sunshine of such gods is regarded as desirable in
itself, and the real pain of Homeric men is caused by parting from it, especially by early
parting: so that now, reversing the wisdom of Silenus, we might say of the Greeks that
"to die soon is worst of all for them, the next worst—to die at all." Once heard, it will
ring out again; do not forget the lament of the short-lived Achilles, mourning the
leaflike change and vicissitudes of the race of men and the decline of the heroic age. It
is not unworthy of the greatest hero to long for a continuation of life, even though he
lived as a day laborer. At the Apollinian stage of development, the "will" longs so
vehemently for this existence, the Homeric man feels himself so completely at one
with it, that lamentation itself becomes a song of praise. . . .

The Homeric "naïveté" can be understood only as the complete victory of Apollinian illusion: this is one of those illusions which nature so frequently employs to
achieve her own ends. The true goal is veiled by a phantasm: and while we stretch out
our hands for the latter, nature attains the former by means of our illusion. In the
Greeks the "will" wished to contemplate itself in the transfiguration of genius and the
world of art; in order to glorify themselves, its creatures had to feel themselves worthy
of glory; they had to behold themselves again in a higher sphere, without this perfect
world of contemplation acting as a command or a reproach. This is the sphere of
beauty, in which they saw their mirror images, the Olympians. With this mirroring of
beauty the Hellenic will combated its artistically correlative talent for suffering and for
the wisdom of suffering—and, as a monument of its victory, we have Homer, the naïve
artist.

Now the dream analogy may throw some light on the naïve artist. Let us imagine the
dreamer: in the midst of the illusion of the dream world and without disturbing it, he
calls out to himself: "It is a dream, I will dream on." What must we infer? That he
experiences a deep inner joy in dream contemplation; on the other hand, to be at all
able to dream with this inner joy in contemplation, he must have completely lost sight
of the waking reality and its ominous obtrusiveness. Guided by the dream-reading
Apollo, we may interpret all these phenomena in roughly this way.

Though it is certain that of the two halves of our existence, the waking and the
dreaming states, the former appeals to us as infinitely preferable, more important,
excellent, and worthy of being lived, indeed, as that which alone is lived—yet in
relation to that mysterious ground of our being of which we are the phenomena, I
should, paradoxical as it may seem, maintain the very opposite estimate of the value of
dreams. For the more clearly I perceive in nature those omnipotent art impulses, and
in them an ardent longing for illusion, for redemption through illusion, the more I feel
myself impelled to the metaphysical assumption that the truly existent primal unity,
eternally suffering and contradictory, also needs the rapturous vision, the pleasurable
illusion, for its continuous redemption. And we, completely wrapped up in this
illusion and composed of it, are compelled to consider this illusion as the truly
nonexistent—i.e., as a perpetual becoming in time, space, and causality—in other

words, as empirical reality. If, for the moment, we do not consider the question of our own "reality," if we conceive of our empirical existence, and of that of the world in general, as a continuously manifested representation of the primal unity, we shall then have to look upon the dream as a *mere appearance of mere appearance*, hence as a still higher appeasement of the primordial desire for mere appearance. And that is why the innermost heart of nature feels that ineffable joy in the naïve artist and the naïve work of art, which is likewise only "mere appearance of mere appearance."

In a symbolic painting, *Raphael*, himself one of these immortal "naïve" ones, has represented for us this demotion of appearance to the level of mere appearance, the primitive process of the naïve artist and of Apollinian culture. In his *Transfiguration*, the lower half of the picture, with the possessed boy, the despairing bearers, the bewildered, terrified disciples, shows us the reflection of suffering, primal and eternal, the sole ground of the world: the "mere appearance" here is the reflection of eternal contradiction, the father of things. From this mere appearance arises, like ambrosial vapor, a new visionary world of mere appearances, invisible to those wrapped in the first appearance—a radiant floating in purest bliss, a serene contemplation beaming from wide-open eyes. Here we have presented, in the most sublime artistic symbolism, that Apollinian world of beauty and its substratum, the terrible wisdom of Silenus; and intuitively we comprehend their necessary interdependence. Apollo, however, again appears to us the apotheosis of the *principium individuationis*, in which alone is consummated the perpetually attained goal of the primal unity, its redemption through mere appearance. With his sublime gestures, he shows us how necessary is the entire world of suffering, that by means of it the individual may be impelled to realize the redeeming vision, and then, sunk in contemplation of it, sit quietly in his tossing bark, amid the waves.

If we conceive of it all as imperative and mandatory, this apotheosis of individuation knows but one law—the individual, i.e., the delimiting of the boundaries of the individual, *measure* in the Hellenic sense. Apollo, as ethical deity, exacts measure of his disciples, and, to be able to maintain it, he requires self-knowledge. And so, side by side with the aesthetic necessity for beauty, there occur the demands "know thyself" and "nothing in excess"; consequently overweening pride and excess are regarded as the truly hostile demons of the non-Apollinian sphere, hence as characteristics of the pre-Apollinian age—that of the Titans; and of the extra-Apollinian world—that of the barbarians. Because of his titanic love for man, Prometheus must be torn to pieces by vultures; because of his excessive wisdom, which could solve the riddle of the Sphinx, Oedipus must be plunged into a bewildering vortex of crime. Thus did the Delphic god interpret the Greek past.

The effects wrought by the *Dionysian* also seemed "titanic" and "barbaric" to the Apollinian Greek; while at the same time he could not conceal from himself that he, too, was inwardly related to these overthrown Titans and heroes. Indeed, he had to recognize even more than this: despite all its beauty and moderation, his entire existence rested on a hidden substratum of suffering and of knowledge, revealed to him by the Dionysian. And behold: Apollo could not live without Dionysus! The "titanic" and the "barbaric" were in the last analysis as necessary as the Apollinian.

And now let us imagine how into this world, built on mere appearance and moderation and artificially dammed up, there penetrated, in tones ever more bewitching and alluring, the ecstatic sound of the Dionysian festival; how in these strains all of nature's *excess* in pleasure, grief, and knowledge became audible, even in piercing shrieks; and let us ask ourselves what the psalmodizing artist of Apollo, with his phantom harp-sound, could mean in the face of this demonic folk-song! The muses of the arts of "illusion" paled before an art that, in its intoxication, spoke the truth. The wisdom of Silenus cried "Woe! woe!" to the serene Olympians. The individual, with all his restraint and proportion, succumbed to the self-oblivion of the Dionysian states, forgetting the precepts of Apollo. *Excess* revealed itself as truth. Contradiction, the bliss born of pain, spoke out from the very heart of nature. And so, wherever the Dionysian prevailed, the Apollinian was checked and destroyed. But, on the other hand, it is equally certain that, wherever the first Dionysian onslaught was successfully withstood, the authority and majesty of the Delphic god exhibited itself as more rigid and menacing than ever. For to me the *Doric* state and Doric art are explicable only as a permanent military encampment of the Apollinian. Only incessant resistance to the titanic-barbaric nature of the Dionysian could account for the long survival of an art so defiantly prim and so encompassed with bulwarks, a training so warlike and rigorous, and a political structure so cruel and relentless.

Up to this point we have simply enlarged upon the observation made at the beginning of this essay: that the Dionysian and the Apollinian, in new births ever following and mutually augmenting one another, controlled the Hellenic genius; that out of the age of "bronze," with its wars of the Titans and its rigorous folk philosophy, the Homeric world developed under the sway of the Apollinian impulse to beauty; that this "naïve" splendor was again overwhelmed by the influx of the Dionysian; and that against this new power the Apollinian rose to the austere majesty of Doric art and the Doric view of the world. If amid the strife of these two hostile principles, the older Hellenic history thus falls into four great periods of art, we are now impelled to inquire after the final goal of these developments and processes, lest perchance we should regard the last-attained period, the period of Doric art, as the climax and aim of these artistic impulses. And here the sublime and celebrated art of *Attic tragedy* and the dramatic dithyramb presents itself as the common goal of both these tendencies whose mysterious union, after many and long precursory struggles, found glorious con-summation in this child—at once Antigone and Cassandra.

We must now avail ourselves of all the principles of art considered so far, in order to find our way through the labyrinth, as we must call it, of *the origin of Greek tragedy*. I do not think I am unreasonable in saying that the problem of this origin has as yet not even been seriously posed, to say nothing of solved, however often the ragged tatters of ancient tradition have been sewn together in various combinations and torn apart again. This tradition tells us quite unequivocally *that tragedy arose from the tragic chorus*, and was originally only chorus and nothing but chorus. Hence we consider it our duty to look into the heart of this tragic chorus as the real proto-drama, without resting satisfied with such arty clichés as that the chorus is the "ideal spectator" or that it represents the people in contrast to the aristocratic region of the scene. . . .

* * *

It is indeed an "ideal" domain, as Schiller correctly perceived, in which the Greek satyr chorus, the chorus of primitive tragedy, was wont to dwell. It is a domain raised high above the actual paths of mortals. For this chorus the Greek built up the scaffolding of a fictitious *natural state* and on it placed fictitious *natural beings*. On this foundation tragedy developed and so, of course, it could dispense from the beginning with a painstaking portrayal of reality. Yet it is no arbitrary world placed by whim between heaven and earth; rather it is a world with the same reality and credibility that Olympus with its inhabitants possessed for the believing Hellene. The satyr, as the Dionysian chorist, lives in a religiously acknowledged reality under the sanction of myth and cult. That tragedy should begin with him, that he should be the voice of the Dionysian wisdom of tragedy, is just as strange a phenomenon for us as the general derivation of tragedy from the chorus.

Perhaps we shall have a point of departure for our inquiry if I put forward the proposition that the satyr, the fictitious natural being, bears the same relation to the man of culture that Dionysian music bears to civilization. Concerning the latter, Richard Wagner says that it is nullified by music just as lamplight is nullified by the light of day. Similarly, I believe, the Greek man of culture felt himself nullified in the presence of the satyric chorus; and this is the most immediate effect of the Dionysian tragedy, that the state and society and, quite generally, the gulfs between man and man give way to an overwhelming feeling of unity leading back to the very heart of nature. The metaphysical comfort—with which, I am suggesting even now, every true tragedy leaves us—that life is at the bottom of things, despite all the changes of appearances, indestructibly powerful and pleasurable—this comfort appears in incarnate clarity in the chorus of satyrs, a chorus of natural beings who live ineradicably, as it were, behind all civilization and remain eternally the same, despite the changes of generations and of the history of nations.

With this chorus the profound Hellene, uniquely susceptible to the tenderest and deepest suffering, comforts himself, having looked boldly right into the terrible destructiveness of so-called world history as well as the cruelty of nature, and being in danger of longing for a Buddhistic negation of the will.[5] Art saves him, and through art—life.

For the rapture of the Dionysian state with its annihilation of the ordinary bounds and limits of existence contains, while it lasts, a *lethargic* element in which all personal experiences of the past become immersed. This chasm of oblivion separates the worlds of everyday reality and of Dionysian reality. But as soon as this everyday reality re-enters consciousness, it is experienced as such, with nausea: an ascetic, will-negating mood is the fruit of these states.

In this sense the Dionysian man resembles Hamlet: both have once looked truly into the essence of things, they have *gained knowledge*, and nausea inhibits action; for their action could not change anything in the eternal nature of things; they feel it to be ridiculous or humiliating that they should be asked to set right a world that is out of joint. Knowledge kills action; action requires the veils of illusion: that is the doctrine of Hamlet, not that cheap wisdom of Jack the Dreamer who reflects too much and, as it were, from an excess of possibilities does not get around to action. Not reflection,

[5]Here Nietzsche's emancipation from Schopenhauer becomes evident, and their difference from each other concerns the central subject of the whole book: the significance of tragedy. Nietzsche writes about tragedy as the great life-affirming alternative to Schopenhauer's negation of the will. One can be as honest and free of optimistic illusions as Schopenhauer was, and still celebrate life as fundamentally powerful and pleasurable as the Greeks did.

no—true knowledge, an insight into the horrible truth, outweighs any motive for action, both in Hamlet and in the Dionysian man.

Now no comfort avails any more; longing transcends a world after death, even the gods; existence is negated along with its glittering reflection in the gods or in an immortal beyond. Conscious of the truth he has once seen, man now sees everywhere only the horror or absurdity of existence; now he understands what is symbolic in Ophelia's fate; now he understands the wisdom of the sylvan god, Silenus: he is nauseated.

Here, when the danger to his will is greatest, *art* approaches as a saving sorceress, expert at healing. She alone knows how to turn these nauseous thoughts about the horror or absurdity of existence into notions with which one can live: these are the *sublime* as the artistic taming of the horrible, and the *comic* as the artistic discharge of the nausea of absurdity. The satyr chorus of the dithyramb is the saving deed of Greek art; faced with the intermediary world of these Dionysian companions, the feelings described here exhausted themselves.[6]

* * *

Such magic transformation is the presupposition of all dramatic art. In this magic transformation the Dionysian reveler sees himself as a satyr, *and as a satyr, in turn, he sees the god,* which means that in his metamorphosis he beholds another vision outside himself, as the Apollinian complement of his own state. With this new vision the drama is complete.

In the light of this insight we must understand Greek tragedy as the Dionysian chorus which ever anew discharges itself in an Apollinian world of images. Thus the choral parts with which tragedy is interlaced are, as it were, the womb that gave birth to the whole of the so-called dialogue, that is, the entire world of the stage, the real drama. In several successive discharges this primal ground of tragedy radiates this vision of the drama which is by all means a dream apparition and to that extent epic in nature; but on the other hand, being the objectification of a Dionysian state, it represents not Apollinian redemption through mere appearance but, on the contrary, the shattering of the individual and his fusion with primal being. Thus the drama is the Dionysian embodiment of Dionysian insights and effects and thereby separated, as by a tremendous chasm, from the epic.

* * *

Let us array ourselves in the armor of the insights we have acquired. In contrast to all those who are intent on deriving the arts from one exclusive principle, as the necessary vital source of every work of art, I shall keep my eyes fixed on the two artistic deities of the Greeks, Apollo and Dionysus, and recognize in them the living and conspicuous representatives of *two* worlds of art differing in their intrinsic essence and in their

---

[6]Having finally broken loose from Schopenhauer, Nietzsche for the first time shows the brilliancy of his own genius. It is doubtful whether anyone before him had illuminated *Hamlet* so extensively in so few words: the passage invites comparison with Freud's great footnote on *Hamlet* in the first edition of *Die Traumdeutung* (interpretation of dreams), 1900. Even more obviously, the last three paragraphs invite comparison with existentialist literature, notably, but by no means only, Sartre's *La Nausée* (1938).

highest aims. I see Apollo as the transfiguring genius of the *principium individuationis* through which alone the redemption in illusion is truly to be obtained; while by the mystical triumphant cry of Dionysus the spell of individuation is broken, and the way lies open to the Mothers of Being, to the innermost heart of things. This extraordinary contrast, which stretches like a yawning gulf between plastic art as the Apollinian, and music as the Dionysian art, has revealed itself to only one of the great thinkers, to such an extent that, even without this clue to the symbolism of the Hellenic divinities, he conceded to music a character and an origin different from all the other arts, because, unlike them, it is not a copy of the phenomenon, but an immediate copy of the will itself, and therefore complements *everything physical in the world* and every phenomenon by representing *what is metaphysical*, the thing in itself.

* * *

From the nature of art as it is usually conceived according to the single category of appearance and beauty, the tragic cannot honestly be deduced at all; it is only through the spirit of music that we can understand the joy involved in the annihilation of the individual. For it is only in particular examples of such annihilation that we see clearly the eternal phenomenon of Dionysian art, which gives expression to the will in its omnipotence, as it were, behind the *principium individuationis*, the eternal life beyond all phenomena, and despite all annihilation. The metaphysical joy in the tragic is a translation of the instinctive unconscious Dionysian wisdom into the language of images: the hero, the highest manifestation of the will, is negated for our pleasure, because he is only phenomenon, and because the eternal life of the will is not affected by his annihilation. "We believe in eternal life," exclaims tragedy; while music is the immediate idea of this life. Plastic art has an altogether different aim: here Apollo overcomes the suffering of the individual by the radiant glorification of the *eternity of the phenomenon:* here beauty triumphs over the suffering inherent in life; pain is obliterated by lies from the features of nature. In Dionysian art and its tragic symbolism the same nature cries to us with its true, undissembled voice: "Be as I am! Amid the ceaseless flux of phenomena I am the eternally creative primordial mother, eternally impelling to existence, eternally finding satisfaction in this change of phenomena!"

Dionysian art, too, wishes to convince us of the eternal joy of existence: only we are to seek this joy not in phenomena, but behind them. We are to recognize that all that comes into being must be ready for a sorrowful end; we are forced to look into the terrors of the individual existence—yet we are not to become rigid with fear: a metaphysical comfort tears us momentarily from the bustle of the changing figures. We are really for a brief moment primordial being itself, feeling its raging desire for existence and joy in existence; the struggle, the pain, the destruction of phenomena, now appear necessary to us, in view of the excess of countless forms of existence which force and push one another into life, in view of the exuberant fertility of the universal will. We are pierced by the maddening sting of these pains just when we have become, as it were, one with the infinite primordial joy in existence, and when we anticipate, in Dionysian ecstasy, the indestructibility and eternity of this joy. In spite of fear and pity, we are the happy living beings, not as individuals, but as the *one* living being, with whose creative joy we are united.

* * *

It is an eternal phenomenon: the insatiable will always find a way to detain its creatures in life and compel them to live on, by means of an illusion spread over things. One is chained by the Socratic love of knowledge and the delusion of being able thereby to heal the eternal wound of existence; another is ensnared by art's seductive veil of beauty fluttering before his eyes; still another by the metaphysical comfort that beneath the whirl of phenomena eternal life flows on indestructibly—to say nothing of the more vulgar and almost more powerful illusions which the will always has at hand. These three stages of illusion are actually designed only for the more nobly formed natures, who actually feel profoundly the weight and burden of existence, and must be deluded by exquisite stimulants into forgetfulness of their displeasure. All that we call culture is made up of these stimulants; and, according to the proportion of the ingredients, we have either a dominantly *Socratic* or *artistic* or *tragic* culture; or, if historical exemplifications are permitted, there is either an Alexandrian or a Hellenic or a Buddhistic culture.

* * *

Suppose a human being has thus put his ear, as it were, to the heart chamber of the world will and felt the roaring desire for existence pouring from there into all the veins of the world, as a thundering current or as the gentlest brook, dissolving into a mist—how could he fail to break suddenly? How could he endure to perceive the echo of innumerable shouts of pleasure and woe in the "wide space of the world night," enclosed in the wretched glass capsule of the human individual, without inexorably fleeing toward his primordial home, as he hears this shepherd's dance of metaphysics? But if such a work could nevertheless be perceived as a whole, without denial of individual existence; if such a creation could be created without smashing its creator— whence do we take the solution of such a contradiction?

Here the tragic myth and the tragic hero intervene between our highest musical emotion and this music—at bottom only as symbols of the most universal facts, of which only music can speak so directly. But if our feelings were those of entirely Dionysian beings, myths as a symbol would remain totally ineffective and unnoticed, and would never for a moment keep us from listening to the re-echo of the *universalia ante rem*. Yet here the *Apollinian* power erupts to restore the almost shattered individual with the healing balm of blissful illusion. . . .

Should our analysis have established that the Apollinian element in tragedy has by means of its illusion gained a complete victory over the primordial Dionysian element of music, making music subservient to its aims, namely, to make the drama as vivid as possible—it would certainly be necessary to add a very important qualification: at the most essential point this Apollinian illusion is broken and annihilated. The drama that, with the aid of music, unfolds itself before us with such inwardly illumined distinctness in all its movements and figures, as if we saw the texture coming into being on the loom as the shuttle flies to and fro—attains as a whole an effect that transcends *all Apollinian artistic effects*. In the total effect of tragedy, the Dionysian predominates once again. Tragedy closes with a sound which could never come from the realm of Apollinian art. And thus the Apollinian illusion reveals itself as what it really is—the veiling during the performance of the tragedy of the real Dionysian effect; but the latter is so powerful that it ends by forcing the Apollinian drama itself into a sphere where it begins to speak with Dionysian wisdom and even denies itself and its Apollinian visibility. Thus the intricate relation of the Apollinian and the Dionysian in tragedy may really be symbolized by a fraternal union of the two deities: Dionysus speaks the language of Apollo; and Apollo, finally the language of Dionysus; and so the highest goal of tragedy and of all art is attained.

                                    *   *   *

That life is really so tragic would least of all explain the origin of an art form— assuming that art is not merely imitation of the reality of nature but rather a metaphysical supplement of the reality of nature, placed beside it for its overcoming. The tragic myth, too, insofar as it belongs to art at all, participates fully in this metaphysical intention of art to transfigure. But what does it transfigure when it presents the world of appearance in the image of the suffering hero? Least of all the "reality" of this world of appearance, for it says to us: "Look there! Look closely! This is your life, this is the hand on the clock of your existence. . . ."

Here it becomes necessary to take a bold running start and leap into a metaphysics of art, by repeating the sentence written above, that existence and the world seem justified only as an aesthetic phenomenon. In this sense, it is precisely the tragic myth that has to convince us that even the ugly and disharmonic are part of an artistic game that the will in the eternal amplitude of its pleasure plays with itself. But this primordial phenomenon of Dionysian art is difficult to grasp, and there is only one direct way to make it intelligible and grasp it immediately: through the wonderful significance of *musical dissonance*. Quite generally, only music, placed beside the world, can give us an idea of what is meant by the justification of the world as an aesthetic phenomenon. The joy aroused by the tragic myth has the same origin as the joyous sensation of dissonance in music. The Dionysian, with its primordial joy experienced even in pain, is the common source of music and tragic myth.

                                    *   *   *

Music and tragic myth are equally expressions of the Dionysian capacity of a people, and they are inseparable. Both derive from a sphere of art that lies beyond the Apollinian; both transfigure a region in whose joyous chords dissonance as well as the terrible image of the world fade away charmingly; both play with the sting of displeasure, trusting in their exceedingly powerful magic arts; and by means of this play both justify the existence of even the "worst world." Thus the Dionysian is seen to be, compared to the Apollinian, the eternal and original artistic power that first calls the whole world of phenomena into existence—and it is only in the midst of this world that a new transfiguring illusion becomes necessary in order to keep the animated world of individuation alive.

If we could imagine dissonance become man—and what else is man?—this dissonance, to be able to live, would need a splendid illusion that would cover dissonance with a veil of beauty. This is the true artistic aim of Apollo in whose name we comprehend all those countless illusions of the beauty of mere appearance that at every moment make life worth living at all and prompt the desire to live on in order to experience the next moment.

Of this foundation of all existence—the Dionysian basic ground of the world—not one whit more may enter the consciousness of the human individual than can be overcome again by this Apollinian power of transfiguration. Thus these two art drives must unfold their powers in a strict proportion, according to the law of eternal justice. Where the Dionysian powers rise up as impetuously as we experience them now, Apollo, too, must already have descended among us, wrapped in a cloud; and the next generation will probably behold his most ample beautiful effects.

ATTEMPT AT A SELF-CRITICISM (1886)

Whatever may be at the bottom of this questionable book, it must have been an exceptionally significant and fascinating question, and deeply personal at that: the time in which it was written, in *spite* of which it was written, bears witness to that—the exciting time of the Franco-Prussian War of 1870/71. As the thunder of the battle of Wörth was rolling over Europe, the muser and riddle-friend who was to be the father of this book sat somewhere in an Alpine nook, very bemused and beriddled, hence very concerned and yet unconcerned, and wrote down his thoughts about the *Greeks*—the core of the strange and almost inaccessible book to which this belated preface (or postscript) shall now be added. A few weeks later—and he himself was to be found under the walls of Metz, still wedded to the question marks that he had placed after the alleged "cheerfulness" of the Greeks and of Greek art. Eventually, in that month of profoundest suspense when the peace treaty was being debated at Versailles, he, too, attained peace with himself and, slowly convalescing from an illness contracted at the front, completed the final draft of *The Birth of Tragedy out of the Spirit of Music.*—Out of music? Music and tragedy? Greeks and the music of tragedy? Greeks and the art form of pessimism? The best turned out, most beautiful, most envied type of humanity to date, those most apt to seduce us to life, the Greeks—how now? They of all people should have *needed* tragedy? Even more—art? For what—Greek art?

You will guess where the big question mark concerning the value of existence had thus been raised. Is pessimism *necessarily* a sign of decline, decay, degeneration, weary and weak instincts—as it once was in India and now is, to all appearances, among us, "modern" men and Europeans? Is there a pessimism of *strength*? An intellectual predilection for the hard, gruesome, evil, problematic aspect of existence, prompted by well-being, by overflowing health, by the *fullness* of existence? . . .

Still, I do not want to suppress entirely how disagreeable it now seems to me, how strange it appears now, after sixteen years—before a much older, a hundred times more demanding, but by no means colder eye which has not become a stranger to the task which this audacious book dared to tackle for the first time: *to look at science in the perspective of the artist, but at art in that of life.*

To say it once more: today I find it an impossible book: I consider it badly written, ponderous, embarrassing, image-mad and image-confused, sentimental, in places saccharine to the point of effeminacy, uneven in tempo, without the will to logical cleanliness, very convinced and therefore disdainful of proof, mistrustful even of the *propriety* of proof, a book for initiates, "music" for those dedicated to music, those who are closely related to begin with on the basis of common and rare aesthetic experiences, "music" meant as a sign of recognition for close relatives *in artibus*[7]—an arrogant and rhapsodic book that sought to exclude right from the beginning the *profanum vulgus*[8] of "the educated" even more than "the mass" or "folk." Still, the effect of the book proved and proves that it had a knack for seeking out fellow-rhapsodizers and for luring them on to new secret paths and dancing places. What found expression here was anyway—this was admitted with as much curiosity as antipathy—a *strange* voice, the disciple of a still "unknown God," one who concealed himself for the time being under the scholar's hood, under the gravity and dialectical ill humor of the German, even under the bad manners of the Wagnerian. Here was a spirit with strange, still nameless needs, a memory bursting with questions, experiences, concealed things after which the name of Dionysus was added as one more question mark. What spoke here—as was admitted, not without suspicion—was something like a mystical, almost maenadic soul that stammered with difficulty, a feat of the will, as in a strange tongue, almost undecided whether it should communicate or conceal itself. It should have *sung*, this "new soul"—and not spoken! What I had to say then—too bad that I did not dare say it as a poet: perhaps I had the ability. Or at least as a philologist: after all, even today practically everything in this field remains to be discovered and dug up by philologists! Above all, the problem that there *is* a problem here—and that the Greeks, as long as we lack an answer to the question "what is Dionysian?" remain as totally un-comprehended and unimaginable as ever.[9]

[7]In the arts.

[8]The profane crowd.

[9]The conception of the Dionysian in *The Birth* differs from Nietzsche's later conception of the Dionysian. He originally introduced the term to symbolize the tendencies that found expression in the festivals of Dionysus, and contrasted the Dionysian with the Apollinian; but in his later thought the Dionysian stands for the creative employment of the passions and the affirmation of life in spite of suffering—as it were, for the synthesis of the Dionysian, as originally conceived, with the Apollinian—and it is contrasted with the Christian negation of life and extirpation of the passions. In the *Twilight of the Idols*, written in 1888, the outlook of the old Goethe can thus be called Dionysian (section 49).

Richard Schacht

NIETZSCHE ON ART
IN *THE BIRTH OF TRAGEDY*

No higher significance could be assigned to art than that which Nietzsche assigns to it in the opening section of *The Birth of Tragedy** (hereafter BT): "The arts generally" are said to "make life possible and worth living" (p. 35).[1] Art is never far from Nietzsche's mind, even when he is dealing with matters seemingly far removed from it. Thus, for example, he some years later characterized his "view of the world" as "anti-metaphysical" to be sure, "but an artistic one"; and he even went so far on another subsequent occasion as to speak of "the world as a work of art which gives birth to itself."[2] He also includes a number of artists among the "higher men" whom he takes to stand out from the greater part of mankind hitherto and likens to artists both the "philosophers of the future" he envisages and the "overman" he declares to be "the meaning of the earth." Indeed, he even aspired to art himself, investing much effort and a good deal of himself in poetic and musical composition.

His views with respect to art and artists underwent a number of changes in the course of his productive life; but he by no means abandoned either his early concern with it nor the whole of his initial understanding and estimation of it in his later years. It would be an error to take the position set forth in BT to be "Nietzsche's philosophy of art"; but it is with this book (purporting in the very first sentence to make a major contribution to "the science of aesthetics") that his efforts along these lines began. It amply warrants extended discussion on a number of counts; for, while it constitutes his first word about art rather than his last, it is not only of intellectual-biographical significance but also of considerable interest in its own right and has long been recognized as a classic contribution to the philosophical literature on art.[3]

**This essay was written for the first edition of this collection and is being reprinted here in an abridged form.*
   [1]All page references and quotations, unless otherwise indicated, are to and from Walter Kaufmann's translation of BT (New York: Random House/Vintage, 1967).
   [2]In notes published in *The Will to Power*, Walter Kaufmann, ed., translated by Walter Kaufmann and R. J. Hollingdale (New York: Random House/Vintage, 1967), numbered 1048 and 796.
   [3]For a discussion of Nietzsche's later thinking with respect to art, see my *Nietzsche* (London: Routledge & Kegan Paul, 1983), pp. 508–29.

I

Nietzsche's interest in art was by no means either exclusively academic or merely personal; and the urgency he felt with respect to the task to which he refers was not at all simply a function of his belief that Greek art and art generally had not previously been adequately understood by his fellow classical philologists and aestheticians. In his original preface to the book, he speaks disparagingly of readers who may "find it offensive that an aesthetic problem should be taken so seriously," and who are unable to consider art more than a "pleasant sideline, a readily dispensable tinkling of bells that accompanies the 'seriousness of life.' " . . . Against them, he advances the startling contention that "art represents the highest task and the truly metaphysical activity of this life" (pp. 31–32). And it has been observed, he goes on to maintain, that "the arts generally" serve to "make life possible and worth living" (p. 35).

It remains to be seen what he has in mind in speaking of art making life "possible" and, further, "worth living," as well as in terming art "the truly metaphysical activity of this life." But these passages provide an ample indication of the centrality of art both in the cluster of issues he deals with in BT and also in his thinking about them. And it is well worth noting that, while "tragedy" is singled out from among the other arts in the title of the book (with music also receiving special mention), it is art generally with which he is actually concerned. To be sure, Nietzsche insists upon the necessity of distinguishing and differentially analyzing various art forms and attaches special significance to tragic art (and Greek tragedy in particular, though not exclusively) among them. And it remains to be considered whether he regards "art" as anything more than a mere "common term" (p. 33) for a number of entirely different things. But it is "the arts" with which he deals, not tragic art alone, and it is with his treatment of this larger subject that I shall be concerned in this essay.

Nietzsche makes no attempt to conceal the influence of Schopenhauer on both his conception of reality and his thinking about the arts. This influence is so considerable that some preliminary remarks about it are a virtual necessity here, particularly in view of the fact that Nietzsche makes little independent effort to justify those aspects of his thinking deriving from this remarkable predecessor.

Schopenhauer may fairly be said to have been Nietzsche's primary philosophical inspiration, in a twofold way. On the one hand, Nietzsche was initially convinced of the soundness of much of what Schopenhauer had to say about the world, life, and the arts; of this, more in a moment. But, on the other hand, he was deeply unsettled by Schopenhauer's dark conclusions with respect to "the value of existence" and the worth of living. Most of his contemporaries tended to dismiss Schopenhauer as a morbidly pessimistic crank even while being appreciative of his stylistic brilliance. But Nietzsche saw that he had raised profoundly serious questions about life, which could no longer be answered as theologians and philosophers traditionally had answered them, and to which new answers had to be found if those given by Schopenhauer himself were not to prevail. Schopenhauer had concluded that existence is utterly unjustifiable and valueless, except in the negative sense that the inevitable preponderance of suffering endows it with an actual disvalue; and that, for anyone who considered the matter soberly and clearsightedly, oblivion had to be acknowledged to be preferable to life.

Schopenhauer's reason for taking his darkly pessimistic position was, briefly put, that in his view existence in general and life in particular are characterized by ceaseless struggle and striving, inevitably resulting in destruction and (among sentient forms of life) involving incessant suffering of one sort or another. The whole affair, as he saw it, is quite pointless, since nothing of any value is thereby attained (the perpetuation of life merely continuing the striving and suffering). No transcendent purposes are thereby served; no pleasures, enjoyments, or satisfactions attainable can suffice to overbalance the sufferings life involves, thus excluding a hedonic justification of living; and so life stands condemned at the bar of evaluative judgment. It is, in a word, absurd. Ceaseless striving, inescapable suffering, inevitable destruction—all pointless, with no meaning and no justification, no redemption or after worldly restitution, and with the only deliverance being that of death and oblivion: this is Schopenhauer's world as *Wille und Vorstellung*[4]—the pre-Christian apprehension of life attributed by Nietzsche in BT to the Greeks, recurring again in the modern world as Christianity enters its death throes.

Nietzsche does not question the soundness of this picture in BT; and, even though he later rejected the Schopenhauerian metaphysics, which he here accepts, he continued to concur with this general account of the circumstances attending life in the world. To live is to struggle, suffer, and die; and, while there is more to living than that, no amount of "progress" in any field of human enterprise can succeed in altering these basic parameters of individual human existence. Even more significantly, for Nietzsche as well as for Schopenhauer and Nietzsche's Greeks, it is not possible to discern any teleological *justification* of what the individual is thus fated to undergo, either historically or supernaturally. We can look neither to a future utopia nor to a life hereafter that might serve to render endurable and meaningful "the terror and horror of existence."

How can one manage to endure life in a world of the sort described by Schopenhauer, once one recognizes it for what it is—endure it, and beyond that *affirm* it as desirable and worth living despite the "terrors and horrors" that are inseparable from it? "Suppose a human being has thus put his ear, as it were, to the heart chamber of the world will," Nietzsche writes, "how could he fail to *break*?" (p. 127). He terms this general recognition of the world's nature and of the fate of the individual within it "Dionysian wisdom"; and he compares the situation of the Greek who attained it to that of Hamlet—and implicitly to that of modern man (with a Schopenhauerian-existentialist world view) as well:

> In this sense the Dionysian man resembles Hamlet: both have once looked truly into the essence of things, they have *gained knowledge*, and nausea inhibits action; for their action could not change anything in the external nature of things. . . .
>
> Now no comfort avails any more. . . . Conscious of the truth he has once seen, man now sees everywhere only the horror or absurdity of existence . . . . : he is nauseated (p. 60).

Nietzsche desperately wanted to find some sort of solution to this predicament—though he cloaked his longing in the guise of a more detached interest in the question of how it has been possible for "life" to manage to "detain its creatures in existence" even when the erroneous beliefs which commonly shield them are no longer in operation. For this reason his attention was drawn to a people who were already very much on his mind owing to his professional concerns and who constituted a perfect

---

[4]Arthur Schopenhauer, *The World as Will and Idea*, translated by R. B. Haldane and J. Kemp (London: Routledge & Kegan Paul, 1964), Fourth Book; see, for example, § 71.

subject for a case study along these lines: the early Greeks. There were no brute savages, mindlessly and insensitively propelled through life by blind instinctive urges; rather, they were highly intelligent, sensitive, and cognizant of the ways of the world. And what is more, they were sustained neither by anything like Judeo-Christian religious belief nor by any myth of historical progress and human perfectibility. Yet they did not succumb to Schopenhauerian pessimism; on the contrary, they were perhaps the most vigorous, creative, life-affirming people the world has known. And thus Nietzsche was drawn irresistibly to them, asking of them, how did they do it? What was the secret of their liberation from the action- and affirmation-inhibiting nausea which seemingly ought to have been the result of their own Dionysian wisdom?

The answer, he believed, lay in that which was the most striking and glorious achievement of their culture: their art. Thus the passage cited continues,

> Here, where the danger to [the] will is greatest, *art* approaches as a saving sorceress, expert at healing. She alone knows how to turn these nauseous thoughts about the horror or absurdity of existence into notions with which one can live (p. 60).

This is the guiding idea of Nietzsche's whole treatment of art in general, as well as tragedy in particular, in BT. The main themes of this work are summarized in the following lines from its concluding section, which expand upon this idea of making reference to the key concepts of the "Dionysian" and "Apollinian" and bring to the fore the most central and crucial notions in Nietzsche's entire philosophy of art—the notions of *overcoming* and *transfiguration*:

> Thus the Dionysian is seen to be, compared to the Apollinian, the eternal and original artistic power that first calls the whole world of phenomena into existence—and it is only in the midst of this world that a new transfiguring illusion becomes necessary in order to keep the animated world of individuation alive. . . .

> Of this foundation of all existence—the Dionysian basic ground of the world—not one whit more may enter the consciousness of the human individual than can be overcome again by this Apollinian power of transfiguration (p. 143).

II

Before turning to a closer consideration of these conceptions, a fundamental ambivalence in Nietzsche's thinking about the relation between art and life in BT must be noted. And in this connection I shall refer briefly to Nietzsche's thinking about art after as well as in BT.

From first to last, he was deeply convinced that art requires to be understood not as a self-contained and self-enclosed sphere of activity and experience detached from the rest of life, but rather as intimately bound up with life and as having the greatest significance in and for it. This is reflected in his later observation (in his "Self-Criticism") that art in BT is viewed "in the perspective of life"—a circumstance he regards as one of the signal merits of the work, its many inadequacies not withstanding. And it is one of the most decisive and distinctive features of his general philosophical position that its development is characterized by a kind of dialectic between his understanding of life and the world and his understanding of art—each affecting the other and bringing about changes in the other as the other worked changes upon it.

The underlying unity of the nations of art and life in Nietzsche's thinking is to be seen in BT in his treatment of the basic impulses operative in art—the Dionysian and the Apollinian—as identical with basic tendencies discernible in man and nature alike. And the consequences of his conviction of the existence of this unity are apparent in the subsequent development of the two notions which gradually move to the center of his discussions of man, life, and the world in his later writings: the "overman" and the "will to power." For I would suggest that the latter is to be understood as an outgrowth of the dual notions of the Dionysian and Apollinian "art impulses of nature," in which they are *aufgehoben* in the threefold Hegelian sense of this term (in a manner lending itself to a further union with Nietzsche's successor conception to Schopenhauer's world will, his world of "energy-quanta"). And I would also suggest that the "overman" is to be construed as a symbol of human life raised to the level of art, in which crude self-assertive struggle is sublimated into creativity that is no longer subject to the demands and limitations associated with the "human, all-too-human."

The overcoming of the initial meaningless and repugnant character of existence, through the creative transformation of the existing, cardinally characterizes both art and life as Nietzsche ultimately comes to understand them. And this means for him both that life is essentially artistic and that art is an expression of the fundamental nature of life. "Will to power" is properly understood only if it is conceived as a disposition to effect such creatively transformative overcoming, in nature, human life generally, and art alike. And the overman is the apotheosis of this fundamental disposition, the ultimate incarnation of the basic character of reality generally to which all existence, life, and art are owing.

In BT, of course, neither "will to power" nor "overman" makes an appearance, and the relation between art and life is discussed in other terms. One of the most notable features of the discussion, however, is Nietzsche's readiness to employ the term "art" not only to refer in a conventional manner to sculpture, music, and the other standard "art forms" (kinds of work of art, their production, and their experience), but also in a broader, extended sense. For example, Nietzsche suggests that "every man is truly an artist" to the extent that it is part of the experience of everyone to engage in the "creation" of "the beautiful illusion" of "dream worlds" (p. 34), even though no "works of art" in the usual sense are thereby produced. Furthermore, turning his attention from such (Apollinian) "dreaming" to the experience of what he calls "Dionysian ecstasies," Nietzsche speaks of the Dionysian throng as *being* "works of art" themselves: here "man . . . is no longer an artist, he has become a work of art. . . . The noblest clay, the costliest marble, man, is here kneaded and cut . . ." (p. 37).

Most strikingly of all, however, Nietzsche refers constantly to "nature" herself as "artistic" and terms both the Apollinian and the Dionysian tendencies "art-impulses" of *nature*. Thus he initially presents them "as artistic energies which burst forth from nature herself, without the mediation of the human artist," and goes on to say, "With reference to these immediate art-states of nature every artist is an 'imitator' " (p. 38). And he is not merely suggesting that nature is thus "artistic" as well as man, albeit in different ways; for he contends that these two "art-states of nature" are "the only two art impulses" (p. 83), and he even goes so far as to attribute the true authorship of *all* art to "nature" rather than to human agency considered in its own right. "One thing above all must be clear to us. The entire comedy of art is neither performed for our betterment or education, nor are we the true authors of this art world." The human artist is said to be merely "the medium through which the one truly existent subject celebrates his release in appearance." Artists and the rest of us alike are "merely images and artistic projections for the true author," which is the fundamental principle of reality—the world will—itself; and we "have our highest dignity in our significance as works of art," as creations of this ultimate "artist," rather than as producers and appreciators of art objects (p. 52).

Yet Nietzsche also speaks of art very differently, and in a way that suggests a much less direct and even contrasting relation between it and the world. Thus, for example, he writes that "the highest, and indeed the truly serious task of art" is "to save the eye from grazing into the horrors of night and to deliver the subject by the healing balm of illusion from the spasms of the agitations of the will" (p. 118).

Again and again, he asserts that art in all of its forms deals in "illusion" and even "lies." Art spreads a "veil of beauty" over a harsh reality—and, when Nietzsche speaks of it as a "transfiguring mirror" (p. 43), the emphasis belongs not on the latter term but rather on the former, which does away with any accurate reflection. Thus he writes that "art is not merely imitation of the reality of nature but rather a metaphysical supplement of the reality of nature, placed beside it for its overcoming" (p. 140). And here the concluding passage of the entire work, cited earlier, should be recalled, in which Nietzsche returns to this theme of the necessity of overcoming whatever consciousness of the world's nature is attained by means of an art of "transfiguration" capable of covering over what has been glimpsed with a "splendid illusion" (p. 143). It was the "terror and horror of existence" from which the Greeks needed to be saved; and "it was in order to be able to live" that they developed their art: "all this was again and again overcome by the Greeks with the aid of the Olympian *middle world* of art; or at any rate it was veiled and withdrawn from sight" (p. 42). Nor does this apply only to nontragic art forms; for Nietzsche asserts that "the tragic myth too, insofar as it belongs to art at all, participates fully in this metaphysical intention of art to transfigure" (p. 140).

Even while thinking along these lines, however, Nietzsche envisages a fundamental link between "art" and "life," in that the latter is held to have been the source of the Greek's salvation from the desperate situation in which it also placed him: "Art saves him, and through art—life" (p. 59). Life thus is cast in a dual role, with the consequence that the relation of art to it is also a dual one.

Can the world of art in the narrower sense be thought of as a world "supplementing the reality of nature, placed beside it for its overcoming," and therefore distinct from it and contrasting to it—and at the same time as the creation of this very nature itself, expressing its own basic "artistic impulses," and therefore fundamentally homogeneous and identical to it? In BT, Nietzsche tries to have it both ways, but it is far from clear that it is possible to do so.

III

In any event, it should be clear by now that Nietzsche thinks of what art *is* in terms of *what art does* and *how art does it*; and that for him the answers to these two questions are to be given in terms of the notions of *overcoming (Überwindung)* and *transfiguration (Verklärung)*. These two notions recur repeatedly throughout BT and figure centrally in most of his major pronouncements about art—regardless of what art forms he may be considering and notwithstanding any basic differences between them.

It should further be evident that the former is to be understood in relation to certain human needs which Nietzsche regards as fundamental and profoundly compelling, thereby endowing art with an extraordinary importance transcending that of mere enjoyment or satisfaction derived from self-expression. And his interpretation of art in terms of the latter notion also clearly involves him in a fundamental break with Schopenhauer and all other cognitivist philosophers of art; for, if art is essentially a matter of transfiguration, its ministrations to our needs will necessarily proceed otherwise than by heightening our powers of insight and understanding.

Nietzsche's frequent references to "illusions" in a number of contexts make this obvious, but the point applies even where this latter notion does not (notably, in the case of music). Otherwise put, even where some sort of "truth" about reality is purported to come through in art, Nietzsche takes it to be essential to the artistic character of the expression that a transfiguration of the "true" content has occurred in its artistic treatment—and its artistic character and quality attaches entirely to the element of transfiguration, rather than to this content and its transmission. On this point, however, more shall be said later.

It is important to bear in mind the general applicability of the notions of overcoming and transfiguration when turning to Nietzsche's discussion of the art impulses and art forms he is intent upon distinguishing, both to properly interpret what he says about them individually and to avoid the error of supposing that he takes them to be entirely different phenomena united by nothing more than a shared name. For, while he begins by speaking of "the science of aesthetics" and of "the continuous development of art," thereby implying some degree of unity of both the discipline and its subject, he immediately introduces the notion of "the *Apollinian* and *Dionysian* duality," asserts that "art" is but a "common term" until the two are "coupled with each other" (p. 33), and goes on to analyze them along very different lines—even to the point of maintaining that these notions represent "*two* worlds of art differing in their intrinsic essence and in their highest aims" (p. 99). These "art impulses" and "worlds of art," however, while very different indeed for Nietzsche, are nonetheless both "*art* impulses" and "worlds *of art*." That they have more than merely this same "art" denomination in common is testified to by the fact that their "coupling" had a fruitful artistic issue (tragedy).

According to Nietzsche, neither in Apollinian nor in Dionysian art do we encounter unvarnished representations of the world, as it is in itself, as it presents itself to us in experience, or as it might be conceived by a thinker concerned with the natures of the types to which all existing things belong. The impulses to the creation of art for him are not cognitive impulses of any sort; rather, if they stand in any relation at all to knowledge, he holds that this relation may best be conceived as an *antidotal* one. And it is undoubtedly in part to stress the extent of his departure from any cognitively oriented interpretation of art that Nietzsche introduces his discussion of the Apollinian and the Dionysian by dwelling upon their connection with the phenomena of dreaming and intoxication. Each of these phenomena, he maintains, manifests a deeply rooted and profoundly important aspect of man's nature, and each answers to a powerful need. And the strength of the hold art exerts upon us can be understood only if it is recognized that the different art forms have their origins in these basic impulses and emerge in answer to these strong needs.

Nietzsche's discussion of Apollinian and Dionysian duality in BT is intended to bring out both the radical difference between what he thus takes to be the two basic life-serving and art-generating impulses these names designate as well as the possibility of their interpenetration and, further, the great importance (for "life" and art alike) of the results when this occurs. At the outset of his discussion of the Apollinian and Dionysian duality, Nietzsche singles out two art forms as paradigms of each—"the Apollinian art of sculpture and the nonimagistic, Dionysian art of music" (p. 33)—but then moves immediately to a consideration of the more fundamental experiential "states" (also termed Apollinian and Dionysian) to which he takes all such art forms to be related: dreaming and intoxication.

He contends that human beings are so constituted as to be impelled to each by deeply rooted dispositions and to respond to each with powerful but differing positive feelings. Thus he suggests that there is something in "our innermost being" which "experiences dreams with profound delight and joyous necessity" (p. 35), while it is likewise the case that "paroxysms of intoxication" are accompanied by a "blissful ecstasy that wells up from the innermost depths of man, indeed of nature . . ." (p. 36).

It is these feelings of "profound delight" on the one hand and of "blissful ecstasy" on the other which are held to characterize the experience of the respective Apollinian and Dionysian art forms. These forms touch the same deep chords in our nature and so produce the same sort of response. And this is taken to be the key to understanding how it is that they are able to perform their life-sustaining functions (to the extent that they manage to do so).

As Nietzsche views them, dreaming and intoxication are not merely analogs to art, or pre-forms of art, or even experiential sources of artistic activity. Rather, there is an important sense in which they themselves *are* artistic phenomena—only the "artist" in these cases is no human being but, rather, "nature," working in the medium of human life. In this context, the Dionysian and Apollinian require to be conceived "as artistic energies which burst forth from nature herself, without the mediation of the human artist—energies in which nature's art impulses are satisfied in the most immediate and direct way" (p. 38). Nietzsche does not mean this to be construed merely metaphorically; for it is his contention that human artistic activities are to be regarded as of a piece with these more basic life processes—developments of them, to be sure, but outgrowths sufficiently similar to them fundamentally to warrant regarding "every artist as an 'imitator' " in relation to "these immediate art-states of nature." Thus he also contends that "only insofar as the genius in the act of artistic creation coalesces with this primordial artist of the world, does he learn anything of the eternal essence of art . . ." (p. 52).

It may be noted in this connection that for Nietzsche it is in this respect—and only in this respect—that art may properly be conceived as involving "the imitation of nature." That is, art imitates nature in that the same sort of thing goes on in the former instance as goes on (among other things) in the latter. But, precisely because creative transformation is involved in the former no less than in the latter (as part of the very "imitation" in question), true art no more involves the attempt exactly to represent nature as it confronts us than dreaming and intoxication faithfully record it—nor yet again does true art merely give expression to the contents of experiences had while in these states.

Having said this, it must immediately be granted that Nietzsche does employ the language of "representation" in speaking of the relation between both Apollinian and Dionysian art forms and the content of what might be termed the "visions" associated with both Apollinian and Dionysian experiential states more broadly and fundamentally conceived. It has already been noted that he is willing to speak with Schopenhauer of (Dionysian) music as a "copy" of the "primal unity" underlying all appearances (p. 49). It has also been observed that he conceives of Dionysian art as effecting a kind of identification of the individual with this underlying reality through a captivating revelation of its nature as conveyed by "the Dionysian artist" who has glimpsed it and "identified himself with" it (p. 49). To this it must be added that he also speaks of the employment of "the best of rhythm" and tonal architectonics in Apollinian music "for the representation of Apollinian states" (p. 40). And, while it is "mere appearances" rather than the reality underlying them with which all such states are held to be concerned, the "beautiful illusions" of Apollinian plastic art are suggested to be, if not such appearances themselves, at any rate "appearances of" *those* appearances (p. 45).

In short, Nietzsche holds that there is at least a kind of "mirroring" relation between what is discerned in Dionysian states and what one finds in Dionysian art, and also between what is envisaged in Apollinian states and what one finds in Apollinian art. Indeed, it can even be said that for Nietzsche the efforts of artists of both sorts serve at once to share and to heighten experiences centering upon the contents of the respective sorts of vision. Were this not so, the "joy in existence" deriving from the "blissful ecstasy" generated by the one and the "profound delight" arising from the other (through the generation and intensification of which these types of art are held to perform their life-sustaining function) could not be stimulated by art.

The solution to this difficulty is to be found in the fact that for Nietzsche art transforms even as it thus "represents," that it is no simple faithful mirror of the contents of these states but, rather, "a transfiguring mirror" (p. 43). And it is one of the central points of his discussion of these two types of art that they not only transfigure even as they mirror but, moreover, that they transfigure the already dissimilar contents of the visions associated with the two kinds of state in quite different ways. In view of this double difference, it is perhaps understandable that Nietzsche could have been moved to speak of "two worlds of art differing in their intrinsic essence" (p. 99).

The basic contrast he is concerned with establishing here may be expressed in terms of the distinction between *images* and *symbols*, and the double difference just mentioned bears importantly upon it. In the case of what Nietzsche calls Apollinian art, the chaotic play of crude and ephemeral appearances associated with such basic Apollinian experiential states as dreaming and imagination undergoes a transformative process, issuing in the creation of enduring, idealized images—"beautiful illusions," as Nietzsche often terms them, illusory because nothing either in the flux of appearance or beyond it corresponds to them, and of greater beauty than the haphazardly constituted contents of this flux. They are transfigurations of appearances, images akin to the stuff of dreams but also contrasting markedly to them.

In the case of Dionysian art, on the other hand, the transformation from which it issues is of the experience of the inexhaustible, dynamic "primal unity" that is "beyond all phenomena and despite all annihilation" associated with such basic Dionysian states as intoxication and orgiastic revelry. What *this* transformation gives rise to is "a new world of symbols," in which "the essence of nature is now . . . expressed symbolically" (p. 40); and it is the resulting *symbolic forms* in which Dionysian art consists. These symbolic forms are transfigurations of ecstatic states—expressions akin to immediate Dionysian ecstasy but, again, differing markedly from it, no less than from the underlying reality glimpsed in it. Thus Nietzsche holds that "Dionysian art . . . gives expression to the will in its omnipotence, at it were, behind the *principium individuationis*" (p. 104)—and yet insists that even so paradigmatic a case of such art as music is not to be thought of as identical with this will: "music, according to its essence, cannot possibly be will. To be will it would have to be wholly banished from the realm of art" (p. 55). For were it the same as will, it would lack the transfigured character definitive of all art.

In short, it is Nietzsche's contention that there is one sort of art in which the works produced have a symbolically expressive character and another sort in which the works produced do not, having instead the character of idealized images or "beautiful illusions." And it is one of the seemingly curious but important points of his analysis that the kinds of art generally regarded as most clearly "representational" fall largely into the latter category, while those generally thought of as primarily "non-representational" belong in the former. The idealized images of Apollinian art are not to be thought of as having the function either of faithfully representing or of symbolically expressing anything at all. They are rather to be thought of as beautiful illusions to be contemplated simply for what they are in themselves and to be enjoyed solely on account of their intrinsic beauty. They are, as Nietzsche says, a "supplement of the reality of nature, placed beside it for its overcoming" (p. 140). And, if there is any significant relation between them and this "reality," it does not consist in their genetic link to the experiential phenomena of which they are transfigurations but, rather, in their ability to lead us to think better of the world of ordinary experience by regarding it in the "transfiguring mirror" they constitute, "surrounded with a higher glory" (p. 43). Through Apollinian art, the world of ordinary experience is not actually transformed and its harshness eliminated. But, to the extent that the idealized images created through the transformative activity of the Apollinian artist admit to association with that which we encounter in this world, our attitude toward the latter benefits from this association, as our delight in these images carries over into our general disposition toward anything resembling them.

Once again, however, it is not knowledge that we thereby attain but, rather, only an altered state of mind, brought about by "recourse to the most forceful and pleasurable illusions" and "seducing one to a continuation of life" (p. 43). One may have reservations about the psychological validity of these latter contentions, or about the effectiveness of the process indicated (as indeed Nietzsche himself has and sets forth later in his analysis). These reservations do not touch Nietzsche's main point here, however, concerning the status of those works of art he terms Apollinian. They are beautiful illusions, idealized images which neither represent nor symbolize but, rather, delight precisely by virtue of the beauty they possess as a result of the creative transfiguration accomplished in their production.

In the case of Dionysian art, matters stand quite differently. The Dionysian artist too is creative, and not merely someone with insight and the ability to communicate it—notwithstanding Nietzsche's assertion that, in the paradigm case of such art, "he produces [a] copy of [the] primal unity as music" (p. 49). It may be that there is a kind of "re-echoing" of the nature of this fundamental reality in instances of Dionysian art, as Nietzsche goes on alternately to put the point (p. 50). In terms of this metaphor, however, such art is no less a "transfiguring echo-chamber" than Apollinian art is a "transfiguring mirror," for the artistic "re-echoing" does not stand in the same near-immediate relation of identity to this "primal unity" as does the more basic, Dionysian phenomenon of intoxication but, rather, comes back in an altered form, the creative production of which involves "the greatest exaltation of all [man's] symbolic faculties."

Thus, Nietzsche goes on to say, "the essence of nature is now to be expressed symbolically; we need a new world of symbols" (p. 40)—and it is this "new world of symbols" which constitutes both the language and the substance of Dionysian art. The issue is somewhat confused by Nietzsche's use of the term Dionysian to refer to the "primal unity" itself ("the Dionysian basic ground of the world," etc.) and also to insight into its nature and the plight of the individual in such a world ("Dionysian wisdom"), as well as to such art, which draws upon man's "symbolic powers" and thereby transfigures even while giving expression to the former. But, once again, it must be borne in mind that for Nietzsche, like other art forms, "it belongs to art at all" only insofar as it "participates fully in this metaphysical intention of art to transfigure" (p. 140).

The symbolism of which Nietzsche is speaking here, however, is of a rather special sort. At least in its origins, it is neither conventional nor intentional and is far removed from the use of words to formulate and express thoughts. Thus, in discussion the "Dionysian dithyramb" (which he takes to be the proto-form of Dionysian art), he writes that in order to develop the "new world of symbols" needed to be able to express "the essense of nature" symbolically,

> . . . the entire symbolism of the body is called into play . . . , the whole pantomine of dancing, forcing every member into rhythmic movement. Then the other symbolic powers suddenly press forward, particularly those of music, in rhythmics, dynamics, and harmony (p. 50).

The development of Dionysian art is thus a matter of the refinement and elaboration of those symbolic forms answering to the "symbolic powers" and resources available to the human artist and serving to give expression to the nature of the reality encountered when one penetrates beyond and beneath all individuated appearances and all perceptible images, idealized or "real." And, to avoid misunderstanding Nietzsche's meaning in speaking of symbolization here, it is important to see that he takes these art forms to express "the essence of nature" symbolically, not on the level of any specific "content" that may be discerned in cases of various instances of them but, rather, on the deeper level of the general character of these art forms. Some sorts and even some instances of (Dionysian) music and dance may be superior to others in terms of the adequacy with which they perform this expressive function, but it is essentially the character of these art forms as such that accounts for their symbolic significance and their ability to perform this function.

Thus music is both more and less than that which Nietzsche takes it to express; it is sound, while the "primal unity" is not, and the "art world" of musical sounds is in a significant sense other than "the essence of nature." And it is no mere transparent medium through which the latter is brought before us distinctly and unadorned; while not opaque, as Apollinian art may be said to be in this context, it is at most only translucent. Neither the fact of its mere translucency, however, nor the fact of the transformation it involves is considered by Nietzsche to be detrimental to its mediating function. On the contrary, he takes them actually to enhance it. For he believes that we could not endure the full glare of an unmediated encounter with the world's essential nature and that it is only *as transfigured* through its expression in the entrancing symbolic forms of the Dionysian arts that a nondestructive identification with it is possible.

In short, in these arts the world's nature is expressed in a form that attracts rather than repels us—a symbolic form, the attractiveness of which is bound up with the transfiguration involved in this symbolization and made possible by the character of the "new world of symbols" under consideration. Dionysian art does not have the character of a "veil of illusion" radically different from the reality of nature and "placed alongside it for its overcoming," as does Apollinian art for Nietzsche. Yet it does have a somewhat analogous character and function in that it expresses the reality of nature in a manner enabling us to overcome our abhorrence of it and derive "joy in existence" from identification with it, by means of a quasi-"illusory" *medium* of transfiguring symbolic forms.

The most fundamental and crucial ideas Nietzsche seeks to advance in this connection are that art is essentially not representational (or imitative) with respect to the world either as we perceive it or as it is apprehended in cognition but, rather, that it is transfigurative; that, on the other hand, the transfigurations it involves are more than mere pleasing expressions of emotions or fancies in sensuous form; and that they are not all of the same kind. One does not have to subscribe to the version of the appearance/reality distinction which he accepts here (but later rejects), or to his contention that art is the "highest task and truly metaphysical activity of this life," or to his conviction that it has the purpose of performing the kind of "overcoming" function he describes in relation to the "terror and horror of existence" to follow him this far—and farther still.

IV

Nietzsche does not take the notions of transfiguration and illusion to apply only to works of Apollinian and Dionysian art conceived as objects of aesthetic experience but, rather, also to the subjects of such experience insofar as they become absorbed in them. This point is of great importance in connection with his treatment of tragic art, as well as in his analysis of these two art forms. And for this reason it warrants close attention. The entire significance of art is missed, for Nietzsche, if one does not recognize that the consciousness of those experiencing these art forms undergoes a transformation analogous to that occurring in their creation—and that, with this transformation, the experiencing subject's very psychological identity is in a sense transfigured, even if only temporarily and in a way that does not alter the basic reality of his human nature and of his existence in the world. The latter circumstance is what renders it appropriate to speak of illusion here—though Nietzsche is no less concerned to indicate the value of such illusion "for life" than he is to point out its illusory character.

The subjective transformation associated with the objective one involved in the creation of the work of art, however, has a very different character in the two general sorts of cases under consideration. Thus Nietzsche contends that they constitute two fundamentally distinct stratagems by means of which "the insatiable will" at the heart of nature conspires to "detain its creatures in life and compel them to live on" (p. 109). He discusses them in terms of what occurs in the case of the Dionysian man and in the case of the Apollinian man, and for the sake of convenience I shall follow him in this—with the understanding, however, that these expressions refer to contrasting types of psychological states rather than to distinct groups of human beings.

That an inward transformation occurs in the course of the kind of experience appropriate to Dionysian art has already been intimated in Nietzsche's observation that one in the grip of the "paroxysms of intoxication" in which the Dionysian impulse primordially manifests itself "has become a work of art" (p. 37). It has also been suggested that he takes Dionysian art to mediate an identification of the individual with the reality underlying the appearances whose nature is expressed symbolically in it. It is a common observation that art has the remarkable power to *transport* us, not only into the domain established through artistic creation, but also out of our ordinary selves and everyday lives. Nietzsche seizes upon this idea and elaborates it—in a manner, it may be remarked, influenced significantly by Schopenhauer. Schopenhauer had contrasted our normal condition as creatures and captives of will, absorbed in the constant struggle for existence characterizing all life in the world, with a radically different condition purported to be temporarily attainable through aesthetic experience; "he who is sunk in this perception is no longer individual," Schopenhauer had written, but rather "is pure, will-less, painless, timeless subject of knowledge."[5]

Nietzsche modifies this suggestion and expands it so that it applies both to the contemplation of idealized images that elevates one above the world of ordinary experience and action and to the experience of enrapturing symbolic expressions of the reality underlying this phenomenal world that carries one beyond it. Yet in either event he agrees with Schopenhauer that one so affected is "no longer individual" or at any rate ceases for the moment to have the psychological identity associated with his ordinary individual existence. The transformation undergone by the Apollinian man (which is most akin to that indicated by Schopenhauer) will be considered shortly. That transformation undergone by the Dionysian man was not envisioned by Schopenhauer, at least in connection with art, for it involves not the attainment of contemplative will-lessness but, rather, the effecting of a far deeper psychological union with the world will than that which is merely a matter of our being its creatures and having to live under the conditions it imposes upon all its particular instances.

The Dionysian man does not exchange his physiological and sociocultural identity and situation in the world for another or escape them altogether in the course of the "destruction of the *principium individuationis*" of which Nietzsche speaks. As an experiental phenomenon, however, this destruction is very real: the Dionysian man is psychologically transformed into one for whom the only reality of which he is aware—and therefore that with which he himself identifies—is that which is expressed in the movements, tonalities, or other symbolic forms in which he is immersed. Thus Nietzsche contends that, through the experience of Dionysian art, "we are really for a brief moment primordial being itself, feeling its raging desire for existence and joy in existence; the struggle, the pain, the destruction of phenomena, now appear necessary

---

[5]Schopenhauer, *The World as Will and Idea*, § 34.

for us . . ." (p. 104). As one in a state of intoxication may be said (quite appropriately, even if only psychologically) not to "be himself," one immersed in the surge and flow of an instance of this type of aesthetic experience "loses himself" in it. His consciousness is caught up in it and his self-consciousness is altered accordingly, whether this transformation manifests itself behaviorally in an enraptured cessation of ordinary activity, in outward inaction making inward tumult, or in entrance into overt participation in the event as well. Such experience is of being blissful, but also in the original and literal sense of the term *ekstasis*, which denotes a standing out from, beside, beyond (oneself).

To the extent that one's own existence may be conceived as being actually a moment of the reality expressed in Dionysian art and with which one thus comes to feel at one through its mediation, this transformation may be said to have the significance of a dispelling of the illusion involved in one's ordinary consciousness of oneself as something distinct from it and to be characterized in other terms. But, to the extent that such experience leads one to identify oneself so completely with this reality that one feels oneself to enjoy even those of its features that actually characterize it only as a whole, with which one is not truly identical, this transformation may also be said to have the significance of the fostering of another, different illusion. Thus Nietzsche suggests that, here no less than in the case of Apollinian art, we are dealing with a way in which, "by means of an illusion," life conspires "to detain its creatures in existence" despite the harshness of the conditions it imposes upon them—in this instance, through "the metaphysical comfort that beneath the whirl of phenomena eternal life flows on indestructibly" (pp. 109–10).

The illusion in question is not that "life flows on indestructibly" despite the ephemerality of phenomena—for it does. We may be "comforted" (and more) through the transformation of our psychological identity enabling us to achieve a sense of unity with this indestructible and inexhaustible underlying reality, of which we are truly manifestations. But, while such comfort may be termed metaphysical, this transfiguration is not, for it leaves our actual status in the world unchanged and the basic conditions of our human existence unaltered—as we discover that when the moment passes the Dionysian aesthetic experience comes to an end, and we "return to ourselves," our psychological identities transformed back gain into their original non-Dionysian state. The only enduring confort is the recollection of the rapture of the Dionysian experience and the knowledge that it remains available to us. But a profound danger attends this kind of "overcoming," of which Nietzsche is acutely aware: the letdown may be great, the disparity between Dionysian states and ordinary life distressing, the illusion discerned, and its recognition found disconcerting—and thus the long-term effect of such experience may be detrimental rather than conducive to life (pp. 59–60). It is for this reason, more than any other, that Nietzsche has reservations about Dionysian art and experience generally, despite the evident fascination they have for him.

These reservations would appear to be well founded. And as Nietzsche also observes, in connection with the historical supersession of Dionysianism by other cultural forms, Dionysian art may no longer perform the larger function in human life which he takes to have called it into existence. Yet it by no means follows that it constitutes a closed chapter in the development of art. Its capacity to move us, enrapture us, transport us, and transform our sense of identity is in Nietzsche's view ensured by very basic features of our human nature, and it does not succumb to the passing of the ability of a people to live under its immediate spell. The psychological transfiguration Nietzsche describes is one which he takes to occur not merely in those who meet this description but, rather, in all of us when we open ourselves to the experience of Dionysian art. To the extent that we do so, when we do, we approach the condition of Nietzsche's Dionysian man; indeed, we are changed and *become* as Dionysian man, if only in these moments.

Nietzsche's Apollinian man constitutes a very different case, being the product of quite another kind of psychological transformation. As in the previous case, this transcendence is held to be not only merely temporary but also fundamentally illusory, and the resulting transformation only psychological rather than genuinely ontological. Here, too, Nietzsche sees the cunning hand of nature at work, in this instance "detaining its creatures in life" through rendering the Apollinian man "ensnared by art's seductive veil of beauty fluttering before his eyes" (p. 109).

The realm of Apollinian art is a kind of "dream world, an Olympian *middle world* of art" (p. 43) that is neither the everyday world nor the underlying world of will but, rather, a created world by means of which the latter is "veiled and withdrawn from sight" and the former is supplanted as the focus of concern. And entrance into this world is possible, Nietzsche holds, only for a kind of dreamer, or Olympian spectator, detached from the kinds of involvements and concerns that both characterize the everyday world and endow us with our ordinary psychological identities. Indeed, it requires that one *become* such a "pure spectator"—or, rather, that the images presented are such that they induce a kind of contemplative consciousness through which one's psychological identity is transformed into that of such a subject. They stand outside of time and change, need and strife, and to become absorbed in them is for Nietzsche to have one's consciousness comparably transformed. If, in the experience of Dionysian art, one is enraptured, one may be said here to be entranced. And, in a state of such entrancement, it is as if one had become a part of this world of images—not as one of them, but as a placeless, disembodied center of awareness, a subject fit for such objects and answering to their nature.

While Apollinian art involves "the arousing of delight in beautiful forms" (p. 100), this is not to be construed merely in the sense of providing us with pleasure but, rather, in terms of an overcoming of the distress associated with our human condition through what is felt to be a kind of redemption from it. "Here Apollo overcomes the suffering of the individual by the radiant glorification of the *eternity of the Phenomenon*; here beauty triumphs over the suffering inherent in life" (p. 104), for the Apollinian man "is absorbed in the pure contemplation of images" (p. 50), the beauty of which strongly attracts us and brings us under their spell, causing us to banish all else from our minds and seemingly to become nothing but the delighted awareness of them. Our delight is genuine, and our psychological transformation real—even though on a more fundamental level both the objects of such consciousness and this self-consciousness are merely two aspects of the Apollinian illusion, which is but "one of those illusions which nature so frequently employs to achieve her own ends" (p. 44).

This illusion, however, is by no means as insubstantial as the term might seem to suggest. One indication of this, on Nietzsche's account, is the very fact that it is powerful enough to enable "nature" to achieve her end of "seducing one to a continuation of life" by means of it (p. 43). And if it is the case, as Nietzsche claims in this same sentence, that Apollinian art is thus "called into being, as the complement and consummation of existence," it follows that it is no *mere* illusion which leaves the reality of human life unaffected. It may not alter the human condition. But, if it is in some significant sense the "consummation of existence," it may be truly said to effect a significant transformation of "existence," or at least that portion of it which is the reality of human life. Art may be created by man, but man is also recreated or transfigured by art.

The kind of experience and spirituality which become attainable in relation to the idealized images of Apollinian art may not constitute an elevation of those who attain to them entirely beyond the reach of the entanglements of ordinary life and the deeper harsh realities of existence in this world. Yet they do render the existence of those attaining to them qualitatively different from that of those who remain entirely immersed in the former or who further succeed only in finding occasional respite through Dionysian experience. It is Nietzsche's appreciation of the magnitude of this qualitative difference that accounts for his celebration of the achievement of the archaic Greeks in their creation of Apollinian art, both plastic and epic.

Life cannot in the end be lived merely on the plane of Apollinian aesthetic experience, or even simply in the radiation of the reflected glory with which Apollinian art is capable of lighting the world of ordinary experience. The human condition is too recalcitrant, and the undercurrent of the "Dionysian ground of existence" too strong, for the psychological transformation involved in the ascent into the realm of Apollinian art prevails indefinitely. Absorbing and delightful as this kind of experience is, it suffers from the fatal weakness of failing to come to terms with basic aspects of human life in the world that do not disappear when veiled, despite "recourse to the most forceful and pleasurable illusions" (p. 43). Yet Nietzsche is by no means disposed to conclude that what might be termed "the Apollinian experiment" is to be regarded as a mere blind alley, to be abandoned in favor of the Dionysian alternative. For these two alternatives to life lived solely on the plane of dull immersion in the affairs of everyday existence, and also to reversion "to the tiger and the ape" and Schopenhauerian ascetic withdrawal, are not the only ones. There remains at least one other, which Nietzsche associates with the phenomenon of tragic art. And in this connection his suggestion should be kept in mind that the "Apollinian illusion" is a development in which there is to be found the "consummation of existence," for, "illusion" though it may be, the kind of transfiguration it involves—both of the objects and the subjects of experience— is of the utmost importance in the emergence alike of tragic art and the more viable form of human existence he associates with it.

V

Thus, BT's full original title *(The Birth of Tragedy, Out of the Spirit of Music)* notwithstanding, Nietzsche conceives tragic art to be no less Apollinian than Dionysian in origin and nature. At the very outset of the book, he advances this contention with respect to the archetype of it, asserting that "by a metaphysical miracle of the Hellenic 'will,'" the "tendencies" associated with each "appear coupled with each other, and through this coupling ultimately generate an equally Dionysian and Apollinian form of art—Attic tragedy" (p. 33). The burden of his entire discussion of it is that its emergence presupposed not only the prior development of the art of Dionysian transfiguration, but also the *retransfiguration* of the latter under the influence of the likewise previously developed art of Apollinian transfiguration.

The birth of tragedy for Nietzsche was an event of the greatest actual and possible future significance, for it did not merely involve the appearance of a qualitatively new art form, thus opening another chapter in the development of art. It also made possible a further qualitative transformation of human life, which he conceives to have been and to be of far greater moment than is generally recognized. "Tragic art" and "Attic tragedy" are by no means synonymous for him; the latter is without question a paradigm case of the former, and there may be no better way to approach the former than by the course Nietzsche follows in BT, of investigating the latter. But the possibility of tragic art did not end with the expiration of Attic tragedy and is not wedded to the dramatic form of the works produced by the classical tragedians. Nor is Nietzsche here thinking in addition merely of Elizabethan tragic drama, together with the tragic opera of his own time, but rather of what he characterizes more generally as *tragic myth*.

Moreover, and even more importantly, he does not conceive of tragic art as a phenomenon the significance of which is confined to but a single sphere of human experience and cultural life. Rather, he views it as the potential foundation and guiding force of an entire form of culture and human existence, which alone is capable of filling the void left by the collapse of "optimistic" life-sustaining myths (both religious and philosophical-scientific). And he looks to it to assume anew the function of "making life possible and worth living," which neither Apollinian nor Dionysian art as such is capable any longer of performing. The former may continue to entrance and delight us, and the latter to enrapture and excite us, and both may continue to transport and transform us in their respective fashions, but the power of the illusions they involve to sustain us has been lost.

Aristotle had maintained that the tragedian constructs a dramatic means of enabling us to be purged of the feelings of fear and pity arising in connection with our recognition of our own plight in this world and threatening to paralyze us, by arousing such feelings directed toward a tragic figure and discharging them upon this figure. In this way, our capacity to feel them for ourselves is held to be diminished (at least for a time), thus enabling us to return to the world of action temporarily unimpaired by them.

Nietzsche says something of a similar nature, in connection with comedy as well as tragedy. One who "sees everywhere only the horror or absurdity of existence" may be beyond the reach of the consolations of lesser art forms, but even here, "when the danger to his will is greatest," art still has the capacity to save him, for it—and it alone—is able to "turn these nauseous thoughts . . . into notions with which one can live: These are the *sublime* as the artistic taming of the horrible, and the *comic* as the artistic discharge of absurdity." The details of his account differ from those of Aristotle's, but Nietzsche is close to him when he concludes that the effect of this "saving deed of Greek art" upon the Greeks who were thus endangered was that "the feelings described here exhausted themselves" (p. 60).

However, to say this much is by no means to say enough, for, if one confines one's attention to this aspect of the experience of tragic art alone, one misses something of even greater significance than the discharge or exhaustion of such negative feelings—

namely, the powerful *positive* feelings generated at the same time, which are akin to those associated with Dionysian aesthetic experience.

In a word, what is absent from the above account is reference to the tremendous *exhilaration* that tragic art serves to inspire, notwithstanding the distressing fate of the central tragic figures. This exhilaration is much more than a mere feeling of relief from the torment occasioned by the negative feelings of which one is purged. And it is also different in both magnitude and kind from the delight associated with Apollinian aesthetic experience, even though certain aspects of works of tragic art may occasion such delight, or at least admit of being experienced in an Apollinian manner. Thus Nietzsche contends that "the drama . . . attains as a whole an effect that transcends *all* Apollinian effects" (p. 130).

There may be those whom tragedy does not affect in this way; but that, for Nietzsche, says something about *them* rather than about the nature of tragic art. Exhilaration is, in his view, an essential feature of the proper effect such art should have, and this phenomenon both renders comprehensible why he attaches such great significance to tragic art and guides his interpretation of it—for it is his conviction that it holds the key to the understanding of the nature of this art form and that no analysis of tragic art can be considered sound or adequate that does not do justice to it.

In this connection it is both crucial and illuminating to bear in mind the passage cited earlier from the last section of the book, in which Nietzsche contends—clearly with tragic art specifically in mind—that, with respect to the underlying nature and character of the world and existence in it, "not one whit more may enter the consciousness of the human individual than can be overcome again by [the] Apollinian power of transfiguration" (p. 143). To be able to endure the consciousness of them of which we are capable and which cannot in the long run be prevented from emerging, and to be able further to embrace and affirm life despite the attainment of such an awareness, a transformation of this consciousness is necessary. In its starkest, simplest and most vivid form, according to Nietzsche, it would be overwhelmingly horrible, "nauseating," paralyzing and unendurable, save in temporary transports of Dionysian ecstatic self-trancendence which cannot be sustained and so constitute no adequate long-term recourse.

For Nietzsche, tragic art alone is truly equal to this task, and thus the problem before us is to determine how his conception of its nature enables him to so regard it. As has been seen, he holds that it enables us to experience the terrible not as merely terrible but, rather, as sublime and that it achieves something akin to a Dionysian effect upon us, which however is not identical with it—for it does not take the kind of life-endangering toll that Dionysian intoxication does, inducing an experiential state that differs as significantly from such intoxication as it does from Apollinian dreaming. In the long run it has the character of a tonic rather than a depressant; its aftermath is held to be exhilaration, rather than either the overall exhaustion which follows upon Dionysian excitement or the exasperation which Apollinian exaltation leaves in its train. And, considered more immediately, it might be said to enthrall, rather than to entrance *or* enrapture. So to describe what tragic art does is not to give an analysis of it, though Nietzsche's conception of its nature requires to be comprehended in the light of this understanding of its effects.

Tragic art too, for Nietzsche, may be said to constitute a kind of "transfiguring mirror." It is a mirror, however, in which we see reflected neither "appearances" idealizingly transfigured nor the character of the reality underlying them symbolically expressed. We are confronted instead with "images of life"—reflections of the human (and our) condition, highlighting both the individuation it involves and the fate bound up with the latter in a world in which all individual existence is ephemeral, harsh, and ridden with strife and suffering. What we encounter, however, is not a stark and brutally "realistic" portrayal of this condition as such. We see it in transfigured form—even though this transfiguration of it does not consist in its radical transmutation into a merely imaginary idealized condition *contrasting* to the actual human condition on these counts. And it likewise does not involve the effective obliteration of the salient features of human life through the diversion of attention from the entire domain of individuation to the collective, the impersonal, the merely vital and the enduring aspects of life underlying it. Rather, the kind of transfiguration occurring here is one which pertains to our perception of individual human existence—*as* existence that is individual rather than merely a part of an inexhaustible and in-destructible flow of life and that is human rather than above and beyond the conditions to which man is subject.

This transfiguration pertains first to the character of the dramatic figures with which we are confronted—or, rather, it comes about first in the context of our confrontation with them, but it does not remain confined to this encounter, serving rather to alter our apprehension of the human condition more generally. It is in this sense above all that tragic art may be said to serve as a transfiguring mirror: it works a transformation upon our consciousness of the human reality that is also our own, at the same time as it reflects that reality for us to behold. The fate of the tragic figure takes on the aspect of something sublime rather than merely horrible, and thus, without being denied or glossed over, it ceases to inspire mere "nausea," moving us instead to fascination and awe. The life of the tragic figure is endowed with a significance that entirely alters its aspect, and what might seem from a simple recitation of the brute facts of the matter to be a merely wretched and distressing tale emerges as an enthralling and moving spectacle.

Tragic art presents us neither with an ideal to be admired and emulated nor with an avenue by means of which to escape all thought of the hard realities of life. The latter are very much in evidence, and the tragic figure caught up in them is one with whom, as an individual, we empathize but with whom, as a character, we do not identify. Yet the manner of presentation of such figures, which renders them tragic and not merely pathetic, does much more than merely purge us of our self-directed feelings of fear and pity through an empathic discharge. It can have a powerful positive impact upon the way in which we perceive our human condition and experience the reality of our own lives, by revealing them to us in a very different light from that in which we would otherwise tend to view them. The point might be put by saying that the tragic artist, not through the persona of the tragic figure per se but in the larger structure of the tragic drama, interposes a medium between us and the reality of human existence which does more than simply give expression to the latter, for the medium further shapes and colors our consciousness of reality and is able to help us attain an affirmative attitude toward it precisely by virtue of doing so.

In short, tragic art provides us with a way of apprehending this reality that enables us to come to terms with it—and not only to endure but also to affirm what we thereby see, as we thereby learn to see it. In this way it resembles Dionysian art. And for

Nietzsche this similarity of tragic art to the Dionysian arts is by no means merely fortuitous. In tragic myth, as in music and dance, something transcending mere appearances is symbolically expressed—and in being so expressed is transformed for our consciousness. Here, however, the symbolic forms employed are not primarily those characteristic of these Dionysian art forms but, rather, are drawn from the initially nonsymbolic domain of Apollinian art.

Life regarded as tragic is no longer life seen as merely wretched and pathetic; and the "displeasure" associated with "the weight and burden of existence" is overshadowed and forgotten when the latter takes on the aspect of tragic fate rather than mere senseless suffering and annihilation. The fate of the tragic figure, when nobly met rather than basely suffered, enhances rather than detracts from his stature, and the figure serves as a symbolic medium through which individual existence more generally is enhanced for us. It is in these terms that the exquisite stimulant distinctively characteristic of tragic art is to be conceived, even though it is strongly supplemented by the presence of that which is characteristic of Dionysian art as well.

The unique achievement of tragic art is thus held to be that it fundamentally alters our apprehension of human existence and the circumstances associated with it, which result in the suffering and destruction of even such extraordinary figures as the central characters of tragic drama and myth. Through it, these circumstances cease to stand as *objections* to human life and its worth and emerge instead as features of it which—as part of the larger whole human lives are and can be—actually contribute to its overall significance and attractiveness. And thus, Nietzsche suggests, it serves to bring it about that existence can "seem justified" *aesthetically* "only as an aesthetic phenomenon" (p. 141). Nietzsche's use of the term "only" here is highly important, for his general point is that it is *only* in this way, in the last analysis, that it is possible for us to find human life and our own existence endurable and worthwhile without recourse to illusions which radically misrepresent the actual nature of our human reality and the world more generally.

VI

As has been observed in connection with Apollinian and Dionysian art, there is for Nietzsche a significant sense in which all images, like appearances more generally, are to be considered illusory. And so, for that matter, are all symbols, for neither may be supposed to correspond even approximately, let alone exactly, to the actual nature of reality. No relation of resemblance obtains between these sorts of experiential phenomena and the consitution of this underlying reality itself; the difference is qualitative, and profound. But it is by no means only in this very basic (and relatively uninteresting) respect that Nietzsche takes tragic art too to involve the generation of illusion.

It has already been observed that this illusion centers on the "image of life" with which we are confronted in the tragic figure. While such figures are not simply "realistically" drawn, or fictitious but true-to-life individuals, or representatives of the elemental characteristics of "Dionysian universality" (as is the chorus), they are not mere Apollinian beautiful illusions either. Like Apollinian idealized images, however, they constitute something on the order of a "supplement of the reality of nature," and of that of ordinary human existence along with it, "placed beside it for its overcoming" (p. 140). The "core of life they contain" is the same as our own, but this core is artistically transformed into images of life expressing possibilities which are more human than mere glorious appearances, and yet which differ markedly from the commonplace, in ways moreover answering to no predetermined human essence or foreordained human ideal. They thus can in no sense be said to confront us with the "truth" of human existence. And, since what they confront us with is something other than truth, they may be said to present us with a kind of illusion. It is in this sense that Nietzsche's remarks to this effect are to be understood.

Yet this illusion is no *mere* illusion, and the transformed consciousness of ourselves which emerges when we view our own lives in the light of the manner of those of these tragic figures is not *merely* illusory, for the creations in which they consist are not distorted or erroneous representations of something that has a fixed and immutable character and cannot be otherwise. And they also are not simply imaginary substitutes temporarily usurping a position in our consciousness that is normally and more properly occupied by our ordinary conception of our own mundane reality. Rather, they are symbols of *human* possibility. And as such they serve to carry us beyond the mere acknowledgment of intractable aspects of the human condition, enabling us to discern ways in which the latter may be confronted and transformed into occasions for the endowment of life with grandeur and dignity.

By means of these symbols, human life thus may come to take on an aesthetic significance sufficing to overcome the distressing character of its harsh basic features. It stands revealed as a potentially aesthetic phenomenon, "justifiable" accordingly in our estimation even in the face of its hardest circumstances. And of paramount importance for Nietzsche is the fact that tragic art works this feat in a non-Apollinian way; it does not confine this perception of the tragic figure themselves, while precluding its application to our lives. These figures stand as symbols serving to facilitate our apprehension of the possibilities they express, together with "the core of life they contain," as our own—and so to alter the aspect of our own lives.

To say that this is all illusion, as Nietzsche does, is neither to deny the reality of this alteration nor to downplay its significance. Rather, it is to make the point that our lives thus acquire an experiential character which is no part of their fundamental objective nature and that this occurs through the transforming mediation of created images enabling us to discern aesthetic significance in human existence, notwithstanding that its basic circumstances warrant the attribution to it of no significance whatsoever.

The principal feature of tragic art thus is not the chorus (or its counterparts in instances of it other than Greek tragedy), through which "Dionysian wisdom" is given expression, considered simply as such. Neither is it the tragic figure regarded apart from this Dionysian background, in all his "epic clearness and beauty" or as a glorious appearance fated for annihilation. To be sure, both are essential elements of tragic art, and it is further the case for Nietzsche that "*tragic myth* is to be understood only as a symbolization of Dionysian wisdom through Apollinian artifices" (p. 131). But even this characterization of the relation effected between these two elements does not adequately convey the nature of the result. Nietzsche does contend that "the highest goal of tragedy and of all art is attained" when it thus comes about that "Dionysus speaks the language of Apollo; and Apollo, finally, the language of Dionysus" (p. 130). Yet it would be an error to suppose that this goal consists merely in the supersession of

Apollinian and ordinary forms of consciousness alike by a triumphantly reascendant Dionysianism.

This point can hardly be overemphasized, for it is of the greatest importance. What is at issue here, once again, is the "aesthetic justification" not simply of the world generally, but also of human existence, as we do and must live it—and this is something that presupposes the supersession of Dionysian as well as Apollinian (and also ordinary) consciousness. Tragic art is held to be capable of accomplishing this result only by virtue of the "fraternal union of Apollo and Dionysus" occurring in it, not by a victory of the latter over the former. The quasi-Apollinian tragic figure may be "annihilated," but the entire Apollinian element is not. And, while "the Dionysian predominates" in "the total effect of the tragedy" (p. 130), it does not emerge in sole possession of the field. If human existence is to be "justified" *despite* its inescapable harsh conditions and fate, it cannot be exhibited in such a way that only the suffering and destruction it involves are made to stand as its final truth, with all aesthetically justifying characteristics being reserved to the "primordial unity" that flows on beneath the surface of individuation and appearance.

In tragic art the Apollinian is neither merely assimilated into the Dionysian, nor is it the fundamental import of tragedy that the true status and meaning of human existence is to be conceived exclusively in terms of the nature of Dionysian reality, which gives the lie to all Apollinian transfiguration. The Apollinian is transformed through being brought into relation with the Dionysian, but not shattered and banished or deprived of all significance. On the contrary, Nietzsche contends that it thereby "receives wings from the spirit of music and soars" (p. 139) more powerfully than it ever can otherwise—and leaves its mark on the Dionysian, which is likewise transformed in this "union." To be sure, the underlying character of the world itself and of the human condition is not thereby altered, but the aspect of human existence is, even while it is apprehended against the background of this Dionysian reality.

The consciousness of human existence and of ourselves which Nietzsche terms "tragic" is neither purely Apollinian nor merely Dionysian, for the tragic myth in accordance with which it is shaped places this existence we share in a new and different light. A new way of seeing it becomes possible, in that our relation to the reality that is at once the ground and the abyss in our existence comes to be regarded as amenable to Apollinian transformation. Here our own existence as individuals is not something to which it is necessary to be oblivious to experience aesthetic enjoyment, as in the cases of Apollinian delight and Dionysian rapture in their separate and more basic aesthetic forms. Rather, human life itself becomes the focus of a kind of aesthetic satisfaction identical with neither but related to both through its treatment in a way that brings our capacity for responses of both sorts into play in relation to it.

While the last word in tragedy might seem to belong to Dionysian reality and Dionysian wisdom, therefore, it in fact does not—even if it does not belong to Apollinian ideality and optimism either. The former is as hopelessly pessimistic with respect to human existence as it actually can and must be lived as the latter is naive and unrealistic—whereas tragedy is neither but, rather, is fundamentally and strongly affirmative in relation to it. In the attainment of a tragic sense of life, the "terror and horror of existence" are surmounted through the remarkable alchemy of tragic art which transmutes the terrible and horrible into the sublime and magnificent. And the key to this transmutation is not the quickening of that sense of "metaphysical comfort" that "beneath the whirl of phenomena eternal life flows on indestructibly—though this too occurs. It is rather the "Apollinian power of transfiguration," which alone enables us to endure and affirm the existence that is ours as parts of this "whirl," not only in moments of Dionysian rapture, self-abnegation and obliviousness to the human condition, but also when we acknowledge our individuality and confront the circumstances of human life.

Nietzsche may often seem to be more concerned with what might be termed the ecstatic component of the experience of tragic art than with this companion feature of it. Yet it is the latter which he finally stresses, when he concludes his discussion by emphasizing that "of this foundation of all existence—the Dionysian basic ground of the world—not one whit more may enter the consciousness of the human individual than can be overcome again by this Apollinian power of transfiguration" (p. 143). This power must be brought to bear upon our consciousness of our existence as human individuals, not merely upon our awareness of "the Dionysian basic ground of the world" as such, if we are to be able to find our lives endurable and worth living. It would avail us little to regard the world generally as justified if no comparable justification were discernible when we turned to a consideration of our own existence.

In a sense, tragic art may thus be said to accomplish the Apollinianization of the Dionysian, in our consciousness of the latter if not also in its actual nature. But it may perhaps more appropriately be said to accomplish a complex and radical transformation of something else, in a less one-sided manner: the aspect of our human existence, at once along partly Apollinian and partly Dionysian lines. What is thus transformed is not tragedy, for the accomplishment of tragic art is not the transformation of tragedy into something else. Tragedy, rather, is the *issue* of this artistic transformation, through which existence comes to be experienced as tragic. This is indeed an artistic accomplishment, since tragedy no less than beauty may be said to exist only in the eye of the beholder, whose sensibility has been formed and cultivated by art. It is no brute fact of human existence but, rather, an acquired aspect it may come to bear through the transfiguring agency of the tragic artist.

It is in this way that the tragic myth comes to be endowed with what Nietzsche terms its "intense and convincing metaphysical significance" (p. 126)—and also its most profoundly illusory character, for it leads us to feel something to be the deepest and highest "truth" of human existence—the tragic character it is capable of coming to bear, with all the sublimity and majesty devolving upon it therefrom—which is no part of either its fundamental nature or any intrinsic essence legitimately attributable to it. We are led to view life as though it were a means to the end of actualizing the aesthetic values associated with human existence as it is revealed in the transfiguring mirror of tragic myth.

In BT, Nietzsche places his hope for a revitalization of Western civilization, in the face of the collapse of both other worldly religiousness and rationalistic-scientific optimism, in a re-emergence of a tragic sense of life. But, as he readily acknowledges, such a view of life cannot be sustained in the absence of tragic myth and an acceptance of the understanding of human existence associated with some instance of it. It is for this reason that he devotes so much discussion in this work to the importance of myth and to the need for a new and compelling form of tragic myth in the modern Western world.

Nietzsche obviously thought, when he wrote BT, that Wagner was well on the way to accomplishing the task he thus envisaged. The details of his discussion of this and related matters, however, are of relatively little intrinsic interest—especially since he soon after lost his enthusiasm for Wagner and abandoned his commitment to the ultimacy and indispensability of that form of art he associates here with tragic myth. He further seems to have become convinced that art generally has a significance in relation to life and that it also has a variety of features to which his analysis of it in BT does not do justice. In any event, he subsequently approached the arts somewhat differently, placing less emphasis upon differences between the various art forms and the kinds of experience associated with them and concerning himself more with the phenomenon of artistic creativity generally.

Although he devoted at least some (and often considerable) attention to art in nearly all of his later writings, however, he never again subjected it to a comparably comprehensive, intensive, and sustained analysis or treated it with a similar breadth of vision. Although he subsequently deepened and modified his understanding of art in certain important ways and recast his views with respect to it in the light of basic alterations in his understanding of the natures of man, life, and reality, he retained most of the fundamental notions in terms of which he interprets it in BT, in one form or another, and continued to give them central roles in his subsequent discussions of it. Finally, it should be clear that, however unsatisfactory, questionable, and excessive some of what he says in BT may be, he is to be credited in this early effort with a number of extremely valuable insights concerning such things as the relation between art and life, the transfigurative character of art, the nature of artistic creation, the distinction between imagistic and symbolically expressive art forms, and the distinctive character and impact of tragic art.

It may be that few classics in the literature of the philosophy of art are as flawed in as many particular respects as is BT. Yet it is also the case that few so richly reward patience with their flaws and close attention to their substance.

THE THEORY OF THE PLASTIC ARTS: PAINTING AND ARCHITECTURE

One of the great contributions of the art historian E. H. Gombrich is that he has shown the complexity of works of art even on a very basic level. His inquiries have given rise to important philosophical questions about the nature of the resemblance of signs to objects in the visual arts. Gombrich asks how, fundamentally, a shape can stand for a cat or dog, a question that leads him to dismiss a resemblance theory of representation. When an artist undertakes to represent something, according to Gombrich, he or she is not merely trying to copy what is seen. Instead, visual representation involves the manipulation of signs or "schemata" that can be recognized as standing for particular objects. For example, a stick drawing of a woman does not in the strict sense resemble a woman, although it can be used to represent one because it works in this way as a sign. Thus, Gombrich maintains that reference to things does not depend upon resemblance, a view that leads to the consequence that art is a kind of language of conventional signs or symbols rather than a relationship based on resemblances or natural causes.

On the naive view of representation, it is believed that artists look at things and then try to reproduce them in an appropriate visual medium. But this is a mistake, according to Gombrich. Artists do not possess an "innocent eye"; rather, they employ schemata or vocabularies (circles, squares, etc.) that have developed within a cultural and social context. If we consider the way in which a cat is visually depicted, we will find that artists begin with a certain visual form that they progressively refine until it resembles the animal in question. The refinements arise through a manipulation of what has been *made* (a circular form) rather than by trying to match what is seen. This Gombrich calls the "process of 'making and matching', 'schema and correction.' " In place of a resemblance theory of representation, Gombrich supports a substitution theory in which items substitute for things depending on our needs and purposes. As a result, he argues that human psychology plays an important role in the symbols that we use to render nature. It is in this sense that pictures are "stand-ins" for things.

Richard Wollheim's "Reflections on *Art and Illusion*" is a critical discussion of Gombrich's views on representation. Gombrich's fundamental question is: Why has representative art a history? Why have different painters depicted the visible world in such radically different ways? Clearly, an important aim of pictorial art is the rendering of reality with naturalistic accuracy. Wollheim refers to and refutes three different theories that attempt to explain why art has a history: the perceptual theory, the technological theory, and the theory of "seeing and knowing," each of which is an unsuccessful account of artistic change.

Is naturalism in representational art really possible? "Neutral naturalism" for Gombrich is the mistaken view that works can depict the world without any reference to style or convention. Wollheim enumerates Gombrich's several arguments against "neutral naturalism." Gombrich thus attempts to redefine naturalism in terms of the information conveyed by a picture. To say that a drawing or painting is truthful means that those who understand the notation will derive *no false information* from it. Wollheim points up two merits of this definition: first, it relates truth and falsehood to statements rather than objects, and second, it emphasizes the conventional element in any form of naturalism.

Gombrich thus draws the consequences that there is no unique form of naturalistic art toward which all forms of representational painting approximate to a greater or lesser degree, and that a correct form of art can only be the result of a long process of trial and error. Gombrich's theory of "making and matching" mentioned above is intended to account for the evolution of representational art. The artist begins with a crude model or schema that is matched against the object and gradually corrected as the history of art evolves until a full-fledged naturalism, an art of verisimilitude, is attained.

Wollheim also deals with the problem of Gombrich's view that "naturalism" and "illusion" are interchangeable. Gombrich holds that naturalism *is* illusion, and that the more naturalistic a painting is, the more effectively it creates an illusion. However, Wollheim shows for a variety of reasons that total effectiveness is seldom possible. As a result, in practice naturalism is a partial illusion, one that is as successful as the medium permits. But this view is untenable, according to Wollheim, for it is inconsistent with Gombrich's notion of art as conventional in nature. On Wollheim's view, different interpretations of a picture are possible; we may see a picture of an object sometimes as a picture and sometimes merely as that object.

Wollheim concludes with a discussion of the two major themes of *Art and Illusion*: the necessary connection between the progress of representation in art, and the employment of pictorial schemata toward that end. Wollheim is adept at pointing up the ambiguities in Gombrich's understanding of a schema. Moreover, Wollheim demonstrates that Gombrich's theory of perception is incompatible with his general view of pictorial representation as the progressive refinement of schemata. Despite these serious shortcomings, Wollheim considers Gombrich's work to be an important and novel contribution to the subject.

Nelson Goodman's "How Buildings Mean" is an application of Goodman's general theory of symbols to architecture. Goodman notes, first, that architecture has a close affinity with music insofar as both arts are seldom descriptive or representational. Moreover, architecture is distinguishable from many of the other arts by virtue of its absence of definite practical functions. The question then naturally arises: What is the distinctively aesthetic function of architectural works? Goodman answers by referring to the *symbolic* function of buildings, which is often obscured by their dedication to practical purposes. However, not all symbolic functioning is aesthetic, and Goodman seeks to uncover important ways in which buildings are able to symbolize.

For Goodman, the varieties of reference may be grouped under four headings: "denotation," "exemplification," "expression," and "mediated reference." Goodman thus turns to exemplification as a kind of reference characteristic of much architecture. He argues that "formalist architecture" is frequently designed to refer explicitly to certain properties of its structure, and in this way exemplifies the structure of a building.

In Goodman's view, not all the properties a building refers to are among those that literally apply to it. The organization of a building may be dynamic, but this is so in a metaphorical rather than literal sense. "A building may express feelings it does not feel, ideas that it cannot think or state, activities it cannot perform." However, such metaphorical description does not imply falsity, for metaphorical as well as literal ascriptions may be true. Goodman thus stresses the role of exemplification in architecture because it "picks out, points to, *refers to*, some of its properties but not others," which are also properties of other things associated with the work.

Finally, Goodman discusses opposing views of the interpretation of buildings. He rejects both the "absolutist" view that only one interpretation of a building is correct, as well as the contentions of a "radical relativism" that regards any interpretation as acceptable. His own position is that judgments of rightness often involve "some sort of good fit," a notion that has itself evolved historically. "The fit in question," writes Goodman, "is of exemplified forms to each other and into the form exemplified by the whole." Thus, buildings mean by entering into different ways in which we conceive and comprehend the world in general; they advance our understanding and enable us to participate in our continual making of a world.

E. H. Gombrich

TRUTH AND THE STEREOTYPE:
FROM *ART AND ILLUSION*

> The schematism by which our understanding deals with the phenomenal
> world . . . is a skill so deeply hidden in the human soul that we shall hardly
> guess the secret trick that Nature here employs.
>
> IMMANUEL KANT, Kritik der reinen Vernunft

In his charming autobiography, the German illustrator Ludwig Richter relates how he
and his friends, all young art students in Rome in the 1820's, visited the famous beauty
spot of Tivoli and sat down to draw. They looked with surprise, but hardly with
approval, at a group of French artists who approached the place with enormous
baggage, carrying large quantities of paint which they applied to the canvas with big,
coarse brushes. The Germans, perhaps roused by this self-confident artiness, were
determined on the opposite approach. They selected the hardest, best-pointed pencils,
which could render the motif firmly and minutely to its finest detail, and each bent
down over his small piece of paper, trying to transcribe what he saw with the utmost
fidelity. "We fell in love with every blade of grass, every tiny twig, and refused to let
anything escape us. Everyone tried to render the motif as objectively as possible."

Nevertheless, when they then compared the fruits of their efforts in the evening,
their transcripts differed to a surprising extent. The mood, the color, even the outline
of the motif had undergone a subtle transformation in each of them. Richter goes on to
describe how these different versions reflected the different dispositions of the four
friends, for instance, how the melancholy painter had straightened the exuberant
contours and emphasized the blue tinges. We might say he gives an illustration of the
famous definition by Emile Zola, who called a work of art "a corner of nature seen
through a temperament."

It is precisely because we are interested in this definition that we must probe it a little further. The "temperament" or "personality" of the artist, his selective preferences, may be one of the reasons for the transformation which the motif undergoes under the artist's hands, but there must be others—everything, in fact, which we bundle together into the word "style," the style of the period and the style of the artist. When this transformation is very noticeable we say the motif has been greatly "stylized," and the corollary to this observation is that those who happen to be interested in the motif, for one reason or another, must learn to discount the style. This is part of that natural adjustment, the change in what I call "mental set," which we all perform quite automatically when looking at old illustrations. We can "read" the Bayeux tapestry without reflecting on its countless "deviations from reality." We are not tempted for a moment to think the trees at Hastings in 1066 looked like palmettes and the ground at that time consisted of scrolls. It is an extreme example, but it brings out the all-important fact that the word "stylized" somehow tends to beg the question. It implies there was a special activity by which the artist transformed the trees, much as the Victorian designer was taught to study the forms of flowers before he turned them into patterns. It was a practice which chimed in well with ideas of Victorian architecture, when railways and factories were built first and then adorned with the marks of a style. It was not the practice of earlier times.

The very point of Richter's story, after all, is that style rules even where the artist wishes to reproduce nature faithfully, and trying to analyze these limits to objectivity may help us get nearer to the riddle of style. One of these limits . . . is indicated in Richter's story by the contrast between coarse brush and fine pencil. The artist, clearly, can render only what his tool and his medium are capable of rendering. His technique restricts his freedom of choice. The features and relationships the pencil picks out will differ from those the brush can indicate. Sitting in front of his motif, pencil in hand, the artist will, therefore, look out for those aspects which can be rendered in lines—as we say in a pardonable abbreviation, he will tend to see his motif in terms of lines, while, brush in hand, he sees it in terms of masses.

The question of why style should impose similar limitations is less easily answered, least of all when we do not know whether the artist's intentions were the same as those of Richter and his friends.

. . . Take the image on the artist's retina. It sounds scientific enough, but actually there never was *one* such image which we could single out for comparison with either photograph or painting. What there was was an endless succession of innumerable images as the painter scanned the landscape in front of him, and these images sent a complex pattern of impulses through the optic nerves to his brain. Even the artist knew nothing of these events, and we know even less. How far the picture that formed in his mind corresponded to or deviated from the photograph it is even less profitable to ask. What we do know is that these artists went out into nature to look for material for a picture and their artistic wisdom led them to organize the elements of the landscape into works of art of marvelous complexity that bear as much relationship to a surveyor's record as a poem bears to a police report.

Does this mean, then, that we are altogether on a useless quest? That artistic truth differs so much from prosaic truth that the question of objectivity must never be asked? I do not think so. We must only be a little more circumspect in our formulation of the question.

* * *

Logicians tell us—and they are not people to be easily gainsaid—that the terms "true" and "false" can only be applied to statements, propositions. And whatever may be the usage of critical parlance, a picture is never a statement in that sense of the term. It can no more be true or false than a statement can be blue or green. Much confusion has been caused in aesthetics by disregarding this simple fact. It is an understandable confusion because in our culture pictures are usually labeled, and labels, or captions, can be understood as abbreviated statements. When it is said "the camera cannot lie," this confusion is apparent. Propaganda in wartime often made use of photographs falsely labeled to accuse or exculpate one of the warring parties. Even in scientific illustrations it is the caption which determines the truth of the picture. In a *cause célèbre* of the last century, the embryo of a pig, labeled as a human embryo to prove a theory of evolution, brought about the downfall of a great reputation. Without much reflection, we can all expand into statements the laconic captions we find in museums and books. When we read the name "Ludwig Richter" under a landscape painting, we know we are thus informed that he painted it and can begin arguing whether this information is true or false. When we read "Tivoli," we infer the picture is to be taken as a view of that spot, and we can again agree or disagree with the label. How and when we agree, in such a case, will largely depend on what we want to know about the object represented. The Bayeux tapestry, for instance, tells us there was a battle at Hastings. It does not tell us what Hastings "looked like."

Now the historian knows that the information pictures were expected to provide differed widely in different periods. Not only were images scarce in the past, but so were the public's opportunities to check their captions. How many people ever saw their ruler in the flesh at sufficiently close quarters to recognize his likeness? How many traveled widely enough to tell one city from another? It is hardly surprising, therefore, that pictures of people and places changed their captions with sovereign disregard for truth. The print sold on the market as a portrait of a king would be altered to represent his successor or enemy.

There is a famous example of this indifference to truthful captions in one of the most ambitious publishing projects of the early printing press, Hartmann Schedel's so-called "Nuremberg Chronicle" with woodcuts by Dürer's teacher Wolgemut. What an opportunity such a volume should give the historian to see what the world was like at the time of Columbus! But as we turn the pages of this big folio, we find the same woodcut of a medieval city recurring with different captions as Damascus, Ferrara, Milan, and Mantua. Unless we are prepared to believe these cities were as indistinguishable from one another as their suburbs may be today, we must conclude that neither the publisher nor the public minded whether the captions told the truth. All they were expected to do was to bring home to the reader that these names stood for cities.

These varying standards of illustration and documentation are of interest to the historian of representation precisely because he can soberly test the information supplied by picture and caption without becoming entangled too soon in problems of aesthetics. Where it is a question of information imparted by the image, the comparison with the correctly labeled photograph should be of obvious value. Three topographical prints representing various approaches to the perfect picture post card should suffice to exemplify the results of such an analysis.

The first shows a view of Rome from a German sixteenth-century newssheet reporting a catastrophic flood when the Tiber burst its banks. Where in Rome could the artist have seen such a timber structure, a castle with black-and-white walls, and a steep roof such as might be found in Nuremberg? Is this also a view of a German town with a misleading caption? Strangely enough, it is not. The artist, whoever he was, must have made some effort to portray the scene, for this curious building turns out to be the Castel Sant' Angelo in Rome, which guards the bridge across the Tiber. A comparison with a photograph shows that it does embody quite a number of features which belong or belonged to the castle: the angel on the roof that gives it its name, the main round bulk, founded on Hadrian's mausoleum, and the outworks with the bastions that we know were there.

I am fond of this coarse woodcut because its very crudeness allows us to study the mechanism of portrayal as in a slow-motion picture. There is no question here of the artist's having deviated from the motif in order to express his mood or his aesthetic preferences. It is doubtful, in fact, whether the designer of the woodcut ever saw Rome. He probably adapted a view of the city in order to illustrate the sensational news. He knew the Castel Sant' Angelo to be a castle, and so he selected from the drawer of his mental stereotypes the appropriate cliché for a castle—a German *Burg* with its timber structure and high-pitched roof. But he did not simply repeat his stereotype—he adapted it to its particular function by embodying certain distinctive features which he knew belonged to that particular building in Rome. He supplies some information over and above the fact that there is a castle by a bridge. . . .

I do not want to be misunderstood here. I do not want to prove by these examples that all representation must be inaccurate or that all visual documents before the advent of photography must be misleading. Clearly, if we had pointed out to the artist his mistake, he could have further modified his scheme and rounded the windows. My point is rather that such matching will always be a step-by-step process—how long it takes and how hard it is will depend on the choice of the initial schema to be adapted to the task of serving as a portrait. I believe that in this respect these humble documents do indeed tell us a lot about the procedure of any artist who wants to make a truthful record of an individual form. He begins not with his visual impression but with his idea or concept: the German artist with his concept of a castle that he applies as well as he can to that individual castle. . . . The individual visual information, those distinctive features I have mentioned, are entered, as it were, upon a pre-existing blank or formulary. And, as often happens with blanks, if they have no provisions for certain kinds of information we consider essential, it is just too bad for the information.

The comparison, by the way, between the formularies of administration and the artist's stereotypes is not my invention. In medieval parlance there was one word for both, a *simile*, or pattern, that is applied to individual incidents in law no less than in pictorial art.

And just as the lawyer or the statistician could plead that he could never get hold of the individual case without some sort of framework provided by his forms or blanks, so the artist could argue that it makes no sense to look at a motif unless one has learned how to classify and catch it within the network of a schematic form. This, at least, is the conclusion to which psychologists have come who knew nothing of our historical series but who set out to investigate the procedure anyone adopts when copying what is called a "nonsense figure," an inkblot, let us say, or an irregular patch. By and large, it appears, the procedure is always the same. The draftsman tries first to classify the blot and fit it into some sort of familiar schema—he will say, for instance, that it is triangular or that it looks like a fish. Having selected such a schema to fit the form approximately, he will proceed to adjust it, noticing for instance that the triangle is rounded at the top, or that the fish ends in a pigtail. Copying, we learn from these experiments, proceeds through the rhythms of schema and correction. The schema is not the product of a process of "abstraction," of a tendency to "simplify"; it represents the first approximate, loose category which is gradually tightened to fit the form it is to reproduce.

* * *

The study of pathology is meant to increase our understanding of health. The sway of schemata did not prevent the emergence of an art of scientific illustration that sometimes succeeds in packing more correct visual information into the image than even a photograph contains. But the diagrammatic maps of muscles in our illustrated anatomies are not "transcripts" of things seen but the work of trained observers who build up the picture of a specimen that has been revealed to them in years of patient study.

Now in this sphere of scientific illustration it obviously makes sense to say that . . . Vuillard himself could not have done what the modern illustrator can do. They lacked the relevant schemata, their starting point was too far removed from their motif, and their style was too rigid to allow a sufficiently supple adjustment. For so much certainly emerges from a study of portrayal in art: you cannot create a faithful image out of nothing. You must have learned the trick if only from other pictures you have seen.

In our culture, where pictures exist in such profusion, it is difficult to demonstrate this basic fact. There are freshmen in art schools who have facility in the objective rendering of motifs that would appear to belie this assumption. But those who have given art classes in other cultural settings tell a different story. James Cheng, who taught painting to a group of Chinese trained in different conventions, once told me of a sketching expedition he made with his students to a famous beauty spot, one of Peking's old city gates. The task baffled them. In the end, one of the students asked to be given at least a picture post card of the building so that they would have something to copy. It is stories such as these, stories of breakdowns, that explain why art has a history and artists need a style adapted to a task.

I cannot illustrate this revealing incident. But luck allows us to study the next stage, as it were—the adjustment of the traditional vocabulary of Chinese art to the unfamiliar task of topographical portrayal in the Western sense. For some decades Chiang Yee, a Chinese writer and painter of great gifts and charm, has delighted us with contemplative records of the Silent Traveller, books in which he tells of his encounters with scenes and people of the English and Irish countryside and elsewhere. I take an illustration from the volume on the English Lakeland.

It is a view of Derwentwater. Here we have crossed the line that separates documentation from art. Mr. Chiang Yee certainly enjoys the adaptation of the Chinese idiom to a new purpose; he wants us to see the English scenery for once "through Chinese eyes." But it is precisely for this reason that it is so instructive to compare his view with a typical "picturesque" rendering from the Romantic period. We see how the relatively rigid vocabulary of the Chinese tradition acts as a selective screen which admits only the features for which schemata exist. The artist will be attracted by motifs which can be rendered in his idiom. As he scans the landscape, the sights which can be matched successfully with the schemata he has learned to handle will leap forward as centers of attention. The style, like the medium, creates a mental set which makes the artist look for certain aspects in the scene around him that he can render. Painting is an activity, and the artist will therefore tend to see what he paints rather than to paint what he sees.

It is this interaction between style and preference which Nietzsche summed up in his mordant comment on the claims of realism:

> "All Nature faithfully"—But by what feint
> Can Nature be subdued to art's constraint?
> Her smallest fragment is still infinite!
> And so he paints but what he likes in it.
> What does he like? He likes, what he can paint!

There is more in this observation than just a cool reminder of the limitations of artistic means. We catch a glimpse of the reasons why these limitations will never obtrude themselves within the domain of art itself. Art presupposes mastery, and the greater the artist the more surely will he instinctively avoid a task where his mastery would fail to serve him. The layman may wonder whether Giotto could have painted a view of Fiesole in sunshine, but the historian will suspect that, lacking the means, he would not have wanted to, or rather that he could not have wanted to. We like to assume, somehow, that where there is a will there is also a way, but in matters of art the maxim should read that only where there is a way is there also a will. The individual can enrich the ways and means that his culture offers him; he can hardly wish for something that he has never known is possible.

The fact that artists tend to look for motifs for which their style and training equip them explains why the problem of representational skill looks different to the historian of art and to the historian of visual information. The one is concerned with success, the other must also observe the failures. But these failures suggest that sometimes we assume a little rashly that the ability of art to portray the visible world developed, as it were, along a uniform front. We know of specialists in art—of Claude Lorrain, the master of landscape whose figure paintings were poor, of Frans Hals who concentrated almost exclusively on portraits. May not skill as much as will have dictated this type of preference? Is not all naturalism in the art of the past selective?

A somewhat Philistine experiment would suggest that it is. Take the next magazine containing snapshots of crowds and street scenes and walk with it through any art gallery to see how many gestures and types that occur in life can be matched from old paintings. Even Dutch genre paintings that appear to mirror life in all its bustle and variety will turn out to be created from a limited number of types and gestures, much as the apparent realism of the picaresque novel or of Restoration comedy still applies and modifies stock figures which can be traced back for centuries. There is no neutral naturalism. The artist, no less than the writer, needs a vocabulary before he can embark on a "copy" of reality.

Everything points to the conclusion that the phrase the "language of art" is more than a loose metaphor, that even to describe the visible world in images we need a developed system of schemata. This conclusion rather clashes with the traditional distinction, often discussed in the eighteenth century, between spoken words which are conventional signs and painting which uses "natural" signs to "imitate" reality. It is a plausible distinction, but it has led to certain difficulties. If we assume, with this tradition, that natural signs can simply be copied from nature, the history of art represents a complete puzzle. It has become increasingly clear since the late nineteenth century that primitive art and child art use a language of symbols rather than "natural signs." To account for this fact it was postulated that there must be a special kind of art grounded not on seeing but rather on knowledge, an art which operates with "conceptual images." The child—it is argued—does not look at trees; he is satisfied with the "conceptual" schema of a tree that fails to correspond to any reality since it does not embody the characteristics of, say, birch or beech, let alone of individual trees. This reliance on construction rather than on imitation was attributed to the peculiar mentality of children and primitives who live in a world of their own.

But we have come to realize that this distinction is unreal. Gustaf Britsch and Rudolf Arnheim have stressed that there is no opposition between the crude map of the world made by a child and the richer map presented in naturalistic images. All art originates in the human mind, in our reactions to the world rather than in the visible world itself, and it is precisely because all art is "conceptual" that all representations are recognizable by their style.

Without some starting point, some initial schema, we could never get hold of the flux of experience. Without categories, we could not sort our impressions. Paradoxically, it has turned out that it matters relatively little what these first categories are. We can always adjust them according to need. Indeed, if the schema remains loose and flexible, such initial vagueness may prove not a hindrance but a help. An entirely fluid system would no longer serve its purpose; it could not register facts because it would lack pigeonholes. But how we arrange the first filing system is not very relevant.

The progress of learning, of adjustment through trial and error, can be compared to the game of "Twenty Questions," where we identify an object through inclusion or exclusion along any network of classes. The traditional initial scheme of "animal, vegetable, or mineral" is certainly neither scientific nor very suitable, but it usually serves us well enough to narrow down our concepts by submitting them to the corrective test of "yes" or "no." The example of this parlor game has become popular of late as an illustration of that process of articulation through which we learn to adjust ourselves to the infinite complexity of this world. It indicates, however crudely, the way in which not only organisms but even machines may be said to "learn" by trial and error. Engineers at their thrilling work on what they call "servo mechanisms," that is, self-adjusting machines, have recognized the importance of some kind of "initiative" on the part of the machine. The first move such a machine may make will be, and indeed must be, a random movement, a shot in the dark. Provided a report of success or failure, hit or miss, can be fed back into the machine, it will increasingly avoid the wrong moves and repeat the correct ones. One of the pioneers in this field has recently described this machine rhythm of schema and correction in a striking verbal formula: he calls all learning "an arboriform stratification of guesses about the world." Arboriform, we may take it, here describes the progressive creation of classes and subclasses such as might be described in a diagrammatic account of "Twenty Questions."

We seem to have drifted far from the discussion of portrayal. But it is certainly possible to look at a portrait as a schema of a head modified by the distinctive features about which we wish to convey information. The American police sometimes employ draftsmen to aid witnesses in the identification of criminals. They may draw any vague face, a random schema, and let witnesses guide their modifications of selected features simply by saying "yes" or "no" to various suggested standard alterations until the face is sufficiently individualized for a search in the files to be profitable. This account of portrait drawing by remote control may well be over-tidy, but as a parable it may serve its purpose. It reminds us that the starting point of a visual record is not knowledge but a guess conditioned by habit and tradition.

Need we infer from this fact that there is no such thing as an objective likeness? That it makes no sense to ask, for instance, whether Chiang Yee's view of Derwentwater is more or less correct than the nineteenth-century lithograph in which the formulas of classical landscapes were applied to the same task? It is a tempting conclusion and one which recommends itself to the teacher of art appreciation because it brings home to the layman how much of what we call "seeing" is conditioned by habits and ex-pectations. It is all the more important to clarify how far this relativism will take us. I believe it rests on the confusion between pictures, words, and statements which we saw arising the moment truth was ascribed to paintings rather than to captions.

If all art is conceptual, the issue is rather simple. For concepts, like pictures, cannot be true or false. They can only be more or less useful for the formation of descriptions. The words of a language, like pictorial formulas, pick out from the flux of events a few signposts which allow us to give direction to our fellow speakers in that game of "Twenty Questions" in which we are engaged. Where the needs of users are similar, the signposts will tend to correspond. We can mostly find equivalent terms in English, French, German, and Latin, and hence the idea has taken root that concepts exist independently of language as the constituents of "reality." But the English language erects a signpost on the roadfork between "clock" and "watch" where the German has only "Uhr." The sentence from the German primer, *Meine Tante hat eine Uhr,* leaves us in doubt whether the aunt has a clock or a watch. Either of the two translations may be wrong as a description of a fact. In Swedish, by the way, there is an additional roadfork to distinguish between aunts who are "father's sisters," those who are "mother's sisters," and those who are just ordinary aunts. If we were to play our game in Swedish we would need additional questions to get at the truth about the timepiece.

This simple example brings out the fact, recently emphasized by Benjamin Lee Whorf, that language does not give name to pre-existing things or concepts so much as it articulates the world of our experience. The images of art, we suspect, do the same. But this difference in styles or languages need not stand in the way of correct answers and descriptions. The world may be approached from a different angle and the information given may yet be the same.

From the point of view of information there is surely no difficulty in discussing portrayal. To say of a drawing that it is a correct view of Tivoli does not mean, of course, that Tivoli is bounded by wiry lines. It means that those who understand the notation will derive *no false information* from the drawing—whether it gives the contour in a few lines or picks out "every blade of grass" as Richter's friends wanted to do. The complete portrayal might be the one which gives as much correct information about the spot as we would obtain if we looked at it from the very spot where the artist stood.

Styles, like languages, differ in the sequence of articulation and in the number of questions they allow the artist to ask; and so complex is the information that reaches us from the visible world that no picture will ever embody it all. This is not due to the subjectivity of vision but to its richness. Where the artist has to copy a human product he can, of course, produce a facsimile which is indistinguishable from the original. The forger of banknotes succeeds only too well in effacing his personality and the limitations of a period style.

But what matters to us is that the correct portrait, like the useful map, is an end product on a long road through schema and correction. It is not a faithful record of a visual experience but the fruitful construction of a relational model.

Neither the subjectivity of vision nor the sway of conventions need lead us to deny that such a model can be constructed to any required degree of accuracy. What is decisive here is clearly the word "required." The form of representation cannot be divorced from its purpose and the requirements of the society in which the given visual language gains currency.

Richard Wollheim

REFLECTIONS ON *ART AND ILLUSION*

There is a question that few of those who feel a concern with painting and have the habit of looking at pictures cannot have asked themselves at some moment or other. The moment most likely was an early one in their experience of art when, on opening some illustrated history of art or trailing through the long endless galleries of a museum, they first became aware of the astounding variety of styles, modes, manners in which at different times different artists have recorded the one unique unchanging reality. Once asked, however, the question is usually put aside, quite rapidly, probably with embarrassment, as revealing a naïvety or literal-mindedness quite unsuitable in a serious and sophisticated lover of the arts.

It is around this question that *Art and Illusion*[1] has been constructed. And if I may for a moment contravene the self-denying ordinance that I have for the course of this lecture passed upon myself and indulge in a brief tribute to the author of the book, I should like to say that I regard it as typical of the fundamental and radical character of Professor Gombrich's thinking that he should take as his starting-point a question that nearly all of us find it natural to raise, but then, instead of, as many do, thinking it superior to ignore it and pass on, he should prefer to press into the service of answering it a formidable and dazzling erudition.

The question might be put like this: Why has representative art a history? Why did Duccio and Rubens, Van Eyck and Monet, Uccello and Watteau, all of whom, it must be granted, were interested in depicting the visible world, depict it in such different, such bewilderingly different, ways—so different, indeed, that we have no method, even in the mind's eye, of abstracting these differences, but invariably see the manner as part of the picture, take in the subject together with the style? Are these differences, we might ask, essential or merely accidental? Could, for instance, the Egyptians have depicted the human body in the way the Florentines did, and could the Florentines have anticipated the Impressionists in the representation of nature? If the

From On Art and the Mind *by Richard Wollheim (Cambridge: Harvard University Press, 1974). Reprinted by permission of Harvard University Press. Copyright © 1974 by Richard Wollheim.*
[1]E. H. Gombrich, *Art and Illusion* [A & I] (London, 1960, second edition 1962). All page references are to the second edition.

answer is yes, in what sense could they have done this? If the answer is no, how and why was the possibility closed to them?

To some these questions will seem quaint, even obsolete. For they carry with them, do they not?, the suggestion of a single end towards which all pictorial art has been directed—the representation of appearances—and in consequence a single criterion— naturalistic accuracy—by reference to which all its efforts are to be judged. Yet today we have outgrown these conceptions. We no longer esteem representational accuracy in our own art, and we are also able to see, by a kind of natural extension, that the hold that it had over earlier art has been much exaggerated. Indeed, so removed are we from this pictorial aim that we can no longer take seriously the problems associated with it. But to such objections Gombrich has his reply. If it is true that the representation of appearances was never the sole aim that earlier artists set themselves, it was certainly one aim and moreover an aim of singular and impressive cogency. And this cogency had much to do with the enormous practical difficulties to which its implementation gave rise. Indeed, the fact that as an aim it no longer commands general assent—or perhaps assent of any kind whatsoever—may very well be because these difficulties have now been largely overcome. They could not arise for the modern artist with the same acuteness with which they were experienced in earlier ages. Effects that would have been taken by the Greeks as indicative of powers of a divine order are now within the reach of any competent commercial artist: we overlook the fact that the "crude coloured renderings we find on a box of breakfast cereal would have made Giotto's contemporaries gasp."[2] But, if this is so, it looks as though an understanding of representation and its problems might be helpful for the understanding, not only of the art of the past, but also of the art of the present in so far as that defines itself in opposition to that of the past. Furthermore, it may well be the case, Gombrich argues, that there are other problems related to our understanding of art, specifically of non-representational or at any rate non-figurative art, that are inherently linked to that of representation. An example might be the highly contemporary problem of expression, and it is significant that *Art and Illusion* ends on a brief, a tantalizingly brief, but stimulating, discussion of expression and the issues that expression raises.

2. The question why art has a history does not itself fall within the domain of art-history. Art-history, at any rate as traditionally conceived, is complete when it has recorded the changes that constitute the history of art and, perhaps, gone some way towards offering an explanation why these changes occurred. If we now want to ask why there has been change at all, then we stand in need of some more general body of theory to which we can appeal. There is, however, both in the literature of the subject, to which, indeed, the more philosophical art-historians have made a distinguished contribution, and in ordinary reflective thought, a number of theories which set out to answer our question, and as good a way as any to approach Gombrich's book is via a consideration of them: not only because Gombrich has something to say about each of them but because, in an uncertain terrain, they provide fixed points by reference to which his theory can be plotted. They form the natural background to *Art and Illusion*.

The first theory I shall consider is what might be called the *perceptual theory* of artistic change. According to this theory, each painter paints the world as he sees it, but

<hr>

[2] *A & I*, p. 7.

each painter sees the world for himself, idiosyncratically, so that the various man-ifestations of representational art can be accounted for in terms of the varieties of human perception. Giotto, Velazquez, Van Gogh painted things differently because, and to the degree to which, they saw things differently. Secondly, there is what might be called the *technological theory* of artistic change, so called because, according to it, the course of art follows the history of technical advance in the skill of representation. It is to specific inventions and discoveries that we can attribute the capacity of successive painters to render effects of likeness or to encompass tricks of verisimilitude that lay quite outside the competence of their predecessors. On this theory, Egyptian art has a childlike character because Egyptian artists could do no better: by contrast, in later art, say in that of the Quattrocento or the High Renaissance or the nineteenth century, we see the consequences of an ever-increasing body of representational skill and technique. Later, we might say, means better. And, thirdly, there is the *theory of "seeing and knowing,"* felt by many to be the most sophisticated account of the matter obtainable, according to which artists across the ages have been involved in a kind of continuous and collusive enterprise to rid themselves of the burden of knowledge in their effort to portray the world as it presents itself. For knowledge of how things really are—for instance, that the face is symmetrical along the axis of the nose—is necessarily an obstacle in the way of depicting things as they appear to be—with, for instance, only half the face visible when seen from the side. To achieve a truly visual art what is required is to see the world directly, without preconceptions, and it is this struggle against the corrupting influence of knowledge, this sustained effort to capture the vision of the innocent eye, that accounts for the evolution of the pictorial arts from, say, the highly "conceptual" art of the Old Kingdom to the totally "perceptual" art of the Impressionists.

None of these theories is, in Gombrich's eyes, without interest or indeed without its element of truth: but against each of them as it stands, he brings, either implicitly or explicitly, what amounts to a fatal objection.

The perceptual theory is defective because, even if true, it would account only for the fact that art displays diversity, and not for the further fact that it possesses a coherent history. For, if the varieties of art were merely expressive of the varieties of vision, we should have no right to assume, as we do, certainly in connoisseurship, that pictures produced in spatial proximity to one another would be marked by natural likeness, nor should we have any reason to anticipate the temporal evolution of style, which is not just an assumption, but a fact, about the course of painting. To remedy this defect in the perceptual theory some writers of a more speculative temper have postulated a history for human vision, for "seeing" itself, tracing its evolution from the simple schematic vision to be found at the dawn of culture to the subtle and sensitive perceptions of modern man: the idea being that, once the history of vision is made out, art could then be geared to this history and so, indirectly, acquire one of its own. But any such supplementary hypothesis either straightway takes us out of the empirical world into a realm of unverifiable entities, or else degenerates into narrow circularity. For when we ask for the evidence in favour of the hypothesis, either we are given empty speculation or we are referred back to those changes in artistic style which the hypothesis was introduced to explain.

By contrast the technological theory has the dual virtue both of accounting for the historical character of art and of admitting into its framework of explanation only identifiable entities. On the debit side, however, it can be said that the technological theory allows art a history at the expense of denying it value: and, while we are all agreed that art possesses a history, we also all believe that it possesses value. Yet, if the story of art is to be interpreted purely as a story of technical advance, of accumulating skill in the production of certain desired effects, it is hard to see why anyone should esteem the outmoded experiments of the past. They might have archaeological interest or the charm of a lost way of life, but certainly no intrinsic value. Furthermore, though the technological theory gives us a historical account of artistic production, it leads to what might reasonably be thought of as an excessively a-historical conception of artistic psychology. For, according to the theory, Giotto differs from Michelangelo and Michelangelo differs from Degas in that Giotto couldn't do what Michelangelo could do and Michelangelo couldn't do what Degas could do. But this allows the possibility that Giotto might have wanted to do what Michelangelo did, perhaps even what Degas did. But the conception of earlier painters haunted by images which only later painters were able to realize, forming these images in the mind's eye with a clarity and a fineness of execution that unfortunately outstripped the technical resources that they had at their disposal—such a conception is surely the product of a quite disordered historical imagination.

And then there is the theory of "seeing and knowing." In various ways an advance upon its rivals, able at once to provide an explanation of the phenomena of pictorial evolution and also to furnish a terminology in which they can be profitably discussed, it runs into difficulties because of its attachment to the unexamined distinction between an art based on what we really see and an art to which non-perceptual factors contribute. But notice that the acceptance of this distinction is not peculiar to the theory of "seeing and knowing," though in this theory it comes to the fore. Both the technological and the perceptual theories of artistic change involve, in their different ways, reference to a kind of art which embodies the direct transcription of what the artist sees, free from any ancillary content. In the case of one theory, such an art appears as the aim, in the case of the other, it appears as the norm, of pictorial art. According to the technological theory, a thoroughly naturalistic art is that towards which all the ages aspire; according to the perceptual theory, it is that which they all effortlessly achieve. The question to which the two latter theories presuppose an answer arises in an explicit and inescapable fashion for anyone who takes seriously the theory of seeing and knowing. That question is, Is naturalism possible? For it is on this possibility that all three theories seem to be founded.

3. To the question, Is naturalism possible? Gombrich's answer might be said to be yes and no. Yes, naturalism is possible; but no, what is commonly assumed to be naturalism is impossible. I shall take the second part of Gombrich's answer, or his attack upon what he calls "neutral naturalism," first. By "neutral naturalism" Gombrich would have us understand a form of art within which individual works can, outside any reference to style or convention, be regarded as *the* portrayal of a particular scene or incident, in which every stroke of the pen or brush is uniquely determined by what is given to the senses. Such a form of art is, Gombrich maintains, a fiction. "There is no neutral naturalism," he writes.[3] And to establish this point, which

[3]*A & I*, p. 75.

engages him intermittently through *Art and Illusion*, he uses three different kinds of argument.

In the first place Gombrich employs arguments—most of them familiar enough but here restated with fine lucidity—which relate to the limitation of the artist's media. Take, for instance, the essential problem of colour. Nature produces, as we are all aware, a vast range of chromatic effects, and to achieve this she has at her disposal two variables: local colour, that is the actual colour of the object, and light, the ever-changing light that plays on the object. The painter, by contrast—and this is a fact of which we sometimes lose sight—has only one resource: the actual colour of his pigment, which is always seen in, or at any rate as if it were in, standard conditions. The light in a gallery or a drawing-room may vary, brighten and fade, but such fluctuations are something with which the picture has to contend, not something that the painter can make use of. However, even if *per impossibile* the painter were able to match what he sees area for area, it still does not follow that there would be an identity of colour, or match, between the picture and the scene it depicts. For to assume this in the first place ignores the fact that (apparent) tone varies with size, so that a small patch painted with one pigment will most likely not resemble a larger patch painted with the same pigment:[4] and it is of course most unlikely that a painting will be life-size with its subject. Secondly, the "mosaic theory of representation," as Gombrich calls it at one point,[5] leaves out of account the further fact that (apparent) tone is affected by the relations between the areas.[6] In this context Gombrich cites the "spreading effect" in the famous Von Bezold arabesque. But this is only a singularly striking demonstration of the more general truth that, if you alter the relation between two shapes, they will look different even if they are of the same local colour. And it seems inevitable that the relation between two shapes on a flat canvas will be different from those which exist between the two elements in reality that they are supposed to represent.

The second set of arguments that Gombrich employs against neutral naturalism relate to the phrase "what we really see." For it must be evident that the artistic ideal of portraying things as we really see them, or of setting down what we really see—and it is around this ideal that neutral naturalism is constructed—could not long survive a demonstration that the phrase "what we really see" has no clear reference. It seems to be an aim of Gombrich's to provide such a demonstration.

I must say now that I do not follow all of Gombrich's argument on this point, but I get the impression that much of it does not really engage the target upon which he wishes to direct it. For whereas what he claims to be attacking is the proposition that in all cases of seeing there is something that we really see, the proposition that much of the time he in fact attacks is a more specific one: namely, that there is some *one* thing that in all cases of seeing is what we really see. In other words, Gombrich flings down his challenge in the direction of the very general thesis that all our vision has a determinate object. But the thesis that he actually fights and (I would say) conclusively defeats is one that accepts this and then goes on to identify this object in a special way with a configuration of flat coloured patches lying in a two-dimensional field. And this

[4] *A & I*, pp. 262–3.
[5] *A & I*, p. 263.
[6] *A & I*, pp. 259–62.

is, of course, merely a particular version or interpretation of the more general thesis. One could continue to think that in all cases of vision there *is* something that we really see, without thinking that it is always something of a specific and identical kind and *a fortiori* without thinking that it is of the kind that, traditionally, empiricist philosophers and psychologists have thought it to be. One could agree (and I am sure one should) with Gombrich that, "We do not observe the appearance of colour patches and then proceed to interpret their meaning,"[7] without being forced to maintain that there is nothing that we really observe.

There are passages in *Art and Illusion* where Gombrich certainly shows himself aware of the difference between the avowed and the real object of his criticism. So, for instance, he writes, "We 'really' see distance not changes in size: we 'really' see light, not modifications of tone; and most of all we really see a brighter face and not a change in muscular contractions";[8] and championing Constable's naturalism he writes, "What Constable 'really' saw in Wivenhoe Park was surely a house across a lake"[9] as opposed presumably to a "flat patchwork of colours" which Gombrich had just denounced as being a fabrication of false theory. Now in these passages Gombrich explicitly admits that there is something we really see, and if he still insists on placing inverted commas around the word "really," this is no more than a pious tribute he pays to the more extreme thesis that he advocates elsewhere: namely, that whenever we see, there is nothing at all of which it can properly be said that it is what we really see.

Of this more extreme thesis I shall have something to say later. Here I shall only point out a feature of Gombrich's presentation that facilitates the confusion between them. And that is his use of one and the same formulation to cover the limited and the extreme thesis: namely, that all seeing is interpretation. What suitability this phrase has for expressing the more far-reaching thesis I shall consider when I come to consider that thesis. The justice that the phrase does to the more moderate thesis is that it catches the fact, presumably essential to that thesis, that what we see is always partly determined by the concept or concepts that we bring to the perception. It is because of this that (as the thesis maintains) there is not one thing that we always see, which might have been plausible if what we saw were entirely determined by the brute facts of the case.

On the question whether the limited thesis is in any way fatal to neutral naturalism I find it difficult to arrive at a stable opinion: partly because the theory of neutral naturalism is itself somewhat indeterminate. What the thesis certainly does is to weaken the naturalistic ideal considerably, by breaking any connection that one might have supposed to exist between it and a specific or identifiable style—for instance, Impressionism. For, if there is no one kind of thing that we really see whenever we see, then the art that sets out to depict what we really see will not have any consistent look; there is no pictorial manner in which we can say *a priori* that a naturalistic painter should work. It certainly seems as though in the three theories of artistic change that we have considered there was such an assumption: and, moreover, that this assumption is also at work in calling naturalism "neutral."

The third and final line of argument that Gombrich brings against neutral naturalism derives from the role of projection in our vision of art. For, even if the artist were able to set down on the canvas an image that literally resembled exactly what he had

[7]*A & I*, p. 219.
[8]*A & I*, p. 282.
[9]*A & I*, p. 278.

seen, there would be no certainty as to how the spectator would see the image. For the image would be ambiguous: and ambiguous not just in the theoretical sense that it *could be* seen in different ways, but in the practical sense (though Gombrich is not always careful to keep these two senses apart) that it almost certainly *would be* seen in different ways. Strictly speaking, this fact need not be seen as an objection to neutral naturalism when this is defined, as it was above, as a form of art in which every stroke was uniquely determined by what was given to the eye. But such a definition, I suggest, seemed satisfactory because it seemed natural to assume that if there was a one–one correspondence between what the eye saw and what the hand did in obedience to it, there would also be a one–one correspondence between what the hand had done and what the eye would then see of what it had done. If what is uniquely transcribed may be ambiguously perceived, naturalism as a pictorial aim has lost much of its point.

4. At this stage of the argument, however, when naturalism appears to be fatally trapped, Gombrich suddenly calls off the chase. For has not the argument gone too far? "The old insight that it is naïve to demand that a painting should look real is gradually giving way to the conviction that it is naïve to believe any painting can ever look real."[10] And such a conviction, however ingeniously argued for, must ultimately be absurd. For do we not unhesitatingly regard some painters as more realistic than others—Masaccio, say, than Cimabue, or Gainsborough than Perugino? Are there not even certain painters, like Constable or Monet, whom we consider to have achieved about as much in the mastery of appearance as is humanly possible?

The problem, then, is not so much the existence as the definition of naturalism: for if there is a respectable form of naturalism, it cannot be the neutral naturalism whose discomfiture we have observed. At this juncture Gombrich suggests a redefinition of naturalism in terms of the information that the picture conveys. To say, for instance, that a drawing of Tivoli is correct or truthful means "that those who understand the notation will derive *no false information* from the drawing."[11]

This redefinition has two great merits. In the first place it respects the simple logical point that truth and falsehood cannot properly be predicated of objects: strictly speaking, they are properties of statements and, if we loosely talk of a picture as correct or truthful, this is an oblique way of talking about a certain set of assertions that can be derived from the picture.[12] The question then arises, What assertions are we entitled to derive from a picture?—or, to put it another way, How much of the picture are we justified in interpreting or decoding? And this connects with the second merit of Gombrich's redefinition, namely that it emphasizes the "conventional" element in any form of naturalism. For, in order to know how much of the picture is to be decoded, we must be acquainted with the convention or—to use a locution which Gombrich at one point[13] insists is "more than a loose metaphor"—with the "language" or "vocabulary" in which the picture is composed. For instance, it would be quite erroneous to infer from the fact that our drawing of Tivoli is correct "that Tivoli is bounded by wiry lines."[14] To make such an inference would be to misunderstand the contour-convention in a drawing.

[10]A & I, p. 209.
[11]A & I, p. 78; cf. p. 252.
[12]A & I, p. 59.
[13]A & I, p. 76.
[14]A & I, p. 78.

From Gombrich's redefinition of naturalism two consequences important for his general theory are derived. The first is that, though certain forms of art are clearly non-naturalistic, there is no unique form of naturalistic art towards which all forms of representational painting approximate to a greater or lesser degree. To posit the existence of such a style would be to make two further assumptions. First, that the conveying of information is a simple cumulative task, so that a picture containing a certain amount of information could always be revised so as to convey some further piece of information. But it may be that some information can be conveyed only at the expense of omitting other information: in constructing a picture we may have to make a choice. Indeed, Gombrich points out not merely that this may be so, but that in fact it is so—and he illustrates his point ingeniously by comparing three representations of a boat, one by Duccio, one by Constable and one by Turner, and he shows how, as we cast our eye across the paintings in historical sequence, we get progressively more information about the appearance of the boat as at a certain moment and in a certain light, and progressively less information about the structure of the boat. We are told new things at the price of having to take familiar things for granted. And the second assumption that seems to be involved in the idea of a unique naturalistic art is that there is only one way of conveying a given piece of information. But this also is clearly false. "The world may be approached from a different angle and the information given may yet be the same."[15]

The other consequence of this revised conception of naturalism is that we can now see that a "correct" or "truthful" form of art could not conceivably have been the starting-point of artistic evolution. Defined as it is, it could only be "the end product" of a long process of trial and error.

And here at last we have the stage set for Gombrich's account of the evolution of representational art: the theory of "making and matching." In the beginning, the artist makes a diagram of what he wants to depict—a crude model which, for those who understand it, succeeds in conveying a modicum of information about its object: a schema. Gradually, however, as the schema is matched against the object, deficiencies in its informativeness are brought to light. Suggestions are made as to how these deficiencies could be made good, and both the accuracy and the amount of the information it provided be increased; and so we have the schema corrected. The corrected schema, however, also has its deficiencies, and so the process of making and matching, of schema and correction, unfolds itself. At each step the resultant schema can always be said to be more lifelike than the schema of which it is a correction. And so it might seem that, as the process enters an advanced stage, we attain to an art of verisimilitude, a fully fledged naturalism. And so, in an historical sense, we do. But we should not conclude from this that, if only we had used our eyes properly in the first place, this kind of naturalism could have come into being without the long, painful struggle that led up to it. For such a conclusion would not merely be false: it would be absurd.

5. But, we might reasonably ask, Absurd in what sense? What kind of impropriety would attach to the supposition that representational art did not evolve in accordance with the principle of schema and correction? In other words, what is the status of Gombrich's hypothesis?

[15]*A & I*, p. 78.

It must be admitted at the outset that on this point Gombrich himself is by and large unenlightening. In various places he talks of the "psychology" of artistic procedure as though his theory were a contribution to our understanding of how the artists's mind actually works. But I do not think that this could really be his intention, for, if it were, one consequence would be that his hypothesis would be purely empirical. It would rest simply on observed fact, and would be overthrown if it could be shown that some artists worked or had worked in a way other than that of schema and correction. But I do not think that Gombrich really envisages the possibility of a counter-example to his hypothesis, and this suggests that he puts it forward as a logical not as a psychological theory.

In the preface to the second edition of *Art and Illusion* Gombrich addresses himself to the problem, and what he says is revealing. "I am grateful," he writes,

> to one of my painter friends who helped me to formulate my problem afresh by asking me to tell quite simply what would be the opposite of the view I hold. It would be a state of affairs in which every person wielding a brush could always achieve fidelity to nature. The mere desire to preserve the likeness of a beloved person or of a beautiful view would then suffice for the artist to "copy what he sees."[16]

Now here Gombrich seems to suggest that things might have been otherwise than as they are, that there is a constructable alternative to the situation that obtains: in fact we cannot achieve instant fidelity to nature, but that possibility isn't ruled out as a matter of logic. Such seems to be Gombrich's suggestion. But if the argument of *Art and Illusion* has established anything so far, it is, surely, that the notion of fidelity to nature, taken in some absolute sense, i.e. otherwise than by relation to some prior process of schema and correction, must be absurd. And, if this is so, then any account that includes this notion must be absurd. So, in purporting to answer his friend's question, Gombrich is in effect saying that there is no fully coherent opposite of the view that he holds. For, in the ultimate analysis, the idea of representation necessarily involves the idea of trial and error. It is not merely that in the history of art, as we have it, making always does in point of fact precede matching, but that making must precede matching.

But, if making must precede matching, what this means is that we cannot have matching without (i.e. without being preceded by) making. But it does not mean that we cannot have making without (i.e. without being succeeded by) matching. Now, this asymmetry is of great importance to Gombrich, for it is in virtue of it that the hypothesis of making and matching acquires its secondary role in his system: that of an historical as well as a logical principle. In Chapters IV and V Gombrich attempts to define certain very general phases in the history of art by reference to the degree to which making was linked with matching.

In Egyptian art making was virtually independent of matching. And this was because of the peculiar function that the Egyptians attached to the image. As far as we can reconstruct the situation their main concern would seem to have been not to secure a representation of an aspect or element of life—which would naturally have led them to correct the image, once they had made it, in the interests of verisimilitude—but simply to make an object. It is only with "the Greek revolution" that we have the desire for an

---

[16]*A & I*, p. xii.

image that not merely existed but was "convincing," that not merely stood for itself but also spoke of things outside itself; and it is at this juncture that, for the first time, we come across the restless, dissatisfied reappraisal of the object with the constant aim of bringing it closer and closer to the reality it attempts to mirror.

Again, Gombrich suggests that the connection between making and matching can be used to bring out the difference between medieval and post-medieval art. For in the Middle Ages the impact of "the Greek revolution" was comparatively spent. The image was still regarded as primarily representational, but there was no longer that burning discontent with each and every effort to make it convey information about the world. For this we have to wait till the Renaissance. "To the Middle Ages," Gombrich writes, "the schema is the image; to the post-medieval artist, it is the starting point for corrections, adjustments, adaptations, the means to probe reality and to wrestle with the particular."[17] Between the Middle Ages and the world of the contemporary artist there lies a period where not only is matching always preceded by making (as it must be), but making is always followed by matching. In this period occurred the apogee of European naturalism.

6. This highly compressed summary of Gombrich's doctrine might suggest an obvious title for his book: *Art and Naturalism.* Yet if we look to the book, we find it called something quite different: *Art and Illusion.* Nor is this a mere vagary. For when we go on to examine the text itself we find that, throughout, the two sets of terms, "naturalism," "naturalistic" on the one hand, "illusion," "illusionistic" on the other, are used interchangeably. And there corresponds to this linguistic practice a substantive doctrine. It appears to be Gombrich's considered view that, within certain limitations, naturalism *is* illusion, and that a painting is to be regarded as more naturalistic the more effective it is in creating its illusion.

Total effectiveness will of course seldom be within its reach: "that such illusions are rarely complete goes without saying," Gombrich concedes.[18] And there are reasons for this, some of which at any rate in no way reflect upon the skill of the artist. In the first place, there is the setting or context in which the work of art is displayed, which almost invariably will provide a contrast with the work itself. As the eye passes over the picture, across the frame, to the wall on which it is placed, it cannot but become aware, however cunning the painting may be, of a discrepancy or discontinuity which is fatal to the illusion. In this connection Gombrich refers to the work of Baroque decorators or *quadratisti,* who were as successful as anyone could be in overcoming these difficulties: and he points out how their choice of subject-matter—the sky, a frieze, a cornice, always something which might actually have existed in the very place where it is portrayed—was guided by their determination to reduce or blur as much as possible "the transition between the solidly built and the flatly painted."[19]

Secondly, there is the fact that a two-dimensional illusion can only ever work for a stationary eye. Not only must the eye not take in the setting or context of the picture, but it must not move either inside the picture or relative to the picture. For then the illusion could be maintained only be ever-shifting modifications in the perspectival profiles of what is depicted, which of course will not occur. "As soon as we move,"

[17]*A & I,* p. 148.
[18]*A & I,* p. 234.
[19]*A & I,* p. 221.

Gombrich writes apropos of a Fantin-Latour, "the illusion must disappear, since the objects in the still life will not shift in relation to each other."[20]

Finally, even if the visual illusion is complete—that is, it works for a stationary eye whose field of vision is wholly contained within the picture frame—it is unlikely to be accompanied by all those other "expectations" which are, according to Gombrich, an integral part of our recognizing or identifying something as an object of a certain kind: expectations of what we would see if we moved, of what we would feel if we reached out our hand. "All perceiving relates to expectations," Gombrich writes,[21] and he describes how all painters from the Greeks onwards have struggled to supplement the direct pictorial effects that were within their power with induced expectations. Yet these expectations, even when induced, hang by the slightest thread. We might feel that, if we craned our neck a little, the dinner plate would then look circular, or that, if we reached out our hand, we could succeed in touching the bloom—but we have only to try to crane our neck or to contemplate reaching out our hand, we have only to test the expectations the smallest bit and they evaporate and with them the completeness of the illusion.

Gombrich allows, then, that very few naturalistic paintings are totally illusionistic. "Only in extreme cases . . . are the illusions of art illusions about our real environment."[22] But this seems not to go against the view, for he continues to adhere to it, that naturalism depends upon illusion. The illusion may invariably break down: but then who says that a painting is ever totally naturalistic? It would seem an accurate formulation of Gombrich's thought to say that for him naturalism is an approximation to illusion, so that the more naturalistic a painting is, the more illusionistic it is, but that in practice naturalism is partial illusion—an illusion, that is, as successful and sustained as the medium permits.

Such a conception of naturalism is, it seems to me, quite untenable. In the first place it is clearly impossible for Gombrich to hold to such a conception, for it is quite inconsistent with the rest of his thought. Not merely is it out of line with his general notion of art as something conventional, which, for instance, offers up its secrets only to those who "understand the notation,"[23] but more specifically it makes total nonsense of the definition he offers elsewhere of naturalism. For a picture, it will be recalled, is said to be naturalistic in so far as it conveys (or, more precisely, in so far as there can be derived from it) correct information. But how can we be said to gain information about an object from something that we take to be that object? A *trompe l'œil* painting of a duck, for instance, cannot, at least as long as it succeeds in being *trompe l'œil*, tell us anything about a duck: it is no more informative about a duck than the duck itself would be. If we are to talk meaningfully of information, we must be able to discriminate between, on the one hand, the medium of communication and, on the other hand, the referent or what is communicated.

But quite apart from issues of consistency within a particular system, which relate specifically to Gombrich, there are other and stronger reasons for rejecting the equation of naturalism with illusion: if, that is to say, we take illusion literally, which I

---

[20] *A & I*, p. 234.
[21] *A & I*, p. 254.
[22] *A & I*, p. 234.
[23] *A & I*, p. 90.

maintain we are required to do by the theory. In the first place such an equation completely distorts the attitude that we adopt to naturalistic painting.[24] It is surely quite untrue to suggest that, in looking at the masterpieces of Constable or Monet, we have any temptation, even a partial or inhibited temptation, to react towards them in a way similar to that in which we would to the objects they represent: that we in any way wish to stretch out a hand and join in the picnic, or to assume dark glasses against the glare of the sun.

Not only is Gombrich's conception of naturalism false to our ordinary attitude to paintings of this kind, but also—more seriously I should say—it conceals or distorts the kind of admiration that we feel for them. When we admire the great achievements of naturalistic art we do so because we think of them as very lifelike representations of objects in the real world: but to think of them in this way is clearly quite incompatible with taking them to be or seeing them as (in, if you like, the most attenuated sense of either of these two expressions) the objects themselves. Indeed, if we took the picture of an object to be that object, what would there be left for us to admire?

Of course, Gombrich does not explicitly deny what he appears to be denying: namely, that we admire naturalistic pictures as pictures. Yet, I maintain, in substance he does—at any rate in the sections about illusion—and I think that why he is able to do this is because of the particular analysis he gives of what it is to see something as a picture of an object. For Gombrich, to see something as a picture of an object is to see it sometimes as a picture and sometimes as that object. To admire something as a good or naturalistic picture of an object is to say something about the speed or facility with which we can move between these two different ways of seeing it.

But now we must ask, Why does Gombrich analyse what it is to see something as a picture of an object in this particular way? And to understand his answer here—which is, roughly, that any other suggestion would be absurd or self-contradictory—we must consider a notion that plays an important role at this stage in the argument: and this is what Gombrich calls "the inherent ambiguity of all images."[25] We have already touched on this point, but we now need to look at it in greater detail.

For part of the time what Gombrich means by talking of ambiguity is quite clear. He introduces the notion at the very beginning of the book by a consideration of the now famous duck-rabbit figure: a drawing which originally appeared in *Die Fliegenden Blätter* and which can, when accurately reproduced, indifferently be seen as a duck (turned to the left) or a rabbit (turned to the right).

Later on Gombrich illustrates the notion by reference to the outline drawing of a hand, of which it is impossible to tell whether it is a right hand seen from the front or a left hand seen from the back. Having introduced the notion of "ambiguity" by means of these special cases, Gombrich then goes on to point out[26] that in one significant respect all configurations drawn on a flat surface are ambiguous. For, if we take any given configuration, there is an infinity of shapes in space of which it is the correct

---

[24]I mean by this the psychological attitude that we adopt. My argument would not be affected by any demonstration that, in looking at a picture where a river is depicted as being behind a tree, the eye makes the same kind of accommodation movement as if the river were actually farther away than the tree. (This note is stimulated by an observation made by Gombrich in private discussion.)

[25]*A & I*, p. 211.

[26]*A & I*, pp. 209–17.

Duck-rabbit figure

perspectival profile. Of course, if the angle and distance from the spectator are known, the shape is determined—just as ordinarily, assuming the shape to be a conventional or familiar one, we can work out the angle and distance. But, if the angle and distance are not determined, we must in principle allow the shape to have any one of an infinite number of values. In this sense, then, all configurations are ambiguous.

So far, I think, everything is clear. Starting from a few particular cases which he characterizes as being ambiguous, Gombrich soon extends the application of the concept. But in doing so he extends only its denotation, and he leaves its meaning or its connotation intact. The feature in virtue of which the duck-rabbit figure, or the drawing of a hand, or all perspectival profiles, can be described as ambiguous is in each case the same: that is, that the figure can be seen in two or more ways, but that it cannot be seen in more than one way at once. This point is expressed by Gombrich at several places by saying that "ambiguity . . . can never be seen as such."[27]

But from the very beginning of the book Gombrich assimilates to these cases, and wishes to subsume under the concept of ambiguity, another feature that is universally possessed by images: namely, that they are both pictures (canvas) and of things (nature). Just as the duck-rabbit figure can be seen sometimes as a duck and sometimes as a rabbit, so a picture can be seen sometimes as canvas and sometimes as nature. It was the achievement of the earliest artists, Gombrich writes, that "instead of playing 'rabbit or duck' they had to invent the game of 'canvas or nature' ":[28] and he thereby suggests that the two games are identical in structure. Later the point is made more specifically. "Is it possible," he asks,

> to "see" both the plane surface and the battle horse at the same time? If we have been right so far, the demand is for the impossible. To understand the battle horse is for a moment to disregard the plane surface. We cannot have it both ways.[29]

But why does Gombrich assume that we can no more see a picture simultaneously as canvas and as nature than we can see the duck-rabbit figure simultaneously as a duck and as a rabbit? Because—it might be said—canvas and nature are different in-

[27]*A & I*, p. 211; cf. pp. 198, 200, 223.
[28]*A & I*, p. 24.
[29]*A & I*, p. 237.

terpretations. But, if this is Gombrich's argument, it is invalid. For the reason why we cannot see the duck-rabbit figure simultaneously as a duck and as a rabbit is not because "duck" and "rabbit" are two different interpretations, it is because they are two incompatible interpretations. Gombrich is correct when he writes, "We can train ourselves to switch more rapidly, indeed to oscillate between readings, but we cannot hold conflicting interpretations."[30] But it does not follow from this that we cannot hold different interpretations. For Gombrich's specific argument about canvas or nature to be effective, he requires a criterion for distinguishing between conflicting or (as I have called them) incompatible interpretations and merely different interpretations. Gombrich offers no such criterion and, in its absence, he has no right to insist, against common sense, that seeing something as a picture of an object *must be* sometimes to see it as a picture and sometimes to see it as that object. He has no right, in other words, to assert that the picture is ambiguous in the sense in which the figure in the picture is: for so far all he has established about what the two cases have in common is that in both multiple interpretation is possible.

Finally, I should like to consider two lines of thought in Gombrich's book which more indirectly relate to his equation of naturalism with illusion: one which might have led him into the belief, the other which might have helped to sustain him in it. The first is to do with Gombrich's use of the notion of "projection." For Gombrich emphasizes, surely rightly, the immense importance of projection in the viewing of naturalistic art. But under the general heading of projection he brings together (I want to suggest) phenomena which, though they can be arranged on a scale, need also to be distinguished rather carefully: by assimilating the phenomena that lie on one end of the scale to those which lie on the other, Gombrich finds support for his view that naturalism is illusion. The variety of phenomenon he has in mind is illustrated by the three examples that he gives of projection. First, the case of Shadow Antiqua lettering, in which letters are indicated only by what would be their shaded side if they were formed of ribbons standing up, but where we tend to see a top to each letter. Secondly, there is the case of the Giandomenico.

ILLUSION

Shadow Antiqua

Tiepolo etching where we read the garments of St. Joseph and the Virgin Mary as coloured (even if indeterminately coloured). And finally there is the case of *all* representative painting,[31] of Frith as well as of Manet,[32] of Van Eyck[33] as well as the Impressionists, for throughout we project on to the dabs of paint people and objects as they exist in the world. But "projection" here has no single simple core of meaning, though all the cases may have what is called a family resemblance. In the case of the Shadow Antiqua lettering we see something that definitely is not there: in the case of

[30]*A & I*, p. 198.
[31]*A & I*, pp. 158, 170, 191.
[32]*A & I*, p. 181.
[33]*A & I*, p. 184.

Van Eyck, or even Manet, the most that can be said is that we would not see what we do if it were not for something outside, or in addition to, the "visual situation." In the first kind of case there is a genuine deception: in that the beliefs of the man who makes the projection will be incompatible with those of the man who does not. In the third kind of case there is no such deception: and correspondingly there is no divergence in belief between the man who makes the projection and the man who cannot make head or tail of an Impressionist or even of a Quattrocento painting. By assimilating the latter kind of case to the former, by subsuming all cases of projection under the single pattern provided by the reading of Shadow Antiqua, Gombrich is drawn towards the view that to look at naturalistic art is to experience a kind of illusion.

The second line of thought to which it seems to me some responsibility must be attributed for Gombrich's equation of naturalism with illusion, at least in that it sustains him in this position, is connected with a view of his about perception, which I have already referred to but so far delayed considering. I referred to it as the more extreme version of the thesis that all seeing is interpretation, and I said that this is a view to which Gombrich adheres some of the time but not all the time. In the next section I shall consider the view itself in some detail, but I want here to anticipate that discussion to the extent of pointing out one consequence that the view would appear to have. If we accept the view, then we seem committed to assigning to perception, in part at least, a subjective or arbitrary character: it cannot, in its entirety, be checked against experience. If I am right in this, then it would look as though someone inclined to accept this view would be comparatively undisturbed by one kind, and perhaps the most obvious kind, of objection to the equation of naturalism with illusion. That the perception of pictures should involve deception will seem much easier to accept if it has already been conceded that deception is something in which all perception participates to some degree or other.—But now I can delay no longer considering that view of perception which has this for its consequence.

7. In any comprehensive analysis of *Art and Illusion*, it is not possible to pass over Gombrich's more extreme theory of perception. For though it is in itself only a minor theme in the book, as well as one to which Gombrich is only intermittently committed, it emerges from, and remains so entwined with, the major theme, that if it were ignored, the examination of the other would be incomplete.

By the major theme of *Art and Illusion*, I mean Gombrich's account of artistic change, or his answer to the question, Why has art a history? As we have seen, his account is that aesthetic change occurs by means of the mechanism of schema and correction. Without some initial schema, which gradually, step by step, we correct and refine, we would never arrive at anything reasonably naturalistic in the arts.

However, having set out this account of artistic change, Gombrich then goes on to propose a parallel account of perception: an account, that is, according to which perception displays the same pattern. We acquire visual knowledge of the world by first applying schemata to it and then correcting and refining them in accordance with anticipations rewarded or frustrated, until we arrive at an undisturbed or, as we might say, "naturalistic" vision. "The very process of perception," Gombrich writes, "is based on the same rhythm that we found governing the process of representation: the rhythm of schema and correction."[34]

---

[34]*A & I*, p. 231.

The question arises, What is the relation between these two isomorphic theories? At first it might seem that this more general theory about schema and correction provides some kind of confirmation for the specific theory. For, if the phenomenon of schema and correction is very widespread, as widespread as vision itself, it is not surprising—one might think—that it is to be found also in the more limited domain of art. Gombrich himself is sometimes of this view: and it is, of course, when he is of this view that he is particularly inclined to assert the schema-correction theory of perception. Against this I want to argue that, if we believe perception to embody the process of schema and correction—where (note) these two latter notions are used in just the same sense as that in which they are said to determine artistic change—then, in the first place, so far from having a theory that gives support to the theory of artistic change, we will have one that is incompatible with it, and, secondly, the theory that we get will be quite inadequate to perception. The two points are related.

The theory of artistic change asserts that we move towards naturalism in art by means of the progressive correction of schematic images. We make a schema that is intended to represent a certain object: we observe the schema and then correct it so as to bring it more into line with the object. Now, for such a theory to hold good, there must at some point be what we might call an "exit to the object." Without such a possibility any progression within representational art towards verisimilitude would be purely coincidental, and so, in at least one important respect, Gombrich's theory of artistic change would have failed to explain what it was devised to explain. Now, the natural place to locate this exit to the object would be in perception. And this certainly fits in with our ordinary view of perception. Accordingly, if, as I shall argue, the theory that perception too proceeds in accordance with schema and correction means that perception cannot provide this exit to the object, we can see how the theory is at one and the same time at odds with the theory of artistic change advanced in *Art and Illusion* and false to the nature of perception.

So the question arises whether it is indeed the case that, if the schema-correction process is thought to give the nature of perception, this would have the effect of enclosing perception within itself, of denying it its essential character. I think that there are two ways—both perhaps somewhat oblique—of showing that some such consequence holds.

The first is to contrast the analysis of perception in terms of schema and correction with the corresponding analysis of representation. I have already said something about this: The analysis fits for representation because we can assign a clear meaning to the notion of correction. If we are to talk of the correction of schemata, then there must be available an appeal to something outside the circle of *those* schemata: when the schemata in question are representational, we can clearly envisage such a possibility, and it is consequently on this possibility that the fittingness of the analysis to representation rests. However, when the analysis is re-applied to perception, the situation is radically transformed. For now there seems no possibility of an appeal to anything outside the circle of schemata that the analysis proposes. The only appeal that seems possible is one within the circle, i.e. from one perceptual schema to another. And this, which seems to have no claim to be thought of as correction, will ensure that perception is a purely hermetic activity. At this stage it might be argued that we should understand the notion of schema altogether differently in the context of perception from how we do in the context of representation: but that is to go outside the original terms of the argument. The charm, and the value, of a unitary analysis has been lost. The situation might be put more generally, thus: Representation is a parasitic phenomenon, and that is one reason why the schema-correction analysis suits it. Perception— which is that on which representation is parasitic—is a self-correcting phenomenon. And it is inadequate to apply the analysis that fits the former kind of phenomenon to the latter kind, with simply the adjustment that, in the new case, any reference to anything outside the phenomenon is blocked. For we haven't thereby arrived at a self-correcting process, we have, rather, an incorrigible process.

The second way of bringing out the unacceptable consequences of analysing perception in terms of schema and correction is to contrast this analysis of perception with another analysis of perception. The other analysis is one which, as we have already seen, Gombrich accepts for much of the time. I have referred to it as the more limited version of the thesis that seeing is interpretation, and we are now in a position to recognize that the schema-correction analysis of perception can be equated with the more extreme version of the thesis—though some of the difficulty in *Art and Illusion* comes from the fact that Gombrich does not always recognize the difference between the two analyses.

Now, on the first analysis—or the more moderate version of the thesis that seeing is interpretation—it follows that when I see x, I always see x as y: where, of course, x and y may be identical. On the extreme version of the thesis—or the schema-correction analysis of perception—it follows that when I see x, I always see a schema of x: where *ex hypothesi* x and a schema of x cannot be identical. Now, the first of these two views clearly allows for correction. For when I see x as y, I might learn that I am committing an error, i.e. in how I see x: for the fact that I see x provides me with grounds for such correction. But (apart from its internal incoherence) the second analysis cuts me off from any such possibility. For when I see a schema of x, I don't see x—if, that is, x and the schema of x can never be identical.

Someone, it is true, might take up this last point and suggest, very reasonably, that, when "I see a schema of x" is given as the analysis of "I see x," it must be wrong to understand "a schema of x" in such a way that x and a schema of x can never be identical. And the suggestion might be made that an adequate account of perception could be made out in terms of schema and correction, if "a schema of x" were understood as more or less synonymous with "a schematized x." And taken in this way, the analysis clearly would provide for what in principle it insists on: namely, the possibility of correction. However, while I am in sympathy with this suggestion it does not preserve the parallelism between the schemata of representation and the schemata of perception which is central to Gombrich's case. For the schemata in terms of which representation is analysed cannot be understood in a parallel way. Clearly it could be no part of an analysis, or indeed explanation, of representation to say that when I represent x, I set down a schematized x. For "setting down a schematized x" still contains within it the problematic notion of representation: for the only sense in which, when I represent x, I set down "an x" (schematized or otherwise) is that in which I set down a representation of an x. I conclude, therefore, that if we adhere to a consistent interpretation of the notions of schema and correction, we have once again reason for thinking that we cannot interpret perception as well as representation in terms of them without making perception a hermetic process: which would make not merely perception directly, but representation indirectly, incomprehensible.

8. The strength of *Art and Illusion* must, then, rest upon its major theme: that of the necessary connection between the progress of representation in art, on the one hand, and the employment of pictorial schemata, on the other.

How effective the thesis is for resolving Gombrich's central problem is something that we have already considered. The thesis provides a clue to the question why representational art has a history—though, of course, it makes no attempt to answer the more specific question why art has the particular history that it has. But, even within this limited, though by no means narrow, context the thesis still has at least one residual difficulty. Representational art owes its history, we are told, to the use of pictorial schemata. But what is a schema? Now it is fairly clear what Gombrich does not mean by talking of a "schema." And it is fairly clear what, in a very rough way, he does mean. But to say exactly what he means is not without its difficulties. I am not going to say that Gombrich uses the word in different senses. That would be un-warranted. But what I think would be true to say is that at different times he seems to be working under different conceptions of what a typical instance of a schema would be, and these different conceptions lead to an elusiveness in the thesis taken as a whole.

(i) The most ordinary and the most evident thing that Gombrich has in mind when he talks of "a schema" is any form or configuration that an artist uses to represent, depict, portray an object in the world. In this context a schema has no special degree of complexity or sophistication; it can vary from the simple diagrammatic shapes em-ployed by Gombrich's niece in her delightful copy after Wivenhoe Park to the minutely detailed (though, as it turned out, quite inaccurate) image of the whale which figures in the two engravings (c. 1600), one Italian, one Dutch, which Gom-brich reproduces. It is in this general, extended usage of "schemata" that Morellian connoisseurship might be said to be characteristically concerned with the morphology of a particular sub-set of schemata: roughly, those used to portray certain parts of the body (notably, the hand and ear) or certain natural objects.

(ii) At other times, Gombrich in talking of schemata has in mind forms or con-figurations that satisfy a further condition: namely, that they are highly simplified. The divided oval or egg-shape as an abbreviation of the human head—a matter on which Gombrich has some highly illuminating things to say[35]—is a typical example of a schema in this sense; and it is, I think, very significant that in so far as Gombrich writes or thinks under the direction of this conception of the typical schema, he identifies "schematic" art with what used to be called "conceptual" art.[36]

(iii) At yet other times Gombrich works with a very different conception indeed of what a schema is, and this is when he identifies schemata with those very general and elusive elements which conjointly make up what we call a style. For instance, in the course of describing Constable's artistic evolution, Gombrich talks of the painter's "dissatisfaction with ready-made idyllic schemata, his wish to go beyond them and discover visual truth."[37] But what are these "idyllic schemata" which Constable rejected? It is evident from the discussion that they are not to be narrowly identified with particular pictorial devices for portraying such things as distant mountains or spreading oaks and ilex. They are to be taken much more broadly and include things as general and as "non-formal" as the choice of subject-matter, the atmosphere in which

[35]A & I, pp. 144–8.
[36]A & I, e.g. pp. 121–3, 247.
[37]A & I, p. 325.

the subject is invested, and the preference for a kind of all-over finish, or the lack of it, in a composition.

Of course, Gombrich, by employing the word "schema" so generously, brings home to us how different elements in a picture can have a common function. But at a price. At the price, that is, of making the thesis of schema and correction a bit imprecise.

Basically, the hypothesis of schema and correction relates to the first usage of "schema" as equivalent to any configuration employed to represent an object. But the existence of the other two usages I have specified leads to confusion in the following ways. First of all, by not distinguishing clearly between schema as *any* inherited or invented configuration and schema as always an abbreviated or simplified configuration, Gombrich slides from the general view that representation always begins with some configuration into the more specific view that representation always begins with a simplified configuration. In other words, setting out to explain why art has a history at all, he commits himself in an entirely *a priori* way to a specific, though still very broad, account of what that history was: namely, that in the beginning there were simple forms. This commitment emerges clearly in Gombrich's discussion of Palaeolithic art, where he treats the complex cave-paintings of Lascaux as though they provided a *prima facie* counter-example to the thesis of schema and correction: and he feels that he can get around this difficulty and save his thesis only by postulating "thousands of years of image-making" which must have preceded these seemingly early works.[38]

Secondly, Gombrich's use of "schema" to pick out certain highly general pictorial elements such as the preference for one kind of subject-matter or method of illumination rather than another, makes it difficult to see how much of the phenomenon of art Gombrich thinks his thesis covers. For instance, does the hypothesis of schema and correction provide an over-all explanation of "stylistic" change? Whether it does or does not depends, presumably, on the prior question whether a style can be analysed without remainder into a set of schemata. I am sure that, on the whole, Gombrich thinks that it cannot be. But there are passages where he suggests that it can. Until such problems are resolved, the scope of Gombrich's hypothesis remains indeterminate, and to this extent its utility is impaired. . . .

[38]*A & I*, p. 91.

Nelson Goodman

HOW BUILDINGS MEAN

1. Architectural Works

Arthur Schopenhauer ranked the several arts in a hierarchy, with literary and dramatic arts at the top, music soaring in a separate even higher heaven, and architecture sinking to the ground under the weight of beams and bricks and mortar.[1] The governing principle seems to be some measure of spirituality, with architecture ranking lowest by vice of being grossly material.

Nowadays such rankings are taken less seriously. Traditional ideologies and mythologies of the arts are undergoing deconstruction and disvaluation, making way for a neutral comparative study that can reveal a good deal not only about relations among the several arts[2] but also about the kinships and contrasts between the arts, the sciences, and other ways that symbols of various kinds participate in the advancement of the understanding.

In comparing architecture with the other arts, what may first strike us, despite Schopenhauer, is a close affinity with music: architectural and musical works, unlike paintings or plays or novels, are seldom descriptive or representational. With some interesting exceptions, architectural works do not denote—that is, do not describe, recount, depict, or portray. They mean, if at all, in other ways.

On the other hand, an architectural work contrasts with other works of art in scale. A building or park or city[3] is not only bigger spatially and temporally than a musical performance or painting, it is bigger even than we are. We cannot take it all in from a single point of view; we must move around and within it to grasp the whole. Moreover, the architectural work is normally fixed in place. Unlike a painting that may be

Nelson Goodman, "How Buildings Mean," from Reconceptions in Philosophy and Other Arts and Sciences *by Nelson Goodman and Catherine Z. Elgin (Cambridge and Indianapolis: Hackett, 1988).*

Laurie Olin and John Whiteman have given valuable help with the literature of architecture.

[1]See Bryan Magee, *The Philosophy of Schopenhauer* (Oxford: Oxford University Press, 1983), pp. 176–178.

[2]A recent contribution is *Das Laokoon-Projekt*, ed. Gunter Gebauer (Stuttgart: J. V. Metzler, 1984); see especially Gebauer's own essay, "Symbolstrukturen und die Grenzen der Kunst: Zu Lessings Kritik der Darstellungsfähigkeit künstlerischer Symbole," pp. 137–165.

[3]Hereafter I shall ordinarily use "building" as the generic term for all such cases.

reframed or rehung or a concerto that may be heard in different halls, the architectural work is firmly set in a physical and cultural environment that alters slowly.

Finally, in architecture as in few other arts, a work usually has a practical function, such as protecting and facilitating certain activities, that is no less important than, and often dominates, its aesthetic function. The relationship between these two functions ranges from interdependence to mutual reinforcement to outright contention, and can be highly complex.

Before considering some consequences of and questions raised by these characteristics of architecture, perhaps we should ask what a work of architectural art is. Plainly, not all buildings are works of art, and what makes the difference is not merit. The question "What is art?" must not be confused with the question "What is good art?" for most works of art are bad. Nor does being a work of art depend upon the maker's or anyone else's intentions but rather upon how the object in question functions. A building is a work of art only insofar as it signifies, means, refers, symbolizes in some way. That may seem less than obvious, for the sheer bulk of an architectural work and its daily dedication to a practical purpose often tend to obscure its symbolic function. Moreover, some formalist writers preach that pure art must be free of all symbolism, must exist and be looked upon solely in and for itself, and that any reference beyond it amounts virtually to pollution. But this contention, as we shall see, rests upon a cramped conception of reference.

Of course, not all symbolic functioning is aesthetic. A scientific treatise signifies abundantly but is not thereby a work of literary art; a painted sign giving directions is not thereby a work of pictorial art. And a building may mean in ways unrelated to being an architectural work—may become through association a symbol for sanctuary, or for a reign of terror, or for graft. Without attempting to characterize in general the features of symbolic function that distinguish works of art, we can proceed to look at some pertinent ways that architectural works as such symbolize.

2. *Ways of Meaning*

I am neither an architect nor a historian or critic of architecture. My undertaking here is not to evaluate works or to provide canons for evaluation or even to say what is meant by particular works of architecture, but rather to consider how such works may mean, how we determine what they mean, how they work, and why it matters.

The vocabulary of reference and related terms is vast: within a few brief passages from a couple of essays on architecture, we may read of buildings that allude, express, evoke, invoke, comment, quote; that are syntactical, literal, metaphorical, dialectical; that are ambiguous or even contradictory! All these terms and many more, have to do in one way or another with reference and may help us to grasp what a building means. Here I want to outline some distinctions and interrelations among such terms (*Of Mind and Other Matters*, 51–71; *The Roots of Reference*, 141–154). To begin with, the varieties of reference may be grouped under four headings: "denotation," "exemplification," "expression," and "mediated reference."

Denotation includes naming, predication, narration, description, exposition, and also portrayal and all pictorial representation—indeed, any labeling, any application of a symbol of any kind to an object, event, or other instance of it. "Berlin" and a certain postcard both denote Berlin, and so does "city," even though this word denotes other places as well. "Word" denotes many things, including itself.

Buildings are not texts or pictures and usually do not describe or depict. Yet representation does occur in salient ways in some architectural works, notably in Byzantine churches with mosaic-covered interiors and in Romanesque facades that consist almost entirely of sculpture (see Fig. 1). Perhaps even in such cases, we are inclined to say that prominent *parts* of the building represent rather than that the building itself or as a whole represents. As buildings that themselves depict, we may think first of shops that represent a peanut or an ice cream cone or a hot dog, but not all cases are so banal, Jørn Utzon's Opera House (1973) in Sydney is almost as literal a depiction of sailboats, though with a primary concern for form (see Fig. 2). In Arland Dirlam's First Baptist Church (1964) in Gloucester, Massachusetts, a traditional peaked roof is modified and accentuated to reflect the forms of sailboats as we approach from the east; and the frame of the nave, made of curved wood beams, is an inverted image of the skeletons of fishing boats often seen under construction in nearby Essex. Again, the weird towers of Antonio Gaudí's church of the Sagrada Familia (Fig. 3), in Barcelona, are revealed as startling representations when we come upon the tapering conical mountains a few miles away at Montserrat.

Yet since few architectural works depict either as wholes or in part, directly or indirectly, architecture never had to undergo the trauma brought on by the advent of modern abstractionism in painting. In painting, where representation was customary, the absence of representation sometimes left a sense of deprivation and gave rise to both acrid accusations and defiant defenses of meaninglessness; but where representation is not expected, we readily focus upon other kinds of reference. These are no less important in painting or literature—indeed, their presence is a major feature distinguishing literary from nonliterary texts—but they are often somewhat obscured by our concern with what is depicted or described or recounted.

Whether or not a building represents anything, it may exemplify or express certain properties. Such reference runs, not as denotation does, from symbol to what it applies to as label, but in the opposite direction, from symbol to certain labels that apply to it or to properties possessed by it.[4] A commonplace case is a swatch of yellow plaid woolen serving as a sample. The swatch refers not to anything it pictures or describes or otherwise denotes but to its properties of being yellow, plaid, and woolen, or to the words "yellow," "plaid," and "woolen" that denote it. But it does not so exemplify all its properties nor all labels applying to it—not, for instance, its size or shape. The lady who ordered dress material "exactly like the sample" did not want it in two-inch-square pieces with zigzag edges.

Exemplification is one of the major ways that architectural works mean. In formalist architecture it may take precedence over all other ways. According to William H. Jordy, the Dutch architect Gerrit Reitveld (see Fig. 4) "fragmented architecture into primal linear elements (columns, beams, and framing elements for openings) and

---

[4] I shall speak indifferently of properties or labels as being exemplified. For a discussion of this matter, see *Languages of Art*, pp. 54–57.

Figure 1.
Saint Nicholas Church,
Civray, France, 12th Century.
From Nelson Goodman, "How
Buildings Mean," from
Reconceptions in Philosophy
and Other Arts and Sciences
by Nelson Goodman and
Catherine Z. Elgin (Cambridge
and Indianapolis: Hackett,
1988), reprinted with permis-
sion.

Figure 2.
Jørn Utzon,
Opera House, Sydney, 1973.
From Nelson Goodman, "How
Buildings Mean," from
Reconceptions in Philosophy
and Other Arts and Sciences
by Nelson Goodman and
Catherine Z. Elgin (Cambridge
and Indianapolis: Hackett,
1988), reprinted with permis-
sion.

Figure 3.
Antonio Gaudí,
Sagrada Familia Church,
Barcelona, 1882–1930. From
Nelson Goodman, "How
Buildings Mean," from
Reconceptions in Philosophy
and Other Arts and Sciences
by Nelson Goodman and
Catherine Z. Elgin (Cambridge
and Indianapolis: Hackett,
1988), reprinted with permission.

Figure 4.
Gerrit Reitveld, Schroder
House (model), Utrecht, 1924.
From Nelson Goodman, "How
Buildings Mean," from
Reconceptions in Philosophy
and Other Arts and Sciences
by Nelson Goodman and
Catherine Z. Elgin (Cambridge
and Indianapolis: Hackett,
1988), reprinted with permission.

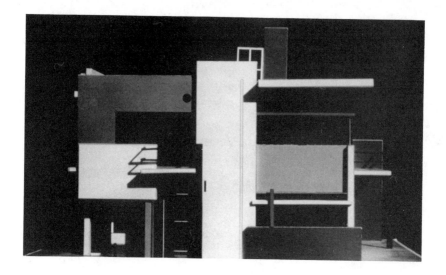

Figure 5.
Balthasar Neumann, Vierzehnheiligen Church, Bamberg, 1743–1772. From Nelson
Goodman, "How Buildings Mean," from Reconceptions in Philosophy and Other Arts and
Sciences *by Nelson Goodman and Catherine Z. Elgin (Cambridge and Indianapolis:*
Hackett, 1988), reprinted with permission.

planes (wall increments) in order to make visible the 'build' of the building."[5] That is,
the building is designed to refer effectively to certain characteristics of its structure. In
other buildings made of columns, beams, frames, and walls, the structure is not thus
exemplified at all, serving only practical and perhaps also other symbolic functions.
But exemplifications of structure may accompany, and either take precedence over or
be subordinate to, other ways of meaning. For instance, reference to structure is not
the primary symbolic function of a church but may play a notable supporting role. Of
the Vierzehnheiligen pilgrimage church near Bamberg (Figs. 5, 6), Christian Norberg-
Schulz writes:

> Analysis shows that two systems have been combined in the layout: a biaxial organism . . . and
> a conventional Latin cross. As the centre of the biaxial layout does not coincide with the
> crossing, an exceptionally strong syncopation results. Over the crossing, where traditionally
> the centre of the church ought to be, the vault is eaten away by the four adjacent baldachins.
> The space defined by the groundplan is thereby transposed relative to space defined by the

[5]William H. Jordy, "Aedicular Modern: The Architecture of Michael Graves," *New Criterion* 2 (October
1983) 46.

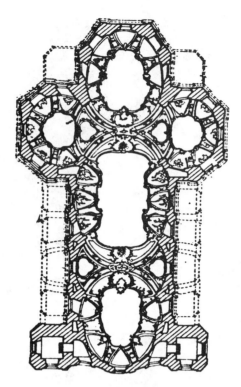

Figure 6.
Ground plan, Vierzehnheiligen Church. From Nelson Goodman, "How Buildings Mean,"
from Reconceptions in Philosophy and Other Arts and Sciences *by Nelson Goodman and*
Catherine Z. Elgin (Cambridge and Indianapolis: Hackett, 1988), reprinted with
permission.

vault and the resulting syncopated interpenetration implies a spatial integration more intimate
than ever before in the history of architecture. This dynamic and ambiguous system of main
spaces is surrounded by a secondary, outer zone, derived from the traditional aisles of the
basilica.[6]

The shape of the church might have been correctly described in many alternative
ways—the ground plan as a highly complex polygon, and so on. But, induced by the
greater familiarity of oblongs and crosses and by the long preceding history of basilicas
and cruciform churches, what comes forth, what is exemplified here, is the structure as
derivative from these simpler forms. The vault likewise tells not as a single undulating
shell but as a smooth shape interrupted by others. The syncopation and dynamism
mentioned depend upon the interrelation not of formal properties that the building
merely possesses but of properties it exemplifies.

Not all the properties (or labels) that a building refers to are among those it literally
possesses (or that literally apply to it). The vault in the Vierzehnheiligen church is not
literally eaten away; the spaces do not actually move; and their organization is not
literally but rather metaphorically dynamic. Again, although literally a building blows
no brass and beats no drums, some buildings are aptly described as "jazzy." A building

[6]Christian Norberg-Schulz, *Meaning in Western Architecture* (New York: Praeger, 1975), p. 311.

may express feelings it does not feel, ideas it cannot think or state, activities it cannot perform. That the ascription of certain properties to a building in such cases is metaphorical does not amount merely to its being literally false, for metaphorical truth is as distinct from metaphorical falsity as is literal truth from literal falsity. A Gothic cathedral that soars and sings does not equally droop and grumble. Although both descriptions are literally false, the former but not the latter is metaphorically true.

Reference by a building to properties possessed either literally or metaphorically is exemplification, but exemplification of metaphorically possessed properties is what we more commonly call "expression." To mark the distinction, I ordinarily use "exemplification" as short for "literal exemplification" and reserve "expression" for the metaphorical cases, although in much writing "expression" is used for cases of both sorts. For instance, we often read of a building's "expressing" its function, but since a factory has the function of manufacturing, its exemplification of that function is of a property literally possessed. Only if the factory were to exemplify the function of, say, marketing, would it in my terminology be expressing that function. But distinguishing between exemplification and expression matters less than recognizing literal exemplification as an important variety of reference, especially in architecture. A purely formal building that neither depicts anything nor expresses any feelings or ideas is sometimes held not to function as a symbol at all. Actually, it exemplifies certain of its properties, and only so distinguishes itself from buildings that are not works of art at all.

I stress the role of exemplification, for it is often overlooked or even denied by writers who insist that the supreme virtue of a purely abstract painting or a purely formal architectural work lies in its freedom from all reference to anything else. But such a work is not an inert unmeaning object, nor does it refer solely (if at all) to itself. Like the swatch of cloth, it picks out, points to, *refers* to some of its properties but not others. And most of these exemplified properties are also properties of other things which are thus associated with, and may be indirectly referred to by, the work.

An architectural work may of course both literally exemplify some properties and express others. Of the facade of San Miniato al Monte outside Florence, Rudolph Arnheim writes that it "expresses its character as a self-contained object dependent on . . . the earth; but it also symbolizes the human mind's struggle for maintaining its own centered integrity against the interference by outer powers."[7] In my vocabulary the facade *exemplifies* the first (literal) property and *expresses* the second (metaphorical) one.

3. Ramifications

Representation, exemplification, and expression are elementary varieties of symbolization, but reference by a building to abstruse or complicated ideas sometimes runs along more devious paths, along homogeneous or heterogeneous chains of elementary referential links. For instance, if a church represents sailboats, and sailboats exemplify freedom from earth, and freedom from earth in turn exemplifies spirituality, then the church refers to spirituality via a three-link chain. Parts of a Michael Graves building may exemplify keystonelike and other forms depicted or exemplified by Egyptian or Greek architecture and, thus, indirectly refer to such buildings and in turn to proper-

[7] Rudolph Arnheim, "The Symbolism of Centric and Linear Composition," *Perspecta* 20 (1983) 142.

ties these exemplify and express.[8] Such indirect or mediate reference is often termed "allusion," as when "The Five" architects are described as making "allusions to ancient and Renaissance classicism" and as being "attracted by Le Corbusier's witty introduction of collage allusion into his buildings."[9] And when Robert Venturi writes of "contradiction" in architecture, he is not supposing that a building can actually assert a self-contradictory sentence, but is speaking of exemplification by a building of forms that give rise when juxtaposed, because they are also severally exemplified in architecture of contrasting kinds (for example, classical and baroque), to expectations that contravene each other.[10] The "contradiction" thus arises from indirect reference.

Not all chains consisting of referential links conduct reference from one end to the other. The name of the name of the rose is not the name of the rose; and "Gaudí's famous church in Barcelona" refers to a certain building, not to the mountains that that building refers to. On the other hand, a symbol that refers via a chain may also refer directly to the same thing; and sometimes where reference via a given chain becomes common, short-circuiting occurs. For instance, if a building alludes to Greek temples that in turn exemplify classical proportions that it does not itself possess, it may come to express these proportions directly. Moreover, reference by a work via a chain is seldom unique; a building may reach symbolically to the same referent along several routes. The reader will find his own examples.

Sometimes other relationships a building may stand in—for instance, to effects or causes of it—are mistaken for reference. What an architectural work means cannot in general be identified either with thoughts it inspires and feelings it arouses or with circumstances responsible for its existence or design. Although "evocation" is sometimes used almost interchangeably with "allusion" or "expression," it should be distinguished from them; for while some works allude to or express feelings they evoke, not all do. A building of an earlier era does not always express the nostalgia it evokes, nor does a skyscraper in a New England town always refer to the fury, however widespread and lasting, it may arouse. Equally, allusion and all other reference must be distinguished from causation. Even if in some cases "an epoch is inscribed in its monuments [so] architecture is not neutral[;] it expresses political, social, economic, and cultural 'finalities' "[11] still, an architectural work does not always refer to economic or social or psychological or other factors or ideas that brought about its construction or affected its design.

Even when a building does mean, that may have nothing to do with its architecture. A building of any design may come to stand for some of its causes or effects, or for some historical event that occurred in it or on its site, or for its designated use; any abattoir may symbolize slaughter, and any mausoleum, death; and a costly county courthouse may symbolize extravagance. To mean in such a way is not thereby to function as an architectural work.

[8]Although a link in an ordinary chain is nondirectional, one element in a referential link may refer to but not be referred to by the other. Where one element exemplifies the other, however, reference runs in both directions, for the exemplified element denotes what exemplifies it.

[9]Jordy, "Aedicular Modern," p. 45.

[10]See Robert Venturi, *Complexity and Contradiction in Architecture* (Garden City, N.Y.: Doubleday, 1966).

[11]François Mitterand, quoted in Julia Trilling, "Architecture as Politics," *Atlantic Monthly* (October 1983) 35.

4. Architectural Judgment

So much for some of the ways that architectural works as such do mean and some they do not. But when does a work actually mean as such? Some writing about architecture may give the impression that prose is as prominent an ingredient in architecture as steel and stone and cement. Does a work mean just whatever anyone says it means, or is there a difference between right and wrong statements about how and what it means?

On one view, correct interpretation is unique; there are no alternatives, and rightness is tested by accord with the artist's intentions. Obviously, drastic adjustments in this are needed to accommodate works that fail to realize the artist's intentions or that exceed or diverge from them: not only the road to hell is paved with unfulfilled intentions, and great works are often full of unintended realizations. Moreover, we are seldom utterly at a loss to interpret a prehistoric or other work when virtually nothing is known of the artist or his intentions. But the main fault I find in this view lies in its absolutism rather than in the particular test of rightness specified. A work of art typically means in varied and contrasting and shifting ways and is open to many equally good and enlightening interpretations.

At the opposite extreme from such absolutism is a radical relativism that takes any interpretation to be as right or wrong as any other. Everything goes if anything does. All interpretations are extraneous to the work, and the critic's function is to strip them off. A work means whatever it may be said to mean—or, in other words, it does not mean at all. No difference between rightness and wrongness of interpretation is recognized. So stated, this view obviously involves a gross oversimplification. More than any other art, architecture makes us aware that interpretation cannot be so easily distinguished from the work. A painting can be presented all at once—though our perception of it involves synthesizing the results of scanning—but a building has to be put together from a heterogeneous assortment of visual and kinesthetic experiences: from views at different distances and angles, from walks through the interior, from climbing stairs and straining necks, from photographs, miniature models, sketches, plans, and from actual use. Such construction of the work as known is itself of the same sort as interpretation and will be affected by our ideas about the building and by what it and its parts mean or are coming to mean. The same altar may be a central pivot or an incidental deviation. A mosque will not have the same structure for a Muslim, a Christian, an atheist. Stripping off or ripping out *all* construals (that is, all interpretation and construction) does not leave a work cleansed of all encrustation but demolishes it (*Of Mind and Other Matters*, 33–36).

The resolute deconstructionist will not flinch at this. He will dismiss unconstrued works as will-o-the-wisps and treat interpretation not as *of* anything but as mere storytelling. He is thus released from any stereotyped conception of a work and from the hampering and hopeless search for the single right interpretation. A heady freedom replaces oppressive obligation. But the freedom is bought at the price of inconsequence. Whatever may be said counts as a right interpretation of any work.

Thus both the absolutist's view that a work is and means what the architect intended and the extreme relativist's view that a work is and means whatever anyone happens to say have serious shortcomings. A third view that might be called constructive relativism takes deconstruction as a prelude to *re*construction and insists on recognition that

Figure 7.
Charles Garnier, Opéra House, Avenue de l'Opéra, Paris, 1861–1874. From Nelson Goodman, "How Buildings Mean," from Reconceptions in Philosophy and Other Arts and Sciences *by Nelson Goodman and Catherine Z. Elgin (Cambridge and Indianapolis: Hackett, 1988), reprinted with permission.*

among the many construals of a work some—even some that conflict with one another—are right while others are wrong. Consideration of what constitutes the difference thus becomes obligatory.

This question is formidable; for a work may be right or wrong in many different ways, and rightness reaches far beyond truth which pertains to verbal statements only. Obviously, no full and final answer to this question will be forthcoming. Not only is any search for a ready and conclusive test of rightness (for a key, no less, to all knowledge!) patently absurd, but even a pat and satisfying definition can hardly be expected. The particular determination of which works are right and which wrong is no more the philosopher's responsibility than is the determination of which statements are true in a particular science or of what are the facts of life. Those who are most concerned must apply and constantly develop their own procedures and sensibilities. The philosopher is no expert in all fields or, indeed, in any. His role is to study particular judgments made and general principles proposed on the basis of them and examine how tensions between particular judgments and general principles are resolved—sometimes by altering a principle, sometimes by changing a judgment. All I can offer here are some reflections on the *nature* of rightness and on factors affecting our tentative decisions concerning what versions are right or more nearly right than others (WW, 109–140).

Judgments of rightness of a building as a work of architecture (of how well it works as a work of art) are often in terms of some sort of good fit—fit of the parts together and of the whole to context and background. What constitutes such fit is not fixed but evolves. As illustrated in the case of "contradiction" in architecture, drastic changes in standards of fit start from and are effected against some concepts and expectations that give way slowly. *Entrenchment* established by habit is centrally involved in the determination of rightness and is, indeed, the basis that makes innovation possible. In Venturi's words, "Order must exist before it can be broken."[12]

As an example of the judgment of rightness in terms of fit, consider Julia Trilling's discussion of Charles Garnier's Opéra in Paris (Fig. 7):

> Even Haussmann didn't always get the proportions right. The Garnier opera house, while indisputably monumental itself, doesn't really work to complete the Avenue de l'Opéra. It is too wide for its site, spilling over the sides of the frame defined by the buildings adjoining the avenue. In the case of the Place de la Bastille, the correct site for the new opera house would not be the designated one, on the old railway yards, but adjacent to it on the canal that completes Haussmann's Boulevard Richard-Lenoir.[13]

What is being discussed here is not physical fit; there is no complaint of blocked access of light or of intrusion into the public way. The fit in question is of exemplified forms to each other and into the form exemplified by the whole. It thus depends upon what the components and the whole signify in one way or another—in this case, primarily by exemplification. In other cases, fit may depend upon what is expressed or denoted or referred to via complex chains. And I am not suggesting that all rightness is a matter of fit.

To summarize briefly, I have tried to suggest some of the ways buildings may mean and ways that their meaning is involved in factors that affect judgment of their effective functioning as works of art. I have not tried to say how to determine what and how particular buildings mean, for we have no general rules for this any more than for determining what a text means or a drawing depicts; but I have tried to give some examples of the kinds of meaning involved. As for the further question, why it matters how and when a building means, I think that a work of architecture, or any other art, works as such to the extent that it enters into the way we see, feel, perceive, conceive, comprehend in general. A visit to an exhibition of paintings may transform our vision, and I have argued elsewhere that excellence of a work is a matter of enlightenment rather than of pleasure. A building, more than most works, alters our environments physically; but moreover, as a work of art it may through various avenues of meaning, inform and reorganize our entire experience. Like other works of art—and like scientific theories, too—it can give new insight, advance understanding, participate in our continual remaking of a world.

[12]Venturi, *Complexity and Contradiction in Architecture*, p. 46.
[13]Trilling, "Architecture as Politics", pp. 33–34.

THE THEORY OF FILM:
METAPHYSICAL REFLECTIONS

In many ways film is unique among the arts. Writing in the 1930s, the great art historian Erwin Panofsky noted, "Film art is the only art the development of which men now living have witnessed from the very beginnings." Panofsky and subsequent writers on film have taken advantage of this fact, investigating both historically and philosophically the idea of artistic origins. These investigations have produced some of the most stimulating work in the philosophy of art in recent decades.

The theories of film we have selected for this text—by Cavell, Bates, and Sesonske—represent the second stage in the development of a classic conception of the subject. This stage, which can be thought of as its middle period, subscribes to a conception of film that relates it directly to the physical world. In the words of Panofsky, "The medium of the movies is physical reality as such. . . . Its [the moving picture's] substance remains a series of visual sequences held together by an uninterrupted flow of movement and space." Stanley Cavell represents the culmination of this tradition, giving us a philosophically sophisticated orchestration of this classic theme: "The material basis of the media of movies . . . is a succession of automatic world projections."

Cavell's understanding of the medium of movies as a succession of "automatic world projections" brings him to consider in a subtle and complex way the relationship of photography to film. As Stanley Bates notes, Cavell's reflections on the role of reality in photography and film has its basis in the historical tradition, beginning with Plato, in which philosophers have attempted to understand our relationship to "reality." Cavell capitalizes on the contrast between the production of an "image of the world" by means of automatism and that of representational painting. More importantly, he discusses this question in the context of the uniqueness of the film-goer's situation—"at some point the unhinging of our consciousness from the world interposed our sub-jectivity between us and our presentness to the world." The result is that Cavell raises in a unique way the question of how the self is related to the world via the film experience.

Moreover, Cavell's account is perhaps the most sophisticated statement within the tradition of Bazin, Kracauer, and Panofsky insofar as he aims at avoiding the pitfalls of metaphysical theorizing about film while at the same time capturing what is ontologi-cally unique about the medium. In this respect Cavell's discussion of the distinctive-ness of film by comparison with other art forms such as photography and painting is a useful addition to the literature of the subject.

In his paper "Movies Viewed: Cavell on Medium and Motion Pictures," Stanley Bates offers a clear account of Cavell's objectives in *The World Viewed*. Bates pursues a number of lines of inquiry that Cavell's text opens up, including Cavell's account of the "ontology" of photograph and film and his reflections on the concept of medium; finally, Bates considers Cavell's understanding of modernism in motion pictures. Bates's account of Cavell's ontology has already been discussed here. But Bates is also most helpful in clarifying Cavell's account of the medium of motion pictures. On the one hand, Bates shows how Cavell combines the traditional notion of the medium of an art as the material in which it is embodied and on the other hand he points up Cavell's identification of medium with genre or form or type. While Cavell sometimes distinguishes these two senses, he often juxtaposes them, as in his important statement, "The material basis of the media of movies . . . is . . . a *succession of automatic world projections.*" Thus, Bates argues that his discussion of the "material basis of film" is immediately relevant to his account of the ontology of film. In particular, Cavell's account of the media can be contrasted with Panofsky's, who had viewed the medium in terms of possibilities which could be discovered, described, and then exploited. But for Cavell, Bates maintains, the possibilities of a medium are not givens; they can only be discerned after they have been exploited.

Finally, Bates produces a lively account of Cavell's view of modernism in film. He maintains that for Cavell modernism implies the condition of self-consciousness in the artist, resulting in distinctive possibilities for artistic creativity. This means, among other things, that the period of which Cavell writes (1925–1960) contained cycles and genres of movies which he calls the "myths" of film. The problem Cavell pinpoints is our inability to believe in these myths and in turn to find new ways in which to create significance in movies after the myths have ended. These different themes in Cavell's aesthetics of film are lucidly expressed in Bates' exegesis.

By contrast, Alexander Sesonske's "Aesthetics of Film, or A Funny Thing Happened on the Way to the Movies" represents an approach to film aesthetics implicitly opposed to Cavell's. Sesonske's article "Aesthetics of Film" is both an engaging discussion of the critical differences between film and some of the other arts, such as painting and drama, and more importantly an exposition of the "formal categories" unique to film—space, time, and motion. According to Sesonske, the "creative possibilities [of film] . . . are at least as great as in any art." Sesonske demonstrates this claim by arguing for the uniqueness of space, time, and motion in film.

In the first part of Sesonske's paper, he distinguishes between the character of film and such apparently related arts as painting, music, and drama. In each case, he shows convincingly that cinema is irreducible to these other arts, and that while its "formal possibilities" (the use of space, time, and motion) are similar, the *modes* of such forms differ radically in cinema as opposed to other arts. For example, the use of space in painting has nothing like the dynamism and discontinuity which we find in film; this is also true for the temporal character of music, in which there are no similar discontinuities resulting from the manipulation of time and motion on the movie screen.

The remainder of Sesonske's paper consists of an illuminating discussion of the distinctiveness of space, time, and motion in cinema. He contrasts the familiar space of our lives with *cinema space*, which is wholly and only visual, and goes on to characterize it as a three-dimensional space, an *action-space*, in which we perceive characters, actions, and events. Sesonske further characterizes this action space as discontinuous with that of our normal world, discontinuous in itself and as experienced within an unlimited frame. Similarly he contrasts time and cinema with the other arts and clarifies two aspects of cinema time which he calls "viewing time" and "dramatic time." He argues that the discontinuity of dramatic time allows for remarkable possibilities in cinema inaccessible to any other art. In addition, our experience of motion in film "imparts a definiteness in direction and magnitude lacking in normal experience." As a result, movement becomes an element of composition in cinema that is treated in a distinctive way—"the experience created by camera movement is something entirely new under the sun."

Sesonske concludes his essay with some comments about the use of sound in cinema and the way in which it is employed in conjunction with space, time, and motion. He concludes by maintaining that while character and action are what interest us in films, it is the expressive qualities of the underlying form that are crucial to our experience of film. And these expressive qualities are made possible by the extraordinary use to which space, time, and motion are put by the filmmaker.

Stanley Cavell

SIGHTS AND SOUNDS:
FROM *THE WORLD VIEWED*

. . . What is film?

The beginning of an answer is given by the two continuously intelligent, interesting, and to me useful theorists I have read on the subject. Erwin Panofsky puts it this way: "The medium of the movies is physical reality as such."[1] André Bazin emphasizes essentially this idea many times and many ways: at one point he says, "Cinema is committed to communicate only by way of what is real"; and then, "The Cinema [is] of its essence a dramaturgy of Nature."[2] "Physical reality as such," taken literally, is not correct: that phrase better fits the specialized pleasures of *tableaux vivants*, or formal gardens, or Minimal Art. What Panofsky and Bazin have in mind is that the basis of the medium of movies is photographic, and that a photograph is *of* reality or nature. If to this we add that the medium is one in which the photographic image is projected and gathered on a screen, our question becomes: What happens to reality when it is projected and screened?

That it is reality that we have to deal with, or some mode of depicting it, finds surprising confirmation in the way movies are remembered, and misremembered. It is tempting to suppose that movies are hard to remember the way dreams are, and that is not a bad analogy. As with dreams, you do sometimes *find* yourself remembering moments in a film, and a procedure in *trying* to remember is to find your way back to a characteristic mood the thing has left you with. But, unlike dreams, other people can help you remember, indeed are often indispensable to the enterprise of remembering. Movies are hard to remember, the way the actual events of yesterday are. And yet, again like dreams, certain moments from films viewed decades ago will nag as vividly as moments of childhood. It is as if you had to remember what happened *before* you slept. Which suggests that film awakens as much as it enfolds you.

From The World Viewed: Reflections on the Ontology of Film *(New York: Viking Press, 1971), chaps. 2, 3, 4, 5, and 6. Reprinted with permission of the author.*
    [1]Erwin Panofsky, "Style and Medium in the Moving Pictures," in Daniel Talbot, ed., *Film* (New York: Simon and Schuster, 1959), p. 31.
    [2]André Bazin, *What Is Cinema?*, trans. Hugh Gray (Berkeley: University of California Press, 1967), p. 110.

It may seem that this starting point—the projection of reality—begs the question of the medium of film, because movies, and writing about movies, have from their beginnings also recognized that film can depict the fantastic as readily as the natural.[3] What is true about that idea is not denied in speaking of movies as "communicating by way of what is real": the displacement of objects and persons from their natural sequences and locales is itself an acknowledgement of the physicality of their existence. It is as if, for all their insistence on the newness of the medium, the anti-realist theorists could not shake the idea that it was essentially a form of painting, for it was painting which had visually repudiated—anyway, forgone—the representation of reality. This would have helped them neglect the differences between representation and projection. But an immediate fact about the medium of the photograph (still or in motion) is that it is not painting. (An immediate fact about the *history* of photography is that this was not at first obvious.)

What does this mean—not painting? A photograph does not present us with "likenesses" of things; it presents us, we want to say, with the things themselves. But wanting to say that may well make us ontologically restless. "Photographs present us with things themselves" sounds, and ought to sound, false or paradoxical. Obviously a photograph of an earthquake, or of Garbo, is not an earthquake happening (fortunately), or Garbo in the flesh (unfortunately). But this is not very informative. And, moreover, it is no less paradoxical or false to hold up a photograph of Garbo and say, "That is not Garbo," if all you mean is that the object you are holding up is not a human creature. Such troubles in notating so obvious a fact suggest that we do not know what a photograph is; we do not know how to place it ontologically. We might say that we don't know how to think of the *connection* between a photograph and what it is a photograph of. The image is not a likeness; it is not exactly a replica, or a relic, or a shadow, or an apparition either, though all of these natural candidates share a striking feature with photographs—an aura or history of magic surrounding them.

One might wonder that similar questions do not arise about recordings of sound. I mean, on the whole we would be hard put to find it false or paradoxical to say, listening to a record, "That's an English horn"; there is no trace of temptation to add (as it were, to oneself), "But I know it's really only a recording." Why? A child might be very puzzled by the remark, said in the presence of a photograph. "That's an English horn," if something else had already been pointed out to him as an English horn. Similarly, he might be very puzzled by the remark, said of a photograph, "That's your grandmother." Very early, children are *no longer* puzzled by such remarks, luckily. But that doesn't mean we know why they were puzzled, or why they no longer are. And I am suggesting that we don't know either of these things about ourselves.

Is the difference between auditory and visual transcription a function of the fact that we are fully accustomed to hearing things that are invisible, not present to us, not present with us? We would be in trouble if we weren't so accustomed, because it is the nature of hearing that what is heard comes *from* someplace, whereas what you can see you can look *at*. It is why sounds are warnings, or calls; it is why our access to another world is normally through voices from it; and why a man can be spoken to by God and

---

[3]Certainly I am not concerned to deny that there may be, through film, what Paul Rotha in his *The Film Till Now* (first published in 1930) refers to as "possibilities . . . open for the great sound and visual [i.e., non-dialogue sound, and perhaps non-photographically visual] cinema of the future." But in the meantime the movies have been what they have been.

survive, but not if he sees God, in which case he is no longer in *this* world. Whereas we are not accustomed to seeing things that are invisible, or not present to us, not present with us; or we are not accustomed to acknowledging that we do (except for dreams). Yet this seems, ontologically, to be what is happening when we look at a photograph: we see things that are not present.

Someone will object: "That is playing with words. We're not seeing something not present; we are looking at something perfectly present, namely, a *photograph*." But that is affirming something I have not denied. On the contrary, I am precisely describing, or wishing to describe, what it means to say that there is this photograph here. It may be felt that I make too great a mystery of these objects. My feeling is rather that we have forgotten how mysterious these things are, and in general how *different* things are from one another, as though we had forgotten how to value them. This is in fact something movies teach us.

Suppose one tried accounting for the familiarity of recordings by saying, "When I say, listening to a record, 'That's an English horn,' what I really mean is, 'That's the *sound* of an English horn'; moreover, when I am in the presence of an English horn playing, I still don't literally hear the horn, I hear the sound of the horn. So I don't worry about hearing a horn when the horn is not present, because *what* I hear is exactly the same (ontologically the same, and if my equipment is good enough, empirically the same) whether the thing is present or not." What this rigmarole calls attention to is that sounds can be perfectly copied, and that we have various interests in copying them. (For example, if they couldn't be copied, people would never learn to talk.) It is interesting that there is no comparable rigmarole about visual transcriptions. The problem is not that photographs are not visual copies of objects, or that objects can't be visually copied. The problem is that even if a photograph were a copy of an object, so to speak, it would not bear the relation to its object that a recording bears to the sound it copies. We said that the record reproduces its sound, but we cannot say that a photograph reproduces a sight (or a look, or an appearance). It can seem that language is missing a word at this place. Well, you can always invent a word. But one doesn't know what to pin the word *on* here. It isn't that there aren't sights to see, nor even that a sight has by definition to be especially *worth* seeing (hence could not be the sort of thing we are *always* seeing), whereas sounds are being thought of here, not unplausibly, as what we always hear. A sight *is* an object (usually a very large object, like the Grand Canyon or Versailles, although small southern children are frequently held, by the person in charge of them, to be sights) or an extraordinary happening, like the aurora borealis; and what you see, when you sight something, is an object—anyway, not the sight of an object. Nor will the epistemologist's "sense-data" or "surfaces" provide correct descriptions here. For we are not going to say that photographs provide us with the sense-data of the objects they contain, because if the sense-data of photographs were the same as the sense-data of the objects they contain, we couldn't tell a photograph of an object from the object itself. To say that a photograph is of the surfaces of objects suggests that it emphasizes texture. What is missing is not a word, but, so to speak, something in nature—the fact that objects don't *make* sights, or *have* sights. I feel like saying: Objects are too *close* to their sights to give them up for reproducing; in order to reproduce the sights they (as it were) make, you have to reproduce *them*—make a mold, or take an impression. Is that what a photograph does? We might, as Bazin does on occasion, try thinking of a photograph as a visual mold or a visual impression. My dissatisfaction with that idea is, I think, that physical molds and impressions and imprints have clear procedures for getting *rid* of their originals, whereas in a photograph, the original is still as present as it ever was. Not present as it once was to the camera; but that is only a mold-machine, not the mold itself.

Photographs are not *hand*-made; they are manufactured. And what is manufactured is an image of the world. The inescapable fact of mechanism or automatism in the making of these images is the feature Bazin points to as "[satisfying], once and for all and in its very essence, our obsession with realism."[4]

It is essential to get to the right depth of this fact of automatism. It is, for example, misleading to say, as Bazin does, that "photography has freed the plastic arts from their obsession with likeness,"[5] for this makes it seem (and it does often look) as if photography and painting were in competition, or that painting had wanted something that photography broke in and satisfied. So far as photography satisfied a wish, it satisfied a wish not confined to painters, but the human wish, intensifying in the West since the Reformation, to escape subjectivity and metaphysical isolation—a wish for the power to reach this world, having for so long tried, at last hopelessly, to manifest fidelity to another. And painting was not "freed"—and not by photography—from its obsession with likeness. Painting, in Manet, was *forced* to forgo likeness exactly because of its own obsession with reality, because the illusions it had learned to create did not provide the conviction in reality, the connection with reality, that it craved.[6] One might even say that in withdrawing from likeness, painting freed photography to be invented.

And if what is meant is that photography freed painting from the idea that a painting had to be a picture (that is, of or *about* something else), that is also not true. Painting did not free itself, did not force itself to maintain itself apart from *all* objective reference until long after the establishment of photography; and then not because it finally dawned on painters that paintings were not pictures, but because that was the way to maintain connection with (the history of) the art of painting, to maintain conviction in its power to create paintings, meaningful objects in paint.

And are we sure that the final denial of objective reference amounts to a complete yielding of connection with reality—once, that is, we have given up the idea that "connection with reality" is to be understood as "provision of likeness"? We can be sure that the view of painting as dead without reality, and the view of painting as dead with it, are both in need of development in the views each takes of reality and of painting. We can say, painting and reality no longer *assure* one another.

It could be said further that what painting wanted, in wanting connection with reality, was a sense of *presentness*[7]—not exactly a conviction of the world's presence to us, but of our presence to it. At some point the unhinging of our consciousness from the world interposed our subjectivity between us and our presentness to the world. Then our subjectivity became what is present to us, individuality became isolation.

[4]Bazin, *op cit.*, p. 12.

[5]*Loc. cit.*

[6]See Michael Fried, *Three American Painters* (Cambridge, Mass.: Fogg Art Museum, Harvard University, 1965), n. 3; and "Manet's Sources," *Artforum*, March 1969, pp. 28–79.

[7]See Michael Fried, "Art and Objecthood," *Artforum*, June 1967; reprinted in Gregory Battrock, ed., *Minimal Art* (New York: E. P. Dutton, 1968), pp. 116–47.

The route to conviction in reality was through the acknowledgment of that endless presence of self. What is called expressionism is one possibility of representing this acknowledgment. But it would, I think, be truer to think of expressionism as a representation of our *response* to this new fact of our condition—our terror of ourselves in isolation—rather than as a representation of the world from within the condition of isolation itself. It would, to that extent, not be a new mastery of fate by creating selfhood against no matter what odds; it would be the sealing of the self's fate by theatricalizing it. Apart from the wish for selfhood (hence the always simultaneous granting of otherness as well), I do not understand the value of art. Apart from this wish and its achievement, art is exhibition.

To speak of our subjectivity as the route back to our conviction in reality is to speak of romanticism. Perhaps romanticism can be understood as the natural struggle between the representation and the acknowledgment of our subjectivity (between the acting out and the facing off of ourselves, as psychoanalysts would more or less say). Hence, Kant and Hegel; hence Blake secreting the world he believes in; hence Wordsworth competing with the history of poetry by writing out himself, writing himself back into the world. A century later Heidegger is investigating Being by investigating *Dasein* (because it is in *Dasein* that Being shows up best, namely as questionable), and Wittgenstein investigates the world ("the possibilities of phenomena") by investigating what we say, what we are inclined to say, what our pictures of phenomena are, in order to wrest the world from our possessions so that we may possess it again. Then the recent major painting which Fried describes as objects of *presentness* would be painting's latest effort to maintain its conviction in its own power to establish connection with reality—by permitting us presentness to ourselves, apart from which there is no hope for a world.

Photography overcame subjectivity in a way undreamed of by painting, a way that could not satisfy painting, one which does not so much detect the act of painting as escape it altogether: by *automatism*, by removing the human agent from the task of reproduction.

One could accordingly say that photography was never in competition with painting. What happened was that at some point the quest for visual reality, or the "memory of the present" (as Baudelaire put it), split apart. To maintain conviction in our connection with reality, to maintain our presentness, painting accepts the recession of the world. Photography maintains the presentness of the world by accepting our absence from it. The reality in a photograph is present to me while I am not present to it; and a world I know, and see, but to which I am nevertheless not present (through no fault of my subjectivity), is a world past.

Photograph and Screen

Let us notice the specific sense in which photographs are of the world, of reality as a whole. You can always ask, pointing to an object in a photograph—a building, say—what lies behind it, totally obscured by it. This only accidentally makes sense when asked of an object in a painting. You can always ask, of an area photographed, what lies adjacent to that area, beyond the frame. This generally makes no sense asked of a painting. You can ask these questions of objects in photographs because they have answers in reality. The world of a painting is not continuous with the world of its frame; at its frame, a world finds its limits. We might say: A painting *is* a world; a photograph is *of* the world. What happens in a photograph is that *it* comes to an end. A photograph is cropped, not necessarily by a paper cutter or by masking but by the camera itself. The camera crops it by predetermining the amount of view it will accept; cutting, masking, enlarging predetermine the amount after the fact. (Something like this phenomenon shows up in recent painting. In this respect, these paintings have found, at the extremest negation of the photographic, media that achieve the condition of photographs.) The camera, being finite, crops a portion from an indefinitely larger field; continuous portions of that field could be included in the photograph in fact taken; in principle, it could all be taken. Hence objects in photographs that run past the edge do not feel cut; they are aimed at, shot, stopped live. When a photograph is cropped, the rest of the world is cut *out*. The implied presence of the rest of the world, and its explicit rejection, are as essential in the experience of a photograph as what it explicitly presents. A camera is an opening in a box: that is the best emblem of the fact that a camera holding on an object is holding the rest of the world away. The camera has been praised for extending the senses; it may, as the world goes, deserve more praise for confining them, leaving room for thought.

The world of a moving picture is screened. The screen is not a support, not like a canvas; there is nothing to support, that way. It holds a projection, as light as light. A screen is a barrier. What does the silver screen screen? It screens me from the world it holds—that is, makes me invisible. And it screens that world from me—that is, screens its existence from me. That the projected world does not exist (now) is its only difference from reality. (There is no feature, or set of features, in which it differs. Existence is not a predicate.) Because it is the field of a photograph, the screen has no frame; that is to say, no border. Its limits are not so much the edges of a given shape as they are the limitations, or capacity, of a container. The screen *is* a frame; the frame is the whole field of the screen—as a frame of film is the whole field of a photograph, like the frame of a loom or a house. In this sense, the screen-frame is a mold, or form.[8]

---

[8]When painting found out how to acknowledge the fact that paintings had shapes, shapes became forms, not in the sense of patterns, but in the sense of containers. A form then could *give* its shape to what it contained. And content could transfer its significance as painting to what contains it. Then shape *pervades*, like gravity, or energy, or air. (See Michael Fried, "Shape as Form," *Artforum*, November 1966; reprinted in Henry Geldzahler's catalogue, *New York Painting and Sculpture: 1940–1970* [New York: E. P. Dutton, 1969].)

This is not, as far as we yet know, a possibility of the film or screen frame—which only repeats the fact that a film is not a painting. The most important feature of the screen format remains what it was from the beginning of movies—its scale, its absolute largeness. Variation of format—e.g., CinemaScope—is a matter determined, so far as I can tell, by questions of convenience and inconvenience, and by fashion. Though perhaps, as in painting, the declaration of color as such required or benefited from the even greater expanses of wider screens.

The idea may seem obviously false or foolish that the essential ontological difference between the world as it is and as it is screened is that the screened world does not exist; because this overlooks—or perhaps obscurely states—a fully obvious difference between them, *viz.*, that the screened world is two-dimensional. I do not deny the obscurity, but better a real obscurity than a false clarity. For *what* is two-dimensional? The world which is screened is not; its objects and motions are as three-dimensional as ours. The screen itself, then? Or the images on it? We seem to understand what it means to say that a painting is two-dimensional. But that depends on our understanding that the support on which paint is laid is a three-dimensional object,

(*continued*)

The fact that in a moving picture successive film frames are fit flush into the fixed screen frame results in a phenomenological frame that is indefinitely extendible and contractible, limited in the smallness of the object it can grasp only by the state of its technology, and in largeness only by the span of the world. Drawing the camera back, and panning it, are two ways of extending the frame; a close-up is of a part of the body, or of one object or small set of objects, supported by and reverberating the whole frame of nature. The altering frame is the image of perfect attention. Early in its history the cinema discovered the possibility of *calling* attention to persons and parts of persons and objects; but it is equally a possibility of the medium not to call attention to them but, rather, to let the world happen, to let its parts draw attention to themselves according to their natural weight. This possibility is less explored than its opposite. Dreyer, Flaherty, Vigo, Renoir, and Antonioni are masters of it.

Audience, Actor, and Star

The depth of the automatism of photography is to be read not alone in its mechanical production of an image of reality, but in its mechanical defeat of our presence to that reality. The audience in a theater can be defined as those to whom the actors are present while they are not present to the actors.[9] But movies allow the audience to be mechanically absent. The fact that I am invisible and inaudible to the actors, and fixed in position, no longer needs accounting for; it is not part of a convention I have to comply with; the proceedings do not have to make good the fact that I do nothing in the face of tragedy, or that I laugh at the follies of others. In viewing a movie my helplessness is mechanically assured: I am present not at something happening, which I must confirm, but at something that has happened, which I absorb (like a memory). In this, movies resemble novels, a fact mirrored in the sound of narration itself, whose tense is the past.

It might be said: "But surely there is the obvious difference between a movie house and a theater that is not recorded by what has so far been said and that outweighs all this fiddle of differences. The obvious difference is that in a theater we are in the presence of an actor, in a movie house we are not. You have said that in both places the actor is in our presence and in neither are we in his, the difference lying in the mode of our absence. But there is also the plain fact that in a theater a real man is *there*, and in a movie no real man is there. That is obviously essential to the differences between our responses to a play and to a film." What that means must not be denied; but the fact remains to be understood. Bazin meets it head on by simply denying that

---

and that the description of *that* object will not (except in an exceptional or vacuous sense) be the description of a painting. More significantly, it depends on our understanding of the support as *limiting* the extent of the painting in two dimensions. This is not the relation between the screen and the images projected across it. It seems all right to say that the screen is two-dimensional, but it would not follow that what you see there has the same dimensionality—any more than in the case of paint, its support, and the painting. Shadows are two-dimensional, but they are cast by three-dimensional objects—tracings of opacity, not gradations of it. This suggests that phenomenologically the idea of two-dimensionality is an idea of either transparency or outline. Projected images are not shadows; rather, one might say, they are shades.

[9]This idea is developed to some extent in my essays on *Endgame* and *King Lear* in *Must We Mean What We Say?* (New York: Scribner's, 1969).

"the screen is incapable of putting us 'in the presence of' the actor"; it, so to speak, relays his presence to us, as by mirrors.[10] Bazins' idea here really fits the facts of live television, in which the thing we are presented with is happening simultaneously with its presentation. But in live television, what is present to us while it is happening is not the world, but an event standing out from the world. Its point is not to reveal, but to cover (as with a gun), to keep something on view.

It is an incontestable fact that in a motion picture no live human being is up there. But a human *something* is, and something unlike anything else we know. We can stick to our plain description of that human something as "in our presence while we are not in his" (present *at* him, because looking at him, but not present *to* him) and still account for the difference between his live presence and his photographed presence to us. We need to consider what is present or, rather, since the topic is the human being, *who* is present.

One's first impulse may be to say that in a play the character is present, whereas in a film the actor is. That sounds phony or false: one wants to say that both are present in both. But there is more to it, ontologically more. Here I think of a fine passage of Panofsky's:

> Othello or Nora are definite, substantial figures created by the playwright. They can be played well or badly, and they can be "interpreted" in one way or another; but they most definitely exist, no matter who plays them or even whether they are played at all. The character in a film, however, lives and dies with the actor. It is not the entity "Othello" interpreted by Robeson or the entity "Nora" interpreted by Duse, it is the entity "Greta Garbo" incarnate in a figure called Anna Christie or the entity "Robert Montgomery" incarnate in a murderer who, for all we know or care to know, may forever remain anonymous but will never cease to haunt our memories.[11]

If the character lives and dies with the actor, that ought to mean that the actor lives and dies with the character. I think that is correct, but it needs clarification. Let us develop it slightly.

For the stage, an actor works himself into a role; for the screen, a performer takes the role onto himself. The stage actor explores his potentialities and the possibilities of his role simultaneously; in performance these meet at a point in spiritual space—the better the performance, the deeper the point. In this respect, a role in a play is like a position in a game, say, third base: various people can play it, but the great third baseman is a man who has accepted and trained his skills and instincts most perfectly and matches them most intimately with his discoveries of the possibilities and necessities of third base. The screen performer explores his role like an attic and takes stock of his physical and temperamental endowment; he lends his being to the role and accepts only what fits; the rest is nonexistent. On the stage there are two beings, and the being of the character assaults the being of the actor; the actor survives only by yielding. A screen performance requires not so much training as planning. Of course, both the actor and the performer require, and can make use of, experience. The actor's role is his subject for study, and there is no end to it. But the screen performer is essentially not an actor

---

[10]Bazin, *op. cit.*, p. 97.
[11]Panofsky, *op. cit.*, p. 28.

at all: he *is* the subject of study, and a study not his own. (That is what the content of a photograph is—its subject.) On a screen the study is projected; on a stage the actor is the projector. An exemplary stage performance is one which, for a time, most fully creates a character. After Paul Scofield's performance in *King Lear*, we know who King Lear is, we have seen him in flesh. An exemplary screen performance is one in which, at a time, a star is born. After *The Maltese Falcon* we know a new star, only distantly a person. "Bogart" *means* "the figure created in a given set of films." His presence in those films is who he is, not merely in the sense in which a photograph of an event is that event; but in the sense that if those films did not exist, Bogart would not exist, the name "Bogart" would not mean what it does. The figure it names is not only in our presence; we are in his, in the only sense we could ever be. That is all the "presence" he has.

But it is complicated. A full development of all this would require us to place such facts as these: Humphrey Bogart was a man, and he appeared in movies both before and after the ones that created "Bogart." Some of them did not create a new star (say, the stable groom in *Dark Victory*), some of them defined stars—anyway meteors—that may be incompatible with Bogart (e.g., Duke Mantee and Fred C. Dobbs) but that are related to that figure and may enter into our later experience of it. And Humphrey Bogart was both an accomplished actor and a vivid subject for a camera. Some people are, just as some people are both good pitchers and good hitters; but there are so few that it is surprising that the word "actor" keeps on being used in place of the more beautiful and more accurate word "star"; the stars are only to gaze at, after the fact, and their actions divine our projects. Finally, we must note the sense in which the creation of a (screen) performer is also the creation of a character—not the kind of character an author creates, but the kind that certain real people are: a type.

Types; Cycles as Genres

Around this point our attention turns from the physical medium of cinema in general to the specific forms or genres the medium has taken in the course of its history.

Both Panofsky and Bazin begin at the beginning, noting and approving that early movies adapt popular or folk arts and themes and performers and characters: farce, melodrama, circus, music hall, romance, etc. And both are gratifyingly contemptuous of intellectuals who could not come to terms with those facts of life. (Such intellectuals are the alter egos of the film promoters they so heartily despise. Roxy once advertised a movie as "Art, in every sense of the word"; his better half declaims, "That is not art, in any sense of the word.") Our question is, why did such forms and themes and characters lend themselves to film? Bazin, in what I have read of him, is silent on the subject, except to express gratitude to film for revivifying these ancient forms, and to justify in general the legitimacy of adaptation from one art to another. Arnold Hauser, if I understand him, suggests wrong answers, in a passage that includes the remark "Only a young art can be popular,"[12] a remark that not only is in itself baffling (did Verdi and Dickens and Chaplin and Frank Loesser work in young arts?) but suggests that it was only natural for the movies to pick up the forms they did. It *was*

---

[12]"The Film Age," in Talbot, *op. cit.*, p. 74.

natural—anyway it happened fast enough—but not because movies were destined to popularity (they were at first no more popular than other forms of entertainment). In any case, popular arts are likely to pick up the forms and themes of high art for their material—popular theater naturally *burlesques*. And it means next to nothing to say that movies are young, because we do not know what the normal life span of an art is supposed to be, nor what would count as a unit of measure. Panofsky raises the question of the appropriateness of these original forms, but his answer is misleading.

> The legitimate paths of evolution [for the film] were opened, not by running away from the folk art character of the primitive film but by developing it within the limits of its own possibilities. Those primordial archetypes of film productions on the folk art level—success or retribution, sentiment, sensation, pornography, and crude humor—could blossom forth into genuine history, tragedy and romance, crime and adventure, and comedy as soon as it was realized that they could be transfigured—not by an artificial injection of literary values but by the exploitation of the unique and specific possibilities of the new medium.[13]

The instinct here is sound, but the region is full of traps. What are "the unique and specific possibilities of the new medium"? Panofsky defines them as dynamization of space and spatialization of time—that is, in a movie things move, and you can be moved instantaneously from anywhere to anywhere, and you can witness successively events happening at the same time. He speaks of these properties as "self-evident to the point of triviality" and, because of that, "easily forgotten or neglected." One hardly disputes this, or its importance. But we still do not understand what makes these properties "the possibilities of the medium." I am not now asking how one would know that these are *the* unique and specific possibilities (though I will soon get back to that); I am asking what it means to call them possibilities at all.

Why, for example, didn't the medium begin and remain in the condition of home movies, one shot just physically tacked on to another, cut and edited simply according to subject? (Newsreels essentially did, and they are nevertheless valuable, enough so to have justified the invention of moving pictures.) The answer seems obvious: narrative movies emerged because someone "saw the possibilities" of the medium—cutting and editing and taking shots at different distances from the subject. But again, these are mere actualities of film mechanics: every home movie and newsreel contains them. We could say: To make them "possibilities of the medium" is to realize what will give them *significance*—for example, the narrative and physical rhythms of melodrama, farce, American comedy of the 1930s. It is not as if film-markets saw these possibilities and then looked for something to apply them to. It is truer to say that someone with the wish to make a movie saw that certain established forms would give point to certain properties of film.

This perhaps sounds like quibbling, but what it means is that the aesthetic possibilities of a medium are not givens. You can no more tell what will give significance to the unique and specific aesthetic possibilities of projecting photographic images by thinking about them or seeing some, than you can tell what will give significance to the possibilities of paint by thinking about paint or by looking some over. You have to think about painting, and paintings; you have to think about motion pictures. What does this "thinking about them" consist in? Whatever the useful criticism of an art

[13]Panofsky, *op. cit.*, p. 18.

consists in. (Painters before Jackson Pollock had dripped paint, even deliberately. Pollock made dripping into a medium of painting.) I feel like saying: The first successful movies—i.e., the first moving pictures accepted as motion pictures—were not applications of a medium that was defined by given possibilities, but the *creation of a medium* by their giving significance to specific possibilities. Only the art itself can discover its possibilities, and the discovery of a new possibility is the discovery of a new medium. A medium is something through which or by means of which something specific gets done or said in particular ways. It provides, one might say, particular ways to get through to someone, to make sense; in art, they are forms, like forms of speech. To discover ways of making sense is always a matter of the relation of an artist to his art, each discovering the other.

Panofsky uncharacteristically skips a step when he describes the early silent films as an "unknown language . . . forced upon a public not yet capable of reading it."[14] His notion is (with good reason, writing when he did) of a few industrialists forcing their productions upon an addicted multitude. But from the beginning the language was not "unknown"; it was known to its creators, those who found themselves speaking it; and in the beginning there was no "public" in question; there were just some curious people. There soon was a public, but that just proves how easy the thing was to know. If we are to say that there was an "unknown" something, it was less like a language than like a fact—in particular, the fact that something is intelligible. So while it may be true, as Panofsky says, that "for a Saxon peasant of around 800 it was not easy to understand the meaning of a picture showing a man as he pours water over the head of another man," this has nothing special to do with the problems of a moviegoer. The meaning of that act of pouring in certain communities is still not easy to understand; it was and is impossible to understand for anyone to whom the practice of baptism is unknown. Why did Panofsky suppose that comparable understanding is essential, or uniquely important, to the reading of movies? Apparently he needed an explanation for the persistence in movies of "fixed iconography"—"the well-remembered types of the Vamp and the Straight Girl . . . the Family Man, and the Villain," characters whose conduct was "predetermined accordingly"—an explanation for the persistence of an obviously primitive or folkloristic element in a rapidly developing medium. For he goes on, otherwise inexplicably, to say that "devices like these became gradually less necessary as the public grew accustomed to interpret the action by itself and were virtually abolished by the invention of the talking film." In fact such devices persist as long as there are still Westerns and gangster films and comedies and musicals and romances. *Which* specific iconography the Villain is given will alter with the times, but that his iconography remains specific (i.e., operates according to a "fixed attitude and attribute" principle[15]) seems undeniable: if Jack Pallance in *Shane* is not a Villain, no honest home was ever in danger. Films have changed, but that is not because we don't need such explanations any longer; it is because we can't *accept* them.

These facts are accounted for by the actualities of the film medium itself: types are exactly what carry the forms movies have relied upon. These media created new types, or combinations and ironic reversals of types; but there they were, and stayed. Does

[14]*Ibid.*, p. 24.
[15]*Ibid.*, p. 25.

this mean that movies can never create individuals, only types? What it means is that this is the movies' way of creating individuals: they create *individualities*. For what makes someone a type is not his similarity with other members of that type but his striking separateness from other people.

Until recently, types of black human beings were not created in film: black people were stereotypes—mammies, shiftless servants, loyal retainers, entertainers. We were not given, and were not in a position to be given, individualities that projected particular *ways* of inhabiting a social role; we recognized only the role. Occasionally the humanity behind the role would manifest itself; and the result was a revelation not of a human individuality, but of an entire realm of humanity becoming visible. When in *Gone with the Wind* Vivien Leigh, having counted on Butterfly McQueen's professed knowledge of midwifery, and finding her as ignorant as herself, slaps her in rage and terror, the movement can stun us with a question: What was the white girl assuming about blackness when she believed the casual claim of a black girl, younger and duller and more ignorant than herself, to know all about the mysteries of childbirth? The assumption, though apparently complimentary, is dehumanizing—with such creatures knowledge of the body comes from nowhere, and in general they are to be trusted absolutely or not at all, like lions in a cage, with whom you either do or do not know how to deal. After the slap, we are left with two young girls equally frightened in a humanly desperate situation, one limited by a distraction which expects and forgets that it is to be bullied, the other by an energetic resourcefulness which knows only how to bully. At the end of Michael Curtiz' *Breaking Point*, as the wounded John Garfield is carried from his boat to the dock, awaited by his wife and children and, just outside the circle, by the other woman in his life (Patricia Neal), the camera pulls away, holding on the still waiting child of his black partner, who only the unconscious Garfield knows has been killed. The poignance of the silent and unnoticed black child overwhelms the yarn we had been shown. Is he supposed to symbolize the fact of general human isolation and abandonment? Or the fact that every action has consequences for innocent bystanders? Or that children are the real sufferers from the entangled efforts of adults to straighten out their lives? The effect here is to rebuke Garfield for attaching so much importance to the loss of his arm, and generally to blot out attention to individual suffering by invoking a massive social evil about which this film has nothing to say.

The general difference between a film type and a stage type is that the individuality captured on film naturally takes precedence over the social role in which that individuality gets expressed. Because on film social role appears arbitrary or incidental, movies have an inherent tendency toward the democratic, or anyway the idea of human equality. (But because of film's equally natural attraction to crowds, it has opposite tendencies toward the fascistic or populistic.) This depends upon recognizing film types as inhabited by figures we have met or may well meet in other circumstances. The recognized recurrence of film performers will become a central idea as we proceed. At the moment I am emphasizing only that in the case of black performers there was until recently no other place for them to recur in, except just the role within which we have already met them. For example, we would not have expected to see them as parents or siblings. I cannot at the moment remember a black person in a film making an ordinary purchase—say of a newspaper, or a ticket to a movie or for a train, let alone writing a check. (*Pinky* and *A Raisin in the Sun* prove the rule: in the former, the making of a purchase is a climactic scene in the film; in the latter, it provides the whole subject and structure.)

One recalls the lists of stars of every magnitude who have provided the movie camera with human subjects—individuals capable of filling its need for individualities, whose individualities in turn, whose inflections of demeanor and disposition were given full play in its projection. They provided, and still provide, staples for impersonators: one gesture or syllable of mood, two strides, or a passing mannerism was enough to single them out from all other creatures. They realized the myth of singularity—that we can still be found, behind our disguises of bravado and cowardice, by someone, perhaps a god, capable of defeating our self-defeats. This was always more important than their distinction by beauty. Their singularity made them more like us—anyway, made their difference from us less a matter of metaphysics, to which we must accede, than a matter of responsibility, to which we must bend. But then that made them even more glamorous. That they should be able to stand upon their singularity! If one did that, one might be found, and called out, too soon, or at an inconvenient moment.

What was wrong with type-casting in films was not that it displaced some other, better principle of casting, but that factors irrelevant to filmmaking often influenced the particular figures chosen. Similarly, the familiar historical fact that there are movie cycles, taken by certain movie theorists as in itself a mark of unscrupulous commercialism, is a possibility internal to the medium; one could even say, it is the best emblem of the fact that a medium had been created. For a cycle is a genre (prison movies, Civil War movies, horror movies, etc.); and a genre is a medium.

As Hollywood developed, the original types ramified into individualities as various and subtle, as far-reaching in their capacities to inflect mood and release fantasy, as any set of characters who inhabited the great theaters of our world. We do not know them by such names as Pulcinella, Crispin, Harlequin, Pantaloon, the Doctor, the Captain, Columbine; we call them the Public Enemy, the Priest, James Cagney, Pat O'Brien, the Confederate Spy, the Army Scout, Randolph Scott, Gary Cooper, Gable, Paul Muni, the Reporter, the Sergeant, the Sheriff, the Deputy, the D.A., the Quack, the Shyster, the Other Woman, the Fallen Woman, the Moll, the Dance Hall Hostess. Hollywood was the theater in which they appeared, because the films of Hollywood constituted a world, with recurrent faces more familiar to me than the faces of the neighbors of all the places I have lived.

The great movie comedians—Chaplin, Keaton, W. C. Fields—form a set of types that could not have been adapted from any other medium. Its creation depended upon two conditions of the film medium mentioned earlier. These conditions seem to be necessities, not merely possibilities, so I will say that two necessities of the medium were discovered or expanded in the creation of these types. First, movie performers cannot project, but are projected. Second, photographs are of the world, in which human beings are not ontologically favored over the rest of nature, in which objects are not props but natural allies (or enemies) of the human character. The first necessity—projected visibility—permits the sublime comprehensibility of Chaplin's natural choreography; the second—ontological equality—permits his Proustian or Jamesian relationships with Murphy beds and flights of stairs and with vases on runners on tables on rollers: the heroism of momentary survival, Nietzsche's man on a tightrope across an abyss. These necessities permit not merely the locales of Keaton's extrications, but the philosophical mood of his countenance and the Olympic resourcefulness of his body; permit him to be perhaps the only constantly beautiful and continuously hilarious man ever seen, as though the ugliness in laughter should be redeemed. They permit Fields to mutter and suffer and curse obsessively, but heard and seen only by us; because his attributes are those of the gentleman (confident swagger and elegant manners, gloves, cane, outer heartiness), he can manifest continuously, with the remorselessness of nature, the psychic brutalities of bourgeois civilization.

Ideas of Origin

It is inevitable that in theorizing about film one at some point speculates about its origins, because despite its recentness, its origin remains obscure. The facts are well enough known about the invention and the inventors of the camera, and about improvements in fixing and then moving the image it captures. The problem is that the invention of the photographic picture is not the same thing as the creation of photography as a medium for making sense. The historical problem is like any other: a chronicle of the facts preceding the appearance of this technology does not explain why it happened when and as it did. Panofsky opens his study of film by remarking, "It was not an artistic urge that gave rise to the discovery and gradual perfection of a new technique; it was a technical invention that gave rise to the discovery and gradual perfection of a new art." We seem to understand this, but do we understand it? Panofsky assumes we know what it is that at any time has "given rise" to a "new art." He mentions an "artistic urge," but that is hardly a candidate to serve as an explanation; it would be about as useful as explaining the rise of modern science by appealing to "a scientific urge." There may be such urges, but they are themselves rather badly in need of explanation. Panofsky cites an artistic urge explicitly as the occasion for a new "technique." But the motion picture is not a new *technique*, any more than the airplane is. (What did we use to do that such a thing enables us to do better?) Yet some idea of flying, and an urge to do it, preceded the mechanical invention of the airplane. What is "given rise to" by such inventions as movable type or the microscope or the steam engine or the pianoforte?

It would be surprising if the history of the establishment of an artistic medium were less complex a problem for the historical understanding than (say) the rise of modern science. I take Bazin to be suggesting this when he reverses the apparent relation between the relevant technology and the idea of cinema, emphasizing that the idea preceded the technology, parts of it by centuries, and that parts of the technology preceded the invention of movies, some of it by centuries. So what has to be explained is not merely how the feat was technically accomplished but, for example, what stood in the way of its happening earlier. Surprisingly, Bazin, in the selection of essays I have read, does not include the contemporary condition of the related arts as a part of the ideological superstructure that elicited the new material basis of film. But it is certainly relevant that the burning issue during the latter half of the nineteenth century, in painting and in the novel and in the theater, was realism. And unless film captured possibilities opened up by the arts themselves, it is hard to image that its possibilities as an artistic medium would have shown up as, and as suddenly as, they did.

The idea of and wish for the world re-created in its own image was satisfied *at last* by cinema. Bazin calls this the myth of total cinema. But it had always been one of the myths of art; each of the arts had satisfied it in its own way. The mirror was in various hands held up to nature. In some ways it was more fully satisfied in theater. (Since theater is on the whole not now a major art for us, it on the whole no longer makes contact with its historical and psychological sources; so we are rarely gripped by the trauma we must once have suffered when the leader of the chorus stopped contributing to a narrative or song and turned to face the others, suffering incarnation.)

What is cinema's way of satisfying the myth? Automatically, we said. But what does that mean—mean mythically, as it were? It means satisfying it without *my* having to do anything, satisfying it *by* wishing. In a word, *magically*. I have found myself asking: How could film be art, since all the major arts arise in some way out of religion? Now I can answer: Because movies arise out of magic; from *below* the world.

The better a film, the more it makes contact with this source of its inspiration; it never wholly loses touch with the magic lantern behind it. This suggests why movies of the fantastic *(The Cabinet of Dr. Caligari, Blood of a Poet)* and filmed scenes of magic (say, materialization and dematerialization), while they have provided moods and devices, have never established themselves as cinematic media, however strongly this "possibility" is suggested by the physical medium of film: they are technically and psychologically trivial compared with the medium of magic itself. It is otherwise if the presented magic is itself made technically or physically interesting *(The Invisible Man, Dr. Jeckyll and Mr. Hyde, Frankenstein, 2001: A Space Odyssey)*, but then that becomes another way of confirming the physicality of our world. Science presents itself, in movies, as magic, which was indeed one source of science. In particular, projected science retains magic's mystery and forbiddenness. Science-fiction films exploit not merely certain obvious aspects of adventure, and of a physicality that special effects specialize in, but also the terrific mumbo-jumbo of hearsay science: "My God, the thing is impervious to the negative beta ray! We must reverse the atom recalcitration spatter, before it's too late!" The dialogue has the surface of those tinbox-and-lever contraptions that were sufficiently convincing in prime *Flash Gordon*. These films are carried by the immediacy of the fantasy that motivates them (say, destruction by lower or higher forms of life, as though the precariousness of human life is due to its biological stage of development); together with the myth of the one way and last change in which the (external) danger can be averted. And certainly the beauty of forms and motions in Frankenstein's laboratory is essential to the success of *Frankenstein*; computers seem primitive in comparison. It always made more sense to steal from God than to try to outwit him.

How do movies reproduce the world magically? Not by literally presenting us with the world, but by permitting us to view it unseen. This is not a wish for power over creation (as Pygmalion's was), but a wish not to need power, not to have to bear its burdens. It is, in this sense, the reverse of the myth of Faust. And the wish for invisibility is old enough. Gods have profited from it, and Plato tells it at the end of the *Republic* as the Myth of the Ring of Gyges. In viewing films, the sense of invisibility is an expression of modern privacy or anonymity. It is as though the world's projection explains our forms of unknownness and of our inability to know. The explanation is not so much that the world is passing us by, as that we are displaced from our natural habitation within it, placed at a distance from it. The screen overcomes our fixed distance; it makes displacement appear as our natural condition.[16]

[16]Within that condition, objects as such may seem displaced; any close-up of an object may render it *trouvé*. Dadaists and surrealists found in film a direct confirmation of their ideologies or sensibilities, particularly in film's massive capacities for nostalgia and free juxtaposition. This confirmation is, I gather, sometimes taken to mean that dadaist and surrealist films constitute the *avant-garde* of film-making. It might equally be taken to show why film made these movements obsolete, as the world has. One might say: Nothing is more surrealist than the ordinary events of the modern world; and nothing less reveals that fact than a surrealist attitude. This says nothing about the value of particular surrealist films, which must succeed or fail on the same terms as any others.

Ideas of displacement (or contrasted position), of privacy, and of the inability to know are linked in my study of the problem of other minds, "Knowing and Acknowledging," in *Must We Mean What We Say?*

Stanley Bates

MOVIES VIEWED: CAVELL ON MEDIUM AND MOTION PICTURES

Since its publication, Stanley Cavell's *The World Viewed* has caused difficulty, even for would-be sympathetic readers, as Cavell himself has acknowledged.[1] His writing has its difficulties, although I believe that the reward for meeting these difficulties is genuine—an encounter with an authentic philosophical voice meditating on the nature of art, the concept of medium, the meaning of modernism, and, above all, the ontology and phenomenology of the art an understanding of which is likely to shed light on the previous topics. I am less inclined to locate the problems of understanding this work in the admittedly difficult topics and the allusive style of its author, than in the expectations of its audience. Cavell is a philosopher, maintaining his own fidelity to the tradition of philosophy by transforming and re-forming it. His first book on movies bears about the same relationship to the dominant philosophical tradition of the time of its initial publication as Nietzsche's *The Birth of Tragedy* bore to the dominant philological practice of *his* own time. This is to say that the work was not received as a work of philosophy initially; like many major works, it had to begin to produce its own audience.

There was, however, another potential audience for this book, one made up of practitioners and students of Film Studies—a relatively new but now flourishing branch of the academy. There was much interest in this book from this community, but here again many had trouble placing the concerns and views of the text. I think that this was the case for two reasons. First, even though the subtitle of the work is "Reflections on the Ontology of Film," I think the real topic of this book is not "film" or "cinema" but rather "movies" (and, often, "talkies"). Let me make a preliminary distinction between these two topics here, and later return to this issue in a discussion of Cavell's view of medium.

Many film theories begin from an abstract consideration of the properties of film; the supposition is that such a consideration can be helpful in determining what the specific

---

This essay was written for the second edition of this collection and is being published for the first time.

[1]Stanley Cavell, *The World Viewed: Reflections on the Ontology of Film* (Cambridge: Harvard University Press, 1979), p. 162. Page numbers in parentheses in text refer to this work.

defining characteristics of film are, and, therefore, what can properly be thought of as "cinematic." Such an account begins from the supposition that what is of aesthetic interest is what all screened sequences of light projected through exposed (or manipulated, or sometimes unexposed) film have in common. A film theory must understand, e.g., conventional narrative films, avant-garde cinema (including abstract sequences of dark and light frames), claymation, and animated cartoons, together. Cavell's procedure is almost the reverse of this; he begins from his experience of significance in his viewing of movies and a conviction in the value of that experience. Without such a conviction, why would one undertake any theorizing at all? His attempt is then to understand, and to account for, this experience. However, I wrote "almost the reverse" because, of course, he does not presume that there is some pure "natural" response to the movies that is independent of the structures and practices of our lives as human beings. He is aware of what he calls "the natural circle of theory and evidence." (p. 9) Perhaps the word "circle" is too static, since the movement from evidence to theory to evidence again may be a dialectical one, but the interdependence of theory and critical judgment is made clear.

Now, I can say why the real topic of this book is "movies" rather than "film." The evidence Cavell seeks to understand is the body of his own critical judgments of movies, above all (but not exclusively) Hollywood movies of roughly the quarter century from 1935 to 1960. In seeking to understand that experience, he of course considers other historical periods of American movies, the movies of foreign directors (especially Antonioni, Godard, and Renoir), and the relationship of the movies to other arts. In one sense, this might seem to make the project of the work modest: to account for a limited, though important, subset of films—traditional, narrative, story-telling movies. The real claim, though, is much stronger: that the possibility for creating an art form from the physical (or material) basis of the media of movies has been realized in this kind of film. Cavell does not deny the possibility of other kinds of art in film, though he does say, "But, in the meantime the movies have been what they have been." (p. 232) I shall return to this issue in discussing his account of the concept of medium.

I said above that there were two reasons why those in Film Studies had difficulty in "placing" Cavell's work. The second reason is that Cavell's meditations occur on a level that in my experience is not usual in film theory. A field of study often presupposes the importance of, and the nature of, what it studies. Most works in film theory can (perfectly reasonably) presuppose a shared understanding of an existing practice, and raise questions within this practice. These questions are often concerned with the "how" of films, and answers are possible in, for example, technical terms concerning the process of filming or in semiotic explanations of meaning. Cavell rather raises questions about the nature of movies from outside of our shared presuppositions and familiarity with them. He asks about the "what" and the "why" of them. He seeks to make the familiar unfamiliar, to reveal to us the amazing power of movies, a power into which we are initiated so thoroughly that we can fail to be aware of it. Cavell's work is overtly nontechnical; how what gets on the screen gets there is of less interest to him than the issues of what is on the screen (the ontology of movies) and why and how we take an interest in what is on the screen (the phenomenology of movies).

Let me now turn to the substance of Cavell's account. I shall be less concerned with criticizing it than with attempting to present my understanding of his procedures and conclusions. In this brief paper I shall confine myself to three topics, leaving aside a number of fascinating lines of inquiry his text opens up. First, I shall discuss his account of the "ontology" of photograph and film; then I want to look at his reflections on the concept of medium; finally, I shall briefly consider his understanding of modernism and motion pictures.

The Ontology of Movies

Cavell begins from the reflections on movies of Erwin Panofsky and André Bazin. This places him in a tradition of thought that acknowledges a special role for *reality* in photography and in motion pictures, and this, in turn, leads him to reflect both on what this special role is and also on how photography and movies *differ* from other arts—especially from painting and from theater. Cavell is careful in this discussion to attempt both to voice statements he is tempted to make about photographs and about movies that will sound paradoxical, and to explore their supposed paradoxicality. Thus, he says that what seems to happen when we view a photograph is that "we see things that are not present." To the doggedly commonsensical answer to this that there is something present—a *photograph*—he responds:

> But that is affirming something I have not denied. On the contrary, I am precisely describing, or wishing to describe, what it means to say that there is a photograph here. It may be felt that I make too great a mystery of these objects. My feeling is rather that we have forgotten how mysterious these things are. (pp. 18–19)

Here we have a good example of what I called the level at which Cavell's inquiry operates. It is exactly what constitutes an *answer* to a question for some that for him *is* the problem.

The problem of the role of reality in photography and motion pictures is compounded when we recall that the tradition of reflection on what we call the arts, going back at least to Plato, has proposed some account of the relationship of art (say painting or sculpture or poetry) to reality—for example, that art is an imitation of reality. The relationship of the world to us, and of us to the world, has always been at issue in the histories of various of the arts. How then is photography different from these other arts? Cavell's answer is that at the core of the photographic process the production of the image of the world occurs via a "mechanism" or "automatism." This need not be taken to deny the obvious facts of decisions that must be made by the photographer (e.g., of film speed, exposure time, aperture setting, focus, object to be photographed, etc.) and the printer. There is more than enough room for an art of photography that would be consistent with Cavell's claim of automatism. Nonetheless, the difference between the relationships of a representational painting to that of which it is a representation, and of a photograph to that of which it is a photograph, seems clear.

Cavell here contests a not uncommon view of the relationship between the history of painting and the invention of photography. In that view the photograph represents the ideal to which, so to speak, painting had aspired. When photography was invented, it freed painting for abstraction and nonrepresentation. Both for historical and conceptual reasons, this view will not do for Cavell: for historical reasons because abstraction and nonrepresentation come too long after the invention of photography, and because they are better understood as part of the internal history of painting; for conceptual reasons because this view assumes uninvestigated conceptions of reality and of painting that if brought to consciousness would be seen to be highly contestable.

Why, however, even if we grant the characteristic of automatism to photography, is this so important? It is here that Cavell connects the history of photography to what I shall call the dialectic of human consciousness. He says the wish that photography satisfied was the wish "to escape subjectivity and metaphysical isolation." (p. 21) Here Cavell may be assuming too much from the average reader: nothing less than an acquaintance with the history of modern philosophy and with romanticism. The varying conceptions of self and world and of the relationship of self to world in, e.g., Descartes, Hume, Kant, Hegel, and the romantics lie just below, and occasionally break through, the surface of the last seven paragraphs of the section called "Sights and Sounds." Very roughly, I think what he has in mind is something like the following sketch. At some point in the history of human thinking, thought attempts to take itself for its own object (for convenience here, let us locate a beginning of this project in Descartes). Ironically, this begins as an attempt to present a connection of the self to the world that can be felt as *certain*; but, of course, this very attempt creates a problem in the relationship between self and world. This problem becomes the threat of skepticism as it is variously conceived and addressed in the history of modern philosophy. It is to this that Cavell refers when he writes, "At some point the unhinging of our consciousness from the world interposed our subjectivity between us and our present-ness to the world." (p. 22)

Cavell sees much of the art of the last two centuries as best understood as imbedded in this dialectic of the human mind and in the issue of the *presentness* of world to self and self to world. Located in this way, the origin of photography with the feature of *automatism*, which here means the absence of the human agent from the central part of the linkage between photograph and what a photograph is a photograph of, is now understood by him to avoid this problem of skepticism. This does not, of course, mean that the existence of a photograph is a *refutation* of skepticism, or that pictures can't involve some form of deception. It means that the philosophical issue of subjectivity is bypassed. However, this is at a price. The world of the photograph that is present to us is, necessarily, a world from which we are absent. (This is, of course, true even if the photograph happens to be of the person viewing the photograph.) Our condition when we encounter a photograph or a movie is that of viewer; our relationship to the world of the photograph or movie is therefore the very relationship Descartes thinks of us as having to our own subjectivity.

I have focused here on Cavell's account of the ontology of the photograph because photography provides the material basis for movies. However, what Cavell means by that should be presented in an account of his treatment of the concept of medium.

The Medium of Motion Pictures

The concept of medium in art can be considered at more than one level. Often in traditional writing on the arts, the medium is identified with the physical material in which the work of art is embodied. (This pretty obviously doesn't work well for literature, although attempts have been made to stretch it there.) In this conception a medium of painting might be oil paint on canvas or fresco or watercolor. A medium of sculpture might be marble to be chiseled, or wood to be carved, or metal to be welded. It is sometimes believed that useful thinking about the possibilities of an art can be based on a consideration of the properties of its medium (and the way in which those physical properties might differ from some other medium).

There is another way to think about "medium." In this conception a medium of painting might be a portrait or a history painting or a landscape or a series of related abstractions. A medium of sculpture might be a memorial bust or a public monument. This sense of "medium" is close to the idea of genre or form or type. It is this sense of "medium" that Cavell is using when he writes, "A medium is something through which or by means of which something specific gets done or said in particular ways. It provides, one might say, particular ways to get through to someone, to make sense; in art they are forms, like forms of speech." (p. 32)

Now Cavell usually distinguishes, but sometimes self-consciously joins, these two senses of "medium" in his account of motion pictures. He writes, "The material basis of the media of movies (as paint on a flat delimited support is the material basis of the media of painting), is, in the terms which have so far made their appearance, *a succession of automatic world projections*" [emphasis by Cavell]. (p. 72) In this very important quotation, Cavell distinguishes between "the material basis of the media" (roughly my first sense of "medium" above) and the "media of movies" (roughly my second sense of "medium" above). Much of his discussion of the ontology of film is relevant to the working out of this idea of "material basis." Indeed, the quotation above is central both in position and in importance to *The World Viewed*, for it explicitly relates his discussion of the ontology of film and the phenomenology of viewing to his account of what have been the media of movies in his discussions of types, cycles, genres, and the myths of film. (It also structures the remainder of the first edition of his book, as he investigates, successively, aspects of each of the elements of his account of the material basis of movies in an attempt to assess the changed state of motion pictures at the time he was writing from that earlier period when he had amassed the body of viewing to which his account of the media of movies had attempted to be faithful.)

Let me now turn to Cavell's discussion of the media of movies, in order to try to situate that part of his work. The first thing that should be noted is the historical character of this discussion. He is not trying to write a history of the movies, but rather to describe certain characteristics of the body of movies through a particular historical period. The media of the movies are the ways that have been found to utilize the material basis of movies to make sense—to communicate. (Perhaps this is what produces the nearly irresistible urge to speak of a "language of film" or a "language of movies," and perhaps, depending on your view of language, the urge for this metaphor need not be resisted.) Cavell contrasts his position with Panofsky's here. Panofsky had written of the "unique and specific possibilities of the new medium" as though these could be first discovered, then described, then exploited. For Cavell, the "possibilities of a medium" cannot be described or specified prior to the actual achievement of someone making sense in a particular way:

> The aesthetic possibilities of a medium are not givens. You can no more tell what will give significance to the unique and specific aesthetic possibilities of projecting photographic

images by thinking about them or seeing some, than you can tell what will give significance to the possibilities of paint by thinking about paint or by looking some over. You have to think about painting, and paintings; you have to think about motion pictures. (p. 31)

It is precisely *this* thinking about movies in which Cavell is engaged.

The acts of giving and finding significance by, say, the director and the critic in some use of the material basis of movies are, of course, carried out against the background of all the previous acts of direction and criticism. There is no need to suppose that there is any *a priori* limitation on the possibilities of significance established by what has already been done. Much of it couldn't have been done had there been such limitations imposed by what had gone before it. When Cavell discusses "Types: Cycles as Genres," therefore, he is not saying that the existing types that he mentions constitute an exhaustive list of the possibilities of the medium. Indeed, he is saying just the opposite. However, he is also surveying a large number of films and asking why did these types (of films and of stars) achieve their significance, and what does it mean if these types can no longer achieve significance for us?

Modernism and Motion Pictures

Cavell raises the question of how movies (and he here presupposes that this includes valuable works of art) for so long remained traditional, when it was characteristic of the other arts in the twentieth century to exist in a state of modernism. (Now that we have reached not only postmodernism, but post-postmodernism, that question may not interest some. Whether it interests you will depend upon what you believe modernism—and postmodernism—to be.) I believe that this question presupposes a value judgment about the relative worth of the (mostly) Hollywood movies Cavell discusses as compared with an avant-garde tradition that has claimed to be modernism in film. A part of his answer depends upon his account of the ontology of film discussed above—that we are situated as viewers relative to film automatically. Modernism in art means for Cavell the coming into self-consciousness of the artist of the condition of his or her art as such, and the acknowledgment of that condition. (Such self-consciousness, and such attempted acknowledgment, provide no guarantee of quality for the work that expresses them. It does mean that failure in modernist terms is more complete than in traditional art, for it is failure to be a part of the art at all.) Cavell writes:

Modernism signifies not that the powers of the arts are exhausted, but on the contrary that it has become the immediate task of the artist to achieve in his art the muse of the art itself—to declare, from itself, the art as a whole for which it speaks, to become a present of that art. One might say that the task is no longer to produce another instance of an art but a new medium within it. (p. 103)

This has not been the condition of movies for the period of which Cavell mainly writes. In that period there were cycles, genres, types of movies that embodied what Cavell calls the myths of film. I won't try to recount what he says about those myths, but the burden of his account, and its outcome, is that the myths are over. They are over for reasons both internal to, and external to, the history of the movies. One way of putting this would be to say that though movies secured our condition of viewing a world automatically, we can no longer believe in the types of world the traditional movies allowed us to view.

"Automatism" functions for Cavell at both levels of the concept of medium I discussed earlier. It figures in his summary account of the material basis of the media of movies, and it also becomes a term nearly equivalent to "genre." He acknowledges the possibility of confusion in his bringing together these two different senses, which he had carefully tried to distinguish, but he claims that this is justified by the way modernism has seemed to need to collapse the distinction.

> It has to do with the fate of modernist art generally—that its awareness and responsibility for the physical basis of its art compel it at once to assert and deny the control of its art by that basis. This is also why, although I am trying to free the idea of a medium from its confinement in referring to the physical bases of various arts, I go on using the same word to name those bases as well as to characterize modes of achievement within the arts. (p. 105)

Much of the final part of the original version of *The World Viewed* is devoted to looking at ways in which people try to create significance in movies after the myths have ended. Whether this actually means that the movies are now in the condition of modernism, I won't try to judge. What Cavell says is:

> What has made the movie a candidate for art is its natural relation to its traditions of automatism. The lapse of conviction in its traditional uses of its automatism forces it into modernism, its potentiality for acknowledging that lapse in ways that will redeem its power makes modernism an option for it. (p. 103)

What is important to remember is that our judgments about quality and worth of movies cannot be made on the basis of any *a priori* criteria derived from aesthetic theory or a theory of modernism. Such judgments must be made on the basis of our experience of the significance of a movie—an experience informed by our broad acquaintance with what the movies have been, and what they are now.

As can be seen from this relatively brief survey, which can only touch upon themes in Stanley Cavell's book, *The World Viewed* is a rich source for reflection not only on the nature of movies, but also on art more generally, and even on the nature of philosophy itself.

Alexander Sesonske

AESTHETICS OF FILM, OR A FUNNY THING HAPPENED ON THE WAY TO THE MOVIES

The history of aesthetics displays two rather divergent tendencies in our attitude toward theories about art. One, expressed in the question, What is art? sees all the arts as one and seeks to formulate a theory applying equally well to architecture and poetry, painting and dance. It takes aesthetics proper to be concerned only with analyses or arguments related to these conclusions about art in general or "aesthetic experience" or "the creative process," while any claim about a particular art has only the status of "criticism." The opposing tendency presumes that all generalizations about art are suspect and would have us talk only about particular arts, music, drama, sculpture, if we are to speak sensibly or defensibly—a poetics or a theory of film is plausible, whereas aesthetics, unqualified, is not. At the limit of this urge stands the claim that every individual work of art is unique in ways which render useless even any attempt to talk generally about paintings or poems, since every work must be considered by itself and "in its own terms"—whatever that may mean.

These tendencies diverge from what is perhaps the core of traditional aesthetics, the view that both a general theory and an analysis of individual arts fall within the province of philosophy and jointly constitute the major goals of aesthetics. In a significant strand of the tradition repeated attempts to classify the arts on the basis of a general theory have issued in schemata of a hierarchy of the arts. But such enterprises have not been much in fashion in twentieth-century America. . . .

Like most of those who have been teaching aesthetics in the past two decades, I have tended to talk both about art and painting, to assert generalizations about expression or form or disinterestedness, then to wander into talk about "the aesthetics of"—painting or architecture or poetry, without ever wondering much about what the relation between these might really be. And as long as the discussions at either end were plausible and interesting, no one else seemed to wonder either.

But in recent years my concern with the arts has settled rather exclusively on

Alexander Sesonske, "Aesthetics of Film, or A Funny Thing Happened on the Way to the Movies," from Journal of Aesthetics and Art Criticism 33, no. 1 (Fall 1974): 51–57. Reprinted by permission of the American Society of Aesthetics and the author.

cinema. In order to be able to talk about what most intrigued me, I invented a course entitled "Aesthetics of Film," aiming to create students able to see a film as a work of art and discuss it in appropriate terms. I do not claim to have invented the subject, but after having devoted considerable time to it over several years, it finally occurred to me to wonder exactly what it was I thought I was doing. What I knew about others' work in this alleged field did not help, for everyone who taught a film class seemed to do it quite differently. The traditional problem of the basis of our distinctions between the arts poses the question of what one might reasonably mean by "the aesthetics of *x*," where *x* is some particular art. I had avoided this in the past by assuming that any theoretical discussion of an art fell somewhere within the province of aesthetics. But now my compulsion to talk about film seemed to lead toward a systematic sorting out of the grab bag of aesthetics and an attempt to map the province in a way which displayed both the differences and connections between the arts.

It is appropriate, I think, that this should all come from worrying about films. For our ways of talking about other arts are so securely rooted in tradition that we hardly think of questioning them; the distinctions are so old they seem natural and obvious. All these arts, architecture, sculpture, painting, music, literature, drama, dance, had already reached some stage of maturity in ancient Greece. Centuries of careful thought precede our own. But Hegel's hierarchy of the arts does not include cinema, nor is it mentioned in Aristotle's *Poetics*. And the place of this newcomer in a schemata of the arts is not at all obvious—one striking fact in the short history of cinema is the divergence between what theoretical writers said that film was and the things that film makers were taking it to be.

In theory, we find attempts to assimilate film to almost every other art. One talks of "cinema as a graphic art," taking its essential connection to be with painting and its central aesthetic focus the compositional construction of the shot. An influential theory identifies the creative element in cinema as editing, with the work of art emerging when one joins together the separate strips of film we call shots, which may be likened to either the words of a poem or the notes of a musical composition. Film has been called both visual poetry and visual music; experimental film makers have tried to show the correctness of each of these assimilations. Again, though its basis is probably more financial than aesthetic, a current effort within the American film scene seeks to recognize film as a subcategory of literature by assigning the major credit for a film to its writer rather than to the director. Pauline Kael's rather lengthy *New Yorker* article circling around what many still consider the greatest American sound film seems allied to this effort insofar as it repeatedly suggests that it is really Herman Mankiewicz's *Citizen Kane*.

The only major theory that grants film an independence from the traditional arts often seems so independent as to deny that film is art at all. This view stresses the development of cinema from photography, perhaps citing Erwin Panofsky's remark that contrary to precedent "it was not an artistic urge that gave rise to the discovery and gradual perfection of a new technique; it was a technical invention that gave rise to the discovery and gradual perfection of a new art." Its core is the claim that the natural function of photography is to reproduce images of physical reality, hence only those films which exploit this "realistic tendency" are truly cinematic. Other types of film "fail to exploit camera reality," with such a failure considered a betrayal of the medium. Siegfried Kracauer, of course, has put forth the most ambitious version of this view in his *Theory of Film*.

Meanwhile, back at the academy, a university catalogue describes a course entitled "Film Aesthetics" in these terms: "A study of the aesthetics of film. Symbolism, realism, expressionism, abstraction and other forms of film art will be studied in relation to the great schools and theoreticians in the field." One wonders what this has to do with any of the familiar views of the nature of film.

But the "theory" which has dominated film production differs from all this. Shortly after the technical invention occurred, someone noted that actors could act out a story before a camera, thus transforming film from an interesting novelty into a means of expression or communication. Since then commercial film producers have treated film as obviously a type of drama, an offshoot of the theater. Much of the film audience shares this view. Scores of the most successful films have been adapted from the stage, and many people probably still think Laurence Olivier's film versions of Shakespeare rank among cinema's finest moments.

But theorists deplore the assumption that film and theater are companion arts. Some treat the whole history of cinema as a sort of mistake and talk as if *true* movies were yet to be born, and this only when film is finally freed of all theatrical elements. Such talk points in one direction toward the mere play of visual forms, as in some films by Norman McLaren or John Whitney, in the other toward early Warhol, films which present a recognizable world but are wholly devoid of any dramatic action or interest. So called experimental films vibrate between these poles; the thought that either represents genuine cinema or the true future of film, I find quite depressing.

Given this range of opinions, how can one decide what film really is and what an aesthetic of film might properly be? Each claim about the relation of cinema to other arts has some support in our experience of films, but how could one tell whether painting or music or literature or drama really provides the proper basis for the art of cinema, or, indeed, whether film is to be seen as an independent art?

My proposal is neither surprising nor very original, though I think its details differ somewhat from what has been said before. The problem lies not so much in seeing in what direction to go, as in going resolutely once we have seen. It seems obvious that the basic distinctions between arts are to be made out in formal terms; that is, they are differences in form and, particularly, differences in the range of formal possibilities open to an art. It follows, I think, that as its first and fundamental task the aesthetics of any art must specify and describe or analyze what I will call the effective formal categories or dimensions of the art. The familiar distinction between spatial and temporal arts already begins this work, but I have in mind a much more fully worked out specification than this, one which not merely identifies space as the primary formal category of painting, sculpture, and architecture but will then describe the *modes* of space which define these arts. Scholastic terminology seems unavoidable; different arts often share one or more primary formal categories and their differences must then be made out within these categories by describing the range of forms accessible to each art. Thus painting and architecture both have space as their fundamental formal category, but the modes of space present and experienced in each are wholly distinct. We often call painting two-dimensional but this only loosely identifies its characteristic mode of space. For a painting may appear on the curved surface of an amphora, with the curve being a significant element within the painting, or a heavy impasto may create a sort of low relief. But these three-dimensional aspects occur within the spatial mode articulated in painting, which I call that of *visual surface space* (meaning simply that the space of a painting is a purely visual space, i.e., to experience it as painting is to experience it visually, and that it is only the space of surfaces). But this mode, visual surface space, occurs only as detail for architecture, whose own task is to articulate *action space*.

Each architectural work creates a space to contain, facilitate, and express some determinate forms of action and can be fully judged as architecture only when we have moved or acted within its space, and not merely seen an exterior. These mere beginnings of an aesthetic of painting and architecture may suggest perhaps the first consequences of such an enterprise, i.e., to show the falsity of our habit of classing painting, sculpture, and architecture together as *visual arts*. Of these three only painting is truly a visual art, in this respect being more like pantomime than architecture. The traditional talk of visual arts tends to make us regard architecture as a sort of large-scale sculpture and sculpture as a sort of three-dimensional painting. But they are not! This may seem obvious, but were it taken seriously we might have been spared such disasters as Frank Lloyd Wright's Guggenheim Museum—a building whose design makes it impossible to perform properly the actions it was built to contain.

But what, in these terms, is film? I can only begin an answer here and go far enough, perhaps, to show that film is, indeed, an independent art. Much of what I say may seem obscure, but one reason for saying it is the hope of moving toward greater clarity.

The primary formal categories of cinema are space, time, and motion. Sound, a fourth major category, differs in that a film may be quite complete without sound, whereas a necessary condition for the existence of a film is that some mode of space, of time, and of motion be actualized and that some particular spaces, some particular time sequences, and some particular motions (or at least changes) be presented. Yet when a film has sound our experience of its space, time, and motion depends upon the relation of sound to image in the film. Also, of course, the pattern of sound itself constitutes one of the dominant formal structures of the film.

Merely listing those formal categories suffices to show the independence of film from drama. For the fundamental categories of drama are nothing like space, time, and motion, but are rather character and action. Space and time, of course, are necessary conditions for the presentation of a drama on the stage, but are merely that rather than being themselves essential constituents of the work. One indication of this is the fact that a play need not be seen or heard to be fully experienced and understood, but can be read. Indeed some critics believe that some plays are impossible to stage adequately and can *only* be properly experienced when read. In contrast, a film cannot be read. Reading a film script is a way of finding out something about the film but not a way of experiencing it; our direct apprehension of space, time, and motion is an essential constituent in our experience of a film. Not only can a film be quite complete and absorbing, yet contain neither characters nor actions, but our perception and interpretation of character and action is shaped by the treatment of space, time, and motion and their interrelations within the film. Space is as essential to film as it is to painting; time is as essential to film as it is to music; motion is as essential to film as it is to dance! The characteristic way we experience cinema, with both its immediacy and its dreamlike quality, is rooted in the modes of space actualized in film. Our feeling of participation in the world of the film and our assurance about this world depend greatly upon the treatment of space, time, and motion in that film.

The complexity apparent here on the level of formal categories seems one source of the temptation to assimilate film to other arts. For example, since time is a primary formal category of film we think that cinema could be like music, a sequence of distinct simple elements given form through their arrangement in time. And of course it could, but why think that would be the highest achievement of cinema?

But the uniqueness of cinema emerges quickly when we turn from formal categories to their modes. In each category the forms possible in film can be achieved in no other medium. When we view a film our experience of space, time, and motion differs from any other context of our lives. Let us begin to see what the possibilities are:

The "natural" space of our lives is continuous in three dimensions, with objects and areas in it experienced tactually and kinesthetically as well as visually. The familiar spaces in which we live are familiar as much from our touching or moving within them as from our seeing. In contrast *cinema space* is wholly and only visual: a space given to a single sense, vision. Any tactual or kinesthetic awareness we seem to have derives from our seeing. This purely visual nature of cinema space makes possible its other major characteristics. Fundamental among these is its duality; we experience a film as a two-dimensional design on a flat surface and a three-dimensional space within which the action of the film occurs. Cinema shares this duality of its space with painting, of course, where we are often aware of both a two-dimensional design on the flat canvas and a three-dimensional visual space in which objects are arranged in depth, with some sort of tension or interaction between these two spatial aspects of the painting often playing a significant role in our experience of it. In painting the three-dimensional space is only picture-space; it affords only a greater realism and complexity of composition. But the occurrence of motion in cinema makes its three-dimensional space a genuine visual action-space, where we perceive not merely compositions but characters, actions, and events. And this action-space is itself most unusual. 1) It is discontinuous with the space of our normal world. We cannot go from any point in normal space to any point in the action-space of a film by traversing the intermediate space, for there is none. There is no fixed distance between a point in action-space and any point in ordinary space. Hence we can experience the events in a film from within its action-space and have the sense of moving through it, while, of course, also remaining in our seat in the theater. 2) The action-space of a film is discontinuous in itself. Characters in a film and viewers of it can instantaneously go from one point in action-space to any other without traversing any intervening space. Or they can be simultaneously in two different locations, etc. 3) The action-space of a film is experienced as confined within a frame yet as unlimited. I cannot overstate the importance of the frame to our experience of cinema. This usually rectangular shape gives to the surface design on the screen all the dynamics of the space of painting. It also contains objects and events in the action-space as elements of composition; a composition which frequently lends character to these objects and events. Yet the flow of action in and out of the frame leaves no doubt as to the openness of the space; we do not perceive it as ending at the frame line but as extending indefinitely in all directions.

These characteristics define the normal mode of space in cinema. But it need not be just like this. Some films have only a two-dimensional space; most frequently these are animated cartoons. Or a film may be made so that the action-space seems confined within a limited area, or even within the frame. A change in the focal length of camera lenses alters the very form of a film's action-space. Long focus lenses flatten the space along the axis perpendicular to the screen; motion along this axis then appears very different from motion parallel to the screen. Short focal length lenses stretch the space, accelerate motion along the perpendicular axis so that a runner may almost disappear from sight in ten steps. Thus great variations in the formal properties of the space of a film are possible as well as great variations in the "feel" of the space in any of these forms, i.e., the space may feel empty or cluttered, open or confined, etc. The essential fact about the space of a film is that it is *created*; there is not simply a determinate dimension waiting to be instantiated.

Time in cinema, as in music, dance, and staged drama, is controlled in the sense that the artist determines temporal order and duration; we must see the work at its own pace, not ours. We cannot alter its order or duration without damaging or changing the work. In the category of time we find again a duality in cinema. There is both the temporal sequence and duration of our experience—the order of shots in the film and their running time—and the order, duration, and location in time of the events within the world of the film. These may coincide, but very rarely do in feature films. I call these two aspects of cinema time "viewing time" and "dramatic time." Viewing time is, of course, the time of our ordinary experience, measurable on a watch, constant in rate and direction, though with variations in felt duration; that is, a measurable segment of time, three seconds or twenty minutes, may seem shorter or longer depending upon its context. In its ability to alter felt duration film does not differ greatly from other temporal arts; it is rather in presentation of dramatic time that its remarkable possibilities appear. Dramatic time, like action-space in cinema, is discontinuous, its order created by the maker of the film; any segment of time within the world of the film may follow any other, and with equal immediacy. The process of editing allows a film to move freely in dramatic time in a manner not equalled in any other art; even literature cannot accomplish temporal transitions as quickly and freely as film. Past, present, and future within the world of the film can be brought together in any way the film maker desires. He can combine several distinct temporal periods in a single shot if he wishes, show past and present in a single frame, or leap from the prehistoric past to a distant future without even interrupting the continuity of motion. Or one can change the very nature of time itself within the world of the film, reverse its direction, accelerate or retard its rate of flow, make it circular or cyclical. These changes are accomplished, of course, by changing the rate and order of movement as projected on the screen and often appear as just that. But they can be so achieved as to render our experience that of a change in the form of time. A freeze frame, for example, is often not experienced as a mere cessation of motion; rather, we feel that within the world of the film time itself has stopped.

Juggling these aspects of time in a movie may seem mere trickery, but the very stuff of cinema is the expansion or contraction of dramatic time in the ordinary flow of action in a film. In a minute and a half we can witness an event which takes, say, ten or twenty minutes in the normal and natural world, yet feel that we have seen it all. The truth is, perhaps, that we have seen everything important, but a skillfully made film may convince us that nothing at all has been left out. The normal mode of time in cinema is a discontinuous, condensed time experienced as an uninterrupted flow.

Despite the uniqueness of space and time in film, we may only seldom notice that they vary much from the space and time of ordinary events. Motion, though, is so significant in movies that it is rather more difficult not to be aware of. Of course we constantly see objects moving in the world, in just the way they move before the camera when a film is made. But when seen in the film, something has changed. We see the movement in relation not only to surrounding objects but also to the frame; this imparts a definiteness in direction and magnitude lacking in normal experience. Thus the movement becomes an element of composition and compositions themselves shift and change as objects move. Or a moving object may be caught, as it were, in an unchanging composition, creating a tension between the perceived motion and the stability of the composition which can become a major element in the expressive force of a scene. Or, again, a movement so small we would hardly notice it can be made the center of all our attention and endowed with the significance of the voice of God. Very often the camera seems to find in moving objects a life of their own that wholly escapes us otherwise.

The camera's treatment of object movement is perhaps only an apotheosis of the ordinary. In contrast the experience created by camera movement is something genuinely new under the sun. We do, of course, move through the world—walk, ride, run—looking as we go, and thus have a sort of moving panoramic view. But the view through the lens of a camera transforms this familiar experience. Once again the frame plays a major role in creating this change. It renders perspectival differences in size much more noticeable and, more importantly, transforms the panorama into a flow of composition. When the camera moves, the frame itself seems to be in motion and the whole compositional structure of the shot becomes alive. In the hands of such masters as Renoir, Kurosawa, or Fellini the resulting flow of action in the context of design in motion may almost leave us breathless in admiration. All of the vectors which lead us to talk about movement in painting can be activated within the two-dimensional rectangle of the screen; when they are augmented by actual movement in the three-dimensional action-space we have the possibility for expressive action of a force and immediacy not equalled in any other medium. By combining camera movement, object movement, and editing, a continuous flow of motion can be achieved which bridges discontinuities of space and time, or highly complex rhythms of movement may pulse through large sections of a film. Such organizations of movement within a film become dominant factors in our experience of some films, creating a felt unity that pervades and shapes our perception of every other aspect of the work.

The normal mode of space in film allows for a much greater range in our relation to the motion we perceive than occurs in any other art. Since we seem to view the events in a film from within its action-space, we may, for example, see a movement at a great distance, suddenly be quite engulfed by it, then find ourselves moving with it through the world of the film. We may be thrust into the very heart of a whirl of motion, as in the battle scenes of Seven Samurai where we almost expect to be splashed by the mud or, instead, see it from a point of view that renders it as almost abstract design. The expressive possibilities of motion in film seem almost unlimited.

In each of these formal categories, space, time, and motion, the modes that can be realized in cinema are unique to cinema. And though it is sometimes suggested that cinema must be inferior as an art because of its dependence on mechanical devices, we might note here that the creative possibilities in film are at least as great as in any art.

As in literature, the whole of the world of the work is to be created, not only the characters and their actions but the very forms of space and time in which they act.

I conclude with a word about sound. The sounds we may hear in a film are not, of course, unique to film. Any sound or pattern of sound presented in a film could be heard in other contexts quite independent of cinema. But what is peculiar and important for film is that the sound is always heard in conjunction with an image and that any sound can be conjoined to any image. The creative and expressive aspect of sound in film lies here, in control of this relation of sound to image, a more precise control with greater possibilities than in any other art. The sound may be heard as outside, inside, or part of the action, or it may by itself convey all of the action we perceive. Its effective coordination may be with the events or incidents of the narrative or with the formal structure of the image. It may confirm, augment, qualify, or contradict what we see. As with every other formal category, I can merely indicate the complexity of formal relationships it allows and hint at the expressive possibilities inherent in these.

The obscure answer I have offered to the question, What is film? is that it is an art form which conveys its contents within these formal modes, i.e., space, time, motion, and sound as here described. As such it is quite different from any other art and reducible to none of them. The accuracy of this analysis is, perhaps, confirmed by the intuitions of those early film makers who felt that the chase was somehow the heart of cinema and concluded every film with a long chase scene; for the chase exploits exactly those modes of space, time, and motion that are distinctive of film.

Nothing I have said should be understood as advising you, when you go to a movie, to attend only to the forms of space, time, and motion presented. What interests us in films, usually, is character and action, the world of the film and the events it unfolds for us—and rightly so. I suggest, rather, that if you wonder what makes the world of the film be what it is, be as fascinating as it is, or how the characters and actions acquire the power to engulf us as they do and have the qualities we see them as having, then, ultimately—in the films I love, at least—you will find these rooted in the expressive qualities of the underlying form. A further elaboration of my "aesthetic of film" would begin to show how this happens, how form does shape and inform the world of the film.

THE THEORY OF MUSIC:
EXPRESSIVENESS IN MUSIC

The conflict between formalists and expressionists has been a recurrent theme throughout this text. In Part One Clive Bell sets forth a classic statement of the formalist position, while such writers as Tolstoy and Collingwood defend different versions of expressionism. This controversy has been no less prevalent in the aesthetics of music. Among formalists, the theory that music is purely a succession of sounds and silences that appeal to our aesthetic interest may be contrasted with the expressionist view that emotions are inextricably bound up with the qualities of the music or of the composer who articulates them. In this section, Eduard Hanslick argues for a version of musical formalism, as does Renee Cox in a modern idiom. Edward T. Cone, by contrast, offers an interesting exposition of an expressionist theory of music.

According to Hanslick, the material of music, in the sense of the stuff out of which music is made, is "the entire system of tones, with their latent possibilities for melodic, harmonic, and rhythmic variety." By "tones" Hanslick means something much more specific than "sounds." He means the degree of the major and minor (i.e., diatonic) scales, with all their intervals and relationships, and the various degrees of tension or repose of which these are capable, in actual or imagined sound. A piece of music is a tonal construction, tones in various combinations, produced according to the laws of the art, in the composer's imagination, and contemplated in the listener's. The composer is prompted to compose, not by some emotional event or state, but by an "inner singing." The listener who responds sensuously or emotionally is not responding aesthetically, since aesthetic response to music is, like composing itself, an activity of the human intellect, not a passive surrender to sensation or feeling. Only such hearers as possess the requisite musical cultivation are capable of attending to music aesthetically, says Hanslick.

The material of music (i.e., the tones) possesses its own logic, based on laws of nature and of human nature; it is intrinsically both formal and expressive. Hence, musical compositions communicate both thought and feeling, but *exclusively* musical thought and feeling, not translatable into words and not subordinate to the requirements of literary or pictorial representation.

Hence, according to Hanslick, it is not the essential purpose of music to portray scenes or events from ordinary life, or to express or arouse feelings. It obviously can do these things, but only incidentally, not essentially. Music is essentially purposeless, which is not to say that it is mere play. Far from it: of all human productions, music most directly manifests thought itself, and the activity of thinking is what distinguishes humankind from all other creatures. Thus, Hanslick cannot be considered a formalist in the usual sense as he attributes the musical work to an expressive activity on the part of the musical artist.

Edward T. Cone, in *The Composer's Voice*, defends an expressionist theory of music, although one that involves a number of subtle distinctions. While Cone does not subscribe to a straightforward version of the expression theory, which holds that the artist's own emotions are directly expressed in his work, he nonetheless maintains that music is expressive by virtue of a vicarious or "implied" voice. It is this voice that is the persona in a musical composition.

Essentially, Cone considers music to be a language of gesture. By contrast with everyday speech, which has a semantic as well as a gestural aspect, music is symbolic purely as gesture. According to Cone, "both the verbal gestures of poetry and the bodily gestures of the dance are symbolized in the medium of pure sound." A musical gesture, however, has no specific reference and conveys no specific message; it can fit into many contexts that explain its significance. Without such a context, a musical gesture cannot express anything; it is only potentially expressive.

Musical content, then, is entirely dependent upon context. And content, according to Cone, refers to "humanly expressive content." In vocal music we associate musical motion with human emotion, but in purely instrumental music the music itself must realize its expressive potential. This is a key concept for Cone, and it recurs in his discussion of vocal compositions, program music, and purely instrumental music. In each case "we subconsciously ascribe to the music a content based on the correspondence between musical gestures and their patterns on the one hand, and isomorphically analogous experiences, inner or outer, on the other." It is therefore unavoidable for us to comprehend music without drawing from our background of previous experience which suggests numerous associations.

Thus, Cone is at odds with a formalist position that attempts to restrict our comprehension of music to the interrelationships of sounds and silences devoid of human and personal content. Each listener is linked, despite a divergence of contexts, by a "common ground of expression" that suggests the nature of the music's expressive potential. The total potential content is thus located in the relationship among all its contents and in the illumination bestowed on that relationship by the musical structure that unites them. As opposed to formalism, Cone insists that the musical context and the human context are inseparable; where there is a context, there is always a *human* context.

Renée Cox contests the assumption that Cone and others make, that music can express emotion. In "Varieties of Musical Expressionism" she argues that if music makes us feel emotions, if music seems to embody emotion, or if musical motion seems emotional in nature, it is inevitably because we associate the music with actual emotional experiences. When we associate music with emotion, it is often because the music accompanies an emotional text, title, program, drama, or situation. But music is also often associated with emotional personal experiences of our own. Music is always heard within the context of our lives, and is sometimes difficult to separate from these contexts. If purely instrumental music seems emotional and we are not affected emotionally while listening, the "emotion" is most likely the result of a past association. If newly heard instrumental music seems emotional, it is because we have associated similar music with emotion in the past. When we make these associations, the music seems to swallow them up, as if it were a vacuum in need of filling. But just as an object is reflected in a mirror only when near the mirror, music seems emotional only when emotional subject matter is or has been brought to bear on it.

Eduard Hanslick

A MUSICAL THEORY OF SOUND AND MOTION:
FROM ON THE MUSICALLY BEAUTIFUL

. . . What kind of beauty is the beauty of a musical composition?

It is a specifically musical kind of beauty. By this we understand a beauty that is self-contained and in no need of content from outside itself, that consists simply and solely of tones and their artistic combination. Relationships, fraught with significance, of sounds which are in themselves charming—their congruity and opposition, their separating and combining, their soaring and subsiding—this is what comes in spontaneous forms before our inner contemplation and pleases us as beautiful.

The primordial stuff of music is regular and pleasing sound. Its animating principle is rhythm: rhythm in the larger scale as the co-proportionality of a symmetrical structure; rhythm in the smaller scale as regular alternating motion of individual units within the metric period. The material out of which the composer creates, of which the abundance can never be exaggerated, is the entire system of tones, with their latent possibilities for melodic, harmonic, and rhythmic variety. Unconsumed and inexhaustible, melody holds sway over all, as the basic form of musical beauty. Harmony, with its thousandfold transformations, inversions, and augmentations, provides always new foundations. The two combined are animated by rhythm, the artery which carries life to music, and they are enhanced by the charm of a diversity of timbres.

If now we ask what it is that should be expressed by means of this tone-material, the answer is musical ideas. But a musical idea brought into complete manifestation in appearance is already self-subsistent beauty; it is an end in itself, and it is in no way primarily a medium or material for the representation of feelings or conceptions.

The content of music is tonally moving forms.

How music is able to produce beautiful forms without a specific feeling as its content is already to some extent illustrated for us by a branch of ornamentation in the visual arts, namely arabesque. We follow sweeping lines, here dipping gently, there boldly soaring, approaching and separating, corresponding curves large and small, seemingly incommensurable yet always well connected together, to every part a counterpart, a

From On the Musically Beautiful, *translated and edited by Geoffrey Payzant (Indianapolis: Hackett, 1986), pp. 28–44. Reprinted with permission of Hackett Publishing Company. (Footnotes omitted).*

collection of small details but yet a whole. Now let us think of an arabesque not dead and static, but coming into being in continuous self-formation before our eyes. How the lines, some robust and some delicate, pursue one another! How they ascend from a small curve to great heights and then sink back again, how they expand and contract and forever astonish the eye with their ingenious alternation of tension and repose! There before our eyes the image becomes ever grander and more sublime. Finally, let us think of this lively arabesque as the dynamic emanation of an artistic spirit who unceasingly pours the whole abundance of his inventiveness into the arteries of this dynamism. Does this mental impression not come close to that of music?

As children, all of us have much enjoyed the play of colour and shape in a kaleidoscope. Music is a kind of kaleidoscope, although it manifests itself on an incomparably higher level of ideality. Music produces beautiful forms and colours in ever more elaborate diversity, gently overflowing, sharply contrasted, always coherent and yet always new, self-contained and self-fulfilled. The main difference between such a musical, audible kaleidoscope and the familiar visible one is that the former presents itself as the direct emanation of an artistically creative spirit, while the latter is no more than a mechanically ingenious plaything. If, not merely in thought but in actuality, we want to raise colour to the level of music, we get involved in the tasteless frivolity of colour organs and the like. The invention of these devices, for all that, does at least show how the formal aspects of both music and colour rest on the same basis. . . .

If people do not acknowledge the abundance of beauty residing in the purely musical, one may blame the undervaluation of the sensuous, which we find in the older systems of aesthetics favouring morality and aesthetic sensitivity and in Hegel's system favouring the "Idea." Every art originates from and is active within the sensuous. The feeling theory fails to recognize this; it ignores hearing entirely and goes directly to feeling. Music creates for the heart, they say; the ear is of no consequence. Indeed, for what they call the ear, namely the labyrinth or the eardrum, no Beethoven composes. The auditory imagination, however, which is something entirely different from the sense of hearing regarded as a mere funnel open to the surface of appearances, enjoys in conscious sensuousness the sounding shapes, the self-constructing tones, and dwells in free and immediate contemplation of them.

It is extraordinarily difficult to describe this specifically musical, autonomous beauty. Since music has no prototype in nature and expresses no conceptual content, it can be talked about only in dry technical definitions or with poetical fictions. Its realm is truly not of this world. All the fanciful portrayals, characterizations, circumscriptions of a musical work are either figurative or perverse. What in every other art is still description is in music already metaphor. Music demands once and for all to be grasped as music and can be only from itself understood and in itself enjoyed.

In no way is the specifically musically beautiful to be understood as mere acoustical beauty or as symmetry of proportion—it embraces both as ancillary—and still less can we talk about an ear-pleasing play of tones and other such images, by which the lack of a mental source of animation tends to become emphasized. Thus, in order to make our case for musical beauty, we have not excluded ideal content but, on the contrary, have insisted on it. For we acknowledge no beauty without its full share of ideality. Basically what we have done is to transfer the beauty of music to tonal forms. This already implies that the ideal content of music is in the most intimate relationship with these forms. In music the concept of "form" is materialized in a specifically musical way. The forms which construct themselves out of tones are not empty but filled; they are not mere contours of a vacuum but mind giving shape to itself from within. Accordingly, by contrast with arabesque, music is actually a picture, but one whose subject we cannot grasp in words and subsume under concepts. Music has sense and logic—but musical sense and logic. It is a kind of language which we speak and understand yet cannot translate. It is due to a kind of subconscious recognition that we speak of musical "thoughts," and, as in the case of speech, the trained judgment easily distinguishes between genuine thoughts and empty phrases. In the same way, we recognize the rational coherence of a group of tones and call it a sentence, exactly as with every logical proposition we have a sense of where it comes to an end, although what we might mean by "truth" in the two cases is not at all the same thing.

The gratifying reasonableness which can be found in musical structures is based upon certain fundamental laws of nature governing both the human organism and the external manifestations of sound. It is mainly the law of harmonic progression (an analogue to the circle in the visual arts) which produces the nucleus of the most significant musical development and the explanation (itself unfortunately almost inexplicable) of the various musical relationships.

All musical elements have mysterious bonds and affinities among themselves, determined by natural laws. These, imperceptibly regulating rhythm, melody, and harmony, require obedience from human music, and they stamp as caprice and ugliness every noncompliant relationship. They reside, though not in a manner open to scientific investigation, instinctively in every cultivated ear, which accordingly perceives the organic, rational coherence of a group of tones, or its absurdity and unnaturalness, by mere contemplation, with no concept as its criterion or *tertium comparationis*.

This negative, intrinsic rationality is inherent in the tonal system by natural law. In it is grounded the further capacity of tones for entering into the positive content of the beautiful.

Composing is a work of mind upon material compatible with mind. This material is immensely abundant and adaptable in the composer's imagination, which builds, not like the architect, out of crude, ponderous stone, but out of the aftereffects of audible tones already faded away. Being subtler and more ideal than the material of any other art, the tones readily absorb every idea of the composer. Since tonal connections, upon the relationships of which musical beauty is based, are achieved not through being linked up mechanically into a series, but by spontaneous activity of the imagination, the spiritual energy and distinctiveness of each composer's imagination make their mark upon the product as character. Accordingly, as the creation of a thinking and feeling mind, a musical composition has in high degree the capability to be itself full of ideality and feeling. This ideal content we demand of every musical artwork. It is to be found only in the tone-structure itself, however, and not in any other aspect of the work. Concerning the place of ideality and feeling in a musical composition, our view is to the prevailing view as the notion of immanence is to that of transcendence.

Every art has as its goal to externalize an idea actively emerging in the artist's imagination. In the case of music, this idea is a tonal idea, not a conceptual idea which has first been translated into tones. The starting point of all the creative activity of the composer is not the intention to portray a specific feeling but the devising of a particular melody. Through this deep-seated, mysterious power, into the workings of which the human eye will never penetrate, there resounds in the mind of the composer a theme, a motive. We cannot trace this first seed back to its origins; we have to accept it simply as given. Once it has occurred in the composer's imagination, his activity begins, which, starting from this principle theme or motive and always in relation to it, pursues the goal of presenting it in all its relationships. The beauty of a self-subsistent, simple theme makes itself known in aesthetical awareness with an immediacy which permits no other explanation than the inner appropriateness of the phenomenon, the harmony of its parts, without reference to any external third factor. It pleases us in itself, like the arabesque, the ornamental column, or like products of natural beauty such as leaves and flowers.

Nothing could be more misguided and prevalent than the view which distinguishes between beautiful music which possesses ideal content and beautiful music which does not. This view has a much too narrow conception of the beautiful in music, representing both the elaborately constructed form and the ideal content with which the form is filled as self-subsistent. Consequently this view divides all compositions into two categories, the full and the empty, like champagne bottles. Musical champagne, however, has the peculiarity that it grows along with the bottle.

One particular musical conception is, taken by itself, witty; another is banal. A particular final cadence is impressive; change two notes, and it becomes insipid. Quite rightly we describe a musical theme as majestic, graceful, tender, dull, hackneyed, but all these expressions describe the musical character of the passage. To characterize this musical expressiveness of a motive, we often choose terms from the vocabulary of our emotional life: arrogant, peevish, tender, spirited, yearning. We can also take our descriptions from other realms of appearance, however, and speak of fragrant, vernal, hazy, chilly music. Feelings are thus, for the description of musical characteristics, only one source among others which offer similarities. We may use such epithets to describe music (indeed we cannot do without them), provided we never lose sight of the fact that we are using them only figuratively and take care not to say such things as "This music portrays arrogance," etc.

Detailed examination of all the musical determinations of a theme convinces us, however, that, despite the inscrutableness of the ultimate ontological grounds, there is a multitude of proximate causes with which the ideal expression of a piece of music is in precise correlation. Each individual musical element (i.e., each interval, tone-colour, chord, rhythmic figure, etc.) has its own characteristic physiognomy, its specific mode of action. The artist is inscrutable, but the artwork is not.

One and the same melody will not sound the same when accompanied by a triad as when accompanied by a chord of the sixth. A melodic interval of a seventh is wholly unlike a sixth. The accompanying rhythm of a motive, whether loud or soft, on whatever kind of musical instrument, modifies the motive's specific colouration. In brief, each individual factor in a musical passage necessarily contributes to its taking on its own unique ideal expression and having its effect upon the listener in this way and no other. What makes Halévy's music bizarre and Auber's charming, what brings about the peculiarities by which we at once recognize Mendelssohn and Spohr, can be traced to purely musical factors without reference to the obscurities of the feelings.

Why Mendelssohn's numerous six-five chords and narrow diatonic themes, Spohr's chromaticisms and enharmonic relations, Auber's short, bipartite rhythms, etc., produce just these specific, unequivocal impressions: These questions, of course, neither psychology nor physiology can answer.

If, however, we are asking about proximate causes (and this is a matter of importance especially in connection with the arts), the powerful effect of a theme comes not from the supposed augmentation of anguish in the composer but from this or that augmented interval, not from the trembling of his soul but from the drumstrokes, not from his yearning but from the chromaticism. The correlation of the two we shall not ignore; on the contrary, we shall soon examine it more closely. We should keep in mind, however, that scientific examination of the effect of a theme can only be done with those aforementioned invariable and objective data, never with the supposed state of mind which the composer externalizes by means of them. If we want to reason from that state of mind directly to the effects of the work or to explain the latter in terms of the former, we might perhaps arrive at a correct conclusion but will have omitted the most important thing, the middle term of the syllogism, namely, the music itself.

The proficient composer possesses a working knowledge, be it more by instinct or by deliberation, of the character of every musical element. Nevertheless, a theoretical knowledge of these characters, from their most elaborate constructions to the least discriminable element, is required for scientific explanation of the various musical effects and impressions. The particular feature by which a melody has its power over us is not merely some kind of obscure miracle of which we can have no more than an inkling. It is rather the inevitable result of musical factors which are at work in the melody as a particular combination of those factors. Tight or broad rhythm, diatonic or chromatic progression, each has its characteristic feature and its own kind of appeal. That is why a trained musician, from a printed account of an unfamiliar composition, will get a much better idea of it if he reads, for example, that diminished sevenths and tremolos predominate, than from the most poetical description of the emotional crisis through which the reviewer went as a result of listening to it.

Investigation of the nature of each separate musical element and its connection with a specific impression (just of the facts of the matter, not of the ultimate principles) and finally the reduction of these detailed observations to general laws: that would be the philosophical foundation of music for which so many authors are yearning (without, incidentally, telling us what they really understand by the expression "philosophical foundation of music"). The psychological and physical effect of each chord, each rhythm, each interval, however, is by no means explained by saying that this is red, the other green, this is hope, the other discontent, but only by subsuming the particular musical qualities under general aesthetical categories and these in turn under a supreme principle. If, in the former manner, the separate factors were explained in their isolation, it would then have to be shown how they determine and modify each other in their various combinations. Most musically learned people have granted to harmony and contrapuntal accompaniment the preeminent position as the ideal content of a composition. In making this claim, however, they have proceeded much too superficially and atomistically. Some people have settled upon melody as the prompting of genius, as the vehicle for sensuousness and feeling (the Italians are famous for this); harmony has been cast opposite melody in the role of vehicle for the genuine content, being learnable and the product of deliberation. It is curious the way people keep going along with such a superficial way of looking at things. There is basic truth in both claims, but neither at this level of generality nor in isolation do they carry weight. The mind is a unity, and so is the musical creation of an artist. A theme emerges fully armed with its melody and its harmony, together, out of the head of the composer. Neither the principle of subordination nor that of opposition applies to the essence of the relation of harmony to melody. Both can in one place pursue their own lines of development and in another place readily subordinate one to the other. In either case, the highest degree of ideal beauty can be achieved. Is it perhaps the (very sketchy) harmony in the principle themes of Beethoven's "Coriolanus" overture and Mendelssohn's "Hebrides" which confers upon them the expression of brooding melancholy? Would Rossini's "Oh, Matilda" or a Neapolitan folksong achieve more spirit if a basso continuo or a complicated chord sequence replaced the sparse harmonic background? Each melody must be thought up along with its own particular harmony, with its own rhythm and sonority. The ideal content is due only to the conjunction of them all; mutilation of any one part damages also the expression of the remainder. That melody or harmony or rhythm should be able to predominate is to the advantage of all, and to consider on the one hand all genius to be in chords, and on the other all triviality to be in the lack of them, is sheer pedantry. . . .

So the "philosophical foundation of music" would have to try first of all to find out which necessary ideal determinants are connected with each musical element, and in what manner they are connected. The double requirement of a strictly scientific framework and the most elaborate casuistics makes the task a very formidable but not quite insurmountable one: to strive for the ideal of an "exact" science of music after the model of chemistry or of physiology.

The manner in which the creative act takes place in the mind of the composer of instrumental music gives us the most reliable insight into the nature of musical beauty. A musical idea simply turns up in the composer's imagination; he elaborates it. It takes shape progressively, like a crystal, until imperceptibly the form of the completed product stands before him in its main outlines, and there remains only to realize it artistically, checking, measuring, revising. The composer of a piece of instrumental music does not have in mind the representation of a specific content. If he does this, he places himself at a wrong standpoint, more alongside music than within it. His composition becomes the translation of a program into tones which then are unintelligible without the program. We neither deny nor underestimate the conspicuous talent of Berlioz if we mention his name here. Liszt has emulated him with his much feebler "symphonic poems."

Just as out of the same marble one sculptor carves ravishing forms, the other clumsy botchings, so the musical scales in different hands take on the form of a Beethoven overture or one by Verdi. What makes the difference between these two compositions? That the one represents a heightened emotion, perhaps, or the same emotion more faithfully? No, rather that it is constructed in more beautiful tone-forms. This alone makes a piece of music good or bad, that one composer puts in a theme sparkling with genius, the other a commonplace one; that the former works everything out in new and significant relationships, while the latter always makes his (if anything) worse. The harmony of the one unfolds eventually and with originality, while that of the other turns out to be not so much flawed as impoverished; the rhythm in the one throbs with life; in the other, it thumps like a military tattoo.

There is no art which wears out so many forms so quickly as music. Modulations, cadences, intervallic and harmonic progressions all in this manner go stale in fifty, nay, thirty years, so that the gifted composer can no longer make use of them and will be forever making his way to the discovery of new, purely musical directions. Without inaccuracy we may say, of many compositions which were outstanding in their own day, that once upon a time they were beautiful. Out of the primordially obscure connections of musical elements and their innumerable possible combinations, the imagination of the gifted composer will bring to light the most elegant and recherché. It will construct tone-forms which appear to be devised out of free choice yet are all necessarily linked together by an imperceptible, delicate thread. Such works or details we do not hesitate to call works of genius. . . .

Like its beauty, the laws of the construction of a piece of music are grounded exclusively in its musical determinants. Concerning this there are many fluctuating and absurd views, of which we will bring up only one here. This is precisely the view arising out of the generally accepted idea of sonata and symphony which comes from the feeling theory. According to this view, the composer has to represent four separate and distinct states of mind which, in the separate movements of the sonata, must nevertheless together be a coherent whole (how?). In order to justify the undeniable coherence of the movements and to explain the different impressions they make upon us, we in effect compel the listener to impute to them specific feelings as their content. The explanation is sometimes appropriate, more often not, and never is it so by necessity. But this will always occur by necessity: that four musical movements which mutually contrast and enhance one another, according to musical-aesthetical laws, are combined into a single whole. . . .

It is often said that Beethoven, while sketching many of his compositions, must have thought of specific events or states of mind. Where Beethoven or any other composer followed this procedure, he used it merely as a device whereby the coherence of an external event makes it easier to keep hold of the musical entity. If Berlioz, Liszt, etc., believed they got more than this out of the poem, the title, or the experience, this was a self-delusion. It is the unity of musical impression which characterizes the four movements of a sonata as organically unified, not the connection with objects thought of by the composer. Where such poetical leading-strings as these are denied and purely musical ones devised, there we will find no other unity of the parts than a musical unity. Aesthetically it is a matter of indifference whether Beethoven had to adopt such specific subjects even for all his compositions; we do not know what they were, hence so far as the work is concerned they do not exist. Apart from all interpretation, it is the work itself which is under consideration. And as the jurist pretends that whatever is not in the evidence is not in the world, so for aesthetic judgment nothing is available which is not in the work of art. If the parts of a composition appear unified to us, this unity must have its basis in musical determinants.

Finally we shall head off a possible misunderstanding by investigating our concept of the musically beautiful according to three of its facets.

The musically beautiful, in the specific meaning we have adopted, is not limited to music in the so-called "classical" style, nor does it include a preference for the classical over the romantic. It applies to the one as to the other: to Bach as well as Beethoven, to Mozart as well as Schumann. So our thesis contains no hint of partisanship. The whole drift of the present inquiry avoids questions of what ought to be and considers only what is. From this it deduces no particular musical ideal as the only genuine beauty but merely establishes in the same way for all schools what the beautiful is in each, even the most antagonistic.

It is only recently that people have begun looking at artworks in relation to the ideas and events of the times which produced them. In all likelihood this undeniable connection also applies to music. Being a manifestation of the human mind, it must, of course, also stand in interrelation with the other activities of mind: with contemporaneous productions of the literary and visual arts, the poetic, social, scientific conditions of its time, and ultimately with the individual experiences and convictions of the composer. The examination and demonstration of this interrelation are therefore warranted with regard to individual composers and works, and they are truly profitable. Yet we must always keep in mind that drawing such a parallel between artistic matters and special historical circumstances is an art-historical and not at all an aesthetical procedure. While the connection between art history and aesthetics seems necessary from the methodological point of view, yet each of these two sciences must preserve unadulterated its own unique essence in the face of unavoidable confusion of one with the other. The historian, interpreting an artistic phenomenon in its wider context, might see in Spontini the expression of the French Empire period, in Rossini the political restoration. The aesthetician, however, has to limit himself exclusively to the works of these men, to inquire what in these works is beautiful and why. Aesthetical inquiry does not and should not know anything about the personal circumstances and historical background of the composer; it hears and believes only what the artwork itself has to say. It will accordingly discover in Beethoven's symphonies (the identity and biography of the composer being unknown) turbulence, striving, unappeasable longing, vigorous defiance; but that the composer had republican sympathies, was unmarried and becoming deaf, and all the other features which the art historian digs up as illuminating it will by no means glean from the works and may not be used for the evaluation of them. To compare differences in world view between Bach, Mozart, and Haydn and then go back to the differences between their compositions may count as a very attractive and meritorious exercise, yet it is infinitely complicated and will be the more prone to fallacies, the stricter the causal connection it seeks to establish. The danger of exaggeration as a result of accepting this principle is extraordinarily great. We can all too easily interpret the most incidental contemporary influence as a matter of inherent necessity and interpret the perpetually untranslatable language of music any way we like. It is purely on account of quick-witted delivery that the same paradox spoken by a clever person sounds like wisdom but, spoken by a simple person, sounds like nonsense.

Even Hegel, in discussing music, often misled in that he tacitly confused his predominantly art-historical point of view with the purely aesthetical and identified in music certainties which music itself never possessed. Of course there is a connection between the character of every piece of music and that of its author, but for the aesthetician this is not open to view. The idea of necessary connection between all phenomena can in its actual application be exaggerated to the point of caricature. Nowadays it takes real heroism to declare, in opposition to this pleasantly stimulating and ingeniously represented trend, that historical comprehension and aesthetical judgment are two different things. It is objectively certain, first, that the variety of impressions of the various works and schools is based upon crucially dissimilar arrangements of the musical elements, and second, that what rightly pleases in a composition, be it the strictest fugue of Bach or the dreamiest nocturne of Chopin, is *musically* beautiful.

Even less than with the classical can the musically beautiful be equated with the architectonic, which includes the musically beautiful as one of its branches. The rigid grandeur of superimposed towering figurations, the elaborate entwining of many voices, of which none is free and independent because all of them are—these have their own ageless rightness. Yet those marvellously sombre vocal pyramids of the old Italians and Netherlanders are just one small part of the realm of the musically beautiful, just as are the many exquisitely wrought saltcellars and silver candelabra of the venerable Sebastian Bach.

Many aestheticians consider that musical enjoyment can be adequately explained in terms of regularity and symmetry. But no beauty, least of all musical beauty, has ever consisted entirely in these. The most insipid theme can be constructed with perfect symmetry. *Symmetry* is merely a relational concept; it leaves open the question: What is it, then, that appears symmetrical? Orderly structure may be detected among the trivial, shabby fragments of even the most pathetic compositions. The musical sense of the word demands always new symmetrical creations.

Most recently Oersted has expounded this Platonic view in connection with music by means of the example of the circle, for which he claims positive beauty. We may suppose that he had no firsthand experience of such an atrocity as an entirely circular composition.

Perhaps more out of caution than from need, we may add in conclusion that the musically beautiful has nothing to do with mathematics. This notion, which laymen (sensitive authors among them) cherish concerning the role of mathematics in music, is a remarkably vague one. Not content that the vibrations of tones, the spacing of intervals, and consonances and dissonances can be traced back to mathematical proportions, they are also convinced that the beauty of a musical work is based on number. The study of harmony and counterpoint is considered a kind of cabala which teaches compositional calculus.

Even though mathematics provides an indispensable key for the investigation of the physical aspects of musical art, its importance with regard to completed musical works ought not to be overrated. In a musical composition, be it the most beautiful or the ugliest, nothing at all is mathematically worked out. The creations of the imagination are not sums. All monochord experiments, acoustic figures, proportions of intervals, and the like, are irrelevant: The domain of aesthetics begins where these elementary relationships, however important, have left off. Mathematics merely puts in order the rudimentary material for artistic treatment and operates secretly in the simplest relations. Musical thought comes to light without it, however. I confess that I do not understand it when Oersted asks: "Would the lifetime of several mathematicians be enough to calculate all the beauties of a Mozart symphony?" What is there that should or can be calculated? Perhaps the ratio of the vibrations of each tone with those of the next or the lengths of individual phrases or sections with relation to each other? What makes a piece of music a work of art and raises it above the level of physical experiment is something spontaneous, spiritual, and therefore incalculable. In the musical artwork, mathematics has just as small or great a share as in the productions of the other arts. For ultimately mathematics must also guide the hand of the painter and sculptor; mathematics is involved in the measures of verses, in the structures of the architect, and in the figures of the dancer. In every precise study, the application of mathematics, as a function of reason, must find a place. Only we must not grant it an actual, positive, creative power, as so many musicians and aesthetical conservatives would cheerfully have it. Mathematics is in a way like the production of feelings in the listener: It occurs in all the arts, but only in the case of music is a big fuss made about it.

Likewise some people have frequently drawn a parallel between speech and music and have tried to lay down the laws of the former as the laws of the latter. The kinship of song with speech is close enough that one might go along with the similarity of physiological conditions or with their common characteristics as revealing the inner self through the human voice. The analogical relationships are so striking that there is no need for us to go into the matter here. So we would just grant explicitly that, wherever music actually deals just with the subjective revealing of an inner longing, the laws governing speech will in fact to some extent be decisive for song.

That the person who gets into a rage raises the pitch of his voice, while the voice of a speaker who is recovering his composure descends; that sentences of particular gravity will be spoken slowly, and casual ones quickly: These and their like the composer of songs, particularly of dramatic songs, ignores at his peril. However, some people have not been content with these limited analogies but consider music itself to be a kind of language (though more unspecific or more refined), and now they want to abstract the laws of its beauty from the nature of language and trace back every attribute and effect of music to its affinity with language. We take the view that, where the specifics of an art are concerned, their differences with regard to respective domains are more important than their similarities. Such analogies are often enticing but are not at all appropriate to the actual essence of music. Undistracted by them, aesthetical research must push unrelentingly on to the point where language and music part irreconcilably. Only from this point will the art of music be able to germinate truly fruitful aesthetical principles. The essential difference is that in speech the sound is only a sign, that is, a means to an end which is entirely distinct from that means, while in music the sound is an object, i.e., it appears to us as an end in itself. The autonomous beauty of tone-forms in music and the absolute supremacy of thought over sound as merely a means of expression in spoken language are so exclusively opposed that a combination of the two is a logical impossibility.

The essential centre of gravity thus lies entirely differently in language and music, and around these centres all other characteristics arrange themselves. All specifically musical laws will hinge upon the autonomous meaning and beauty of the tones, and all linguistic laws upon the correct adaptation of sound to the requirements of expression.

The most harmful and confused views have arisen from the attempt to understand music as a kind of language; we see the practical consequences every day. Above all, it must seem appropriate to composers of not much creative power to regard autonomous musical beauty (which to them is inaccessible) as a false, materialistic principle and to opt for the programmatic significance of music. Quite apart from Richard Wagner's operas, we often come across interruptions in the melodic flow of even the most insignificant instrumental pieces, due to disconnected cadences, recitatives, and the like. These startle the hearer and behave as if they signify something special, but in fact they signify nothing but ugliness. Some people have taken to praising modern compositions which keep breaking up the overall rhythm and developing inexplicable bumps and heaped-up contrasts. Thus they would have music strive to burst forth from its narrow limits and elevate itself to speech. To us this kind of commendation has always seemed equivocal. The limits of music are by no means narrow, but they are very precisely drawn. Music can never be "elevated" to the level of speech (strictly speaking, from the musical standpoint, one must say "lowered"), since music obviously would have to be an elevated kind of speech.

Even our singers forget this, who in deeply moving passages bellow words, indeed phrases, as if speaking them, and believe they have thereby demonstrated the highest degree of intensification of music. They fail to notice that the transition from singing to speaking is always a descent, so that the highest normal tone in speech sounds even deeper than the deepest sung tone of the same voice. Just as bad as these practical consequences, indeed worse, because they cannot be experimentally refuted, are theories which would foist upon music the laws of development and construction of speech, as had been attempted in earlier times by Rousseau and Rameau and more recently by the disciples of R. Wagner. The true heart of music, the formal beauty which gratifies in itself, would thereby be pierced through, and the chimera of "meaning" pursued. An aesthetics of musical art must therefore take as its most important task to set forth unrelentingly the basic distinction between the essence of music and that of language and in all deductions hold fast to the principle that, where the specifically musical is concerned, the analogy with language does not apply.

Edward T. Cone

EXPRESSIVENESS IN MUSIC:
FROM *THE COMPOSER'S VOICE*

Even the most sympathetic reader of the foregoing pages will no doubt be dissatisfied, and on two counts. In the first place, he may contend that the discussion primarily develops an elaborate figure of speech, and that conclusions based on analogies cannot be trusted.

He would be right. Yet I do not see how an attempt to interpret nonverbal and unverbalizable phenomena can proceed otherwise than by metaphor and analogy. No doubt, at every point along the way I should have posted a little sign reading So To Speak, or As It Were, but this would soon have proved tiresome to the reader. So I depend on his indulgence, hoping that I have not used my metaphors illegitimately. It is true that argument of this kind cannot lead to conclusions as firm as those of deductive logic, but it is not true that it cannot lead to reasonable and even convincing conclusions. Its method is not proof but persuasion. So, although I freely grant that I have proved nothing, I hope that I have persuaded some readers of the reasonableness of some of the results of my investigations.

The second hypothetical complaint refers to subject matter, not method. Here is a book, one may say, that apparently promises to deal with music as a medium of communication. Yet it never comes to grips, except briefly and almost peripherally, with the basic question of what music means or expresses.

To this charge, too, I plead guilty; and again the guilt is deliberately incurred. The subject of my study is not what music is about but rather how one might profitably think about music. More specifically, my task has been to consider what it means to say that music is a form of utterance, and not to determine what such utterance might be trying to say. A number of interesting essays on the latter subject—sometimes called musical semantics—have appeared over the past few years.[1] These differ widely from

From The Composer's Voice *(Berkeley: University of California Press, 1974), pp. 159–175. Reprinted with permission of the University of California Press.*
    [1]E.g.: Wilson Coker, *Music and Meaning* (New York: The Free Press, 1972); Donald N. Ferguson, *Music and Metaphor* (Minneapolis: University of Minnesota Press, 1960); Terence McLaughlin, *Music and Communication* (London: Faber and Faber, 1970); Leonard B. Meyer, *Emotion and Meaning in Music* (Chicago: University of Chicago Press, 1956).

one another in their methods and in their conclusions, but all of them seem either to ignore problems that I deem basic to all such investigations, or to take their solutions for granted.

My study, then, is meant to be prefatory to any theory of musical meaning or musical expression, and I have tried to keep it broad enough to serve as a framework for almost any such theory—even that of the pure formalist. For most of the categories of my dramatistic analysis, as I have pointed out, become formal categories when observed from another point of view. The formalist need only reinterpret them thus in the case of absolute music. The extramusical implications of program music he can dismiss as illusory, and he can insist that the verbal expression of song is only conventionally associated with the music. Or, applying a more sophisticated technique, he can look in both program and text for patterns that, by their relations to the purely musical design, can add a new dimension of structural complexity.

It should be clear, though, that I do not accept the formalist's premises; and at this point it is perhaps only fair to state what my own are. I do so tentatively, for these matters are highly speculative. I put forward the following, then, as the view that seems to me the most reasonable at the moment.

My investigation has developed the picture of music as a form of utterance, to be compared and contrasted with the verbal utterances of ordinary speech and of imaginative literature. If a sample of ordinary speech is an actual utterance, then a literary production is a simulated utterance: it is not to be construed as the utterance of a real person, living or dead, but as that of a persona or character who is an imaginary creation of the literary work itself—indeed, who subsists only by virtue of the literary utterance. (One could make a further distinction between simulated utterances on the page and in performance—as read and as heard. But, as in music, reading is a kind of performance, albeit a silent one. Hence I find the distinction unnecessary. In this connection one must remember that the performed utterance is not the utterance of the performer, but of the character he portrays.)

The medium of musical utterance, like that of speech, consists of purposefully organized sounds, produced or producible by actual performers. But except in the special case of natural song, the utterances themselves, like those of literature, are artistic creations to be construed as simulated—as emanating from personas or characters who subsist only by virtue of the musical composition. But musical sounds, unlike those of speech, are basically nonverbal. Song, of course, makes use of verbal utterance; but even in unaccompanied song one can distinguish between the verbal and vocal levels of expression. Qua poetry, a song is a kind of verbal utterance; qua music, its medium is the human voice, independent of verbal meaning—a vocal, symbolic, nonverbal utterance. Instrumental music, whether alone or accompanying the voice, goes one step further in the direction of abstraction from the word and constitutes a form of purely symbolic utterance, an utterance by analogy with song.

Has musical utterance any meaning? The answer naturally depends on what one means by "meaning," and what one means by the question. For example, it can be contended that no piece of music has a meaning because no work of art has a meaning—*a* meaning, of which one can say, "This is the meaning of the work of art." For, although a work of art may have meaning, or meanings, it is never its function—as it is the function of a piece of expository prose—merely to convey information that can be identified as its meaning.

The question whether music has meaning is usually intended, however, to compare or to contrast music with poetry, not with expository prose. A poem, whether or not it has *a* meaning, normally has both meaning—that is, paraphrasable content—and meanings—that is, the connotations and denotations of its words and phrases. On both counts music fails. True, music has its own syntax. But it has no content that can be paraphrased in other music, or in words, or in any other medium; and its elements—notes, chords, motifs—normally have no referents. (Here, of course, is where the metaphor of music as a language completely fails.)

One might offer Wagner's leitmotifs as counterexamples; but the objects, characters, etc., with which the motifs are associated hardly ever function analogously to semantic referents. In some cases, the musical idea has merely been *named* in accordance with a presumable dramatic counterpart. That is, if a motif is frequently associated with dramatic situations involving X, and if the motif sounds expressively appropriate to X, then it is convenient to give it the same name as X. This is the case with many of Wagner's motifs, the names of which vary from commentator to commentator according to their interpretations of the situations in question. In other examples, the musical idea seems to have been designed as a suggestive *representation* of X. But such a representation no more *means* X than a portrait *means* its sitter. As usual, Berlioz is on the right track. The musical *idée fixe* of the *Fantastic Symphony* is a melody that is always associated in the mind of the hero with the image of his beloved. Whenever he thinks of her, the melody appears. But the melodic image in his mind's ear does not *mean* "the Beloved" any more than the visual image in his mind's eye does.

To be sure, once one has accepted a definite name for a motif, it is hard to keep from thinking of that name whenever the motif is sounded. The referent of the name does then become an artificial referent of the motif. Exploitation of this reaction can lead to a kind of arbitrary symbolism that some composers have deliberately employed—usually at the expense of more typically musical values. Even Berlioz may have gone too far in this direction when he inserted the *idée fixe* at the end of the "March to the Scaffold." Certainly Strauss relied on the method in the mechanical exposition of leitmotifs in his melodrama "Enoch Arden." So did Puccini when he allowed the conventional associations of a familiar theme to inform his audience of the nationality of *Madama Butterfly's* hero-villain. To most listeners today, "Enoch Arden" seems overly contrived, and Puccini's use of "The Star-Spangled Banner" downright ludicrous. Referents may thus be attached to musical ideas, but always at the risk of doing violence to the medium.

Words do not always have referents. "Hey-diddle-diddle" is a word, or phrase, used in a well-known poem, but it is entirely meaningless. We need not restrict ourselves to nonsense syllables. Words like "oh" and "ah," while perfectly intelligible in context, have no core of meaning that can be independently conveyed. "Oh" can express astonishment, delight, regret, fear, and so on. That is, in context the single word can mean "I am astonished," "I am delighted," "I am sorry," or "I am afraid." Although these shades of meaning can be indicated to some extent by a speaker's tone of voice, they can be interpreted with certainty only by one who is familiar with the context. In this sense, then, words like "oh" and "ah" are meaningless—but meaningful! They function as pure gesture—to borrow a term used by R. P. Blackmur.[2] For language has a gestural as well as a strictly semantic aspect. Semantically a verbal utterance conveys a conceptual content; gesturally, it functions as an expressive action. Like physical gesture, verbal gesture communicates the speaker's (or the writer's) attitude toward what he is saying; or it tries to influence his hearers (or readers), not by the sense of the discourse, but by its intensity.

Especially in dramatic poetry, even words of normal signification can be used to produce almost pure gestural effects that depend less on the specific meanings of the words than on the modes of performance—the kinds of expression—they imply. This is true, for example, in those reiterative passages so characteristic of Shakespeare, in which a word or phrase will be repeated long after it has done its semantic work, or even without regard for that work. The context determines the tempo, the tone of voice, and the inflections, that must be used in order to convey the appropriate intensity, for the words in themselves reveal little. Such passages as the following are merely silly when presented in isolation:

> "Tomorrow, and tomorrow, and tomorrow . . ."
> "Howl, howl, howl, howl!"
> "Never, never, never, never, never!"

Yet in context they are extremely powerful, for they articulate attitudes that are usually only suggested by half-articulate interjections, or else relegated to the realm of the completely inarticulate—sighs, groans, cries of pain, snarls of rage. A level of half-conscious, almost involuntary utterance is raised to the level of fully realized poetic expression.

Not all poetry, and very little prose, can exploit the potentialities of language as gesture to the extent of the quoted passages. But the gestural aspect is often present when unsuspected—concealed, perhaps, in the syntax or the word order. In the best poetry—in the best prose, for that matter—gesture and meaning complement and reinforce each other.

It is the gestural aspect of utterance that is simulated, and symbolized, by music. If music is a language at all, it is a language of gesture: of direct actions, of pauses, of startings and stoppings, of rises and falls, of tenseness and slackness, of accentuations. These gestures are symbolized by musical motifs and progressions, and they are given structure by musical rhythm and meter, under the control of musical tempo. The vocal utterance of song emphasizes, even exaggerates, the gestural potentialities of its words. Instrumental utterance, lacking intrinsic verbal content, goes so far as to constitute what might be called a medium of pure symbolic gesture.

The gestures of music can be interpreted as symbolic of physical as well as verbal gestures. For a physical gesture is an action that emulates an utterance—an action that tries to speak (hence our admiration of the "eloquent gesture"). If music resembles utterance in being sound, it resembles physical gesture in being speechless. Once

---

[2]See the title essay in R. P. Blackmur, *Language as Gesture* (New York: Harcourt Brace, 1952), pp. 3–24. My discussion is greatly indebted to Blackmur's.

more, in music symbolic utterance and symbolic gesture come together. Indeed, in music symbolic utterance *is* symbolic gesture.

Another way of putting the same point is to say that music is both poetry and dance. This is not meant to imply a theory of the origin of music, but to suggest that in music both the verbal gestures of poetry and the bodily gestures of the dance are symbolized in the medium of pure sound. The present study has approached its subject mainly from the direction of poetry. No doubt a similar investigation could start with the dance. I should expect it to come to similar conclusions.

The symbolic gestures of music, like the verbal gestures cited above, are both meaningless and meaningful. This apparent contradiction arises, of course, from a play on words. In the same spirit we might also say: musical gestures lack signification, but they can be significant. Like a sigh, a musical gesture has no specific referent, it conveys no specific message. But like a sigh, it can prove appropriate to many occasions; it can fit into many contexts, which in return can explain its significance. The expressive content of the musical gesture, then, depends on its context. Deprived of context, the gesture expresses nothing; it is only potentially expressive.

No context, no content. Almost all musicians would agree with this dictum when interpreted in a strictly formal way to mean that only the syntactical and formal context supplied by a specific compositional situation can reveal the significance of a musical idea. Only the die-hard Wagnerian would maintain the contrary. But I mean something stronger. Significance must include the significance of the entire composition as well as of each motif. And content refers to humanly expressive content. I use that somewhat pretentious term for want of a better. "Emotional content" is too restrictive, and it begs the question of what music expresses. "Extramusical content" implies something adventitious, not really connected with the music. So I come back to "humanly expressive content": whatever of human importance a musical composition may express, not only through each individual gesture, but also through the totality of gestures that constitutes its form. "No context, no content," then, means: a composition represents a human action, and only in a context of wider human activity is its content revealed.

Context in this sense is most obviously provided by words that are actually sung. These can, for example, tell us whether a musical sigh—perhaps a downward slur—is one of relief or of despondency. They can define the change of mood implied by a modulation. They can explain a rapid movement as the result of impetuosity, or fear, or sheer good spirits. They can, in short, associate each musical motion with a human emotion—or mood, or activity, or attitude. When the gestures of the music are closely analogous to those implied by the words, we are tempted to say that the music expresses the emotion, mood, activity, or attitude revealed by the text. Perhaps it does, but if so only contingently, not necessarily. It would therefore be more accurate to say that the music appropriates the emotion, etc., of the text, and through this borrowed meaning it realizes some part of its expressive potential. (Yet the music pays well for the privilege, as I point out in chapter 2.) It is thus wrong to conclude that the emotion—or any other state of mind, idea, or image, derived from the poetry—constitutes the content of the song. The content emerges from the mutual relations of words and musical gestures, and from the light they throw on each other. A song is thus a kind of metaphor, an equation whose significance consists, not in what it states about either of the two members, but in the coupling itself—in the fact that the equality is asserted.

The suggestion that music does not express emotions but appropriates them gains some plausibility from the existence of strophic song—one might say, with reference to examples from *Die schöne Müllerin*, the triumphant existence. The fact that a given musical setting can be applied to a number of different stanzas need not mean that the music is expressively neutral, since for any of the Schubert examples it would be easy to find stanzas that would fit metrically but would not work because of expressive disparity. What strophic song suggests is that a piece of music allows a wide but not unrestricted range of possible expression: this is what I call its expressive potential. A given text specifies one possibility, or at most a relatively narrow range of possibility, its verbal formulation providing the immediate context that renders the musical gestures emotionally, etc., expressive.

At the same time, a text can do something more. Its content—the states of mind, ideas, and images it communicates—can be taken as an example of the kind of human content that can properly be associated with the music; and by this exemplification it can suggest a broad span of the entire range of expression available to that music. In a successful strophic song, every stanza offers such an example, each throwing its own light on the whole field of the expressive potential.

Words, then, do not limit the potential of music; rather, by specification and exemplification, they may render it more easily comprehensible. The situation is not very different when the words are only implied, as in chorale-preludes or transcriptions. The connotations of a known text and of its associated melody can be just as vivid to the informed listener as if they were actually being sung.

Another way in which music can be supplied with a human context is by a program, and the most convincing justification of program music rests on an argument similar to the preceding. A program can specify a general mood to be associated with the movement of the music, or it can follow—or direct—the course of the music more closely through the succession of sounds, actions, tensions, and relaxations that its narrative suggests. The effectiveness of a program depends on the degree to which it is felt to be figuratively isomorphic with the form of the composition—the extent to which the pattern of activity suggested by the program corresponds to the pattern of symbolic gestures created by the music. Naturally, the less detailed the program is, the easier it is for the listener to imagine such correspondence. This is probably the reason why composers who do not normally utilize explicit programs are willing to imply vague ones by suggestive titles: Funeral March, Ballade, Nocturne, and the like.

To what extent does the program influence the content of the composition? The content of song is to be found in the mutual illumination of text and music; but there the words are an integral part of the complete composition. The music, that is to say, is heard in a specific verbal context. A program, however, is merely an adjunct to the music with which it is associated. Words and music are not sounded together; and since they are not synchronized, it is fruitless even to try to imagine them as sounding together. In fact, the exact words are of little importance; the program consists of the ideas the words convey. A program, then, gives a composition a conceptual, not a verbal, context. Its content, like that of a song text, can serve as an example of the expressive possibilities of the music. But whereas the words of the song provide a context that is both specifically relevant to the music and exemplary, the context provided by the program is only exemplary. That is why it is usually considered a fault to include in a composition details that are related only programmatically to the structure as a whole. These fasten on the composition an interpretation that should be at most suggestive of the total expressive potential.

An example or two may clarify this point. Debussy has given us every encouragement, by his title and by his directions to the pianist, to hear "Des pas sur la neige" as depicting a wintry landscape. But one can imagine a number of other desolate scenes to which the music would be equally appropriate. Or one can think in more abstract terms of loneliness and regret. Finally, one can simply try to let the music communicate its expressive message through one's subconscious associations with its symbolic gestures. If one applies these levels of abstraction to "Feux d'artifice," however, one is always brought up short by the quotation from "La Marseillaise" at the end. Here is a formally gratuitous detail that gains significance most readily from the assumption that the piece really depicts the fireworks at a public celebration, and that we hear the music of a band dying away in the distance. On this literal level the passage is effective and amusing, but it limits the possible significance of the music and discourages one from taking it very seriously.

The best program music can thus be heard as absolute music. Absolute music lacks specific verbal or conceptual context, but this does not mean that it lacks context. As in the more abstract approaches to program music, so here each listener supplies his own context, out of the store of his own experience. He may do this consciously and verbally, finding in the first movement of Beethoven's Fifth Symphony a struggle against Fate, and in the finale a triumphant victory. Such interpretations, however, often divert one's attention from the course of the music. Moreover, one tends to take one's own interpretation as more than merely exemplary, and to consider it as the true context—even the true content—of the music. More sophisticated listeners therefore eschew such verbalization. Many of them claim to enjoy music as pure structure alone. I doubt whether this is ever possible, for even when our conscious attention is entirely occupied with following the formal design, our subconscious, in Proustian fashion, is still creating a context—nonverbal but highly personal. We subconsciously ascribe to the music a content based on the correspondence between musical gestures and their patterns on the one hand, and isomorphically analogous experiences, inner or outer, on the other. So long as we do not—or cannot—express these experiences or explain their correspondence with the music in words, we cannot be tempted to maintain that they restrictively define the context of the composition. The danger is rather that, unaware of the power of this level of musical comprehension, we adopt the formalist position. But is this so dangerous after all? The claim of the strict formalist is but the extreme version of an important truth: that only by concentrating on the structure of a composition can we allow our subconscious complete freedom to adduce, from its fund of knowledge and experience, the appropriate associations that will suggest, by exemplification, the full range of the composition's expressive potential.

This view seems reasonable in the light of a situation familiar to many music lovers. Few of us try to define our reactions to a given composition in terms of mood or emotion, but whenever we are asked point-blank to do so, we discover that our subconscious has already done the job. We know what the piece is "about," and we know that we know, but we usually have to grope for a way to express it. Often the verbalization we come up with will not be abstract but related to specific kinds of personal experience.

Sometimes the principle works in the opposite direction. Young pianists often fail to give convincing accounts of the last Beethoven sonatas not because of technical deficiency or lack of intellectual understanding but because of insufficient emotional maturity. Their personal histories offer them no parallel to help them gauge the expressive potential of the music. And it not infrequently happens—as attested by more than one eminent musician—that in the course of events one encounters situations that startlingly illuminate, and are illuminated by, such a composition hitherto imperfectly grasped. For our musical sensibility is affected by our experience—and not just our musical experience. The capacity for seemingly perpetual self-renewal that characterizes the greatest music is only partially due to the fact that we keep finding in it new patterns of structural relationships; in fact, this is not always the case. But we do, continually though subconsciously, bring new personal experiences to bear on it, finding in them new exemplifications of an ever-widening range of expressive possibilities.

Because each listener's reconstruction of the human context must be in terms of his own experience, attempts at verbal formulation of that context vary—sometimes widely. Nor, if we could read the subconscious reactions of which the words are only imperfect and incomplete reports, would we find any more unanimity. This does not condemn us to complete relativism, however. For the context is not the content, it is only the necessary vehicle of the content. The content of a song is not revealed by the words alone but by the quasi-metaphorical relation between words and music. In the same way, the content of instrumental music is revealed to each listener by the relation between the music and the personal context he brings to it. Since each such context can be only exemplary, the resulting content can be only partial. The total content of a complex and profound composition is thus probably beyond the comprehension of any individual listener; it is a potential content matching the entire expressive potential. If the context a hearer adduces is related to the composition analogically, through isomorphic resemblance to its gestures and their structural pattern, and not adventitiously, through arbitrary choice or chance connection, then that context will contribute legitimately and appropriately to the total potential. Superficially divergent as one listener's context may seem from another's, they will be linked by their common isomorphism with the musical structure, and hence with each other. And deeper analysis should reveal, beneath the surface differences, some common ground of expression that in turn suggests the nature of the complete potential. Here, finally, is where the total potential content of any musical work is located: in the relationship among all its contexts and in the illumination thrown on that relationship by the musical structure that unites them.

It is therefore possible for a complex work like Mozart's Symphony No. 40 to receive such diverse, even contradictory characterizations as "heroically tragic"[3] and "[exhibiting] the poised gracefulness of Greece."[4] We must assume that any serious listener who reports a reaction of this kind has brought to bear on his interpretation those of his own experiences that seem to fit the patterns of the music. Owing to a combination of

---

[3]Alfred Einstein, *Mozart, His Character, His Work*, trans. Arthur Mendel and Nathan Broder (New York: Oxford University Press, 1945), p. 235.

[4]"Nun vergleiche man die Mozartsche G-moll-Symphonie, diese griechisch-schwebende Grazie," Robert Schumann, "Characteristik der Tonarten," in *Gesammelte Schriften über Musik und Musiker*, 5th edition, Martin Kreisig, ed. (Leipzig: Breitkopf und Härtel, 1914), Vol. I, p. 105.

temperament and personal history, one such listener may find that the sum of the adduced associations suggests heroism in defeat; for the same reasons, another invokes an image of contentment in a classical setting. If we could examine and analyze the relevant experiences of both, we should no doubt come to the conclusion that the common ground of context uniting them and relating them to the music is not necessarily attached to any mood. It might, for example, be a pattern of restrained impulses and controlled energies, which some may associate with tragic resignation and others with temperate joy. A more philosophically disposed listener might recognize both possibilities. For him the content of the movement would derive from the discovery of the basic likenesses revealed by the music as underlying two apparently opposed states of mind. Even this would be a partial content, however. A still more profound view of the movement might find its expressive potential in a general attitude applicable to a broad spectrum of moods and emotional reactions—for example, an essential serenity despite superficial agitation, based on a realistic acceptance of whatever comes. Yet even this might not yield the total content. The expressive potential of Mozart's music is so broad that one understands immediately what W. J. Turner has in mind when he compares it to "a still, bright, perfect, cloudless day. . . . Such a day does not provoke or in the faintest degree suggest one mood rather than another. It is infinitely protean. It means just what you mean. It is intangible, immaterial—fitting your spirit like a glove."[5]

For the musician, the fact that he can never satisfactorily formulate the content of a composition in words is no disadvantage. Why should he try? For him the gestures of music are second nature. They are a part of his subconscious as well as his conscious mind. They are, in fact, an important segment of that store of experience that subconsciously creates a context for music. For the musician, that is, the context created by his memory is largely, although never entirely, a musical context. When he tries to verbalize the significance of a certain composition, he often does so by relating it to other musical works.

In a more general sense, the same is true of every informed listener. In order to understand any piece of music, he must place it in the context of a musical style and its conventions—again, by relating it to other works. When he cannot make such connections, as when an untrained Westerner hears music of the Orient, he fails to recognize the content, or else he grossly misinterprets it.

The formalist goes one step further and insists that the only context, or the only legitimate context, of music is other music. For him its apparent human content is factitious, arising solely from the traditional and arbitrary associations of stylistic convention. But such generalization is unwarranted. True, musical expression does rely heavily on convention, but music is not alone among the arts in this respect. An appreciation of their conventional aspects is essential to an understanding of all of them—even of the verbal and representational arts, to which the power of expressing human content is usually conceded. For stylistic conventions are not necessarily arbitrary. They arise for both expressive and formal reasons, and they serve both expressive and formal purposes. The supposed distinction between the emotional effects of major and minor in modern Western music is a case in point. The distinction

[5]W. J. Turner, *Mozart: The Man and His Works* (New York: Knopf, 1938), pp. 380–381.

rests on a convention, true, but on a convention that developed naturally out of the structure of the tonal system and fulfilled an important expressive need.

A more specific example may make this point clearer. It might be argued that the expressive associations of the Funeral March from Chopin's Sonata in B-flat minor depend on mere convention—on the fact that we recognize the combination of common meter, slow tempo, ponderous beat, and somber color, as adding up to a conventional symbol that reads: Funeral March. But, leaving aside the question of how such a symbol could have been established without the existence of compositions (such as Chopin's!) that are supposed to exemplify it, one can reply that the convention is not an arbitrary one. It arose in response to the demands of a specific kind of occasion for which music served a functional purpose, and hence the same convention can be used artistically to evoke a similar occasion in the imagination. The convention thus places the composition in a musical context that includes, in this case, the demands of a familiar human situation. It is to this situation, and to the (imagined) function that it calls on the music to perform, that the expressive associations of the Chopin movement should be attributed.

The formalist forgets, moreover, that even a purely musical context can be determined by expressive as well as formal factors. When we try to explain the content of one composition in terms of others, we often rely on stylistic resemblances—but not always. Sometimes we find kinship among works that have nothing—at least nothing obvious—in common with respect to technique, form, or style. What they seem to share is a large area of what I have called expressive potential. One's sense of this type of relationship must necessarily be highly subjective, but I suggest as an example Bartók's Sixth Quartet, which I hear as defining an area of content near that of the last quartets of Beethoven. In particular, the fourfold Mesto of the Bartók seems to me close in expressive effect—although neither in idiom nor in structure—to the opening fugue of Beethoven's Op. 131.

The formalist is justified in demanding a purely musical context for music only if he recognizes that (above all for the musician) the musical context and the human context are inextricably intertwined. John O'Hara was right: "Music . . . is to be enjoyed, and we might as well face it: it must have human associations if it is to be enjoyed."[6] In other words: no context, no content. But there is always a context, and there is always a content.

[6]John O'Hara, *Butterfield 8* (New York: Harcourt Brace, 1935), p. 131.

Renée Cox

VARIETIES OF MUSICAL EXPRESSIONISM

The statement "music expresses emotion" is interpreted in a variety of ways. Some of the interpretations that have been offered focus on music perceivers or makers:

a. Music can evoke emotions in listeners, or can enhance or deepen emotions felt by listeners.[1]

b. Composers or performers can somehow vent or communicate their emotions with music.[2]

In order for either of these positions to be viable, it must be accompanied by a theory that explains how or why music can evoke or communicate emotion. Even when such an explanation is given, many theorists consider the emotions of music makers and perceivers irrelevant to musical expression. For it is often the case that perceivers regard music as expressive even when they do not react emotionally to the music; and it is clear that music makers do not have to feel emotion while composing or performing in order for their music to be regarded as expressive of emotion. Hence there are expressionist theories that focus not on music's relation to the emotions of particular persons, but on music's relation to emotion in general. According to Harold Osborne, Susanne Langer, and Peter Kivy respectively, to say that music expresses emotion is to say that:

c. music can actually embody feeling.[3]

d. music symbolizes emotion through its resemblance of emotion's dynamic properties.[4]

This essay was written for the second edition of this collection and is being published for the first time. An earlier version of this paper was presented at the October 1987 meeting of the American Society for Aesthetics.

[1]The view that expression is what the perceiver takes away from the experience is proposed by John Hospers as one of four interpretations of expression in "The Concept of Artistic Expression," *Introductory Readings in Aesthetics*, ed. Hospers (New York: Macmillan, 1969), pp. 142–166.

[2]This interpretation of "expression" is characteristic of J. W. N. Sullivan's *Beethoven: His Spiritual Development* (New York: Vintage Books, 1960).

[3]See Harold Osborne, "Expressiveness: Where Is the Feeling Found?" *British Journal of Aesthetics* 23, no. 2 (1983): 112–23, and his "Expressiveness in the Arts," *Journal of Aesthetics and Art Criticism* 41, no. 1 (1982): 19–26.

[4]See Susanne Langer, *Philosophy in a New Key: A Study in the Symbolism of Reason, Rite, and Art* (New York: New American Library, 1952). Langer later substituted the term "signal" for "symbol."

e.   music sounds emotional through its resemblance of expressive speech or gesture.[5]

Even when taken together or in various combinations, these positions are insufficient to account for the "emotional" nature of music. It will be argued below that if music seems emotional or makes us emotional, it is inevitably because we associate it with emotional situations in our own lives or the lives of others. Before advancing this position, I would like to consider briefly the merits of the ones listed above.

What is it about instrumental music that can make some people emotional? Some listeners say they can be touched by the sheer beauty of music. Leonard Meyer has suggested that people can get emotional when music inhibits their musical tendencies. When a listener is uncertain about what sort of consequent will follow a musical antecedent, or expects a particular consequent and is surprised by another, the ambiguity or conflict involved may give rise to negative emotion (or "affect"), and a subsequent resolution of the ambiguity or conflict may give rise to positive emotion.[6] In other words, we tend to react emotionally to problems we cannot solve, even if these problems are musical ones that have no bearing on our personal lives. We may also become emotional through sympathy with an expressive performer. (Here we move outside the music itself to the world of human expression.) If a performer is tearful, has a pained expression, or moves expressively while performing, some sensitive people may identify with the intensity of the expression and become emotional themselves. This is most likely to happen if the dynamic properties of the music somehow conform to the movements and expressions the performer is making.

If a performer feels emotional while performing, and this emotion has an impact on the way the music is played, it seems appropriate to say that the performer is expressing his or her emotion. If aggressive movements can be considered expressions of anger outside of aesthetic experience, then aggressive violin playing by an angry player could be considered an expression of anger as well. (Of course, a performer may also play aggressively for purely musical reasons.) Similarly, a composer's emotion may have an impact on the nature of a composition or on the compositional process. Tchaikovsky considered his Symphony No. 6 (Pathétique) to be a reflection of his grief and desolation. The 125 songs that Robert Schumann composed in 1840 were probably motivated by his joy at the opportunity to marry Clara Wieck. Performers or composers can also attempt to express an emotion that they are not feeling while playing or writing. If expression is considered to be a kind of communication, these sorts of expression are inexact at best. Performers, who can use facial expressions and bodily movements, have a much better chance at success. To what extent a composer can communicate an emotion without words (texts, titles, performance instructions, etc.) depends on the extent to which composer and audience share expressive conventions. If both composer and audience consider soft, slow, minor music to be expressive of sadness, then the composer can express sadness musically. But most expressive con-

---

[5]See Peter Kivy, *The Corded Shell: Reflections on Musical Expression* (Princeton: Princeton University Press, 1980), p. 14. Jerrold Levinson has noted that expressionists sometimes do not distinguish clearly between what "expression" *means* or amounts to, and what the *causes* of expression are. Peter Kivy, he points out, concentrates exclusively on the latter, while Nelson Goodman (see below, note 25) is concerned with the former. See Levinson's review of *The Corded Shell* in *Canadian Philosophical Reviews* (Winter 1981), p. 150.

[6]Leonard Meyer, *Emotion and Meaning in Music* (Chicago: Chicago University Press, 1956), chap. 1.

ventions are not codified and thus difficult to establish, and expressive conventions in general are rejected as irrelevant to instrumental music by many composers and listeners.

Harold Osborne, who has advanced position c above, maintains that music cannot embody an emotion, which requires a real-life situation or object, but believes that it can embody the feeling accompanying emotional experience. He concurs with Vincent Tomas that "from the phenomenological point of view, feeling is literally in aesthetic objects in precisely the same sense that colors are."[7] I'm not sure what is meant here by "the phenomenological point of view." If it is being suggested that feelings can exist outside of people, the position is strongly counterintuitive. For if feelings were literally in aesthetic objects, more perceivers would be able to detect them. The fact is that while everyone not color-blind agrees that blood (seen in the light) is red, not everyone perceives music—any music—as an embodiment of emotion or feeling. This cannot be due to any musical deficiency; Stravinsky, who has written music many regard as highly expressive, was one listener who believed there is no emotion in music to be found.

But there is a sense in which emotion can be embodied in music, and that is if we consider music to be essentially a mental phenomenon.[8] By this account, sounds are external to humans, but the aesthetic tone-conceiving and systemic relating of tones that is music takes place only in human minds. During this process, the sounds and the music seem fused; there is not objective sound on one hand and subjective tone-relating on the other, there is only the experience of music. When an emotion is related to the music, or when music reminds us of emotion associated in the past, the emotion can seem fused with the music as well. But emotion does not actually fuse with the sounds external to us. Like music itself, emotion in music is something we bring to sound, a way of making sense of sound.

If a composer should want to express an emotion suggested by a text or other subject matter associated with the music, one of the best ways to do so is to compose music that has dynamic properties similar to the dynamic properties of the felt emotion, or to speech and gestures characteristic of the emotion. If, when we are angry, our heads seem to race, our actions are quick and forceful, and our speech loud and clipped, a composer will do well to compose fast, loud, staccato music to express this emotion. Analogies such as these will be discussed further below. Important as these analogies are, they are not the only factors that make particular musics seem suitable for particular subjects. As any one who watches television or movies can attest, timbre, texture, and pitch frequency have come to be used quite effectively in this regard. Much of what is considered as expressive in music relates to musical ambiguity and clarity, stability and instability.

Dissonance and chromaticism have traditionally been regarded as systemically unstable, at least before the twentieth century, and used in the extreme, they are disturbing to some listeners. (What is regarded as dissonant, however, varies culturally and changes over time.) The minor mode is ambiguous relative to the major. While there is only one major mode, there are three minor ones (pure, harmonic, and

---

[7]Harold Osborne, "The Concept of Expression in Art," in *Philosophy Looks at the Arts*, ed. Joseph Margolis (New York: Scribner, 1962).
[8]See my "A Defence of Musical Idealism," *British Journal of Aesthetics* 26, no. 2 (1986): 133–42.

melodic), and it is often unclear which form will ensue in a given minor passage.[9] The minor third (6:5), which gives the minor triad its quality, is slightly more dissonant than the major. Also, the major triad appears intact in the natural overtone series, and the minor triad does not. This has led Paul Hindemith to claim that the major triad is "one of the most impressive phenomena of nature, simple and elemental as rain, snow and wind," and that the minor triad is simply a "clouding" of the major.[10] Whether the relative dissonance, ambiguity, and "unnatural" character of minor can be detected by the average listener would be difficult to determine. But it is clear that composers and theorists throughout history were aware of these characteristics. And because ambiguity and instability are associated with negative emotions, composers have traditionally associated minor modes, dissonance, and chromaticism with negative emotions in texts, programs, and the like.

How widespread such expressive conventions were throughout music history is difficult to ascertain; the concepts of major and minor were not firmly established until the eighteenth century, and their associations with positive and negative emotions respectively probably came even later. But it seems clear these expressive conventions exist, and are having an impact on contemporary listeners. Instability, clarity, and ambiguity are not emotions, however, and they are not sufficient to make music emotional. Musical motion will seem like emotion only if emotional subject matter is brought to bear.

And so it is with all musical expression. If music makes us emotional, if composers or performers can express emotions musically, if music and emotion seem fused, or if musical motion or quality seems emotional, it is inevitably because we associate the music with human emotional experience. When we associate music with emotion, it is often because the music accompanies an emotional text, title, program, drama, or situation. But music is also often associated with emotional personal experiences of our own. Music is always heard within the contexts of our lives, and is sometimes difficult to separate from these contexts. If purely instrumental music seems emotional and we are not emotional while listening, it is because we have associated that music with emotion in the past. If newly heard instrumental music seems emotional, it is because we have associated similar music with emotion in the past. When we make these associations, the music seems to swallow them up, as if it were a vacuum in need of filling. And as Osborne has noted, it seems best at swallowing up not emotional circumstances but the feeling that accompanied these circumstances; it is the feeling that we are most likely to be reminded of when music is heard at a later date. But just as an object is reflected in a mirror only when near the mirror, music is expressive of emotion only when emotional subject matter is or has been brought to bear. The advantage of such a position lies in its ability to explain why different listeners find the same music expressive of different emotions, and why some listeners insist that music cannot express emotion. Different listeners bring different emotional contexts to bear, and some listeners will be disinclined to bring any contexts to music at all. Apart from the bringing to bear of these contexts, a musical work has only musical properties.

A recent work that argues otherwise is Peter Kivy's beautifully written monograph *The Corded Shell: Reflections on Musical Expression*. Kivy holds that music's resem-

---

[9]Leonard Meyer, *Emotion and Meaning in Music*, pp. 222–229.
[10]*The Craft of Musical Composition*, 2 vols., tr. Arthur Mendel (London: Schott, 1942), I: 22, 78.

blance to "attitudes of face and body and voice" is sufficient to make it expressive of emotion. Unlike Susanne Langer, who believes that music's "ambivalence of content" prevents it from expressing any particular emotion we can identify verbally, Kivy believes that music can express individual or particular emotions—not the grief of any one in particular, but the particular emotion of grief nonetheless. It does so through "contour" (music's resemblance to human gesture and utterance) and "convention" (such as our convention of associating sadness with the minor mode). Expressiveness by convention may seem arbitrary, but such conventions are rooted, Kivy suggests, in expressiveness by contour. [11] Expressive conventions come into play only for a competent listener within a particular cultural context. And Kivy is careful to point out, as Alan Tormey has before him, [12] that music ordinarily does not express emotion, but rather is "expressive of" emotion. The clenched fist of an angry man actually expresses the man's anger. But the sad-looking face of a St. Bernard is not necessarily expressing the dog's sadness, for the dog may not be sad. Because the face resembles a sad human face, however, it is nonetheless expressive of sadness regardless of what or if the dog is feeling. Similarly, music, as a result of its resemblance to sad gesture and utterance, can be expressive of sadness even though it cannot experience sadness, or even though it may not be expressing sadness of the composer. [13]

Kivy qualifies his position on musical expressiveness in a chapter entitled "Tone, Text, and Title." Here he asserts that pure instrumental music is "expressively ambiguous" and capable of expressing only "gross distinctions" among emotions. Hence the opening of Mozart's G Minor Symphony is "surely melancholy, or sad, or serious, and certainly not spritely or gay or exuberant or joyous," but to get any more specific would require a verbal component. [14] Thus it is not surprising that of the twenty or so musical examples provided in *The Corded Shell*, virtually all have texts or are from texted compositions. As a result of this qualification, Kivy suggests that in a texted work it is the work—a combination of text and music—that expresses something or other in particular, and not just the music. At the same time, he asserts that music "maintains whatever expressiveness it may (or may not) have had apart from the text." [15]

Kivy assumes that we can associate musical contour with emotions because we can distinguish the real-life expressive behaviors the contour resembles. But even in real life, gestures and nonverbal utterances must be taken in context in order to be interpreted with any precision. We interpret weeping differently if it is the result of the death of a loved one than if it is the result of the birth of a child. And emotional people are not altogether consistent in the gestures used to express a particular emotion. Even if we can distinguish emotional behaviors in real life, however, it seems rare that a particular piece of music resembles enough nonverbal utterances and/or gestures to be able to remind us of emotions. For most of the behavior that music can resemble is not specifically expressive. Music can resemble sighs and wails, but musical ones are few and far between, and because a composer must consider aesthetic factors as well as the

---

[11] Kivy, *The Corded Shell*, chap. 3.
[12] Alan Tormey, *The Concept of Expression: A Study in Philosophical Psychology and Aesthetics* (Princeton: Princeton University Press, 1971), chap. 2.
[13] Kivy, *The Corded Shell*, pp. 12–13.
[14] Ibid., pp. 101–102.
[15] Ibid., p. 108.

process of imitation, sighs are not imitated exactly in music and are ordinarily recognized as such only in conjunction with a text.

What are other gestures and utterances associated with sadness? One of the main ways we are able to identify sadness is from facial expressions, and music can hardly resemble these. We may move slowly when we are sad; we may slouch or fall down; we may speak slowly and in soft, low tones. Music, analogously, can move slowly, descend, and be soft and low. But these characteristics are not specifically expressive, even when taken together. Slow, soft, descending, low-ranged music does not necessarily, or perhaps even usually, sound sad, even when "sighs" are added. And so it is with practically all music deemed emotional. Certainly musical contour can enhance emotional subject matter. But except in rare cases of near-exact imitation of expressive utterance (which probably limits the aesthetic value of the piece), extramusical associations, whether from a mode, text, title, screen, or past experience, are necessary before musical contour is related to emotion.

Why is it that Kivy believes that music's resemblance to expressive behavior is sufficient to make it expressive of emotion? And why do we not consider music expressive of other phenomena it resembles, such as the waves of the ocean or the rise and fall of the stock market? Kivy's response is as follows:

> The answer to this objection is simply that music might well be expressive of other things that it resembles, or things related to them, but only if certain other conditions were satisfied. One of these conditions, a "logical" one, is that it makes sense to say of the thing, "the music is expressive of that." One would hardly say that a kidney-shaped swimming pool is expressive of kidneys, or organs. A second condition, a frankly empirical one, is just that there be some psychological link between the music and what it expresses. Music is expressive of the emotions not just because it resembles expressive behavior, or that it, in addition, makes sense to say that something is expressive of emotions, but, as has been argued above, because we, for whatever reason, tend to animate our perceptions, and cannot but see expressiveness in them, any more than we can help seeing expressiveness in the Saint Bernard's face.[16]

Kivy does not elaborate on why he believes there is a psychological link between music and emotion, why we are more likely to see (or hear) expressiveness in music than in other perceptual phenomena. A possible explanation is that music often accompanies texts, and texts often suggest or evoke emotion. (If musical texts referred to the rise and fall of the stock market as often as they referred to emotion, music would probably express that too.) We are inclined to make sounds, to cry out when we feel deeply, and the first songs may have been intimately connected to such expressive utterance. And it seems clear that music can enrich considerably our emotional lives. But the fact remains that there are many listeners who do not find music emotional. And some of the listeners most likely to deny that music can express emotion are trained musicians.

Musicologists and theorists tend to prefer formal or syntactic interpretations of music to expressive ones because the former are more objective, dependable, comprehensive, and verifiable. This is not to say that all theorists analyze music in the same way from era to era or within one; an analysis by Leonard Meyer looks quite different from a Schenkerian one of the same work. But there are considerable degrees of overlap in

[16]Ibid., p. 62.

analyses, and points of contention or differences of emphasis can be meaningfully discussed or championed owing to common knowledge of the musical system in question. Expressive musical conventions, in contrast, are rather colloquial, usually uncodified, and tend to be more variable and less conventional than formal considerations. Of course, the relation of expressive word and tone in a texted work can be quite pertinent to a work. But many musicians find expressive conventions, even fairly established ones like the association of the minor mode with negative emotions, to be essentially superfluous or trivial to abstract music. The main reason expressive interpretations seem trivial, I believe, is that they tend to be a reaction only to surface features of music. One seldom hears about the expressiveness of a brilliant musical structure. There is nothing wrong with focusing on music's surface (the moment-to-moment experience of melodic, rhythmic, and simple harmonic features), but theorists are inclined to combine this mode of listening with a sort of structural hearing that tends to diminish the perception of music as expressive. Theorist Benjamin Boretz goes so far as to say that expressive interpretation is worse than trivial:

> The only problem with "sad" is that we simply have nothing observational to tie it to in either music or painting, and so it makes no difference to the music or painting—identity of anything. In use, however, such proper names have negative value, since they serve to perpetuate the internalization of a perceiver's theoretical scheme and, hence, to minimize his competence. The world of the average listener contains very little music and a great deal of noise, a gap which he tends to cover by the invocation of picturesque place-holding slogans.
>
> But to a sophisticated observer, the space thus straddled is filled with so many determinate particulars producing such particular identities that the sloganizing terms actually do seem hopelessly inapplicable. [17]

Lately, however, there are a few musicians who are turning against this sort of strict formalism, and offering more humanistic analysis and criticism. Their analyses include expressive terminology, but only when formal elements of works are related explicitly to human experience. A notable argument for work along these lines is presented in Anthony Newcomb's "Sound and Feeling." [18] Newcomb rejects the idea that formal or purely musical properties and structures are more "independent" or "objective" than expressive properties. Both expressive interpretation and technical analysis, he believes, are simply interactions "of properties of the work with culturally learned conventions brought to it by the listener-interpreter." [19] (In analysis these conventions include the concepts of contrast, motive, development, dominant chord, etc.) Newcomb acknowledges that there are not, and probably cannot be, strict rules of reference for expressive interpretation, but he feels that this in no way invalidates it. Indeed, for Newcomb "the lack of strict rules of reference . . . lies at the very basis of the richness of artistic expressiveness." [20]

Newcomb finds several problems with traditional expressive interpretation. One problem is the tendency of some musical expressionists to focus on musical detail, particularly melodic detail, in determining musical meaning. He quotes Edward Cone

---

[17]"Nelson Goodman's *Languages of Art* from a Musical Point of View," *Journal of Philosophy* 67 (1979): 548.

[18]Newcomb, "Sound and Feeling," *Critical Inquiry* 10 (1984): 614–643. This article provides excellent summaries of Kivy's and several other expressionist theories.

[19]Newcomb, "Sound and Feeling," p. 636.

[20]Ibid.

as pointing out that a composition may express "not only through each individual gesture, but also through the totality of gestures that constitutes its form."[21] Music, Newcomb stresses, must be taken as successiveness, as a temporal unfolding, as a large-scale process, and expressive analysis must reflect this. A related problem with traditional expressive interpretations is the tendency to summarize lengthy passages, movements, or entire works with a single word or phrase. The second movement of the *Eroica* may be sad, but it is vacuous and uninteresting to say simply that. Complex musical structures require complex verbal explanations. Third, expressive interpretations should not be limited only to emotive terms. Newcomb approves of Nelson Goodman's use of physical properties (brittle), plastic shapes (curvilinear), and natural phenomena (electric) in expressive interpretation, and of Wilson Coker's use of active verbs and words borrowed from architecture and mathematics.[22]

For Newcomb, expressiveness results from "the metaphorical resonances or analogies that a viewer-listener-reader finds between properties that an object possesses and properties of experience outside the object itself."[23] Although the properties of experience are brought to bear by a perceiver, this sort of expressiveness is not purely subjective, for it is based, in the case of music, on intrinsic musical properties of the work. Newcomb's position is indebted to what Jan Broeckx calls "creative metaphor making" in response to an artwork, to Nelson Goodman's theory of metaphorical exemplification, and to the work of music theorist Edward Cone. Broeckx believes that expression lies not exclusively in an artwork, but in the interaction between work and perceiver. He is concerned with identifying time-and-place-specific meaning codes that we bring to works in order to understand their properties as expressive.[24] For Goodman, music does not literally possess emotional properties, but acquires them from "foreign realms of discourse"—that is, by metaphorical transfer. Newcomb concurs with Goodman, for the most part, that emotions are not simply denoted by music but metaphorically exemplified by it. In simple reference or denotation, attention is directed away from the sign to the signified; in exemplification, the reference flows in both directions. Thus music can metaphorically exemplify sadness, and the label "sadness" can also refer to the expressive property of the music.[25]

Another departure from musical formalism has been offered by Cone in *The Composer's Voice*. Cone suggests that the potential "content" of a musical work is a function of "the relationship among all its contexts and . . . the illumination thrown on that relationship by the musical structure that unites them."[26] Contexts are brought to music by texts, programs, titles, or in the case of instrumental music, the life experience of the individual listener. These subjective contexts might vary widely, or even be contradictory; Cone points out that descriptions of Mozart's Symphony No. 40 have ranged from "heroically tragic" to "exhibiting the poised gracefulness of ancient

[21]Ibid., p. 627; from Edward Cone, *The Composer's Voice* (Berkeley: University of California Press, 1974), p. 171.

[22]Newcomb, "Sound and Feeling," pp. 627, 632.

[23]Ibid., p. 625.

[24]Jan L. Broeckx, "De mythe van der specifek muzikale expressive: Naar aanleiding van Alan Tormey's *Concept of Expression* toegepast op de muziek," *Revue belge de musicologie* 32–33 (1979–80): 1232–1250. Discussed in Newcomb, "Sound and Feeling," pp. 620–621.

[25]Nelson Goodman, *Language of Art: An Approach to a Theory of Symbols* (Indianapolis: Hackett Publishing Co., 1968). Discussed in Newcomb, "Sound and Feeling," pp. 621–624.

[26]Cone, *The Composer's Voice*, p. 171.

Greece."[27] But the number of possible contexts is not unrestricted, for the contexts must be congruous with the musical structure. Together the contexts allowed by the structure make up what Cone calls the "expressive potential" of the piece.

Cone is careful to point out that, without context, there is no (extramusical) content. Like Kivy after him, Cone considers music's resemblance to human gesture and utterance an important factor in musical expressiveness. But Cone believes that gesture and utterance themselves are meaningless apart from context. "Oh" and "ah" can express astonishment, delight, fear, or regret; a sigh can express relief or despondency. Only through context can the expressive potential of gestures and utterances be realized, in life or in music.[28] But according to Cone, there is always a context, and always a content. He doubts that it is possible to listen to pure musical structure alone; for even when our conscious attention is directed exclusively to formal design, our subconscious is creating a nonverbal but highly personal context.[29]

An example of the application of context to musical structure favored by Cone and Newcomb is presented in "Schubert's Promissory Note."[30] In a superb analysis of Schubert's Moment Musical in A-flat, op. 94, no. 6, Cone discusses how Schubert's treatment of a nonharmonic E-natural disrupts the stability of the tonic A-flat. This disruption or "imbalance" is felt throughout the structure, at first being only hinted at, later appearing with more emphasis but again being suppressed, and finally returning in an unexpected way, and "with terrifying intensity," before the imbalance is finally resolved. Apart from a few terms such as "terrifying intensity," "troubling element," and "devastating in its effect," Cone's analysis is purely formal or technical. But he then proceeds to relate the analysis to a human context:

> As I apprehend the work, it dramatizes the injection of a strange, unsettling element into an otherwise peaceful situation. At first ignored and suppressed, that element persistently returns. It not only makes itself at home but even takes over the direction of events in order to reveal unsuspected possibilities. When the normal state of affairs eventually returns, the originally foreign element seems to have been completely assimilated. But that appearance is deceptive. The element has not been tamed; it bursts out with even greater force, revealing itself as basically inimical to its surroundings, which it proceeds to demolish.[31]

Cone then provides an even more specific context, comparing the disruptive element to a vice:

> A vice, as I see it, begins as a novel and fascinating suggestion, not necessarily dangerous though often disturbing. It becomes dangerous, however, as its increasing attractiveness encourages investigation and experimentation, leading to possible obsession and eventual addiction. If one now apparently recovers self-control, believing that the vice has been mastered, it is often too late; either the habit returns to exert its domination in some fearful form, or the effects of the early indulgence have left their indelible and painful marks on the personality—and frequently, of course, on the body as well.[32]

Finally, Cone reminds us of a disruptive element that was taking its toll on Schubert's

[27]Ibid., p. 172.
[28]Ibid., pp. 162–166.
[29]Ibid., p. 169.
[30]*Nineteenth Century Music* 5 (1982): 233–241.
[31]Ibid., pp. 239–240.
[32]Ibid., p. 240.

mind and body at the time he was writing the Moment Musical in question: the disruptive element of syphilis.

While Cone does not assign a particular emotion to the work, the work becomes expressive of intense, negative emotions once his contexts are brought to bear. The contexts conform beautifully to Schubert's musical structure, and give the piece a human element that perhaps even Hanslick, if not Boretz, could appreciate. Now, it is probably not necessary to have a context that conforms to music's structure in order for music to seem expressive; music can swallow up contexts whether or not they conform to its dynamic properties. By providing expressive contexts that conform to a work's structure, however, Cone and Newcomb provide a means for expressive terminology to make sense in music criticism: sections of a narrative may be related to sections of a composition or analysis. Yet it is important to note that expressive conventions and extramusical contexts are never essential to interpretation of an instrumental work. Newcomb suggests that expressive interpretation is no less objective than technical analysis in that both are interactions of the work's properties with cultural conventions brought by listeners. Yet technical components are more objective than expressive ones, not because they exist independently of people, but because they are codified and highly conventional. And formal aspects, unlike expressive ones, are essential to a work; they make the work what it is. Without them, the "work" would be only meaningless sounds. (Because formal relationships can be conceived even without knowledge of the theoretical terminology used to describe them, untrained listeners can have knowledge of works.) Cone claims we will always bring extramusical contexts to works, even if only subconsciously. I am in no position to determine what we can or cannot bring to music subconsciously. But even if we do inevitably bring human contexts to music, surely they are not necessarily expressive ones. And the reality is that many listeners report deeply moving musical experiences while concentrating on structure and syntax alone. Perhaps music is inevitably enhanced by bringing human contexts to it. But it is too strong to suggest, as Cone does by quoting John O'Hara, that "music is to be enjoyed, and we might as well face it: it must have human associations if it is to be enjoyed."[33]

Why is Osborne convinced that there are emotions in music, while Stravinsky denies it? Why are Berlioz, Wagner, and Berg so much more concerned with extramusical content than Brahms and Webern, and why does Cone consider extramusical contexts inevitable, while Hanslick and Boretz are content to consider instrumental music apart from any such associations? It appears that recent brain research may provide at least a partial answer to such questions. As a result of tests on brain-damaged patients, most researchers agree that the left hemisphere of the brain tends to control language and sequential, digital, and temporal processes, while the right hemisphere tends to control visuo-spatial abilities and simultaneous and analogic processes.[34] (These abilities or processes are often not strongly lateralized.) In light of this research, it is significant that psychologist Thomas G. Bever has reported that melodies are most likely to be processed in the right hemisphere (left ear) by nonmusi-

---

[33]Quoted in Cone, *The Composer's Voice*, p. 175. From *Butterfield 8* (New York: Harcourt Brace, 1935), p. 131.

[34]Sally P. Springer and Georg Deutch, *Left Brain, Right Brain* (San Francisco: Freeman, 1981), p. 185.

cians, but more likely to be processed in the left hemisphere (right ear) by musicians.[35] Bever's theoretical position is that musicians, because of their theoretical training, process melodies analytically or relationally, and thus better in the left hemisphere, while nonmusicians without the relational techniques process them holistically, or in the right hemisphere.

Other research has shown a connection between right-hemisphere, holistic processing and emotions: as Sally P. Springer and Georg Deutch have put it, there "appears to be a good case for believing that the right hemisphere is involved both in the processing of emotional information and in the production of emotional expressions to a greater degree than the left."[36] Given this, it seems reasonable to speculate that people processing music in the right hemisphere are more likely than trained musicians to associate emotion with music. These two groups cannot be sharply delineated, of course, for there are theoretically trained expressionists and formalists with no such training. But the research could account for what seem to be very real differences in the musical response. The research might also account for the fact that some pieces seem more emotional to expressionists than others: perhaps highly "emotional" music is music that lends itself particularly well to right-hemisphere processing.

But why are some musicians with a great deal of theoretical training, like Newcomb, Cone, and many composers, disinclined to limit themselves to pure structure when listening to or composing music? Bever's research sheds light on this question as well. For while it is the case, according to Bever, that musicians are more likely to listen with the right ear than nonmusicians, the musician is nonetheless perfectly able to listen with the left ear. Thus it is most accurate to say not that musicians are more left-hemisphered for music, but rather that they are "more differentiated hemispherically." In view of this, Bever postulates "a developmental pattern in which people oscillate between first treating a skill holistically, then relationally as experience with it increases, and then holistically again (with higher-order holistic templates the second time)."[37] If it is the case that holistic, right-hemisphered processing is more conducive to expressive interpretation of music, it may be that those inclined to characterize complex music in simple emotive terms are processing music principally with the right hemisphere, those interested only in music's structure are processing it principally in the left, and those inclined to construct complex expressive analyses based on musical structure are processing in a more integrated way.

Can music express emotion? Only if we mean by this that music can seem expressive when we associate it with emotion, or that music can remind us of emotion we associated it with in the past. It serves these purposes well because it is pure form and has "room" for extramusical content, because it often accompanies emotional texts, and because it has dynamic properties analogous to those of our emotions and expressive behavior. When we relate emotion to music, the two can seem fused. But

[35]Reported in Bever, "Broca and Lashley Were Right: Cerebral Dominance Is an Accident of Growth," in *Biological Studies of Mental Processes*, ed. David Caplan (Cambridge: MIT Press, 1980), pp. 186–230.
[36]Springer and Deutch, *Left Brain, Right Brain*, p. 171.
[37]Bever, "Cerebral Dominance," p. 206. For more on music and the brain, including the impact of brain damage on musical ability, see Howard Gardner's *Art, Mind, and Brain* (New York: Basic Books, 1982), and his *The Shattered Mind* (New York: Random House, 1976).

there is nothing about abstract, instrumental music itself that is sufficient to express emotion apart from the process of association.

When is expressive terminology appropriate for analysis and criticism? Certainly expressive aspects are relevant to works when they are specified: when there is an emotional text, title, or program; expressive terminology in performance instructions; conventional motives that symbolize emotion, etc. And expressive terminology can become relevant to instrumental music when an extramusical context is brought to bear, preferably one that is historically pertinent and that conforms to the work's structure. But it is important to remember that the number of contexts that can be assigned is infinite, and the very assignment of a context is optional. One of the reasons music can mean so much to us is that we can bring our own personal contexts and emotions to it. To insist on a particular context or emotion for an instrumental work is needlessly limiting. Music is also valued because we can use it to escape from our lives, emotional or otherwise, and focus briefly on pure form. Listeners can approach an abstract instrumental work in terms of formal and syntactic aspects alone and not miss anything essential.

THE THEORY OF DANCE:
WHAT IS GOING ON IN A DANCE?

The past decade has witnessed a growing interest among aestheticians in dance. This recent development was inaugurated with the publication of *Dance Illuminations* in 1984, which contains a number of important philosophical essays on dance. More recently, the publication of monographs by Sondra H. Fraleigh and Francis Sparshott have attested to a genuine concern on the part of aestheticians with dance. This has been due in no small measure to the development of contemporary dance itself, which has revitalized interest in it as an important art form.

Francis Sparshott's "Why Philosophy Neglects the Dance" attempts to explain the lack of an influential historical literature in the aesthetics of dance. Sparshott raises the controversial question "Is dance a feminine art?" and answers it in the negative. Despite the fact that the rise of contemporary dance has been dominated by female artists, Sparshott insists that dance is a universal phenomenon and not a distinctively female art. He also dismisses the explanation for a neglect of the dance by philosophers on the grounds that dance is a bodily art, and that philosophers despise the body.

According to Sparshott, for an art to be of central philosophical interest, it must possess a culturally significant position in society or be capable of being assimilated into that society's dominant ideology. He maintains that this situation has not existed for dance for the most part in Western European societies. In this connection, Sparshott discusses both the system of the fine arts articulated by Diderot in the seventeenth century as well as Hegel's account of the interrelationships of the arts in the early nineteenth century. Each of these systems, Sparshott believes, is unconsciously at the root of our thinking about the arts. In the case of the former system, the arts are viewed as essentially imitative in nature, and dance an art of imitation. On the Hegelian scheme, dance could have found a place alongside architecture as a symbolic art, on the one hand, or with sculpture, which is an art of the human body, on the other. But neither option was really open to Hegel because his own experience of dance was so impoverished. Moreover, since the time of Hegel, no subsequent developments in dance have enabled it to assume a status akin to that of the other major arts. Finally, Sparshott argues, philosophers cannot create importance for an art form; they can only accept it as a datum to be interpreted. And dance does not currently enjoy the status of a major art form in our culture. However, Sparshott does not discuss in detail the significance of the rise of contemporary dance and the extent of its philosophical importance. Rather, he seems to imply that it does not carry the *conviction* essential to establish it now as a major art form in our culture.

Monroe C. Beardsley's "What Is Going On in a Dance?" is concerned with the problem of defining the art of dance. Beardsley draws upon action theory in order to clarify our understanding of dance. He distinguishes between mere bodily motion on the one hand and dance itself which is generated by those motions. Thus, dance is "movings"—actions that have the character of a dance—that are "sortally generated by bodily motions" (including bodily pauses or rests, which are part of the dance). Beardsley thus characterizes dance as a kind of act-generation, "a transformation of motions into movings."

In order to clear the ground for his theory, Beardsley considers a number of candidates for a definition of dance, each of which he dismisses. Finally, Beardsley considers a definition of dance in which motion does not generate practical actions. While he does not subscribe in its entirety to this characterization, he nonetheless concludes that dance as an art form must be independent to some degree of any practical function. He concludes that the "overflow or superfluity of expressiveness" is what distinguishes the domain of dance. Thus, the achievement of expressiveness to a high degree (zest, vigor, fluency, etc.) is the distinguishing mark of dance movements.

Noël Carroll and Sally Banes offer a critical response to Beardsley's essay in their "Working and Dancing: A Response to Monroe Beardsley's 'What Is Going On in a Dance?' " Carroll and Banes interpret Beardsley's basic claim to be that a "superfluity of expressiveness" is a defining feature of dance movement. However, this claim is rejected as being neither a necessary nor a sufficient condition of dance. First, they argue that many practical activities, such as patriotic marches, that involve expressive movement are not properly classifiable as dances. However, Beardsley's definition not only fails to be sufficiently exclusive but also is not inclusive enough. Carroll and Banes discuss a number of "incontestable examples" of dance in which there is no apparent superfluity of expressiveness, such as *Room Service* by Yvonne Rainer. In such dances, which are paradigm cases of "postmodern" dance, the aim is simply to make ordinary movement perceptible. Often, such dances involve no more than the carrying out of ordinary, everyday tasks. As Carroll and Banes put it, *Room Service* is a dance "because through its aesthetic context, it transforms an ordinary working . . . into an object for close scrutiny." Thus, the emphasis of the dance is on the working human body rather than on any attempt to attain expressiveness. In this regard, Carroll and Banes compare much postmodern dance with the anti-illusionist theories of Jasper Johns and Andy Warhol. In each case, there is no intent to *represent* objects, nor to realize the formal and expressive qualities that characterize ballet and much of modern dance. As a result, Carroll and Banes insist that *Room Service* is undeniably a major work of postmodern dance but at the same time possesses none of the necessary qualities required by Beardsley's conception.

Francis Sparshott

WHY PHILOSOPHY NEGLECTS THE DANCE

The 1960's saw an immense increase of interest in dance in the United States—an interest soon reflected in sociological and anthropological studies that now begin to be plentifully published. This situation drew attention to a strange state of affairs in aesthetics. A venerable tradition regards dance as one of the most basic of arts, and this tradition was strengthened in the early years of the present century by evolutionary notions that remarked the ubiquity of dance in primitive cultures and singled out dance-like behavior among primates as one of the principal animal antecedents of human art. But philosophers of art, contenting themselves with this lip-service, had done little work on the aesthetics of the art thus determined as fundamental. Examples of general points in aesthetics were and are seldom drawn from dance, and separate articles and monographs on dance aesthetics are few. Moreover, though there is an extensive early literature on dance, that literature is little known to the learned and literary worlds at large. One wonders why this should be so.

One suggestion is that dance is a female art, and our civilization has been patriarchal. But that is not so. World-wide, men dance as much as women do, and sometimes more. To assert that, despite this, dance is somehow an expression of the truly feminine aspects of the human psyche is to remove oneself from the domain of responsible discourse. And if dance here and now is in some respects institutionally associated with femininity, that is a contingent phenomenon calling for historical explanation rather than itself an explanation for the larger currents of thought.

Another explanation is that dance is corporeal, and philosophers fear and hate the body. That may explain why philosophers are seldom athletes, but dance as an art or arts is not, from the standpoint of observer or critic, significantly more bodily and less spiritual than other arts tangibly embodied.

A third suggestion is that examples of dance have not until the advent of TV and videotape been generally accessible, so that few philosophers could acquaint themselves with much dance or rely on such acquaintance in their readers; and that the lack of a generally readable dance notation rendered dances themselves ephemeral. That is true, but does not explain what needs explaining, for aesthetics has never depended on a common stock of specific instances.

To be surprised that little has been written on the philosophy of dance is to be naive about the conditions in which philosophies of specific arts get written. That an art exists, and that admired works are created in it, has never sufficed to generate a philosophy of that art. It is necessary that the art should occupy at the relevant time a culturally central position, or that the ideology of the art could be integrated with a culturally prevalent ideology. Thus, theories of literature abound because poets have been thought crucial figures in the culture of their times, and because vernacular literatures played key ideological roles in the rise of European nationalism. Philosophies of music reflect an era when music was allowed so central a role in education that its importance became not something to be established but a datum to be explained. Theories of cinema were developed in acknowledgement of the fact that the movies for some decades dominated even sophisticated imaginations, and this domination needed to be explored from within. But when we turn to dance we find, first, that for various reasons the ideologies available to the other arts have not been available to it, so that philosophers could not bring it into their general theories of the arts; and second, that dance has at no convenient time been a culturally central art. It may attain centrality in small non-literate ("primitive") societies, but their ways of doing things are not imaginatively accessible to us—nothing like them belongs anywhere in our imagined heritage. Dance was also a focus of interest in the personal monarchies of the sixteenth and seventeenth centuries, but this association with courts has itself sufficed to remove it from centrality in any contemporary western society. Attempts to find other contexts in which dance as an art might achieve the centrality one might expect it to possess have not yet succeeded. For instance, Isadora Duncan and others in the early years of this century thought dance might be the natural expression of Whitmanian democracy, the spirit of the healthy individual in open spaces; but the replacement of the frontier mentality by a disillusioned one-small-world-ism has woken us from that dream. Again, Diaghilev's Ballets Russes nearly succeeded in tearing ballet (still the only highly developed dance in the west) loose from its monarchical associations and making it a *Gesamtkunstwerk* that would rival Wagnerian opera, but in the end it did not come about. World War I shifted the balance of artistic acceptability towards less opulent forms; Wagner was in any case there first; and, perhaps most important, Diaghilev failed to establish a strong choreography at the core of his enterprise, which never fully established itself as dance rather than miscellaneous spectacle. Most recently, a new dance associated with such names as John Cage and Merce Cunningham has offered itself as the pure and necessary art of the moving body. But it turned out that there was no place for it to fill. As art for an alternative culture its place was preempted by the artistically unprecedented and unexpected outbursting of popular musics, a worldwide cultural revolution whose measure we have yet to take; and within its own solemn circle of art, as the name of John Cage reminds us, it did not establish a cultural presence and function separate from that of avant-garde music, para-theater, and "art" generally.

The upshot of the history summarized above is that there has been nothing for a philosophy of the dance to be about. Indeed, the very idea of an art of dance as such, distinct from mime and pageantry, is new and perhaps unstable. The prestigious court ballet of Louis XIV and his predecessors was less like anything we would call dance than like a pageant or a homecoming parade. The dances available from classical antiquity as imaginary exemplars for those who would dignify the dance were either pure mime, whose values were entirely those of expression and communication, or choric maneuverings whose value lay in the ceremony of which they formed part. The *ballet d'action* of Noverre and his contemporaries was again mimetic in its emphasis. Even Isadora Duncan at one time denounced the idea of a pure dance, saying that the value of her dances lay in their fidelity to the music for the sake of which they were created. Dance as dance, the rhythmically patterned movements of the body, was at all these times decried as a mere capering. The objection was not to its physicality but to its lack of meaning. Natural movements of the living body are motivated; unmotivated movements are mere swingings, jerkings, twitchings. The invention of a pure art of dance depends on the development of a characteristic system of motivation of its own, or something that will do duty for that. Till then, however many beautiful dances we have, there can be no philosophy of dance, because their significances remain indefeasibly miscellaneous. Only their beauty unites them. Beauty justifies dances, dancers, dancing, and the dance, but little can be said about it.

In order to vindicate a place for an art (such as dance) among the serious cultural concerns either of mankind or of our civilization, one must define a place that only it can fill, or that it fills in a distinctive way. To do that convincingly, it is advisable to construct a survey of real or possible arts among which the art in question is determinately located. Many such "systems of the arts" have been constructed. Some of these cover the whole range of human skills or a large part of that range, and others confine themselves to anatomizing the practices and skills that we lump together as "art" without relating art as a whole to any similarly articulated scheme for other areas of human activity. Many such systems, notably that of S. K. Langer, do make a place for dance. But only two such systems have been so widely accepted that our own spontaneous thinking still shows their influence, because they form part of the tradition within which our minds work. And neither of these two preferred systems assigns a place to dance. Since philosophers of art, like other philosophers, spend most of their time (and most of them spend all their time) examining particular problems within unexamined frames of reference, these omissions go far to explain why philosophers neglect the dance. Of course, the prevalence of these two schematisms is not itself an ultimate datum, but demands explanation. Such explanation would include a demonstration of how each schema articulated the most pressing relevant concerns of the most influential ideologists of its age, and an explanation of that influence. No such explanation can even be sketched here; we will only note that the successful promulgation of a system of the arts from which dance was omitted shows either that dance was felt to lack significance at the relevant time or that its significance was not felt to lie within the proper scope of the system.

The two prevailing schemata of the arts to which I refer are the system of the "fine arts" as arts of imitation, derived via Aristotle from the Platonic *Epinomis* and developed in the sixteenth to early eighteenth century, and the system of the arts articulated by Hegel in his lectures on aesthetics and found at the basis of much nineteenth-century writing. Neither scheme commands the assent of serious thinkers today, but no other scheme of comparable mesmeric power has displaced them, so that they remain detectable as unquestioned operative assumptions in shaping the ways we still frame our questions.

The system of the "Fine Arts" is, for our purposes, best examined in the shallow but sophisticated version presented by D'Alembert in his "Preliminary Discourse" to Diderot's *Encyclopédie* (1751), where it forms part of a classification of the kinds of human knowledge.[1] "Another kind of reflective knowledge," he writes, ". . . consists of the ideas which we create for ourselves by imagining and putting together beings similar to those which are the object of our direct ideas" (p. 37). Among these arts of imitation painting and sculpture are primary because "it is in those arts above all that imitation best approximates the objects represented and speaks most directly to the senses" (ibid.); architecture does the same sort of thing only not so well; "Poetry, which comes after painting and sculpture, . . . speaks to the imagination rather than to the senses"; and music "holds the last place in the order of imitation" because it lacks a developed vocabulary, though it is nowadays evolving into a "kind of discourse" expressing the passions of the soul (p. 38). But, significantly from our point of view, "Any music that does not portray something is only noise" (p. 39). All these arts that "undertake the imitation of Nature" are called the Fine Arts "because they have pleasure for their principal object" (p. 43); they could all be included "under the general title of Painting" because they differ from that art only in their means (p. 55), or could be considered forms of poetry if "poetry" is taken in its old broad sense of "invention or creation." In the whole of this discussion, D'Alembert never mentions dance. Why not? Presumably because what he is classifying is forms of *knowledge*. Any dance which is not a variety of representational theater, and hence a form of "Painting," is mere movement in the same way that non-expressive music is "only noise," hence not a branch of knowledge and not to be included among the arts. What makes D'Alembert's exclusion of dance particularly remarkable is that his enumeration of great artists gives pride of place to those active at the court of that passionate practitioner and devotee of dance, Louis XIV; he even mentions Lully, Louis' great ballet impresario, but mentions him only as a musician. Yet the ballets of Louis' court were great public occasions, assigned high symbolic importance by their devisers and commentators. How could D'Alembert have overlooked them? A possible explanation is that opera (in which dance interludes were a normal component) was originally devised as a re-creation of Greek tragedy and inherited tragedy's traditional place among arts that "imitate Nature"; but the court ballet, in which Prince and nobility took part, found its ancestry in a different region of Platonic thought, in the choric dances in which the city expressed its unity and its symbolic equivalence with the hierarchy of the cosmos. Thus its strictly choreographic component (always subsidiary in the whole design) was as such below the level of art, its theatrical component is categorized as a continuation of painting by other means, and its inner significance lies in a mode of imitation radically other than that which the fine arts exemplify. There was thus no way in which the court ballet could be assigned a distinctive place among the fine arts, and its successors suffered the same difficulty.

In face of this exclusion it is easy to see what apologists of dance should do: they should say that dance stands alongside painting and poetry as an independent mode of

---

[1]Jean Le Rond D'Alembert, *Preliminary Discourse to the Encyclopedia of Diderot*, trans. by Richard Schwab and Walter Rex, Indianapolis, Bobbs-Merrill, 1963.

imitation. And so they did. Noverre, among others, took just that line.[2] But the move never won general acceptance, because it was not as "imitation of Nature" that significant dance was significant.

The other schematism of arts that has dominated our minds is Hegel's. It goes like this. The fine arts are arts that produce beauty. Beauty is the adequation of a form to an idea, so that a fine art embodies ideas in forms adequate to them. As civilization advances, arts become more refined. Symbolic arts in which spirit partly informs matter give way to classical arts in which spirit and matter are perfectly fused, and these in turn yield to romantic arts in which spirit dominates its material embodiment. After that, spirit assumes autonomous forms and art as a whole is superseded. The paradigm of a symbolic art is architecture; of a classical art, sculpture; the romantic arts are typically painting, music, and poetry. Sculpture is the central art, the most artistic of the arts; among romantic arts music is central, the most romantic, but poetry is the most spiritual and the most advanced.

One might have looked for dance in two places in Hegel's scheme. On the one hand, since the central place assigned to sculpture rests on the old thesis that of all natural forms only the human body, the favorite subject of sculpture, gives natural expression to "the Idea" because it is the body of the only theorizing animal, one might have expected dance, which sets actual human bodies in graceful motion, to join sculpture at the center. That place had been prepared for it by the Fine Arts schematism, but Hegel leaves it empty. On the other hand, dance might have been set alongside architecture as the primitive art, in which the actual materiality of the body is partly infused with formally significant properties in the same way that an architect gives a significant form to actual materials in all their solid strength. Why does Hegel refuse to make either of these obvious moves?

So far as Hegel knew, architecture of the appropriate heavy and symbolizing sort did dominate the early civilizations of Egypt and India; and sculpture, since Winckelmann, was taken to epitomize Greek civilization. But no civilized era had expressed its characteristic orientation in dance. Dance belonged to savages, and to primitive men whose expression was inarticulate. As a means of expression it is subhuman and pre-artistic. Apes and peacocks dance. Long after Hegel's death, as we have seen, such animal behavior would be assigned to the ancestry of art.

The supposed facts of history may have sufficed, but another thing that might make dance an unlikely partner for sculpture would be that the body made by God in His own image must already be expressive in the only way in which it can be expressive. The dancer as dancer can express no idea higher than the personality and full humanity his life should already more fully and perfectly show. An idealization of gesture could not be more eloquently expressive of humanity, but only an attenuation and trivialization.

What, then, of the analogy of architecture? The dancer's agility and grace imperfectly animate his real corporeal presence, the sweating and straining body, as an architect imparts an illusory lightness to the vault that sustains and is confirmed by the loads imposed on it. Even if no advanced civilization has taken dance as its central expression, should we not recognize that dance, like architecture, is an inevitable and

---

[2]Jean-Georges Noverre, *Letters on Dancing and Ballets* (1760), trans. by Cyril Beaumont, New York, Dance Horizons, 1966.

basic art—that human beings will always build, and will always dance, and it will always matter to them how they do so? If the origins of dance are prehistoric and even prehuman, what is at the origin is not necessarily superseded, or if it is so is superseded only by losing its place at the focus of concern. It was in this sense that Hegel thought all art was superseded: science and philosophy must from now on always be more central to the concerns of humanity, but art has by no means completed its mission.

Hegel's relegation of architecture to the past corresponds to a historical fact. The architecture of his day was bankrupt, reduced to exploiting a repertory of forms of which the original significance was lost, in desperate search for any sort of authentic or persuasive style. Similarly, nothing in Hegel's day suggested any inevitable importance for an art of dance. The *ballet d'action* of Noverre and his contemporaries had quickly relapsed into the formalism they had protested against, and the dance of Hegel's day had nothing more significant to show than Vigano's *choreo-drammi* at Milan— magnificent spectacle, but mere spectacle. In Hegel's terms, spectacle is not art. A modern art, a living art, had in Hegel's day to be a romantic art; and it was not until the year of Hegel's death (1831) that the dance of the nuns in *Robert le Diable* revealed the possibilities—quickly followed up—of a romantic art of dance.

Hegel will acknowledge no split between the rational and the real, and therefore always bases his schematizations on something very solid and closely observed in history. Dance in his place and time offered no such basis to observation, and to have claimed for it any systematic significance would have been pure ideology.

Dance as romantic art is born in the romantic ballet of Paris immediately after Hegel's death, and it is this ballet that still typifies the art of dance in the general mind. Such a dance, culturally prestigious and ideologically significant, might have won a posthumous place in the Hegelian system. But it did not. As Ivor Guest shows the inner meaning of that ballet was a yearning for the unattainable as symbolized in a man's hopeless love for a fairy being, an etherealized woman.[3] But not only is that sort of "idealism" a weak escapism, incapable of bearing any but the most vapid symbolism; more seriously, the artistic fact it corresponded to was the cult of the ballerina, of Marie Taglioni and her rivals and successors down to Pavlova—and of the ballerina as kept or keepable woman, whose body was central only as fetish for the Jockey Club. The idealization of the feminine is the degradation of the female. So far from vindicating for ballet a place among the arts in which the human spirit finds its defining form, this social attitude excludes ballet from art and confines it within the luxury trades. Association with ballet has meant the stigma of spiritual sickness, and for a while it seemed that the only hope for a serious art of dance was to repudiate ballet utterly. Unfortunately, no technique of comparable development, and no tradition of comparable weight, existed in the west or (because of the rigors of training, if nothing else) was importable from the east.

What this all amounts to is that there has not yet been any available basis for a philosophy of dance. Nor can such a basis be invented by philosophers. Philosophers cannot invent or bestow seriousness; they can only explain it.[4]

---

[3]Ivor Guest, *Romantic Ballet in Paris*, Middletown, Conn., Wesleyan University Press, 1966.
[4]Most of this essay is condensed from a longer paper, "On the Question: 'Why Do Philosophers Neglect the Aesthetics of the Dance?" to appear in *Dance Research Journal.*

Monroe C. Beardsley

WHAT IS GOING ON IN A DANCE?

I begin these rather tentative and exploratory reflections by calling upon some provocative remarks by George Beiswanger, from an essay written some years ago and later reprinted:

> Muscular capacity is the physical means by which dances are made. But the means becomes available to the choreographic imagination only through the operation of a metaphor, a metaphor by which a *moving* in the muscular sense takes on the character of a *doing* or *goings on*. . . . Strictly speaking, then, dances are not made out of but *upon* movement, movement being the poetic bearer, the persistent metaphor, by which muscular material is made available for the enhanced, meaningful, and designed *goings-on* that are dance.[1]

Though this passage summarizes a view that I shall try to defend and articulate, the attempt to apply the concept of metaphor troubles me: it seems a strained extension of an otherwise reasonably clear and useful term. So instead of Beiswanger's rather mysterious "operation of a metaphor," I shall suggest that we employ some concepts and principles borrowed from the philosophical theory of action. But I still like his favored expression for what we are all trying to understand better—those special "goings-on" that constitute dance.

A partial, though basic, description of what is going on would be to say, using terms provided by Beiswanger (but I am also borrowing language from legal theorists such as John Austin and Oliver Wendell Holmes), that there are willed muscular contractions that cause changes of position in human bodies or parts of bodies. Such caused changes we may agree to call "bodily motions," or simply *motions*, assuming them to be—with surely few exceptions—voluntary. (For even if push comes to shove in a certain symbolic sense, I take it that no one is actually knocked off balance. But for a dancer to be lifted up or carried from one location to another is not a motion, in my sense, of that dancer, though it requires motions by other dancers.)

Monroe C. Beardsley, "What Is Going On in a Dance?" from Dance Research Journal, *15 (1982):31–37. Reprinted with permission of the author's estate.*

[1]"Chance and Design in Choreography," reprinted from the *Journal of Aesthetics and Art Criticism* 21 (1962):14–17, in *The Dance Experience: Readings in Dance Appreciation*, rev. ed., ed. Howard Nadel and Constance Nadel Miller (New York: Universe Books, 1978), 88.

Bodily motions are actions; they are, in one sense, basic actions, the foundation of all other actions, at least as far as we are concerned today; for even if there are such things as purely *mental* actions, in which no muscle is disturbed, these cannot be the stuff or raw material of dance. But as Beiswanger says, bodily motions are not themselves the goings-on we label *Afternoon of a Faun* or *Jewels*. It is actions of another sort that we witness and wonder at; how, then, are these related to bodily motions?

An extremely fruitful discovery of philosophical action theory is that actions build upon, or grow out of, each other in certain definable ways. The wielding of a hammer, say, can become, in capable hands, the driving of a nail, and that in turn a step in the building of a house. One action, in a technical sense, is said to "generate" another action that is its fruition or even its aim. Thus we can analyze and come to understand certain actions by examining their *generating conditions*—that is, the conditions that are to be fulfilled in order for act A to generate act B. This is easy in some cases; clearly it is the presence of the nail and the wood, in proper relationship, that converts the swinging of a hammer into the driving of a nail and that enables the former action to generate the latter action: *in* or *by* swinging the hammer, the carpenter drove the nail. Now there is, of course, an endless variety of such sets of generating conditions; however, they fortunately fall into a limited number of classes, and these classes themselves belong to two fundamental categories. The first is *causal generation*. Since the swinging of the hammer *causes* the nail to penetrate the two-by-four studding, the swinging of the hammer *generates* the (act of) driving the nail into the wood. If the hammer misses or the nail is balked by a knot, this act-generation does not occur.

In this first category of act-generation, one action generates a second action that is numerically distinct from it: swinging the hammer is not the same action as driving the nail (or building the house). In the second category, no new action, yet a different kind of action, is generated. If a person mistakenly believes that his or her divorce is final and legal and so marries a second spouse, that person has (unintentionally) committed bigamy; given the generating conditions (the persisting legal bond), the act of marrying generates the act of committing bigamy. The person has not done two things, but two kinds of things: the same action was both an act of marrying and an act of bigamy. This I call *sortal generation*: the act-generation that occurs when an action of one sort becomes also (under the requisite conditions) an action of another sort—without, of course, ceasing to be an action of the first sort as well.

These concepts, simple as they are, can help us clarify idioms sometimes used by dance theorists. Thus when George Beiswanger says that "dances are not made out of but *upon* movement" (and remember he is using the term *movement* the way I am using the term *motion*), we can interpret him, I think, as saying that a dance is not composed of, does not have as its parts or elements, bodily motions, but rather is in some way sortally generated by those motions: under certain conditions, the motion "takes on the character" (as he says) of a dance-movement. And if I may be permitted the license, I should like to take advantage of the dancer's cherished special use of the word *moving* and use it in a nominative form to refer to *actions that have the character of a dance:* I shall call them *movings*. Thus when Beiswanger adds, "Dance does consist of *goings-on* in the act of coming to be," I shall adopt a somewhat more cautious paraphrase: *in a dance, movings are sortally generated by bodily motions*. And this proposition must be supplemented at once to forestall an imminent objection:

certainly there are rests in dance as well as doings, and these, however passive, are part and parcel of what is happening (it happens for a time that nothing happens). Muscular contractions may be needed to maintain a position as well as to change one—especially if it is to stand on tiptoe with arm and leg outstretched. So, besides motions we shall have to include *bodily pauses* or cessations of motion; and we can add that just as motions can generate movings, so pauses can generate *posings* (using this term for peculiarly dance states of affairs). Thus we may now propose the following: *dancing is sortally generating movings by bodily motions and posings by bodily pauses.*

Thus I find myself in disagreement—not wholly verbal, I think—with a recent valuable essay by Haig Khatchadourian.[2] It has been effectively criticized on several points by Julie Van Camp,[3] and I shall not review her objections here but only call attention to a few other matters. According to Khatchadourian, "Dancing consists of movements and not, or not also, of actions of some kind or other."[4] First, although this distinction—which I hope to clarify shortly—may seem oversubtle, I believe (with Beiswanger) that dancing consists not in what Khatchadourian calls movements—that is, motions—but in actions generated by them. And second, I think it is a mistake— and there seems no warrant for this in action theory—to divide bodily motions from actions: they *are* actions of a certain kind, though in themselves generally not as interesting as the actions they generate. However, Khatchadourian's distinction be- tween (as I would say) bodily motions and *other* actions is important; but then the distinguishing features of these other actions need to be spelled out.

Taking off from the first of these two objections to Khatchadourian, I must now try to explain why I say that movings are more than motions: that there is indeed act-generation, a transformation of motions into movings. I have two main reasons.

My first reason rests on two propositions that will probably not be challenged. (1) It seems we do not dance all of the time—not every motion is dancing—so there must be some difference between the motions that generate dancing and those that don't, however difficult it may be to get a fix on. (2) It seems there is nothing in the nature of motions themselves that marks off those that can be dance from those that can't; practically any kind is available. Some insight into the puzzles here may be derived from Marcia Siegel's discussion of Anna Sokolow's *Rooms*. She describes the various motions of the performers—for example,

> Then, drooping across the chair seats, they lower their heads to the floor, lift their arms to the side and let them drop, slapping against the floor with a dead sound. . . . Slowly they lean forward and back in their seats, staring at the audience.
>
> None of this can be called dance movement, but neither is it merely the prosaic activity that it seems to be at first. Sokolow gives these ordinary movements a dancelike character by exaggerating the dynamics and the timing, sometimes beyond "natural" limits. Instead of just raising or lowering a hand, someone might take a very long time to raise it, giving the gesture great importance, then drop it suddenly and heavily, as if, having made all that effort to

[2]"Movement and Action in the Performing Arts," *Journal of Aesthetics and Art Criticism* 37 (1978): 25–36.
[3]See Haig Khatchadourian, "Movement and Action in Film," *British Journal of Aesthetics* 20 (1980):349–55. In writing this essay I have benefitted much from studying Julie Van Camp's dissertation, "Philosophical Problems of Dance Criticism" (Ph.D., Temple University, 1981), and also from her helpful comments on an earlier draft of my essay.
[4]Khatchadourian, "Movement and Action in the Performing Arts," 25.

prepare, there was nothing worth doing with the hand after all. Besides the intensified way everything is carried out, each move or repeated series of moves is a separate gesture that finishes in some way before the next series is undertaken.[5]

I am not sure I fully understand this passage, which is not as clear as Siegel's writing usually is. When she says that "none of this can be called dance movement," she is apparently not denying that what is going on is a dance; I think she means that these motions are not the usual stuff of dance, not conventionally used in dancing. When she adds that "Sokolow gives these ordinary movements a dancelike character," I take this to mean that Sokolow shapes the motions so that they actually *are* dance, not merely *like* dance. Of course this kind of performance is difficult to talk about, but if I understand her, Siegel is marking an important distinction. Of two motions, abstractly classified as, say, "raising an arm," one may be a dance and the other not, depending on some distinguishing feature contributed by the choreographer—so that, more concretely described, they may be somewhat different motions, though they belong to the same shared type. One motion generates moving, in my sense of the term, and the other doesn't. (Some would add that merely transferring an "ordinary" movement to a stage, under a bright spotlight, could give it a quality that makes it a dance.)

My second reason for distinguishing the concept of *motion* from that of *moving* is that this very distinction seems to be deeply embedded in a large special or technical vocabulary that is used for talking about dancing. Take the term *pirouette*, for example. We can explain "how you do" a pirouette, and we can say that in turning rapidly on her toe, the dancer pirouetted. A turning of a certain sort generated a pirouetting, and they were the same event; yet if we first describe the event as a rapid turning on the toe we are adding something to this description when we say that it was also a pirouette, for that is to say it was dancing. So with numerous other familiar terms: *jeté, glissade, demi-plié, sissone fermé, pas de bourrée*. (And, since we must not forget to include posings as well as movings, we should add *arabesque*.) My thesis is that all these terms refer to movings as such, not to the motions that generate them. When the technical terms are supplemented by other words, borrowed from ordinary speech—*leap, lope, skip, run*—these take on a second sense in the context of dance description, though I do not think this is a case of metaphor.

The question that looms next is evidently this: how does it come about that—or what are the generating conditions that make—motions and pauses become the movings and poses of dance? Without pretending to offer much of an argument, I will illustrate some features of action theory by reflecting briefly on a few possible answers to this rather large question.

First, then, let us consider an answer that is not without plausibility and is in fact suggested by Marcia Siegel. You will recall her remark that a dancer in *Rooms* "might take a very long time to raise [his or her hand], giving the gesture great importance, then drop it suddenly and heavily, as if . . . there was nothing worth doing with the hand after all." She speaks of "the intensified way everything is carried out." If we are wary, I think we can make do with the word *expressive* to mark her meaning—and mine. When I use the word in this context, I refer to *regional qualities* of a motion or

---

[5]Marcia B. Siegel, *The Shapes of Change: Images of Modern Dance* (Boston: Houghton Miffli. 1979), 280.

sequence of motions: it has an air of momentousness or mystery or majesty; it is abrupt, loose, heavy, decisive, or languid. To say that the motion is expressive is just to say that it has some such quality to a fairly intense degree. And this is *all* I mean by "expressive." We might then try formulating our first answer in this way: *When a motion or sequence of motions is expressive, it is dance.*

Selma Jeanne Cohen, in her well-known essay,[6] apparently holds that expressiveness is present in all true dance—though her defense of this view is, I think, marred by a tendency to confuse expressiveness with other things I shall shortly touch on, such as representation and signalling. Khatchadourian, in reply, says that expressiveness is not a necessary condition of dance but a criterion of *good* dance.[7] An objection to making it a *sufficient* condition is, for example, that an actress in a play might appropriately make exactly the same expressive motion as Sokolow's dancers yet would not be bursting into dance but dramatically revealing a mental state or trait of personality. Thus to make the first answer work we would need to introduce further restrictions on the range of regional qualities that are to be taken into account. If we look about in writings on dance, we find a diversity of terms but some convergence of meaning; take two examples from rather different quarters. As is well known, Susanne Langer speaks of "virtual powers" as the "primary illusion" of dance; and though I don't see the need for talking about illusions, I think "powers" conveys some general truth. Then there is a remark by Merce Cunningham, reported by Calvin Tomkins:

> He has remained firmly committed to dance as dance, although he acknowledges that the concept is difficult to define. "I think it has to do with amplification, with enlargement," he said recently. "Dancing provides something—an amplification of energy—that is not provided any other way, and that's what interests me."[8]

This remark is noteworthy in part because of what it tells about Cunningham's own taste and preferences, but I think "amplification of energy" conveys a general truth.

To put my suggestion briefly, and all too vaguely: in dance the forms and characters of voluntary motion (the generating base) are encouraged to allow the emergence of new regional qualities, which in turn are lifted to a plane of marked perceptibility; they are exhibited or featured. It is the featuring specifically of the qualities of *volition*, of willing to act, that makes movings of motions. This is most obviously true when we see power, energy, force, zest, and other positive qualities of volition; but it also applies to such qualities as droopy exhaustion and mechanical compulsion—weaknesses of the will, as well as strengths. Dances of course may be expressive in other ways, have other qualities besides these volitional qualities. But the first answer to our basic question might be reformulated this way: *When a motion or sequence of motions is expressive in virtue of its fairly intense volitional qualities, it is dance.*

Some will say that this sounds like sport, and the proposal does seem to extend beyond dance. Not that it is necessarily a mistake to find an affinity, but it seems we

---

[6]"A Prolegomenon to an Aesthetics of Dance," *Journal of Aesthetics and Art Criticism* 21 (1962):19–26, reprinted in several places, including Nadel and Miller, *Dance Experience*, and *Aesthetic Inquiry: Essays on Art Criticism and the Philosophy of Art*, ed. M. C. Beardsley and H. M. Schueller (Belmont, Calif.: Dickenson, 1967).

[7]P. 36, n. 13.

[8]Calvin Tomkins, "An Appetite for Motion," reprinted from the *New Yorker* (1968) in Nadel and Miller, *Dance Experience*, 273.

must continue our search. There are of course several familiar suggestions, which are
dogged by equally familiar objections. Some of them are rather nicely brought together
in this passage from St. Augustine:

> Suppose there is no actual work in hand and no intention to make anything, but the motions
> of the limbs are done for pleasure, that will be dancing. Ask what delights you in dancing and
> number will reply, "Lo, here am I." Examine the beauty of bodily form, and you will find that
> everything is in its place by number. Examine the beauty of bodily motion, and you will find
> everything in its due time by number.[9]

Some of these ideas are worth following up, when the opportunity presents itself.
There is, for example, the suggestion that what transforms motions into dance is a
certain *intention* that accompanies them: the intention to perform the motions for the
sake of pleasure (I suppose, either of the performer or of the audience). This seems too
narrow a restriction, even if it applies to most dancing; other intentions can be
prominent. There is also the suggestion that the relevant pleasure is one derived from
mathematically ordered motion (i.e., pulse and rhythm, which together form meter).
This, too, has been regarded as central to dance (by both Khatchadourian and Cohen,
for example), but we cannot take it as a necessary or sufficient condition, even if it may
be a very useful criterion of dancehood. (St. Augustine, at some stages of his thought,
was a bit obsessed with number.) There is also the suggestion that it is somehow the
absence of practical intent ("no actual work in hand," he says) that distinguishes dance
from other actions. This calls for another look, after we have gained a clearer notion of
what "actual work" might encompass.

To get to this topic, we may take a short detour by way of another answer to our basic
question, one that tries to capture an essence of dance through the concept of
representation. Consider an *act-type* (that is, a kind of action, having numerous actual
instances): say, snow shovelling. This involves, for effectiveness and efficiency, certain
characteristic *motion-types*. If we select certain of these motion-types that distinguish
snow shovelling from other activities and perform them for the benefit of someone
else, we may enable the other person to recognize the action-type from which the
motions have been derived. This, roughly put, is the representation (or depiction) of
one action-type by an action of another type—for in representing snow shovelling, we
are not actually doing it (the actor smoking a pipe onstage does not represent a man
smoking a pipe, for he is one; but he may represent a detective smoking a pipe, which
he is not).

Now representation by motions clearly comes in many degrees of abstraction, of
which we can perhaps distinguish three degrees in a standard way. In *playacting* (as in
drama) we have the most realistic degree: the actor may wield a shovel, and the director
may even call for artificial snow for the actor to push about. In *miming*, we dispense
with props and verbal utterance, and we allow room for witty exaggeration: the mime
would be rushing about the stage, busily moving his arms in shovelling motions,
stopping to blow on his fingers or to rub his aching back. In *suggesting*, we merely
allude to the original action-type, borrowing a motion or two, sketching or outlining,
and mingling these motions with others, such as whirling or leaping. This might be the

---

[9]*De Libero Arbitrio*, 2.16.42; trans. H. S. Burleigh, in *The Library of Christian Classics*, vol. 6
(Philadelphia: Westminster Press, 1955).

Snow-shovelling Dance, to be performed, of course, after the actual job has been done, by way of celebrating the victory of humankind over one more assault of nature. Playacting, taken quite narrowly, must be comparatively rare in dance, miming much more common, though in short stretches, I should think. Suggesting, on the other hand, is pervasive; it appears in many of the most striking and cogent movings.[10]

Indeed, it is this pervasiveness that prompts another answer to our question: *When a motion, or sequence of motions, represents actions of other types in the mode of suggestion, it is dance.* This will undoubtedly cover a lot of ground, but it will not, of course, be satisfactory to all dancers today. For beyond the third degree of abstraction in representation there lies a fourth degree, where representation disappears; we have loping-back-and-forth and panting dancers, sitting and bending dancers, who don't represent anything. Or pirouetting dancers. Now one could argue that these fragments of moving only become dance when embedded in larger sequences that do represent by suggestion. But I should think many a pas de deux as well as many a contemporary dance episode is utterly nonrepresentational.

Snow shovelling is an example of a class of actions in which we effect a change in the physical world outside our skins; it is causally generated. Many of these actions have their own characteristic, and therefore imitable, forms of motion: corn planting, baby rocking, knitting, hammering. I should like to call such actions *workings*, because they perform work in the physicist's sense—even though some of them would ordinarily be called play: kicking a field goal or sinking a putt. It is plain that dances include many representations of working actions, nearly always at a fairly high degree of abstraction. And this contributes to their expressiveness: seen as baby rocking, the motions may yield a more intense quality of gentleness.

Besides workings, we may take note of two other broad classes of action that have some bearing upon the subject of this inquiry. In one of these we are concerned, not with physical states of the world, but (indirectly) with mental states of other persons. The actions I refer to, when they are performed with the help of, or by means of, verbal utterances, are called "illocutionary actions," and they are generally of familiar types: asserting, greeting, inviting, thanking, refusing, insisting. These types have subtypes: insisting on being paid time-and-a-half for last week's overtime, for example, is a subtype that may have numerous instances. Many of these same types of action can also be performed without words; we can greet by gestures as well, or sometimes better. Nodding, shrugging, winking, bowing, kneeling might be called "para-illocutionary actions" when they are done with this sort of significance; so biting the thumb generates insulting, as in act 1, scene 2 of *Romeo and Juliet*. With or without words, such actions can be called *signallings* or *sayings*, in acknowledgment of the messages they carry. I choose the latter term, and the way to put it is: in waving a hand a certain way, the infant is saying good-bye. Sayings, like workings, are representable: in waving his or her hand, the dancer is representing someone saying good-bye. And, like working-representations, saying-representations can contribute much to the expressiveness of motions in dance. The quality of that waving, as a moving, may be intensified by its semantic aspect. The dancer summons up and draws into the texture of his or her

---

[10]Where playacting or miming is prominent, we are tempted to say what Anna Kisselgoff wrote of a Jerome Robbins work: "The line between dance and nondance has been obliterated in *Watermill*" (*New York Times*, 27 May 1979).

moving something of the sorrow or finality of the action-type he or she is representing. Sayings involve a form of sortal generation, what is (very broadly) called "conventional generation." It is the existence of a social convention that enables arm waving to generate good-bying; the dancer does not make use of that convention to say anything, but recalls it to intensify expressiveness.

This raises an important question that there is no time to do more than glance at now: do dances not only represent, but also constitute sayings? That is, can motions that generate movings also generate sayings? I have read an odd remark attributed to John Cage: "We are not, in these dances, saying something. We are simple-minded enough to think that if we were saying something we would use words."[11] This is indeed simple-minded, given the extraordinary richness of bodily motions as generators of para-illocutionary actions. It might even be argued that representations of para-illocutionary actions can hardly help but be para-illocutionary actions themselves, since by selecting the suggestive elements and giving them a different context we may seem to comment on the sayings we quote. But this claim goes beyond what I am prepared to argue for at the moment.

The third class of actions I shall call attention to consists of motions that are goal-directed, though not necessarily goal-attaining, and that have a point or purpose, even though they move neither other bodies nor other minds. Take, for example, running a race (with the aim of winning), or reaching out, or shrinking away. We might call these actions "strivings." They are generated by the presence of mental states, such as intentions (a form of "circumstantial generation"). Of course strivings, too, can be represented.

Workings, sayings, and strivings seem to belong together at some level of abstraction, as entering into social interactions that have a function, that end in achievement or are so aimed. If it is not too misleading, we may use the label "practical" for them all—and at least we will have tried to delimit the scope of this notorious weasel word somewhat more scrupulously than is usual. With its help, as so defined, we can state St. Augustine's proposal in what seems to be its most plausible form: *When a motion, or sequence of motions, does not generate practical actions, and is intended to give pleasure through perception of rhythmic order, it is dance.* But even at its best the proposal will not serve. Perhaps if we were to add a suitable insistence on expressiveness as another source of the pleasure, we would come close to an adequate characterization of dance as an art. But I assume that we do not wish to limit our concept of dance in this way. Suppose the pueblo corn dance, for example, is not only performed in order to aid the growth of corn but is actually effective; then it is a working, just as much as seed planting or hoeing. Dance shades off into and embraces some part of ritual, which is a kind of saying. If the dance is done at a festival in competition for first prize (although that may be opposed to the true spirit of dance), I suppose it is no less a dance for being at the same time a striving.

Thus we cannot define dance in this negative way as excluding motions that generate practical actions. Yet there is something to this opposition, something about dancing that is different, even if those other actions can be, in their various ways, expressive. Perhaps we can come nearer to it in one final line of thought. If *every*

[11]Quoted by Erica Abel in "The New Dance," reprinted from *Dance Scope* 2 (1965):21–26, in Nadel and Miller, *Dance Experience*, 117.

motion of the corn dance is prescribed in detail by magical formulas or religious rules to foster germination, growth, or a fruitful harvest, we might best regard it as pure ritual, however expressive it may be as a *consequence* of its mode of working. Like soldiers on parade or priests officiating at Mass, the participants would verge on dance but they would not really be dancing. But if some part of what goes on in the ritual helps it to achieve expressiveness (of volitional qualities) that is to some degree independent of any practical function, then whatever else it may be, it is also a moving. If, in other words, there is more zest, vigor, fluency, expansiveness, or stateliness than appears necessary for practical purposes, there is an overflow or superfluity of expressiveness to mark it as belonging to its own domain of dance.

Noël Carroll and Sally Banes

WORKING AND DANCING: A RESPONSE TO MONROE BEARDSLEY'S "WHAT IS GOING ON IN A DANCE?"

Professor Beardsley's paper is distinguished by his customary clarity. Many of the distinctions he draws will undoubtedly be useful not only for dance theoreticians, but for dance critics as well. Nevertheless, the way that these distinctions are placed in the service of a putative characterization of what constitutes a dance "moving" seems to us problematic. This brief note will be devoted to exploring the adequacy of Professor Beardsley's proposal.

Beardsley appears to conclude his paper by stating a condition requisite for a motion to be counted as a dance "moving." He writes,

> If, in other words, there is more zest, vigor, fluency, expansiveness, or stateliness than appears necessary for its practical purposes, there is an overflow or superfluity of expressiveness to mark it as belonging to its own domain of dance.[1]

We interpret Beardsley's basic point here as the claim that a superfluity of expressiveness (above the requirements of practical exigencies) is a defining feature of a dance "moving." However, in our opinion, this attribute represents neither a necessary nor a sufficient condition of dance.

First of all, "superfluity of expressiveness" is not exclusive enough to define a dance moving. We often hear of the fervor of socialist volunteers, urbanites, who travel to rural areas to help with a harvest and boost productivity. Imagine a truck-load of such

Noël Carroll and Sally Banes, "A Response to Monroe Beardsley's 'What Is Going On in a Dance?' " from Dance Research Journal, 15 (1982):37–42. Reprinted by permission of the authors.

This paper was originally an invited response to Monroe Beardsley's paper for the expanded proceedings of the "Illuminating Dance" conference. The authors wish to express their gratitude to Monroe Beardsley, Maxine Sheets-Johnstone, Selma Jeanne Cohen, Adina Armelagos, and Anne Hatfield for their careful readings of this paper.

[1]Monroe C. Beardsley, "What Is Going On in a Dance?" All mentions of Beardsley refer to this paper, given at a conference entitled "Illuminating Dance: Philosophical Inquiry and Aesthetic Criticism," co-sponsored by CORD and the Dance Department of Temple University, held at Temple University, May 5, 1979.

patriotic workers arriving at a cane field somewhere in Cuba. Some of them may even be professional dancers. They raise their machetes much higher than necessary, use more force than is required by their task, and perhaps their swinging becomes rhythmic. Their activity is expressive of patriotic zest and revolutionary zeal, but it is not dance. Here we have an overflow of expressiveness, and it is not related to the practical purpose of the event, which is aimed at increasing productivity, not at displaying class solidarity. Of course, a journalist might describe the harvest as a dance, but we would have to understand this as poetic shorthand, meaning "dance-like." To take the term "dance" literally in referring to such an event would commit us to such unlikely ballets as some sweeping infantry maneuvers and the dramatic tantrums of an adolescent. If a dance critic were to review these events, we would be very surprised.

Undoubtedly, a choreographer could take our truckload of harvesters, place them on a proscenium stage, and transform their enthusiasm into a dance. But in such a case, it seems to us that it is the choreographer's act of framing, or recontextualizing, rather than an intrinsic quality of the movement, that is decisive. In general, whether one is speaking about art dance or social dance, the context of the event in which the movement is situated is more salient than the nature of the movement itself in determining whether the action is dance.

Professor Beardsley's definition not only fails to be exclusive enough, but also falters in inclusiveness. There are, we believe, incontestable examples of dance in which there is no superfluity of expressiveness in the movement. One example is *Room Service* by Yvonne Rainer, which was first performed at the Judson Church in 1963 and again the next year at the Institute of Contemporary Art in Philadelphia. Rainer describes it as "a big sprawling piece with three teams of people playing follow-the-leader through an assortment of paraphernalia which is arranged and rearranged by a guy and his two assistants."[2] Part of the dance includes climbing up a ladder to a platform and jumping off. A central segment of the Philadelphia performance (and of particular interest for this paper) was the activity of two dancers carrying a mattress up an aisle in the theater, out one exit, and back in through another.

Although *Room Service* may appear similar to a dance Beardsley discusses—Anna Sokolow's *Rooms*—it differs from it in important ways. The ordinary movement in *Room Service* is not marked by "the intensified way"[3] in which it is carried out. The point of the dance is to make ordinary movement *qua* ordinary movement perceptible. The audience observes the performers navigating a cumbersome object, noting how the working bodies adjust their muscles, weights, and angles. If the dance is performed correctly, there can be no question of superfluity of expression over the requirements of practical purposes, because the *raison d'être* of the piece is to display the practical

---

[2]Yvonne Rainer, "Some retrospective notes on a dance for 10 people and 12 mattresses called *Parts of Some Sextets,* performed at the Wadsworth Atheneum, Hartford, Connecticut, and Judson Memorial Church, New York, in March, 1965," *Tulane Drama Review* 10 (Winter 1965): 168. Reprinted in Yvonne Rainer, *Work 1961–73* (Halifax, Nova Scotia: The Press of the Nova Scotia College of Art and Design: New York: New York University Press, 1974), p. 45. In her discussions of *Room Service* in *Work 1961–73* on pp. 45 and 294, Rainer may give the impression that the first performance of the work was the one in Philadelphia in April 1964. However, it was first performed as a choreographic collaboration between Rainer and sculptor Charles Ross at Concert of Dance 13, on November 10–12, 1963, at the Judson Memorial Church in New York City.

[3]Quoted from Marcia B. Siegel by Professor Beardsley in order to show why the movement in *Rooms* is dance.

intelligence of the body in pursuit of a mundane, goal-oriented type of action—moving a mattress. That is, the subject of the dance is the functional economy of a movement in the performance of bodies involved in what Beardsley calls a working. *Room Service* is not a representation of a working; it *is* a working. But it is also a dance—partially because through its aesthetic context it transforms an ordinary working (the sort of thing whose kinetic intricacies usually go unnoticed or ignored) into an object for close scrutiny. Rainer immediately went on to make another dance, *Parts of Some Sextets*, comprising a variety of activities involving ten dancers, twelve mattresses, and gears, string, rope, and buffers. Again, the emphasis in the dance is on the working human body.

Room Service is not an atypical dance. It is an example of a genre of avant-garde performance that might loosely be referred to as task dances, which have been made continuously since the Sixties. The roster of task dances includes other works by Rainer, Trisha Brown's Equipment Pieces and her *Rulegame 5* (1964), and Simone Forti's "dance construction" *Slant Board* (1961), in which three or four people move constantly across a wooden ramp slanted against a wall at a 45° angle to the floor, by means of knotted ropes.[4] The existence of this genre is an important motive in writing this reply to Professor Beardsley, because we fear that his definition is unwittingly conservative, operating to exclude prescriptively some of the most exciting work of contemporary choreographers.

Of course, Beardsley may wish to defend his definition by arguing that *Room Service*, and works like it, are not dances. This seems ill-advised for several reasons. First, the dance shares a set of recognized aesthetic preoccupations with contemporary fine art. For example, it is what has been called "anti-illusionist." That is, it attempts to close the conceptual gap between artworks and real things—a major theme of modernist sculpture and painting. In this vein, Jasper Johns reportedly has said that "people should be able to look at a painting "the same way you look at a radiator.' "[5] Johns's flag paintings, especially *Flag* (1955, Museum of Modern Art), ingeniously implement this "demystifying" attitude toward artworks, since in certain pertinent respects the painting is a flag (or one side of one), rather than a representation (or "illusion") of one; schoolchildren could pledge to it with no loss of allegiance. Johns's bronzed beer cans or his Savarin can with paint brushes are sculptures that likewise attempt to narrow the categorical distinction between mundane objects and works of art.

The choice of ordinary working movement as the subject of *Room Service* is on a par with the "demythologizing" tendency toward fine art that one finds in many of Jasper Johns's pieces. Stated formulaically, we might say that "ordinary object" in art is equivalent to "ordinary movement" in dance. Now, Johns's work is (rightfully, we believe) considered among the major accomplishments of the art of the Fifties, Sixties, and early Seventies. There can be little doubt that it is art or that his patterned canvases are paintings. Why? One answer is that his works are the intelligible products of a

---

[4]Trisha Brown's Equipment Pieces are well documented in Sally R. Sommer, "Equipment Dances: Trisha Brown," *The Drama Review* 16 (September 1972, T-55): 135–141. Simone Forti writes about her dance constructions and other works in her *Handbook in Motion* (Halifax, Nova Scotia: The Press of the Nova Scotia College of Art and Design; New York: New York University Press, 1974). See also the chapters on Trisha Brown and Simone Forti in Sally Banes, *Terpsichore in Sneakers: Post-Modern Dance* (Boston: Houghton Mifflin, 1980).

[5]Michael Crichton, *Jasper Johns* (New York: Harry N. Abrams, 1977), p. 31.

Jasper Johns, Flag, 1955. Encaustic, oil and collage on canvas, 42¼ × 60⅝". Collection, The Museum of Modern Art, New York. Gift of Philip Johnson in honor of Alfred H. Barr, Jr.

century of animated interplay between art making and art theorizing. Since the rise of photography, anti-illusionist arguments for the role and destiny of painting abound. Part of the rhetoric of this theorizing is that a painting is essentially an object (a "real" object), like any other (e.g., a radiator or beer can), rather than a cypher (a virtual object) standing for real objects. The Johns examples, as well as Warhol's Brillo boxes, attempt to literalize this type of theory by proposing master-pieces that in terms of certain relevant features are indistinguishable from everyday objects. *Room Service* bears a *strict genetic resemblance* to the above cases of modernist painting and sculpture. If they are full-blooded examples of painting and sculpture, as we believe their position in the history of twentieth-century art establishes, then *Room Service* is a dance.

Specifically, it is an art dance, since the tradition it directly emerges from is that of the artworld rather than custom, ritual, or popular culture. Indeed, it is an art dance in a triple sense. First, it is presented to the spectator as an object of aesthetic contemplation and not as a social or ritual activity. Second, and more importantly, it mimes (or, less metaphorically, transposes) the theoretical *données* of fine art in the medium of dance. And third, in doing this it is also in the domain of art dancing proper, since both the balletic and modern traditions of dance have always made a practice of exploring other arts for inspiration and invention.

In making this argument, we hasten to add that we do not believe that it is necessary for the anti-illusionist theories that form the conceptual background of Johns, of Warhol, or of Rainer to be true or even compelling philosophically in order that the putative paintings, sculptures, and dances be classified as paintings, sculptures, and dances. It is enough that the theories have currency in their appropriate communities of discourse and that the works in question can be seen as their consequences. We are assuming this on the grounds that a genetic link between an evolving artistic tradition (including theory, practice, and the cross-fertilization between the two) and a candidate for inclusion in that tradition is a *prima facie* reason for classifying the candidate as part of the tradition. *Room Service* is both art and art dance because of such genetic links. Indeed, insofar as it is even less ambiguously an ordinary working than painting the design of the Stars and Stripes is a flag, it is perhaps a more effective implementation of modernist concerns than the Johns example. In terms of our use of *Room Service*, and dances like it, as counterexamples to Beardsley's characterization of dance, it is important to iterate that these dances are able to articulate the modernist theme of anti-illusionism precisely because their movements are completely practical—a literal performance of a task—with no superfluity of expressiveness.

A related, though less persuasive reason to believe that *Room Service* is a dance (specifically, an art dance) is that it performs a major (though not essential) function of art in general and art dancing in particular. Namely, it symbolically reflects major values and preoccupations of the culture from which it emerged. In other words, it behaves the way we expect dances to behave. Its anti-illusionist stance and its disavowal of representation, formal decorativeness, and the kinds of expressiveness found in most modern dance (e.g., Graham, Humphrey, and Limon) evince a reductive bias, a quest to get down to basics, to eschew the layers of convention, coded symbolism, and elaborate structure that "obstruct" the spectator's perception of movement. This search for fundamentals is in many respects utopian. Nevertheless, it does reflect a particular post-war mood—a positivist search for the hard facts of dance, bereft of illusionist "nonsense." Again, whether there are such hard facts is beside the point; it is the quest implied by this dance that reflects the temper of the times. And, to return to Beardsley's definition, *Room Service* reflects the values and prejudices of its cultural context because of the sheer practicality of its movement. (Interestingly, a Labananalysis of Rainer's non-task dances of this period shows a striking similarity between the efficient motions used in work and those used in the dances: a somewhat narrow and medium level stance, an even flow of energy, and sagittal gestures—in two planes, forward and backward plus up and down—rather than the three-dimensional shaping, gathering, and scattering movements of much modern dance.)[6]

Admittedly, *Room Service* is an extremely complex dance, with several levels of symbolic import. It is not our intention to argue that it is not expressive. For example, it communicates a conception of dance, albeit a reductive one, and, as the previous paragraph argues, it espouses identifiable values. However, this sense of expression is different from Beardsley's. It is not a matter of the movement having intensified, nonpractical qualities, but of the movement implying certain polemical commitments, easily statable in propositions, due to the art-historical and cultural contexts in which the dance was produced. Here the propositional import of the dance hinges on the practicality of the movement; this level of expression, in other words, cannot be mapped in terms of an overflow of intensified qualities, above and beyond the

---

[6]For an analysis of the workly movements of Rainer's *Trio A*, see "Yvonne Rainer: The Aesthetics of Denial," in Banes, *Terpsichore in Sneakers*, pp. 41–55.

Room Service by Yvonne Rainer and Charles Ross, in its first performance at Concert of Dance #13. Judson Memorial Church, November 20, 1963. © *1963 by Peter Moore.*

functional. Though *Room Service* has propositional meaning, it is not what Beardsley calls a saying, nor is it a representation of a saying. Professor Beardsley's sayings are highly conventionalized signals, e.g., a wave of the hand is regularly associated with "hello." However, we do not "read" the significance of the movement in *Room Service*, but infer it as the best explanation of Rainer's choreographic choices within a specific historical context.

Room Service might also be called expressive in the sense that the choreography metaphorically possesses certain anthropomorphic qualities; we have already called it "positivist." It might also be called factual or objective. But each of these labels fits the dance specifically because of the theoretically "hard-minded," anti-illusionist position it promotes. That the subject is work in the context of a culture that often identifies art and dance with play also has expressive repercussions: the choreography is "serious" rather than "sentimental" or "frivolous" (in the idiom of the Protestant ethic). Again, it is the choice of unadorned workings as its subject that is the basis of its expressive effect as well as the basis, as previously argued, of its being recognizable as an art dance. Given this, Professor Beardsley's stipulation, identifying dance with a superfluity of expressiveness above practical purposes, does not seem to fit the facts of a major work of post-modern dance and, by extension, a genre of which it is a primary example.

Professor Beardsley's paper also raises issues relevant to post-modern choreography in the section where he argues that the basic constituents of dance are not bodily motions as such. Instead, Beardsley holds that dances are composed of actions that he calls "movings" and "posings." It is interesting to note that in certain post-modern dances and dance theorizing it is presupposed that dance is fundamentally bodily motion and that the function of a dance is to make the spectator see bodily motions as such. The motive behind this enterprise derives from the modernist bias outlined earlier. In brief, in contemporary theoretical discussions of fine art, the conception of a painting as an *ordinary* object easily becomes associated with the idea that it is an object as such. It is a surface. Thus, the role of an artist like Jules Olitski is seen as acknowledging the flat surface of the painting. Painters are cast in a role akin to nuclear physicists, exploring the basic physical constituents of their medium, as if plumbing the mysteries of the atom. The result is paintings "about" paint or, to change media, films "about" celluloid. This anti-illusionist move is also in evidence in post-modern dance. Dances like Trisha Brown's *Accumulation* identify dance as a concatenation of physical motions without any ostensible formal, conventional, expressive, or representational unity. *Accumulation* is a list of abstract gestures—simple rotations, bends, and swings of the joints and limbs—that are accumulated by repeating the first gesture several times, adding the second gesture and repeating gestures one and two several times, and so on. There are no transitions between gestures. *Accumulation* suggests a position about the nature of the basic elements of dance, a position which holds that dance consists of bodily motions.

The philosophical problems raised by dances like *Accumulation* can be quite vexing.[7] But in our opinion, such dances are not counter-examples to Beardsley's claim that dances are made up of actions and never mere bodily motions. Our reasons for believing this are, for the most part, contained in our gloss of *Room Service*. We have admitted that the search for the fundamentals of dance by post-modern choreographers is utopian. Making dances like *Accumulation*, which are designed to *imply* that dance essentially consists of bodily motions, requires that the basic movements chosen for the dance be purposively made so that a) they are not straightforwardly classifiable in terms of traditional categories of dance actions (e.g., Beardsley's "suggestings") and b) they are intelligible, due to their historical context, as rejections of the traditional categories. In meeting the first requirement, each movement is a type of action—namely, a *refraining*. Specifically, each movement is *a studied omission* of the movement qualities found in ballet and modern dance.[8] In the context of the Sixties, this sort of refraining implied a commitment to the idea that dance consists primarily of bodily motions. However, the movements used to articulate that position were actually anything but mere bodily motions. They were actions, refrainings whose implicit disavowal of the traditional qualities of dance movements enabled them to be understood as polemical. Thus, though we feel that certain developments in post-modern dance, specifically task dances, threaten Professor Beardsley's concept of dance, we do not believe that the existence of dances like *Accumulation* challenge Beardsley's point that dances consist of actions rather than mere bodily motions.

---

[7]Some of these problems are examined in Noël Carroll's "Post-Modern Dance and Expression," a paper delivered at the American Dance Festival at Duke University in July 1979, published in *Philosophical Essays in Dance*, ed. Gordon Fancher and Gerald Myers (Brooklyn: Dance Horizons, 1981), pp. 95–104.

[8]We are indebted to Paul Ziff for the suggestion that concepts like omission, forbearance, and refraining, as used in both legal theory and action theory, would be useful in the description of avant-garde dance.

SELECTED BIBLIOGRAPHY

The editors have made no attempt to construct a comprehensive bibliography of writings in aesthetics prior to the publication of the first edition. For such an extensive bibliography, readers are referred to the first edition of Dickie/Sclafani, which contains a useful bibliography into 1976. Here, we restrict the bibliography primarily to writings published during the past decade. In addition, where possible, we highlight books containing extensive bibliographies on a specific subject with an *asterisk*(*). Second, a number of important studies that antedate 1980, such as Monroe Beardsley's *The Possibility of Criticism*, are included because of their particular relevance to the subject in a specific section. In Part Five the bibliographies are limited primarily to the topics included in that part. Readers wishing further bibliographic information in the literature of aesthetics should consult *The Philosophers' Index*.

APQ American Philosophical Quarterly
BJA British Journal of Aesthetics
CC Communication and Cognition
CI Critical Inquiry
ISP International Studies in Philosophy
JAAC Journal of Aesthetics and Art Criticism
JAE Journal of Aesthetic Education
JCLA Journal of Comparative Literature and Aesthetics
JHI Journal of the History of Ideas
JHP Journal of the History of Philosophy
JP Journal of Philosophy
PAS Proceedings of the Aristotelian Society
PASS Proceedings of the Aristotelian Society Supplemental
PEW Philosophy East and West
PI Philosophical Investigations
PL Philosophy in Literature
PPQ Pacific Philosophical Quarterly
PPR Philosophy and Phenomenological Research
PQ Philosophical Quarterly
PS Philosophical Studies
RM Review of Metaphysics

Part One: Traditional Theories of Art and Contemporary Critiques of These Theories

Plato and Aristotle

Alexandrakis, A. "A Differing View: Plato's Books III and X of *The Republic*." *Diotima* 8 (1980).
Alexandrakis, A., and Knoblock, J. "The Aesthetic Appeal of Art in Plato and Aristotle." *Diotima* 6 (1978).

Barnes, J., et al., eds. *Articles on Aristotle: 4 Psychology and Aesthetics.* London, 1979.

Belfiore, E. "Plato's Greatest Accusation Against Poetry." *Canadian Journal of Philosophy* 19 (1983).

————. "Pleasure, Tragedy, and Aristotelian Psychology." *Classical Quarterly* 35 (1985).

————. "The Role of the Visual Arts in Plato's Ideal State." *The Journal of the Theory and Criticism of the Visual Arts* 1 (1981).

Eden, K. "Poetry and Equity: Aristotle's Defense of Fiction." *Traditio* 38 (1982).

Elias, J. A. *Plato's Defense of Poetry.* Albany, 1984.

Else, G. F. *The Structure and Date of Book X of Plato's "Republic."* Heidelberg, 1972.

————. *Plato and Aristotle on Poetry.* Chapel Hill, 1987.

*Else, G. F., and Burian, P., eds. *Plato and Aristotle on Poetry.* Chapel Hill, 1987.

Faas, E. "From Mimesis to Kinesis: The Aristotelian Dramatic Matrix, Psychoanalysis, and Some Recent Alternatives." *Process Studies* 13 (1983).

Finnegan, J. D. "Aristotelian Causality and the Teaching of Literary Theory." *JAE* 16 (1982).

Fisher, J. "Did Plato Have a Theory of Art?" *PPQ* 63 (1982).

————. "Plato's Use of Poetry." *JCLA* 2 (1979–80).

Fortenbaugh, W. W. *Aristotle on Emotion.* London, 1975.

Goodrich, R. A. "Plato on Poetry and Painting." *BJA* 22 (1982).

Gould, T. "Plato's Hostility to Art." *Arion* 3 (1964). (Reprinted in *Essays on Classical Literature,* ed. N. Rudd. Cambridge, 1972.)

Griswold, C. "The Ideas and the Criticism of Poetry in Plato's *Republic,* Book 10." *JHP* 19 (1981).

Gravel, P., and Reiss, J. *Tragedy and the Tragic in Western Culture.* Montreal, 1983.

Grube, G. M. A. *Aristotle on Poetry and Style.* New York, 1958.

————. *The Greek and Roman Critics.* London, 1965.

Halliwell, S. *Aristotle's Poetics.* Chapel Hill, 1986.

*————. *The Poetics of Aristotle.* Chapel Hill, 1987.

Hantz, H. D. "Plato's Ambivalence Toward the Arts." *Diotima* 13 (1985).

Hutton, J. *Aristotle's Poetics.* New York, 1982.

Hwang, P. H. "Poetry in Plato's *Republic.*" *Apeiron* 15 (1981).

Kemal, S. "Arabic Poetics and Aristotle's *Poetics.*" *BJA* 26 (1986).

Keuls, E. C. *Plato and Greek Painting.* Leiden, 1978. *Antika* 10 (1960).

Misra, K. S. *Modern Tragedies and Aristotle's Theory.* Atlantic Highlands, 1981.

Moles, J. "Notes on Aristotle: *Poetics* 13 and 14." *Classical Quarterly* 29 (1979).

————. "Philanthropia in the *Poetics.*" *Phoenix* 38 (1984).

Moravscik, J., and Temko, P., eds. *Plato on Beauty, Wisdom, and the Arts.* New Jersey, 1982.

Packer, M. "The Conditions of Aesthetic Feeling in Aristotle's *Poetics.*" *BJA* 24 (1984).

Papanoutsos, E. P. "The Aristotelian Katharsis." *BJA* 17 (1977).

Pollitt, J. J. *The Ancient View of Greek Art.* Student ed. New Haven, 1974.

Potts, L. J. *Aristotle on the Art of Fiction.* 2nd ed. Cambridge, 1959.

Riola, J. "The Unresolved Paradox in Plato's Aesthetics." *Dialogue* 20 (1978).

Roochnik, D. L. "Plato's Critique of Postmodernism." *PL* 11 (1987).

Russell, D. A. *Criticism in Antiquity.* London, 1981.

Russell, D. A., and Winterbottom, M., eds. *Ancient Literary Criticism.* Oxford, 1972.

Santoro, L. "Aristotle and Contemporary Aesthetics." *Diotima* 10 (1982).

Smithson, I. "The Moral View of Aristotle's *Poetics.*" *JHI* 44 (1983).

Snoeyenbos, M., and Frederic, R. "Aristotle and Freud on Art." *JCLA* 2 (1978–80).

Sorbom, G. *Mimesis and Art.* Stockholm, 1966.

Verdenius, W. J. *Mimesis: Plato's Doctrine of Artistic Imitation and Its Meaning to Us.* Leiden, 1949: reprinted 1972.

Yanal, R. "Aristotle's Definition of Poetry." *Nous* 16 (1982).

Tolstoy, Bell, and Collingwood

Armstrong, A. M. "The Primrose Path to Philistinism." *BJA* 23 (1983).

Bell, C. *Art.* New York, 1912.

Black, D. W. "Collingwood on Corrupt Consciousness" *JAAC* 40 (1980).

Bywater, W. J., Jr. *Clive Bell's Eye.* Detroit, 1975.

Collingwood, R. G. *The Principles of Art.* Oxford, 1938.

Curtin, D. W. "Varieties of Aesthetic Formalism." *JAAC* 40 (1982).

Diffey, T. J. "Art and Goodness: Collingwood's Aesthetics and Moore's Ethics Compared." *BJA* 25 (1985).

———. *Tolstoy's "What Is Art?"* London, 1985.

Donagan, A., ed. *Essays in the Philosophy of Art.* Bloomington, 1964.

Donagan, A. *The Later Philosophy of R. G. Collingwood* (Oxford, 1988)

Dowling, D. *Bloomsbury Aesthetics and the Novels of Forster and Woolf.* New York, 1985.

Duran, J. "Collingwood and Intentionality." *BJA* 27 (1987).

Fethe, C. B. "Craft and Art: A Phenomenological Distinction." *BJA* 17 (1977).

Grant, J. "On Reading Collingwood's Principles of Art." *JAAC* 46 (1987).

Hagberg, G. "Art as Thought: The Inner Conflicts of Aesthetic Idealism." *PI* 9 (1986).

Ingram, P. T., "Art, Language, and Community in Collingwood's *Principles of Art.*" *JAAC* 37 (1978).

Kiros, T. "Alienation and Aesthetics in Marx and Tolstoy: A Comparative Analysis." *Man and World* 18 (1985).

*Krausz, M. *Critical Essays in the Philosophy of R. G. Collingwood.* Oxford, 1972.

Martienssen, H. "A Note on Formalism." *BJA* 19 (1979).

McLaughlin, T. M. "Clive Bell's Aesthetic: Tradition and Significant Form." *JAAC* 35 (1977).

Mink, L. O. *Mind, History, and Dialectic: The Philosophy of R. G. Collingwood.* Bloomington, 1969.

Thomas, J. A. "Tolstoy's Expressionism: How is Agreement in Our Emotional Response Explained?" *De Philosophia* 6 (1987).

Tolstoy, L. *What Is Art?* Indianapolis, 1960.

Whittick, A. "Towards Precise Distinctions of Art and Craft." *BJA* 24 (1984).

Part Two: Contemporary Theories of Art and Contemporary Critiques of These Theories

*Aagard-Mogenson, L., ed. *Culture and Art.* Atlantic Highlands, 1976.

———. "The Definition of 'Art.' " *Dialogos* 2 (1974).

Aagard-Mogenson, L., and Hermerén, G. *Contemporary Aesthetics in Scandinavia.* Doxa, 1980.

Aldrich, V. "McGregor on Dickie's Institutionalized Aesthetic." *JAAC* 36 (1977).

Arnheim, R. "Art among the Objects." *CI* 13 (1987).

Bachrach, J. E. "Dickie's Institutional Definition of Art: Further Criticism." *JAE* 11 (1977).

Balis, A., et al., eds. *Art in Culture.* 3 vols. Ghent, 1985.

Bartel, T. W. "Appreciation and Dickie's Definition of Art." *BJA* 19 (1979).

Beardsley, M. C. "Art and Its Cultural Context." *CC* 17 (1984).

Binkley, T. "Piece: Contra Aesthetics." *JAAC* 35 (1976).

Blizek, W. L. "An Institutional Theory of Art." *BJA* 14 (1974).

Brand, P. Z. "Lord, Lewis, and the Institutional Theory of Art." *JAAC* 40 (1982).

Brook, D. "A New Theory of Art." *BJA* 20 (1980).

Burgin, V. *The End of Art Theory: Criticism and Modernity.* Atlantic Highlands, 1986.

Carney, J. D. "What Is a Work of Art?" *JAE* 16 (1982).

Cohen, T. "The Possibility of Art: Remarks on a Proposal by Dickie." *Philosophical Review* 82 (1973).

Cormier, R. "Art as a Social Institution." *The Personalist* 58 (1977).

Crowther, P. "Art and Autonomy." *BJA* 21 (1981).

Curtler, H., ed. *What Is Art?* New York, 1983.

Danto, A. "Aesthetic Responses and Works of Art." *Philosophical Exchange* 3 (1981).

———. "Art, Evolution, and the Consciousness of History." *JAAC* 44 (1986).

———. "Deep Interpretation." *JP* (1978).

———. "The Appreciation and Interpretation of Works of Art." In *Relativism in the Arts*, ed. B. J. Craig. Athens, Ga., 1983.

———. *The Philosophical Disenfranchisement of Art.* New York, 1986.

———. *The State of the Art.* New York, 1987.

———. *The Transfiguration of the Commonplace.* New York, 1981.

Devereaux, D. "Artifacts, Natural Objects, and Works of Art." *Analysis* 37 (1977).

Dickie, G. *Art and the Aesthetic.* Ithaca, 1974.

———. "An Earnest Reply to Professor Stalker." *Philosophia* 8 (1979).

———. "The Actuality of Art." In *Aesthetics: A Critical Anthology*, ed. G. Dickie and R. Sclafani. New York, 1977.

———. *The Art Circle: A Theory of Art.* New York, 1984.

———. "The Return to Aesthetic Theory." In *Modern Trends in Philosophy*, vol. 2. Tel Aviv, 1983.

Diffey, T. J. "On Defining Art." *BJA* 17 (1977).

———. "The Idea of Art." *BJA* 17 (1977).

Donnell—Kotrozo, C. "In Defense of George Dickie." *JAE* 16 (1982).

Dorter, K. "Sparshott's Theory of the Arts." *BJA* 27 (1987).

Dziemidok, B. "Institutional Definition of a Work of Art." *Philosophical Inquiry* 2 (1980).

Eaton, M. M. *Art and Nonart.* East Brunswick, 1983.

Eldridge, R. "Form and Content: An Aesthetic Theory of Art." *BJA* 25 (1985).

Elgin, C. G. and Goodman, N. "Changing the Subject." *JAAC* (1987).

Fletcher, J. J. "Artifactuality Broadly and Narrowly Speaking." *Southern Journal of Philosophy* 20 (1982).

Goldsmith, S. "The Readymades of Marcel Duchamp: The Ambiguities of an Aesthetic Revolution." *JAAC* 42 (1982).

Hermerén, G. *Aspects of Aesthetics.* Lund, 1984.

Humble, P. N. "Duchamp's Readymades: Art and Anti-Art." *BJA* 22 (1982).

Johannessen, K. S., and Nordenstam, T., eds. *Wittgenstein: Aesthetics and Transcendental Philosophy.* Vienna, 1981.

Korsmeyer, C. "Wittgenstein and the Ontological Problem of Art." *The Personalist* 59 (1978).

Krukowski, L. "A Basis for Attributions of 'Art.' " *JAAC* 39 (1980).

———. *Art and Concept.* Amherst, 1987.

Kushner, T. "The Question of Definition Revisited." *Journal of Critical Analysis* 8 (1979).

Lang, B., ed. *The Death of Art.* New York, 1984.

Lansing, K. M. "Is a Definition of Art Necessary for the Teaching of Art?" *JAE* 14 (1980).

Lind, R. "Why Isn't Minimal Art Boring?" *JAAC* 45 (1986).

Lipman, N. "Definition and Status in Aesthetics." *Philosophical Forum* 7 (1975).

Lord, C. "Convention and Dickie's Institutional Theory of Art." *BJA* 20 (1980).

———. "Indexicality, Not Circularity: Dickie's New Definition of Art." *JAAC* 45 (1987).

*Margolis, J. *Art and Philosophy*, (Atlantic Heights 1980).

———. "Artworks and the History of Production" *CC* 17 (1984).

———. "Meyer Schapiro and the Science of Art History." *BJA* 21 (1981).

———. "Puzzles Regarding the Cultural Link between Artworks and Criticism." *JAE* 15 (1981).

————. "A Strategy for a Philosophy of Art." *JAAC* 37 (1979).

McCormick, P., ed. *The Reasons of Art*. Ottawa, 1987.

McFee, G. "Wollheim and the Institutional Theory of Art." *PQ* 35 (1985).

McGregor, R. " 'Art'-Again." *CI* 5 (1979).

————. R. "Dickie's Institutionalized Aesthetic." *BJA* 17 (1977).

Mendenhall, V. "Dickie and Cohen on What Art Is." *JAE* 16 (1982).

Mitias, M. "The Institutional Theory of the Aesthetic Object." *The Personalist* 58 (1977).

————. "The Institutional Theory of Artistic Creativity." *BJA* 18 (1978).

Morawski, S. "Contemporary Approaches to Aesthetic Inquiry: Absolute Demands and Limited Possibilities" *CI* 4 (1977).

Morawski, S. *Inquiries into the Fundamentals of Aesthetics*. Cambridge, 1974.

Nash, R. "Dickie: Defining Art and Falsifying Dada." *JAE* 15 (1981).

Osborne, H. "What Is a Work of Art?" *BJA* 21 (1981).

Platt, R. "Aesthetic Crisis and Artwork." *JAAC* 44 (1986).

Rudinow, J. "Duchamp's Mischief." *CI* 7 (1981).

Sankowski, E. "Free Action, Social Institutions, and the Definition of 'Art.' " *PS* 37 (1980).

Shusterman, R. S. "Analytic Aesthetics: Retrospect and Prospect" *JAAC* (1987).

Silvers, A. "Letting the Sun Shine In: Has Analysis Made Aesthetics Clear?" *JAAC* (1987).

*Sparshott, F. *The Theory of the Arts*. Princeton, 1983.

————. "What Works of Art Are." *PPQ* 61 (1980).

Stalker, D. F. "The Importance of Being an Artifact." *Philosophia* 8 (1979).

Stolnitz, J. "You Can't Separate the Work of Art from the Artist." *PL* 8 (1984).

Tilghman, B. R. *But Is It Art?* Oxford, 1984.

————. "Danto and the Ontology of Literature." *JAAC* 40 (1982).

Todd, G. F. "Art and the Concept of Art." *PPR* 44 (1983).

Tollefsen, O. "The Family Resemblances Argument and Definitions of Art." *Journal of Metaphysics* 7 (1976).

Tormey, J. F. and Tormey, A. "Art and Ambiguity." *Leonardo* 16 (1983).

Von Morstein, P. *On Understanding Works of Art: An Essay in Philosophical Analysis*. Lewiston, 1986.

————. "Understanding Works of Art: Universality, Unity, and Uniqueness." *Dialectical Humanism* 8 (1981).

Walhout, D. *A Festival of Aesthetics*. Washington, D.C., 1978.

————. "The Nature and Function of Art." *BJA* 26 (1986).

Wartofsky, M. W. "Art, Artworlds, and Ideology" *JAAC* 38 (1980).

————. "The Liveliness of Aesthetics." *JAAC* (1987).

Welsh, P. "George Dickie and the Definition of a Work of Art." *Acta Philosophica Fennica* 32 (1981).

Werhane, P. H. "Evaluating the Classificatory Process." *JAAC* 37 (1979).

Wieand, J. "Can There Be an Institutional Theory of Art?" *JAAC* 39 (1981).

————. "Critical Response: Duchamp and the Artworld." *CI* 8 (1981).

————. "Defining Art and Artifacts." *PS* 38 (1980).

Wollheim, R. *On Art and the Mind*. Cambridge, 1974.

————. "The Institutional Theory of Art." In *Art and Its Objects*. Cambridge, 1980.

Wolterstorff, N. *Art in Action: Toward a Christian Aesthetic*. Grand Rapids, 1980.

————. "The Philosophy of Art after Analysis and Romanticism." *JAAC* (1987).

————. *Works and Worlds of Art*. Oxford, 1980.

Yanal, R. "The Institutional Theory of the Aesthetic Object: A Reply to Michael Mitias." *The Personalist* 58 (1977).

Zangwill, N. "Aesthetics and Art." *BJA* 26 (1986).

Ziff, P. *Antiaesthetics*. (Dordrecht, 1984).

Part Three: Traditional Theories of the Aesthetic and Contemporary Discussions of These Theories

The British Enlightenment

Carroll, N. "Hume's Standard of Taste." *JAAC* 43 (1984).

Hester, M. "Hume on Principles and Perceptual Ability." *JAAC* 37 (1979).

Hipple, W. *The Beautiful, the Sublime, and the Picturesque in Eighteenth Century Aesthetic Theory.* (Carbondale, 1967).

Jensen, H. "Comments on Peter Jones' 'Hume on Art, Criticism, and Language: Debts and Premises.' " *PS* 33 (1978).

Jones, P. "Hume's Aesthetics Reassessed." *PQ* 26 (1977).

Kivy, P., ed. *Francis Hutcheson: An Inquiry Concerning Beauty, Order, Harmony, and Design.* The Hague, 1973.

——. *The Seventh Sense: A Study of Francis Hutcheson's Aesthetics and Its Influence in Eighteenth Century Britain.* New York, 1976.

——. "Thomas Reid and the Expression Theory of Art." *The Monist* 61 (1978).

Korsmeyer, C. "Hume and the Foundations of Taste." *JAAC* 35 (1976).

MacLachlan, C. "Hume and the Standard of Taste." *Hume Studies* 12 (1986).

MacMillan, C. "Hume, Points of View, and Aesthetic Judgments." *Journal of Value Inquiry* 20 (1986).

Michael, E. "Francis Hutcheson on Aesthetic Perception and Aesthetic Pleasure." *BJA* 25 (1984).

Roderick, R. "Hume on Beauty, Ideal Observers, and the Justification of Aesthetic Judgment." *Dialogue* 22 (1979).

Ross, S. "The Picturesque: An Eighteenth Century Debate." *JAAC* 46 (1987).

Townsend, D. "Archibald Alison: Aesthetic Experience and Emotions." *BJA* 28 (1988).

——. "From Shaftesbury to Kant: The Development of the Concept of Aesthetic Experience." *JHI* 48 (1987).

——. "Shaftesbury's Aesthetic Theory." *JAAC* 41 (1982).

Weiand, J. "Hume's Two Standards of Taste." *PQ* 34 (1984).

Kant

Ameriks, K. "How to Save Kant's Deduction of Taste." *Journal of Value Inquiry* 16 (1982).

——. "Kant and the Objectivity of Taste." *BJA* 23 (1983).

——. *Kant's Theory of Mind.* Oxford, 1982.

Aquila, R. E. "A New Look at Kant's Aesthetic Judgment." *Kant-Studien* 70 (1979).

Beardsley, M. C. *Aesthetics from Classical Greece to the Present.* New York, 1966.

Beck, L. W. *Early German Philosophy: Kant and His Predecessors.* Cambridge, 1969.

——. "Kant on the Uniformity of Nature." *Synthese* 47 (1981).

Cassirer, H. W. *A Commentary on Kant's "Critique of Judgment."* New York, 1970.

*Cohen, T., and Guyer, P., eds. *Essays in Kant's Aesthetics.* Chicago, 1982.

Coleman, F. X. *The Harmony of Reason: A Study in Kant's Aesthetics.* Pittsburgh, 1974.

Cox, J. G. "The Single Power Thesis in Kant's Theory of the Faculties." *Man and World* 16 (1983).

Crawford, D. W. *Kant's Aesthetic Theory.* Madison, 1974.

——. "Kant's Principles of Judgment and Taste." *Proceedings of the Sixth International Kant Congress* (1988).

Crowther, P. "Fundamental Ontology and Transcendental Beauty: An Approach to Kant's Aesthetics." *Kant-Studien* 76 (1985).

————. "Kant and Greenberg's Varieties of Aesthetic Formalism." *JAAC* 42 (1984).

Fisher, J., ed. *Essays on Aesthetics*. Philadelphia, 1983.

Guyer, P. *Kant and the Claims of Taste*. Cambridge, 1979.

————. "Autonomy and Integrity in Kant's Aesthetics." *Monist* 66 (1983).

————. "Kant's Distinction between the Beautiful and the Sublime." *RM* 35 (1982).

Harroll, J. G. "Kant's A Priori in *Critique of Judgment*." *JAAC* 39 (1980).

Hund, W. B. "Kant and A. Lazaroff on the Sublime." *Kant-Studien* 73 (1982).

————."The Sublime and God in Kant's *Critique of Judgment*." *The New Scholasticism* 57 (1983).

*Kant, I. *Critique of Judgment*. Translated by W. S. Pluhar. Indianapolis, 1987.

Kemal, S. "Aesthetic Necessity, Culture, and Epistemology." *Kant-Studien* 74 (1983).

————."The Importance of Artistic Beauty." *Kant-Studien* 71 (1980).

————. "Kant and the Production of Fine Art." *Proceedings of the Sixth International Kant Congress* (1988).

Kennington, R. *The Philosophy of Immanuel Kant*. Washington, D.C., 1985.

Knox, I. *The Aesthetic Theories of Kant, Hegel, and Schopenhauer*. New York, 1958.

MacMillan, C. "Kant's Deduction of Pure Aesthetic Judgments." *Kant-Studien* 76 (1985).

*Mothersill, M. *Beauty Restored*. Oxford, 1984.

O'Farrell, F. "Problems of Kant's Aesthetics." *Gregorianum* 57 (1976).

————. "System and Reason for Kant." *Gregorianum* 62 (1981).

Padro, M. *The Manifold in Perception: Theories of Art from Kant to Hildebrand*. Oxford, 1972.

Rogerson, K. F. "The Meaning of Universal Validity in Kant's Aesthetics." *JAAC* 40 (1981).

Savile, A. "Objectivity in Aesthetic Judgment: Eva Schaper on Kant." *BJA* 21 (1981).

————. "What Is a Judgment of Taste?" *Proceedings of the Sixth International Kant Congress* (1988).

Scarre, G. "Kant on Free and Dependent Beauty." *BJA* 21 (1981).

Schaper, E. *Studies in Kant's Aesthetics*. Edinburgh, 1979.

Warnock, M. *Imagination*. Berkeley, 1976.

Werkmeister, W. H. *Kant: The Architectonic and Development of His Philosophy*. London, 1980.

White, D. A. "On Bridging the Gulf between Nature and Morality in *Critique of Judgment*." *JAAC* 38 (1979).

Zeldin, M. B. "Formal Purposiveness and the Continuity of Kant's Argument in *Critique of Judgment*." *Kant-Studien* 74 (1983).

————. *Freedom and the Critical Undertaking: Essays on Kant's Later Critiques*. Ann Arbor, 1983.

Part Four: Contemporary Theories of the Aesthetic and Contemporary Critiques of These Theories

Aldrich, V. C. "Aesthetic Perception and Objectivity." *BJA* 18 (1978).

Armstrong, A. M. "Shapeliness a Clue to Aesthetics." *BJA* 27 (1987).

*Beardsley, M. C. *Aesthetics: Problems in the Philosophy of Criticism*. Indianapolis, 1981.

————. *The Aesthetic Point of View*. Edited by M. Wreen and D. Callen. London, 1982.

Blocker, H. G. "A New Look at Aesthetic Distance." *BJA* 17 (1977).

Bolton, G. M. "Psychical Distance and Acting." *BJA* 17 (1977).

Bourdieu, P. "The Historical Genesis of a Pure Aesthetics." *JAAC* (1987).

Bullough, E. *Aesthetics*. London, 1958.

Cecato, S. "The Aesthetic Attitude and the Artistic Values: An Analysis in Terms of Operations." *Diotima* 5 (1977).

Coleman, E. J. "On Saxena's Defense of the Aesthetic Attitude." *PEW* 29 (1979).
———, ed. *Varieties of Aesthetic Experience*. Lanham, 1983.
Crowther, P. "Aesthetic Aspects." *BJA* 27 (1987).
Dempster, D. J. "Aesthetic Experience and Psychological Definitions of Art." *JAAC* 44 (1985).
Dickie, G. "Beardsley, Sibley and Critical Principles." *JAAC* 46 (1987).
———. "Stolnitz's Attitude: Taste and Perception." *JAAC* 43 (1984).
Dziemidok, B. "Main Problems in the Theory of the Aesthetic Attitude." *Philosophical Inquiry* 1 (1978).
Eldridge, R. "Form and Content: An Aesthetic Theory of Art." *BJA* 25 (1985).
Feezell, R. "The Aesthetic Attitude Debate: Some Remarks on Saxena, Coleman, and a Phenomenological Approach to the Issue." *PEW* 30 (1980).
Fisher, J., ed. *Essays on Aesthetics: Perspectives on the Work of Monroe C. Beardsley*. Philadelphia, 1983.
Galard, J. "Remarks on the Broadening of Esthetic Experience." *Diogenes* 119 (1982).
Gordon, D. "The Aesthetic Attitude and the Hidden Curriculum." *JAE* 15 (1981).
Hyde, W. H. "What *Else* Makes Aesthetic Terms *Aesthetic?*" *PPR* 39 (1978).
Hyman, L. "A Defense of Aesthetic Experience: In Reply to George Dickie." *BJA* 26 (1986).
Iseminger, G. "Aesthetic Appreciation." *JAAC* 39 (1981).
Kasprisin, L. "The Concept of Distance: A Conceptual Problem in the Study of Literature." *JAE* 18 (1984).
Kelly, E. "Philosophy, Aesthetic Experience, and the Liberal Arts." *JAE* 17 (1983).
Kivy, P. "Aesthetic Concepts: Some Fresh Considerations." *JAAC* 37 (1979).
———. "Secondary Senses and Aesthetic Concepts: A Reply to Professor Tilghman." *PI* 4 (1981).
Korsmeyer, C. "On Distinguishing 'Aesthetic' from 'Artistic.' " *JAE* 11 (1977).
Kupfer, J. *Experience as Art: Aesthetics in Everyday Life*. Albany, 1983.
———. "Teaching Aesthetics Aesthetically." *JAAC* 41 (1982).
Lind, R. W. "Attention and the Aesthetic Object." *JAAC* 39 (1980).
Lofton, R. W. "Psychical Distance and the Aesthetic Appreciation of Wilderness." *International Journal of Applied Philosophy* 13 (1986).
MacKenzie, I. "Wittgenstein and Aesthetic Responses." *PL* 11 (1987).
Margolis, J. "Aesthetic Appreciation and the Imperceptible." *BJA* 16 (1976).
McAdoo, N. "Aesthetic Education and the 'Antinomy of Taste.' " *BJA* 27 (1987).
McGregor, R. "Art and the Aesthetic." *JAAC* 32 (1974).
Mitias, M. H. *The Aesthetic Object: Critical Studies*. Washington, D.C., 1977).
———. ed. *Possibility of the Aesthetic Experience*. Dordrecht, 1986).
———. "What Makes an Experience Aesthetic?" *JAAC* 41 (1982).
Mitscherling, J. "The Aesthetic Experience and the 'Truth' of Art." *BJA* 28 (1988).
Morreall, J. S. "Aldrich and Aesthetic Perception." *BJA* 17 (1977).
Mothersill, M. *Beauty Restored*. Oxford, 1984.
New, C. "Scruton on the Aesthetic Attitude." *BJA* 19 (1979).
Olen, J. "Perception, Inference, and Aesthetic Qualities." *The Monist* 62 (1980).
Osborne, H. "Aesthetic and Other Forms of Order." *BJA* 22 (1982).
Pandit, S. "In Defense of Psychical Distance." *BJA* 16 (1976).
Price, K. "The Truth about Psychical Distance." *JAAC* 35 (1977).
———. "What Makes an Experience Aesthetic?" *BJA* 19 (1979).
Rogerson, K. F. "Dickie's Disinterest." *Philosophia* 17 (1987).
Rose, M. C. "Nature as an Aesthetic Concept." *BJA* 16 (1976).
Saxena, S. K. "The Aesthetic Attitude." *PEW* 28 (1978).
———. "The Aesthetic Attitude Debate: Reply to Some New Criticisms." *PEW* 30 (1980).
———. "Reply to My Critics." *PEW* 29 (1979).

Schaper, E., ed. *Pleasure, Preference, and Value: Studies in Philosophical Aesthetics.* Cambridge, 1983.

Schiff, R. "Art and Life: A Metaphoric Relationship." *CI* 5 (1979).

Schlesinger, G. "Aesthetic Experience and the Definition of Art." *BJA* 19 (1979).

Schultz, R. A. "Does Aesthetics Have Anything to Do with Art?" *JAAC* 36 (1978).

Snoeyenbos, M. "Attitudes and Aesthetic Theory." *The Personalist* 60 (1979).

———. "On the Possibility of Theoretical Aesthetics." *Journal of Metaphysics* 9 (1978).

———. "Saxena on the Aesthetic Attitude." *PEW* 29 (1979).

Stolnitz, J. *Aesthetics and Philosophy of Art.* Boston, 1960.

———. " 'The Aesthetic Attitude' in the Rise of Modern Aesthetics." *JAAC* 36 (1978).

———. "Afterwords: 'The Aesthetic Attitude' in the Rise of Modern Aesthetics—Again." *JAAC* 43 (1984).

———. "The Artistic and the Aesthetic 'In Interesting Times.' " *JAAC* 37 (1979).

Suter, R. *Six Answers to the Problem of Taste.* Washington, D.C., 1979.

Talmor, S. "Bullough's 'Psychical Distance' and Its Critics." *Philosophical Studies (Ireland)* 25 (1977).

Tilghman, B. R. "Aesthetic Descriptions and Secondary Senses." *PI* 3 (1980).

———. "Reply to Professor Kivy's Comment on Secondary Senses and Aesthetic Concepts." *PI* 4 (1981).

Tolhurst, W. "Toward an Aesthetic Account of the Nature of Art." *JAAC* 42 (1984).

Part Five: Theories of the Individual Arts

Literature

Aagard-Mogensen, L., and DeVos, L., eds. *Text, Literature, and Aesthetics.* Rodolpi, 1986.

Banfield, A. *Unspeakable Sentences: Narration and Representation in the Language of Fiction.* Boston, 1982.

Baxter, L. "Recent Music: The Intentional Fallacy Restored." *JAAC* 39 (1980).

Beardsley, M. C. "Intentions and Interpretations: A Fallacy Revived." *The Aesthetic Point of View: Selected Essays.* Ithaca, 1982.

———. *The Possibility of Criticism.* Detroit, 1970.

Bruns, J. L. "Intention, Authority, and Meaning." *CI* 7 (1980).

Carrier, D. "Artist's Intentions and Art Historians Interpretation of the Artwork." *Leonardo* 19 (1984).

Cascardi, A. J., ed. *Literature and the Question of Philosophy.* Baltimore, 1987.

Chatman, S., ed. *Literary Style: A Symposium* (Oxford, 1971).

Chatterjee, M. "Must We Be For or Against 'Intention' in Art?" *Diotima* 9 (1981).

Cioffi, F. "Intention and Interpretation in Criticism." *PAS* 64 (1963–64).

Davies, S. "The Aesthetic Relevance of Authors and Painters." *JAAC* 40 (1982).

Davis, S. "A Note on Feagin's 'On Defining and Interpreting Art Intentionalistically.' " *BJA* 27 (1987).

Demetz, P., et al., eds. *The Discipline of Criticism.* New Haven, 1968.

Donnell-Kotrozo, C. "Counterword on Intentions." *JAE* 17 (1983).

———. "The Intentional Fallacy: An Applied Reappraisal." *BJA* 20 (1980).

Dundas, J. "Style and the Mind's Eye." *JAAC* 37 (1979).

Gendin, S. "The Artist's Intentions." *JAAC* 23 (1964).

Genova, J. "The Significance of Style." *JAAC* 37 (1979).

Goodman, N. *Ways of Worldmaking.* Indianapolis, 1978.

Gribble, J. "Literary Intention and Literary Education." *Journal of Philosophical Education* 15 (1981).

Heath, J. M., and Payne, M., eds. *Text, Interpretation Theory: Bucknell Review, Volume 29.* Lewisburg, 1985.

Hermerén, G. "Intention and Interpretation in Literary Criticism." *New Literary History* 7 (1975–76).

Hirsch, E. D., Jr. *The Aims of Interpretation.* Chicago, 1976.

———. *Validity in Interpretation.* New Haven, 1967.

Hyslop, A. "The Correct Reading of a Literary Work of Art." *Australian Journal of Philosophy* 61 (1983).

Kastely, J. L. "Convention, Necessity, and the Concept of Literature." *JAAC* 45 (1987).

Kemp, J. "The Work of Art and the Artist's Intentions." *BJA* 4 (1964).

Lang, B. "The Intentional Fallacy Revisited." *BJA* 14 (1974).

———. "Style as Instrument, Style as Person." *CI* 4 (1978).

Laroque, J., ed., *Philosophy and Literature.* Edinburgh, 1983.

Lyas, C. "Anything Goes: The Intentional Fallacy Revisited." *BJA* 23 (1983).

Margolis, J. *Art and Philosophy.* Atlantic Highlands, 1980.

Marshall, D. G., ed. *Literature as Philosophy/Philosophy as Literature.* New York, 1987.

Matthews, R. J. "Literary Works and Institutional Practices." *BJA* 21 (1981).

Meiland, J. "The Meaning of a Text." *BJA* 21 (1981).

Nathan, D. O. "Irony and the Artist's Intentions." *BJA* 22 (1982).

Newton-de Molina, D. *On Literary Intention.* Edinburgh, 1976.

Ohmann, R. "Speech Acts and the Definition of Literature." *Philosophy and Rhetoric* 4 (1971).

———. "Speech, Literature, and the Space Between." *New Literary History* 5 (1874).

Olsen, S. H. "Authorial Intention." *BJA* 13 (1973).

———. "Interpretation and Intention." *BJA* 27 (1977).

Pearce, D. "Intension and the Nature of a Musical Work." *BJA* 28 (1988).

Pratt, M. L. *Toward a Speech Act Theory of Literary Discourse.* Bloomington, 1977.

Raval, S. "Intention and Contemporary Literary Theory." *JAAC* 38 (1980).

Robinson, J. "General and Individual Style in Literature." *JAAC* 43 (1984).

———. "Style and Significance in Art History and Art Criticism." *JAAC* 40 (1981).

Rothschild, L. "Aesthetics and the Artist's 'Intention.' " *JAAC* 38 (1979).

Roy, P. K. "The Concept of Intentionality and the Problem of Aesthetic Response." *Indian Philosophical Quarterly* 12 (1986).

Savile, A. "The Place of Intention in the Concept of Art." *PAS* 69 (1968–69).

Sharpe, R. A. *Contemporary Aesthetics: A Philosophical Analysis.* New York, 1983.

Shiner, R. "The Mental Life of Works of Art." *JAAC* 40 (1982).

Silvers, A. "The Secret of Style." *JAAC* 39 (1981).

Sirridge, M. "Artistic Intention and Critical Prerogative." *BJA* 18 (1978).

Tilghman, B. R. "The Best of Intentions." *JAE* 16 (1982).

Tolhurst, W. "On What a Text Is and How It Means." *BJA* 29 (1979).

Wimsatt, W., Jr. "Genesis of Fallacy Revisited." In *The Discipline of Criticism*, ed. P. Demetz et al. New Haven, 1968.

———. *The Verbal Icon.* Lexington, 1954.

Zumbach, C. "Artistic Functions and the Intentional Fallacy." *APQ* 21 (1984).

Nietzsche and Tragedy

Alderman, H. G. *Nietzsche's Gift.* Columbus, 1977.

Alison, D. B., ed. *The New Nietzsche: Contemporary Styles of Interpretation.* New York, 1977.

Blosser, P. E. "Tragic Myth and the Malady of Nietzsche's Europe." *Dialogos* 19 (1984).

Chessick, R. D. A *Brief Introduction to the Genius of Nietzsche*. Lanham, 1983.

Copleston, F. *Friedrich Nietzsche: Philosopher of Culture*. London, 1942.

————. "Schopenhauer and Nietzsche." In *Schopenhauer: His Philosophical Achievement*, ed. M. Fox. Brighton, 1980.

Danto, A. C. *Nietzsche as Philosopher*. New York, 1965.

Davey, N. "Nietzsche's Aesthetics and the Question of Hermeneutic Interpretation." *BJA* 26 (1986).

Degenaar, J. J. "Nietzsche's View of the Aesthetic." *South African Journal of Philosophy* 4 (1985).

Grimm, R. H. *Nietzsche's Theory of Knowledge*. Berlin, 1977.

Harper, R. *The Seventh Solitude*. Baltimore, 1965.

Hayman, R. *Nietzsche: A Critical Life*. New York, 1980.

Heidegger, M. *Nietzsche. Vol. 1: The Will to Power as Art*. Translated by D. Krell. New York, 1979.

Hollingdale, R. J. *Nietzsche*. London, 1973.

————. *Nietzsche: The Man and His Philosophy*. Baton Rouge, 1965.

Jaspers, K. *Nietzsche: An Introduction to the Understanding of His Philosophical Activity*. Translated by C. F. Wallraff and F. J. Schmitz. Chicago, 1961.

————. *Nietzsche and Christianity*. Translated by E. B. Ashton. Chicago, 1961.

Kaufmann, W. *Nietzsche: Philosopher, Psychologist, Anti-Christ*. 4th ed. Princeton, 1974.

Lea, F. A. *The Tragic Philosopher: A Study of Friedrich Nietzsche*. London, 1957.

Lenson, D. *"The Birth of Tragedy": A Commentary*. Boston, 1987.

Love, F. *The Young Nietzsche and the Wagnerian Experience*. Chapel Hill, 1963.

Lowith, K. *From Hegel to Nietzsche*. Translated by D. Green. Garden City, 1967.

Magnus, B. *Nietzsche's Existential Imperative*. Bloomington, 1978.

Manthey-Zorne, O. *Dionysus: The Tragedy of Nietzsche*. Amherst, 1956.

McGinn, R. "Culture as Prophylactic: Nietzsche's *Birth of Tragedy* as Cultural Criticism." *Nietzsche-Studien* 4 (1975).

Megill, A. "Nietzsche as Aestheticist." *PL* 5 (1981).

Morgan, G. A., Jr. *What Nietzsche Means*. New York, 1965.

Nehamas, A. *Nietzsche: Life as Literature*. Harvard, 1985.

Neville, M. "Nietzsche on Beauty and Taste: The Problem of Aesthetic Evaluations." *ISP* 16 (1984).

O'Flaherty, J. C.; Sellnert, T. F.; and Helm, R. M., eds. *Studies in Nietzsche and the Classical Tradition*. Chapel Hill, 1979.

Risser, J. "Nietzsche's View of Philosophical Style: Comments." *ISP* 18 (1986).

*Schacht, R. *Nietzsche*. London, 1983.

————. "Nietzsche's Second Thoughts about Art." *The Monist* 64 (1981).

Silk, M. S., and Stern, J. P. *Nietzsche on Tragedy*. Cambridge, 1981.

Solomon, R. C., ed. *Nietzsche: A Collection of Critical Essays*. Garden City, 1973.

Stambaugh, J. *Nietzsche's Thought of Eternal Return*. Baltimore, 1972.

Stern, J. P. *A Study of Nietzsche*. Cambridge, 1979.

Strong, T. *Friedrich Nietzsche and the Politics of Transfiguration*. Berkeley, 1975.

Weiss, D. D. "Nietzsche on the Joys of Struggle: Some Remarks in Response to Professor Neville." *ISP* 16 (1984).

West, S. K. "Nietzsche on Artistic Reality and Artistic Motivation." *Philosophy Today* 25 (1981).

White, R. "Art and the Individual in Nietzsche's *Birth of Tragedy*." *BJA* 28 (1988).

Wilcox, J. T. *Truth and Value in Nietzsche*. Ann Arbor, 1974.

Williams, W. D. *Nietzsche and the French*. Oxford, 1952.

Wurzer, W. S. "Nietzsche's Return to an Absolute Beginning." *Man and World* 11 (1978).

The Visual Arts

Abercrombie, S. *Architecture as Art: An Esthetic Analysis.* New York, 1984.
Altieri, C. "Representation, Representativeness, and 'Non-Representational' Art." *JCLA* (1982).
Arrell, D. "What Goodman Should Have Said about Representation." *JAAC* 46 (1987).
Battin, M. P. "Exact Replication of the Visual Arts." *JAAC* 38 (1979).
Baxandall, L. *Patterns of Intention.* (New Haven, 1985).
Brook, D. "Painting, Photography, and Representation." *JAAC* 42 (1983).
Bryson, N. *Vision and Painting: The Logic of the Gaze.* New Haven, 1983.
Carney, J. D. "Wittgenstein's Theory of Picture Representation." *JAAC* 40 (1981).
Carrier, D. *Artwriting* (Amherst, 1987).
————. "The Presentness of Painting: Adrian Stokes as Aesthetician." *CI* 12 (1986).
Deregowski, J. B. *Distortion in Art: The Eye and the Mind.* Boston, 1984.
Eaton, M. M. "Truth in Pictures." *JAAC* 39 (1980).
Fisher, J., ed. *Perceiving Artworks.* Philadelphia, 1980.
Gibson, J. J. *The Ecological Approach to Visual Perception.* Boston, 1979.
————. "The Information Available in Pictures." *Leonardo* 4 (1971).
————. *The Senses Considered as Perceptual Systems.* Boston, 1966.
Gilmour, J. *Picturing the World.* Albany, 1986.
Gombrich, E. *Art and Illusion.* London, 1960.
————. *Ideals and Idols.* (Oxford, 1979).
————. *Meditations on a Hobby Horse and Other Essays on the Theory of Art.* London, 1963.
————. "Representation and Misrepresentation." *CI* 2 (1984).
————. "Standards of Truth: The Arrested Image and the Moving Eye." *CI* 7 (1980).
————. *The Image and the Eye: Further Studies in the Psychology of Pictorial Representation.* Ithaca, 1982.
————. *The Sense of Order: A Study in the Psychology of Decorative Art.* Ithaca, 1979.
Gombrich, E.; Hochberg, J.; and Black, M. *Art, Perception, and Reality.* Baltimore, 1972.
Goodman, N. *Of Mind and Other Matters.* Cambridge, 1984.
————. *Languages of Art.* Indianapolis, 1968.
————. "Roots of Reference." *CI* 8 (1981).
————. *Ways of Worldmaking.* Indianapolis, 1978.
Goodman, N., and Elgin, C. I. "Interpretation and Identity: Can the Work Survive the World?" *CI* 12 (1986).
Goodrich, R. A. "Goodman on Representation and Resemblance." *BJA* 28 (1988).
Gosselin, M. "Conventionalism Versus Realism in Pictorial Art: Is Perception Basically Particular or General?" *CC* 17 (1984).
————. "Conventionalism Versus Realism: Perspective." *CC* 17 (1984).
Gregory, R. L., and Gombrich, E. *Illusion in Nature and Art.* London, 1973.
Hagen, M. A., ed. *The Perception of Pictures.* 2 vols. New York, 1980.
Hermerén, G. "Depiction: Some Formal and Conceptual Problems." *JAAC* 37 (1978).
————. *Representation and Meaning in the Visual Arts.* Lund, 1969.
Jones, R. K. "A Three Point Perspective on Pictorial Representation: Wartofsky, Goodman, and Gibson on Seeing Pictures." *Erkenntis* 15 (1980).
Korsmeyer, C. "Pictorial Assertion." *JAAC* 43 (1985).
Krieger, M. "The Ambiguities of Representation and Illusion: An E. H. Gombrich Retrospective." *CI* 2 (1984).
Marshall, D. G. "Aristotelian 'Imitation' as Non-Positivist Representation." *Annals of Scholarship* 2 (1981).
Maynard, P. "Depiction, Vision, and Convention." *APQ* 9 (1972).
Mitchell, W. J. *Iconology: Image, Text, Ideology.* Chicago, 1986.

Neander, K. "Pictorial Representation: A Matter of Resemblance." *BJA* 27 (1987).

Nodine, C. F., and Fisher, D. F., eds. *Perception and Pictorial Representation*. New York, 1979.

Novitz, D. "Conventions and the Growth of Pictorial Style." *BJA* 16 (1976).

———. *Pictures and Their Use in Communications*. Gravenhage, 1977.

———. "Pictures, Fiction, and Resemblance." *BJA* 22 (1982).

Peetz, D. "Some Current Theories of Pictorial Representation." *BJA* 27 (1987).

Pitkanen, R. "On the Analysis of Pictorial Representation." *Acta Philosophica Fennica* 31 (1980).

———. "The Resemblance View of Pictorial Representation." *BJA* 16 (1976).

Richter, P. "On Professor Gombrich's Model of Schema and Correction." *BJA* 16 (1976).

Ricoeur, P. "Mimesis and Representation." *Annals of Scholarship* 2 (1981).

Robinson, J. "Representation in Music and Painting." *Philosophy* 56 (1981).

———. "Some Remarks on Goodman's Language Theory of Pictures." *BJA* 19 (1979).

Rogers, L. R. "Representation and Schemata." *BJA* 5 (1965).

Roskill, M., and Carrier, D. *Truth and Falsehood in Visual Images*. Amherst, 1983.

Ross, S. D. "Representation and Paradigms." *Annals of Scholarship* 2 (1981).

Rudner, R., and Scheffler, I., eds. *Logic in Art*. Indianapolis, 1972.

Schier, F. *Deeper into Pictures: An Essay on Pictorial Representation*. Cambridge, 1986.

Scruton, R. "Photography and Representation." *CI* 7 (1981).

Todd, J. "The Roots of Pictorial Reference." *JAAC* 39 (1980).

Walsh, D. "Some Functions of Pictorial Representation." *BJA* 21 (1981).

Walton, K. L. "Transparent Pictures: On the Nature of Photographic Realism." *CI* 11 (1984).

Watkins, E. W. "Point of View in Depictive Representation." *Nous* 13 (1979).

Wilkerson, T. "Representation, Illusion, and Aspects." *BJA* 18 (1978).

Wilson, C. "Illusion and Representation." *BJA* 22 (1982).

Wollheim, R. "Imagination and Pictorial Understanding." *PASS* 60 (1986).

Woodfield, R. "Gombrich on Language and Meaning." *BJA* 25 (1985).

———. "Words and Pictures." *BJA* 26 (1986).

Zemach, E. M. "Description and Depiction." *Mind* 84 (1977).

Film

Arnheim, R. *Film as Art*. Berkeley, 1958.

Balazs, B. *Theory of the Film*. New York, 1970.

Barthes, R. *Camera Lucida*. New York, 1981.

———. *Semiology of the Cinema*. Boston, n.d.

Bazin, A. *What Is Cinema?* Berkeley, 1971.

Brannigan, E. R. *Point of View in the Cinema: A Theory of Narrative and Subject in Classical Film*. Berlin, 1984.

Carroll, N. "Address to the Heathen." *Dialectics in Humanism* 23 (1982).

———. "Film History and Film Theory: An Outline for an Institutional Theory of Film." *Film Reader* 4 (1979).

———. *Philosophical Problems of Classical Film Theory*. New York, 1988.

———. *Mystifying Movies: Fads and Fallacies in Contemporary Film Theory*. New York, 1988.

Casebier, A. *Film Appreciation*. New York, 1976.

Cavell, S. "More of the World Viewed." *Georgia Review* 38 (1980).

———. *Pursuits of Happiness: The Hollywood Comedy of Remarriage*. Cambridge, 1981.

———. "What Becomes of Things on Film?" *PL* 2 (1978).

*Cohen, M., and Mast, G., eds. *Film Theory and Criticism*. New York, 1979.

Danto, A. "Moving Pictures." *Quarterly Review of Film Studies* 4 (1979).

Dickinson, T. *A Discovery of Cinema*. London, 1971.
Dudley, A. *The Major Film Theories*. New York, 1976.
———. *André Bazin*. New York, 1978.
———. *Concepts in Film Theory*. New York, 1987.
Eisenstein, S. *Film Form: Essays in Film Theory*. New York, 1949.
Ellis, J. *Visible Fictions: Cinema, TV, Video*. London, 1982.
Heath, S. *Questions of Cinema*. Bloomington, 1981.
Holland, N. N. "I-ing Film." *CI* 12 (1986).
Hudlin, E. "Film Language." *JAE* 33 (1975).
Jarvie, I. C. *Movies and Society*. New York, 1983.
*———. *The Philosophy of the Film*. New York, 1987.
Khatchadourian, H. "Film as Art." *JAAC* 33 (1975).
———. *Music, Film, and Art*. New York, 1985.
Kracauer, S. *Theory of Film: The Redemption of Physical Reality*. Princeton, 1965.
Lackey, D. P. "Reflection on Cavell's Ontology of Film." *JAAC* 32 (1973).
Linden, G. *Reflections on the Screen*. San Francisco, 1970.
Mast, G. *Film/Cinema/Movie*. New York, 1977.
———. "On Framing." *CI* 11 (1984).
Metz, C. *Film Language: A Semiotics of the Cinema*. New York, 1974.
———. *The Imaginary Signifier*. Bloomington, 1982.
Nichols, B., ed. *Movies and Methods*. Berkeley, 1976.
Pudovkin, V. I. *Film Technique and Film Acting*. New York, 1960.
*Rosen, P., ed. *Narrative, Apparatus, Ideology*. New York, 1987.
Sesonske, A. "Cinema Space." *Explorations in Phenomenology*. The Hague, 1973.
———. "The World Viewed." *Georgia Review* 38 (1980).
———. "Time and Tense in Cinema." *JAAC* 38 (1980).
Sparshott, F. "Basic Film Aesthetics." *JAE* 5 (1971).
Stephenson, R., and Debrix, J. R. *The Cinema as Art*. Baltimore, 1976.
Thomas, S., ed. *Film/Culture*. Metuchen, 1982.
Tudor, A. *Theories of Film*. New York, 1973.
Weiss, P. *Cinematics*. Carbondale, 1975.

Music

Alperson, P. " 'Musical Time' and Music as an 'Art of Time.' " *JAAC* 38 (1980).
*———, ed. *What Is Music?* New York, 1988.
Booth, M. W. *The Experience of Song*. New Haven, 1981.
Budd, M. "Hanslick on Music: The Repudiation of Emotion." *BJA* 20 (1980).
———. "Motion and Emotion in Music: How Music Sounds." *BJA* 23 (1983).
———. *Music and the Emotions*. London, 1985.
Callen, D. "The Sentiment in Musical Sensibility." *JAAC* 40 (1982).
Coker, W. *Music and Meaning: A Theoretical Introduction to Musical Aesthetics*. New York, 1972.
Cone, E. T. *Musical Form and Musical Performance*. New York, 1968.
———. *The Composer's Voice*. Berkeley, 1974.
Cooke, D. *The Language of Music*. Oxford, 1959.
Davies, S. "The Expression of Emotion in Music." *Mind* 89 (1980).
———. "Is Music a Language of the Emotions?" *BJA* 23 (1983).
Dufrenne, M. *The Phenomenology of Aesthetic Experience*. Evanston, 1973.
Ferguson, D. *Music as Metaphor: The Elements of Expression*. Minneapolis, 1963.
Finkelstein, S. *How Music Expresses Ideas*. New York, 1976.

Gurney, E. *The Power of Sound*. London, 1980.

Hall, R. "On Hanslick's Supposed Formalism in Music." *JAAC* 25 (1967).

Hagberg, G. "Music and Imagination." *Philosophy* 61 (1986).

Hansen, F. "The Adequacy of Verbal Articulation of Emotions." *JAAC* 31 (1972).

———. "Ferguson's Dissonant Expressionism." *JAAC* 32 (1974).

Hanslick, E. *On the Musically Beautiful*. Translated by G. Payzant. Indianapolis, 1987.

Hoaglund, J. "Music as Expressive." *BJA* 20 (1980).

Howard, V. A. *Artistry: The Work of Artists*. Indianapolis, 1982.

———. "On Musical Expression." *BJA* 11 (1971).

———. "On Representational Music." *Nous* 6 (1972).

Khatchadourian, H. *Music, Film, and Art*. London, 1985.

Kivy, P. *The Corded Shell: Reflections on Musical Expression*. Princeton, 1980.

———. *Sound and Semblance: Reflections and Musical Representation*. Princeton, 1984.

Langer, S. K. *Mind: An Essay on Human Feeling*. Vol. 1. Baltimore, 1970.

Levinson, J. "Music and Negative Emotion." *PPQ* 63 (1982).

———. "What a Musical Work Is." *JP* 77 (1980).

Lippman, E. A. *Musical Aesthetics: A Historical Reader*. Vol. 1. New York, 1986.

Mark, T. "The Work of Virtuosity." *JP* 77 (1980).

Meidner, O. C. "Motion and E-Motion in Music." *BJA* 25 (1985).

Meu, P. "The Musical Arousal of Emotions." *BJA* 25 (1985).

———. "The Expression of Emotion in Music." *BJA* 26 (1986).

Meyer, L. *Emotion and Meaning in Music*. Chicago, 1956.

———. *Explaining Music*. Chicago, 1973.

———. "Exploiting Limits: Creation, Archetypes, and Style Change." *Daedalus* 119 (1980).

———. *Music, History, and Ideas*. Chicago, 1962.

Newcomb, A. "Sound and Feeling." *CI* 10 (1984).

Payne, E. "The Nature of Musical Emotion and Its Place in the Appreciative Experience." *BJA* 13 (1973).

Payzant, G. "Essay: Towards a Revised Reading of Hanslick." *On the Musically Beautiful*. Indianapolis, 1986.

———. *Glenn Gould: Music and Mind*. Toronto, 1978.

———. "Hanslick, Sams, Gay, and 'tonend bewegte Foremen.' " *JAAC* 40 (1981).

Price, K., ed. *On Criticizing Music: Five Philosophical Perspectives*. Baltimore, 1981.

Ridley, A. "Mr. Meu on Music." *BJA* 26 (1986).

Scruton, R. "Analytic Philosophy and the Meaning of Music." (1987).

———. *The Aesthetic Imagination*. London, 1984.

———. *The Aesthetic Understanding*. London, 1983.

Sharpe, R. A. "Is There a Language of Music?" *Journal of the British Society for Phenomenology* 1 (1970).

Sparshott, F. E. "Aesthetics of Music." In *The New Grove Dictionary of Music and Musicians*. Vol. 6. London, 1981.

———. *The Theory of the Arts*. Princeton, 1982.

Speck, S. " 'Arousal Theory' Reconsidered." *BJA* 28 (1988).

Sullivan, J. W. N. *Beethoven: His Spiritual Development*. New York, 1960.

Swanick, K. "Music and the Education of the Emotions." *BJA* 14 (1974).

Dance

Arnold, P. J. "Creativity, Self-Expression, and Dance" *JAE* 20 (1986).

Banes, S. *Democracy's Body: Judson Dance Theater, 1962–1964*. Ann Arbor, 1983.

———. *Terpsichore in Sneakers: Post-Modern Dance*. New York, 1980.

Best, D. "The Aesthetics of Dance." *Dance Research Journal* 7 (1975).
————. *Philosophy and Human Movement.* London, 1978.
Carr, D. "Thought and Action in the Art of Dance." *BJA* 87 (1987).
Cohen, S. J., ed. *The Modern Dance: Seven Statements of Belief.* Middletown, 1966.
————. *Next Week, Swan Lake: Reflections on Dance and Dances.* Middletown, 1982.
*Copeland, R., and Cohen, M., eds. *What Is Dance?* New York, 1983.
Croce, A. *Afterimages.* New York, 1978.
Ellfeldt, L. *Dance from Magic to Art.* Dubuque, 1976.
Fancher, G., and Myers, G., eds. *Philosophical Essays on Dance.* Brooklyn, 1981.
Fraleigh, S. *Dance and the Lived Body.* Pittsburgh, 1987.
Gordon, S. *Off Balance: The Real World of Ballet.* New York, 1983.
Hanna, J. L. *The Performer-Audience Connection: Emotion to Metaphor in Dance and Society.*
        Austin, 1983.
————. *To Dance Is Human: A Theory of Non-Verbal Communication.* Austin, 1979.
Hood, H. *The Scenic Art.* Toronto, 1984.
Jowitt, D. *The Dance in Mind.* Boston, 1985.
Kaprelian, M. H. *Aesthetics for Dancers.* Washington, D.C., 1976.
Keller, E. F. *A Feeling for the Organism.* New York and San Francisco, 1983.
Kendall, E. *Where She Danced.* New York, 1979.
Levin, D. M. "Philosophers and the Dance." *Ballet Review* 6 (1977–78).
Louis, M. *Inside Dance.* New York, 1980.
Margolis, J. "The Autographic Nature of the Dance." *JAAC* 29 (1981).
Miller, J. *Measures of Wisdom: The Cosmic Dance in Classical and Christian Antiquity.*
        Toronto, 1986.
Murray, J. *Dance Now.* London, 1979.
*Nadel, M. H., and Nadel, G. C., eds. *The Dance Experience.* New York, 1970.
Newman, B. *Striking a Balance: Dancers Talk about Dancing.* Boston, 1982.
Percival, J. *Modern Ballet.* Rev. ed. London, 1980.
*Redfern, B. *Dance, Art, and Aesthetics.* London, 1983.
Royce, A. P. *Movement and Meaning: Creativity and Interpretation in Ballet and Mime.*
        Bloomington, 1984.
Sheets-Johnstone, M. "An Account of Recent Changes in Dance in the U.S.A." *Leonardo* 11
        (1978).
————, ed. *Illuminating Dance.* Lewisburg, 1984.
Shelton, S. *Divine Dancer: A Biography of Ruth St. Denis.* Garden City, 1981.
Siegel, M. B. *Watching the Dance Go By.* Boston, 1977.
————. *The Shapes of Change: Images of American Dance.* Berkeley, 1985.
Sirridge, M., and Armelagos, A. "The In's and Out's of Dance: Expression as an Aspect of
        Style." *JAAC* 36 (1977).
Snoeyenbos, M. "Three Aspects of Meaning in Dance." *JCLA* 3 (1981–82).
*Sparshott, F. *Off the Ground: First Steps to a Philosophical Consideration of the Dance.*
        Princeton, 1988.
————. "On the Question: 'Why Do Philosophers Neglect the Dance?' " *Dance Research
        Journal* 15 (1982).
Suits, B. *The Grasshopper.* Toronto, 1978.
Wigman, M. *The Mary Wigman Book.* Edited by W. Sorell. Middletown, 1975.

NOTES ON THE CONTRIBUTORS

ARISTOTLE (384–322 B.C.) ranks with Plato as one of the most important thinkers in Western civilization. The *Poetics* has probably been the most influential work in the history of Western literary criticism.

SALLY BANES is editor of *Dance Research Journal*, senior critic for *Dance* Magazine, and the author of *Terpsichore in Sneakers: Post-Modern Dance* (1980). She teaches dance history and theory at Cornell University.

STANLEY BATES is chair of the Department of Philosophy at Middlebury College, Vermont. He writes in ethics and other philosophical areas as well as in aesthetics.

MONROE C. BEARDSLEY was late professor of philosophy at Temple University. He is one of the best-known writers in aesthetics in the Anglo-American world. His major work, *Aesthetics: Problems in the Philosophy of Criticism*, was published in 1958 and has had an enormous influence on the subject.

CLIVE BELL was a highly influential critic and member of the famous Bloomsbury group, which included such figures as Virginia Woolf, John Maynard Keynes, and G. E. Moore. His collaboration with Roger Fry was enormously influential in changing the course of art appreciation and criticism toward a formalist aesthetics.

EDWARD BULLOUGH (1880–1934) late professor of Italian literature at Cambridge University. He is most famous, however, for his aesthetic writings and his coining of the term "psychical distance."

NOËL CARROLL is an associate professor of theatre arts at Cornell University. He is author of *Philosophical Problems of Classical Film Theory* (1988) and *Mystifying Movies: Fads and Fallacies in Contemporary Film Theory* (1988). He is completing a book entitled *The Philosophy of Horror*.

STANLEY CAVELL is Walter M. Cabot Professor of Aesthetics and General Theory of Value at Harvard University. He has published a number of highly influential essays in aesthetics, some of which are collected under the title *Must We Mean What We Say?*

TED COHEN is professor of philosophy at the University of Chicago. He is an eminent scholar of Kant's aesthetics and has written influential articles in diverse areas of aesthetics as well as on the philosophical writings of J. L. Austin.

R. G. COLLINGWOOD was late Waynflete Professor of Metaphysics at Oxford University. He published extensively in philosophy as well as history. In addition to *The Principles of Art* (1934), his major contribution to the theory of art, he wrote *Outlines of a Philosophy of Art* and numerous articles in aesthetics.

EDWARD T. CONE is professor of music at Princeton University. He is a composer as well as a frequent contributor to musical journals and is the author of *Musical Form and Musical Performance* (1968) and *The Composer's Voice* (1974).

RENÉE COX has taught music history and double bass at the University of Tennessee since 1976. She has published articles in the *Journal of Aesthetics and Art Criticism* and *British Journal of Aesthetics*.

ARTHUR DANTO is Johnsonian Professor of Philosophy at Columbia University. He has published widely in all areas of philosophy, including important works in the analytical tradition as well as books on Nietzsche and Sartre. His major publications in aesthetics include *The Transfiguration of the Commonplace* (1981) and *The Philosophical Disenfranchisement of Art* (1986).

GEORGE DICKIE is professor of philosophy at the University of Illinois, Chicago Circle campus. His work in aesthetics over the last twenty-five years includes *Aesthetics: A Critical Introduction* (1970), *Art and the Aesthetic: An Institutional Analysis* (1974), and *The Art Circle* (1986), among numerous other contributions to the field. His most recent book is on the subject of aesthetic evaluation.

E. H. GOMBRICH is director of the Warburg Institute, London. He is the author of *The Story of Art*, *Art and Illusion*, *Meditations on a Hobby Horse*, and *The Sense of Order*, among other major theoretical and critical essays on the visual arts.

NELSON GOODMAN is professor of philosophy at Harvard University. He is the author of a number of important books, including *Languages of Art* (second edition, 1976), *Ways of Worldmaking* (1978), *Of Mind and Other Matters* (1984), and most recently *Reconceptions in Philosophy and Other Arts and Sciences* with Catherine Z. Elgin (1988).

PAUL GUYER is professor of philosophy at the University of Pennsylvania. His extensive contributions to aesthetics include *Kant and the Claims of Taste* (1984). He is an eminent scholar of Kant's philosophy.

EDUARD HANSLICK, born in Prague in 1825, was professor of music at the University of Vienna and music critic for the famous journal *Wiener Zeitung*. Aesthetically, he championed Brahms and scorned Wagner. His influence among his contemporaries was as strong as a critic's influence has ever been.

DAVID HUME (1711–1776) is, in the opinion of many, the greatest philosopher in the British tradition. His *Treatise of Human Nature* and *Enquiries* are philosophical classics. "On the Standard of Taste" is a brief essay that remains a primary source on the subject of taste.

FRANCIS HUTCHESON (1694–1746) was one of the first British empiricist philosophers who wrote on beauty and morals. Hutcheson's work is currently undergoing a revival. New editions of his work continue to appear, and philosophers and scholars are once again paying him serious notice.

IMMANUEL KANT (1724–1804) was one of the greatest philosophers in the Western tradition. Kant's three critiques are perennial sources of philosophical scholarship, commentary, and analysis. The *Critique of Judgment* contains Kant's contribution to aesthetics and is a source of continuing interpretation and study.

PETER KIVY is professor of philosophy at Rutgers University, New Brunswick, campus. He is an associate editor of *The Journal of Aesthetics and Art Criticism*. A leading scholar in eighteenth-century British aesthetics who has written a book on Hutcheson, Kivy is in addition the author of several important books on the aesthetics of music.

COLIN LYAS has taught at the University of Lancaster, England, since 1966. In 1987 he was Cowling Professor of Philosophy at Carleton College, Minnesota. He edited *Philosophy and Linguistics* (1971) and is the author of numerous articles and reviews, including several important essays on the intentional fallacy. He has recently completed a new edition of the Theoria of Benedetto Croce's *Esthetica*.

MAURICE MANDELBAUM is professor emeritus of philosophy at Johns Hopkins University. He is a well-known philosophical figure in America who has long contributed books and essays to the subject.

MARY MOTHERSILL is professor of philosophy and department chair at Barnard College, where she has taught since 1963. Her most recent contribution to aesthetics is *Beauty Restored* (1984). She is the editor of *Aesthetics and Theory of Criticism: Selected Essays of Arnold Isenberg* (1973). In addition, she has published widely in the areas of moral and social philosophy.

FRIEDRICH NIETZSCHE, the noted late nineteenth-century German philosopher, is often called a nihilist. He continues to be a major influence in Continental European philosophy as well as on thinkers within the Anglo-American tradition.

PLATO (427/8–348/7 B.C.) stands at the foot of the Western philosophical tradition. His dialogues are of perennial philosophical interest, and the issues he raised are as central today as they were to his fellow Athenians. Among his most important contributions to aesthetics are *The Republic*, *Symposium*, *Phaedrus*, *Ion*, and *Hippias Major*.

JENEFER M. ROBINSON is professor of philosophy at the University of Cincinnati. Her work has appeared in *Philosophical Review*, *Philosophical Quarterly*, *Erkenntnis*, *Journal of Aesthetics and Art Criticism*, *British Journal of Aesthetics*, and elsewhere.

RICHARD SCHACHT is professor of philosophy at the University of Illinois at Urbana-Champaign. He is the author of *Alienation* (1970), *Hegel and After* (1975), *Classical Modern Philosophers* (1985), and a major study of Nietzsche's philosophical thought, *Nietzsche* (1983).

EVA SCHAPER is professor of philosophy

at the University of Glasgow, Scotland. Among her numerous contributions to aesthetics are *Prelude to Aesthetics* (1969) and *Studies in Kant's Aesthetics* (1979). Most recently, she is the editor of the book *Pleasure, Preference, and Value* (1986).

ALEXANDER SESONSKE is professor in the Film Studies Program at the University of California, Santa Barbara. He is best known for his writings in the aesthetics of film, including "Time and Tense in Cinema" and "Cinema Space," and has edited an important anthology entitled *What Is Art?* (1965).

FRANK N. SIBLEY is professor emeritus of philosophy at the University of Lancaster, England. He is a well-known writer in the analytical tradition and has published several highly influential articles on the concept of the aesthetic.

ANITA SILVERS is professor of philosophy at San Francisco State University. She is a member of the Boards of both the American Philosophical Association and the American Society for Aesthetics. The author of articles in several areas of aesthetics, she is working on a book-length treatment of art-historical methodology.

FRANCIS SPARSHOTT is University Professor and professor of philosophy at Victoria College in the University of Toronto. Among his numerous publications in aesthetics are *The Structure of Aesthetics* (1963), *The Concept of Criticism* (1967), *The Theory of the Arts* (1982), and a forthcoming book on the aesthetics of dance. He is the author of several books of poetry.

ROBERT STECKER is an assistant professor in the Philosophy Department at Central Michigan University. He has published in a variety of areas in aesthetics in such journals as *The British Journal of Aesthetics*.

JEROME STOLNITZ is professor of philosophy at Lehman College, City University of New York. He is well known for

his scholarly and philosophical work on aesthetics, especially for his important book *Aesthetics and the Philosophy of Art Criticism*.

BENJAMIN R. TILGHMAN is professor of philosophy at Kansas State University. He is the editor of *Language and Aesthetics* (1976) and the author of *But Is It Art?* (1986). His interests are primarily in aesthetics, in which he has written extensively, and the philosophy of Wittgenstein.

LEO TOLSTOY's (1828–1910) importance as a novelist is world famous. Among his greatest works of fiction are *War and Peace* and *Anna Karenina*. In *What Is Art?* (1898) he investigates the moral, social, and religious significance of the arts.

ALAN TORMEY is professor of philosophy at the University of Maryland, Baltimore County. He is the author of *The Concept of Expression* (1971) and has written extensively in many areas of the subject, including the aesthetics of music.

KENDALL L. WALTON is professor of philosophy at the University of Michigan. He has authored a number of very important articles in aesthetics and is at work on a book in the field.

MORRIS WEITZ is the late Richard Koret Professor of Philosophy, Brandeis University. Among his numerous writings in the philosophy of art are *Philosophy of the Arts* (1950), *Philosophy in Literature* (1963), *Hamlet and the Philosophy of Literary Criticism* (1964), and *The Opening Mind* (1977).

WILLIAM K. WIMSATT, Jr., is the late professor of English at Yale University. He is the author of *Philosophic Words* (1948) and *The Verbal Icon* (1954), and coauthor of *Literary Criticism* (1957).

RICHARD WOLLHEIM is professor of philosophy, Columbia University. He is among the most eminent British aestheticians. His writings include the influential *Art and Its Objects* (1968, 1980), *On Art and the Mind* (1973), and most recently *Painting as an Art* (1987).

INDEX OF NAMES